The Baseball Necrology

The Baseball Necrology

The Post-Baseball Lives and Deaths of Over 7,600 Major League Players and Others

Bill Lee

McFarland & Company, Inc., Publishers
Jefferson, North Carolina, and London

LIBRARY OF CONGRESS CATALOGUING-IN-PUBLICATION DATA

Lee, Bill, 1937–
The baseball necrology : the post-baseball lives and deaths
of over 7,600 major league players and others / Bill Lee.
p. cm.
Includes bibliographical references.

ISBN 0-7864-1539-8 (illustrated case binding : 50# alkaline paper) ∞

1. Baseball players — United States — Obituaries. I. Title.
GV865.A1L42 2003 796.357'092'2 — dc21 2002156689

British Library cataloguing data are available

Manufactured in the United States of America

McFarland & Company, Inc., Publishers
Box 611, Jefferson, North Carolina 28640
www.mcfarlandpub.com

ACKNOWLEDGMENTS

The compilation of *The Baseball Necrology* required the assistance of too many people to list individually. I am fearful of leaving some out and also mindful of keeping the size of the book at a manageable level. They include librarians and staff at state libraries, state historical societies, state university libraries, and local city and county libraries. They also include personnel in county courthouses, especially in California, cemetery caretakers all over the United States, and funeral directors all over the country as well. Please accept my sincerest statement of gratitude.

Spending over six months a year for five years traveling to gather the information in *The Baseball Necrology*, I also thank those doing their everyday jobs in RV parks, restaurants, grocery stores and service stations who helped make our traveling experience a pleasant one.

Last, and certainly not least, I thank LaVonne Lee, my best friend and wife of over 30 years, who was by my side throughout this project, lending her support, clerical help, and editing, and even spending a great deal of time looking at microfilm for hard to find obituaries. Without her encouragement and support *The Baseball Necrology* would not be possible. It is to LaVonne that I dedicate this work.

Table of Contents

INTRODUCTION

During a baseball player's career as a player, everything he did is well documented. Every at bat — every hit — every pitch. This information is written about, talked about, hashed and rehashed, sometimes for years afterward. But the reflexes slow, the eyes grow dim, or the arm gets sore. The crowd quits cheering and the ballplayer's days in the limelight are over. Unlike most other professions, the baseball player's career is over at an age when most other careers are just beginning. Sometime between age 25 and age 45, usually in the early 30's, the ballplayer is through as a performer, but he still has twenty to forty useful years ahead of him. What did the ballplayers of the past do with those twenty to forty years? *The Baseball Necrology* addresses this subject on more than 7600 now deceased baseball players, as well as other personalities in the game of baseball, giving their cause of death and the location of their final resting place.

The vast majority of information contained in *The Baseball Necrology* came from newspaper obituaries. The United States Newspaper Project (USNP), a cooperative national effort among the states and the federal government, funded by the National Endowment for the Humanities, has located, cataloged and preserved on microfilm, newspapers published in the United States from the 18th century to present. Each state has one, and in a few instances more than one, central repository, or newspaper morgue, of this microfilm. These are usually at a state library, a state historical library, a state university, or as in the case of Massachusetts, the Boston Public Library. Using various versions of the baseball encyclopedia as a guide, between 1997 and 2001, I visited each of these locations at least once, and some two or more times, gathering data for *The Baseball Necrology*. Supplementing the obituary research, I also used information from public records, cemetery records, many calls to cemetery caretakers and funeral directors and, occasionally, visits to local libraries — especially in Texas.

Information in obituaries varies greatly from a single line that may only list the name of the decedent and the funeral director to pages of biographical information, some of which is of little interest for the purposes of *The Baseball Necrology*. Obituary information in large city newspapers is usually the most sparse, while those of smaller towns are more wordy. Consequently, the short descriptive entries in *The Baseball Necrology* vary according to what information was available. In a good many cases an obituary might give a blow-by-blow description of the decedent's baseball career, information that is not included in

The Baseball Necrology, but little insight regarding what he did in the thirty years following his baseball days.

A large portion of obituaries in the large cities of California, where over 11 percent of the population of late ballplayers died, fit the category of having only single line entries. Fortunately, in California death records are available to the public at County Recorder offices. Consequently, I visited most of California's 58 county courthouses at least once, some of them twice, in order to gather the desired information.

A special mention must also be made about my chosen home state of Texas. The central repository of newspapers in Texas is the Center for American History in Austin. Even though this library is one of the leading benefactors of funds from the USNP, it has one of the poorest collections of newspapers encountered on this project, not even having good coverage for some of the state's major cities. This made it necessary to visit many local libraries throughout one of the largest states in order to do justice to the nearly 5 percent of ballplayers who died in Texas.

In about 10 percent of the population of deceased major league ballplayers I was unable to locate an obituary of any sort, or any indication that the person ever lived or died. This could be for several reasons.

A good many of them died in the Latin countries of North, Central and South America. Because of cultural and language barriers no attempt was made to research outside the United States. This is left for the research of some ambitious person in the future. Other reasons for missing obituaries are that a newspaper was not readily available in the location the person died, or because I didn't have the correct death place or date. It could be that the person was at a location he wasn't known when he died and that an obituary exists somewhere in another area, or that there just wasn't an obituary printed. In some instances I was unable to locate a newspaper for the time and place where the person died.

A good many of the ballplayers listed in *The Baseball Necrology* played in only one season, some maybe in only a single game or just part of an inning. Even though such players may be somewhat obscure, the decision was made early in the course of my research to include every person who ever played in a major league game. The reason for this was twofold. First, where does one draw the line — be it more than one season — more than two seasons — more than a single game? Wherever the line was drawn, someone of some importance to someone would be left out, so all are included. Second, the major leagues are the utopia of baseball — the goal of every ballplayer who ever played the game. In order for that ballplayer to have made it to the major leagues he had to be pretty good and well known at some level, and therefore included in this history of deceased major league baseball players. There were many really good minor league players who never made it to the major leagues, but they are not included for the very reason that they did not ever play in the major leagues.

Some people who have reviewed my manuscript have been critical of the fact that I do not indicate who the player played for. This is for many reasons. First, this is not a baseball book. It is a book about baseball players — what they did after their baseball playing days were over, cause of death, and where they are buried. What they did as baseball players is well documented in various versions of the *Baseball Encyclopedia*, and I strongly recommend that every true baseball fan own the latest version of this outstanding reference work. Also, the size of *The Baseball Necrology* has always been a major concern, and therefore including more baseball related information would only make it larger and more unwieldy. Finally, also size related, some of these ballplayers played for many teams during their careers — some for several teams in just a single season.

The Baseball Necrology includes all of the following information I could locate for any deceased person who ever played in a major league baseball game, and also some other baseball personalities such as umpires, managers, owners, administrators, announcers, sportswriters and those who played in the Negro Leagues:

Player — The number of years played in the major leagues and the primary position played. The number of years as a field manager (if applicable)
Hall of Fame indication
Date and place of birth
Date and place of death
Military Service, when found
Obituary information about his after-baseball career
Cause of death
Burial place

In rare instances, an interesting piece of baseball trivia was found in an obituary that I have included, thinking that it could be lost if I didn't capture it. If the number of years and primary position are excluded, it was because the person was a baseball personality and not a player. Some parts of the above information might be, and in a good many instances is, missing. If I couldn't find it, I was unable to include it.

The very sizeable appendix presents burial locations for all players and personalities for whom I could find information, arranged by state, then city and then cemetery.

As with any research project of this size, there are errors. These may be clerical errors, errors of interpretation or errors of omission. The compiler has made every effort to keep these to a minimum, but they are there, and with the reader's support they can be corrected in future editions. Please write in care of the publisher and let me know what needs to be corrected and what is the accurate information. If a reply is requested, please enclose a stamped, self-addressed envelope.

Bill Lee

The Necrology

A

Tommie Aaron—7 Years Infielder (b. 5 Aug 1939 Mobile AL–d. 16 Aug 1984 Emory University Hospital, Atlanta GA) He worked his entire life in the Braves organization as a player, coach and minor league manager. Died from leukemia. Buried Catholic Cemetery, Mobile AL.

Ed Abbaticchio—9 Years Infielder (b. 15 Apr 1877 Latrobe PA–d. 6 Jan 1957 Fort Lauderdale FL) He was the first proprietor of the Abbaticchio Hotel before retiring to Florida about 1941. Died from cancer. Buried St Mary's Cemetery, Latrobe PA.

Bert Abbey—5 Years Pitcher (b. 29 Nov 1869 Essex VT–d. 11 Jun 1962 Fanny Allen Hospital, Essex Junction VT) He helped his son operate Gardenside Nurseries at Shelburne VT. Buried Mountain View Cemetery, Essex Center VT.

Charlie Abbey—5 Years Outfielder (b. 14 Oct 1866 near Salem NE–d. 2 May 1926 Park Emergency Hospital, San Francisco CA) His baseball career came to an abrupt end in 1897 when he was accidentally run over in Washington DC, causing the amputation of an arm. He was a newspaper vender when he died. Died from the rupture of an aortic aneurysm. Buried Steele Cemetery, Falls City NE.

Dan Abbott—1 Year Pitcher (b. 16 May 1862 Portage OH–d. 13 Feb 1930 Ottawa Lake MI) Buried Weston Cemetery, Weston OH.

Fred Abbott—3 Years Catcher (b. 22 Oct 1874 Versailles OH–d. 11 Jun 1935 at his home in Los Angeles CA) He owned and operated a gas station. Died from a heart attack. Buried Valhalla Memorial Park, North Hollywood CA.

Ody Abbott—1 Year Outfielder (b. 5 Sep 1886 New Eagle PA–d. 13 Apr 1933 Walter Reed Hospital, Washington DC) Served in the U.S. Army during World War I. He was deputy sheriff, then sheriff, and deputy sheriff again, of Washington County, PA. Died from heart trouble and complications after three months of hospitalization. Buried Monongahela Cemetery, Monongahela PA.

Al Aber—6 Years Pitcher (b. 31 Jul 1927 Cleveland OH–d. 20 May 1993 Marymount Hospital, Garfield Heights OH) Served in the U.S. Army in Germany. He was a sales rep for Myron Nickman Corporation and Professional Housewares Distributors, both Cleveland-based distributors of housewares. Died from a chronic heart problem, collapsing while shopping for plants for his backyard. Cremated.

Woody Abernathy—2 Years Pitcher (b. 1 Feb 1915 Forest City NC–d. 5 Dec 1994 at his home in Louisville KY) He was a retired loom repairman for Reeves Brothers Textile Company in South Carolina. Buried Resthaven Memorial Park, Louisville KY.

Cliff Aberson—3 Years Outfielder (b. 28 Aug 1921 Chicago IL–d. 23 Jun 1973 Kaiser Hospital, Vallejo CA) Also a professional football player, he lived in Fairfield CA and was a real estate agent there. Died from cancer of the esophagus. Buried Suisun-Fairfield Cemetery, Fairfield CA.

Harry Ables—3 Years Pitcher (b. 4 Oct 1884 Terrell TX–d. 8 Feb 1951 San Antonio TX) He managed the Builder's Lumber Company. Buried San Jose Burial Park, San Antonio TX.

Cal Abrams—8 Years Outfielder (b. 2 Mar 1924

Philadelphia PA–d. 25 Feb 1997 North Ridge Med Center, Fort Lauderdale FL) He owned several cocktail lounges on Long Island and worked for New York City's off-track betting before retiring to Florida in 1984. Died after suffering a heart attack five days earlier. Buried Star of David Memorial Gardens, North Lauderdale FL.

George Abrams—1 Year Pitcher (b. 9 Nov 1897 Seattle WA–d. 5 Dec 1986 Morton Plant Hospital, Clearwater FL) For 28 years he was a district manager for Acushnet Company of New Bedford MA. An avid golfer, he retired to Clearwater from Evanston IL in 1951. Buried Sylvan Abbey Memorial Park, Clearwater FL.

Joe Abreu—1 Year Infielder (b. 24 May 1913 Oakland CA–d. 17 Mar 1993 St Rose Nursing Facility, Hayward CA) Served in the U.S. Navy during World War II. Died from congestive heart failure, but suffered from diabetes. Cremated. Buried Evergreen-Washelli Cemetery, Seattle WA.

Bill Abstein—3 Years Infielder (b. 2 Feb 1885 St Louis MO–d. 8 Apr 1940 St Louis MO) In addition to baseball he was also an accomplished soccer star. Died following a lingering illness. Buried Bethlehem Cemetery, Bellefontaine Neighbors MO.

Jose Acosta—3 Years Pitcher (b. 4 Mar 1891 Havana, Cuba–d. 16 Nov 1977 Havana, Cuba).

Merito Acosta—5 Years Outfielder (b. 2 Jun 1896 Havana, Cuba–d. 16 Nov 1963 Miami FL).

Jerry Adair—13 Years Infielder (b. 17 Dec 1936 Sand Springs OK–d. 31 May 1987 Tulsa OK) He coached for the A's. Died from liver cancer. Buried Woodland Cemetery, Sand Springs OK.

Jimmy Adair—1 Year Infielder (b. 25 Jan 1907 Waxahachie TX–d. 9 Dec 1982 Dallas TX) He spent 48 years in baseball as a player, coach, scout and minor league manager. Buried Hillcrest Memorial Park, Dallas TX.

Babe Adams—19 Years Pitcher (b. 18 May 1882 Tipton IN–d. 27 Jul 1968 at his home in Silver Spring MD) He farmed near Mount Moriah MO until 1958 when he retired to Silver Spring. Died after a long illness.

Bert Adams—8 Years Catcher (b. 21 Jun 1891 Wharton TX–d. 24 Jun 1940 Hollywood Hospital, Los Angeles CA) He was a grip at Paramount Studios for 17 years. Died from pneumonia following an intestinal ailment. Buried Hollywood Memorial Park Cemetery, Los Angeles CA.

Bob Adams—2 Years Pitcher (b. 20 Jan 1907 Birmingham AL–d. 6 Mar 1970 Jacksonville FL) Living in Jacksonville more than 40 years, he was a mail foreman with the Jacksonville Terminal Company. Buried Restlawn Memorial Park, Jacksonville FL.

Bob Adams—1 Year Pitcher (b. 24 Jul 1901 Holyoke MA–d. 17 Oct 1996 Lemoyne PA).

Bobby Adams—14 Years Infielder (b. 14 Dec 1921 Tuolumne CA–d. 13 Feb 1997 Gig Harbor WA).

Buster Adams—6 Years Outfielder (b. 24 Jun 1915 Trinidad CO–d. 1 Sep 1990 Eisenhower Medical Center, Rancho Mirage CA) Died from congestive heart failure. Buried Eternal Hills Memorial Park, Oceanside CA.

Dan Adams—2 Years Pitcher (b. 19 Jun 1887 St Louis MO–d. 6 Oct 1964 St Louis MO) Buried Resurrection Cemetery, St Louis MO.

Joe Adams—1 Year Pitcher (b. 28 Oct 1877 Cowden IL–d. 8 Oct 1952 at his home in Montgomery City MO) He operated a dog kennel at Herrick IL for several years. Buried Myers Cemetery, Herrick IL.

Karl Adams—2 Years Pitcher (b. 11 Aug 1891 Columbus GA–d. 17 Sep 1967 at a hospital in Everett WA) Served in the U.S. Army during World War I. A retired pipefitter, he had lived in Everett 27 years. Prior to that he was a golf pro in Illinois and Kentucky. Died following an extended illness. Cremated. Buried Cypress Lawn Memorial Park, Everett WA.

Rick Adams—1 Year Pitcher (b. 24 Dec 1878 Paris TX–d. 10 Mar 1955 at his home in Paris TX) Died unexpectedly from a heart attack. Buried Providence Cemetery, Paris TX .

Sparky Adams—13 Years Infielder (b. 26 Aug 1894 Newtown PA–d. 24 Feb 1989 Good Samaritan Hospital, Pottsville PA) He owned and operated a service station in Schuykill County, PA, until his retirement. Buried Reformed Cemetery, Tremont PA.

Spencer Adams—4 Years Infielder (b. 21 Jun 1897 Layton UT–d. 25 Nov 1970 Salt Lake City UT) He retired from Hill Air Force Base at

Ogden UT. Died from natural causes. Buried Kaysville-Layton Memorial Park, Layton UT.

Willie Adams—5 Years Pitcher (b. 27 Sep 1890 Clearfield PA–d. 18 Jun 1937 at his home in Albany NY) His baseball career was shortened by a heart attack in 1922. He worked in the shop for the New York Central Railroad. Buried Philipsburg PA.

Joe Adcock—17 Years Infielder 1 Year Manager (b. 30 Oct 1927 Coushatta LA–d. 3 May 1999 Coushatta LA) He was one of the leading breeders of thoroughbred horses in Louisiana. Died from the complications of Alzheimer's disease. Buried Holly Springs Cemetery, Martin LA.

Bob Addie—Hall of Fame (b. abt 1910 New York City NY–d. 18 Jan 1982 Suburban Hospital, Bethesda MD) Served in Europe for the U.S. Army Air Corps during World War II. He was a sportswriter for a number of newspapers, including the *Washington Post*, from the 1930s until retiring in 1977. Died from cardiorespiratory arrest after a number of strokes. Buried St Gabriel's Cemetery, Potomac MD.

Bob Addy—2 Years Outfielder 1 Year Manager (b. 1838 Rochester NY–d. 9 Apr 1910 Pocatello ID) He was one of the early settlers in Pocatello ID where he owned and operated a hardware store. Died from a stroke of apoplexy. Buried Mountain View Cemetery, Pocatello ID.

Morrie Aderholt—5 Years Outfielder (b. 13 Sep 1915 Mt Olive NC–d. 18 Mar 1955 Sarasota FL) He managed minor league teams and scouted for the Senators. Died following a heart attack. Buried Appomattox Cemetery, Hopewell VA.

Dick Adkins—1 Year Infielder (b. 3 Mar 1920 Electra TX–d. 12 Sep 1955 Electra Hospital, Electra TX) He lived at Clovis NM eight years and was a warehouseman for the Clovis Air Force Supply Department there. Died from brain cancer. Buried Electra Memorial Park, Electra TX.

Doc Adkins—2 Years Pitcher (b. 5 Aug 1872 Troy WI–d. 21 Feb 1934 Durham NC).

Grady Adkins—2 Years Pitcher (b. 29 Jun 1897 Jacksonville AR–d. 31 Mar 1966 at his home in Little Rock AR) He played in the American Association, Texas League and Southern Association and served as a deputy sheriff in Pulaski County, AR, for 20 years. Later he was a bondsman and also a court bailiff. Buried Pine Crest Memorial Park, Alexander AR.

Henry Adkinson—1 Year Outfielder (b. 1 Sep 1874 Chicago IL–d. 1 May 1923 Salt Lake City UT) He was a miner after his baseball days were over. Buried Oak Woods Cemetery, Chicago IL.

Tommie Agee—12 Years Outfielder (b. 9 Aug 1942 Magnolia AL–d. 22 Jan 2001 New York City NY) He worked for Stewart Title Insurance Company in New York City. Died from a heart attack while leaving his office. Buried Pine Crest Cemetery, Mobile AL.

Harry Agganis—2 Years Infielder (b. 20 Apr 1930 Lynn MA–d. 27 Jun 1955 Santa Maria Hospital, Cambridge MA) He died at the height of his baseball career from a massive pulmonary embolism following pneumonia and a lung infection. Buried Pine Grove Cemetery, Lynn MA.

Joe Agler—3 Years Infielder (b. 12 Jun 1889 Coshocton OH–d. 26 Apr 1971 City Hospital, Massillon OH) He owned a retail grocery store in Canton OH before operating a service station and motel on Highway 62 near there. He was also active in Canton city politics. Died following a brief illness. Buried Warstler Church Cemetery, Canton OH.

Sam Agnew—7 Years Catcher (b. 12 Apr 1887 Farmington MO–d. 19 Jul 1951 Valley District Hospital, Sonoma CA) He owned a service station at Boyes Hot Springs CA. Died from a stroke brought on by a heart condition. Cremated. Buried Chapel of the Chimes, Santa Rosa CA.

Hank Aguire—16 Years Pitcher (b. 31 Jan 1931 Azusa CA–d. 5 Sep 1994 at his home in Bloomfield Hills MI) He owned and operated Mexican Industries, a multi-million dollar auto parts manufacturing company from 1979 until his death. It was the largest Hispanic business in Michigan. Died from prostate cancer. Buried San Gabriel Mission Cemetery, San Gabriel CA.

Eddie Ainsmith—15 Years Catcher (b. 4 Feb 1890 Cambridge MA–d. 6 Sep 1981 Fort Lauderdale FL).

Raleigh Aitchison—3 Years Pitcher (b. 5 Dec 1887 Tyndall SD–d. 26 Sep 1958 Columbus City Hospital, Columbus KS) For 18 years he worked for the Columbus police and was a deputy sheriff for Cherokee County, KS, at one time. He worked for the Spencer Chemical Company from 1948 until he retired in 1955. A well-known trainer of bird dogs, he enjoyed hunting and fishing. Died after an illness of two years. Buried Columbus City Cemetery, Columbus KS.

George Aiton—1 Year Outfielder (b. 29 Dec 1890 Kingman KS–d. 16 Aug 1976 Valley Palms Conv Hosp, North Hollywood CA) He was a security guard at Desert Inn Hotel. Died from generalized arteriosclerotic heart disease and dementia. Cremated.

John Ake—1 Year Infielder (b. 29 Aug 1861 Altoona PA–d. 11 May 1887 La Crosse WI) He died at the height of his baseball career by drowning in the Mississippi River in a boating accident. His body was never recovered.

Bill Akers—4 Years Infielder (b. 25 Dec 1904 Chattanooga TN–d. 13 Apr 1962 at a hospital in Chattanooga TN) He was a retired Air Force Sergeant. Buried Chattanooga National Cemetery, Chattanooga TN.

Jerry Akers—1 Year Pitcher (b. 1 Nov 1887 Shelbyville IN–d. 15 May 1979 Veteran's Hospital, Bay Pines FL) World War I veteran. He managed a Robert Hall clothing store in Columbus OH until 1953 when he retired to Florida. Died from heart disease. Buried Garden of Memories, Tampa FL.

Cy Alberts—1 Year Pitcher (b. 14 Jan 1882 Grand Rapids MI–d. 27 Aug 1917 St Joseph Hospital, Fort Wayne IN) He conducted a saloon in Fort Wayne. Died from ulcers of the kidneys. Buried Catholic Cemetery, Fort Wayne IN.

Gus Alberts—3 Years Infielder (b. 1860 Reading PA–d. 8 May 1912 Idaho Springs CO) He mined in the Idaho Springs area while living at Alice CO. Died from asthma. Buried Mount Olivet Cemetery, Wheat Ridge CO.

Ed Albrecht—2 Years Pitcher (b. 28 Feb 1929 St Louis MO–d. 29 Dec 1979 Centreville Hospital, Centreville IL) He was a truck driver. Died from a heart attack. Buried St Joseph Cemetery, Dupo IL.

Jack Albright—1 Year Infielder (b. 30 Jun 1921 St Petersburg FL–d. 22 Jul 1991 Sharp Knollwood Conv Hosp, San Diego CA) World War II veteran. For 30 years he was a security officer. Died from head injuries suffered in a fall at his home. Cremated. Buried Fort Rosecrans National Cemetery, Point Loma CA.

Scotty Alcock—1 Year Infielder (b. 29 Nov 1885 Wooster OH–d. 30 Jan 1973 Wooster OH).

Dale Alderson—2 Years Pitcher (b. 9 Mar 1918 Belden NE–d. 12 Feb 1982 Palm Harbor General Hosp, Garden Grove CA) He was a school teacher at Cherokee IA for 30 years. Died from a heart attack. Buried Alderson Family Cemetery, Belden NE.

Vic Aldridge—9 Years Pitcher (b. 25 Oct 1893 Indian Springs IN–d. 17 Apr 1973 St Anthony Hospital, Terre Haute IN) Served in the U.S. Navy during World War I. He entered law school after retiring from baseball, and was admitted to the Indiana bar. He served 12 years as a senator in the Indiana legislature. Buried Trinity Springs Cemetery, Trinity Springs IN.

Bob Alexander—2 Years Pitcher (b. 7 Aug 1922 Vancouver, British Columbia, Canada–d. 7 Apr 1993 Tri-City Medical Center, Oceanside CA) World War II veteran. He was a salesman for S & H Green Stamps for 20 years. Died from a heart attack. He was cremated and his ashes scattered off the coast of Point Loma CA.

Dale Alexander—5 Years Infielder (b. 26 Apr 1903 Greenville TN–d. 2 Mar 1979 Laughlin Memorial Hospital, Greenville TN) He spent his entire adult life in baseball as a player, coach, scout and minor league manager. Buried Shiloh Cemetery, Tusculum TN.

Grover Alexander—20 Years Pitcher Hall of Fame (b. 26 Feb 1887 Elba NE–d. 4 Nov 1950 in his room at St Paul NE) World War I veteran. Died from a heart ailment. Buried Elmwood Cemetery, St Paul NE.

Hugh Alexander—1 Year Outfielder (b. 10 Jul 1917 Buffalo MO–d. 25 Nov 2000 Oklahoma City OK) He scouted 61 years in the major leagues, including time with the Cubs, Indians, White Sox, Dodgers and Phillies. His playing career ended abruptly in 1937 when his left hand was severed while he was working at an Oklahoma oil well. Buried Maple Grove Cemetery, Seminole OK.

Nin Alexander—1 Year Catcher (b. 24 Nov 1858 Pana IL–d. 22 Dec 1933 at his home in Pana IL) A prominent citizen of Pana IL, he worked in the newspaper business, ran a meat market, was postmaster four years, served as mayor and was a city councilman. Died from pneumonia. Buried West Mound Cemetery, Pana IL.

Walt Alexander—5 Years Catcher (b. 5 Mar 1891 Atlanta GA–d. 29 Dec 1978 Fort Worth TX) He managed several minor league teams in

Texas before working in construction in the Dallas area. He lived in Dallas 50 years before moving to Fort Worth in 1966. Buried Grove Hill Memorial Park, Dallas TX.

Bob Allen—7 Years Infielder 1 Year Manager (b. 10 Jul 1867 Marion OH–d. 14 May 1943 at a hospital in Little Rock AR) He was known as the "Dean of Southern Association baseball." At different times he owned the Montgomery, Nashville, Little Rock and Knoxville teams in that league. Buried Roselawn Memorial Park, Little Rock AR.

Bob Allen—1 Year Outfielder (b. 13 Oct 1894 Muscoda WI–d. 18 Dec 1975 Naperville IL).

Ethan Allen—13 Years Outfielder (b. 1 Jan 1904 Cincinnati OH–d. 15 Sep 1993 Crescent City Hospital, Brookings OR) He coached baseball at Yale University, directed ten films for the National League and invented the game "All-Star Baseball."

Frank Allen—6 Years Pitcher (b. 26 Aug 1888 Newbern AL–d. 30 Jul 1933 Gainesville AL) Died from a heart attack at the home of his father-in-law while enroute from his home in Newbern to Meridian MS.

Hezekiah Allen—1 Year Catcher (b. 25 Feb 1863 Westport CT–d. 21 Sep 1916 at his home in Saugatuck CT) For years he was the constable of Westport. Died after a year's illness. Buried Willowbrook Cemetery, Westport CT.

Horace Allen—1 Year Outfielder (b. 11 Jun 1899 DeLand FL–d. 5 Jul 1981 Canton NC) He played professional football as well as baseball and retired from baseball in 1926 in order to devote full-time to professional golf. He owned the College Arms Country Club in De Land FL from 1946 to 1955. Died from cancer. Buried Oakdale Cemetery, De Land FL.

Jack Allen—1 Year Infielder (b. 2 Oct 1855 Woodstock IL–d. 21 Apr 1915 Girard PA).

John Allen—1 Year Pitcher (b. 27 Oct 1890 Berkeley Springs WV–d. 24 Sep 1967 Hagerstown MD) Served in Europe during World War I. He retired from Fairchild Aircraft in 1959 after working there 17 years. Died enroute to the hospital from a heart attack. Buried Rose Hill Cemetery, Hagerstown MD.

Johnny Allen—13 Years Pitcher (b. 30 Sep 1905 Lenoir NC–d. 29 Mar 1959 at his home in St Petersburg FL) He moved to St Petersburg in 1933 and dealt in real estate there. Died from a heart attack. Buried Forest Lawn Cemetery, Greensboro NC.

Lee Allen—(b. 15 Jan 1915 Cincinnati OH–d. 20 May 1969 St Joseph's Hospital, Syracuse NY) Starting as a public relations man for the Cincinnati Reds before working for several newspapers and radio stations, he was an historian for the National Baseball Hall of Fame at Cooperstown NY when he died. Died from a heart attack when he was returning to Cooperstown after a trip to Cincinnati. Buried Boca Raton Cemetery, Boca Raton FL.

Mel Allen—Hall of Fame (b. 14 Feb 1913 Johns AL–d. 16 Jun 1996 at his home in Greenwich CT) He was the radio announcer for the New York Yankees from 1939 to 1964 and had a syndicated television show from 1977 to 1995. Died from a heart attack. Buried Beth El Cemetery, Stamford CT.

Myron Allen—4 Years Outfielder (b. 22 Mar 1854 Kingston NY–d. 8 Mar 1924 City Hospital, Kingston NY) He was a caretaker at the Central Post Office in Kingston. Died after suddenly becoming ill at work two days earlier. Buried Rhinebeck Cemetery, Rhinebeck NY.

Newt Allen—21 Years Infielder 1 Year Manager (b. 19 May 1901 Austin TX–d. 11 Jun 1988 Cincinnati OH) He played in the negro leagues.

Nick Allen—6 Years Catcher (b. 14 Sep 1888 Udall KS–d. 16 Oct 1939 Hines Memorial Hospital, Chicago IL) He managed teams in the American Association.

Pete Allen—1 Year Catcher (b. 1 May 1868 Columbiana OH–d. 16 Apr 1946 Jefferson Hospital, Philadelphia PA) A medical doctor, he was an assistant professor of proctology at Jefferson Medical College from 1936 until his death. Died after a short illness.

Sled Allen—1 Year Catcher (b. 23 Aug 1886 West Plains MO–d. 16 Oct 1959 West Texas Hospital, Lubbock TX) He managed some minor league baseball. For 27 years he promoted sports, especially wrestling, in Lubbock. Owned Allen's Arena in Lubbock. Died from bone cancer. Buried Lubbock City Cemetery, Lubbock TX.

Art Allison—1 Year Outfielder (b. 29 Jan 1849 Philadelphia PA–d. 25 Feb 1916 Casualty Hospital, Washington DC) He worked in the monotype section of the government printing office. Killed when he was run over by a truck while walking to work in a blinding snowstorm.

Bob Allison—12 Years Outfielder (b. 11 Jul 1934 Raytown MO–d. 10 Apr 1995 at his home in Rio Verde AZ) He was a salesman for Coca-Cola Midwest. Died from olivopontocerebellar atrophy, a form of ataxia. Ataxia is a neurological disease causing degeneration of motor activities. He spent his last few years in a wheel-chair. Cremated.

Doug Allison—5 Years Catcher (b. 1846 Philadelphia PA–d. 19 Dec 1916 Washington DC) Civil War veteran. He worked for the Post Office in Washington DC. Dropped dead while leaving his home for work.

Mack Allison—3 Years Pitcher (b. 23 Jan 1887 Owensboro KY–d. 12 Mar 1964 Mount Vernon MO) He spent 27 years in professional baseball. He was a jailor in St Joseph MO before moving to United States Engineering Company in 1940, working there as a pipefitter. Buried Mount Washington Cemetery, Independence MO.

Milo Allison—4 Years Outfielder (b. 16 Oct 1889 Elk Rapids MI–d. 18 Jun 1957 at a hospital in Kenosha WI) He worked for an extended period for the Jenor Lodge at Maiden Lake. Died after a four-year bout with cancer. Buried Community Bible Church Cemetery, Lakewood WI.

Mel Almada—7 Years Outfielder (b. 7 Feb 1913 Hwatabampo, Mexico–d. 13 Aug 1988 Hermosillo, Mexico).

Rafael Almeida—7 Years Outfielder (b. 30 Jul 1887 Havana, Cuba–d. 19 Mar 1968 Havana, Cuba).

Luis Aloma—4 Years Pitcher (b. 23 Jul 1923 Havana, Cuba–d. 7 Apr 1997 Park Ridge IL).

Whitey Alperman—4 Years Infielder (b. 11 Nov 1879 Etna PA–d. 25 Dec 1942 St Margaret's Hospital, Pittsburgh PA) Buried Mount Royal Cemetery, Glenshaw PA.

Tom Alston—4 Years Infielder (b. 31 Jan 1926 Greensboro NC–d. 30 Dec 1993 Human Service Alliance, Winston-Salem NC) Served in the U.S. Navy during World War II. Buried New Goshen Church Cemetery, Greensboro NC.

Walter Alston—1 Year Infielder 23 Years Manager Hall of Fame (b. 1 Dec 1911 Venice OH–d. 1 Oct 1984 McCullough-Hyde Memorial Hosp, Oxford OH) He spent his entire life in baseball. Died from heart disease after suffering a heart attack early in 1983. Buried Darrtown Cemetery, Darrtown OH.

Ernie Alten—1 Year Pitcher (b. 1 Dec 1894 Avon OH–d. 9 Sep 1981 Queen of the Valley Hospital, Napa CA) Served in the U.S. Army in France and Germany during World War I. He worked for the Alaska Packers cannery in Alameda CA before becoming a security guard at the Oakland Naval Air Station, retiring in 1960. Died from a ruptured aortic aneurysm, but also suffered from bladder cancer. Buried Yountville Cemetery, Yountville CA.

Jesse Altenburg—2 Years Outfielder (b. 2 Jan 1893 Ashley MI–d. 12 Mar 1973 at a hospital in Lansing MI) World War I veteran. He managed some minor league baseball. Lived 50 years in Lansing and directed teams in the city recreation league there. Buried North Star Cemetery, North Star MI.

Dave Altizer—6 Years Infielder (b. 6 Nov 1876 Pearl IL–d. 14 May 1964 Pleasant Hill IL) He served in the U.S. Army and saw action during the Boxer Rebellion in China in 1900. Buried Crescent Heights Cemetery, Pleasant Hill IL.

George Alton—1 Year Outfielder (b. 29 Dec 1890 Kingman KS–d. 16 Aug 1976 Van Nuys CA).

Nick Altrock—19 Years Pitcher (b. 15 Sep 1876 Cincinnati OH–d. 20 Jan 1965 Doctor's Hospital, Washington DC) He was a coach known for his pregame clowning with comic Al Schacht. Died from uremia after suffering a stroke two and a half years earlier. Buried Vine Street Hill Cemetery, Cincinnati OH.

Wayne Ambler—3 Years Infielder (b. 8 Nov 1915 Abington PA–d. 3 Jan 1998 Ponte Vedra Beach FL) Served as a gunnery officer in the U.S. Navy on a merchant ship during World War II. He worked 10 years for Container Corporation and 35 years for Standard Press Steel and Pier I Imports, retiring to Ponte Vedra Beach in 1986.

Red Ames—17 Years Pitcher (b. 2 Aug 1882 Warren OH–d. 8 Oct 1936 Warren OH) He operated a bowling alley in Warren for many years and later went into the dairy business. Died from pulmonary failure due to asthma. Buried Oakwood Cemetery, Warren OH.

Doc Amole—2 Years Pitcher (b. 5 Jul 1878 Coatesville PA–d. 7 Mar 1912 at his home in Wilmington DE) He was a carpenter. Died from congestion of the lungs.

Sandy Amoros—7 Years Outfielder (b. 30 Jan 1930 Havana, Cuba–d. 27 Jun 1992 Jackson Memorial Hospital, Miami FL) Nearly destitute and in failing health he died from pneumonia. He had lost a leg to diabetes and had battled circulatory problems. Buried Woodlawn Park Cemetery, Miami FL.

Walter Ancker—1 Year Pitcher (b. 10 Apr 1894 New York City NY–d. 13 Feb 1954 Englewood Hospital, Englewood NJ) World War I veteran. He was associated with the Bergen County, NJ, adjuster's office for many years. Buried George Washington Memorial Park, Paramus NJ.

Alf Anderson—3 Years Infielder (b. 28 Jan 1914 Gainesville GA–d. 23 Jun 1985 Albany GA) Buried Crown Hill Cemetery, Albany GA.

Andy Anderson—2 Years Infielder (b. 13 Nov 1922 Bremerton WA–d. 18 Jul 1982 Seattle WA) Served in the U.S. Army during World War II and was a Prisoner of War. Buried Evergreen-Washelli Cemetery, Seattle WA.

Bill Anderson—1 Year Pitcher (b. 3 Dec 1895 Boston MA–d. 13 Mar 1983 Lawrence Memorial Hospital, Medford MA) Served in the U.S. Army during World War II. He was a clerk for the Boston Market Terminal and the New England Produce Company. Buried Forest Hill Cemetery, Derry NH.

Dave Anderson—2 Years Pitcher (b. 10 Oct 1868 Chester PA–d. 22 Mar 1897 Chester PA) Buried Chester Rural Cemetery, Chester PA.

Ferrell Anderson—2 Years Catcher (b. 9 Jan 1918 Maple City KS–d. 12 Mar 1978 St John's Medical Center, Joplin MO) World War II veteran. He played professional baseball 17 years. His last 17 years were spent as a general agent for Occidental Life Insurance Company. Died after a year of ill health. Buried Ozark Memorial Park Cemetery, Joplin MO.

Fred Anderson—7 Years Pitcher (b. 11 Dec 1885 Calahan NC–d. 8 Nov 1957 at his home in Winston-Salem NC) Served in the U.S. Army during World War I. He was a dentist in Winston-Salem from 1920 until he retired in 1948. He had been in ill health two years when he died from a self-inflicted shotgun blast to the chest. Buried Salem Cemetery, Winston-Salem NC.

George Anderson—3 Years Outfielder (b. 26 Sep 1889 Cleveland OH–d. 28 May 1962 Warrensville Heights OH) He was a deputy sheriff in Cuyahoga County, OH. Buried Calvary Cemetery, Cleveland OH.

Goat Anderson—1 Year Outfielder (b. 13 Jan 1880 Cleveland OH–d. 15 Mar 1923 Epworth Hospital, South Bend IN) He operated a cigar store in South Bend, and later, a soft drink and lunch room there. Died from stomach cancer. Buried Atlantic Cemetery, Atlantic PA.

Hal Anderson—1 Year Outfielder (b. 10 Feb 1904 St Louis MO–d. 1 May 1974 St Louis MO) Buried Calvary Cemetery, St Louis MO.

Harry Anderson—5 Years Outfielder (b. 10 Sep 1931 North East MD–d. 11 Jun 1998 at his home in Greenville DE) Died from a heart attack. Buried Wilmington-Brandywine Cemetery, Wilmington DE.

John Anderson—14 Years Outfielder (b. 14 Dec 1873 Sasbourg, Norway–d. 23 Jul 1949 Worcester MA) For about five years he was a policeman for the Worcester Police Department, then went back into baseball where he was a minor league coach. Buried Swedish Cemetery, Worcester MA.

Red Anderson—3 Years Pitcher (b. 19 Jun 1912 Lawton IA–d. 7 Aug 1972 at a hospital in Sioux City IA) Served in the U.S. Navy during World War II. He was a foreman for the Concrete Pipe Machinery Company. Died after a six-month illness. Buried Memorial Park Cemetery, Sioux City IA.

Rick Anderson—2 Years Pitcher (b. 25 Dec 1953 Inglewood CA–d. 23 Jun 1989 at his home in Wilmington CA) He was a truck driver for five years. Died from heart disease. Cremated.

Varney Anderson—4 Years Pitcher (b. 18 Jun 1866 Geneva IL–d. 5 Nov 1941 St Anthony Hospital, Rockford IL) For many years he was foreman of the jeweling room at the Rockford Watch Factory until it closed. He then opened his own watch shop in Rockford. Died following a brief illness. Buried Willwood Burial Park, Rockford IL.

Walter Anderson—2 Years Pitcher (b. 25 Sep 1897 Grand Rapids MI–d. 6 Jan 1990 Veteran's

Hospital, Battle Creek MI) Served in France for the U.S. Navy during World War I. He was involved in the furniture finishing business. Buried Fair Plains Cemetery, Grand Rapids MI.

Wingo Anderson—1 Year Pitcher (b. 13 Aug 1886 Alvarado TX–d. 19 Dec 1950 Fort Worth TX) He was a former Alvardo farmer and the sheriff of Hall County, TX, from 1937 to 1947. Died after he had been ill several months. Buried Crown Hill Cemetery, Dallas TX.

John Andre—1 Year Pitcher (b. 3 Jan 1923 Brockton MA–d. 25 Nov 1976 Centerville Nursing Home, Centerville MA) He worked at Dunfey's Restaurant in Hyannis MA. Died following a long illness. Buried People's Cemetery, Chatham MA.

Ed Andrews—8 Years Outfielder (b. 5 Apr 1859 Painesville OH–d. 12 Aug 1934 at a hospital in West Palm Beach FL) An early promoter, developer and entrepreneur in South Florida, he developed real estate in Palm Beach, owned a water company and wrote articles for outdoor and yachting magazines. Died two days after suffering a heart attack. Buried Woodlawn Cemetery, West Palm Beach FL.

Elbert Andrews—1 Year Pitcher (b. 11 Dec 1901 Greenwood SC–d. 25 Nov 1979 Self Memorial Hospital, Greenwood SC) He worked in the wholesale grocery business from 1915 to 1933 and was general manager of Long Motor Lines from 1938 to 1944. He then owned and managed the DeVore Andrews Company in Greenwood. He was also mayor of Greenwood for two terms. Died after a brief illness. Buried Edgewood Cemetery, Greenwood SC.

Ivy Andrews—8 Years Pitcher (b. 6 May 1907 Dora AL–d. 24 Nov 1970 Carraway Methodist Hospital, Birmingham AL) Died following a series of heart attacks. Buried Shanghi Cemetery, Quinton AL.

Jim Andrews—1 Year Outfielder (b. 5 Jun 1865 Shelburne Falls MA–d. 27 Dec 1907 Chicago IL) He was known for his expertise in Cook County, IL, estate. Died from lung trouble.

Nate Andrews—8 Years Pitcher (b. 30 Sep 1913 Pembroke NC–d. 26 Apr 1991 Baptist Hospital, Winston-Salem NC) Buried Rowland Cemetery, Rowland NC.

Stan Andrews—4 Years Catcher (b. 17 Apr 1917 Lynn MA–d. 10 Jun 1995 Bradenton FL).

Wally Andrews—3 Years Infielder (b. 18 Sep 1859 Philadelphia PA–d. 20 Jan 1940 at his home in Indianapolis IN) For 30 years he was timekeeper for the Indianapolis City Street Commission. Died following an illness of seven weeks. Buried Memorial Park Cemetery, Indianapolis IN.

Bill Andrus—2 Years Infielder (b. 25 Jul 1907 Beaumont TX–d. 12 Mar 1982 Washington DC).

Fred Andrus—2 Years Outfielder (b. 23 Aug 1850 Washington MI–d. 10 Nov 1937 Henry Ford Hospital, Detroit MI) He was connected with the management of the David Whitney estate for 35 years. Died from lobar pneumonia. Buried Woodlawn Cemetery, Detroit MI.

Tom Angley—1 Year Catcher (b. 2 Oct 1904 Baltimore MD–d. 26 Oct 1952 St Francis Hospital, Wichita KS) He moved to Wichita in 1941 and played semipro baseball almost until his death. Buried Wichita Park Cemetery, Wichita KS.

Pat Ankenman—3 Years Infielder (b. 23 Dec 1912 Houston TX–d. 13 Jan 1989 Houston TX) He managed some minor league baseball before owning and operating Camp Ozark from 1952 until retiring in 1985. Buried Memorial Oaks Cemetery, Houston TX.

Bill Annis—1 Year Outfielder (b. 8 Mar 1857 Stoneham MA–d. 10 Jun 1923 at his brother's home in Kennebunkport ME).

Cap Anson—22 Years Infielder 20 Years Manager Hall of Fame (b. 17 Apr 1852 Marshalltown IA–d. 14 Apr 1922 St Luke's Hospital, Chicago IL) Died following surgery for glandular trouble. Buried Oak Woods Cemetery, Chicago IL.

John Antonelli—2 Years Infielder (b. 15 Jul 1915 Memphis TN–d. 18 Apr 1990 at his home in Memphis TN) He was a salesman in the wine and liquor business between two careers in baseball as a player, minor league manager and coach—first as a youth, then later in life. Died after a lengthy illness. Buried Calvary Cemetery, Memphis TN.

Bill Antonello—1 Year Outfielder (b. 19 May 1927 Brooklyn NY–d. 4 Mar 1993 Fridley MN) World War II veteran. He was a steamfitter on the Alaskan pipeline and in St Paul MN. Buried Fort Snelling National Cemetery, Minneapolis MN.

Fred Applegate—1 Year Pitcher (b. 9 May 1879 Bradford PA–d. 21 Apr 1968 Divine Providence Hospital, Williamsport PA) He served as a Lycoming County, PA, commissioner from 1920 into the 1930s and later was county auditor. Buried Wildwood Cemetery, Williamsport PA.

Ed Appleton—2 Years Pitcher (b. 29 Feb 1892 Arlington TX–d. 27 Jan 1932 Arlington TX) World War I veteran. He was a special agent for the MKT Railway Company in Dallas TX. He dropped dead suddenly from apoplexy while training a bird dog in a field three miles north of Arlington. Buried Arlington Cemetery, Arlington TX.

Pete Appleton—14 Years Pitcher (b. 20 May 1904 Terryville CT–d. 18 Jan 1974 St Francis Hospital, Trenton NJ) He coached and scouted for the Twins almost up until his death. Buried St Gertrude's Cemetery, Colonia NJ.

Luke Appling—20 Years Infielder 1 Year Manager Hall of Fame (b. 2 Apr 1907 High Point NC–d. 3 Jan 1991 Lakeside Community Hospital, Cumming GA) Known as "Old Aches and Pains," he worked his entire life in baseball as a player, coach, manager and minor league manager. Up until 1990 he was a hitting instructor for the Braves. Died suddenly from an abdominal aneurysm. Buried Sawnee View Memorial Gardens, Cumming GA.

Angel Aragon—3 Years Infielder (b. 2 Aug 1893 Havana, Cuba–d. 24 Jan 1952 New York City NY).

Jack Aragon—1 Game Pinch Runner (b. 20 Nov 1915 Havana, Cuba–d. 4 Apr 1988 Morton Plant Hospital, Clearwater FL) Served in the U.S. Navy during World War II. He was a senior vice-president of Founder's Life Assurance Co, retiring to Clearwater from Greensboro NC in 1970. Buried Serenity Gardens Memorial Park, Largo FL.

Maurice Archdeacon—3 Years Outfielder (b. 14 Dec 1898 St Louis MO–d. 5 Sep 1954 St Louis MO) He scouted for the Yankees and Browns. Died following a long illness. Buried Memorial Park Cemetery, St Louis MO.

Fred Archer—2 Years Pitcher (b. 7 Mar 1912 Johnson City TN–d. 31 Oct 1981 Charlotte Memorial Hospital, Charlotte NC) He was a retired textile worker. Buried West Lawn Memorial Park, Landis NC.

Jimmy Archer—12 Years Catcher (b. 13 May 1883 Dublin, Ireland–d. 29 Mar 1958 St Mary's Hospital, Milwaukee WI) He was one of the first catchers to throw from a squatting position, and was feared by base runners because of his strong and accurate arm. Died from a heart ailment following surgery for tuberculosis of the spine. Buried Sacred Heart Cemetery, Boone IA.

Joe Ardner—2 Years Infielder (b. 27 Feb 1858 Mt Vernon OH–d. 15 Sep 1935 City Hospital, Cleveland OH) He was a theatre stageman. Died from broncho-pneumonia and heart failure. Buried Woodland Cemetery, Cleveland OH.

Frank Arellanes—3 Years Pitcher (b. 28 Jan 1882 Santa Cruz CA–d. 13 Dec 1918 at his home in San Jose CA) Died from pneumonia, brought on by influenza. Buried Oak Hill Memorial Park, San Jose CA.

Buzz Arlett—1 Year Outfielder (b. 3 Jan 1899 Elmhurst CA–d. 16 May 1964 Northwestern Hospital, Minneapolis MN) He played 20 years in the minor leagues, most of them in the American Association, and compiled a lifetime .341 minor league batting average while hitting 432 home runs. Died from a heart attack. Buried Lakewood Cemetery, Minneapolis MN.

Orville Armbrust—1 Year Pitcher (b. 2 Mar 1910 Beirne AR–d. 2 Oct 1967 at his home in Mobile AL) He lived at Mobile for 27 years. Buried Magnolia Cemetery, Mobile AL.

Charlie Armbruster—3 Years Catcher (b. 30 Aug 1880 Cincinnati OH–d. 7 Oct 1964 Grants Pass OR) Buried Granite Hill Cemetery, Grants Pass OR.

Harry Armbruster—1 Year Outfielder (b. 20 Mar 1882 Cincinnati OH–d. 11 Dec 1953 Cincinnati OH).

Bill Armour—5 Years Manager (b. 3 Sep 1869 Homestead PA–d. 2 Dec 1922 Swedish Hospital, Minneapolis MN) He is credited with finding several future hall of famers, including Ty Cobb. He conducted a restaurant in Minneapolis. Died following a stroke. Buried Homestead PA.

George Armstrong—1 Year Catcher (b. 3 Jun 1924 Orange NJ–d. 24 Jul 1993 Memorial Hospital, Orange NJ) For 35 years he was a fireman for the East Orange Fire Department, retiring in 1987. Cremated.

Howard Armstrong—1 Year Pitcher (b. 2 Dec 1889 East Claridon OH–d. 8 Mar 1926 St James Hospital, Hornell NY) He was the foreman of the printing room at the Up-to-Date Advertising Company at Canisteo NY. Died from pneumonia that developed after a severe case of blood poisoning. Buried Woodlawn Cemetery, Canisteo NY.

Harry Arndt—4 Years Infielder (b. 12 Feb 1879 South Bend IN–d. 24 Mar 1921 Healthwin Hospital, South Bend IN) He was active in baseball as a player, coach and minor league manager until health forced him to quit. Died from tuberculosis. Buried Cedar Grove Cemetery, South Bend IN.

Morrie Arnovich—7 Years Outfielder (b. 20 Nov 1910 Superior WI–d. 20 Jul 1959 at his home in Superior WI) After retiring as a player he was the co-owner of a sporting goods store, and also worked as a baseball scout. He was in apparent good health when he died from a coronary occlusion. Buried Hebrew Cemetery, Superior WI.

Orie Arntzen—1 Year Pitcher (b. 18 Oct 1909 Beverly IL–d. 28 Jan 1970 Cedar Rapids IA) He was the 1949 Minor League Player of the Year, and worked for Iowa Manufacturing Company. Died after a brief illness. Buried Cedar Memorial Park Cemetery, Cedar Rapids IA.

Harry Arundel—2 Years Pitcher (b. 1855 Philadelphia PA–d. 25 Mar 1904 Cleveland OH).

Tug Arundel—4 Years Catcher (b. 1863 Auburn NY–d. 5 Sep 1912 at a hospital in Ovid NY) Buried St Joseph's Cemetery, Auburn NY.

Jim Asbell—1 Year Outfielder (b. 22 Jun 1914 Dallas TX–d. 6 Jul 1967 Mills Memorial Hospital, San Mateo CA) He lived in San Mateo since 1949, working as West Coast public relations manager for Container Corporation of America until 1963 when he formed his own real estate investment and insurance firm. Died from a cerebral aneurysm. Buried Woodlawn Memorial Park, Daly City CA.

Asby Asbjornson—4 Years Catcher (b. 19 Jun 1909 Concord MA–d. 21 Jan 1970 Williamsport Hospital, Williamsport PA) He worked at Avco in Williamsport. Buried Wildwood Cemetery, Williamsport PA.

Ken Ash—4 Years Pitcher (b. 16 Sep 1901 Anmoore WV–d. 15 Nov 1979 United Hospital Center, Clarksburg WV) He retired from Union Carbide Corporation after 25 years service. Died following a three-month illness. Buried Elk View Masonic Cemetery, Clarksburg WV.

Richie Ashburn—15 Years Outfielder Hall of Fame (b. 20 Mar 1927 Tilden NE–d. 9 Sep 1997 New York City NY) He broadcast the Phillies games for 35 years. Died from a heart attack in a New York City hotel when the Phillies were on the road, playing the Mets. Buried United Methodist Church Cemetery, Gladwyne PA.

Emmett Ashford—(b. 23 Nov 1914 CA–d. 1 Mar 1980 Marina Mercy Hospital, Marina del Rey CA) The first black umpire in the major leagues, he umpired in the American League from 1965 to 1970. He had a showmanship flair in his style that kept the crowd entertained. After 1970 he worked in the commissioner's office and did some officiating of college sports in the Pac 10. Died from a heart attack. Cremated.

Tom Asmussen—1 Year Catcher (b. 26 Sep 1876 Chicago IL–d. 21 Aug 1963 Arlington Heights IL) Buried Ridgewood Cemetery, Des Plaines IL.

Charlie Atherton—1 Year Infielder (b. 19 Oct 1873 New Brunswick NJ–d. 19 Dec 1934 Vienna, Austria).

Tommy Atkins—2 Years Pitcher (b. 9 Dec 1887 Ponca NE–d. 7 May 1956 St Luke's Hospital, Cleveland OH) He was a maintenance man at the state highway garage. Died from a heart ailment.

Lefty Atkinson—1 Game Pinch Hitter (b. 4 Jun 1904 Chicago IL–d. 12 Feb 1961 Chicago IL) Buried Mount Carmel Cemetery, Hillside IL.

Al Atkisson—3 Years Pitcher (b. 9 Mar 1861 Clinton IL–d. 17 Jun 1952 at his home in McNatt MO) Well-known as an artist, he painted scenes of the Ozarks and was also an expert wood carver. Buried Macedonia Cemetery, Stella MO.

Dick Attreau—2 Years Infielder (b. 8 Apr 1897 Chicago IL–d. 5 Jul 1964 Chicago IL) Buried Mount Olivet Cemetery, Chicago IL.

Bill Atwood—5 Years Catcher (b. 25 Sep 1911 Rome GA–d. 14 Sep 1993 Snyder TX).

Jake Atz—4 Years Infielder (b. 1 Jul 1880 Washington DC–d. 22 May 1945 New Orleans LA) He spent his entire life in baseball as a player, umpire, minor league manager and executive. He won six straight pennants while managing Fort Worth in the Texas League from 1920 to 1925. Died after being ill several years. Buried Hope Mausoleum, New Orleans LA.

Harry Aubrey—1 Year Infielder (b. 5 Jul 1880 St Joseph MO–d. 18 Sep 1953 at his home in Baltimore MD) Buried Loudon Park National Cemetery, Baltimore MD.

Jimmy Austin—18 Years Infielder 3 Years Manager (b. 8 Dec 1879 Swansea, Wales–d. 6 Mar 1965 St Joseph Hospital, Orange CA) He coached for the White Sox. Died from a heart attack. Buried Melrose Abbey Cemetery, Orange CA.

Chick Autry—2 Years Infielder (b. 2 Jan 1885 Humboldt TN–d. 16 Jan 1976 at his home in Santa Rosa CA) He worked 34 years for the Light Oil Division of Standard Oil Company, retiring as an assistant superintendent. Died from a heart attack. Cremated. Buried Chapel of the Chimes, Santa Rosa CA.

Gene Autry—(b. 29 Sep 1907 Tioga TX–d. 2 Oct 1998 at his home in Studio City CA) Served in the Army Air Corps as a pilot in the Pacific during World War II. A famous cowboy movie star known as the "Singing Cowboy," he made 94 movies and used his show business earnings to invest in oil wells, radio and television stations and hotels. He owned the Angels from 1961 to 1995. Died from lymphoma. Buried Forest Lawn-Hollywood Hills, Los Angeles CA.

Martin Autry—6 Years Catcher (b. 5 Mar 1903 Martindale TX–d. 26 Jan 1950 at a hospital in Savannah GA) He managed minor league baseball up until his death. Died from a heart attack suffered two weeks earlier at his winter home on Colonel's Island, Georgia. Buried La Rosa Cemetery, Woodsboro TX.

Earl Averill—13 Years Outfielder Hall of Fame (b. 21 May 1902 Snohomish WA–d. 16 Aug 1983 Providence Hospital, Everett WA) He hit the linedrive that broke Dizzy Dean's toe in the 1937 All-Star Game—shortening Dean's career. He owned a flower shop in Snohomish WA for eight years before operating a motel there for 20 years, retiring in 1970. Died from pneumonia. Buried Grand Army of the Republic Cemetery, Snohomish WA.

Jay Avrea—1 Year Pitcher (b. 6 Jul 1920 Cleburne TX–d. 26 Jun 1987 Dallas TX) Buried Laurel Land Memorial Park, Dallas TX.

Jake Aydelott—2 Years Pitcher (b. 6 Jul 1861 North Manchester IN–d. 22 Oct 1926 Detroit MI).

Bill Ayers—1 Year Pitcher (b. 27 Sep 1919 Newnan GA–d. 24 Sep 1980 Newnan GA) Served in the U.S. Army during World War II. He was a route mail clerk for the U.S. Postal Service. Died from a heart attack while golfing. Buried Oakhill Cemetery, Newnan GA.

Doc Ayers—9 Years Pitcher (b. 20 May 1890 Fancy Gap VA–d. 26 May 1968 General Hospital, Pulaski VA) He managed minor league and semi-pro baseball before spending the rest of his life farming. Died from a heart attack. Buried Grantham Cemetery, Draper VA.

Dick Aylward—1 Year Catcher (b. 4 Jun 1925 Baltimore MD–d. 11 Jun 1983 at his home in Spring Valley CA) He was a truck driver for 20 years. Died from gastric cancer. Buried Glen Abbey Memorial Park, Bonita CA.

B

Charlie Babb—3 Years Infielder (b. 20 Feb 1873 Milwaukie OR–d. 19 Mar 1954 at his home in Portland OR) He managed minor league baseball. Cremated. Buried Portland Memorial, Portland OR.

Loren Babe—2 Years Infielder (b. 11 Jan 1928 Pisgah IA–d. 14 Feb 1984 at his home in Omaha NE) He spent his entire life in baseball as a coach, scout and minor league manager. Died from lung cancer. Buried Calvary Cemetery, Omaha NE.

Charlie Babington—1 Year Outfielder (b. 4 May 1895 Cranston RI–d. 22 Mar 1957 Providence RI) Died from injuries suffered in a fall.

Les Backman—2 Years Pitcher (b. 20 Mar 1888 Cleves OH–d. 8 Nov 1975 Cincinnati OH) Buried Spring Grove Cemetery, Cincinnati OH.

Eddie Bacon—1 Year Pitcher (b. 8 Apr 1898 Frankfort KY–d. 2 Oct 1963 Veteran's Hospital, Louisville KY) World War I veteran. Died following a short illness. Buried Peak's Mill Cemetery, Frankfort KY.

Fred Baczewski—3 Years Pitcher (b. 15 May 1926 St Paul MN–d. 14 Nov 1976 Brotman Memorial Hospital, Culver City CA) For 15 years he was a foreman for ARCO. Died from lung cancer. Buried Holy Cross Cemetery, Culver City CA.

Art Bader—1 Year Outfielder (b. 21 Sep 1886 St Louis MO–d. 5 Apr 1957 Missouri Baptist Hospital, St Louis MO) He retired from baseball early because of an injury, but used the money he had earned to put himself through law school. He practiced law in St Louis until 1929 when he was appointed as Circuit Court Judge. Served as St Louis Excise Commissioner from 1941 until his death. Died from a heart ailment. Buried Valhalla Cemetery, St Louis MO.

Loren Bader—3 Years Pitcher (b. 27 Apr 1888 Bader IL–d. 2 Jun 1973 LeRoy KS) World War I veteran. He was the Coffey County, KS, WPA director during the 1930s, and later managed a farm. Buried LeRoy Cemetery, LeRoy KS.

Red Badgro—2 Years Outfielder (b. 1 Dec 1902 Orilla WA–d. 13 Jul 1998 Kent WA) Also a professional football player, he was selected to the All-NFL team four years and was inducted into the Professional Football Hall of Fame in 1981. He was an assistant football coach at Columbia University and at the University of Washington. Buried Hillcrest Burial Park, Kent WA.

Ed Baecht—6 Years Pitcher (b. 15 May 1907 Paden OK–d. 15 Aug 1957 at his home in Grafton IL) He was a practicing physician at Grafton for a number of years before opening a restaurant and tavern there. Died following an extended period of ill health. Buried Oak Grove Cemetery, Jerseyville IL.

Jim Bagby—9 Years Pitcher (b. 5 Oct 1889 Barnett GA–d. 28 Jul 1954 Kennestone Hospital, Marietta GA) He was the first pitcher to hit a homerun in a World Series game. He umpired some minor league baseball until suffering a stroke in 1942. After that he was a guard at an ordinance plant. Died after suffering another stroke less than a week earlier. Buried Westview Cemetery, Atlanta GA.

Jim Bagby, Jr—10 Years Pitcher (b. 8 Sep 1916 Cleveland OH–d. 2 Sep 1988 Marietta GA) He was the starting pitcher for Cleveland the night Joe Dimaggio's 56 game hitting streak ended.

Bill Bagwell—2 Years Outfielder (b. 24 Feb 1896 Choudrant LA–d. 5 Oct 1976 Glenwood Hospital, West Monroe LA) World War I veteran. He was a civic leader in Choudrant. Buried Sibley Cemetery, Sibley LA.

Grover Baichley—1 Year Pitcher (b. 10 Dec 1889 Toledo IL–d. 28 Jun 1956 San Jose CA) World War I veteran. He was a retired accountant for Western Electric. He apparently died from a self-inflicted pistol wound. Buried Golden Gate National Cemetery, San Bruno CA.

Bill Bailey—1 Year Outfielder (b. 19 Nov 1881 Shawnee OH–d. 27 Oct 1967 at a nursing home in Seattle WA) He moved from Dayton OH to Seattle in 1953 and was associated with his two sons in Bailey Hardware there. Buried Acacia Cemetery, Seattle WA.

Bill Bailey—11 Years Pitcher (b. 12 Apr 1889 Fort Smith AR–d. 2 Nov 1926 Baptist Hospital, Houston TX) During a 20 year minor league career he won 242 games while compiling an ERA of 2.87. Died shortly after retiring from baseball from a ruptured vessel in his stomach caused by a baseball injury. Buried Omaha NE.

Fred Bailey—3 Years Outfielder (b. 16 Aug 1895 Mt Hope WV–d. 16 Aug 1972 Huntington WV) He operated a real estate brokerage business and insurance agency in Huntington and was involved in real estate development. Died following a three-month illness. Buried Spring Hill Cemetery, Huntington WV.

Gene Bailey—5 Years Outfielder (b. 25 Nov 1893 Pearsall TX–d. 14 Nov 1973 at a hospital in Houston TX) Living in Houston 71 years, he managed in the minor leagues and coached baseball at Rice University. Buried Hollywood Cemetery, Houston TX.

Harvey Bailey—2 Years Pitcher (b. 24 Nov 1877 Adrian MI–d. 10 Jul 1922 State Hospital, Toledo OH) He was a dentist. Died from generalized paralysis and dementia. Buried Greenlawn Cemetery, Delta OH.

King Bailey—1 Year Pitcher (b. 18 Nov 1870–d. 19 Nov 1917 Macon Hospital, Macon GA) He coached college baseball for a time, then managed the southern headquarters of National Casualty Insurance Company of Chicago in Macon. Died from blood poisoning. Buried Riverside Cemetery, Macon GA.

Sweetbreads Bailey—3 Years Pitcher (b. 12 Feb 1895 Joliet IL–d. 27 Sep 1939 at the home of his sister in Joliet IL) World War I veteran. He played in the Texas League and Southern Association and worked for the Phoenix Horseshoe Company in Joliet. Died after being ill for several years. Buried Elmhurst Cemetery, Joliet IL.

Loren Bain—1 Year Pitcher (b. 4 Jul 1922 Staples MN–d. 24 Nov 1996 Lakeview Medical Center, Rice Lake WI) For 25 years he was a bottler for Coca-Cola in Minneapolis MN, retiring to Chetek WI in 1978. Cremated.

Al Baird—2 Years Infielder (b. 2 Jun 1895 Cleburne TX–d. 27 Nov 1976 Schumpert Medical Center, Shreveport LA) Served in the U.S. Navy during World War I. He was involved in the oil and gas business, and was chairman of the civil service commission. Died following a short illness. Buried Forest Park Cemetery, Shreveport LA.

Bob Baird—2 Years Pitcher (b. 16 Jan 1942 Knoxville TN–d. 11 Apr 1974 Erlanger Hospital, Chattanooga TN) He was a traveling salesman for Tie Bracket Company, a Cincinnati OH distributor. Died from complications after being shot by a woman in a Chattanooga motel nine days earlier. Buried Lynnhurst Cemetery, Knoxville TN.

Doug Baird—6 Years Infielder (b. 27 Sep 1891 St Charles MO–d. 13 Jun 1967 Thomasville GA).

Jersey Bakely—6 Years Pitcher (b. 17 Apr 1864 Blackwood NJ–d. 17 Feb 1915 at his home in Philadelphia PA) Died suddenly. Buried Greenmount Cemetery, Philadelphia PA.

Al Baker—1 Year Pitcher (b. 28 Feb 1906 Batesville MS–d. 6 Nov 1982 Restful Acres Nursing Home, Kenedy TX) He was a retired farmer and rancher. Died from chronic obstructive lung disease and cardio-respiratory failure. Buried Butler Family Cemetery, Kenedy TX.

Bock Baker—1 Year Pitcher (b. 17 Jul 1878 Troy NY–d. 17 Aug 1940 New York City NY).

Charlie Baker—1 Year Outfielder (b. 15 Jan 1856 Sterling MA–d. 15 Jan 1937 at a hospital in Manchester NH) Died after an illness of five weeks. Buried Hudson MA.

Del Baker—3 Years Catcher 6 Years Manager (b. 3 May 1892 Sherwood OR–d. 11 Sep 1973 at his home in San Antonio TX) Served in the U.S. Navy during World War I. He retired in 1960 after a 51 year career in baseball as a player, manager, coach and minor league manager. Buried Sunset Memorial Park, San Antonio TX.

Ernie Baker—1 Year Pitcher (b. 8 Aug 1875 Concord MI–d. 25 Oct 1945 at his home in Homer MI) He lived in the Homer area for about 25 years. Buried Maple Grove Cemetery, Concord MI.

Frank Baker—13 Years Infielder Hall of Fame (b. 13 Mar 1886 Trappe MD–d. 26 Jun 1963 at his home in Trappe MD) He retired to his boyhood home on the eastern shore of Chesapeake Bay. Died after suffering a stroke two weeks earlier. Buried Spring Hill Cemetery, Easton MD.

Gene Baker—8 Years Infielder (b. 15 Jun 1925 Davenport IA–d. 1 Dec 1999 Genesis Medical Center, Davenport IA) Served in the U.S. Navy during World War II. He played in the negro leagues, managed minor league baseball and scouted for the Pirates, retiring in 1992. He was an avid golfer. Buried Rock Island National Cemetery, Rock Island IL.

Howard Baker—3 Years Infielder (b. 1 Mar 1888 Bridgeport CT–d. 16 Jan 1964 St Vincent's Hospital, Bridgeport CT) He was a metal roller for the Stanley Works in Bridgeport. Buried St Michael's Cemetery, Bridgeport CT.

Jesse Baker—1 Year Infielder (b. 9 Feb 1897 New York City NY–d. 25 Jun 1960 Valley Community Hospital, Pomona CA) He was a rangeman for Southern California Edison Company for 37 years. Died from a heart attack. Buried Pomona Cemetery, Pomona CA.

Jesse Baker—1 Year Pitcher (b. 3 Jun 1888 Steilacoom WA–d. 26 Sep 1972 Tacoma WA) He was a logger for Aloha Lumber Company after years of stardom as a pitcher in the Pacific Coast League. Buried Mountain View Memorial Park, Tacoma WA.

Kirtley Baker—5 Years Pitcher (b. 24 Jun 1869 Aurora IN–d. 13 Apr 1927 Booth Memorial Hospital, Covington KY) Died from a pulmonary embolism. Buried Greendale Cemetery, Greendale IN.

Neal Baker—1 Year Pitcher (b. 30 Apr 1904 LaPorte TX–d. 5 Jan 1982 Houston TX) Buried Woodlawn Garden of Memories, Houston TX.

Norm Baker—3 Years Pitcher (b. 14 Oct 1864 Philadelphia PA–d. 20 Feb 1949 Hurffville NJ) Buried Wenonah Cemetery, Wenonah NJ.

Phil Baker—3 Years Infielder (b. 19 Sep 1856 Philadelphia PA–d. 4 Jun 1940 Washington DC) Died at his daughter's home after a long illness. Buried Glenwood Cemetery, Washington DC.

Tom Baker—1 Year Pitcher (b. 6 May 1934 Port Townsend WA–d. 9 Mar 1980 at his home in Port Townsend WA) Served in the U.S. Army during the Korean War. He was a deputy assessor for Jefferson County, WA. Buried Laurel Grove Cemetery, Port Townsend WA.

Tom Baker—4 Years Pitcher (b. 11 Jun 1913 Nursery TX–d. 3 Jan 1991 Fort Worth TX) Buried Greenwood Memorial Park, Fort Worth TX.

Tracy Baker—1 Year Infielder (b. 7 Nov 1891 Pendleton OR–d. 14 Mar 1975 Marshall Hospital, Placerville CA) Retiring from construction work after 35 years, he had lived in California 50 years and in El Dorado County 34 years. Died from heart failure. Buried Westwood Hills Memorial Park, Placerville CA.

Bobby Balcena—1 Year Outfielder (b. 1 Aug 1925 San Pedro CA–d. 5 Jan 1990 at his home in San Pedro CA) Served in World War II. He was a longshoreman for 24 years. Died from a heart attack while suffering from the flu. He was cremated and his ashes scattered off the coast of Santa Monica CA.

Harry Baldwin—2 Years Pitcher (b. 30 Jun 1900 Baltimore MD–d. 23 Jan 1958 Baltimore MD) Buried Oak Lawn Cemetery, Baltimore MD.

Henry Baldwin—1 Year Infielder (b. 13 Jun 1894 Chadds Ford PA–d. 24 Feb 1964 Chester County Hospital, West Chester PA) He owned and operated a dairy farm near West Chester where he also raised fox hunting dogs and show horses. He was well-known throughout the county for his fox hunters and horses. Died from cancer. Buried Birmingham-Lafayette Cemetery, West Chester PA.

Kid Baldwin—7 Years Catcher (b. 1 Nov 1864 Newport KY–d. 10 Jul 1897 Cincinnati OH) Died shortly after being committed to Longview Insane Asylum. Dissipation had caused him to be nearly blind and he had become a tramp. Buried Longview Asylum Cemetery, Cincinnati OH.

Lady Baldwin—6 Years Pitcher (b. 10 Apr 1859 Ormel NY–d. 7 Mar 1937 at his home in Hastings MI) Died from heart disease. Buried Riverside Cemetery, Hastings MI.

Mark Baldwin—7 Years Pitcher (b. 29 Oct 1865 Pittsburgh PA–d. 10 Nov 1929 Passavant Hospital, Pittsburgh PA) He became a doctor and practiced medicine in Pittsburgh 30 years. Died following a long illness.

Orson Baldwin—1 Year Pitcher (b. 3 Nov 1881 Carson City MI–d. 16 Feb 1942 at his home in Los Angeles CA) Died when he hung himself from a pipe. Cremated.

Mike Balenti—2 Years Infielder (b. 3 Jul 1886 Calumet OK–d. 4 Aug 1955 Memorial Hospital, Altus OK) Died after suffering a heart attack at his home. Buried Altus Cemetery, Altus OK.

Art Ball—2 Years Infielder (b. 1873 Chicago IL–d. 26 Dec 1915 Chicago IL) Buried Mount Olivet Cemetery, Chicago IL.

Jim Ball—2 Years Catcher (b. 22 Feb 1884 Hartford MD–d. 7 Apr 1963 Glen Manor Convalescent Hosp, Glendale CA) He was a purchasing agent for Lockheed Aircraft in Burbank CA. Died from colon cancer. Buried Calvary Cemetery, Los Angeles CA.

Neal Ball—7 Years Infielder (b. 22 Apr 1881 Grand Haven MI–d. 15 Oct 1957 at his home in Bridgeport CT) In 1909 he was the first major league player to make an unassisted triple play. He managed minor league baseball for a time, then managed a bowling alley in Bridgeport until an extended illness forced his retirement. Buried Mountain Grove Cemetery, Bridgeport CT.

Philip DeCatesby Ball—(d. 22 Oct 1933 St Louis MO) A prominent industrialist, he owned the St Louis Browns as a hobby. Died from blood poisoning. Buried Bellefontaine Cemetery, St Louis MO.

Pelham Ballenger—1 Year Infielder (b. 6 Feb 1894 Gilreath Mill SC–d. 8 Dec 1948 Greenville SC) Served in the U.S. Army during World

War I. He worked in the maintenance department for Duncan Mill, and played and managed semi-pro baseball up until his last year. Died from a sudden illness. Buried Graceland Cemetery, Greenville SC.

Win Ballou —4 Years Pitcher (b. 30 Nov 1897 Mount Morgan KY–d. 29 Jan 1963 General Hospital, San Francisco CA) Died from a liver ailment. Buried Woodlawn Memorial Park, Daly City CA.

Dave Bancroft —16 Years Infielder 4 Years Manager Hall of Fame (b. 20 Apr 1891 Sioux City IA–d. 9 Oct 1972 at a hospital in Superior WI) He worked for Lakehead Pipe Company in Superior WI. Died after a lengthy illness. Buried Greenwood Cemetery, Superior WI.

Frank Bancroft —9 Years Manager (b. 9 May 1846 Lancaster MA–d. 31 Mar 1921 Deaconess Hospital, Cincinnati OH) Served in the Union Army during the Civil War. He was business manager for the Reds from 1890 until he died from pneumonia after an illness of neuritis. Buried Spring Grove Cemetery, Cincinnati OH.

Dan Bankhead —3 Years Pitcher (b. 3 May 1920 Empire AL–d. 2 May 1976 Veteran's Hospital, Houston TX) He was the first black pitcher in the major leagues. Died from lung cancer.

Bill Banks —2 Years Pitcher (b. 26 Feb 1873 Danville PA–d. 8 Sep 1936 at his daughter's home in Danville PA) He umpired in the minor leagues for a few years, then became an iron worker. Died from a heart attack. Buried Odd Fellows Cemetery, Danville PA.

George Banks —5 Years Infielder (b. 24 Sep 1938 Pacolet Mills SC–d. 1 Mar 1985 Spartanburg SC) Died after a long illness. Buried Pacolet Memorial Gardens, Pacolet SC.

Bill Bankston —1 Year Outfielder (b. 25 May 1893 Barnesville GA–d. 26 Feb 1970 Spaulding County Hospital, Griffin GA) Buried Fredonia Church Cemetery, Barnesville GA.

Jimmy Bannon —4 Years Outfielder (b. 5 May 1871 Amesbury MA–d. 24 Mar 1948 General Hospital, Paterson NJ) He managed minor league baseball and coached baseball at Lehigh University and the University of New Hampshire. Later he went into the hotel business and served in the New Hampshire legislature. Died after a brief illness. Buried St Mary's Cemetery, Rochester NH.

Tom Bannon —2 Years Outfielder (b. 8 May 1869 South Groveland MA–d. 25 Jan 1950 at his home in Lynn MA) He worked for General Electric at Lynn. Died after an illness of nearly two years. Buried St Joseph Cemetery, Lynn MA.

Walter Barbare —8 Years Infielder (b. 11 Aug 1891 Greenville SC–d. 28 Oct 1965 at a nursing home in Greenville SC) World War I veteran. He coached high school baseball and basketball, and managed some minor league baseball. Died after an illness of five months. Buried Graceland Cemetery, Greenville SC.

Jap Barbeau —4 Years Infielder (b. 10 Jun 1882 New York City NY–d. 10 Sep 1969 St Joseph's Hospital, Milwaukee WI) Buried Holy Cross Cemetery, Milwaukee WI.

Dave Barbee —2 Years Outfielder (b. 7 May 1905 Greensboro NC–d. 1 Jul 1968 at his home in Albemarle NC) Buried Guilford Memorial Park, Greensboro NC.

Charlie Barber —1 Year Infielder (b. 1854 Martinsburg PA–d. 23 Nov 1910 Philadelphia PA).

Red Barber —Hall of Fame (b. 17 Feb 1908 Columbus MS–d. 22 Oct 1992 Tallahassee FL) He was a broadcaster for 33 years. Died from complications following surgery for an intestinal blockage. Cremated.

Turner Barber —9 Years Outfielder (b. 9 Jul 1893 Lavinia TN–d. 20 Oct 1968 Milan Hospital, Milan TN) He played in the International League and the Southern League for several years. Died following a heart attack suffered while attending church. Buried Oakwood Cemetery, Milan TN.

Frank Barberich—2 Years Pitcher (b. 3 Feb 1882 New Town NY–d. 1 May 1965 Munroe Memorial Hospital, Ocala FL) Buried Greenfield Cemetery.

Curt Barclay —3 Years Pitcher (b. 22 Aug 1931 Chicago IL–d. 25 Mar 1985 St Patrick's Hospital, Missoula MT) Served two years in the armed forces. He was the plywood division superintendent for Evans Company for 22 years and worked for Champion International in the same capacity. Died from cancer. Cremated.

George Barclay —4 Years Outfielder (b. 16 May 1876 Millville PA–d. 3 Apr 1909 University Hospital, Philadelphia PA) He practiced medicine in Philadelphia for three years and at one time was the acting football coach at Lafayette College. Died from peritonitis shortly after undergoing surgery to remove his appendix. Buried Easton Cemetery, Easton PA.

Ray Bare—5 Years Pitcher (b. 15 Apr 1949 Miami FL–d. 29 Mar 1994 Baptist Hospital, Miami FL) He was a manufacturer's representative for John Gabrick and Associates. Died from leukemia. Buried Miami Memorial Park, Miami FL.

Clyde Barfoot—3 Years Pitcher (b. 8 Jul 1891 Richmond VA–d. 11 Mar 1971 at his home in Highland Park CA) He was a bartender at the Palladium. Died from heart disease. Buried Forest Lawn Memorial Park, Glendale CA.

Carl Barger—(b. abt 1932 Lewistown PA–d. 9 Dec 1992 Humana Hospital, Louisville KY) He was president of the Pittsburgh Pirates and, later, the Florida Marlins. Died from a ruptured aortic aneurysm.

Cy Barger—7 Years Pitcher (b. 18 May 1885 Jamestown KY–d. 23 Sep 1964 Adair Memorial Hospital, Columbia KY) He coached baseball at the University of Kentucky. Died following an illness of several months. Buried Columbia City Cemetery, Columbia KY.

Sam Barkley—6 Years Infielder 1 Year Manager (b. 24 May 1858 Wheeling WV–d. 20 Apr 1912 Wheeling WV) He died from a complication of diseases he had suffered from for some time.

Al Barlick—Hall of Fame (b. 2 Apr 1915 Springfield IL–d. 27 Dec 1995 Memorial Medical Center, Springfield IL) Served in the U.S. Coast Guard during World War II. He was a National League umpire from 1940 until he retired in 1971. Died from cardiac arrest. Cremated.

Babe Barna—5 Years Outfielder (b. 2 Mar 1915 Clarksburg WV–d. 18 May 1972 General Hospital, Charleston WV) He operated the B and H Club in Charleston. Died following a stroke suffered a week earlier. Buried Mountain View Memorial Park, Dunbar WV.

Charlie Barnabe—2 Years Pitcher (b. 12 Jun 1900 Russell Gulch CO–d. 16 Aug 1977 at a hospital in Waco TX) Buried Rosemound Cemetery, Waco TX.

Ernest Barnard—(b. abt 1875–d. 27 Mar 1931 Mayo Clinic, Rochester MN) He was a sportswriter early in his career, and was president of the Cleveland Indians before becoming the second president of the American League in 1927, a position he held until his death. Died from a heart attack. Buried Knollwood Cemetery, Mayfield OH.

Bob Barnes—1 Year Pitcher (b. 6 Jan 1902 Washburn IL–d. 8 Dec 1993 Methodist Medical Center, Peoria IL) He practiced law in Lacon IL from 1925 until 1993. Buried Lacon Cemetery, Lacon IL.

Eppie Barnes—2 Years Infielder (b. 1 Dec 1900 Ossining NY–d. 17 Nov 1980 Nassau Hospital, Mineola NY) He was a real estate executive until 1939 when he returned to Colgate University. There he coached baseball from 1939 to 1956 and was athletic director from 1956 to 1968. Died from a heart attack.

Frank Barnes—2 Years Pitcher (b. 9 Jan 1900 Dallas TX–d. 27 Sep 1967 Houston TX) He lived in Houston 40 years and was a Harris County, TX, deputy sheriff before becoming assistant manager of the W P Hobby International Airport. Buried Forest Park East, Houston TX.

Honey Barnes—1 Year Catcher (b. 29 Jan 1900 Fulton NY–d. 18 Jun 1981 Lockport NY) He worked for Bell Aircraft and later for Harrison Radiator. Most recently he worked for the State Department of Social Services in Lockport. Died after a short illness. Buried St Mary's Cemetery, Fulton NY.

Jesse Barnes—13 Years Pitcher (b. 26 Aug 1892 Perkins OK–d. 9 Sep 1961 Guadalupe General Hospital, Santa Rosa NM) A retired police officer, living at Midway City CA, he died from a heart seizure while passing through Santa Rosa, returning to California after a trip to the east. Buried Westminster Memorial Park, Westminster CA.

Junie Barnes—1 Year Pitcher (b. 11 Dec 1911 Churchland NC–d. 31 Dec 1963 Onslow Hospital, Jacksonville NC) He graduated from Southeastern Seminary in 1958 and was pastor at Bethlehem Baptist Church in Jacksonville from then until his death. Died following an illness of several months. Buried Barnes Family Cemetery, Churchland NC.

Red Barnes—4 Years Outfielder (b. 25 Dec 1903 Suggsville AL–d. 3 Jul 1959 at an infirmary in Mobile AL) He operated a small store and a post office in Suggsville. Died after a long illness. Buried Suggsville Cemetery, Suggsville AL.

Ross Barnes—4 Years Infielder (b. 8 May 1850 Mt Morris NY–d. 5 Feb 1915 in his apartment, Wicklow Hotel, Chicago IL) He was a bookkeeper for the People's Gas, Light and Coke Company. Died from heart trouble. Buried Greenwood Cemetery, Rockford IL.

Sam Barnes—1 Year Infielder (b. 18 Dec 1899 Suggsville AL–d. 19 Feb 1981 at a hospital in Montgomery AL) Died from cancer. Buried Fairmount Memorial Cemetery, Red Level AL.

Virgil Barnes—9 Years Pitcher (b. 5 Mar 1897 Ontario KS–d. 24 Jul 1958 V A Hospital, Wichita KS) Served as a bugler in the U.S. Army during World War I. He moved to Wichita about 1937. Died from a heart condition. Buried Holton Cemetery, Holton KS.

Ed Barney—2 Years Outfielder (b. 23 Jan 1890 Amery WI–d. 4 Oct 1967 Rice Lake WI).

Rex Barney—6 Years Pitcher (b. 19 Dec 1924 Omaha NE–d. 12 Aug 1997 at his home in Baltimore MD) He worked at radio jobs, bartending and for a liquor distributor before becoming public address announcer for the Orioles in 1974, remaining in that job until his death. Died from a heart attack. Buried Lorraine Park Cemetery, Baltimore MD.

Clyde Barnhart—9 Years Outfielder (b. 29 Dec 1895 Buck Valley PA–d. 21 Jan 1980 Washington County Hospital, Hagerstown MD) He retired after working 18 years for the Maryland Correctional Institution. Buried Cedar Lawn Memorial Park, Hagerstown MD.

Ed Barnhart—1 Year Pitcher (b. 16 Sep 1904 Providence MO–d. 14 Sep 1984 Columbia Regional Hospital, Columbia MO) He owned a billiard parlor in Columbia. Buried Memorial Park Cemetery, Columbia MO.

Les Barnhart—2 Years Pitcher (b. 23 Feb 1905 Hoxie KS–d. 7 Oct 1971 Scottsdale AZ) Buried East Resthaven Park Cemetery, Phoenix AZ.

Dave Barnhill—10 Years Pitcher (b. 30 Oct 1914 Greenville NC–d. 8 Jan 1983 at his home in Miami FL) He played in the negro leagues and was a clerk and truck driver for the Miami Parks Department from 1953 until he retired in 1980. Buried Brownhill Cemetery, Greenville NC.

George Barnicle—3 Years Pitcher (b. 26 Aug 1917 Fitchburg MA–d. 10 Oct 1990 Largo FL).

Billy Barnie—2 Years Catcher and 12 Years Manager (b. 26 Jan 1852 New York City NY–d. 15 Jul 1900 at his brother-in-law's home in Hartford CT) He spent his entire life in baseball as both a major and minor league manager, and as a minor league team owner and executive. Died from pneumonia and asthmatic bronchitis. Buried Greenwood Cemetery, Brooklyn NY.

Bob Barr—5 Years Pitcher (b. 1856 Washington DC–d. 11 Mar 1930 Gallinger Hospital, Washington DC) He was the chief clerk of the Washington DC engineering department from 1896 until he died from uremic poisoning. Buried Oak Hill Cemetery, Washington DC.

Scotty Barr—2 Years Outfielder (b. 6 Oct 1886 Bristol TN–d. 2 Dec 1934 Fort Smith AR) He was an independent oil dealer. Died from complications following an appendectomy two months earlier. Buried Rose Hill Memorial Park, Fort Worth TX.

Bill Barrett—9 Years Outfielder (b. 28 May 1900 Cambridge MA–d. 26 Jan 1951 Cambridge MA) He was a member and former chairman of the Cambridge recreation department. Died suddenly. Buried Cambridge Cemetery, Cambridge MA.

Bob Barrett—5 Years Infielder (b. 27 Jan 1899 Atlanta GA–d. 18 Jan 1982 Atlanta GA) He was a retired steamfitter. Buried Westview Cemetery, Atlanta GA.

Dick Barrett—5 Years Pitcher (b. 28 Sep 1906 Montoursville PA–d. 7 Nov 1966 at his home in Seattle WA) He pitched for years for Seattle in the Pacific Coast League. During a minor league career that lasted from 1925 until 1953 he won 325 games while losing 257. He lived in Seattle for 30 years. Died in his sleep. Buried Holyrood Cemetery, Seattle WA.

Frank Barrett—5 Years Pitcher (b. 1 Jul 1913 Fort Lauderdale FL–d. 6 Mar 1998 Leesburg FL) After coaching and managing minor league baseball he owned and operated Red Barrett's Drive-in Restaurant in Leesburg from 1953 to 1966 and the Phillips 66 service station in Leesburg from 1954 to 1978. Buried Hillcrest Memorial Gardens, Leesburg FL.

Jimmy Barrett—10 Years Outfielder (b. 28 Mar 1875 Athol MA–d. 24 Oct 1921 at his office in Detroit MI) He was a senior partner in the real estate firm of Barrett and Walsh in Detroit. Died from a stroke of apoplexy. Buried Mount Olivet Cemetery, Detroit MI.

Johnny Barrett—5 Years Outfielder (b. 18 Dec 1915 Lowell MA–d. 17 Aug 1974 at his summer home in Seabrook Beach NH) He was a salesman for a brewery from 1951 to 1961 when he was appointed superintendent of the Essex County (MA) Training School, a job he held until his sudden death. Buried Ridgewood Cemetery, North Andover MA.

Marty Barrett—1 Year Catcher (b. Nov 1860 Port Huron NY–d. 29 Jan 1910 at his home in Holyoke MA) He tended bar and was employed by S J Wolohan and Company. Died after a short illness. Buried St Jerome Cemetery, Holyoke MA.

Red Barrett—11 Years Pitcher (b. 14 Feb 1915 Santa Barbara CA–d. 28 Jul 1990 at his home in Wilson NC) He holds the record for the fewest number of pitches thrown in a nine inning game—58 in 2–0 shutout in 1944, facing only 27 batters. After baseball he worked for Sealtest. Died after a long illness. Buried Evergreen Memorial Garden, Wilson NC.

Francisco Barrios—7 Years Pitcher (b. 10 Jun 1953 Hermosillo, Mexico–d. 9 Apr 1982 Hermosillo, Mexico).

Frank Barron—1 Year Pitcher (b. 6 Aug 1890 St Marys WV–d. 18 Sep 1964 St Marys WV) Served in the U.S. Army during World War I. He was a prominent St Marys attorney, serving 14 years as city attorney, 12 years as Pleasants County, WV, prosecuting attorney and represented the Baltimore and Ohio Railroad several years. Died after a lengthy illness. Buried Odd Fellows Cemetery, St Marys WV.

Red Barron—1 Year Outfielder (b. 21 Jun 1900 Clarksville GA–d. 4 Oct 1982 Atlanta GA) He devoted his life to education and was a member of the Board of Regents of the University of Georgia system. Buried Clarksville City Cemetery, Clarksville GA.

Ed Barrow—5 Years Manager Hall of Fame (b. 10 May 1868 Springfield IL–d. 15 Dec 1953 Port Chester United Hosp, Port Chester NY) He started life as a newspaperman and took a fling in the soap business before buying an interest in a minor league team in West Virginia. Worked as an executive for the Tigers and Red Sox before becoming general manager for the Yankees in 1920. He is generally credited with building the Yankee dynasty. Spent 52 years in baseball, retiring in 1947. Died from cancer. Buried Kensico Cemetery, Valhalla NY.

Cuke Barrows—4 Years Outfielder (b. 20 Oct 1883 Gray ME–d. 10 Feb 1955 at his home in Gorham ME) He played one year after injuring his ankle, breaking a bone and pulling several tendons. He then retired to Gorham where he helped his wife operate a greenhouse business she had established there. Buried Eastern Cemetery, Portland ME.

Ed Barry—3 Years Pitcher (b. 2 Oct 1882 Madison WI–d. 19 Jun 1920 Farren Hospital, Montague MA) He traveled for an aluminum goods company. Buried Resurrection Catholic Cemetery, Madison WI.

Hardin Barry—1 Year Pitcher (b. 26 Mar 1891 Susanville CA–d. 5 Nov 1969 at a hospital in Carson City NV) A prominent lawyer in Susanville for many years, he retired in 1967. Buried Susanville Cemetery, Susanville CA.

Jack Barry—11 Years Infielder 1 Year Manager (b. 26 Apr 1887 Meriden CT–d. 23 Apr 1961 Shrewsbury MA) He spent 56 years in baseball, the last 40 as coach at College of the Holy Cross. Died from lung cancer while enroute to the hospital. Buried Sacred Heart Cemetery, Meriden CT.

Shad Barry—10 Years Outfielder (b. 27 Oct 1878 Newburgh NY–d. 27 Nov 1936 Verdugo Hills Sanitarium, Los Angeles CA) He was a security officer at a bank. Died from prostate cancer. Buried Calvary Cemetery, Los Angeles CA.

Tom Barry—1 Year Pitcher (b. 10 Apr 1879 St Louis MO–d. 4 Jun 1946 St Louis MO) Buried Calvary Cemetery, St Louis MO.

Dick Bartell—18 Years Infielder (b. 22 Nov 1907 Chicago IL–d. 4 Aug 1995 Hillhaven Convalscent Hospital, Alameda CA) Served in World War II. He managed in the minor leagues until 1956 and coached ten years. Died from a heart attack and pneumonia five days after suffering a stroke. He also suffered from Alzheimer's disease. Cremated. Buried Chapel of the Chimes, Oakland CA.

John Barthold—1 Year Pitcher (b. 14 Apr 1882 Philadelphia PA–d. 4 Nov 1946 Fairview Village

PA) He worked a number of years for the Philadelphia Police Department, becoming a captain of Special Squad # 1 in 1929, involved in prohibition policing. In 1932 he resigned and went to work for Beck Engraving Company where he stayed until his death. Died from a heart attack while hunting. Buried St Mary's Cemetery, Philadelphia PA.

Les Bartholomew—2 Years Pitcher (b. 4 Apr 1903 Madison WI–d. 19 Sep 1972 Barrington IL).

Bill Bartley—3 Years Pitcher (b. 8 Jan 1885 Cincinnati OH–d. 17 May 1965 Jewish Hospital, Cincinnati OH) He worked for the Cincinnati police department from 1918 until he retired in 1950. Died from congestive heart failure. Buried St Joseph New Cemetery, Cincinnati OH.

Irv Bartling—1 Year Infielder (b. 27 Jun 1914 Bay City MI–d. 12 Jun 1973 Westland MI) Buried Grand Lawn Cemetery, Detroit MI.

Harry Barton—1 Year Catcher (b. 20 Jan 1875 Chester PA–d. 25 Jan 1955 Crozer Hospital, Upland PA) He was in charge of production schedules in the equipment division of the S S White Dental Manufacturing Company, retiring in 1951. Buried Arlington Cemetery, Drexel Hill PA.

Vince Barton—2 Years Outfielder (b. 1 Feb 1908 Edmonton, Alberta, Canada–d. 13 Sep 1973 St Joseph's Hospital, Toronto, Canada) Cremated.

Charlie Bartson—1 Year Pitcher (b. 13 Mar 1865 Peoria IL–d. 9 Jun 1936 at his home in Peoria IL) He owned and managed the Peoria team of the Western League briefly. Active in civic affairs, he served as a Peoria city official in many capacities and was chairman of the city's Republican Central Committee for a while. He was working for the Empire Cigar Store in Peoria when he died. Died from heart disease. Buried Springdale Cemetery, Peoria IL.

Al Bashang—2 Years Outfielder (b. 22 Aug 1888 Cincinnati OH–d. 23 Jun 1967 Jewish Hospital, Cincinnati OH) He owned and operated a restaurant. Buried Vine Street Hill Cemetery, Cincinnati OH.

Walt Bashore—1 Year Outfielder (b. 6 Oct 1909 Harrisburg PA–d. 26 Sep 1984 Highlands General Hospital, Sebring FL) He was a passenger trainmaster for the Penn Central Railroad.

Jim Baskette—3 Years Pitcher (b. 10 Dec 1887 Athens TN–d. 30 Jul 1942 Foree Hospital, Athens TN) He pitched in the Southern League. His baseball career ended when he injured a hip. He was known for his love of fox hunting and the breeding of Walker fox hounds. Died from cancer of the kidney. Buried Cedar Grove Cemetery, Athens TN.

Dick Bass—1 Year Pitcher (b. 7 Jul 1906 Rogersville TN–d. 3 Feb 1989 Graceville FL).

Doc Bass—2 Games Pinch Hitter (b. 4 Dec 1899 Macon GA–d. 12 Jan 1970 Macon GA) He was the shop foreman for Steve M Solomon Motor Company in Macon. Buried Mount Zion Baptist Church Cemetery, Macon GA.

Charley Bassett—9 Years Infielder (b. 9 Feb 1863 Central Falls RI–d. 28 May 1942 Pawtucket RI) Buried Moshassuck Cemetery, Central Falls RI.

Johnny Bassler—9 Years Catcher (b. 3 Jun 1895 Mechanics Grove PA–d. 29 Jun 1979 City Hospital, Santa Monica CA) Died from congestive heart failure. Buried Woodlawn Cemetery, Santa Monica CA.

Charlie Bastian—8 Years Infielder (b. 4 Jul 1860 Philadelphia PA–d. 18 Jan 1932 at his home in Merchantville NJ) He was a carpenter. Died from chronic heart disease. Buried Holy Cross Cemetery, Yeadon PA.

Emil Batch—4 Years Infielder (b. 21 Jan 1880 Brooklyn NY–d. 23 Aug 1926 Brooklyn NY).

Joe Batchelder—3 Years Pitcher (b. 11 Jul 1898 Wenham MA–d. 5 May 1989 Beverly MA) Served in the U.S. Army during World War I. He worked over 25 years for the USM Corporation. Buried Hamilton Cemetery, Hamilton MA.

John Bateman—10 Years Catcher (b. 21 Jul 1940 Kileen TX–d. 3 Dec 1996 Sand Springs TX).

Bud Bates—1 Year Outfielder (b. 16 Mar 1912 Los Angeles CA–d. 29 Apr 1987 Palmcrest Medallion Hospital, Long Beach CA) He was the golf starter clerk at the Ironwood Nine for 22 years. Died from a heart attack. Cremated.

Charlie Bates—1 Year Outfielder (b. 17 Sep 1907 Philadelphia PA–d. 29 Jan 1980 at a hospital in Topeka KS) He worked many years for the State of Kansas and lived in the Topeka and Lake Waubaunsee areas 34 years. Buried Memorial Park Cemetery, Topeka KS.

Johnny Bates—9 Years Outfielder (b. 10 Jan 1884 Steubenville OH–d. 10 Feb 1949 Gill Memorial Hospital, Steubenville OH) He was a glass worker before serving a time as a deputy sheriff of Jefferson County, OH. Died 10 days after suffering a heart attack while shoveling snow. Buried Union Cemetery, Steubenville OH.

Ray Bates—2 Years Infielder (b. 8 Feb 1890 Paterson NJ–d. 15 Aug 1970 Tucson AZ) Veteran of World War I. He moved to Tucson in 1934 and was a dispatcher for Tucson Gas and Electric Company. Buried Holy Hope Cemetery, Tucson AZ.

Bill Batsch—1 Game Pinch Hitter (b. 18 May 1892 Mingo Junction OH–d. 31 Dec 1963 Aultman Hospital, Canton OH) He was a car salesman for Ewing Chevrolet in Canton, retiring in 1958. Buried West Lawn Cemetery, Canton OH.

Larry Battam—1 Year Infielder (b. 1 May 1878 Brooklyn NY–d. 27 Jan 1938 Brooklyn NY) He retired as a patrolman from the New York City Police Department. Buried Holy Cross Cemetery, Brooklyn NY.

George Batten—1 Year Infielder (b. 7 Oct 1891 Haddonfield NJ–d. 4 Aug 1972 New Port Richey FL).

Joe Battin—6 Years Infielder 2 Years Manager (b. 11 Nov 1851 Philadelphia PA–d. 10 Dec 1937 St Thomas Hospital, Akron OH) A retired bricklayer, he died from broncho pneumonia and senility. Buried Glendale Cemetery, Akron OH.

Jim Battle—1 Year Infielder (b. 26 Mar 1901 Celeste TX–d. 30 Sep 1965 Enloe Memorial Hospital, Chico CA) For 14 years he was a clerk at the Cork and Bottle liquor store in Chico. Died from a heart attack. Buried Glen Oaks Memorial Park, Chico CA.

Lou Bauer—1 Year Pitcher (b. 30 Nov 1898 Egg Harbor City NJ–d. 4 Feb 1979 Atlantic City Medical Center, Pomona NJ) He retired after owning the Ford dealership at Egg Harbor City 40 years. Buried Egg Harbor City Cemetery, Egg Harbor City NJ.

Al Bauers—2 Years Pitcher (b. abt 1841 Columbus OH–d. 6 Sep 1913 at his home in Wilkes-Barre PA) Civil War veteran. He was the groundskeeper at the local ballpark. Died suddenly from a heart attack while eating breakfast. Buried Hollenback Cemetery, Wilkes-Barre PA.

Russ Bauers—8 Years Pitcher (b. 10 May 1914 Townsend WI–d. 1 Jan 1995 Hines Memorial Hospital, Chicago IL).

Paddy Baumann—7 Years Infielder (b. 20 Dec 1885 Indianapolis IN–d. 20 Nov 1969 University Heights Hosp, Indianapolis IN) He played in the American Association, International League and Texas League, and managed in the Texas League. He also umpired four years in the Three-I League before going to work in the maintenance department of J I Holcomb Company. Buried Crown Hill Cemetery, Indianapolis IN.

Jim Baumer—2 Years Infielder (b. 29 Jan 1931 Tulsa OK–d. 8 Jul 1996 at his home in Paoli PA) He worked his entire life in baseball, retiring as vice-president of player development for the Phillies in 1993. Before spending 14 years with the Phillies he was general manager of the Brewers for six years. Died after a long illness. Buried St Peter and St Paul Cemetery, Springfield PA.

George Baumgardner—5 Years Pitcher (b. 22 Jul 1891 Barboursville WV–d. 13 Dec 1970 at his home in Barboursville WV) Served in the U.S. Army during World War I. Buried Barboursville Cemetery, Barboursville WV.

Harry Baumgartner—1 Year Pitcher (b. 8 Oct 1892 South Pittsburg TN–d. 3 Dec 1930 at an infirmary in Augusta GA) World War I veteran. He was an immigration inspector for the U.S. Coast Guard. Buried City Cemetery, South Pittsburg TN.

Stan Baumgartner—8 Years Pitcher (b. 14 Dec 1894 Houston TX–d. 4 Oct 1955 at his home in Philadelphia PA) For 25 years he was a sportswriter and baseball authority for the Philadelphia *Inquirer*. Died after being in poor health for a year. Buried Holy Sepulchre Cemetery, Philadelphia PA.

Frank Baumholtz—10 Years Outfielder (b. 7 Oct 1918 Midvale OH–d. 14 Dec 1997 Winter Springs FL) Served in the U.S. Navy during World II. He was a food broker.

George Bausewine—1 Year Pitcher (b. 22 Mar 1869 Philadelphia PA–d. 29 Jul 1947 at his home in Norristown PA) He had been a member of the Philadelphia police force 29 years when he took the Chief of Police job at Norristown in 1929. He held that job until he resigned in 1944 after he was convicted on bribery charges in a slot machine scam. The State Supreme Court overturned the conviction in 1946. Died in his sleep after suffering from heart troubles and arthritis for ten years. Buried Arlington Cemetery, Drexel Hill PA.

Jim Baxes —1 Year Infielder (b. 5 Jul 1928 San Francisco CA–d. 14 Nov 1996 Garden Grove CA) For 33 years he was a sheet metal worker for a heating and air conditioning company. Died from heart failure. Cremated. Buried Magnolia Memorial Park, Garden Grove CA.

Moose Baxter —1 Year Infielder (b. 27 Jul 1876 Chippewa Falls WI–d. 7 Aug 1926 at a hospital in Portland OR) He was engaged in the hotel business in Aberdeen WA. Buried Greenwood Memorial Terrace, Spokane WA.

Harry Bay —8 Years Outfielder (b. 17 Jan 1878 Pontiac IL–d. 20 Mar 1952 Peoria IL) He was the secretary to the fire chief for several years, and later was switchboard operator at the Peoria Fire Department. He was a highly successful musician and stage performer in the Peoria area. Found dead in his home. Buried Parkview Cemetery, Peoria IL.

Burley Bayer —1 Year Infielder (b. 19 Dec 1875 Louisville KY–d. 30 May 1933 at his home in Louisville KY) For 20 years he was a foreman for the Kentucky and Indiana Terminal Railroad. Died after a seven-month illness. Buried Portland Cemetery, Louisville KY.

Dick Bayless —1 Year Outfielder (b. 6 Sep 1883 Joplin MO–d. 16 Dec 1920 Santa Rita NM) He was a powder man for the Chino Copper Company at the Santa Rita mine. Killed instantly when a charge of powder he was setting exploded. Buried Forest Park Cemetery, Joplin MO.

Bill Bayne —9 Years Pitcher (b. 18 Apr 1899 Pittsburgh PA–d. 22 May 1981 St Louis MO) Died after a long illness. Buried Bellefontaine Cemetery, St Louis MO.

Jack Beach—1 Year Outfielder (b. abt 1862 Alexandria VA–d. 23 Jul 1896 at his home in Alexandria VA) Died from Bright's disease.

Johnny Beall —4 Years Outfielder (b. 12 Mar 1882 Beltsville MD–d. 13 Jun 1926 Beltsville MD) Buried St John's Cemetery, Beltsville MD.

Walter Beall —5 Years Pitcher (b. 29 Jul 1899 Washington DC–d. 28 Jan 1959 Suitland MD).

Tommy Beals —1 Year Outfielder (b. abt 1855 Hartford CT–d. 2 Oct 1915 San Francisco CA) Cremated. Buried Cypress Lawn Memorial Park, Colma CA.

Alex Beam —1 Year Pitcher (b. 21 Nov 1870 Johnstown PA–d. 17 Apr 1938 at his home in Nogales AZ) He lived in Nogales from 1919 until his death, working in mining. Died from the effects of a stroke suffered three years earlier. Buried Nogales City Cemetery, Nogales AZ.

Ernie Beam —1 Year Pitcher (b. 17 Mar 1867 Mansfield OH–d. 12 Sep 1918 Mansfield OH) He was a patrolman for the Mansfield Police Department. Died from cancer of the brain. Buried Mansfield Cemetery, Mansfield OH.

Belve Bean —5 Years Pitcher (b. 23 Apr 1905 Mullin TX–d. 1 Jun 1988 Western Hills Nursing Home, Comanche TX) He had a ranch near Comamche where he raised cattle and later operated a dairy. From 1957 to 1965 he was the sheriff of Comanche County, TX. Died from cardiac arrest. Buried White Point Cemetery, Comanche TX.

Joe Bean —1 Year Infielder (b. 18 Mar 1874 Boston MA–d. 15 Feb 1961 at his home in Atlanta GA) He coached baseball from 1914 to 1917 at the University of Georgia, and 1917 to 1922 at Georgia Tech. He then coached baseball, football, basketball and track from 1922 to 1950 at Marist College. He was also the sports instructor at the Atlanta Athletic Club. Died in his sleep. Buried Westview Cemetery, Atlanta GA.

Ollie Beard —3 Years Infielder (b. 2 May 1864 Lexington KY–d. 28 May 1929 Cincinnati OH) Died from a heart attack. Cremated.

Larry Bearnarth—5 Years Pitcher (b. 11 Sep 1941 New York City NY–d. 31 Dec 1999 St Anthony's Hospital, St Petersburg FL) He worked his entire life in baseball as a pitching coach and scout. Died from a heart attack. Buried Memorial Park Cemetery, St Petersburg FL.

Eb Beatin —5 Years Pitcher (b. 10 Aug 1866 Baltimore MD–d. 9 May 1925 Baltimore MD).

Des Beatty —1 Year Infielder (b. 7 Apr 1893 Baltimore MD–d. 6 Oct 1969 at a hospital in Norway ME) World War I veteran. He worked at a number of jobs, including several years in the food brokerage business. He was a business analyst for the Office of Price Stabilization. Died following a brief illness. Buried Pine Grove Cemetery, Falmouth ME.

Ginger Beaumont—12 Years Outfielder, (b. 20 Jun 1876 Rochester WI–d. 10 Apr 1956 Burlington Memorial Hospital, Burlington WI.) He was the first batter to hit in a World Series game. Member of the Wisconsin Hall of Fame. Died following an extended illness. He was stricken by bronchopneumonia and was in a coma his last three weeks. Buried Rochester Cemetery, Rochester WI.

Johnny Beazley—6 Years Pitcher (b. 25 May 1918 Nashville TN–d. 21 Apr 1990 at his home in Nashville TN) Served in the U.S. Navy during World War II. A Nashville civic leader, he owned and operated the Falstaff beer distributorship there, retiring in 1972. Died after an extended battle with cancer. Buried Mount Olivet Cemetery, Nashville TN.

Buck Becannon—3 Years Pitcher (b. 22 Aug 1859 New York City NY–d. 5 Nov 1923 at his home in New York City NY) Died suddenly.

Boom-Boom Beck—12 Years Pitcher (b. 16 Oct 1904 Decatur IL–d. 7 May 1987 Burnham Hospital, Champaign IL) He was a scout and pitching coach in the minor and major leagues. Died from a heart attack. Buried Lutheran Cemetery, Decatur IL.

Clyde Beck—6 Years Infielder (b. 6 Jan 1900 Bassett CA–d. 15 Jul 1988 City Convalescent Hospial, Temple City CA) He was a motor rewinder for 25 years. Died from a heart attack and kidney failure. Cremated.

Erve Beck—3 Years Infielder (b. 19 Jul 1878 Toledo OH–d. 23 Dec 1916 Toledo OH) He was a clerk. Died from heart disease. Buried St Mary's Catholic Cemetery, Toledo OH.

Fred Beck—5 Years Infielder (b. 17 Nov 1886 Havana IL–d. 12 Mar 1962 Mason District Hospital, Havana IL) World War I veteran. He played in the Three-I League, American Association and Western League. Buried Laurel Hills Cemetery, Havana IL.

George Beck—1 Year Pitcher (b. 21 Feb 1890 South Bend IN–d. 29 Oct 1973 Carlyle Nursing Home, South Bend IN) World War I veteran. Died after a six-week illness. Buried Riverside Cemetery, South Bend IN.

Zinn Beck—5 Years Infielder (b. 30 Sep 1885 Steubenville OH–d. 19 Mar 1981 West Palm Beach FL) For 51 years he was a scout, 45 of them for the Senators/Twins. Buried Evergreen Cemetery, West Palm Beach FL.

Heinie Beckendorf—2 Years Catcher (b. 15 Jun 1884 New York City NY–d. 15 Sep 1949 at his home in Jackson Heights NY) Buried Long Island National Cemetery, Farmingdale NY.

Beals Becker—8 Years Outfielder (b. 5 Jul 1886 El Dorado KS–d. 16 Aug 1943 at his home in Huntington Park CA) He was a saw worker in an aircraft factory. Died from bladder cancer. Buried Inglewood Park Cemetery, Inglewood CA.

Bob Becker—2 Years Pitcher (b. 15 Aug 1875 Syracuse NY–d. 11 Oct 1951 at his home in Syracuse NY) Buried Assumption Cemetery, Syracuse NY.

Charlie Becker—2 Years Pitcher (b. 14 Oct 1888 Washington DC–d. 30 Jul 1928 at his home in Washington DC) He was a news photographer. Served in the Ambulance Corps during World War I and was gassed during the war. His death was attributed to effects from the gas. Buried Arlington National Cemetery, Arlington VA.

Heinz Becker—4 Years Infielder (b. 26 Aug 1915 Berlin, Germany–d. 11 Oct 1991 Dallas TX) Buried Restland Memorial Park, Dallas TX.

Joe Becker—2 Years Catcher (b. 25 Jun 1908 St Louis MO–d. 11 Jan 1998 Sunset Hills MO).

Marty Becker—1 Year Outfielder (b. 25 Dec 1893 Tiffin OH–d. 25 Sep 1957 at his home in Cincinnati OH) He managed in the minor leagues 15 years before managing a bowling alley in Norwood OH during World War II. He then owned a publicity and advertising agency for more than 20 years. Cremated.

Jake Beckley—20 Years Infielder Hall of Fame (b. 4 Aug 1867 Hannibal MO–d. 25 Jun 1918 at his home in Kansas City MO) After his 20 year major league career he played minor league baseball another three years, until 1910. He umpired some and played semi-pro ball after that. He was known for his bunting ability, which he did with the bat handle out. Died from heart disease. Buried Riverside Cemetery, Hannibal MO.

Bill Beckman—4 Years Pitcher (b. 8 Dec 1907 Clayton MO–d. 2 Jan 1990 Villa at Riverwood, Florissant MO) Died from a blood clot. Buried Calvary Cemetery, St Louis MO.

Jim Beckman —2 Years Pitcher (b. 1 Mar 1905 Cincinnati OH–d. 5 Dec 1974 at his home in Montgomery OH) Died suddenly. Buried Gate of Heaven Cemetery, Cincinnati OH.

Gene Bedford —1 Year Infielder (b. 2 Dec 1896 Dallas TX–d. 6 Oct 1977 San Antonio TX) Buried Sunset Memorial Park, San Antonio TX.

Jim Bedford —1 Year Infielder (b. 25 May 1904 Hudson NY–d. 27 Jun 1962 Vassar Hospital, Poughkeepsie NY) He conducted an insurance business in Poughkeepsie. Died suddenly. Buried Cedar Park Cemetery, Hudson NY.

Phil Bedgood —2 Years Pitcher (b. 8 Mar 1899 Harrison GA–d. 8 May 1927 Fort Pierce Hospital, Fort Pierce FL) He sold Studebakers in Fort Pierce before becoming an assistant manager at the Fort Pierce Hudson-Essex dealership. Died from complications following surgery for appendicitis. Buried Baptist Church Cemetery, Harrison GA.

Hugh Bedient —4 Years Pitcher (b. 23 Oct 1889 Gerry NY–d. 21 Jul 1965 W C A Hospital, Jamestown NY) He retired from the Harbison-Carborudum Corporation in Falconer NY. Died from arteriosclerotic heart disease. Buried Levant Cemetery, Falconer NY.

Andy Bednar —2 Years Pitcher (b. 16 Aug 1908 Streator IL–d. 25 Nov 1937 near Graham TX) He had just begun working for his uncle in the oil fields when he was killed in a one-car accident 25 miles south of Graham. Buried Nokomis IL.

Fred Beebe —7 Years Pitcher (b. 31 Dec 1880 Lincoln NE–d. 30 Oct 1957 LaGrange IL) He coached baseball and track at Indiana University two years before becoming associated with People's Gas Company in Chicago IL where he worked until 1937 when he was forced to retire because of ill health. Buried Parkholm Cemetery, LaGrange Park IL.

Ed Beecher —4 Years Outfielder (b. 2 Jul 1859 Guilford CT–d. 12 Sep 1935 St Francis Hospital, Hartford CT) He worked for the Hartford Police Department. Died after a long illness. Buried Mount St Benedict Cemetery, Bloomfield CT.

Roy Beecher —2 Years Pitcher (b. 10 May 1884 Swanton OH–d. 11 Oct 1952 Toledo OH) He was a meat cutter 45 years at the Toledo State Hospital. Died from a heart attack while working. Buried Swanton Cemetery, Swanton OH.

Joe Beggs —9 Years Pitcher (b. 4 Nov 1910 Rankin PA–d. 19 Jul 1983 St Vincent Hospital, Indianapolis IN) Served as a lieutenant in the U.S. Navy during World War II. He taught history and geography at several Kentucky schools before taking a job as director of urban renewal in Newport KY. He worked on that job six years before returning to teaching, retiring in 1970. Cremated.

Ed Begley —2 Years Pitcher (b. 1863 New York City NY–d. 24 Jul 1919 at his home in Waterbury CT) Buried Old St Joseph's Cemetery, Waterbury CT.

Jim Begley —1 Year Infielder (b. 19 Sep 1903 San Francisco CA–d. 22 Feb 1957 Fort Miley Hospital, San Francisco CA) He also played professional basketball even though he was only 5' 7" tall. After his sports career he was an attorney. Died from cancer. Buried Golden Gate National Cemetery, San Bruno CA.

Petie Behan —3 Years Pitcher (b. 11 Dec 1887 Dallas City PA–d. 22 Jan 1957 Bradford PA) He clerked for H A Spencer and Company grocery store and later worked for the Dresser Manufacturing Division until his health failed. Died after being in failing health two years. Buried St Bernard's Cemetery, Bradford PA.

Steve Behel —2 Years Outfielder (b. 6 Nov 1860 Earlville IL–d. 15 Feb 1945 at his home in Los Angeles CA) He was a watchman superintendent for a petroleum company. Died from a heart condition. Buried Inglewood Park Cemetery, Inglewood CA.

Hank Behrman —4 Years Pitcher (b. 27 Jun 1921 Brooklyn NY–d. 20 Jan 1987 New York City NY).

Ollie Bejma —4 Years Infielder (b. 12 Sep 1907 South Bend IN–d. 3 Jan 1995 at his home in South Bend IN) He worked for Studebaker in South Bend, the University of Notre Dame security department and the Indiana License Bureau in Mishawaka IN. An avid bowler, he won several city and state bowling championships. Buried St Joseph Cemetery, South Bend IN.

Mark Belanger —18 Years Infielder (b. 8 Jun 1944 Pittsfield MA–d. 6 Oct 1998 New York City NY) He was a key figure in the MLB Player's Association. Died from lung cancer. Buried St Joseph's Cemetery, Pittsfield MA.

Wayne Belardi—6 Years Infielder (b. 5 Sep 1930 St Helena CA–d. 21 Oct 1993 Dominican Hospital, Santa Cruz CA) He owned and operated a bar and restaurant for five years. Died from a heart attack but suffered from cirrhosis of the liver. He was cremated and his ashes scattered off the coast of Santa Cruz.

Ira Belden—1 Year Outfielder (b. 16 Apr 1874 Cleveland OH–d. 15 Jul 1916 Lakewood OH).

Bo Belinsky—8 Years Pitcher (b. 7 Dec 1936 New York City NY–d. 23 Nov 2001 Las Vegas NV) Died from a heart attack.

Beau Bell—7 Years Outfielder (b. 20 Aug 1907 Bellville TX–d. 14 Sep 1977 at a hospital in College Station TX) He coached baseball at Texas A & M from 1951 to 1958 and was working at the physical plant there when he retired. Died after a brief illness. Buried Restever Memorial Park, Bryan TX.

Bill Bell—2 Years Pitcher (b. 24 Oct 1933 Goldsboro NC–d. 11 Oct 1962 V A Hospital, Durham NC) He was an automobile salesman at Fort Myers FL. He never regained consiousness after an automobile accident in Fort Myers, and died ten months later. Buried Willow Dale Cemetery, Goldsboro NC.

Charlie Bell—2 Years Pitcher (b. 12 Aug 1868 Cincinnati OH–d. 7 Feb 1937 General Hospital, Cincinnati OH) He was a police patrolman from 1900 until retiring in 1925. Died from emphysema following bronchopneumonia. Buried Baltimore Pike Cemetery, Cincinnati OH.

Cool Papa Bell—25 Years Outfielder Hall of Fame (b. 17 May 1903 Starkville MS–d. 7 Mar 1991 St Louis University Hospital, St Louis MO) He played in the negro leagues. Said to be the fastest man to ever play baseball. One story says that when he turned the light out at night, he could be in bed before it got dark. Another story says that once, as he rounded second base, he was hit by a ball he had hit up the middle. After retiring from baseball he worked at the St Louis City Hall, first as a janitor and, later, as a security guard, until his retirement in 1973. Died after suffering a heart attack. Buried St Peter's Cemetery, St Louis MO.

Frank Bell—1 Year Catcher (b. 1863 Cincinnati OH–d. 14 Apr 1891 Cincinnati OH) He was a private security guard. He was intoxicated when he was shot to death at a saloon in a brawl over a card game. Buried Wesleyan Cemetery, Cincinnati OH.

George Bell—5 Years Pitcher (b. 2 Nov 1874 Bronx NY–d. 25 Dec 1941 New York City NY).

Gus Bell—15 Years Outfielder (b. 15 Nov 1928 Louisville KY–d. 7 May 1995 Bethesada North Hospital, Montgomery OH) Died following a heart attack. Buried Gate of Heaven Cemetery, Cincinnati OH.

Hi Bell—8 Years Pitcher (b. 16 Jul 1899 Louisville KY–d. 7 Jun 1949 at his home in Glendale CA) He operated a restaurant in Glendale. Died from a heart attack. Buried Calvary Cemetery, Los Angeles CA.

Les Bell—9 Years Infielder (b. 14 Dec 1901 Harrisburg PA–d. 26 Dec 1985 Hershey Medical Center, Hershey PA) He managed minor league baseball. Buried East Harrisburg Cemetery, Harrisburg PA.

Ralph Bell—1 Year Pitcher (b. 16 Nov 1891 Kohoka MO–d. 18 Oct 1959 Mercy Hospital, Burlington IA) Died after being in failing health for a few months. Buried St Peter's Catholic Church Cemetery, Keokuk IA.

Rudy Bell—1 Year Outfielder (b. 1 Jan 1881 Wausau WI–d. 28 Jul 1955 at his home in Albuquerque NM) He umpired in the minor leagues for several years. Buried Sunset Memorial Park, Albuquerque NM.

John Bellman—1 Year Catcher (b. 4 Mar 1864 Taylorsville KY–d. 8 Dec 1931 at his home in Louisville KY) He worked for the Louisville Gas and Electric Company for 41 years. Died following a stroke. Buried Calvary Cemetery, Louisville KY.

Harry Bemis—9 Years Catcher (b. 1 Feb 1874 Farmington NH–d. 23 May 1947 at his home in Cleveland OH) He worked in the shipping department of a furniture company. Died from a heart attack. Buried Elmhurst Park Cemetery, Avon OH.

Chief Bender—16 Years Pitcher Hall of Fame (b. 5 May 1883 Brainerd MN–d. 22 May 1954 Graduate Park Hospital, Philadelphia PA) A full-blooded Chippewa Indian, he had been a coach for the Philadelphia Athletics. Died from a heart attack while being treated for cancer. Buried Hillside Cemetery, Roslyn PA.

Art Benedict—1 Year Infielder (b. 31 Mar 1862 Cornwall IL–d. 20 Jan 1948 Denver CO).

Joe Benes—1 Year Infielder (b. 8 Jan 1901 Long Island City NY–d. 7 Mar 1975 Elmhurst NY).

Ray Benge—12 Years Pitcher (b. 22 Apr 1902 Jacksonville TX–d. 27 Jun 1997 Centerville TX) Served in the U.S. Navy during World War II. He coached baseball at Sam Houston University until retiring to his Leon County, TX, ranch in 1968. Buried Concord Cemetery, Concord TX.

Benny Bengough—10 Years Catcher (b. 27 Jul 1898 Niagara Falls NY–d. 22 Dec 1968 Philadelphia PA) He coached for the Phillies and was a noted banquet speaker. Died from a heart attack. Buried St Dominic Cemetery, Philadelphia PA.

Henry Benn—1 Year Pitcher (b. 25 Jan 1890 Viola WI–d. 4 Jun 1967 Madison WI) Buried Viola Cemetery, Viola WI.

Bugs Bennett—2 Years Pitcher (b. 19 Apr 1892 Wier KS–d. 21 Nov 1957 Noel MO) He moved to Noel in 1939 and was the owner/operator of the Red Top Tourist Courts there. Died from a heart attack. Buried White Rose Cemetery, Bartlesville OK.

Charlie Bennett—15 Years Catcher (b. 21 Nov 1854 New Castle PA–d. 24 Feb 1927 at his home in Detroit MI) After the baseball season of 1894 he lost both legs in a railroad accident while on a hunting trip. Provided with artificial limbs he was able to get around with a cane. He took up painting china, first as a hobby, later as a livelihood. Died after an illness of a year. Buried Woodmere Cemetery, Detroit MI.

Frank Bennett—2 Years Pitcher (b. 27 Oct 1904 Mardela Springs MD–d. 18 Mar 1966 General Hospital, Wilmington DE) He became a pipe fitter for Pure-Oil Corporation in Marcus Hook PA. From 1948 to 1958 he worked as a piping superintendent on construction projects for duPont Company and later was associated with Pipe Fitter's Union Local #80. Died from a heart attack. Buried Gracelawn Memorial Park, New Castle DE.

Fred Bennett—2 Years Outfielder (b. 15 Mar 1902 Atkins AR–d. 12 May 1957 Atkins AR) He operated a men's clothing store at Atkins. Died from a heart attack. Buried Atkins City Cemetery, Atkins AR.

Herschel Bennett—5 Years Outfielder (b. 21 Sep 1896 Elwood MO–d. 9 Sep 1964 Kimbrough Nursing Home, Springfield MO) Served in the U.S. Navy during World War I. He was the Commissioner of Revenue for the City of Springfield from 1934 until 1946. He had been ill since 1950. Buried Greenlawn Memorial Gardens, Springfield MO.

Joe Bennett—1 Year Infielder (b. 2 Jul 1900 New York City NY–d. 11 Jul 1987 Pacific Care Center, Morro Bay CA) He retired from the U.S. Army in 1955 after 38 years, serving during both World Wars I and II and the Korean War. Died from prostate cancer. Buried Cedar Park Cemetery, Paramus NJ.

Pug Bennett—2 Years Infielder (b. 20 Feb 1874 Ponca NE–d. 10 Sep 1935 at his home in Kirkland WA) He worked at the county sheds. Died suddenly, apparently from a heart condition. Buried Kirkland WA.

Jack Bentley—9 Years Pitcher (b. 8 Mar 1895 Sandy Spring MD–d. 24 Oct 1969 Montgomery General Hospital, Olney MD) He was bedridden the last few years of his life with arthritis. Buried Friend Cemetery, Sandy Spring MD.

Al Benton—14 Years Pitcher (b. 18 Mar 1911 Noble OK–d. 14 Apr 1968 St Francis Hospital, Lynwood CA) He was a motel manager. Died from burns caused by an accidental explosion in a motel room. Buried Park Lawn Memorial Park, Bell Gardens CA.

Larry Benton—13 Years Pitcher (b. 20 Nov 1897 St Louis MO–d. 3 Apr 1953 Cincinnati OH) He was a supervisor for Cincinnati Transit Company. Died from a heart attack while golfing. Buried St Joseph Old Catholic Cemetery, Cincinnati OH.

Rube Benton—15 Years Pitcher (b. 27 Jun 1887 Clinton NC–d. 12 Dec 1937 Dothan AL) He died in an automobile accident in which one other person was killed. Buried Baptist Church Cemetery, Salemburg NC.

Sid Benton—1 Year Pitcher (b. 4 Aug 1894 Buckner AR–d. 8 Mar 1977 at a hospital in Fayetteville AR) Buried Evergreen Cemetery, Fayetteville AR.

Stan Benton—1 Year Infielder (b. 29 Sep 1901 Cannel City KY–d. 7 Jun 1984 Mesquite TX).

Joe Benz—9 Years Pitcher (b. 21 Jan 1886 New

Alsace IN–d. 22 Apr 1957 St George Hospital, Chicago IL) He was a custodian at St Killian's Church and later worked at O'Hare Field. Died following a stroke. Buried Holy Sepulchre Cemetery, Worth IL.

Johnny Berardino—11 Years Infielder (b. 1 May 1917 Los Angeles CA–d. 19 May 1996 at his home in Los Angeles CA) World War II veteran. He became a noted actor, starring 33 years in "General Hospital" on TV. Died from cancer. Buried Holy Cross Cemetery, Culver City CA.

Moe Berg—15 Years Catcher (b. 2 Mar 1902 New York City NY–d. 29 May 1972 Maass Memorial Hospital, Belleville NJ) Known for his scholarly credentials and linguistic abilities, he had command of ten languages. He worked for the Office of Strategic Services as a linguist during World War II. He was cremated and his ashes scattered in Israel.

Augie Bergamo—2 Years Outfielder (b. 14 Feb 1918 Detroit MI–d. 19 Aug 1974 at his home in Grosse Point City MI) For 20 years he was a manufacturer's representative. Died following a brief illness. Buried Forest Lawn Cemetery, Detroit MI.

Bill Bergen—11 Years Catcher (b. 13 Jun 1873 North Brookfield MA–d. 19 Dec 1943 City Hospital, Worcester MA) He managed and coached in the minor leagues and in semi-pro baseball. Died after a long illness. Buried St John's Cemetery, Worcester MA.

Marty Bergen—4 Years Catcher (b. 25 Oct 1871 North Brookfield MA–d. 19 Jan 1900 North Brookfield MA) He died at the height of his baseball career when he killed his wife and two children with an ax, then himself by cutting his throat with a razor. Buried St Joseph Cemetery, North Brookfield MA.

Boze Berger—6 Years Infielder (b. 13 May 1910 Baltimore MD–d. 2 Nov 1992 Bethesda MD) Buried Baltimore Cemetery, Baltimore MD.

Clarence Berger—1 Year Outfielder (b. 1 Nov 1894 Cleveland OH–d. 30 Jun 1959 at his home in Washington DC) Buried Mount Olivet Cemetery, Frederick MD.

Heinie Berger—4 Years Pitcher (b. 7 Jan 1882 LaSalle IL–d. 10 Feb 1954 at his home in Lakewood OH) He was a shipping clerk at the Bing Furniture Company. Died from a heart attack. Buried Lake View Cemetery, Cleveland OH.

Joe Berger—2 Years Infielder (b. 20 Dec 1886 St Louis MO–d. 5 Mar 1956 at his home in Rock Island IL) He managed minor league teams in the Western League from 1917 to 1929. After that he was a guard at the International Harvestor plant in Rock Island until he retired in 1954. Died after a three-month illness. Buried Memorial Park Cemetery, Rock Island IL.

Johnny Berger—2 Years Catcher (b. 27 Aug 1901 Philadelphia PA–d. 7 May 1979 at a hospital in Lake Charles LA) He managed minor league baseball four years before working 25 years for United Gas Corporation in Lake Charles. Buried Graceland Cemetery, Lake Charles LA.

Tun Berger—3 Years Infielder (b. 6 Dec 1867 Pittsburgh PA–d. 11 Jun 1907 at his home in Allegheny PA) He was a glass blower. Died from kidney disease.

Wally Berger—11 Years Outfielder (b. 10 Oct 1905 Chicago IL–d. 30 Nov 1988 South Bay Hospital, Redondo Beach CA) Died from complications of diabetes. Buried Inglewood Park Cemetery, Inglewood CA.

John Bergh—2 Years Catcher (b. 8 Oct 1857 Boston MA–d. 16 Apr 1883 at his home in Boston MA) He died at the height of his career from consumption. Buried Holyhood Cemetery, Brookline MA.

Marty Berghammer—4 Years Infielder (b. 18 Jan 1886 Pittsburgh PA–d. 21 Dec 1957 at his home in Pittsburgh PA) He managed minor league baseball for a time, then opened a tavern in Pittsburgh. Died from a heart attack. Buried St Martin's Cemetery, Pittsburgh PA.

Al Bergman—1 Year Infielder (b. 27 Sep 1890 Peru IN–d. 21 Jun 1961 Irene Bryan Hospital, Fort Wayne IN) He lettered in four sports at Notre Dame and played on the same team as Knute Rockne. He was plant manager of the American Stationery Company plant in Peru until he was forced to retire because of tuberculosis. He spent his last 18 years hospitalized with the disease. Buried St Charles Cemetery, Peru IN.

Jack Berly—4 Years Pitcher (b. 24 May 1903 Natchitoches LA–d. 26 Jun 1977 at his home in Houston TX) He lived in Houston 67 years. Buried Hollywood Cemetery, Houston TX.

Bob Berman—1 Year Catcher (b. 24 Jan 1899 New York City NY–d. 2 Aug 1988 Bridgeport

CT) Buried Gate of Heaven Cemetery, Hawthorne NY.

Curt Bernard—2 Years Outfielder (b. 18 Feb 1878 Parkersburg WV–d. 10 Apr 1955 at a hospital in Culver City CA) An osteopathic physician and surgeon, he had lived in Santa Monica CA 28 years. Buried Inglewood Park Cemetery, Inglewood CA.

Joe Bernard—1 Year Pitcher (b. 24 Mar 1882 Brighton IL–d. 22 Sep 1960 at his home in Springfield IL) He owned and operated Bernard Investment Company in Springfield for over 50 years. Buried Calvary Cemetery, Springfield IL.

Bill Bernhard—9 Years Pitcher (b. 16 Mar 1871 Clarence NY–d. 30 Mar 1949 Balboa Hospital, San Diego CA) Died from leukemia. Cremated.

Walter Bernhardt—1 Year Pitcher (b. 20 May 1893 Pleasant Valley PA–d. 26 Jul 1958 Watertown NY) He was a prominent dentist in Webster NY for 39 years. Died on the seventh hole of the Ives Hill Country Club while golfing. Buried Webster Rural Cemetery, Webster NY.

Carlos Bernier—1 Year Outfielder (b. 28 Jan 1929 Juana Diaz, Puerto Rico–d. 6 Apr 1989 Juana Diaz, Puerto Rico) He hung himself.

Johnny Bero—2 Years Infielder (b. 22 Dec 1922 Gary WV–d. 11 May 1985 at his home in Gardena CA) World War II veteran. For ten years he was maintenance supervisor for the City of Gardena. Died from lung cancer that had spread to his brain. Buried Holy Cross Cemetery, Culver City CA.

Denny Berran—1 Year Outfielder (b. 1887 Merrimac MA–d. 28 Apr 1943 Boston MA) Buried New Calvary Cemetery, Mattapan MA.

Charlie Berry—1 Year Infielder (b. 6 Sep 1860 Elizabeth NJ–d. 22 Jan 1940 at his home in Phillipsburg NJ) He worked for Ingersoll-Rand Company, retiring in 1929. Died from a cerebral embolism. Buried Mount Olivet Cemetery, Elizabeth NJ.

Charlie Berry—11 Years Catcher (b. 18 Oct 1902 Phillipsburg NJ–d. 6 Sep 1972 Evanston Hospital, Evanston IL) An All-American football player prior to his baseball career, and an American League umpire from 1942 to 1962, he also officiated in the National Football League. Died from a heart attack. Buried Belvidere Cemetery, Belvidere NJ.

Claude Berry—5 Years Catcher (b. 14 Feb 1880 Losantville IN–d. 1 Feb 1974 Heritage House Nursing Home, Richmond IN) He played organized baseball 17 years before becoming a realtor in Richmond in 1920, working in real estate 50 years. Buried Earlham Cemetery, Richmond IN.

Joe Berry—1 Year Catcher (b. 10 Sep 1872 Wheeling WV–d. 13 Mar 1961 Philadelphia PA) He owned and operated Berry and Son, a Philadelphia bookbinding firm. Buried Westminster Cemetery, Bala Cynwyd PA.

Joe Berry—4 Years Pitcher (b. 16 Dec 1904 Huntsville AR–d. 27 Sep 1958 Memorial Hospital, Anaheim CA) He was a calendar man for a rubber company. Died without regaining consiousness following an auto accident. His skull was fractured when he was thrown from his car. Buried Huntsville Cemetery, Huntsville AR.

Joe Berry—2 Years Infielder (b. 31 Dec 1894 Philadelphia PA–d. 27 Apr 1976 at his home in Philadelphia PA) Served in the U.S. Army during World War I, and later retired from the U.S. Marine Corps. A figure in Republican Party circles and a leader in veteran's organizations, he was a property assessor for the Philadelphia Board of Revision of Taxes. Buried West Laurel Hill Cemetery, Bala Cynwyd PA.

Harry Berte—1 Year Infielder (b. 10 May 1872 Covington KY–d. 6 May 1952 Los Angeles CA) A retired clerk for the Los Angeles County (CA) Health Department, he died from heart disease. Buried Valhalla Memorial Park, North Hollywood CA.

Bob Bescher—11 Years Outfielder (b. 25 Feb 1883 London OH–d. 29 Nov 1942 London OH) Known for his love of the outdoors, he was an avid big game hunter. Killed when his car was struck by a train. Buried Kirkwood Cemetery, London OH.

Herman Besse—5 Years Pitcher (b. 16 Aug 1911 St Louis MO–d. 13 Aug 1972 Los Angeles CA) He was a newspaper dealer for the Los Angeles *Times* for 16 years. Died from pancreatic cancer. Buried Calvary Cemetery, St Louis MO.

Don Bessent—4 Years Pitcher (b. 13 Mar 1931 Jacksonville FL–d. 7 Jul 1990 Jacksonville FL) A lifelong resident of Jacksonville, he was a retired sales manager for Pepsi-Cola Bottling Company there. Buried Oaklawn Cemetery, Jacksonville FL.

Frank Betcher—1 Year Infielder (b. 15 Feb 1888 Philadelphia PA–d. 27 Nov 1981 Wynnewood PA).

Larry Bettencourt—3 Years Outfielder (b. 22 Sep 1905 Centerville CA–d. 16 Sep 1978 New Orleans LA) He lived in New Orleans 40 years. Buried Lake Lawn Mausoleum, New Orleans LA.

Hal Betts—2 Years Pitcher (b. 14 Jun 1881 Alliance OH–d. 22 May 1946 San Antonio TX).

Huck Betts—10 Years Pitcher (b. 18 Feb 1897 Millsboro DE–d. 13 Jun 1987 at his home in Millsboro DE) Served in the U.S. Army during World War I. He owned and operated the Ball Theatre, a movie house, in Millsboro, selling it in 1971. Died from a heart attack. Buried Millsboro Cemetery, Millsboro DE.

Bruno Betzel—5 Years Infielder (b. 6 Dec 1894 Chattanooga OH–d. 7 Feb 1965 at a hospital in West Hollywood FL) He managed minor league baseball and scouted for several teams, spending his entire life in baseball. Buried North Grove Cemetery, Celina OH.

Hal Bevan—3 Years Infielder (b. 15 Nov 1930 New Orleans LA–d. 5 Oct 1968 Baptist Hospital, New Orleans LA) When his mobility was hampered by a broken leg he played several years in the Pacific Coast League. Scouted for the Braves. Died from a kidney infection. Buried Greenwood Cemetery, New Orleans LA.

Bill Bevans—4 Years Pitcher (b. 20 Oct 1916 Hubbard OR–d. 26 Oct 1991 Salem OR) He managed the Pacific Intermountain Express Trucking Company terminal at Salem for 27 years. Died from heart disease and diabetes. Buried Restlawn Memory Gardens, Salem OR.

Lou Bevil—1 Year Pitcher (b. 27 Nov 1922 Nelson IL–d. 1 Feb 1973 K S B Hospital, Dixon IL) Served in Europe for the U.S. Army during World War II. He was a division road master for the railroad. Died following a long illness. Buried Oakwood Cemetery, Dixon IL.

Charlie Beville—1 Year Pitcher (b. 28 Aug 1877 Colusa CA–d. 5 Jan 1937 Veteran's Hospital, Yountville CA) Spanish-American War and World War I veteran. He worked a number of years for the government at Pittsburg CA. Died from alcoholic poisoning. Buried Colusa Cemetery, Colusa CA.

Monte Beville—2 Years Catcher (b. 24 Feb 1875 Dublin IN–d. 24 Jan 1955 at his home in Grand Rapids MI) Buried Oakwood Cemetery, Muskegon MI.

Hugo Bezdek—3 Years Manager (b. 1 Apr 1883 Prague, Czechoslovakia–d. 19 Sep 1952 City Hospital, Atlantic City NJ) He was an All-American football player at the Univ of Chicago, coached college football at Arkansas, Oregon and Penn State, coached the Cleveland Rams and was the athletic director at Penn State. Died from a heart attack. Buried Whitemarsh Memorial Cemetery, Prospectville PA.

Hank Biasatti—1 Year Infielder (b. 14 Jan 1922 Beano, Italy–d. 20 Apr 1996 Dearborn MI).

Vern Bickford—7 Years Pitcher (b. 17 Aug 1920 Hellier KY–d. 6 May 1960 McGuire V A Hospital, Richmond VA) He was an automobile dealer, traveling salesman and a carpenter. Died from cancer. Buried Zion Baptist Church Cemetery, North Garden VA.

Dan Bickham—1 Year Pitcher (b. 31 Oct 1864 Dayton OH–d. 3 May 1951 Dayton OH).

Oscar Bielaski—1 Year Outfielder (b. 21 Mar 1847 Washington DC–d. 8 Nov 1911 Washington DC) He worked at the Navy yard in Washington DC. Died from a heart attack enroute to Casualty Hospital. Buried Arlington VA.

Harry Biemiller—2 Years Pitcher (b. 9 Oct 1897 Baltimore MD–d. 25 May 1965 Orlando FL) He retired from the Baltimore Police Department in 1950 and moved to Orlando. Buried Glen Haven Memorial Park, Winter Park FL.

Lou Bierbauer—13 Years Infielder (b. 28 Sep 1865 Erie PA–d. 31 Jan 1926 at his home in Erie PA) He was a molder before spending his last eight years as a night watchman at the Oden Stove plant. Died from pneumonia. Buried Erie Cemetery, Erie PA.

Carson Bigbee—11 Years Outfielder (b. 31 Mar 1895 Sweet Home OR–d. 17 Oct 1964 Portland OR) Served in the U.S. Army during World War I. He lived his entire life in Portland where he was in the automobile business. Buried Willamette National Cemetery, Portland OR.

Lyle Bigbee—2 Years Pitcher (b. 22 Aug 1893 Sweet Home OR–d. 3 Aug 1942 Portland OR) He worked in a Portland shipyard when he died from a self-inflicted gunshot wound. Earlier he had farmed in Pleasant Valley. Buried Liberty Cemetery, Sweet Home OR.

Elliott Bigelow—1 Year Outfielder (b. 13 Oct 1898 Tarpon Springs FL–d. 10 Aug 1933 Tampa Hospital, Tampa FL) Died from cerebral meningitis shortly after retiring from baseball. Buried Cycadia Cemetery, Tarpon Springs FL.

Charlie Biggs—1 Year Pitcher (b. 15 Sep 1906 French Lick IN–d. 24 May 1954 French Lick Hospital, French Lick IN) He was a farmer and part-time bartender. Died following a stroke. Buried Mount Lebanon Cemetery, French Lick IN.

Pete Bigler—1 Game Pinch Runner (b. 13 Dec 1892 Bradford OH–d. 1 Apr 1975 Coldwater MI).

George Bignal—1 Year Catcher (b. 18 Jul 1858 Taunton MA–d. 16 Jan 1925 Rhode Island Hospital, Providence RI) Died after an illness of four weeks. Buried St Joseph Cemetery, Taunton MA.

Helene Bigsby—(b. 1888–d. 8 Jan 1950 at her home in Philadelphia PA) She was the first woman to own a baseball team, the St Louis Cardinals, from 1912 to 1918. Buried Lake View Cemetery, Cleveland OH.

Jim Bilbrey—1 Year Pitcher (b. 20 Apr 1924 Rickman TN–d. 26 Dec 1985 Mercy Hospital, Toledo OH) Served in the U.S. Navy during World War II. He was sales manager for a Buick dealership from 1959 to 1972 and a Pontiac dealership from 1972 until he retired in 1978. Buried New Belleville Cemetery, Dowling OH.

Emil Bildilli—5 Years Pitcher (b. 16 Sep 1912 Diamond IN–d. 16 Sep 1946 Blackford County Hospital, Hartford City IN) He was a fireman at Muncie IN. Died as a result of a skull fracture suffered in a one-car accident north of Hartford City when he apparenty went to sleep while driving. Buried Roselawn Memorial Park, Terre Haute IN.

Steve Bilko—10 Years Infielder (b. 13 Nov 1928 Nanticoke PA–d. 7 Mar 1978 Mercy Hospital, Wilkes-Barre PA) He worked 11 years for the Dana Perfume Company at Mountain Top PA, retiring in 1977. Buried St Joseph Church Cemetery, Nanticoke PA.

Harry Billiard—3 Years Pitcher (b. 11 Nov 1883 Monroe IN–d. 3 Jun 1923 at his home in Wooster OH) He was a car salesman. Died from typhoid fever and pneumonia. Buried Wooster Cemetery, Wooster OH.

Haskell Billings—3 Years Pitcher (b. 27 Sep 1907 New York City NY–d. 26 Dec 1983 Marin General Hospital, Greenbrae CA) He lived in Marin County, CA, 35 years and was a well-known homebuilder there. Died from a heart attack. Cremated.

Josh Billings—11 Years Catcher (b. 30 Nov 1891 Grantville KS–d. 30 Dec 1981 City Hospital, Santa Monica CA) He was a real estate broker for 33 years. Died from heart disease and donated his body to the UCLA Medical School.

Steve Biras—1 Year Infielder (b. 26 Feb 1922 East St Louis IL–d. 21 Apr 1965 St Louis MO) Died from a cerebral hemorrhage. Buried Mount Carmel Cemetery, Belleville IL.

Jud Birchall—3 Years Outfielder (b. 1858 Philadelphia PA–d. 22 Dec 1887 Philadelphia PA).

Frank Bird—1 Year Catcher (b. 10 Mar 1869 Spencer MA–d. 20 May 1958 St Francis Home, Worcester MA) He became paralyzed during an exhibition game at age 24, for no apparent reason, and was a semi-invalid the rest of his life. Died after a long illness. Buried Holy Rosary-St Mary's Cemetery, Spencer MA.

Red Bird—1 Year Pitcher (b. 25 Apr 1890 Stephenville TX–d. 23 Mar 1972 Murfeesboro Hospital, Murfeesboro AR) World War I veteran. He was a retired government engineer. Buried Oakdale Cemetery, Murfeesboro AR.

Ralph Birkofer—5 Years Pitcher (b. 5 Nov 1908 Cincinnati OH–d. 16 Mar 1971 at his home in Cincinnati OH) He worked for the Coca-Cola Bottling Company, retiring in 1964. Buried St Mary Cemetery, Cincinnati OH.

Joe Birmingham—9 Years Outfielder 4 Years Manager (b. 6 Aug 1884 Elmira NY–d. 24 Apr 1946 Tampico, Mexico).

Frank Biscan—3 Years Pitcher (b. 13 Mar 1920 Mount Olive IL–d. 22 May 1959 Veteran's Hospital, St Louis MO) Served in the U.S. Navy during World War II. Died from heart disease. Buried Jefferson Barracks National Cemetery, St Louis MO.

John Bischoff—2 Years Catcher (b. 28 Oct 1894 Edwardsville IL–d. 28 Dec 1981 St Elizabeth Medical Ctr, Granite City IL) He was a carpenter for Nesco Barrel 27 years before retiring in 1960. Buried Sunset Hill Memorial Estates, Edwardsville IL.

Bill Bishop —1 Year Pitcher (b. 22 Oct 1900 Clearfield PA–d. 14 Feb 1956 at a hospital in St Joseph MO) A retired coal miner, he had lived in St Joseph four years. He was forced to give up his baseball career in the 1930s due to rheumatism. Buried Memorial Park Cemetery, St Joseph MO.

Bill Bishop —3 Years Pitcher (b. 27 Dec 1869 Adamsburg PA–d. 15 Dec 1932 at his home in Pittsburgh PA) Died after a paralytic stroke suffered four months earlier.

Charlie Bishop —4 Years Pitcher (b. 1 Jan 1924 Atlanta GA–d. 5 Jul 1993 Lawrenceville GA) He operated Bishop and Company, a medical insurance investigation firm. Buried White Chapel Memorial Gardens, Duluth GA.

Frank Bishop —1 Year Infielder (b. 21 Sep 1860 Belvidere IL–d. 18 Jun 1929 Chicago IL) Buried Oak Woods Cemetery, Chicago IL.

Jim Bishop —2 Years Pitcher (b. 28 Jan 1898 Montgomery City MO–d. 20 Sep 1973 Audrain Medical Center, Mexico MO) He was associated with the MFA Insurance Company in Montgomery City. Buried Montgomery City Cemetery, Montgomery City MO.

Lloyd Bishop —1 Year Pitcher (b. 25 Apr 1890 Conway Springs KS–d. 18 Jun 1968 Terrace Gardens Nursing Center, Wichita KS) He was an officer in several Kansas banks. Died from cancer. Buried Clearwater Cemetery, Clearwater KS.

Max Bishop —12 Years Infielder (b. 5 Sep 1899 Waynesboro PA–d. 24 Feb 1962 Waynesboro PA) He coached the baseball team at the U.S. Naval Academy from 1938 until his death, and was due to retire four days after he died in his sleep from a heart condition. Buried Woodlawn Cemetery, Gwynn Oak MD.

Rivington Bisland —3 Years Infielder (b. 17 Feb 1890 New York City NY–d. 11 Jan 1973 Salzburg, Austria).

Del Bissonette —5 Years Infielder 1 Year Manager (b. 6 Sep 1899 Winthrop ME–d. 9 Jun 1972 Augusta General Hospital, Augusta ME) His playing career ended when he spiked himself in the achilles tendon. After that he managed several minor league teams. He retired to Winthrop in 1952. Died from a stroke following a self-inflicted gunshot wound to the stomach. Buried Glenside Cemetery, Winthrop ME.

Hi Bithorn —4 Years Pitcher (b. 18 Mar 1916 Santurce, Puerto Rico–d. 1 Jan 1952 El Mante, Mexico) He was shot by a Mexican policeman.

Red Bittmann —1 Year Infielder (b. 22 Jul 1862 Cincinnati OH–d. 8 Nov 1929 Cincinnati OH) He was a custodian at the armory. Died from liver cancer. Buried Vine Street Hill Cemetery, Cincinnati OH.

Jim Bivin —1 Year Pitcher (b. 11 Dec 1909 Jackson MS–d. 7 Nov 1982 Parkview Episcopal Hospital, Pueblo CO) Served in the U.S. Marine Corps during World War II. He was the last pitcher to face Babe Ruth and managed minor league baseball 23 years. Died from a heart attack. Buried Imperial Memorial Gardens, Pueblo CO.

Bill Black —1 Year Infielder (b. 12 Aug 1899 Philadelphia PA–d. 14 Jan 1968 St Mary's Hospital, Philadelphia PA) He was a retired clerk in the Philadelphia City Traffic Court. Buried East Cedar Hill Cemetery, Philadelphia PA.

Bob Black —1 Year Outfielder (b. 10 Dec 1862 Cincinnati OH–d. 21 Mar 1933 at his home in Sioux City IA) He was involved in local baseball activities his entire life. Died from the effects of a stroke suffered two weeks earlier while playing pool at the Martin Hotel. Buried Graceland Cemetery, Sioux City IA.

Dave Black —3 Years Pitcher (b. 19 Apr 1892 Chicago IL–d. 25 Oct 1936 at his home in Pittsburgh PA) Buried Union Dale Cemetery, Pittsburgh PA.

Don Black —6 Years Pitcher (b. 20 Jul 1916 Salix IA–d. 21 Apr 1959 at his home in Cuyahoga Falls OH) He was an automobile and insurance salesman. Buried Good Shepherd Church Cemetery, McKenney VA.

Jack Black —1 Year Infielder (b. 23 Feb 1890 Covington KY–d. 20 Mar 1962 Rutherford NJ).

Joe Black —6 Years Pitcher (b. 8 Feb 1924 Plainfield NJ–d. 17 May 2002) Played in the Negro Leagues. He was the first black pitcher to win a World Series game. Died from prostate cancer.

Babe Blackburn—2 Years Pitcher (b. 6 Jan 1895 Chicago IL–d. 9 Mar 1984 New Port Richey FL) A retired foreign service officer for the U.S. Dept of Agriculture, he moved from Washington DC to Florida about 1961. Cremated. Buried Irving Park Cemetery, Chicago IL.

Earl Blackburn—5 Years Catcher (b. 1 Nov 1892 Leesville OH–d. 3 Aug 1966 General Hospital, Mansfield OH) He worked over 25 years for Mansfield Tire and Rubber Company. Died following a two-week illness. Buried Massillon Cemetery, Massillon OH.

Jim Blackburn—2 Years Pitcher (b. 19 Jun 1924 Warsaw KY–d. 26 Oct 1969 Cincinnati OH) Buried Spring Grove Cemetery, Cincinnati OH.

Ron Blackburn—2 Years Pitcher (b. 23 Apr 1935 Mount Airy NC–d. 29 Apr 1998 at his home in Morganton NC) He retired from the North Carolina Department of Corrections as recreation director. Died after a period of declining health. Buried Carolina Memorial Park, Concord NC.

Lena Blackburne—8 Years Infielder 2 Years Manager (b. 23 Oct 1886 Clifton Heights PA–d. 29 Feb 1968 Zurbrugg Memorial Hospital, Riverside NJ) He spent 60 years associated with baseball as a player, manager, coach and supplier of "Delaware River Mud" to rub down balls used in every official game. Buried Morgan Cemetery, Cinnaminson NJ.

George Blackerby—1 Year Outfielder (b. 10 Oct 1903 Luther OK–d. 30 May 1987 Wichita Falls TX).

Ewell Blackwell—10 Years Pitcher (b. 23 Oct 1922 Fresno CA–d. 29 Oct 1996 at his home in Hendersonville NC) He was called "The Whip" for his sidearm fastball that approached 100 mph. Died from cancer.

Fred Blackwell—3 Years Catcher (b. 7 Sep 1895 Bowling Green KY–d. 8 Dec 1975 Morgantown KY).

Ray Blades—10 Years Outfielder 2 Years Manager (b. 6 Aug 1896 Mount Vernon IL–d. 18 May 1979 Lincoln Memorial Hospital, Lincoln IL) Served in France for the U.S. Army during World War I. He worked his entire life in baseball, coaching for several teams and managing in the minor leagues. Buried IOOF Cemetery, McLeansboro IL.

George Blaeholder—11 Years Pitcher (b. 26 Jan 1904 Orange CA–d. 29 Dec 1947 at his home in Garden Grove CA) Died from liver cancer. Buried Westminster Memorial Park, Westminster CA.

Rae Blaemire—1 Year Catcher (b. 8 Feb 1911 Gary IN–d. 23 Dec 1975 Burnham City Hospital, Champaign IL) He was a partner in the Blaemire-Saddoris Implement Company, and later worked for Hannagan Implement Company and for Reigel Motors until his retirement in 1975. He was an executive in the Eastern Illinois Baseball League and president of the league from 1962 until 1965.

Bill Blair—1 Year Pitcher (b. 17 Sep 1863 Pittsburgh PA–d. 22 Feb 1890 at the home of his parents in Pittsburgh PA).

Buddy Blair—1 Year Infielder (b. 10 Sep 1910 Columbia MS–d. 7 Jun 1996 Monroe LA).

Footsie Blair—3 Years Infielder (b. 13 Jul 1900 Interprise OK–d. 1 Jul 1982 at a hospital in Texarkana TX) He operated a service station in Texarkana where he had lived 70 years. Died after a lengthy illness. Buried Hillcrest Memorial Park, Texarkana TX.

Walter Blair—7 Years Catcher 1 Year Manager (b. 13 Oct 1883 Arnot PA–d. 20 Aug 1948 Lewisburg PA) He managed minor league baseball until 1917 when he became the baseball coach at the University of Pittsburgh. In 1925 he moved to Bucknell University where he stayed until he died from a heart attack. Buried Lewisburg Cemetery, Lewisburg PA.

Dick Blaisdell—1 Year Pitcher (b. 18 Jun 1862 Bradford MA–d. 20 Aug 1886 Malden MA).

Harry Blake—6 Years Outfielder (b. 16 Jun 1874 Portsmouth OH–d. 14 Oct 1919 Chicago IL) Burned to death in a rooming house fire. Buried Greenlawn Cemetery, Portsmouth OH.

Sheriff Blake—10 Years Pitcher (b. 17 Sep 1899 Ansted WV–d. 31 Oct 1982 Beckley WV) He is a member of the West Virginia Sportswriter's Hall of Fame. Died after a long illness. Buried Sunset Memorial Park, Beckley WV.

Link Blakely—1 Year Outfielder (b. 12 Feb 1912 Oakland CA–d. 28 Sep 1976 at his home in Oakland CA) He owned a liquor store in Oakland for 12 years. Died from the effects of a broken hip and prostate cancer. Buried Mountain View Cemetery, Oakland CA.

Bob Blakiston—3 Years Outfielder (b. 2 Oct 1855 San Francisco CA–d. 25 Dec 1918 San Francisco CA) He was a janitor. Died from pulmonary tuberculosis. Buried Holy Cross Catholic Cemetery, Colma CA.

Al Blanche—2 Years Pitcher (b. 21 Sep 1909 Somerville MA–d. 2 Apr 1997 Melrose MA) Served in the U.S. Army during World War II. Buried Woodlawn Cemetery, Everett MA.

Fred Blanding—5 Years Pitcher (b. 8 Feb 1888 Redlands CA–d. 16 Jul 1950 at his home in Salem VA) He was in the automobile business in Roanoke VA from 1935 until his death, except for the World War II years when he worked at the Radford Arsenal. Died from a heart attack. Buried Franklin Cemetery, Franklin MI.

Coonie Blank—1 Year Catcher (b. 18 Oct 1892 St Louis MO–d. 8 Dec 1961 St Louis MO) Buried New St Marcus Cemetery, St Louis MO.

Fred Blank—1 Year Pitcher (b. 18 Jun 1874 DeSoto MO–d. 5 Feb 1936 at the Model Hotel in St Louis MO) Buried DeSoto MO.

Cliff Blankenship—3 Years Catcher (b. 10 Apr 1880 Columbus GA–d. 26 Apr 1956 Veteran's Hospital, Oakland CA) A Spanish-American War veteran, he managed some minor league baseball and operated a bowling alley in Oakland. Died from cancer of the pharynx. Cremated.

Homer Blankenship—3 Years Pitcher (b. 4 Aug 1902 Bonham TX–d. 21 Jun 1974 at a hospital in Gladewater TX) He retired from Mobil Oil Company and lived in White Oak TX 12 years. Buried Spring Hill Cemetery, Longview TX.

Ted Blankenship—9 Years Pitcher (b. 10 May 1901 Bonham TX–d. 14 Jan 1945 Atoko OK) He was a prominent stockman in the Atoko area. Died from pneumonia and a liver ailment. Buried Atoko Cemetery, Atoko OK.

Cy Blanton—9 Years Pitcher (b. 6 Jul 1908 Waurika OK–d. 13 Sep 1945 at a hospital in Norman OK) Died during his baseball career from a liver ailment. Buried Tecumseh Cemetery, Shawnee OK.

Henry Blauvelt—1 Year Pitcher (b. 8 Apr 1873 Nyack NY–d. 28 Dec 1926 Portland OR) He was a well-known insurance man in Portland. Dropped dead from a stroke of apoplexy at his desk in the office of Oregon Life Insurance Company in the Corbett Building. Cremated.

Marv Blaylock—4 Years Infielder (b. 30 Sep 1929 Fort Smith AR–d. 23 Oct 1993 Conway AR) He lived in Little Rock AR 33 years where he was an agent for New York Life Insurance Company. Died from respiratory complications following heart bypass surgery. Buried Pine Crest Memorial Park, Alexander AR.

Ray Blemker—1 Year Pitcher (b. 9 Aug 1937 Huntingburg IN–d. 15 Feb 1994 St Mary's Medical Center, Evansville IN) Buried Fairmount Cemetery, Huntingburg IN.

Clarence Blethen—2 Years Pitcher (b. 11 Jul 1893 Dover-Foxcroft ME–d. 11 Apr 1973 Memorial Hospital, Frederick MD) Served in the U.S. Army during World War I. He pitched equally well left or right handed. An avid hunter, he worked many years for the City of Frederick. Died after a lengthy illness. Buried Mount Olivet Cemetery, Frederick MD.

Bob Blewett—1 Year Pitcher (b. 28 Jun 1877 Fond du Lac WI–d. 17 Mar 1958 Sedro Wooley WA).

Ned Bligh—4 Years Catcher (b. 30 Jun 1864 Brooklyn NY–d. 18 Apr 1892 at his home in Brooklyn NY) Died suddenly from typhoid fever.

Elmer Bliss—2 Years Outfielder (b. 9 Mar 1875 Penfield PA–d. 18 Mar 1962 Bradford Hospital, Bradford PA) He was a retired insurance and bonding company executive. Died after becoming seriously ill a month earlier. Buried Oak Hill Cemetery, Bradford PA.

Frank Bliss—1 Year Infielder (b. 15 Feb 1844 Mount Carmel IL–d. 24 Jul 1919 Janesville WI) After retiring from baseball he operated a wholesale saddlery and hardware business. For six years he was superintentent of the Wisconsin State School for the Blind, and later was managing editor of the Janesville (WI) *Gazette*. Died after months of patient suffering. Buried Oak Hill Cemetery, Janesville WI.

Jack Bliss—5 Years Catcher (b. 9 Jan 1882 Vancouver WA–d. 23 Oct 1968 at his home in Temple City CA) For 40 years he was a rancher, growing oranges. Died from pancreatic cancer. Cremated.

Bruno Block—5 Years Catcher (b. 14 Mar

1885 Wisconsin Rapids WI–d. 6 Aug 1937 South Milwaukee WI) He was a salesman for the Miller Brewing Company for 22 years. Died from tuberculosis after being confined to his bed four months. Buried St Adalbert's Cemetery, Milwaukee WI.

Joe Blong—2 Years Outfielder (b. 17 Sep 1853 St Louis MO–d. 17 Sep 1892 at his home in St Louis MO) Buried Calvary Cemetery, St Louis MO.

Jack Blott—1 Year Catcher (b. 24 Aug 1902 Girard OH–d. 11 Jun 1964 at his home in Ann Arbor MI) He was an All-American football player at the Univ of Michigan and assistant football coach there for 23 years. During World War II he worked for the Ford Motor Company and later managed the university's ice rink and golf service. Died from a heart attack. Cremated.

Bert Blue—1 Year Catcher (b. 14 Dec 1876 Bettsville OH–d. 2 Sep 1929 Detroit MI).

Lu Blue—13 Years Infielder (b. 5 Mar 1897 Washington DC–d. 28 Jul 1958 at his home in Alexandria VA) Served in the U.S. Army during World War I. He conducted baseball schools throughout the country in the 1940s. Died from a heart attack. Buried Arlington National Cemetery, Arlington VA.

Ossie Bluege—18 Years Infielder 5 Years Manager (b. 24 Oct 1900 Chicago IL–d. 14 Oct 1985 at his home in Edina MN) He was an executive for the Minnesota Twins. Buried Lakewood Cemetery, Minneapolis MN.

Otto Bluege—2 Years Infielder (b. 20 Jul 1909 Chicago IL–d. 28 Jun 1977 Bethany Methodist Hospital, Chicago IL) He was a scout for the Senators (later Twins) for 25 years. Cremated.

Jim Bluejacket—3 Years Pitcher (b. 8 Jul 1887 Adair OK–d. 26 Mar 1947 Pekin Hospital, Pekin IL) He was a welder foreman for Standard Oil of New Jersey, including a tour of duty in the Dutch West Indies where he worked on the large oil refinery there. Died following an illness of several months. Buried St Joseph Cemetery, West Peoria IL.

Red Bluhm—1 Game Pinch Hitter (b. 27 Jun 1893 Cleveland OH–d. 7 May 1952 at his home in Flint MI) He worked for General Motors Corporation from 1927 until his death — three years for Buick and the rest for Fisher Body. Died from a heart attack. Buried Sunset Hills, Flint MI.

Clint Blume—2 Years Pitcher (b. 17 Oct 1900 Brooklyn NY–d. 12 Jun 1973 at his summer home in Islip NY) Served in the U.S. Navy during World War I. A real estate broker in New York City, he was president of his own real estate company for 20 years and president of the New York Real Estate Board from 1953 to 1955. Buried Ferncliff Cemetery, Hartsdale NY.

Chet Boak—2 Years Infielder (b. 19 Jun 1935 New Castle PA–d. 28 Nov 1983 Emporium PA) He was a mold maker for Universal Rundle Corporation. Died from a heart attack while hunting. Buried St Phillip and James Church Cemetery, New Castle PA.

Charlie Boardman—3 Years Pitcher (b. 27 Mar 1893 Seneca Falls NY–d. 10 Aug 1968 County Hospital, Sacramento CA) He was a car salesman for 23 years. Died from a sudden heart attack. Cremated.

Randy Bobb—2 Years Catcher (b. 1 Jan 1948 Los Angeles CA–d. 13 Jun 1982 near Carnelian Bay CA) He was a self-employed carpenter at Bullhead City AZ. Died in an automobile accident while on a camping trip at Lake Tahoe. Cremated.

Ping Bodie—9 Years Outfielder (b. 8 Oct 1887 San Francisco CA–d. 17 Dec 1961 Notre Dame Hospital, San Francisco CA) He was an electrician at Universal Studios in Hollywood for 32 years, retiring in 1960. Died from lung cancer. Buried Holy Cross Catholic Cemetery, Colma CA.

Tony Boeckel—6 Years Infielder (b. 25 Aug 1892 Los Angeles CA–d. 16 Feb 1924 La Jolla Sanitarium, La Jolla CA) Died at the height of his career from injuries suffered when his car collided with a truck two days earlier. Buried Inglewood Park Cemetery, Inglewood CA.

George Boehler—9 Years Pitcher (b. 2 Jan 1892 Lawrenceburg IN–d. 23 Jun 1958 at his home in Lawrenceburg IN) Between 1911 and 1930 he won 248 games as a minor league pitcher. Buried Greendale Cemetery, Greendale IN.

Joe Boehling—7 Years Pitcher (b. 20 Mar 1891 Richmond VA–d. 8 Sep 1941 St Luke's Hospital, Richmond VA) For 21 years he was a partner with his brother in a feed and seed business in Richmond. Died from chest injuries suffered in a fall from a second story porch at his home. Buried Holy Cross Cemetery, Richmond VA.

Larry Boerner —1 Year Pitcher (b. 21 Jan 1905 Staunton VA–d. 16 Oct 1969 Staunton VA).

John Bogart —1 Year Pitcher (b. 21 Sep 1900 Bloomsburg PA–d. 7 Dec 1986 Clarence NY).

Dusty Boggess —(b. abt 1904–d. 8 Jul 1968 Dallas TX) A National League umpire from 1944 to 1962, he also officiated more than 2800 basketball games and 500 football games and was a professional football scout for the Steelers. Died from chronic lung disease. Buried Hillcrest Memorial Park, Dallas TX.

Ray Boggs —1 Year Pitcher (b. 12 Dec 1904 Reamsville KS–d. 27 Nov 1989 St Mary's Hospital, Grand Junction CO) Living in Grand Junction 52 years, he owned and operated Boggs and Fuller Implement Company. Prior to that he installed windmills, conducted funerals, worked in the oil fields, managed a hardware store and worked for International Harvestor. Buried Municipal Cemetery, Grand Junction CO.

Pat Bohen —2 Years Pitcher (b. 30 Sep 1890 Oakland IA–d. 8 Apr 1942 Napa County Infirmary, Napa CA) He was a retired machinist at Mare Island. Died from bronchopneumonia after overexposure. Buried Tulocay Cemetery, Napa CA.

Charlie Bohn —1 Year Outfielder (b. 1857 Cleveland OH–d. 1 Aug 1903 at his home in Cleveland OH) Buried Woodland Cemetery, Cleveland OH.

Sammy Bohne —7 Years Infielder (b. 22 Oct 1894 Palo Alto CA–d. 23 May 1977 Sharon Heights Conv Hospital, Menlo Park CA) He was a self-employed investment broker for 30 years. Died from a heart attack. Cremated.

Bob Boken —2 Years Infielder (b. 23 Feb 1908 Maryville IL–d. 8 Oct 1988 Las Vegas NV) He was a 41 year resident of Las Vegas. Buried Memory Gardens Cemetery, Las Vegas NV.

Joe Bokina —1 Year Pitcher (b. 4 Apr 1910 Northampton MA–d. 25 Oct 1991 at a hospital in Chattanooga TN) He lived in Chattanooga most of his life and was owner and operator of Joe Bokina Trucking Company there. Buried Lake Hills Memorial Gardens, Trenton GA.

Bernie Boland —7 Years Pitcher (b. 21 Jan 1892 Rochester NY–d. 12 Sep 1973 Mount Carmel Hospital, Detroit MI) He opened Tiger Construction Company, a cement firm in Detroit. Later he was construction foreman for Detroit's Department of Public Works, retiring in 1957. Died following a three-week illness. Buried St Hedwig Cemetery, Dearborn Heights MI.

Ed Boland —3 Years Outfielder (b. 18 Apr 1908 Long Island City NY–d. 5 Feb 1993 Clearwater FL).

Charlie Bold —1 Year Infielder (b. 27 Oct 1894 Karlskrong, Sweden–d. 29 Jan 1978 Chelsea MA).

Bill Bolden —1 Year Pitcher (b. 9 May 1893 Dandridge TN–d. 8 Dec 1966 Milligan Clinic, Jefferson City TN) Died after a brief illness. Buried Hillcrest Memorial Cemetery, Dandridge TN.

Stew Bolen —4 Years Pitcher (b. 12 Oct 1902 Jackson AL–d. 30 Aug 1969 at an infirmary in Mobile AL) He was the Jackson Town Marshall until a police department was established there in 1947. He then became Jackson's first Chief of Police, working for the police department until he retired in 1965. He was also a noted amateur golfer. Died after a long illness. Buried Pine Crest Cemetery, Mobile AL.

Joe Boley —6 Years Infielder (b. 19 Jul 1896 Mahanoy City PA–d. 30 Dec 1962 Locust Mountain Hosp, Shenandoah Heights PA) He managed minor league baseball and scouted for the Athletics. During World War II he worked for the Cressona (PA) Alcoa Works. Buried St Mary's Slovak Church Cemetery, Mahanoy City PA.

Jack Bolling —2 Years Infielder (b. 20 Feb 1917 Mobile AL–d. 13 Apr 1998 at a hospital in Panama City FL) Buried Forest Lawn Memorial Cemetery, Panama City FL.

Don Bollweg —5 Years Infielder (b. 12 Feb 1921 Wheaton IL–d. 26 May 1996 Wheaton IL) Served in the U.S. Army during World War II. He worked for the DuPage County, IL, Board of Elections from 1981 to 1993.

Cecil Bolton —1 Year Infielder (b. 13 Feb 1904 Booneville MS–d. 25 Aug 1993 Manhattan Health Care Center, Jackson MS) Served in Italy for the U.S. Army during World War II. He managed minor league baseball for a short while before becoming director for Wells Funeral Home. Died from heart failure. Buried Greenville Cemetery, Greenville MS.

Cliff Bolton—7 Years Catcher (b. 10 Apr 1907 High Point NC–d. 21 Apr 1979 at his home in Lexington NC) He was a retired employee of Ragan Knitting Company. Buried Holly Hill Memorial Park, Thomasville NC.

Tommy Bond—8 Years Pitcher 1 Year Manager (b. 2 Apr 1856 Granard, Ireland–d. 24 Jan 1941 at his daughter's home in Boston MA) He went into the leather business for a few years before going to work in the assessor's office at Boston City Hall in 1891, retiring in 1926. Buried Forest Hills Cemetery, Boston MA.

Walt Bond—6 Years Outfielder (b. 19 Oct 1937 Denmark TN–d. 14 Sep 1967 Methodist Hospital, Houston TX) Died from leukemia at the height of his baseball career. Buried Houston National Cemetery, Houston TX.

George Bone—1 Year Infielder (b. 28 Aug 1876 New Haven CT–d. 26 May 1918 West Haven CT) Also a professional roller polo player, he played roller polo up until he died from complications of a bronchial nature. Buried Oak Grove Cemetery, West Haven CT.

Julio Bonetti—3 Years Pitcher (b. 14 Jul 1911 Genoa, Italy–d. 17 Jun 1952 at his home in Belmont CA) He was a carpenter. Died from a sudden heart attack. Buried Holy Cross Catholic Cemetery, Colma CA.

Ernie Bonham—10 Years Pitcher (b. 16 Aug 1913 Ione CA–d. 15 Sep 1949 Pittsburgh PA) Died at the height of his baseball career, a week after surgery for cancer. Buried St Mary's Cemetery, Sacramento CA.

Luther Bonin—2 Years Outfielder (b. 13 Jan 1889 Green Hill IN–d. 3 Jan 1966 at his home in Sycamore OH) A retired farmer, he died from a heart condition after being in failing health eight years and seriously ill four years. Buried Bethel Cemetery, McCutchenville OH.

Frank Bonner—6 Years Infielder (b. 20 Aug 1869 Lowell MA–d. 31 Dec 1905 St Joseph's Hospital, Kansas City MO) Died from blood poisoning. Buried St Mary's Cemetery, Kansas City MO.

Bill Bonness—1 Year Pitcher (b. 15 Dec 1923 Cleveland OH–d. 3 Dec 1977 St John's Hospital, Cleveland OH) Served in the U.S. Army during World War II. He was a field inspector for the Cuyahoga County, OH, engineer's office. Died from injuries suffered at home when he fell down his basement stairs carrying a box of tools. Buried Elmhurst Park Cemetery, Avon OH.

Gus Bono—1 Year Pitcher (b. 29 Aug 1894 Doe Run MO–d. 3 Dec 1948 Dearborn MI) He was a millwright at Great Lakes Steel Company. Buried Grand Lawn Cemetery, Detroit MI.

Zeke Bonura—7 Years Infielder (b. 20 Sep 1908 New Orleans LA–d. 9 Mar 1987 Mercy Hospital, New Orleans LA) Died after suffering a stroke and a ruptured aneurysm. Buried Metairie Cemetery, Metairie LA.

Everett Booe—2 Years Outfielder (b. 28 Sep 1890 Mocksville NC–d. 21 May 1969 Kenedy TX) A World War I veteran, he owned and operated the Booe Lumber Company. Died from a heart attack. Buried Kenedy City Cemetery, Kenedy TX.

Al Bool—3 Years Catcher (b. 24 Aug 1897 Lincoln NE–d. 27 Sep 1981 Lincoln NE) Buried Raymond Cemetery, Raymond NE.

Red Booles—1 Year Pitcher (b. 14 Jul 1880 Bernice LA–d. 16 Mar 1955 Monroe LA) Died following a long illness. Buried Shiloh Cemetery, Bernice LA.

Danny Boone—4 Years Pitcher (b. 19 Jan 1895 Samantha AL–d. 11 May 1968 Druid City Hospital, Tuscaloosa AL) He managed minor league baseball for a short time before becoming a cotton farmer in Deering MO. He retired to Northport AL. Died after a long illness. Buried Memory Hill Gardens Cemetery, Tuscaloosa AL.

George Boone—1 Year Pitcher (b. 1 Mar 1871 Louisville KY–d. 24 Sep 1910 at his country home near Louisville KY) He was a prominent Louisville banker and businessman. Died from an overdose of medication taken to relieve sleeplessness. Buried Cave Hill Cemetery, Louisville KY.

Ike Boone—8 Years Outfielder (b. 17 Feb 1897 Samantha AL–d. 1 Aug 1958 Northport AL) He played several years in the minor leagues and had a lifetime .370 minor league batting average. He managed minor league baseball for a short time and was the director of plant security at Central Foundry. Died after suffering a heart attack while mowing his yard. Buried Tuscaloosa Memorial Park, Tuscaloosa AL.

Lute Boone—5 Years Infielder (b. 6 May 1890 Pittsburgh PA–d. 21 Aug 1982 Pittsburgh PA).

Amos Booth—4 Years Catcher (b. 14 Sep 1853 Cincinnati OH–d. 1 Jul 1921 Miamisburg OH) Died from cerebral apoplexy. Buried Woodland Cemetery, Dayton OH.

John Boozer—7 Years Pitcher (b. 6 Jul 1939 Red Bank SC–d. 24 Jan 1986 at his home in Lexington SC) He was executive director of the Lexington County (SC) Recreation Commission. Died from liver cancer. Buried Pilgrim Lutheran Church Cemetery, Lexington SC.

George Borchers—2 Years Pitcher (b. 18 Apr 1869 Sacramento CA–d. 24 Oct 1938 County Hospital, Sacramento CA) He operated a dairy farm in the Natonias district for more than 40 years. Died from heart disease. Buried City Cemetery, Sacramento CA.

Frenchy Bordagaray—11 Years Outfielder (b. 3 Jan 1910 Coalinga CA–d. 15 Apr 2000 Coalinga CA) Buried Pleasant View Cemetery, Coalinga CA.

Joe Borden—1 Year Pitcher (b. 9 May 1854 Jacobstown NJ–d. 14 Oct 1929 at his daughter's home in Yeadon PA) He was a retired officer of Guarantee Trust and Safe Deposit Company.

Babe Borton—4 Years Infielder (b. 14 Aug 1888 Marion IL–d. 29 Jul 1954 at a rest home in Berkeley CA) A World War I veteran, he worked as a process operator for Standard Oil in Richmond CA, living in Berkeley CA 27 years. Buried Mountain View Cemetery, Oakland CA.

Harley Boss—4 Years Infielder (b. 19 Nov 1908 Hodge LA–d. 14 May 1964 at his home in Nashville TN) He played baseball for 19 years before coaching baseball at Vanderbilt University. Buried Woodlawn Memorial Park, Nashville TN.

Mel Bosser—1 Year Pitcher (b. 8 Feb 1914 Johnstown PA–d. 26 Mar 1986 Cumberland Medical Center, Crossville TN) Served in the U.S. Army during World War II. He was a salesman. Buried Crossville City Cemetery, Crossville TN.

Henry Bostick—1 Year Infielder (b. 11 Jan 1895 Boston MA–d. 16 Sep 1968 Denver CO).

Lyman Bostock—4 Years Outfielder (b. 22 Nov 1950 Birmingham AL–d. 23 Sep 1978 Gary IN) Killed at the height of his career by a shotgun blast fired by a man who was shooting at his estranged wife who was riding in a car with Bostock. Buried Inglewood Park Cemetery, Inglewood CA.

Andy Boswell—1 Year Pitcher (b. 5 Sep 1874 New Gretna NJ–d. 3 Feb 1936 at his home in Ocean City NJ) Considered an expert on municipal law, for 26 years he was the city solicitor for Ocean City. Died after being bedridden four years with chronic arthritis, but had continued his law practice up until his death. Buried Riverview Cemetery, Lambertville NJ.

John Bottarini—1 Year Catcher (b. 14 Sep 1908 Crockett CA–d. 8 Oct 1976 Jemez Springs NM).

Jim Bottomley—16 Years Infielder 1 Year Manager Hall of Fame (b. 23 Apr 1900 Oglesby IL–d. 11 Dec 1959 St Louis MO) After retiring as a player he managed some in the minor leagues and scouted. He farmed near Bourbon MO for a time. Died from a heart attack in a downtown parking lot while Christmas shopping. Buried IOOF Cemetery, Sullivan MO.

Al Boucher—1 Year Infielder (b. 13 Nov 1881 Franklin MA–d. 23 Jun 1974 Bay Crest Convalescent Hosp, Torrance CA) Living 35 years in Gardena CA, he was the recreational supervisor for Northrup Aircraft Company. Died from a heart attack. Buried Holy Cross Cemetery, Culver City CA.

Medric Boucher—1 Year Catcher (b. 12 Mar 1886 St Louis MO–d. 12 Mar 1974 Martinez CA).

Lou Boudreau—15 Years Infielder 16 Years Manager Hall of Fame (b. 17 Jul 1917 Harvey IL–d. 10 Aug 2001 St James Hospital, Olympia Falls IL) He was a color analyst for the Cubs on WGN in Chicago for over 25 years. Died from heart failure brought on by complications of diabetes. Buried Pleasant Hill Cemetery, Frankfort IL.

Jake Boultes—3 Years Pitcher (b. 6 Aug 1884 St Louis MO–d. 24 Dec 1955 St Louis MO) He was a clerk for the St Louis City Recorder of Deeds. Died from a heart ailment. Buried Resurrection Cemetery, St Louis MO.

Benny Bowcock—1 Year Infielder (b. 28 Oct 1879 Fall River MA–d. 16 Jun 1961 at a rest home in New Bedford MA) He was a machinist for Morse Twist Drill Company in New Bedford.

Died after a long illness. Buried St Mary's Cemetery, New Bedford MA.

Tim Bowden—1 Year Outfielder (b. 15 Aug 1891 McDonough GA–d. 25 Oct 1949 Emory University Hospital, Atlanta GA) Served in France for the U.S. Army during World War I. Also served in World War II. He was a division manager for Armour Fertilizer Works in North Carolina. Died from a self-inflicted gunshot wound. Buried Bethany Baptist Church Cemetery, McDonough GA.

Chick Bowen—1 Year Outfielder (b. 26 Jul 1897 New Haven CT–d. 9 Aug 1948 St Raphael's Hospital, New Haven CT) An educator, he coached and taught at New Haven High School from 1922 until his death. He had risen to the position of assistant principal when he died from a broken neck, pneumonia and other complications a week after falling from a window at the school. Buried St Lawrence Cemetery, West Haven CT.

Cy Bowen—1 Year Pitcher (b. 12 Feb 1872 Kingston IN–d. 25 Jan 1925 at his home in Greensburg IN) He owned a grocery store in Greensburg. Died following an attack of acute indigestion. He had been in poor health for some time. Buried Kingston Cemetery, Kingston IN.

Frank Bowerman—15 Years Catcher 1 Year Manager (b. 5 Dec 1868 Romeo MI–d. 30 Nov 1948 at his farm home near Romeo MI) Buried Romeo Cemetery, Romeo MI.

Billy Bowers—1 Year Outfielder (b. 25 Mar 1922 Parkin AR–d. 17 Sep 1996 Wynne AR) He was a retired maintenance worker for the Wynne School System. Buried Cogbill Cemetery, Wynne AR.

Frank Bowes—1 Year Catcher (b. 1865 Bath NY–d. 21 Jan 1895 New York City NY) He was shot to death over a disagreement arising from an 80 cent pay discrepancy at an off-season job.

Grant Bowler—2 Years Pitcher (b. 24 Oct 1907 Denver CO–d. 25 Jun 1968 in his sleep at home in Denver CO) He was a Denver police detective for over 25 years. Died from a heart attack. Buried Mount Olivet Cemetery, Wheat Ridge CO.

Emmett Bowles—1 Year Pitcher (b. 2 Aug 1898 Wanette OK–d. 3 Sep 1959 Flagstaff AZ) World War I veteran. He was a miner at Madrid NM, retiring to Albuquerque NM in 1956. Died from a heart attack. Buried Mount Calvary Cemetery, Albuquerque NM.

Abe Bowman—2 Years Pitcher (b. 25 Jan 1893 Greenup IL–d. 11 Oct 1979 at his home in Longview TX) He lived in Longview since 1926 and once managed the Longview minor league team of the East Texas League. Later he was the sales manager for Kelly Plow Company in Longview. Died after a lengthy illness. Buried Memory Park Cemetery, Longview TX.

Bill Bowman—1 Year Catcher (b. 1869 Chicago IL–d. 6 Apr 1918 Arlington Heights IL).

Bob Bowman—4 Years Pitcher (b. 3 Oct 1910 Keystone WV–d. 4 Sep 1972 Bluefield Sanitarium, Bluefield WV) He worked 12 years for the Fort Lauderdale FL recreation department. Died following a brief illness. Buried Woodlawn Memorial Park, Bluewell WV.

Elmer Bowman—2 Games Pinch Hitter (b. 19 Mar 1897 Proctor VT–d. 17 Dec 1985 Kaiser Hospital, Los Angeles CA) For 36 years he was an electrical technician in the movie industry. Died from kidney disease. Cremated.

Joe Bowman—11 Years Pitcher (b. 17 Jun 1916 Kansas City KS–d. 22 Nov 1990 St Joseph Hospital, Kansas City MO) The starting pitcher for the Phillies in the first night game in the major leagues in 1935, he spent over 50 years in baseball as a player, scout and executive, retiring in 1988. Buried Resurrection Cemetery, Lenexa KS.

Roger Bowman—5 Years Pitcher (b. 18 Aug 1927 Amsterdam NY–d. 21 Jul 1997 Longwood Manor Conv Hosp, Los Angeles CA) Served in the military. For 45 years he owned and operated Roger Bowman Upholstery. He suffered from Parkinson's disease but died from pneumonia and cardiopulmonary arrest. Buried Hagamans Mills Cemetery, Amsterdam NY.

Sumner Bowman—2 Years Pitcher (b. 9 Feb 1867 Millersburg PA–d. 11 Jan 1954 Millersburg PA) He was a practicing attorney from 1892 until a few months before his death. He rose to the rank of major while serving in the Judge Advocate General's office during World War I. Buried Oakhill Cemetery, Millersburg PA.

Red Bowser—1 Year Outfielder (b. 20 Sep 1881 Freeport PA–d. 22 May 1943 at his home in Moundsville WV) He lived in Moundsville about 30 years and worked at the Fostoria glass plant there. Died unexpectedly. Buried Greensburg PA.

Frank Boyd—1 Year Catcher (b. 2 Apr 1868 West Middletown PA–d. 17 Dec 1937 at his home in Oil City PA) He managed minor league baseball for a short while before going to work in the land title and tax dept of South Penn Oil Company in 1901, retiring in 1933. Died following an illness of 18 months duration. Buried St Joseph's Cemetery, Oil City PA.

Jake Boyd—3 Years Outfielder (b. 19 Jan 1874 Martinsburgh WV–d. 12 Aug 1932 Gettysburg PA) Buried Evergreen Cemetery, Gettysburg PA.

Ray Boyd—2 Years Pitcher (b. 11 Feb 1887 Hortonville IN–d. 17 Feb 1920 Hortonville IN) Died from the effects of influenza, after a brief illness. Buried Westfield Cemetery, Westfield IN.

Ken Boyer—15 Years Infielder 3 Years Manager (b. 20 May 1931 Liberty MO–d. 7 Sep 1982 St Louis MO) He was a scout for the Cardinals. Died from lung cancer. Buried Friend's Cemetery, Purcell MO.

Buzz Boyle—5 Years Outfielder (b. 9 Feb 1908 Cincinnati OH–d. 12 Nov 1978 Christ Hospital, Cincinnati OH) He managed minor league baseball before scouting 21 years for the Reds and six years for other teams, retiring in 1974. Died from lung cancer. Buried St Joseph New Cemetery, Cincinnati OH.

Eddie Boyle—1 Year Catcher (b. 8 May 1874 Cincinnati OH–d. 9 Feb 1941 Cincinnati OH) After a foot ailment forced him from baseball he operated a cafe in downtown Cincinnati until his death. Died from a heart attack. Buried St Joseph New Cemetery, Cincinnati OH.

Henry Boyle—6 Years Pitcher (b. 20 Sep 1860 Philadelphia PA–d. 25 May 1932 Philadelphia PA) Buried Holy Cross Cemetery, Yeadon PA.

Jack Boyle—13 Years Catcher (b. 22 Mar 1867 Cincinnati OH–d. 6 Jan 1913 at his home in Cincinnati OH) He owned a saloon. Died from chronic Bright's disease. Buried St Joseph New Cemetery, Cincinnati OH.

Jack Boyle—1 Year Infielder (b. 9 Jul 1889 Morris IL–d. 3 Apr 1971 Pompano Beach FL) Served in the U.S. Army during World War I. He was an attorney in Chicago from 1924 until 1940 when he moved to New York City. There he was an executive vice-president for W T Grant Company, in charge of real estate, retiring to Florida in 1951. Died from a heart attack. Buried Hillside Cemetery, Ogema WI.

Jim Boyle—1 Year Catcher (b. 19 Jan 1904 Cincinnati OH–d. 24 Dec 1958 at his home in Cincinnati OH) For 26 years he was a sales manager for Aluminum Industries, Inc., and from 1953 until his death was director of sales for Zollner Machine Works in Fort Wayne IN. Buried St Joseph New Cemetery, Cincinnati OH.

Gene Brabender—5 Years Pitcher (b. 16 Aug 1941 Madison WI–d. 27 Dec 1996 at a hospital in Madison WI) Served two years in the U.S. Army. He was involved in the mobile home and construction business. Died from a heart attack. Buried St Barnabas Cemetery, Mazomanie WI.

Gib Brack—3 Years Outfielder (b. 29 Mar 1908 Chicago IL–d. 20 Jan 1960 Greenville TX) He worked for Lone Star Steel at Longview TX. He was found dead in his car at a roadside park from a gunshot wound. Ruled a suicide. Buried Memoryland Memorial Park, Greenville TX.

Jack Bracken—1 Year Pitcher (b. 14 Apr 1881 Cleveland OH–d. 16 Jul 1954 Highland Park MI) He lived at Highland Park for 35 years and was a scout for the Indians until 1949. He then joined Aldrich Industrial Oil Company of Cleveland as a representative in the Detroit area. Died from a heart attack. Buried Holy Sepulchre Cemetery, Southfield MI.

John Brackinridge—1 Year Pitcher (b. 24 Dec 1880 Harrisburg PA–d. 20 Mar 1953 at the home of an aunt in Harrisburg PA) He was a deputy commissioner for the Pennsylvania State Athletic Commission and was assistant circulation manager for the Harrisburg *Patriot* newspaper. He was also a scout for the Pirates and Cardinals. Buried Harrisburg Cemetery, Harrisburg PA.

Larry Bradford—4 Years Pitcher (b. 21 Dec 1949 Chicago IL–d. 11 Sep 1998 Atlanta GA) He coached high school baseball and taught physical education classes. Died from a heart attack in the lobby of the Braves' offices at Turner Field. Buried Jackson City Cemetery, Jackson GA.

Vic Bradford—1 Year Outfielder (b. 15 Mar 1915 Brownsville TN–d. 10 Jun 1994 Good Samaritan Hospital, Lexington KY) Served in the U.S. Navy during World War II. He was an assistant football coach at Kansas, Navy, Baylor and Kentucky until the 1950s. He then entered the family's Sipple Brick Company business as a vice-president in charge of marketing, retiring in 1972. Buried North Middletown Cemetery, North Middletown KY.

Alva Bradley—(b. 29 Feb 1884 Cleveland OH–d. 29 Mar 1953 Delray Beach FL) A wealthy Cleveland businessman with interests in real estate, coal and transportation, he owned the Indians from 1927 to 1946. Died from a heart attack. Buried Lake View Cemetery, Cleveland OH.

Bill Bradley—14 Years Infielder 1 Year Manager (b. 13 Feb 1878 Cleveland OH–d. 11 Mar 1954 Ingleside Hospital, Cleveland OH) For more than 25 years he was a scout and advisor for the Indians. Died from pneumonia. Buried Calvary Cemetery, Cleveland OH.

Foghorn Bradley—1 Year Pitcher (b. 1 Jul 1855 Milford MA–d. 3 Apr 1900 Philadelphia PA).

George Bradley—1 Year Outfielder (b. 1 Apr 1914 Greenwood AR–d. 19 Oct 1982 at his home in Lawrenceburg TN) World War II veteran. He was a retired employee of Jobber's Supply. Died after a sudden illness. Buried Lawrence County Memorial Gardens, Lawrenceburg TN.

George Bradley—10 Years Pitcher (b. 13 Jul 1852 Reading PA–d. 2 Oct 1931 Philadelphia PA) He was the first man to pitch an official no-hit no-run game in major league baseball. He retired from the Philadelphia Police Department in 1930. Buried Northwood Cemetery, Philadelphia PA.

Herb Bradley—3 Years Pitcher (b. 3 Jan 1903 Agenda KS–d. 16 Oct 1959 Clay County Hospital, Clay Center KS) He owned and operated the Bradley Motor Company in Clay Center from 1941 until his death. Died unexpectedly in the hospital while awaiting surgery. Buried Greenwood Cemetery, Clay Center KS.

Hugh Bradley—5 Years Infielder (b. 23 May 1885 Grafton MA–d. 26 Jan 1949 City Hospital, Worcester MA) A professional entertainer and singer, he also was a playground director at Logan Field. Died from a heart attack. Buried St John's Cemetery, Worcester MA.

Jack Bradley—1 Year Catcher (b. 20 Sep 1893 Denver CO–d. 18 Mar 1969 at a hospital in Tulsa OK) He worked in the lubricating oil blending business at Tulsa and served as a district foreman for Service Pipe Line Company before becoming an independent oil operator in Tulsa. Died after an 11-week illness. Buried Calvary Cemetery, Tulsa OK.

Dallas Bradshaw—1 Year Infielder (b. 23 Nov 1895 Herrin IL–d. 11 Dec 1939 at his home in Herrin IL) He operated the family insurance business in Herrin for 15 years. Died from liver cancer. Buried Herrin City Cemetery, Herrin IL.

George Bradshaw—1 Year Catcher (b. 12 Sep 1924 Salisbury NC–d. 4 Nov 1994 at his home in Hendersonville NC) Served in the U.S. Marine Corps during World War II. He was a leasing director at Parkland Corporation in Asheville NC. Buried Western Carolina Veteran's Cemetery, Black Mountain NC.

Joe Bradshaw—1 Year Pitcher (b. 17 Aug 1897 Dyersburg TN–d. 30 Jan 1985 Tavares FL).

Bob Brady—2 Years Catcher (b. 8 Nov 1922 Lewistown PA–d. 22 Apr 1996 Manchester CT) He retired from the purchasing department of the State of Connecticut in 1983. Buried East Cemetery, Manchester CT.

Cliff Brady—1 Year Infielder (b. 6 Mar 1897 St Louis MO–d. 25 Sep 1974 St Elizabeth Hospital, Belleville IL) He played in the International League and the Pacific Coast League. Later he was an assistant yardmaster for a steel company. Died from a heart attack. Buried Calvary Cemetery, St Louis MO.

King Brady—2 Years Pitcher (b. 28 May 1881 Monroeville NY–d. 21 Aug 1947 Memorial Hospital, Albany NY) For many years he operated King Brady's Grill next to his home in Albany, where he lived for 31 years.

Neal Brady—3 Years Pitcher (b. 4 Mar 1897 Covington KY–d. 19 Jun 1947 at his home in Fort Mitchell KY) He was personnel manager for the Coca Cola Company in Cincinnati OH. Buried St Mary's Cemetery, Fort Mitchell KY.

Steve Brady—4 Years Outfielder (b. 14 Jul 1851 Worcester MA–d. 1 Nov 1917 at his home in Hartford CT) Died after being ill eight weeks. Buried Mount St Benedict Cemetery, Bloomfield CT.

Dick Braggins—1 Year Pitcher (b. 25 Dec 1879 Mercer PA–d. 16 Aug 1963 Lake Wales FL).

Dave Brain—7 Years Infielder (b. 24 Jan 1879 Hereford, England–d. 25 May 1959 at his home in Los Angeles CA) He was credit manager for Standard Oil Company for 20 years. Died from congestive heart failure. Cremated.

Fred Brainerd—3 Years Infielder (b. 17 Jan 1892 Champaign IL–d. 17 Apr 1959 Galveston TX).

Al Braithwood—1 Year Pitcher (b. 15 Feb 1892 Braceville IL–d. 24 Nov 1960 Rowlesburg WV) He retired from the Baltimore and Ohio Railroad as an engineer and opened the Buffalo Inn at Macomber WV. Died from a heart attack. Buried Aurora Cemetery, Aurora WV.

Erv Brame—5 Years Pitcher (b. 12 Oct 1901 Big Rock TN–d. 22 Nov 1949 in his room at Hopkinsville KY) He managed some minor league baseball before buying a Kentucky farm. His last job was with the Eastern Dark Fired Tobacco Grower's Assn. Died from a heart attack. Buried Powell Cemetery, La Fayette KY.

Art Bramhall—1 Year Infielder (b. 22 Feb 1909 Oak Park IL–d. 4 Sep 1985 at a hospital in Madison WI) He played major league baseball, basketball and football. Later he was a prominent radio sports broadcaster, mostly as the voice of the University of Wisconsin football and basketball. Buried Resurrection Catholic Cemetery, Madison WI.

Norm Branch—2 Years Pitcher (b. 22 Mar 1915 Spokane WA–d. 21 Nov 1971 Grimes County Hospital, Navasota TX) World War II veteran. He was a rural mail carrier. Died from cirrhosis of the liver. Buried Montgomery Cemetery, Montgomery TX.

Chick Brandom—3 Years Pitcher (b. 31 Mar 1887 Oklahoma City OK–d. 7 Oct 1958 Santa Ana CA) He was a press operator for Brandom Manufacturing Corporation, a cabinet manufacturing company, for 11 years. Died from a heart attack in his doctor's office. Buried Fairhaven Memorial Park, Santa Ana CA.

Bill Brandt—3 Years Pitcher (b. 21 Mar 1918 Aurora IN–d. 16 May 1968 Lutheran Hospital, Fort Wayne IN) Served in the U.S. Navy during World War II. He worked for General Electric 17 years. Buried Concordia Cemetery, Fort Wayne IN.

Ed Brandt—11 Years Pitcher (b. 17 Feb 1905 Spokane WA–d. 1 Nov 1944 Spokane WA) He operated a hunting lodge in western Montana and owned a tavern in Clayton WA. Killed when he was struck by car while crossing a Spokane street. Buried Fairmount Memorial Park, Spokane WA.

Otis Brannan—2 Years Infielder (b. 13 Mar 1899 Greenbrier AR–d. 6 Jun 1967 at his home in Conway AR) He played for Hollywood in the Pacific Coast League and was a steamfitter. Buried Spring Hill Cemetery, Greenbrier AR.

Dudley Branom—1 Year Infielder (b. 30 Nov 1897 Sulphur Springs TX–d. 4 Feb 1980 Beverly Manor, Sun City AZ) He served 16 years as sheriff of Garfield County, OK. Cremated. Buried Memorial Park Cemetery, Enid OK.

Kitty Bransfield—12 Years Infielder (b. 7 Jan 1876 Worcester MA–d. 1 May 1947 at his home in Worcester MA) He managed and umpired minor league baseball for a time, and scouted. Later he was a watchman from 1925 until he died following a brief illness. Buried St John's Cemetery, Worcester MA.

Kitty Brashear—1 Year Infielder (b. 27 Aug 1877 Mansfield OH–d. 22 Dec 1934 California Hospital, Los Angeles CA) He managed minor league baseball before owning and operating a popular Los Angeles restaurant for 15 years. Died from a hemorrhaging duadenal ulcer. Cremated.

Roy Brashear—2 Years Infielder (b. 3 Jan 1874 Ashtabula OH–d. 20 Apr 1951 at his home in Los Angeles CA) He umpired several years in the Pacific Coast League and was the owner and operator of a cafe. Died from a heart attack. Cremated.

Joe Bratcher—1 Year Outfielder (b. 22 Jul 1898 Grand Saline TX–d. 13 Oct 1977 at a hospital in Fort Worth TX) He umpired and managed minor league baseball before becoming a dining car official for the Fort Worth and Denver Railroad. Buried Mount Olivet Cemetery, Fort Worth TX.

Fred Bratchi—3 Years Outfielder (b. 16 Jan 1892 Alliance OH–d. 10 Jan 1962 Massillon OH) He worked ten years for a Standard Oil storage station before opening his own service station in Massillon, operating it 16 years. Died from a suicidal ingestion of battery acid. Buried Rose Hill Memorial Park, Massillon OH.

Garland Braxton—10 Years Pitcher (b. 10 Jun 1900 Snow Camp NC–d. 25 Feb 1966 at his home in Norfolk VA) Died after suffering 10 years from a heart ailment. Buried Woodlawn Memorial Gardens, Norfolk VA.

Buster Bray—1 Year Outfielder (b. 1 Apr 1913 Birmingham AL–d. 4 Sep 1982 Welborn Baptist Hospital, Evansville IN) He worked for Republic Aviation during World War II and for George Koch Sons in Evansville from 1946 until he retired in 1978. Died from a heart attack. Buried Locust Hill Cemetery, Evansville IN.

Frank Brazill—2 Years Infielder (b. 11 Aug 1899 Spangler PA–d. 3 Nov 1976 Oakland CA) He scouted for the Giants and managed several minor league teams. Later he was a foreman for Rigney Tile Company for 30 years. Died from a heart attack. Cremated.

Al Brazle—10 Years Pitcher (b. 19 Oct 1914 Loyal OK–d. 24 Oct 1973 Veteran's Hospital, Grand Junction CO) Served in the U.S. Army during World War II. He played baseball 22 years before going into business in Florida from 1956 until 1970. He then retired to Cortez CO. Buried Fairview Cemetery, Yellow Jacket CO.

Bill Breckinridge—1 Year Pitcher (b. 27 Oct 1907 Tulsa OK–d. 23 Aug 1958 at a hospital in Tulsa OK) Served for the U.S. Army in Europe during World War II. A Tulsa attorney since 1933, he was the Democratic candidate for U.S. Congress in 1938. His wife was the daughter of the founder of Phillips 66. Died from a heart ailment. Buried Memorial Park, Tulsa OK.

Alonzo Breitenstein—1 Year Pitcher (b. 9 Nov 1857 Utica NY–d. 19 Jun 1932 at a hospital in Utica NY) He was a butcher before going to Oneida Lake in 1887. There he operated a hotel for 25 years, and in later life he was a janitor for the City of Utica. Died after an illness of more than two months. Buried Forest Hill Cemetery, Utica NY.

Ted Breitenstein—11 Years Pitcher (b. 1 Jun 1869 St Louis MO–d. 3 May 1935 at field house in Forest Park, St Louis MO) He pitched in the Southern Association for ten years and umpired in the minor leagues for another ten years. He then engaged in business for a while and, finally, was a laborer for the St Louis City Parks Department. Died from heart disease. Buried St Peter's Cemetery, St Louis MO.

Herb Bremer—3 Years Catcher (b. 25 Oct 1913 Chicago IL–d. 28 Nov 1979 St Francis Hospital, Columbus GA) A World War II veteran, he worked as an engineer for the Central of Georgia Railway. Buried Parkhill Cemetery, Columbus GA.

Sam Brenegan—1 Year Catcher (b. 1 Sep 1890 Galesville WI–d. 20 Apr 1956 at the home of a sister in Galesville WI) World War I veteran. He once caught two no-hitters thrown by the same pitcher in a minor league double header. Buried Pine Cliff Cemetery, Galesville WI.

Ad Brennan—7 Years Pitcher (b. 18 Jul 1881 LaHarpe KS–d. 7 Jan 1962 Kansas City MO) He worked with youth in the Ban Johnson leagues in Kansas City from 1931 until 1948. Buried Forest Hill Cemetery, Kansas City MO.

Don Brennan—5 Years Pitcher (b. 2 Dec 1903 Augusta ME–d. 26 Apr 1953 Boston MA).

Jim Brennan—5 Years Catcher (b. abt 1865 St Louis MO–d. 17 Oct 1904 at his home in Philadelphia PA) He was the proprietor of the "Light Bar" saloon in downtown Philadelphia. Died suddenly from neuralgia of the heart while sitting in his easy chair. Buried Holy Cross Cemetery, Yeadon PA.

Bert Brenner—1 Year Pitcher (b. 18 Jul 1887 Minneapolis MN–d. 11 Apr 1971 St Louis Park MN) Buried Lakewood Cemetery, Minneapolis MN.

Lynn Brenton—4 Years Pitcher (b. 7 Oct 1889 Peoria IL–d. 14 Oct 1968 at his home in Los Angeles CA) He was a self-employed chiropractor for 40 years. Died from heart disease. Cremated.

Bill Brenzel—3 Years Catcher (b. 3 Mar 1910 Oakland CA–d. 12 Jun 1979 Merritt Hospital, Oakland CA) A scout for the Dodgers, he was associated with baseball 53 years. Died from a heart attack. Buried Mountain View Cemetery, Oakland CA.

Roger Bresnahan—17 Years Catcher, 5 Years Manager. Hall of Fame (b. 11 Jun 1879 Toledo OH–d. 4 Dec 1944 at his home in Toledo OH) He owned the Toledo Mud Hens in the American Association from 1916 to 1924. After that he was a salesman for Buckeye Brewing Company. Died from a heart attack. Buried Calvary Cemetery, Toledo OH.

Rube Bressler—19 Years Outfielder (b. 23 Oct 1894 Coder PA–d. 7 Nov 1966 Cincinnati OH) Rube also pitched, winning 26 games as a pitcher. He operated a restaurant in Cincinnati for many years. Died from cancer. Buried Mount Moriah Cemetery, Withamsville OH.

Jim Breton—3 Years Infielder (b. 15 Jul 1891 Chicago IL–d. 30 May 1973 Beloit Memorial Hospital, Beloit WI) World War I veteran. He was a design engineer. Buried Mount Thabor Cemetery, Beloit WI.

Herb Brett—2 Years Pitcher (b. 23 May 1900 Lawrenceville VA–d. 25 Nov 1974 St Petersburg FL) He managed minor league baseball and founded the Carolina League. Buried Highland Burial Park, Danville VA.

Marv Breuer—5 Years Pitcher (b. 29 Apr 1914 Rolla MO–d. 17 Jan 1991 Phelps Regional Hospital, Rolla MO) He worked for the U.S. Geological Survey 31 years, retiring in 1976. Buried Rolla Cemetery, Rolla MO.

Jim Brewer—17 Years Pitcher (b. 14 Nov 1937 Merced CA–d. 16 Nov 1987 Medical Center Hospital, Tyler TX) He coached baseball at Oral Roberts University and at Northwestern. He was a minor league pitching coach for the Dodgers when he died following a head-on automobile accident near Carthage TX. Buried Floral Haven Memorial Gardens, Broken Arrow OK.

Fred Brickell—8 Years Outfielder (b. 9 Nov 1906 Saffordville KS–d. 8 Apr 1961 at his home in Wichita KS) He was the manager of Wichita Hegman, Inc, a cigar and tobacco firm. Died from a heart attack. Buried Old Mission Cemetery, Wichita KS.

Fritzie Brickell—3 Years Infielder (b. 19 Mar 1935 Wichita KS–d. 15 Oct 1965 Wichita KS) He was in the sporting goods business in Wichita. Died from cancer. Buried Memorial Park Cemetery, St Joseph MO.

Jack Brickhouse—Hall of Fame (b. 24 Jan 1916 Peoria IL–d. 6 Aug 1998 St Joseph Hospital, Chicago IL) The Cubs' broadcaster from 1941 to 1981, and White Sox broadcaster from 1940 to 1967, he also broadcast the Chicago Bears games for 24 years, the Bulls games and the football Cardinals games for a short while. He also broadcast wrestling matches for nine years. Died from the effects of a stroke suffered seven months earlier. Buried Rosehill Cemetery, Chicago IL.

George Brickley—1 Year Outfielder (b. 19 Jul 1894 Everett MA–d. 23 Feb 1947 at his home in Everett MA) Served in the U.S. Navy during World War I. He coached high school baseball and football and was active in civic affairs. He worked his last six years at the Boston MA Navy Yard. Died suddenly.

Ralph Brickner—1 Year Pitcher (b. 2 May 1925 Cincinnati OH–d. 9 May 1994 Bridgetown OH) He was credit manager for Rauh Company and office manager for the Mack Shirt Company before spending 25 years in the Hamilton County, OH, clerk of courts office, retiring as the head cashier there. Died suddenly from a heart attack. Buried St Aloysius Cemetery, Cincinnati OH.

Jim Brideweser—7 Years Infielder (b. 13 Feb 1927 Lancaster OH–d. 24 Aug 1989 El Toro CA) World War II veteran. He taught at Saddleback College in Irvine CA. Died from respiratory failure. He was cremated and his ashes scattered off the coast near Dana Point CA.

Marshall Bridges—7 Years Pitcher (b. 2 Jun 1931 Jackson MS–d. 3 Sep 1990 University Medical Center, Jackson MS) Died from cancer. Buried Garden Memorial Park, Jackson MS.

Tommy Bridges—16 Years Pitcher (b. 28 Dec 1906 Gordonsville TN–d. 19 Apr 1968 Parkview Hospital, Nashville TN) Served with the Office of Strategic Service during World War II. He was a salesman for Tires, Inc, of Lakeland FL. Died from cancer. Buried Ridgewood Cemetery, Carthage TN.

Al Bridwell—11 Years Infielder (b. 4 Jan 1884 Friendship OH–d. 23 Jan 1969 Mercy Hospital, Portsmouth OH) He served two terms as Scioto County (OH) sheriff becoming a security policeman at the steel plant. He had been in the hospital two months when he died. Buried Greenlawn Cemetery, Portsmouth OH.

Bunny Brief—4 Years Infielder (b. 3 Jul 1892 Remus MI–d. 10 Feb 1963 at his home in Milwaukee WI) A longtime minor league player, he holds the American Association record of 191 RBIs, set in 1921, a lifetime .331 minor league batting average and 340 minor league home runs. He supervised the Milwaukee Recreation Dept baseball program. Died from cancer after a two-year battle. Buried Oakwood Cemetery, Milwaukee WI.

Buttons Briggs—5 Years Pitcher (b. 8 Jul 1876 Poughkeepsie NY–d. 18 Feb 1911 at his home in Cleveland OH) Died from phthisis. Buried Calvary Cemetery, Cleveland OH.

Grant Briggs—4 Years Catcher (b. 16 Mar 1865 Pittsburgh PA–d. 31 May 1928 at his home in Pittsburgh PA).

Walter O Briggs, Jr—(b. 20 Jan 1912 Detroit MI–d. 3 Jul 1970 William Beaumont Hospital, Royal Oak MI) Served in the U.S. Army Air Force during World War II. He owned the Tigers from 1952 to 1956, taking control of them, and other Briggs' concerns, upon the death of his father. Died from a heart attack after being in ill health a number of years. Buried Holy Sepulchre Cemetery, Southfield MI.

Walter O Briggs, Sr—(b. 27 Feb 1872–d. 17 Jan 1952 at his winter home in Miami Beach FL) A well-known industrialist, he formed Briggs' Manufacturing Company, a manufacturer of plumbing and bathroom fixtures, in 1909. He was part-owner of the Detroit Tigers from 1903 until Frank Navin's death in 1935, and full owner until his own death. Died from complications of a kidney infection. Buried Holy Sepulchre Cemetery, Southfield MI.

Frank Brill—1 Year Pitcher (b. 30 Mar 1864 Astoria NY–d. 19 Nov 1944 Flushing NY) Buried Flushing Cemetery, Flushing NY.

Jim Brillheart—4 Years Pitcher (b. 28 Sep 1903 Dublin VA–d. 2 Sep 1972 Community Hospital, Radford VA) He was a retired iron worker. Buried Dublin Cemetery, Dublin VA.

Bill Brinker—1 Year Outfielder (b. 30 Aug 1884 Warrensburg MO–d. 5 Feb 1965 Arcadia CA) World War I veteran. For 45 years he was a lawyer in the securities investment business. Died from a heart attack. Cremated.

Fatty Briody—8 Years Catcher (b. 13 Sep 1858 Lansingburg NY–d. 22 Jun 1903 Chicago IL) Buried St John's Cemetery, Troy NY.

Gus Brittain—1 Year Catcher (b. 29 Nov 1909 Wilmington NC–d. 16 Feb 1974 Cape Fear Memorial Hospital, Wilmington NC) He worked for the North Carolina State Port Authority at Wilmington. Died following a short illness. Buried Oakdale Cemetery, Wilmington NC.

Jack Brittin—2 Years Pitcher (b. 4 Mar 1924 Athens IL–d. 5 Jan 1994 Memorial Medical Center, Springfield IL) Served in the U.S. Navy during World War II. He taught at Butler School before working 27 years in special education for the State of Illinois, retiring in the late 1980s. Buried Brittin Cemetery, Sherman IL.

Gil Britton—1 Year Infielder (b. 21 Sep 1891 Parsons KS–d. 20 Jun 1983 Presbyterian Manor, Parsons KS) He owned and operated the Britton Coal Company in Parsons for many years. Buried Memorial Lawn Cemetery, Parsons KS.

Johnny Broaca—5 Years Pitcher (b. 3 Oct 1909 Lawrence MA–d. 16 May 1985 at his home in Lawrence MA) Buried Immaculate Conception Cemetery, Lawrence MA.

John Brock—2 Years Catcher (b. 16 Oct 1896 Hamilton IL–d. 27 Oct 1951 at a hospital in Clayton MO) He operated a greeting card and gift shop in the Arcade Building for 15 years. Died after a three-month illness. Buried Lakewood Park Cemetery, St Louis MO.

Lew Brockett—3 Years Pitcher (b. 13 Jul 1880 Brownsville IL–d. 19 Sep 1960 Ferrell Hospital, Eldorado IL) He managed some minor league baseball and coached college baseball. Buried Odd Fellows Cemetery, Norris City IL.

Matt Broderick—1 Year Infielder (b. 1 Dec 1877 Lattimer Mines PA–d. 26 Feb 1940 at his sister's home in Freeland PA) He managed minor league baseball. Died after a short illness. Buried St Ann's Cemetery, Woodside PA.

Steve Brodie—12 Years Outfielder (b. 11 Sep 1868 Warrenton VA–d. 30 Oct 1935 Baltimore MD) He worked for the Baltimore Park Board from 1922 until he died from a heart ailment. Buried Woodlawn Cemetery, Baltimore MD.

Herman Bronkie—7 Years Infielder (b. 30 Mar 1885 South Manchester CT–d. 27 May 1968 Somers CT) He managed minor league baseball and coached at Trinity College before spending 20 years as a salesman for Berkshire Chemical Company. Buried West Cemetery, Somers CT.

Bobby Brooks—4 Years Outfielder (b. 1 Nov 1945 Los Angeles CA–d. 11 Oct 1994 at his home in Harbor City CA) Died from the effects of multiple sclerosis. Buried Inglewood Park Cemetery, Inglewood CA.

Harry Brooks—1 Year Pitcher (b. 30 Nov 1865 Philadelphia PA–d. 5 Dec 1945 Philadelphia PA) Buried North Cedar Hill Cemetery, Philadelphia PA.

Mandy Brooks—2 Years Outfielder (b. 18 Aug 1898 Milwaukee WI–d. 17 Jun 1962 Kirkwood MO).

Siggy Broskie—1 Year Catcher (b. 23 Mar 1911 Iselin PA–d. 17 May 1975 Timken Mercy Hospital, Canton OH) Served in the U.S. Navy during World War II. He lived in Canton 35 years and worked for the Timken Company police department 27 years, retiring in 1973. Died from a heart attack. Buried Forest Hill Cemetery, Canton OH.

Tony Brottem—3 Years Catcher (b. 30 Apr 1892 Halstead MN–d. 5 Aug 1929 Chicago IL) He was found dead in his hotel room with his throat slashed. His death was ruled a suicide.

Cal Broughton—4 Years Catcher (b. 28 Dec 1860 Magnolia WI–d. 15 Mar 1939 at the home of a nephew in Evansville WI) He was Chief of Police at Evansville for 17 years, and later Assistant Chief of Police. Died following a stroke suffered six weeks earlier. He had been an invalid for three years. Buried Maple Hill Cemetery, Evansville WI.

Heywood C Broun—Hall of Fame (b. 7 Dec 1888 Brooklyn NY–d. 18 Dec 1939 Columbia-Pres Medical Ctr, New York City NY) He was a columnist for a number of New York City newspapers writing about several topics, including baseball. He started with the *Tribune* in 1912 and later worked for the *World-Telegram* and, finally, for the *Post*, for whom he wrote just one article, published the day of his death. Died from pneumonia. Buried Gate of Heaven Cemetery, Hawthorne NY.

Art Brouthers—1 Year Infielder (b. 25 Nov 1882 Montgomery AL–d. 28 Sep 1959 at his home in Charleston SC) Buried Magnolia Cemetery, Charleston SC.

Dan Brouthers—19 Years Infielder Hall of Fame (b. 8 May 1858 Sylvan Lake NY–d. 2 Aug 1932 at his home in East Orange NJ) He scouted for the Giants for a short time. Later he was a night watchman at the Polo Grounds in New York City and watched over the press gate there. Died from a heart attack. Buried St Mary's Cemetery, Wappinger Falls NY.

Joe Brovia—21 Game Pinch Hitter (b. 18 Feb 1922 Davenport CA–d. 15 Aug 1994 Dominican Hospital, Santa Cruz CA) Served in World War II. He was one of the Pacific Coast League's most feared hitters. He drove a truck for a Santa Cruz beer distributor and worked weekends at the Santa Cruz amusement park. Died from kidney cancer. Buried Holy Cross Cemetery, Santa Cruz CA.

Frank Brower—5 Years Outfielder (b. 26 Mar 1893 Gainesville VA–d. 20 Nov 1960 Johns Hopkins Hospital, Baltimore MD) He was a grain dealer on Maryland's Eastern Shore. Buried Sudlersville Cemetery, Sudlersville MD.

Louis Brower—1 Year Infielder (b. 1 Jul 1900 Cincinnati OH–d. 4 Mar 1994 Tyler TX).

Bill Brown—1 Year Outfielder (b. 8 Jul 1893 Coleman TX–d. 13 May 1965 West Texas Hospital, Lubbock TX) World War I veteran. He owned and operated the Busy Bee restaurant in Lubbock from 1922 to 1924 and the Duck Inn from 1925 until he retired in 1940. Buried Resthaven Memorial Park, Lubbock TX.

Boardwalk Brown—5 Years Pitcher (b. 20 Feb 1889 Woodbury NJ–d. 8 Feb 1977 Burlington NJ).

Bob Brown—7 Years Pitcher (b. 1 Apr 1911 Dorchester MA–d. 3 Aug 1990 North River Nursing Home, Pembroke MA) He was an ironworker with Union Local # 7 in Boston. Died after a short illness. Buried St Joseph's Cemetery, West Roxbury MA.

Buster Brown—9 Years Pitcher (b. 31 Aug 1882 Prairie City IA–d. 9 Feb 1914 St Joseph Hospital, Sioux City IA) Died at the height of his career following surgery for the inflamation of the lymph glands under his left arm, believed to be caused by overtraining. Buried Onawa Cemetery, Onawa IA.

Clint Brown—15 Years Pitcher (b. 8 Jul 1903 Guys Mills PA–d. 31 Dec 1955 Rocky River OH) He was a sales representative in the foundry and die casting industry. Died from a heart attack. Buried Lakewood Park Cemetery, Cleveland OH.

Curly Brown—4 Years Pitcher (b. 9 Dec 1888 Spring Hill KS–d. 10 Jun 1968 Spring Hill KS) Buried Spring Hill Cemetery, Spring Hill KS.

Delos Brown—1 Game Pinch Hitter (b. 4 Oct 1892 Anna IL–d. 21 Dec 1964 Doctor's Hospital, Carbondale IL) He lived in Pueblo CO the last 50 years of his life. World War I veteran. Buried Roselawn Cemetery, Pueblo CO.

Dick Brown—9 Years Catcher (b. 17 Jan 1935 Shinnston WV–d. 17 Apr 1970 U.S. Public Health Hospital, Baltimore MD) His playing career was ended by brain cancer from which he died after a four-year struggle. Buried Lake Worth FL.

Drummond Brown —3 Years Catcher (b. 31 Jan 1885 Los Angeles CA–d. 27 Jan 1927 Parkville MO).

Eddie Brown —7 Years Outfielder (b. 17 Jul 1891 Milligan NE–d. 10 Sep 1956 Vallejo CA) World War I veteran. He was a retired carpenter from the Mare Island Naval Ammunition Depot. Buried Golden Gate National Cemetery, San Bruno CA.

Elmer Brown —5 Years Pitcher (b. 25 Mar 1883 Southport IN–d. 23 Jan 1955 at his home in Indianapolis IN) During World War I he worked at the Nordyke and Marmon Company. He managed the old Capitol Bowling Alley in Indianapolis and later worked as a millwright for Evans Milling Company. Buried Greenwood Cemetery, Greenwood IN.

Fred Brown —2 Years Outfielder (b. 12 Apr 1879 Ossipee NH–d. 3 Feb 1955 Somersworth NH) An attorney, he served as Governor of New Hampshire and as a United States Senator. Died after a lengthy illness. Buried Ossipee Cemetery, Ossipee NH.

Freeman Brown —2 Years Manager (b. 31 Jan 1845 Hubbardstown MA–d. 27 Dec 1916 at his home in Worcester MA) Died from an apoplectic stroke. Buried Hope Cemetery, Worcester MA.

Jake Brown —1 Year Outfielder (b. 22 Mar 1946 Sumrall MS–d. 18 Dec 1981 Houston TX) Died from leukemia. Buried Paradise Cemetery, Houston TX.

Jim Brown —2 Years Pitcher (b. 12 Dec 1860 Clinton County PA–d. 6 Apr 1908 Williamsport PA) He was a bookkeeper for the Lycoming Rubber Company from 1897 until his death. Died following a month's illness. Buried Highland Cemetery, Lock Haven PA.

Jimmy Brown —8 Years Infielder (b. 25 Apr 1910 Jamesville NC–d. 29 Dec 1977 Bath NC).

Joe Brown —2 Years Pitcher (b. 4 Apr 1859 Warren PA–d. 28 Jun 1888 Warren PA).

Joe Brown —1 Year Pitcher (b. 3 Jul 1900 Little Rock AR–d. 7 Mar 1950 Los Angeles CA) He was a laborer. Died from cirrhosis of the liver. Buried Forest Lawn Memorial Park, Glendale CA.

Jumbo Brown —12 Years Pitcher (b. 30 Apr 1907 Greene RI–d. 2 Oct 1966 Freeport NY).

Larry Brown —26 Years Catcher 11 Years Manager (b. 5 Sep 1905 Pratt City AL–d. 7 Apr 1972 Methodist Hospital, Memphis TN) He played in the negro leagues, and was a cook in a Memphis hotel. Buried New Park Cemetery, Memphis TN.

Lew Brown —7 Years Catcher (b. 1 Feb 1858 Leominster MA–d. 16 Jan 1889 City Hospital, Boston MA) He worked as a clerk for a sporting house in Boston when he was hospitalized for an injury received in a friendly wrestling bout. Pneumonia set in and he died. Buried Forest Hills Cemetery, Boston MA.

Lindsay Brown —1 Year Infielder (b. 22 Jul 1911 Mason TX–d. 1 Jan 1967 Santa Rosa Hospital, San Antonio TX) Buried Gooch Cemetery, Mason TX.

Lloyd Brown —12 Years Pitcher (b. 25 Dec 1904 Beeville TX–d. 14 Jan 1974 at his home in Opa-Locka FL) Living in the Miami FL area 40 years, he was a scout for the Senators and Phillies. Cremated.

Myrl Brown —1 Year Pitcher (b. 10 Oct 1894 Waynesboro PA–d. 23 Feb 1981 Polyclinic Medical Center, Harrisburg PA) Served in the U.S. Army during World War I. He taught biology at William Penn High School from 1936 until he retired. Buried Paxtang Cemetery, Harrisburg PA.

Norm Brown —2 Years Pitcher (b. 1 Feb 1919 Evergreen NC–d. 31 May 1995 Bennettsville SC) Served in the U.S. Army during World War II. He owned Brownie's Mens Store in Bennettsville. Buried Sunset Hill Memorial Park, Bennettsville SC.

Ray Brown —1 Year Pitcher (b. 31 Jan 1889 Chicago IL–d. 29 May 1955 General Hospital, Los Angeles CA) World War I veteran. He was an electrical appliance salesman. Died from heart disease. Buried Forest Lawn Memorial Park, Glendale CA.

Sam Brown —2 Years Catcher (b. 21 May 1878 West Newton PA–d. 8 Nov 1931 at his home in Trauger PA) He was the superintendent of the H C Frick Coke Company in Trauger for 22 years. Died from a heart attack.

Stub Brown —3 Years Pitcher (b. 3 Aug 1870 Baltimore MD–d. 10 Mar 1948 Baltimore MD) Died after being ill only a few days. Buried Green Mount Cemetery, Baltimore MD.

Three Finger Brown—14 Years Pitcher 1 Year Manager Hall of Fame (b. 19 Oct 1876 Nyesville IN–d. 14 Feb 1948 Union Hospital, Terre Haute IN) He lost part of an index finger in a farm accident when a boy, thus the name "Three Finger." After baseball he lived on oil interests and investments. Died from complications of diabetes. Buried Roselawn Memorial Park, Terre Haute IN.

Tom Brown—17 Years Outfielder 2 Years Manager (b. 21 Sep 1860 Liverpool, England–d. 25 Oct 1927 Tuberculosis Hospital, Washington DC) He owned a cigar store in Washington DC his last four or five years. Died from tuberculosis. Buried Fort Lincoln Cemetery, Brentwood MD.

Walter Brown—1 Year Pitcher (b. 23 Apr 1915 Jamestown NY–d. 3 Feb 1991 Westfield NY).

Warren Brown—Hall of Fame (d. 20 Nov 1978 at his home in Forest Park IL) He played baseball briefly in the Pacific Coast League before launching a six-decade career as a sportswriter. He worked for the San Francisco *Call-Post* before becoming sports editor for the New York *Evening Mail.* Later he worked for several Chicago newspapers. Buried Queen of Heaven Cemetery, Hillside IL.

Willard Brown—7 Years Infielder (b. 1866 San Francisco CA–d. 20 Dec 1897 at his home in San Francisco CA) Died at the height of his career. Buried Mount Calvary Cemetery, San Francisco CA.

Willard Brown—1 Year Outfielder (b. 26 Jun 1915 Shreveport LA–d. 8 Aug 1996 Houston TX) Buried Houston National Cemetery, Houston TX.

Earl Browne—4 Years Outfielder (b. 5 Mar 1911 Louisville KY–d. 12 Jan 1993 Berryman Healthcare Unit, Whittier CA) For 20 years he was an inspector for a fire insurance company in Little Rock AR. Died from a heart attack, but suffered from prostate cancer. Buried Pine Crest Memorial Park, Alexander AR.

George Browne—12 Years Outfielder (b. 12 Jan 1876 Richmond VA–d. 9 Dec 1920 Hyde Park NY) Buried St Peter's Cemetery, Poughkeepsie NY.

Pidge Browne—1 Year Infielder (b. 21 Mar 1929 Peekskill NY–d. 3 Mar 1997 Houston TX) Buried Earthman Rest Haven, Houston TX.

Frank Browning—1 Year Pitcher (b. 29 Oct 1882 Falmouth KY–d. 19 May 1948 San Antonio TX) Died in a fire that consumed his home. Buried Mission Burial Park, San Antonio TX.

Pete Browning—13 Years Outfielder (b. 17 Jun 1861 Louisville KY–d. 10 Sep 1905 City Hospital, Louisville KY) He owned and operated a saloon in Louisville and later worked as a cigar drummer. He was committed to a Kentucky assylum for a short time. Died from mastoiditis following ear surgery. Buried Cave Hill Cemetery, Louisville KY.

Bill Brubaker—10 Years Infielder (b. 7 Nov 1910 Cleveland OH–d. 2 Apr 1978 Saddleback Community Hosp, Laguna Hills CA) He was a foreman for the Coachella Valley Water District. Died from prostate cancer. Cremated.

Lou Bruce—1 Year Outfielder (b. 16 Jan 1877 St Regis NY–d. 9 Feb 1968 Ilion NY) A dentist and Methodist minister, he practiced denistry for several years in Syracuse and served a number of churches in Northern New York State, retiring in 1949. Buried Lake View Cemetery, Richfield Springs NY.

Earle Brucker—5 Years Catcher 1 Year Manager (b. 6 May 1901 Albany NY–d. 8 May 1981 Grossmont Hospital, San Diego CA) Died from lung cancer. Buried Greenwood Memorial Park, San Diego CA.

Andy Bruckmiller—1 Year Pitcher (b. 1 Jan 1882 McKeesport PA–d. 12 Jan 1970 McKeesport Hospital, McKeesport PA) He was a retired plumbing inspector for the City of Clairton. Died after a brief illness. Buried Elizabeth Cemetery, Elizabeth PA.

Frank Bruggy—5 Years Catcher (b. 4 May 1891 Elizabeth NJ–d. 5 Apr 1959 Alexian Brother's Hospital, Elizabeth NJ) For 27 years he was a detective in the Union County, NJ, prosecuter's office. Died after a brief illness. Buried St Gertrude's Cemetery, Colonia NJ.

Roy Bruner—3 Years Pitcher (b. 10 Feb 1917 Cecilia KY–d. 30 Nov 1986 Humana Hospital-Suburban, St Mathews KY) Served in the Army Air Corps during World War II. He owned Bruner Aluminum Company. Buried Resthaven Memorial Park, Louisville KY.

George Brunet—15 Years Pitcher (b. 8 Jun 1935 Houghton MI–d. 25 Oct 1991 Poza Rica,

Mexico) He won 244 games as a minor league pitcher between 1953 and 1985.

Bob Brush—1 Year Infielder (b. 8 Mar 1875 Osage IA–d. 2 Apr 1944 Charity Hospital, San Bernardino CA) Died from a cerebral hemorrhage. Cremated.

John T Brush—(d. 26 Nov 1912 near Louisiana MO) He was president of the New York Giants. Died in private train car while on a journey west for his his health. Buried Crown Hill Cemetery, Indianapolis IN.

Bill Bruton—12 Years Outfielder (b. 9 Nov 1925 Panola AL–d. 5 Dec 1995 Marshallton DE) Served in the U.S. Army during World War II. He owned a Chrysler dealership and had a long career with Chrysler in advertising, promotion, customer service and financing. Suffered a heart attack and died when his car hit a power pole while he was driving near his home. Buried Gracelawn Memorial Park, New Castle DE.

Ed Bruyette—1 Year Outfielder (b. 31 Aug 1879 Wanawa WI–d. 5 Aug 1940 Peshastin WA) He was in the grocery business in Seattle WA until 1913 when he moved to Peshastin. There he owned an apple orchard and worked as a grading foreman at the local packing plant. Died from a heart attack while tending the sprayer in his orchard. Cremated.

George Bryant—1 Year Infielder (b. 10 Feb 1857 Bridgeport CT–d. 12 Jun 1907 Roxbury MA).

Charlie Brynan—2 Years Pitcher (b. Jul 1863 Philadelphia PA–d. 10 May 1925 Philadelphia PA) Buried Fernwood Cemetery, Fernwood PA.

Hal Bubser—3 Games Pinch Hitter (b. 28 Sep 1895 Chicago IL–d. 22 Jun 1959 Melrose Park IL).

Johnny Bucha—3 Years Catcher (b. 22 Jan 1925 Allentown PA–d. 28 Apr 1996 St Luke's Hospital, Bethlehem PA) Served in the U.S. Navy during World War II. An iron-worker in construction, he also operated a small farm near Danielsville. Died from a heart attack. Buried Cedar Hill Memorial Park, Allentown PA.

Jim Buchanan—1 Year Pitcher (b. 1 Jul 1876 Chatham Hill VA–d. 15 Jun 1949 at a hospital in Norfolk NE) He was a farmer near Randolph NE. Died after becoming seriously ill the night before. Buried Randolph Cemetery, Randolph NE.

Jack Buck—Hall of Fame (b. 21 Aug 1924 Holyoke MA–d. 18 Jun 2002 Barnes-Jewish Hospital, St Louis MO) He was wounded while serving in Germany for the U.S. Army during World War II. A radio and television broadcaster for the Cardinals from 1954 until a year before his death, he also announced 17 Super Bowls and several championship bowling tournaments. Undergoing surgery for lung cancer the prior December, he also suffered from Parkinson's disease and had been hospitalized over five months for a variety of complications when he died. Buried Jefferson Barracks National Cemetery, St Louis MO.

Al Buckenberger—9 Years Manager (b. 31 Jan 1861 Detroit MI–d. 1 Jul 1917 Syracuse NY).

Garland Buckeye—5 Years Pitcher (b. 16 Oct 1897 Heron Lake MN–d. 14 Nov 1975 at his home at Stone Lake WI) He also played professional football. As a baseball pitcher he struck out Babe Ruth twice. He operated a Ford dealership at Toledo OH for several years. Buried Ottawa Hills Memorial Park, Toledo OH.

Ed Buckingham—1 Year Pitcher (b. 12 May 1874 Metuchen NJ–d. 30 Jul 1942 Bridgeport Hospital, Bridgeport CT) An attorney, he was active in civic affairs in Bridgeport, serving three terms as mayor. He was compensation commissioner in Fairfield County, CT, when he died. Died after an illness of several weeks. Buried Lawncroft Burial Cemetery, Fairfield CT.

Jess Buckles—1 Year Pitcher (b. 20 May 1890 LaVerne CA–d. 2 Aug 1975 Community Hospital, Westminster CA) He was a deputy sheriff for the Orange County, CA, Sheriff's Department for 20 years. Died from a heart attack. Buried Good Shepherd Cemetery, Huntington Beach CA.

Dick Buckley—8 Years Catcher (b. 21 Sep 1858 Troy NY–d. 12 Dec 1929 at his home in Pittsburgh PA) Buried West View Cemetery, Pittsburgh PA.

John Buckley—1 Year Pitcher (b. 20 Mar 1870 Marlboro MA–d. 4 May 1942 Boston MA) Buried Immaculate Conception Cemetery, Marlboro MA.

Charlie Buelow—1 Year Infielder (b. 12 Jan 1877 Dubuque IA–d. 4 May 1951 at his home in Dubuque IA) Died after being ill for several years. Buried Linwood Cemetery, Dubuque IA.

Fritz Buelow—9 Years Catcher (b. 13 Feb 1876 Berlin, Germany–d. 27 Dec 1933 Grace Hospital, Detroit MI) He worked at various jobs for Ford Motor Company and as a gateman at Navin Field (later Briggs Stadium, then Tiger Stadium) and was proprietor of a rooming house. Died following a long illness. Buried Woodlawn Cemetery, Detroit MI.

Art Bues—2 Years Infielder (b. 3 Mar 1888 Milwaukee WI–d. 7 Nov 1954 at his home in Whitefish Bay WI) He spent most of his baseball career in the three triple A leagues. Died from a heart attack. Buried Pinelawn Memorial Park, Milwaukee WI.

Charlie Buffinton—11 Years Pitcher 1 Year Manager (b. 14 Jun 1861 Fall River MA–d. 23 Sep 1907 Dr Aldrich's Hospital, Fall River MA) A principal in the Bowenville Coal Company in Fall River, he became active in its operations. Died from fatty degeneration of the heart. Buried Oak Grove Cemetery, Fall River MA.

Bob Buhl—15 Years Pitcher (b. 12 Aug 1928 Saginaw MI–d. 16 Feb 2001 at his home in Titusville FL) Died from pneumonia and emphysema.

Harry Buker—1 Year Infielder (b. 1859 Chicago IL–d. 10 Aug 1899 at a friend's home in Chicago IL) He worked in the real estate business, and for the last year had been an acting manager of a lyceum bureau. Buried Rosehill Cemetery, Chicago IL.

Morgan G Bulkeley—Hall of Fame (b. abt 1838 East Haddam CT–d. 6 Nov 1922 Hartford CT) The president of Aetna Life Insurance Company, he was a former governor of Connecticut, U.S. Senator and mayor of Hartford. He was one of the founders of the National League and its first president. Died after being ill with a hard cold for two weeks. Buried Cedar Hill Cemetery, Hartford CT.

Sim Bullas—1 Year Catcher (b. 10 Apr 1861 Cleveland OH–d. 14 Jan 1908 at his home in Cleveland OH).

Red Bullock—1 Year Pitcher (b. 12 Oct 1911 Biloxi MS–d. 27 Jun 1988 Singing River Hospital, Pascagoula MS) He worked 40 years in education as a coach, principal and superintendent, retiring in 1977 as superintendent of the Moss Point MS schools. Buried Griffin Cemetery, Moss Point MS.

Josh Bunce—1 Year Outfielder (b. 10 May 1847 Manhattan NY–d. 28 Apr 1912 at his home in Brooklyn NY) He worked 16 years for the New York *Journal* and was a member of the Brooklyn Volunteer Firemen's Association. Buried Greenwood Cemetery, Brooklyn NY.

Al Burch—6 Years Outfielder (b. 7 Oct 1883 Albany NY–d. 5 Oct 1926 Brooklyn NY).

Ernie Burch—3 Years Outfielder (b. 1858 DeKalb County, IL–d. 8 Nov 1933 Evanston IL).

Fred Burchell—4 Years Pitcher (b. 14 Jul 1879 Perth Amboy NJ–d. 20 Nov 1951 at his home in Jordan NY) He managed minor league baseball for a short while and owned the Syracuse NY Stars at one time. Later he worked for the New York State Highway Department until a year before his death when he was forced to retire because of illness. Buried St Patrick Cemetery, Jordan NY.

Bill Burdick—2 Years Pitcher (b. 11 Oct 1859 Austin MN–d. 23 Oct 1949 at his home in Spokane WA) He was a railroad man before operating Burdick's Resort on Newman Lake for many years. Buried St Thomas Cemetery, Coeur d'Alene ID.

Jack Burdock—14 Years Infielder 1 Year Manager (b. 1851 Brooklyn NY–d. 27 Nov 1931 at his home in Brooklyn NY) Died after a short illness. Buried Holy Cross Cemetery, Brooklyn NY.

Pete Burg—1 Year Infielder (b. 4 Jun 1882 Chicago IL–d. 28 Apr 1969 Joliet IL).

Smoky Burgess—18 Years Catcher (b. 6 Feb 1927 Caroleen NC–d. 15 Sep 1991 Rutherford Hospital, Asheville NC) He lived in Forest City NC and was a scout several years for the Braves. Died from unreported causes. Buried Sunset Memorial Park, Spindale NC.

Bill Burgo—2 Years Outfielder (b. 15 Nov 1919 Johnstown PA–d. 19 Oct 1988 Morgan City LA).

Si Burick—Hall of Fame (b. 14 Jun 1909 Dayton OH–d. 10 Dec 1986 Good Samaritan Hospital, Dayton OH) Sports editor for the Dayton *Daily News* for nearly 58 years, he also had a daily sports show on radio and later on television. Died after suffering a massive stroke. Buried Beth Abraham Cemetery, Dayton OH.

Sandy Burk—5 Years Pitcher (b. 22 Apr 1887 Columbus OH–d. 11 Oct 1934 Brooklyn NY).

Chris Burkam—1 Game Pinch Hitter (b. 13 Oct 1892 Benton Harbor MI–d. 9 May 1964 Kalamazoo MI) He worked 15 years for the U.S. government, and retired from Western Michigan University in 1956. Buried Mount Ever-Rest Cemetery, Kalamazoo MI.

Elmer Burkart—4 Years Pitcher (b. 1 Feb 1917 Torresdale PA–d. 6 Feb 1995 Baltimore MD) Buried Dulaney Valley Memorial Garden, Timonium MD.

Bill Burke—1 Year Pitcher (b. Nov 1865 Cincinnati OH–d. 17 Mar 1939 Atchison KS).

Billy Burke—2 Years Pitcher (b. 11 Jul 1889 Clinton MA–d. 9 Feb 1967 at his home in Worcester MA) Served in the U.S. Marines during World War I. He was a hearing officer for the State Registry of Motor Vehicles for 29 years, retiring in 1955. Buried St John's Cemetery, Lancaster MA.

Bobby Burke—10 Years Pitcher (b. 23 Jan 1907 Joliet IL–d. 8 Feb 1971 Stuart FL) Served in the U.S. Navy during World War II. He owned and operated Bob Burke's Plainfield Fishing Resort. Died suddenly. Buried St Patrick's Cemetery, Joliet IL.

Dan Burke—2 Years Outfielder (b. Mar 1869 Whitman MA–d. 20 Mar 1933 at his home in Taunton MA) Died after a short illness. Buried St Patrick's Cemetery, Rockland MA.

Eddie Burke—8 Years Outfielder (b. 6 Oct 1866 Northumberland PA–d. 26 Nov 1907 General Hospital, Utica NY) He was a cook for a section gang of the New York Central Railway.

Frank Burke—2 Years Outfielder (b. 16 Feb 1880 Carbon County PA–d. 17 Sep 1946 at his home in Los Angeles CA) He owned and operated a billiard parlor. Died from a heart attack. Buried Holy Cross Cemetery, Culver City CA.

Glenn Burke—4 Years Outfielder (b. 16 Nov 1952 Oakland CA–d. 30 May 1995 Fairmont Hospital, San Leandro CA) An acknowledged gay, he spent 17 months, during the early 1990s, in San Quentin State Prison for false imprisonment, grand theft, drug abuse and parole violations. Upon release he spent time on the San Francisco CA streets as a homeless person. Died from AIDS. Buried Mountain View Cemetery, Oakland CA.

Jimmy Burke—6 Years Infielder 4 Years Manager (b. 12 Oct 1874 St Louis MO–d. 26 Mar 1942 St John's Hospital, St Louis MO) He managed minor league teams and coached for several major league teams until he was paralysed by a stroke in 1929. Died from pneumonia. Buried Calvary Cemetery, St Louis MO.

John Burke—2 Years Outfielder (b. 27 Jan 1877 Hazleton PA–d. 4 Aug 1950 St Francis Hospital, Jersey City NJ) Served as a chaplin during World War I. Ordained as a Catholic priest in 1908, he served congregations in New York and New Jersey, the church in Keyport NJ from 1929 until his death. Died after a prolonged illness. Buried St Joseph's Cemetery, Keyport NJ.

Les Burke—4 Years Infielder (b. 18 Dec 1902 Lynn MA–d. 6 May 1975 Hunt Memorial Hospital, Danvers MA) He retired in 1968 after working many years as a gear shaver at the General Electric River Works in Lynn. Collapsed from a heart attack while golfing. Buried Swampscott Cemetery, Swampscott MA.

Michael Burke—(b. 1916 Enfield CT–d. 5 Feb 1987 Ireland) Served during World War II with the U.S. Office of Strategic Services. He was Chief Executive Officer of the Yankees from 1966 to 1973 when CBS owned the team. Died from cancer. Buried Enfield CT.

Mike Burke—1 Year Infielder (b. 1855 Cincinnati OH–d. 4 Jun 1889 Albany NY).

Pat Burke—1 Year Infielder (b. 13 May 1901 St Louis MO–d. 7 Jul 1965 St Louis MO) Buried Resurrection Cemetery, St Louis MO.

Walter Burke—4 Years Pitcher (b. abt 1852 CA–d. 3 Mar 1911 Memphis TN) He was a book dealer at Memphis. Died from Bright's disease. Buried Calvary Cemetery, Memphis TN.

Jesse Burkett—16 Years Outfielder Hall of Fame (b. 4 Dec 1870 Wheeling WV–d. 27 May 1953 Belmont Hospital, Worcester MA) He managed minor league baseball, coached and scouted for the Giants and coached college baseball at Holy Cross and Assumption College. Buried St John's Cemetery, Worcester MA.

Hercules Burnett—2 Years Outfielder (b. 13 Aug 1865 Louisville KY–d. 4 Oct 1936 at his home in Louisville KY) He worked for the Louisville and Nashville Railroad for 47 years. Buried Eastern Cemetery, Louisville KY.

Jack Burnett—1 Year Outfielder (b. 2 Dec 1889 MO–d. 8 Sep 1929 Taft CA) He was an oil worker. Died from a self-inflicted poisoning. Buried Union Cemetery, Bakersfield CA.

Johnny Burnett—9 Years Infielder (b. 1 Nov 1904 Bartow FL–d. 12 Aug 1959 at a hospital in Tampa FL) Died from leukemia. Buried Garden of Memories, Tampa FL.

Watch Burnham—1 Year Manager (b. 20 May 1860 Saline MI–d. 18 Nov 1902 Dearborn MI) A National League umpire six years between 1883 and 1895, he later engaged in advertising. Died at a retreat after suffering a mental collapse. Buried Oakwood Cemetery, Saline MI.

Bill Burns—5 Years Pitcher (b. 27 Jan 1880 San Saba TX–d. 7 Jun 1953 Trammell Rest Home, Ramona CA) Died from a heart attack. Buried Holy Cross Cemetery, San Diego CA.

Charlie Burns—1 Game Pinch Hitter (b. 15 May 1879 Bay View MD–d. 6 Jun 1968 Harford Memorial Hosp, Havre de Grace MD). Buried Angel Hill Cemetery, Havre de Grace MD.

Denny Burns—2 Years Pitcher (b. 24 May 1898 Tiff City MO–d. 21 May 1969 at a hospital in Tulsa OK) He played and managed in the minor leagues for 21 years before coaching baseball at the University of Tulsa one year. He then worked in the real estate business in Tulsa and Miami OK while doing ministerial work for the Jehovah's Witnesses. Buried Rest Haven Cemetery, Sperry OK.

Dick Burns—3 Years Outfielder (b. 26 Dec 1863 Holyoke MA–d. 16 Nov 1937 Holyoke MA) For many years he was connected with the Kaffir Cigar Company and later operated a cigar store in Holyoke, retiring in 1930. He entered politics and was elected to the Board of Aldermen. Died after a short illness. Buried Calvary Cemetery, Holyoke MA.

Ed Burns—7 Years Catcher (b. 31 Oct 1888 San Francisco CA–d. 30 May 1942 Monterey CA) He was a popular Monterey clothing merchant for 23 years. Died from a heart attack. Buried San Carlos Catholic Cemetery, Monterey CA.

Edward H Burns—(b. 17 Jan 1891 Frankfort IN–d. 27 Jan 1955 Chicago IL) Served in the U.S. Army during World War I. He worked for the *Chicago Tribune* 37 years, the last 27 as a sportswriter. Collapsing while on an assignment, he had been in a coma for three weeks when he died. Buried Rosehill Cemetery, Chicago IL.

George Burns—16 Years Infielder (b. 31 Jan 1893 Niles OH–d. 7 Jan 1978 Evergreen Hospital, Kirkland WA) A retired King County, WA, deputy sheriff, he died from cancer. Buried Calvary Cemetery, Seattle WA.

George Burns—15 Years Outfielder (b. 24 Nov 1889 Utica NY–d. 15 Aug 1966 at his home in Gloversville NY) He was a paymaster for G Levor Company, retiring in 1957. Died after being in ill health six years. Buried Mount Carmel Cemetery, Johnstown NY.

Jack Burns—7 Years Infielder (b. 31 Aug 1907 Cambridge MA–d. 18 Apr 1975 at his home in Allston MA) He spent his entire life in baseball, managing minor league baseball ten years, working as third base coach five years for the Red Sox and scouting 15 years for the Red Sox. Buried Evergreen Cemetery, Brighton MA.

Jack Burns—2 Years Infielder (b. 13 May 1880 Avoca PA–d. 24 Jun 1957 at his home in Waterford CT) He was assistant superintendent for the New London CT office of Metropolitan Life Insurance Company and operated a real estate and insurance business before becoming postmaster at Waterford in 1933, retiring in 1948. Died suddenly. Buried Jordan Cemetery, Waterford CT.

Joe Burns—2 Years Outfielder (b. 26 Mar 1889 Ipswich MA–d. 12 Jul 1987 Ledgewood Nursing Center, Beverly MA) Served in the U.S. Navy during World War I. He worked for New England Carbide Company before retiring. Buried Highland Cemetery, Ipswich MA.

Joe Burns—3 Years Infielder (b. 17 Jun 1916 Bryn Mawr PA–d. 24 Jun 1974 Bryn Mawr PA) He died suddenly. Buried St Dennis Church Cemetery, Havertown PA.

Joe Burns—1 Year Catcher (b. 25 Feb 1900 Trenton NJ–d. 7 Jan 1986 St Francis Medical Center, Trenton NJ) He retired as a sales executive for New Jersey Manufacturer's Insurance Company in 1985. Buried St Mary's Cemetery, Trenton NJ.

Oyster Burns—11 Years Outfielder (b. 6 Sep 1864 Philadelphia PA–d. 11 Nov 1928 Victory Memorial Hospital, Brooklyn NY) A National League umpire in 1899, he owned and operated a cafe in Brooklyn before becoming an agent for a cigar manufacturer. He was a corporation inspector for the borough of Brooklyn when he died following a stroke. Buried Holy Cross Cemetery, North Arlington NJ.

Tom Burns—13 Years Infielder 3 Years Manager (b. 30 Mar 1857 Honesdale PA–d. 19 Mar 1902 Jersey City NJ) He was president of the Eastern League, and managed minor league baseball until his death. Died from heart failure at the home of Pat Powers as he prepared for the upcoming Eastern League season. Buried St Michael's Cemetery, Springfield MA.

Alex Burr—1 Year Outfielder (b. 1 Nov 1893 Chicago IL–d. 1 Nov 1918 Cazaux, France) He was killed in action during World War I.

Buster Burrell—4 Years Catcher (b. 8 Dec 1866 East Weymouth MA–d. 8 May 1962 at a nursing home in South Weymouth MA) He worked for the Edwin Clapp Shoe Company in Weymouth from 1902 until he retired in 1957. Just named the oldest living major leaguer, he died after a long illness. Buried Fairmount Cemetery, Weymouth MA.

Harry Burrell—1 Year Pitcher (b. 1866 East Weymouth MA–d. 11 Dec 1914 Omaha NE).

Al Burris—1 Year Pitcher (b. 28 Jan 1874 Warwick MD–d. 24 Mar 1938 Peninsula General Hospital, Salisbury MD) He practiced general medicine in Salisbury and for many years was superintendent of the Pine Bluff Sanitorium there. He was also the proprietor of a drug store. Died after a series of strokes. Buried Hollywood Cemetery, Harrington DE.

John Burrows—2 Years Pitcher (b. 30 Oct 1913 Winnfield LA–d. 27 Apr 1987 Coal Run OH) Died in a fire that consumed his home. Cremated.

Dick Burrus—6 Years Infielder (b. 29 Jan 1898 Hatteras NC–d. 2 Feb 1972 Albemarle Hospital, Elizabeth City NC) He was the Texaco distributor at Hatteras until his retirement in 1962. Buried New Hollywood Cemetery, Elizabeth City NC.

Bill Burwell—3 Years Pitcher 1 Year Manager (b. 27 Mar 1895 Jarbalo KS–d. 11 Jun 1973 at his home in Daytona Beach FL) World War I veteran. He lived in Daytona Beach for 35 years and was a consultant for the Pirates. Buried Bellevue Memory Gardens, Daytona Beach FL.

Jim Busby—13 Years Outfielder (b. 8 Jan 1927 Kenedy TX–d. 8 Jul 1996 University Hospital, Augusta GA) Served in the U.S. Army during World War II. He spent over 30 years in major league baseball as a player and coach. Died from a heart attack. Buried Millen Cemetery, Millen GA.

Ed Busch—3 Years Infielder (b. 16 Nov 1917 Lebanon IL–d. 17 Jan 1987 Scott AFB Medical Center, Scott AFB IL) He worked for the City of O'Fallon IL. Buried O'Fallon City Cemetery, O'Fallon IL.

August Busch, Jr—(b. 28 Mar 1899 St Louis MO–d. 29 Sep 1989 on his estate at Grant's Farm, St Louis MO) He was the owner of the St Louis Cardinals from 1953 until his death. Also the owner of the Anheuser-Busch Brewing Company, he was a member of the family that founded the brewery. Served in the U.S. Army during World War II. Died from pneumonia. Buried Sunset Memorial Park, Affton MO.

Guy Bush—17 Years Pitcher (b. 23 Aug 1901 Aberdeen MS–d. 2 Jul 1985 North Mississippi Medical Ctr, Shannon MS) Died after a sudden illness. Buried Shannon Cemetery, Shannon MS.

Joe Bush—17 Years Pitcher (b. 27 Nov 1892 Brainerd MN–d. 1 Nov 1974 Fort Lauderdale FL) Cremated.

Ownie Bush—16 Years Infielder 7 Years Manager (b. 8 Oct 1887 Indianapolis IN–d. 28 Mar 1972 St Vincent Hospital, Indianapolis IN) He had a 65 year career in baseball as a player, owner, manager and executive. At the time of his death he was a scout for the White Sox, and was the oldest man working actively in the game. Buried Holy Cross Cemetery, Indianapolis IN.

Jack Bushelman—3 Years Pitcher (b. 29 Aug 1885 Cincinnati OH–d. 26 Oct 1955 at his home in Gate City VA) Buried Gate City VA.

Frank Bushey—2 Years Pitcher (b. 1 Aug 1906 Wheaton KS–d. 18 Mar 1972 at a hospital in Topeka KS) He operated a grocery store and other businesses at St Marys KS before retiring shortly before his death. Died from cancer. Buried Mount Calvary Cemetery, St Marys KS.

Doc Bushong—12 Years Catcher (b. 10 Jan 1856 Philadelphia PA–d. 19 Aug 1908 at his home in Brooklyn NY) He was a dentist. Buried Holy Cross Cemetery, Brooklyn NY.

Joe Buskey—1 Year Infielder (b. 18 Dec 1902 Cumberland MD–d. 11 Apr 1949 Cumberland MD) Served in the U.S. Army. During World War II he was in the Merchant Marines. He worked for Potomac Edison Co and Railway Express before spending his last five years as a cellarman for Queen City Brewing Company. Died at the brewery from a heart attack shortly after going to work. Buried St Peter's and St Paul's Cemetery, Cumberland MD.

Hank Butcher—2 Years Outfielder (b. 12 Jul 1886 Chicago IL–d. 28 Dec 1979 Hazel Crest IL) Buried St Mary Cemetery, Evergreen Park IL.

Max Butcher—10 Years Pitcher (b. 21 Sep 1910 Holden WV–d. 15 Sep 1957 General Hospital, Logan WV) Died from a liver ailment. Buried Forest Lawn Cemetery, Pecks Mill WV.

Bill Butland—4 Years Pitcher (b. 22 Mar 1918 Terre Haute IN–d. 19 Sep 1997 Union Hospital, Terre Haute IN) Served in the U.S. Army during World War II. He was a machine operator for Ethel Visqueen and retired from Commercial Solvents Corporation as a pipefitter. Buried Roselawn Memorial Park, Terre Haute IN.

Art Butler—6 Years Infielder (b. 19 Dec 1887 Fall River MA–d. 7 Oct 1984 Fall River MA) He was the oldest living former major leaguer at the time of his death. Died from a heart attack. Buried Notre Dame Cemetery, Fall River MA.

Charlie Butler—1 Year Pitcher (b. 12 May 1905 Green Cove Springs FL–d. 10 May 1964 at a hospital in Brunswick GA) He was director of the Glynn County (GA) Recreation Department for 15 years when he died. Buried Christ Churchyard Cemetery, Saint Simons Island GA.

Frank Butler—1 Year Outfielder (b. 18 Jul 1866 Savannah GA–d. 10 Jul 1945 Jacksonville FL) A longtime employee of the *Florida Times-Union* newspaper, he was a solicitor in the circulation department. Died following a brief illness. Buried St Mary's Section-Evergreen Cemetery, Jacksonville FL.

Frank Butler—1 Year Outfielder (b. 1862 Boston MA–d. 9 Apr 1921 at his home in South Boston MA) He worked at the Boston baseball parks at the ticket gates. Died after a month's illness with throat trouble. Buried Mount Calvary Cemetery, Roslindale MA.

Ike Butler—1 Year Pitcher (b. 22 Aug 1873 Langston MI–d. 17 Mar 1948 Oakland CA) He was a bartender. Died from a heart attack. Cremated.

John Butler—4 Years Catcher (b. 26 Jul 1879 Boston MA–d. 2 Feb 1950 Dorchester MA) Buried Mount Calvary Cemetery, Roslindale MA.

Johnny Butler—4 Years Infielder (b. 20 Mar 1893 Eureka KS–d. 29 Apr 1967 Woodruff Community Hospital, Long Beach CA) He was a sound technician for a movie studio for 20 years. Died from a heart attack. Buried Rosedale Cemetery, Los Angeles CA.

Kid Butler—1 Year Infielder (b. 9 Aug 1887 Franklin PA–d. 22 Feb 1964 at a hospital in Richmond CA) World War I veteran. He was a retired assistant manager of the Richmond Housing Authority and a part-time scout for several teams. Buried Golden Gate National Cemetery, San Bruno CA.

Ormond Butler—1 Year Manager (b. 18 Nov 1854 WV–d. 12 Sep 1915 at his home in Baltimore MD) He was connected with the business end of theatricals in Baltimore for 40 years. Died after a lingering illness of one year. Buried Mount Olivet Cemetery, Frederick MD.

Ralph Buxton—2 Years Pitcher (b. 7 Jun 1914 Rainton, Saskatchewan, Canada–d. 6 Jan 1988 at his home in San Leandro CA) He was a self-employed furniture finisher. Died from a heart attack. Cremated.

Bill Byers—1 Year Catcher (b. 3 Oct 1877 Bridgetown IN–d. 8 Sep 1948 Baltimore MD) Buried Loudon Park National Cemetery, Baltimore MD.

Harry Byrd—7 Years Pitcher (b. 3 Feb 1925 Darlington SC–d. 14 May 1985 at a hospital in Darlington SC) Served in the U.S. Army during World War II. He worked 12 years for Goodson Construction Co in Darlington, retiring as a foreman. Died after a long illness. Buried Darlington Memory Gardens, Hartsville SC.

Sammy Byrd—8 Years Outfielder (b. 15 Oct 1906 Bremen GA–d. 11 May 1981 Mesa AZ).

Bobby Byrne—11 Years Infielder (b. 31 Dec 1884 St Louis MO–d. 31 Dec 1964 Caley Nursing Manor, Wayne PA) In addition to baseball, he also excelled in soccer, golf and bowling, and ran a bowling alley for a time. Buried Calvary Cemetery, St Louis MO.

Charlie Byrne—3 Years Manager (b. Sep 1843 New York City NY–d. 4 Jan 1898 at his home in New York City NY) He organized the first Brooklyn baseball team. Died from a complication of diseases. Buried Calvary Cemetery, Woodside NY.

Jerry Byrne—1 Year Pitcher (b. 2 Feb 1907 Parnell MI–d. 11 Aug 1955 at a hospital in Lansing MI) His baseball career was cut short when he injured his arm throwing to first base. He was personnel director for Reo Motors, Inc, in Lansing from 1945 until his death. He was active in civic affairs there. Died from cancer. Buried Oakwood Cemetery, Grand Ledge MI.

Jim Byrnes—1 Year Catcher (b. 5 Jan 1880 San Francisco CA–d. 31 Jul 1941 St Mary's Hospital, San Francisco CA) He was elected as a California state assemblyman, and from 1934 until his death he was a deputy parole officer for the State of California. Died from heart disease. Buried Holy Cross Catholic Cemetery, Colma CA.

Milt Byrnes—3 Years Outfielder (b. 15 Nov 1916 St Louis MO–d. 1 Feb 1979 St Louis MO) Buried Our Redeemer Cemetery, Affton MO.

C

Leon Cadore—10 Years Pitcher (b. 20 Nov 1890 Chicago IL–d. 16 Mar 1958 V A Hospital, Spokane WA) He pitched the longest game in major league history, a 26 inning 1 to 1 tie, for the Dodgers in 1920. He married Charlie Ebbets' daughter, and was a New York stock broker until the 1929 crash. He then moved to Hope ID, living there and at Spokane the rest of his life. Died from cancer. Buried Pinecrest Memorial Park, Sandpoint ID.

Charlie Cady—2 Years Pitcher (b. Dec 1865 Chicago IL–d. 9 Jun 1909 Kankakee IL).

Hick Cady—8 Years Catcher (b. 26 Jan 1886 Bishop Hill IL–d. 3 Mar 1946 Cedar Rapids IA) He caught Babe Ruth when Ruth first joined the Red Sox as a pitcher. He umpired in the minor leagues for 18 years. Died from suffocation in a fire in his room at the Alliance Hotel. The fire was caused by an electric heater he forgot to turn off when he went to bed. Cremated.

Tom Cafego—1 Year Outfielder (b. 21 Aug 1911 Whipple WV–d. 29 Oct 1961 Detroit MI) Died from a heart attack. Buried Cadillac Memorial Gardens, Westland MI.

Ben Caffyn—1 Year Outfielder (b. 10 Feb 1880 Peoria IL–d. 22 Nov 1942 Proctor Hospital, Peoria IL) Veteran of the Spanish-American War and World War I. He worked 14 years for the Peoria Fire Department, retiring in 1935. Buried Springdale Cemetery, Peoria IL.

John Cahill—3 Years Outfielder (b. Philadephia PA–d. 1 Nov 1901 Pleasanton CA) He was one of several players purported to be the original "Casey at the Bat" depicted in the Earnest Thayer poem. Died from consumption.

Tom Cahill—1 Year Catcher (b. Oct 1868 Fall River MA–d. 25 Dec 1894 Scranton PA) He was studying medicine during the off-season when he died at the height of his baseball career from hemorrhages caused by consumption. Buried Fall River MA.

Bob Cain—6 Years Pitcher (b. 16 Oct 1924 Longford KS–d. 7 Apr 1997 University Hospital, Euclid OH) He was the pitcher that walked Eddie Gaedel, the St Louis Browns midget, on four pitches in 1951. Served in the U.S. Army during World War II. He owned and operated a dry cleaning plant in Parma OH. Died from cancer. Cremated.

Sugar Cain—7 Years Pitcher (b. 5 Apr 1907 Macon GA–d. 3 Apr 1975 Atlanta GA) Cremated.

George Caithamer—1 Year Catcher (b. 22 Jul 1910 Chicago IL–d. 1 Jun 1954 Chicago IL) Buried Bohemian National Cemetery, Chicago IL.

Bruce Caldwell—2 Years Outfielder (b. 8 Feb 1906 Ashton RI–d. 15 Feb 1959 Veteran's Hospital, West Haven CT) Served in the U.S. Navy during World War II. An attorney in New Haven CT, he was also an elected selectman and town judge. Died from cancer. Buried Swan Point Cemetery, Providence RI.

Charlie Caldwell —1 Year Pitcher (b. 2 Aug 1901 Bristol VA–d. 1 Nov 1957 Princeton Hospital, Princeton NJ) He coached football at Princeton University. Died from cancer. Cremated.

Earl Caldwell —8 Years Pitcher (b. 9 Apr 1905 Sparks TX–d. 15 Sep 1981 Mission Municipal Hospital, Mission TX) He lived in the Rio Grande Valley of Texas since 1929 and in Mission since 1954. Buried Valley Memorial Gardens, Pharr TX.

Ralph Caldwell —2 Years Pitcher (b. 18 Jan 1884 Philadelphia PA–d. 5 Aug 1969 at his home in Trenton NJ) He coached baseball at Lehigh University and other colleges while teaching in Pennsylvania. In 1918 he joined the Trenton High School faculty and retired in 1948. While there he founded Caldwell Supply Company, a supplier of all kinds of farm equipment. Buried Ewing Church Cemetery, Trenton NJ.

Ray Caldwell —12 Years Pitcher (b. 26 Apr 1888 Corydon PA–d. 17 Aug 1967 District Hospital, Salamanca NY) He was a telegrapher for the B R and P Railway. Buried Randolph Cemetery, Randolph NY.

Bill Calhoun —1 Year Infielder (b. 23 Jun 1890 Rockmart GA–d. 28 Jan 1955 Rawlings Sanitarium, Sandersville GA) A civil engineer, he worked several years for the Goodyear Mills in Rockmart. Died after an illness of several months. Buried Rose Hill Cemetery, Rockmart GA.

John Calhoun —1 Year Infielder (b. 14 Dec 1879 Pittsburgh PA–d. 27 Feb 1947 Mercy Hospital, Cincinnati OH) He managed minor league teams before going into police work. He was chief of police at Daytona Beach FL from 1928 to 1946, and at Hamilton OH when he died from a heart attack. Cremated and his ashes taken to Pittsburgh PA.

Marty Callaghan —4 Years Outfielder (b. 9 Jun 1900 Norwood MA–d. 23 Jun 1975 at a hospital in Norfolk MA) He coached in the minor leagues for some years, later working for Plimpton Press in Norwood before retiring. Buried Highland Cemetery, Norwood MA.

Dave Callahan —2 Years Outfielder (b. 20 Jul 1888 Seneca IL–d. 28 Oct 1969 Ottawa IL).

Jim Callahan —1 Year Outfielder (b. 12 Jan 1879 Alegheny County, PA–d. 9 Mar 1968 Carnegie PA).

Joe Callahan —2 Years Pitcher (b. 8 Oct 1916 East Boston MA–d. 24 May 1949 at his home in West Roxbury MA) He worked for the Firestone Rubber Company. Died after a two-day illness. Buried New Calvary Cemetery, Mattapan MA.

Leo Callahan —2 Years Outfielder (b. 9 Aug 1890 Jamaica Plain MA–d. 2 May 1982 Veteran's Hospital, Erie PA) Served in the U.S. Navy during World War I. He managed minor league baseball for a few years following World War I. Buried Calvary Cemetery, Oil City PA.

Nixey Callahan —13 Years Outfielder 7 Years Manager (b. 18 Mar 1874 Fitchburg MA–d. 4 Oct 1934 at his apartment in Boston MA) A successful contractor in Chicago, he executed the contract for the complete waterworks at the Great Lakes Naval Station near there. Died from heart failure while visiting friends in Boston. Buried Fitchburg MA.

Pat Callahan —1 Year Infielder (b. 15 Oct 1866 Cleveland OH–d. 4 Feb 1940 Louisville KY) A well known Louisville industrialist, churchman and crusader, he owned and operated the Louisville Varnish Company, the world's largest maker of varnishes. Recognized as one of the nation's most distinguished citizens. Buried Calvary Cemetery, Louisville KY.

Ray Callahan —1 Year Pitcher (b. 28 Aug 1891 Portage WI–d. 23 Jan 1973 at a hospital in Olympia WA) He operated an automobile dealership in Centralia WA until retiring in 1950. Buried Olympia Cemetery, Olympia WA.

Wes Callahan —1 Year Infielder (b. 3 Jul 1888 Lyons IN–d. 13 Sep 1953 at a hospital in Dayton OH) He was a salesman. Buried Cincinnati OH.

Will Callahan —2 Years Pitcher (b. 1869 Rochester NY–d. 20 Dec 1917 St Mary's Hospital, Rochester NY) Died from pneumonia after a short illness.

Frank Callaway —2 Years Infielder (b. 26 Feb 1898 Knoxville TN–d. 21 Aug 1987 at his home in Knoxville TN) He was the board chairman for the Athletic House in Knoxville. Buried Highland Memorial Cemetery, Knoxville TN.

Jack Calvo —2 Years Outfielder (b. 11 Jun 1894 Havana, Cuba–d. 15 Jun 1965 Miami FL).

Hank Camelli —5 Years Catcher (b. 12 Dec 1914 Gloucester MA–d. 14 Jul 1996 at his home in Wellesley MA) Served in the U.S. Army during World War II. He ran a sporting goods store with Earl Torgeson for many years. Later he retired as a contractor's salesman for Grossman's of Braintree MA. Buried Woodlawn Cemetery, Wellesley MA.

John Cameron —1 Year Outfielder (b. 1 Aug 1879 Truro, Nova Scotia, Canada–d. 15 Jun 1964 at a nursing home in West Roxbury MA) He was a retired cable splicer for James Sugden Company of Boston MA. Buried Spring Grove Cemetery, Andover MA.

Dolph Camilli —12 Years Infielder (b. 23 Apr 1907 San Francisco CA–d. 21 Oct 1997 Hillsdale Extended Care, San Mateo CA) He was a coach, scout and minor league manager. Died from recurrent pneumonia following surgery for an epidermal abscess. Buried Cypress Lawn Memorial Park, Colma CA.

Bill Cammeyer —1 Year Manager (b. 20 Mar 1821 New York City NY–d. 4 Sep 1898 at his home in Brooklyn NY) An early pioneer in baseball, he established the Union Baseball Ground for playing baseball in New York City in 1861. He retired in 1876 after making a fortune, but lost it all while experimenting with explosives in a fruitless effort to blast the rock at Hell Gate in the East River. Buried Greenwood Cemetery, Brooklyn NY.

Harry Camnitz —2 Years Pitcher (b. 26 Oct 1884 McKinney KY–d. 6 Jan 1951 Kentucky Baptist Hospital, Louisville KY) From 1917 until 1931 he operated an automobile dealership in South Carolina. In 1931 he returned to Louisville where he worked as an automobile salesman, operated a used-car business and, finally, worked for Rodes-Rapier Company. He suffered a heart attack two years before his death. Buried Cave Hill Cemetery, Louisville KY.

Howie Camnitz —11 Years Pitcher (b. 22 Aug 1881 Covington KY–d. 2 Mar 1960 at his home in Louisville KY) He was sales manager at a Louisville Chevrolet dealership. Buried Cave Hill Cemetery, Louisville KY.

Howie Camp —1 Year Outfielder (b. 1 Jul 1893 Munford AL–d. 8 May 1960 Eastaboga AL) His major league baseball career cut short by a broken arm, he managed minor league baseball for a few years, then spent the rest of his career as a minor league umpire. Died suddenly.

Kid Camp —2 Years Pitcher (b. 2 Jan 1870 Columbus OH–d. 2 Mar 1895 at his home in Omaha NE) Buried Forest Lawn Memorial Park, Omaha NE.

Llewellan Camp —3 Years Infielder (b. 22 Feb 1868 Columbus OH–d. 1 Oct 1948 at his home in Omaha NE) He carried mail 33 years in Omaha, retiring in 1932. His death was unexpected as he had not been ill. Buried Forest Lawn Memorial Park, Omaha NE.

Roy Campanella —10 Years Catcher Hall of Fame (b. 19 Nov 1921 Philadelphia PA–d. 26 Jun 1993 Woodland Hills CA) His career was ended by an auto accident in 1958 that left him paralyzed from the chest down. He worked as an executive for the Dodgers until he died from a heart attack. Cremated. Buried Forest Lawn-Hollywood Hills, Los Angeles CA.

Al Campanis —1 Year Infielder (b. 2 Nov 1916 Kos, Greece–d. 21 Jun 1998 at his home in Fullerton CA) He coached and scouted for the Dodgers before becoming their general manager in 1968, a job he held until 1987 when he was fired for making a racially insensitive remark. Died from heart disease. Buried Loma Vista Memorial Park, Fullerton CA.

Count Campau —3 Years Outfielder 1 Year Manager (b. 17 Oct 1863 Detroit MI–d. 3 Apr 1938 at his home in New Orleans LA) He lived many years in New Orleans. Buried Metairie Cemetery, Metairie LA.

Archie Campbell —3 Years Pitcher (b. 20 Oct 1903 Maplewood NJ–d. 22 Dec 1989 Sierra Health Care Center, Sparks NV) He lived at Sparks from 1947 until his death. Buried Sierra Memorial Gardens, Reno NV.

Billy Campbell —4 Years Pitcher (b. 4 Nov 1873 Pittsburgh PA–d. 7 Oct 1957 Deaconess Hospital, Cincinnati OH) He was associated with a number of firms, retiring as a salesman for Wassler Meat Company in Cincinnati. Buried Spring Grove Cemetery, Cincinnati OH.

Bruce Campbell —13 Years Outfielder (b. 20 Oct 1909 Chicago IL–d. 17 Jun 1995 Fort Myers Beach FL) He moved to Fort Myers Beach in 1940. Cremated.

Gilly Campbell—5 Years Catcher (b. 13 Feb 1908 Kansas City KS–d. 21 Feb 1973 Hollywood Presbyterian Hosp, Los Angeles CA) He played for years in the Pacific Coast League before working as a grip in the movie studios. Died from cancer of the esophogus. Buried San Fernando Mission Cemetery, Mission Hills CA.

John Campbell—1 Year Pitcher (b. 13 Sep 1907 Washington DC–d. 24 Apr 1995 Daytona Beach FL) Served in the U.S. Navy during World War II. He worked for the Daytona Beach Golf and Country Club, living in Daytona Beach 84 years. Cremated. Buried Cedar Hill Memory Gardens, Daytona Beach FL.

Marc Campbell—1 Year Infielder (b. 29 Nov 1884 Punxsutawney PA–d. 13 Feb 1946 at his home in New Bethlehem PA) He was engaged in the coal business. Died suddenly from a heart attack. Buried New Bethlehem Cemetery, New Bethlehem PA.

Vin Campbell—6 Years Outfielder (b. 30 Jan 1888 St Louis MO–d. 16 Nov 1969 Towson MD).

Sal Campfield—1 Year Pitcher (b. 19 Feb 1868 Meadville PA–d. 16 May 1952 Spencer Hospital, Meadville PA) He owned and operated the Arthur Bates Stock Farm at Guys Mills for nearly 50 years, retiring in 1946. Buried Saegertown Cemetery, Saegertown PA.

Hugh Canavan—1 Year Pitcher (b. 13 May 1897 Worcester MA–d. 4 Sep 1967 Veteran's Hospital, Jamaica Plain MA) Served in the U.S. Army during World War I. He was a retired chef. Buried St John's Cemetery, Worcester MA.

Jimmy Canavan—5 Years Outfielder (b. 26 Nov 1866 New Bedford MA–d. 26 May 1949 New Bedford MA) Buried St Mary's Cemetery, New Bedford MA.

Milo Candini—8 Years Pitcher (b. 3 Aug 1917 Manteca CA–d. 17 Mar 1998 CareWest Convalescent Hospital, Manteca CA) Served in the U.S. Army during World War II. He owned and operated Milo's Liquors in Manteca from 1962 until 1979. Died from prostate cancer. Buried Park View Cemetery, Manteca CA.

Buck Canel—Hall of Fame (b. 1906 Buenos Aires, Argentina–d. 9 Apr 1980 at his home in Croton-on-Hudson NY) From the late 1930s until he retired in 1972 he was known as the "Latin-American Voice" of baseball on radio. Died from emphysema.

Rip Cannell—2 Years Outfielder (b. 23 Jan 1880 South Bridgton ME–d. 26 Aug 1948 Bridgton ME).

Dick Cannon—(b. 10 Apr 1910 New York City NY–d. 4 Dec 1973 at his apartment in Manhattan NY) He was a sports columnist for a number of New York City newspapers in a career that started in 1926 and lasted until his death. Died from complications of a stroke. Buried Calvary Cemetery, Woodside NY.

Joe Cantillon—3 Years Manager (b. 19 Aug 1861 Janesville WI–d. 31 Jan 1930 at his home in Hickman KY) He worked in baseball for 52 years, starting as a batboy in 1878. He was a player, manager, umpire, owner, secretary and scout. Buried Mount Olivet Cemetery, Janesville WI.

Guy Cantrell—3 Years Pitcher (b. 9 Apr 1904 Clarita OK–d. 31 Jan 1961 McAlester OK).

Ben Cantwell—11 Years Pitcher (b. 13 Apr 1902 Milan TN–d. 4 Dec 1962 at his home in Salem MO) He coached baseball and moved to Salem 14 years before his death to assist with a baseball camp there. Died after an illness of several months. Buried North Lawn Cemetery, Salem MO.

Mike Cantwell—3 Years Pitcher (b. 15 Jan 1896 Washington DC–d. 5 Jan 1953 Oteen NC).

Tom Cantwell—2 Years Pitcher (b. 23 Dec 1888 Washington DC–d. 1 Apr 1968 Providence Hospital, Washington DC) Buried Mount Olivet Cemetery, Washington DC.

Bart Cantz—3 Years Catcher (b. 29 Jan 1860 Philadelphia PA–d. 12 Feb 1943 Philadelphia PA) Buried Holy Redeemer Cemetery, Philadelphia PA.

Pat Capri—1 Year Infielder (b. 27 Nov 1918 New York City NY–d. 14 Jun 1989 New York City NY).

Ralph Capron—2 Years Outfielder (b. 16 Jun 1889 Minneapolis MN–d. 19 Sep 1980 Los Angeles CA) Buried Forest Lawn-Hollywood Hills, Los Angeles CA.

Pat Caraway—3 Years Pitcher (b. 26 Sep 1908 Gordon TX–d. 9 Jun 1974 Southwestern General Hospital, El Paso TX) He was a locomotive engineer for the Texas Pacific Railroad, retiring in 1971. Died from complications of cirrhosis of the liver. Buried Gordon Cemetery, Gordon TX.

John Carbine—1 Year Infielder (b. 12 Oct 1855 Syracuse NY–d. 11 Sep 1915 Chicago IL) Buried Calvary Cemetery, Evanston IL.

John Carden—1 Year Pitcher (b. 19 May 1921 Killeen TX–d. 8 Feb 1949 near Mexia TX) Served in the U.S. Marines during World War II. Died instantly at the height of his baseball career when he came in contact with a high voltage line while working on a telephone line with his father-in-law. Buried Mexia City Cemetery, Mexia TX.

Ben Cardoni—3 Years Pitcher (b. 21 Aug 1920 Jessup PA–d. 1 Apr 1969 Jessup PA) He managed minor league baseball a short time before operating a tavern in Jessup. Died in his car from a heart attack. Buried St John's Cemetery, Jessup PA.

Harry Carey—Hall of Fame (b. 1914 St Louis MO–d. 18 Feb 1998 Eisenhower Medical Center, Rancho Mirage CA) A broadcaster from 1941 until his death, he broadcast Cardinal games from 1945 until 1969, A's games in 1970, White Sox games from 1971 until 1981 and Cub games from 1982 through 1997. Not only did Harry call the games, he became an integral part of the games. Died from brain damage caused by a serious heart attack. Buried All Saints Cemetery, Des Plaines IL.

Max Carey—20 Years Outfielder 2 Years Manager Hall of Fame (b. 11 Jan 1890 Terre Haute IN–d. 30 May 1976 at his home in Miami Beach FL) He helped with the organization of the women's professional baseball league during World War II and was a member of the Florida State Racing Commission. Died from natural causes. Buried Woodlawn Park Cemetery, Miami FL.

Scoops Carey—4 Years Infielder (b. 4 Dec 1870 East Liverpool OH–d. 17 Dec 1916 City Hospital, East Liverpool OH) He was a painter. Died from heart disease. Buried Spring Grove Cemetery, East Liverpool OH.

Tom Carey—8 Years Infielder (b. 11 Oct 1908 Hoboken NJ–d. 21 Feb 1970 Rochester NY) Buried Holy Sepulchre Cemetery, Rochester NY.

Tom Carey—4 Years Infielder 2 Years Manager (b. 1849 Brooklyn NY–d. 13 Feb 1899 Los Angeles CA) Died from lung congestion in his hotel room while visiting in Los Angeles.

Chick Cargo—1 Year Infielder (b. 1871 Pittsburgh PA–d. 27 Apr 1904 Atlanta GA) He was a wallpaper hanger during the off-season. Died from typhoid pneumonia while preparing for another season with the Atlanta Crackers of the Southern Association. Buried St Mary's Cemetery, Pittsburgh PA.

Fred Carisch—8 Years Catcher (b. 14 Nov 1881 Fountain City WI–d. 19 Apr 1977 Alderwood Manor Conv Hosp, San Gabriel CA) He was a salesman for White Truck Company, a maker of large trucks, for 20 years. Died from heart disease. Cremated.

Fred Carl—1 Year Outfielder (b. 1856 Germany–d. 4 May 1919 Emergency Hospital, Washington DC) A first class machinist and model maker, he conducted a machine shop in Washington DC. Many of his models were used in court to validate claims of inventors. Died from a stroke of apoplexy. Cremated.

Tex Carleton—8 Years Pitcher (b. 19 Aug 1906 Comanche TX–d. 11 Jan 1977 at his home in Fort Worth TX) Buried Oakwood Cemetery, Comanche TX.

Walter Carlisle—1 Year Outfielder (b. 6 Jul 1882 Yorkshire, England–d. 27 May 1945 at his home in Los Angeles CA) He was a painter for an oil company. Died from a heart attack. Buried Inglewood Park Cemetery, Inglewood CA.

Hal Carlson—14 Years Pitcher (b. 17 May 1892 Rockford IL–d. 28 May 1930 Chicago IL) World War I veteran. Died from a stomach hemorrhage at the height of his career. Buried Arlington Memorial Park Cemetery, Rockford IL.

Leon Carlson—1 Year Pitcher (b. 17 Feb 1895 Jamestown NY–d. 15 Sep 1961 at his home in Jamestown NY) Served in the U.S. Army during World War I. He was the founder of Laco Roofing Asbestos Company and Laco Applicator, Inc, and operated the companies for 29 years. He was an avid fisherman. Buried Sunset Hill Cemetery, Lakewood NY.

Swede Carlstrom—1 Year Infielder (b. 26 Oct 1890 Elizabeth NJ–d. 28 Apr 1935 St Elizabeth Hospital, Elizabeth NJ) He served in Europe for the U.S. Army during World War I and contracted rheumatism there that ended his baseball career. He then worked as a bartender. Died from spinal meningitis. Buried Evergreen Cemetery, Hillside NJ.

Cleo Carlyle —1 Year Outfielder (b. 7 Sep 1902 Fairburn GA–d. 12 Nov 1967 Hollywood West Hospital, Los Angeles CA) He was a stockroom clerk in the missile department of Douglas Aircraft Company. Died from internal complications following acute appendicitis. Buried Forest Lawn Memorial Park, Glendale CA.

Roy Carlyle —2 Years Outfielder (b. 10 Dec 1900 Buford GA–d. 22 Nov 1956 Norcross GA) He purportedly hit a home run 618 feet at Oakland CA while playing in the Pacific Coast League in 1929. He operated a hardware store in Norcross. Died after being ill a year. Buried Norcross Cemetery, Norcross GA.

George Carman —1 Year Infielder (b. 29 Mar 1866 Philadelphia PA–d. 16 Jun 1929 Lancaster PA) The proprietor of hotels, cafes and private clubs in the Lancaster area, he was manager of the Hotel Brunswick there when he died. Died from a heart attack. Buried Woodward Hill Cemetery, Lancaster PA.

Chet Carmichael —1 Year Pitcher (b. 9 Jan 1888 Muncie IN–d. 23 Aug 1960 Rochester NY) Buried Honeoye Falls Cemetery, Honeoye Falls NY.

John Carmichael —Hall of Fame (b. 16 Oct 1902 Madison WI–d. 6 Jun 1986 Columbus Hospital, Chicago IL) He was a sportswriter for the *Chicago Daily News* from 1932 to 1972. He had been in failing health after suffering a stroke several years before his death. Cremated. Buried All Saints Cemetery, Des Plaines IL.

Bill Carney —1 Year Outfielder (b. 25 Mar 1874 St Paul MN–d. 31 Jul 1938 Hopkins MN) A National League umpire, he later worked as a deputy sheriff in Hennepin County, MN, and also as a game warden. Died from heart disease. Buried Grand-View Park Cemetery, Hopkins MN.

Jack Carney —3 Years Infielder (b. 10 Nov 1867 Salem MA–d. 19 Oct 1925 at his home in Litchfield NH) He coached baseball at a number of schools, including Phillips Exeter Academy, Boston University and Cornell University. Raised a rare specimen of rabbits. Died from heart failure. Buried Pine Grove Cemetery, Manchester NH.

Pat Carney —4 Years Outfielder (b. 7 Aug 1876 Holyoke MA–d. 9 Jan 1953 at his home in Worcester MA) He practiced medicine in Worcester from 1907 until he retired in 1949. He also coached baseball four years at the College of Holy Cross, and was the house physician at Holy Cross and the team physician for their athletic teams. Died after a long illness. Buried St John's Cemetery, Worcester MA.

Hick Carpenter —12 Years Infielder (b. 16 Aug 1855 Grafton MA–d. 18 Apr 1937 San Diego CA) Died from a heart attack. Buried Mount Hope Cemetery, San Diego CA.

Lew Carpenter —1 Year Pitcher (b. 16 Aug 1913 Woodstock GA–d. 25 Apr 1979 Marietta GA).

Paul Carpenter —1 Year Pitcher (b. 12 Aug 1894 Granville OH–d. 14 Mar 1968 Licking County Memorial Hospital, Newark OH) Served in France for the U.S. Army during World War I. He worked for the street department of the City of Newark from 1928 to 1944 and for the route marking department of the Ohio State Highway Department from 1944 until he retired in 1954. Buried Wilson Cemetery, St Louisville OH.

Robert Carpenter, Jr —(b. abt 1916–d. 8 Jul 1990 at his home in Montchanin DE) An heir of the duPont family, he owned the Phillies from 1943 to 1972. Died from cancer of the lung linings.

Charlie Carr —7 Years Infielder (b. 27 Dec 1876 Coatesville PA–d. 25 Nov 1932 Baptist Hospital, Memphis TN) He manufactured athletic equipment. Died from a coronary embolism while on a business trip. Buried Crown Hill Cemetery, Indianapolis IN.

Lew Carr —1 Year Infielder (b. 15 Aug 1872 Union Springs NY–d. 15 Jun 1954 at his home in Moravia NY) He coached baseball at Syracuse University from 1909 until he retired in 1945, and was inducted into the College Baseball Hall of Fame two weeks before he died in his sleep. Buried Indian Mound Cemetery, Moravia NY.

Alex Carrasquel —8 Years Pitcher (b. 24 Jul 1912 Caracas, Venezuela–d. 19 Aug 1969 Caracas, Venezuela).

Cam Carreon —8 Years Catcher (b. 6 Aug 1937 Colton CA–d. 2 Sep 1987 Tucson AZ) U.S. Army veteran. He was a groundskeeper at the El Rio Golf Course in Tucson. Died from cirrhosis of the liver after being in a coma for eight days. Buried Hermosa Cemetery, Colton CA.

Bill Carrick—5 Years Pitcher (b. 5 Sep 1873 Erie PA–d. 7 Mar 1932 at his home in Frankford PA) Died from heart disease. Buried Oakwood Cemetery, Adrian MI.

Bill Carrigan—10 Years Catcher 7 Years Manager (b. 22 Oct 1883 Lewiston ME–d. 8 Jul 1969 Central Maine General Hospital, Lewiston ME) He caught Babe Ruth when Ruth first came to the Red Sox as a pitcher, and also managed him there. After leaving baseball he went into banking in his hometown of Lewiston. Buried Riverside Cemetery, Lewiston ME.

Chick Carroll—1 Year Outfielder (b. 1868 AR–d. 13 Jul 1908 Chicago IL).

Cliff Carroll—11 Years Outfielder (b. 18 Oct 1859 Clay Grove IA–d. 12 Jun 1923 at his home in Portland OR) Buried Mount Scott Park Cemetery, Portland OR.

Dick Carroll—1 Year Pitcher (b. 21 Jul 1884 Cleveland OH–d. 22 Nov 1945 at his sister's home in Cleveland OH) He managed in the International League until he returned to Cleveland to sell tractors and trailers. In 1930 he moved to New York City where he engaged in the oil business. He was visiting his sister when he died. Buried Calvary Cemetery, Cleveland OH.

Dixie Carroll—1 Year Outfielder (b. 19 May 1891 Paducah KY–d. 13 Oct 1984 at his home in Jacksonville FL) Living in Jacksonville since 1912, he founded Dixie Carroll Electric Company there in 1930, retiring in 1960. Buried Evergreen Cemetery, Jacksonville FL.

Doc Carroll—1 Year Catcher (b. 28 Dec 1891 Worcester MA–d. 27 Jun 1983 City Hospital, Worcester MA) A dentist, he was on the staff at St Vincent's Hospital and the Forsythe Dental Infirmary for children in Boston MA. Buried St John's Cemetery, Worcester MA.

Ed Carroll—1 Year Pitcher (b. 27 Jul 1907 Baltimore MD–d. 13 Oct 1984 Franklin Square Hospital, Rossville MD) He was a milkman for Western Maryland Dairy before spending many years as a payroll clerk for Bethlehem Steel Corporation at Sparrows Point, retiring in 1962. Died from cancer. Buried Gardens of Faith Memorial Gardens, Baltimore MD.

Fred Carroll—8 Years Catcher (b. 2 Jul 1864 Sacramento CA–d. 7 Nov 1904 San Rafael CA) Died from "the athletic heart." Cremated. Buried Odd Fellows Columbarium, San Francisco CA.

Ownie Carroll—9 Years Pitcher (b. 11 Nov 1902 Kearny NJ–d. 8 Jun 1975 St Mary's Hospital, Orange NJ) He coached baseball at Seton Hall University and was the physical education director 37 years at the Newark (NJ) Police Academy. Buried Gate of Heaven Catholic Cemetery, East Hanover NJ.

Pat Carroll—1 Year Catcher (b. Philadelphia PA–d. 11 Feb 1916 Philadelphia PA) Buried Holy Cross Cemetery, Yeadon PA.

Scrappy Carroll—3 Years Outfielder (b. 15 Aug 1860 Buffalo NY–d. 14 Nov 1942 Buffalo NY) Buried Mount Olivet Cemetery, Buffalo NY.

Kid Carsey—10 Years Pitcher (b. 22 Oct 1870 New York City NY–d. 29 Mar 1960 Miami FL).

Alex Carson—1 Year Pitcher (b. 22 Aug 1882 Chicago IL–d. 26 Nov 1962 at his home in San Diego CA) Spanish-American War veteran. For 26 years he was a policeman for the San Diego Police Department. Died from stomach cancer. Buried Cypress View Cemetery, San Diego CA.

Kit Carson—2 Years Outfielder (b. 15 Nov 1912 Colton CA–d. 21 Jun 1983 Willow Lake Convalescent Ctr, Long Beach CA) For 27 years he was equipment manager at Long Beach City College, retiring in 1972. Died from complications of diabetes. Buried Forest Lawn Memorial Park, Cypress CA.

Arnold Carter—2 Years Pitcher (b. 14 Mar 1918 Rainelle WV–d. 12 Apr 1989 at his home in Louisville KY) He retired as a painter for Ford Motor Company. Buried Evergreen Cemetery, Louisville KY.

Blackie Carter—2 Years Outfielder (b. 30 Sep 1902 Langley SC–d. 10 Sep 1976 Greenville SC) A scout for the Dodgers, he refereed industrial league basketball games. He worked for Dodenhoff Company and at the time of his death he was with the Slip Not Belting Company of Kingsport TN. Buried Woodlawn Memorial Park, Greenville SC.

Howie Carter—1 Year Infielder (b. 13 Oct 1904 New York City NY–d. 24 Jul 1991 at his home in New York City NY) A trial lawyer for

30 years, he was U.S. Attorney for Manhattan and a founding partner in a leading New York City law firm. Died from cancer. Buried Gate of Heaven Cemetery, Hawthorne NY.

Nick Carter—1 Year Pitcher (b. 19 May 1879 Oatlands VA–d. 23 Nov 1961 Grasonville MD) He moved to Queen Anne's County, MD, in 1915 and took up farming. Buried Wye Cemetery, Wye Mills MD.

Paul Carter—7 Years Pitcher (b. 1 May 1894 Lake Park GA–d. 11 Sep 1984 at his home in Lake Park GA) He owned and operated the Lake Park Peat Moss Company. Buried Lake Park Cemetery, Lake Park GA.

Alexander J Cartwright—Hall of Fame (d. 12 Jul 1892 Honolulu HI) A surveyor by trade, he is usually given credit for framing the first standard set of rules for the game that was adopted in 1845. Buried Nouanu Cemetery, Honolulu HI.

Ed Cartwright—5 Years Infielder (b. 3 Oct 1859 Pittsburgh PA–d. 3 Sep 1933 at his home in St Petersburg FL) Died from pneumonia. Buried Oak Hill Cemetery, Youngstown OH.

Bob Caruthers—10 Years Outfielder (b. 5 Jan 1864 Memphis TN–d. 5 Aug 1911 St Francis Hospital, Peoria IL) After his playing career he umpired in the Three-I League. Died following a nervous breakdown. Buried Graceland Cemetery, Chicago IL.

Charlie Case—4 Years Pitcher (b. 7 Sep 1879 Rural OH–d. 16 Apr 1964 Clermont OH) Buried Spring Grove Cemetery, Cincinnati OH.

George Case—11 Years Outfielder (b. 11 Nov 1915 Trenton NJ–d. 23 Jan 1989 Mercer Medical Center, Trenton NJ) He spent his entire life in baseball, managing minor league baseball, coaching at Rutgers Univ from 1946 to 1960 and coaching for several major league teams. Buried Ewing Church Cemetery, Trenton NJ.

Bob Casey—1 Year Infielder (b. 1859 Canada–d. 28 Nov 1936 Syracuse NY).

Dan Casey—7 Years Pitcher (b. 2 Oct 1865 Binghamton NY–d. 8 Feb 1943 George Washington Univ Hosp, Washington DC) He was one of those credited with being "Casey at the Bat" in Ernest Thayer's classic poem. Died following a siege of illness. Buried Fort Lincoln Cemetery, Brentwood MD.

Dennis Casey—2 Years Outfielder (b. 30 Mar 1858 Binghamton NY–d. 19 Jan 1909 at his home in Maine NY) Buried Catholic Cemetery, Lestershire NY.

Doc Casey—10 Years Infielder (b. 15 Mar 1871 Lawrence MA–d. 30 Dec 1936 at his home in Detroit MI) He owned a drug store in Detroit. Later he was a permit inspector at City Hall and a building guard at the Municipal Court Building. Buried Mount Olivet Cemetery, Detroit MI.

Hugh Casey—9 Years Pitcher (b. 14 Oct 1913 Atlanta GA–d. 3 Jul 1951 Atlantan Hotel, Atlanta GA) He ran a bar and grill in Brooklyn NY. Died from a self-inflicted shotgun blast while his estranged wife listened on the phone. He had been despondent after losing a paternity suit that had been brought against him. Buried Mount Parran Cemetery, Atlanta GA.

Joe Casey—4 Years Catcher (b. 15 Aug 1887 Boston MA–d. 2 Jun 1966 Melrose-Wakefield Hospital, Melrose MA) He was a playground director for the Wakefield MA Recreation Commission. Died after a brief illness. Buried St Patrick's Cemetery, Stoneham MA.

Norm Cash—17 Years Infielder (b. 10 Nov 1934 Justiceburg TX–d. 12 Oct 1986 Beaver Island MI) He was a manufacturer's representative and a televison baseball commentator in Detroit. Drowned in northern Lake Michigan when he slipped on a dock, falling into the lake. Buried Pine Lake Cemetery, West Bloomfield MI.

Jay Cashion—4 Years Pitcher (b. 6 Jun 1891 Mecklenburg NC–d. 17 Nov 1935 Lake Millicent WI) He went to work at the Globe Shipyard in Superior WI in 1916 and later was an inspector for the Coalerator Corporation in Duluth MN. Died from a heart attack while spending a weekend with friends on the lake. Buried Greenwood Cemetery, Superior WI.

Ed Caskin—7 Years Infielder (b. 30 Dec 1851 Danvers MA–d. 9 Oct 1924 Danvers MA) Died after a long illness. Buried St Mary's Cemetery, Danvers MA.

Ed Cassian—1 Year Pitcher (b. 8 Nov 1867 Wilbraham MA–d. 10 Sep 1918 Meriden CT).

Harry Cassidy—2 Years Outfielder (b. 20 Jul 1880 Bellflower IL–d. 19 Apr 1969 St Agnes Hospital, Fresno CA) He moved to Fresno in 1928 and worked as an agent for Equitable Life

Insurance Company. Died after suffering a stroke. Cremated.

Joe Cassidy—2 Years Infielder (b. 8 Feb 1883 Chester PA–d. 25 Mar 1906 at his home in Chester PA) He died at the height of his career from acute malaria. Buried Immaculate Heart of Mary Cemetery, Linwood PA.

John Cassidy—10 Years Outfielder (b. 1857 Brooklyn NY–d. 2 Jul 1891 Brooklyn NY) Buried Flatbush Cemetery, Brooklyn NY.

Pete Cassidy—2 Years Infielder (b. 8 Apr 1873 Wilmington DE–d. 9 Jul 1929 St Francis Hospital, Wilmington DE) He owned the Hotel Cassidy in Wilmington. He had been in ill health some time when he became affected by the heat and died. Buried Cathedral Cemetery, Wilmington DE.

George Caster—12 Years Pitcher (b. 4 Aug 1907 Colton CA–d. 18 Dec 1955 Seaside Hospital, Long Beach CA) He was a milling machine operator for Douglas Aircraft Company. Died from a heart attack suffered while attending a company Christmas party. Buried Sunnyside Cemetery, Long Beach CA.

Vince Castino—3 Years Catcher (b. 11 Oct 1917 Willisville IL–d. 6 Mar 1967 Sutter Memorial Hospital, Sacramento CA) He worked 13 years as a district circulation manager for the *Sacramento Bee* newspaper. Died after a lingering bout with lung cancer. Buried St Mary's Cemetery, Sacramento CA.

John Castle—1 Year Outfielder (b. 1 Jun 1883 Honeybrook PA–d. 13 Apr 1929 at his home in Philadelphia PA) He managed and umpired in the minor leagues before becoming a passenger car inspector for the Pennsylvania Railroad shortly before his death. Died from pneumonia. Buried St Dennis Church Cemetery, Havertown PA.

Slick Castleman—6 Years Pitcher (b. 8 Sep 1913 Donelson TN–d. 2 Mar 1998 at his home in Nashville TN) He was appointed state travel representative with the Tennessee Tourism Development staff. Buried Woodlawn Memorial Park, Nashville TN.

Roy Castleton—3 Years Pitcher (b. 26 Jul 1885 Salt Lake City UT–d. 24 Jun 1967 Doctor's Hospital, Los Angeles CA) He was an inspector for a water heater manufacturer. Died from a cerebral hemorrhage and complications of diabetes. Buried Salt Lake City Cemetery, Salt Lake City UT.

Paul Castner—1 Year Pitcher (b. 16 Feb 1897 St Paul MN–d. 3 Mar 1986 St Paul MN) Buried Calvary Cemetery, St Paul MN.

Eli Cates—1 Year Pitcher (b. 26 Jan 1877 Greensfork IN–d. 29 May 1964 Community Hospital, Anderson IN) He played in the Pacific Coast League. For 17 years he worked at the Eagle Home, retiring in 1944. Died following a lengthy illness. Buried East Maplewood Cemetery, Anderson IN.

Ted Cather—4 Years Outfielder (b. 20 May 1889 Chester PA–d. 9 Apr 1945 Union Hospital, Elkton MD) He engaged in the mercantile business for some years in Charlestown MD. Buried Charlestown Cemetery, Charlestown MD.

Hardin Cathey—1 Year Pitcher (b. 6 Jul 1919 Burns TN–d. 27 Jul 1997 Knowles Home for the Aged, Nashville TN) Died from heart failure. Buried Middle Tennessee Veteran's Cemetery, Nashville TN.

Buster Caton—4 Years Infielder (b. 16 Jul 1896 Zanesville OH–d. 8 Jan 1948 at his home in Zanesville OH) World War I veteran. He worked for the maintenance section of the Zanesville City Water Department and was groundskeeper at the municipal stadium. Died from a heart attack. Buried Greenwood Cemetery, Zanesville OH.

John Cattanach—1 Year Pitcher (b. 10 May 1863 Providence RI–d. 10 Nov 1926 at a rooming house in Providence RI) Died after a three-month illness.

Tom Catterson—2 Years Outfielder (b. 25 Aug 1884 Warwick RI–d. 5 Feb 1920 at his home in Portland ME) He worked for the customs service, and later as a clerk for the Grand Trunk Railroad in Portland. Died from pneumonia.

John Caulfield—1 Year Infielder (b. 23 Nov 1917 Los Angeles CA–d. 16 Dec 1986 Children's Hospital, San Francisco CA) He was an inspector for the San Francisco Police Department for 30 years. Died from colon cancer. Buried Holy Cross Catholic Cemetery, Colma CA.

Red Causey—5 Years Pitcher (b. 11 Aug 1893 Seville FL–d. 11 Nov 1960 Walker Memorial Hospital, Avon Park FL) For several years he was the assistant custodian at the Sebring FL Post Office. Died following amputation of his right leg because of a diabetic condition. Buried Oak Hill Cemetery, Lake Placid FL.

John Cavanaugh—1 Year Infielder (b. 5 Jun 1900 Scranton PA–d. 14 Jan 1961 Middlesex Hospital, New Brunswick NJ) He worked as a grinder for Sorbo-Cast Corporation in New Brunswick NJ. Buried Cathedral Cemetery, Scranton PA.

Ike Caveney—4 Years Infielder (b. 10 Dec 1894 San Francisco CA–d. 6 Jul 1949 San Francisco CA) Died from tuberculosis. Buried Holy Cross Catholic Cemetery, Colma CA.

Pug Cavet—3 Years Pitcher (b. 26 Dec 1889 McGregor TX–d. 4 Aug 1966 General Hospital, San Luis Obispo CA) He was a warehouseman for the National Guard at Camp San Luis Obispo for 15 years. Died from a heart attack. Buried Odd Fellows Cemetery, San Luis Obispo CA.

Ollie Caylor—3 Years Manager (b. 14 Dec 1849 Dayton OH–d. 19 Oct 1897 Winona MN) He was a lawyer until he became interested in baseball. One of the founders of the Cincinnati Red Stockings, he later went into newspaper work and was the baseball writer for the *New York Herald.* Died from consumption and blood poisoning. Buried Woodland Cemetery, Dayton OH.

Rex Cecil—2 Years Pitcher (b. 8 Oct 1917 Lindsay OK–d. 23 Oct 1966 V A Hospital, Bellflower CA) World War II veteran. He was a roofer for a construction company. Died from liver disease. Buried Westminster Memorial Park, Westminster CA.

Ed Cermak—1 Year Outfielder (b. 23 Jul 1881 Cleveland OH–d. 22 Nov 1911 Cleveland OH) He was a minor league umpire. Died from pulmonary tuberculosis. Buried Woodland Cemetery, Cleveland OH.

Elio Chacon—3 Years Infielder (b. 26 Oct 1936 Caracas, Venezuela–d. 24 Apr 1992 Caracas, Venezuela).

Chet Chadbourne—5 Years Outfielder (b. 28 Oct 1884 Parkman ME–d. 21 Jun 1943 Georgia Street Hospital, Los Angeles CA) He was a bartender. Died from a self-inflicted gunshot wound to the head. Cremated.

Henry Chadwick—Hall of Fame (b. 5 Oct 1824 Exeter, England–d. 20 Apr 1908 at his home in Brooklyn NY) A writer and statistician, he is known as the "Father of Baseball." He was the first baseball writer, working for the *Brooklyn Eagle* from 1856 to 1894. He wrote 13 years for the *New York World* and six years for the *New York Sun.* From 1881 until his death he edited the *Spalding Baseball Guide.* Buried Greenwood Cemetery, Brooklyn NY.

Leon Chagnon—6 Years Pitcher (b. 28 Sep 1902 Pittsfield NH–d. 30 Jul 1953 Amesbury Hospital, Amesbury MA) He worked for several shops in the Amesbury area, and was last working for General Electric in Lynn MA. Died after a brief illness. Buried Mount Prospect Cemetery, Amesbury MA.

George Chalmers—7 Years Pitcher (b. 7 Jun 1888 Edinburgh, Scotland–d. 5 Aug 1960 Bronx NY) Died following a series of strokes. Buried Lutheran Cemetery, Middle Village NY.

Bill Chamberlain—1 Year Pitcher (b. 21 Apr 1909 Stoughton MA–d. 6 Feb 1994 Brockton MA).

Icebox Chamberlain—10 Years Pitcher (b. 5 Nov 1867 Warsaw NY–d. 22 Sep 1929 Baltimore MD).

Joe Chamberlain—1 Year Infielder (b. 10 May 1910 San Francisco CA–d. 28 Jan 1983 Laguna Honda Hospital, San Francisco CA) For 25 years he was a laborer on construction jobs. Died from lung cancer. Buried Holy Cross Catholic Cemetery, Colma CA.

Bill Chambers—1 Year Pitcher (b. 13 Sep 1889 Cameron WV–d. 27 Mar 1962 St Joseph Hospital, Fort Wayne IN) He worked for Western Gas Company in Fort Wayne 27 years and for Hillman's China Warehouse in Fort Wayne 22 years, retiring in 1958. Buried Covington Memorial Gardens, Fort Wayne IN.

John Chambers—1 Year Pitcher (b. 9 Sep 1910 Copperhill TN–d. 11 May 1977 near his home in Satsuma FL) Drowned in Lake George. Buried Oaklawn Cemetery, Jacksonville FL.

Rome Chambers—1 Year Pitcher (b. 31 Aug 1875 Weaverville NC–d. 30 Aug 1902 Weaverville NC).

Frank Chance—17 Years Infielder 11 Years Manager Hall of Fame (b. 9 Sep 1877 Fresno CA–d. 14 Sep 1924 at a hospital in Los Angeles

CA) He worked in baseball his entire life as a player and manager. Died from complications of influenza. Buried Rosedale Cemetery, Los Angeles CA.

A B "Happy" Chandler—Hall of Fame (b. 14 Jul 1898 Corydon KY–d. 15 Jun 1991 Versailles KY) The baseball commissioner from 1945 until 1951, he served terms as governor of Kentucky and was elected twice to the U.S. Senate. Died from a heart attack. Buried Pisgah Presbyterian Church Cemetery, Versailles KY.

Spud Chandler—11 Years Pitcher (b. 12 Sep 1907 Commerce GA–d. 9 Jan 1990 Manor Nursing Home, South Pasadena FL) World War II veteran. He managed minor league baseball and was a coach and scout for several teams. Died after a series of strokes. Buried Woodlawn Memory Gardens, St Petersburg FL.

Estey Chaney—2 Years Pitcher (b. 29 Jan 1891 Hadley PA–d. 5 Feb 1952 at his home in Cleveland OH) For 30 years he was a locomotive engineer for the New York Central Railway. Died following a heart attack. Buried Hadley Cemetery, Hadley PA.

Les Channell—2 Years Outfielder (b. 3 Mar 1886 Crestline OH–d. 7 May 1954 Denver General Hospital, Denver CO) He played baseball for 12 years and lived on a ranch near Fort Morgan CO for 10 years. He was police chief at Aurora CO and also worked for Denver Dry Goods Company. He had been ill for several months and suffered a fall shortly before his death. Buried Fairmount Cemetery, Denver CO.

Ed Chaplin—3 Years Catcher (b. 25 Sep 1893 Pelzer SC–d. 15 Aug 1978 Sanford FL) Served in the U.S. Navy during World War I. He lived in Florida since 1916 and owned Chaplin Concrete Company in Sanford. Buried Oaklawn Park Cemetery, Lake Mary FL.

Tiny Chaplin—4 Years Pitcher (b. 13 Jul 1905 Los Angeles CA–d. 25 Mar 1939 Elwyn Sanitarium, National City CA) He was killed at the height of his baseball career when a car in which he was a passenger hit a car that was stalled on the road south of National City. Buried Woodlawn Park North Cemetery, Miami FL.

Ben Chapman—15 Years Outfielder 4 Years Manager (b. 25 Dec 1908 Nashville TN–d. 7 Jul 1993 at his home in Hoover AL) He was the first batter to hit in an All-Star game. Died from a heart attack. Buried Elmwood Cemetery, Birmingham AL.

Calvin Chapman—2 Years Outfielder (b. 20 Dec 1910 Courtland MS–d. 1 Apr 1983 Batesville MS).

Fred Chapman—1 Year Pitcher (b. 25 Nov 1872 Little Cooley PA–d. 14 Dec 1957 Union City PA) Buried Evergreen Cemetery, Union City PA.

Fred Chapman—3 Years Infielder (b. 17 Jul 1916 Liberty SC–d. 27 Mar 1997 Kannapolis NC) Buried Carolina Memorial Park, Concord NC.

Glenn Chapman—1 Year Outfielder (b. 21 Jan 1906 Cambridge City IN–d. 5 Nov 1988 Reid Memorial Hospital, Richmond IN) He played in the American Association and the Pacific Coast League. Buried Lutheran Cemetery, Pershing IN.

Harry Chapman—5 Years Catcher (b. 26 Oct 1885 Severance KS–d. 21 Oct 1918 Nevada MO) He lived at Springfield MO where he was engaged in stock raising. Died from influenza. Buried McPherson Cemetery, McPherson KS.

Jack Chapman—1 Year Outfielder 10 Years Manager (b. 8 May 1843 Brooklyn NY–d. 10 Jun 1916 at his home in Brooklyn NY) He organized several minor league teams in New England and managed minor league teams until retiring from baseball in the 1890s. Died suddenly. Buried Greenwood Cemetery, Brooklyn NY.

John Chapman—1 Year Infielder (b. 15 Oct 1899 Centralia PA–d. 3 Nov 1953 Univ of Pennsylvania Hosp, Philadelphia PA) He conducted a hotel business in Philadelphia until 1941 when he sold out and moved to Frackville PA where he was a liquor salesman. Died from a kidney ailment. Buried St Joseph's Cemetery, Fountain Springs PA.

Ray Chapman—9 Years Infielder (b. 15 Jan 1891 Beaver Dam KY–d. 17 Aug 1920 New York City NY) Died when hit in the head by a pitch thrown by Carl Mays of the Yankees. Buried Lake View Cemetery, Cleveland OH.

Larry Chappell—5 Years Outfielder (b. 19 Feb 1890 McCluskey IL–d. 8 Nov 1918 Letterman Hospital, San Francisco CA) He was serving in the U.S. Army Medical Corps during World War I when he died from pneumonia caused by influenza. Buried Oak Grove Cemetery, Jerseyville IL.

Bill Chappelle—3 Years Pitcher (b. 22 Mar 1884 Waterloo NY–d. 31 Dec 1944 Mineola NY) Spanish-American War veteran.

Chappy Charles—3 Years Infielder (b. 25 Mar 1881 Phillipsburg NJ–d. 4 Aug 1959 at his home in Bethlehem PA) He worked for Bethlehem Steel Corporation until 1946 when he retired because of illness.

Oscar Charleston—23 Years Outfielder 9 Years Manager Hall of Fame (b. 14 Oct 1896 Indianapolis IN–d. 6 Oct 1954 General Hospital, Philadelphia PA) Played in the negro leagues. Served in the Philippines for the U.S. Army from 1911 to 1915. He spent his entire life in baseball. Buried Floral Park Cemetery, Indianapolis IN.

Mike Chartak—4 Years Outfielder (b. 28 Apr 1916 Brooklyn NY–d. 25 Jul 1967 Cedar Rapids IA) His baseball career was cut short by tuberculosis. Died after a long illness. Buried Mount Calvary Cemetery, Cedar Rapids IA.

Hal Chase—15 Years Infielder 2 Years Manager (b. 13 Feb 1883 Los Gatos CA–d. 18 May 1947 Colusa Memorial Hospital, Colusa CA) Died from nephritis and heart failure. Buried Oak Hill Memorial Park, San Jose CA.

Ken Chase—8 Years Pitcher (b. 6 Oct 1913 Oneonta NY–d. 16 Jan 1985 Oneonta NY) Buried Laurel Land Memorial Park, Dallas TX.

Buster Chatham—2 Years Infielder (b. 25 Dec 1901 West TX–d. 15 Dec 1975 at a hospital in Waco TX) He managed minor league baseball and scouted for the Pirates and Rangers. Died from a heart condition. Buried Oakwood Cemetery, Waco TX.

Jim Chatterton—1 Year Outfielder (b. 14 Oct 1864 Brooklyn NY–d. 18 Dec 1944 Malden MA).

Nestor Chavez—1 Year Pitcher (b. 6 Jul 1947 Chacao Miranda, Venezuela–d. 16 Mar 1969 Maracaibo, Venezuela) Killed in the crash of a Venezuelan jetliner at the height of his baseball career.

Charlie Chech—4 Years Pitcher (b. 27 Apr 1878 Madison WI–d. 31 Jan 1938 at his home in Los Angeles CA) Died from a heart attack. Buried Calvary Cemetery, Los Angeles CA.

Harry Cheek—1 Year Catcher (b. 1879 Sedalia MO–d. 25 Jun 1956 Bergen Pines Hospital, Paramus NJ) Buried George Washington Memorial Park, Paramus NJ.

Virgil Cheeves—6 Years Pitcher (b. 12 Feb 1901 Oklahoma City OK–d. 5 May 1979 Dallas TX) Buried Laurel Land Memorial Park, Dallas TX.

Italo Chelini—3 Years Pitcher (b. 10 Oct 1914 San Francisco CA–d. 25 Aug 1972 at his home in San Francisco CA) He was a bartender at the Press Club for 20 years. Died suddenly from a heart attack after leaving work. Buried Holy Cross Catholic Cemetery, Colma CA.

Larry Cheney—9 Years Pitcher (b. 2 May 1886 Belleville KS–d. 6 Jan 1969 Halifax Hospital, Daytona Beach FL) He managed minor league baseball and was a scout for the Yankees. Buried Shadyrest Cemetery, Daytona Beach FL.

Paul Chervinko—2 Years Catcher (b. 23 Jul 1910 Trauger PA–d. 3 Jun 1976 St Elizabeth Hospital, Danville IL) Served in the U.S. Air Force during World War II. He was in organized baseball 20 years as a player and minor league manager. He retired after working 17 years for Olin-Mathieson Company at Covington IN. Buried Calvary Cemetery, Witt IL.

Jack Chesbro—11 Years Pitcher Hall of Fame (b. 5 Jun 1874 North Adams MA–d. 6 Nov 1931 at his chicken farm in Conway MA) The winner of 41 games in 1904, he coached pitchers intermittently while raising chickens in the heart of the Berkshire Hills where he was born and raised. Died from a heart attack. Buried Howland Cemetery, Conway MA.

Bob Chesnes—3 Years Pitcher (b. 6 May 1921 Oakland CA–d. 23 May 1979 at a hospital in Everett WA) Died from a heart attack. Cremated. Buried Evergreen Cemetery, Everett WA.

Mitch Chetkovich—1 Year Pitcher (b. 21 Jul 1917 Fairpoint OH–d. 24 Aug 1971 Grass Valley CA) Served in the U.S. Army during World War II. He lived in Grass Valley 20 years, and was a carpenter there. Died from a heart attack. Buried St Patrick's Cemetery, Grass Valley CA.

Harry Child—1 Year Pitcher (b. 23 May 1905 Baltimore MD–d. 8 Nov 1972 Alexandria Hospital, Alexandria VA) He was a Red Cross field representative during World War II. In 1938 he was director of the Alexandria Boy's Club, and worked ten years for the Alexandria School

Board. Buried Mount Comfort Cemetery, Alexandria VA.

Cupid Childs—13 Years Infielder (b. 14 Aug 1868 Calvert County MD–d. 8 Nov 1912 St Agnes Hospital, Baltimore MD) Died from Bright's disease. Buried Loudon Park Cemetery, Baltimore MD.

Pete Childs—2 Years Infielder (b. 15 Nov 1871 Philadelphia PA–d. 15 Feb 1922 at his home in Philadelphia PA) He managed minor league baseball for a few years and was selling Christmas trees near the ballpark the December before he died. Buried West Laurel Hill Cemetery, Bala Cynwyd PA.

Eddie Chiles—(b. 11 May 1910 Itasca TX–d. 22 Aug 1993 Fort Worth TX) A Texas oilman, he was the owner of the Texas Rangers from 1980 to 1989. Buried Greenwood Memorial Park, Fort Worth TX.

Dino Chiozza—1 Year Infielder (b. 30 Jun 1914 Memphis TN–d. 23 Apr 1972 Methodist Hospital, Memphis TN) He was co-owner of a liquor store with his brother, Lou. Honored for his activities in the Catholic Church. Buried Calvary Cemetery, Memphis TN.

Lou Chiozza—6 Years Infielder (b. 11 May 1910 Tallulah LA–d. 28 Feb 1971 St Joseph's Hospital, Memphis TN) He represented a wholesale liquor firm in Memphis before opening a liquor store there. He also broadcast baseball games for the Memphis Chicks of the Southern League for a number of years. Buried Calvary Cemetery, Memphis TN.

Bob Chipman—12 Years Pitcher (b. 11 Oct 1918 Brooklyn NY–d. 8 Nov 1973 Huntington NY) Buried Cemetery of Holy Rood, Westbury NY.

Walt Chipple—1 Year Outfielder (b. 26 Sep 1918 Utica NY–d. 8 Jun 1988 Kenmore Mercy Hospital, Tonawanda NY) Served in the U.S. Navy during World War II. He managed minor league baseball. Died after a long illness. Buried Elmwood Cemetery, Kenmore NY.

Felix Chouinard—4 Years Outfielder (b. 5 Oct 1887 Chicago IL–d. 28 Apr 1955 Hines Memorial Hospital, Chicago IL).

Chief Chouneau—1 Year Pitcher (b. 2 Sep 1889 Cloquet MN–d. 17 Sep 1948 Cloquet MN).

Harry Chozen—1 Year Catcher (b. 27 Sep 1915 Winnebago MN–d. 16 Sep 1994 Houston TX).

Lloyd Christenbury—4 Years Outfielder (b. 19 Oct 1893 Mecklenburg County NC–d. 13 Dec 1944 Birmingham AL) Buried Forest Hill Cemetery, Birmingham AL.

Cuckoo Christensen—2 Years Outfielder (b. 24 Oct 1899 San Francisco CA–d. 20 Dec 1984 Sharon Heights Conv Hospital, Menlo Park CA) For 25 years he was a machinist for Caterpiller Tractor Company. Died from pneumonia following a heart attack. Cremated.

Bob Christian—3 Years Outfielder (b. 17 Oct 1945 Chicago IL–d. 20 Feb 1974 Kaiser Hospital, La Mesa CA) Died from leukemia at the height of his career. Buried Alpine Cemetery, Alpine CA.

Mark Christman—9 Years Infielder (b. 21 Oct 1913 Maplewood MO–d. 9 Oct 1976 at his home in St Louis MO) He managed some minor league baseball before scouting for the Yankees and Dodgers. He was an executive for an insurance agency. Died from a heart attack. Buried Resurrection Cemetery, St Louis MO.

Loyd Christopher—2 Years Outfielder (b. 13 Dec 1919 Richmond CA–d. 5 Sep 1991 at his home in Richmond CA) He was a scout for the Angels. Died from prostate cancer. Cremated.

Russ Christopher—7 Years Pitcher (b. 12 Sep 1917 Richmond CA–d. 5 Dec 1954 Brookside Hospital, Richmond CA) He played baseball until rheumatic heart disease forced his retirement shortly before his death. Died from the heart condition. Buried Sunset Mausoleum, Kensington CA.

Len Church—1 Year Pitcher (b. 21 Mar 1942 Chicago IL–d. 22 Apr 1988 Richardson TX).

John Churry—4 Years Catcher (b. 26 Nov 1900 Johnstown PA–d. 8 Feb 1970 Bethesda Hospital, Zanesville OH) He was a tavern operator in Corning OH for 45 years. Died after being in failing health ten months. Buried Maplewood Cemetery, New Lexington OH.

Nestor Chylak—Hall of Fame (b. 11 May 1922 Olyphant PA–d. 17 Feb 1982 at his home in Dunmore PA) Purple Heart recipient while in the U.S. Army during World War II. Buried St Cyril and Methodius Cemetery, Peckville PA.

He was an American League umpire 1954 to 1978 and the supervisor of American League umpires from 1979 until his death.

Larry Ciaffone—1 Year Outfielder (b. 17 Aug 1924 Brooklyn NY–d. 14 Dec 1991 Brooklyn NY) Buried Greenwood Cemetery, Brooklyn NY.

Joe Cicero—3 Years Outfielder (b. 18 Nov 1910 Atlantic City NJ–d. 30 Mar 1983 at his home in Clearwater FL) He was a security officer for the Panama Canal Company in the Canal Zone, retiring to Clearwater about 1973. Cremated. Buried Curlew Hills Memory Gardens, Palm Harbor FL.

Al Cicotte—5 Years Pitcher (b. 23 Dec 1929 Melvindale MI–d. 29 Nov 1982 Westland MI) He was a self-employed insurance agent. Buried Holy Sepulchre Cemetery, Southfield MI.

Eddie Cicotte—14 Years Pitcher (b. 19 Jun 1884 Detroit MI–d. 5 May 1969 Henry Ford Hospital, Detroit MI) He was banned from baseball for his involvement in the Black Sox Scandal. He worked at Ford Motor Company until retiring in 1944. Died from cancer. Buried Parkview Memorial Cemetery, Livonia MI.

Ed Cihocki—2 Years Infielder (b. 9 May 1907 Wilmington DE–d. 9 Nov 1987 Christiana Hospital, Delaware City DE) For 30 years he was a pipe fitter for Hercules Company in Wilmington, retiring in 1972. Died from heart failure. Buried All Saints Cemetery, Newark DE.

Lou Ciola—1 Year Pitcher (b. 6 Sep 1922 Norfolk VA–d. 18 Oct 1981 Austin MN) He was a foreman in the transportation department for Hormel Company and co-owner of the Golden Parrot Restaurant in Austin. Died from a heart attack while golfing at the Austin Country Club. Buried Calvary Cemetery, Austin MN.

Bill Cissell—9 Years Infielder (b. 3 Jan 1904 Perryville MO–d. 15 Mar 1949 Mercy Hospital, Chicago IL) He was destitute and penniless when he died from a heart ailment. Buried Mount Hope Cemetery, Perryville MO.

Moose Clabaugh—1 Year Outfielder (b. 13 Nov 1901 Albany MO–d. 11 Jul 1984 Tucson AZ) Served in the U.S. Navy. He was Chief of Security for the U.S. Army Corp of Engineers. Died from a heart attack. Cremated.

Bobby Clack—1 Year Outfielder (b. 1851 Brooklyn NY–d. 22 Oct 1933 Danvers MA).

Danny Claire—1 Year Infielder (b. 18 Nov 1897 Ludington MI–d. 24 Mar 1929 Battle Creek MI) He managed some minor league baseball before becoming a millwright for Kellogg Company in Battle Creek. He also umpired amateur baseball. Died from injuries suffered when a gasoline tank on a car exploded. Buried Ludington Cemetery, Ludington MI.

Al Clancy—1 Year Infielder (b. 14 Aug 1888 Santa Fe NM–d. 17 Oct 1951 Las Cruces NM) He was an Assistant U.S. District Attorney. Dropped dead from a heart attack while having breakfast in a cafe. Buried Fairview Cemetery, Santa Fe NM.

Bill Clancy—1 Year Infielder (b. 12 Apr 1878 Redfield NY–d. 10 Feb 1948 at his home in Oriskany NY) He worked for the Rome Manufacturing Division of Revere Copper and Brass Company for several years. He was also a deputy sheriff for a short time before his death. Buried Mount Olivet Cemetery, Whitesboro NY.

Bud Clancy—9 Years Infielder (b. 15 Sep 1900 Odell IL–d. 27 Sep 1968 St Joseph Hospital, Ottumwa IA) He was a quality inspector for John Deere in Ottumwa and a scout for the White Sox for many years. Died following an illness of several weeks. Buried St Paul Cemetery, Odell IL.

Uke Clanton—1 Year Infielder (b. 19 Feb 1898 Powell MO–d. 24 Feb 1960 Antlers OK) He managed minor league baseball for a time. An insurance man in the Ada OK area, he was president of the Sooner State Baseball League from 1952 to 1955. Died from injuries suffered in a head-on automobile collision. Buried Memorial Park Cemetery, Ada OK.

Aaron Clapp—1 Year Infielder (b. Jul 1856 Ithaca NY–d. 13 Jan 1914 Sayre PA).

John Clapp—7 Years Catcher 4 Years Manager (b. 17 Jul 1851 Ithaca NY–d. 17 Dec 1904 Ithaca NY) A National League umpire in 1897, he opened a cafe in New York City that failed. He then returned to Ithaca where he painted houses for a while, and had just gone to work for the Ithaca police force as a patrolman when he collapsed and died from a stroke after carrying a drunk several blocks to the jail.

Bill Clark—1 Year Infielder (b. 11 Apr 1875 Circleville OH–d. 15 Apr 1959 Los Angeles CA) World War I veteran. He was secretary of the

Association of Professional Baseball Players of America from 1938 until he died from a heart attack. The last seven years he worked from a wheelchair due to having both his legs amputated because of a severe diabetic attack. Cremated.

Bob Clark—7 Years Catcher (b. 18 May 1864 Covington KY–d. 21 Aug 1919 at his home in Covington KY) He umpired in the Southern League for a few years before working at a chemical factory in Cincinnati OH. Died from complications of severe burns received on his job some months earlier. Buried St Mary's Cemetery, Fort Mitchell KY.

Bob Clark—2 Years Pitcher (b. 22 Aug 1897 Newport PA–d. 18 May 1944 in a hospital in Carlsbad NM) World War I veteran. He was a warehouse and loading foreman for Potash Company of America in Carlsbad from 1934 until his death. Died following a one month illness. Buried Carlsbad Cemetery, Carlsbad NM.

Cap Clark—1 Year Catcher (b. 19 Sep 1906 Snow Camp NC–d. 16 Feb 1957 Fayetteville NC) He owned and operated Clark's Sporting Goods Store in Fayetteville. Died from a heart attack. Buried Lafayette Memorial Park, Fayetteville NC.

Danny Clark—3 Years Infielder (b. 18 Jan 1895 Meridian MS–d. 23 May 1937 Riley Hospital, Meridian MS) He played in the Texas League and the Three-I League. Died from a stroke suffered several days earlier. Buried Magnolia Cemetery, Meridian MS.

Earl Clark—8 Years Outfielder (b. 6 Nov 1907 Washington DC–d. 16 Jan 1938 Washington DC) He had just retired from baseball to take a job with the FBI when he was killed instantly when his car was hit by a streetcar. Buried Cedar Hill Cemetery, Suitland MD.

Fred Clark—1 Year Infielder (b. 16 Jul 1873 San Francisco CA–d. 26 Jul 1956 St Benedict's Hospital, Ogden UT) He was station master for the Ogden Railway and Depot Company from 1900 to 1943 when he retired. Died after an illness of several weeks. Buried Ogden City Cemetery, Ogden UT.

George Clark—1 Year Pitcher (b. 19 May 1891 Smithland IA–d. 14 Nov 1940 at a hospital in Sioux City IA) Served as a 2nd Lieutenant in the U.S. Army during World War I. He worked in real estate sales in the Sioux City area. Died after an illness of one month. Buried Graceland Cemetery, Sioux City IA.

Ginger Clark—1 Year Pitcher (b. 7 Mar 1879 Wooster OH–d. 10 May 1943 Lake Charles LA).

Jim Clark—2 Years Outfielder (b. 26 Dec 1887 Brooklyn NY–d. 20 Mar 1969 St Elizabeth Hospital, Beaumont TX) Served in France for the U.S. Army during World War I. He moved to Beaumont in the early 1920s, working at the Magnolia Refinery and in the Southern Pacific freight office. Later he was a distributor for the Beaumont newspaper until retiring. Died after a long illness. Buried Forest Lawn Memorial Park, Beaumont TX.

Jim Clark—1 Year Infielder (b. 21 Sep 1927 Baggaley PA–d. 24 Oct 1990 at his home in Santa Monica CA) He owned and operated an apartment building for 15 years. Died from arteriosclerotic heart disease. He was cremated and his ashes scattered off the coast of Long Beach CA.

Mike Clark—2 Years Pitcher (b. 12 Feb 1922 Camden NJ–d. 25 Jan 1996 Camden NJ) Buried St Mary's Cemetery, Bellmawr NJ.

Pep Clark—1 Year Infielder (b. 18 Mar 1883 Union City OH–d. 8 Jun 1965 County General Hospital, Milwaukee WI) He played and managed for the Milwaukee Brewers of the American Association for years. He died from bronchopneumonia after being in ill health in recent years. Buried Valhalla Memorial Cemetery, Milwaukee WI.

Royal Clark—1 Year Outfielder (b. 11 May 1874 New Haven CT–d. 1 Nov 1925 at his home in Bridgeport CT) Formerly the secretary of the YMCA at Bridgeport, he was a representative for Traveler's Insurance when he died unexpectedly, even though he had been ill for some time. Buried Mountain Grove Cemetery, Bridgeport CT.

Spider Clark—2 Years Outfielder (b. 16 Sep 1867 Brooklyn NY–d. 8 Feb 1892 Brooklyn NY).

Watty Clark—12 Years Pitcher (b. 16 May 1902 St Joseph LA–d. 4 Mar 1972 Morton Plant Hospital, Clearwater FL) He operated a vegetable plant growing and shipping business in Omaha TX from 1939 until 1946 when he moved to Clearwater. There he went into the construction business and in 1962 formed Clark and Logan General Contractors, retiring in 1967. Buried Dunedin Cemetery, Dunedin FL.

Willie Clark—5 Years Infielder (b. 16 Aug 1872 Pittsburgh PA–d. 13 Nov 1932 at his home in Pittsburgh PA) Died after a long illness.

Alan Clarke—1 Year Pitcher (b. 8 Mar 1896 Clarksville MD–d. 11 Mar 1975 Cheverly MA).

Archie Clarke—2 Years Catcher (b. 6 May 1865 Brookline MA–d. 14 Nov 1949 Brookline MA) An attorney, he practiced law for many years in Boston MA before retiring about 1940.

Boileryard Clarke—13 Years Catcher (b. 18 Oct 1868 New York City NY–d. 29 Jul 1959 Princeton Hospital, Princeton NJ) Over a 47 year period he coached baseball at Princeton University for 34 years. Died from complications and shock following a hip fracture. Buried Druid Ridge Cemetery, Pikesville MD.

Dad Clarke—7 Years Pitcher (b. 7 Jan 1865 Oswego NY–d. 3 Jun 1911 St Joseph's Hospital, Lorain OH) He was a bartender. Died from a cerebral hemorrhage suffered a week earlier. Buried Calvary Cemetery, Lorain OH.

Fred Clarke—21 Years Outfielder 19 Years Manager Hall of Fame (b. 3 Oct 1872 Winterset IA–d. 14 Aug 1960 St Mary's Hospital, Winfield KS) He owned the Pirates from 1900 to 1915 and operated a 1320 acre ranch near Winfield. Died from pneumonia. Buried St Mary's Cemetery, Winfield KS.

Grey Clarke—1 Year Infielder (b. 26 Sep 1912 Fulton AL–d. 25 Nov 1993 Kannapolis NC).

Harry Clarke—1 Year Outfielder (b. 13 Jan 1863 NY–d. 3 Mar 1923 Angeles Hospital, Los Angeles CA) He was an actor. Died from liver cancer. Cremated.

Henry Clarke—2 Years Pitcher (b. 4 Aug 1875 Bellevue NE–d. 28 Mar 1950 Colorado Springs CO) An Omaha NE attorney, he represented the Omaha Grain Exchange for many years. He was also chairman of the Nebraska State Railway Commission. Buried Forest Lawn Memorial Park, Omaha NE.

Josh Clarke—5 Years Outfielder (b. 8 Mar 1879 Winfield KS–d. 2 Jul 1962 Camarillo State Hospital, Camarillo CA) He managed and umpired minor league baseball. Died from heart disease. Buried Ivy Lawn Memorial Park, Ventura CA.

Nig Clarke—9 Years Catcher (b. 15 Dec 1882 Amherstburg, Ontario, Canada–d. 15 Jun 1949 at his home in Detroit MI) He once hit eight homeruns in a minor league game. Served in the U.S. Marines during World War I. He worked at the Whitehead and Kales plant in River Rouge MI. Cremated. Buried Woodmere Cemetery, Detroit MI.

Rufe Clarke—2 Years Pitcher (b. 13 Apr 1900 Estill SC–d. 8 Feb 1983 Manor Care Center, Columbia SC) He was in the banking business, spending about 30 years with the Federal Land Bank, including a period of time as president of that group, retiring in 1962. He also served on the Columbia City Council. Buried Elmwood Cemetery, Columbia SC.

Stu Clarke—2 Years Infielder (b. 24 Jan 1906 San Francisco CA–d. 26 Aug 1985 Hayward CA) Served in the U.S. Navy during World War II. Buried Holy Sepulchre Cemetery, Hayward CA.

Sumpter Clarke—3 Years Outfielder (b. 18 Oct 1897 Savannah GA–d. 16 Mar 1962 Fort Sanders Hospital, Knoxville TN) A representative for a rubber company, he lived in Knoxville for 20 years. Died from a heart seizure. Buried Estill SC.

Tommy Clarke—10 Years Catcher (b. 9 May 1888 New York City NY–d. 14 Aug 1945 Corona NY) He managed minor league baseball, coached and scouted for the Giants until 1938. He then bought the M & M Restaurant in Corona, which he operated until his death. Died from a heart attack while tending bar at his restaurant. Buried St John's Cemetery, Middle Village NY.

Webbo Clarke—1 Year Pitcher (b. 8 Jun 1928 Cristobal, Canal Zone–d. 14 Jun 1970 Cristobal, Canal Zone).

Bill Clarkson—3 Years Pitcher (b. 27 Sep 1898 Portsmouth VA–d. 27 Aug 1971 Raleigh NC) Buried Montlawn Memorial Park, Raleigh NC.

Buzz Clarkson—1 Year Infielder (b. 13 Mar 1918 Hopkins SC–d. 18 Jan 1989 Monsour Medical Center, Jeanette PA) Served in the U.S. Army during World War II and played 14 years in the Negro Leagues. He was a retired glass worker for A S G Industries of Jeanette. Died from cancer. Buried Brush Creek Cemetery, Irwin PA.

Dad Clarkson—6 Years Pitcher (b. 31 Aug 1866 Cambridge MA–d. 5 Feb 1911 at a hospital in North Cambridge MA) He was engaged in the tailoring business, dealing mostly with Harvard students. Died after surgery the day before for stomach trouble. Buried Mount Auburn Cemetery, Cambridge MA.

John Clarkson—12 Years Pitcher Hall of Fame (b. 1 Jul 1861 Cambridge MA–d. 4 Feb 1909 McLean Hospital, Belmont MA) He was in the pipe and tobacco business in Bay City MI, but was forced to retire because of ill health. Died from a severe attack of pneumonia. Buried Mount Auburn Cemetery, Cambridge MA.

Walter Clarkson—5 Years Pitcher (b. 3 Nov 1878 Cambridge MA–d. 10 Oct 1946 at his home in Cambridge MA) He worked for the U.S. government. Died suddenly. Buried Cambridge Cemetery, Cambridge MA.

Gowell Claset—1 Year Pitcher (b. 16 Nov 1907 Battle Creek MI–d. 8 Mar 1981 St Petersburg FL) He was a pattern maker for General Electric in Elmira NY, retiring to Florida in 1973. Cremated.

Fritz Clausen—4 Years Pitcher (b. 26 Apr 1869 New York City NY–d. 11 Feb 1960 Shelby County Hospital, Memphis TN) He pitched in the Southern League. Living at Memphis for 33 years, he was a carpenter there until he retired in 1950. Buried Forest Hill Cemetery, Memphis TN.

Al Clauss—1 Year Pitcher (b. 24 Jun 1891 New Haven CT–d. 13 Sep 1952 Veteran's Hospital, Newington CT) World War I veteran. Died after a long illness. Buried St Lawrence Cemetery, West Haven CT.

Bill Clay—1 Year Outfielder (b. 23 Nov 1874 Baltimore MD–d. 12 Oct 1917 at his home in York PA) A Spanish-American War veteran. He engaged in the fish and produce business in York. Died from heart disease. Buried Prospect Hill Cemetery, York PA.

Dain Clay—4 Years Outfielder (b. 10 Jul 1919 Hicksville OH–d. 28 Aug 1994 Scripps Memorial Hospital, Chula Vista CA) He was a self-employed real estate agent. Died from pneumonia and respiratory failure while suffering from pancreatitis. Buried Glen Abbey Memorial Park, Bonita CA.

Bob Clemens—1 Year Outfielder (b. 9 Aug 1886 Mount Hebron MO–d. 5 Apr 1964 Fitzgibbon Hospital, Marshall MO) Died after being ill about a year. Buried Ridge Park Cemetery, Marshall MO.

Clem Clemens—3 Years Catcher (b. 21 Nov 1886 Chicago IL–d. 2 Nov 1967 St Petersburg FL) World War I veteran. He was a retired attorney. Buried St Mary Cemetery, Evergreen Park IL.

Bill Clemensen—3 Years Pitcher (b. 20 Jun 1919 New Brunswick NJ–d. 18 Feb 1994 at his home in Alta CA) Served in World War II. For 27 years he was a superintendent for the California Youth Authority. Died from a heart attack. Buried Memorial Lawn Cemetery, Sacramento CA.

Wally Clement—2 Years Outfielder (b. 21 Jul 1881 Auburn ME–d. 1 Nov 1953 Coral Gables FL).

Roberto Clemente—18 Years Outfielder Hall of Fame (b. 18 Aug 1934 Carolina, Puerto Rico–d. 31 Dec 1972 San Juan, Puerto Rico) Died in the crash of a cargo plane, carrying relief supplies to earthquake victims in Managua, Nicaragua. His body was never recovered.

Jack Clements—17 Years Catcher (b. 24 Jun 1864 Philadelphia PA–d. 23 May 1941 State Hospital, Norristown PA) For years he worked at the A J Reach Company in Philadelphia. After the plant closed he worked at a baseball factory in Perkasie PA. Died from a heart ailment. Buried Arlington Cemetery, Drexel Hill PA.

Verne Clemons—7 Years Catcher (b. 8 Sep 1891 Clemons IA–d. 5 May 1959 Bay Pines Veteran's Hosp, St Petersburg FL) World War I veteran. Died from lung cancer. Buried Bay Pines National Cemetery, Bay Pines FL.

Elmer Cleveland—3 Years Infielder (b. 15 Sep 1862 Washington DC–d. 8 Oct 1913 at his hotel in Zimmerman PA) In the hotel business many years, he conducted the St Charles Hotel in Johnstown PA, and at the time of his death he was running the Merchant's Hotel in Zimmerman. Buried Grandview Cemetery, Johnstown PA.

Harland Clift—12 Years Infielder (b. 12 Aug 1912 El Reno OK–d. 27 Apr 1992 St Elizabeth Medical Center, Yakima WA) He coached and managed in the minor leagues and scouted for the Tigers until the early 1950s. At that time he moved to Yakima where he lived the rest of his life, raising cattle and guiding tours for hunting trips. Died from cancer. Cremated.

Flea Clifton—4 Years Infielder (b. 12 Dec 1909 Cincinnati OH–d. 22 Dec 1997 Franciscan Hospital-W Hills, Cincinnati OH) He worked 40 years for George R Hammerlein Insurance in Cincinnati, retiring as a vice-president. Died after suffering a stroke three days earlier. Buried Bridgetown Cemetery, Cincinnati OH.

Monk Cline—5 Years Outfielder (b. 3 Mar 1858 Louisville KY–d. 23 Sep 1916 at his home in Louisville KY) He played baseball for 14 years. For 12 years he worked for the Louisville Fire Department, once serving as captain. Died from liver complications and other ailments. Buried Cave Hill Cemetery, Louisville KY.

Billy Clingman—10 Years Infielder (b. 21 Nov 1869 Louisville KY–d. 14 May 1958 Bethesda Hospital, Cincinnati OH) He managed some minor league baseball before entering the printing business, owning Clingman Engraving Company in Louisville. He retired in 1947. Buried Cave Hill Cemetery, Louisville KY.

Jim Clinton—6 Years Outfielder 1 Year Manager (b. 10 Aug 1850 New York City NY–d. 3 Sep 1921 Brooklyn NY).

Lou Clinton—8 Years Outfielder (b. 13 Oct 1937 Ponca City OK–d. 6 Dec 1997 Wichita KS) He owned and operated Clinton Production, Inc. Buried Lakeview Cemetery, Wichita KS.

Ed Clough—3 Years Outfielder (b. 11 Oct 1905 Wiconisco PA–d. 30 Jan 1944 Harrisburg PA).

Bill Clowers—1 Year Pitcher (b. 1898 San Marcos TX–d. 13 Jan 1978 Sweeney TX).

Bill Clymer—1 Year Infielder (b. 18 Dec 1873 Philadelphia PA–d. 26 Dec 1936 Philadelphia PA) He was well-known as a minor league manager, winning seven league championships in his long career. He coached briefly in the majors. Died from cirrhosis of the liver. Buried North Cedar Hill Cemetery, Philadelphia PA.

Otis Clymer—6 Years Outfielder (b. 27 Jan 1880 Pine Grove PA–d. 27 Feb 1926 St Paul MN) He owned a Ford dealership in Hudson WI. Killed in an automobile accident. Buried Willow River Cemetery, Hudson WI.

Andy Coakley—9 Years Pitcher (b. 20 Nov 1882 Providence RI–d. 27 Sep 1963 Mary Manning Walsh Home, New York City NY) He coached baseball at Columbia University from 1914 until 1951 and discovered Lou Gehrig there. He was also an agent for Mutual Insurance Company for 40 years. Died from the effects of a stroke suffered nine months earlier. Buried Kensico Cemetery, Valhalla NY.

George Cobb—1 Year Pitcher (b. 25 Sep 1865 Independence IA–d. 19 Aug 1926 Pomona CA) He lived in Pomona and was secretary of the Los Angeles County Fair for 27 years. Died after a year-long illness. Buried Evergreen Memorial Park, Riverside CA.

Herb Cobb—1 Year Pitcher (b. 6 Aug 1904 Pinetops NC–d. 8 Jan 1980 Tarboro NC) Buried Pinetops Cemetery, Pinetops NC.

Joe Cobb—1 Game Pinch Hitter (b. 24 Jan 1895 Hudson PA–d. 24 Dec 1947 Allentown PA).

Ty Cobb—24 Years Outfielder 6 Years Manager Hall of Fame (b. 18 Dec 1886 Narrows GA–d. 17 Jul 1961 Emery University Hospital, Atlanta GA) A shrewd investor, he lived off his stock investments and became a millionaire, living in a ranch-type mansion at Atherton CA and a Lake Tahoe retreat in Nevada. Died from prostate cancer. Buried Rose Hill Cemetery, Royston GA.

Gordon Cobbledick—Hall of Fame (b. 31 Dec 1898 Cleveland OH–d. 2 Oct 1969 Tucson Medical Center, Tucson AZ) He was a sportswriter and columnist for the Cleveland *Plain Dealer* for 41 years. Died from cancer. He had suffered a stroke two years earlier. Buried East Lawn Cemetery, Tucson AZ.

Dave Coble—1 Year Catcher (b. 24 Dec 1912 Monroe NC–d. 16 Oct 1971 Orlando FL) World War II veteran. He was a real estate salesman. Buried Lakeland Memorial Park, Monroe NC.

Al Cochran—1 Year Pitcher (b. 31 Jan 1891 Concord GA–d. 23 May 1947 in a private hospital in Atlanta GA) He worked for the Atlanta Fire Department and for the Fulton County, GA, marshall's office. At one time he was the baseball coach at Georgia Tech University and for the Atlanta city schools. Died after a long illness. Buried College Park Cemetery, College Park GA.

George Cochran—1 Year Infielder (b. 12 Feb 1889 Rusk TX–d. 21 May 1960 Kaiser Hospital,

Harbor City CA) He was a retail clerk at a market. Died from heart disease. Cremated.

Mickey Cochrane—13 Years Catcher 5 Years Manager Hall of Fame (b. 6 Apr 1903 Bridgewater MA–d. 28 Jun 1962 Lake Forest Hospital, Lake Forest IL) Died after a long illness. He was cremated and his ashes scattered over Lake Michigan.

Jim Cockman—1 Year Infielder (b. 26 Apr 1873 Guelph, Ontario, Canada–d. 28 Sep 1947 Guelph, Ontario, Canada).

Phil Cockrell—17 Years Pitcher (b. abt 1892 Augusta GA–d. 31 Mar 1951 Misericordia Hospital, Philadelphia PA) Played in the negro leagues. He was a bartender at a Philadelphia taproom when he was assaulted on his way home from work. Died as a result of seven stab wounds suffered from an assailant who apparently mistook Cockrell as his wife's lover. Buried Mount Lawn Cemetery, Sharon Hill PA.

Gene Cocreham—3 Years Pitcher (b. 14 Nov 1884 Luling TX–d. 27 Dec 1945 Luling TX) He coached baseball at Texas A & M while earning a degree in horticulture. He managed the planting and budding of pecan and fruit trees for McKean Orchards. Later he raised broiler chickens. He had been in ill health several years and hospitalized three months when he died. Buried Luling City Cemetery, Luling TX.

Jack Coffey—2 Years Infielder (b. 28 Jan 1887 New York City NY–d. 14 Feb 1966 at a nursing home in Bronx NY) He was the baseball coach and athletic director at Fordham University for 37 years, retiring in 1959. Died after a long illness. Buried Calvary Cemetery, Woodside NY.

Dick Coffman—15 Years Pitcher (b. 18 Dec 1906 Veto AL–d. 24 Mar 1972 Athens Nursing Home, Athens AL) Buried Athens City Cemetery, Athens AL.

Dick Cogan—3 Years Pitcher (b. 5 Dec 1871 Paterson NJ–d. 2 May 1948 Paterson NJ) Active in local politics, he was the first to hold the office of Registrar of Deeds and Mortgages in Passaic County, NJ. Died following a lengthy illness. Buried Holy Sepulchre Cemetery, Totowa NJ.

Ed Cogswell—3 Years Infielder (b. 25 Feb 1854 England–d. 27 Jul 1888 at his mother's home in Fitchburg MA) He worked several years as an overseer at the Fitchburg Worsted Mill.

Andy Cohen—3 Years Infielder 1 Year Manager (b. 25 Oct 1904 Baltimore MD–d. 29 Oct 1988 El Paso TX) He managed minor league baseball and founded the University of Texas-El Paso baseball program in 1960 coaching there until 1976. Died after several medical setbacks in his last years. Buried B'nai Zion Cemetery, El Paso TX.

Syd Cohen—3 Years Pitcher (b. 7 May 1908 Baltimore MD–d. 9 Apr 1988 El Paso TX) He managed in the minor leagues and was the pitching coach at University of Texas-El Paso in the 1960s and 1970s. Buried B'nai Zion Cemetery, El Paso TX.

Francisco Coimbre—4 Years Outfielder (b. 29 Jan 1909 Coamo, Puerto Rico–d. 8 Nov 1989 Ponce, Puerto Rico) He played in the negro leagues.

Jimmie Coker—9 Years Catcher (b. 28 Mar 1936 Holly Hill SC–d. 29 Oct 1991 at his home in Throckmorton TX) He was a cattle rancher in the Throckmorton area and was on the Board of Directors of the Texas and Southwestern Cattle Raisers Association and a local bank. Died from a heart attack. Buried Throckmorton Cemetery, Throckmorton TX.

Tom Colcolough—4 Years Pitcher (b. 8 Oct 1870 Charleston SC–d. 10 Dec 1919 Roper Hospital, Charleston SC) He was in the produce business for a while before becoming an acetylene welder at the Charleston Navy Yard. Died suddenly. Buried St Lawrence Cemetery, Charleston SC.

Bert Cole—6 Years Pitcher (b. 1 Jul 1896 San Francisco CA–d. 30 May 1975 Mills Memorial Hospital, San Mateo CA) He umpired in the Pacific Coast League and was a warehouse foreman for U.S. Plywood Corporation for ten years. Died from a heart attack. Buried Cypress Lawn Memorial Park, Colma CA.

King Cole—6 Years Pitcher (b. 15 Apr 1886 Toledo IA–d. 6 Jan 1916 at his home in Bay City MI) Died from lung cancer at the height of his career. Buried Woodlawn Cemetery, Toledo IA.

Willis Cole—2 Years Outfielder (b. 6 Jan 1882 Milton Junction WI–d. 11 Oct 1965 University Hospital, Madison WI) He worked for American Motors in Kenosha WI. Died after suffering failing health for a year. Buried Milton Junction Cemetery, Milton Junction WI.

Bob Coleman—3 Years Catcher 2 Years Manager (b. 26 Sep 1890 Huntingburg IN–d. 16 Jul 1959 Peter Bent Brigham Hospital, Boston MA) He managed minor league baseball and coached in the majors. His final years were spent as a scout for the Braves. Died from cancer.

Curt Coleman—1 Year Infielder (b. 18 Feb 1887 Salem OR–d. 1 Jul 1980 Yaquina Care Center, Newport OR) He was a farmer most of his life. Buried St Paul Cemetery, St Paul OR.

Ed Coleman—5 Years Outfielder (b. 1 Dec 1902 Canby OR–d. 5 Aug 1964 at a hospital in Oregon City OR) Died following a long illness. Buried Zion Memorial Park, Canby OR.

Gordy Coleman—9 Years Infielder (b. 5 Jul 1934 Rockville MD–d. 12 Mar 1994 Providence Hospital, Cincinnati OH) He was director of the Reds' speakers bureau, traveling about 40000 miles a year in Ohio, Indiana, Kentucky and West Virginia, making some 200 appearances and speeches a year. Died from a heart attack. Buried Arlington Memorial Gardens, Cincinnati OH.

Joe Coleman—10 Years Pitcher (b. 30 Jul 1922 Medford MA–d. 9 Apr 1997 Fort Myers FL) Buried Memorial Gardens, Fort Myers FL.

John Coleman—8 Years Outfielder (b. 6 Mar 1863 Saratoga Springs NY–d. 31 May 1922 Receiving Hospital, Detroit MI) He worked at bowling alleys in the Detroit area. Died after being struck by a car.

Percy Coleman—2 Years Pitcher (b. 15 Oct 1876 Mason OH–d. 16 Feb 1948 V A Hospital, Van Nuys CA) Spanish-American War veteran. He was a paint salesman. Died from a cerebral hemorrhage. Buried Los Angeles National Cemetery, Los Angeles CA.

Cad Coles—1 Year Outfielder (b. 17 Jan 1889 Rock Hill SC–d. 30 Jun 1942 at sea near Miami FL) He drowned in the Atlantic Ocean.

Chuck Coles—1 Year Outfielder (b. 27 Jun 1931 Fredericktown PA–d. 25 Jan 1996 Myrtle Beach SC) Served in the U.S. Army during the Korean War. A mill-wright, he worked in construction on power plants, electric generators and turbines. He enjoyed bowling, camping, hunting, fishing and golfing. Died from a heart attack while golfing. Buried Greene County Memorial Park, Waynesburg PA.

Bill Colgan—1 Year Catcher (b. East St Louis IL–d. 8 Aug 1895 Great Falls MT) He worked for the railroad and was accidentally killed while coupling railroad cars.

Bill Coliver—1 Year Outfielder (b. 1867 Detroit MI–d. 24 Mar 1888 St Mary's Hospital, Detroit MI) He died at the height of his career following surgery for a spinal disorder. Buried McPherson Cemetery, Clyde OH.

Allan Collamore—3 Years Pitcher (b. 5 Jun 1887 Worcester MA–d. 8 Aug 1980 Leila Hospital, Battle Creek MI) He was a machinist for Clark Equipment Company, retiring in 1954. In 1978 he was inducted into the Wisconsin Athletic Hall of Fame. Buried Oak Hill Cemetery, Battle Creek MI.

Hap Collard—3 Years Pitcher (b. 29 Aug 1898 Williams AZ–d. 7 Jul 1968 at his home in Jamestown CA) He was a cattle rancher in Tuolumne County, CA, and the longtime owner of the Smoke Cafe in Jamestown. Died from a heart attack. Buried Casa Bonita Mausoleum, Stockton CA.

Orlin Collier—1 Year Pitcher (b. 17 Feb 1907 East Prairie MO–d. 9 Sep 1944 Baptist Memorial Hospital, Memphis TN) He lived at Paragould AR where he operated a dry cleaning establishment. Died from a coronary occlusion. Buried Linwood Cemetery, Paragould AR.

Harry Colliflower—1 Year Pitcher (b. 11 Mar 1869 Petersville MD–d. 14 Aug 1961 at his home in Washington DC) Buried Mount Olivet Cemetery, Washington DC.

Bill Collins—3 Years Catcher (b. 1867 Dublin, Ireland–d. 8 Jun 1893 at his home in Brooklyn NY) He died at the height of his baseball career from complications of a severe cold and typhoid fever. Buried Mount Olivet Cemetery, Maspeth NY.

Bill Collins—4 Years Outfielder (b. 27 Mar 1882 Chestertown IN–d. 26 Jun 1961 County Hospital, San Bernardino CA) For 14 years he was head switchman for Kaiser Steel Corporation at Fontana CA. Died from pneumonia brought on by a diabetic condition. Buried Bellevue Memorial Gardens, Ontario CA.

Bob Collins—2 Years Catcher (b. 18 Sep 1909 Pittsburgh PA–d. 19 Apr 1969 Pittsburgh PA) Buried Jefferson Memorial Park, Pleasant Hills PA.

Chub Collins—2 Years Infielder (b. 1862 Dundas, Ontario, Canada–d. 20 May 1914 Dundas, Ontario, Canada).

Cyril Collins—2 Years Outfielder (b. 7 May 1889 Pulaski TN–d. 28 Feb 1941 Fort Sanders Hospital, Knoxville TN) Coaching athletic teams at Knoxville High School for 14 years, he was one of the outstanding athletes, coachs and officials of the south. Died from a heart ailment. Buried Maplewood Cemetery, Pulaski TN.

Dan Collins—1 Year Outfielder (b. 12 Jul 1854–d. 21 Sep 1883 New Orleans LA) Died at the height of his baseball career.

Eddie Collins—25 Years Infielder 2 Years Manager Hall of Fame (b. 2 May 1887 Millerton NY–d. 25 Mar 1951 Peter Bent Brigham Hospital, Boston MA) He spent his entire life in baseball as a player, manager and executive. His last 18 years he was a Red Sox vice-president. Died from a series of heart attacks suffered during his last two weeks. Buried Linwood Cemetery, Weston MA.

Hub Collins—7 Years Infielder (b. 15 Apr 1864 Louisville KY–d. 21 May 1892 Brooklyn NY) Died from typhoid pneumonia at the height of his career. Buried Cave Hill Cemetery, Louisville KY.

Jimmy Collins—14 Years Infielder 6 Years Manager Hall of Fame (b. 16 Jan 1870 Buffalo NY–d. 6 Mar 1943 Millard Fillmore Hospital, Buffalo NY) He was president of the Buffalo Municipal Leagues for 22 years. Died from pneumonia. Buried Holy Cross Cemetery, Lackawanna NY.

Joe Collins—10 Years Infielder (b. 3 Dec 1922 Scranton PA–d. 30 Aug 1989 Union NJ) He was a pilot in the U.S. Navy during World War II, and vice-president of People's Express Trucking Company in Newark NJ, retiring in 1987. Died following a brief illness. Buried Fairview Cemetery, Westfield NJ.

Orth Collins—2 Years Outfielder (b. 27 Apr 1880 Lafayette IN–d. 15 Dec 1949 Broward General Hosp, Fort Lauderdale FL) He was a retired house painter. Buried Evergreen Cemetery, Fort Lauderdale FL.

Pat Collins—10 Years Catcher (b. 13 Sep 1896 Sweet Springs MO–d. 20 May 1960 at his apartment in Kansas City KS) He was being treated for a heart condition when he died. Buried Memorial Park Cemetery, Kansas City KS.

Phil Collins—8 Years Pitcher (b. 27 Aug 1901 Chicago IL–d. 14 Aug 1948 Cook County Hospital, Chicago IL) He was a guard at the House of Corrections. Died from cancer. Buried Holy Cross Cemetery, Hammond IN.

Ray Collins—7 Years Pitcher (b. 11 Feb 1887 Colchester VT–d. 9 Jan 1970 at a hospital in Burlington VT) He coached the University of Vermont baseball team from 1923 to 1926. After that he ran the family farm near Colchester. He was a member of the University of Vermont Hall of Fame. Buried Colchester Village Cemetery, Colchester VT.

Rip Collins—11 Years Pitcher (b. 26 Feb 1896 Weatherford TX–d. 27 May 1968 at a hospital in Bryan TX) Served in the U.S. Army during World War I. He was a law enforcement officer in Bryan. Buried City Cemetery, College Station TX.

Ripper Collins—9 Years Infielder (b. 30 Mar 1904 Altoona PA–d. 16 Apr 1970 at his home in New Haven NY) He managed minor league baseball and coached for the Cubs. Died from a heart condition. Buried Mexico Village Cemetery, Mexico NY.

Shano Collins—16 Years Outfielder 2 Years Manager (b. 4 Dec 1885 Charlestown MA–d. 10 Sep 1955 at his home in Newton MA) He managed minor league baseball. Died from a heart seizure. Buried St Mary's Cemetery, Needham MA.

Zip Collins—5 Years Outfielder (b. 2 May 1892 Brooklyn NY–d. 19 Dec 1983 Prince William Hospital, Manassas VA) He was a salesman for Consolidated Edison in New York City. During World War II he was an inspector at a defense plant in New Jersey, retiring to Bethpage NY after the war and moving to Virginia about 1958. Died from a heart ailment. Buried Cemetery of Holy Rood, Westbury NY.

Frank Colman—6 Years Outfielder (b. 2 Mar 1918 London, Ontario, Canada–d. 19 Feb 1983 London, Ontario, Canada).

Earle Combs—12 Years Outfielder Hall of Fame (b. 14 May 1899 Pebworth KY–d. 21 Jul 1976 Pattie A Clay Hospital, Richmond KY) He retired from baseball to a 400 acre farm in eastern Kentucky in 1955. For 19 years he served on the Eastern Kentucky University Board of Regents. He also was a Kentucky State Banking

Commissioner and had other business interests. Died after a long illness. Buried Richmond Cemetery, Richmond KY.

Merrill Combs—5 Years Infielder (b. 11 Dec 1919 Los Angeles CA–d. 7 Jul 1981 Community Hospital, Riverside CA) He was a scout for the Indians. Died from lung cancer that had spread to his brain. Cremated.

Charlie Comiskey—13 Years Infielder 11 Years Manager Hall of Fame (b. 15 Aug 1859 Chicago IL–d. 26 Oct 1931 at his summer home near Eagle River WI) He was the owner of the Chicago White Sox. Died from nephritis, pneumonia and heart trouble. Buried Calvary Cemetery, Evanston IL.

Grace Lou Comiskey—(b. abt 1920–d. 15 Jun 1952 Chicago IL) She was part owner of the Chicago White Sox. Died from a heart attack. Buried Calvary Cemetery, Evanston IL.

Adam Comorosky—10 Years Outfielder (b. 9 Dec 1904 Swoyerville PA–d. 2 Mar 1951 at his home in Swoyerville PA) He owned and operated a store in Swoyerville. Died from heart failure brought on by syphilis. Buried St Ignatius Cemetery, Pringle PA.

Jack Compton—1 Year Pitcher (b. 9 Mar 1882 Lancaster OH–d. 4 Jul 1974 Fairfield County Hospital, Lancaster OH) He was a painter. Buried Hitler-Ludwig Cemetery, Circleville OH.

Pete Compton—6 Years Outfielder (b. 28 Sep 1889 San Marcos TX–d. 3 Feb 1978 St Luke's Hospital, Kansas City MO) Cremated.

Ralph Comstock—3 Years Pitcher (b. 24 Nov 1890 Sylvania OH–d. 13 Sep 1966 Cherry Hill Nursing Home, Toledo OH) He was a traveling insurance agent for Mutual of Omaha, retiring in 1946. Died after a long illness. Buried Toledo Memorial Park, Sylvania OH.

Bob Cone—1 Year Pitcher (b. 27 Feb 1894 Galveston TX–d. 24 May 1955 at his home in Galveston TX) A professor of urology at the University of Texas Medical School at Galveston from 1920 until his death, he was also one of the owners and a director of Woodley Petroleum Company of Houston TX. Buried Galveston Memorial Park, Hitchcock TX.

Bunk Congalton—4 Years Outfielder (b. 24 Jan 1878 Guelph, Ontario, Canada–d. 19 Aug 1937 at his home in Cleveland OH) He was a laborer at the Cleveland City Waterworks. Died from a heart attack. Buried Crown Hill Cemetery, Twinsburg OH.

Dick Conger—4 Years Pitcher (b. 3 Apr 1921 Los Angeles CA–d. 16 Feb 1970 at his home in Arcadia CA) He was a production foreman in the newspaper business for the Times-Mirror Company. Buried Live Oak Memorial Park, Monrovia CA.

Tony Conigliaro—8 Years Outfielder (b. 7 Jan 1945 Revere MA–d. 24 Feb 1990 Salem MA) His baseball career was shortened by vision problems after being hit by a pitch. Died from kidney failure. Buried Holy Cross Cemetery, Malden MA.

Allen Conkwright—1 Year Pitcher (b. 4 Dec 1896 Sedalia MO–d. 30 Jul 1991 California Special Care Hosp, La Mesa CA) World War I veteran. He was a foreman for Texaco Corporation for 35 years. Died from cardio-respiratory failure and arteriosclerotic heart disease. Buried All Souls Cemetery, Long Beach CA.

Jocko Conlan—2 Years Outfielder Hall of Fame (b. 6 Dec 1899 Chicago IL–d. 16 Apr 1989 Scottsdale Memorial Hospital, Scottsdale AZ) Served in the U.S. Navy during World War I. He was a National League umpire for 24 years. Died from unreported causes. Buried Green Acres Cemetery, Scottsdale AZ.

Ed Conley—1 Year Pitcher (b. 10 Jul 1864 Sandwich MA–d. 16 Oct 1894 at his home in Valley Falls RI) Died after a lingering illness. Buried Mount Calvary Cemetery, Cumberland RI.

Snipe Conley—3 Years Pitcher (b. 25 Apr 1894 Cressona PA–d. 7 Jan 1978 DeSoto TX) Died from a heart attack. Buried Wheatland Cemetery, Dallas TX.

Art Conlon—1 Year Infielder (b. 10 Dec 1897 Woburn MA–d. 5 Aug 1987 Falmouth MA).

Bert Conn—3 Years Infielder (b. 22 Sep 1879 Philadelphia PA–d. 2 Nov 1944 at his home in Philadelphia PA) Buried Oakland Cemetery, Philadelphia PA.

Sarge Connally—12 Years Pitcher (b. 31 Aug 1898 McGregor TX–d. 27 Jan 1978 at a hospital in Houston TX) World War I veteran. Buried Harris Creek Cemetery, McGregor TX.

Tom Connally—1 Year Infielder (b. 30 Dec 1892 Boston MA–d. 14 May 1966 Boston MA).

Bruce Connatser—2 Years Infielder (b. 19 Sep 1902 Sevierville TN–d. 27 Jan 1971 St Anthony Hospital, Terre Haute IN) He was active in baseball 43 years as a player, scout and minor league manager. He scouted 13 years for the Tigers and 18 years for the Phillies. Died from a heart attack suffered at an Exchange Club luncheon. Buried Highland Lawn Cemetery, Terre Haute IN.

Frank Connaughton—3 Years Infielder (b. 1 Jan 1869 Clinton MA–d. 1 Dec 1942 City Hospital, Boston MA) Died from injuries received in an auto accident.

Gene Connell—1 Year Catcher (b. 10 May 1906 Hazleton PA–d. 31 Aug 1937 Elmira NY) Died in an automobile crash. Buried St Gabriel's Cemetery, Hazleton PA.

Joe Connell—2 Games Pinch Hitter (b. 16 Jan 1902 Bethlehem PA–d. 21 Sep 1977 Mosser Nursing Home, Trexlertown PA) He owned and operated the Connell Coal Company in Bethlehem and later was a clothing salesman for the Hess Department Store there. Served in the U.S. Army during World War I. Buried Fairview Cemetery, Whitehall PA.

Bill Connelly—4 Years Pitcher (b. 29 Jun 1925 Alberta VA–d. 27 Nov 1980 Richmond VA) Earned a Purple Heart while in the U.S. Navy during World War II. He worked for the State of Virginia Beverage Control Board. Buried Crestview Memorial Park, La Crosse VA.

Tom Connelly—2 Years Outfielder (b. 20 Oct 1897 Chicago IL–d. 18 Feb 1941 Hines Memorial Hospital, Chicago IL) Buried Calvary Cemetery, Evanston IL.

Bud Connolly—1 Year Infielder (b. 25 Apr 1901 San Francisco CA–d. 12 Jun 1964 at his home in Berkeley CA) World War II veteran. He worked nine years on the maintenance staff at St Jerome's School. Died from a heart attack. Buried St Mary's Cemetery, Oakland CA.

Ed Connolly—4 Years Catcher (b. 17 Jul 1908 Brooklyn NY–d. 12 Nov 1963 near Pittsfield MA) Served in the U.S. Navy during World War II. He worked for the Massachusetts State Dept of Natural Resources, and collapsed and died while at work in the Pittsfield State Forest. Buried St Joseph's Cemetery, Pittsfield MA.

Ed Connolly—2 Years Pitcher (b. 3 Dec 1939 Brooklyn NY–d. 1 Jul 1998 New Canaan CT) He was a senior vice-president of Paine-Webber in New York City. Died after suffering a heart attack while driving his car. Buried Lakeview Cemetery, New Canaan CT.

Joe Connolly—4 Years Outfielder (b. 4 Jun 1896 San Francisco CA–d. 30 Mar 1960 San Francisco CA) World War I veteran. He was a checker in the Ship Clerk's Union on the San Francisco waterfront. Died from a heart attack while working. Buried Golden Gate National Cemetery, San Bruno CA.

Joe Connolly—4 Years Outfielder (b. 12 Feb 1886 North Smithfield RI–d. 1 Sep 1943 at his home in North Smithfield RI) He coached baseball at Providence College and Sacred Heart Academy in Woonsocket RI. Later he was an investigator for the Rhode Island State Board of Milk Control and represented North Smithfield in the state legislature four years. Died from a heart condition. Buried St Charles Cemetery, Blackstone MA.

Red Connolly—1 Year Outfielder (b. abt 1857 New York City NY–d. 2 Mar 1896 New York City NY) He umpired minor league baseball up until he died from pneumonia.

Thomas Connolly, Sr—Hall of Fame (b. abt 1870 Manchester, England–d. 28 Apr 1961 Natick MA) An American League umpire from 1901 to 1931, he was the first umpire inducted into baseball's Hall of Fame. Buried St Patrick's Cemetery, Natick MA.

Jim Connor—4 Years Infielder (b. 11 May 1865 Port Jervis NY–d. 4 Sep 1950 St Joseph's Hospital, Providence RI) He managed a short while in the minor leagues and umpired for a brief period before becoming a janitor at the Ruggles Street School in Providence. Buried Mount St Mary's Cemetery, Pawtucket RI.

Joe Connor—3 Years Catcher (b. 8 Dec 1874 Waterbury CT–d. 8 Nov 1957 at his home in Waterbury CT) He worked in the packing department of the Waterbury Manufacturing Company at one time, and was a roofer for Waterbury Roofing Company. He retired in 1946 after serving as a messenger for the Superior Court in Waterbury. Died suddenly from natural causes. Buried Old St Joseph's Cemetery, Waterbury CT.

John Connor—2 Years Pitcher (b. 1853 Glasgow, Scotland–d. 13 Oct 1932 Dorchester MA) Buried New Calvary Cemetery, Mattapan MA.

Roger Connor—18 Years Infielder 1 Year Manager Hall of Fame (b. 1 Jul 1857 Waterbury CT–d. 4 Jan 1931 at his daughter's home in Waterbury CT) He retired in 1920 after spending seven years as a school inspector in Waterbury. Died after a lingering illness following surgery for a stomach ailment a year earlier. Buried Old St Joseph's Cemetery, Waterbury CT.

Chuck Connors—2 Years Infielder (b. 10 Apr 1921 Brooklyn NY–d. 10 Nov 1992 Los Angeles CA) Better known as an actor in "The Rifleman" televison show, he also played pro basketball. Died from lung cancer. Buried San Fernando Mission Cemetery, Mission Hills CA.

Ted Conovar—1 Year Pitcher (b. 10 Mar 1868 Lexington KY–d. 27 Jul 1910 at his home in Lexington KY) Died after a brief illness. Buried Lexington Cemetery, Lexington KY.

Ben Conroy—1 Year Infielder (b. 14 Mar 1871 Philadelphia PA–d. 25 Nov 1937 Philadelphia PA) He worked 32 years for the Philadelphia Gas Works Company. Died after an illness of three years. Buried Old Cathedral Cemetery, Philadelphia PA.

Bill Conroy—6 Years Catcher (b. 26 Feb 1915 Bloomington IL–d. 13 Nov 1997 at his home in Citrus Heights CA) Served in World War II. He was a technician for the Alameda County (CA) School District. Died from congestive heart failure and other complications from diabetes. Buried Mount Vernon Memorial Park, Fair Oaks CA.

Pep Conroy—1 Year Infielder (b. 9 Jan 1899 Chicago IL–d. 23 Jan 1970 Chicago IL) Buried Holy Sepulchre Cemetery, Worth IL.

Wid Conroy—11 Years Infielder (b. 5 Apr 1877 Camden NJ–d. 6 Dec 1959 Burlington County Hospital, Mount Holly NJ) He coached for a while. Buried Mount Carmel Cemetery, Moorestown NJ.

Bill Conway—2 Years Catcher (b. 28 Nov 1861 Lowell MA–d. 18 Dec 1943 Somerville MA).

Charlie Conway—1 Year Outfielder (b. 28 Apr 1886 Youngstown OH–d. 12 Sep 1968 Northside Hospital, Youngstown OH) He was secretary to the Youngstown chief of police and a county deputy sheriff before spending 30 years as an agent for the Youngstown Humane Society, retiring in 1962. Died from arteriosclerosis. Buried Lake Park Cemetery, Youngstown OH.

Dick Conway—3 Years Pitcher (b. 1865 Lowell MA–d. 9 Sep 1926 at his home in Lowell MA) Died after an illness of several weeks. Buried St Mary's Cemetery, Lawrence MA.

Jack Conway—4 Years Infielder (b. 30 Jul 1918 Bryan TX–d. 11 Jun 1993 Waco TX) Served in the U.S. Navy during World War II. He managed in the minor leagues and was a house parent for several years at the State Home and at the Methodist Home. For his last ten years he was a bus driver for Midway Schools. Buried Rosemound Cemetery, Waco TX.

Owen Conway—1 Year Infielder (b. 23 Oct 1890 New York City NY–d. 12 Mar 1942 Philadelphia PA).

Pat Conway—1 Year Pitcher (b. 7 Jun 1901 Holyoke MA–d. 16 Apr 1980 at a nursing home in Holyoke MA) He was district sales manager for Schaefer Brewing Co. Buried St Jerome Cemetery, Holyoke MA.

Pete Conway—5 Years Pitcher (b. 30 Oct 1866 Burmont PA–d. 13 Jan 1903 Clifton Heights PA) Died from neuralgia of the heart.

Rip Conway—1 Year Infielder (b. 18 Apr 1896 White Bear MN–d. 3 Dec 1971 St Paul MN).

Ed Conwell—1 Year Infielder (b. 29 Jan 1890 Chicago IL–d. 1 May 1980 Norwood Park IL).

Herb Conyers—1 Year Infielder (b. 8 Jan 1921 Cowgill MO–d. 16 Sep 1964 Glenville Hospital, Cleveland OH) Served as a U.S. Army Air Corps navigator during World War II. He taught mathematics and coached in a Cleveland area high school for 12 years. Buried Knollwood Cemetery, Mayfield OH.

Joe Conzelman—3 Years Pitcher (b. 14 Jul 1885 Bristol CT–d. 17 Apr 1979 Mountain Brook AL) Served as a pilot during World War I. Buried Elmwood Cemetery, Birmingham AL.

Dale Coogan—1 Year Infielder (b. 14 Aug 1930 Los Angeles CA–d. 8 Mar 1989 Mission Hospital, Mission Viejo CA) Served in the military and worked 22 years as a school teacher. He was superintendent of the Oceanview School District. Died from lung cancer. Buried Pacific View Memorial Park, Newport Beach CA.

Dan Coogan—1 Year Infielder (b. 16 Feb 1875 Philadelphia PA–d. 28 Oct 1942 General Hospital, Philadelphia PA) Served as physical director for the Canadian armies during World War I. He coached college sports at Penn, Cornell, Bowdoin College and Georgetown University. Died after a long illness. Buried Holy Cross Cemetery, Yeadon PA.

Doc Cook—4 Years Outfielder (b. 24 Jun 1886 Witt TX–d. 30 Jun 1973 Lawrence County Hospital, Lawrenceburg TN) Buried Lawrence County Memorial Gardens, Lawrenceburg TN.

Earl Cook—1 Year Pitcher (b. 10 Dec 1908 Stouffville, Ontario, Canada–d. 21 Nov 1996 Markham, Ontario, Canada).

Jim Cook—1 Year Outfielder (b. 10 Nov 1879 Dundee IL–d. 16 Jun 1949 at his home in St Louis MO) He coached baseball and football at Soldan High School in St Louis from 1914 until 1935, and taught mechanical and architectural drawing there until his death. Died from heart disease. Buried Dundee IL.

Paul Cook—7 Years Catcher (b. 5 May 1863 Caledonia NY–d. 25 May 1905 St Mary's Hospital, Rochester NY) He conducted a saloon in Rochester for several years before opening the Oasis Cafe there. Died after an illness of several months. Buried Holy Sepulchre Cemetery, Rochester NY.

Rollin Cook—1 Year Pitcher (b. 5 Oct 1890 Toledo OH–d. 11 Aug 1975 City Hospital, Toledo OH) Served in the U.S. Army during both World Wars I and II. He was a mechanical engineer for a number of firms, including Willys Corporation, before becoming a partner in Riley and Cook Paving Contractors for ten years, retiring in 1958. Buried Woodlawn Cemetery, Toledo OH.

Dusty Cooke—8 Years Outfielder 1 Year Manager (b. 23 Jun 1907 Swepsonville NC–d. 21 Nov 1987 Raleigh NC) He was a co-owner of Mobley's Art Supply in Raleigh. Buried Westview Memorial Gardens, Lillington NC.

Duff Cooley—13 Years Outfielder (b. 14 Mar 1873 Dallas TX–d. 9 Aug 1937 Parkland Hospital, Dallas TX) Died from the effects of heat prostration. Buried Grove Hill Memorial Park, Dallas TX.

Bobby Coombs—2 Years Pitcher (b. 2 Feb 1908 Lyman ME–d. 21 Oct 1991 Ogunquit ME) Served in the U.S. Navy during World War II. He coached baseball at Williams College in Williamstown MA from 1946 until retiring in 1974. Died after a brief illness. Buried Riverside Cemetery, Ogunquit ME.

Cecil Coombs—1 Year Outfielder (b. 18 Mar 1888 Moweaqua IL–d. 25 Nov 1975 Fort Worth TX) Living in Fort Worth over 50 years, he was the business manager of the Fort Worth Cats of the Texas League during the 1930s. Buried Mount Olivet Cemetery, Fort Worth TX.

Jack Coombs—14 Years Pitcher 1 Year Manager (b. 18 Nov 1882 LeGrand IA–d. 15 Apr 1957 at his home in Palestine TX) The winner of the longest complete game (24 innings) in American League history, he also pitched three complete games during a five day period in the 1910 World Series, winning them all. He was active in banking and real estate in Maine and in Palestine TX. Died from a heart attack. Buried St Joseph Cemetery, Palestine TX.

Bill Cooney—2 Years Pitcher (b. 4 Apr 1887 Boston MA–d. 6 Nov 1928 at his sister's home in Roxbury MA) He umpired in the minor leagues for many years and later was an inspector in the power department for the City of Boston. Died suddenly. Buried New Calvary Cemetery, Mattapan MA.

Bob Cooney—2 Years Pitcher (b. 12 Jul 1907 Glens Falls NY–d. 4 May 1976 Glens Falls hospital, Glens Falls NY) Served in the Pacific during World War II. He worked with his wife in the real estate business for 42 years. Died following a long illness. Buried St Mary's Cemetery, South Glens Falls NY.

Jimmy Cooney—3 Years Infielder (b. 9 Jul 1865 Cranston RI–d. 1 Jul 1903 Cranston RI) He died from pneumonia. Buried St Ann's Cemetery, Cranston RI.

Jimmy Cooney—7 Years Infielder (b. 24 Aug 1894 Cranston RI–d. 7 Aug 1991 Brentwood Nursing Home, Warwick RI) Served in the U.S. Army during World War I. He worked 25 years for the Cranston Print Works, retiring in 1960. Buried St Ann's Cemetery, Cranston RI.

Johnny Cooney—20 Years Outfielder 1 Year Manager (b. 18 Mar 1901 Cranston RI–d. 8 Jul 1986 Sarasota Memorial Hospital, Sarasota FL) He coached for the Braves and White Sox. Buried Manasota Memorial Park, Sarasota FL.

Phil Cooney—1 Year Infielder (b. 14 Sep 1886 Paterson NJ–d. 6 Oct 1957 New York City NY).

William Coons—1 Year Outfielder (b. 21 Mar 1855 Philadelphia PA–d. 30 Aug 1915 Burlington NJ) He worked for the government postal service. Buried Odd Fellows Cemetery, Burlington NJ.

Andy Cooper—11 Years Pitcher 8 Years Manager (b. 4 Mar 1896 Waco TX–d. 10 Jun 1941 Waco TX) He played in the negro leagues.

Cal Cooper—1 Year Pitcher (b. 11 Aug 1922 Great Falls SC–d. 4 Jul 1994 Clinton SC) Served in the U.S. Navy during World War II. He was personnel director at Clinton Mills and a member of Laurens County School Board for 28 years. He had been in declining health a number of weeks when he died. Buried Pinelawn Memory Gardens, Clinton SC.

Claude Cooper—5 Years Outfielder (b. 1 Apr 1892 Troupe TX–d. 21 Jan 1974 Nichols Memorial Hospital, Plainview TX) World War I veteran. Died from pneumonia, caused by emphysema. Buried Plainview Cemetery, Plainview TX.

Guy Cooper—2 Years Pitcher (b. 28 Jan 1893 Rome GA–d. 2 Aug 1951 General Hospital, Los Angeles CA) Serving in the U.S. Army during World War I, he also served in the U.S. Navy. He lived in Santa Monica CA since 1919. Died from a stroke. Buried Woodlawn Cemetery, Santa Monica CA.

Mort Cooper—11 Years Pitcher (b. 2 Mar 1913 Atherton MO–d. 17 Nov 1958 St Vincent's Hospital, Little Rock AR) He managed some minor league baseball and was active with boy's clubs. He worked for the security division of Sheffield Steel Company in Houston TX. Died from cirrhosis of the liver and a pulmonary staphylococcal infection. Buried Salem Cemetery, Independence MO.

Pat Cooper—2 Years Pitcher (b. 26 Nov 1917 Albemarle NC–d. 15 Mar 1993 Carolinas Medical Center, Charlotte NC) Served in the U.S. Army during World War II. He was a retired contractor. Buried Sharon Memorial Park, Charlotte NC.

Walker Cooper—18 Years Catcher (b. 8 Jan 1915 Atherton MO–d. 11 Apr 1991 Scottsdale AZ).

Wilbur Cooper—15 Years Pitcher (b. 24 Feb 1892 Bearsville WV–d. 7 Aug 1973 West Valley Community Hospital, Encino CA) He was a real estate salesman. Died from a heart attack. Cremated.

Mays Copeland—1 Year Pitcher (b. 31 Aug 1913 Mountain View AR–d. 29 Nov 1982 Indio CA) For 27 years he was superintendent for Massey Sand and Rock in Indio. Died from a heart attack. Buried Coachella Valley Cemetery, Coachella CA.

Henry Coppola—2 Years Pitcher (b. 6 Aug 1912 East Douglas MA–d. 10 Jul 1990 Norfolk MA).

Joe Corbett—4 Years Pitcher (b. 4 Dec 1877 San Francisco CA–d. 2 May 1945 San Francisco CA) The brother of heavyweight champion Jim Corbett, he was a retired clerk from Tidewater Associated Oil Company. Died from a heart attack. Buried Holy Cross Catholic Cemetery, Colma CA.

Claude Corbitt—4 Years Infielder (b. 21 Jul 1915 Sunbury NC–d. 1 May 1978 St Francis Hospital, Cincinnati OH) For 23 years he was a traffic manager for the H S Pogue Company in Cincinnati. Died following a long illness. Buried Arlington Memorial Gardens, Cincinnati OH.

Art Corcoran—1 Year Infielder (b. 23 Oct 1894 Roxbury MA–d. 27 Jul 1958 at the Soldier's Home in Chelsea MA) He was a Navy aviator during World War I. A football coach, he was an assistant coach at Columbia, Navy and the University of Virginia, and head coach at Holy Cross and Harvard. After retiring from coaching he directed the sandlot baseball program in Boston MA 14 years. Died after an illness of several months.

John Corcoran—1 Year Infielder (b. 1873 Cincinnati OH–d. 1 Nov 1901 at his sister's home in Cincinnati OH) Died from consumption.

Larry Corcoran—8 Years Pitcher (b. 10 Aug 1859 Brooklyn NY–d. 14 Oct 1891 at his home in Newark NJ) He umpired in the minor leagues until he became ill. Died from Bright's disease. Buried Holy Sepulchre Cemetery, East Orange NJ.

Mickey Corcoran—1 Year Infielder (b. 26 Aug 1884 Buffalo NY–d. 9 Dec 1950 at his home in Buffalo NY) He played professional baseball for 22 years. Buried Holy Cross Cemetery, Lackawanna NY.

Tommy Corcoran—18 Years Infielder (b. 4 Jan 1869 New Haven CT–d. 25 Jun 1960 at a convalescent home in Plainfield CT) He umpired and managed in the minor leagues. Buried Pachaug Cemetery, Pachaug CT.

Ed Corey—1 Year Pitcher (b. 13 Jul 1897 Chicago IL–d. 17 Sep 1970 St Catherine's Hospital, Kenosha WI) He managed the Town Casino for a number of years. Later he worked for American Motors, Inc. Died following a long illness. Buried Sunset Ridge Memorial Park, Kenosha WI.

Fred Corey—7 Years Infielder (b. 1857 South Kingston RI–d. 26 Nov 1912 Providence RI) Died when he was asphyxiated by illuminating gas from a jet in his room. It was not possible to determine if it was an accident or suicide.

Chuck Corgan—2 Years Infielder (b. 4 Dec 1902 Wagoner OK–d. 13 Jun 1928 Wagoner OK) Died at the height of his baseball career from cancer. Buried Elmwood Cemetery, Wagoner OK.

Roy Corhan—2 Years Infielder (b. 21 Oct 1887 Indianapolis IN–d. 24 Nov 1958 at his home in San Francisco CA) He was a retired postmaster of Pinecrest CA. Died from a heart attack. Buried Holy Cross Catholic Cemetery, Colma CA.

Pop Corkhill—10 Years Outfielder (b. 11 Apr 1858 Parkesburg PA–d. 4 Apr 1921 Pennsauken NJ) He was a machinist in a furniture factory. Died from kidney cancer. Buried Bethel Memorial Park, Pennsauken NJ.

Red Corriden—5 Years Infielder 1 Year Manager (b. 4 Sep 1887 Logansport IN–d. 28 Sep 1959 Community Hospital, Indianapolis IN) He worked in baseball as a player, coach, manager or scout from 1908 until 1958, except for 1920 when he sat out because of bad health. Died from a heart attack. Buried St Vincent Cemetery, Indianapolis IN.

Frank Corridon—6 Years Pitcher (b. 25 Nov 1880 Newport RI–d. 21 Feb 1941 Syracuse NY).

Shine Cortazzo—1 Game Pinch Hitter (b. 26 Sep 1904 Wilmerding PA–d. 4 Mar 1963 General Hospital, Braddock PA) He worked for the Westinghouse Air Brake Company in Wilmerding PA. Buried St Joseph's Cemetery, East McKeesport PA.

Joe Coscarart—2 Years Infielder (b. 18 Nov 1909 Escondido CA–d. 5 Apr 1993 Sequim WA) Buried Dungeness Cemetery, Sequim WA.

Howard Cosell—(b. 25 Mar 1918 Winston-Salem NC–d. 23 Apr 1995 New York City NY) Educated as an attorney, he was best known as an outspoken and controversial sports commentator. Died from a heart embolism.

Dan Costello—4 Years Outfielder (b. 9 Sep 1895 Jessup PA–d. 26 Mar 1936 St Francis Hospital, Pittsburgh PA) Died from pneumonia. Buried St Mary's Cemetery, St Marys PA.

Henry Cote—2 Years Catcher (b. 20 Dec 1864 Troy NY–d. 28 Apr 1940 at his home in Troy NY) He retired from professional baseball at age 48, going to work for Cluett, Peabody and Company, Inc, where he stayed several years. Buried St Joseph's Cemetery, Troy NY.

Pete Cote—2 Games Pinch Hitter (b. 30 Aug 1902 Cambridge MA–d. 17 Oct 1987 at his home in Middleton MA) He was a retired liquor salesman. Died after a sudden illness. Buried St Paul Cemetery.

Dan Cotter—1 Year Pitcher (b. 14 Apr 1867 Boston MA–d. 4 Sep 1935 Dorchester MA) Buried Mount Benedict Cemetery, West Roxbury MA.

Dick Cotter—2 Years Catcher (b. 12 Oct 1889 Manchester NH–d. 4 Apr 1945 Brooklyn NY) Buried Holy Cross Cemetery, Brooklyn NY.

Ed Cotter—1 Year Infielder (b. 4 Jul 1904 Hartford CT–d. 14 Jun 1959 at his home in Hartford CT) Served in the U.S. Navy during World War II. He was associated for 30 years as a broker for S Jackson Company in Hartford. Buried Mount St Benedict Cemetery, Bloomfield CT.

Harvey Cotter—2 Years Infielder (b. 22 May 1900 Holden MO–d. 6 Aug 1955 Doctor's Hospital, Los Angeles CA) He was the owner and operator of an apartment building. Died following emergency abdominal surgery. Buried Forest Lawn Memorial Park, Glendale CA.

Tom Cotter—1 Year Catcher (b. 30 Sep 1866 Waltham MA–d. 22 Nov 1906 Corey Hill Hospital, Brookline MA) He was noted as a rower and polo player. Died from pneumonia, but was being treated for necrosis of the bone. Buried Calvary Cemetery, Waltham MA.

Ensign Cottrell—5 Years Pitcher (b. 29 Aug 1888 Hoosick Falls NY–d. 27 Feb 1947 Crouse-Irving Hospital, Syracuse NY) He was a self-employed civil engineer and surveyor. Buried Morningside Cemetery, Syracuse NY.

Johnny Couch—5 Years Pitcher (b. 31 Mar 1891 Vaughn MT–d. 8 Dec 1975 Stanford University Hospital, Palo Alto CA) Served in Europe for the U.S. Army during World War I. A patrolman for the California Highway Patrol for 25 years, he retired about 1955. Died from heart disease. Buried Alta Mesa Memorial Park, Palo Alto CA.

Bill Coughlin—9 Years Infielder (b. 12 Aug 1877 Scranton PA–d. 7 May 1943 at his home in Scranton PA) He coached baseball at Lafayette College from 1919 until his death. Died after being ill three years, but his condition turned for the worse the last month. Buried Cathedral Cemetery, Scranton PA.

Ed Coughlin—1 Year Pitcher (b. 5 Aug 1861 Hartford CT–d. 25 Dec 1952 at his home in Hartford CT) He worked 35 years for the Hartford Electric Light Company, retiring as traffic manager in 1946. Died suddenly. Buried Mount St Benedict Cemetery, Bloomfield CT.

Roscoe Coughlin—2 Years Pitcher (b. 15 Mar 1868 Walpole MA–d. 20 Mar 1951 at the Soldier's Home in Chelsea MA) Buried St Patrick's Cemetery, Lowell MA.

Bob Coulson—4 Years Outfielder (b. 17 Jun 1887 Courtney PA–d. 11 Sep 1953 Washington Hospital, Washington PA) Active in local politics, he was the Washington County, PA, Registrar of Wills from 1928 to 1936, and an inspector for the Pennsylvania Department of Labor and Industry. He worked for the County Assessments Office when he died from a coronary thrombosis. Buried Beallsville Cemetery, Beallsville PA.

Fritz Coumbe—8 Years Pitcher (b. 13 Dec 1889 Antrim PA–d. 21 Mar 1978 Feather River Hospital, Paradise CA) For ten years he was a carpenter for Corning Glass Works in Whittier CA. Died from bronchopneumonia six days after breaking ribs in a fall at his home. Buried Paradise Cemetery, Paradise CA.

Clint Courtney—11 Years Catcher (b. 16 Mar 1927 Hall Summit LA–d. 16 Jun 1975 Rochester NY) He managed minor league baseball at the time of his death. Died from a heart attack he suffered in his hotel room when the team he was managing was on the road. Buried Mount Zion Cemetery, Hall Summit LA.

Ernie Courtney—6 Years Infielder (b. 20 Jan 1875 Los Angeles CA–d. 29 Feb 1920 Buffalo NY).

Henry Courtney—4 Years Pitcher (b. 19 Nov 1898 Asheville NC–d. 11 Dec 1954 Lyme CT).

Dee Cousineau—3 Years Catcher (b. 16 Dec 1898 Watertown MA–d. 14 Jul 1951 at his home in Watertown MA) He engaged in the insurance business until health forced his retirement. He also served Watertown as superintendent of playgrounds. Died suddenly after suffering ten years with an asthmatic heart. Buried St Patrick's Cemetery, Watertown MA.

Harry Coveleski—9 Years Pitcher (b. 23 Apr 1886 Luke Fidler PA–d. 4 Aug 1950 State Hospital, Shamokin PA) He was a slate picker and later a miner at Luke Fidler Colliery. Died after a series of strokes. Buried St Stanislaus Cemetery, Shamokin PA.

Stan Coveleski—14 Years Pitcher Hall of Fame (b. 13 Jul 1889 Shamokin PA–d. 20 Mar 1984 South Bend IN) He lived in South Bend 55 years and operated a service station there. Died after a brief illness. Buried St Joseph Cemetery, South Bend IN.

John Coveney—1 Year Catcher (b. 10 Jun 1880 South Natick MA–d. 28 Mar 1961 at his home in Wellesley MA) For 30 years he was an engineer at Dana Hall School, retiring in 1950. Buried St Patrick's Cemetery, Natick MA.

Chet Covington—1 Year Pitcher (b. 6 Nov 1910 Jackson TN–d. 11 Jun 1976 Hallandale FL) He worked as a radio announcer, clerk, deputy sheriff and plumbing supply distributor. He retired in 1970 as a truck driver for Terminal Transport Company. Died suddenly. Buried Vista Memorial Gardens, Hialeah FL.

Sam Covington—3 Years Infielder (b. 17 Dec 1892 Henryville TN–d. 4 Jan 1963 Denison TX) Died from a heart attack. Buried Oakwood Cemetery, Denison TX.

Tex Covington—2 Years Pitcher (b. 19 Mar 1887 Henryville TN–d. 10 Dec 1931 Denison TX) Buried Fairview Cemetery, Denison TX.

Bill Cox—5 Years Pitcher (b. 23 Jun 1913 Ashmore IL–d. 16 Feb 1988 at his home in Charleston IL) Served in Germany for the U.S. Army during World War II. Active in local politics, he was Coles County (IL) sheriff from 1958 to 1962, county treasurer 1962 to 1966, state representative 1966 to 1974 and a Coles County chairman. He also officiated basketball games for a number of years. Buried Ashmore Cemetery, Ashmore IL.

Billy Cox—11 Years Infielder (b. 29 Aug 1919 Newport PA–d. 30 Mar 1978 Polyclinic Hospital, Harrisburg PA) Served in the U.S. Army during World War II. He was a steward at a club in Newport. Died from cancer. Buried Newport Cemetery, Newport PA.

Dick Cox—2 Years Outfielder (b. 30 Sep 1895 Pasadena CA–d. 1 Jun 1966 Morro Bay CA) World War I veteran. For 30 years he was a grip for Hal Roach Studios in Hollywood. Died from a heart attack. Buried Mountain View Cemetery, Altadena CA.

Ernie Cox—1 Year Pitcher (b. 19 Feb 1894 Birmingham AL–d. 29 Apr 1974 at a hospital in Birmingham AL) Buried Forest Hill Cemetery, Birmingham AL.

Frank Cox—1 Year Infielder (b. 29 Aug 1859 Waltham MA–d. 24 Jun 1928 Hartford CT).

George Cox—1 Year Pitcher (b. 15 Nov 1904 Sherman TX–d. 17 Dec 1995 Bedford TX).

Larry Cox—9 Years Catcher (b. 11 Sep 1947 Bluffton OH–d. 17 Feb 1990 Bellefontaine OH) He managed minor league baseball five years for the Cubs and was the bullpen coach for the Cubs when he died. Died unexpectedly from a heart attack while playing racquetball. Buried Gethsemane Cemetery, Lima OH.

Les Cox—1 Year Pitcher (b. 14 Aug 1905 Junction TX–d. 14 Nov 1934 San Angelo TX).

Red Cox—1 Year Pitcher (b. 16 Feb 1895 Laurel Springs NC–d. 15 Oct 1984 Roanoke VA) Served in the U.S. Marines during World War I. Buried Mountain View Cemetery, Vinton VA.

Toots Coyne—1 Year Infielder (b. 20 Oct 1894 St Louis MO–d. 18 Sep 1939 St Louis MO) Buried Valhalla Cemetery, St Louis MO.

Jim Crabb—1 Year Pitcher (b. 23 Aug 1890 Monticello IA–d. 30 Mar 1940 at the Burke Hotel in Lewistown MT) A well-known painter in the area, he lived at Lewistown 16 years. Died in his hotel apartment following 18 months of illness caused primarily from an old chest injury from his baseball days. Buried Lewistown City Cemetery, Lewistown MT.

Estel Crabtree—8 Years Outfielder (b. 19 Aug 1903 Crabtree OH–d. 4 Jan 1967 Hocking Valley Community Hospital, Logan OH) He was associated with Gem Coal Company of Nelsonville OH a number of years before becoming an interviewer at the Logan office of the Ohio State Employment Service in 1963. Buried Green Lawn Cemetery, Nelsonville OH.

Walter Craddock—3 Years Pitcher (b. 25 Mar 1932 Willis Branch WV–d. 6 Jul 1980 Parma Heights OH) He was a general foreman for Ford Motor Company. Died from a heart attack. Buried Blue Ridge Memorial Gardens, Prosperity WV.

Harry Craft—6 Years Outfielder 7 Years Manager (b. 19 Apr 1915 Ellisville MS–d. 3 Aug 1995 Conroe TX) He coached and managed major league baseball from 1955 to 1964. Cremated.

Molly Craft—4 Years Pitcher (b. 28 Nov 1895 Portsmouth VA–d. 25 Oct 1978 V A Hospital, Los Angeles CA) He worked for the Maritime Commission. Died from liver cancer. Cremated.

Howard Craghead—2 Years Pitcher (b. 25 May 1908 Selma CA–d. 15 Jul 1962 San Diego CA) Served in the U.S. Navy during World War II. A resident of San Diego since 1936, he was the corporate secretary for San Diego Gas and Electric Company. Died from a heart attack while golfing at Balboa Park. Buried Fort Rosecrans National Cemetery, Point Loma CA.

George Craig—1 Year Pitcher (b. 15 Nov 1887 Philadelphia PA–d. 23 Apr 1911 Indianapolis IN) Killed by a burglar, at the height of his baseball career, in his room at the Mineral Springs resort. Buried Fernwood Cemetery, Fernwood PA.

Bill Cramer—1 Year Pitcher (b. 21 May 1891 Bedford IN–d. 11 Sep 1966 St Joseph Hospital, Fort Wayne IN) Buried Greenlawn Memorial Park, Fort Wayne IN.

Dick Cramer—1 Year Outfielder (b. Brooklyn NY–d. 12 Aug 1885 Camden NJ).

Doc Cramer—20 Years Outfielder (b. 22 Jul 1905 Beach Haven NJ–d. 9 Sep 1990 at his home in Manahawkin NJ) He coached baseball for a short while, then worked as a carpenter. Buried Greenwood Cemetery, Cedar Run NJ.

Doc Crandall—10 Years Pitcher (b. 8 Oct 1887 Wadena IN–d. 17 Aug 1951 Mission Hospital, Bell CA) He pitched 13 years for the Los Angeles Angels in the Pacific Coast League, winning 224 games while losing only 147 with an ERA of 2.92. In recent years he had been paralyzed by a series of strokes. Buried Inglewood Park Cemetery, Inglewood CA.

Cannonball Crane—9 Years Pitcher (b. May 1862 Boston MA–d. 19 Sep 1896 at a boarding house in Rochester NY) Taking his own life by drinking a bottle of chloral, his death was ruled accidental. He had been despondent and drinking heavily, and had been told he had to move due to arrearages in his rent. Buried Holyhood Cemetery, Brookline MA.

Sam Crane—7 Years Infielder (b. 13 Sep 1894 Harrisburg PA–d. 12 Nov 1955 Presbyterian Hospital, Philadelphia PA) He served 13 years in prison for the 2nd degree murder of his sweetheart, Della Lyter, and her escort at a Harrisburg saloon in 1929. Paroled in 1944, he died after a long illness.

Sam Crane—7 Years Infielder 2 Years Manager (b. 2 Jan 1854 Springfield MA–d. 26 Jun 1925 at his home in New York City NY) After his baseball career he was a sportswriter, his last 25 years spent with the *New York Evening Journal.* In his day he was known as the "dean of baseball writers." Died from pneumonia. Buried Lutheran Cemetery, Middle Village NY.

Gavvy Cravath—11 Years Outfielder 2 Years Manager (b. 23 Mar 1881 Escondido CA–d. 23 May 1963 at his home in Laguna Beach CA) He served 36 years as Justice of the Peace at Laguna Beach. He was the last judge to serve in Orange County, CA, who was not a member of the bar, and the county's last JP. Died in his sleep from heart failure. Buried Melrose Abbey Cemetery, Orange CA.

Bill Craver—2 Years Infielder 3 Years Manager (b. 13 Jun 1844 Troy NY–d. 17 Jun 1901 at his home in Troy NY) Civil War veteran. He was a policeman for the Troy Police Department from 1893 until his death. Died from heart trouble after being ill some time.

Forrest Crawford—2 Years Infielder (b. 10 May 1881 Rockdale TX–d. 29 Mar 1908 at his home in Austin TX) Died from an injury on his side at the height of his baseball career. Buried Oakwood Cemetery, Austin TX.

Glenn Crawford—2 Years Outfielder (b. 2 Dec 1913 North Branch MI–d. 2 Jan 1972 General Hospital, Saginaw MI) He lived in North Branch his entire life except from 1938 to 1952 when he played organized baseball. Buried Greenwood Cemetery, North Branch MI.

Ken Crawford—1 Year Infielder (b. 31 Oct 1894 South Bend IN–d. 11 Nov 1976 Pittsburgh PA).

Larry Crawford—1 Year Pitcher (b. 27 Apr 1914 Swissvale PA–d. 20 Dec 1994 Hanover PA).

Pat Crawford—4 Years Infielder (b. 28 Jan 1902 Society Hill SC–d. 25 Jan 1994 Morehead City NC).

Sam Crawford—19 Years Outfielder Hall of Fame (b. 18 Apr 1880 Wahoo NE–d. 15 Jun 1968 Hollywood Community Hosp, Los Angeles CA) He was known as "Wahoo Sam". Died from a heart attack. Buried Inglewood Park Cemetery, Inglewood CA.

George Creamer—7 Years Infielder 1 Year Manager (b. 1855 Philadelphia PA–d. 27 Jun 1886 Philadelphia PA).

Birdie Cree—8 Years Outfielder (b. 22 Oct 1882 Khedive PA–d. 8 Nov 1942 Packer Hospital, Sunbury PA) He worked for the First National Bank in Sunbury from 1919 until his death, the last 11 years as cashier. Died after a ten-week illness centering around his stomach and abdomen. Buried Pomfret Manor Cemetery, Sunbury PA.

Connie Creeden—5 Games Pinch Hitter (b. 21 Jul 1915 Danvers MA–d. 30 Nov 1969 Community Hospital, Santa Ana CA) For 30 years he was a self-employed musician. Died from a heart attack. Buried Good Shepherd Cemetery, Huntington Beach CA.

Pat Creeden—1 Year Outfielder (b. 23 May 1906 Newburyport MA–d. 20 Apr 1992 Cushing General Hospital, Brockton MA) Served in the U.S. Navy during World War II. Active in sports his entire life, he coached college, high school and semi-pro football and baseball teams. He later worked for the Massachusetts State Department of Youth Services, retiring in 1972. Died after a short illness. Buried Calvary Cemetery, Brockton MA.

Marty Creegan—1 Year Outfielder (b. County Limerick, Ireland–d. 14 Mar 1941 San Francisco

CA) Buried Holy Cross Catholic Cemetery, Colma CA.

Gus Creely—1 Year Infielder (b. 6 Jun 1870 Florissant MO–d. 22 Apr 1934 St Louis MO) Buried Calvary Cemetery, St Louis MO.

Pete Cregan—2 Years Outfielder (b. 13 Apr 1875 Kingston NY–d. 18 May 1945 New York City NY) Buried Calvary Cemetery, Woodside NY.

Creepy Crespi—5 Years Infielder (b. 16 Feb 1918 St Louis MO–d. 1 Mar 1990 Florissant MO) Buried Calvary Cemetery, St Louis MO.

Walker Cress—2 Years Pitcher (b. 6 Mar 1917 Ben Hur VA–d. 21 Apr 1996 Baton Rouge LA).

Tim Crews—6 Years Pitcher (b. 3 Apr 1961 Tampa FL–d. 23 Mar 1993 Regional Medical Center, Orlando FL) Died at the height of his career from head and lung injuries suffered the day before in a boating accident on Little Lake Nellie. Buried Woodlawn Cemetery, Orlando FL.

Lou Criger—16 Years Catcher (b. 6 Feb 1872 Elkhart IN–d. 14 May 1934 at his home in Tucson AZ) He lived in Tucson the last ten years of his life. Buried Evergreen Cemetery, Tucson AZ.

Pat Crisham—1 Year Infielder (b. 4 Jun 1877 Amesbury MA–d. 12 Jun 1915 Syracuse NY).

Joe Crisp—2 Years Catcher (b. 8 Jul 1889 Higginsville MO–d. 5 Feb 1939 St Mary's Hospital, Kansas City MO) He was the County Recorder for Jackson County, MO. Died from a heart ailment. Buried Forest Hill Cemetery, Kansas City MO.

Dode Criss—4 Years Pitcher (b. 12 Mar 1885 Sherman MS–d. 7 Sep 1955 Sanatorium MS) He was a retired standard tower builder. Died following an illness of a year. Buried Sherman Cemetery, Sherman MS.

Ches Crist—1 Year Catcher (b. 10 Feb 1882 Cozaddale OH–d. 7 Jan 1957 at his home in Milford OH) He lived in Milford 30 years, farming and working as a carpenter up until his death. Died from a heart attack. Buried Greenlawn Cemetery, Milford OH.

Bill Cristall—1 Year Pitcher (b. 12 Sep 1878 Odessa, Russia–d. 28 Jan 1939 Buffalo NY) He pitched 27 years in the minor leagues with stints in the Pacific Coast League, American Association, International League and Southern League. Later he was a minor league umpire.

Leo Cristante—2 Years Pitcher (b. 10 Dec 1926 Detroit MI–d. 24 Aug 1977 Oakwood Hospital, Dearborn MI) He was a quality inspector for Ford Motor Company. Buried Our Lady of Hope Cemetery, Wyandotte MI.

Morrie Critchley—1 Year Pitcher (b. 26 Mar 1850 New London CT–d. 6 Mar 1910 at his home in Pittsburgh PA) He went into the saloon and hotel business in Pittsburgh. Died from heart disease.

Hughie Critz—12 Years Infielder (b. 17 Sep 1900 Starkville MS–d. 10 Jan 1980 Greenwood MS) He was the owner and president of Hugh Critz Motor Company of Greenwood. Buried Odd Fellows Cemetery, Greenwood MS.

Davey Crockett—1 Year Infielder (b. 15 Oct 1876 Roanoke VA–d. 23 Feb 1961 Martha Jefferson Hosp, Charlottesville VA) Buried Memorial Cemetery.

Art Croft—2 Years Infielder (b. 23 Jan 1855 St Louis MO–d. 16 Mar 1884 St Louis MO) Buried Calvary Cemetery, St Louis MO.

Henry Croft—2 Years Outfielder (b. 1 Aug 1875 Chicago IL–d. 11 Dec 1933 Oak Park IL) Buried Mount Carmel Cemetery, Hillside IL.

Fred Croluis—2 Years Outfielder (b. 16 Dec 1876 Jersey City NJ–d. 25 Aug 1960 in a nursing home in Ormond Beach FL) He was a consulting engineer in Pittsburgh PA before retiring to Florida in 1956. Cremated.

Herb Crompton—2 Years Catcher (b. 7 Nov 1911 Taylor Ridge IL–d. 5 Aug 1963 Public Hospital, Moline IL) He worked in baseball 20 years as a player, scout and minor league manager. In 1953 he went to work in the mixed-car warehouse for John Deere and Company. Died after being in ill health 18 months. Buried Memorial Park Cemetery, Rock Island IL.

Ned Crompton—2 Years Outfielder (b. 12 Feb 1889 Liverpool, England–d. 28 Sep 1950 Aspinwall PA).

Bill Cronin—4 Years Catcher (b. 26 Dec 1902 West Newton MA–d. 26 Oct 1966 Newton-Wellesley Hospital, Newton MA) He worked for the Star Market in Newton. Died after a long illness. Buried Newton Cemetery, Newton MA.

Dan Cronin—1 Year Outfielder (b. 1857 Boston MA–d. 30 Nov 1885 Boston MA) Buried Mount Calvary Cemetery, Roslindale MA.

Jim Cronin —1 Year Infielder (b. 7 Aug 1905 Richmond CA–d. 10 Jun 1983 Concord CA) Buried St Joseph Cemetery, San Pablo CA.

Joe Cronin —20 Years Infielder 15 Years Manager Hall of Fame (b. 12 Oct 1906 San Francisco CA–d. 7 Sep 1984 at his home in Osterville MA) He spent his entire life in baseball as a player, manager and executive and was president of the American League from 1959 to 1973. Buried St Francis Xavier Cemetery, Barnstable MA.

John Cronin —7 Years Pitcher (b. 26 May 1874 Staten Island NY–d. 13 Jul 1929 Middletown NY) Died after suffering a stroke while working in his garden. Buried Valhalla Burial Park, Staten Island NY.

Jack Crooks —8 Years Infielder (b. 9 Nov 1865 St Paul MN–d. 2 Feb 1918 Insane Asylum, St Louis MO) He once hit four homeruns and a single for 17 total bases in an American Association game. He was a salesman until he became afflicted with elephantiasis. He died from the disease and weighed over 300 pounds when he died. Buried St Louis MO.

Tom Crooks —2 Years Infielder (b. Washington DC–d. 5 Apr 1929 Quantico Hospital, Quantico VA) He managed a minor league team in 1916, and umpired minor league baseball from 1917 until his death. Died from injuries received when the bus carrying him and the Cornell University baseball team crashed while enroute from Quantico to Washington DC. Buried Mount Olivet Cemetery, Washington DC.

George Crosby —1 Year Pitcher (b. 1860 Chicago IL–d. 9 Jan 1913 St Mary's Hospital, San Francisco CA) He was a teamster. Died from cancer of the pylorus. Buried Cypress Lawn Memorial Park, Colma CA.

Frankie Crosetti —17 Years Infielder (b. 4 Oct 1910 San Francisco CA–d. 11 Feb 2002 Stockton CA) He was the Yankees' third base coach for 20 years. Died of complications from a fall suffered a month earlier.

Powel Crosley, Jr —(b. 18 Sep 1887 Cincinnati OH–d. 28 Mar 1961 at his home in Cincinnati OH) He was a manufacturer of refrigerators, radios and even a small car — the Crosley. He also owned a radio station, and from 1934 to 1961 he owned the Reds. Died from a heart attack. Buried Spring Grove Cemetery, Cincinnati OH.

Amos Cross —3 Years Catcher (b. abt 1863 Czechoslovakia–d. 17 Jul 1888 at his home in Cleveland OH) Died at the height of his career from consumption. Buried Riverside Cemetery, Cleveland OH.

Clarence Cross —2 Years Infielder (b. 4 Mar 1856 St Louis MO–d. 23 Jun 1931 Harborview Hospital, Seattle WA) Cremated.

Frank Cross —1 Year Outfielder (b. 29 Jan 1873 Cleveland OH–d. 2 Nov 1932 at his home in Geauga Lake OH) Died from leukemia. Buried Riverside Cemetery, Cleveland OH.

Jeff Cross —4 Years Infielder (b. 28 Aug 1918 Tulsa OK–d. 23 Jul 1997 Huntsville TX) He worked 40 years in the insurance business at Houston TX, retiring in 1988. Buried Memorial Oaks Cemetery, Houston TX.

Lave Cross —21 Years Infielder 1 Year Manager (b. 12 May 1866 Milwaukee WI–d. 6 Sep 1927 Toledo OH) He was a machinist for Willy's Overland. Died from heart disease on his way to work. Buried Woodlawn Cemetery, Toledo OH.

Lew Cross —2 Years Pitcher (b. 9 Jan 1872 Sanbornton NH–d. 9 Oct 1930 Manchester NH) He was a master mechanic at F M Hoyt Shoe Company at Manchester. Died suddenly from natural causes. Buried Pine Grove Cemetery, Manchester NH.

Monte Cross —15 Years Infielder (b. 31 Aug 1869 Philadelphia PA–d. 21 Jun 1934 at his home in Philadelphia PA) He managed minor league baseball for a while before becoming a clothing salesman at the Gimble Brother's store in Philadelphia. He also umpired college and local games and was an accomplished bowler. Died suddenly from a heart attack. Buried Arlington Cemetery, Drexel Hill PA.

Frank Crossin —3 Years Catcher (b. 15 Jun 1891 Avondale PA–d. 6 Dec 1965 Nesbitt Memorial Hospital, Kingston PA) Served overseas for the U.S. Army during World War I. He operated a business in Swoyersville PA, retiring several years earlier. Died after being hospitalized five days. Buried St Mary's Cemetery, Wilkes-Barre PA.

Doug Crothers —2 Years Pitcher (b. 16 Nov 1859 Natchez MS–d. 29 Mar 1907 St Louis MO) He played in the Southern Association and the Texas League and was involved in political work in the St Louis area. Died from tuberculosis. Buried Bellefontaine Cemetery, St Louis MO.

Joe Crotty—4 Years Catcher (b. 24 Dec 1860 Cincinnati OH–d. 22 Jun 1926 at his home in Minneapolis MN) He was the proprietor of the Crotty Credit Clothing Store in Minneapolis for 30 years. Died from a heart attack. Buried St Mary's Cemetery, Minneapolis MN.

Bill Crouch—1 Year Pitcher (b. 3 Dec 1886 Marshallton DE–d. 22 Dec 1945 at his home in Highland Park MI) He worked for the Cadillac Division of General Motors.

Bill Crouch—3 Years Pitcher (b. 20 Aug 1910 Wilmington DE–d. 26 Dec 1980 Howell MI) He was baseball coach at Eastern Michigan University. Buried Lakeview Cemetery, Howell MI.

Jack Crouch—3 Years Catcher (b. 20 Feb 1906 Salisbury NC–d. 25 Aug 1972 Leesburg FL) He was a retired manufacturing agent for a lumber products company.

Frank Croucher—4 Years Infielder (b. 23 Jul 1914 San Antonio TX–d. 21 May 1980 Houston TX) He was a lifelong resident of Houston. Buried Forest Park of Lawndale, Houston TX.

Buck Crouse—8 Years Catcher (b. 6 Jan 1897 Anderson IN–d. 23 Oct 1983 Ball Hospital, Muncie IN) He worked at Hemingray Glass Company and Acme-Lees Division of Serrick Company in Muncie. Died following a brief illness. Buried Elm Ridge Memorial Park, Muncie IN.

General Crowder—11 Years Pitcher (b. 11 Jan 1899 Winston-Salem NC–d. 3 Apr 1972 Forsyth Memorial Hospital, Winston-Salem NC) World War I veteran. He owned the Winston-Salem minor league team in the late 1930s and early 1940s. Buried Forsyth Memorial Park, Winston-Salem NC.

Billy Crowell—2 Years Pitcher (b. 6 Nov 1865 Cincinnati OH–d. 23 Jul 1935 at a hospital in Fort Worth TX) He operated an army surplus store in Fort Worth, retiring in 1925. Died from the effects of a surgery performed three months earlier.

Cap Crowell—2 Years Pitcher (b. 5 Sep 1892 Roxbury MA–d. 30 Sep 1962 at his home in Central Falls RI) He worked 40 years for E L Freeman Company, a printing firm, and was vice-president and secretary when he died. Active in civic and fraternal organizations. Buried Swan Point Cemetery, Providence RI.

Bill Crowley—7 Years Outfielder (b. 8 Apr 1857 Philadelphia PA–d. 14 Jul 1891 Gloucester City NJ) Buried St Mary's Cemetery, Philadelphia PA.

Ed Crowley—1 Year Infielder (b. 6 Aug 1906 Watkinsville GA–d. 14 Apr 1970 Birmingham AL) Widely known in the petroleum industry, he was a sales representative for Texaco. Died from a heart attack. Buried Westview Cemetery, Atlanta GA.

John Crowley—1 Year Catcher (b. 12 Jan 1862 Lawrence MA–d. 23 Sep 1896 at his home in Lawrence MA) Died from tuberculosis. Buried St Mary's Cemetery, Lawrence MA.

Woody Crowson—1 Year Pitcher (b. 9 Sep 1918 Fuquay Springs NC–d. 14 Aug 1947 Mayodan NC) Died when the team bus he was riding in sideswiped a watermelon truck. He was the only person injured in the bus-truck accident. Buried Springfield Friends Church Cemetery, High Point NC.

Walt Cruise—10 Years Outfielder (b. 6 May 1890 Childersburg AL–d. 9 Jan 1975 Sylacauga AL) World War I veteran. He was a retired superintendent of the Sylacauga Water Department. Died after a long illness. Buried Evergreen Memorial Cemetery, Sylacauga AL.

Cal Crum—2 Years Pitcher (b. 27 Jul 1892 Mattoon IL–d. 7 Dec 1945 at a hospital in Tulsa OK) He sold jewelry and cars before going to work for Tulsa County, OK, as deputy court clerk in 1930. Elected as court clerk in 1936, he held that job until his death. Died suddenly from a lung hemorrhage after a week's illness. Buried Memorial Park, Tulsa OK.

Buddy Crump—1 Year Outfielder (b. 29 Nov 1901 Norfolk VA–d. 7 Sep 1976 Raleigh NC).

Roy Crumpler—2 Years Pitcher (b. 8 Jul 1896 Clinton NC–d. 6 Oct 1969 V A Hospital, Fayetteville NC) Buried Crumpler Family Cemetery, Bearskin NC.

Dick Crutcher—2 Years Pitcher (b. 25 Nov 1889 Frankfort KY–d. 19 Jun 1952 at his home in Frankfort KY) He managed a motor company in Kenosha WI before he went to work for the Kentucky Highway Department. His death was believed to have been from a heart attack. Buried Frankfort Cemetery, Frankfort KY.

Press Cruthers—2 Years Infielder (b. 8 Sep 1890 Marshallton DE–d. 27 Dec 1976 Brookside

Care Center, Kenosha WI) He was a pattern maker at Simmons Company and for 28 years the Town Clerk of Pleasant Prairie WI. Died after a long illness. Buried Sunset Ridge Memorial Park, Kenosha WI.

Tony Cuccinello —15 Years Infielder (b. 8 Nov 1907 Long Island City NY–d. 21 Sep 1995 St Joseph Hospital, Tampa FL) He coached for the Reds, Indians and White Sox, retiring to Tampa in 1968. There he became an accomplished senior golfer. Died from congestive heart failure. Buried Garden of Memories, Tampa FL.

Cookie Cuccurullo —3 Years Pitcher (b. 8 Feb 1918 Asbury Park NJ–d. 23 Jan 1983 at his home in West Orange NJ) He owned Art Cuccurullo and Sons Landscapers in West Orange for 25 years, retiring in 1972. He was also a standout amateur golfer. Buried Rosedale Cemetery, Orange NJ.

Jim Cudworth—1 Year Infielder (b. 22 Aug 1858 Fairhaven MA–d. 21 Dec 1943 at his home in Lakeville MA) Buried Clark Cemetery, Lakeville MA.

Charlie Cuellar —1 Year Pitcher (b. 23 Aug 1917 Ybor City FL–d. 11 Oct 1994 Tampa FL) He was a self-employed builder and master craftsman. Buried Centro Asturiano Cemetery, Tampa FL.

Manuel Cueto —4 Years Outfielder (b. 8 Feb 1892 Havana, Cuba–d. 29 Jun 1942 Havana, Cuba).

Leon Culberson —6 Years Outfielder (b. 6 Aug 1918 Hall's Station GA–d. 17 Sep 1989 at a hospital in Rome GA) For 32 years he worked for General Electric Company in Rome, retiring in 1983. He officiated 12 years of high school basketball and football in northeast Georgia and was a prominent amateur golfer. Buried Oaknoll Memorial Gardens, Rome GA.

John Cullen —1 Year Outfielder (b. 2 Feb 1870 New York City NY–d. 19 Apr 1941 St Mary's Hospital, San Francisco CA) He was a boilermaker. Died from a heart attack. Buried Holy Cross Catholic Cemetery, Colma CA.

Roy Cullenbine —10 Years Outfielder (b. 18 Oct 1913 Nashville TN–d. 28 May 1991 Mount Clemens MI) Died from a lingering heart ailment. Buried Christian Memorial Cultural Cemetery, Rochester MI.

Dick Culler —8 Years Infielder (b. 25 Jan 1915 High Point NC–d. 16 Jun 1964 North Carolina Mem Hosp, Chapel Hill NC) He operated Autographed Ball, Inc. and Coin Banks, Inc. in High Point and was director of the nonprofit Downtown Development Corporation. Died after being in declining health 15 months. Buried Floral Garden Park Cemetery, High Point NC.

Nick Cullop —5 Years Outfielder (b. 16 Oct 1900 St Louis MO–d. 8 Dec 1978 Westerville OH) He played minor league baseball from 1920 until 1944, compiling a lifetime .312 minor league batting average. He then managed minor league baseball for several years in the 1940s and 1950s. Buried Mifflin Cemetery, Mifflin OH.

Nick Cullop —6 Years Pitcher (b. 17 Sep 1887 Chilhowie VA–d. 15 Apr 1961 Tazewell VA).

Bud Culloton —2 Years Pitcher (b. 19 May 1896 Kingston NY–d. 9 Nov 1976 Kingston NY) Served in the U.S. Army during both World Wars I and II. An attorney, he maintained a private practice until his death. He was a Kingston City Judge and chairman of the county Democratic Party. In a legal capacity he represented the New York Motor Vehicle Department and the New York State Department of Taxation and Finance, as well as other state offices. Died suddenly. Buried St Mary's Cemetery, Kingston NY.

Bill Culp —1 Year Pitcher (b. 11 Jun 1887 Bellaire OH–d. 3 Sep 1969 Arnold PA) He was a glass cutter for American Window Glass Company in Arnold. Buried Plum Creek Cemetery, New Kensington PA.

Candy Cummings —2 Years Pitcher Hall of Fame (b. 13 Oct 1848 Ware MA–d. 16 May 1924 at his son's home in Toledo OH) It is claimed that he threw the first curve ball. Died from exhaustion and senile dementia. Buried Aspen Grove Cemetery, Ware MA.

Jack Cummings —4 Years Catcher (b. 1 Apr 1904 Pittsburgh PA–d. 5 Oct 1962 Pittsburgh PA) He was a salesman. Died from cancer. Buried North Side Catholic Cemetery, Pittsburgh PA.

Bert Cunningham —12 Years Pitcher (b. 25 Nov 1866 Wilmington DE–d. 14 May 1952 at his home in Cragmere DE) He umpired for a short time before he was a salesman in the typewriter division of Remington-Rand Company for 38 years, retiring in 1944. Died after a two-month illness. Buried Lawn Croft Cemetery, Linwood PA.

Bill Cunningham—4 Years Outfielder (b. 30 Jul 1895 San Francisco CA–d. 26 Sep 1953 Colusa CA) He coached baseball at the University of San Francisco. Died from a heart attack shortly after the exertion and excitement of catching a 28 pound salmon in the Sacramento River. Buried Holy Cross Catholic Cemetery, Colma CA.

Bill Cunningham—3 Years Infielder (b. 9 Jun 1888 Schenectady NY–d. 21 Feb 1946 Schenectady NY) He worked for General Electric at Schenectady. Died suddenly. Buried St John's Cemetery, Schenectady NY.

Bruce Cunningham—4 Years Pitcher (b. 29 Sep 1905 San Francisco CA–d. 8 Mar 1984 at his home in Hayward CA) For 20 years he was a police inspector for the Oakland CA Police Department. Retired, he died from lung cancer. Cremated.

George Cunningham—5 Years Pitcher (b. 14 Jul 1894 Sturgeon Lake MN–d. 10 Mar 1972 at his home in Chattanooga TN) He pitched for the Chattanooga Lookouts in the Southern League. Buried Chattanooga Memorial Park, Chattanooga TN.

Mike Cunningham—1 Year Pitcher (b. 14 Jun 1882 Lancaster SC–d. 10 Dec 1969 at a hospital in Lancaster SC) Buried Bethlehem Baptist Church Cemetery, Lancaster SC.

Nig Cuppy—10 Years Pitcher (b. 4 Jul 1868 Eaton OH–d. 27 Jul 1922 at his home near Elkhart IN) He engaged in retail tobacco and billiard business in Elkhart for 20 years. Died from pneumonia, but was seriously ill with Bright's disease. Buried Rice Cemetery, Elkhart IN.

Doc Curley—1 Year Infielder (b. 12 Mar 1874 Upton MA–d. 23 Sep 1920 Belmont Hospital, Worcester MA) He practiced medicine ten years at Framingham MA. Died following a three-year illness. Buried St Mary's Catholic Cemetery, Milford MA.

Sam Curran—1 Year Pitcher (b. 30 Oct 1874 Dorchester MA–d. 19 May 1936 Dorchester MA) A physician for 35 years, he served in the Medical Corps during World War I. Died after being in ill health since Jan 1935 when he fell on an icy sidewalk. Buried Holy Cross Cemetery, Malden MA.

Clarence Currie—2 Years Pitcher (b. 30 Dec 1878 Glencoe, Ontario, Canada–d. 15 Jul 1941 Little Chute WI).

Murphy Currie—1 Year Pitcher (b. 31 Aug 1893 Fayetteville NC–d. 22 Jun 1939 Asheboro NC).

George Curry—1 Year Pitcher (b. 21 Dec 1888 Bridgeport CT–d. 5 Oct 1963 Veteran's Hospital, West Haven CT) World War I veteran. He retired from Carpenter Steel Company. Buried Lakeview Cemetery, Bridgeport CT.

Jim Curry—3 Years Infielder (b. 10 Mar 1893 Camden NJ–d. 2 Aug 1938 Camden County General Hospital, Grenloch NJ) He was a policeman. Died from a cerebral embolism. Buried Lakeview Memorial Park, Cinnaminson NJ.

Wes Curry—1 Year Pitcher (b. 1 Apr 1860 Wilmington DE–d. 19 May 1933 Philadelphia PA) Buried Arlington Cemetery, Drexel Hill PA.

Cliff Curtis—5 Years Pitcher (b. 3 Jul 1881 Delaware OH–d. 23 Apr 1943 at his home in Utica OH) He was a Ford dealer in Utica for 20 years. Died from a heart attack. Buried Oak Grove Cemetery, Delaware OH.

Fred Curtis—1 Year Infielder (b. 30 Oct 1880 Beaver Lake MI–d. 5 Apr 1939 Minneapolis MN) Buried Sunset Memorial Park, Minneapolis MN.

Gene Curtis—1 Year Outfielder (b. 5 May 1883 Bethany WV–d. 1 Jan 1919 Follansbee WV) He was the chief of the mill police at the Follansbee Brother's plant in Follansbee. Died from pneumonia superinduced by influenza. Buried Brooke Cemetery, Wellsburg WV.

Harry Curtis—1 Year Catcher (b. 19 Feb 1883 Portland ME–d. 1 Aug 1951 St Francis Hospital, Evanston IL) He was an All-American football player at Syracuse University before embarking on a baseball career. Later he worked for John Sexton and Company, a wholesale grocery firm. Buried Calvary Cemetery, Evanston IL.

Vern Curtis—3 Years Pitcher (b. 24 May 1920 Cairo IL–d. 24 Jun 1992 Cairo IL).

Jim Curtiss—1 Year Outfielder (b. 27 Dec 1861 Coldwater MI–d. 14 Feb 1945 North Adams MA) He went into the poolroom and bowling business in Savannah GA and later in Connecticut before managing the Casino Lanes in North Adams for several years. He later opened a poolroom there. Died after three weeks of illness. Buried Hillside Cemetery, North Adams MA.

Guy Curtright—4 Years Outfielder (b. 18 Oct 1912 Holliday MO–d. 23 Aug 1997 Sun City Center FL) He was a high school athletic director in Denver CO, retiring to Tampa FL in 1983. Cremated.

Charlie Cushman—1 Year Manager (b. 25 May 1850 New York City NY–d. 29 Jun 1909 at a hospital in Milwaukee WI) He worked in baseball most of his life. When he died he had been ailing for some time. Buried Calvary Catholic Cemetery, Milwaukee WI.

Ed Cushman—6 Years Pitcher (b. 27 Mar 1852 Eaglesville OH–d. 26 Sep 1915 at his home in Erie PA) He was a conductor for the New York Central Railroad before owning a restaurant in Erie. Died after an illness of more than four months. Buried Erie Cemetery, Erie PA.

Harv Cushman—1 Year Pitcher (b. 10 Jul 1877 Rockland ME–d. 27 Dec 1920 Emsworth PA).

Jack Cusick—2 Years Infielder (b. 12 Jun 1928 Weehawken NJ–d. 17 Nov 1989 Edgewood NJ) He was a lieutenant with the New Jersey State Police where he worked 26 years. Buried George Washington Memorial Park, Paramus NJ.

Tony Cusick—4 Years Catcher (b. 1867 Limerick, Ireland–d. 6 Aug 1929 Chicago IL) Buried Mount Olivet Cemetery, Chicago IL.

Ned Cuthbert—5 Years Outfielder 1 Year Manager (b. 20 Jun 1845 Philadelphia PA–d. 6 Feb 1905 St Louis MO) He was superintendent of the original Sportsman's Park before he opened a saloon in St Louis, which he operated until he became ill. Died from the effects of a stroke suffered some months earlier. Buried Bellefontaine Cemetery, St Louis MO.

George Cutshaw—12 Years Infielder (b. 29 Jul 1886 Wilmington IL–d. 22 Aug 1973 Point Loma Conv Hospital, Point Loma CA) An Imperial Valley rancher, he also owned and operated a Texaco service station in Brawley CA for years. Died from heart disease. Cremated.

Kiki Cuyler—18 Years Outfielder Hall of Fame (b. 30 Aug 1899 Harrisville MI–d. 11 Feb 1950 Ann Arbor MI) He managed minor league baseball and was a coach for the Red Sox when he died from a heart attack. He was dead-on-arrival at University Hospital. Buried St Ann's Cemetery, Harrisville MI.

Mike Cvengros—6 Years Pitcher (b. 1 Dec 1900 Pana IL–d. 2 Aug 1970 at a hospital in Hot Springs AR) He lived in Hot Springs the last three years of his life. Buried Calvary Cemetery, Hot Springs AR.

Al Cypert—1 Year Infielder (b. 7 Aug 1889 Little Rock AR–d. 9 Jan 1973 Washington DC) Served in the U.S. Army during World War I. Buried National Memorial Park, Falls Church VA.

D

Pete Dagila—1 Year Pitcher (b. 28 Feb 1907 Napa CA–d. 11 Mar 1952 Howard Memorial Hospital, Willits CA) He was a liquor salesman. Buried Tulocay Cemetery, Napa CA.

Jay Dahl—1 Year Pitcher (b. 6 Dec 1945 San Bernardino CA–d. 20 Jun 1965 Salisbury NC) Killed instantly, near the beginning of his career, when the car in which he was riding failed to negoiate a curve and crashed into a tree. Buried Montecito Memorial Park, Colton CA.

Bill Dahlen—21 Years Infielder 4 Years Manager (b. 5 Jan 1870 White Plains NY–d. 5 Dec 1950 Kings' County Hospital, Brooklyn NY) He was a scout for many years. Died after a long illness. Buried Evergreen Cemetery, Brooklyn NY.

Babe Dahlgren—12 Years Infielder (b. 15 Jun 1912 San Francisco CA–d. 4 Sep 1996 at his home in Arcadia CA) He is best known as the man who took Lou Gehrig's place at the end of Gehrig's consecutive game stint. Died from a heart attack, but suffered from prostate cancer. Buried Forest Lawn Memorial Park, Glendale CA.

Sam Dailey—1 Year Pitcher (b. 31 Mar 1904 Oakford IL–d. 2 Dec 1979 Columbia SC).

Con Daily—13 Years Catcher (b. 11 Sep 1864 Blackstone MA–d. 14 Jun 1928 Kings' County

Hospital, Brooklyn NY) He had his baseball career terminated when he fractured his spinal cord while saving a drowning child on the beach at Coney Island.

Ed Daily—7 Years Outfielder (b. 7 Sep 1862 Providence RI–d. 21 Oct 1891 Washington DC) He managed a saloon in Washington DC. Died from quick consumption.

Vince Daily—1 Year Outfielder (b. 25 Dec 1864 Osceola PA–d. 14 Nov 1919 St James Mercy Hospital, Hornell NY) For 14 years he was a patrolman for the Hornell Police Department before becoming a watchman at the Huguet Silk Company plant in Hornell. At the time of his death he was working for the Erie Railway when he fell from the top of the Erie roundhouse. He died two days later. Buried Rural Cemetery, Hornell NY.

Gene Dale—4 Years Pitcher (b. 16 Jun 1889 St Louis MO–d. 20 Mar 1958 St Louis MO) He was a plater for Steel Products Company.

Bill Daley—3 Years Pitcher (b. 27 Jun 1868 Poughkeepsie NY–d. 4 May 1922 Poughkeepsie NY) He worked at the rolling mill and at the opera house in Poughkeepsie. Found dead in his home where he had died several days earlier from heart disease.

John Daley—1 Year Infielder (b. 25 May 1887 Pittsburgh PA–d. 31 Aug 1988 Woodlawn Nursing Home, Mansfield OH) He worked 43 years for Mansfield Tire and Rubber Company, retiring in 1958. Before he died, at age 101, he was the oldest living former major league player. Buried Mansfield Catholic Cemetery, Mansfield OH.

Jud Daley—2 Years Outfielder (b. 14 Mar 1884 South Coventry CT–d. 26 Jan 1967 East Gadsden AL).

Tom Daley—4 Years Outfielder (b. 13 Nov 1885 DuBois PA–d. 2 Dec 1934 Los Angeles CA) He was an insurance agent. Died from heart disease. Buried Calvary Cemetery, Los Angeles CA.

Dom Dallessandro—8 Years Outfielder (b. 3 Oct 1913 Reading PA–d. 29 Apr 1988 at his home in Indianapolis IN) World War II veteran. He played several years in the Pacific Coast League and the American Association. Buried St Joseph Cemetery, Indianapolis IN.

Abner Dalrymple—12 Years Outfielder (b. 19 Sep 1857 Gratiot WI–d. 25 Jan 1939 Warren IL) He was a brakeman, and later a conductor, for the Northern Pacific Railroad, retiring in 1928. Died after a short illness, although he had been in failing health for some time. Buried Elmwood Cemetery, Warren IL.

Bill Dalrymple—1 Year Infielder (b. 7 Feb 1891 Baltimore MD–d. 14 Jul 1967 Sharp Memorial Hospital, San Diego CA) For 33 years he was sales manager for Eastman Mfg Co, a manufacturer of pressure hoses and couplings. Died from Addison's disease. Buried Greenwood Memorial Park, San Diego CA.

Bert Daly—1 Year Infielder (b. 8 Apr 1881 Bayonne NJ–d. 3 Sep 1952 Bayonne NJ) He had been a political power in Bayonne since 1910 when he was elected to the city council. He resigned as mayor in 1947. Buried Holy Name Cemetery, Jersey City NJ.

George Daly—1 Year Pitcher (b. 28 Jul 1887 Buffalo NY–d. 12 Dec 1957 Our Lady of Victory Hosp, Lackawanna NY) Served in the U.S. Navy during World War I. He was a physical education director for the Buffalo City Division of Recreation from 1912 until his death. Died after experiencing ill health for two years.

Joe Daly—3 Years Outfielder (b. 21 Sep 1868 Philadelphia PA–d. 21 Mar 1943 Philadelphia PA) Buried Holy Sepulchre Cemetery, Philadelphia PA.

Sun Daly—1 Year Outfielder (b. 6 Jan 1865 Port Henry NY–d. 30 Apr 1938 at his home in Albany NY) He was a clerk in the state engineer's office before spending several years as a watchman for the Gibson Snow Company, retiring in 1930. Died from a cerebral hemorrhage.

Tom Daly—8 Years Catcher (b. 12 Dec 1891 St John, New Brunswick, Canada–d. 7 Nov 1946 at his home in Medford MA) He managed minor league baseball and was a coach for the Red Sox from 1932 to 1945, leaving his coaching job because of the long illness he died from. Buried Oak Grove Cemetery, Medford MA.

Tom Daly—16 Years Infielder (b. 7 Feb 1866 Philadelphia PA–d. 29 Oct 1938 at his home in Brooklyn NY) He coached for the Yankees. Died after a protracted illness.

Bill Dam—1 Year Outfielder (b. 4 Apr 1885 Cambridge MA–d. 22 Jun 1930 Quincy City Hospital, Quincy MA) Buried Mount Wollaston Cemetery, Quincy MA.

Bill Damman —3 Years Pitcher (b. 9 Aug 1872 Chicago IL–d. 6 Dec 1948 at his home in Lynnhaven VA) Buried Eastern Shore Chapel Cemetery, Virginia Beach VA.

Harry Damrau —1 Year Infielder (b. 11 Sep 1890 Newburgh NY–d. 21 Aug 1957 Staten Island NY).

Ray Dandridge —16 Years Infielder Hall of Fame (b. 31 Aug 1913 Richmond VA–d. 12 Feb 1994 Palm Bay FL) He played in the negro leagues, and was considered by many to be the finest third baseman to play the game. Died from prostate cancer. Buried Fountainhead Memorial Park, Palm Bay FL.

Lee Daney —1 Year Pitcher (b. 9 Jul 1905 Talihina OK–d. 11 Mar 1988 Phoenix AZ) Buried Green Acres Cemetery, Scottsdale AZ.

Dave Danforth —10 Years Pitcher (b. 7 Mar 1890 Granger TX–d. 19 Sep 1970 Shangri-La Nursing Home, Baltimore MD) He also had an illustrious minor league career in the International League and coached baseball at Loyola College in the 1930s. After that he practiced denistry in Baltimore from 1932 until retiring in 1960. Died after a brief illness. Buried Loudon Park National Cemetery, Baltimore MD.

Dan Daniel —Hall of Fame (b. 1890 Springfield MA–d. 1 Jul 1981 Cypress Community Hosp, Pompano Beach FL) A sportswriter, he was known as the "Dean of American Baseball Writers." Died from cancer. Buried Forest Lawn Memorial Gardens, Pompano Beach FL.

Jake Daniel —1 Year Infielder (b. 22 Apr 1911 Roanoke AL–d. 23 Apr 1996 LaGrange GA).

Bert Daniels —5 Years Outfielder (b. 31 Oct 1882 Danville IL–d. 6 Jun 1958 at his home in Cedar Grove NJ) He coached baseball at Manhattan College nine years. Later he was a building inspector at Cedar Grove. Buried Immaculate Conception Cemetery, Montclair NJ.

Charlie Daniels —1 Year Pitcher (b. 1 Jul 1861 Roxbury MA–d. 9 Feb 1938 at the Home for Aged Men in Boston MA) Buried Mount Hope Cemetery, Boston MA.

Law Daniels —2 Years Catcher (b. 14 Jul 1862 Newton MA–d. 7 Jan 1929 Waltham MA) For many years he was a foreman in the die making department at the J L Thompson Manufacturing Company. Died after a short illness. Buried Calvary Cemetery, Waltham MA.

Pete Daniels —2 Years Pitcher (b. 8 Apr 1864 County Cavan, Ireland–d. 13 Feb 1928 Indianapolis IN) Died suddenly at his brother's home. Buried Holy Cross Cemetery, Indianapolis IN.

Buck Danner —1 Year Infielder (b. 8 Jun 1891 Dedham MA–d. 21 Sep 1949 Pratt Hospital, Boston MA) He worked as a maintenance man at Milton Academy. Buried Brookdale Cemetery, Dedham MA.

Ike Danning —1 Year Catcher (b. 20 Jan 1905 Los Angeles CA–d. 30 Mar 1983 St John's Hospital, Santa Monica CA) He was the head of transportation for Twentieth Century Fox movie studios. Died from lung cancer. Buried Hillside Memorial Park, Los Angeles CA.

Fats Dantonio —2 Years Catcher (b. 31 Dec 1918 New Orleans LA–d. 28 May 1993 New Orleans LA).

Babe Danzig —1 Year Infielder (b. 30 Apr 1887 Binghamton NY–d. 14 Jul 1931 at his home in San Francisco CA) Died from toxic poisoning—the result of an old baseball injury. Cremated.

George Darby —1 Year Pitcher (b. 6 Feb 1869 Kansas City MO–d. 25 Feb 1937 Sutter Hospital, Sacramento CA) A boilermaker, he owned a large boiler and metal company in Los Angeles CA before retiring and moving to Dixon CA. Died from kidney disease. Buried Dixon Cemetery, Dixon CA.

Cliff Daringer —1 Year Infielder (b. 10 Apr 1885 Hayden IN–d. 26 Dec 1971 Mercy Hospital, Sacramento CA) He was a salesman at a Sacramento department store for 26 years. Died from kidney failure. Buried East Lawn Memorial Park, Sacramento CA.

Rolla Daringer —2 Years Infielder (b. 15 Nov 1888 Hayden IN–d. 23 May 1974 Jackson County Memorial Hosp, Seymour IN) Served in the U.S. Army after World War I. Died after a long illness. Buried Hayden Cemetery, Hayden IN.

Dell Darling —6 Years Catcher (b. 21 Dec 1861 Erie PA–d. 20 Nov 1904 at his home in Erie PA) He owned and operated a lucrative restaurant in Erie before working nine years for Scott Coal Company. Died from complications of an old baseball injury after being in poor health for six months. Buried Trinity Cemetery, Erie PA.

Bob Darnell —2 Years Pitcher (b. 6 Nov 1930 Wewoka OK–d. 1 Jan 1995 Fredericksburg TX).

Mike Darr—1 Year Outfielder (b. abt 1977–d. 15 Feb 2002 near Peoria AZ) Killed when the vehicle he was riding in rolled over on an interstate highway.

Jack Darragh—1 Year Infielder (b. 17 Jul 1866 Ebensburg PA–d. 12 Aug 1939 Rochester NY).

George Darrow—1 Year Pitcher (b. 12 Jul 1903 Beloit KS–d. 24 Mar 1983 St Joseph's Hospital, Phoenix AZ) He was a supervisor for Pacific Maritime Association and retired to Sun City AZ in 1969. Buried Sunland Memorial Park, Sun City AZ.

Wally Dashiell—1 Year Infielder (b. 9 May 1901 Jewett TX–d. 20 May 1972 at his home in Pensacola FL) He managed some minor league baseball, moving to Pensacola in 1938 where he was the owner-manager of the minor league team there. He opened an insurance agency in 1945 and ran it until retiring. Died after a two-year illness. Buried Bayview Memorial Park, Pensacola FL.

Lee Dashner—1 Year Pitcher (b. 25 Apr 1887 Renault IL–d. 16 Dec 1959 El Dorado KS).

Dan Daub—6 Years Pitcher (b. 12 Jan 1868 Cotton Run OH–d. 26 Mar 1951 Bradenton FL) Once a coach at the University of Delaware and Amherst College, he was a retired general superintendent of a cash register manufacturer in Dayton OH. Buried Hickory Flats Cemetery, Overpeck OH.

Harry Daubert—1 Game Pinch Hitter (b. 19 Jun 1892 Columbus OH–d. 8 Jan 1944 Receiving Hospital, Detroit MI) Buried Forest Lawn Cemetery, Detroit MI.

Jake Daubert—15 Years Infielder (b. 7 Apr 1884 Shamokin PA–d. 9 Oct 1924 Good Samaritan Hospital, Cincinnati OH) Died at the height of his career from acute appendicitis. Buried Charles Baber Cemetery, Pottsville PA.

Bob Daughters—He was a retired fabric salesman for Union Carbide. (b. 5 Aug 1914 Cincinnati OH–d. 22 Aug 1988 Southbury CT) Served in the U.S. Navy during World War II. Buried St Patrick's Cemetery, Watertown MA.

Hooks Dauss—15 Years Pitcher (b. 22 Sep 1889 Indianapolis IN–d. 27 Jul 1963 Firmin Desdose Hospital, St Louis MO) Died following a lengthy illness. Buried Sunset Memorial Park, Affton MO.

Claude Davenport—1 Year Pitcher (b. 28 May 1898 Runge TX–d. 13 Jun 1976 at a hospital in Corpus Christi TX) A retired farmer, he had lived in Corpus Christi since 1931. Died from injuries suffered in an automobile accident in Robstown TX three days earlier. Buried Robstown Memorial Park, Robstown TX.

Dave Davenport—6 Years Pitcher (b. 20 Feb 1890 DeRidder LA–d. 16 Oct 1954 at a hospital in El Dorado AR) He drove a taxi at El Dorado at the time of his death. Died after an illness of six weeks. Buried Arlington Cemetery, El Dorado AR.

Lum Davenport—4 Years Pitcher (b. 27 Jun 1900 Tucson AZ–d. 21 Apr 1961 Dallas TX) From 1928 until his death he was a technical claims coordinator for Texas Employers' Insurance Association and Employers' Casualty Company in Dallas. Died from a heart attack. Buried Hillcrest Memorial Park, Dallas TX.

Bill Davidson—3 Years Outfielder (b. 10 May 1884 Lafayette IN–d. 23 May 1954 Lincoln NE) He was a retired employee of the Nebraska State Department of Roads and Irrigation. Buried Rose Hill Cemetery, Waverly NE.

Claude Davidson—2 Years Infielder (b. 13 Oct 1896 Boston MA–d. 18 Apr 1956 South Shore Hospital, Weymouth MA) A self-employed consulting engineer, he was at one time president of the New England Baseball League and scouted for the Braves and Red Sox. Died after a brief illness. Buried Blue Hill Cemetery, Braintree MA.

Homer Davidson—1 Year Catcher (b. 14 Oct 1884 Cleveland OH–d. 26 Jul 1948 at his home in Detroit MI) He started Hydraulic Steel Company of Cleveland and became manager of Automotive Credit Service, Inc, after moving to Detroit in 1927. He was a leading figure in the financial reorganization of several large corporations during the depression years. Buried Grand Lawn Cemetery, Detroit MI.

Mordecai Davidson—1 Year Manager (b. 30 Nov 1846 Port Washington OH–d. 6 Sep 1940 at his home in Louisville KY) Served for the Union in the Civil War. Also served in the Spanish-American War. He moved to Louisville KY in 1867 and lived there the rest of his life. Died following a heart attack. Buried Cave Hill Cemetery, Louisville KY.

Chick Davies—4 Years Pitcher (b. 6 Mar 1892 Peabody MA–d. 5 Sep 1973 Middletown CT).

George Davies—3 Years Pitcher (b. 22 Feb 1868 Portage WI–d. 22 Sep 1906 in his office in Waterloo WI) After retiring from baseball he became a doctor, and was one of the best known physicians in the Waterloo area. Died from an overdose of medicine he was taking as a sedative. Buried Waterloo Cemetery, Waterloo WI.

Bud Davis—1 Year Pitcher (b. 7 Dec 1889 Merry Point VA–d. 26 May 1967 at his home in Williamsburg VA) A commercial fisherman and farmer, he lived in Williamsburg his last 26 years. Buried Williamsburg Memorial Park, Williamsburg VA.

Cherokee Davis—9 Years Outfielder (b. 6 Feb 1918 Newark NJ–d. 17 Nov 1982 Fort Lauderdale FL) He played in the negro leagues. Cremated.

Curt Davis—13 Years Pitcher (b. 7 Sep 1903 Greenfield MO–d. 12 Oct 1965 Inter-Community Hospital, Covina CA) He was a self-employed real estate broker for 15 years. Died from a heart attack. Buried Oakdale Memorial Park, Glendora CA.

Daisy Davis—2 Years Pitcher (b. 28 Nov 1858 Boston MA–d. 5 Nov 1902 Lynn MA).

Dixie Davis—10 Years Pitcher (b. 12 Oct 1892 Wilson Mills NC–d. 4 Feb 1944 Raleigh NC) He pitched more than 20 years in professional baseball including several seasons in the American Association. He lived at Oxford NC where he was engaged in the tobacco business. Died from a cerebral hemorrhage. Buried Christian Church Cemetery, Virgilina VA.

George Davis—20 Years Infielder 3 Years Manager Hall of Fame (b. 23 Aug 1870 Cohoes NY–d. 17 Oct 1940 Philadelphia PA) Buried Fernwood Cemetery, Fernwood PA.

George Davis—4 Years Pitcher (b. 9 Mar 1890 Lancaster NY–d. 4 Jun 1961 at his home in Buffalo NY) Served in the U.S. Army during World War II. He studied law in the off-season during his baseball career, and quit baseball at age 27 when he received his degree. He was an attorney and a nationally known amateur astronomer. Died by hanging himself. Buried Lancaster Cemetery, Lancaster NY.

Harry Davis—22 Years Infielder 1 Year Manager (b. 10 Jul 1873 Philadelphia PA–d. 11 Aug 1947 at his home in Philadelphia PA) He was a coach, scout, iron merchant, railroad man, accountant, member of Philadelphia's old Common Council and, during World War II, a defense guard. When he died he was a watchman for Burns Detective Agency at the *Philadelphia Inquirer*'s newspaper plant. Died from a stroke. Buried Westminster Cemetery, Bala Cynwyd PA.

Harry Davis—3 Years Infielder (b. 7 May 1908 Shreveport LA–d. 3 Mar 1997 Shreveport LA).

Ike Davis—3 Years Infielder (b. 14 Jun 1895 Pueblo CO–d. 2 Apr 1984 Tucson AZ) Cremated.

Ira Davis—1 Year Infielder (b. 8 Jul 1870 Philadelphia PA–d. 21 Dec 1942 Brooklyn NY) He umpired in the minor leagues and worked his last ten years in a branch of Bonds clothing stores. Buried Lutheran Cemetery, Middle Village NY.

Jim Davis—4 Years Pitcher (b. 15 Sep 1924 Red Bluff CA–d. 30 Nov 1995 at his home in San Mateo CA) Served in World War II. For 27 years he was in business for himself, operating Jim Davis Enterprises. Died from advanced lung cancer. Cremated.

Jumbo Davis—7 Years Infielder (b. 5 Sep 1861 St Louis MO–d. 14 Feb 1921 St Louis MO) Buried Calvary Cemetery, St Louis MO.

Kiddo Davis—8 Years Outfielder (b. 12 Feb 1902 Bridgeport CT–d. 4 Mar 1983 Golden Heights Conv Hospital, Bridgeport CT) He was a retired CPA. Buried Park Cemetery, Bridgeport CT.

Lefty Davis—4 Years Outfielder (b. 4 Feb 1875 Nashville TN–d. 4 Feb 1919 Collins NY).

Peaches Davis—4 Years Pitcher (b. 31 May 1905 Glen Rose TX–d. 28 Apr 1995 Duncan OK) He was a real estate developer and building contractor in Duncan, retiring in 1977. Buried Duncan Cemetery, Duncan OK.

Piper Davis—9 Years Infielder 3 Years Manager (b. 3 Jul 1917 Piper AL–d. 21 May 1997 Baptist Medical Center, Birmingham AL) Played in the negro leagues. In 1950 he was the first black player signed by the Red Sox, but he never played in the major leagues. In the 1970s and 1980s he was a scout for the Tigers, Cardinals and Expos. Died from a heart attack. Buried Elmwood Cemetery, Birmingham AL.

Ron Davis—5 Years Outfielder (b. 21 Oct 1941 Roanoke Rapids NC–d. 5 Sep 1992 Houston TX) A resident of Houston 30 years, he spent 20 of those years in the computer and import business. Died from complications of diabetes. Buried Davis Family Cemetery, Jackson NC.

Spud Davis—16 Years Catcher 1 Year Manager (b. 4 Dec 1904 Birmingham AL–d. 14 Aug 1984 St Vincent's Hospital, Birmingham AL) He coached and scouted for several major league teams. Died following back surgery performed several weeks earlier. Buried Elmwood Cemetery, Birmingham AL.

Tod Davis—2 Years Infielder (b. 24 Jul 1924 Los Angeles CA–d. 31 Dec 1978 West Covina CA) He was sales manager for Paramount Equipment Company, a manufacturer of water trucks, for ten years. Died from heart disease. Buried Rose Hills Memorial Park, Whittier CA.

Wiley Davis—1 Year Pitcher (b. 1 Aug 1875 Seymour TN–d. 22 Sep 1942 at his home in Detroit MI) Died suddenly from a heart attack. Buried Detroit MI.

Joe Dawson—4 Years Pitcher (b. 1897 Bow WA–d. 4 Jan 1978 at a hospital in Longview TX) Served in both the U.S. Army and U.S. Navy during World War I. A noted aviator, he owned a flying school in Pittsburgh PA and operated the airport there. He later operated a tourist resort at Port O'Connor TX. Died after a lengthy illness. Buried Lakeview Memorial Gardens, Longview TX.

Rex Dawson—1 Year Pitcher (b. 10 Feb 1889 Mount Vernon WA–d. 20 Oct 1958 at his home in Indianapolis IN) Served as a lieutenant in the U.S. Naval Air Corps during World War I. For 20 years he managed an office of Remedial Finance Corporation, and was a partner in a Ford dealership. Died from a heart attack. Buried Crown Hill Cemetery, Indianapolis IN.

Bill Day—2 Years Pitcher (b. 28 Jul 1867 Wilmington DE–d. 16 Aug 1923 Delaware Hospital, Wilmington DE) Died after a second stroke of apoplexy. Buried Cathedral Cemetery, Wilmington DE.

John Day—1 Year Manager (b. 23 Sep 1847 Colchester MA–d. 25 Jan 1925 Cliffside NJ) A prosperous tobacco merchant, he was the founder of the Giants in 1883. He spent a fortune trying to keep them in the National League and died in poverty in a barber's chair from a stroke. He had been a hopeless cripple from paralysis for years. Buried Fairmount Cemetery, Newark NJ.

Leon Day—8 Years Pitcher Hall of Fame (b. abt 1916–d. 13 Mar 1995 St Agnes Hospital, Baltimore MD) Played in the negro leagues. Known for his no-windup delivery, he was often compared to Satchel Paige. Died from heart ailments, diabetes and gout, less than a week after being selected for baseball's Hall of Fame. Buried Arbutus Memorial Park, Baltimore MD.

Pea Ridge Day—4 Years Pitcher (b. 27 Aug 1899 Pea Ridge AR–d. 21 Mar 1934 Kansas City MO) Known as a country bumpkin and pitching comedian, he owned two farms and a filling station in Pea Ridge. Took his own life by slashing his throat with a hunting knife at the home of a former teammate. Buried Pea Ridge Cemetery, Pea Ridge AR.

Tommy de la Cruz—1 Year Pitcher (b. 18 Sep 1914 Marianao, Cuba–d. 6 Sep 1958 Havana, Cuba).

Ren Deagle—2 Years Pitcher (b. 26 Jun 1858 New York City NY–d. 24 Dec 1936 at his home in Kansas City MO) He worked for the American Railway Express Company. Buried Elmwood Cemetery, Kansas City MO.

Charlie Deal—10 Years Infielder (b. 30 Oct 1891 Wilkinsburg PA–d. 16 Sep 1979 Rowland Convalescent Hospital, Covina CA) For 32 years he was a special agent for Southern California Gas Company. Partially paralyzed, he died from pneumonia. Cremated. Buried Pasadena Mausoleum, Pasadena CA.

Lindsay Deal—1 Year Outfielder (b. 3 Sep 1911 Lenoir NC–d. 18 Apr 1979 Little Rock AR) He played 14 years in the Southern League, American Association and International League. After baseball he worked for the Pulaski County, AR, sheriff's office and was an Arkansas state trooper before working as a deputy U.S. marshall for 25 years, retiring in 1976. Buried Pine Crest Memorial Park, Alexander AR.

Snake Deal—1 Year Infielder (b. 21 Jan 1879 Lancaster PA–d. 9 May 1944 Harrisburg PA) He worked for the Capitol Police at the state capitol in Harrisburg. Died from a heart attack while at work in the police headquarters at the capitol. Buried Florin Cemetery, Marietta PA.

Pat Dealy—5 Years Catcher (b. Moosup CT–d. 16 Dec 1924 Buffalo NY) He was a bricklayer.

Chubby Dean—8 Years Pitcher (b. 24 Aug 1916 Mount Airy NC–d. 21 Dec 1970 at his home in Riverside NJ) Buried St Peter's Cemetery, Riverside NJ.

Dizzy Dean—12 Years Pitcher Hall of Fame (b. 16 Jan 1911 Lucas AR–d. 17 Jul 1974 St Mary's Hospital, Reno NV) After his playing career was shortened by a broken toe, suffered in the 1937 All-Star game, he turned to baseball broadcasting. Died three days after suffering a heart attack while in Reno, enjoying a couple of weeks of fun and golf. Buried Bond Cemetery, Bond MS.

Dory Dean—1 Year Pitcher (b. 6 Nov 1852 Cincinnati OH–d. 4 May 1935 at his son's home in Nashville TN) One of the first to throw a curve ball, his career was shortened when he injured his arm while experimenting with the curve. Later he worked for the Dixie Electrotype Company in Nashville. Buried Woodlawn Memorial Park, Nashville TN.

Harry Dean—1 Year Pitcher (b. 12 May 1915 Rockmart GA–d. 1 Jun 1960 at a hospital in Rockmart GA) He worked for a textile firm in Dalton GA. He played and refereed various sports locally. Died after an extended illness. Buried Rose Hill Cemetery, Rockmart GA.

Paul Dean—9 Years Pitcher (b. 14 Aug 1913 Lucas AR–d. 17 Mar 1981 Springdale Memorial Hospital, Springdale AR) World War II veteran. He was the brother of Dizzy Dean, and was known as "Daffy." He is a member of Ohio and Oklahoma halls of fame. He owned several minor league teams and conducted baseball schools. Died from a massive heart attack. Buried Oakland Cemetery, Clarksville AR.

Wayland Dean—4 Years Pitcher (b. 20 Jun 1902 Richwood WV–d. 10 Apr 1930 Huntington WV) Died at the height of his baseball career from tuberculosis. Buried Spring Hill Cemetery, Huntington WV.

Buddy Dear—1 Year Infielder (b. 1 Dec 1905 Norfolk VA–d. 29 Aug 1989 Radford VA).

Charlie DeArmond—1 Year Infielder (b. 13 Feb 1877 Okeana OH–d. 17 Dec 1933 Morning Sun OH) Died from lobar pneumonia. Buried Shandon Cemetery, Shandon OH.

Jim Deasley—1 Year Infielder (b. abt 1860 Philadelphia PA–d. 25 Dec 1910 Philadelphia PA).

Pat Deasley—8 Years Catcher (b. 17 Nov 1857 Ireland–d. 1 Apr 1943 at his home in Philadelphia PA) His baseball career ended abruptly when he was hit in the head by a pitched ball. Buried Mount Moriah Cemetery, Philadelphia PA.

Hank DeBerry—11 Years Catcher (b. 29 Dec 1893 Savannah TN–d. 10 Sep 1951 at his home in Savannah TN) Served in the U.S. Navy during World War I. He was a scout and farm manager for the New York Giants and served as a representative in the Tennessee State Assembly. He was also a bank director and owned extensive real estate in Savannah TN. Died from a heart ailment. Buried Savannah Cemetery, Savannah TN.

Joe DeBerry—2 Years Pitcher (b. 29 Nov 1896 Mount Gilead NC–d. 9 Oct 1944 at his home in Southern Pines NC) For 22 years he was a buyer for American Tobacco Company. Died from a heart attack. Buried Mount Hope Cemetery, Southern Pines NC.

Adam DeBus—1 Year Infielder (b. 7 Oct 1892 Chicago IL–d. 13 May 1977 Chicago IL) Buried St Boniface Cemetery, Chicago IL.

Art Decatur—6 Years Pitcher (b. 14 Jan 1894 Cleveland OH–d. 23 Apr 1966 at his home in Talladega AL) He served 16 years as city clerk of Talladega, one year as administrator of Citizens Hospital in Talladega, and as president of Talladega National Bank from 1956 until his death. Died from a heart attack. Buried Oak Hill Cemetery, Talladega AL.

Frank Decker—2 Years Infielder (b. 26 Feb 1853 St Louis MO–d. 5 Feb 1940 Missouri Baptist Hospital, St Louis MO) He retired as general superintendent of Meyer Brother's Drug Company in 1932 after 50 years of service. Died from a heart ailment. Buried Valhalla Cemetery, St Louis MO.

George Decker—8 Years Outfielder (b. 1 Jun 1866 York PA–d. 8 Jun 1909 Compton CA) Died from consumption. Buried Woodlawn Memorial Park, Compton CA.

Artie Dede—1 Year Catcher (b. 12 Jul 1895 Brooklyn NY–d. 6 Sep 1971 Elliot Community Hospital, Keene NH) World War I veteran. He was a scout for the Brooklyn Dodgers, and later for the New York Yankees. Buried Evergreen Cemetery, Brooklyn NY.

Shorty Dee—1 Year Infielder (b. 4 Oct 1889 Halifax, Canada–d. 12 Aug 1971 Jamaica Plains MA) Buried St Patrick's Cemetery, Lowell MA.

Dummy Deegan—1 Year Pitcher (b. 16 Nov 1874 Bronx NY–d. 1 May 1957 Bronx NY).

John Deering—1 Year Pitcher (b. 25 Jun 1878 Lynn MA–d. 15 Feb 1943 Beverly MA) He was a retired employee of Pope Lumber Co in Beverly. Buried St Mary's Cemetery, Beverly MA.

Tony DeFate—1 Year Infielder (b. 22 Feb 1898 Kansas City MO–d. 3 Sep 1963 New Orleans LA).

Rube DeGroff—2 Years Outfielder (b. 2 Sep 1879 Hyde Park NY–d. 17 Dec 1955 St Francis Hospital, Poughkeepsie NY) He operated a busline between Poughkeepsie and Hyde Park during the 1930s. Later he was a night watchman at Schatz Manufacturing Company. He was on his way to work when he was killed in a head-on collision with a car being driven on the wrong side of the road. Buried St James Churchyard, Hyde Park NY.

Dutch Dehlman—2 Years Infielder 1 Year Manager (b. 1850 Catasauqua PA–d. 13 Mar 1885 at his home in Wilkes-Barre PA) Died from peritonitis at the height of his career.

Pep Deininger—3 Years Outfielder (b. 10 Oct 1877 Wasseralfingen, Germany–d. 25 Sep 1950 Boston MA) Buried Forest Hills Cemetery, Boston MA.

Pat Deisel—2 Years Catcher (b. 9 Apr 1876 Ripley OH–d. 17 Apr 1948 at his home in Cincinnati OH) He operated a sporting goods store in Cincinnati before becoming a clerk with the Hamilton County, OH, Board of Elections. Died from a heart attack. Buried Spring Grove Cemetery, Cincinnati OH.

Mike Dejan—1 Year Outfielder (b. 13 Jan 1915 Cleveland OH–d. 2 Feb 1953 V A Hospital, Los Angeles CA) World War II veteran. He was a processor for Aire-Research Corporation. Died from Hodgkin's disease. Buried Los Angeles National Cemetery, Los Angeles CA.

Bill DeKoning—1 Year Catcher (b. 19 Dec 1918 Brooklyn NY–d. 26 Jul 1979 Palm Harbor FL) He was a retired president and business manager for the International Union of Operating Engineers at Farmingdale NY. Buried Curlew Hills Memory Gardens, Palm Harbor FL.

Ed Delahanty—16 Years Outfielder Hall of Fame (b. 30 Oct 1867 Cleveland OH–d. 2 Jul 1903 Niagara Falls NY) Died at the height of his baseball career when he tumbled off a bridge into the Niagara River. His body was recovered a week later after washing over Niagara Falls. He had been put off a train near Buffalo NY for rowdy behavior. Buried Calvary Cemetery, Cleveland OH.

Frank Delahanty—6 Years Outfielder (b. 29 Dec 1885 Cleveland OH–d. 22 Jul 1966 Cleveland OH) He was a street inspector for the City of Cleveland. Buried Calvary Cemetery, Cleveland OH.

Jim Delahanty—13 Years Infielder (b. 20 Jun 1879 Cleveland OH–d. 17 Oct 1953 St John's Hospital, Cleveland OH) He was a foreman on the street paving crew for the City of Cleveland. Died after being ill several months. Buried Calvary Cemetery, Cleveland OH.

Joe Delahanty—3 Years Outfielder (b. 18 Oct 1876 Cleveland OH–d. 29 Jan 1936 at his home in Cleveland OH) He was a deputy sheriff for Cuyahoga County, OH. Died from a cerebral hemorrhage. Buried Calvary Cemetery, Cleveland OH.

Tom Delahanty—3 Years Infielder (b. 9 Mar 1872 Cleveland OH–d. 10 Jan 1951 at a hospital in Sanford FL) He was a toolmaker for Kilbee Tool Company in Cleveland before retiring to Florida in 1928. There he operated the Shoal Fishing Camp on the St Johns River for 20 years. Died following a brief illness. Buried All Souls Cemetery, Sanford FL.

Bill DeLancey—4 Years Catcher (b. 28 Nov 1901 Greensboro NC–d. 28 Nov 1946 at his home in Phoenix AZ) He managed in the minor leagues for a short while before moving to Phoenix AZ in 1936. There he ranched and was a sporting goods salesman. Died from tuberculosis. Buried St Francis Catholic Cemetery, Phoenix AZ.

Art Delaney—3 Years Pitcher (b. 5 Jan 1895 Greensboro NC–d. 2 May 1970 Blossom Convalescent Hospital, Hayward CA) He spent 14 years as a production worker for Friden Calculator Company. Died from pneumonia, but suffered from chronic organic brain syndrome. Cremated. Buried Chapel of the Chimes, Hayward CA.

Bill Delaney—1 Year Infielder (b. 4 Mar 1863 Cincinnati OH–d. 1 Mar 1942 at his home in Canton OH) He operated the Barnett Cafe in Canton for many years. Died from a cerebral hemorrhage. Buried St John's Cemetery, Canton OH.

Flame Delhi—1 Year Pitcher (b. 2 Nov 1890 Harqua Hala AZ–d. 9 May 1966 Marin General Hospital, San Rafael CA) He was a consulting engineer in the steel business for 50 years. Died following a heart attack. Buried Mount Tamalpais Cemetery, San Rafael CA.

Eddie Delker—4 Years Infielder (b. 17 Apr 1906 Palo Alto CA–d. 14 May 1997 Pottsville Hospital, Pottsville PA) He was the caretaker at the Odd Fellows Cemetery in St Clair PA. Buried Odd Fellows Cemetery, St Clair PA.

Wheezer Dell—4 Years Pitcher (b. 11 Jun 1886 Tuscarora NV–d. 24 Aug 1966 Southern Inyo Hospital, Lone Pine CA) Buried Inglewood Park Cemetery, Inglewood CA.

Bert Delmas—1 Year Infielder (b. 20 May 1911 San Francisco CA–d. 4 Dec 1979 Inter-Community Hosp, Huntington Beach CA) For 47 years he was an insurance agent. Died from heart disease. Buried Pacific View Memorial Park, Newport Beach CA.

Fred Demarais—1 Year Pitcher (b. 1 Nov 1866 Canada–d. 6 Mar 1919 at his brother's home in Stamford CT) He was a bartender. Died from pulmonary tuberculosis. Buried St John's Cemetery, Darien CT.

Al Demaree—8 Years Pitcher (b. 8 Sep 1884 Quincy IL–d. 30 Apr 1962 County Hospital, Los Angeles CA) He was a syndicated cartoonist for 25 years. Died from intestinal hemorrhaging and heart disease. Buried Harbor Rest Memorial Park, Costa Mesa CA.

Frank Demaree—12 Years Outfielder (b. 10 Jun 1910 Winters CA–d. 30 Aug 1958 Temple Hospital, Los Angeles CA) He managed some minor league baseball before working as a grip for United Artists in Studio City CA. Died from an intestinal hemorrhage. Cremated.

Harry DeMiller—1 Year Infielder (b. 12 Nov 1867 Wooster OH–d. 19 Oct 1928 at his home in Santa Ana CA) He was a merchant. Died from a cerebral hemorrhage. Buried Fairhaven Memorial Park, Santa Ana CA.

Ray Demmitt—7 Years Outfielder (b. 2 Feb 1884 Illiopolis IL–d. 19 Feb 1956 Glen Ellyn IL) He was an inspector for the U.S. Naval Ordnance plant in St Charles IL. Died suddenly at his home. Buried Mount Pulaski Cemetery, Mount Pulaski IL.

Gene DeMontreville—11 Years Infielder (b. 26 Mar 1874 St Paul MN–d. 18 Feb 1935 at his home on the fairgrounds, Memphis TN) He was a player and manager in the Southern League for several years before he became involved with the Tri-State Fair project, an activity he continued until his death. Died from a coronary thrombosis. Buried Glenwood Cemetery, Washington DC.

Lee DeMontreville—1 Year Infielder (b. 23 Sep 1879 St Paul MN–d. 22 Mar 1962 Pelham Manor NY).

Bingo DeMoss—12 Years Infielder 4 Years Manager (b. 5 Sep 1889 Topeka KS–d. 26 Jan 1965 Chicago IL) He played in the negro leagues.

Ben DeMott—2 Years Pitcher (b. 2 Apr 1889 Green Village NJ–d. 5 Jul 1963 Somerset Hospital, Somerville NJ) World War I veteran. Died after a long illness. Buried Evergreen Cemetery, Basking Ridge NJ.

Tod Dennehey—1 Year Outfielder (b. 12 May 1899 Philadelphia PA–d. 8 Aug 1977 Philadelphia PA).

Otto Denning—2 Years Pitcher (b. 28 Dec 1912 Hays KS–d. 25 May 1992 at his home in Chicago IL) He managed minor league baseball. Died after suffering a heart attack. Buried St Joseph Cemetery, River Grove IL.

Jerry Denny—13 Years Infielder (b. 16 Mar 1859 New York City NY–d. 16 Aug 1927 Houston TX) Playing baseball before gloves were used, he was considered the best bare-handed player of the game. Buried Holy Cross Cemetery, Houston TX.

Eddie Dent—3 Years Pitcher (b. 8 Dec 1887 Baltimore MD–d. 25 Nov 1974 Birmingham AL).

Roger Denzer—2 Years Pitcher (b. 5 Oct 1871 LeSeuer MN–d. 18 Sep 1949 at his home in

LeSeuer MN) When he developed a sore arm he retired to the family farm in Minnesota. Buried Mound Cemetery, LeSeuer MN.

Mike DePangher —1 Year Catcher (b. 11 Sep 1858 Marysville CA–d. 7 Jul 1915 San Francisco Hospital, San Francisco CA) Died from a cerebral neoplasm. Buried Holy Cross Catholic Cemetery, Colma CA.

Tony DePhillips —1 Year Catcher (b. 20 Sep 1912 New York City NY–d. 5 May 1994 Port Jefferson NY).

Gene Derby —1 Year Catcher (b. Feb 1860 NH–d. 12 Oct 1928 Dr Pierce's Invalid Hospital, Buffalo NY) He owned and operated Derby's Bakery in Glens Falls NY. Died following a surgery he failed to recover from. Buried Glens Falls Cemetery, Glens Falls NY.

George Derby —3 Years Pitcher (b. 6 Jul 1857 Webster MA–d. 4 Jul 1925 Philadelphia PA).

Claud Derrick —5 Years Infielder (b. 11 Jun 1886 Burton GA–d. 15 Jul 1974 at his home in Clayton GA) He was a prominent businessman in Clayton, owning Clayton Ford Motor Company from 1921 to 1956, and serving as vice-president of the Bank of Clayton. He was also the mayor of Clayton at one time. Died after a long illness. Buried Clayton Cemetery, Clayton GA.

Paul Derringer —15 Years Pitcher (b. 17 Oct 1906 Springfield KY–d. 17 Nov 1987 Sarasota Memorial Hospital, Sarasota FL) He was the winning pitcher in the major league's first night game. Cremated.

Joe DeSa —1 Year Outfielder (b. 7 Jul 1959 Honolulu, Hawaii–d. 20 Dec 1986 Ponce, Puerto Rico) He was killed at the height of his baseball career when his car collided with another car while returning to his hotel following a winter league game. Buried Hawaiian Memorial Park Cemetery, Kaneohe HI.

Gene Desautels —13 Years Catcher (b. 13 Jun 1907 Worcester MA–d. 5 Nov 1994 Hurley Medical Center, Flint MI) He managed minor league baseball and was a coach and scout before going to work for the Mott Foundation. He retired in 1972 as a counselor for Southwestern High School in Flint. Buried New Calvary Catholic Cemetery, Flint MI.

Jimmy DeShong —7 Years Pitcher (b. 30 Nov 1909 Harrisburg PA–d. 16 Oct 1993 Lower Paxton PA).

Shorty DesJardien —1 Year Pitcher (b. 24 Aug 1893 Coffeyville KS–d. 7 Mar 1956 at his home in Monrovia CA) He was an All-American center in football at the Univ of Chicago. He retired as a Los Angeles manufacturing executive. Died from a cerebral thrombosis. Cremated.

Rube Dessau —2 Years Pitcher (b. 29 Mar 1883 New Galilee PA–d. 6 May 1952 York Hospital, York PA) World War I veteran. He managed minor league baseball a number of years before becoming employment manager for the American Chain plant in York. Died following a lingering illness. Buried Grove Cemetery, New Brighton PA.

George DeTore —2 Years Infielder (b. 11 Nov 1906 Utica NY–d. 7 Feb 1991 St Elizabeth Hospital, Utica NY) He worked 47 years in baseball as a player, coach and minor league manager. Buried Calvary Cemetery, Utica NY.

Jim Devine —2 Years Pitcher (b. 5 Oct 1858 Navarino NY–d. 11 Jan 1905 at his home in Syracuse NY) A barred attorney, he practiced law in Syracuse from 1886 until his death. Died after suffering four years from consumption. Buried St Agnes Cemetery, Syracuse NY.

Mickey Devine —3 Years Catcher (b. 9 May 1892 Albany NY–d. 1 Oct 1937 at his home in Albany NY) He worked in the publicity department of the WPA at Albany. Died from a heart attack. Buried Our Lady of Angels Cemetery, Albany NY.

Hal Deviney —1 Year Pitcher (b. 1891 Newton MA–d. 4 Jan 1933 at his home in Westwood MA) He worked for Martin Sorenson, a tree warden. Died suddenly. Buried Brookdale Cemetery, Dedham MA.

Bernie DeViveiros —2 Years Infielder (b. 19 Apr 1901 Oakland CA–d. 5 Jul 1994 Summit Medical Center, Oakland CA) He spent 60 years in baseball as a player, teacher, scout and minor league manager. He was a scout many years for the Tigers. Died from congestive heart failure and acute renal failure. Buried Mountain View Cemetery, Oakland CA.

Art Devlin —10 Years Infielder (b. 16 Oct 1879 Washington DC–d. 17 Sep 1948 Medical Center, Jersey City NJ) Died after a two-month illness. Buried Congressional Cemetery, Washington DC.

Jim Devlin —2 Years Pitcher (b. 1849 Philadelphia PA–d. 10 Oct 1883 at his home in Philadelphia PA) He was a patrolman for the Philadelphia Police Department. Died from consumption.

Jim Devlin—4 Years Pitcher (b. 16 Apr 1866 Troy NY–d. 18 Dec 1900 at his home in Troy NY) Engaged in the cigar business, he was also an officer in the Rensselaer County, NY, Supreme Court. Died from typhoid pneumonia. Buried St John's Cemetery, Troy NY.

Rex DeVogt—1 Year Catcher (b. 4 Jan 1889 Clare MI–d. 9 Nov 1935 near Ithaca MI) He was sales manager for a company that manufactured illuminated highway signs in Alma MI, where he lived. Killed when he crashed his car into the rear of a moving truck on Highway 27 south of Ithaca. Buried Riverside Cemetery, Alma MI.

Josh Devore—7 Years Outfielder (b. 13 Nov 1887 Murray City OH–d. 5 Oct 1954 Chillicothe Hospital, Chillicothe OH) World War I veteran. He operated cafes and lunchrooms in Chillicothe. Buried New Marshfield Cemetery, New Marshfield OH.

Al DeVormer—5 Years Catcher (b. 19 Aug 1891 Grand Rapids MI–d. 29 Aug 1966 St Mary's Hospital, Grand Rapids MI) Died after an illness of several weeks. Buried Fair Plains Cemetery, Grand Rapids MI.

Walt Devoy—1 Year Outfielder (b. 14 Mar 1885 St Louis MO–d. 17 Dec 1953 at his home in St Louis MO) He was a secretary for Plumber's Supply Company of St Louis. Died from a heart attack. Buried Calvary Cemetery, St Louis MO.

Charlie DeWald—1 Year Pitcher (b. 22 Sep 1867 Newark NJ–d. 22 Aug 1904 at his home in Cleveland OH) He was superintendent of cemeteries for the City of Cleveland until he resigned because of ill health 18 months before his death.

William DeWitt—(b. 3 Aug 1902 St Louis MO–d. 3 Mar 1982 at his home in Cincinnati OH) Part-owner of the Browns from 1949 to 1951 and the Reds from 1961 to 1966, he was also an executive for the Cardinals, Tigers and Yankees. Died from cancer. Buried Oak Grove Cemetery, St Louis MO.

Charlie Dexter—8 Years Outfielder (b. 15 Jun 1876 Evansville IN–d. 9 Jun 1934 St Luke's Hospital, Cedar Rapids IA) After his baseball career he owned and operated a restaurant. He also worked in clothing stores. Died when he shot himself in the head with a .38 caliber revolver in a room at the Pullman Hotel. Buried Glendale Cemetery, Des Moines IA.

Bo Diaz—13 Years Catcher (b. 23 Mar 1953 Cua, Venezuela–d. 23 Nov 1990 Caracas, Venezuela).

Pedro Dibut—2 Years Pitcher (b. 18 Nov 1892 Cienfuegos, Cuba–d. 4 Dec 1979 Hialeah FL) He worked in a sugar mill, retiring and moving to Hialeah in 1968. Buried Vista Memorial Gardens, Hialeah FL.

Leo Dickerman—3 Years Pitcher (b. 31 Oct 1896 DeSoto MO–d. 30 Apr 1982 St Mary's Hospital, Atkins AR) He lived his last 55 years at Atkins where he had a large farm. Buried Atkins City Cemetery, Atkins AR.

Buttercup Dickerson—7 Years Outfielder (b. 11 Oct 1858 Tyaskin MD–d. 23 Jul 1920 Baltimore MD) Buried Loudon Park Cemetery, Baltimore MD.

George Dickerson—1 Year Pitcher (b. 1 Dec 1892 Renner TX–d. 9 Jul 1938 Los Angeles CA) Died from tuberculosis. Buried Frankford Cemetery, Carrollton TX.

Bill Dickey—17 Years Catcher 1 Year Manager Hall of Fame (b. 6 Jun 1907 Bastrop LA–d. 12 Nov 1993 Little Rock AR) Served in the U.S. Navy during World War II. After retiring as a player he coached for a few years, then was a securities representative for an investment firm until retiring in 1977. He is a member of the New York, Arkansas and Louisiana sports halls of fame. Buried Roselawn Memorial Park, Little Rock AR.

George Dickey—6 Years Catcher (b. 10 Jul 1915 Kensett AR–d. 16 Jun 1976 DeWitt AR) Served in the U.S. Navy during World War II. He was an expert on bond issues and an executive for a large investment firm. Died from a heart attack while on a fishing trip. Buried Roselawn Memorial Park, Little Rock AR.

Emerson Dickman—5 Years Pitcher (b. 12 Nov 1914 Buffalo NY–d. 27 Apr 1981 Memorial-Sloan-Kettering, New York City NY) Served in the U.S. Navy during World War II. He coached ten years at Princeton University before becoming a manufacturer's representative in New York City for a furniture company, retiring in 1980. Died after a brief illness. Buried George Washington Memorial Park, Paramus NJ.

Johnny Dickshot—6 Years Outfielder (b. 24 Jan 1910 Waukegan IL–d. 4 Nov 1997 at his home in Waukegan IL) He owned and operated the Dugout Saloon in Waukegan from 1947 until 1977 and tended bar at the Lithuanian Hall in Waukegan after selling his saloon in 1977. Buried Ascension Cemetery, Libertyville IL.

Murry Dickson—18 Years Pitcher (b. 21 Aug 1916 Tracy MO–d. 21 Sep 1989 Bethany Medical Center, Kansas City MO) He lived near Leavenworth KS the last 20 years of his life, and suffered from emphysema. Buried Sunset Memory Gardens, Leavenworth KS.

Walt Dickson—5 Years Pitcher (b. 3 Dec 1878 New Summerfield TX–d. 9 Dec 1918 Ardmore OK).

Harry Diddlebock—1 Year Manager (b. 27 Jun 1854 Philadelphia PA–d. 5 Feb 1900 Philadelphia PA) He was the sports editor for the *Philadelphia Inquirer* before and after managing the Browns in 1896. Died after a brief, but painful, illness of muscular rheumatism. Buried West Laurel Hill Cemetery, Bala Cynwyd PA.

Ernie Diehl—4 Years Outfielder (b. 2 Oct 1874 Cincinnati OH–d. 6 Nov 1958 Miami FL) He moved to Miami about 1918 and was in the real estate business there. Buried Spring Grove Cemetery, Cincinnati OH.

George Diehl—2 Years Pitcher (b. 25 Feb 1918 Emmaus PA–d. 24 Aug 1986 at his home in Kingsport TN) Living at Kingsport since 1939, he had been in the mortgage banking business for 36 years. Died from a heart attack. Buried Oak Hill Cemetery, Kingsport TN.

Bill Dietrich—16 Years Pitcher (b. 29 Mar 1910 Philadelphia PA–d. 20 Jun 1978 at his home in Philadelphia PA) He was a salesman for Frankford-Unity Grocery Stores, retiring in 1957. Died suddenly.

Bill Dietrick—2 Years Infielder (b. 20 Apr 1902 Hanover County VA–d. 6 May 1946 U.S. Naval Hospital, Bethesda MD) He worked in the trust department of Chase National Bank until 1937 when he joined the American Cyanamid and Chemical Company of Bluefield WV. A Lieutenant Commander in the U.S. Navy, he took part in the Iwo Jima, Okinawa and Japan occupations during World War II. Died following surgery. Buried Arlington National Cemetery, Arlington VA.

Dutch Dietz—4 Years Pitcher (b. 12 Feb 1912 Cincinnati OH–d. 29 Oct 1972 Baptist Hospital, Beaumont TX) He was recreation director for the City of Beaumont from 1950 until 1962, and personnel director for the city from 1962 until his death. Buried Forest Lawn Memorial Park, Beaumont TX.

Reese Diggs—1 Year Pitcher (b. 22 Sep 1915 Mathews VA–d. 30 Oct 1978 Baltimore MD) Buried Gwynn's Island Cemetery, Mathews VA.

Steve Dignan—1 Year Outfielder (b. 16 May 1859 Boston MA–d. 11 Jul 1881 Boston MA) Died at the height of his career from consumption. Buried Mount Calvary Cemetery, Roslindale MA.

Martin Dihigo—12 Years Infielder Hall of Fame (b. 25 May 1905 Matanzas, Cuba–d. 20 May 1971 Cienfuegos, Cuba) He played in the negro leagues. Buried Cienfuegos Cemetery, Cienfuegos, Cuba.

Pat Dillard—1 Year Outfielder (b. 12 Jun 1874 Chattanooga TN–d. 22 Jul 1907 at the Oakes Home in Denver CO) Died at the height of his career from tuberculosis. Buried Forest Hills Cemetery, Chattanooga TN.

Pickles Dillhoefer—5 Years Catcher (b. 13 Oct 1894 Cleveland OH–d. 22 Feb 1922 St John's Hospital, St Louis MO) Died from typhoid fever at the height of his career, just one month after he had married. Buried Magnolia Cemetery, Mobile AL.

Harley Dillinger—1 Year Pitcher (b. 30 Oct 1894 Pomeroy OH–d. 8 Jan 1959 St Luke's Hospital, Cleveland OH) World War I veteran. For 30 years he was a sales agent for Consolidation Coal Company. Died following a long illness. Buried Calvary Cemetery, Cleveland OH.

Pop Dillon—5 Years Infielder (b. 17 Oct 1873 Normal IL–d. 12 Sep 1931 Pasadena CA) He managed in the Pacific Coast League ten years before going into ranching and the wholesale tire business, dividing his time between the two pursuits. Died after a protracted illness. Buried Forest Lawn Memorial Park, Glendale CA.

Joe DiMaggio—13 Years Outfielder Hall of Fame (b. 25 Nov 1914 Martinez CA–d. 8 Mar 1999 at his home in Hollywood FL) He had an interest in a restaurant on Fisherman's Wharf in San Francisco and did endorsements for selected products. Died following a six-month struggle with lung cancer. Buried Holy Cross Catholic Cemetery, Colma CA.

Vince DiMaggio —10 Years Outfielder (b. 6 Sep 1912 Martinez CA–d. 3 Oct 1986 at his home in North Hollywood CA) The oldest of three baseball-playing DiMaggio brothers, he was a bartender, carpenter, milkman, liquor salesman and, finally, a Fuller Brush salesman. Died from colon cancer. Cremated. Buried Valhalla Memorial Park, North Hollywood CA.

Vance Dinges —2 Years Outfielder (b. 29 May 1915 Elizabeth NJ–d. 4 Oct 1990 Liberty House Nursing Home, Harrisonburg VA) He managed minor league baseball and was a salesmam at a Chevrolet dealership. Later he was steward at the Harrisonburg Moose Lodge and drove a chuck wagon. Died from complications of Alzheimer's disease after being ill ten years. Buried Cedar Wood Cemetery, Edinburg VA.

Bill Dinneen —12 Years Pitcher (b. 5 Apr 1876 Syracuse NY–d. 13 Jan 1955 Syracuse NY) He was an American League umpire from 1909 to 1937. After retiring as an umpire he worked part-time in a brewery owned by his wife's family. Died from heart failure and congestion of the lungs. Buried St Agnes Cemetery, Utica NY.

George Disch —1 Year Pitcher (b. 15 Mar 1879 Lincoln MO–d. 25 Aug 1950 at his home in Rapid City SD) Buried Mountain View Cemetery, Rapid City SD.

Dutch Distel —1 Year Infielder (b. 15 Apr 1896 Madison IN–d. 12 Feb 1967 at his home in Madison IN) He played baseball in a number of minor leagues from 1914 to 1930 and owned and operated Distel's Tavern in Madison from 1932 until retiring in 1951. Buried St Patrick's Cemetery, Madison IN.

Moxie Divis —1 Year Outfielder (b. 16 Jan 1894 Cleveland OH–d. 19 Dec 1955 at his home in Lakewood OH) For 32 years he was a district circulation manager for the *Cleveland Plain Dealer*. He had worked the day before he died. Died in his sleep from a heart attack. Buried Holy Cross Cemetery, Cleveland OH.

Leo Dixon —4 Years Catcher (b. 6 Sep 1896 Chicago IL–d. 11 Apr 1984 Chicago IL) Buried Holy Sepulchre Cemetery, Worth IL.

Rap Dixon —12 Years Outfielder (b. 2 Sep 1902 Kingston GA–d. 20 Jul 1945 Detroit MI) He played in the negro leagues.

Bill Doak —16 Years Pitcher (b. 28 Jan 1891 Pittsburgh PA–d. 26 Nov 1954 at his home in Bradenton FL) He moved to Bradenton in 1925 and was in the real estate business until 1941 when he opened Bill Doak's Sweet Shop there. He operated the confectionary store until his death. Died from a heart attack. Cremated.

Walt Doane —2 Years Pitcher (b. 12 Mar 1887 Bellevue ID–d. 20 Oct 1935 at his farm home near Coatesville PA) Died suddenly from a heart attack while reading the newspaper. Buried East Cain Friend's Burying Ground, Coatesville PA.

John Dobb —1 Year Pitcher (b. 15 Nov 1901 Muskegon MI–d. 31 Jul 1991 Muskegon MI) He was a superintendent at Norge Corporation, and later worked for Certified Concrete. Buried Mona View Jewish Cemetery, Muskegon MI.

John Dobbs —5 Years Outfielder (b. 3 Jun 1876 Chattanooga TN–d. 9 Sep 1934 Charlotte Sanitarium, Charlotte NC) He worked his entire life in baseball as a player, manager and owner. He managed several years in the Southern Association and was part-owner of the Charlotte minor league team when he died. Died from a heart attack. Buried Forest Hills Cemetery, Chattanooga TN.

Ray Dobens —1 Year Pitcher (b. 28 Jul 1906 Nashua NH–d. 21 Apr 1980 at a hospital in Stuart FL) Served in China for the U.S. Navy during World War II. He worked 35 years in civil service with duty for the Tobacco Tax Division of the U.S. Treasury, as an IRS tax agent and as recreation supervisor for the Manchester NH VA Hospital. After retiring from the government he operated an income tax service and went into commercial real estate. Died after a short illness. Buried Mount Calvary Cemetery, Manchester NH.

Jess Dobernic —3 Years Pitcher (b. 20 Nov 1917 Mount Olive IL–d. 16 Jul 1998 St Louis MO).

Joe Dobson —14 Years Pitcher (b. 20 Jan 1917 Durant OK–d. 23 Jun 1994 at his home in Bayard FL) World War II veteran. He was the general manager of the Red Sox minor league team at Winterhaven FL from 1954 until retiring in 1978. Died from cancer. Buried Evergreen Cemetery, Jacksonville FL.

George Dockins —2 Years Pitcher (b. 5 May 1917 Clyde KS–d. 22 Jan 1997 at his home in

Clyde KS) He had careers in several fields including carpentry, co-op elevator and dairy production. Retired from Hutchinson Manufacturing in Clay Center KS in 1980. Buried Mount Hope Cemetery, Clyde KS.

Ona Dodd—1 Year Infielder (b. 14 Sep 1889 Bagwell TX–d. 31 Mar 1929 Gray Sanitarium, Newport AR) He played in the Texas League and was engaged in farming. While serving in World War I he received poison gas injuries that eventually contributed to his death. Died from pneumonia following a bout with influenza. Buried Dodd Family Cemetery, Detroit TX.

John Dodge—2 Years Infielder (b. 27 Apr 1889 Bolivar TN–d. 19 Jun 1916 Mobile AL) Died instantly when hit in the head with a pitched ball during a Southern Association game. Buried Cave Hill Cemetery, Louisville KY.

Sam Dodge—2 Years Pitcher (b. 9 Dec 1889 Neath PA–d. 5 Apr 1966 at his home in Utica NY) He worked for the Earl Fletcher Company at Tupper Lake. Died from heart disease. Buried New Forest Cemetery, Utica NY.

Al Doe—1 Year Pitcher (b. 18 Apr 1864 Rockport MA–d. 4 Oct 1938 at his home in Atlantic MA) A noted roller polo player, he also umpired minor league baseball for a time. Buried Oak Grove Cemetery, Gloucester MA.

Ed Doheny—9 Years Pitcher (b. 24 Nov 1874 Northfield VT–d. 29 Dec 1916 Medfield MA) Died from complications following a nervous breakdown.

Edward S Doherty, Jr—(b. abt 1900–d. 8 Jul 1971 Winchester Hospital, Winchester MA) Served in the U.S. Navy during World War II. Enjoying a 57 year career as a baseball executive, he was general manager for the Senators from 1960 to 1963 and headed up the Red Sox farm system. He was president of the American Association at one time. Died following a long illness. Buried St Joseph Cemetery, Oascoag RI.

Biddy Dolan—1 Year Infielder (b. 9 Jul 1881–d. 15 Jul 1950 Indianapolis IN).

Cozy Dolan—7 Years Outfielder (b. 23 Dec 1889 Oshkosh WI–d. 10 Dec 1958 Resurrection Hospital, Chicago IL) He was banished from baseball in 1924 for allegedly "taking it easy" while playing the game. He operated night clubs in Chicago and was later a municipal court bailiff and a precinct captain. Died after an illness of one year. Buried All Saints Cemetery, Des Plaines IL.

Cozy Dolan—9 Years Outfielder (b. 3 Dec 1872 Cambridge MA–d. 29 Mar 1907 Norton Memorial Infirmary, Louisville KY) Died from typhoid fever at the height of his career. Buried St Paul's Cemetery, Arlington MA.

Joe Dolan—5 Years Infielder (b. 24 Feb 1873 Baltimore MD–d. 24 Mar 1938 at a hospital in Omaha NE) For 30 years he was a flagman for the Burlington Railway in Omaha. Died after an illness of six months. Buried Holy Sepulchre Cemetery, Omaha NE.

John Dolan—5 Years Pitcher (b. 12 Sep 1867 Newport KY–d. 8 May 1948 Springfield OH).

Tom Dolan—7 Years Catcher (b. 10 Jan 1859 Buffalo NY–d. 16 Jan 1913 St Louis MO) He worked for the St Louis Fire Department. Died from a complication of diseases. Buried Calvary Cemetery, St Louis MO.

Frank Doljack—6 Years Outfielder (b. 5 Oct 1907 Cleveland OH–d. 23 Jan 1948 at his home in Cleveland OH) He worked for the State of Ohio Liquor Department. Died from a heart attack. Buried Calvary Cemetery, Cleveland OH.

Art Doll—3 Years Pitcher (b. 7 May 1913 Chicago IL–d. 28 Apr 1978 Calumet City IL).

Jiggs Donahue—9 Years Infielder (b. 13 Jul 1879 Springfield OH–d. 19 Jul 1913 State Hospital, Columbus OH) He spent his last year confined in the State Hospital at Columbus. Died from paresis, dementia paralysis and complications from syphilis. Buried Calvary Cemetery, Springfield OH.

Jim Donahue—5 Years Catcher (b. 8 Jan 1862 Lockport IL–d. 19 Apr 1935 at his home in Lockport IL) He owned and operated a retail liquor store in Lockport for several years before retiring in 1919. Died after a lingering illness. Buried South Lockport Cemetery, Lockport IL.

John Donahue—1 Year Outfielder (b. 19 Apr 1894 Roxbury MA–d. 3 Oct 1949 at his home in Roxbury MA).

Pat Donahue—3 Years Catcher (b. 3 Nov 1884 Springfield OH–d. 31 Jan 1966 City Hospital, Springfield OH) He spent 64 years in baseball, umpiring minor league baseball from 1921 to 1928 and after that scouting for several teams.

Died after a two-year illness. Buried St Ambrose Cemetery, Des Moines IA.

Red Donahue—13 Years Pitcher (b. 23 Jan 1873 Waterbury CT–d. 25 Aug 1913 at his home in Philadelphia PA) He owned and operated a saloon in Philadelphia. He also coached baseball at LaSalle Univ and Yale Univ. Died from tuberculosis. Buried St Joseph's Cemetery, Waterbury CT.

She Donahue—1 Year Infielder (b. 29 Jun 1877 Oswego NY–d. 28 Aug 1947 Fordham Hospital, New York City NY) He worked 40 years for the postal service in New York City, retiring in 1940. Died after a year's illness. Buried St Paul's Cemetery, Oswego NY.

Tim Donahue—8 Years Catcher (b. 8 Jun 1870 Raynham MA–d. 12 Jun 1902 at his home in Taunton MA) He died at the height of his career from an exhausted condition brought on by kidney and stomach troubles. Buried St Joseph Cemetery, Taunton MA.

Atley Donald—8 Years Pitcher (b. 19 Aug 1910 Morton MS–d. 19 Oct 1992 West Monroe LA) Died after battling cancer for a year.

Ed Donalds—1 Year Pitcher (b. 22 Jun 1885 Bidwell OH–d. 3 Jul 1950 at his home in Columbus OH) Buried Forest Lawn Memorial Gardens, Columbus OH.

Mike Donlin—12 Years Outfielder (b. 30 May 1878 Erie PA–d. 24 Sep 1933 at his home in Los Angeles CA) He played character parts in movies for ten years. Died from heart disease. Cremated.

Blix Donnelly—8 Years Pitcher (b. 21 Jan 1914 Olivia MN–d. 20 Jun 1976 Renville County Hospital, Olivia MN) Buried St Aloysius Catholic Church Cemetery, Olivia MN.

Ed Donnelly—2 Years Pitcher (b. 29 Jul 1880 Hampton NY–d. 28 Nov 1957 Rutland Hospital, Rutland VT) He worked in the slate manufacturing business at Rutland and operated a service station there. Died after a brief illness. Buried St Raphael Cemetery, Poultney VT.

Ed Donnelly—1 Year Pitcher (b. 10 Dec 1932 Allen MI–d. 25 Dec 1992 St Luke's Hospital, Houston TX) He worked for Exxon. Buried St Michael Catholic Cemetery, Weimer TX.

Frank Donnelly—1 Year Pitcher (b. 7 Oct 1869 Tamaroa IL–d. 3 Feb 1953 Graham Hospital, Canton IL) He played in the Three-I League and the Southern Association. He operated a taxi in Havana IL until ill health forced the amputation of both legs in 1947. Died from a stroke. Buried Laurel Hills Cemetery, Havana IL.

Jim Donnelly—11 Years Infielder (b. 19 Jul 1865 New Haven CT–d. 5 Mar 1915 New Haven CT).

Pete Donohue—12 Years Pitcher (b. 5 Nov 1900 Athens TX–d. 23 Feb 1988 Fort Worth TX) He was a retired co-owner of Berry Brothers and Donohue Cleaners in Fort Worth. Buried Greenwood Memorial Park, Fort Worth TX.

Lino Donoso—2 Years Pitcher (b. 23 Sep 1922 Havana, Cuba–d. 13 Oct 1990 Vera Cruz, Mexico).

Bill Donovan—2 Years Pitcher (b. 6 Jul 1916 Maywood IL–d. 25 Sep 1997 Maywood IL) Buried Chapel Hill Gardens West, Oakbrook Terrace IL.

Dick Donovan—15 Years Pitcher (b. 7 Dec 1927 Boston MA–d. 6 Jan 1997 South Shore Hospital, Weymouth MA) He was an investment broker for Eastman & Dillon in Boston and for Bache & Company in Boston. He later opened his own real estate appraisal office in Quincy, retiring in 1994. Buried Woodside Cemetery, Cohasset MA.

Fred Donovan—1 Year Catcher (b. 4 Jul 1864 NH–d. 7 Mar 1916 St John's Hospital, Springfield IL) He played and umpired in the Three-I League. When he died he was working at the Illinois Watch Factory in Springfield. Died from Bright's disease. Buried Oak Ridge Cemetery, Springfield IL.

Jerry Donovan—1 Year Catcher (b. 24 Aug 1875 Lock Haven PA–d. 27 Jun 1938 St Petersburg FL) For many years he was associated with H J Bressler in the wholesale and retail tobacco business at Williamsport PA. Died following a stroke suffered a week earlier. Buried St Mary's Cemetery, Lock Haven PA.

Mike Donovan—2 Years Infielder (b. 13 Oct 1883 New York City NY–d. 3 Feb 1938 New York City NY) Died after being shot to death by a fellow employee. Buried Calvary Cemetery, Woodside NY.

Patsy Donovan—17 Years Outfielder 11 Years Manager (b. 16 Mar 1865 County Cork, Ireland–d. 25 Dec 1953 at his home in Lawrence MA) He was a scout for the Yankees, retiring in 1940. Died following a short illness. Buried St Mary's Cemetery, Lawrence MA.

Tom Donovan—1 Year Outfielder (b. 7 Jul 1879 Lock Haven PA–d. 20 Feb 1955 at his home in Williamsport PA) He umpired minor league and college baseball. Later he was an assistant foreman in the Penn Railroad car shops at Tyrone PA until 1919. He then moved to Williamsport where he operated a retail tobacco store and a Coca-Cola distributorship, retiring in 1938. Died after a four-year illness, the last two years spent in bed. Buried St Mark's Cemetery, Lock Haven PA.

Tom Donovan—1 Year Outfielder (b. 1 Jan 1873 West Troy NY–d. 25 Mar 1933 at his home in Watervliet NY) He was a stove mounter for the Empire Furnace Company of Albany NY. Died after a long illness. Buried St Patrick's Cemetery, Watervliet NY.

Wild Bill Donovan—18 Years Pitcher 4 Years Manager (b. 13 Oct 1876 Lawrence MA–d. 9 Dec 1923 Forsyth NY) He worked his entire life in baseball as a player and manager. He was managing a minor league team in Connecticut when he was killed in a train wreck. Buried Holy Cross Cemetery, Yeadon PA.

Red Dooin—15 Years Catcher 5 Years Manager (b. 12 Jun 1879 Cincinnati OH–d. 14 May 1952 Rochester NY) He worked the vaudeville circuit as a singer with a tenor voice. Died from a heart attack. Buried Holy Sepulchre Cemetery, Rochester NY.

Mickey Doolan—13 Years Infielder (b. 7 May 1880 Ashland PA–d. 1 Nov 1951 at a hospital in Orlando FL) A dentist, he coached baseball before going into denistry. Buried Greenwood Cemetery.

Jack Dooms—1 Year Outfielder (b. 30 Jan 1867 St Louis MO–d. 14 Dec 1899 St Louis MO) Died from gastroenteritis.

Bill Doran—1 Year Infielder (b. 14 Jun 1898 San Francisco CA–d. 9 Mar 1978 St John's Hospital, Santa Monica CA) He was an umpire in the Pacific Coast League for 17 years. Died from a heart attack. Cremated.

Tom Doran—3 Years Catcher (b. 2 Feb 1880 Westchester County NY–d. 22 Jun 1910 New York City NY).

Jerry Dorgan—4 Years Outfielder (b. 1856 Meriden CT–d. 10 Jun 1891 at the jail in Middletown CT) Found drunk in a livery stable the night before, he died from acute alcoholism. Buried St John's Cemetery, Middletown CT.

Mike Dorgan—10 Years Outfielder 1 Year Manager (b. 2 Oct 1853 Middletown CT–d. 25 Apr 1909 St Francis Hospital, Hartford CT) He operated a saloon. Died from blood poisoning following surgery to repair an injured knee. Buried St Agnes Cemetery, Syracuse NY.

Harry Dorish—10 Years Pitcher (b. 13 Jul 1921 Swoyersville PA–d. 29 Dec 2000 Wilkes-Barre PA) Buried St Mary's Annunciation Church Cemetery, Pringle PA.

Charlie Dorman—1 Year Catcher (b. 23 Apr 1898 San Francisco CA–d. 15 Nov 1928 St Mary's Hospital, San Francisco CA) He was a San Francisco police officer. Died from an embolism in the coronary artery caused by a fracture of the left patella while playing baseball. Buried Woodlawn Memorial Park, Daly City CA.

Red Dorman—2 Years Outfielder (b. 3 Oct 1900 Jacksonville IL–d. 7 Jul 1974 Beverly Manor Convalescent Hosp, Anaheim CA) He was a fireman for 35 years. Died from kidney failure. Buried Westminster Memorial Park, Westminster CA.

Gus Dorner—6 Years Pitcher (b. 18 Aug 1876 Chambersburg PA–d. 4 May 1956 Chambersburg Hospital, Chambersburg PA) He managed minor league baseball a few years before working at Schael's Garage in Chamdersburg from 1918 until retiring in 1950. Died after a protracted illness. Buried Corpus Christi Cemetery, Chambersburg PA.

Bert Dorr—1 Year Pitcher (b. 22 Feb 1862 New York City NY–d. 16 Jun 1914 Dickinson Township NY).

Cal Dorsett—3 Years Pitcher (b. 10 Jun 1913 Greenville TX–d. 22 Oct 1970 Community Hospital, Elk City OK) Served for the U.S. Marines in the Pacific during World War II. He managed the Dr Pepper bottling plant in Elk City from 1955 until his death. Died from a heart attack. Buried Fairlawn Cemetery, Elk City OK.

Jerry Dorsey—1 Year Pitcher (b. 1854 Auburn NY–d. 3 Nov 1938 at his home in Auburn NY)

Died from a heart attack. Buried St Joseph's Cemetery, Auburn NY.

Herm Doscher—3 Years Infielder (b. 20 Dec 1852 New York City NY–d. 19 Mar 1934 Buffalo NY) He managed minor league baseball and umpired, including three years in the National League, before spending 20 years in the restaurant business in the Buffalo area. Buried Elmlawn Cemetery, Kenmore NY.

Jack Doscher—5 Years Pitcher (b. 27 Jul 1880 Troy NY–d. 27 May 1971 Meyer's Sanitorium, Park Ridge NJ) Politically active in the Democratic Party for more than 40 years, he was a Bergen County, NJ, undersheriff in the 1930s. Buried Mount Carmel Cemetery, Tenafly NJ.

Babe Doty—1 Year Pitcher (b. 17 Dec 1867 Genoa OH–d. 20 Nov 1929 St Vincent Hospital, Toledo OH) He was a carpenter for Ohio Public Service. Died from colon cancer. Buried Clay Township Cemetery, Genoa OH.

Abner Doubleday—(b. 1819–d. 26 Jan 1893 at his home in Mendham NJ) Served in the U.S. Army during the Mexican War and the Civil War. He is credited as one of the fathers of baseball. Died from Bright's disease. Buried Arlington National Cemetery, Arlington VA.

Charlie Dougherty—1 Year Infielder (b. 7 Feb 1862 Darlington WI–d. 18 Feb 1925 at his home in Milwaukee WI) Buried Forest Home Cemetery, Milwaukee WI.

Patsy Dougherty—10 Years Outfielder (b. 27 Oct 1876 Andover NY–d. 30 Apr 1940 at his home in Bolivar NY) For 23 years he was assistant cashier at the State Bank of Bolivar. Died suddenly from a heart ailment. Buried Catholic Cemetery, Bolivar NY.

Tom Dougherty—1 Year Pitcher (b. 30 May 1881 Chicago IL–d. 6 Nov 1953 St Mary's Hospital, Milwaukee WI) He pitched in the American Association for 12 years. He had both legs amputated due to arteriosclerosis in 1947 and 1949. Died from a heart attack. Buried Wisconsin Memorial Park, Brookfield WI.

John Douglas—1 Year Infielder (b. 14 Sep 1917 Thayer WV–d. 11 Feb 1984 Baptist Hospital, Miami FL) He lived in Coral Gables 42 years and was associated with the greyhound racetracks in Florida 35 years. Buried Woodlawn Park Cemetery, Miami FL.

Larry Douglas—1 Year Pitcher (b. 5 Jun 1890 Jellico TN–d. 4 Nov 1949 at his home in Jellico TN) Buried Jellico Cemetery, Jellico TN.

Phil Douglas—9 Years Pitcher (b. 17 Jun 1890 Cedartown GA–d. 1 Aug 1952 Sequatchie TN) He was banned from baseball in 1922 for a threatened breech of contract. Died from a stroke. Buried Tracy City Cemetery, Tracy City TN.

Astyanax Douglass—2 Years Catcher (b. 19 Sep 1897 Covington TX–d. 26 Jan 1975 at his apartment in El Paso TX) World War I veteran. He coached at Amarillo High School and was the original founder of the Furniture Warehouse stores in El Paso. Died from a heart attack after suffering from emphysema for 20 years. Buried Evergreen East Cemetery, El Paso TX.

Klondike Douglass—9 Years Infielder (b. 10 May 1872 Boston PA–d. 1 Oct 1953 Bend OR).

Taylor Douthit—11 Years Outfielder (b. 22 Apr 1901 Little Rock AR–d. 28 May 1986 at his home in Fremont CA) For 37 years he was a self-employed insurance broker in Oakland CA, retiring in 1966. Died from bronchial pneumonia and generalized heart disease. Cremated.

Clarence Dow—1 Year Outfielder (b. 11 Oct 1854 Charlestown MA–d. 11 Mar 1893 Somerville MA) He was a baseball writer for the *Boston Globe.* Died from consumption. Buried Woodlawn Cemetery, Everett MA.

Skip Dowd—1 Year Pitcher (b. 16 Feb 1889 Holyoke MA–d. 20 Dec 1960 Providence Hospital, Holyoke MA) A prominent insurance executive in Holyoke, he was the senior member in Dowd and Sons Insurance Company, as well as being active in civic, religious and fraternal organizations. Died after a short illness. Buried St Jerome Cemetery, Holyoke MA.

Snooks Dowd—2 Years Infielder (b. 20 Dec 1898 Springfield MA–d. 4 Apr 1962 Veteran's Hospital, Leeds MA) Served in the U.S. Army during World War I. Buried St Michael's Cemetery, Springfield MA.

Tommy Dowd—10 Years Outfielder 2 Years Manager (b. 20 Apr 1869 Holyoke MA–d. 2 Jul 1933 Holyoke MA) Died by drowning. Buried Calvary Cemetery, Holyoke MA.

Joe Dowie—1 Year Outfielder (b. 1866 New Orleans LA–d. 4 Mar 1917 at his home in New

Orleans LA) Shot by an assailant on the street on 3 Sep 1893, he recovered to work as a screwman foreman for Kent and Sons on the New Orleans riverfront. Died suddenly from a hemorrhage. Buried Soniat Street Cemetery, New Orleans LA.

Pete Dowling—4 Years Pitcher (b. St Louis MO–d. 30 Jun 1905 Hot Lake OR) At the height of his career he was decapitated when hit by a train while walking from Hot Lake to LaGrande OR. Buried Odd Fellows Cemetery, LaGrande OR.

Red Downey—1 Year Outfielder (b. 6 Feb 1889 Aurora IN–d. 10 Jul 1949 Detroit MI) A graduate of Georgetown University Law School, he was the general purchasing agent for Chrysler Corporation until 1928 when he became vice-president of the Dodge Division, in charge of trucks, retiring in 1940. Died following a long illness. Buried Woodlawn Cemetery, Detroit MI.

Tom Downey—6 Years Infielder (b. 1 Jan 1884 Lewiston ME–d. 3 Aug 1961 Passaic NJ).

Red Downs—3 Years Infielder (b. 23 Aug 1883 Neola IA–d. 19 Oct 1939 Council Bluffs IA) Died after a long illness. Buried Neola Township Cemetery, Neola IA.

Tom Dowse—3 Years Catcher (b. 12 Aug 1867 Ireland–d. 14 Dec 1946 County Hospital, Riverside CA) He was a retired salesman. Died from bronchopneumonia brought on by chronic pyelonephritis. Buried Evergreen Memorial Park, Riverside CA.

Carl Doyle—4 Years Pitcher (b. 30 Jul 1912 Knoxville TN–d. 4 Sep 1951 General Hospital, Knoxville TN) He was a Knoxville policeman from 1942 until his death. Died after an illness of several months. Buried Lynnhurst Cemetery, Knoxville TN.

Conny Doyle—1 Year Outfielder (b. 26 Sep 1857 South Hampton MA–d. 6 Oct 1938 at his home in West Springfield MA) He worked 17 years for the Springfield Street Railway Company and at one time drove the first horse car in West Springfield. He then owned the Orchard Farm in Westfield MA for eight years before working 25 years as the custodian at the West Springfield Public Library. Buried St Thomas Cemetery, West Springfield MA.

Conny Doyle—2 Years Outfielder (b. 1862 Ireland–d. 29 Jul 1921 El Paso TX).

Ed Doyle—1 Year Pitcher (b. abt 1850 IL–d. 6 Feb 1929 Havre MT) He moved from St Paul MN to Havre while working for the Great Northern Railway. There he operated a hand laundry eight years, then a soda pop bottling company another nine years. In 1899 he was elected the first mayor of Havre and served two more terms on the city council. Died following an illness of several weeks. Buried Calvary Cemetery, Havre MT.

Jack Doyle—17 Years Infielder 2 Years Manager (b. 25 Oct 1869 Killorgin, Ireland–d. 31 Dec 1958 Providence Hospital, Holyoke MA) He spent more than 70 years in organized baseball as a player, manager, umpire and scout. He retired as a scout for the Cubs in 1948, after 28 years with the club, but remained in an advisory capacity. Died from a heart attack. Buried St Jerome Cemetery, Holyoke MA.

Jess Doyle—4 Years Pitcher (b. 14 Apr 1898 Knoxville TN–d. 15 Apr 1961 Memorial Hospital, Belleville IL) World War I veteran. He operated a tavern in Belleville for many years. Died from an internal hemorrhage. Buried Walnut Hill Cemetery, Belleville IL.

Jim Doyle—2 Years Infielder (b. 25 Dec 1881 Detroit MI–d. 1 Feb 1912 St Joseph's Hospital, Syracuse NY) Died at the height of his baseball career from blood poisoning following surgery for appendicitis. Buried St Agnes Cemetery, Syracuse NY.

Joe Doyle—1 Year Manager (b. 9 Apr 1838 New York City NY–d. 7 Jan 1906 Elberon Hotel, White Plains NY) The original organizer of the Brooklyn baseball team, for his last 15 years he was the proprietor of the Elberon Hotel in White Plains. Died from pneumonia.

John Doyle—1 Year Outfielder (b. Nova Scotia–d. 24 Dec 1915 Providence RI).

Larry Doyle—14 Years Infielder (b. 31 Jul 1886 Caseyville IL–d. 1 Mar 1974 Saranac Lake NY) Buried St Bernard's Church Cemetery, Saranac Lake NY.

Slow Joe Doyle—5 Years Pitcher (b. 15 Sep 1881 Leonardville KS–d. 21 Nov 1947 Tannersville NY) He conducted a summer garage business in Haines Falls NY and traveled widely during the winters, spending part of the time in Florida. Died from a heart attack. Buried Evergreen Cemetery, Tannersville NY.

Bill Drake—9 Years Pitcher (b. 8 Jun 1895 Sedalia MO–d. 30 Oct 1977 St Louis MO) He played in the negro leagues.

Delos Drake—3 Years Outfielder (b. 3 Dec 1886 Girard OH–d. 3 Oct 1965 Findlay OH) Buried St Michael's Cemetery, Findlay OH.

Larry Drake—2 Years Outfielder (b. 4 May 1921 McKinney TX–d. 14 Jul 1985 Houston TX) He was a division manager of Western Company of North America. Buried Memorial Park Cemetery, Tyler TX.

Logan Drake—3 Years Pitcher (b. 26 Dec 1900 Spartanburg SC–d. 1 Jun 1940 Columbia Hospital, Columbia SC) Died after being ill two days. Buried Elmwood Cemetery, Columbia SC.

Tom Drake—2 Years Pitcher (b. 7 Aug 1914 Birmingham AL–d. 2 Jul 1988 Birmingham AL) Buried Marvin's Chapel Cemetery, Pinson AL.

John Drebinger—Hall of Fame (b. abt 1891 New York City NY–d. 23 Oct 1979 at a nursing home in Greensboro NC) For 40 years he was a sportswriter for the *New York Times,* retiring in 1964. After retiring he did public relations work for the Yankees. Cremated.

Bill Dreesen—1 Year Infielder (b. 26 Jul 1904 New York City NY–d. 9 Nov 1971 Mount Vernon NY).

Bill Drescher—3 Years Catcher (b. 23 May 1921 Congers NY–d. 15 May 1968 Haverstraw NY).

Chuck Dressen—8 Years Infielder 16 Years Manager (b. 20 Sep 1898 Decatur IL–d. 10 Aug 1966 Henry Ford Hospital, Detroit MI) He spent his entire life in baseball as a player, coach and manager. He went to the hospital for a kidney infection, but died there from heart failure. Buried Forest Lawn Memorial Park, Glendale CA.

Lee Dressen—2 Years Infielder (b. 23 Jul 1888 Ellinwood KS–d. 30 Jun 1931 at a hospital in Odell NE) Died after a long illness. Buried Prairie Home Cemetery, Diller NE.

Bob Dresser—1 Year Pitcher (b. 4 Oct 1878 Newton MA–d. 27 Jul 1924 Duxbury MA).

Frank Drews—2 Years Infielder (b. 25 May 1916 Buffalo NY–d. 22 Apr 1972 Buffalo General Hospital, Buffalo NY) He worked for the Chevrolet Motor Division's forge plant in the Town of Tonawanda NY from 1953 to 1969. He was a member of the Western New York Softball Hall of Fame. Buried St Stanislaus Cemetery, Buffalo NY.

Karl Drews—8 Years Pitcher (b. 22 Feb 1920 Staten Island NY–d. 15 Aug 1963 Dania FL) Killed instantly when he was hit by a car while attempting to get help on Florida Hwy 1 after his car had stalled. Buried Memorial Gardens Cemetery, Hollywood FL.

Barney Dreyfuss—(b. 23 Feb 1865–d. 5 Feb 1932) He owned the Pirates from 1900 until his death. Buried West View Cemetery, Pittsburgh PA.

Florence Dreyfuss—(b. abt 1882–d. 12 May 1950 Montefiore Hospital, Pittsburgh PA) She owned the Pirates from 1932, when her husband died, until 1946. Her husband owned the team from 1900 until his death. Died after an illness of three weeks. Buried West View Cemetery, Pittsburgh PA.

Lew Drill—4 Years Catcher (b. 9 May 1877 Browerville MN–d. 4 Jul 1969 St Paul MN) After his baseball career he was athletic director at Hamline University, an attorney, and a U.S. District Court Judge. Died following a brief illness. Buried Sunset Memorial Park, Minneapolis MN.

Denny Driscoll—5 Years Pitcher (b. 19 Nov 1855 Lowell MA–d. 11 Jul 1886 Lowell MA) Died from consumption.

Mike Driscoll—1 Year Pitcher (b. 19 Oct 1892 Rockland MA–d. 21 Mar 1953 Foxboro MA) Buried Immaculate Conception Cemetery, Easton MA.

Paddy Driscoll—1 Year Infielder (b. 11 Jan 1895 Evanston IL–d. 28 Jun 1968 Illinois Masonic Hospital, Chicago IL) An all-around athlete, he stared in baseball, football and basketball while attending college and played professional football. He coached both professional and college football and was an advisor for the Chicago Bears when he died. Buried All Saints Cemetery, Des Plaines IL.

Mike Drissel—1 Year Catcher (b. 19 Dec 1865 St Louis MO–d. 26 Feb 1913 St Louis MO) Buried SS Peter and Paul Cemetery, St Louis MO.

Tom Drohan—1 Year Pitcher (b. 26 Aug 1888 Fall River MA–d. 17 Sep 1926 St Francis Hospital, Kewanee IL) He worked his last seven years for the Kewanee Fire Department. Died from uremic poisoning. Buried Pleasant View Cemetery, Kewanee IL.

Dick Drott—7 Years Pitcher (b. 1 Jul 1936 Cincinnati OH–d. 16 Aug 1985 at his home in Glendale Heights IL) He was a supervisor and baseball coordinator for the Chicago IL Park District from 1965 until his death. Died from stomach cancer. Buried Queen of Heaven Cemetery, Hillside IL.

Louis Drucke—4 Years Pitcher (b. 3 Dec 1888 Waco TX–d. 22 Sep 1955 at his home in Waco TX) Served for the U.S. Army in Europe during World War I. After hurting his back in a subway accident he retired from baseball at age 24 and entered the cotton business. Buried Holy Cross Cemetery, Waco TX.

Carl Druhot—2 Years Pitcher (b. 1 Sep 1882 OH–d. 5 Feb 1918 Good Samaritan Hospital, Portland OR) Died from head injuries suffered several weeks earlier in an industrial accident at the Northwest Steel plant. Buried Mount Scott Park Cemetery, Portland OR.

Cal Drummond—(b. 29 Jun 1917 Ninety Six SC–d. 3 May 1970 Des Moines IA) World War II veteran. He was an American League umpire from 1960 to 1969. Died from a cerebral hemorrhage while umpiring an American Association game. He had brain surgery the year before after being hit in the head by a foul ball. He was scheduled to return to the American League the next day. Buried Greenwood Memorial Gardens, Greenwood SC.

Charles Dryden—Hall of Fame (b. abt 1859–d. 11 Feb 1931 at his winter cottage in Ocean Springs MS) A well-known humorist, poet, traveler and sportswriter, he worked several years for Chicago newspapers — the *Tribune*, *Herald* and *Examiner*. He had been an invalid several years, suffering a stroke ten years earlier. Buried Monmouth City Cemetery, Monmouth IL.

Don Drysdale—14 Years Pitcher Hall of Fame (b. 23 Jul 1936 Van Nuys CA–d. 3 Jul 1993 Montreal, Canada) For 23 years he was an announcer for the Angels, Expos and Dodgers. Died from a heart attack in his hotel room. Buried Forest Lawn Memorial Park, Glendale CA.

Monk Dubiel—7 Years Pitcher (b. 12 Feb 1919 Hartford CT–d. 23 Oct 1969 Hartford Hospital, Hartford CT) He worked for Rockwell Manufacturing Company and later for the Hartford Post Office. Died from cirrhosis of the liver. Buried Rose Hill Memorial Park, Rocky Hill CT.

Jean Dubuc—9 Years Pitcher (b. 15 Sep 1888 Nashua NH–d. 28 Aug 1958 Lee Memorial Hospital, Fort Myers FL) He managed minor league baseball, coached and scouted for some years before working 20 years as a salesman for Braden-Sutphin Ink Company. He also coached baseball at Brown Univ. Died after a series of strokes. Buried Fort Myers Memorial Gardens, Fort Myers FL.

Clise Dudley—5 Years Pitcher (b. 8 Aug 1903 Graham NC–d. 12 Jan 1989 Berkeley Convalescent Ctr, Moncks Corner SC) Buried Lake City Memorial Park, Lake City SC.

Jim Dudley—(b. 1909 Alexandria VA–d. 12 Feb 1999 Tucson AZ) Served in the U.S. Army Air Corps during World War II. The radio voice of the Indians for 20 years, starting in 1948, he greeted fans tuning in on the radio with, "Hello baseball fans everywhere." Died following a stroke, after suffering from Alzheimer's disease, and spending his last two years in a special care home.

John Dudra—1 Year Infielder (b. 27 May 1916 Assumption IL–d. 24 Oct 1965 Huber Memorial Hospital, Pana IL) Awarded five major battle stars for action in the European Theater during World War I. He was a coal miner at the Pana Refinery and later worked for the Christian County Highway Department. Died from diabetes. Buried Calvary Cemetery, Pana IL.

Larry Duff—1 Year Pitcher (b. 30 Nov 1896 Radersburg MT–d. 10 Nov 1969 Bend OR).

Pat Duff—1 Game Pinch Hitter (b. 6 May 1875 Providence RI–d. 11 Sep 1925 Providence RI) He was the first baseball coach at Providence College, coaching there two years. Died after a lingering illness.

Charlie Duffee—5 Years Outfielder (b. 27 Jan 1866 Mobile AL–d. 24 Dec 1894 Mobile AL) After leaving baseball because of ill health he worked one year in the saloon business at

Mobile before dying from a lingering bout with lung trouble. Buried Magnolia Cemetery, Mobile AL.

Bernie Duffy—1 Year Pitcher (b. 18 Aug 1893 Vinson OK–d. 9 Feb 1962 St Ann Hospital, Abilene TX) He was an independent oil operator in West Texas and Oklahoma. Died from cancer. Buried Elmwood Memorial Park, Abilene TX.

Hugh Duffy—17 Years Outfielder 8 Years Manager Hall of Fame (b. 26 Nov 1866 Cranston RI–d. 19 Oct 1954 at his home in Brighton MA) He has the all-time high batting average for a single season of .438 in 1894. He was a scout for the Red Sox until 1953. Buried Mount Calvary Cemetery, Roslindale MA.

Dan Dugan—2 Years Pitcher (b. 22 Feb 1907 Plainfield NJ–d. 25 Jun 1968 Green Brook NJ).

Ed Dugan—1 Year Pitcher (b. abt 1861 LaCrosse WI–d. 19 Jul 1943 at his home in Sea Cliff NJ) He was one of the founders of Dugan Brothers, Inc, a New York City based baking company. Died following several heart attacks. Buried Mount Olivet Cemetery, Maspeth NY.

Joe Dugan—14 Years Infielder (b. 12 May 1897 Pottsville PA–d. 8 Jul 1982 Norwood MA) Died from pneumonia after suffering a stroke. Buried Mount Calvary Cemetery, Roslindale MA.

Gus Dugas—4 Years Outfielder (b. 24 Mar 1907 Quebec, Canada–d. 14 Apr 1997 Colchester Nursing Center, Colchester CT) He worked 25 years for the Plastic Wire and Cable Company in Jewett City CT, retiring in 1972. Died two weeks after suffering a stroke. Buried St Joseph's Cemetery, Colchester CT.

Dan Dugdale—2 Years Catcher (b. 28 Oct 1864 Peoria IL–d. 9 Mar 1934 Providence Hospital, Seattle WA) Widely known as the "Father of Northwest Baseball," he at one time owned the Seattle franchise in the old Northwest League. He served part of a term as a Washington State legislator. Died after being hit by a truck while walking across the street. Buried Calvary Cemetery, Seattle WA.

Oscar DuGey—6 Years Infielder (b. 25 Oct 1887 Palestine TX–d. 1 Jan 1966 Dallas TX) Died at the Ambassador Hotel where he lived. Buried Oakland Cemetery, Dallas TX.

Jim Duggan—1 Year Infielder (b. 1 Jun 1885 Franklin IN–d. 5 Dec 1951 Indianapolis IN) World War I veteran. Buried Holy Cross Cemetery, Indianapolis IN.

Bill Duggleby—8 Years Pitcher (b. 16 Mar 1874 Utica NY–d. 30 Aug 1944 at his sister's home in Redfield NY) He worked for the Savage Arms Corporation at Rome NY. Died from heart trouble. Buried Redfield Cemetery, Redfield NY.

Martin Duke—1 Year Pitcher (b. Columbus OH–d. 31 Dec 1898 City Hospital, Minneapolis MN) At the time of his death he was working as a saloon porter in Minneapolis.

George Dumont—5 Years Pitcher (b. 13 Nov 1895 Minneapolis MN–d. 13 Oct 1956 Minneapolis MN) Buried Lakewood Cemetery, Minneapolis MN.

Nick Dumovich—1 Year Pitcher (b. 2 Jan 1902 Sacramento CA–d. 12 Dec 1979 Laguna Hills CA).

Frank Duncan—22 Years Catcher 8 Years Manager (b. 14 Feb 1901 Kansas City MO–d. 4 Dec 1973 Veteran's Hospital, Kansas City MO) He played in the negro leagues. Served in the U.S. Army during World War II. After his playing days were over he was known as one of the most competent umpires in the negro leagues. Later he was a bondsman for Passantio Bonding Company in Kansas City. Buried Highland Park Cemetery, Kansas City MO.

Jim Duncan—1 Year Catcher (b. 1 Jul 1871 Oil City PA–d. 16 Oct 1901 Foxburg PA) A boilermaker by trade, he had recently retired from baseball and was working as an inspector of boilers for the P & W Railway. He drowned with two companions when his boat capsized while fishing. His body was not recovered.

Pat Duncan—7 Years Outfielder (b. 6 Oct 1893 Coalton OH–d. 17 Jul 1960 Jackson OH) Served in the U.S. Army during World War I. Buried Fairmount Cemetery, Jackson OH.

Vern Duncan—3 Years Outfielder (b. 6 Jan 1890 Clayton NC–d. 1 Jun 1954 Daytona Beach FL) He was an antique dealer. Died unexpectedly while enroute to Halifax Hospital. Buried Hillside Cemetery, Ormond Beach FL.

Ed Dundon—2 Years Pitcher (b. 10 Jul 1859 Columbus OH–d. 18 Aug 1893 at his home in Columbus OH) He was known as the famous mute pitcher. Died at the height of his career from consumption. Buried Mount Calvary Cemetery, Columbus OH.

Gus Dundon—3 Years Infielder (b. 10 Jul 1874 Columbus OH–d. 1 Sep 1940 at his home in Pittsburgh PA) He managed minor league baseball several years. Died from a stroke. Buried North Side Catholic Cemetery, Pittsburgh PA.

Sam Dungan—5 Years Outfielder (b. 29 Jan 1866 Ferndale CA–d. 16 Mar 1939 at his home in Santa Ana CA) He was a rancher for 32 years. Died from heart disease. Buried Fairhaven Memorial Park, Santa Ana CA.

Lee Dunham—1 Year Infielder (b. 9 Jun 1902 Atlanta IL–d. 11 May 1961 enroute to Lincoln Mem Hospital, Lincoln IL) An attorney, he was serving his second elected term as Logan County, IL, judge when he died from a heart attack. Buried Atlanta Cemetery, Atlanta IL.

Wiley Dunham—1 Year Pitcher (b. 30 Jan 1877 Piketon OH–d. 16 Jan 1934 Lakeside Hospital, Cleveland OH) He was an insurance salesman. Died from lobar pneumonia. Buried Mound Cemetery, Piketon OH.

Davey Dunkle—5 Years Pitcher (b. 19 Aug 1872 Philipsburg PA–d. 19 Nov 1941 at his home in Lock Haven PA) He worked 30 years in the pipe shop of a paper mill in Lock Haven. Died from an illness that had kept him bedfast his last five months. Buried Highland Cemetery, Lock Haven PA.

Bill Dunlap—2 Years Outfielder (b. 1 May 1909 Three Rivers MA–d. 29 Nov 1980 Community General Hospital, Reading PA) He was a steelworker for Carpenter Technology Corp and, later, for Bethlehem Steel Corp. Died after six days in the hospital. Buried Charles Evans Cemetery, Reading PA.

Fred Dunlap—12 Years Infielder 1 Year Manager (b. 21 May 1859 Philadelphia PA–d. 1 Dec 1902 Philadelphia PA) Died from a rectal disorder. Buried Odd Fellows Cemetery, Rockledge PA.

Jack Dunleavy—3 Years Outfielder (b. 14 Sep 1879 Norwalk CT–d. 11 Apr 1944 South Norwalk CT) Died from a heart attack while waiting for a train to Danbury CT. Buried St Mary's Cemetery, Norwalk CT.

George Dunlop—2 Years Infielder (b. 19 Jul 1888 Meriden CT–d. 12 Dec 1972 Meriden CT).

Jack Dunn—8 Years Infielder (b. 6 Oct 1872 Meadville PA–d. 22 Oct 1928 Towson MD) He owned and managed the minor league Orioles from 1910 until his death. Died from a heart attack while horseback riding. Buried St Mary's Cemetery, Baltimore MD.

James C Dunn—(b. 11 Sep 1866 near Marshalltown IA–d. 9 Jun 1922 Chicago IL) Earning his fortune in railroad construction work, he was the owner of the Cleveland Indians from 1916 until his death. Buried Riverside Cemetery, Marshalltown IA.

Joe Dunn—2 Years Catcher (b. 11 Mar 1885 Springfield OH–d. 19 Mar 1944 at his home in Springfield OH) He managed minor league baseball a number of years before going to work for Shell Oil Company. Later he was a timekeeper for Robbins and Myers, Inc. Died from a heart attack. Buried Calvary Cemetery, Springfield OH.

Steve Dunn—1 Year Infielder (b. 21 Dec 1858 London, Ontario, Canada–d. 5 May 1933 London, Ontario, Canada).

Andy Dunning—2 Years Pitcher (b. 12 Aug 1871 New York City NY–d. 21 Jun 1952 New York City NY).

Mike Dupaugher—1 Year Catcher (b. 11 Sep 1858 Marysville CA–d. 7 Jul 1915 San Francisco CA) Buried Holy Cross Catholic Cemetery, Colma CA.

Frank Dupee—1 Year Pitcher (b. 29 Apr 1877 Monkton VT–d. 14 Aug 1956 Portland ME) He injured his arm early in his career, but was able to pitch 15 years in the minor leagues. After retiring from baseball he was a Maine guide for over 30 years. Buried Pine Grove Cemetery, Falmouth ME.

Kid Durbin—3 Years Outfielder (b. 10 Sep 1886 Lamar KS–d. 11 Sep 1943 Kirkwood MO) Buried St Peter's Cemetery, St Louis MO.

Bull Durham—4 Years Pitcher (b. 27 Jun 1876 New Oxford PA–d. 28 Jun 1960 Bentley KS) A retired geologist, he had lived in Bentley 18 years. Buried Pleasant Valley Cemetery, Bentley KS.

Ed Durham—5 Years Pitcher (b. 17 Aug 1907 Chester SC–d. 27 Apr 1976 Chester County Hospital, Chester SC) He owned and operated the Ed Durham Service Station in Blackstock SC for 25 years, retiring in 1972. Died after an illness of several days. Buried Presbyterian Church Cemetery, Blackstock SC.

Jimmy Durham —1 Year Pitcher (b. 7 Oct 1881 Douglass KS–d. 7 May 1949 Coffeyville KS) He operated a drugstore in Douglass until retiring in 1942, after which he served as a substitute pharmacist at a drugstore in Wichita KS for six years. He moved to Coffeyville in 1949. Died from a heart ailment. Buried Douglass Cemetery, Douglass KS.

Dick Durning —2 Years Pitcher (b. 10 Oct 1892 Louisville KY–d. 23 Sep 1948 Veteran's Hospital, Castle Point NY) Served in World War I. Buried Zachary Taylor National Cemetery, Louisville KY.

George Durning —4 Years Outfielder (b. 9 May 1898 Philadelphia PA–d. 18 Apr 1986 Tampa FL).

Leo Durocher —17 Years Infielder 24 Years Manager Hall of Fame (b. 27 Jul 1905 West Springfield MA–d. 7 Oct 1991 Desert Hospital, Palm Springs CA) Known as "The Lip," he coined the phrase, "Nice guys finish last." He worked in baseball 48 years as a player, coach, manager and broadcaster. Died from complications of abdominal hemorrhaging. Buried Forest Lawn-Hollywood Hills, Los Angeles CA.

Red Durrett —2 Years Outfielder (b. 3 Feb 1921 Sherman TX–d. 17 Jan 1992 Waxahachie TX) Served at Guadalcanal for the U.S. Marine Corps during World War II. He retired from the U.S. Postal Servive in 1982. Buried Laurel Land Memorial Park, Dallas TX.

Cedric Durst —7 Years Outfielder (b. 23 Aug 1896 Austin TX–d. 16 Feb 1971 Mercy Hospital, San Diego CA) He managed in the Pacific Coast League and was a security guard at the Convair aircraft factory in San Diego. Died from a stroke. Buried El Camino Memorial Park, San Diego CA.

Jesse Duryea —5 Years Pitcher (b. 7 Sep 1859 Osage IA–d. 19 Aug 1942 at his home in Algona IA) His baseball career ended suddenly when he was hit in the face with a pitched ball, damaging his eyesight. He operated hotels in Britt IA and in Algona from 1895 to 1915. For years he worked at the Barry Recreation Parlor in Algona, retiring in 1938. Died after a long illness. Buried Riverview Cemetery, Algona IA.

Erv Dusak —9 Years Outfielder (b. 29 Jul 1920 Chicago IL–d. 6 Nov 1994 Glendale Heights IL) Buried Woodlawn Cemetery, Forest Park IL.

Bill Duzen —1 Year Pitcher (b. 21 Feb 1870 Buffalo NY–d. 11 Mar 1944 at his home in Buffalo NY) He was a patrolman for the Buffalo NY police force for 44 years before retiring in 1940. Died from a heart attack. Buried White Chapel Memorial Park, Amherst NY.

Ward Dwight —1 Year Catcher (b. 4 Jan 1856 New York City NY–d. 20 Feb 1903 San Francisco CA) He was a merchant. Died from heart disease. Cremated.

Double Joe Dwyer —12 Games Pinch Hitter (b. 27 Mar 1903 Orange NJ–d. 21 Oct 1992 Mountainside Hospital, Glen Ridge NJ) For many years he was a security guard for Carteret Savings and Loan in Newark NJ. Buried Gate of Heaven Catholic Cemetery, East Hanover NJ.

Frank Dwyer —12 Years Pitcher 1 Year Manager (b. 25 Mar 1868 Lee MA–d. 4 Feb 1943 House of Mercy Hospital, Pittsfield MA) He conducted a coal business in Geneva NY for over 50 years. Umpired in the American League in 1904 and was the New York State Boxing Commissioner from 1916 to 1922. Died from a heart attack while visiting his family in Massachusetts. Buried St Patrick's Cemetery, Geneva NY.

Ben Dyer —6 Years Infielder (b. 13 Feb 1893 Chicago IL–d. 7 Aug 1959 Kenosa Hospital, Kenosha WI) Served in the U.S. Navy during World War I. He worked for Simmons Company for several years. Died following a long illness. Buried Green Ridge Cemetery, Kenosha WI.

Eddie Dyer —6 Years Pitcher 5 Years Manager (b. 11 Oct 1900 Morgan City LA–d. 20 Apr 1964 Methodist Hospital, Houston TX) He was a partner in an insurance firm and had extensive holdings in oil and other business enterprises. Died after being in ill health since suffering a stroke two years earlier. Buried Garden of Gethsemani, Houston TX.

Jimmy Dygert —6 Years Pitcher (b. 5 Jul 1884 Utica NY–d. 7 Feb 1936 New Orleans LA) He lived in New Orleans 30 years, working as a repair foreman for New Orleans Public Service, Inc. Died from pneumonia. Buried Greenwood Cemetery, New Orleans LA.

Jimmy Dykes —22 Years Infielder 21 Years Manager (b. 10 Nov 1896 Philadelphia PA–d. 15 Jun 1976 Hahnemann Hospital, Philadelphia PA) Served in the U.S. Army during World War I. He spent his entire life in baseball as a player, coach and manager. Buried St Dennis Church Cemetery, Havertown PA.

E

Bad Bill Eagan—3 Years Infielder (b. 1 Jun 1869 Camden NJ–d. 14 Feb 1905 Denver County Hospital, Denver CO) He went to Denver for his health, but failed to rally. He was penniless when he died from consumption.

Truck Eagan—1 Year Infielder (b. 10 Aug 1876 San Francisco CA–d. 19 Mar 1949 at his home in San Francisco CA) He was a retired warehouseman. Died from heart disease. Buried Greenlawn Memorial Park, Daly City CA.

Bill Eagle—1 Year Outfielder (b. 25 Jul 1877 Comus MD–d. 27 Apr 1951 at his son's home in Churchtown MD) He entered railway police work with the Baltimore and Ohio Railway in 1900 and retired as captain of police for the Southern Railway System in 1942. Buried Union Cemetery, Rockville MD.

Charlie Eakle—1 Year Infielder (b. 27 Sep 1887 Baltimore MD–d. 15 Jun 1959 Baltimore MD) Buried New Cathedral Cemetery, Baltimore MD.

Howard Earl—2 Years Outfielder (b. 27 Feb 1869 Palmyra NY–d. 22 Dec 1916 at his home in North Bay NY) He managed minor league baseball and was a scout for the Pirates. He was sick but one week when he died from an attack of stomach and bowell trouble. Buried New York City NY.

Billy Earle—5 Years Catcher (b. 10 Nov 1867 Philadelphia PA–d. 30 May 1946 Omaha NE) Buried Forest Lawn Memorial Park, Omaha NE.

Arnie Earley—8 Years Pitcher (b. 4 Jun 1933 Lincoln Park MI–d. 29 Sep 1999 at his home in Flint MI) He worked for the Genesee County (MI) Sheriff's Department from 1969 to 1977. Buried Sunset Hills, Flint MI.

Tom Earley—6 Years Pitcher (b. 18 Apr 1917 Roxbury MA–d. 5 Apr 1988 at his apartment in Nantucket MA) Served in the U.S. Navy during World War II. He was an expediter for the Fafnir Bearing Company in New Britain CT for 28 years. Died from a heart attack. Buried St Mary's Cemetery, Nantucket MA.

Jake Early—9 Years Catcher (b. 19 May 1915 King's Mountain NC–d. 31 May 1985 Holmes Regional Med Center, Melbourne FL) He worked as a groundskeeper for the Twins before retiring to Florida in 1963. Buried Brevard Memorial Park, Cocoa FL.

George Earnshaw—9 Years Pitcher (b. 15 Feb 1900 New York City NY–d. 1 Dec 1976 at a hospital in Little Rock AR) He was awarded the Bronze Star for his service during World War II. In 1952 he moved to Hot Springs AR and retired as personnel director for Dierk's Forests in 1962. Buried Memorial Gardens Cemetery, Hot Springs AR.

Mal Eason—6 Years Pitcher (b. 13 Mar 1879 Brookville PA–d. 16 Apr 1970 Douglas AZ) Died in a fire at his home. Buried Black Oak Cemetery, Camille (south of Elgin) AZ.

Carl East—2 Years Outfielder (b. 27 Aug 1894 Marietta GA–d. 15 Jan 1953 at his farm home near Whitesburg GA) World War I veteran. He managed minor league baseball for a short while before opening an insurance office for Gulf Life in 1935. Buried Mount Pleasant Church Cemetery, Clem GA.

Hugh East—3 Years Pitcher (b. 7 Jul 1918 Birmingham AL–d. 2 Nov 1981 Charleston SC) World War II veteran. For 25 years he was an insurance salesman for Liberty National Life Insurance Company. Buried Valhalla Cemetery, Bessemer AL.

Luke Easter—6 Years Infielder (b. 4 Aug 1915 St Louis MO–d. 29 Mar 1979 Euclid OH) He worked for TRW, Inc. in Euclid. Died after being shot by two men during a robbery outside a bank. He had just cashed some of his fellow worker's paychecks, as a favor, and was carrying several thousand dollars. Buried Highland Park Cemetery, Cleveland OH.

Henry Easterday—4 Years Infielder (b. 16 Sep 1864 Philadelphia PA–d. 30 Mar 1895 Philadelphia PA) Buried Fernwood Cemetery, Fernwood PA.

Paul Easterling—3 Years Outfielder (b. 28 Sep 1905 Reidsville GA–d. 15 Mar 1993 Tattnall Nursing Home, Reidsville GA) He was a retired service station attendant. Died after a long illness. Buried Reidsville City Cemetery, Reidsville GA.

Ted Easterly—7 Years Catcher (b. 20 Apr 1885 Lincoln NE–d. 6 Jul 1951 at his home in Clear Lake Highlands CA) A carpenter, he had lived in the Clear Lake area since 1926. Died from bladder cancer. Buried Lower Lake Cemetery, Lower Lake CA.

Roy Easterwood—1 Year Catcher (b. 12 Jan 1915 Waxahachie TX–d. 24 Aug 1984 Cedar Oaks Nursing Home, Graham TX) Died from cardiac arrest. Buried Pioneer Cemetery, Graham TX.

Jack Easton—5 Years Pitcher (b. 28 Feb 1867 Bridgeport OH–d. 28 Nov 1903 at his apartment in Steubenville OH) He was a glass finisher at the Jefferson Glass Works. Died from stomach trouble after an illness of four or five months. Buried Indian Mound Cemetery, Tiltonsville OH.

Zeb Eaton—2 Years Pitcher (b. 2 Feb 1920 Cooleemee NC–d. 17 Dec 1989 West Palm Beach FL).

Vallie Eaves—5 Years Pitcher (b. 6 Sep 1911 Allen OK–d. 19 Apr 1960 Oklahoma State Hospital, Norman OK) Died from cancer. Buried Connerville Cemetery, Connerville OK.

Eddie Eayrs—3 Years Outfielder (b. 10 Nov 1890 Blackstone MA–d. 30 Nov 1969 Kent County Memorial Hospital, Warwick RI) Served in the U.S. Navy during World War I. He coached baseball at Brown University two years and was a broker in Providence RI. He also was a cashier at Lincoln Park RI and Narragansett RI. Died after a brief illness. Buried Swan Point Cemetery, Providence RI.

Charlie Ebbets—1 Year Manager (b. 29 Oct 1859 New York City NY–d. 18 Apr 1925 Waldorf-Astoria Hotel, New York City NY) He was part-owner of the Brooklyn Robins (later called Dodgers). Died from heart disease. Buried Greenwood Cemetery, Brooklyn NY.

Hi Ebright—1 Year Catcher (b. 12 Jun 1859 Lancaster County PA–d. 23 Oct 1916 Milwaukee WI) Buried Evergreen Cemetery, Milwaukee WI.

Harry Eccles—1 Year Pitcher (b. 9 Jul 1893 Kennedy NY–d. 2 Jun 1955 General Hospital, Jamestown NY) Served in France for the U.S. Army during World War I. He was a rural mail carrier for 36 years and a volunteer fireman. Died following a heart attack suffered a week earlier. Buried Riverside Cemetery, Kennedy NY.

Johnny Echols—2 Games Pinch Runner (b. 9 Jan 1917 Atlanta GA–d. 12 Nov 1972 Atlanta GA) He was a salesman for a wholesale electrical company. World War II veteran. Died from cancer. Buried Greenwood Cemetery, Atlanta GA.

Al Eckert—3 Years Pitcher (b. 17 May 1906 Milwaukee WI–d. 20 Apr 1974 Milwaukee WI) He was a foreman at the Pabst Brewery in Milwaukee. Buried Good Hope Cemetery, Milwaukee WI.

Charlie Eckert—3 Years Pitcher (b. 8 Aug 1897 Philadelphia PA–d. 22 Aug 1986 at his home in Bensalem PA) He managed minor league baseball two years before working for the Ford Motor plant in Chester PA from 1938 until his retirement. Died following a lengthy illness. Buried Forest Hills Cemetery, Philadelphia PA.

William Eckert—(b. 20 Jan 1909–d. 16 Apr 1971 Freeport, Bahamas) Served in World War II as commander of a bomber group and chief of flight maintenance for the Ninth Air Force in Europe. He retired from the U.S. Air Force in 1961 as a lieutenant general and was baseball commissioner from 1965 until 1968. Died from a heart attack while playing tennis. Buried Arlington National Cemetery, Arlington VA.

Ox Eckhardt—2 Years Outfielder (b. 23 Dec 1901 Yorktown TX–d. 22 Apr 1951 at his home near Yorktown TX) He played 16 years of minor league baseball, compiling a lifetime .367 minor league batting average. He then became known throughout Texas as an outstanding cattleman. Died from a heart attack. Buried Oakwood Cemetery, Austin TX.

Ed Edelen—1 Year Pitcher (b. 16 Mar 1912 Bryantown MD–d. 1 Feb 1982 Physician's Memorial Hospital, LaPlata MD) He practiced general medicine in Charles County, MD, from 1938 until his death. Buried St Ignatius Church Cemetery, Port Tobacco MD.

Charlie Eden—4 Years Outfielder (b. 18 Jan 1855 Lexington KY–d. 17 Sep 1920 Cincinnati OH) He was a conductor for the New York Central Railway. Died from a stroke. Cremated.

Stump Edington—1 Year Outfielder (b. 4 Jul 1891 Koleen IN–d. 29 Nov 1969 Bastrop LA) World War I veteran. He was a deputy sheriff in Beaumont TX for a short time before moving to Bastrop where he was an optometrist. Died after a long illness. Buried Prairie Chapel Cemetery, Lyons IN.

George Edmondson—3 Years Pitcher (b. 18 May 1896 Waxahachie TX–d. 11 Jul 1973 at a hospital in Waco TX) He was a farmer. Buried Restland Cemetery, Lubbock TX.

Paul Edmondson—1 Year Pitcher (b. 12 Feb 1943 Kansas City KS–d. 13 Feb 1970 Santa Barbara CA) He and a passenger were killed when he lost control of his car on a wet road, sliding into oncoming traffic, causing a fiery head-on collision. Buried Valley Oaks Memorial Park, Westlake Village CA.

Sam Edmondston—2 Years Pitcher (b. 30 Aug 1883 Washington DC–d. 12 Apr 1979 Midicenter Nursing Home, Corpus Christi TX) He was an insurance salesman for 35 years in Washington DC, working 20 years for Banker's Life of Des Moines and the remainder for New England Mutual, retiring in 1954. Died from arteriosclerotic heart disease. Buried Washington DC.

Eddie Edmonson—1 Year Outfielder (b. 20 Nov 1889 Hopewell PA–d. 10 May 1971 Leesburg FL).

Bob Edmundson—1 Year Outfielder (b. 30 Apr 1879 Paris KY–d. 14 Aug 1931 at his home near Lawrence KS) Buried Oak Hill Cemetery, Lawrence KS.

Bruce Edwards—10 Years Catcher (b. 15 Jul 1923 Quincy IL–d. 25 Apr 1975 Mercy Hospital, Sacramento CA) For 13 years he was an inventory control analyst before becoming a projectionist at various Sacramento movie theatres. Died from a heart attack. Buried Memorial Lawn Cemetery, Sacramento CA.

Foster Edwards—5 Years Pitcher (b. 1 Sep 1903 Holstein IA–d. 4 Jan 1980 Cape Cod Hospital, Hyannis MA) Served in the U.S. Army during World War II. He was a personnel director for A and P Tea Company.

Hank Edwards—11 Years Outfielder (b. 29 Jan 1919 Elmwood Place OH–d. 22 Jun 1988 General Hospital, Anaheim CA) He was a guard for an armored car company. Suffering from colon cancer, he hung himself. Buried Fairhaven Memorial Park, Santa Ana CA.

Jim Joe Edwards—6 Years Pitcher (b. 14 Dec 1894 Banner MS–d. 19 Jan 1965 Sarepta MS) He taught school for a short while until he was named postmaster at Pontotoc MS. Later he worked on a rural mail delivery route until he retired about 1961. Died in an automobile accident. Buried Pontotoc Cemetery, Pontotoc MS.

Ralph Edwards—1 Year Infielder (b. 14 Dec 1882 Brewster NY–d. 5 Jan 1949 White Plains NY).

Sherman Edwards—1 Year Pitcher (b. 25 Jul 1909 Mount Ida AR–d. 8 Mar 1992 at a hospital in El Dorado AR) A retired supervisor for Montsanto Chemical Company, he lived in El Dorado nearly 60 years. Buried Woodlawn Cemetery, El Dorado AR.

Harry Eells—1 Year Pitcher (b. 14 Feb 1882 Ida Grove IA–d. 15 Oct 1940 San Francisco CA).

Ben Egan—4 Years Catcher (b. 20 Nov 1883 Augusta NY–d. 18 Feb 1968 Sherrill NY) Working many years for Oneida Silversmiths, he retired about 1957. Died after a lengthy illness. Buried St Helena Church Cemetery, Sherrill NY.

Dick Egan—9 Years Infielder (b. 23 Jun 1884 Portland OR–d. 7 Jul 1947 at his home in Oakland CA) Died from a liver ailment. Buried St Helena Catholic Cemetery, St Helena CA.

Jim Egan—1 Year Outfielder (b. 1858 Derby CT–d. 26 Sep 1884 in the county jail at New Haven CT) Died from brain fever while incarcerated for theft.

Rip Egan—1 Year Pitcher (b. 9 Jul 1871 Philadelphia PA–d. 22 Dec 1950 Cranston RI) He spent 55 years in baseball as a player, minor league manager, college coach, umpire and scout. He umpired in the American League nine years. Died after six weeks of ill health. Buried St Ann's Cemetery, Cranston RI.

Wish Egan—3 Years Pitcher (b. 16 Jun 1881 Evart MI–d. 13 Apr 1951 Henry Ford Hospital, Detroit MI) Working his entire life in baseball, he was a scout for the Tigers from 1913 until his death, and was responsible for finding the majority of their talent during that time. Buried Woodmere Cemetery, Detroit MI.

Elmer Eggert—1 Year Infielder (b. 29 Jan 1902 Rochester NY–d. 9 Apr 1971 Rochester NY)

World War II veteran. He was a mail carrier for the U.S. Postal Service. Buried Mount Hope Cemetery, Rochester NY.

Dave Eggler—6 Years Outfielder (b. 30 Apr 1851 Brooklyn NY–d. 5 Apr 1902 Buffalo NY) He was an expressman for American Express for 15 years. Died when a train rolled over him at Central Station as he was crawling under the train for no explicable reason. Buried Holy Cross Cemetery, Lackawanna NY.

Howard Ehmke—15 Years Pitcher (b. 24 Apr 1894 Silver Creek NY–d. 17 Mar 1959 Germantown Hospital, Philadelphia PA) Served in the U.S. Navy during World War I. He owned and operated a canvas fabricating business in Philadelphia, featuring covers for sports fields. Died suddenly from an unannounced ailment.

Red Ehret—11 Years Pitcher (b. 31 Aug 1868 Louisville KY–d. 28 Jul 1940 General Hospital, Cincinnati OH) For several years he was a minor league umpire and for four years a National League umpire. Died from rectal cancer. Buried Baltimore Pike Cemetery, Cincinnati OH.

Rube Ehrhardt—6 Years Pitcher (b. 20 Nov 1894 Beecher IL–d. 27 Apr 1980 St James Hospital, Chicago Heights IL) Served in the U.S. Navy during World War I. He worked at Republic Steel. Buried Trinity Lutheran Cemetery, Crete IL.

Hack Eibel—2 Years Outfielder (b. 6 Dec 1893 Brooklyn NY–d. 16 Oct 1945 Macon GA) He operated billiard parlors and amusement centers in Atlanta GA and in Macon. He had been in ill health several months when he took his own life with a self-inflicted gunshot wound at his Macon sports palace. Buried Westview Cemetery, Atlanta GA.

Fred Eichrodt—4 Years Outfielder (b. 6 Jan 1903 Chicago IL–d. 14 Jul 1965 Community Hospital, Indianapolis IN) He owned and operated Eichrodt's Restaurant, a popular eating place and rendezvous in Indianapolis, for 28 years, selling it in 1957. Buried Memorial Park Cemetery, Indianapolis IN.

Jake Eisenhart—1 Year Pitcher (b. 3 Oct 1922 Perkasie PA–d. 20 Dec 1987 Blair Memorial Hospital, Huntingdon PA) Served in the U.S. Army during World War II. An educator, he taught mathematics and coached basketball, football and baseball at Bordentown Military Institute from 1945 to 1953 and at Pennsbury High School from 1953 until retiring in 1982. Buried Mount Union Cemetery, Mount Union PA.

Ed Eiteljorg—2 Years Pitcher (b. 14 Oct 1871 Berlin, Germany–d. 5 Dec 1942 at his son's home in Greencastle IN) He served as sheriff of Putnam County, IN, four years and, later, as deputy sheriff. He was also a county commissioner. Died from the effects of high blood pressure. Buried Forest Hill Cemetery, Greencastle IN.

Kid Elberfeld—14 Years Infielder 1 Year Manager (b. 13 Apr 1875 Pomeroy OH–d. 13 Jan 1944 Erlanger Hospital, Chattanooga TN) He managed several years for a number of teams in the Southern League. Died from bronchopneumonia after battling a cold for a week. Buried Chattanooga Memorial Park, Chattanooga TN.

Heinie Elder—1 Year Pitcher (b. 23 Aug 1890 Seattle WA–d. 13 Nov 1958 Long Beach CA) World War II veteran. He was a self-employed real estate broker. Died from a heart attack. Buried Los Angeles National Cemetery, Los Angeles CA.

Pete Elko—2 Years Infielder (b. 17 Jun 1918 Wilkes-Barre PA–d. 17 Sep 1993 at his home in Wilkes-Barre PA) He was a coal miner for the Dorrance Colliery of the Lehigh Valley Coal Company and an engineer for Rohm-Haas International Corporation in Bristol. Buried SS Peter and Paul Parish Cemetery, Plains PA.

Roy Ellam—2 Years Infielder (b. 8 Feb 1886 Conshohocken PA–d. 28 Oct 1948 Conshohocken PA) He managed minor league baseball before becoming a plumbing and heating contractor. Killed on the job when a counterbalance weight fell on him as he lowered a fire escape ladder.

Hod Eller—5 Years Pitcher (b. 5 Jul 1894 Muncie IN–d. 18 Jul 1961 Indianapolis IN) He won two games for Cincinnati in the infamous 1919 World Series against the "Black" Sox. For 22 years he was a patrolman for the Indianapolis Police Department and later was a security guard. Died from cancer. Buried Crown Hill Cemetery, Indianapolis IN.

Frank Ellerbe—6 Years Infielder (b. 25 Dec 1895 Marion County, SC–d. 7 Jul 1988 Latta SC) Served in the U.S. Navy during World War I. He returned to South Carolina in 1925 and worked the family farm. From 1927 to 1928 he served in the South Carolina House of Representatives and was chairman of the World War II Selective Service Board for eight years. He was an avid golfer, hunter and angler. Buried Haselden Family Cemetery, Sellers SC.

Joe Ellick—3 Years Outfielder 1 Year Manager (b. 3 Apr 1854 Cincinnati OH–d. 21 Apr 1923 at his home in Kansas City KS) He was a cigar maker. Buried Mount Calvary Cemetery, Kansas City KS.

Allen Elliott—2 Years Infielder (b. 25 Dec 1897 St Louis MO–d. 6 May 1979 St Louis MO) Buried Laurel Hill Memorial Gardens, Pagedale MO.

Bob Elliott—15 Years Infielder 1 Year Manager (b. 26 Nov 1916 San Francisco CA–d. 4 May 1966 Mercy Hospital, San Diego CA) He managed minor league baseball for a few years, then worked for a beer distributor in Indio CA. Died from a ruptured vein in his lower windpipe, but suffered from pancreatic cancer. Buried Greenwood Memorial Park, San Diego CA.

Carter Elliott—1 Year Infielder (b. 29 Nov 1893 Atchison KS–d. 21 May 1959 at his home in Palm Springs CA) He was a self-employed security investor for 37 years. Died from a heart attack. Buried Welwood Murray Cemetery, Palm Springs CA.

Claude Elliott—2 Years Pitcher (b. 17 Nov 1876 Pardeeville WI–d. 23 Jun 1923 at the home of his mother in Pardeeville WI) He pitched in the minor leagues for 15 years and umpired for 12 years. Later he managed a garage in Minneapolis MN. Buried Pardeeville Cemetery, Pardeeville WI.

Gene Elliott—1 Year Outfielder (b. 8 Feb 1889 Fayette City PA–d. 5 Jan 1976 Blair Memorial Hospital, Huntingdon PA) He managed minor league baseball and later worked as a carpenter. Buried Riverview Cemetery, Huntingdon PA.

Glenn Elliott—3 Years Pitcher (b. 11 Nov 1919 Sapulpa OK–d. 27 Jul 1969 Providence Hospital, Portland OR) He was a scout for the Phillies. Died from a brain tumor. Buried Odd Fellows Cemetery, Myrtle Creek OR.

Hal Elliott—4 Years Pitcher (b. 29 May 1899 Mount Clemens MI–d. 25 Apr 1963 Honolulu HI).

Jumbo Elliott—10 Years Pitcher (b. 22 Oct 1900 St Louis MO–d. 7 Jan 1970 Terre Haute IN) He operated a garage in Terre Haute before he was a deputy sheriff in Vigo County, IN, for 25 years, retiring in 1966. He was dead-on-arrival at St Anthony Hospital after being in poor health for some time. Buried Roselawn Memorial Park, Terre Haute IN.

Rowdy Elliott—5 Years Catcher (b. 4 Mar 1890 Kokomo IN–d. 12 Feb 1934 Harbor Hospital, San Francisco CA) He managed in the Pacific Coast League. Died after he fell one story into an apartment well while intoxicated. Buried San Francisco National Cemetery, San Francisco CA.

Rube Ellis—4 Years Outfielder (b. 17 Nov 1886 Downey CA–d. 13 Mar 1938 at his home near Rivera CA) He was a farmer in the citrus business. Died from a heart attack. Buried Rose Hills Memorial Park, Whittier CA.

Babe Ellison—5 Years Infielder (b. 15 Nov 1896 Ola AR–d. 11 Aug 1955 San Francisco CA) World War I veteran. He managed three years in the Pacific Coast League before spending 20 years as an appraiser for the U.S. Customs Service. Died from a heart attack during removal of an obstructed esophagus. Buried Golden Gate National Cemetery, San Bruno CA.

George Ellison—1 Year Pitcher (b. 24 Jan 1895 CA–d. 20 Jan 1978 Laguna Honda Hospital, San Francisco CA) Died from arteriosclerotic heart disease and inanition. Cremated.

Verdo Elmore—1 Year Outfielder (b. 10 Dec 1899 Gordo AL–d. 5 Aug 1969 V A Hospital in Birmingham AL) An attorney in Gordo, he served a ten year period as circuit court judge in Pickens, Fayette and Lamar counties in Alabama. Buried Gordo Cemetery, Gordo AL.

Roy Elsh—3 Years Outfielder (b. 1 Mar 1892 Pennsgrove NJ–d. 12 Nov 1978 Philadelphia PA).

Bob Elson—Hall of Fame (b. abt 1903–d. 10 Mar 1981 Augustana Hospital, Chicago IL) Served in the U.S. Navy during World War II. A radio announcer more than 40 years, he broadcast the Cubs games and, later, the White Sox games. Died from heart trouble. Buried Queen of Heaven Cemetery, Hillside IL.

Don Elston—9 Years Pitcher (b. 6 Apr 1929 Campbellstown OH–d. 2 Jan 1995 Evanston

Hospital, Evanston IL) He managed briefly in the minor leagues before becoming a regional sales manager for Danley Die Set, a tool and die manufacturer in Chicago. Died after suffering a heart attack. Cremated.

Bones Ely—14 Years Infielder (b. 7 Jun 1863 Girard PA–d. 10 Jan 1952 Napa State Hospital, Napa CA) Died from dementia after being confined in the state hospital four months. Cremated.

Red Embree—8 Years Pitcher (b. 30 Aug 1917 El Monte CA–d. 24 Sep 1996 Eugene OR) Served in the U.S. Army during World War II. Died from complications of Alzheimer's disease. Buried Crescent City CA.

Slim Embry—1 Year Pitcher (b. 17 Aug 1901 Columbia TN–d. 10 Oct 1947 at his home in Nashville TN) He studied law at Vanderbilt University and quit baseball to practice law in Nashville. Died from a heart attack. Buried Mount Olivet Cemetery, Nashville TN.

Chester Emerson—2 Years Outfielder (b. 27 Oct 1889 Stow ME–d. 2 Jul 1971 Augusta ME).

Spoke Emery—1 Year Outfielder (b. 10 Dec 1898 Bay City MI–d. 2 Jun 1975 Cape Canaveral FL).

Charlie Emig—1 Year Pitcher (b. 5 Apr 1875 Cincinnati OH–d. 2 Oct 1975 Oklahoma City OK) Buried Memorial Park Cemetery, Edmond OK.

Frank Emmer—2 Years Infielder (b. 17 Feb 1896 Crestline OH–d. 18 Oct 1963 at his home in Homestead FL) For 28 years he was the chief of police at the Westinghouse plant in Mansfield OH, retiring to Florida in 1961. Died from a heart attack.

Bob Emmerich—1 Year Outfielder (b. 1 Aug 1897 New York City NY–d. 23 Nov 1948 at his home in Bridgeport CT) He managed minor league baseball for a time. He was the custodian at Lincoln School in Bridgeport when he died after being ill several months. Buried Lakeview Cemetery, Bridgeport CT.

Bob Emslie—3 Years Pitcher (b. 27 Jan 1859 Guelph, Ontario, Canada–d. 26 Apr 1943 St Thomas, Ontario, Canada).

Joe Engel—7 Years Pitcher (b. 12 Mar 1893 Washington DC–d. 12 Jun 1969 Campbell General Hospital, Chattanooga TN) He owned the Chattanooga Lookouts of the Southern League and operated a baseball school. Buried Forest Hills Cemetery, Chattanooga TN.

Charlie Engle—3 Years Infielder (b. 27 Aug 1903 New York City NY–d. 12 Oct 1983 Humana Hospital, San Antonio TX) He coached in the minor leagues for the White Sox and owned the Main Bar, a tavern and restaurant in San Antonio, until 1976. Died following a heart attack. Buried Sunset Memorial Park, San Antonio TX.

Clyde Engle—8 Years Outfielder (b. 19 Mar 1884 Dayton OH–d. 26 Dec 1939 at the Hotel Lenox in Boston MA) He coached baseball at the University of Vermont in 1921 and 1922, then moved to Yale University where he coached the freshman baseball team 17 years until his death. Died from a heart attack.

Gil English—6 Years Infielder (b. 2 Jul 1909 Glenola NC–d. 31 Aug 1996 Gray Brier Nursing Center, Trinity NC) He was a scout for the Braves, Yankees and Giants. Died after being in declining health several months. Buried Mount Vernon Methodist Church Cemetery, Archdale NC.

Woody English—12 Years Infielder (b. 2 Mar 1907 Fredonia OH–d. 26 Sep 1997 Arlington Nursing Home, Newark AR) He managed a women's team in the All-American Baseball League in the early 1950s. Later he was a night supervisor at the State Farm Insurance Company in Newark, retiring in 1971. Died after a brief illness. Buried Fredonia Cemetery, Fredonia OH.

Del Ennis—14 Years Outfielder (b. 8 Jun 1925 Philadelphia PA–d. 8 Feb 1996 Huntingdon Valley PA) Served in the U.S. Navy during World War II. He co-owned and operated Del Ennis Lanes, a bowling facility in Rockledge PA. Died of complication from diabetes. Buried Hillside Cemetery, Roslyn PA.

Russ Ennis—1 Year Catcher (b. 10 Mae 1897 Superior WI–d. 21 Jan 1949 at a hospital in Superior WI) Served in France and Germany for the U.S. Army during both World War I and World War II. Buried Calvary Cemetery, Superior WI.

Jack Enright—1 Year Pitcher (b. 25 Nov 1895 Fort Worth TX–d. 18 Aug 1975 Pompano Beach FL) Buried Forest Lawn Central, Fort Lauderdale FL.

Jewel Ens—4 Years Infielder 3 Years Manager (b. 24 Aug 1889 St Louis MO–d. 17 Jan 1950

University Hospital, Syracuse NY) World War I veteran. He managed minor league baseball until his death. Died from pneumonia after being ill 11 days. Buried Calvary Cemetery, St Louis MO.

Mutz Ens —1 Year Infielder (b. 8 Nov 1884 St Louis MO–d. 28 Jun 1950 St Louis MO) Spent most of his baseball career in the American Association. He was a salesman for the Anheuser-Busch brewery. Buried Memorial Park Cemetery, St Louis MO.

Charlie Enwright —1 Year Infielder (b. 6 Oct 1886 Sacramento CA–d. 19 Jan 1917 Sister's Hospital, Sacramento CA) He was a member of the Sacramento Civil Service Commission and a merchant with the firm Miller and Enright. Died from blood poisoning after an abscess of the ear. Buried St Joseph's Cemetery, Sacramento CA.

Jack Enzenroth—2 Years Catcher (b. 4 Nov 1885 Mineral Point WI–d. 21 Feb 1944 Detroit MI).

Johnny Enzmann —4 Years Pitcher (b. 4 Mar 1890 Brooklyn NY–d. 14 Mar 1984 Riverhead NY).

Aubrey Epps —1 Year Catcher (b. 3 Mar 1912 Memphis TN–d. 13 Nov 1984 Choctaw County Hospital, Ackerman MS) Served in the U.S. Marines during World War II. He was a deputy sheriff in Shelby County, TN. Buried Concord Cemetery, Ackerman MS.

Joe Erautt —2 Years Catcher (b. 1 Sep 1921 Vibank, Saskatchewan, Canada–d. 6 Oct 1976 at a hospital in Portland OR) Served in Italy and Algiers for the U.S. Army during World War II. For seven years he was a milk salesman for Carnation Company in Seattle WA. Buried Willamette National Cemetery, Portland OR.

Eric Erickson —7 Years Pitcher (b. 13 Mar 1892 Gothenburg, Sweden–d. 19 May 1965 W C A Hospital, Jamestown NY) World War I veteran. He operated a farm near Jamestown and was widely known for his berries and garden produce. He also worked in the shipping department of Art Metal, Inc, retiring in 1958. Buried Sunset Hill Cemetery, Lakewood NY.

Hank Erickson —1 Year Catcher (b. 11 Nov 1907 Chicago IL–d. 13 Dec 1964 St Anthony Hospital, Louisville KY) His baseball career ended because of injuries suffered in an automobile accident. He was a stock manager for the City of Louisville stores warehouse. Buried Glen Oak Cemetery, Hillside IL.

Tex Erwin —6 Years Catcher (b. 22 Dec 1885 Forney TX–d. 5 Apr 1953 Strong Memorial Hospital, Rochester NY) He operated an insurance agency and was a Rochester City Councilman for 12 years. He suffered from arthritis. Buried Holy Sepulchre Cemetery, Rochester NY.

Jim Eschen —1 Year Outfielder (b. 21 Aug 1891 Brooklyn NY–d. 27 Sep 1960 Sloatsburg NY).

Jimmy Esmond —4 Years Infielder (b. 8 Oct 1889 Albany NY–d. 26 Jun 1948 Troy Hospital, Troy NY) Died from marked cerebral edema following an operation performed several weeks earlier. Buried St Agnes Cemetery, Menands NY.

Duke Esper —9 Years Pitcher (b. 28 Jul 1868 Salem NJ–d. 31 Aug 1910 at his home in Philadelphia PA) He ran a restaurant in Philadelphia. Died from Bright's disease.

Nino Espinosa —8 Years Pitcher (b. 15 Aug 1953 Villa Altagracia, Dominican Republic–d. 24 Dec 1987 Villa Altagracia, Dominican Republic) Died from a heart attack.

Bill Essick —2 Years Pitcher (b. 18 Dec 1880 Grand Ridge IL–d. 12 Oct 1951 Fairview Sanitarium, Los Angeles CA) He was a scout 25 years for the Yankees, retiring in 1950. He was known as one of the architects of the Yankee dynasty of the 1930s, 1940s and 1950s. Died in his sleep from a heart condition. Buried Inglewood Park Cemetery, Inglewood CA.

Bobby Estalella —9 Years Outfielder (b. 25 Apr 1911 Cardenas, Cuba–d. 6 Jan 1991 Hialeah FL) Buried Vista Memorial Gardens, Hialeah FL.

Dude Esterbrook —11 Years Infielder 1 Year Manager (b. 20 Jun 1860 Staten Island NY–d. 30 Apr 1901 Thrall Hospital, Middletown NY) Mentally troubled, he plunged to his death from a window of a moving train while enroute to the state hospital.

Oscar Estrada —1 Year Pitcher (b. 15 Feb 1904 Havana, Cuba–d. 2 Jan 1978 Havana, Cuba).

Buck Etchison —2 Years Infielder (b. 27 Jan 1915 Baltimore MD–d. 24 Jan 1980 East New Market MD) He farmed in Howard County, MD, until he retired to East New Market in 1968. Died from a heart condition enroute to the hospital. Buried St Louis Cemetery, Clarksville MD.

Nick Etten—9 Years Infielder (b. 19 Sep 1913 Spring Grove IL–d. 18 Oct 1990 at his home in Hinsdale IL) He was president of Carroll Construction Company in Chicago IL. Buried Queen of Heaven Cemetery, Hillside IL.

John Eubank—3 Years Pitcher (b. 9 Sep 1872 Servia IN–d. 3 Nov 1958 Bellevue MI) Buried Riverside Cemetery, Bellevue MI.

Uel Eubanks—1 Year Pitcher (b. 14 Feb 1903 Quinlan TX–d. 21 Nov 1954 at a hospital in Dallas TX) A lifelong resident of Dallas, he was in the construction business. Died after a brief illness. Buried Laurel Land Memorial Park, Dallas TX.

Ferd Eunick—1 Year Infielder (b. 22 Apr 1896 Baltimore MD–d. 9 Dec 1959 Baltimore MD) Died suddenly. Buried Loudon Park National Cemetery, Baltimore MD.

Frank Eustace—1 Year Infielder (b. 7 Nov 1873 New York City NY–d. 16 Oct 1932 near Cressona PA) He managed minor league baseball for a time and worked at the steel mill in Pottsville PA before becoming an odd job worker in the area. He was killed instantly when he accidentally fell from a railroad bridge to the state highway below. Buried Mount Laurel Cemetery, Pottsville PA.

Al Evans—12 Years Catcher (b. 28 Sep 1916 Kenly NC–d. 6 Apr 1979 Memorial Hospital, Wilson NC) Served in the U.S. Navy during World War II. He scouted for the Twins and Giants, retiring in 1965. Buried Kenly Cemetery, Kenly NC.

Art Evans—1 Year Pitcher (b. 3 Aug 1911 Elvins MO–d. 8 Jan 1952 Wesley Hospital, Wichita KS) He was a supervisor in the tool planning department at the Boeing plant in Wichita. Buried Sterling Cemetery, Sterling KS.

Bill Evans—3 Years Pitcher (b. 10 Feb 1893 Reidsville NC–d. 21 Dec 1946 Burlington NC) He was a salesman. Died from a heart attack. Buried Pine Hill Cemetery, Burlington NC.

Bill Evans—2 Years Pitcher (b. 25 Mar 1919 Childress TX–d. 30 Nov 1983 Grand Junction CO).

Billy Evans—Hall of Fame (b. 10 Feb 1884 Chicago IL–d. 23 Jan 1956 North Shore Hospital, Miami FL) Working in baseball 45 years as an umpire, league president, club administrator and writer, he umpired in the American League from 1906 to 1927. Died from a stroke. Buried Knollwood Cemetery, Mayfield OH.

Chick Evans—2 Years Pitcher (b. 15 Oct 1889 Arlington VT–d. 2 Sep 1916 Ellis Hospital, Schenectady NY) He worked in the munitions department at General Electric. Died from heart trouble. Buried Bennington VT.

Ford Evans—1 Year Manager (d. 14 Oct 1884 Akron OH).

Jake Evans—7 Years Outfielder (b. Sep 1856 Baltimore MD–d. 16 Jan 1907 Baltimore MD).

Joe Evans—11 Years Outfielder (b. 15 May 1895 Meridian MS–d. 8 Aug 1953 Gulfport MS) He interned at various hospitals between seasons to complete his medical training and practiced as a physician and surgeon at Gulfport. Died following an illness of several months.

Red Evans—2 Years Pitcher (b. 12 Nov 1906 Chicago IL–d. 18 Jun 1982 at his home in Lakeview AR) Served in the U.S. Navy during World War II. He retired from his job as a testing engineer for Johnson Motor Company in 1969 and moved to Lakeview. Buried Tucker Memorial Cemetery, Mountain Home AR.

Roy Evans—5 Years Pitcher (b. 19 Mar 1874 Knoxville TN–d. 15 Aug 1915 Galveston TX).

Steve Evans—8 Years Outfielder (b. 17 Feb 1885 Cleveland OH–d. 28 Dec 1943 St John's Hospital, Cleveland OH) He was a supervisor for the State of Ohio. Died from a heart attack. Buried Calvary Cemetery, Cleveland OH.

Bill Everett—7 Years Infielder (b. 13 Dec 1868 Fort Wayne IN–d. 19 Jan 1938 at his home in Denver CO) Called the greatest bunter of his time, he was president of the Colorado Wrecking Company. Died from diabetes. Buried Crown Hill Cemetery, Denver CO.

Hoot Evers—12 Years Outfielder (b. 8 Feb 1921 St Louis MO–d. 25 Jan 1991 Houston TX) Served in the U.S. Army Air Corps during World War II. He was director of the Indian farm system until he took over the Tiger farm system. After 1983 he was a special assignment scout for the Tigers. Buried Memorial Oaks Cemetery, Houston TX.

Joe Evers—1 Game Pinch Runner (b. 10 Sep 1892 Troy NY–d. 4 Jan 1949 Memorial Hospital, Albany NY) He operated a sporting goods store with his brother. Died from an abscess of the liver. Buried St Agnes Cemetery, Menands NY.

Johnny Evers—18 Years Infielder 3 Years Manager Hall of Fame (b. 21 Jul 1881 Troy NY–d. 28 Mar 1947 St Peter's Hospital, Albany NY) A member of the famed double play combination that prompted the poem "Baseball's Sad Lexicon," he operated a sporting goods store. Died after a cerebral hemorrhage. Buried St Mary's Cemetery, Troy NY.

Tom Evers—2 Years Infielder (b. 31 Mar 1852 Troy NY–d. 21 Mar 1925 at his home in Washington DC) He worked for the government 41 years. Died after a protracted illness. Buried Oak Hill Cemetery, Washington DC.

Bob Ewing—11 Years Pitcher (b. 24 Apr 1873 New Hampshire OH–d. 20 Jun 1947 at his home in Wapakoneta OH) He farmed near New Hampshire OH for a number of years and served as sheriff of Auglaize County, OH, for two terms. He also managed several businesses. Buried Walnut Hill Cemetery, New Hampshire OH.

Buck Ewing—18 Years Catcher 7 Years Manager Hall of Fame (b. 25 Dec 1859 Hoagland OH–d. 20 Oct 1906 at his home in Cincinnati OH) Died from Bright's disease. Buried Mount Washington Cemetery, Cincinnati OH.

John Ewing—6 Years Pitcher (b. 1 Jun 1863 Cincinnati OH–d. 23 Apr 1895 Denver CO) Died from tuberculosis. Buried Mount Washington Cemetery, Cincinnati OH.

Reuben Ewing—1 Year Infielder (b. 30 Nov 1899 Odessa, Russia–d. 5 Oct 1970 at his home in West Hartford CT) He was a retired realtor. Buried Emmanuel Cemetery, Wethersfield CT.

Art Ewoldt—1 Year Infielder (b. 8 Jan 1892 Paullina IA–d. 8 Dec 1977 Des Moines IA) He played in the minor leagues 25 years before working another 25 years for the U.S. Post Office. Died after a long illness. Buried Glendale Cemetery, Des Moines IA.

Homer Ezzell—3 Years Infielder (b. 28 Feb 1896 Victoria TX–d. 3 Aug 1976 San Antonio TX) He was a lifelong resident of San Antonio. Buried Mission Burial Park, San Antonio TX.

F

Jay Faatz—4 Years Infielder 1 Year Manager (b. 24 Oct 1860 Weedsport NY–d. 10 Apr 1923 Syracuse NY).

Red Faber—20 Years Pitcher Hall of Fame (b. 6 Sep 1888 Cascade IA–d. 25 Sep 1976 Chicago IL) He worked on a county highway surveying crew into his 70s. Died from a heart attack. Buried Acacia Park Cemetery, Chicago IL.

Bunny Fabrique—2 Years Infielder (b. 23 Dec 1887 Clinton MI–d. 10 Jan 1960 Veteran's Hospital, Ann Arbor MI) Served in the U.S. Navy during World War I. He worked for Ford Motor Company in Dearborn MI and for Clinton Machine Company in Clinton, retiring in 1956. Buried Riverside Cemetery, Clinton MI.

Tony Faeth—2 Years Pitcher (b. 9 Jul 1893 Aberdeen SD–d. 22 Dec 1982 St Paul MN) Buried Calvary Cemetery, St Paul MN.

Bill Fagan—2 Years Pitcher (b. 15 Feb 1869 Troy NY–d. 21 Mar 1930 at his home in Troy NY) He was engaged in brush making at Lansingburg NY, but since 1912 he had been confined to his home with neuritis. Died from chronic nephritis. Buried St Agnes Cemetery, Menands NY.

Everett Fagan—2 Years Pitcher (b. 13 Jan 1918 Pottersville NJ–d. 16 Feb 1983 Memorial Hospital, Morristown NJ) Served in Europe for the U.S. Army during World War II. He operated his own plumbing business in Peapack NJ from 1955 to 1980. Died after a long illness. Cremated.

Paul Fagan—(b. abt 1890 Alameda CA–d. 18 Dec 1960 Hillsborough CA) Served as a Captain in the Army Air Corps during World War I. He earned his fortune in the import-export business. He owned the San Francisco Seals of the Pacific Coast League from 1945 to 1953, and was a leader in the efforts to bring major league baseball to the west coast. Died in his sleep. Cremated. Buried Cypress Lawn Memorial Park, Colma CA.

Frank Fahey—1 Year Outfielder (b. 22 Jan 1896 Milford MA–d. 19 Mar 1954 Veteran's Hospital, Boston MA) World War I veteran. He worked for the Bachmann Uxbridge Worsted Company in Uxbridge MA and the Whiten Machine Works in Whitinsville MA. Died after a long illness. Buried St Mary's Cemetery, Uxbridge MA.

Howard Fahey—1 Year Infielder (b. 24 Jun 1892 Medford MA–d. 24 Oct 1971 Clearwater FL) World War I veteran. He was a retired engineer for American Telephone and Telegraph. Buried Oak Grove Cemetery, Medford MA.

Pete Fahrer—1 Year Pitcher (b. 10 Mar 1890 Holgate OH–d. 10 Jun 1967 Fremont MI) For 17 years he was a guide on the Muskegon River and played for dances in the Oldtime Croton String Band. He was a deputy sheriff in Newaygo County, MI, for some time. Buried Big Prairie-Everitt Cemetery, White Cloud MI.

George Fair—1 Year Infielder (b. 14 Jan 1856 Boston MA–d. 12 Feb 1939 Roslindale MA).

Jim Fairbank—2 Years Pitcher (b. 17 Mar 1881 Deansboro NY–d. 27 Dec 1955 Memorial Hospital, Utica NY) He went into the cigar business in Oneida Square and worked for Savage Arms before he was an agent for John Hancock Life Insurance Company for many years. He had retired when he died following an illness of two weeks. Buried New Forest Cemetery, Utica NY.

Rags Faircloth—1 Year Pitcher (b. 19 Aug 1892 Kenton TN–d. 5 Oct 1953 at a hospital in Tucson AZ) Served in the U.S. Navy during World War I. He was a sales engineer for Westinghouse in East Orange NJ, retiring in 1951, and moving to Tucson. Buried Evergreen Cemetery, Tucson AZ.

Anton Falch—1 Year Outfielder (b. 4 Dec 1860 Milwaukee WI–d. 31 Mar 1936 Wauwatosa WI) Buried Union Cemetery, Milwaukee WI.

Bibb Falk—12 Years Outfielder (b. 27 Jan 1899 Austin TX–d. 8 Jun 1989 Brackenridge Hospital, Austin TX) World War I veteran. He managed minor league baseball for a short time, then coached baseball at the University of Texas from 1940 to 1967, winning all or part of 20 Southwest Conference championships and two College World Series. Died from a heart ailment. Buried Austin Memorial Park Cemetery, Austin TX.

Chet Falk—3 Years Pitcher (b. 15 May 1905 Austin TX–d. 7 Jan 1982 Austin TX) Buried Austin Memorial Park Cemetery, Austin TX.

Cy Falkenberg—12 Years Pitcher (b. 17 Dec 1880 Chicago IL–d. 15 Apr 1961 San Francisco CA) An avid bowler, he worked briefly for the Ukiah CA Chamber of Commerce before operating several bowling establishments in the San Francisco Bay Area. Died suddenly from a heart attack. Buried Holy Cross Catholic Cemetery, Colma CA.

Ed Fallenstin—2 Years Pitcher (b. 22 Dec 1908 Newark NJ–d. 24 Nov 1971 Memorial Hospital, Orange NJ) He owned Ronnie's Tavern in Maplewood NJ before working for Paul's Tavern in Newark. His last three years he was an investigator for the Newark antipoverty program. Buried Hollywood Memorial Park, Union NJ.

Charlie Fallon—1 Game Pinch Runner (b. 7 Mar 1881 New York City NY–d. 10 Jun 1960 Kings Park NY).

George Fallon—4 Years Infielder (b. 8 Jul 1914 Jersey City NJ–d. 25 Oct 1994 Lake Worth FL) He worked 25 years for the Remington Shaver Company in Connecticut. Died after an extended illness. Buried Palm Beach Memorial Park, Lantana FL.

Pete Falsey—3 Games Pinch Hitter (b. 24 Apr 1891 New Haven CT–d. 23 May 1976 at his home in Los Angeles CA) Died from heart disease. Buried St Bernard's Cemetery, West Haven CT.

Gus Falzer—(b. 21 Jul 1884 Bavaria, Germany–d. 26 Jan 1953 at his home in Orange NJ) A broadcaster, sportswriter and columnist for nearly 50 years, he worked on four New Jersey newspapers. He is credited with the first coast-to-coast broadcast of the World Series in 1921. Died from a heart attack. Buried Fairmount Cemetery, Newark NJ.

Cliff Fannin—8 Years Pitcher (b. 13 May 1924 Louisa KY–d. 11 Dec 1966 Sandusky OH) Died from a heart attack. Buried Toledo OH.

Jack Fanning—2 Years Pitcher (b. abt 1865 South Orange NJ–d. 10 Jun 1917 near Humptulips WA) He worked as a flagman for the

Aberdeen Lumber and Shingle Company and was said to have a timber claim in the area. Died following a violent coughing spell.

Harry Fanwell—1 Year Pitcher (b. 16 Oct 1886 Patapsco MD–d. 16 Jul 1965 Baltimore MD) Buried Woodlawn Cemetery, Baltimore MD.

Alex Farmer—1 Year Catcher (b. 9 May 1880 New York City NY–d. 5 Mar 1920 New York City NY).

Jack Farmer—2 Years Infielder (b. 14 Jul 1892 Granville TN–d. 21 May 1970 Columbia LA).

Sid Farrar—8 Years Infielder (b. 10 Aug 1859 Paris Hill ME–d. 7 May 1935 Roosevelt Hospital, New York City NY) The father of famed opera star, Geraldine Farrar, he lived on a farm near Ridgefield CT, raising turkeys. Died a week after undergoing surgery. Buried Stamford CT.

Dick Farrell—14 Years Pitcher (b. 8 Apr 1934 Boston MA–d. 10 Jun 1977 Great Yarmouth, England) He was an oil rig foreman in the North Sea for Brown and Root Oil Company of Houston TX. Killed in an automobile accident. Buried Forest Park Westheimer Cemetery, Houston TX.

Doc Farrell—9 Years Infielder (b. 26 Dec 1901 Johnson City NY–d. 20 Dec 1966 St Bernard's Medical Center, Livingston NJ) He practiced denistry in Newark NJ from 1936 until his death. Buried Calvary Cemetery, Johnson City NY.

Duke Farrell—18 Years Catcher (b. 31 Aug 1866 Oakdale MA–d. 15 Feb 1925 Carney Hospital, Boston MA) He coached and scouted for the Braves and Yankees and served as a deputy U.S. Marshall in Boston during World War I. Died following surgery ten days earlier for a stomach disorder. Buried Immaculate Conception Cemetery, Marlboro MA.

Frank Farrell—(d. 10 Feb 1926 Ritz Carlton Hotel, Atlantic City NJ) A bartender, bookmaker, gambling house proprietor and real estate magnate, he was the original owner of the Yankees, forming them in 1903 and selling them to Colonel Ruppert in 1915. Died from chronic valular heart disease. Buried Calvary Cemetery, Woodside NY.

Jack Farrell—2 Years Infielder (b. 16 Jun 1892 Chicago IL–d. 24 Mar 1918 at his home in Chicago IL) He played in the Western League and the Nebraska State League. Died at the height of his baseball career from pneumonia. Buried Mount Olivet Cemetery, Chicago IL.

Jack Farrell—11 Years Infielder (b. 5 Jul 1857 Newark NJ–d. 9 Feb 1914 Essex County Hospital, Cedar Grove NJ) He was a hospital attendant. Died from a heart attack. Buried Holy Sepulchre Cemetery, East Orange NJ.

Joe Farrell—4 Years Infielder (b. 1858 Brooklyn NY–d. 18 Apr 1893 Brooklyn NY).

John Farrell—5 Years Infielder (b. 4 Dec 1876 Covington KY–d. 13 May 1921 St Joseph's Hospital, Kansas City MO) Buried Forest Hill Cemetery, Kansas City MO.

Kerby Farrell—2 Years Infielder 1 Year Manager (b. 3 Sep 1913 Leapwood TN–d. 17 Dec 1975 at his home in Nashville TN) He played, coached or managed baseball his entire life and is a member of the Tennessee Sports Hall of Fame. Died from a heart attack. Buried Woodlawn Memorial Park, Nashville TN.

John Farrow—1 Year Catcher (b. 1852 Verplanck's Point NY–d. 31 Dec 1914 Perth Amboy NJ) He was a retired hotelkeeper. Died from cirrhosis of the liver. Buried Holy Sepulchre Cemetery, East Orange NJ.

Jim Faulkner—3 Years Pitcher (b. 27 Jul 1899 Beatrice NE–d. 1 Jun 1962 at his home in West Palm Beach FL) Prior to World War II he operated a flying school and was an avid bowler. Died suddenly. Buried Pinecrest Cemetery, Lake Worth FL.

Buck Fausett—1 Year Infielder (b. 8 Apr 1908 Sheridan AR–d. 2 May 1994 at his home in College Station TX) Buried Restlawn Memorial Park, Sulphur Springs TX.

Charlie Faust—1 Year Pitcher (b. 9 Oct 1880 Marion KS–d. 18 Jun 1915 Steilacoom WA) Died from tuberculosis. Buried West Washington State Hosp Cemetery, Steilacomm WA.

Joe Fautsch—1 Game Pinch Hitter (b. 28 Feb 1887 Minneapolis MN–d. 16 Mar 1971 Newhope MN) Buried St Mary's Cemetery, Minneapolis MN.

Cayt Fauver—1 Year Pitcher (b. 1 Aug 1872 North Eaton OH–d. 3 Mar 1942 Chatsworth Hotel, Chatsworth GA) An attorney, he practiced law in Cleveland from 1902 to 1916 while also serving as a professor and secretary of Western Reserve Law School. In 1916 he opened his own law office in New York City, serving as legal advisor for several corporations in the import and export trades. Returning to Oberlin OH in 1933, he was the investment executive for Oberlin College and president of Oberlin Savings Bank. Died suddenly from a heart attack while enroute from Ohio to Florida. Buried Westwood Cemetery, Oberlin OH.

Vern Fear—1 Year Pitcher (b. 8 Aug 1925 Everly IA–d. 6 Sep 1976 Spencer Municipal Hospital, Spencer IA) Served in the U.S. Navy during World War II. After retiring from baseball he worked 22 years for Terrace Park in Spencer. Buried Lakeland Memorial Gardens, Spirit Lake IA.

Jack Fee—1 Year Pitcher (b. 1870 Carbondale PA–d. 3 Mar 1913 Emergency Hospital, Carbondale PA) He had been ill for some time and had recently had an operation for kidney trouble. Buried St Rose Cemetery, Carbondale PA.

Chub Feeney—(b. 31 Aug 1921 South Orange NJ–d. 10 Jan 1994 Calif Pacific Med Center, San Francisco CA) World War II veteran. He was general manager of the Giants before serving as National League President from 1970 to 1986. Died after two heart attacks. Buried Skylawn Memorial Park, San Mateo CA.

Eddie Feinberg—2 Years Infielder (b. 29 Sep 1918 Philadelphia PA–d. 20 Apr 1986 Hollywood FL).

Harry Feldman—6 Years Pitcher (b. 10 Nov 1919 New York City NY–d. 16 Mar 1962 at a hospital in Fort Smith AR) Following his baseball career he owned and operated Elmore's Record Shop and Hank's Record Bar in Fort Smith. Died following a heart attack. Buried Rose Lawn Cemetery, Fort Smith AR.

Gus Felix—5 Years Outfielder (b. 24 May 1895 Cincinnati OH–d. 12 May 1960 Montgomery AL) He worked in the maintenance department at Maxwell Air Force Base for 18 years before taking a job as head of the Children's Home in Montgomery in 1949, a job he held until his death. Died from a heart attack while golfing. Buried Greenwood Cemetery, Montgomery AL.

Harry Felix—2 Years Pitcher (b. 1870 Brooklyn NY–d. 17 Oct 1961 Miami FL).

Happy Felsch—6 Years Outfielder (b. 22 Aug 1891 Milwaukee WI–d. 17 Aug 1964 St Francis Hospital, Milwaukee WI) He was banned from baseball for his involvement in the Black Sox Scandal of 1919. Later he was a crane operator and then owned a tavern and grocery store in Milwaukee. Died after being ill for some time with a liver ailment. Buried Wisconsin Memorial Park, Brookfield WI.

Frank Fennelly—7 Years Infielder (b. 18 Feb 1860 Fall River MA–d. 4 Aug 1920 at his home in Fall River MA) He was engaged in various lines of business in Fall River and served his district four years in the state legislature. Died suddenly. Buried St Patrick's Cemetery, Fall River MA.

Hod Fenner—1 Year Pitcher (b. 12 Jul 1897 Martin MI–d. 20 Nov 1954 at his home in Detroit MI) He worked for the Kalamazoo Vegetable Parchment Company. Buried Riverside Cemetery, Kalamazoo MI.

Stan Ferens—2 Years Pitcher (b. 5 Mar 1915 Wendel PA–d. 7 Oct 1994 Greensburg Nursing Center, Greensburg PA) He retired as a coal miner from the Consolidated Coal Company at the Hutchinson Mine. Cremated.

Alex Ferguson—10 Years Pitcher (b. 16 Feb 1897 Montclair NJ–d. 26 Apr 1976 V A Hospital, Los Angeles CA) He was a co-owner of a tavern for ten years. Died from heart disease. Buried Conejo Mountain Memorial Park, Camarillo CA.

Bob Ferguson—9 Years Infielder 16 Years Manager (b. 31 Jan 1845 Brooklyn NY–d. 3 May 1894 at his home in Brooklyn NY) He umpired, including three years in the National League, until retiring permanently from the game in 1890. Died from a stroke of apoplexy. Buried Cypress Hills Cemetery, Brooklyn NY.

Charlie Ferguson—4 Years Pitcher (b. 17 Apr 1863 Charlottesville VA–d. 29 Apr 1888 Philadelphia PA) Died at the height of his career from typhoid fever. Buried Charlottesville VA.

Charlie Ferguson—1 Year Pitcher (b. 10 May 1875 Okemos MI–d. 17 May 1931 Sault Ste Marie MI).

George Ferguson—6 Years Pitcher (b. 19 Aug 1886 Terre Haute IN–d. 5 Sep 1943 near Monteverde FL) He is credited with introducing shin guards used by catchers. An osteopath in Miami, he was well-known for treating the aches and pains of many top ballplayers. Died from a heart attack while on a fishing trip. Buried Woodlawn Park Cemetery, Miami FL.

Ed Fernandes—2 Years Catcher (b. 11 Mar 1918 Oakland CA–d. 27 Nov 1968 Kaiser Hospital, Hayward CA) Served in the U.S. Navy during World War II. He managed some minor league baseball before working 15 years as a shipping clerk for the Matson Ship Line. Died suddenly from complications of diabetes. Buried Holy Sepulchre Cemetery, Hayward CA.

Nanny Fernandez—4 Years Infielder (b. 25 Nov 1918 Wilmington CA–d. 19 Sep 1996 Kaiser Foundation Hospital, Harbor City CA) He was a longshoreman for 30 years and suffered from hepatitis C for ten years. Died from nonalcoholic cirrhois of the liver. Buried Green Hills Memorial Park, Rancho Palos Verdes CA.

Bill Ferrazzi—1 Year Pitcher (b. 19 Apr 1907 West Quincy MA–d. 10 Aug 1993 Gainesville FL) Served in the U.S. Navy during World War II. He coached high school football in Gainesville before spending 24 years as a manager for the Prudential Life Insurance Company in Gainesville and Mobile AL, retiring in 1972. Died after a short illness. Buried Forest Meadows Memorial Park Central, Gainesville FL.

Rick Ferrell—18 Years Catcher Hall of Fame (b. 12 Oct 1905 Durham NC–d. 27 Jul 1995 William Beaumont Hospital, Royal Oak MI) He worked in various capacities for the Tigers, starting in 1950. Died from arrhythmia. Buried New Garden Cemetery, Greensboro NC.

Wes Ferrell—15 Years Pitcher (b. 2 Feb 1908 Greensboro NC–d. 9 Dec 1976 Sarasota Memorial Hospital, Sarasota FL) A low handicap golfer and an expert fisherman, he owned a string of fishing lakes on his farm near Guilford Station NC. Died during kidney surgery. Buried New Garden Cemetery, Greensboro NC.

Tom Ferrick—9 Years Pitcher (b. 6 Jan 1915 New York City NY–d. 15 Oct 1996 Riddle Memorial Hospital, Lima PA) Served in the U.S. Navy during World War II. He was associated with professional baseball as a player, coach and scout for over 50 years. Died from heart failure after suffering a heart attack, stroke and fractured hip. Buried St Peter and St Paul Cemetery, Springfield PA.

Hobe Ferris—9 Years Infielder (b. 7 Dec 1877 Providence RI–d. 18 Mar 1938 at his home in Detroit MI) Died following a heart attack.

Cy Ferry—2 Years Pitcher (b. 1 Feb 1877 Hudson NY–d. 27 Sep 1938 St Luke's Hospital, Pittsfield MA) He managed minor league baseball and did some scouting. Later he worked in the steel construction business. Died following a stroke suffered two days earlier. Buried St Joseph's Cemetery, Pittsfield MA.

Jack Ferry—4 Years Pitcher (b. 7 Apr 1887 Pittsfield MA–d. 29 Aug 1954 St Luke's Hospital, Pittsfield MA) He coached high school baseball for a time, then went into the painting and paper hanging business. He served several terms on the city council. Died after a short illness. Buried St Joseph's Cemetery, Pittsfield MA.

Alex Ferson—3 Years Pitcher (b. 14 Jul 1866 Philadelphia PA–d. 5 Dec 1957 Boston MA) He operated restaurants in Worcester MA and Dorchester MA. Buried Manchester NH.

Lou Fette—5 Years Pitcher (b. 15 Mar 1907 Alma MO–d. 3 Jan 1981 Johnson County Mem Hospital, Warrensburg MO) He lived at Warrensburg for 40 years, farming in the area. Buried Sunset Hills Cemetery, Warrensburg MO.

Dick Fettelbach—3 Years Outfielder (b. 26 Jun 1929 New Haven CT–d. 26 Jan 1995 East Harwich MA).

John Fetzer—(b. 25 Mar 1901 Decatur IN–d. 21 Feb 1991 at his home in Honolulu HI) A broadcasting pioneer, he owned radio and television stations and was owner of the Tigers from 1961 to 1983. Died from pneumonia, but suffered from a heart condition. Buried Mountain Home Cemetery, Kalamazoo MI.

Willy Fetzer—1 Game Pinch Hitter (b. 24 Jun 1883 Concord NC–d. 3 May 1959 at a hospital in Chapel Hill NC) He coached baseball and football at Davidson College, University of North Carolina and North Carolina State University. For years he owned and operated Camp Sapphire at Brevard NC. Died from a heart attack. Buried Oakwood Cemetery, Concord NC.

Chick Fewster—11 Years Infielder (b. 10 Nov 1895 Baltimore MD–d. 16 Apr 1945 Mercy Hospital, Baltimore MD) Served in the U.S. Merchant Marines during World War II. He operated a private baseball field and trained baseball players at Brooklyn NY. Died from a heart attack. Buried St John's Cemetery, Waverly MD.

John Fick—1 Year Pitcher (b. 18 May 1921 Baltimore MD–d. 9 Jun 1958 Somers Point NJ).

Clarence Fieber—1 Year Pitcher (b. 4 Sep 1913 San Francisco CA–d. 20 Aug 1985 Kaiser Hospital, Redwood City CA) He was a longshoreman for 35 years. Died from kidney disease. Cremated.

Jim Field—5 Years Infielder (b. 24 Apr 1863 Philadelphia PA–d. 13 May 1953 City Hospital, Atlantic City NJ) He owned and operated a tavern near Connie Mack Stadium in Philadelphia. Died from injuries received when he fell down the steps of his home three weeks earlier. Buried Holy Cross Cemetery, Yeadon PA.

Sam Field—1 Year Catcher (b. 12 Oct 1848 Philadelphia PA–d. 28 Oct 1904 Sinking Spring PA) He spent 30 years in the hotel business, ten in Reading and 20 in Sinking Spring. He was also one of the organizers of the Liberty Fire Company in Sinking Spring and held the position of chief for five years. Died after being ill ten months and bedfast six months. Buried Aulenbach's Cemetery, Mount Penn PA.

Jocko Fields—6 Years Outfielder (b. 20 Oct 1864 Cork, Ireland–d. 14 Oct 1950 Medical Center, Jersey City NJ) From 1900 to 1933 he worked for Railway Express. After 1933 he was a utilityman for Hudson County, NJ, retiring in 1947.

Lou Fiene—4 Years Pitcher (b. 29 Dec 1884 Fort Dodge IA–d. 22 Dec 1964 Chicago IL) Buried Calvary Cemetery, Evanston IL.

Jack Fifield—3 Years Pitcher (b. 5 Oct 1871 Enfield NH–d. 27 Nov 1939 Syracuse NY).

Frank Figgemeier—1 Year Pitcher (b. 22 Apr 1874 St Louis MO–d. 15 Apr 1915 St Louis MO) Died following a short illness. Buried Calvary Cemetery, St Louis MO.

Eddie Files—1 Year Pitcher (b. 19 May 1883 Portland ME–d. 10 May 1954 at his home in Cornish ME) He taught German, English and Latin, and coached sports in high school. Later he worked as a bond salesman. Died after an illness of several months. Buried Riverside Cemetery, Cornish ME.

Steve Filipowicz—3 Years Outfielder (b. 28 Jun 1921 Kulpmont PA–d. 21 Feb 1975 Veteran's Hospital, Wilkes-Barre PA) Served in the U.S. Marines during World War II. Also a professional football player, he coached basketball, baseball and football one year at St Mary's College in Emmitsburg MD. For 17 years he was a corporate tax officer for the Pennsylvania Bureau of Revenue in Harrisburg PA. Buried St Casimer's Church Cemetery, Kulpmont PA.

Marc Filley—1 Year Pitcher (b. 28 Feb 1912 Lansingburgh NY–d. 20 Jan 1995 Brentwood Rehab Center, Yarmouth ME) An attorney, he maintained a private law office in Troy NY from 1940 until his retirement in 1990. From 1954 to 1971 he served as a family court judge in Rensselaer County, NY. Died following a long illness. Buried Oakwood Cemetery, Troy NY.

Dana Fillingim—8 Years Pitcher (b. 6 Nov 1893 Columbus GA–d. 3 Feb 1961 Tuskegee AL) He worked more than 20 years for the State of Alabama ABC Department. Died from a heart seizure. Buried Tuskegee Cemetery, Tuskegee AL.

Bill Fincher—1 Year Pitcher (b. 26 May 1894 Atlanta GA–d. 7 May 1946 Schumpert Sanitarium, Shreveport LA) He was a salesman for Standard Oil Company. Despondent over ill health, he died five hours after shooting himself in the head with a .32 caliber pistol. Buried Greenwood Cemetery, Shreveport LA.

Jim Finigan—6 Years Infielder (b. 19 Aug 1928 Quincy IL–d. 16 May 1981 at his home in Quincy IL) He coached minor league and college baseball and also sold life insurance. Died from a massive heart attack. Buried St Peter's Cemetery, Quincy IL.

Herman Fink—3 Years Pitcher (b. 22 Aug 1911 Concord NC–d. 24 Aug 1980 Rowan Memorial Hospital, Salisbury NC) He worked in the plumbing department at Canon Mills in Landis NC until he retired. Buried Carolina Memorial Park, Concord NC.

Pembroke Finlayson—2 Years Pitcher (b. 31 Jul 1888 Cheraw SC–d. 6 Mar 1912 Norwegian Hospital, Brooklyn NY) Died at the height of his baseball career from peritonitis of the heart, brought on by an injury he received while pitching.

Bill Finley—1 Year Outfielder (b. 4 Oct 1863 New York City NY–d. 6 Oct 1912 at his home in Asbury Park NJ) Died in his sleep from valvular heart disease. Buried Calvary Cemetery, Woodside NY.

Bob Finley—2 Years Catcher (b. 25 Nov 1915 Ennis TX–d. 2 Jan 1986 Queen of the Valley Hosp, West Covina CA) He was vice-president of an industrial rubber company for 25 years. Died from a heart attack. Buried Grove Hill Memorial Park, Dallas TX.

Charles O Finley—(b. 22 Feb 1918 Ensley AL–d. 19 Feb 1996 Northwestern Memorial Hospital, Evanston IL) He was the founder and president of the world's largest insurance brokerage firm and owned the Kansas City (later Oakland Athletics) from 1960 to 1980. Died from heart and vascular ailments. Buried Calumet Park Cemetery, Merrillville IN.

Mickey Finn—4 Years Infielder (b. 24 Jan 1904 New York City NY–d. 7 Jul 1933 Sacred Heart Hospital, Allentown PA) Died at the height of his baseball career following surgery for chronic duodenal ulcers that had obstructed his plyorus. Buried Calvary Cemetery, Woodside NY.

Happy Finneran—5 Years Pitcher (b. 29 Oct 1891 East Orange NJ–d. 3 Feb 1942 St Mary's Hospital, Orange NJ) He was a funeral director for 21 years. Died from pneumonia. Buried Gate of Heaven Catholic Cemetery, East Hanover NJ.

Hal Finney—5 Years Catcher (b. 30 Jul 1905 Lafayette AL–d. 26 Dec 1991 Lafayette AL) He farmed in the Lafayette area most of his life and served 18 years as a county commissioner. Buried Chapel Hill Cemetery, Lafayette AL.

Lou Finney—15 Years Outfielder (b. 13 Aug 1910 Buffalo AL–d. 22 Apr 1966 Chambers County Hospital, Lafayette AL) He managed minor league baseball before returning to his home area to be the owner and manager of Chambers County Feed and Seed Store in Lafayette. Died from a heart attack. Buried Chapel Hill Cemetery, Lafayette AL.

Ted Firth—1 Year Pitcher (b. Philadelphia PA–d. 23 Jun 1902 Tewksberry MA) He was murdered.

Bill Fischer—5 Years Catcher (b. 2 Mar 1891 New York City NY–d. 4 Sep 1945 Richmond VA).

Carl Fischer—7 Years Pitcher (b. 5 Nov 1905 Ridgeway NY–d. 10 Dec 1963 at his home in Medina NY) Served in the U.S. Army Air Force during World War II. He operated the Main Street Newsroom in Albion NY from 1948 until his death. Died following a heart attack. Buried Mount Ridge Cemetery, Royalton NY.

Sam Fishburn—1 Year Infielder (b. 18 May 1893 Haverhill MA–d. 11 Apr 1965 St Luke's Hospital, Bethlehem PA) For 37 years he was a realtor, retiring in 1962. Buried Cedar Hill Memorial Park, Allentown PA.

Leo Fishel—1 Year Pitcher (b. 13 Dec 1877 Babylon NY–d. 19 May 1960 Hempstead NY) Buried Babylon Cemetery, Babylon NY.

Bob Fisher—7 Years Infielder (b. 3 Nov 1887 Nashville TN–d. 4 Aug 1963 at a hospital in Jacksonville FL) From 1925 until his death he lived in Jacksonville where he worked for the city recreation department and managed the Lackawanna Pool. Died after an illness of several months. Buried Evergreen Cemetery, Jacksonville FL.

Chauncey Fisher—5 Years Pitcher (b. 8 Jan 1873 Anderson IN–d. 25 Apr 1939 Hollywood Hospital, Los Angeles CA) The owner of a wrecking business in Anderson for 30 years, he retired to the Los Angeles area in 1934. Died from a massive pulmonary embolism caused by prostate cancer that had spread to his lung. Buried Anderson IN.

Cherokee Fisher—3 Years Pitcher (b. Dec 1845 Philadelphia PA–d. 26 Sep 1912 New York City NY).

Clarence Fisher—2 Years Pitcher (b. 27 Aug 1898 Letart WV–d. 2 Nov 1965 Holzer Hospital, Gallipolis OH) He was a toll collector on the Silver Bridge and operated service stations in Point Pleasant. For ten years he farmed near Bucyrus OH. Died after being in ill health from an automobile accident three years earlier. Buried Suncrest Cemetery, Point Pleasant WV.

Don Fisher—1 Year Pitcher (b. 6 Feb 1916 Cleveland OH–d. 29 Jul 1973 Hillcrest Hospital, Mayfield Heights OH) He worked 37 years in the trouble shooting department of power and line maintenance for CEI. Died from congestive heart failure. Buried Whitehaven Park, Mayfield Village OH.

Ed Fisher—1 Year Pitcher (b. 31 Oct 1876 Wayne MI–d. 24 Jul 1951 at his son's home in Spokane WA) A medical doctor, he was appointed head of the Dearborn Health Department in 1946. He was also president of the City of Dearborn from 1922 to 1926 and was a Michigan state representative for 12 years. Buried Glenwood Cemetery, Wayne MI.

Gus Fisher—2 Years Catcher (b. 21 Oct 1885 Pottsboro TX–d. 8 Apr 1972 at a convalescent hospital in Portland OR) He played minor league baseball in Portland ten years, retiring from baseball in 1922 to live in Portland. Buried Riverview Cemetery, Portland OR.

Harry Fisher—2 Years Pitcher (b. 3 Jan 1926 Newbury, Ontario, Canada–d. 20 Sep 1981 Waterloo, Ontario, Canada).

Ike Fisher—1 Year Catcher (b. 28 Jul 1874 Chattanooga TN–d. 28 Feb 1947 Norwood Park IL) Buried Holy Sepulchre Cemetery, Worth IL.

Ray Fisher—10 Years Pitcher (b. 4 Oct 1887 Middlebury VT–d. 3 Nov 1982 Ann Arbor MI) Served in the U.S. Army during World War I. He was baseball coach at the University of Michigan from 1921 to 1958. The baseball stadium there was named for him in 1970. Buried Washtenong Memorial Park, Ann Arbor MI.

Red Fisher—1 Year Outfielder (b. 22 Jun 1887 Pittsburgh PA–d. 1 Feb 1940 at his home in Louisville KY) He was a night watchman for Henry Bickel Company. Died from a heart attack. Buried Walnut Ridge Cemetery, Jeffersonville IN.

Showboat Fisher—4 Years Outfielder (b. 16 Jan 1899 Wesley IA–d. 15 May 1994 St Cloud Hospital, St Cloud MN) He owned and operated Fisher's Club in Avon from 1935 until he retired in 1960. Buried St Benedict's Catholic Church Cemetery, Avon MN.

Tom Fisher—1 Year Pitcher (b. 1 Nov 1880 Anderson IN–d. 3 Sep 1972 Anderson IN) He started a feed and coal business that operated in Anderson for many years. Prior to retirement he worked for Union Grain Company. Died after being in failing health for a year. Buried East Maplewood Cemetery, Anderson IN.

Wilbur Fisher—1 Game Pinch Hitter (b. 18 Jul 1894 Green Bottom WV–d. 24 Oct 1960 Pageton WV) For 13 years he was a general mine foreman for Page Coal and Coke Company. Died after being in failing health for five years. Buried Spring Hill Cemetery, Huntington WV.

Max Fiske—1 Year Pitcher (b. 10 Oct 1889 Chicago IL–d. 28 May 1928 Chicago IL).

Wes Fisler—1 Year Outfielder (b. 5 Jul 1841 Camden NJ–d. 25 Dec 1922 Presbyterian Hospital, Philadelphia PA) He entered the haberdashery business and later was a clerk for one of Philadelphia's leading attorneys. Died from pneumonia.

Paul Fittery—2 Years Pitcher (b. 10 Oct 1887 Lebanon PA–d. 28 Jan 1974 at a hospital in Cartersville GA) He was a fireman at Fort McPherson. Died suddenly. Buried White Cemetery, White GA.

Charlie Fitzberger—7 Games Pinch Hitter (b. 13 Feb 1904 Baltimore MD–d. 25 Jan 1965 Baltimore MD) Buried Oak Lawn Cemetery, Baltimore MD.

Dennis Fitzgerald—1 Year Infielder (b. Mar 1865 England–d. 16 Oct 1936 at his home in New Haven CT) He was a carpenter. Buried Mount St Peter's Cemetery, Derby CT.

Howie Fitzgerald—3 Years Outfielder (b. 16 May 1902 Eagle Lake TX–d. 27 Feb 1959 Matthews TX) He was a farmer and owned a cleaning and pressing business. Killed in a one-car accident when he lost control of his truck and ran off the road. Buried Masonic Cemetery, Eagle Lake TX.

John Fitzgerald—2 Years Pitcher (b. 30 May 1870 Natick MA–d. 31 Mar 1921 Roxbury MA) Buried New Calvary Cemetery, Mattapan MA.

Matty Fitzgerald—2 Years Catcher (b. 31 Aug 1880 Albany NY–d. 22 Sep 1949 at the home of his son in Albany NY) Claimed to be the first catcher to wear shinguards, he coached baseball at Union College and was the superintendent at Lincoln Park in Albany for several years. Died from generalized arteriosclerosis. Buried St Agnes Cemetery, Menands NY.

Mike Fitzgerald—2 Years Outfielder (b. 26 Jun 1891 San Mateo CA–d. 18 Jan 1945 Mills Memorial Hospital, San Mateo CA) He coached baseball at Santa Clara University four years before becoming a building inspector for the City of San Mateo. He was also a San Mateo city councilman. Died following surgery for a duadenal ulcer. Buried St Johns Cemetery, San Mateo CA.

Ray Fitzgerald—1 Game Pinch Hitter (b. 5 Dec 1904 Chicopee MA–d. 6 Sep 1977 Noble Hospital, Westfield MA) Died after a long illness. Buried St Mary's Cemetery, Westfield MA.

Warren Fitzgerald—2 Years Pitcher (b. 18 Apr 1872 PA–d. 7 Nov 1930 at his home in Phoenix

AZ) He worked in a laundry. Died from broncho asthma. Buried Salt Lake City UT.

Paul Fitzke—1 Year Pitcher (b. 30 Jul 1900 LaCrosse WI–d. 30 Jun 1950 at his home in Sacramento CA) He coached baseball and football at Sacramento High School before becoming a chiropractor. Died from lymphocytic leukemia. Buried Morris Hill Cemetery, Boise ID.

Ed Fitzpatrick—3 Years Infielder (b. 9 Dec 1889 Lewiston PA–d. 23 Oct 1965 Muhlenberg Medical Center, Bethlehem PA) He was a foreman in the packaging department for Baker Chemical Company for 28 years before retiring in 1952. Died after spending nine years in the hospital. Buried Fairmount Cemetery, Phillipsburg NJ.

Freddie Fitzsimmons—19 Years Pitcher 3 Years Manager (b. 28 Jul 1901 Mishawaka IN–d. 18 Nov 1979 at his home in Yucca Valley CA) He worked for the Cubs. Died from a self-inflicted gunshot wound to the head. Cremated. Buried Montecito Memorial Park, Colton CA.

Tom Fitzsimmons—1 Year Infielder (b. 6 Apr 1890 Oakland CA–d. 20 Dec 1971 Hillhaven Convalescent Hospital, Oakland CA) Served in France during World War I. He practiced denistry in Oakland for 21 years before becoming active in politics. Elected to the Oakland City Council from 1934 to 1941 when he became Alameda County, CA, Recorder, retiring in 1962. He and his wife died the same day, in separate Oakland rest homes. Buried St Mary's Cemetery, Oakland CA.

Max Flack—12 Years Outfielder (b. 5 Feb 1890 Belleville IL–d. 31 Jul 1975 Memorial Hospital, Belleville IL) He played for two teams the same day, the Cubs in the morning, then the Cardinals, to whom he had been traded, that afternoon. He was a custodian at a high school in East St Louis IL. Buried Walnut Hill Cemetery, Belleville IL.

Wally Flager—1 Year Infielder (b. 3 Nov 1921 Chicago Heights IL–d. 16 Dec 1990 Keizer OR) Served in the U.S. Army during World War II. He worked for the McDonald Candy Company and the Stiff Furniture Company in Salem OR. Buried Restlawn Memory Gardens, Salem OR.

Ira Flagstead—13 Years Outfielder (b. 22 Sep 1893 Montague MI–d. 13 Mar 1940 at his home in Olympia WA) He worked in the Olympia brewery. Died in his sleep. Buried Masonic Memorial Park, Olympia WA.

Martin Flaherty—1 Year Outfielder (b. 24 Sep 1853 Worcester MA–d. 10 Jun 1920 Providence RI) A bookmaker for horse races, he was a lover of hunting and fishing and was fond of hunting dogs.

Pat Flaherty—1 Year Infielder (b. 31 Jan 1876 St Louis MO–d. 28 Jan 1946 Chicago IL) Buried Calvary Cemetery, Evanston IL.

Patsy Flaherty—9 Years Pitcher (b. 29 Jun 1876 Carnegie PA–d. 23 Jan 1968 Alexandria LA).

Al Flair—1 Year Infielder (b. 24 Jul 1916 New Orleans LA–d. 26 Jul 1988 New Orleans LA) Served in the Pacific for the U.S. Army during World War II. He owned Al Flair Company, a sanitary supply firm, until selling it to Manny's Sanitary Supply, where he worked until his retirement. Buried Metairie Cemetery, Metairie LA.

Charlie Flanagan—1 Year Outfielder (b. 13 Dec 1891 Oakland CA–d. 8 Jan 1930 San Francisco CA) He worked for the San Francisco Police Department. Buried San Francisco National Cemetery, San Francisco CA.

Ed Flanagan—2 Years Infielder (b. 15 Sep 1861 Lowell MA–d. 10 Nov 1926 at his home in Lowell MA) He was a member of the Lowell Police Department 29 years and president of the Massachusetts State Police Association. Died suddenly. Buried St Patrick's Cemetery, Lowell MA.

Steamer Flanagan—1 Year Outfielder (b. 20 Apr 1881 Kingston PA–d. 21 Apr 1947 at his home in Wilkes-Barre PA) He engaged in a number of business ventures in the Wilkes-Barre area, all involving the coal business. Died following a stroke suffered the day before. Buried St Mary's Cemetery, Wilkes-Barre PA.

Ray Flanigan—1 Year Pitcher (b. 8 Jan 1923 Morgantown WV–d. 28 Mar 1993 Baltimore MD) He was a mechanic. Cremated. Buried Moreland Memorial Park, Parkville MD.

Ray Flaskamper—1 Year Infielder (b. 31 Oct 1901 St Louis MO–d. 3 Feb 1978 San Antonio TX) He lived in San Antonio 52 years. Buried Sunset Memorial Park, San Antonio TX.

Jack Flater—1 Year Pitcher (b. 22 Sep 1883

Sandymount MD–d. 20 Mar 1970 Carroll County General Hosp, Westminster MD) He was a retired carpenter. Buried Pleasant Grove Cemetery, Sandymount MD.

Les Fleming—7 Years Infielder (b. 7 Aug 1915 Singleton TX–d. 5 Mar 1980 Cleveland TX) For 17 years he was a pipe foreman for Brown and Root in Baytown TX. Buried Forest Lawn Memorial Park, Beaumont TX.

Tom Fleming—3 Years Outfielder (b. 20 Nov 1873 Philadelphia PA–d. 26 Dec 1957 Winthrop MA) He scouted for the Athletics and Phillies. Died after a brief illness.

Art Fletcher—13 Years Infielder 5 Years Manager (b. 5 Jan 1885 Collinsville IL–d. 6 Feb 1950 Los Angeles CA) He worked in baseball as a coach until 1945 when he retired because of poor health. Died from a heart attack while waiting in his car at a traffic signal. Buried Glenwood Cemetery, Collinsville IL.

Elbie Fletcher—12 Years Infielder (b. 18 Mar 1916 Milton MA–d. 9 Mar 1994 Milton Hospital, Milton MA) Served in the U.S. Navy during World War II. He was the recreational director for the City of Melrose MA from 1958 until retiring in 1981. Buried Milton Cemetery, Milton MA.

Frank Fletcher—1 Game Pinch Hitter (b. 6 Mar 1891 Hildreth IL–d. 7 Oct 1974 St Petersburg FL) A retired hotel clerk, he owned Orangewood Apartments in St Petersburg where he had lived 54 years. Buried Royal Palm Cemetery, St Petersburg FL.

Elmer Flick—13 Years Outfielder Hall of Fame (b. 11 Jan 1876 Bedford OH–d. 9 Jan 1971 Municipal Hospital, Bedford OH) He was a retired contractor. Died after a long illness. Buried Crown Hill Cemetery, Twinsburg OH.

Lew Flick—2 Years Outfielder (b. 18 Feb 1915 Bristol TN–d. 7 Dec 1990 Weber City VA) He worked for Munford Do-it-Yourself Stores at Kingsport TN. Died after a brief illness. Buried Oak Hill Cemetery, Kingsport TN.

Don Flinn—1 Year Outfielder (b. 17 Nov 1892 Bluffdale TX–d. 8 Mar 1959 Waco TX) Buried Hucksby Cemetery, Stephenville TX.

Silver Flint—12 Years Catcher (b. 3 Aug 1855 Philadelphia PA–d. 14 Jan 1892 Chicago IL) Died at his ex-wife's home from consumption. Buried Bellefontaine Cemetery, St Louis MO.

Mort Flohr—1 Year Pitcher (b. 15 Aug 1911 Canisteo NY–d. 2 Jun 1994 Mercy Care Nursing Facility, N Hornell NY) He owned and operated Flohr's Tavern in Canisteo from 1949 to 1983. Died following an extended illness. Buried Woodlawn Cemetery, Canisteo NY.

Curt Flood—15 Years Outfielder (b. 18 Jan 1938 Houston TX–d. 20 Jan 1997 UCLA Medical Center, Los Angeles CA) He's best known for his challenge of baseball's Reserve Clause. Died from throat cancer. Buried Inglewood Park Cemetery, Inglewood CA.

Tim Flood—3 Years Infielder (b. 13 Mar 1877 Montgomery City MO–d. 15 Jun 1929 St Louis MO) Died from a heart attack as he drove his car to the curb in downtown St Louis. Buried Calvary Cemetery, St Louis MO.

Paul Florence—1 Year Catcher (b. 22 Apr 1900 Chicago IL–d. 28 May 1986 Gainesville FL).

Jesse Flores—7 Years Pitcher (b. 2 Nov 1914 Guadalajara, Mexico–d. 17 Dec 1991 St Joseph Hospital, Orange CA) He scouted 27 years for the Twins and three years for the Pirates. Died from respiratory failure 13 days after knee replacement surgery. Buried Queen of Heaven Cemetery, Rowland Heights CA.

Jake Flowers—10 Years Infielder (b. 16 Mar 1902 Cambridge MD–d. 27 Dec 1962 Clearwater FL) He worked his entire life in baseball as a player, coach, scout, minor league manager and executive. Died from a heart attack. Buried Cambridge Cemetery, Cambridge MD.

Wes Flowers—2 Years Pitcher (b. 13 Aug 1913 Vanndale AR–d. 31 Dec 1988 Wynne AR) Served in the U.S. Navy during World War II. He retired as a wildlife officer from the Arkansas Game and Fish Commission. Buried Cogbill Cemetery, Wynne AR.

John Fluhrer—1 Year Outfielder (b. 3 Jan 1894 Adrian MI–d. 17 Jul 1946 University Hospital, Columbus OH) He operated athletic supply stores in Toledo OH and Columbus before becoming involved in politics. He then worked for the state highway department and in the state attorney general's office. Died from a heart attack suffered two days earlier. Buried St Joseph Cemetery, Lockbourne OH.

Carney Flynn—2 Years Pitcher (b. 23 Jan 1875 Cincinnati OH–d. 10 Feb 1947 Cincinnati

OH) Buried St Joseph New Cemetery, Cincinnati OH.

George Flynn—1 Year Outfielder (b. 24 May 1871 Chicago IL–d. 28 Dec 1901 at his mother's home in Chicago IL) He was a commercial traveler. Died from a hemorrhage in his lungs.

Jocko Flynn—2 Years Pitcher (b. 30 Jun 1864 Lawrence MA–d. 30 Dec 1907 Lawrence MA) He worked as a clerk at the Franklin House, was in the liquor business for himself and worked for the state liquor board. Died after ailing for some time. Buried Immaculate Conception Cemetery, Lawrence MA.

John Flynn—3 Years Infielder (b. 7 Sep 1883 Providence RI–d. 23 Mar 1935 Providence RI) He managed minor league baseball and coached baseball at Providence College ten years. He also assisted his brothers in their law practices. Died after a year's illness. Buried St Francis Cemetery, Pawtucket RI.

Stu Flythe—1 Year Pitcher (b. 5 Dec 1911 Conway NC–d. 18 Oct 1963 V A Hospital, Durham NC) He was a sales representative for Maola Milk and Ice Cream Company in New Bern NC. Buried Cedar Grove Cemetery, New Bern NC.

Jim Fogarty—7 Years Outfielder 1 Year Manager (b. 12 Feb 1864 San Francisco CA–d. 20 May 1891 St Joseph Hospital, Philadelphia PA) Died at the height of his career from consumption.

Joe Fogarty—1 Year Outfielder (b. 8 Nov 1868 San Francisco CA–d. 28 Mar 1918 City Hospital, San Francisco CA) He was a clerk. Died from pulmonary tuberculosis. Buried Holy Cross Catholic Cemetery, Colma CA.

Horace Fogel—2 Years Manager (b. 2 Mar 1861 Macungie PA–d. 15 Nov 1928 at his home in Philadelphia PA) He was president of the Phillies from 1909 to 1912, but was best known as a sportswriter and baseball authority for Philadelphia newspapers. Died from a stroke after being in poor health his last six years. Buried Mount Peace Cemetery, Philadelphia PA.

Lee Fohl—2 Years Catcher 11 Years Manager (b. 28 Nov 1876 Lowell OH–d. 30 Oct 1965 at his home in Cleveland OH) He operated several filling stations in the Cleveland area and for his last 17 years was a ticket taker at the Highland Park golf course. Buried Calvary Cemetery, Cleveland OH.

Curry Foley—5 Years Outfielder (b. 14 Jan 1856 Milltown, Ireland–d. 20 Oct 1898 at his home in Boston MA) He had been sick with various diseases since he retired from baseball in 1883, and died as a result. Buried Mount Calvary Cemetery, Roslindale MA.

Ray Foley—2 Games Pinch Hitter (b. 23 Jun 1906 Naugatuck CT–d. 22 Mar 1980 Indian River Memorial Hosp, Vero Beach FL) He was an educator at Naugatuck High School from 1932 until he retired in 1969, working his way from teaching to athletic advisor, athletic director, principal and eventually superintendent. Died after a brief illness. Buried St James Cemetery, Naugatuck CT.

Will Foley—6 Years Infielder (b. 15 Nov 1855 Chicago IL–d. 13 Nov 1916 Chicago IL) He was found dead in his brother's barn, probably dying from heart trouble and exposure.

Lew Fonseca—12 Years Infielder 3 Years Manager (b. 21 Jan 1899 Oakland CA–d. 26 Nov 1989 at his home in Ely IA) He spent 60 years in baseball as a player, manager, coach and promoter. After his playing career he produced baseball promotional films for 35 years. Died following an extended illness. Buried All Saints Cemetery, Des Plaines IL.

Davy Force—10 Years Infielder (b. 27 Jul 1849 New York City NY–d. 21 Jun 1918 Englewood NJ) Died from a cerebral thrombosis. Buried Brookside Cemetery, Englewood NJ.

Gene Ford—2 Years Pitcher (b. 23 Jun 1912 Fort Dodge IA–d. 7 Sep 1970 Palo Alto County Hospital, Emmetsburg IA) He farmed in the Emmetsburg area from 1944 until his death. Died shortly after admission to the hospital. Buried Corpus Christi Cemetery, Fort Dodge IA.

Gene Ford—1 Year Pitcher (b. 16 Apr 1881 Milton, Nova Scotia, Canada–d. 23 Aug 1973 Apollo Medical Center, Dunedin FL) A commercial artist in Minneapolis MN, he retired to Dunedin in 1952. Buried Sylvan Abbey Memorial Park, Clearwater FL.

Hod Ford—15 Years Infielder (b. 23 Jul 1897 New Haven CT–d. 29 Jan 1977 Winchester MA) He owned a restaurant in Winchester for many years and sold real estate there. He was also a director of the Winchester Country Club and for more than 20 years was a director of the

Winchester Trust Company. Died after an illness of one year. Buried Wildwood Cemetery, Winchester MA.

Russ Ford—7 Years Pitcher (b. 25 Apr 1883 Brandon, Manitoba, Canada–d. 24 Jan 1960 Memorial Hospital, Rockingham NC) He was known for perfecting the "emery ball." He managed the Rockingham Hotel, was a teller at a Rockingham bank and, later, worked in the shipping department of a mill. He moved to New York City in 1933 where he was a craftsman for an engineering firm, returning to Rockingham in 1958. Died from a heart attack. Cremated. Buried Leak Family Cemetery, Rockingham NC.

Wenty Ford—1 Year Pitcher (b. 25 Nov 1946 Nassau, Bahamas–d. 8 Jul 1980 Nassau, Bahamas).

Bill Foreman—2 Years Pitcher (b. 10 Oct 1886 Vernango PA–d. 2 Oct 1958 Uniontown Hospital, Uniontown PA) He taught school 42 years in Pennsylvania, Oklahoma, Iowa and West Virginia, retiring in 1948. After that he conducted a remedial reading clinic in his home until his death. Buried Lafayette Memorial Park, Brier Hill PA.

Brownie Foreman—2 Years Pitcher (b. 6 Aug 1875 Baltimore MD–d. 10 Dec 1926 Baltimore MD).

Frank Foreman—11 Years Pitcher (b. 1 May 1863 Baltimore MD–d. 19 Nov 1957 Baltimore MD) Died after being bedridden for 18 months. Buried St Mary's Cemetery, Baltimore MD.

Happy Foreman—2 Years Pitcher (b. 20 Jul 1897 Memphis TN–d. 13 Feb 1953 Kings' County Hospital, New York City NY) Served in the U.S. Marines during World War I. Managing minor league baseball, he lived in Shreveport LA and was visiting a sister in Brooklyn NY when he died. Died after undergoing throat surgery a year earlier. Buried Beth David Cemetery, Elmont NY.

Mike Fornieles—12 Years Pitcher (b. 18 Jan 1932 Havana, Cuba–d. 11 Feb 1998 St Petersburg FL).

Tom Forster—4 Years Infielder (b. 1 May 1859 New York City NY–d. 17 Jul 1946 Fordham Hospital, Bronx NY) He worked more than 20 years for Consolidated Edison, retiring about 1934.

Ed Forsythe—1 Year Infielder (b. 30 Apr 1887 Kingston NY–d. 22 Jun 1956 St Mary's Hospital, Hoboken NJ) He retired from the Hoboken Police Department in 1940 after 20 years service. After retiring he worked as a security guard at Bankers Trust Company of New York until 1955. Buried Holy Name Cemetery, Jersey City NJ.

Gary Fortune—3 Years Pitcher (b. 11 Oct 1894 High Point NC–d. 23 Sep 1955 Georgetown Hospital, Washington DC) He lived in Washington DC since 1935 and worked for the Grain Division of the Department of Agriculture. Died after being hospitalized for a month. Buried Kenly Cemetery, Kenly NC.

George Foss—1 Year Infielder (b. 13 Jun 1898 Register GA–d. 10 Nov 1969 Brandon FL) Buried Limona Cemetery, Brandon FL.

Andrew "Rube" Foster—Hall of Fame (b. 17 Sep 1879 Calvert TX–d. 9 Dec 1930 Chicago IL) A black baseball player, he was responsible for founding the Negro National League in 1920. He was president of the league from 1920 until his health forced him to retire in 1928. Died after an illness of two years. Buried Lincoln Cemetery, Chicago IL.

Bill Foster—15 Years Pitcher Hall of Fame (b. 12 Jun 1904 Calvert TX–d. 16 Sep 1978 Lorman MS) He played in the negro leagues.

Eddie Foster—13 Years Infielder (b. 13 Feb 1888 Chicago IL–d. 15 Jan 1937 Casualty Hospital, Washington DC) He conducted a metal welding business in Washington DC. Died from injuries suffered in a hit-and-run automobile accident a week earlier. Buried Columbia Gardens Cemetery, Arlington VA.

Elmer Foster—6 Years Outfielder (b. 15 Aug 1861 Minneapolis MN–d. 22 Jul 1946 Minneapolis MN) Buried Lakewood Cemetery, Minneapolis MN.

Pop Foster—4 Years Outfielder (b. 8 Apr 1878 New Haven CT–d. 16 Apr 1944 Princeton NJ) He managed minor league baseball a short while before coaching at a number of colleges. In 1924 he moved to Princeton University where he was a member of the Dept of Health and Physical Education, teaching corrective and developmental gymnastics and coaching wrestling. Died after a long illness. Buried Princeton Cemetery, Princeton NJ.

Reddy Foster—1 Game Pinch Hitter (b. 1867 Richmond VA–d. 19 Dec 1908 Richmond VA) He stuck a shotgun in his mouth and pulled the trigger, blowing off his head, on the banks of the James River during a drinking spree. Buried Oakwood Cemetery, Richmond VA.

Rube Foster—5 Years Pitcher (b. 5 Jan 1889 Lehigh OK–d. 1 Mar 1976 LeFlore County Hospital, Poteau OK) He was a retired farmer. Buried Milton Cemetery, Bokoshe OK.

Slim Foster—1 Year Pitcher (b. 1885 Birmingham AL–d. 1 Mar 1929 at Fresh Air Camp Infirmary, Montgomery AL) Buried Oakwood Cemetery, Montgomery AL.

Bob Fothergill—12 Years Outfielder (b. 16 Aug 1899 Massillon OH–d. 20 Mar 1938 St Joseph's Mercy Hospital, Detroit MI) He worked for Ford Motor Company and had signed to coach baseball at Lawrence Tech in Highland Park MI just before he died following a stroke. Buried Massillon Cemetery, Massillon OH.

Henry Fournier—1 Year Pitcher (b. 8 Aug 1865 Syracuse NY–d. 8 Dec 1945 Detroit MI).

Jack Fournier—15 Years Infielder (b. 28 Sep 1892 Au Sable MI–d. 5 Sep 1973 Tacoma WA) He coached baseball at UCLA three years, managed minor league baseball two years and scouted for the Cubs, Tigers and Reds. Buried Fern Hill Cemetery, Aberdeen WA.

Bill Fouser—1 Year Infielder (b. 1855 Philadelphia PA–d. 1 Mar 1919 Philadelphia PA) For 38 years he was a baggageman on the Reading Railroad. He dropped dead from a heart attack while waiting for a train. Buried Monument Cemetery, Philadelphia PA.

Dave Foutz—13 Years Infielder 4 Years Manager (b. 7 Sep 1856 Carroll County MD–d. 5 Mar 1897 at his mother's home in Waverly MD) Died from asthma. Buried Loudon Park Cemetery, Baltimore MD.

Frank Foutz—1 Year Infielder (b. 8 Apr 1877 Baltimore MD–d. 25 Dec 1961 Lima Memorial Hospital, Lima OH) He was a conductor on the Ohio Electric Railway. Buried Woodlawn Cemetery, Lima OH.

Boob Fowler—4 Years Infielder (b. 11 Nov 1900 Waco TX–d. 8 Oct 1988 Dallas TX) Buried Restland Memorial Park, Dallas TX.

Dick Fowler—10 Years Pitcher (b. 30 Mar 1922 Toronto, Ontario, Canada–d. 22 May 1972 Fox Hospital, Oneonta NY) Served in the Royal Canadian Infantry during World War II. He was a night desk man at the Oneonta Community Hotel. Died after a lingering illness. Buried Oneonta Plains Cemetery, Oneonta NY.

Jesse Fowler—1 Year Pitcher (b. 30 Oct 1898 Spartanburg SC–d. 23 Sep 1973 State Hospital, Columbia SC) Died after a long illness. Buried Zion Hill Baptist Church Cemetery, Spartanburg SC.

Bill Fox—2 Years Infielder (b. 15 Jan 1872 Fiskdale MA–d. 7 May 1946 Minneapolis MN) Buried St Mary's Cemetery, Minneapolis MN.

Henry Fox—1 Year Pitcher (b. 18 Nov 1874 Scranton PA–d. 6 Jun 1927 at his home in Scranton PA) He was a plumber. Died from a stroke of apoplexy after being ill from organic trouble for some time.

Howie Fox—9 Years Pitcher (b. 1 Mar 1921 Coburg OR–d. 9 Oct 1955 San Antonio TX) Stabbed to death while attempting to restore order to his San Antonio tavern. Buried Laurel Hill Cemetery, Eugene OR.

Jack Fox—1 Year Outfielder (b. 21 May 1885 Reading PA–d. 28 Jun 1963 St Joseph's Hospital, Reading PA) For 31 years he was a policeman for the Reading Police Department, retiring in 1946. He had been hospitalized three weeks when he died. Buried Aulenbach's Cemetery, Mount Penn PA.

John Fox—4 Years Pitcher (b. 7 Feb 1859 Roxbury MA–d. 16 Apr 1893 Boston MA) Buried Mount Benedict Cemetery, West Roxbury MA.

Nellie Fox—19 Years Infielder Hall of Fame (b. 25 Dec 1927 St Thomas PA–d. 1 Dec 1975 University Hospital, Baltimore MD) He owned and operated Nellie Fox Bowl, a bowling alley in Chambersburg PA. An avid hunter and outdoorsman, he coached eight years before he became ill and died from widespread skin cancer. Buried St Thomas Cemetery, St Thomas PA.

Paddy Fox—1 Year Infielder (b. 1 Dec 1868 Pottstown PA–d. 8 May 1914 Philadelphia PA).

Pete Fox—13 Years Outfielder (b. 8 Mar 1909 Evansville IN–d. 5 Jul 1966 New Grace Hospital, Detroit MI) He managed minor league baseball for a short time and scouted for the White

Sox and Tigers. Later he was a manufacturer's representative for R B Harper Company in Detroit. Died from cancer. Buried Woodlawn Cemetery, Detroit MI.

Bill Foxen—4 Years Pitcher (b. 31 May 1884 Tenafly NJ–d. 17 Apr 1937 Brooklyn NY).

Jimmie Foxx—20 Years Infielder Hall of Fame (b. 22 Oct 1907 Sudlersville MD–d. 21 Jul 1967 at his brother's home in Miami FL) He coached minor league and college baseball a short while, but died without a job and almost penniless. Died from asphyxiation when he choked on a piece of meat. Buried Flagler Memorial Park, Miami FL.

Joe Foy—6 Years Infielder (b. 21 Feb 1943 New York City NY–d. 12 Oct 1989 at his home in Bronx NY) Died from a heart attack.

Ossie France—1 Year Pitcher (b. 4 Oct 1859 Greentown OH–d. 2 May 1947 City Hospital, Akron OH) He lived in Akron more than 60 years and was a deputy in the county treasurer's office several years before becoming a partner in a paving and construction business. Buried Greensburg Cemetery, North Canton OH.

Ray Francis—3 Years Pitcher (b. 8 Mar 1893 Sherman TX–d. 6 Jul 1934 Atlanta GA) Died on his first day on the Atlanta police patrol. Buried Greenwood Cemetery, Atlanta GA.

Charlie Frank—2 Years Outfielder (b. 30 May 1870 Mobile AL–d. 24 May 1922 at the home of a friend in Memphis TN) He was the first manager of the Memphis Chicks of the Southern League and was active with various minor leagues in the south for 22 years. Died from myocardia and Bright's disease. Buried Forest Hill Cemetery, Memphis TN.

Fred Frank—1 Year Outfielder (b. 11 Mar 1874 Dayton OH–d. 27 Mar 1950 Ashland KY).

Fred Frankhouse—13 Years Pitcher (b. 9 Apr 1904 Port Royal PA–d. 17 Aug 1989 Brookline Manor Conv Home, Mifflintown PA) Served in the U.S. Army during World War II. He worked at Standard Steel and started a Christmas tree farm. Buried New Church Hill Cemetery, Port Royal PA.

Jack Franklin—1 Year Pitcher (b. 20 Oct 1919 Paris IL–d. 15 Nov 1991 at a hospital in Panama City FL) Served in the U.S. Army during World War II. He was a supervisor for the Beaman Corporation in Paris IL before retiring to Florida in 1986. Buried Garden of Memories, Panama City FL.

Murray Franklin—2 Years Infielder (b. 1 Apr 1914 Chicago IL–d. 16 Mar 1978 Kaiser Hospital, Harbor City CA) He was self-employed 25 years in the wholesale leather and shoe business. Died from kidney cancer. Buried Hillside Memorial Park, Los Angeles CA.

Fletcher Franks—1 Game Pinch Hitter (b. 6 Mar 1891 Hindreth IL–d. 7 Oct 1974 St Petersburg FL) A retired hotel clerk, he owned an apartment building and lived in St Petersburg 54 years. Buried Royal Palm Cemetery, St Petersburg FL.

Chick Fraser—14 Years Pitcher (b. 17 Mar 1871 Chicago IL–d. 8 May 1940 St Valentine's Hospital, Wendell ID) He enjoyed a 50-year career in baseball, managing several minor league teams and scouting for a number of major league teams. Died after an illness of nearly a month. Buried Jerome Cemetery, Jerome ID.

George Frazer—1 Year Manager (b. 7 Jan 1861 Syracuse NY–d. 5 Feb 1913 Philadelphia PA).

Vic Frazier—6 Years Pitcher (b. 5 Aug 1904 Ruston LA–d. 10 Jan 1977 Neptune Hospital, Jacksonville TX) He lived in Jacksonville and worked for W H Brown Co. Buried Mount Bethel Cemetery, Gary TX.

Johnny Frederick—6 Years Outfielder (b. 26 Jan 1902 Denver CO–d. 18 Jun 1977 Tigard OR).

Roger Freed—8 Years Outfielder (b. 2 Jun 1946 Los Angeles CA–d. 9 Jan 1995 Chino CA) Died from a heart attack after being hospitalized three weeks for a ruptured appendix.

Buck Freeman—11 Years Outfielder (b. 30 Oct 1871 Catasauqua PA–d. 25 Jun 1949 Mercy Hospital, Wilkes-Barre PA) He coached and managed minor league baseball until he retired in 1935. Died following a series of strokes. Buried Evergreen Cemetery, Shavertown PA.

Buck Freeman—2 Years Pitcher (b. 5 Jul 1893 Mart TX–d. 21 Feb 1953 Fort Sam Houston TX).

Harvey Freeman—1 Year Pitcher (b. 22 Dec 1897 Mottville MI–d. 10 Jan 1970 Kalamazoo MI) He coached basketball, track, golf and football at Kalamazoo's St Augustine High School for 29 years, retiring in 1954. He also owned Portage Lumber Company at one time. Died following a ten-year illness. Buried Mount Olivet Cemetery, Kalamazoo MI.

Jerry Freeman—2 Years Infielder (b. 26 Dec 1879 Placerville CA–d. 30 Sep 1952 Los Angeles CA) World War I veteran. He was a field supervisor for the Rice Grower's Association. Died from a cerebral hemorrhage. Cremated.

John Freeman—1 Year Outfielder (b. 24 Jan 1901 Boston MA–d. 14 Apr 1958 Washington Hospital Center, Washington DC) A sportswriter, government employee and bussinessman, he was a sportswriter for the *Boston American* and the *Washington Times Herald*. He then worked for a Massachusetts congressman for two years and the Federal Housing Administration for ten years. In 1945 he became connected with the lumber industry, working in that field until his death. Died after an illness of two months. Buried St Joseph's Cemetery, West Roxbury MA.

Julie Freeman—1 Year Pitcher (b. 7 Nov 1868 MO–d. 11 Jun 1921 St Louis MO).

Jake Freeze—1 Year Pitcher (b. 25 Apr 1901 Huntington AR–d. 9 Apr 1983 Shannon Hospital, San Angelo TX) A CPA from 1932 until his retirement in 1970, he was chairman of the Texas State Board of Public Accounting for several years. Died after a lengthy illness. Buried Fairmount Cemetery, San Angelo TX.

Vern Freiburger—1 Year Infielder (b. 19 Dec 1923 Detroit MI–d. 27 Feb 1990 at his home in Palm Springs CA) World War II veteran. He drove a bus for the Long Beach Public Transportation Department for 20 years. Died from lymphoma of the neck and brain but also suffered from prostate cancer. Buried Good Shepherd Cemetery, Huntington Beach CA.

Howard Freigau—7 Years Infielder (b. 1 Aug 1902 Dayton OH–d. 18 Jul 1932 Chattanooga TN) Broke his neck and drowned when he struck his head on the bottom of a swimming pool when the team he was playing for, the Knoxville Smokies, was visiting the Chattanooga Lookouts — both teams in the Southern Association. Buried Woodland Cemetery, Dayton OH.

Tony Freitas—5 Years Pitcher (b. 5 May 1908 Mill Valley CA–d. 14 Mar 1994 at his home in Orangevale CA) During a minor league career stretching from 1928 until 1953 he won 342 games while losing 238, compiling an ERA of 3.11 and striking out 2324 batters. Died from a heart attack while working in his yard. Cremated. Buried St Mary's Cemetery, Sacramento CA.

Charlie French—2 Years Infielder (b. 12 Oct 1883 Indianapolis IN–d. 30 Mar 1962 at his home in Indianapolis IN) For 35 years he was a coffee roaster for Kothe-Wells-Bauer, Inc, in Indianapolis. Buried Washington Park East Cemetery, Indianapolis IN.

Larry French—14 Years Pitcher (b. 1 Nov 1907 Visalia CA–d. 9 Feb 1987 Naval Hospital, San Diego CA) Served 27 years in the U.S. Navy, retiring as a Captain in 1969. Died from heart and kidney disease. Buried Visalia Cemetery, Visalia CA.

Pat French—1 Year Outfielder (b. 22 Sep 1893 Dover NH–d. 13 Jul 1969 at a hospital in Bath ME) Served in the U.S. Navy during World War I. He taught and coached high school for 18 years at Lewiston ME before going to work at the Bath Iron Works in 1937. Died from a heart ailment. Buried Dover NH.

Ray French—3 Years Infielder (b. 9 Jan 1897 Alameda CA–d. 3 Apr 1978 at his home in Alameda CA) He played in 3279 games and came to bat 12178 times during a minor league career that lasted 28 years. He also managed some minor league baseball and umpired ten years in the Pacific Coast League before working the rest of his life as a shipping clerk on the Alameda docks. Died from colon cancer. Buried Holy Sepulchre Cemetery, Hayward CA.

Walter French—6 Years Outfielder (b. 12 Jul 1899 Moorestown NJ–d. 13 May 1984 Mountain Home AR) He played both professional baseball and football, and was inducted into the Professional Football Hall of Fame in 1949. He played in both a football and baseball championship game, and was the head baseball coach at West Point from 1936 until 1941. During World War II he was an intelligence officer.

Benny Frey—8 Years Pitcher (b. 6 Apr 1906 Dexter MI–d. 1 Nov 1937 Jackson MI) Took his own life by carbon monoxide poisoning in his car shortly after being released by the Reds. Buried Woodland Cemetery, Jackson MI.

Bernie Friberg—14 Years Infielder (b. 18 Aug 1899 Manchester NH–d. 8 Dec 1958 Swampscott MA) He coached baseball at Saugus (MA) High School before working many years in the transportation department of the General Electric Company River Works. Died when his car left the road, crashing into a stone wall. It was believed he had a heart attack. Buried Pine Grove Cemetery, Lynn MA.

Marion Fricano—4 Years Pitcher (b. 15 Jul 1923 Brant NY–d. 18 May 1976 at a hospital in Tijuana, Mexico) Active in local politics, he was a town supervisor in North Collins NY from 1961 to 1973. Died from cancer while visiting relatives in California. Buried Holy Spirit Cemetery, North Collins NY.

Ford Frick—Hall of Fame (b. abt 1894 near Wawaka IN–d. 8 Apr 1978 Lawrence Hospital, Bronxville NY) He was a sportswriter, broadcaster and publicist for Babe Ruth before becoming National League president from 1934 to 1951 and baseball commissioner from 1951 to 1965. Died following a stroke. Cremated. Buried Christ Church Columbarium, Bronxville NY.

Skipper Friday—1 Year Pitcher (b. 26 Oct 1897 Cherryville NC–d. 25 Aug 1962 Gastonia NC) World War I veteran. He managed the customer's parking lot next to the railroad tracks in Gastonia. Buried Oakwood Cemetery, Gastonia NC.

Cy Fried—1 Year Pitcher (b. 23 Jul 1897 San Antonio TX–d. 10 Oct 1970 at a hospital in San Antonio TX) He was a foreman in the electric meter shop for the San Antonio Public Service Board until he retired in 1962. Buried Sunset Memorial Park, San Antonio TX.

Bob Friedrichs—1 Year Pitcher (b. 30 Aug 1906 Cincinnati OH–d. 15 Apr 1997 Memorial Hospital, Jasper IN) Buried Shiloh Cemetery, Ireland IN.

Bill Friel—3 Years Infielder (b. 1 Apr 1876 Renovo PA–d. 24 Dec 1959 St Louis MO) Served as field director for the Knight's of Columbus during World War I, working with troops in France. He was business manager for the St Louis Browns in 1923 and 1924. Died after a prolonged illness. Buried Resurrection Cemetery, St Louis MO.

Pat Friel—2 Years Outfielder (b. 11 Jun 1860 Lewisburg WV–d. 15 Jan 1924 at his home in Providence RI) For ten years he was the caretaker of the Winthrop Building in Providence. Died after a long illness. Buried St Francis Cemetery, Pawtucket RI.

Danny Friend—4 Years Pitcher (b. 18 Apr 1873 Cincinnati OH–d. 1 Jun 1942 Chillicothe OH) He ran a bowling alley, umpired baseball, was active in local politics and owned a manufacturing company that made rubber mats from used auto tires. Died from a heart attack. Buried Greenlawn Cemetery, Chillicothe OH.

Frank Friend—1 Year Catcher (b. Washington DC–d. 8 Sep 1897 Atlantic City NJ).

Frank Friend—1 Year Catcher (b. 5 Jul 1875 Jeffersonville IN–d. 5 Nov 1933 Jeffersonville IN) He was found dead in his home, probably from a heart attack. Buried Walnut Ridge Cemetery, Jeffersonville IN.

Buck Frierson—1 Year Infielder (b. 29 Jul 1917 Chicota TX–d. 26 Jun 1996 McCuistion Medical Center, Paris TX) A rancher and farmer in Lamar County, TX, he enjoyed hunting. Buried Presbyterian Cemetery, Chicota TX.

Pete Fries—2 Years Pitcher (b. 30 Oct 1857 Scranton PA–d. 29 Jul 1937 Chicago IL) He was a postal clerk at the Grand Crossing Postal Station 40 years before retiring in 1926. Died from a heart attack in his room at the Railton Hotel. Buried Oak Woods Cemetery, Chicago IL.

John Frill—2 Years Pitcher (b. 3 Apr 1879 Reading PA–d. 28 Sep 1918 Westerly RI) Died from influenza. Buried River Bend Cemetery, Westerly RI.

Fred Frink—1 Year Outfielder (b. 25 Aug 1911 Macon GA–d. 19 May 1995 Fairhaven Nursing Center, Miami Springs FL) Served as a U.S. Marine Corps Captain during World War II. The owner and producer of Ball Movie Productions, he filmed Orange Bowl festivities for 29 uears. Buried Woodlawn Park South Cemetery, Miami FL.

Charlie Frisbee—2 Years Outfielder (b. 2 Feb 1874 Dows IA–d. 7 Nov 1954 Alden IA) Buried Alden Cemetery, Alden IA.

Frankie Frisch—19 Years Infielder 16 Years Manager Hall of Fame (b. 9 Sep 1898 Queens NY–d. 12 Mar 1973 Wilmington Medical Center, Wilmington DE) Died from injuries suffered in an automobile accident a month earlier. Buried Woodlawn Cemetery, Bronx NY.

Danny Frisella—10 Years Pitcher (b. 4 Mar 1946 San Francisco CA–d. 1 Jan 1977 Phoenix

AZ) Died in a dune buggy accident at the height of his career. Cremated and scattered at sea.

Emil Frisk—4 Years Outfielder (b. 15 Oct 1874 Kalkaska MI–d. 27 Jan 1922 City Hospital, Seattle WA) Died from a serious illness following surgery. Buried Lake View Cemetery, Seattle WA.

Charlie Fritz—1 Year Pitcher (b. 18 Jun 1882 Mobile AL–d. 30 Jul 1943 at his home in Mobile AL) Buried Magnolia Cemetery, Mobile AL.

Harry Fritz—3 Years Infielder (b. 30 Sep 1890 Philadelphia PA–d. 4 Nov 1974 at his home in Columbus OH) Served in the U.S. Navy during World War I. He was an associate of the National Casket Company. Cremated. Buried Green Lawn Memorial Cemetery, Columbus OH.

Bill Froats—1 Year Pitcher (b. 20 Oct 1930 New York City NY–d. 9 Feb 1998 Minneapolis MN) Buried Gate of Heaven Cemetery, Hawthorne NY.

Sam Frock—4 Years Pitcher (b. 23 Dec 1882 Bronx NY–d. 3 Nov 1925 Baltimore MD) Buried Loudon Park National Cemetery, Baltimore MD.

Ben Froelich—1 Year Catcher (b. 12 Nov 1887 Pittsburgh PA–d. 2 Sep 1916 Pittsburgh PA).

Art Fromme—10 Years Pitcher (b. 3 Sep 1883 Quincy IL–d. 24 Aug 1956 Queen of Angels Hospital, Los Angeles CA) He was an inspector for the engineering department of the City of Los Angeles for 25 years. Died from congestive heart failure and kidney disease. Buried Rose Hills Memorial Park, Whittier CA.

Johnson Fry—1 Year Pitcher (b. 21 Nov 1901 Huntington WV–d. 7 Apr 1959 Carmi Township Hospital, Carmi IL) He worked for Chrysler Corporation in Detroit MI before moving to Carmi. Died from a heart attack. Buried Spring Hill Cemetery, Huntington WV.

Charlie Frye—1 Year Pitcher (b. 17 Jul 1913 Hickory NC–d. 25 May 1945 Memorial Hospital, Hickory NC) Served in the U.S. Army during World War II. Buried Friendship Church Cemetery, Taylorsville NC.

Charlie Fuchs—3 Years Pitcher (b. 18 Nov 1913 Union Hall NJ–d. 10 Jun 1969 Weehawken NJ) Buried George Washington Memorial Park, Paramus NJ.

Judge Fuchs—1 Year Manager (b. 17 Apr 1878 New York City NY–d. 5 Dec 1961 Massachusetts Memorial Hospital, Boston MA) An attorney and New York City magistrate, he owned the Braves from 1923 to 1935. Died after a lengthy illness. Buried Sharon Memorial Park, Sharon MA.

Mickey Fuentes—1 Year Pitcher (b. 10 May 1949 Loiza Aldea, Puerto Rico–d. 29 Jan 1970 Loiza Aldea, Puerto Rico) Died when he was shot in a barroom brawl at his saloon.

Oscar Fuhr—3 Years Pitcher (b. 22 Aug 1893 Defiance MO–d. 27 Mar 1975 Dallas TX) He worked in the production department for Exxon Oil from 1934 to 1958 and was a patrolman for the Dallas Independent School District from 1958 to 1968. Buried Laurel Land Memorial Park, Dallas TX.

Ollie Fuhrman—1 Year Catcher (b. 20 Jul 1896 Jordan MN–d. 11 Jan 1969 Proctor Hospital, Peoria IL) World War I veteran. He worked 34 years in the maintenance department at Caterpiller before retiring in 1962. Buried Spirit Hill Cemetery, Jordan MN.

Dot Fulghum—1 Year Infielder (b. 4 Jul 1900 Valdosta GA–d. 1 Nov 1967 Raleigh NC).

Ed Fuller—1 Year Pitcher (b. 22 Mar 1868 Washington DC–d. 16 Mar 1935 at his home in Hyattsville MD) A barred attorney, he never practiced law, opting instead for the newspaper business. He was the owner and editor of the *Hyattsville Independent* and was active in local politics, being a county treasurer and town councilman. Died suddenly after being ill a week. Buried Fort Lincoln Cemetery, Brentwood MD.

Frank Fuller—3 Years Infielder (b. 1 Jan 1893 Detroit MI–d. 29 Oct 1965 Warren MI) Buried Mount Olivet Cemetery, Detroit MI.

Harry Fuller—1 Year Infielder (b. 5 Dec 1862 Cincinnati OH–d. 12 Dec 1895 at his home in Cincinnati OH) Died from consumption.

Nig Fuller—1 Year Catcher (b. 30 Mar 1879 Toledo OH–d. 12 Nov 1947 Toledo OH) Buried Woodlawn Cemetery, Toledo OH.

Shorty Fuller—9 Years Infielder (b. 10 Oct 1867 Cincinnati OH–d. 11 Apr 1904 at his home in Cincinnati OH).

Curt Fullerton—6 Years Pitcher (b. 13 Sep 1898 Ellsworth ME–d. 2 Jan 1975 Winthrop MA).

Hugh Fullerton—Hall of Fame (b. abt 1904–d. 15 Sep 1965 Albemarle Hospital, Elizabeth City NC) A sportswriter, he covered major sporting events for the Associated Press for 38 years. Died from an obstruction of a blood vessel while vacationing at Nags Head NC. Buried Brookside Cemetery, Englewood NJ.

Chick Fullis—8 Years Outfielder (b. 27 Feb 1904 Girardville PA–d. 28 Mar 1946 Ashland Hospital, Ashland PA) He owned and operated a taproom and hotel in Girardville. Buried Odd Fellows Cemetery, Tamaqua PA.

Chick Fulmer—6 Years Infielder 1 Year Manager (b. 12 Feb 1851 Philadelphia PA–d. 15 Feb 1940 Philadelphia PA) For a time he managed minor league baseball. He had been an invalid since suffering a stroke two years earlier. Buried Fernwood Cemetery, Fernwood PA.

Chris Fulmer—5 Years Catcher (b. 4 Jul 1858 Tamaqua PA–d. 9 Nov 1931 Tamaqua PA).

Dave Fultz—7 Years Outfielder (b. 29 May 1875 Staunton VA–d. 30 Oct 1959 Fish Memorial Hospital, De Land FL) Served in the U.S. Army during World War I. He practiced law before retiring to Lake Helen in Florida in 1947. Buried Oakdale Cemetery, De Land FL.

Liz Funk—4 Years Outfielder (b. 28 Oct 1904 La Cygne KS–d. 16 Jan 1968 Norman OK) Buried Fairlawn Cemetery, Oklahoma City OK.

Carl Furillo—15 Years Outfielder (b. 8 Mar 1922 Stony Creek Mills PA–d. 21 Jan 1989 at his home in Stony Creek Mills PA) Served in the Pacific for the U.S. Army during World War II. He operated a kitchen business and delicatessen grocery in New York City and was an iron worker there before returning to Pennsylvania. There he was a deputy sheriff and watchman, retiring in 1987. Died in his sleep. Buried Forest Hills Memorial Park, Reading PA.

Eddie Fusselbach—4 Years Catcher (b. 17 Jul 1856 Philadelphia PA–d. 14 Apr 1926 Philadelphia PA).

Fred Fussell—4 Years Pitcher (b. 7 Oct 1895 Sheridan MO–d. 23 Oct 1966 St Joseph Hospital, Syracuse NY) World War I veteran. He worked 25 years for Presto-Lite Corporation, retiring in 1963. Died after a heart attack. Buried Geneva Cemetery, Geneva NE.

Les Fusselman—2 Years Catcher (b. 7 Mar 1921 Pryor OK–d. 21 May 1970 V A Hospital, Cleveland OH) Served in the U.S. Army during World War II. He was a driver-salesman for Drenik Beverage Distributing, Inc, in Cleveland from 1955 until his death. Buried Acacia Masonic Memorial Park, Cleveland OH.

G

Frank Gabler—4 Years Pitcher (b. 6 Nov 1911 East Highlands CA–d. 1 Nov 1967 at his home in Long Beach CA) World War II veteran. He was a scout for the Cardinals. Died in his sleep from a heart attack. Cremated.

Ken Gables—3 Years Pitcher (b. 21 Jan 1919 Walnut Grove MO–d. 2 Jan 1960 at his home in Walnut Grove MO) World War II veteran. He played nine years in the Pacific Coast League and served as city marshall and deputy sheriff at Walnut Grove. Buried Rose Hill Cemetery, Willard MO.

John Gaddy—1 Year Pitcher (b. 5 Feb 1914 Wadesboro NC–d. 3 May 1966 Albemarle NC) He was a salesman for Stanley Fixtures Company. Died in a one-car accident when his car left the road, hitting a tree. Buried Fairview Memorial Park, Albemarle NC.

Eddie Gaedel—1 Game Pinch Hitter (b. 8 Jun 1925 Chicago IL–d. 18 Jun 1961 Chicago IL) 3 ft 7 in tall, he was a 65 lb midget. Used as a pinch hitter, he walked in his only at bat. Died from a heart attack after he had been mugged. Buried St Mary Cemetery, Evergreen Park IL.

Fabian Gaffke—6 Years Outfielder (b. 5 Aug 1913 Milwaukee WI–d. 8 Feb 1992 at his home in Milwaukee WI) For 34 years he was an electrical wireman for Allen-Bradley Company in

Milwaukee. Died from complications of a heart condition. Buried St Adalbert's Cemetery, Milwaukee WI.

John Gaffney—2 Years Manager (b. 29 Jun 1855 Roxbury MA–d. 8 Aug 1913 at his home in New York City NY) He umpired in the minor leagues and in the National League nine years between 1884 and 1900. Buried St John's Cemetery, Worcester MA.

Ed Gagnier—2 Years Infielder (b. 16 Apr 1883 Paris, France–d. 13 Sep 1946 Detroit MI) Died from a heart attack. Buried Mount Olivet Cemetery, Detroit MI.

Chick Gagnon—2 Years Infielder (b. 27 Sep 1897 Millbury MA–d. 30 Apr 1970 Memorial Hospital, Wilmington DE) Served in the U.S. Coast Guard during World War I. He coached and taught at Catholic University in Washington DC and North High School in Worcester MA, retiring in 1955. Buried St John's Cemetery, Worcester MA.

Charlie Gagus—1 Year Pitcher (b. 25 Mar 1862 San Francisco CA–d. 16 Jan 1917 at his home in San Francisco CA) He managed in the Pacific Coast League and umpired minor league baseball. Died from pneumonia. Buried Holy Cross Catholic Cemetery, Colma CA.

Nemo Gaines—1 Year Pitcher (b. 23 Dec 1897 Alexandria VA–d. 26 Jan 1979 Warrenton VA) Served in the U.S. Navy from 1921 to 1946, doing duty in Peru during World War II. He operated a hardware store in Alexandria and raised Hereford cattle on his Fauquier County, VA, farm until his death. Died from cancer. Buried Arlington National Cemetery, Arlington VA.

Del Gainor—10 Years Infielder (b. 10 Nov 1886 Montrose WV–d. 28 Jan 1947 Elkins WV) He was a deputy U.S. Marshall 15 years for northern West Virginia. Died from a sudden heart seizure. Buried Maplewood Cemetery, Elkins WV.

Fred Gaiser—1 Year Pitcher (b. 31 Aug 1885 Stuttgart, Germany–d. 9 Oct 1918 Trenton NJ) He was a machinist. Died from bronchopneumonia resulting from Spanish influenza. Buried Riverview Cemetery, Trenton NJ.

Augie Galan—16 Years Outfielder (b. 23 May 1912 Berkeley CA–d. 28 Dec 1993 North Bay Hospital, Fairfield CA) He was a coach for the Athletics for 17 years. Died from a heart attack after suffering an aneurysm. Buried St Joseph Cemetery, San Pablo CA.

Milt Galatzer—5 Years Outfielder (b. 4 May 1907 Chicago IL–d. 29 Jan 1976 St Francis Hospital, San Francisco CA) He was a sales manager at a lumber company. Died from pancreatic cancer. Buried Ridgelawn Cemetery, Chicago IL.

John Galbreath—(b. abt 1898 Derby OH–d. 20 Jul 1988 on his farm near Columbus OH) Served in the U.S. Army during World War I. A real estate developer, he owned the Pirates from 1946 to 1985. Died from heart disease. Buried Sunset Cemetery, Galloway OH.

Denny Galehouse—15 Years Pitcher (b. 7 Dec 1911 Marshallville OH–d. 12 Oct 1998) Buried Chestnut Hill Cemetery, Doylestown OH.

Bill Gallagher—1 Year Infielder (b. 4 Feb 1874 Boston MA–d. 11 Mar 1950 Worcester MA).

Ed Gallagher—1 Year Pitcher (b. 28 Nov 1910 Dorchester MA–d. 22 Dec 1981 Cape Cod Hospital, Hyannis MA) Active politically, he worked for FDR's son at the National Grain Yeast Company in New York and was the Massachusetts state chairman for FDR's 1936 campaign. During the 1950s and 1960s he was president of radio station WROL in Boston MA and president of Wonderland Race Track in Revere MA until 1975. Died after a five-year illness. Buried Mosswood Cemetery, Cotuit MA.

Gil Gallagher—1 Year Infielder (b. 5 Sep 1896 Washington DC–d. 6 Jan 1957 Georgetown Hospital, Washington DC) Served in the U.S. Navy during World War I. For 22 years he was the plumbing foreman at the Capitol House Building. Died from a heart attack suffered two days earlier following gall bladder surgery. Buried Arlington National Cemetery, Arlington VA.

Jackie Gallagher—1 Year Outfielder (b. 28 Jan 1902 Providence RI–d. 10 Sep 1984 Gladwyn PA).

Jim Gallagher—1 Year Infielder (b. Findlay OH–d. 29 Mar 1894 Scranton PA) He worked in the Leggetts Creek coal mine near Scranton. Died from injuries received when he accidentally fell 175 feet down an air shaft in the mine.

Joe Gallagher—2 Years Outfielder (b. 7 Mar

1914 Buffalo NY–d. 25 Feb 1998 at a healthcare facility in Houston TX) He coached college baseball at Stephen Austin State University, Rice University and University of St Thomas. Buried Cushing Cemetery, Cushing TX.

John Gallagher—1 Year Infielder (b. 1894 Pittsburgh PA–d. 30 Mar 1952 Norfolk VA) World War I veteran. He was a supervisor at the Naval Supply Center at Norfolk Naval Base where he had worked nine years. Died after being in failing health about a year. Buried Forest Lawn Cemetery, Norfolk VA.

Shorty Gallagher—1 Year Outfielder (b. 30 Apr 1872 Detroit MI–d. 23 Mar 1924 Detroit MI).

Bert Gallia—9 Years Pitcher (b. 14 Oct 1891 Beeville TX–d. 19 Mar 1976 Devine Nursing Home, Devine TX) A self-employed electrician, he lived in Natalia TX 29 years. Buried St Joseph Cemetery, Devine TX.

John Galligan—1 Year Outfielder (b. 1868 Easton PA–d. 17 Jul 1901 New York City NY) Despondent because of kidney trouble, he took his own life by cutting his throat with a razor.

Phil Gallivan—3 Years Pitcher (b. 29 May 1907 Seattle WA–d. 24 Nov 1969 St Paul MN) He was a scout for the Baltimore Orioles. Buried Willow River Cemetery, Hudson WI.

Bad News Galloway—1 Year Infielder (b. 16 Sep 1887 Iredell TX–d. 3 May 1950 at his home in Fort Worth TX) He played and managed several years in the Texas League before becoming an inspector for the State Liquor Control Board in Fort Worth, Houston and San Angelo. During World War II he was a bedding inspector. Died from a heart attack. Buried Odd Fellows Cemetery, Georgetown TX.

Chick Galloway—10 Years Infielder (b. 4 Aug 1896 Manning SC–d. 7 Nov 1969 at his home in Clinton SC) Served in the U.S. Navy during World War I. His baseball career ended abruptly in 1928 when he was hit in the head by a pitched ball. Later he was a merchant, college baseball coach, insurance agent and scout. Died after a sudden illness. Buried Rosemont Cemetery, Clinton SC.

Jim Galvin—2 Games Pinch Hitter (b. 11 Aug 1907 Somerville MA–d. 30 Sep 1969 Marietta GA). Buried Resthaven Garden of Memories, Decatur GA.

Pud Galvin—14 Years Pitcher 1 Year Manager Hall of Fame (b. 25 Dec 1855 St Louis MO–d. 7 Mar 1902 at his home in Pittsburgh PA) Died from catarrh of the stomach. Buried Calvary Cemetery, Pittsburgh PA.

Lee Gamble—4 Years Outfielder (b. 28 Jun 1910 Renovo PA–d. 5 Oct 1994 Punxsutawney Area Hospital, Punxsutawney PA) Served in the U.S. Army during World War II. For many years he operated a service station in Punxsutawney. Buried Morningside Cemetery, Du Bois PA.

Daff Gammons—1 Year Outfielder (b. 17 Mar 1876 New Bedford MA–d. 24 Sep 1963 at his home near East Greenwich RI) A real estate and insurance man, he was an expert golfer and served a term in the Rhode Island legislature. He retired to his farm near East Greenwich. Died after an illness of five days. Buried Oak Grove Cemetery, New Bedford MA.

Chick Gandil—9 Years Infielder (b. 19 Jan 1888 St Paul MN–d. 13 Dec 1970 Convalescent Hospital, Calistoga CA) He was banned from baseball for his involvement in the Black Sox Scandal. For 14 years he was a self-employed plumber in the Los Angeles and Oakland areas before retiring in 1952 and moving to Calistoga. Died from heart disease. Cremated. Buried St Helena Cemetery, St Helena CA.

Bob Gandy—1 Year Outfielder (b. 25 Aug 1893 Jacksonville FL–d. 19 Jun 1945 Jacksonville FL) He was the paymaster for McGiffin Coal Company at Commodore's Point. Despondent over poor health, he took his own life while sitting in a car in his driveway. Buried Oaklawn Cemetery, Jacksonville FL.

Bob Ganley—5 Years Outfielder (b. 23 Apr 1875 Lowell MA–d. 9 Oct 1945 General Hospital, Lowell MA) Died following two operations for an organic condition. Buried St Patrick's Cemetery, Lowell MA.

Bill Gannon—2 Years Outfielder (b. abt 1876 New Haven CT–d. 26 Apr 1927 Fort Worth TX) He was a minor league umpire. Drowned in Lake Worth.

Gussie Gannon—1 Year Pitcher (b. 26 Nov 1873 Erie PA–d. 12 Apr 1966 St Vincent Hospital, Erie PA) He managed the Lakes Engineering Company. Died after a brief illness. Buried Trinity Cemetery, Erie PA.

Joe Gantenbein—2 Years Infielder (b. 25 Aug

1915 San Francisco CA–d. 2 Aug 1993 Community Hospital, Novato CA) Served in World War II. For 25 years he was a butcher for Debuque Meat Company. Died from colon cancer. Buried Valley Memorial Park, Novato CA.

Babe Ganzel—2 Years Outfielder (b. 22 May 1901 Malden MA–d. 6 Feb 1978 at a hospital in Jacksonville FL).

Charlie Ganzel—14 Years Catcher (b. 18 Jun 1862 Waterford WI–d. 7 Apr 1914 Quincy MA) Died from cancer. Buried Mount Wollaston Cemetery, Quincy MA.

John Ganzel—7 Years Infielder 2 Years Manager (b. 7 Apr 1874 Kalamazoo MI–d. 14 Jan 1959 Orlando FL) He lived at Orlando 34 years and was active as a manager and captain of baseball teams in many cities for 56 years. Died from a heart attack.

Bob Garback—7 Years Catcher (b. 13 Nov 1909 Houston TX–d. 15 Aug 1990 Meadville PA).

Mike Garbark—2 Years Catcher (b. 3 Feb 1916 Houston TX–d. 31 Aug 1994 Carolinas Medical Center, Charlotte NC) He worked 19 years for Southern Wholesale Distributors and was district manager for Carling Black Label Beer for 20 years. He also worked for Harris Teeter Stores. Buried Evergreen Cemetery, Charlotte NC.

Mike Garcia—14 Years Pitcher (b. 17 Nov 1923 San Gabriel CA–d. 13 Jan 1986 at his home in Fairview Park OH) He owned and operated a dry cleaning business at Parma OH. Died from diabetes and kidney failure after a long battle with kidney disease. Buried Visalia Cemetery, Visalia CA.

Art Gardiner—1 Year Pitcher (b. 26 Dec 1899 Brooklyn NY–d. 21 Oct 1954 Copiague NY) Buried Long Island National Cemetery, Farmingdale NY.

Alex Gardner—1 Year Catcher (b. 28 Apr 1861 Toronto, Ontario, Canada–d. 18 Jun 1926 Danvers MA).

Earl Gardner—5 Years Infielder (b. 24 Jan 1884 Sparta IL–d. 2 Mar 1943 Sparta IL) He owned and operated a shoe store in Sparta from 1917 until his death. Dropped dead from a heart attack while opening his store one morning. Buried Caledonia Cemetery, Sparta IL.

Gid Gardner—7 Years Outfielder (b. 1 Aug 1859 Cambridge MA–d. 1 Aug 1914 Cambridge Hospital, Cambridge MA) After baseball he had no steady employment. Died after being confined to the hospital several weeks. Buried Cambridge Cemetery, Cambridge MA.

Glenn Gardner—1 Year Pitcher (b. 25 Jan 1916 Burnsville NC–d. 7 Jul 1964 Northside Hospital, Rochester NY) His baseball career ended abruptly in 1948 when his jaw was broken by a thrown ball during infield practice. He was a bartender in Rochester.

Harry Gardner—2 Years Pitcher (b. 1 Jul 1887 Quincy MI–d. 2 Aug 1961 at his home in Barlow OR) He lived 40 years in Barlow where he farmed and was a watchman at a log truck crossing on occasion. Died after a year's illness, the last two weeks being bedfast. Buried Zion Memorial Park, Canby OR.

Jim Gardner—5 Years Pitcher (b. 4 Oct 1874 Pittsburgh PA–d. 24 Apr 1905 Passavant Hospital, Pittsburgh PA) He worked in the sporting goods department of a downtown Pittsburgh department store. Died following surgery. Buried Homewood Cemetery, Pittsburgh PA.

Larry Gardner—17 Years Infielder (b. 13 May 1886 Enosburg Falls VT–d. 11 Mar 1976 at his home in St George VT) He was coach and athletic director at the University of Vermont from 1942 to 1952. After that he worked at the Camera Shop in Burlington VT until 1974. He is a member of the University of Vermont Hall of Fame. Cremated. Buried Memorial Gardens at St Paul's Cathedral, Burlington VT.

Ray Gardner—2 Years Infielder (b. 25 Oct 1901 Frederick MD–d. 3 May 1968 Memorial Hospital, Frederick MD) He worked 16 years at Fort Detrick. Buried St John's Catholic Cemetery, Frederick MD.

Bill Garfield—2 Years Pitcher (b. 26 Oct 1867 Sheffield OH–d. 16 Dec 1941 Danville IL).

Art Garibaldi—1 Year Infielder (b. 21 Aug 1907 San Francisco CA–d. 19 Oct 1967 at his home in Sacramento CA) World War II veteran. For 25 years he was a bartender. Despondent over ill health, he died from a self-inflicted gunshot wound to the brain. Buried Mount Vernon Memorial Park, Fair Oaks CA.

Lou Garland—1 Year Pitcher (b. 16 Jul 1905 Archie MO–d. 30 Aug 1990 at his home in

Idaho Falls ID) He managed minor league baseball for a short while and was part-owner of the Idaho Falls minor league team. A machinist and sheet metal worker, he worked for Pratt and Whitney Aircraft Company in Kansas City MO during World War II. Returning to Idaho Falls after the war, he was a partner in a machine shop there and, later, worked for Idaho Falls Sheet Metal before retiring. Died from cancer. Cremated.

Debs Garms—12 Years Outfielder (b. 26 Jun 1907 Bangs TX–d. 16 Dec 1984 Marks-English Hospital, Glen Rose TX) A rancher, he also worked 20 years for Texas Lime. Died from pneumonia while suffering from Alzheimer's disease. Buried Squaw Creek Cemetery, Glen Rose TX.

Willie Garoni—1 Year Pitcher (b. 28 Jul 1877 Fort Lee NJ–d. 9 Sep 1914 Fort Lee NJ) He was a contractor, specializing in installing sewers. Died from chronic pulmonary tuberculosis. Buried Fairview Cemetery, Fairview NJ.

Clarence Garrett—1 Year Pitcher (b. 6 Mar 1891 Reader WV–d. 11 Feb 1977 Moundsville WV) He was a retired employee of Mississippi Fuel Company and was dead-on-arrival at Reynolds Memorial Hospital. Buried Big Run Church Cemetery, Cameron WV.

Cecil Garriott—6 Games Pinch Hitter (b. 15 Aug 1916 Harristown IL–d. 20 Feb 1990 Community Conv Center, Lake Elsinore CA) Died from cardio-pulmonary arrest. World War II veteran. Buried Riverside National Cemetery, Riverside CA.

Cliff Garrison—1 Year Pitcher (b. 13 Aug 1906 Belmont OK–d. 25 Aug 1994 Hillhaven Convalescent Hosp, Woodland CA) A Yolo County, CA, farmer for 60 years, he was also a Yolo County deputy sheriff ten years and the Woodland chief of police from 1939 to 1943. Died from congestive heart failure and chronic obstructive lung disease. Buried Capay Cemetery, Capay CA.

Hank Garrity—1 Year Catcher (b. 4 Feb 1908 Boston MA–d. 1 Sep 1962 Veteran's Hospital, Boston MA) For 15 years he was a probation officer at the West Roxbury (MA) District Court. Died from cancer. Buried St Joseph's Cemetery, West Roxbury MA.

Jim Garry—1 Year Pitcher (b. 21 Sep 1870 Great Barrington MA–d. 13 Jan 1917 House of Mercy Hospital, Pittsfield MA) He coached baseball at College of the Holy Cross, managed minor league baseball and did some umpiring. His last two years he worked at the General Electric plant. Died after a brief illness. Buried Fairview Cemetery, Dalton MA.

Ned Garvin—7 Years Pitcher (b. 1 Jan 1874 Navasota TX–d. 16 Jun 1908 at the county hospital in Fresno CA) Died at the height of his career from tuberculosis. Buried Mountain View Cemetery, Fresno CA.

Harry Gaspar—4 Years Pitcher (b. 28 Apr 1883 Kingsley IA–d. 14 May 1940 St Joseph's Hospital, Orange CA) He was a retired citrus rancher. Died from heart disease. Buried Holy Sepulchre Cemetery, Orange CA.

Charlie Gassaway—3 Years Pitcher (b. 12 Aug 1918 Gassaway TN–d. 15 Jan 1992 Miami FL) He spent 35 years in baseball as a player, scout and minor league manager. When he wasn't involved in baseball he was a Tennessee State Trooper. Died from cardiac arrest. Buried Woodlawn Park South Cemetery, Miami FL.

Tommy Gastall—2 Years Catcher (b. 13 Jun 1932 Fall River MA–d. 20 Sep 1956 Riviera Beach MD) He was killed at the beginning of a promising baseball career when a private plane he was piloting crashed into Chesapeake Bay. Buried St Patrick's Cemetery, Fall River MA.

Ed Gastfield—2 Years Catcher (b. 1 Aug 1865 Chicago IL–d. 1 Dec 1899 Chicago IL) Buried Forest Home Cemetery, Forest Park IL.

Alex Gaston—6 Years Catcher (b. 12 Mar 1893 New York NY–d. 8 Feb 1979 Mercy Hospital, Marina del Rey CA) He was a salesman for American District Telegraph Company for 15 years. Died from a heart attack. Cremated.

Milt Gaston—11 Years Pitcher (b. 27 Jan 1896 Ridgefield Park NJ–d. 26 Apr 1996 Hyannis MA) Died after a short illness, and was only the eighth former major leaguer to reach age 100. Buried Tampa FL.

Welcome Gaston—2 Years Pitcher (b. 19 Dec 1872 Senecaville OH–d. 13 Dec 1944 Grant Hospital, Columbus OH) He was a minor league umpire. Died from a heart attack. Buried Northwood Cemetery, Cambridge OH.

Hank Gastright—7 Years Pitcher (b. 29 Mar

1865 Covington KY–d. 9 Oct 1937 Cold Springs KY).

Frank Gatins — 2 Years Infielder (b. 6 Mar 1871 Johnstown PA–d. 8 Nov 1911 Memorial Hospital, Johnstown PA) He died from pneumonia and bowel trouble. Buried Geistown PA.

Mike Gaule — 1 Year Outfielder (b. 4 Aug 1869 Baltimore MD–d. 24 Jan 1918 at his home in Baltimore MD) He worked 17 years for the Baltimore Police Department. Buried New Cathedral Cemetery, Baltimore MD.

Doc Gautreau — 4 Years Infielder (b. 26 Jul 1904 Cambridge MA–d. 23 Aug 1970 Salt Lake City UT) He managed some minor league baseball and was a scout up until his death. Buried Mount Auburn Cemetery, Cambridge MA.

Sid Gautreaux — 2 Years Catcher (b. 4 May 1912 Schriever LA–d. 19 Apr 1980 Lakewood Hospital, Morgan City LA) Buried Garden of Memory Cemetery, Houma LA.

Chippy Gaw — 1 Year Pitcher (b. 13 Mar 1892 Auburndale MA–d. 26 May 1968 at his home in Dorchester MA) He coached baseball at Dartmouth, Princeton and Boston University. Died after a long illness.

Mike Gazella — 4 Years Infielder (b. 13 Oct 1895 Olyphant PA–d. 11 Sep 1978 Odessa TX) He worked for Lockheed Aircraft in California, retiring in 1975 and moving to Odessa. Killed instantly when his import pickup collided with a Pontiac on an Odessa street. Buried Holy Cross Cemetery, Culver City CA.

Dale Gear — 3 Years Outfielder (b. 2 Feb 1872 Lone Elm KS–d. 23 Sep 1951 at his home in Topeka KS) He had a long career in baseball as a player, minor league manager, club owner and executive. He served as president of two minor leagues at the same time. Active in local politics, he served four terms as commissioner of Shawnee County, KS. Died from a heart attack. Buried Mount Hope Cemetery, Topeka KS.

Dinty Gearin — 2 Years Pitcher (b. 15 Oct 1897 Providence RI–d. 11 Mar 1959 at his home in Providence RI) He was associated with the operation of Gearin's Variety Store in Providence. Buried St Francis Cemetery, Pawtucket RI.

Bob Geary — 3 Years Pitcher (b. 10 May 1891 Cincinnati OH–d. 3 Jan 1980 Cincinnati OH) He worked 28 years for Cincinnati Gas and Electric Company in the overhead transmission department. Buried Arlington Memorial Gardens, Cincinnati OH.

Huck Geary — 2 Years Infielder (b. 22 Jan 1917 Buffalo NY–d. 27 Jan 1981 Cuba Memorial Hospital, Cuba NY) Served in the U.S. Navy during World War II. He was assistant parts manager at Maroone Ford Company in Cheektowaga NY. Buried Holy Cross Cemetery, Lackawanna NY.

Elmer Gedeon — 1 Year Outfielder (b. 15 Apr 1917 Cleveland OH–d. 15 Apr 1944 St Pol, France) He was shot down over France during World War II.

Joe Gedeon — 7 Years Infielder (b. 5 Dec 1893 Sacramento CA–d. 19 May 1941 City Hospital, San Francisco CA) Banned from baseball because he had knowledge of the 1919 Black Sox Scandal, he worked as an investigator for the American League. Died from a liver ailment. Buried East Lawn Memorial Park, Sacramento CA.

Johnny Gee — 6 Years Pitcher (b. 7 Dec 1915 Syracuse NY–d. 23 Jan 1988 at his home in Cortland NY) He taught school at Adams NY, Groton NY and Waterloo NY between 1942 and 1960, serving as principal at Groton from 1955 to 1960. He was then principal at Cortland High School from 1960 until he retired in 1977. Cremated.

Billy Geer — 4 Years Infielder (b. 13 Aug 1849 Syracuse NY–d. 5 Jan 1922 Syracuse NY).

Lou Gehrig — 17 Years Infielder Hall of Fame (b. 19 Jun 1903 New York NY–d. 2 Jun 1941 New York NY) Died from amyotrophic lateral sclerosis, a fatal neuro-muscular disease, later known as Lou Gehrig's Disease. Buried Kensico Cemetery, Valhalla NY.

Henry Gehring — 2 Years Pitcher (b. 24 Jan 1881 St Paul MN–d. 18 Apr 1912 St Mary's Hospital, Kansas City MO) Died at the height of his career from uremic poisoning. Buried Forest Cemetery.

Charlie Gehringer — 19 Years Infielder Hall of Fame (b. 11 May 1903 Fowlerville MI–d. 21 Jan 1993 at a nursing home in Bloomfield Hills MI) Served in the U.S. Navy during World War II. Died a month after suffering a stroke. At the time of his death he was the oldest living member of baseball's Hall of Fame. Buried Holy Sepulchre Cemetery, Southfield MI.

Paul Gehrman —1 Year Pitcher (b. 3 May 1912 Marquam OR–d. 23 Oct 1986 Bend OR) World War II veteran. He lived in Bend from 1928 until his death. Died from natural causes. Buried Greenwood Cemetery, Bend OR.

Phil Geier —5 Years Outfielder (b. 3 Nov 1875 Washington DC–d. 25 Sep 1967 at a hospital in Spokane WA) Buried St Joseph Cemetery, Trentwood WA.

Gary Geiger —12 Years Outfielder (b. 4 Apr 1937 Sand Ridge IL–d. 24 Apr 1996 St Joseph Memorial Hospital, Murphysboro IL) Buried Pleasant Grove Memorial Park, Murphysboro IL.

Bill Geis —1 Year Outfielder (b. 15 Jul 1858 Chicago IL–d. 18 Sep 1924 Chicago IL) Buried St Boniface Cemetery, Chicago IL.

Emil Geis —1 Year Infielder (b. 20 Mar 1867 Chicago IL–d. 4 Oct 1911 Chicago IL) Buried St Boniface Cemetery, Chicago IL.

Charley Gelbert —9 Years Infielder (b. 26 Jan 1906 Scranton PA–d. 13 Jan 1967 Easton Hospital, Easton PA) Served in the U.S. Navy during World War II. He coached baseball at Lafayette College from 1946 until his death. Died from a heart attack. Buried Norland Cemetery, Chambersburg PA.

Joe Genewich —9 Years Pitcher (b. 15 Jan 1897 Elmira NY–d. 21 Dec 1985 Mount View Health Facility, Lockport NY) Served in the U.S. Army during both World Wars I and II. Buried Bath NY.

Frank Genins —3 Years Outfielder (b. 2 Nov 1866 St Louis MO–d. 30 Sep 1922 St Louis MO) Cremated.

Sam Gentile —8 Games Pinch Hitter (b. 12 Oct 1916 Charlestown MA–d. 4 May 1998 Everett MA) For 43 years he was recreation director for the City of Everett, and served on the city council from 1988 to 1994. Served in the U.S. Navy during World War II. Buried Woodlawn Cemetery, Everett MA.

Rufe Gentry —5 Years Pitcher (b. 18 May 1918 Daisy Station NC–d. 3 Jul 1997 Forsyth Memorial Hospital, Winston-Salem NC) He was a self-employed brick mason. Died from acute respiratory failure. Buried Gardens of Memory, Walkertown NC.

Bill George —3 Years Pitcher (b. 27 Jan 1865 Bellaire OH–d. 23 Aug 1916 North Hospital, Wheeling WV) He operated the George Cafe in Wheeling. Died one week following a surgery. Buried Mount Calvary Cemetery, Wheeling WV.

Greek George —5 Years Catcher (b. 25 Dec 1912 Waycross GA–d. 30 Jan 1975 St Louis MO) He worked for Anheuser-Busch brewery. Died from a heart attack. Buried New St Marcus Cemetery, St Louis MO.

Lefty George —4 Years Pitcher (b. 13 Aug 1886 Pittsburgh PA–d. 13 May 1955 at his home in York PA) He played professional baseball 40 years, playing last at age 57. After that he was a salesman for a York beverage distributor. Died from sclerosis of the liver. Buried Prospect Hill Cemetery, York PA.

Ben Geraghty —3 Years Infielder (b. 19 Jul 1912 Jersey City NJ–d. 18 Jun 1963 at his home in Jacksonville FL) He managed minor league baseball from the time he retired as a player in 1947 until the day he died from a heart attack. Buried St Mary's Section-Evergreen Cemetery, Jacksonville FL.

Wally Gerber —15 Years Infielder (b. 18 Aug 1891 Columbus OH–d. 19 Jun 1951 at his home in Columbus OH) He worked ten years for the Columbus City Recreation Department, retiring in 1949. Died from heart disease. Buried Green Lawn Memorial Cemetery, Columbus OH.

Joe Gerhardt —12 Years Infielder 2 Years Manager (b. 14 Feb 1855 Washington DC–d. 11 Mar 1922 Middletown NY).

Al Gerheauser —5 Years Pitcher (b. 24 Jun 1917 St Louis MO–d. 28 May 1972 Cox Medical Center, Springfield MO) He was head pitching instructor for the Mickey Owen Baseball School near Miller MO. Died from a heart attack. Buried Mount Hope Cemetery, Webb City MO.

George Gerken —2 Years Outfielder (b. 28 Jul 1903 Chicago IL–d. 23 Oct 1977 Methodist Hospital, Arcadia CA) He owned and operated a tavern for 14 years. Died from lung cancer. Buried Forest Lawn Memorial Park, Covina CA.

Steve Gerkin —1 Year Pitcher (b. 19 Nov 1915 Grafton WV–d. 8 Nov 1978 Veteran's Hospital, Bay Pines FL) Served in the U.S. Army during World War II. He was a chef in Maryland before retiring to Florida in 1968. Cremated.

Les German—6 Years Pitcher (b. 17 Aug 1870 Mechanicsville MD–d. 10 Jun 1934 Lanham MD).

Ed Gerner—1 Year Pitcher (b. 22 Jul 1897 Philadelphia PA–d. 15 May 1970 Philadelphia PA).

Lou Gertenrich—2 Years Outfielder (b. 4 May 1875 Chicago IL–d. 20 Oct 1933 Danish Hospital, Chicago IL) He founded the Gertenrich Candy Company in Chicago and was also president of the Midwest Baseball League.

Lefty Gervais—1 Year Pitcher (b. 6 Jul 1890 Grover WI–d. 19 Oct 1950 Olive View Sanitarium, Los Angeles CA) He was a tool maker in the aircraft business. Died from a heart attack, but had suffered many years from tuberculosis. Buried Calvary Cemetery, Los Angeles CA.

Doc Gessler—8 Years Outfielder 1 Year Manager (b. 23 Dec 1880 Greensburg PA–d. 26 Dec 1924 Pittsburgh PA) He went to medical school while playing baseball and practiced medicine in Tulsa OK from 1915 to 1917, and in Indiana PA from 1917 until his death. Died after a long illness. Buried Catholic Cemetery, Indiana PA.

Charlie Gettig—4 Years Pitcher (b. 1871 Baltimore MD–d. 11 Apr 1935 Baltimore MD) Buried Trinity Cemetery.

Tom Gettinger—1 Year Pitcher (b. 11 Dec 1868 Frederick MD–d. 26 Jul 1943 Pensacola Hospital, Pensacola FL) A retired Pensacola City employee, he was the first to draw a pension from the city, but died just 26 days after retiring. Buried St Michael's Cemetery, Pensacola FL.

Jake Gettman—3 Years Outfielder (b. 25 Oct 1875 Frank, Russia–d. 4 Oct 1956 Denver CO) He came to the United States when he was 10 years old. After baseball he worked as a rancher and farmer. Died after a long illness. Buried Fairmount Cemetery, Denver CO.

Gus Getz—7 Years Infielder (b. 3 Aug 1889 Pittsburgh PA–d. 28 May 1969 Keansburg NJ).

Charlie Getzien—9 Years Pitcher (b. 14 Feb 1868 Chicago IL–d. 19 Jun 1932 Chicago IL) Buried Concordia Cemetery, Forest Park IL.

Rube Geyer—4 Years Pitcher (b. 26 Mar 1884 Allegheny PA–d. 12 Oct 1962 near Wahkon MN) He was a fruit peddler and tree vendor. Died from a heart attack while walking in the woods. He had been in poor health for 20 years. Buried Oakwood Cemetery, Mora MN.

Chappie Geygan—3 Years Infielder (b. 3 Jun 1903 Ironton OH–d. 15 Mar 1966 Riverside hospital, Columbus OH) He managed minor league baseball for a short while before going into the restaurant business in 1942. He worked that business the rest of his life in a number of different capacities from head waiter to manager. Died following an illness of several months. Buried St Joseph Cemetery, Lockbourne OH.

Patsy Gharrity—10 Years Catcher (b. 13 Mar 1892 Parnell IA–d. 10 Oct 1966 Beloit WI) He was a coach and scout. Found laying dead on a Beloit street. Buried Calvary Cemetery, Beloit WI.

Bart Giamatti—(b. 4 Apr 1938 Boston MA–d. 1 Sep 1989 Edgartown MA) A noted scholar of English and comparative literature, he was president of Yale University from 1978 to 1989. The Commissioner of Baseball for five months in 1989, he is best known for suspending Pete Rose from baseball for gambling. Died from a heart attack. Buried Grove Street Cemetery, New Haven CT.

Joe Giannini—1 Year Infielder (b. 8 Sep 1888 San Francisco CA–d. 26 Sep 1942 San Francisco CA) He was an assistant manager at the Bank of America. Died from a heart attack. Buried Holy Cross Catholic Cemetery, Colma CA.

Joe Giard—3 Years Pitcher (b. 7 Oct 1898 Ware MA–d. 10 Jul 1956 City Hospital, Worcester MA) He managed the Federal Bowling Alleys in Ware. Died after a long illness. Buried Mount Carmel Cemetery, Ware MA.

Bob Gibson—1 Year Pitcher (b. 20 Aug 1869 Duncansville PA–d. 19 Dec 1949 at his home in Pittsburgh PA) An attorney, he was Assistant U.S. Attorney from 1903 to 1914 and Assistant District Attorney of Allegheny County, PA, from 1914 to 1922. In 1922 he was appointed to a federal judgeship, a post he held for 27 years. Died after being in ill health for a year. Buried Homewood Cemetery, Pittsburgh PA.

Charlie Gibson—1 Year Catcher (b. 17 Nov 1879 Sharon PA–d. 22 Nov 1954 General Hospital, Sharon PA) For 20 years he was the paymaster for Carnegie Steel Corporation in Sharon before spending several years as chief clerk for Shenango Furnace Company there, retiring in

1947. Died from a heart attack after being in ill health several years. Buried Oakwood Cemetery, Sharon PA.

Charlie Gibson—1 Year Catcher (b. 21 Nov 1899 Sharon PA–d. 18 Dec 1990 Sharon PA).

Frank Gibson—8 Years Catcher (b. 27 Sep 1890 Omaha NE–d. 27 Apr 1961 Edna TX) He worked 30 years in the power department of the City of Austin TX. Buried Edna Cemetery, Edna TX.

George Gibson—14 Years Catcher 7 Years Manager (b. 22 Jul 1880 London, Ontario, Canada–d. 25 Jan 1967 London, Ontario, Canada).

Josh Gibson—16 Years Catcher Hall of Fame (b. 21 Dec 1911 Buena Vista GA–d. 20 Jan 1947 Pittsburgh PA) He played in the negro leagues and was known as the "Black Babe Ruth." Died from a stroke. Buried Allegheny Cemetery, Pittsburgh PA.

Norwood Gibson—4 Years Pitcher (b. 11 Mar 1877 Peoria IL–d. 7 Jul 1959 Bel-Wood Nursing Home, Peoria IL) He was a chemist for the Curtis Candy Company in Chicago IL. Later he was a desk clerk at the New National Hotel in Peoria. Buried Springdale Cemetery, Peoria IL.

Sam Gibson—5 Years Pitcher (b. 5 Aug 1899 King NC–d. 31 Jan 1983 Galilean Extended Care Fac, High Point NC) During a 27 year minor league career from 1923 to 1949 he won 307 games while losing 200 and compiling an ERA of 3.08. Buried Forest Lawn Cemetery, Greensboro NC.

Whitey Gibson—1 Year Catcher (b. 1866 Lancaster PA–d. 11 Oct 1907 at his home in Talmadge PA) He had been ill for some time and his death was not unexpected. Buried Lancaster Cemetery, Lancaster PA.

Joe Giebel—1 Year Catcher (b. 30 Nov 1891 Washington DC–d. 17 Mar 1981 Silver Spring MD) Served in the American Red Cross during World War I and was a stenographer for the U.S. Navy after the war. For more than 20 years he was manager of the Washington DC branch of Mack Truck, retiring in 1957. Died from pneumonia. Buried Gate of Heaven Cemetery, Silver Spring MD.

Jim Gifford—3 Years Manager (b. 18 Oct 1845 Warren NY–d. 19 Dec 1901 at his home in Columbus OH) He was superintendent of the Columbus Union Station mailing room. Died from Bright's disease. Buried Green Lawn Memorial Cemetery, Columbus OH.

Andy Gilbert—2 Years Outfielder (b. 18 Jul 1914 Bradenville PA–d. 29 Aug 1992 Sutter-Davis Hospital, Davis CA) Served in World War II. He spent 40 years in baseball as a player, coach and minor league manager. Died from a massive pulmonary thrombosis and acute respiratory failure, but also suffered from Alzheimer's disease. Buried St Vincent's Cemetery, Latrobe PA.

Billy Gilbert—8 Years Infielder (b. 21 Jun 1876 Trenton NJ–d. 8 Aug 1927 at his home in New York City NY) He worked his entire life in baseball, managing minor league teams and scouting after his playing days were over. Died following a stroke of apoplexy. Buried Gate of Heaven Cemetery, Hawthorne NY.

Charlie Gilbert—6 Years Outfielder (b. 8 Jul 1919 New Orleans LA–d. 13 Aug 1983 Methodist Hospital, New Orleans LA) He was an auctioneer for the New Orleans' Criminal Sheriff's office. Died from a heart attack. Buried Lake Lawn Mausoleum, New Orleans LA.

Harry Gilbert—1 Year Infielder (b. 7 Jul 1868 Pottstown PA–d. 23 Dec 1909 Pottstown PA) He was a clerk at the Pennsylvania Railroad Freight Station in Pottstown until 1904 when he went into the hotel business, buying the Montgomery House there. Died from a heart attack following an attack of acute indigestion. Buried Pottstown Cemetery, Pottstown PA.

Jack Gilbert—2 Years Outfielder (b. 7 Sep 1875 Rhinecliff NY–d. 7 Jul 1941 Memorial Hospital, Albany NY) He worked at the Elk's club in Albany. He fell on the sidewalk, causing head injuries that proved fatal. Buried St Mary's Cemetery, South Glens Falls NY.

John Gilbert—1 Year Infielder (b. 8 Jan 1864 Pottstown PA–d. 12 Nov 1903 Pottstown PA) He conducted the Gilbert Cafe in Pottstown. Died suddenly from a stroke of apoplexy. Buried Pottstown Cemetery, Pottstown PA.

Larry Gilbert—2 Years Outfielder (b. 3 Dec 1891 New Orleans LA–d. 17 Feb 1965 Mercy Hospital, New Orleans LA) He was one of baseball's most successful minor league managers, managing in the Southern Association 26 years, from 1923 to 1948, and winning nine pennants. After 1948 he was general manager and part-owner of the Nashville team, retiring in 1955. Died following a long illness. Buried Greenwood Cemetery, New Orleans LA.

Pete Gilbert—4 Years Infielder (b. 6 Sep 1867 Baltic CT–d. 31 Dec 1911 Springfield MA) Buried St Michael's Cemetery, Springfield MA.

Tookie Gilbert—2 Years Infielder (b. 4 Apr 1929 New Orleans LA–d. 23 Jun 1967 New Orleans LA) He was a realtor for a short while before being elected for two terms as Orleans Parish Civil Sheriff. Died from a heart attack in his car while on duty. Buried Lake Lawn Mausoleum, New Orleans LA.

Wally Gilbert—5 Years Infielder (b. 19 Dec 1900 Oscoda MI–d. 8 Sep 1958 St Luke Hospital, Duluth MN) He played professional football and basketball as well as baseball. Died after a long illness. Buried Sunrise Memorial Park, Duluth MN.

Warren Giles—Hall of Fame (b. 28 May 1896 Tiskilwa IL–d. 7 Feb 1979 Christ Hospital, Cincinnati OH) World War I veteran. He worked 50 years in baseball, all at the executive level. He was an executive with the Reds from 1936 to 1951 and president of the National League from 1951 to 1969. Died from cancer. Buried Riverside Cemetery, Moline IL.

George Gilham—2 Years Catcher (b. 17 Sep 1899 Shamokin PA–d. 25 Apr 1937 Lansdowne PA) Died from Hodgkin's disease. Buried Shamokin Cemetery, Shamokin PA.

Frank Gilhooley—9 Years Outfielder (b. 10 Jun 1892 Toledo OH–d. 11 Jul 1959 Mercy Hospital, Toledo OH) He served 23 years as deputy treasurer for Lucas County, OH. Buried Calvary Cemetery, Toledo OH.

Bob Gilks—5 Years Outfielder (b. 2 Jul 1867 Cincinnati OH–d. 20 Aug 1944 at his home near Brunswick GA) He managed minor league baseball and worked as a scout for the Yankees. Buried Palmetto Cemetery, Brunswick GA.

Ed Gill—1 Year Pitcher (b. 7 Aug 1895 Somerville MA–d. 10 Oct 1995 West Acres Nursing Home, Brockton MA) Served in the U.S. Army during World War I. He was the principal of John Adams School in South Boston, retiring about 1965. Buried Mount Benedict Cemetery, West Roxbury MA.

Haddie Gill—1 Year Pitcher (b. 23 Jan 1899 Brockton MA–d. 1 Aug 1932 Ducy Hospital, Brockton MA) Died at the height of his baseball career following surgery for appendicitis. Buried Calvary Cemetery, Brockton MA.

Johnny Gill—6 Years Outfielder (b. 27 Mar 1905 Nashville TN–d. 26 Dec 1984 Donelson Hospital, Nashville TN) Buried Calvary Cemetery, Nashville TN.

Warren Gill—1 Year Infielder (b. 21 Dec 1878 Ladoga IN–d. 26 Nov 1952 at his home in Laguna Beach CA) Spanish-American War and World War I veteran. He was a self-employed dentist. Cremated.

Sam Gillen—2 Years Infielder (b. 1870 Pittsburgh PA–d. 13 May 1905 at his parent's home in Pittsburgh PA).

Tom Gillen—2 Years Catcher (b. 18 May 1862 Philadelphia PA–d. 26 Jan 1889 Philadelphia PA).

Carden Gillenwater—5 Years Outfielder (b. 13 May 1918 Riceville TN–d. 26 Feb 1978 at a hospital in Bradenton FL) Cremated.

Claral Gillenwater—1 Year Pitcher (b. 20 May 1900 Simes IN–d. 26 Feb 1978 Pensacola FL).

Jim Gillespie—1 Year Outfielder (b. 23 Sep 1858 St Catharines, Ontario, Canada–d. 5 Sep 1921 North Tonawanda NY) He was a prominent lumber dealer in the upper New York state area. Active in civic affairs, he was Police Commissioner of North Tonawanda when he died from complications of a surgery performed three months earlier. Buried Elmlawn Cemetery, Kenmore NY.

John Gillespie—1 Year Pitcher (b. 25 Feb 1900 Oakland CA–d. 15 Feb 1954 General Hospital, Vallejo CA) He was a machinist at the Mare Island Naval Shipyard in Vallejo. Buried St Vincent's Cemetery, Vallejo CA.

Paul Gillespie—3 Years Catcher (b. 18 Sep 1920 Sugar Valley GA–d. 11 Aug 1970 Memorial Hospital, Anniston AL) World War II veteran. He was a sales representative for Adler Typewriter Company. Died after a short illness. Buried Westview Cemetery, Atlanta GA.

Pete Gillespie—8 Years Outfielder (b. 30 Nov 1851 Carbondale PA–d. 5 May 1910 Carbondale PA) Buried St Rose Cemetery, Carbondale PA.

Jim "Junior" Gilliam—14 Years Infielder (b. 17 Oct 1928 Nashville TN–d. 8 Oct 1978 Daniel Freeman Hospital, Inglewood CA) He coached for the Dodgers until his death. Died from cardiac arrest after a stroke suffered at his home five weeks earlier. Buried Inglewood Park Cemetery, Inglewood CA.

Barney Gilligan—10 Years Catcher (b. 3 Jan 1857 Cambridge MA–d. 1 Apr 1934 Lynn MA) He worked 20 years for the Lynn refuse and garbage department. Died from erysipelas after picking a pimple on his face. Buried Pine Grove Cemetery, Lynn MA.

Jack Gilligan—2 Years Pitcher (b. 18 Oct 1884 Chicago IL–d. 19 Nov 1980 Modesto CA) Buried St Stanislaus Catholic Cemetery, Modesto CA.

Grant Gillis—3 Years Infielder (b. 24 Jan 1901 Grove Hill AL–d. 4 Feb 1981 Thomasville Hospital, Thomasville AL) He was a retired coach and teacher. Buried Gosport Cemetery, Gosport AL.

Pit Gilman—1 Year Outfielder (b. 14 Mar 1864 Laporte OH–d. 17 Aug 1950 at his home in Elyria OH) He was a salesman for Robert F Mackenzie Candy Company, retiring in 1925. Died following an illness of a few months. Buried Butternut Ridge Cemetery, North Eaton OH.

Ernie Gilmore—2 Years Outfielder (b. 1 Nov 1888 Chicago IL–d. 25 Nov 1919 Sioux City IA) Buried Oakridge Cemetery, Hillside IL.

Frank Gilmore—3 Years Pitcher (b. 27 Apr 1864 Webster MA–d. 21 Jul 1929 St Francis Hospital, Hartford CT) For several years he was supervisor of the playground at Pope Park in Hartford. Died after suffering from heat prostration two weeks earlier. Buried Mount St Benedict Cemetery, Bloomfield CT.

George Gilpatrick—1 Year Pitcher (b. 28 Feb 1875 Holden MO–d. 14 Dec 1941 General Hospital, Kansas City MO) He played professional baseball for 15 years, pitching in the Texas League and for Portland in the Pacific Coast League. After baseball he operated a laundry in Kansas City until three years before his death. Died a week after falling down his basement stairs, fracturing his skull. Buried Freeman Cemetery, Freeman MO.

John Gilroy—2 Years Pitcher (b. 26 Oct 1869 Washington DC–d. 4 Aug 1897 St Vincent's Hospital, Norfolk VA) Died at the height of his baseball career from inflamation of the stomach following surgery for appendicitis. Buried Mount Olivet Cemetery, Washington DC.

Billy Ging—1 Year Pitcher (b. 7 Nov 1872 Elmira NY–d. 14 Sep 1950 Elmira NY).

Joe Gingras—1 Year Pitcher (b. 10 Jan 1894 New York City NY–d. 6 Sep 1947 at his home in Jersey City NJ) Served in France for the U.S. Army during World War I. He worked for the Loft Candy Company in Jersey City. He was found dead from natural causes by his wife when she returned from a two-week vacation in Connecticut.

Tinsley Ginn—1 Year Outfielder (b. 26 Sep 1891 Royston GA–d. 30 Aug 1931 Georgia Baptist Hospital, Atlanta GA) Served in the U.S. Army during World War I. He owned the Ford dealership in Covington GA for several years and was active in civic affairs there. Died from blood poisoning. Buried Rose Hill Cemetery, Royston GA.

Charlie Girard—1 Year Pitcher (b. 16 Dec 1884 Brooklyn NY–d. 6 Aug 1936 Brooklyn NY).

Jim Gladd—1 Year Catcher (b. 2 Oct 1922 Fort Gibson OK–d. 8 Nov 1977 at his home in Long Beach CA) For 22 years he was vice-president of a lumber and hardware corporation. Died from a heart attack. Buried Citizen Cemetery, Fort Gibson OK.

Fred Glade—6 Years Pitcher (b. 25 Jan 1876 Dubuque IA–d. 21 Nov 1934 at his home in Grand Island NE) He was active in the flour milling business established by his father at Grand Island. Buried Grand Island Cemetery, Grand Island NE.

Roland Gladu—1 Year Outfielder (b. 10 May 1911 Montreal, Quebec, Canada–d. 26 Jul 1994 Montreal, Quebec, Canada).

John Glaiser—1 Year Pitcher (b. 28 Jul 1894 Yoakum TX–d. 7 Mar 1959 at a hospital in Houston TX) He worked 20 years for the Gulf Brewing Company. Buried Forest Park Cemetery, Houston TX.

Tom Glass—1 Year Pitcher (b. 29 Apr 1898 Greensboro NC–d. 15 Dec 1981 Moses Cone Memorial Hospital, Greensboro NC) He was a retired painter. Died after a lengthy illness.

Buried Moriah Methodist Church Cemetery, Greensboro NC.

Jack Glasscock—17 Years Infielder 1 Year Manager (b. 22 Jul 1857 Wheeling WV–d. 24 Feb 1947 Wheeling Hospital, Wheeling WV) He was a carpenter 20 years for W W Woods Contracting Company of Wheeling. Died following an illness of several months. Buried Peninsula Cemetery, Wheeling WV.

Luke Glavenich—1 Year Pitcher (b. 17 Jan 1893 Jackson CA–d. 22 May 1935 St Joseph's Hospital, Stockton CA) He was an assayer for Amador Metals Reduction Company. Died following surgery for appendix removal. Buried Jackson Catholic Cemetery, Jackson CA.

Ralph Glaze—3 Years Pitcher (b. 13 Mar 1881 Denver CO–d. 31 Oct 1968 Sawyer's Convalescent Home, Atascadero CA) For 15 years he was a superintendent for the Boston and Maine Railroad, retiring to Cambria CA in 1952. Died from a heart attack. Cremated.

Whitey Glazner—5 Years Pitcher (b. 17 Sep 1893 Sycamore AL–d. 6 Jun 1989 Orlando FL) He golfed professionally.

Bill Gleason—3 Years Infielder (b. 6 Sep 1894 Chicago IL–d. 9 Jan 1957 Holyoke MA) Served in the U.S. Navy during World War I. He managed minor league baseball for a few years. Appointed as the local juvenile probation officer in 1948, he served in that capacity until his death. Died after an illness of several months duration. Buried St Jerome Cemetery, Holyoke MA.

Bill Gleason—8 Years Infielder (b. 12 Nov 1865 St Louis MO–d. 21 Jul 1932 at his home in St Louis MO) He was a captain in the St Louis Fire Department. Died from the effects of heat prostration suffered while fighting a fire a week earlier. Buried Calvary Cemetery, St Louis MO.

Bill Gleason—1 Year Pitcher (b. 1868 Cleveland OH–d. 2 Dec 1893 at his home in Cleveland OH) Died from consumption.

Harry Gleason—5 Years Infielder (b. 28 Mar 1875 Camden NJ–d. 21 Oct 1961 at his home in Haddonfield NJ).

Jack Gleason—6 Years Infielder (b. 14 Jul 1854 St Louis MO–d. 4 Sep 1944 St Louis MO) He worked for the St Louis Fire Department. Buried Calvary Cemetery, St Louis MO.

Joe Gleason—2 Years Pitcher (b. 9 Jul 1895 Phelps NY–d. 8 Sep 1990 at his home in Phelps NY) Served in the U.S. Army during World War I. He worked for the Seneca Ordinance Depot and Papec in Shortsville NY. Buried St Francis Cemetery, Phelps NY.

Kid Gleason—22 Years Infielder 5 Years Manager (b. 26 Oct 1866 Camden NJ–d. 2 Jan 1933 at his home in Philadelphia PA) He spent his entire life in baseball as a player, coach and manager. Died in his sleep from a complication of diseases. Buried Northwood Cemetery, Philadelphia PA.

Jim Gleeson—5 Years Outfielder (b. 5 Mar 1912 Kansas City MO–d. 1 May 1996 at his home in Kansas City MO) Served in the U.S. Navy during World War II. He was a retired scout for the Brewers. Buried Calvary Cemetery, Kansas City MO.

Frank Gleich—2 Years Outfielder (b. 7 Mar 1894 Columbus OH–d. 27 Mar 1949 at his home in Columbus OH) World War I veteran. He was a police lieutenant for the Pennsylvania Railroad. Died after an illness of four years. Buried St Joseph Cemetery, Lockbourne OH.

Bob Glenalvin—2 Years Infielder (b. 7 Apr 1874 Kalamazoo MI–d. 24 Mar 1944 Detroit MI).

Martin Glendon—2 Years Pitcher (b. 8 Feb 1877 Milwaukee WI–d. 6 Nov 1950 Chicago IL) Buried St Joseph Cemetery, River Grove IL.

Bob Glenn—1 Year Pitcher (b. 16 Jun 1894 West Sunbury PA–d. 3 Jun 1977 at a hospital in Richmond CA) He was a research engineer and the director of the Extension of Institutional Transporation Studies. Cremated.

Ed Glenn—2 Years Infielder (b. 1876 Ludlow KY–d. 7 Dec 1911 at his parent's home in Ludlow KY) He was a locomotive engineer. Died from injuries caused by a fall into a locomotive pit while working. Buried St Joseph New Cemetery, Cincinnati OH.

Ed Glenn—3 Years Outfielder (b. 19 Sep 1860 Richmond VA–d. 10 Feb 1892 at his home in Richmond VA) Died from a lung injury received while playing baseball.

Harry Glenn—1 Year Catcher (b. 9 Jun 1890 Shelburn IN–d. 12 Oct 1918 Overland Aviation School Hosp, St Paul MN) Died from pneumonia caused by Spanish influenza. Buried Highland Lawn Cemetery, Terre Haute IN.

Joe Glenn—8 Years Catcher (b. 19 Nov 1908 Dickson City PA–d. 6 May 1985 at his home in Tunkhannock PA) He was a car salesman for Russell Pontiac and Burne Oldsmobile in Scranton PA. Died suddenly the morning after he was inducted into the Northeastern Pennsylvania Sports Hall of Fame in Scranton. Buried St Mary's Cemetery, Dickson City PA.

John Glenn—2 Years Outfielder (b. 1849 Rochester NY–d. 10 Nov 1888 Glens Falls NY) He died when he was accidentally shot by a policeman who was protecting him from a mob that wished to lynch him for allegedly assaulting a little girl.

Sal Gliatto—1 Year Pitcher (b. 7 May 1902 Chicago IL–d. 2 Nov 1995 Tyler TX) He owned and operated a bowling alley in East Dallas TX. Died in his sleep. Buried Restland Memorial Park, Dallas TX.

Norm Glockson—1 Year Catcher (b. 15 Jun 1894 Blue Island IL–d. 5 Aug 1955 Maywood IL) Buried Mount Greenwood Cemetery, Chicago IL.

Al Glossop—5 Years Infielder (b. 23 Jul 1914 Christopher IL–d. 2 Jul 1991 John Muir Medical Center, Walnut Creek CA) Served in World War II. He owned and operated a retail liquor store for 15 years. Died from a heart attack. Buried Valhalla Gardens of Memory, Belleville IL.

Jot Goar—2 Years Pitcher (b. 31 Jan 1870 New Lisbon IN–d. 4 Apr 1947 at a clinic in New Castle IN) He farmed near New Lisbon. Died after a ten-day illness. Buried New Lisbon Cemetery, New Lisbon IN.

John Gochnaur—3 Years Infielder (b. 12 Sep 1875 Altoona PA–d. 27 Sep 1929 Altoona Hospital, Altoona PA) He umpired minor league baseball until his death. Died from pneumonia. Buried Fairview Cemetery, Altoona PA.

John Godar—1 Year Outfielder (b. 25 Oct 1864 Cincinnati OH–d. 23 Jun 1949 Park Ridge IL) Buried All Saints Cemetery, Des Plaines IL.

John Godwin—2 Years Infielder (b. 10 Mar 1877 East Liverpool OH–d. 5 May 1956 City Hospital, East Liverpool OH) A jiggerman by trade, he last worked for Cronin China Company at New Cumberland OH. Died following a long illness. Buried Spring Hill Cemetery, Wellsville OH.

Ed Goebel—1 Year Outfielder (b. 1 Sep 1899 Brooklyn NY–d. 12 Aug 1959 Long Island College Hospital, Brooklyn NY) He was a broker, retired from E F Hutton and Company. Died from a heart attack. Buried Maple Grove Park Cemetery, Hackensack NJ.

Bill Goeckel—1 Year Infielder (b. 3 Sep 1871 Wilkes-Barre PA–d. 1 Nov 1922 Lankenau Hospital, Philadelphia PA) He was an attorney and leading citizen in Wilkes-Barre community affairs. Died following surgery for a recurring ailment. Buried St Nicholas Cemetery, Shavertown PA.

Mike Golden—1 Year Outfielder (b. 11 Sep 1851 Shirley MA–d. 11 Jan 1929 Rockford IL) He worked more than 30 years for the Rockford Police Department, retiring in 1911. Died from heart disease. Buried St Marys/St James Cemetery, Rockford IL.

Roy Golden—2 Years Pitcher (b. 12 Jul 1888 Madisonville OH–d. 4 Oct 1961 Norwood OH) He was a bookkeeper. Died from a heart attack. Cremated.

Jonah Goldman—3 Years Infielder (b. 29 Aug 1906 New York City NY–d. 17 Aug 1980 at a hospital in Palm Beach FL) He was president of Atlas Men's Stores, retiring to Florida in 1971. Buried Westchester Hills Cemetery, Hastings on Hudson NY.

Gordon Goldsberry—4 Years Infielder (b. 30 Aug 1927 Sacramento CA–d. 23 Feb 1996 Saddleback Medical Center, Laguna Hills CA) He was a scout for the Orioles. Died from a heart attack. Cremated.

Walt Goldsby—3 Years Outfielder (b. 1 Jan 1862 Evansville IN–d. 11 Jan 1914 Dallas TX) Died from a self-inflicted gunshot to the temple at the Campbell House, a Dallas hotel. Buried Oakland Cemetery, Dallas TX.

Fred Goldsmith—6 Years Pitcher (b. 15 May 1852 New Haven CT–d. 28 Mar 1939 at his home in Berkley MI) He claimed to have invented the curve ball. He was the postmaster at Clawson MI for 12 years before operating a general store there. Died from heart disease after an illness of several weeks. Buried Roseland Park Cemetery, Berkley MI.

Hal Goldsmith—4 Years Pitcher (b. 18 Aug 1898 Peconic NY–d. 20 Oct 1985 Riverhead NY).

Izzy Goldstein —1 Year Pitcher (b. 6 Jun 1908 Odessa, Russia–d. 24 Sep 1993 Delray Beach FL) Buried Eternal Light Memorial Gardens, Boynton Beach FL.

Walt Golvin —1 Year Infielder (b. 1 Feb 1894 Hershey NE–d. 11 Jun 1973 Memorial Hospital, Gardena CA) For 20 years he was a lather in the construction business. Died from heart disease. Buried Holy Cross Cemetery, Culver City CA.

Chile Gomez —3 Years Infielder (b. 23 May 1909 Villa Union, Mexico–d. 1 Dec 1992 Nuevo Laredo, Mexico).

Lefty Gomez —14 Years Pitcher Hall of Fame (b. 26 Nov 1909 Rodeo CA–d. 17 Feb 1989 Marin General Hospital, San Rafael CA) He was a public relations representative for Wilson Sporting Goods Company. Died from congestive heart failure. Buried Mount Tamalpais Cemetery, San Rafael CA.

Joe Gonzales —1 Year Pitcher (b. 19 Mar 1915 San Francisco CA–d. 16 Nov 1996 at a hospital in Torrance CA) Served in World War II. He taught high school for 30 years. Died from a heart attack. He was cremated and his ashes scattered off Hermosa Beach CA.

Vince Gonzales —1 Year Pitcher (b. 28 Sep 1925 Quivican, Cuba–d. 11 Mar 1981 Ciudad Del Carmen, Mexico).

Eusebio Gonzalez —1 Year Infielder (b. 13 Jul 1892 Havana, Cuba–d. 14 Feb 1976 Havana, Cuba).

Julio Gonzalez —1 Year Pitcher (b. 20 Dec 1920 Banes, Cuba–d. 15 Feb 1991 Banes, Cuba).

Mike Gonzalez —17 Years Catcher 2 Years Manager (b. 24 Sep 1890 Havana, Cuba–d. 19 Feb 1977 Havana, Cuba) Buried Christopher Columbus Necropolis, Havana, Cuba.

Charlie Gooch—1 Year Infielder (b. 5 Jun 1902 Smyrna TN–d. 30 May 1982 Lanham MD) Buried Fort Lincoln Cemetery, Brentwood MD.

Johnny Gooch—11 Years Catcher (b. 9 Nov 1897 Smyrna TN–d. 15 May 1975 Baptist Hospital, Nashville TN) He played and managed baseball from 1916 until 1942 and operated a baseball bat manufacturing business in Nashville after 1942. He is a member of the Tennessee Sports Hall of Fame. Buried Mount Olivet Cemetery, Nashville TN.

Lee Gooch—2 Years Outfielder (b. 23 Feb 1890 Oxford NC–d. 18 May 1966 Mayview Convalescent Home, Raleigh NC) He was a retired tobacconist in the late 1940s when he took over as coach of the Wake Forest College baseball team. Buried Wake Forest Cemetery, Wake Forest NC.

Gene Good —1 Year Outfielder (b. 13 Dec 1882 Roxbury MA–d. 6 Aug 1947 Boston MA) He worked as an attache of the Municipal Bureau of Vital Statistics for the City of Boston. Also a musician, he was a life member in the Musician's Union. Died after a brief illness. Buried New Calvary Cemetery, Mattapan MA.

Ralph Good —1 Year Pitcher (b. 25 Apr 1886 Monticello ME–d. 24 Nov 1965 Waterville ME).

Wilbur Good —11 Years Outfielder (b. 28 Sep 1885 Punxsutawney PA–d. 30 Dec 1963 Brooksville FL).

Herb Goodall —1 Year Pitcher (b. 10 Aug 1866 Mansfield PA–d. 20 Jan 1938 Mansfield PA) For many years he was engaged in the feed and lumber business at Canoe Camp. Died after a brief illness.

John Goodell —1 Year Pitcher (b. 5 Apr 1907 Muskogee OK–d. 21 Sep 1993 Mesquite TX) He retired to Bella Vista AR where he lived 18 years. Buried Laurel Land Memorial Park, Fort Worth TX.

Bill Goodenough—1 Year Outfielder (b. 1863 St Louis MO–d. 23 May 1905 at the city insane asylum in St Louis MO) Died from a hemorrhage after a month's illness. Buried Calvary Cemetery, St Louis MO.

Mike Goodfellow—2 Years Outfielder (b. 3 Oct 1866 Port Jervis NY–d. 12 Feb 1920 City Hospital, Newark NJ) He was a hatter. Died from chronic heart disease. Buried Fairmount Cemetery, Newark NJ.

Billy Goodman —16 Years Infielder (b. 22 Mar 1926 Concord NC–d. 1 Oct 1984 Sarasota Memorial Hospital, Sarasota FL) Served in the U.S. Navy during World War II. He lived in Sarasota 34 years and was active in youth sport activities in the area. Died after a long battle with cancer. Buried Mount Olivet Methodist Church Cemetery, Concord NC.

Ival Goodman —10 Years Outfielder (b. 23 Jul 1908 Northview MO–d. 25 Nov 1984 Jewish

Hospital, Cincinnati OH) He was a salesman for a chemical company. Died from an intestinal disorder. Buried Oak Hill Cemetery Park, Cincinnati OH.

Jake Goodman —2 Years Infielder (b. 14 Sep 1853 Lancaster PA–d. 9 Mar 1890 at his father's home in Reading PA) He had been of unsound mind with occasional bouts of palsy since being hit in the head by a baseball in 1884. Died following a stroke of palsy that left him unconscious. Buried Charles Evans Cemetery, Reading PA.

Art Goodwin —1 Year Pitcher (b. 27 Feb 1877 Greene County, PA–d. 19 Jun 1943 Greene County Memorial Hosp, Waynesburg PA) Died from complications after an illness of three weeks. Buried Jefferson Cemetery, Jefferson PA.

Clyde Goodwin —1 Year Pitcher (b. 12 Nov 1886 Shade OH–d. 12 Oct 1963 Dayton OH).

Marv Goodwin —7 Years Pitcher (b. 16 Jan 1893 Richmond VA–d. 21 Oct 1925 Houston TX) He managed minor league baseball in the Texas League and was a member of the Ellington Field Squadron, a flying unit of the Texas National Guard. Died from injuries suffered in an airplane crash when he was training three days earlier. Buried Gordonsville VA.

Pep Goodwin —2 Years Infielder (b. 19 Dec 1891 Pocatello ID–d. 15 Feb 1972 Merritt Hospital, Oakland CA) Served in the U.S. Army during World War I. He spent 47 years as an investment broker and was a well-known sports and civic leader. A member of the California State Athletic Commission, Board of Commissioners of the Port of Oakland and the Alameda County (CA) Institutions Commission, he was also president of the Pacific Coast League for a time. Died from heart disease. Cremated.

Glen Gorbous —3 Years Outfielder (b. 8 Jul 1930 Drumheller, Alberta, Canada 12–d. Jun 1990 Calgary, Alberta, Canada).

Joe Gordon —11 Years Infielder 5 Years Manager (b. 18 Feb 1915 Los Angeles CA–d. 14 Apr 1978 Sutter Memorial Hospital, Sacramento CA) He spent his entire life in baseball management. Died from a heart attack. Cremated.

Sid Gordon —13 Years Outfielder (b. 13 Aug 1917 Brooklyn NY–d. 17 Jun 1975 Lenox Hill Hospital, New York City NY) He was a player-coach in the minor leagues before becoming an insurance underwriter for the Mutual of New York Insurance Company. Died from a heart attack. Buried New Montefiore Cemetery, Farmingdale NY.

Ray Gordonier —2 Years Pitcher (b. 11 Apr 1892 Rochester NY–d. 15 Nov 1960 Rochester NY) He operated a milk business. Buried Holy Sepulchre Cemetery, Rochester NY.

George Gore —14 Years Outfielder (b. 3 May 1852 Hartland ME–d. 16 Sep 1933 Masonic Home, Utica NY).

Herb Gorman —1 Game Pinch-Hitter (b. 18 Dec 1925 San Francisco CA–d. 5 Apr 1953 San Diego CA) Served in the U.S. Coast Guard during World War II. He played minor league baseball in the Canadian-American League, Western International League, Western League and Pacific Coast League. Died from a heart attack while playing in a Pacific Coast League game. Buried Oak Hill Memorial Park, San Jose CA.

Howie Gorman —2 Years Outfielder (b. 14 May 1913 Pittsburgh PA–d. 29 Apr 1984 Harrisburg PA) For 42 years he was a yardmaster for the Monongala Connecting Railroad, retiring in 1976. Died while visiting a son. Buried Queen of Heaven Cemetery, Bridgeville PA.

Jack Gorman —2 Years Infielder (b. 1859 St Louis MO–d. 9 Sep 1889 St Louis MO) Died from lung trouble. Buried Calvary Cemetery, St Louis MO.

Tom Gorman —1 Year Pitcher (b. 16 Mar 1916 New York City NY–d. 11 Aug 1986 Closter NJ) Served in the U.S. Army during World War II. He umpired in the National League from 1951 until 1976 when he retired to a job in the league office. Died from a heart attack. Buried George Washington Memorial Park, Paramus NJ.

Tom Gorman —8 Years Pitcher (b. 4 Jan 1925 New York City NY–d. 26 Dec 1992 at his home in Valley Stream NY) Served in the U.S. Navy during World War II. He was a sales representative for F & M Schaefer Brewing Company and for Manhattan Beer Distributors in the Bronx. Died from heart disease. Buried Cemetery of Holy Rood, Westbury NY.

Ed Gormley —1 Year Pitcher (b. Bethlehem PA–d. 2 Jul 1950 at his home in Summit Hill PA) He retired from the Lehigh Navigation Coal Company in 1945. Buried GAR Cemetery, Summit Hill PA.

Hank Gornicki—4 Years Pitcher (b. 14 Jan 1911 Niagara Falls NY–d. 16 Feb 1996 V A Nursing Home, Riviera Beach FL) Served in the U.S. Army during World War II. He taught school in Palm Beach County, FL, many years and was a mail carrier in Palm Beach FL. Buried Royal Palm Memorial Gardens, West Palm Beach FL.

Goose Goslin—18 Years Outfielder Hall of Fame (b. 16 Oct 1900 Salem NJ–d. 15 May 1971 Bridgeton Hospital, Bridgeton NJ) He ran a recreational boating business in Bayside NJ. Buried Baptist Cemetery, Salem NJ.

Howie Goss—2 Years Outfielder (b. 1 Nov 1934 Wewoka OK–d. 31 Jul 1996 Reno NV).

Dick Gossett—2 Years Catcher (b. 21 Aug 1891 Dennison OH–d. 6 Oct 1962 City Hospital, Massillon OH) He was a foreman for the boiler, water and steam division of Republic Steel Corporation in Massillon. Buried Rose Hill Memorial Park, Massillon OH.

Ted Goulait—1 Year Pitcher (b. 11 Aug 1889 St Clair MI–d. 15 Jul 1936 Community Hospital, St Clair MI) He was a conservation officer for the State of Michigan. Died from heart disease. Buried St Mary's Cemetery, St Clair MI.

Al Gould—2 Years Pitcher (b. 20 Jan 1893 Muscatine IA–d. 8 Aug 1982 Plum Tree Convalescent Hosp, San Jose CA) He owned and operated a Texaco service station for 35 years. Died from a heart attack. Cremated. Buried Los Gatos Memorial Park, San Jose CA.

Charlie Gould—2 Years Infielder 2 Years Manager (b. 21 Aug 1847 Cincinnati OH–d. 9 Apr 1917 Flushing Hospital, Flushing NY) A retired Cincinnati businessman, he lived with his son in Flushing. Died following a stroke of paralysis. Buried Spring Grove Cemetery, Cincinnati OH.

Nick Goulish—2 Years Outfielder (b. 13 Nov 1918 Punxsutawney PA–d. 15 May 1984 at his home in Youngstown OH) He owned the Goulish Insurance Agency in Boardman OH from 1950 until he retired in 1976. Died from polyneuritis. Buried Calvary Cemetery, Youngstown OH.

Claude Gouzzie—1 Year Infielder (b. 1871 PA–d. 21 Sep 1907 Denver CO).

Hank Gowdy—17 Years Catcher (b. 24 Aug 1889 Columbus OH–d. 1 Aug 1966 Mount Carmel Hospital, Columbus OH) Served in France during World War I. He worked in baseball as a player, coach and minor league manager until his retirement in 1948. Died following a long illness. Buried Union Cemetery, Columbus OH.

Al Grabowski—2 Years Pitcher (b. 4 Sep 1901 Syracuse NY–d. 29 Oct 1966 Memphis NY) He worked for the Camillus Cutlery Company. Buried Sacred Heart Cemetery, Syracuse NY.

Johnny Grabowski—7 Years Catcher (b. 7 Jan 1900 Ware MA–d. 23 May 1946 St Peter's Hospital, Albany NY) He umpired minor league baseball for a short while. Died from burns suffered when his home in Guilderland NY burned. Buried Park View Cemetery, Schenectady NY.

Reggie Grabowski—3 Years Pitcher (b. 16 Jul 1907 Syracuse NY–d. 2 Apr 1955 at his home in Syracuse NY) He worked for the Syracuse City Traffic and Lighting Department and was well-known in the area as a top amateur bowler. Died following a heart attack. Buried Sacred Heart Cemetery, Syracuse NY.

Earl Grace—8 Years Catcher (b. 24 Feb 1907 Barlow KY–d. 22 Dec 1980 St Joseph's Hospital, Phoenix AZ) In 1935 he caught the game for the Pittsburgh Pirates when Babe Ruth, then with the Boston Braves, hit the last three home runs of his career. He moved to Phoenix when a boy and, after baseball, owned a nursery there. Buried Greenwood Memory Lawn, Phoenix AZ.

Joe Grace—6 Years Outfielder (b. 5 Jan 1914 Gorham IL–d. 18 Sep 1969 Murphysboro IL) He played in the Pacific Coast League several years and worked for the Murphysboro Police Department and the Murphysboro Parks Department before taking a job with the Illinois Youth Commission. He and his wife were killed in a four-car pileup on Hwy 149, west of Murphysboro. Buried Tower Grove Cemetery, Murphysboro IL.

John Grady—1 Year Infielder (b. 1860 Lowell MA–d. 15 Jul 1893 at his home in Lowell MA) Active in civic matters, he had been elected to serve as a city councilman. Died suddenly from a stroke. Buried St Patrick's Cemetery, Lowell MA.

Mike Grady—11 Years Catcher (b. 23 Dec 1869 Kennett Square PA–d. 3 Dec 1943 Kennett Square PA).

Fred Graff—1 Year Infielder (b. 25 Aug 1889 Canton OH–d. 4 Oct 1979 at a hospital in Chattanooga TN) For 66 years he lived in Chattanooga, where he played several years for the Lookouts in the Southern League. Through the years he operated several businesses there. Cremated. Buried Mizpah Cemetery, Chattanooga TN.

Louis Graff—1 Year Catcher (b. 25 Jul 1866 Philadelphia PA–d. 16 Apr 1955 Bryn Mawr Hospital, Bryn Mawr PA) After working two years as a bank clerk he entered the grain trade and became an exporter on a large scale. Known as a leading authority on grain exportation, he was at one time president of the Commercial Exchange.

Mase Graffen—1 Year Manager (b. 1845 Philadelphia PA–d. 18 Nov 1883 Silver City NM).

Barney Graham—1 Year Infielder (b. Philadelphia PA–d. 30 Oct 1886 Providence Infirmary, Mobile AL) Buried Catholic Cemetery, Mobile AL.

Bert Graham—1 Year Infielder (b. 3 Apr 1886 near Tilton IL–d. 19 Jun 1971 Lawrence Memorial Hospital, Cottonwood AZ) He lived in Apache Junction AZ for six years just prior to his death. Buried Valley View Cemetery, Clarkdale AZ.

Bill Graham—3 Years Pitcher (b. 22 Jul 1884 Owosso MI–d. 15 Feb 1936 at his home in Holt MI) He lived 17 years at Holt, working for Reo Motor Car Company in Lansing MI. Buried Maple Ridge Cemetery, Holt MI.

Charlie Graham—1 Year Catcher (b. 24 Apr 1878 Santa Clara CA–d. 29 Aug 1948 Notre Dame Hospital, San Francisco CA) He spent 50 years in baseball as a player, minor league manager and minor league team owner. Died from a virus infection, pneumonia and the effects of gall bladder surgery seven years earlier. Buried Holy Cross Catholic Cemetery, Colma CA.

Frank Graham—Hall of Fame (b. 12 Nov 1893 Harlem NY–d. 9 Mar 1965 Nathan B Etten Hospital, New York City NY) He was a New York City sportswriter for almost 50 years. He had been in ill health for several years but died from the effects of a fractured skull suffered ten days earlier in a fall at his home. Buried Holy Mount Cemetery, Eastchester NY.

Kyle Graham—4 Years Pitcher (b. 14 Aug 1899 Oak Grove AL–d. 1 Dec 1973 at a hospital in Oak Grove AL) He worked for Pullman-Standard at Bessemer AL. Buried Oak Grove Baptist Church Cemetery, Oak Grove AL.

Moonlight Graham—1 Year Outfielder (b. 10 Oct 1879 Fayetteville NC–d. 25 Aug 1965 Chisholm Memorial Hospital, Chisholm MN) After his baseball career he became a medical doctor. He began a blood pressure and heart test program in the schools that was nationally recognized. Best known as a character depicted by Burt Lancaster in the movie *Field of Dreams.* Died after a lingering illness. Buried Calvary Cemetery, Rochester MN.

Oscar Graham—1 Year Pitcher (b. 20 Jul 1878 Plattsmouth NE–d. 15 Oct 1931 Moline IL) He played in the Three-I League and worked in Moline factories. Died from stomach trouble. Buried Riverside Cemetery, Moline IL.

Peaches Graham—7 Years Catcher (b. 23 Mar 1877 Aledo IL–d. 25 Jul 1939 Seaside Hospital, Long Beach CA) He worked 15 years for Shell Oil. Died after suffering a stroke the day before. Cremated.

Roy Graham—2 Years Catcher (b. 22 Feb 1895 San Francisco CA–d. 26 Apr 1933 Manila, Philippines).

Skinny Graham—2 Years Outfielder (b. 12 Aug 1909 Somerville MA–d. 10 Jul 1967 Mount Auburn Hospital, Cambridge MA) Buried Woodlawn Cemetery, Everett MA.

Tiny Graham—1 Year Infielder (b. 9 Dec 1892 Nashville TN–d. 29 Dec 1962 at his home in Nashville TN) Died from a heart attack. Buried Calvary Cemetery, Nashville TN.

Henry Grampp—2 Years Pitcher (b. 28 Sep 1903 New York City NY–d. 24 Mar 1986 New York City NY).

Jack Graney—14 Years Outfielder (b. 10 Jun 1886 St Thomas, Ontario, Canada–d. 20 Apr 1978 Smith-Barr Manor, Louisiana MO) He was a radio announcer for the Cleveland Indians from 1934 until 1954 when he retired, moving to Bowling Green MO. Buried Memorial Garden Cemetery, Bowling Green MO.

Eddie Grant—10 Years Infielder (b. 21 May 1883 Franklin MA–d. 5 Oct 1918 Argonne Forest, France) He was the first major league baseball player killed in World War I.

George Grant—7 Years Pitcher (b. 6 Jan 1903 East Tallassee AL–d. 25 Mar 1986 at a hospital in Montgomery AL) Buried Oak Hill Cemetery, Prattville AL.

Jim Grant—1 Year Pitcher (b. 4 Aug 1894 Coalville IA–d. 30 Nov 1985 Veteran's Medical Center, Des Moines IA) He played in the first night baseball game in the United States at Des Moines. Died from a respiratory ailment. Buried Mount Hope Cemetery, Madrid IA.

Jimmy Grant—3 Years Infielder (b. 6 Oct 1918 Racine WI–d. 8 Jul 1970 St Mary's Hospital, Rochester MN) He was a self-employed contractor in Racine before becoming a foreman for Bukacek Construction Company there, retiring in 1969 because of ill health. Buried West Lawn Memorial Park, Racine WI.

George Grantham—13 Years Infielder (b. 20 May 1900 Galena KS–d. 16 Mar 1954 Mohave General Hospital, Kingman AZ) Served in the U.S. Navy during World War I. He retired from baseball in 1934 and worked for the Central Commercial Company in Kingman until his death. Died from a cerebral hemorrhage suffered at his home. Buried Mountain View Cemetery, Kingman AZ.

Mickey Grasso—7 Years Catcher (b. 10 May 1920 Newark NJ–d. 15 Oct 1975 Palm Springs Hospital, Miami FL) He was a ticket salesman for horse racing tracks in Florida, including Gulfstream, Hialeah and Calder. Died from a heart attack. Cremated.

Joe Graves—1 Year Infielder (b. 27 Feb 1906 Marblehead MA–d. 22 Dec 1980 Salem Hospital, Salem MA) A master plumber, he owned and operated Graves Plumbing and Heating Contractors in Swampscott MA from 1945 to 1971 when he retired. Died following a long illness. Buried Waterside Cemetery, Marblehead MA.

Sid Graves—1 Year Outfielder (b. 30 Nov 1901 Marblehead MA–d. 26 Dec 1983 at a hospital in Biddeford ME) He worked for the U.S. Post Office at Marblehead, retiring in 1963 and moving to Kennebunk ME in 1972. He was inducted into the Maine Baseball Hall of Fame in 1975. Buried Hope Cemetery, Kennebunk ME.

Chummy Gray—1 Year Pitcher (b. 17 Jul 1873 Rockland ME–d. 14 Aug 1913 Rockland ME) He managed some in the minor leagues before operating a billiard parlor in Rockland. Died from pulmonary tuberculosis. Buried Acorn Cemetery, Rockland ME.

Dolly Gray—3 Years Pitcher (b. 4 Dec 1878 Ishpeming MI–d. 3 Apr 1956 at his home in Yuba City CA) He managed a restaurant in Yuba City where he lived 40 years. Buried Sutter Cemetery, Sutter CA.

Jim Gray—1 Year Infielder (b. 7 Aug 1862 Pittsburgh PA–d. 31 Jan 1938 at his home in Pittsburgh PA) He umpired minor league baseball for a short while before starting a 50-year career with the City of Pittsburgh. There he was water assessor before becoming chairman of the Board of Water Assessors in 1906. Died suddenly from a heart attack while visiting with friends. Buried Homewood Cemetery, Pittsburgh PA.

Milt Gray—1 Year Catcher (b. 21 Feb 1914 Louisville KY–d. 30 Jun 1969 Quincy FL) Served in the U.S. Navy during World War II. He was a salesman for U.S. Plywood in Tallahassee FL. Killed instantly when his car was hit by a train. Buried Resthaven Memorial Park, Louisville KY.

Sam Gray—10 Years Pitcher (b. 15 Oct 1897 Van Alstyne TX–d. 16 Apr 1953 Veteran's Hospital, McKinney TX) He managed minor league baseball and operated a baseball school before retiring to his farm southwest of Van Alstyne. Buried Van Alstyne Cemetery, Van Alstyne TX.

Stan Gray—1 Year Infielder (b. 10 Dec 1888 Ladonia TX–d. 11 Oct 1964 at his home in Snyder TX) World War I veteran. He operated Gray's Style Shop in Snyder from 1949 until his death. Died from a heart attack while watching a World Series game on TV. Buried Evergreen Cemetery, Ballinger TX.

Danny Green—8 Years Outfielder (b. 6 Nov 1876 Burlington NJ–d. 8 Nov 1914 Camden NJ) Died from a stroke of apoplexy, probably caused by a beaning suffered while playing baseball. Buried New Camden Cemetery, Camden NJ.

Ed Green—1 Year Pitcher (b. 17 Mar 1852 Toronto, Canada–d. 22 Mar 1917 at his room in the Lincoln Hotel, Ogden UT) For 47 years he was a telegrapher and dispatcher for Southern Pacific Railroad. His record showed not a single accident when he was working at the telegraph. Died from heart failure. Buried Ogden City Cemetery, Ogden UT.

Fred Green—5 Years Pitcher (b. 14 Sep 1933 Titusville NJ–d. 22 Dec 1996 at his home in Titusville NJ) Served in the U.S. Army. He worked for Mill Supply and Hardware in Trenton NJ. Buried Harbourton Cemetery, Lambertville NJ.

Gene Green—7 Years Outfielder (b. 26 Jun 1933 Los Angeles CA–d. 23 May 1981 St Louis MO) Buried Resurrection Cemetery, St Louis MO.

Harvey Green—1 Year Pitcher (b. 9 Feb 1915 Kenosha WI–d. 24 Jul 1970 Franklin LA) He was a compressor operator for Atlantic Oil Company. Died from a heart attack while at work. Buried McGowen Memorial Cemetery, Jeanerette LA.

Joe Green—1 Game Pinch Hitter (b. 17 Sep 1897 Philadelphia PA–d. 4 Feb 1972 at his home in Wynnewood PA) He was the assistant manager of the Prudential Life Insurance Company office in Philadelphia. Buried Arlington Cemetery, Drexel Hill PA.

Julius Green—2 Years Pitcher (b. 26 Jun 1900 Greensboro NC–d. 19 Mar 1974 Glendora Community Hospital, Glendora CA) For 23 years he was a paymaster for the American Red Cross. Died from a heart attack. Cremated.

Hank Greenberg—13 Years Infielder Hall of Fame (b. 1 Jan 1911 New York City NY–d. 4 Sep 1986 at his home in Beverly Hills CA) Captain in the Army Air Corps during World War II. From 1948 to 1960 he was an executive for the White Sox and the Indians, after which he was a self-employed investor. Died from kidney cancer. Buried Hillside Memorial Park, Los Angeles CA.

Nelson Greene—2 Years Pitcher (b. 20 Sep 1900 Philadelphia PA–d. 6 Apr 1983 Lebanon PA).

Willie Greene—2 Years Infielder (b. 20 Mar 1875 Providence RI–d. 20 Oct 1934 Providence RI).

Kent Greenfield—6 Years Pitcher (b. 1 Jul 1902 Guthrie KY–d. 14 Mar 1978 at his home in Guthrie KY) World War II veteran. Buried Guthrie Highland Cemetery, Guthrie KY.

Bill Greenwood—6 Years Infielder (b. 1857 Philadelphia PA–d. 2 May 1902 Philadelphia PA) Buried Mount Moriah Cemetery, Philadelphia PA.

Ed Greer—3 Years Outfielder (b. 1865 Philadelphia PA–d. 4 Feb 1890 Philadelphia PA).

Dave Gregg—1 Year Pitcher (b. 14 Mar 1891 Chehalis WA–d. 12 Nov 1965 Clarkston WA).

Hal Gregg—9 Years Pitcher (b. 11 Jul 1921 Anaheim CA–d. 13 May 1991 at his home in Bishop CA) Cremated.

Vean Gregg—8 Years Pitcher (b. 13 Apr 1885 Chehalis WA–d. 29 Jul 1964 at a nursing home in Aberdeen WA) He farmed in Alberta, Canada, before opening a cigar store in Hoquiam WA. He was inducted into the Washington State Hall of Fame in 1963. Died after a brief illness. Cremated.

Frank Gregory—1 Year Pitcher (b. 25 Jul 1890 Beloit WI–d. 5 Nov 1955 Beloit WI) His body was found in the Rock River. Buried Eastlawn Cemetery, Beloit WI.

Howie Gregory—1 Year Pitcher (b. 18 Nov 1886 Hannibal MO–d. 30 May 1970 at a nursing home in Jenks OK) He was chief criminal deputy in the Tulsa County, OK, sheriff's office and was also undersheriff before retiring after 20 year's service in 1952. Buried Memorial Park, Tulsa OK.

Tim Greisenbeck—1 Year Catcher (b. 10 Dec 1898 San Antonio TX–d. 25 Mar 1953 at a hospital in San Antonio TX) World War I veteran. He owned and operated Greisenbeck Kennels in San Antonio. Buried San Fernando Archdiocesan Cemetery, San Antonio TX.

Ed Gremminger—4 Years Infielder (b. 30 Mar 1874 Canton OH–d. 26 May 1942 Mercy Hospital, Canton OH) He worked for Canton Storage and Transfer Company until 1936 when he went to work for Hygenic Products Company in Canton. Died from a pulmonary embolism following prostate surgery. Buried Forest Hill Cemetery, Canton OH.

Buddy Gremp—3 Years Infielder (b. 5 Aug 1919 Denver CO–d. 30 Jan 1995 St Dominic's Hospital, Manteca CA) For 50 years he was a self-employed auctioneer for a livestock auction. Died from cardiopulmonary arrest. Buried Lakewood Memorial Park, Hughson CA.

Bill Grevell—1 Year Pitcher (b. 5 Mar 1898 Williamstown NJ–d. 21 Jun 1923 Philadelphia PA) Buried M E Church Cemetery, Williamstown NJ.

Bill Grey—5 Years Infielder (b. 15 Apr 1871 Philadelphia PA–d. 8 Dec 1932 Woman's College Hospital, Philadelphia PA) He worked 29 years for the City of Philadelphia and was the chief of one of the water bureau's high pressure stations for 20 years when he died suddenly from a self-inflicted gunshot wound. Buried Ivy Hill Cemetery, Philadelphia PA.

Reddy Grey—1 Year Outfielder (b. 8 Apr 1875 Zanesville OH–d. 8 Nov 1934 Altadena CA) For 12 years he was the business manager for a private estate. Died from heart disease. Buried Mountain View Cemetery, Altadena CA.

Hank Griffin—2 Years Pitcher (b. 11 Jul 1886 Whitehouse TX–d. 11 Feb 1950 Terrell TX) He was the postmaster at Elmo TX for many years. Buried Elmo Cemetery, Elmo TX.

Ivy Griffin—3 Years Infielder (b. 16 Jan 1896 Thomasville AL–d. 25 Aug 1957 Gainesville FL) Died in an automobile accident.

Marty Griffin—1 Year Pitcher (b. 5 Sep 1901 San Francisco CA–d. 19 Nov 1951 Los Angeles CA) He was a press operator at a rubber plant. Died from a heart attack. Buried All Souls Cemetery, Long Beach CA.

Mike Griffin—12 Years Outfielder 1 Year Manager (b. 20 Mar 1865 Utica NY–d. 10 Apr 1908 at his home in Utica NY) He engaged in the brewery business in Utica from 1898 until his death. Died from pneumonia. Buried St Agnes Cemetery, Utica NY.

Pat Griffin—1 Year Pitcher (b. 6 May 1893 Niles OH–d. 7 Jun 1927 City Hospital, Youngstown OH) He was sheet mill superintendent for Youngstown Sheet and Tube Company. Died from acute lobar pneumonia. Buried Calvary Cemetery, Youngstown OH.

Pug Griffin—2 Years Infielder (b. 24 Apr 1896 Lincoln NE–d. 12 Oct 1951 at a hospital in Colorado Springs CO) He managed and owned minor league teams and scouted for several major league teams until his death. Buried Calvary Cemetery, Lincoln NE.

Sandy Griffin—4 Years Outfielder 1 Year Manager (b. 19 Jul 1858 Fayetteville NY–d. 5 Jun 1926 Fayetteville NY).

Tom Griffin—1 Year Infielder (b. abt 1853 Titusville PA–d. 17 Apr 1933 Swedish-American Hospital, Rockford IL) He spent 35 years as a bridge building superintendent for the Chicago and Northwestern Railroad. Died after a prolonged period of ill health. Buried St Marys/St James Cemetery, Rockford IL.

Bert Griffith—3 Years Outfielder (b. 3 Mar 1896 St Louis MO–d. 5 May 1973 Northern Inyo Hospital, Bishop CA) Buried Big Pine Cemetery, Big Pine CA.

Calvin Griffith—(b. 11 Dec 1911 Montreal, Canada–d. 20 Oct 1999 in a nursing home in Melbourne FL) He owned the Washington Senators from 1955 to 1960, moving them to Minneapolis in 1961 where they became the Twins. He owned the Twins until 1984. Died from heart ailments and a kidney infection. Buried Fort Lincoln Cemetery, Brentwood MD.

Clark Griffith—21 Years Pitcher 20 Years Manager Hall of Fame (b. 20 Nov 1869 Stringtown MO–d. 27 Oct 1955 Washington DC) He was one of the founders of the American League and owned the Washington Senators from 1912 until his death. Buried Fort Lincoln Cemetery, Brentwood MD.

Tommy Griffith—13 Years Outfielder (b. 26 Oct 1889 Prospect OH–d. 13 Apr 1967 Jewish Hospital, Cincinnati OH) He worked the vaudeville circuit a couple of years before going into the radio and sporting goods business in Norwood OH and downtown Cincinnati. Afterward he was a clerk for the Hamilton County (OH) Common Pleas Court. Cremated.

Art Griggs—7 Years Infielder (b. 12 Dec 1884 Topeka KS–d. 19 Dec 1938 at his home in Los Angeles CA) He managed minor league teams and was a minor league executive and team owner. Died from Hodgkin's disease. Cremated.

Denver Grigsby—3 Years Outfielder (b. 24 Mar 1901 Hindman KY–d. 10 Nov 1973 Bartlett Memorial Hospital, Sapulpa OK) He operated the Skelly Service Station in Sapulpa for 35 years. Died after a lengthy illness. Buried South Heights Cemetery, Sapulpa OK.

Bob Grim—8 Years Pitcher (b. 8 Mar 1930 New York City NY–d. 23 Oct 1996 Shawnee Mission Medical Center, Shawnee KS) Served in the U.S. Marine Corps during the Korean War. Buried Maple Hill Cemetery, Kansas City KS.

John Grim—11 Years Catcher (b. 9 Aug 1867 Lebanon KY–d. 28 Jul 1961 at a nursing home in Indianapolis IN) He managed in the International League and coached basketball for a year at DePauw University. He then worked for the Indiana State Highway Department. Buried Crown Hill Cemetery, Indianapolis IN.

Burleigh Grimes—19 Years Pitcher 2 Years Manager Hall of Fame (b. 18 Aug 1893 Clear Lake WI–d. 6 Dec 1985 Clear Lake WI) The last legal spitball pitcher, he was a coach and scout until retiring in 1971. Died from cancer. Cremated. Buried Clear Lake Cemetery, Clear Lake WI.

Ed Grimes—2 Years Infielder (b. 8 Sep 1905 Chicago IL–d. 5 Oct 1974 Chicago IL) Buried Rose Hill Memorial Park, Tulsa OK.

John Grimes—1 Year Pitcher (b. 17 Apr 1869 Woodstock MD–d. 17 Jan 1964 at his home in San Francisco CA) Served 30 years in the U.S. Army, retiring with the rank of Captain. He saw action in the Sioux Indian campaign, Spanish-American War and World War I. Died from heart disease. Buried Golden Gate National Cemetery, San Bruno CA.

Oscar Grimes—9 Years Infielder (b. 13 Apr 1915 Minerva OH–d. 19 May 1993 Hanbidge Cemtre, Westlake OH) He was a millwright at Republic Steel in Cleveland OH from 1951 to 1958, and superintendent at a variety of apartment complexes in the western Cleveland suburbs from 1960 until his retirement in 1982. Died from cancer and complications of Alzheimer's disease. Buried Sunset Memorial Park, North Olmsted OH.

Ray Grimes—6 Years Infielder (b. 11 Sep 1893 Bergholz OH–d. 25 May 1953 Minerva OH) Died from a heart attack while at work at the Cronin China Company. Buried East Lawn Cemetery, Minerva OH.

Roy Grimes—1 Year Infielder (b. 11 Sep 1893 Bergholz OH–d. 13 Sep 1954 at his home in Hanoverton OH) He went into partnership with his brother as a paint contractor before operating a boat livery at Guilford Lake. Died from heart disease. Buried East Lawn Cemetery, Minerva OH.

Charlie Grimm—20 Years Infielder 19 Years Manager (b. 28 Aug 1898 St Louis MO–d. 15 Nov 1983 Scottsdale Memorial Hospital, Scottsdale AZ) He worked his entire life in baseball as a player, manager, owner and administrator. Died from cancer. Cremated and his ashes scattered over Wrigley Field.

Moose Grimshaw—3 Years Infielder (b. 30 Nov 1875 St Johnsville NY–d. 11 Dec 1936 at his home in Canajoharie NY) Playing baseball for 17 years, his career ended when he was hit in the head by a pitch. He then worked for the Beech-Nut Packing Company. Buried Fort Plain Cemetery, Fort Plain NY.

Ross Grimsley—1 Year Pitcher (b. 4 Jun 1922 Americus KS–d. 6 Feb 1994 at his home in Memphis TN) He worked in the maintenance department for DuPont. Died after a heart attack. Buried Woodhaven Cemetery, Millington TN.

Dan Griner—6 Years Pitcher (b. 7 Mar 1888 Centerville TN–d. 3 Jun 1950 Bishopville SC) Died from a heart attack. Buried Bethlehem Methodist Cemetery, Bishopville SC.

Lee Grissom—8 Years Pitcher (b. 23 Oct 1907 Sherman TX–d. 4 Oct 1998 at his home in Corning CA) Served in World War II. Died from heart failure and chronic obstructive pulmonary disease. Cremated. Buried Sunset Hill Cemetery, Corning CA.

Connie Grob—1 Year Pitcher (b. 9 Nov 1932 Cross Plains WI–d. 28 Sep 1997 at a hospital in Madison WI) Served two years in the U.S. Army during the Korean War. A respected businessman, he owned and operated Connie's Home Plate in Ashton WI. He loved the outdoors and hunting and fishing. Buried St Francis Xavier Cemetery, Cross Plains WI.

Heinie Groh—16 Years Infielder 1 Year Manager (b. 18 Sep 1889 Rochester NY–d. 22 Aug 1968 Drake Hospital, Cincinnati OH) He was a minor league team manager and owner and scouted for several teams, retiring in 1946. Buried Spring Grove Cemetery, Cincinnati OH.

Lew Groh—1 Year Infielder (b. 16 Oct 1883 Rochester NY–d. 20 Oct 1960 Municipal Hospital, Rochester NY) He worked at the Rochester Post Office. Died from cancer. Buried Mount Hope Cemetery, Rochester NY.

Bob Groom—10 Years Pitcher (b. 12 Sep 1884 Belleville IL–d. 19 Feb 1948 at his home in Belleville IL) He was a coal mine owner and operator. Died after an extended illness. Buried Walnut Hill Cemetery, Belleville IL.

George Grosart—1 Year Outfielder (b. 1879 Meadville PA–d. 18 Apr 1902 Passavant Hospital, Pittsburgh PA) Died at the height of his career from typhoid fever.

Emil Gross—5 Years Catcher (b. 1859 Chicago IL–d. 24 Aug 1921 Eagle River WI) Buried Graceland Cemetery, Chicago IL.

Turkey Gross—1 Year Infielder (b. 23 Feb 1896 Mesquite TX–d. 11 Jan 1936 St Paul Hospital, Dallas TX) World War I veteran. He managed minor league baseball before he owned and operated the Gross Pharmacy in Mesquite from 1928 until his death. Buried Mesquite Cemetery, Mesquite TX.

Ernie Groth—1 Year Pitcher (b. 24 Dec 1885 Cedarburg WI–d. 23 May 1950 at his home in Madison WI) He pitched in the Lake Shore League in Wisconsin from 1906 to 1916. Later he owned and operated a lime quarry in Cedarsburg. Died suddenly from a heart attack. Cremated.

Lefty Grove—17 Years Pitcher Hall of Fame (b. 6 Mar 1900 Lonaconing MD–d. 23 May 1975 Norwalk OH) Died from a heart attack. Buried Frostburg Memorial Park, Frostburg MD.

Orval Grove—10 Years Pitcher (b. 29 Aug 1919 Mineral KS–d. 20 Apr 1992 Mercy American River Hosp, Carmichael CA) For 25 years he owned and operated a car washing facility. Died from a heart attack but suffered from lymphoma. Buried Calvary Cemetery, Sacramento CA.

Charlie Grover—1 Year Pitcher (b. 20 Jun 1891 Vanceton OH–d. 24 May 1971 Kimball Med Care Facility, Battle Creek MI) He played professional baseball 21 years and was a steamfitter for Hunter-Prell Company, retiring in 1965. Died after being in poor health two years. Buried Floral Lawn Memorial Gardens, Battle Creek MI.

Roy Grover—3 Years Infielder (b. 17 Jan 1892 Snohomish WA–d. 7 Feb 1978 at his home in Milwaukie OR).

Harvey Grubb—1 Year Outfielder (b. 18 Sep 1890 Lexington NC–d. 25 Jan 1970 at a hospital in Corpus Christi TX) A retired employee of Aransas Compres, he had lived in Corpus Christi 15 years. Died after a long illness. Buried Oakwood Cemetery, Corsicana TX.

Tom Grubbs—1 Year Pitcher (b. 22 Feb 1894 Mount Sterling KY–d. 28 Jan 1986 V A Hospital, Lexington KY) Served in France for the U.S. Army during World War I. An attorney, he practiced law in Mount Sterling 50 years. He was appointed county judge by the governor in 1947, a position he held over 20 years. Died following a short illness. Cremated. Buried Machpelah Cemetery, Mount Sterling KY.

Frank Grube—7 Years Catcher (b. 7 Jan 1905 Easton PA–d. 2 Jul 1945 New York City NY) He was shot to death by a prowler outside his home. Buried Easton Cemetery, Easton PA.

Henry Gruber—5 Years Pitcher (b. 14 Dec 1864 New Haven CT–d. 26 Sep 1932 at his home in New Haven CT) Died suddenly. Buried St Bernard's Cemetery, West Haven CT.

John Gruber—(b. 22 Sep 1853 New Albany IN–d. 18 Dec 1932 at his home in Pittsburgh PA) A noted baseball historian, he was Pittsburgh's first sports editor, and for 39 years was the official scorer for the Pirates. Died from pneumonia. Buried North Side Catholic Cemetery, Pittsburgh PA.

Sig Gryska—2 Years Infielder (b. 4 Nov 1914 Chicago IL–d. 27 Aug 1994 Hines Memorial Hospital, Chicago IL) World War II veteran. Buried Resurrection Cemetery, Justice IL.

Marv Gudat—2 Years Outfielder (b. 27 Aug 1905 Goliad TX–d. 1 Mar 1954 at his home in Los Angeles CA) Died from complications of an infection that settled at the base of his brain, leaving him invalided the last two years of his life. Buried Meyersville Cemetery, Meyersville TX.

Mike Guerra—9 Years Catcher (b. 11 Nov 1912 Havana, Cuba–d. 9 Oct 1992 Miami Beach FL) Buried Flagler Memorial Park, Miami FL.

Whitey Guese—1 Year Pitcher (b. 24 Jan 1872 New Bremen OH–d. 8 Apr 1951 Auglaize County Home, Wapakoneta OH) Died following an illness of several months. Buried Wheeler Cemetery, Wapakoneta OH.

Ben Guiney—2 Years Catcher (b. 16 Nov 1858 Detroit MI–d. 5 Dec 1930 at his home in Detroit MI) He was purchasing agent and, later, secretary to the president for Kelsey Wheel and Manufacturing Company in Detroit. Active in local politics, he served on the Wayne County (MI) Board of Supervisors, was president of the Water Board and was a member of the Civil

Service Commission. Died following a month's illness. Buried Mount Elliott Cemetery, Detroit MI.

Witt Guise—1 Year Pitcher (b. 18 Sep 1908 Driggs AR–d. 13 Aug 1968 Little Rock AR) A member of the Arkansas National Guard, he worked for the Arkansas Military Department. Buried Little Rock National Cemetery, Little Rock AR.

Lou Guisto—5 Years Infielder (b. 16 Jan 1895 Napa CA–d. 15 Oct 1989 Queen of the Valley Hospital, Napa CA) World War I veteran. He managed some minor league baseball before becoming the baseball coach at St Mary's College, his alma mater. He later owned and operated the student book store there, retiring in 1964. Died from throat cancer. Buried Tulocay Cemetery, Napa CA.

Tom Gulley—3 Years Outfielder (b. 25 Dec 1899 Garner NC–d. 24 Nov 1966 St Charles AR) He was sheriff of Pulaski County, AR, for 12 years and tax collector for six years. He had been elected judge when he drowned, his car accidentally leaving a ferry and plunging into the White River. Buried Roselawn Memorial Park, Little Rock AR.

Ad Gumbert—9 Years Pitcher (b. 10 Oct 1867 Pittsburgh PA–d. 23 Apr 1925 West Penn Hospital, Pittsburgh PA) He was active in Pittsburgh political circles, holding several elected offices, including county sheriff and county commissioner. Died from a tumor on his brain. Buried Homewood Cemetery, Pittsburgh PA.

Billy Gumbert—3 Years Pitcher (b. 8 Aug 1865 Pittsburgh PA–d. 13 Apr 1946 at his home in Pittsburgh PA) Died from generalized arteriosclerosis. Buried Homewood Cemetery, Pittsburgh PA.

Harry Gumbert—15 Years Pitcher (b. 5 Nov 1909 Elizabeth PA–d. 4 Jan 1995 Wimberley TX).

Red Gunkel—1 Year Pitcher (b. 15 Apr 1894 Sheffield IL–d. 19 Apr 1954 Downey Veteran's Hospital, Chicago IL) World War I veteran. He was a general contractor in Sheffield. Buried Sheffield Cemetery, Sheffield IL.

Hy Gunning—1 Year Infielder (b. 6 Aug 1888 Maplewood NJ–d. 28 Mar 1975 V A Hospital, Togus ME) Served in the U.S. Army in World War I. He worked for the Wallace Candy Manufacturing Company in Brooklyn NY, and was president of the company when he retired in 1932, moving to Belgrade ME in 1938. Died following a long illness. Buried Maine Veteran's Memorial Cemetery, Augusta ME.

Tom Gunning—6 Years Catcher (b. 4 Mar 1862 Newmarket NH–d. 17 Mar 1931 at his home in Fall River MA) A medical doctor, he practiced medicine in Fall River from 1891 until his death, and was also the city physician and medical examiner. Died after ailing for a month. Buried North Burial Ground, Fall River MA.

Joe Gunson—4 Years Catcher (b. 23 Mar 1863 Philadelphia PA–d. 15 Nov 1942 at his home in Philadelphia PA) He is credited with inventing the catcher's protective mitt. A detective for many years, he was later a house sergeant for the Philadelphia Bureau of Police. Buried Northwood Cemetery, Philadelphia PA.

Ernie Gust—1 Year Infielder (b. 24 Jan 1888 Bay City MI–d. 26 Oct 1945 at his home in Maupin OR) He operated the Riverside Hotel in Maupin his last four years. Died from a cerebral hemorrhage following a ten-month illness. Buried Elm Lawn Park Cemetery, Bay City MI.

Frankie Gustine—12 Years Infielder (b. 20 Feb 1920 Hoopeston IL–d. 1 Apr 1991 St Luke's Hospital, Davenport IA) He was a partner in the Sheraton Hotel in Pittsburgh PA. Buried Resurrection Cemetery, Coraopolis PA.

Charlie Guth—1 Year Pitcher (b. 1856 Chicago IL–d. 5 Jul 1883 Cambridge MA).

Dick Gyselman—2 Years Infielder (b. 6 Apr 1908 San Francisco CA–d. 20 Sep 1990 Seattle WA) Cremated. Buried Acacia Cemetery, Seattle WA.

H

Bruno Haas—1 Year Pitcher (b. 5 May 1891 Worcester MA–d. 5 Jun 1952 at his home in Sarasota FL) An executive and owner at the minor league level, he founded the Northern League and owned the Winnipeg Blues. About 1932 he moved to Florida, working as a contractor and scouted for the Athletics. Died from injuries suffered when he fell off the roof of a house two months earlier. Buried Hope Cemetery, Worcester MA.

Mule Haas—12 Years Outfielder (b. 15 Oct 1903 Montclair NJ–d. 30 Jun 1974 New Orleans LA) Buried Immaculate Conception Cemetery, Montclair NJ.

Walter Haas, Jr—(b. 24 Jan 1916 San Francisco CA–d. 20 Sep 1995 at his home in San Francisco CA) The principal owner of Levi Strauss, he was the owner of the A's from 1980 to 1994. Died from prostate cancer. Buried Home of Peace Cemetery, San Francisco CA.

Bob Habenicht—2 Years Pitcher (b. 13 Feb 1926 St Louis MO–d. 24 Dec 1980 Richmond VA) A politically active lawyer, he served on the Richmond City Council from 1964 to 1968 and was vice-mayor of Richmond 1966 to 1968. He practiced law in Richmond and in St Louis MO before moving to Richmond. Buried Riverview Cemetery, Richmond VA.

Emil Haberer—3 Years Catcher (b. 2 Feb 1878 Cincinnati OH–d. 19 Oct 1951 at his home in Louisville KY) He was an executive and part-owner of Haberer and Company, the manufacturer of the Cino automobile, in Cincinnati, until the company shutdown in 1932. Buried Spring Grove Cemetery, Cincinnati OH.

Irv Hach—1 Year Infielder (b. 6 Jun 1873 Louisville KY–d. 13 Aug 1936 City Hospital, Louisville KY) He worked on a weed-cutting crew for the City of Louisville. Died from a fractured skull suffered when he fell off a truck he was riding to work on. Buried Cave Hill Cemetery, Louisville KY.

Stan Hack—16 Years Infielder 4 Years Manager (b. 6 Dec 1909 Sacramento CA–d. 15 Dec 1979 Franklin Grove Health Care Center, Dixon IL) He managed minor league baseball several years. After retiring from baseball in 1958 he opened a restaurant in Grand Detour IL. Buried Grand Detour Cemetery, Grand Detour IL.

Charlie Hackett—2 Years Manager (b. abt 1854 Lee MA–d. 1 Aug 1898 Holyoke MA) He worked as a printer for the Holyoke newspaper and was elected city messenger. Died after a long and protracted illness.

Jim Hackett—2 Years Infielder (b. 1 Oct 1877 Jacksonville IL–d. 28 Mar 1961 Douglas Community Hospital, Douglas MI) He ranched in Idaho for many years before moving to California. He moved to Douglas about 1954. Died following a short illness. Buried St Mary Cemetery, Evergreen Park IL.

Mert Hackett—5 Years Catcher (b. 11 Nov 1859 Cambridge MA–d. 22 Feb 1938 at his home in Cambridge MA) He was a patrolman for the Cambridge Police Department from 1893 until he retired in 1935 because of illness. Buried St Paul's Cemetery, Arlington MA.

Walter Hackett—2 Years Infielder (b. 15 Aug 1857 Cambridge MA–d. 2 Oct 1920 at his home in Cambridge MA) He worked 20 years in the proofroom of the *Boston Globe* newspaper, retiring in 1919.

Harvey Haddix—14 Years Pitcher (b. 18 Sep 1925 Medway OH–d. 8 Jan 1994 Community Hospital, Springfield OH) He pitched a perfect game for 12 innings, only to lose the game in the 13th inning. Served in Korea for the U.S. Army. He coached for 13 years. Died from emphysema. Buried Asbury Cemetery, North Hampton OH.

George Haddock—7 Years Pitcher (b. 25 Dec 1866 Portsmouth NH–d. 18 Apr 1926 Roxbury MA) He died suddenly. Buried Forest Hills Cemetery, Boston MA.

Bump Hadley—16 Years Pitcher (b. 5 Jul 1904 Lynn MA–d. 15 Feb 1963 Lynn Hospital, Lynn MA) He was a radio broadcaster for the Braves during the 1940s and in the 1950s was a color commentator for the Braves on TV. Later he was a salesman and a scout for the Yankees. Died from a heart attack. Buried Swampscott Cemetery, Swampscott MA.

Bill Haeffner—3 Years Catcher (b. 18 Jul 1894 Philadelphia PA–d. 27 Jan 1982 Harlee Manor Nursing Home, Springfield PA) Served in the U.S. Navy during World War I. He was a sales agent for Keystone Auto Club from 1938 until he retired in 1970. He also coached baseball at Haverford College from 1928 to 1937, at Drexel Institute from 1938 to 1947 and at LaSalle after that. Buried Mount Peace Cemetery, Philadelphia PA.

Mickey Haefner—8 Years Pitcher (b. 9 Oct 1912 Lenzburg IL–d. 3 Jan 1995 New Athens Home, New Athens IL) He was a laborer. Buried Oakridge Cemetery, New Athens IL.

Bud Hafey—3 Years Outfielder (b. 6 Aug 1912 Berkeley CA–d. 27 Jul 1986 U C Medical Center, Sacramento CA) For 17 years he was chief probation officer in Sierra County, CA, retiring in 1983. Died from a heart attack. Buried St Joseph Cemetery, San Pablo CA.

Chick Hafey—13 Years Outfielder Hall of Fame (b. 12 Feb 1903 Berkeley CA–d. 2 Jul 1973 Convalescent Hospital, Calistoga CA) He lived 35 years in the Calistoga area where he raised cattle and sheep. Died from congestive heart failure. Buried Holy Cross Cemetery, St Helena CA.

Tom Hafey—2 Years Outfielder (b. 12 Jul 1913 Berkeley CA–d. 2 Oct 1996 at his home in El Cerrito CA) For 13 years he was a consultant for Georgia Pacific Paper Company. Died from stomach cancer. Buried Sunset View Cemetery, El Cerrito CA.

Leo Hafford—1 Year Pitcher (b. 17 Sep 1883 Somerville MA–d. 2 Oct 1911 St Joseph's Cemetery, Willimantic CT) He had recently been engaged to coach the football team at Connecticut Agricultural College when he died from typhoid fever. Buried Holy Cross Cemetery, Malden MA.

Art Hagan—2 Years Pitcher (b. 17 Mar 1863 Providence RI–d. 25 Mar 1936 at his home in Providence RI) He was a grocer in Providence for many years, then was a funeral director there. Most recently he was associated with his brothers in the Park Brewing Co.

Casey Hageman—3 Years Pitcher (b. 12 May 1887 Mount Oliver PA–d. 1 Apr 1964 at his home in New Bedford PA) He owned and operated the Youngstown News Agency from 1915 until his retirement in 1956. Died from a heart ailment. Buried Calvary Cemetery, Grand Rapids MI.

Rip Hagerman—4 Years Pitcher (b. 20 Jun 1888 Linden KS–d. 30 Jan 1930 Albuquerque NM) Buried Mount Calvary Cemetery, Albuquerque NM.

Joe Hague—6 Years Infielder (b. 25 Apr 1944 Huntington WV–d. 5 Nov 1994 San Antonio TX) He entered the construction business and was vice-president of Garza Contracting Company when he died. He loved hunting and fishing. Died from cancer. Buried Sunset Memorial Park, San Antonio TX.

Dick Hahn—1 Year Catcher (b. 24 Jul 1916 Canton OH–d. 5 Nov 1992 Orlando FL) Served in the U.S. Navy during World War II. He owned the Island Store on Captiva Island. Buried Woodlawn Memorium, Orlando FL.

Ed Hahn—6 Years Outfielder (b. 27 Aug 1875 Nevada OH–d. 29 Nov 1941 Iowa Lutheran Hospital, Des Moines IA) Died from complications caused by stomach ulcers. Buried Pine Hill Cemetery, Des Moines IA.

Fred Hahn—1 Year Pitcher (b. 16 Feb 1929 Nyack NY–d. 16 Aug 1984 Valhalla NY).

Noodles Hahn—8 Years Pitcher (b. 29 Apr 1879 Nashville TN–d. 6 Feb 1960 at his home in Asheville NC) He was a veterinary inspector for the government in Cincinnati OH, moving to western North Carolina after retiring. Died following a long illness. Buried Forest Lawn Memorial Park, Enka NC.

Hal Haid—6 Years Pitcher (b. 21 Dec 1897 Barberton OH–d. 13 Aug 1952 Queen of Angels Hospital, Los Angeles CA) He worked in the Beverly Hills CA Post Office until shortly before his death. Died from a heart attack. Buried St Vincent's Cemetery, Latrobe PA.

Ed Haigh—1 Year Outfielder (b. 7 Feb 1867 Philadelphia PA–d. 13 Feb 1953 City Hospital, Atlantic City NJ) He died after a long illness. Buried Pleasantville Cemetery, Pleasantville NJ.

Hinkey Haines—1 Year Outfielder (b. 23 Dec 1898 Sharon Hill PA–d. 9 Jan 1979 Sharon Hill PA) Buried Middletown Cemetery, Middletown PA.

Jesse "Pop" Haines—19 Years Pitcher Hall of Fame (b. 22 Jul 1893 Clayton OH–d. 5 Aug

1978 Good Samaritan Hospital, Dayton OH) He was an auditor for Montgomery County, OH, from 1937 until retiring in 1965. Died following a long illness. Buried Bethel Cemetery, Phillipsburg OH.

Sammy Hairston—1 Year Catcher (b. 20 Jan 1920 Crawford MS–d. 31 Oct 1997 Forestdale Health Care Ctr, Birmingham AL) He played in the Negro Leagues and spent 53 years in professional baseball, 47 in the White Sox organization as a player, coach and scout. Died from heart failure. Buried Elmwood Cemetery, Birmingham AL.

Jim Haislip—1 Year Pitcher (b. 4 Aug 1891 Farmersville TX–d. 22 Jan 1970 Dallas TX) Buried Grove Hill Memorial Park, Dallas TX.

George Halas—1 Year Outfielder (b. 2 Feb 1895 Chicago IL–d. 31 Oct 1983 at his apartment in Chicago IL) Known better as player, coach and owner of the Chicago Bears, he was the founder of the Bears and one of the founding fathers of the National Football League. Died from heart disease and other multiple ailments. Buried St Adalbert Cemetery, Niles IL.

Ed Halbriter—1 Year Pitcher (b. 2 Feb 1860 Auburn NY–d. 9 Aug 1936 Los Angeles CA) He worked ten years in real estate sales, retiring in 1916. Died from prostate cancer. Buried Forest Lawn Memorial Park, Glendale CA.

John Haldeman—1 Year Infielder (b. 2 Dec 1855 Pewee Valley KY–d. 17 Sep 1899 at his home in Louisville KY) Died from cerebritis. Buried Cave Hill Cemetery, Louisville KY.

Dad Hale—1 Year Pitcher (b. 18 Feb 1879 Allegan MI–d. 1 Feb 1946 Allegan Health Center, Allegan MI) Buried Oakwood Cemetery, Allegan MI.

George Hale—4 Years Catcher (b. 3 Aug 1894 Dexter KS–d. 1 Nov 1945 at a hospital in Wichita KS) Died from a heart ailment. Buried Dexter KS.

Odell Hale—10 Years Infielder (b. 10 Aug 1908 Hosston LA–d. 9 Jun 1980 at a nursing home in El Dorado AR) Living at El Dorado most of his life, he worked for Monsanto Chemical Company. Died following a long illness. Buried Arlington Cemetery, El Dorado AR.

Sammy Hale—10 Years Infielder (b. 10 Sep 1896 Glen Rose TX–d. 6 Sep 1974 Parkview Hospital, Wheeler TX) An excellent golfer, he played professional golf and worked as a greenskeeper at a number of golf courses in Texas. Died after a long illness. Buried Wheeler Cemetery, Wheeler TX.

Ray Haley—3 Years Catcher (b. 23 Jan 1891 Danbury IA–d. 8 Oct 1973 Bradenton Hospital, Bradenton FL) World War I veteran. He played and managed minor league baseball until 1930. Buried Avon IL.

Tom Haley—1 Year Pitcher (b. 1853 Cranston RI–d. 8 Feb 1891 at the County Jail in Auburn ME) When he died he was serving a 30 day sentence for intoxication.

Al Hall—2 Years Outfielder (b. Worcester MA–d. 10 Feb 1885 Warren PA).

Bert Hall—1 Year Pitcher (b. 15 Oct 1888 Portland OR–d. 11 Sep 1948 Seattle WA) Died by hanging himself.

Bill Hall—3 Years Catcher (b. 30 Jul 1928 Moultrie GA–d. 1 Jan 1986 Colquitt Medical Center, Moultrie GA) He farmed in Colquitt County, GA. Died after an extended illness. Buried New Bethel Cemetery, Meigs GA.

Bill Hall—1 Year Pitcher (b. 22 Feb 1894 Charleston WV–d. 15 Aug 1947 Newport KY) World War I veteran. He was a carpenter for a Cincinnati construction company. Died from a heart attack while at work. Buried Dunbar Memorial Park, Dunbar WV.

Bob Hall—2 Years Outfielder (b. 20 Dec 1878 Baltimore MD–d. 1 Dec 1950 Wellesley MA) For 40 years he was an inspector for the Burroughs Adding Machine Company. Buried Forest Hills Cemetery, Boston MA.

Bob Hall—3 Years Pitcher (b. 22 Dec 1923 Swissvale PA–d. 12 Mar 1983 St Petersburg FL) He worked for Mills Construction Company and was killed when hit by a hit-and-run motorist while directing traffic around a construction site. Cremated and scattered.

Charley Hall—9 Years Pitcher (b. 27 Jul 1884 Ventura CA–d. 6 Dec 1943 County Hospital, Ventura CA) Died from heart disease. Buried Ivy Lawn Memorial Park, Ventura CA.

Charlie Hall—1 Year Outfielder (b. 24 Aug 1863 Toulon IL–d. 24 Jun 1921 Tacoma WA) For years he was the district surgeon for the Chicago, Milwaukee and St Paul Railway. Buried Toulon Municipal Cemetery, Toulon IL.

George Hall—2 Years Outfielder (b. 22 Jun 1849 England–d. 11 Jun 1923 Ridgewood NY) Buried Evergreen Cemetery, Brooklyn NY.

Herb Hall—1 Year Pitcher (b. 5 Jun 1893 Steelville IL–d. 1 Jul 1970 St Agnes Hospital, Fresno CA) He was a cotton broker in Fresno for 30 years before retiring in 1965. Died from a heart attack. Buried Belmont Memorial Park, Fresno CA.

John Hall—1 Year Pitcher (b. 9 Jan 1924 Muskogee OK–d. 17 Jan 1995 Midwest City OK) Served three years in the U.S. Coast Guard during World War II. A civil service worker, he retired after 30 years at Tinker Air Force Base. Buried Sunny Lane Cemetery, Oklahoma City OK.

Marc Hall—3 Years Pitcher (b. 12 Aug 1886 Joplin MO–d. 24 Feb 1915 at his father's home in Joplin MO) Died from Bright's disease at the height of his baseball career. Buried Diamond Cemetery, Diamond MO.

Russ Hall—2 Years Infielder (b. 29 Sep 1871 Shelbyville KY–d. 1 Jul 1937 at his home in Los Angeles CA) He was the secretary of the Association of Professional Baseball Players of America. Died from heart disease. Buried Inglewood Park Cemetery, Inglewood CA.

John Halla—1 Year Pitcher (b. 13 May 1884 St Louis MO–d. 30 Sep 1947 Standard Oil Hospital, El Segundo CA) He worked for the Standard Oil Company. Died from a heart attack. Buried Pacific Crest Cemetery, Redondo Beach CA.

Wild Bill Hallahan—12 Years Pitcher (b. 4 Aug 1902 Binghamton NY–d. 8 Jul 1981 Our Lady of Lourdes Hospital, Binghamton NY) He was the starting pitcher for the National League in the first All-Star Game in 1933. World War II veteran. Buried Calvary Cemetery, Johnson City NY.

Jack Hallett—6 Years Pitcher (b. 13 Nov 1913 Toledo OH–d. 11 Jun 1982 Medical College Hospital, Toledo OH) Served in the U.S. Navy during World War II. For 12 years he was sales manager for a Buick dealership before selling real estate his last six years. Buried United Church of Christ Cemetery, Holgate OH.

Newt Halliday—1 Year Infielder (b. 18 Jun 1896 Chicago IL–d. 6 Apr 1918 Great Lakes IL) He was serving in the U.S. Navy during World War I when he died from pneumonia. Buried St Joseph Cemetery, River Grove IL.

Jocko Halligan—3 Years Outfielder (b. 8 Dec 1867 Avon NY–d. 13 Feb 1945 Buffalo NY) He played baseball for Jersey City of the International League for 15 years. After his playing career was over he umpired and scouted. Buried Mount Olivet Cemetery, Buffalo NY.

Ed Hallinan—2 Years Infielder (b. 23 Aug 1888 San Francisco CA–d. 24 Aug 1940 Dante Sanitarium, San Francisco CA) World War I veteran. For 21 years he was a law clerk in the San Francisco County Clerk's office. Died from rectal cancer. Buried Holy Cross Catholic Cemetery, Colma CA.

Jimmy Hallinan—3 Years Infielder (b. 27 May 1849 Ireland–d. 28 Oct 1879 Chicago IL) Died at the height of his career from inflamation of the bowels. Buried Calvary Cemetery, Evanston IL.

Bill Hallman—14 Years Infielder 1 Year Manager (b. 30 Mar 1867 Pittsburgh PA–d. 11 Sep 1920 Philadelphia PA) He managed minor league baseball several years before becoming involved in the theatrical business in Philadelphia. Died from heart disease. Buried Holy Sepulchre Cemetery, Philadelphia PA.

Bill Hallman—4 Years Outfielder (b. 15 Mar 1876 Philadelphia PA–d. 23 Apr 1950 General Hospital, Philadelphia PA) Died after a long illness. Buried Mount Peace Cemetery, Philadelphia PA.

Charlie Hallstrom—1 Year Pitcher (b. 22 Jan 1864 Jonkaping, Sweden–d. 6 May 1949 Chicago IL) He operated his own tailoring shop in Chicago and was once elected alderman of his ward. Buried Chicago IL.

Jim Halpin—3 Years Infielder (b. 4 Oct 1863 England–d. 4 Jan 1893 Boston MA) Buried Mount Calvary Cemetery, Roslindale MA.

Al Halt—3 Years Infielder (b. 23 Nov 1890 Sandusky OH–d. 22 Jan 1973 Sandusky OH) He was a contractor. Buried Calvary Cemetery, Sandusky OH.

Doc Hamann—1 Year Pitcher (b. 21 Dec 1900 New Ulm MN–d. 11 Jan 1973 Milwaukee WI) He was a machinist. Buried Wisconsin Memorial Park, Brookfield WI.

Charlie Hamburg—1 Year Outfielder (b. 22

Nov 1863 Louisville KY–d. 18 May 1931 at his home in Union NJ) Died following a series of strokes. Buried Evergreen Cemetery, Hillside NJ.

Jim Hamby—2 Years Catcher (b. 29 Jul 1897 Wilkesboro NC–d. 21 Oct 1991 St John's Hospital, Springfield IL) Served in the U.S. Army during World War II. He drove a truck for Meadow Gold Dairy for many years before retiring. Buried Camp Butler National Cemetery, Springfield IL.

John Hamill—1 Year Pitcher (b. 18 Dec 1860 New York City NY–d. 6 Dec 1911 at his sister's home in Bristol RI) Well-known as an expert in rubber, he at one time was the proprietor of a small rubber company in Bristol. He worked for National India Rubber Company, a rubber factory in Liverpool, England, and Chicago Rubber Co in Racine WI. Died after a long illness. Buried North Burial Ground, Bristol RI.

Billy Hamilton—14 Years Outfielder Hall of Fame (b. 16 Feb 1866 Newark NJ–d. 15 Dec 1940 at his home in Worcester MA) He managed minor league baseball for a time, then went to work for Graton and Knight Company in 1915, retiring in 1935. Buried Eastwood Cemetery, Lancaster MA.

Earl Hamilton—14 Years Pitcher (b. 19 Jul 1891 Gibson City IL–d. 17 Nov 1968 Memorial Hospital, Anaheim CA) He was self-employed in the lumber business, retiring in 1956. Died from emphysema and pulmonary insufficiency. Buried Melrose Abbey Cemetery, Orange CA.

Tom Hamilton—2 Years Infielder (b. 29 Sep 1925 Altoona KS–d. 29 Nov 1973 Medical Center Hospital, Tyler TX) He was the athletic director and baseball coach at St Edwards University in Austin TX from 1961 until his death. Died after suffering a cerebral hemorrhage while officiating a high school football game. Buried Capitol Memorial Park, Austin TX.

Luke Hamlin—9 Years Pitcher (b. 3 Jul 1903 Terris Center MI–d. 18 Feb 1978 Clare Nursing Home, Clare MI) Buried East Lawn Memory Gardens, Okemos MI.

Jack Hammond—2 Years Infielder (b. 26 Feb 1891 Amsterdam NY–d. 4 Mar 1942 Kenosha WI) The athletic director at Colgate University during World War I, he moved to Kenosha in 1923 and became a prominently known chemist, working for the Simmons Company. Died after being ill only a short time. Cremated.

Granny Hamner—17 Years Infielder (b. 26 Apr 1927 Richmond VA–d. 12 Sep 1993 Fair Seasons Hotel, Philadelphia PA) He coached for the Phillies and managed minor league baseball. Died from a heart attack while in Philadelphia for a card show. Cremated.

Bert Hamric—2 Years Pinch Hitter (b. 1 Mar 1928 Clarksburg WV–d. 8 Aug 1984 at his home in Springboro OH) He worked 20 years for P H Glatfelter Paper Company in West Carrollton OH. Buried Springboro Cemetery, Springboro OH.

Fred Hancock—1 Year Infielder (b. 28 Mar 1920 Allenport PA–d. 12 Mar 1986 at his home in Clearwater FL) Served in the U.S. Army during World War II. He worked for Rochester Public Utilities in Rochester MN. Cremated.

Jim Handiboe—1 Year Pitcher (b. 19 Jul 1866 Columbus OH–d. 8 Nov 1942 at his home in Columbus OH) Died from chronic nephritis and heart disease. Buried St Joseph Cemetery, Lockbourne OH.

Mike Handiboe—1 Year Outfielder (b. 21 Jul 1887 Washington DC–d. 31 Jan 1953 Savannah GA) Buried Catholic Cemetery, Savannah GA.

Lee Handley—10 Years Infielder (b. 31 Jul 1913 Clarion IA–d. 8 Apr 1970 Presbyterian-University Hosp, Pittsburgh PA) Died following a brief illness. Buried Resurrection Cemetery, Coraopolis PA.

Harry Hanebrink—4 Years Infielder (b. 12 Nov 1927 St Louis MO–d. 9 Sep 1996 DePaul Health Center, Bridgeton MO) Served in the U.S. Navy during World War II. He was a real estate broker for about 20 years with Dolan Realtors in St Louis and a shuttle bus driver for QuickPark at Lambert Field from 1992 until his death. Died from an aneurysm. Buried Jefferson Barracks National Cemetery, St Louis MO.

Fred Haney—7 Years Infielder 10 Years Manager (b. 25 Apr 1898 Albuquerque NM–d. 9 Nov 1977 at his home in Beverly Hills CA) He worked his entire life in baseball as a manager and executive at both the minor league and major league levels. Died from a heart attack. Buried Holy Cross Cemetery, Culver City CA.

Charlie Hanford—2 Years Outfielder (b. 3

Jun 1882 Tunstall, England–d. 19 Jul 1963 St Francis Hospital, Trenton NJ) He retired as superintendent for Trenton Transit Co. Buried St Mary's Cemetery, Trenton NJ.

Pat Hanifin —1 Year Outfielder (b. 1873 Nova Scotia, Canada–d. 5 Nov 1908 at his sister's home in Springfield MA) Buried St Michael's Cemetery, Springfield MA.

Don Hankins —1 Year Pitcher (b. 9 Feb 1902 Pendleton IN–d. 16 May 1963 City Hospital, Winston-Salem NC) He worked for Wilson Products Company in Reading PA and Allied Safety Equipment Company in Houston TX. In 1942 he moved to Winston-Salem and opened West Hankins Realty Company at Fayetteville NC. Died after being in declining health for six months. Buried Forsyth Memorial Park, Winston-Salem NC.

Frank Hankinson —10 Years Infielder (b. 29 Apr 1856 New York City NY–d. 5 Apr 1911 Palisades Park NJ) Died from septic pneumonia and uremia. Buried Greenwood Cemetery, Brooklyn NY.

Jim Hanley —1 Year Pitcher (b. 13 Oct 1885 Providence RI–d. 1 May 1961 Long Island General Hospital, Elmhurst NJ) He retired in 1957 after working 35 years as a civil engineer for the New York City Transit Authority. Died after a month's illness. Buried St Francis Cemetery, Pawtucket RI.

Bill Hanlon —1 Year Infielder (b. 16 Mar 1865 Sacramento CA–d. 18 Mar 1951 Sutter Hospital, Sacramento CA) He owned a grocery store in Sacramento and a restaurant before going into the hotel business, owning or managing a number of hotels in the Sacramento area. In the 1920s he was the California State Boxing Commissioner. Died from bronchopneumonia and causes incident to age. Buried Masonic Lawn Cemetery, Sacramento CA.

Ned Hanlon —13 Years Outfielder 19 Years Manager Hall of Fame (b. 22 Aug 1857 Montville CT–d. 14 Apr 1937 at a daughter's home in Baltimore MD) Known as the "Father of Modern Baseball," he owned the minor league Baltimore Orioles and was a member of the Baltimore Park Board 21 years, and its president from 1931 until his death. Died from a heart attack suffered four days earlier. Buried New Cathedral Cemetery, Baltimore MD.

John Hanna —1 Year Catcher (b. 3 Nov 1863 Philadelphia PA–d. 7 Nov 1930 at his home in Philadelphia PA) He was an inspector for the Pennsylvania Bureau of Highways and the Bureau of Weights and Measures. When he died he was a tipstaff in the Quarter Sessions Court of Philadelphia. Died suddenly. Buried Cedar Hill Cemetery, Philadelphia PA.

Truck Hannah —3 Years Catcher (b. 5 Jun 1889 Larimore ND–d. 27 Apr 1982 Valley Conv Hosp, Huntington Beach CA) Died from a chronic urinary infection and heart disease. Cremated.

Jack Hannifin —3 Years Infielder (b. 25 Feb 1883 Northampton MA–d. 27 Oct 1945 Holyoke MA) Died following a short illness. Buried St Jerome Cemetery, Holyoke MA.

Loy Hanning —2 Years Pitcher (b. 18 Oct 1917 Bunker MO–d. 24 Jun 1986 St John's Mercy Hospital, Washington MO) Served in the U.S. Army during World War II. Buried Anaconda Cemetery, Anaconda MO.

Roy Hansen —1 Year Pitcher (b. 6 Mar 1898 Beloit WI–d. 9 Feb 1977 Beloit Memorial Hospital, Beloit WI) He worked for Fairbanks Morse. Buried Eastlawn Cemetery, Beloit WI.

Snipe Hansen —5 Years Pitcher (b. 21 Feb 1907 Chicago IL–d. 11 Sep 1978 Chicago IL) Buried Rosehill Cemetery, Chicago IL.

Don Hanski —2 Years Infielder (b. 27 Feb 1916 LaPorte IN–d. 2 Sep 1957 Worth IL) Buried Fairmount Willow Hills Park, Willow Springs IL.

Harry Hanson —1 Year Catcher (b. 17 Jan 1896 Elgin IL–d. 5 Oct 1966 Savannah GA) Served in the U.S. Army during both World Wars I and II. He retired after 37 years in the army. Died from a heart attack while golfing at Savannah Golf Club. Buried Bonaventure Cemetery, Savannah GA.

Ollie Hanson —1 Year Pitcher (b. 19 Jan 1896 Holbrook MA–d. 19 Aug 1951 at his home in Clifton NJ) Served in France for the U.S. Army during World War I.

Ed Hanyzewski —5 Years Pitcher (b. 18 Sep 1920 Union Mills IN–d. 8 Oct 1991 Dakota Hospital, Fargo ND) He retired in 1967 after 20 years with the South Bend IN Police Department. He then worked in security for the South

Bend Community School Corporation, retiring to Vergus MN in 1980. Buried St Joseph Cemetery, South Bend IN.

John Happenny—1 Year Infielder (b. 18 May 1901 Waltham MA–d. 29 Dec 1988 Coral Springs FL) He was an engineer and vice-president for Central Public Works of Illinois, retiring to Broward County, FL, in 1960. Died from heart disease. Buried Our Lady Queen of Heaven Cemetery, North Lauderdale FL.

Bill Harbridge—8 Years Outfielder (b. 29 Mar 1855 Philadelphia PA–d. 16 Mar 1924 at his home in Philadelphia PA) Buried Fernwood Cemetery, Fernwood PA.

Scott Hardesty—1 Year Infielder (b. 26 Jan 1870 Bellville OH–d. 29 Oct 1944 City Hospital, Fostoria OH) He was carpenter. Died from pathologic fracture of the lower left femur. Buried Bellville Cemetery, Bellville OH.

Pat Hardgrove—2 Games Pinch Hitter (b. 10 May 1895 Palmyra KS–d. 26 Jan 1973 University Medical Center, Jackson MS) He was a meat broker for Pioneer Beef. World War I veteran. Died from injuries suffered three days earlier in a one-car accident. Buried White Chapel Cemetery, Wichita KS.

Lew Hardie—4 Years Catcher (b. 24 Aug 1864 New York City NY–d. 5 Mar 1929 Oakland CA) He managed the baseball park in San Francisco. Died from pneumonia. Cremated.

Bud Hardin—1 Year Infielder (b. 14 Jun 1922 Shelby NC–d. 28 Jul 1997 Scripps Memorial Hospital, Encinitas CA) Served in the military. He was a grip for MGM Studios in Hollywood for 28 years. Died from an aortic embolism. Cremated. Buried Fort Rosecrans National Cemetery, Point Loma CA.

Jim Hardin—6 Years Pitcher (b. 6 Aug 1943 Morris Chapel TN–d. 9 Mar 1991 Key West FL) He was a salesman for Xerox Corporation in West Palm Beach FL. He and two others died when the plane he was piloting crashed shortly after takeoff from Key West International Airport. They were returning from a fishing trip off the keys. He was cremated and his ashes scattered over Boca Grande Bar, one of his favorite fishing spots.

Charlie Harding—1 Year Pitcher (b. 3 Jan 1891 Nashville TN–d. 30 Oct 1971 Dickson County Mem Hosp, Bold Springs TN) Buried Calvary Cemetery, Nashville TN.

Alex Hardy—2 Years Pitcher (b. 1877 Toronto, Ontario, Canada–d. 22 Apr 1940 Toronto, Ontario, Canada) He was connected with Gooderham and Worts for many years. While playing for Atlanta in the Southern League many years earlier, he contracted malaria in New Orleans, and always suffered from the effects. Buried Memorial Park Cemetery, Scarborough, Ontario, Can.

Harry Hardy—2 Years Pitcher (b. 5 Nov 1875 Steubenville OH–d. 4 Sep 1943 at his home in Steubenville OH) He worked 25 years in security for Wheeling Steel Corporation. Died from a heart attack. Buried Union Cemetery, Steubenville OH.

Jack Hardy—4 Years Catcher (b. 23 Jun 1878 Cleveland OH–d. 20 Oct 1921 Charity Hospital, Cleveland OH) He was in the real estate business. Died from chronic interstitial nephritis. Buried Lakewood Park Cemetery, Cleveland OH.

Bubbles Hargrave—12 Years Catcher (b. 15 Jul 1892 New Haven IN–d. 23 Feb 1969 Emerson A North Hospital, Cincinnati OH) He was a supervisor for the William Powell Valve Company. Buried Union Cemetery, Montgomery OH.

Pinky Hargrave—10 Years Catcher (b. 31 Jan 1896 New Haven IN–d. 3 Oct 1942 Fort Wayne IN) He played in the American Association and International League and worked for Fort Wayne City Utilities. He also assisted with the youth recreation program. Died from a heart attack while working on one of the city's ball fields. Buried Greenlawn Memorial Park, Fort Wayne IN.

Charlie Hargreaves—8 Years Catcher (b. 14 Dec 1896 Trenton NJ–d. 9 May 1979 Jersey Shore Medical Center, Neptune NJ) He worked for the New Jersey Racing Commission. He also managed some minor league baseball and scouted for the Pirates. Buried Riverside Cemetery, Lambertville NJ.

John Harkins—5 Years Pitcher (b. 12 Apr 1859 New Brunswick NJ–d. 18 Nov 1940 at his home in New Brunswick NJ) He was a retired court attendant. Died from a coronary thrombosis. Buried St Peter's Cemetery, New Brunswick NJ.

Specs Harkness—2 Years Pitcher (b. 13 Dec

1887 Los Angeles CA–d. 16 May 1952 Compton CA) He was a superintendent for a rock quarry. Died from a heart attack. Buried Calvary Cemetery, Los Angeles CA.

Dick Harley—7 Years Outfielder (b. 25 Sep 1872 Blue Bell PA–d. 3 Apr 1952 at his home in Philadelphia PA) He coached baseball at the University of Pittsburgh, Penn State and Villanova before going into the restaurant business with a brother. Buried Old Cathedral Cemetery, Philadelphia PA.

Dick Harley—1 Year Pitcher (b. 18 Aug 1874 Springfield OH–d. 16 May 1961 at his home in Springfield OH) He worked 40 years for Robbins and Myers, Inc, retiring in 1958. Died after being in failing health some time. Buried Ferncliff Cemetery, Springfield OH.

Bob Harmon—9 Years Pitcher (b. 15 Oct 1887 Liberal MO–d. 27 Nov 1961 at a hospital in Monroe LA) He engaged in the oil business around Homer LA until 1922. He then bought an 820 acre plantation near Monroe and opened Roselawn Dairy. He was a prominent dairyman for several years. Died unexpectedly. Buried Riverview Burial Park, Monroe LA.

Bill Harper—1 Year Pitcher (b. 14 Jun 1889 Bertrand MO–d. 17 Jun 1951 Armstrong Clinic, Somerville TN) He was the field service director for MidSouth Cotton Growers Association. Died without regaining consciousness following surgery. Buried Memorial Park Cemetery, Memphis TN.

George Harper—11 Years Outfielder (b. 24 Jun 1892 Arlington KY–d. 18 Aug 1978 Magnolia Hospital, Magnolia AR) He was inducted into the Arkansas Hall of Fame in 1970. Buried New Hope Cemetery, Magnolia AR.

George Harper—2 Years Pitcher (b. 17 Aug 1866 Milwaukee WI–d. 11 Dec 1931 Stockton CA) He operated a tailoring business in Stockton until retiring about 1921. Died after a brief illness brought on by a severe cold contracted a few days earlier. Buried Rural Cemetery, Stockton CA.

Harry Harper—10 Years Pitcher (b. 24 Apr 1895 Hackensack NJ–d. 23 Apr 1963 St Vincent's Hospital, New York City NY) He started a small trucking company during baseball off-seasons that grew into the Harper Terminal, Fuel and Supply Company, a major construction firm. Active in the Republican Party, he held several elected and appointed offices, both at the local and state level. Died after undergoing major surgery. Buried Hainesville Cemetery, Layton NJ.

Jack Harper—8 Years Pitcher (b. 2 Apr 1878 Franklin PA–d. 30 Sep 1950 General Hospital, Jamestown NY) He operated Rapid Transit Company in Jamestown until 1937 when he purchased a grill that he ran until 1945. Then, until his final illness, he operated a gas station and store in Jamestown. Buried Holy Cross Cemetery, Jamestown NY.

Jack Harper—1 Year Pitcher (b. 5 Aug 1893 Hendricks WV–d. 18 Jun 1927 Halstead KS).

Ray Harrell—6 Years Pitcher (b. 16 Feb 1912 Petrolia TX–d. 28 Jan 1984 Rapides General Hospital, Alexandria LA) He was a welder. Buried Byers Cemetery, Byers TX.

Slim Harrell—1 Year Pitcher (b. 31 Jul 1890 Grandview TX–d. 30 Apr 1971 Hillsboro TX) For more than 35 years he was a district manager in the Hillsboro area for Texas Power and Light Company. Died from a heart attack. Buried Grandview Cemetery, Grandview TX.

Will Harridge—Hall of Fame (b. 16 Oct 1885 Chicago IL–d. 9 Apr 1971 Presbyterian Home, Evanston IL) He was a passenger agent for the Wabash Railroad when he became Ban Johnson's private secretary. He went on to become American League president from 1931 to 1959. Died following gall bladder surgery. Buried Memorial Park Cemetery, Skokie IL.

Andy Harrington—1 Game Pinch-Hitter (b. 12 Feb 1903 Mountain View CA–d. 26 Jan 1979 at a hospital in Boise ID) For a brief time he managed in the minor leagues before driving a Greyhound bus, working for Sears-Roebuck and selling cars. Buried Morris Hill Cemetery, Boise ID.

Andy Harrington—1 Year Pitcher (b. 13 Nov 1888 Wakefield MA–d. 12 Nov 1938 Malden Hospital, Malden MA) Served in the U.S. Navy during World War I. An attorney, he was secretary of the Wakefield Municipal Light Board and for 15 years had been a lecturer on business law at Harvard University. Buried Mount Calvary Cemetery, Roslindale MA.

Jerry Harrington—4 Years Catcher (b. 12 Aug 1868 Hamden OH–d. 17 Apr 1913 at his home in Keokuk IA) He was a deputy marshall in

Keokuk. Died from a brain concussion suffered three weeks earlier in a fight outside a saloon. Buried Keokuk IA.

Joe Harrington—2 Years Infielder (b. 21 Dec 1869 Fall River MA–d. 13 Sep 1933 Fall River MA) Died after being in failing health for some time. Buried St Patrick's Cemetery, Fall River MA.

Ben Harris—2 Years Pitcher (b. 17 Dec 1889 Donelson TN–d. 29 Apr 1927 St Louis MO) Buried Mount Olivet Cemetery, Nashville TN.

Bill Harris—7 Years Pitcher (b. 23 Jun 1900 Wylie TX–d. 21 Aug 1965 at a hospital in Indian Trail NC) Associated with major league baseball for 36 years, he was a scout for the Giants, Yankees and Senators. Buried Sharon Memorial Park, Charlotte NC.

Bob Harris—4 Years Outfielder (b. 9 Jul 1916 Ames IA–d. 18 Dec 1976 West Palm Beach FL) Served in the U.S. Navy during World War II. He was a mail carrier. Died following a long illness. Buried Hillcrest Memorial Park, West Palm Beach FL.

Bob Harris—5 Years Pitcher (b. 1 May 1917 Gillette WY–d. 8 Aug 1989 North Platte NE) Served in the U.S. Navy during World War II. He managed minor league baseball seven years before becoming an insurance adjuster. Died from cancer. Buried Fort McPherson National Cemetery, Maxwell NE.

Bucky Harris—12 Years Infielder 29 Years Manager Hall of Fame (b. 8 Nov 1896 Port Jervis NY–d. 8 Nov 1977 Bethesda MD) He worked his entire life in baseball as a player, manager and executive. Died from Parkinson's disease. Buried Hughestown Cemetery, Hughestown PA.

Charlie Harris—1 Year Infielder (b. 21 Oct 1877 Macon GA–d. 14 Mar 1963 Alachua General Hospital, Gainesville FL) Died after a brief illness. Buried Evergreen Cemetery, Gainesville FL.

Dave Harris—7 Years Outfielder (b. 27 Jul 1900 Summerville NC–d. 18 Sep 1973 Atlanta GA) He was a patrolman for the Atlanta Police Department for 26 years. Buried Resthaven Garden of Memories, Decatur GA.

Frank Harris—1 Year Infielder (b. 2 Nov 1858 Pittsburgh PA–d. 26 Nov 1939 State Hospital, East Moline IL) Convicted of murdering his wife in 1895 he was sentenced to hang, but his sentence was commuted by the Governor. Released in 1911, he lived at Freeport IL where he was in the tailoring and furrier business. Buried County Home Cemetery, Freeport IL.

Herb Harris—1 Year Pitcher (b. 24 Apr 1913 Chicago IL–d. 18 Jan 1991 Crystal Lake IL).

Joe Harris—10 Years Infielder (b. 20 May 1891 Coulters PA–d. 10 Dec 1959 at his home in Renton PA) Died after a lingering illness. Buried Sunset Hill Memorial Gardens, Cranberry PA.

Joe Harris—3 Years Pitcher (b. 1 Feb 1882 Melrose MA–d. 12 Apr 1966 Melrose-Wakefield Hospital, Melrose MA) He worked for the Melrose Fire Department from 1903 until retiring as 1939. After 1939 he operated a taxi business in Melrose. Died after a lingering illness. Buried Wyoming Cemetery, Melrose MA.

Lum Harris—6 Years Pitcher 8 Years Manager (b. 17 Jan 1915 New Castle AL–d. 11 Nov 1996 Pell City AL) Worked his entire life in baseball as a player, coach, manager and minor league manager. Died from diabetes. Buried Elmwood Cemetery, Birmingham AL.

Mickey Harris—9 Years Pitcher (b. 30 Jan 1917 New York City NY–d. 15 Apr 1971 Farmington MI) Served four years in the U.S. Army Air Force during World War II. He worked in maintenance for Alexander Hamilton Insurance Company in Farmington Hills MI. Died at a bowling alley from a heart attack. Buried Holy Sepulchre Cemetery, Southfield MI.

Spence Harris—4 Years Outfielder (b. 12 Aug 1900 Duluth MN–d. 3 Jul 1982 University Hospital, Minneapolis MN) From 1921 until 1948 he played minor league baseball, compiling a lifetime .318 minor league batting average. After retiring from baseball he worked in a clothing store. Buried Lakewood Cemetery, Minneapolis MN.

Vic Harris—19 Years Outfielder 10 Years Manager (b. 10 Jun 1917 Pensacola FL–d. 23 Feb 1978 Holy Cross Hospital, Mission Hills CA) He played in the negro leagues and was a custodian at a public school in Castaic CA for 12 years. Died from pancreatic cancer. Buried Eternal Valley Memorial Park, Newhall CA.

Slim Harriss—9 Years Pitcher (b. 11 Dec 1896 Brownwood TX–d. 19 Sep 1963 at a hospital in Temple TX) He lived in Brown County, TX, his entire life and was a Brown County commissioner from 1946 to 1958. Died after a lengthy illness. Buried Bangs Cemetery, Bangs TX.

Earl Harrist—5 Years Pitcher (b. 20 Aug 1919 Dubach LA–d. 1 Sep 1998 Simsboro LA).

Oscar Harstad—1 Year Pitcher (b. 24 May 1892 Parkland WA–d. 14 Nov 1985 Corvallis OR) He practiced denistry for more than 50 years in Eastern Oregon. Buried Oaklawn Cemetery, Corvallis OR.

Bill Hart—8 Years Pitcher (b. 19 Jul 1865 Louisville KY–d. 19 Sep 1936 Cincinnati OH) He played and umpired in baseball 32 years, four years as a National League umpire and one as an American League umpire. Later he was an electrotyper. Died from a heart attack. Buried Rest Haven Memorial Park, Cincinnati OH.

Bill Hart—3 Years Infielder (b. 4 Mar 1913 Wiconisco PA–d. 29 Jul 1968 Holy Spirit Hospital, Lykens PA) He worked for the Reifs and Nestor Company of Lykens. Buried Wiconisco Cemetery, Wiconisco PA.

Hub Hart—3 Years Catcher (b. 2 Feb 1878 Everett MA–d. 10 Oct 1960 at his home in Fort Wayne IN) He owned a grill and billiard hall in Fort Wayne for several years. Died from a heart attack. Buried Greenlawn Memorial Park, Fort Wayne IN.

Jim Hart—1 Year Infielder (b. 28 Jun 1870 Brown County MN–d. 29 Jan 1921 Sacramento CA) He was a chauffeur for a transfer and storage company. Died from a heart attack. Buried Auburn WA.

Jim Hart—3 Years Manager (b. 10 Jul 1855 Fairview PA–d. 18 Jul 1919 at his home in Chicago IL) After following mercantile pursuits he was involved in baseball administration for 25 years. Owned the Cubs until 1905. Died from organic heart disease. Cremated. Buried Girard Cemetery, Girard PA.

Tom Hart—1 Year Catcher (b. 15 Jun 1869 Canaan NY–d. 17 Sep 1939 at a hospital in Gardner MA) Died after a short illness. Buried St Bernard's Church Cemetery, Fitchburg MA.

Frank Harter—3 Years Pitcher (b. 19 Sep 1886 Keyesport IL–d. 14 Apr 1959 St John's Hospital, Breese IL) He was a lifelong resident of Keyesport. Buried Kendree Chapel Cemetery, Keyesport IL.

Bruce Hartford—1 Year Infielder (b. 4 May 1892 Chicago IL–d. 25 May 1975 Martin Luther King Hospital, Los Angeles CA) Died from a heart attack. Cremated and his ashes scattered at sea.

Chris Hartje—1 Year Catcher (b. 25 Mar 1915 San Francisco CA–d. 26 Jun 1946 50 miles east of Seattle WA) Died at the height of his career from injuries suffered when the team bus he was riding crashed into a deep ravine in the Cascade Mountains, killing him and eight other team members. Buried Golden Gate National Cemetery, San Bruno CA.

Chick Hartley—1 Year Outfielder (b. 22 Aug 1880 Philadelphia PA–d. 18 Jul 1948 Temple University Hospital, Philadelphia PA) He was a police inspector for the Philadelphia Police Department. Buried Cathedral Cemetery, Wilmington DE.

Grover Hartley—14 Years Catcher (b. 2 Jul 1888 Osgood IN–d. 19 Oct 1964 at a nursing home in Daytona Beach FL) He managed minor league baseball and lived at Daytona Beach from 1948 until his death. Cremated.

Charlie Hartman—1 Year Pitcher (b. 10 Aug 1888 Los Angeles CA–d. 22 Oct 1960 at his home in Los Angeles CA) He was a purchasing agent for a bakery equipment manufacturer for 28 years. Died from a heart attack. Buried Inglewood Park Cemetery, Inglewood CA.

Fred Hartman—6 Years Infielder (b. 25 Apr 1868 Pittsburgh PA–d. 11 Nov 1938 McKeesport PA).

Gabby Hartnett—20 Years Catcher 3 Years Manager Hall of Fame (b. 20 Dec 1900 Woonsocket RI–d. 20 Dec 1972 Lutheran General Hospital, Park Ridge IL) He owned a bowling alley and sporting goods store in Lincolnwood IL for many years. An excellent golfer and bowler, he bowled in a number of Chicago's major bowling leagues. Died from liver and kidney ailments. Buried All Saints Cemetery, Des Plaines IL.

Pat Hartnett—1 Year Infielder (b. 20 Oct 1863 Boston MA–d. 10 Apr 1935 Boston MA).

Ray Hartranft—1 Year Pitcher (b. 19 Sep 1890 Quakertown PA–d. 10 Feb 1955 at his daughter's home in Spring City PA) Buried Fernwood Cemetery, Royersford PA.

Topsy Hartsel—14 Years Outfielder (b. 25 Jun 1874 Polk OH–d. 14 Oct 1944 City Hospital, Toledo OH) He worked for the Community Traction Company in Toledo for years. Died from diabetes mellitus. Cremated. Buried Woodlawn Cemetery, Toledo OH.

Roy Hartzell—11 Years Outfielder (b. 6 Jul 1881 Golden CO–d. 6 Nov 1961 at his home in Golden CO) He was a safety officer for Standard Oil of Indiana at Denver CO, Casper WY and Chicago IL before retiring in 1946. Died following a heart attack. Buried Golden Cemetery, Golden CO.

Luther Harvel—1 Year Outfielder (b. 30 Sep 1905 Cambria IL–d. 10 Apr 1986 Research Medical Hospital, Kansas City MO) He played professional baseball for 14 years and scouted for the A's and the Tigers for 15 years, retiring in 1975. Buried Mount Olivet Cemetery, Kansas City MO.

Erwin Harvey—3 Years Outfielder (b. 5 Jan 1879 Saratoga CA–d. 3 Jun 1954 Riviera Convalescent Hosp, Santa Monica CA) He was a writer. Cremated.

Ziggy Hasbrook—2 Years Infielder (b. 21 Nov 1893 Grundy Center IA–d. 9 Feb 1976 at a hospital in Garland TX) He was a sales engineer for A Y McDonald Manufacturing Company until 1953. Buried Restland Memorial Park, Dallas TX.

Pete Hasney—1 Year Outfielder (b. 26 May 1865 England–d. 24 May 1908 Philadelphia PA) Buried New Cathedral Cemetery, Philadelphia PA.

Bill Hassamaer—3 Years Outfielder (b. 26 Jul 1864 St Louis MO–d. 25 May 1910 St Louis MO) Died from locomotor ataxia. Buried St Louis MO.

Buddy Hassett—7 Years Infielder (b. 5 Sep 1911 New York City NY–d. 23 Aug 1997 Pascack Valley Hospital, Westwood NJ) Served on an aircraft carrier for the U.S. Navy during World War II. For 40 years he was a salesman for Eastern Freightways in Carlstadt NJ. Later he was a consultant for Metropolitan Trucking Company in Fairview NJ. Buried Garden of Memories, Washington NJ.

Joe Hassler—3 Years Infielder (b. 7 Apr 1905 Fort Smith AR–d. 4 Sep 1971 at a hospital in Duncan OK) He worked 35 years for Halliburton Services in Duncan and was maintenance superintendent for them when he retired in 1970. Died following a short illness. Buried Duncan Cemetery, Duncan OK.

Charlie Hastings—4 Years Pitcher (b. 11 Nov 1870 Ironton OH–d. 3 Aug 1934 at his home in Parkersburg WV) He umpired several years in the minor leagues before working six years as a toll collector on the Parkersburg-Belpre Bridge. Died following an illness of four weeks. Buried Odd Fellows Cemetery, Parkersburg WV.

Scott Hastings—2 Years Outfielder 1 Year Manager (b. 10 Aug 1846 Hillsboro OH–d. 14 Aug 1907 Soldier's Home Hospital, Los Angeles CA) Served in the GAR during the Civil War. He was a boxmaker. Died from stomach cancer. Buried Los Angeles National Cemetery, Los Angeles CA.

Bob Hasty—6 Years Pitcher (b. 3 May 1896 Canton GA–d. 28 May 1972 at his home in Dallas GA) World War I veteran. He was a retired employee of Lockheed-Georgia Company. Died from a heart attack. Buried Marietta City Cemetery, Marietta GA.

Fred Hatfield—9 Years Infielder (b. 18 Mar 1925 Lanette AL–d. 22 May 1998 at his home in Tallahassee FL) He coached baseball at Florida State University from 1964 to 1969, managed minor league baseball and was a coach or scout for several teams. Bedridden his last six months, he died after a year-long battle with cancer. Buried Meadowwood Memorial Park, Tallahassee FL.

Gil Hatfield—8 Years Infielder (b. 27 Jan 1855 Hoboken NJ–d. 26 May 1921 at his brother-in-law's office, Hoboken NJ) He was a bank teller at Hudson Trust Company in Hoboken. Died from a heart attack. Buried Fairview Cemetery, Fairview NJ.

John Hatfield—1 Year Infielder (b. 20 Jul 1847 NJ–d. 20 Feb 1909 at his home in Long Island City NY) Died from heart failure. Buried Mount Olivet Cemetery, Maspeth NY.

Joe Hatten—7 Years Pitcher (b. 7 Nov 1916 Bancroft IA–d. 16 Dec 1988 Redding Medical Center, Redding CA) World War II veteran. Died from prostate cancer. Buried Inwood/Ogburn Cemetery, Shingletown CA.

Clyde Hatter—2 Years Pitcher (b. 7 Aug 1908 Poplar Hill KY–d. 17 Oct 1937 Yosemite KY).

Art Haugher—1 Year Outfielder (b. 18 Nov 1896 Delhi OH–d. 2 Aug 1944 at his home in Redwood City CA) Served in the Coast Guard Reserve during World War II. He worked for Western Pipe and Steel in South San Francisco CA while working part time as a scout for the White Sox. Died from a heart attack. Buried Oakmont Cemetery, Waynesburg PA.

Phil Haugstad—4 Years Pitcher (b. 23 Feb 1924 Black River Falls WI–d. 21 Oct 1998 Black River Mem Hosp, Black River Falls WI) Served as an airplane mechanic for the U.S. Army Air Corps during World War II. He owned and operated a logging and pulping business from 1955 until retiring in 1991. Buried Riverside Cemetery, Black River Falls WI.

Arnold Hauser—5 Years Infielder (b. 25 Sep 1888 Chicago IL–d. 22 May 1966 Aurora IL).

Joe Hauser—6 Years Infielder (b. 12 Jan 1899 Milwaukee WI–d. 11 Jul 1997 Sheboygan Retirement Home, Sheboygan WI) He played minor league baseball from 1918 until 1942, hitting 399 minor league home runs, and managed in the minor leagues until 1958. He owned and operated Hauser's Sporting Goods Store in Sheboygan from 1937 until retiring in 1984. Buried Calvary Cemetery, Sheboygan WI.

Clem Hausmann—3 Years Pitcher (b. 17 Aug 1919 Houston TX–d. 29 Aug 1972 Baytown TX) He worked for Enjay Chemical Company. Buried Memory Gardens, Baytown TX.

Charlie Hautz—1 Year Infielder (b. 5 Feb 1852 St Louis MO–d. 24 Jan 1929 St Louis MO) Buried SS Peter and Paul Cemetery, St Louis MO.

Bill Hawes—2 Years Outfielder (b. 24 Nov 1853 Nashua NH–d. 16 Jun 1940 at his home in Lowell MA) He conducted a business in Lowell for 50 years and at one time served as a member of the Board of Cemetery Commissioners. Buried Edson Cemetery, Lowell MA.

Ed Hawk—1 Year Pitcher (b. 11 May 1890 Neosho MO–d. 26 Mar 1936 at his home in Neosho MO) His baseball career ended abruptly when he fell from the fourth story of a hotel in Detroit MI, breaking a leg and suffering internal injuries. He played and managed minor league and semi-pro ball after that. For years he operated a small community grocery store in Neosho, and was known as an expert house painter and decorator. Buried Gibson Cemetery, Neosho MO.

Bill Hawke—3 Years Pitcher (b. 28 Apr 1870 Wilmington DE–d. 12 Dec 1902 Wilmington DE) Died from cancer. Buried Wilmington-Brandywine Cemetery, Wilmington DE.

Thorny Hawkes—2 Years Infielder (b. 15 Oct 1852 Danvers MA–d. 3 Feb 1929 at his home in Danvers MA) He owned and operated a drug store in Danvers. Died after being ill during the last year or two.

Chicken Hawks—2 Years Infielder (b. 3 Feb 1896 San Francisco CA–d. 26 May 1973 Kaiser Hospital, San Rafael CA) He was a ship's clerk for the Pacific Maritime Assn for 15 years. Died from respiratory failure caused by emphysema. Cremated. Buried Cypress Lawn Memorial Park, Colma CA.

Pink Hawley—10 Years Pitcher (b. 5 Dec 1872 Beaver Dam WI–d. 19 Sep 1938 at his home in Beaver Dam WI) He managed a bowling alley in Beaver Dam. Died after suffering failing health for several years. Buried Oakwood Cemetery, Beaver Dam WI.

Scott Hawley—1 Year Pitcher (b. Painesville OH–d. 28 Apr 1904 Alliance OH).

Howie Haworth—1 Year Catcher (b. 27 Aug 1893 Newburg OR–d. 28 Jan 1953 at a sanitarium in Troutdale OR) Died after a long illness. Buried Willamette National Cemetery, Portland OR.

Jack Hayden—3 Years Outfielder (b. 21 Oct 1880 Bryn Mawr PA–d. 3 Aug 1942 at his home in Haverford PA) He was a meat and provision dealer in Philadelphia PA. Buried St Dennis Church Cemetery, Havertown PA.

Frankie Hayes—14 Years Catcher (b. 13 Oct 1914 Jamesburg NJ–d. 22 Jun 1955 Point Pleasant Hospital, Point Pleasant NJ) He was a partner in a sporting goods store at Point Pleasant Beach from 1948 to 1954. Died from acute peritonitis. Buried Fernwood Cemetery, Jamesburg NJ.

Jackie Hayes—14 Years Infielder (b. 19 Jul 1906 Clanton AL–d. 9 Feb 1983 Birmingham AL) Buried Clanton Cemetery, Clanton AL.

Jim Hayes—1 Year Pitcher (b. 25 Feb 1912 Montevallo AL–d. 27 Nov 1993 Decatur GA) Buried Fairview Memorial Gardens, Stockbridge GA.

Joe Haynes—14 Years Pitcher (b. 21 Sep 1917 Lincolnton GA–d. 7 Jan 1967 at his home in Hopkins MN) He was an executive vice-president for the Minnesota Twins. Died from a heart attack. Buried Fort Lincoln Cemetery, Brentwood MD.

Bob Hazle—3 Years Outfielder (b. 9 Dec 1930 Laurens SC–d. 25 Apr 1992 Columbia SC) He worked for Ben Arnold Company in Columbia. Buried Crescent Hill Memorial Gardens, Columbia SC.

Doc Hazleton—1 Year Infielder (b. 28 Aug 1876 Strafford VT–d. 10 Mar 1941 Burlington VT) He coached baseball at the University of Vermont and Dartmouth College. Buried Lakeview Cemetery, Burlington VT.

Ed Head—5 Years Pitcher (b. 25 Jan 1918 Selma LA–d. 31 Jan 1980 Morehouse General Hospital, Bastrop LA) Served in the U.S. Army during World War II. He worked 25 years for International Paper Company. Died following a brief illness. Buried Sardis Cemetery, West Monroe LA.

Ralph Head—1 Year Pitcher (b. 30 Aug 1893 Tallapoosa GA–d. 8 Oct 1962 Muscadine AL) Buried Hollywood Cemetery, Tallapoosa GA.

Tom Healey—1 Year Pitcher (b. 1853 Cranston RI–d. 6 Feb 1891 Lewiston ME).

Egyptian Healy—8 Years Pitcher (b. 27 Oct 1866 Cairo IL–d. 16 Mar 1899 St Louis MO) He was a police officer for the St Louis Police Department. Buried Calvary Cemetery, St Louis MO.

Tom Healy—2 Years Infielder (b. 30 Oct 1895 Altoona PA–d. 15 Jan 1974 Lakewood Hospital, Cleveland OH) Served in the U.S. Army during World War I. He practiced denistry in Cleveland from 1920 until retiring in 1961. He was also head of oral surgery at St John's Hospital there and was supervisor of mouth hygiene in the Cleveland school district until 1966. Buried Calvary Cemetery, Cleveland OH.

Charlie Heard—1 Year Outfielder (b. 30 Jan 1872 Philadelphia PA–d. 20 Feb 1945 at his home in Philadelphia PA) He umpired minor league baseball for a number of years. Then he was a clerk in the Recorder of Deeds office before spending 25 years as a real estate assessor.

Bunny Hearn—4 Years Pitcher (b. 13 Jan 1904 Brooklyn NY–d. 31 Mar 1974 Venice FL) He was a collector for the Union Gas Company of Brooklyn, retiring to Venice in 1969. Buried Gulf Pines Memorial Park, Englewood FL.

Bunny Hearn—6 Years Pitcher (b. 21 May 1891 Chapel Hill NC–d. 10 Oct 1959 at his home in Wilson NC) He coached baseball at the University of North Carolina for 32 years. He suffered a stroke in 1947, but stayed as coach until he retired in 1956. Buried Maplewood Cemetery, Wilson NC.

Ed Hearn—1 Year Infielder (b. 17 Sep 1888 Ventura CA–d. 8 Sep 1952 V A Hospital, Los Angeles CA) World War I veteran. He was a guard at the V A complex in Los Angeles. Buried Los Angeles National Cemetery, Los Angeles CA.

Jim Hearn—13 Years Pitcher (b. 11 Apr 1921 Atlanta GA–d. 10 Jun 1998 Boca Grande FL) Served in the U.S. Army during World War II. Cremated.

Hugh Hearne—3 Years Catcher (b. 18 Apr 1873 Troy NY–d. 22 Sep 1932 at his home in Troy NY) Died after being ill about a month. Buried St Mary's Cemetery, Troy NY.

Jeff Heath—14 Years Outfielder (b. 1 Apr 1915 Fort William, Ontario, Canada–d. 9 Dec 1975 at his home in Seattle WA) He was the color commentator for telecasts of the Seattle Rainiers team in the Pacific Coast League. Died from a heart attack. Buried Lake View Cemetery, Seattle WA.

Mickey Heath—2 Years Infielder (b. 30 Oct 1904 Toledo OH–d. 30 Jul 1986 Dallas TX).

Spencer Heath—1 Year Pitcher (b. 5 Nov 1895 Chicago IL–d. 25 Jan 1930 Chicago IL) Buried St Boniface Cemetery, Chicago IL.

Tommy Heath—3 Years Catcher (b. 18 Aug 1913 Akron CO–d. 26 Feb 1967 Comunnity Hospital, Los Gatos CA) He worked in baseball his entire life as a player, scout and minor league manager. Died from complications after gall bladder surgery 11 days earlier. Buried Sunset Hills Memorial Gardens, Portland OR.

Cliff Heathcote—15 Years Outfielder (b. 24 Jan 1898 Glen Rock PA–d. 19 Jan 1939 at his home in York PA) Traded between games of a doubleheader, he played for two teams on the same day. After retiring from baseball he spent his time hunting and fishing in the summer and bowling in the winter. Died from a pulmonary embolism. Buried Mount Carmel Cemetery, Littlestown PA.

Mike Hechinger—2 Years Catcher (b. 14 Feb 1890 Chicago IL–d. 13 Aug 1967 Chicago IL) Buried St Boniface Cemetery, Chicago IL.

Guy Hecker—9 Years Pitcher 1 Year Manager (b. 3 Apr 1856 Youngville PA–d. 3 Dec 1938 at his home in Wooster OH) He was a lease adjuster for Ohio Fuel Gas Company. He had been in declining health since he was in an automobile accident in 1931, but died from chronic nephritis. Buried Wooster Cemetery, Wooster OH.

Harry Hedgepath—1 Year Pitcher (b. 4 Sep 1888 Fayetteville NC–d. 30 Jul 1966 Richmond VA) Buried Westhampton Memorial Park, Richmond VA.

Don Heffner—11 Years Infielder 1 Year Manager (b. 8 Feb 1911 Rouzerville PA–d. 1 Aug 1989 Huntington Memorial Hospital, Pasadena CA) He worked in baseball 40 years as a player, coach and manager. Died from pneumonia and a heart attack. Cremated. Buried Mountain View Cemetery, Altadena CA.

Jim Hegan—17 Years Catcher (b. 3 Aug 1920 Lynn MA–d. 17 Jun 1984 at his home in Swampscott MA) Served in the U.S. Coast Guard during World War II. He coached for the Yankees and Tigers and scouted for the Yankees. Died from a heart attack shortly after giving an interview to a newspaperman.

Jake Hehl—1 Year Pitcher (b. 8 Dec 1899 Brooklyn NY–d. 4 Jul 1961 Brooklyn NY).

Emmet Heidrick—8 Years Outfielder (b. 9 Jul 1876 Queenstown PA–d. 20 Jan 1916 Clarion PA) An entrepreneuer in the Clarion area, he had interests in railroads, coal, timber, manufacturing and communications, and was a stockholder and executive in several companies. Died suddenly from grippe and pneumonia. Buried Clarion Cemetery, Clarion PA.

Louie Heilbroner—1 Year Manager (b. 4 Jul 1861 Fort Wayne IN–d. 21 Dec 1933 Fort Wayne IN) He published an annual *Baseball Bluebook* that contained information on players, contracts, trades and statistics from 1910 until his death. Died from a heart attack. Buried Lindenwood Cemetery, Fort Wayne IN.

Chink Heileman—1 Year Infielder (b. 10 Aug 1871 Cincinnati OH–d. 19 Jul 1940 at his home in Cincinnati OH) He was a night watchman at the music hall. Died from heart disease. Buried Vine Street Hill Cemetery, Cincinnati OH.

Harry Heilmann—17 Years Outfielder Hall of Fame (b. 3 Aug 1894 San Francisco CA–d. 9 Jul 1951 Henry Ford Hospital, Detroit MI) He sold insurance for a short while before becoming the radio, and later television, announcer for the Tigers for 18 years. Died from lung cancer. Buried Holy Sepulchre Cemetery, Southfield MI.

Fred Heimach—13 Years Pitcher (b. 27 Jan 1901 Camden NJ–d. 1 Jun 1973 Fort Myers FL) He was a policeman for the Miami Beach (FL) Police Department from 1935 to 1955, retiring to Fort Myers in 1963. Buried Fort Myers Memorial Gardens, Fort Myers FL.

Bud Heine—1 Year Infielder (b. 22 Sep 1900 Elmira NY–d. 2 Sep 1976 Fort Lauderdale FL) He was cremated and scattered at sea.

John Heinzman—1 Year Infielder (b. 27 Sep 1865 Louisville KY–d. 10 Nov 1914 at his home in Louisville KY) He worked for the Louisville Police Department for 12 years and was stationkeeper of the Central Police Station the last five years prior to his death. Died from heart disease. Buried St Louis Cemetery, Louisville KY.

Crese Heismann—2 Years Pitcher (b. 16 Apr 1880 Cincinnati OH–d. 19 Nov 1951 Good Samaritan Hospital, Cincinnati OH) He operated a grocery store in Cincinnati for ten years before opening a chain of general stores in Indiana and Ohio, retiring in 1944. Died from a stroke. Buried Spring Grove Cemetery, Cincinnati OH.

Henry Heitman—1 Year Pitcher (b. 6 Oct 1897 New York City NY–d. 15 Dec 1958 Brooklyn NY).

Heinie Heitmiller—2 Years Outfielder (b. 1883 San Francisco CA–d. 8 Oct 1912 Good Samaritan Hospital, Los Angeles CA) Died at the height of his career from typhoid fever. Buried Olivet Memorial Park, Colma CA.

Hank Helf—3 Years Catcher (b. 26 Aug 1913 Austin TX–d. 27 Oct 1984 Austin TX) Served in the U.S. Navy during World War II. He worked for the Austin Police Department and retired after 20 years with Austin National Bank. Buried Capitol Memorial Park, Austin TX.

Al Helfer —(b. 26 Sep 1911 PA–d. 16 May 1975 Mercy San Juan Hospital, Carmichael CA) For 40 years he was a sports announcer for radio and television. He was the announcer for the Dodgers, Giants and Athletics and traveled millions of miles broadcasting Mutual Network's "Game of the Day." Died from lung cancer. Cremated.

Ty Helfrich—1 Year Infielder (b. 9 Oct 1890 Pleasantville NJ–d. 18 Mar 1955 at his home in Pleasantville NJ) He was the athletic director and baseball coach at Pleasantville High School. Died from a heart attack. Buried Greenwood Cemetery, Pleasantville NJ.

Tony Hellman—1 Year Catcher (b. 1861 Cincinnati OH–d. 29 Mar 1898 Cincinnati OH) Died from nephritis. Buried St Mary Cemetery, Cincinnati OH.

Ed Hemingway—3 Years Infielder (b. 8 May 1893 Sheridan MI–d. 5 Jul 1969 East Grand Rapids MI) Buried Sheridan Cemetery, Sheridan MI.

George Hemming—8 Years Pitcher (b. 15 Dec 1868 Carrollton OH–d. 3 Jun 1930 Springfield Hospital, Springfield MA) Buried Oak Grove Cemetery, Springfield MA.

Ducky Hemp—2 Years Outfielder (b. 27 Dec 1867 St Louis MO–d. 3 Mar 1923 St Louis MO) Buried Calvary Cemetery, St Louis MO.

Charlie Hemphill—11 Years Outfielder (b. 20 Apr 1876 Greenville MI–d. 22 Jun 1953 Detroit MI).

Frank Hemphill—2 Years Outfielder (b. 13 May 1878 Greenville MI–d. 16 Nov 1950 Chicago IL).

Rollie Hemsley—19 Years Catcher (b. 24 Jun 1907 Syracuse OH–d. 31 Jul 1972 Washington DC) He was a coach, scout and minor league manager. Later he was a realtor in the Washington DC area. Died from heart failure. Buried George Washington Cemetery, Hyattsville MD.

Bernie Henderson—1 Year Pitcher (b. 12 Apr 1899 Douglassville TX–d. 4 Jun 1966 Municipal Hospital, Linden TX) He was a farmer and rancher in Cass County, TX. Died from cirrhosis of the liver. Buried St Williams Cemetery, Douglasville TX.

Bill Henderson—1 Year Pitcher (b. 4 Nov 1901 Altha FL–d. 6 Oct 1966 at a hospital in Pensacola FL) World War I veteran. He was a retired civil service worker. Buried Bayview Memorial Park, Pensacola FL.

Ed Henderson—1 Year Pitcher (b. 25 Dec 1884 Newark NJ–d. 15 Jan 1964 New York City NY).

Hardie Henderson—6 Years Pitcher (b. 31 Oct 1862 Philadelphia PA–d. 6 Feb 1903 Philadelphia PA) He umpired in the National League in 1895 and 1896 and called college games as well. He was working at Baker's Pool Room in downtown Philadelphia when he was hit by a trolley and killed on his way home from work. Buried Fernwood Cemetery, Fernwood PA.

Harvey Hendrick—11 Years Infielder (b. 9 Nov 1897 Mason TN–d. 29 Oct 1941 at his home in Covington TN) He played in the Southern League and Texas League and was active in several business endeavors, including a gas and oil dealership and in coal, grain and feed. Ended his own life with a .32 caliber revolver. Buried Munford Cemetery, Covington TN.

Ed Hendricks—1 Year Pitcher (b. 20 Jun 1886 Zeeland MI–d. 28 Nov 1930 Mercy Hospital, Jackson MI) Buried Roseland Memorial Gardens, Jackson MI.

Jack Hendricks—2 Years Outfielder 7 Years Manager (b. 9 Apr 1875 Joliet IL–d. 13 May 1943 at his home in Chicago IL) He managed several years in the American Association and was a major league scout. Died from a heart attack. Buried Mount Carmel Cemetery, Hillside IL.

Don Hendrickson—2 Years Pitcher (b. 14 Jul 1915 Rochester IN–d. 19 Jan 1977 Richmond VA).

Claude Hendrix—10 Years Pitcher (b. 13 Apr 1891 Olathe KS–d. 22 Mar 1944 Sacred Heart Hospital, Allentown PA) He owned and operated the AA Cafe in Allentown from 1925 until his death. Died from tuberculosis. Buried Arlington Memorial Park, Allentown PA.

Tim Hendryx—8 Years Outfielder (b. 31 Jan 1891 LeRoy IL–d. 14 Aug 1957 at his home in Corpus Christi TX) He was a retired taxicab driver and paint contractor. Died from a heart attack. Buried Rose Hill Memorial Park, Corpus Christi TX.

Moxie Hengle—2 Years Infielder (b. 7 Oct

1857 Chicago IL–d. 11 Dec 1924 at his home in River Forest IL) A prominent insurance man in Chicago, he enjoyed outdoor life, especially fishing. His pride was a collection of fishing poles he had made himself. Buried Forest Home Cemetery, Forest Park IL.

Lafayette Henion—1 Year Pitcher (b. 7 Jun 1899 Eureka CA–d. 22 Jul 1955 French Hospital, San Luis Obispo CA) He was a truck driver for a construction company. Buried Odd Fellows Cemetery, San Luis Obispo CA.

Weldon Henley—4 Years Pitcher (b. 20 Oct 1880 Jasper GA–d. 17 Nov 1960 Palatka FL) Living in Palatka since 1918, he was at one time a city commissioner. Died after a long illness. Buried West View Cemetery, Palatka FL.

Butch Henline—11 Years Catcher (b. 20 Dec 1894 Fort Wayne IN–d. 9 Oct 1957 at his home in Sarasota FL) He was a National League umpire from 1945 to 1948 and umpired in the minor leagues until 1954. He was in the hotel business a number of years in Florida where he lived about 25 years.

George Hennessey—3 Years Pitcher (b. 28 Oct 1907 Slatington PA–d. 15 Jan 1988 Medical Center, Princeton NJ) He was a retired ironworker. Buried Our Lady of Loardes Cemetery, Trenton NJ.

Les Hennessy—1 Year Infielder (b. 12 Dec 1893 Lynn MA–d. 20 Nov 1976 at a hospital in New York City NY) He was associated with Union News Company, a restaurant chain, retiring in 1956. Died after a brief illness. Buried St Joseph Cemetery, Lynn MA.

Pete Henning—2 Years Pitcher (b. 28 Dec 1887 Crown Point IN–d. 9 Nov 1939 Dyer IN) World War I veteran. He was a service man for the Crown Point Telephone Company. Died when he was hit by an automobile while he was pushing a stalled car, he had stopped to help, on the highway. Buried Maplewood Cemetery, Crown Point IN.

Fritz Henrich—1 Year Outfielder (b. 8 May 1899 Cincinnati OH–d. 1 May 1959 at his home in Philadelphia PA) He was a retired business machine salesman. Buried Holy Sepulchre Cemetery, Philadelphia PA.

Olaf Henriksen—7 Years Outfielder (b. 26 Apr 1888 Kirkerup, Denmark–d. 17 Oct 1962 at his home in Canton MA) He coached at Boston College. Buried St Mary Cemetery, Canton MA.

Dutch Henry—8 Years Pitcher (b. 12 May 1902 Cleveland OH–d. 23 Aug 1968 Huron Road Hospital, Cleveland OH) He worked for the Engineering Department of Cuyahoga County, OH. Buried Calvary Cemetery, Cleveland OH.

George Henry—1 Year Outfielder (b. 10 Aug 1863 Philadelphia PA–d. 30 Dec 1934 Lynn MA).

Jim Henry—3 Years Pitcher (b. 26 Jun 1910 Danville VA–d. 15 Aug 1976 St Joseph's Hospital-East, Memphis TN) He was a furniture salesman. Buried Forest Hill Cemetery, Memphis TN.

John Henry—9 Years Catcher (b. 26 Dec 1889 Amherst MA–d. 23 Nov 1941 Fort Huachuca AZ) He was a minor league umpire. Died from a coronary thrombosis. Buried Evergreen Cemetery, Bisbee AZ.

John Henry—4 Years Outfielder (b. 2 Sep 1864 Springfield MA–d. 11 Jun 1939 at his home in Hartford CT) A policeman for the Hartford Police Department from 1897 until his death, he had worked his way up to the rank of captain. Died after a short illness. Buried Mount St Benedict Cemetery, Bloomfield CT.

Snake Henry—2 Years Infielder (b. 19 Jul 1895 Waynesville NC–d. 12 Oct 1987 Wendell NC) Buried Montlawn Memorial Park, Raleigh NC.

Roy Henshaw—8 Years Pitcher (b. 29 Jul 1911 Chicago IL–d. 8 Jun 1993 Memorial Hospital, LaGrange IL) Buried Mount Hope Cemetery, Chicago IL.

Phil Hensiek—1 Year Pitcher (b. 13 Oct 1901 St Louis MO–d. 21 Feb 1972 St Louis MO) He was an auditor in the St Louis City License Collector's office. Buried Calvary Cemetery, St Louis MO.

Ernie Herbert—3 Years Pitcher (b. 30 Jan 1887 Breckenridge MO–d. 13 Jan 1968 Dallas TX) He lived at Grand Prairie TX and was a retired expeditor for Ling-Temco-Vought Company. Buried Mount Olivet Cemetery, Marceline MO.

Fred Herbert—1 Year Pitcher (b. 4 Mar 1887 LaGrange IL–d. 29 May 1963 Tice FL).

Art Herman—2 Years Pitcher (b. 11 May 1871

Louisville KY–d. 20 Sep 1955 Van Ness Sanitarium, Los Angeles CA) Buried Inglewood Park Cemetery, Inglewood CA.

Babe Herman —13 Years Outfielder (b. 26 Jun 1903 Buffalo NY–d. 27 Nov 1987 Memorial Hospital, Glendale CA) He was a scout for the Giants. Died from pneumonia and complications of a series of strokes suffered three years earlier. Buried Forest Lawn Memorial Park, Glendale CA.

Billy Herman —15 Years Infielder 4 Years Manager Hall of Fame (b. 7 Jul 1909 New Albany IN–d. 5 Sep 1992 Palm Beach FL) Served in the U.S. Navy during World War II. He spent his entire life in baseball as a player, coach and manager, retiring in 1975. Died from cancer. Buried Riverside Memorial Park, Tequesta FL.

Al Hermann —2 Years Infielder (b. 28 Mar 1899 Milltown NJ–d. 20 Aug 1980 Bethany Beach DE).

Chico Hernandez —2 Years Catcher (b. 3 Jan 1916 Havana, Cuba–d. 3 Jan 1986 Havana, Cuba).

Tom Hernon —1 Year Outfielder (b. 4 Nov 1866 East Bridgewater MA–d. 4 Feb 1902 New Bedford MA).

Ed Herr —3 Years Infielder (b. 19 May 1862 St Louis MO–d. 18 Jul 1943 St Anthony Hospital, St Louis MO) Associated with baseball in various capacities from 1899 until his death, he managed in the minor leagues and scouted for several teams. Credited with finding Carl Hubbell. Buried Bellefontaine Cemetery, St Louis MO.

Walt Herrell —1 Year Pitcher (b. 19 Feb 1889 Rockville MD–d. 23 Jan 1949 Front Royal VA).

Mike Herrera —2 Years Infielder (b. 19 Dec 1897 Havana, Cuba–d. 3 Feb 1978 Havana, Cuba).

Art Herring —11 Years Pitcher (b. 10 Mar 1906 Altus OK–d. 2 Dec 1995 Marion General Hospital, Marion IN) Buried Grant Memorial Park, Marion IN.

Bill Herring —1 Year Pitcher (b. 31 Oct 1893 New York City NY–d. 10 Sep 1962 Wayne Memorial Hospital, Honesdale PA) World War I veteran. Buried Pine Grove Cemetery, South Sterling PA.

Herb Herring —1 Year Pitcher (b. 22 Jul 1891 Danville AR–d. 22 Apr 1964 Tucson AZ) World War I veteran. Buried Holy Hope Cemetery, Tucson AZ.

Lefty Herring —2 Years Infielder (b. 4 Mar 1880 Philadelphia PA–d. 11 Feb 1965 Massapequa NY).

LeRoy Herrmann —3 Years Pitcher (b. 27 Feb 1906 Steward IL–d. 3 Jul 1972 at a hospital in Escalon CA) He worked in real estate 15 years at Stockton CA before retiring to Livermore CA in 1966. Buried San Joaquin Catholic Cemetery, Stockton CA.

Marty Herrmann —1 Year Pitcher (b. 10 Jan 1893 Oldenburg IN–d. 11 Sep 1956 at his home in Cincinnati OH) He was a self-employed plumbing contractor. Died from an acute blood disorder. Buried St Mary Cemetery, Cincinnati OH.

Willard Hershberger —3 Years Catcher (b. 28 May 1910 Lemoncove CA–d. 3 Aug 1940 Boston MA) Died at the height of his baseball career, taking his own life by slashing his throat with a razor. Buried Visalia Cemetery, Visalia CA.

Frank Hershey —1 Year Pitcher (b. 13 Dec 1877 Gorham NY–d. 15 Dec 1949 Thompson Hospital, Canandaigua NY) He was a toolmaker. Died after a brief illnes. Buried Gorham Cemetery, Gorham NY.

Buck Herzog —13 Years Infielder 3 Years Manager (b. 9 Jul 1885 Baltimore MD–d. 4 Sep 1953 City Hospital, Baltimore MD) He worked as a passenger agent for the Baltimore and Ohio Railroad, but was penniless and in rags when he died from tuberculosis. Buried Denton Cemetery, Denton MD.

Otto Hess —10 Years Pitcher (b. 13 Nov 1878 Berne, Switzerland–d. 25 Feb 1926 MacArthur Veteran's Hospital, Tucson AZ) Died from tuberculosis. Buried Fairview Cemetery, North Olmsted OH.

Tom Hess —1 Year Catcher (b. 15 Aug 1875 Brooklyn NY–d. 15 Dec 1945 Albany NY) Died after a brief illness.

George Hesselbacher —1 Year Pitcher (b. 18 Jan 1895 Philadelphia PA–d. 18 Feb 1980 Rydal PA) Served as a commanding officer in the U.S. Army during World War I. A professional engineer, he was the engineer for Cheltenham Township from 1931 retiring in 1964. He also served as a township commissioner. Buried Northwood Cemetery, Philadelphia PA.

Larry Hesterfer—1 Year Pitcher (b. 20 Jun 1878 Newark NJ–d. 22 Sep 1943 at his home in Bloomfield NJ) He worked 25 years at the Thomas Oakes Woolen Mills in Bloomfield. Buried Mount Olivet Cemetery, Bloomfield NJ.

Gus Hetling—1 Year Infielder (b. 21 Nov 1885 St Louis MO–d. 13 Oct 1962 at his home in Wichita KS) He was a retired cigar company salesman. Buried Wichita Park Cemetery, Wichita KS.

George Heuble—1 Year Infielder (b. 1849 Paterson NJ–d. 22 Jan 1896 Philadelphia PA).

Ed Heusser—9 Years Pitcher (b. 7 May 1909 Mill Creek UT–d. 1 Mar 1956 at his home in Aurora CO) He was a commission agent for Continental Oil Company. Died from Hodgkin's disease. Buried Bountiful City Park, Bountiful UT.

Joe Heving—13 Years Pitcher (b. 2 Sep 1900 Covington KY–d. 11 Apr 1970 St Elizabeth Hospital, Covington KY) Died from a heart attack. Buried St Mary's Cemetery, Fort Mitchell KY.

Johnnie Heving—8 Years Catcher (b. 29 Apr 1896 Covington KY–d. 24 Dec 1968 Rowan Memorial Hospital, Salisbury NC) World War I veteran. He worked in the pipefitting department of the Southern Railway Spencer Shops and with the Salisbury YMCA. Buried Rowan Memorial Park, Salisbury NC.

Walter Hewett—1 Year Manager (b. 1861 Washington DC–d. 7 Oct 1944 John Dickson Home, Washington DC) Buried Glenwood Cemetery, Washington DC.

Jake Hewitt—1 Year Pitcher (b. 6 Jun 1870 Maidsville WV–d. 18 May 1959 Morgantown WV).

John Heydler—(b. 10 Jul 1869 NY–d. 18 Apr 1956 Mercy Hospital, San Diego CA) The president of the National League from 1918 to 1934, he spent several years as a virtual invalid due to poor health and eyesight. Died from pneumonia after suffering a stroke ten days earlier. Cremated.

Mike Heydon—7 Years Catcher (b. 15 Jul 1874 MO–d. 13 Oct 1913 at his home in Indianapolis IN) Died from the crippling effects of curvature of the spine.

John Hibbard—1 Year Pitcher (b. 2 Dec 1864 Chicago IL–d. 17 Nov 1937 at his home in Los Angeles CA) The Commissioner of the Metal Trades Association of the United States, he retired in 1927. Died from a heart attack. Cremated.

Eddie Hickey—1 Year Infielder (b. 18 Aug 1872 Cleveland OH–d. 25 Mar 1941 at a hospital in Tacoma WA) For many years he worked for the Tacoma *News Tribune* newspaper. He had been in ill health five years. Buried Calvary Cemetery, Tacoma WA.

Jim Hickey—2 Years Pitcher (b. 22 Oct 1920 North Abington MA–d. 20 Sep 1997 Memorial Hospital, Manchester CT) Served in the U.S. Navy during World War II. He worked over 30 years for Pratt & Whitney Aircraft in East Hartford CT, and also owned Hickey Paving Company there. Buried St Patrick's Cemetery, Rockland MA.

John Hickey—1 Year Pitcher (b. 3 Nov 1881 Minneapolis MN–d. 28 Dec 1941 Zenith Sanitarium, Seattle WA) Bedridden several years, he died following a stroke. Buried Calvary Cemetery, Seattle WA.

Mike Hickey—2 Years Infielder (b. 25 Dec 1871 Chicopee MA–d. 11 Jun 1918 Springfield Hospital, Springfield MA) He umpired some in the minor leagues. Died after an illness of four days. Buried Calvary Cemetery, Chicopee MA.

Ernie Hickman—1 Year Pitcher (b. 1856 East Saint Louis IL–d. 18 Nov 1891 East Saint Louis IL) He worked in his father's office as a commission man at the National Stock Yards. Took his own life by shooting himself after shooting his wife. She died three days later. Buried St Peter's Cemetery.

Jim Hickman—5 Years Outfielder (b. 19 May 1894 Johnson City TN–d. 30 Dec 1958 Brooklyn NY).

Piano Legs Hickman—12 Years Infielder (b. 4 Mar 1876 Taylortown PA–d. 19 Apr 1934 at his home in Morgantown WV) He scouted for the Indians and coached baseball at West Virginia University. Active politically, he served three terms as Morgantown mayor, as peace magistrate and as sheriff of Monongalia County, WV. Died from heart disease. Buried East Oak Grove Cemetery, Morgantown WV.

Nat Hicks—2 Years Catcher 1 Year Manager (b. 19 Apr 1845 Hempstead NY–d. 21 Apr 1907 Naegell's Hotel in Hoboken NJ) A noted soloist and choir singer in the Hoboken area, he conducted a billiard room in the Naegell's Hotel. Died when he accidentally left a gas jet to a heating stove open when he retired for the night. Buried St Peter's Cemetery, Jersey City NJ.

Kirby Higbe—12 Years Pitcher (b. 8 Apr 1915 Columbia SC–d. 6 May 1985 Columbia SC) World War II veteran. He coached American Legion baseball and was a scout. Buried Elmwood Cemetery, Columbia SC.

Mahlon Higbee—1 Year Outfielder (b. 16 Aug 1901 Louisville KY–d. 7 Apr 1968 DePauw IN) Died from a heart attack on Indiana State Road 64 near DePauw while returning home to Louisville from Dale IN. Buried Evergreen Cemetery, Louisville KY.

Bill Higdon—1 Year Outfielder (b. 27 Apr 1924 Camp Hill AL–d. 30 Aug 1986 Singing River Hospital, Pascagoula MS) Served in the U.S. Army Air Corps during World War II. He was a lumber broker for Newman Lumber Company in Gulfport MS. Buried Greenwood Cemetery, Montgomery AL.

Irv Higginbotham—3 Years Pitcher (b. 26 Apr 1881 Homer NE–d. 13 Jun 1959 Seattle WA) He was a painter. Died from a heart ailment. Buried Acacia Cemetery, Seattle WA.

Bill Higgins—2 Years Infielder (b. 8 Sep 1861 Wilmington DE–d. 25 Apr 1919 Wilmington DE) Buried Silverbrook Cemetery, Wilmington DE.

Bob Higgins—3 Years Catcher (b. 23 Sep 1886 Fayetteville TN–d. 25 May 1941 at his home in Chattanooga TN) He played, managed and umpired in the Southern League and was a cotton buyer. Died from undetermined causes. Buried Greenwood Cemetery, Chattanooga TN.

Pinky Higgins—14 Years Infielder 8 Years Manager (b. 27 May 1909 Red Oak TX–d. 21 Mar 1969 St Paul Hospital, Dallas TX) He worked his entire life in baseball as a player, manager and scout. Died from a heart attack two days after parole from a four year sentence for vehicular homicide in Los Angeles CA. He had served two months in prison. Buried Hillcrest Memorial Park, Dallas TX.

Thomas Higgins—2 Years Pitcher (b. 18 Mar 1889 Streator IL–d. 14 Feb 1959 Elgin IL).

Andy High—13 Years Infielder (b. 21 Nov 1897 Ava IL–d. 22 Feb 1981 Lake Park Nursing Care Center, Sylvania OH) Served in the U.S. Navy during World War I. He was a scout for the Dodgers until he retired in 1960. Buried Evergreen Cemetery, Webster Groves MO.

Charlie High—2 Years Outfielder (b. 1 Dec 1898 Ava IL–d. 11 Sep 1960 Oak Grove OR) Cremated. Buried Portland Memorial, Portland OR.

Ed High—1 Year Pitcher (b. 26 Dec 1876 Baltimore MD–d. 10 Feb 1926 Baltimore MD) Buried Western Cemetery, Baltimore MD.

Hugh High—6 Years Outfielder (b. 24 Oct 1887 Pottstown PA–d. 16 Nov 1962 Park Lane Hospital, St Louis MO) He took Ty Cobb's place in the Tiger outfield in 1913 when Cobb held out in a salary dispute. He was a plumber. Died after a long illness. Buried Bellefontaine Cemetery, St Louis MO.

Dick Higham—3 Years Outfielder 1 Year Manager (b. 1852 England–d. 18 Mar 1905 St Luke's Hospital, Chicago IL) Died from pneumonia and dropsy.

John Hiland—1 Year Infielder (b. 1861 Philadelphia PA–d. 10 Apr 1901 at his home in Philadelphia PA).

Whitey Hilcher—4 Years Pitcher (b. 28 Feb 1909 Chicago IL–d. 21 Nov 1962 Minneapolis MN) Served in Europe during World War II. He was a partner in the Johnson-Hilcher Plaster Company. Buried Fort Snelling National Cemetery, Minneapolis MN.

George Hildebrand—1 Year Outfielder (b. 6 Sep 1878 San Francisco CA–d. 30 May 1960 City Hospital, Reseda CA) He was an American League umpire from 1912 to 1934. Died from congestive heart failure, but suffered from lymphoma. Buried Valhalla Memorial Park, North Hollywood CA.

Oral Hildebrand—10 Years Pitcher (b. 7 Apr 1907 Bridgeport IN–d. 7 Sep 1977 at his home in Southport IN) He was a tool and die maker for the Link-Belt Division of FMC Corporation, retiring in 1972. Buried Forest Lawn Memory Gardens, Greenwood IN.

Palmer Hildebrand—1 Year Catcher (b. 23 Dec 1884 Schauck OH–d. 25 Jan 1960 North Canton OH) He worked 36 years for Hoover Company in North Canton, retiring in 1953.

Died from a heart attack and was dead-on-arrival at Aultman Hospital. Buried Shauck Cemetery, Johnsville OH.

Belden Hill—1 Year Infielder (b. 24 Aug 1864 Kewanee IL–d. 23 Oct 1934 Cedar Rapids IA) He was known as the "Father of organized baseball" in Cedar Rapids. Died from heart disease. Buried Oak Hill Cemetery, Cedar Rapids IA.

Carmen Hill—10 Years Pitcher (b. 1 Oct 1895 Royalton MN–d. 1 Jan 1990 Indianapolis IN) For 24 years he was a safety inspector at the General Motors plant in Indianapolis, retiring in 1960. Buried Crown Hill Cemetery, Indianapolis IN.

Herbert Hill—1 Year Pitcher (b. 19 Aug 1891 Hutchins TX–d. 1 Sep 1970 Dallas TX).

Herman Hill—2 Years Outfielder (b. 12 Oct 1945 Tuskegee AL–d. 14 Dec 1970 Valencia, Venezuela).

Hugh Hill—2 Years Outfielder (b. 21 Jul 1879 Ringgold GA–d. 6 Sep 1958 Cincinnati OH) Buried Spring Hill Cemetery, Charleston WV.

Hunter Hill—3 Years Infielder (b. 21 Jun 1879 Austin TX–d. 22 Feb 1959 at his home in Austin TX) He was a lifelong resident of Austin. Buried Austin Memorial Park Cemetery, Austin TX.

Jesse Hill—3 Years Outfielder (b. 20 Jan 1907 Yates MO–d. 31 Aug 1993 Pasadena CA) Served in the U.S. Navy during World War II. He is best known as the track coach (1949–1950), football coach (1951–1956) and athletic director (1957–1972) at the University of Southern California. He was the first commissioner of the Pac-8 (now Pac-10) Conference, retiring in 1978. Died from complications of Alzheimers disease. Buried Corona Cemetery, Corona CA.

John Hill—2 Games Pinch Hitter (b. 16 Oct 1909 Powder Springs GA–d. 20 Sep 1970 V A Hospital, Decatur GA) Died from cancer. Buried Douglasville City Cemetery, Douglasville GA.

Red Hill—1 Year Pitcher (b. 20 Jan 1893 Marshall TX–d. 11 Aug 1938 El Paso TX) Served in the U.S. Army during World War I. Died following an appendectomy. Buried Evergreen Cemetery, El Paso TX.

Still Bill Hill—4 Years Pitcher (b. 26 Aug 1874 Chattanooga TN–d. 28 Jan 1938 General Hospital, Cincinnati OH) He was a detective for the Cincinnati police force from 1902 to 1922. Died from a skull fracture suffered when hit by a car while crossing the street. Buried Evergreen Cemetery, Southgate KY.

Homer Hillebrand—3 Years Pitcher (b. 10 Oct 1879 Freeport IL–d. 20 Jan 1974 Lakeview Hospital, Lake Elsinore CA) He was a farmer for 65 years. Died from a heart attack. Buried Elsinore Valley Cemetery, Lake Elsinore CA.

Frank Hiller—7 Years Pitcher (b. 13 Jul 1920 Irvington NJ–d. 8 Jan 1987 at his home at West Chester PA) He retired from Massachusetts Mutual Life Insurance Company in 1981. Cremated.

Hob Hiller—2 Years Infielder (b. 12 May 1893 East Mauch Chunk PA–d. 27 Dec 1956 Gnaden Hutton Memorial Hosp, Lehighton PA) He was a trainman on the CRR of NJ until a rail accident resulted in the amputation of his right leg. He then ran for public office and was Carbon County (PA) Registrar of Wills. Died from heart disease. Buried Evergreen Cemetery, Jim Thorpe PA.

Ed Hilley—1 Year Infielder (b. 17 Jun 1879 Cleveland OH–d. 14 Nov 1956 Huron Road Hospital, Cleveland OH) He worked more than 40 years for Chandler and Rudd Company, a retail grocery chain. He was first a buyer, then managed several stores for them.

Mack Hillis—2 Years Infielder (b. 23 Jul 1901 Cambridge MA–d. 16 Jun 1961 City Hospital, Cambridge MA) For 22 years he was a Cambridge police officer. Died suddenly one day after completing his beat. Buried Cambridge Cemetery, Cambridge MA.

Pat Hilly—1 Year Outfielder (b. 24 Feb 1887 Fostoria OH–d. 25 Jul 1953 Eureka MO) Buried St Wendelin Church Cemetery, Fostoria OH.

Charlie Hilsey—2 Years Pitcher (b. 23 Mar 1864 Philadelphia PA–d. 31 Oct 1918 Philadelphia PA).

Jack Himes—2 Years Outfielder (b. 22 Sep 1878 Bryan OH–d. 16 Dec 1949 Silver Cross Hospital, Joliet IL) He worked in the Rockdale Steel Mills and later for the Texas Company in Lockport IL. Died following a five-year illness. Buried St John's Cemetery, Joliet IL.

Bill Hinchman—10 Years Outfielder (b. 4 Apr 1883 Philadelphia PA–d. 20 Feb 1963 St Raphael's Home, Columbus OH) He was a scout for the

Pirates until retiring in 1954. Except for Connie Mack, he worked longer for the same team than any other man — 50 years for the Pirates. Buried St Joseph Cemetery, Lockbourne OH.

Harry Hinchman —1 Year Infielder (b. 4 Aug 1878 Philadelphia PA–d. 19 Jan 1933 at his home in Toledo OH) He managed minor league baseball for a while before becoming involved in a bowling alley in Toledo. Died from heart disease. Buried Toledo Memorial Park, Sylvania OH.

Hunkey Hines —1 Year Outfielder (b. 29 Sep 1867 Elgin IL–d. 2 Jan 1928 Rockford IL) For a number of years he was a foreman for the Ward Pump Company and later for Roper Construction in Rockford. Died from acute indigestion and heart trouble.

Mike Hines —4 Years Catcher (b. 1864 Ireland–d. 14 Mar 1910 New Bedford MA) He was a painter and decorator in New Bedford. Died after a long illness.

Paul Hines —16 Years Outfielder (b. 1 Mar 1852 Washington DC–d. 10 Jul 1935 Sacred Heart Home, Hyattsville MD) He was deaf and blind in his declining years.

Gordie Hinkle —1 Year Catcher (b. 3 Apr 1905 Toronto OH–d. 19 Mar 1972 Houston TX) He worked for Mobil Oil Company. Buried Woodlawn Garden of Memories, Houston TX.

Dutch Hinrichs —1 Year Pitcher (b. 27 Apr 1889 Orange CA–d. 18 Aug 1972 North Acres Manor Conv Hosp, Kingsburg CA) He was a real estate salesman. Died from a heart attack. Buried Kingsburg Cemetery, Kingsburg CA.

Paul Hinson —3 Games Pinch Runner (b. 9 May 1904 Van Leer TN–d. 23 Sep 1960 at his home in Muskogee OK) A 42-year resident of Muskogee, he worked for the city police force from 1939 to 1957 and was the chief of police at one time. Died from a self-inflicted gunshot wound in the right temple. Buried Greenhill Cemetery, Muskogee OK.

John Hinton —1 Year Infielder (b. 20 Jun 1876 Pittsburgh PA–d. 19 Jul 1920 Braddock PA).

Herb Hippauf —1 Year Pitcher (b. 9 May 1939 New York City NY–d. 17 Jul 1995 Kaiser Hospital, Santa Clara CA) He was a scout for the Rockies. Died from kidney cancer. Cremated. Buried Santa Clara Mission Cemetery, Santa Clara CA.

Jim Hitchcock —1 Year Infielder (b. 28 Jun 1911 Inverness AL–d. 23 Jun 1959 St Margaret's Hospital Montgomery AL) He was the Public Service Commissioner for the State of Alabama. Died from a heart attack. Buried Greenwood Cemetery, Montgomery AL.

Bruce Hitt —1 Year Pitcher (b. 14 Mar 1897 Comanche TX–d. 10 Nov 1973 at a hospital in Portland OR) Served in the U.S. Navy during World War I. He was a physical therapist at the Veteran's Hospital in Roseburg OR before retiring in 1969 and moving to Santa Maria CA. Buried Willamette National Cemetery, Portland OR.

Roy Hitt —1 Year Pitcher (b. 22 Jun 1884 Carleton NE–d. 8 Feb 1956 Valley Community Hospital, Pomona CA) He was a salesman for a meat company. Buried Pomona Cemetery, Pomona CA.

Myril Hoag —13 Years Outfielder (b. 9 Mar 1908 Davis CA–d. 28 Jul 1971 at his home in High Springs FL) World War II veteran. He managed minor league and semi-pro baseball and was an avid golfer and fisherman. Died after an extended illness. Buried High Springs Cemetery, High Springs FL.

Don Hoak —11 Years Infielder (b. 5 Feb 1928 Roulette PA–d. 9 Oct 1969 Pittsburgh PA) Served in the U.S. Marines during World War II. He tried broadcasting Pirate games for a couple of years, then coached for the Phillies before managing minor league baseball. Died from a heart attack while at the wheel of his car, chasing his brother-in-law's stolen car. Buried Allegheny Cemetery, Pittsburgh PA.

Bill Hobbs —2 Years Infielder (b. 7 May 1893 Grant's Lick KY–d. 5 Jan 1945 Hamilton OH) Served in the U.S. Army during World War I. His baseball career was shortened when he was unconsious for 20 hours after being hit in the head by a pitched ball. He operated Hobb's Distributing Company in Hamilton. Accidentally killed when he was shot by his own gun while hunting rabbits. Buried St Stephen's Cemetery, Hamilton OH.

Dick Hoblitzell —11 Years Infielder (b. 26 Oct 1888 Waverly WV–d. 14 Nov 1962 St Joseph's Hospital, Parkersburg WV) Served in the U.S.

Army during World War I. He managed and umpired minor league baseball and managed the family farm in Wood County, WV. Active in local politics, he was Wood County Commissioner from 1942 to 1948 and sheriff from 1952 to 1956. Buried Valley Cemetery, Marietta OH.

Harry Hoch—3 Years Pitcher (b. 9 Jan 1887 Woodside DE–d. 26 Oct 1981 Lewes Convalescent Center, Lewes DE) He was a lawyer from 1915 until he retired in 1962. He served a term as city solicitor for Wilmington DE and 18 months as recorder of deeds for New Castle County, DE. Died after a long illness. Buried Townsend Cemetery, Townsend DE.

Ed Hock—3 Years Outfielder (b. 27 Mar 1899 Franklin Furnace OH–d. 21 Nov 1963 Portsmouth OH) World War I veteran. He worked 20 years for Armco Steel Corporation in Ashland KY. He had been in ill health for some time when he drowned in the Ohio River. His body was found two days after he was missing. Buried St Peters Catholic Church Cemetery, Wheelersburg OH.

Oris Hockett—7 Years Outfielder (b. 29 Sep 1909 Bluffton IN–d. 23 Mar 1969 Harbor General Hospital, Torrance CA) He was a machinist for 30 years. Died from a ruptured aortic aneurysm. Buried Inglewood Park Cemetery, Inglewood CA.

George Hockette—2 Years Pitcher (b. 7 Apr 1908 Perth MS–d. 20 Jan 1974 Plantation FL).

Johnny Hodapp—9 Years Infielder (b. 26 Sep 1905 Cincinnati OH–d. 14 Jun 1980 Cincinnati OH) He was a funeral director at Hodapp Funeral Home in Cincinnati from 1939 until he retired in 1974. Died from prostate cancer. Buried Oak Hill Cemetery Park, Cincinnati OH.

Shovel Hodge—3 Years Pitcher (b. 6 Jul 1893 Mount Andrew AL–d. 31 Dec 1967 Fort Walton Beach FL).

Gil Hodges—18 Years Infielder 9 Years Manager (b. 4 Apr 1924 Princeton IN–d. 2 Apr 1972 West Palm Beach FL) He worked in baseball his entire life. Died following a heart attack. Buried Holy Cross Cemetery, Brooklyn NY.

Russ Hodges—Hall of Fame (b. 18 Jun 1910 Dayton KY–d. 19 Apr 1971 Marin General Hospital, San Rafael CA) A broadcaster 41 years, and for the Giants from 1949 to 1970, he died from a heart attack. Buried Mount Tamalpais Cemetery, San Rafael CA.

Art Hoelskoetter—4 Years Infielder (b. 30 Sep 1882 St Louis MO–d. 3 Aug 1954 Barnes Hospital, St Louis MO) Buried Calvary Cemetery, St Louis MO.

Joe Hoerner—14 Years Pitcher (b. 12 Nov 1936 Dubuque IA–d. 4 Oct 1996 Hermann MO) Killed when the farm tractor he was operating turned over on him. Buried Resurrection Cemetery, St Louis MO.

Fred Hoey—1 Year Manager (b. 1866 New York City NY–d. 7 Dec 1933 Paris, France) A New York turfman, he was widely known in France and the United States. For several years he had looked after the Joseph E Widener racing establishment in Paris. Died after a short illness.

John Hoey—3 Years Outfielder (b. 10 Nov 1881 Watertown MA–d. 11 Nov 1947 Naugatuck CT).

Chet Hoff—4 Years Pitcher (b. 8 May 1891 Ossining NY–d. 18 Sep 1998 Halifax Medical Center, Daytona Beach FL) He worked for Rand McNally in Ossining before retiring to Florida in 1956. Died after falling and breaking a hip a week earlier. Buried Dale Cemetery, Ossining NY.

Bill Hoffer—6 Years Pitcher (b. 8 Nov 1870 Cedar Rapids IA–d. 21 Jul 1959 Cedar Rapids IA) He pitched in the first game ever played in the American League. He worked for the U.S. Post Office and for the Crandic Railroad. Died following a long illness. Buried Linwood Cemetery, Cedar Rapids IA.

Stew Hofferth—3 Years Catcher (b. 27 Jan 1913 Logansport IN–d. 7 Mar 1994 Porter Memorial Hospital, Valparaiso IN) For 37 years he was a steel worker for Inland Steel Company. Buried St Paul Lutheran Cemetery, Kouts IN.

Danny Hoffman—9 Years Outfielder (b. 10 Mar 1880 Canton CT–d. 14 Mar 1922 Buckland CT) Died from tuberculosis. Buried St Michael's Cemetery, Glastonbury CT.

Dutch Hoffman—1 Year Outfielder (b. 28 Jan 1902 Freeburg IL–d. 6 Dec 1962 Memorial Hospital, Belleville IL) He played in the American Association and in the Texas League and was co-owner of the Belleville Bottling Company, a soft drink firm. Died from heart disease. Buried Lake View Memorial Gardens, Belleville IL.

Hickey Hoffman—1 Year Catcher (b. 27 Oct 1856 Cleveland OH–d. 27 Oct 1915 Peoria IL) Died from a coronary embolism while at his job in a saloon.

Izzy Hoffman—2 Years Outfielder (b. 5 Jan 1875 Bridgeport NJ–d. 13 Nov 1942 Jefferson Hospital, Philadelphia PA) He was a topnotch trapshooter. Died from leukemia. Buried North Cedar Hill Cemetery, Philadelphia PA.

Larry Hoffman—1 Year Infielder (b. 18 Jul 1878 Chicago IL–d. 29 Dec 1948 Chicago IL) Buried Bohemian National Cemetery, Chicago IL.

Tex Hoffman—1 Year Infielder (b. 30 Nov 1893 San Antonio TX–d. 19 May 1947 New Orleans LA) He lived in New Orleans 27 years. Buried Carrollton Cemetery, New Orleans LA.

Bill Hoffner—1 Year Pitcher (b. 18 Aug 1871 Danville PA–d. 22 Nov 1946 Geisinger Hospital, Danville PA) He conducted a tobacco store in Danville for many years and was a custodian at the courthouse his last ten years. Buried Odd Fellows Cemetery, Danville PA.

John Hofford—2 Years Pitcher (b. 25 May 1863 Philadelphia PA–d. 16 Dec 1915 Philadelphia PA).

Bobby Hofman—7 Years Infielder (b. 5 Oct 1925 St Louis MO–d. 5 Apr 1994 St Luke's Hospital, Chesterfield MO) Served in the U.S. Army during World War II. He spent over 40 years in baseball as a player, coach, executive and minor league manager, retiring in 1989. Died from cancer. Buried Bethlehem Cemetery, Bellefontaine Neighbors MO.

Solly Hofman—14 Years Outfielder (b. 29 Oct 1882 St Louis MO–d. 11 Mar 1956 St Louis MO) Buried Memorial Park Cemetery, St Louis MO.

Fred Hofmann—9 Years Catcher (b. 10 Jun 1894 St Louis MO–d. 19 Nov 1964 City Sanitarium and Hospital, St Helena CA) A scout for the Orioles, he worked in organized baseball for 50 years. Died following a heart attack. Buried Golden Gate National Cemetery, San Bruno CA.

George Hogan—1 Year Pitcher (b. 25 Sep 1885 Marion OH–d. 22 Feb 1922 Bartlesville Hospital, Bartlesville OK) He was an engineer for the Indian Territory Illuminating Oil Company. Died from tuberculosis. Buried Marion Cemetery, Marion OH.

Happy Hogan—2 Years Outfielder (b. 14 Sep 1884 San Juan CA–d. 28 Sep 1974 Alexian Brother's Hospital, San Jose CA) He was a bartender at various restaurants and bars for 35 years. Died from a heart attack. Buried Oak Hill Memorial Park, San Jose CA.

Harry Hogan—1 Year Outfielder (b. 1 Nov 1875 Syracuse NY–d. 25 Jan 1934 Syracuse NY).

Ken Hogan—3 Years Outfielder (b. 9 Oct 1902 Cleveland OH–d. 2 Jan 1980 at his home in Cleveland OH) He was a building trades laborer for the Cleveland Board of Education. Buried Calvary Cemetery, Cleveland OH.

Marty Hogan—2 Years Outfielder (b. 15 Oct 1869 Staffordshire, England–d. 15 Aug 1923 at his home in Youngstown OH) He was a park supervisor in Youngstown. Injured in an automobile accident several months earlier, he died from heart disease and pneumonia. Buried Calvary Cemetery, Youngstown OH.

Shanty Hogan—13 Years Catcher (b. 21 Mar 1906 Somerville MA–d. 7 Apr 1967 Faulkner Hospital, Jamaica Plain MA) For 14 years he was an inspector for the Public Works Department in Somerville. Died after a long illness. Buried Oak Grove Cemetery, Medford MA.

Bert Hogg—1 Year Infielder (b. 21 Apr 1913 Detroit MI–d. 5 Nov 1973 St John Hospital, Detroit MI) He retired from the Detroit Police Department after 25 years service. Later he was a security guard at General Motors Corporation and at the Willow Run Air Transport facility. Buried Forest Lawn Cemetery, Detroit MI.

Bill Hogg—4 Years Pitcher (b. 1880 Port Huron MI–d. 8 Dec 1909 New Orleans LA) Died from Bright's disease at the height of his career. Buried New York City NY.

Brad Hogg—5 Years Pitcher (b. 26 Mar 1888 Buena Vista GA–d. 2 Apr 1935 at his home near Buena Vista GA) He became one of the prominent lawyers in Georgia. Died from tuberculosis after being in declining health several years. Buried Tazewell Cemetery, Tazewell GA.

George Hogriever—2 Years Outfielder (b. 17 Mar 1869 Cincinnati OH–d. 26 Jan 1961 Appleton WI) Died after a three-month illness. Buried Riverside Cemetery, Appleton WI.

Bobby Hogue—5 Years Pitcher (b. 5 Apr 1921 Miami FL–d. 22 Dec 1987 Miami FL) Served in the U.S. Navy during World War II. He worked three years for the *Miami News* before spending several years working in the circulation department for the *Miami Herald*, retiring in 1986. He enjoyed fishing in the Florida Keys where he made his home. Died after a long battle with cancer.

Bill Hohman—1 Year Outfielder (b. 27 Nov 1903 Brooklyn MD–d. 29 Oct 1968 Baltimore MD) Died suddenly. Buried Cedar Hill Cemetery, Baltimore MD.

Eddie Hohnhurst—2 Years Infielder (b. 31 Jan 1885 Cincinnati OH–d. 28 Mar 1916 St Elizabeth Hospital, Covington KY) He was a Covington policeman. Died from a self-inflicted gunshot wound to the head. He had been despondent since killing a black man while discharging his duties a year earlier.

Bill Holbert—12 Years Catcher (b. 14 Mar 1855 Baltimore MD–d. 20 Mar 1935 Laurel MD) Buried Burtonville MD.

Wally Holborow—3 Years Pitcher (b. 30 Nov 1913 New York City NY–d. 14 Jul 1986 Fort Lauderdale FL) He was a retired worker of the New York City Sanitation Department.

Sammy Holbrook—1 Year Catcher (b. 1 Jul 1910 Meridian MS–d. 10 Apr 1991 V A Hospital, Jackson MS) World War II veteran. He was a salesman. Buried Memorial Park, Meridian MS.

Bill Holden—2 Years Outfielder (b. 7 Sep 1889 Birmingham AL–d. 14 Sep 1971 at a hospital in Pensacola FL) He managed minor league baseball for a time. Buried Pfeiffer Cemetery, Pensacola FL.

Joe Holden—3 Years Catcher (b. 4 Jun 1913 St Clair PA–d. 10 May 1996 at his home in St Clair PA) He was a scout and minor league manager for the White Sox from 1945 to 1957, spent four years running the family insurance business in St Clair, then 14 years as a scout for the Tigers and four years on special assignment for the Phillies, retiring in 1979. He was also active politically, serving on the St Clair city council and as a county commissioner. Buried Queen of the Universe Cemetery, Pottsville PA.

Jim Holdsworth—4 Years Outfielder (b. 14 Jul 1850 New York City NY–d. 22 Mar 1918 New York City NY).

Walter Holke—11 Years Infielder (b. 25 Dec 1892 St Louis MO–d. 12 Oct 1954 Missouti Baptist Hospital, St Louis MO) He coached for the St Louis Browns for a short time. Buried Rose Lawn Memorial Gardens, Festus MO.

Bill Hollahan—1 Year Infielder (b. 22 Nov 1896 New York City NY–d. 27 Nov 1965 New York City NY).

Dutch Holland—3 Years Outfielder (b. 12 Oct 1903 Middlesex NC–d. 16 Jun 1967 Lumberton Hospital, Lumberton NC) Buried Oak Grove Cemetery, Maxton NC.

Mul Holland—3 Years Pitcher (b. 6 Jan 1903 Franklin VA–d. 16 Feb 1969 Winchester VA) Served as a commander with the U.S. Navy in the South Pacific during World War II. He moved to Winchester in 1948, and was a trust officer for Shenandoah Valley National Bank. In 1962 he became a stock broker for an investment firm, retiring in 1968. Died after a lengthy illness. Buried Mount Hebron Cemetery, Winchester VA.

Will Holland—1 Year Infielder (b. Georgetown DE–d. 19 Jul 1930 Philadelphia PA) Buried Montrose Cemetery, Upper Darby PA.

Ed Holley—4 Years Pitcher (b. 23 Jul 1899 Benton KY–d. 26 Oct 1986 Lourdes Hospital, Paducah KY) Buried Mount Carmel Cemetery, Paducah KY.

Bug Holliday—10 Years Outfielder (b. 8 Feb 1867 St Louis MO–d. 15 Feb 1910 at his home in Cincinnati OH) He umpired for a while—in the National League in 1897 and 1903—then became a caller of the horse races at a Cincinnati pool room. Died from gangrene of the foot and leg. Buried Spring Grove Cemetery, Cincinnati OH.

Carl Holling—2 Years Pitcher (b. 9 Jul 1896 Dana CA–d. 18 Jul 1962 Sonoma County Hospital, Santa Rosa CA) He was a watchman at a lumberyard for 14 years. Died from lung cancer that had spread to his brain. Buried Santa Rosa Memorial Park, Santa Rosa CA.

Holly Hollingshead—1 Year Manager (b. 17 Jan 1853 Washington DC–d. 6 Oct 1926 John Dickson Home, Washington DC) Buried Glenwood Cemetery, Washington DC.

Al Hollingsworth—11 Years Pitcher (b. 25 Feb 1908 St Louis MO–d. 28 Apr 1996 Austin TX) He managed minor league baseball and coached for the Cardinals. Buried Wimberly Cemetery, Wimberly TX.

Bonnie Hollingsworth—4 Years Pitcher (b. 26 Dec 1895 Jacksboro TN–d. 2 Jan 1990 Shannondale Healthcare Center, Knoxville TN) For 30 years he was a salesman for Huttig Sash and Door Company. After retiring he established Bonnie Garage Door Installation. Buried Greenwood Cemetery, Knoxville TN.

John Hollison—1 Year Pitcher (b. 3 May 1870 Chicago IL–d. 19 Aug 1969 Chicago IL) He was a medical doctor. Buried Acacia Park Cemetery, Chicago IL.

Stan Hollmig—3 Years Outfielder (b. 2 Jan 1926 Fredericksburg TX–d. 4 Dec 1981 Methodist Hospital, San Antonio TX) He was a scout for the Reds and Astros. Buried Oakridge Cemetery, Hondo TX.

Charlie Hollocher—7 Years Infielder (b. 11 Jun 1896 St Louis MO–d. 14 Aug 1940 Frontenac MO) Retiring from baseball at the height of his career because of stomach problems, he did investigative work for St Louis County, and was also a night watchman. He later owned a tavern in St Louis. Died from a self-inflicted gunshot wound in the neck from a newly purchased shotgun. Buried Oakhill Cemetery, St Louis MO.

Bobo Holloman—1 Year Pitcher (b. 7 Mar 1924 Thomaston GA–d. 1 May 1987 Athens GA) Buried Evergreen Memorial Park, Athens GA.

Jim Holloway—1 Year Pitcher (b. 22 Sep 1908 Plaquermine LA–d. 15 Apr 1997 Baton Rouge LA).

Ken Holloway—9 Years Pitcher (b. 8 Aug 1897 Barwick GA–d. 25 Sep 1968 Archibald Memorial Hospital, Thomasville GA) He operated a sporting goods store near Tallahassee FL. Died after a long illness. Buried Laurel Hill Cemetery, Thomasville GA.

Ed Holly—4 Years Infielder (b. 6 Jul 1879 Chicago IL–d. 27 Nov 1973 Leader Nursing Center, Williamsport PA) He managed minor league baseball and was a scout for several teams, the last ten years for the White Sox, retiring in 1959. Buried Mound Cemetery, Williamsport PA.

Billy Holm—3 Years Catcher (b. 21 Jul 1912 Chicago IL–d. 27 Jul 1977 St Catherine Hospital, East Chicago IN) He managed in the minor leagues for some years before becoming a bus driver for the Portage Township Schools. Buried Calvary Cemetery, Portage IN.

Wattie Holm—7 Years Outfielder (b. 28 Dec 1901 Peterson IA–d. 19 May 1950 in his apartment at Everly IA) He worked at a sporting goods store, and later at a lumber yard in Everly. He killed himself with a revolver after killing his wife and wounding his 14 year-old daughter. Buried Barnes Township Cemetery, Linn Grove IA.

Ducky Holmes—1 Year Catcher (b. 8 Jul 1883 Dayton OH–d. 18 Sep 1945 Dayton OH).

Ducky Holmes—10 Years Outfielder (b. 28 Jan 1869 Des Moines IA–d. 5 Aug 1932 Truro IA) He owned and managed Western League teams at Sioux City IA and Lincoln NE. Death attributable to diabetes. Buried Hartman Cemetery, Truro IA.

Ed Holmes—1 Year Pitcher (b. 22 Mar 1896 Beverly NJ–d. 15 Apr 1954 Our Lady of Loardes Hospital, Camden NJ) He managed the old Heidelberg Inn at Riverside NJ and later operated the Riverview Inn at Centerton NJ. Buried Evergreen Cemetery, Lumberton NJ.

Fred Holmes—2 Years Infielder (b. 1 Jul 1878 Chicago IL–d. 13 Feb 1956 Norwood Park IL).

Jim Holmes—2 Years Pitcher (b. 2 Aug 1882 Lawrenceburg KY–d. 10 Mar 1960 at a hospital in Jacksonville FL) He lived in Jacksonville from 1926 until his death and worked several years for the minor league baseball team there. Later he was active in the retail grocery business. Died after an illness of several months. Buried Riverside Memorial Park, Jacksonville FL.

Tommy Holmes—Hall of Fame (b. abt 1903–d. 25 Mar 1975 Downstate Medical Center, Brooklyn NY) A sportswriter, he covered the Dodgers for more than 30 years, working for the *Brooklyn Eagle* and the *New York Herald-Tribune*. Died from heart disease and circulatory problems. Cremated.

Herm Holshouser—1 Year Pitcher (b. 20 Jan 1907 Rockwell NC–d. 26 Jul 1994 Cabarrus Memorial Hospital, Concord NC) He was a textile worker. Buried Oakwood Cemetery, Concord NC.

Red Holt—1 Year Infielder (b. 25 Jul 1894 Dayton TN–d. 2 Feb 1961 Birmingham AL).

Marty Honan—2 Years Catcher (b. 1870 Chicago IL–d. 20 Aug 1908 Chicago IL) He served in public office in Chicago and was also a singer of some ability. Died from heart disease. Buried Calvary Cemetery, Evanston IL.

Abie Hood—1 Year Infielder (b. 31 Jan 1903 Sanford NC–d. 14 Oct 1988 at a hospital in Chesapeake VA) He worked 30 years for the Norfolk VA Fire Department. Buried Riverside Memorial Park, Norfolk VA.

Wally Hood—3 Years Outfielder (b. 9 Feb 1895 Whittier CA–d. 2 May 1965 at his home in Los Angeles CA) He was an electrician for 40 years. Died from emphysema. Buried Rose Hills Memorial Park, Whittier CA.

Cy Hooker—2 Years Pitcher (b. 28 Aug 1880 Richmond VA–d. 2 Jul 1929 at his home in Richmond VA) He was a detective for the Richmond, Fredericksburg and Potomac Railroad. Died from a heart attack. Buried Riverview Cemetery, Richmond VA.

Alex Hooks—1 Year Infielder (b. 29 Aug 1906 Edgewood TX–d. 19 Jun 1993 Edgewood TX) Served in the U.S. Army during World War II. He coached baseball at Southern Methodist University for 16 years. Died after a lengthy illness. Buried Oak Hill Cemetery, Edgewood TX.

Bob Hooper—6 Years Pitcher (b. 30 May 1922 Ontario, Canada–d. 17 Mar 1980 at his home in New Brunswick NJ) Served in the U.S. Army Air Force during World War II. He was a physical education teacher at New Brunswick until his retirement in 1979. Died from a heart attack. Buried Immaculate Conception Cemetery, Somerville NJ.

Harry Hooper—17 Years Outfielder Hall of Fame (b. 24 Aug 1887 Bell Station CA–d. 18 Dec 1974 Dominican Hospital, Santa Cruz CA) An avid fisherman and bowler, he was in the real estate business at Capitola CA and later served 24 years as postmaster there. Died from an abdominal aneurysm two weeks following surgery. Buried Calvary Cemetery, Aptos CA.

Dick Hoover—1 Year Pitcher (b. 11 Dec 1925 Columbus OH–d. 12 Apr 1981 Lake Placid FL) He retired as a sergeant from the Columbus Police Department. Killed in an automobile accident six miles south of Lake Placid. Buried St Joseph Cemetery, Lockbourne OH.

Joe Hoover—3 Years Infielder (b. 15 Apr 1915 Brawley CA–d. 2 Sep 1965 Los Angeles CA) He owned and operated a delicatessen. Died from a heart attack. Buried Banning-Cabazon Cemetery, Banning CA.

Sam Hope—1 Year Pitcher (b. 4 Dec 1878 Brooklyn NY–d. 30 Jun 1946 Greenport NY) Died after being in failing health several years. Buried Holtsville NY.

Marty Hopkins—2 Years Infielder (b. 22 Feb 1907 Wolfe City TX–d. 20 Nov 1963 Dallas TX) He lived at Dallas 17 years and was a representative for Employer's Casualty Insurance Company from 1953 until his death. Died from a heart attack. Buried Restland Memorial Park, Dallas TX.

Mike Hopkins—1 Year Catcher (b. 1 Nov 1872 Glasgow, Scotland–d. 5 Feb 1952 Pittsburgh PA) He was a retired railroad conductor. Died from a heart condition. Buried Mount Calvary Cemetery, McKees Rocks PA.

Sis Hopkins—1 Year Outfielder (b. 3 Jan 1883 Grafton VA–d. 2 Oct 1929 Phoebus VA) He was known as an expert carpenter in the Phoebus area. Died from a heart attack. Buried Oakland Cemetery, Hampton VA.

Bill Hopper—3 Years Pitcher (b. 26 Aug 1890 Jackson TN–d. 14 Jan 1965 Veteran's Hospital, Dearborn MI) World War I veteran. He was a retired mechanic for Wilson Motor Company in Pontiac MI. Died after a long illness. Buried Brown's Cemetery, Jackson TN.

Jim Hopper—1 Year Pitcher (b. 1 Sep 1919 Charlotte NC–d. 23 Jan 1982 Charlotte NC) He was a retired self-service station operator. Died from lung cancer. Buried Evergreen Cemetery, Charlotte NC.

John Horan—1 Year Pitcher (b. 1863 Ireland–d. 21 Dec 1905 Chicago IL) Buried Calvary Cemetery, Evanston IL.

Shags Horan—1 Year Outfielder (b. 5 Sep 1905 St Louis MO–d. 13 Feb 1969 Riviera Community Hospital, Torrance CA) Died from a heart attack. Buried Angeles Abbey Memorial Park, Compton CA.

Trader Horne—1 Year Pitcher (b. 12 Apr 1899 Bachman OH–d. 3 Feb 1983 at his home in

Franklin OH) Cremated. Buried Woodland Cemetery, Dayton OH.

Jack Horner—1 Year Pitcher (b. 21 Sep 1863 Baltimore MD–d. 14 Jul 1910 New Orleans LA) He umpired in the minor leagues a few years, then was a scout for the Tigers. Died from a fractured skull when he fell from the second floor of the St Charles Hotel. Cremated.

Rogers Hornsby—23 Years Infielder 13 Years Manager Hall of Fame (b. 27 Apr 1896 Winters TX–d. 5 Jan 1963 Wesley Memorial Hospital, Chicago IL) It is said he was the greatest right handed hitter in the game. Died from a heart condition that developed following surgery to remove a cataract four weeks earlier. Buried Hornsby Bend Cemetery, Austin TX.

Joe Hornung—12 Years Outfielder (b. 12 Jun 1857 Carthage NY–d. 30 Oct 1931 Howard Beach NY) Buried Holy Cross Cemetery, Brooklyn NY.

Hanson Horsey—1 Year Pitcher (b. 26 Nov 1889 Elkton MD–d. 1 Dec 1949 at his home in Millington MD) He umpired minor league baseball and taught at the Bill McGowan umpire school in Florida. Died from a heart attack while bringing wood into his kitchen.

Oscar Horstmann—3 Years Pitcher (b. 2 Jun 1891 Alma MO–d. 11 May 1977 Asbury Hospital, Salina KS) Served in the U.S. Army during World War I. A grain inspector, retiring in 1958, he lived in Kansas City MO 40 years before moving to Salina in 1967. Died from a heart attack. Cremated.

Elmer Horton—2 Years Pitcher (b. 4 Sep 1866 Hamilton OH–d. 12 Aug 1920 at his home in North Bay NY) He conducted a small hotel in North Bay. Died suddenly from heart disease.

Dave Hoskins—2 Years Pitcher (b. 3 Aug 1922 Greenwood MS–d. 2 Apr 1970 Hurley Hospital, Flint MI) He worked at a Chevrolet parts and service department and lived in Flint 32 years. Buried River Rest Cemetery, Flint MI.

Gene Host—2 Years Pitcher (b. 1 Jan 1933 Leeper PA–d. 20 Oct 1998 Nashville TN).

Chuck Hostetler—2 Years Outfielder (b. 22 Sep 1903 McClellandtown PA–d. 18 Feb 1971 at his home in Poudre Park CO) He worked for Boeing Aircraft Company. Buried Blue Eye Cemetery, Blue Eye MO.

Pete Hotaling—9 Years Outfielder (b. 16 Dec 1858 Mohawk NY–d. 3 Jul 1928 Cleveland OH) He was a machinist. Died from lobar pneumonia. Buried Lake View Cemetery, Cleveland OH.

Byron Houck—4 Years Pitcher (b. 28 Aug 1887 Prosper MN–d. 17 Jun 1969 Community Hospital, Santa Cruz CA) A salesman for Flintkote Company for ten years, he had retired and moved to Santa Cruz in 1956. Died from septicemia caused by chronic kidney disease. Cremated. Buried Rosedale Cemetery, Los Angeles CA.

Sadie Houck—8 Years Infielder (b. 1856 Washington DC–d. 26 May 1919 St Elizabeth's Hospital, Washington DC) Buried Glenwood Cemetery, Washington DC.

Fred House—1 Year Pitcher (b. 3 Oct 1890 Cabool MO–d. 16 Nov 1923 Kansas City MO) Buried Mount Washington Cemetery, Independence MO.

Charlie Householder—2 Years Infielder (b. 1856 Harrisburg PA–d. 26 Dec 1908 at his home in Harrisburg PA) He took up woodworking, which he followed until his health failed about 1907. Died after being ill eight months.

Ed Householder—1 Year Outfielder (b. 12 Oct 1869 Pittsburgh PA–d. 3 Jul 1924 General Hospital, Los Angeles CA) Died from cancer of the stomach.

John Houseman—2 Years Infielder (b. 10 Jan 1870 Holland–d. 4 Nov 1922 at his home in Chicago IL) Before prohibition he was in the wholesale wine and liquor business and owned the Majestic Bar in Chicago. Buried Mount Washington Cemetery, Independence MO.

Ben Houser—3 Years Infielder (b. 30 Nov 1883 Shenandoah PA–d. 15 Jan 1952 at his home in Augusta ME) He coached baseball and hockey at Bowdoin College from 1918 until 1931, before becoming the golf pro at the Old Orchard Beach (ME) Club, and later at the Wilson Lake Club at Wilton ME. Cremated. Buried New Gloucester Cemetery, New Gloucester ME.

Joe Houser—1 Year Pitcher (b. 3 Jul 1891 Steubenville OH–d. 3 Jan 1953 at a hospital in Orlando FL) He worked 32 years for Timken Roller Bearing Company, retiring in 1945 and moving to Orlando. There he worked for Atco Aluminum Products. Died after a three-week illness. Buried Forest Hill Cemetery, Canton OH.

Fred Houtz—1 Year Outfielder (b. 4 Sep 1875 Connersville IN–d. 15 Feb 1959 Memorial Hospital, St Marys OH) He worked for the Western Ohio Electric Railway and later was a merchant policeman. Buried New St Joseph Cemetery, Wapakoneta OH.

Hick Hovlik—2 Years Pitcher (b. 20 Aug 1891 Cleveland OH–d. 19 Mar 1955 Lake County Memorial Hosp, Painesville OH) He was a machinist for Park Drop Forge Company in Cleveland. Died after a short illness. Buried Perry OH.

Joe Hovlik—3 Years Pitcher (b. 16 Aug 1884 Czechoslovakia–d. 3 Nov 1951 Oxford Junction IA) For 12 years he was a guard at the Anamosa (IA) Reformatory. Died from a heart attack following a long illness. Buried Mayflower Cemetery, Oxford Junction IA.

Dave Howard—2 Years Infielder (b. 1 May 1889 Washington DC–d. 26 Jan 1956 at a hospital in Dallas TX) A civil and chemical engineer, he was an oil and gas consultant. He was also a barred attorney in Oklahoma. Died from a stroke. Buried Calvary Hill Cemetery, Dallas TX.

Del Howard—5 Years Outfielder (b. 24 Dec 1877 Kenney IL–d. 24 Dec 1956 Waldo Hospital, Seattle WA) He was part-owner of the Oakland Acorns in the Pacific Coast League from 1919 to 1937 and was a dock checker for the U.S. government during World War II. In 1942 he moved to Seattle. Cremated.

Earl Howard—1 Year Pitcher (b. 25 Jun 1893 Everett PA–d. 5 Apr 1937 Everett PA) Served in the U.S. Army during World War I. Died from pneumonia. Buried Everett Cemetery, Everett PA.

Elston Howard—14 Years Catcher (b. 23 Feb 1929 St Louis MO–d. 14 Dec 1980 Columbia Medical Center, New York City NY) Served in the U.S. Army. He was the first black to play for the Yankees and was a coach for the Yankees up until his death. Died from heart failure. Buried George Washington Memorial Park, Paramus NJ.

Ivan Howard—4 Years Infielder (b. 12 Oct 1882 Kenney IL–d. 30 Mar 1967 at a convalescent home in Medford OR) He and his brother operated Camp Lowe, near Hornbrook CA, for many years. Buried Henly-Hornbrook Cemetery, Hornbrook CA.

Paul Howard—1 Year Outfielder (b. 20 May 1884 Boston MA–d. 29 Aug 1968 Miami FL) Died suddenly. Buried Winthrop Cemetery, Winthrop MA.

Les Howe—2 Years Pitcher (b. 24 Aug 1895 Brooklyn NY–d. 16 Jul 1976 Woodmere NY) Buried Long Island National Cemetery, Farmingdale NY.

Dixie Howell—6 Years Pitcher (b. 7 Jan 1920 Bowman KY–d. 18 Mar 1960 Hollywood FL) Served in France and Belgium for the U.S. Army during World War II and was a German POW for five months. Died near the end of his baseball career after suffering a heart attack during a spring training workout. Buried Oak Lawn Cemetery, Wilkes-Barre PA.

Dixie Howell—8 Years Catcher (b. 24 Apr 1920 Louisville KY–d. 5 Oct 1990 Binghamton NY).

Harry Howell—13 Years Pitcher (b. 14 Nov 1876 Brooklyn NY–d. 22 May 1956 Spokane WA) He was a retired mining engineer. He had lived in Spokane since 1927. Buried Greenwood Memorial Terrace, Spokane WA.

Red Howell—11 Games Pinch Hitter (b. 29 Jan 1909 Atlanta GA–d. 1 Oct 1950 at his home in Travelers Rest SC) He operated the Lonesome Pines Tourist Camp at Travelers Rest. Died suddenly. Buried Hollywood Cemetery, Atlanta GA.

Roland Howell—1 Year Pitcher (b. 3 Jan 1892 Napoleonville LA–d. 31 Mar 1973 at his home in Baton Rouge LA) World War I veteran. A retired lawyer, he was Assistant City Attorney in New Orleans until 1925. He also served as a member of Louisiana State University Board of Supervisors from 1942 to 1948, and as National Vice-Commander of the American Legion from 1931 to 1932. Buried Roselawn Memorial Park, Baton Rouge LA.

Dan Howley—1 Year Catcher 6 Years Manager (b. 16 Oct 1885 East Weymouth MA–d. 10 Mar 1944 East Weymouth MA) Buried St Francis Xavier Cemetery, Weymouth MA.

Dick Howser—8 Years Infielder 8 Years Manager (b. 14 May 1937 Miami FL–d. 17 Jun 1987 St Luke's Hospital, Kansas City MO) He managed major league baseball up until his death.

Died from brain cancer. Buried Tallahassee Memory Gardens, Tallahassee FL.

Dummy Hoy—14 Years Outfielder (b. 23 May 1862 Houckstown OH–d. 15 Dec 1961 Cincinnati OH) A deaf-mute, he was a farmer. At the time of his death he was the oldest living ex-major league player. Cremated.

Tex Hoyle—1 Year Pitcher (b. 1 Jul 1921 Carbondale PA–d. 4 Jul 1994 Carbondale PA).

Waite Hoyt—21 Years Pitcher Hall of Fame (b. 9 Sep 1899 Brooklyn NY–d. 25 Aug 1984 Jewish Hospital, Cincinnati OH) At age 15 he was one of the youngest to sign a contract. He later was an announcer 25 years for the Reds. Died from a heart attack. Buried Spring Grove Cemetery, Cincinnati OH.

Al Hubbard—1 Year Infielder (b. 9 Dec 1860 Westfield MA–d. 14 Dec 1930 Newton MA) A consulting engineer, he was involved in construction at Yale, Harvard, Wellesley, Mount Holyoke, William and Mary and many public buildings in the Boston MA area. Died from a stroke. Buried Newton Cemetery, Newton MA.

Cal Hubbard—Hall of Fame (b. 31 Oct 1900 Keytesville MO–d. 17 Oct 1977 Hubert Rutland Hospital, St Petersburg FL) An American League umpire from 1936 to 1951, he was chief of American League umpires from 1951 until 1969. He is also a member of two football halls of fame. Died from cancer. Buried Oakwood Cemetery, Milan MO.

Bill Hubbell—7 Years Pitcher (b. 17 Jun 1897 San Francisco CA–d. 3 Aug 1980 Lakewood CO) He worked for the Internal Revenue Service in Denver CO for 32 years. Buried Crown Hill Cemetery, Denver CO.

Carl Hubbell—16 Years Pitcher Hall of Fame (b. 22 Jun 1903 Carthage MO–d. 21 Nov 1988 Scottsdale Memorial Hospital, Scottsdale AZ) Known for his knuckle ball and his 1934 All-Star Game performance when he struck out five of the greatest hitters in baseball history in order. He once won 24 straight games, and pitched 46⅓ consecutive scoreless innings. He was Director of Player Development for the Giants until his retirement in 1977. Died from injuries suffered in an automobile accident three days earlier. Cremated. Buried New Hope Cemetery, Meeker OK.

Ken Hubbs—3 Years Infielder (b. 23 Dec 1941 Riverside CA–d. 15 Feb 1964 near Provo UT) Died early in a promising baseball career when his private airplane crashed in Provo Lake. Buried Montecito Memorial Park, Colton CA.

Clarence Huber—4 Years Infielder (b. 28 Oct 1897 Tyler TX–d. 22 Feb 1965 Mercy Hospital, Laredo TX) World War I veteran. He retired as a U.S. customs inspector in 1963. Buried Laredo City Cemetery, Laredo TX.

Otto Huber—1 Year Infielder (b. 12 Mar 1914 Garfield NJ–d. 9 Apr 1989 Passaic NJ) Served in the U.S. Army during World War II. He was a master plumber for the City of Garfield for 25 years, retiring in 1978. Buried St Nicholas Cemetery, Lodi NJ.

Jimmy Hudgens—3 Years Infielder (b. 24 Aug 1902 Newburg MO–d. 26 Aug 1955 City Hospital, St Louis MO) Buried St Matthew Cemetery, St Louis MO.

Johnny Hudson—7 Years Infielder (b. 30 Jun 1912 Bryan TX–d. 7 Nov 1970 at his home in Bryan TX) He was a scout for the Giants. Died after a long illness. Buried City Cemetery, Bryan TX.

Nat Hudson—4 Years Pitcher (b. 12 Jan 1859 Chicago IL–d. 14 Mar 1928 at his home in Chicago IL) He worked ten years in the collection department of the Commonwealth Edison Company and was active in city affairs in Chicago from 1894 to 1918. Died following a heart attack. Buried Rosehill Cemetery, Chicago IL.

Frank Huelsman—3 Years Outfielder (b. 5 Jun 1874 St Louis MO–d. 9 Jun 1959 Affton MO).

Al Huenke—1 Year Pitcher (b. 26 Jun 1891 New Bremen OH–d. 20 Sep 1974 Joint Township Memorial Hosp, St Marys OH) World War I veteran. Died after an illness of four months. Buried German Protestant Cemetery, New Knoxville OH.

George Huff—1 Year Manager (b. 11 Jun 1872 Champaign IL–d. 1 Oct 1936 Carle Memorial Hospital, Urbana IL) He was associated with the athletic department of the University of Illinois from 1895 until his death, except for a short while in 1907 when he was manager of the Red Sox. He was athletic director for 35 years and baseball coach for 24 years. Died from uremia following surgery to remove a stomach obstruction. Buried Roselawn Cemetery, Champaign IL.

Ed Hug—1 Year Catcher (b. 14 Jul 1880 Fayetteville OH–d. 11 May 1953 St Francis Hospital, Cincinnati OH) He operated an elevator at the Fenwick Club for many years before becoming associated with the Business Men's Club of Fenwick. He had been hospitalized five years when he died. Buried St Joseph Old Catholic Cemetery, Cincinnati OH.

Miller Huggins—13 Years Infielder 17 Years Manager Hall of Fame (b. 19 Apr 1879 Cincinnati OH–d. 25 Sep 1929 St Vincent's Hospital, New York City NY) Died at the height of his managerial career from blood poisoning brought on by an infection under his right eye. Buried Spring Grove Cemetery, Cincinnati OH.

Bill Hughes—2 Years Infielder (b. 25 Nov 1866 Blandensville IL–d. 25 Aug 1943 at his home in Santa Ana CA) He was a rancher. Died from heart disease. Buried Fairhaven Memorial Park, Santa Ana CA.

Bill Hughes—1 Year Pitcher (b. 18 Nov 1896 Philadelphia PA–d. 25 Feb 1963 at his home in Birmingham AL) Buried Elmwood Cemetery, Birmingham AL.

Ed Hughes—3 Years Pitcher (b. 5 Oct 1880 Chicago IL–d. 11 Oct 1927 McHenry IL) Buried Mount Carmel Cemetery, Hillside IL.

Jim Hughes—4 Years Pitcher (b. 23 Jan 1874 Sacramento CA–d. 2 Jun 1924 Sacramento CA) He was a caretaker at a Sacramento ballpark. Died from a fractured skull suffered in a fall from a railroad trestle. Buried St Joseph's Cemetery, Sacramento CA.

Joe Hughes—1 Year Outfielder (b. 21 Feb 1880 Pardoe PA–d. 13 Mar 1951 Cleveland Clinic, Cleveland OH) He was a salesman for Wood Shovel and Tool Company of Piqua OH. Buried Grove Cemetery, Beaver Falls PA.

Long Tom Hughes—13 Years Pitcher (b. 29 Nov 1878 Chicago IL–d. 8 Feb 1956 Cook County Hospital, Chicago IL) Died from pneumonia. Buried St Joseph Cemetery, River Grove IL.

Mickey Hughes—3 Years Pitcher (b. 25 Oct 1866 New York City NY–d. 10 Apr 1931 Medical Center, Jersey City NJ) He was a shipping clerk. Died from a cerebral hemorrhage.

Roy Hughes—9 Years Infielder (b. 11 Jan 1911 Cincinnati OH–d. 5 Mar 1995 at a health care center in Asheville NC) He owned and operated a paving and roofing company in Dayton OH. Buried Guardian Angel Cemetery, Cincinnati OH.

Tom Hughes—9 Years Pitcher (b. 18 Jan 1884 Coal Creek CO–d. 1 Nov 1961 Olive View Hospital, Los Angeles CA) He was a shipping clerk for a retail clothing company. Died from emphysema, but also suffered from prostate cancer. Buried Forest Lawn Memorial Park, Glendale CA.

Tom Hughes—1 Year Outfielder (b. 6 Aug 1907 Emmet AR–d. 10 Aug 1989 Beaumont TX).

Tommy Hughes—5 Years Pitcher (b. 7 Oct 1919 Wilkes-Barre PA–d. 28 Nov 1990 Geisinger Medical Center, Wilkes-Barre PA) Served as a member of the Special Services during World War II. He was an engineer for the Jersey Central Railroad and later for Foster Wheeler Energy Corp and Crestwood Industrial Park, retiring in 1981. Buried Maple Hill Cemetery, Wilkes-Barre PA.

Vern Hughes—1 Year Pitcher (b. 15 Apr 1893 Etna PA–d. 26 Sep 1961 Sewickley Valley Hospital, Sewickley PA) He retired from the American Bridge Company where he worked 47 years. Buried Sylvania Hills Memorial Park, Rochester PA.

Jim Hughey—7 Years Pitcher (b. 8 Mar 1869 Coldwater MI–d. 29 May 1945 Coldwater MI) Buried Lester Cemetery, Coldwater MI.

Tex Hughson—8 Years Pitcher (b. 9 Feb 1916 Buda TX–d. 6 Aug 1993 Central Texas Medical Center, San Marcos TX) Buried San Marcos Cemetery, San Marcos TX.

Emil Huhn—3 Years Infielder (b. 10 Mar 1892 North Vernon IN–d. 5 Sep 1925 Camden SC) Killed late in his career while playing minor league baseball for the Augusta GA team. The car he was driving, with seven team members as passengers, left the road and turned over, killing two and injuring the others. Buried Oakwood Cemetery, Adrian MI.

William A Hulbert—Hall of Fame (b. 30 Oct 1832 Burlington Flats NY–d. 10 Apr 1882 Chicago IL) He was in the wholesale grocery business and the coal business in Chicago when he became interested in baseball and the Chicago White Stockings in 1870. He was involved in the formation of the National League, and is credited with being the "Founder of the National League." Died from heart disease. Buried Graceland Cemetery, Chicago IL.

Billy Hulen—2 Years Infielder (b. 12 Mar 1870 Dixon CA–d. 2 Oct 1947 Sonoma County Hospital, Santa Rosa CA) He was a house painter. Died from bronchial asthma and heart disease. Buried Cypress Hill Memorial Park, Petaluma CA.

Harry Hulihan—1 Year Pitcher (b. 18 Apr 1899 Rutland VT–d. 11 Sep 1980 Rutland Hospital, Rutland VT) Served in the U.S. Army during World War I. His baseball career was ended by a shoulder injury. He then became an executive for 30 years for Aetna Life Insurance Company in New York City. Died after a short illness. Buried Evergreen Cemetery, Rutland VT.

Rudy Hulswitt—7 Years Infielder (b. 23 Feb 1877 Newport KY–d. 16 Jan 1950 at the Federal Building in Louisville KY) He managed teams in the minors and scouted for the Red Sox, Braves and Dodgers. Died from a heart attack. Buried Lakeland FL.

Jim Hulvey—1 Year Pitcher (b. 18 Jul 1897 Mount Sidney VA–d. 9 Apr 1982 at his home in Mount Sidney VA) He farmed near Mount Sidney. Buried Lebanon Church Cemetery, Mount Sidney VA.

John Hummel—12 Years Infielder (b. 4 Apr 1883 Bloomsburg PA–d. 18 May 1959 Mercy Hospital, Springfield MA) He managed minor league baseball before working 26 years for the Diamond Match Company, retiring in 1957. Buried St Jerome Cemetery, Holyoke MA.

Al Humphrey—1 Year Outfielder (b. 28 Feb 1886 Ashtabula OH–d. 13 May 1961 Ashtabula OH).

Bill Humphrey—1 Year Pitcher (b. 17 Jun 1911 Vienna MO–d. 13 Feb 1992 Cox Medical Center South, Springfield MO) He scouted ten years for the Orioles and retired after six years as a scouting supervisor for the Cardinals. Buried Iberia Cemetery, Iberia MO.

Bert Humphries—6 Years Pitcher (b. 26 Sep 1880 California PA–d. 21 Sep 1945 Orlando FL).

John Humphries—2 Years Catcher (b. 15 Nov 1861 North Gower, Ontario, Canada–d. 29 Nov 1933 at his home in Salinas CA) He taught Latin and mathematics at Salinas Union High School for 13 years after teaching at high schools in Pennsylvania and Palo Alto CA. Died from a heart attack. Cremated.

John Humphries—9 Years Pitcher (b. 23 Jun 1915 Clifton Forge VA–d. 24 Jun 1965 Mercy Hospital, New Orleans LA) Died after a brief illness. Buried Metairie Cemetery, Metairie LA.

Bernie Hungling—3 Years Catcher (b. 5 Mar 1896 Dayton OH–d. 30 Mar 1968 Dayton OH) Buried Calvary Cemetery, Dayton OH.

Bill Hunnefield—6 Years Infielder (b. 5 Jan 1899 Dedham MA–d. 28 Aug 1976 Nantucket MA).

Ben Hunt—2 Years Pitcher (b. 10 Nov 1888 Eufaula OK–d. 27 Sep 1927 Greybull WY) Died from tuberculosis.

Joel Hunt—2 Years Outfielder (b. 11 Oct 1905 Texico NM–d. 24 Jul 1978 Teague TX) Buried Greenwood Cemetery, Teague TX.

Ken Hunt—6 Years Outfielder (b. 13 Jul 1934 Grand Forks ND–d. 8 Jun 1997 at his home in Los Angeles CA) He was a self-employed owner of a trucking company. Died from a heart attack. Cremated. Buried Holy Cross Cemetery, Fargo ND.

Bill Hunter—1 Year Outfielder (b. 8 Jul 1886 Buffalo NY–d. 10 Apr 1934 at his home in Buffalo NY) Died after a long illness. Buried Ridge Lawn Cemetery, Cheektowaga NY.

Catfish Hunter—15 Years Pitcher Hall of Fame (b. 18 Apr 1946 Hertford NC–d. 9 Sep 1999 at his home in Hertford NC) He retired to his farm in North Carolina where he died. Died from Lou Gehrig's disease. Buried Cedarwood Cemetery, Hertford NC.

Eddie Hunter—1 Games Infielder (b. 6 Feb 1905 Bellevue KY–d. 14 Mar 1967 Colerain OH) He was a checker for Pepsi-Cola. Buried Gate of Heaven Cemetery, Cincinnati OH.

George Hunter—2 Years Outfielder (b. 9 Jul 1886 Buffalo NY–d. 11 Jan 1968 at a hospital in Harrisburg PA) He worked 27 years for the U.S. Postal Service, retiring in 1956. Buried Rolling Green Memorial Park, Camp Hill PA.

Herb Hunter—4 Years Infielder (b. 25 Dec 1895 Melrose MA–d. 25 Jul 1970 Orlando FL)

Served in the U.S. Navy during both World Wars I and II. A retired hotel manager, he moved to Central Florida in 1937 where he engaged in real estate sales.

Lem Hunter—1 Year Pitcher (b. 14 Jan 1863 Coshocton OH–d. 9 Nov 1956 Rose Lawn Nursing Home, West Lafayette OH) Died following a four-week illness. Buried Fairfield Cemetery, West Lafayette OH.

Newt Hunter—1 Year Infielder (b. 5 Jan 1880 Chillicothe OH–d. 26 Oct 1963 University Hospital, Columbus OH) He worked 50 years in baseball as a player, coach, scout, minor league manager and minor league umpire. Buried Green Lawn Memorial Cemetery, Columbus OH.

Walter Huntzinger—4 Years Pitcher (b. 6 Feb 1899 Pottsville PA–d. 11 Aug 1981 Delaware County Hospital, Drexel Hill PA) He coached basketball at Haverford College before going to work for Adam Scheidt Brewery in Norristown PA. Later he was a court crier in Delaware County (PA) Court of Common Pleas and a township constable. Buried Arlington Cemetery, Drexel Hill PA.

Tom Hurd—3 Years Pitcher (b. 27 May 1924 Danville VA–d. 5 Sep 1982 Scholtz Medical Center, Waterloo IA) He was a foreman at Hawkeye Steel Products. Cremated.

Jerry Hurley—3 Years Catcher (b. 15 Jun 1863 Boston MA–d. 17 Sep 1950 Dorchester MA) He joined the U.S. Immigration Department in 1894, working in Boston and Washington DC, retiring many years later as Deputy Commissioner of the Boston office. Died after a long illness.

Pat Hurley—2 Years Catcher (b. Apr 1875 New York City NY–d. 27 Dec 1919 New York City NY).

Don Hurst—7 Years Infielder (b. 12 Aug 1905 Maysville KY–d. 6 Dec 1952 Los Angeles CA) He worked in maintenance for the Veteran's Memorial Auditorium in Culver City CA. Died from adenocarcinoma while enroute to the hospital after being ill several months. Cremated.

Tim Hurst—1 Year Manager (b. 30 Jun 1865 Ashland PA–d. 4 Jun 1915 at his cousin's home in Minersville PA) He umpired nine years in the National League before going into the real estate business in Far Rockaway NY. He also promoted sports events in New York City. Died suddenly from ptomaine poisoning following an acute attack of indigestion while visiting his cousin. Buried Calvary Cemetery, Woodside NY.

Carl Husta—1 Year Infielder (b. 8 Apr 1902 Egg Harbor NJ–d. 6 Nov 1951 Kingston NY) Died after a lingering illness. Buried Egg Harbor City Cemetery, Egg Harbor City NJ.

Bill Husted—1 Year Pitcher (b. 9 Oct 1867 Gloucester NJ–d. 17 May 1941 Gloucester NJ) Died suddenly. Buried Cedar Grove Cemetery, Gibbsboro NJ.

Bert Husting—3 Years Pitcher (b. 6 Mar 1878 Mayville WI–d. 3 Sep 1948 Columbia Hospital, Milwaukee WI) A Mayville attorney, from 1932 to 1944 he was the United States Attorney for the eastern district of Wisconsin. He was an avid duck hunter. Died from a hemorrhage. Buried Graceland Cemetery, Mayville WI.

Harry Huston—1 Year Catcher (b. 14 Oct 1883 DeGraff OH–d. 13 Oct 1969 Blackwell OK) He coached baseball and football at Southwestern College before becoming coach, history teacher and principal at Blackwell High School in 1915. He was superintendent of the school for 17 years. Buried IOOF Cemetery, Blackwell OK.

Joe Hutcheson—1 Year Outfielder (b. 5 Feb 1905 Springtown TX–d. 23 Feb 1993 Tyler TX).

Johnny Hutchings—6 Years Pitcher (b. 14 Apr 1916 Chicago IL–d. 27 Apr 1963 Methodist Hospital, Indianapolis IN) He worked in or around baseball all his life, most of the time in the American Association. Died from uremic poisoning. Buried Holy Cross Cemetery, Indianapolis IN.

Ed Hutchinson—1 Year Infielder (b. 19 May 1867 Pittsburgh PA–d. 19 Jul 1934 at a hospital in Auburn CA) An iceman, he had lived in Colfax CA since 1914. Died from nephritis. Buried Colfax Cemetery, Colfax CA.

Fred Hutchinson—11 Years Pitcher 12 Years Manager (b. 12 Aug 1919 Seattle WA–d. 12 Nov 1964 Manatee Memorial Hospital, Bradenton FL) World War II veteran. He worked his entire life in baseball. Died from chest cancer. Buried Mount Olivet Cemetery, Renton WA.

Ira Hutchinson—8 Years Pitcher (b. 21 Aug 1910 Chicago IL–d. 21 Aug 1973 Chicago IL) He played and managed in the minor leagues for many years. Died from cancer. Buried Chapel Hill Gardens South, Worth IL.

Jim Hutchinson—1 Year Pitcher (b. 1863–d. 24 Dec 1941 New York City NY) Buried Calvary Cemetery, Woodside NY.

Bill Hutchison—8 Years Pitcher (b. 17 Dec 1859 New Haven CT–d. 19 Mar 1926 Kansas City MO) He was a railroad engineer. Buried Yantic Cemetery, Norwich CT.

Roy Hutson—1 Year Outfielder (b. 27 Feb 1902 Luray MO–d. 20 May 1957 Mercy Hospital, San Diego CA) He was a retired apartment house owner and manager. Died from heart disease. Buried Cypress View Cemetery, San Diego CA.

Ham Hyatt—7 Years Infielder (b. 1 Nov 1884 Buncombe County NC–d. 15 Sep 1963 at a hospital in Spokane WA) A Spokane resident for 25 years, he worked 22 years for the Washington State Patrol. Buried Holy Cross Cemetery, Spokane WA.

Pat Hynes—2 Years Outfielder (b. 12 Mar 1884 St Louis MO–d. 12 Mar 1907 St Louis MO) Shot to death in a bar by the bartender in an argument over the payment for two beers. Buried Calvary Cemetery, St Louis MO.

I

Ham Iburg—1 Year Pitcher (b. 30 Oct 1876 San Francisco CA–d. 11 Feb 1945 San Francisco CA) Died from lymphosarcoma. Buried Holy Cross Catholic Cemetery, Colma CA.

Doc Imlay—1 Year Pitcher (b. 12 Jan 1889 Allentown NJ–d. 7 Oct 1948 Bordentown NJ) He practiced denistry in Bordentown from 1913 until his death. Died suddenly following a heart attack. Buried Christ Churchyard, Bordentown NJ.

Bob Ingersoll—1 Year Pitcher (b. 8 Jan 1883 Rapid City SD–d. 13 Jan 1927 General Hospital, Minneapolis MN) He was a mechanic. Died from pneumonia. Buried Crystal Lake Cemetery, Minneapolis MN.

Scotty Ingerton—1 Year Infielder (b. 19 Apr 1886 Peninsula OH–d. 15 Jun 1956 Fairview Park Hospital, Cleveland OH) For seven years he was a deputy sheriff in Summit County, OH, before opening Scotty's Tavern in Peninsula. He closed the tavern in 1946. Buried St Vincent Cemetery, Akron OH.

Mel Ingram—3 Games Pinch Runner (b. 4 Jul 1903 Asheville NC–d. 28 Oct 1979 Rogue Valley Memorial Hospital, Medford OR) He coached high school sports 40 years, including 1947 to 1968 at Grants Pass High School where he won four state football titles. He had a 40-year record of 220 wins, 77 losses and 22 ties. Died two months after open-heart surgery. Buried Hillcrest Memorial Park, Grants Pass OR.

Bert Inks—5 Years Pitcher (b. 27 Jan 1871 Ligonier IN–d. 3 Oct 1941 at his home in Ligonier IN) He owned the Crystal Theatre in Ligonier from 1907 until his death. Died following a six-month illness. Buried Oak Park Cemetery, Ligonier IN.

Happy Iott—1 Year Outfielder (b. 7 Jul 1876 Houlton ME–d. 17 Feb 1941 Milliken Memorial Hospital, Island Falls ME) Died after suffering from failing health for years. Buried Smyrna Mills ME.

Hooks Iott—2 Years Pitcher (b. 3 Dec 1919 Mountain Grove MO–d. 17 Aug 1980 St Petersburg FL) He managed minor league baseball and worked ten years as a property appraiser for the Pinellas County (FL) Tax Appraiser's Office. He was an avid golfer. Died from a heart attack. Buried Memorial Park Cemetery, St Petersburg FL.

Hal Irelan—1 Year Infielder (b. 5 Aug 1890 Burnettsville IN–d. 16 Jul 1944 Carmel IN) He managed minor league baseball and was a scout for the Indians. Cremated.

Ed Irvin—1 Year Infielder (b. 1882 Philadelphia PA–d. 18 Feb 1916 Philadelphia PA) Died from injuries suffered when he was thrown through a saloon window.

Arthur Irwin —13 Years Infielder 8 Years Manager (b. 14 Feb 1858 Toronto, Ontario, Canada–d. 16 Jul 1921 Atlantic Ocean) He worked his entire life in baseball as a player, manager or executive. He disappeared onboard the cruise steamer *Calvin Austin*, sailing between New York City and Boston, apparently taking his own life by jumping overboard. He had been despondent over ill health and had been treated in a New York City hospital for stomach trouble. His body was never recovered.

Bill Irwin —1 Year Pitcher (b. 16 Sep 1859 Neville OH–d. 8 Aug 1933 Fort Thomas KY).

Charlie Irwin —10 Years Infielder (b. 15 Feb 1869 Clinton IL–d. 21 Sep 1925 Chicago IL) He managed one year in the Pacific Coast League before becoming an umpire in the American Association and the South Atlantic (Sally) League. Killed when he was run over by a city transit bus. Buried Holy Sepulchre Cemetery, Worth IL.

John Irwin —8 Years Infielder (b. 21 Jul 1861 Toronto, Ontario, Canada–d. 28 Feb 1934 St Margaret's Hospital, Dorchester MA) He coached baseball at Bowdoin College for six years, then was associated with Miah Murray in bowling alleys and a billiard parlor. Later he built and maintained a hotel on Pedocks Island until it was closed by military order during World War I. Died from pneumonia following surgery for an intestinal disorder. Buried Mount Hope Cemetery, Boston MA.

Tommy Irwin —1 Year Infielder (b. 20 Dec 1912 Altoona PA–d. 25 Apr 1996 at his home in Altoona PA) For 31 years he was a conductor on the Penn Central Railroad, retiring in 1974. He was also a scout for the Indians. Died following an extended illness. Buried Calvary Cemetery, Altoona PA.

Walt Irwin —4 Games Pinch Hitter (b. 23 Sep 1897 Henrietta PA–d. 18 Aug 1976 Spring Lake MI) He was a millwright for Anderson Bolling, retiring in 1970. World War I veteran. Buried Altoona PA.

James Isaminger —Hall of Fame. Died 1946. He was a sportswriter.

Frank Isbell —10 Years Infielder (b. 21 Aug 1875 Delavan NY–d. 15 Jul 1941 at a hospital in Wichita KS) He owned and managed the Wichita team in the Western League until 1927. Operating a filling station in Wichita, he was also a Sedgwick County Commissioner from 1938 until his death. Died from a heart attack while being prepared for minor surgery. Buried Old Mission Cemetery, Wichita KS.

J

Ray Jablonski —8 Years Infielder (b. 17 Dec 1926 Chicago IL–d. 25 Nov 1985 Rush-Presbyterian St Luke Hosp, Chicago IL) World War II veteran. Died from kidney failure. Buried Resurrection Cemetery, Justice IL.

Fred Jacklitsch—13 Years Catcher (b. 24 May 1876 Brooklyn NY–d. 18 Jul 1937 at his home in Laurelton NY) He coached college baseball at Amherst College from 1919 to 1925 and at Rutgers University from 1926 to 1931. He also worked with youth groups at Prospect Park Parade Grounds. Buried Greenwood Cemetery, Brooklyn NY.

Bill Jackson —2 Years Infielder (b. 4 Apr 1881 Pittsburgh PA–d. 24 Sep 1958 St Francis Hospital, Peoria IL) He was a real estate salesman. Buried Springdale Cemetery, Peoria IL.

Charlie Jackson —2 Years Outfielder (b. 7 Feb 1894 Granite City IL–d. 27 May 1968 Community Hospital, Radford VA) Buried Oak Grove Cemetery, St Louis MO.

Charlie Jackson —1 Year Pitcher (b. 4 Aug 1876 Versailles OH–d. 23 Nov 1957 at a hospital in Scottsbluff NE) Died from exposure after collapsing while pheasant hunting. Buried Fairview Cemetery, Scottsbluff NE.

George Jackson —3 Years Outfielder (b. 2 Jan 1882 Springfield MO–d. 26 Nov 1972 Johnson

County Memorial Hosp, Cleburne TX) A rancher, he lived in Blum TX 84 years. Buried Blum Cemetery, Blum TX.

Henry Jackson—1 Year Infielder (b. 23 Jun 1861 Union City IN–d. 14 Sep 1932 Chicago IL).

Jim Jackson—4 Years Outfielder (b. 28 Nov 1877 Philadelphia PA–d. 8 Oct 1955 at his home in Philadelphia PA) After spending some time managing minor league baseball he conducted a real estate business in Philadelphia for 30 years. Buried Arlington Cemetery, Drexel Hill PA.

Joe Jackson—13 Years Outfielder (b. 16 Jul 1888 Brandon Mills SC–d. 5 Dec 1951 at his home in Greenville SC) He has the third highest lifetime batting average and was banned from baseball due to the Black Sox Scandal. He played and managed semi-pro baseball in South Carolina after he was banned from baseball and owned a liquor store in Greenville. Died from a heart attack. Buried Woodlawn Memorial Park, Greenville SC.

John Jackson—1 Year Pitcher (b. 15 Jul 1909 Wynnefield PA–d. 24 Oct 1956 Somers Point NJ).

Larry Jackson—14 Years Pitcher (b. 2 Jun 1931 Nampa ID–d. 28 Aug 1990 at a care center in Boise ID) He served eight years in the Idaho legislature during the 1970s and was also a member of the Idaho Industrial Commission. In 1978 he campaigned for the Republican nomination for governor and lost. Died after a long bout with cancer. Cremated.

Lou Jackson—3 Years Outfielder (b. 26 Jul 1935 Riverton LA–d. 29 May 1969 Tokyo, Japan) Died after a short illness. Buried Monroe City Cemetery, Monroe LA.

Travis Jackson—15 Years Infielder Hall of Fame (b. 2 Nov 1903 Waldo AR–d. 27 Jul 1987 at his home in Waldo AR) A member of the Arkansas Hall of Fame, he coached for several years. Buried Waldo Cemetery, Waldo AR.

Art Jacobs—1 Year Pitcher (b. 28 Aug 1902 Luckey OH–d. 8 Jun 1967 Centinela Valley Hospital, Inglewood CA) For 30 years he was a studio grip at a motion picture studio. Died from a heart attack. Cremated.

Bucky Jacobs—3 Years Pitcher (b. 21 Mar 1913 Altavista VA–d. 15 Jun 1990 at a hospital in Richmond VA) He worked at Bellwood Arsenal during World War II, then went into the vacuum cleaner business in Richmond. Died after a heart attack. Buried Forestlawn Cemetery, Richmond VA.

Elmer Jacobs—9 Years Pitcher (b. 10 Aug 1892 Salem MO–d. 10 Feb 1958 at his home in Salem MO) He played professional baseball 22 years, some in the Pacific Coast League and Southern Association. Buried Cedar Grove Cemetery, Salem MO.

Mike Jacobs—1 Year Infielder (b. abt 1873–d. 21 Mar 1949 Louisville KY) Died from gas inhalation, an apparent suicide.

Otto Jacobs—1 Year Catcher (b. 19 Apr 1889 Chicago IL–d. 19 Nov 1955 Chicago IL) Buried Acacia Park Cemetery, Chicago IL.

Ray Jacobs—2 Games Pinch-Hitter (b. 2 Jan 1902 Salt Lake City UT–d. 5 Apr 1952 Los Angeles CA) He managed in the minor leagues until 1946 when he went to work as a loader for Standard Oil Company. Died in an automobile accident on the Santa Ana Freeway when he failed to negotiate a curve. Buried Holladay Memorial Park, Holladay UT.

Tony Jacobs—2 Years Pitcher (b. 5 Aug 1925 Dixmoor IL–d. 21 Dec 1980 at an infirmary in Nashville TN) World War II veteran. He worked for the Glass Plant of the Ford Motor Company. Buried Spring Hill Cemetery, Nashville TN.

Baby Doll Jacobson—11 Years Outfielder (b. 16 Aug 1890 Cable IL–d. 16 Jan 1977 Rock Island County Health Center, Orion IL) Served in the U.S. Navy during World War I. He farmed near Coal Valley IL from 1929 to 1960. Buried Dayton Corners Cemetery, Colona IL.

Beany Jacobson—4 Years Pitcher (b. 5 Jun 1881 Port Washington WI–d. 31 Jan 1933 Wabash Employee Hospital, Decatur IL) He was a mechanic at the Wabash shops in Decatur. Died from pneumonia after an illness of three weeks. Buried Fairlawn Cemetery, Decatur IL.

Merwin Jacobson—4 Years Outfielder (b. 7 Mar 1894 New Britain CT–d. 13 Jan 1978 at his home in Baltimore MD) He died from cancer. Buried Govans Presbyterian Cemetery, Baltimore MD.

Larry Jacobus—1 Year Pitcher (b. 13 Dec 1893 Cincinnati OH–d. 19 Aug 1965 at his home in North College Hill OH) He was a custodian at a bowling alley. Buried Spring Grove Cemetery, Cincinnati OH.

Charlie Jaeger —1 Year Pitcher (b. 17 Apr 1875 Ottawa IL–d. 27 Sep 1942 Ryburn-King Hospital, Ottawa IL) He played in the Three-I League, Central League and American Association, and was a foreman at Ottawa Drain Tile Company and National Fireproofing Company. He also was a gateman at the Owens-Ford Glass factory west of Ottawa. Buried Ottawa Avenue Cemetery, Ottawa IL.

Joe Jaeger —1 Year Pitcher (b. 3 Mar 1895 St Cloud MN–d. 13 Dec 1963 Hampton IA) Buried Hampton Cemetery, Hampton IA.

Art Jahn —2 Years Outfielder (b. 5 Dec 1895 Struble IA–d. 9 Jan 1948 at a hospital in Little Rock AR) He played in the Southern Association and Pacific Coast League. A good bowler, he opened a bowling alley in Little Rock in 1932. Later he worked as a hotel clerk. Buried Roselawn Memorial Park, Little Rock AR.

Sig Jakucki —3 Years Pitcher (b. 20 Aug 1909 Camden NJ–d. 28 May 1979 Panama Hotel, Galveston TX) World War II veteran. Died from natural causes. Buried Calvary Cemetery, Galveston TX.

Charlie Jamerson —1 Year Pitcher (b. 26 Jan 1900 Enfield IL–d. 4 Aug 1980 at his home in Mocksville NC) He was a retired employee of Burlington Industries. Cremated.

Bernie James —3 Years Infielder (b. 2 Sep 1905 Angleton TX–d. 1 Aug 1994 San Antonio TX) He played and coached in the Texas League for several years before a brief career as a professional calf roper on the rodeo circuit. Later he ranched near Raymondville TX where he raised cattle and prize-winning quarter horses. Died from complications of emphysema. Buried Holy Cross Cemetery, San Antonio TX.

Bill James —8 Years Pitcher (b. 20 Jan 1887 Ann Arbor MI–d. 25 May 1942 V A Hospital, Los Angeles CA) World War I veteran. He was a foreman for WPA. Died from heart disease. Buried Los Angeles National Cemetery, Los Angeles CA.

Bill James —4 Years Pitcher (b. 12 Mar 1892 Iowa Hill CA–d. 10 Mar 1971 Community Hospital, Oroville CA) He was an appraiser for Butte County, CA. He was also an avid fisherman. Died from a stroke. Buried Memorial Park Cemetery, Oroville CA.

Bob James —1 Year Outfielder (b. 7 Jul 1884 Coopertown TN–d. 2 Jan 1959 at his home in Adairville KY) A prominent farmer in Adairville, he also owned a grocery store there, retiring from the grocery business in 1939. He was a magistrate in the Logan County (KY) fiscal court from 1931 until his death and a director in the First National Bank there since 1944, as well as being active in a number of other civic affairs. Buried Greenwood Cemetery, Adairville KY.

Lefty James —3 Years Pitcher (b. 1 Jul 1889 Glen Roy OH–d. 3 May 1933 at his parent's home in Glen Roy OH) He operated a restaurant and billiard room at New Boston OH. Died from grippe and septic endocarditis. Buried Ridgewood Cemetery, Wellston OH.

Charlie Jamieson —18 Years Outfielder (b. 7 Feb 1893 Paterson NJ–d. 27 Oct 1969 General Hospital, Paterson NJ) He worked for Wright Aeronautical Company until he retired in 1958. After that he was a school-crossing guard in Hawthorne NJ. Died after a five-week illness. Buried Valleau Cemetery, Ridgewood NJ.

Vic Janowicz —2 Years Catcher (b. 26 Feb 1930 Elyria OH–d. 27 Feb 1996 Riverside Methodist Hospital, Columbus OH) The Heisman Trophy winner in 1950, playing football at Ohio State University, he also played pro football. He was an administrative assistant in the Auditor's Office of the State of Ohio. Died after a five-year battle with cancer. Buried St Joseph Cemetery, Lockbourne OH.

Ray Jansen —1 Year Infielder (b. 16 Jan 1889 St Louis MO–d. 19 Mar 1934 Barnes Hospital, St Louis MO) He was sales manager for the Chevrolet Motor Company at Denver CO before moving to a similar position in St Louis shortly before his death. Died following surgery for a brain tumor. Buried Valhalla Cemetery, St Louis MO.

Heinie Jantzen —1 Year Outfielder (b. 9 Apr 1890 Chicago IL–d. 1 Apr 1948 Hines Memorial Hospital, Chicago IL).

Hal Janvrin —10 Years Infielder (b. 27 Aug 1892 Haverhill MA–d. 2 Mar 1962 City Hospital, Boston MA) Served in the U.S. Army during World War I. He coached baseball at Harvard from 1931 to 1934. Owned a bowling alley in Boston prior to World War II when he served as the civilian head of Rowes Wharf in Boston for the Dept of Civil Defense. Later he worked for the Internal Revenue Service in Boston. Buried Exeter NH.

Roy Jarvis—3 Years Catcher (b. 27 Jun 1926 Shawnee OK–d. 13 Jan 1990 at his home in Oklahoma City OK) Served in the U.S. Navy during World War II. He was a salesman. Buried Lofland Cemetery, Wyandotte OK.

Hi Jasper—4 Years Pitcher (b. 24 May 1887 St Louis MO–d. 22 May 1937 St Louis MO) He was a bartender in a St Louis tavern. Killed instantly when the tailboard of a truck, on which he was riding, collapsed, plunging him to the pavement and fracturing his skull.

Al Javery—7 Years Pitcher (b. 5 Jun 1918 Worcester MA–d. 16 Aug 1977 Kimball Hospital, Putnam CT) He worked at a number of jobs including head of the housekeeping unit at a Worcester carecenter, bookkeeper for B and D Distributors in Worcester, manager of a bowling alley and automobile salesman. Died from a heart attack while vacationing in Connecticut. Buried St Roch's Cemetery, Oxford MA.

Tex Jeanes—5 Years Outfielder (b. 19 Dec 1900 Maypearl TX–d. 5 Apr 1973 at a hospital in Longview TX) He lived in Longview 40 years, moving there from Dallas to manage the local minor league baseball team. Died after a lengthy illness. Buried Memory Park Cemetery, Longview TX.

George Jeffcoat—4 Years Pitcher (b. 24 Dec 1913 New Brookland SC–d. 13 Oct 1978 at his home in Leesville SC) He was pastor and training director of the Old Lexington Baptist Church for 17 years. Died from a self-inflicted gunshot wound. Buried Old Lexington Baptist Church Cemetery, Lexington SC.

Irv Jeffries—3 Years Infielder (b. 10 Sep 1905 Louisville KY–d. 8 Jun 1982 Lyndon Lane Nursing Center, Louisville KY) He managed several minor league teams and was a scout for the White Sox. Died after a long illness. Buried Evergreen Cemetery, Louisville KY.

Frank Jelincich—1 Year Outfielder (b. 3 Sep 1917 San Jose CA–d. 27 Jun 1992 St Mary's Hospital, Rochester MN) He was a retired salesman. Buried Oak Hill Memorial Park, San Jose CA.

Fats Jenkins—17 Years Outfielder (b. 19 Jan 1898 New York City NY–d. 4 Dec 1968 Broad Street Med Center, Philadelphia PA) He played in the negro leagues and also played basketball on a black touring team. He was inducted into the Basketball Hall of Fame in 1963. Buried Eden Cemetery, Philadelphia PA.

Joe Jenkins—3 Years Catcher (b. 12 Oct 1890 Shelbyville TN–d. 21 Jun 1974 at his home in Fresno CA) He was a vineyard rancher for 30 years. Died from a heart attack. Buried Belmont Memorial Park, Fresno CA.

John Jenkins—1 Year Infielder (b. 7 Jul 1896 Bosworth MO–d. 3 Aug 1968 Ellis Fischel Hospital, Columbia MO) Died after being a patient in the hospital for three months. Buried Van Horn Cemetery, Tina MO.

Tom Jenkins—6 Years Outfielder (b. 10 Apr 1898 Camden AL–d. 3 May 1979 South Shore Hospital, Weymouth MA) He was a shop worker at the Allis-Chalmers plant in Bostom MA for 16 years, retiring in 1963. Died unexpectedly. Buried Pine Hill Cemetery, Quincy MA.

Alamazoo Jennings—1 Year Catcher (b. 30 Nov 1851 Newport KY–d. 2 Nov 1894 City Hospital, Cincinnati OH) He was a policeman for a short while before becoming a minor league umpire. Buried Evergreen Cemetery, Southgate KY.

Hughie Jennings—17 Years Infielder 14 Years Manager Hall of Fame (b. 2 Apr 1869 Pittston PA–d. 1 Feb 1928 at his home in Scranton PA) He spent most of his life in baseball as a player, coach and manager. Died from meningitis. Buried St Catherine's Cemetery, Moscow PA.

Bill Jensen—2 Years Pitcher (b. 17 Nov 1889 Philadelphia PA–d. 27 Mar 1917 Philadelphia PA).

Jackie Jensen—11 Years Outfielder (b. 9 Mar 1927 San Francisco CA–d. 14 Jul 1982 University Hospital, Charlottesville VA) An All-American halfback at the Univ of California, he was the only person to play in the Rose Bowl, the East-West Shrine Game, the World Series and baseball's All-Star Game. Served in the U.S. Navy during World War II. He coached baseball at the University of Nevada and the University of California before moving to Virginia in 1977 to operate a Christmas tree farm and run a baseball camp. Died from a heart attack. Buried Amherst Cemetery, Amherst VA.

Dan Jessee—1 Game Pinch Runner (b. 22 Feb 1901 Olive Hill KY–d. 30 Apr 1970 at his home in Venice FL) A college professor and coach, he retired to Venice from Hartford CT in 1968. Cremated.

Augie Johns —2 Years Pitcher (b. 10 Sep 1899 St Louis MO–d. 12 Sep 1975 San Antonio TX).

Ollie Johns —1 Year Pitcher (b. 21 Aug 1879 Trenton OH–d. 17 Jun 1961 Sunnybreeze Convalscent Home, Hamilton OH) He owned and operated a hardware implement and feed store in Trenton and Dayton OH for many years. Died after being in failing health for 18 months. Buried Miltonville Cemetery, Miltonville OH.

Pete Johns —2 Years Infielder (b. 17 Jan 1889 Cleveland OH–d. 9 Aug 1964 Hanna House Hospital, Cleveland OH) Died from cancer. Buried Knollwood Cemetery, Mayfield OH.

Abbie Johnson —2 Years Infielder (b. 26 Jul 1872 Chicago IL–d. 28 Nov 1960 Detroit MI).

Adam Johnson —3 Years Pitcher (b. 4 Feb 1888 Burnet TX–d. 2 Jul 1972 Lysock View, Williamsport PA) Buried Montoursville Cemetery, Montoursville PA.

Arnold Johnson —(b. 11 Jan 1907 Chicago IL–d. 10 Mar 1960 West Palm Beach FL) The owner of the Kansas City Athletics from 1954 to 1960, he had extensive real estate holdings, including Yankee Stadium, which he sold when he bought the Athletics. He also had interests in the publishing business. Died from a stroke. Cremated.

Art Johnson —1 Year Pitcher (b. 15 Feb 1897 Warren PA–d. 7 Jun 1982 Sarasota Memorial Hospital, Sarasota FL) He worked 27 years as a salesman for Metropolitan Life Insurance Company and was the sports editor for the *Jamestown* (NY) *Post* before retiring to Florida in 1965. Cremated.

Ban Johnson —Hall of Fame (b. Jan 1865 Norwalk OH–d. 28 Mar 1931 St John's Hospital, St Louis MO) Educated as an attorney, he worked as a sportswriter until he was instrumental in the formation of the Western League in 1893 and, finally, the American League in 1901. He was president of the American League from 1901 to 1927. Died from diabetes. Buried Riverside Cemetery, Spencer IN.

Bill Johnson —2 Years Outfielder (b. 18 Oct 1892 Chicago IL–d. 5 Nov 1950 V A Hospital, Los Angeles CA) World War I veteran. He was a laborer at a motion picture studio. Died from congestive heart failure. Buried Los Angeles National Cemetery, Los Angeles CA.

Bob Johnson —13 Years Outfielder (b. 26 Nov 1906 Pryor OK–d. 6 Jul 1982 Tacoma WA) He was inducted into the Washington State Sports Hall of Fame. Died from heart failure. Cremated. Buried Mountain View Memorial Park, Tacoma WA.

Charlie Johnson —1 Year Outfielder (b. 12 Mar 1885 Slatington PA–d. 28 Aug 1940 Marcus Hook PA).

Chet Johnson —1 Year Pitcher (b. 1 Aug 1917 Redmond WA–d. 10 Apr 1983 Seattle WA) He pitched for years in the Pacific Coast League, retiring in 1955. He retired as a salesman for Cudahy-Bar S Products in Seattle in 1982. Died after an extended illness. Cremated.

Chief Johnson —3 Years Pitcher (b. 25 Mar 1887 Winnebago NE–d. 12 Jun 1922 Des Moines IA) An Indian, he was shot to death after a quarrel over a dice game. Buried Agency Cemetery, Winnebago NE.

Deron Johnson —16 Years Infielder (b. 17 Jul 1938 San Diego CA–d. 23 Apr 1992 at his home in Poway CA) He spent his entire life in baseball as a player and coach. Died from lung cancer. Buried Dearborn Memorial Park, Poway CA.

Earl Johnson —8 Years Pitcher (b. 2 Apr 1919 Redmond WA–d. 3 Dec 1994 Seattle WA) A highly decorated World War II veteran, he was an avid bowler and fisherman. For 44 years he was associated with the Red Sox as a player and scout.

Ed Johnson —1 Year Outfielder (b. 31 Mar 1899 Morganfield KY–d. 3 Jul 1975 Union County Hospital, Morganfield KY) He played baseball for 12 years before he surveyed for gas transmission lines in Indiana and Kentucky. In 1932 he entered the theater business at Sturgis KY, working in that business until his death. Died after suffering from failing health for years. Buried St Ann's Cemetery, Morganfield KY.

Ellis Johnson —3 Years Pitcher (b. 8 Dec 1892 Minneapolis MN–d. 14 Jan 1965 Minneapolis MN) World War I veteran. He was a plumber for Dayton Company. Buried Hillside Cemetery, Minneapolis MN.

Elmer Johnson —1 Year Catcher (b. 12 Jun 1884 Beard IN–d. 31 Oct 1966 Gulf Crest Nursing Home, Hollywood FL) Until his retirement he was an employee of Indiana Brass Company. Died after being in failing health for some time. Buried Bunnell Cemetery, Frankfort IN.

Ernie Johnson—10 Years Infielder (b. 29 Apr 1888 Chicago IL–d. 1 May 1952 at a sanitarium in Monrovia CA) A minor league manager and a scout for the Red Sox since 1930, he signed players like Ted Williams, Bobby Doerr and Johnny Pesky. Died from bronchial asthma. Buried Fairhaven Memorial Park, Santa Ana CA.

Fred Johnson—4 Years Pitcher (b. 5 Mar 1897 Hanley TX–d. 14 Jun 1973 V A Hospital, Kerrville TX) Buried Sunset Memorial Park, San Antonio TX.

Hank Johnson—12 Years Pitcher (b. 21 May 1906 Bradenton FL–d. 20 Aug 1982 Manatee Memorial Hospital, Bradenton FL) He was a constable and worked in the Manatee County, FL, tax office. Buried Fogartyville Cemetery, Bradenton FL.

Jing Johnson—5 Years Pitcher (b. 9 Oct 1894 Parker Ford PA–d. 6 Dec 1950 Pottstown PA) He coached college baseball before becoming co-manager of the McCarraher Brothers Store in Pottstown. He was killed instantly in a two-car accident. Buried Parker Ford Baptist Cemetery, Parker Ford PA.

John Johnson—1 Year Pitcher (b. 18 Nov 1869 North Cohocton NY–d. 28 Jan 1941 Kansas City MO) Buried Floral Hills Memorial Gardens, Kansas City MO.

Johnny Johnson—2 Years Pitcher (b. 29 Sep 1914 Belmore OH–d. 26 Jun 1991 Iron Mountain MI).

Judy Johnson—18 Years Infielder Hall of Fame (b. 26 Oct 1899 Snow Hill MD–d. 15 Jun 1989 Terrace Nursing Home in Wilmington DE) Played in the negro leagues. He worked for the Continental Can Company and operated a general store with his brother. Later he was a major league coach and scout. Buried Silverbrook Cemetery, Wilmington DE.

Lloyd Johnson—1 Year Pitcher (b. 24 Dec 1910 Santa Rosa CA–d. 8 Oct 1980 at a hospital in Stockton CA) An ARCO petroleum products dealer in Stockton, he retired about 1978. Buried Cherokee Memorial Park, Lodi CA.

Otis Johnson—1 Year Infielder (b. 5 Nov 1883 Fowler IN–d. 9 Nov 1915 Johnson City NY) He was killed accidentally at the height of his career when he tripped and fell on his gun during a fox chase. He worked as a shoemaker during the off-season. Buried Floral Park Cemetery, Johnson City NY.

Paul Johnson—2 Years Outfielder (b. 2 Sep 1896 North Grosvenordale CT–d. 14 Feb 1973 General Hospital, McAllen TX) World War I veteran. He lived in the Rio Grande Valley of Texas for 50 years and was a retired oil field gauger. Died from a cerebral hemorrhage. Buried Laurel Hill Cemetery, Mission TX.

Roy Johnson—10 Years Outfielder 1 Year Manager (b. 23 Feb 1903 Pryor OK–d. 11 Sep 1973 at his home in Tacoma WA) He was a laborer. Died from a heart attack after years of chronic alcoholism. Cremated.

Roy Johnson—1 Year Pitcher (b. 1 Oct 1895 Madill OK–d. 10 Jan 1986 Pueblo Norte Nursing Center, Scottsdale AZ) He coached for the Cubs for 20 years, and was a scout for them another 20 years. He moved to Scottsdale AZ in 1964. Cremated, and his ashes scattered on Camelback Mountain in Phoenix.

Si Johnson—17 Years Pitcher (b. 5 Oct 1906 Danway IL–d. 12 May 1994 at his home in Sheridan IL) Served in the U.S. Navy during World War II. He is best known for striking out Babe Ruth the day before Ruth retired. He was a fireman at the Sheridan Correctional Center. Buried Elerding Cemetery, Sheridan IL.

Syl Johnson—19 Years Pitcher (b. 31 Dec 1900 Portland OR–d. 20 Feb 1985 Portland OR) He managed one year in the minor leagues and was a scout for the Yankees and Dodgers, retiring in 1970. Buried Portland Memorial, Portland OR.

Walter Johnson—21 Years Pitcher 7 Years Manager Hall of Fame (b. 6 Nov 1887 Humboldt KS–d. 10 Dec 1946 Georgetown Hospital, Washington DC) He farmed near Georgetown MD. Died from a brain tumor. Buried Union Cemetery, Rockville MD.

Youngy Johnson—2 Years Pitcher (b. 22 Jul 1877 San Francisco CA–d. 28 Aug 1936 Berkeley CA) Buried Holy Cross Catholic Cemetery, Colma CA.

Dick Johnston—8 Years Outfielder (b. 6 Apr 1863 Kingston NY–d. 3 Apr 1934 at his son's home in Detroit MI) He was superintendent of the Freeman Job Printing Plant in Kingston until he moved to Detroit about 1921. There he worked at the House of Corrections. Died from cancer of the throat. Buried St Mary's Cemetery, Kingston NY.

Doc Johnston—11 Years Infielder (b. 9 Sep 1887 Cleveland TN–d. 17 Feb 1961 at a hospital in Chattanooga TN) He was a plant manager for Sinclair Oil and Refining Company. Died after an extended illness. Buried Brainerd Methodist Cemetery, Chattanooga TN.

Fred Johnston—1 Year Infielder (b. 9 Jul 1901 Pineville NC–d. 14 Jul 1959 Mother Frances Hospital, Tyler TX) He was a real estate agent. Died from a heart attack. Buried Oakwood Cemetery, Tyler TX.

James Johnston—(b. 8 Dec 1895 Chapel Hill NC–d. 28 Dec 1967 at his home in Washington DC) Served in France and Germany for the U.S. Army Air Service during World War I. He was an investment banker and Chairman of the Board for the Washington Senators from 1965 to 1967. Died from cancer. Buried New Hope Church Cemetery, Chapel Hill NC.

Jimmy Johnston—13 Years Infielder (b. 10 Dec 1889 Cleveland TN–d. 14 Feb 1967 Hutcheson Memorial Hospital, Chattanooga TN) He once stole 124 bases in one season for the Pacific Coast League's San Francisco Seals and played and managed in the Southern League. From 1941 until 1959 he was the park superintendent at the Chattanooga baseball park. Buried Forest Hills Cemetery, Chattanooga TN.

Johnny Johnston—1 Year Outfielder (b. 28 Mar 1890 Longview TX–d. 7 Mar 1940 Quintard Hospital, San Diego CA) He was a timekeeper for San Diego Gas and Electric Company. Died from throat cancer. Cremated.

Roy Joiner—3 Years Pitcher (b. 30 Oct 1906 Red Bluff CA–d. 26 Dec 1989 St Elizabeth Hospital, Red Bluff CA) Served in World War II. He ranched near Vina CA for 45 years. Died from pneumonia and arteriosclerotic heart disease. Cremated. Buried Vina-Carter Cemetery, Vina CA.

Stan Jok—2 Years Infielder (b. 3 May 1926 Buffalo NY–d. 6 Mar 1972 Buffalo NY) Served in the U.S. Navy during World War II. He was a commercial distributor for Petroleum Sales and Service of Buffalo. Buried St Stanislaus Cemetery, Buffalo NY.

Smead Jolley—4 Years Outfielder (b. 14 Jan 1902 Wesson AR–d. 17 Nov 1991 South Shore Convalescent Hosp, Alameda CA) He played minor league baseball 17 years, compiling a lifetime .367 minor league batting average and hitting 336 home runs. Died from a stroke. He was cremated and his ashes scattered in the Pacific Ocean, three miles west of the Golden Gate Bridge.

Dave Jolly—5 Years Pitcher (b. 14 Oct 1924 Stony Point NC–d. 27 May 1963 V A Hospital, Durham NC) Served in Europe with the U.S. Army during World War II. He worked for John Boyle and Company in Statesville NC until he had surgery for a brain tumor in July 1962, never fully recovering. Buried Stony Point Cemetery, Stony Point NC.

Alex Jones—4 Years Pitcher (b. 25 Dec 1867 Pittsburgh PA–d. 4 Apr 1941 Woodville PA) Died after a long illness. Buried Homestead Cemetery, Munhall PA.

Art Jones—1 Year Pitcher (b. 7 Feb 1906 Kershaw SC–d. 25 Nov 1980 V A Hospital, Columbia SC) World War II veteran. For 35 years he was an attorney in Kershaw. He represented Kershaw County (SC) in the South Carolina House of Representatives for several terms and was mayor of Kershaw for over 20 years. Buried Kershaw City Cemetery, Kershaw SC.

Bill Jones—2 Years Outfielder (b. 8 Apr 1887 Hartland, New Brunswick, Canada–d. 10 Oct 1946 Boston MA).

Binky Jones—1 Year Infielder (b. 11 Jul 1899 St Louis MO–d. 13 May 1961 St Louis MO) Buried Resurrection Cemetery, St Louis MO.

Bob Jones—9 Years Infielder (b. 2 Dec 1889 Clayton CA–d. 30 Aug 1964 Casa Blanca Convalescent Home, San Diego CA) He operated a Shell service station for 20 years. Died from cirrhosis of the liver. Buried El Camino Memorial Park, San Diego CA.

Broadway Jones—1 Year Pitcher (b. 15 Nov 1898 Millsboro DE–d. 7 Sep 1977 at his home in Lewes DE) He was a salesman for Swift and Company, retiring in 1964. Died from natural causes. Buried Millsboro Cemetery, Millsboro DE.

Bumpus Jones—2 Years Pitcher (b. 1 Jan 1870 Cedarville OH–d. 25 Jun 1938 Green County Hospital, Xenia OH) Died from syphilis tabes dorsalis. Buried North Cemetery, Cedarville OH.

Charlie Jones—5 Years Outfielder (b. 2 Jun 1876 Butler PA–d. 2 Apr 1947 Two Harbors Hospital, Two Harbors MN) He was known far and wide in Cook County, MN, as a master sign painter. Earlier he had worked 14 years for the U.S. Internal Revenue Service in Minneapolis MN. Died following an illness of three weeks. Buried Lutsen MN.

Cobe Jones—2 Years Infielder (b. 21 Aug 1907 Denver CO–d. 3 Jun 1969 Denver CO) He coached high school baseball and football. Buried Mount Olivet Cemetery, Wheat Ridge CO.

Cowboy Jones—4 Years Pitcher (b. 23 Aug 1874 Golden CO–d. 8 Feb 1958 Community Hospital, Gardena CA) He was an engineer for the water department of the State of Colorado. Died from complications of pernicious anemia. Buried Golden Cemetery, Golden CO.

Dale Jones—1 Year Pitcher (b. 17 Dec 1918 Marquette NE–d. 8 Nov 1980 Orlando FL) He was a scout for the Phillies and Dodgers. Died from a heart attack at an awards banquet shortly after receiving a special plaque. Buried Arlington National Cemetery, Arlington VA.

Davy Jones—14 Years Outfielder (b. 30 Jun 1880 Cambria WI–d. 30 Mar 1972 at his home in Mankato MN) He helped organize the forerunner of present-day Baseball Player's Association in 1912. He was an attorney before switching to pharmacy, owning a chain of drug stores in the Detroit area. Selling his last store in 1956, he traveled extensively after that. Buried Roseland Park Cemetery, Berkley MI.

Deacon Jones—3 Years Pitcher (b. 20 Dec 1893 Oskaloosa MO–d. 28 Dec 1952 Mount Carmel Hospital, Pittsburg KS) He was a coal miner before spending ten years as a brakeman for the Kansas City Southern Railroad. Buried LeRoy Cemetery, Oskaloosa KS.

Dick Jones—2 Years Pitcher (b. 22 May 1902 Meadville MS–d. 2 Aug 1994 CareWest Medical Center, Burlingame CA) He was a soil tester for the Soil Division of the U.S. Army Corps of Engineers for 30 years. Died from congestive heart failure. Buried Mount Zion Cemetery, Meadville MS.

Earl Jones—1 Year Pitcher (b. 11 Jun 1919 Fresno CA–d. 24 Jan 1989 St Agnes Hospital, Fresno CA) He spent 50 years in baseball as a player, coach and scout and for 20 years was an engineer for the Fresno Fire Department. Died from lung cancer and a heart attack. Buried Belmont Memorial Park, Fresno CA.

Elijah Jones—2 Years Pitcher (b. 27 Jan 1882 Oakwood MI–d. 28 Apr 1943 Pontiac MI) Died at work in the Fisher Body plant from a heart attack. Buried Oxford Cemetery, Oxford MI.

Fielder Jones—15 Years Outfielder 10 Years Manager (b. 13 Aug 1871 Shinglehouse PA–d. 13 Mar 1934 Good Samaritan Hospital, Portland OR) He was in the lumber business in Portland. Died from a heart ailment. Cremated. Buried Portland Memorial, Portland OR.

Frank Jones—1 Year Outfielder (b. 25 Aug 1859 Princeton IL–d. 6 Feb 1936 Marietta OH) Died from apoplexy. Buried Valley Cemetery, Marietta OH.

Gordon Jones—11 Years Pitcher (b. 2 Apr 1930 Portland OR–d. 25 Apr 1994 Lodi Memorial Hospital, Lodi CA) Served in the Korean War. He was a sales representative for a wholesale electrical dealer. Died from a heart attack, but suffered from diabetes. Buried East Lawn Sierra Hill Memorial Park, Sacramento CA.

Henry Jones—1 Year Outfielder (b. 10 May 1857 New York City NY–d. 31 May 1955 County Convalescent Home, Manistee MI) He was a railroad engineer. Died from senility. Buried Oak Grove Cemetery, Manistee MI.

Howie Jones—1 Year Outfielder (b. 1 Mar 1897 Irwin PA–d. 15 Jul 1972 Jeanette PA).

Jim Jones—3 Years Outfielder (b. 25 Dec 1876 London KY–d. 6 May 1953 Marymount Hospital, London KY) He managed minor league baseball before he was elected Laurel County (KY) Clerk, serving for 16 years. Later he was the London City Clerk. Died following a heart attack. Buried A R Dyche Memorial Park, London KY.

John Jones—2 Years Outfielder (b. 13 May 1901 Wagontown PA–d. 3 Nov 1956 at his home in Baltimore MD) Identified with the U.S. Department of Commerce and Agriculture, he served as head of Farm and Labor Bureaus from 1941 to 1945. He then worked in the scrap iron business with Luria Brothers and Sharon Steel Company. From 1951 to 1956 he was a real estate broker in Baltimore. Died from a heart attack while tinkering with his car. Buried Fairview Cemetery, Coatesville PA.

Johnny Jones—2 Years Pitcher (b. 25 Aug 1894 Arcadia LA–d. 5 Jun 1980 Ruston LA) He was a retired building and grounds superintendent at Louisiana State University. Buried Greenwood Cemetery, Ruston LA.

Jumping Jack Jones—1 Year Pitcher (b. 23 Oct 1860 Litchfield CT–d. 19 Oct 1936 at the Masonic Home in Wallingford CT) He practiced denistry in East Haven CT from 1889 until failing health forced his retirement in 1935. Buried East Lawn Cemetery, East Haven CT.

Ken Jones—2 Years Pitcher (b. 13 Apr 1903 Dover NJ–d. 15 May 1991 Hartford Hospital, Hartford CT) He was a quality control supervisor for Continental Can Corporation in Paterson NJ for 25 years before retiring in 1970. He then operated Jonesey's, a snack bar at the Avon Golf Club for 19 years. Died from lymphoma. Cremated.

Mike Jones—1 Year Pitcher (b. Hamilton, Ontario, Canada–d. 24 Mar 1894 Hamilton, Ontario, Canada).

Nippy Jones—8 Years Infielder (b. 29 Jun 1925 Los Angeles CA–d. 3 Oct 1995 at his home in Sacramento CA) Served in the U.S. Marine Corps during World War II. He worked in public relations for a Sacramento title company before becoming a fishing guide. Died from a heart attack. Buried Southeast Lawn Memorial Park, Sacramento CA.

Oscar Jones—3 Years Pitcher (b. 21 Jan 1879 London Grove PA–d. 8 Oct 1946 Perkasie PA) He was a watchman for the Royal Parts Manufacturing Company. Died from a heart attack after having 13 teeth extracted and while waiting in the meat line at the grocery store.

Percy Jones—9 Years Pitcher (b. 28 Oct 1899 Harwood TX–d. 18 Mar 1979 at a hospital in Dallas TX) Served in the U.S. Navy during World War I. He was injured while playing for the Columbus (OH) minor league team in 1931 and spent the rest of his life confined to a wheelchair. Buried Grove Hill Memorial Park, Dallas TX.

Red Jones—1 Year Outfielder (b. 2 Nov 1911 Timpson TX–d. 30 Jun 1974 at his home in Lincoln CA) For ten years he was a carpenter, working in the construction business. Died from acute leukemia. Cremated.

Sad Sam Jones—22 Years Pitcher (b. 26 Jul 1892 Woodsfield OH–d. 6 Jul 1966 Barnesville Hospital, Barnesville OH) He was president of Woodsfield Savings and Loan Association. Buried Oak Lawn Cemetery, Woodsfield OH.

Sam Jones—12 Years Pitcher (b. 14 Dec 1925 Stewartsville OH–d. 5 Nov 1971 West Virginia Univ Hosp, Morgantown WV) He coached minor league baseball. Died from cancer. Buried Woodlawn Cemetery, Fairmont WV.

Samuel "Butch" Jones—(b. abt 1852 PA–d. 12 Aug 1919 Philadelphia PA) An early owner of the Athletics, he entered the notion business when a youth and, later, was an editor for United Press and Associated Press from 1877 to 1906 when he bought a quarter interest in the Athletics. He sold to Connie Mack in 1912. Died after a long illness. Buried West Laurel Hill Cemetery, Bala Cynwyd PA.

Sheldon Jones—8 Years Pitcher (b. 2 Feb 1922 Tecumseh NE–d. 18 Apr 1991 Greenville NC).

Tex Jones—1 Year Infielder (b. 4 Aug 1885 Marion KS–d. 26 Feb 1938 Wichita KS) A prominent oilman, he associated with his brother-in-law in the oil business for more than 20 years. Although he had been in failing health for a long time, his untimely death was a shock to everyone. Buried Old Mission Cemetery, Wichita KS.

Tom Jones—8 Years Infielder (b. 22 Jan 1877 Honesdale PA–d. 21 Jun 1923 Danville PA).

Willie Jones—15 Years Infielder (b. 16 Aug 1925 Dillon SC–d. 18 Oct 1983 Christ Hospital, Cincinnati OH) He was a car salesman in the Cincinnati area. Died from cancer of the lymph glands. Buried Hillside Memorial Park, Laurinburg NC.

Bubber Jonnard—6 Years Catcher (b. 23 Nov 1897 Nashville TN–d. 23 Aug 1977 New York City NY) He was a scout for the Mets. Buried Hillcrest Memorial Park, Dallas TX.

Claude Jonnard—6 Years Pitcher (b. 23 Nov 1897 Nashville TN–d. 27 Aug 1959 Baptist Hospital, Nashville TN) He played baseball for 25 years before managing several minor league teams and scouting. He was in charge of the Giants' training base in Florida for a time and had a sporting goods store in Florida for a short while before he became associated with a firm that did research work on guided missles. Died during surgery to remove a clot from his heart. Buried Mount Olivet Cemetery, Nashville TN.

Buck Jordan—10 Years Infielder (b. 16 Jan 1907 Cooleemee NC–d. 18 Mar 1993 Rowan Memorial Hospital, Salisbury NC) He farmed near Salisbury. Buried Chestnut Hills Cemetery, Salisbury NC.

Charlie Jordan—1 Year Pitcher (b. 4 Oct 1871 Philadelphia PA–d. 1 Jun 1928 at his home in Hazleton PA) Buried Vine Street Cemetery, Hazleton PA.

Dutch Jordan—2 Years Infielder (b. 5 Jan 1880 Pittsburgh PA–d. 24 Dec 1972 Allegheny Hospital, Pittsburgh PA) He was the police chief of Brentwood PA from 1925 until he retired in 1959. Died after a three-year illness. Buried Jefferson Memorial Park, Pleasant Hills PA.

Harry Jordan—2 Years Pitcher (b. 14 Feb 1873 Pittsburgh PA–d. 2 Mar 1920 at his home in Pittsburgh PA) He worked in the accounting department of the Westinghouse Electric Company.

Jimmy Jordan—4 Years Infielder (b. 13 Jan 1908 Tucapau SC–d. 4 Dec 1957 at a hospital in Gastonia NC) He was a salesman for Sanders Distributing Company. Buried Forest Lawn Cemetery, Charlotte NC.

Mike Jordan—1 Year Outfielder (b. 7 Feb 1862 Lawrence MA–d. 25 Sep 1940 at his home in Lawrence MA) He worked as a woolsorter in various textile plants before becoming involved in local politics, winning seats on the General Court and the State House of Representatives. Later he worked as an investigator for the state's attorney general. Died suddenly from coronary disease. Buried Immaculate Conception Cemetery, Lawrence MA.

Milt Jordan—1 Year Pitcher (b. 24 May 1927 Mineral Springs PA–d. 13 May 1993 Tompkin's Community Hospital, Ithaca NY) Served in the U.S. Army Air Corps during World War II. He worked in the salt mines. Died following a long illness. Cremated.

Rip Jordan—2 Years Pitcher (b. 28 Sep 1889 Portland ME–d. 5 Jun 1960 at his home in Meriden CT) He managed minor league baseball. Buried Center Conway Cemetery, Conway NH.

Slats Jordan—2 Years Outfielder (b. 26 Sep 1879 Baltimore MD–d. 7 Dec 1953 Catonsville MD) Buried Loudon Park National Cemetery, Baltimore MD.

Tim Jordan—7 Years Infielder (b. 14 Feb 1879 New York City NY–d. 13 Sep 1949 at his home in Bronx NY) He was a special policeman for the Hudson and Manhattan Railroad, retiring in 1942.

Arndt Jorgens—11 Years Catcher (b. 18 May 1905 Modum, Norway–d. 1 Mar 1980 at his home in Wilmette IL) He retired in 1968 as president of Schultz Brothers Variety Stores, headquartered in Lake Zurich IL, a firm he had worked for since 1940. Buried Memorial Park Cemetery, Skokie IL.

Orville Jorgens—3 Years Pitcher (b. 4 Jun 1908 Rockford IL–d. 11 Jan 1992 Colorado Springs CO).

Newt Joseph—12 Years Infielder (b. 27 Oct 1899 Montgomery AL–d. 18 Jan 1953 Kansas City MO) He played in the negro leagues.

Rick Joseph—5 Years Infielder (b. 24 Aug 1940 San Pedro de Macoris, Dominican Republic–d. 8 Sep 1979 Santo Domingo, Dominican Republic) Died from the effects of diabetes.

Duane Josephson—8 Years Catcher (b. 3 Jun 1942 New Hampton IA–d. 30 Jan 1997 at his home in New Hampton IA) He coached high school basketball before becoming a realtor in New Hampton. Died from heart disease. Buried New Hampton City Cemetery, New Hampton IA.

Addie Joss—9 Years Pitcher Hall of Fame (b. 12 Apr 1880 Juneau WI–d. 14 Apr 1911 at his home in Toledo OH) Died at the height of his baseball career from tubercular meningitis. Buried Woodlawn Cemetery, Toledo OH.

Ted Jourdan—4 Years Infielder (b. 5 Sep 1895 New Orleans LA–d. 23 Sep 1961 V A Hospital, New Orleans LA) Died following a heart attack. Buried Hope Mausoleum, New Orleans LA.

Pop Joy—1 Year Infielder (b. 11 Jun 1860 Washington DC–d. 28 Jun 1937 at his home in Washington DC) He operated a confectionary in Washington DC, and as he became increasingly prosperous he gave large amounts of money to charity. He spent his last 20 years as superintendent of the Knights of Columbus Home in Washington DC. Buried Mount Olivet Cemetery, Washington DC.

Bill Joyce—8 Years Infielder 3 Years Manager (b. 21 Sep 1865 St Louis MO–d. 8 May 1941 City Hospital, St Louis MO) He ran a tavern in downtown St Louis before buying a minor league team. Subsequent to that he scouted for a short time, then went to work for St Louis City. Died after a three-month illness. Buried Bellefontaine Cemetery, St Louis MO.

Bob Joyce—2 Years Pitcher (b. 14 Jan 1915 Stockton CA–d. 10 Dec 1981 Children's Hospital, San Francisco CA) He was a liquor salesman for Foremost-McKesson for 28 years. Died from circulation problems. Buried San Joaquin Catholic Cemetery, Stockton CA.

Oscar Judd—8 Years Pitcher (b. 14 Feb 1908 London, Ontario, Canada–d. 27 Dec 1995 Ingersoll, Ontario, Canada).

Ralph Judd—3 Years Pitcher (b. 7 Dec 1901 Perrysburg OH–d. 6 May 1957 Lapeer County Convalescent Ctr, Lapeer MI) Died from a liver ailment. Buried Oregon Township Cemetery, Lapeer MI.

Frank Jude—1 Year Outfielder (b. 1885 Mahnomen MN–d. 4 May 1961 Mercy Hospital, Brownsville TX) Buried Rose Lawn Memorial Gardens, Brownsville TX.

Joe Judge—20 Years Infielder (b. 25 May 1894 Brooklyn NY–d. 11 Mar 1963 at his home in Washington DC) He coached baseball at Georgetown University from 1936 to 1958, except for 1945 and 1946 when he was a coach for the Senators. Died from a heart attack after shoveling snow. Buried Gate of Heaven Cemetery, Silver Spring MD.

Walt Judnich—7 Years Outfielder (b. 24 Jan 1916 San Francisco CA–d. 10 Jul 1971 Memorial Hospital, Glendale CA) He worked 16 years for Lockheed Aircraft in Burbank CA before retiring. Died from colon cancer and liver failure. Buried Grand View Memorial Park, Glendale CA.

Lyle Judy—1 Year Infielder (b. 15 Nov 1913 Lawrenceville IL–d. 15 Jan 1991 Memorial Hospital, Ormond Beach FL) He was a draftsman for the Florida East Coast Railroad. Buried San Lorenzo Cemetery, St Augustine FL.

Red Juelich—1 Year Infielder (b. 20 Sep 1916 St Louis MO–d. 25 Dec 1970 St Mary's Hospital, St Louis MO) World War II veteran. He was part owner of a pizza parlor and cocktail lounge. Died from cancer. Buried SS Peter and Paul Cemetery, St Louis MO.

George Jumonville—2 Years Infielder (b. 16 May 1917 Mobile AL–d. 12 Dec 1996 at a nursing home in Mobile AL) Served in the U.S. Navy during World War II. He spent many years in the grocery and produce business, retiring from Fruit Distributing/Sysco in 1985. Buried Magnolia Cemetery, Mobile AL.

Ken Jungels—5 Years Pitcher (b. 23 Jun 1916 Aurora IL–d. 9 Sep 1975 St Joseph's Hospital, West Bend WI) World War II veteran. He pitched in Canada and in the Three-I League. He owned and operated a tavern near County Stadium in Milwaukee WI. Died after suffering a stroke at his home the day before. Buried Wisconsin Memorial Park, Brookfield WI.

Billy Jurges—17 Years Infielder 2 Years Manager (b. 9 May 1908 Bronx NY–d. 3 Mar 1997 Clearwater FL) He coached for the Cubs and Senators.

Al Jurisich—4 Years Pitcher (b. 25 Aug 1921 New Orleans LA–d. 3 Nov 1981 New Orleans LA) Died following a heart attack. Buried Greenwood Cemetery, New Orleans LA.

Walt Justis—1 Year Pitcher (b. 17 Aug 1883 Moores Hill IN–d. 4 Oct 1941 at his home in Greendale IN) He worked in the maintenance department at the Old Quaker Distillery. Died from a heart attack. Buried Greendale Cemetery, Greendale IN.

Earl Juul—1 Year Pitcher (b. 21 May 1893 Chicago IL–d. 4 Jan 1942 Hines Hospital, Chicago IL) Served in the Army Air Corps during World War I. He was a salesman. Buried Mount Olive Cemetery, Chicago IL.

Herb Juul—1 Year Pitcher (b. 2 Feb 1886 Chicago IL–d. 14 Nov 1928 Norwegian-American Hospital, Chicago IL) World War I veteran. He was the director of Republican Headquarters in a Chicago ward for the 1928 election. Died following surgery for gallstones. Buried Mount Olivet Cemetery, Chicago IL.

K

Jack Kading—2 Years Infielder (b. 27 Nov 1884 Waukesha WI–d. 2 Jun 1964 Illinois Masonic Hospital, Chicago IL) He was a typesetter 32 years for the *Chicago American*, retiring in 1957. Buried St Boniface Cemetery, Chicago IL.

Harold Kaese—Hall of Fame (b. abt 1908–d. 10 May 1975 Massachusetts General Hospital, Boston MA) For 30 years he was a sports columnist for the Boston Globe, retiring in 1973. Died from a heart attack. Buried Puritan Lawn Memorial Park, Peabody MA.

Jake Kafora—2 Years Catcher (b. 16 Oct 1888 Chicago IL–d. 23 Mar 1928 at his home in Chicago IL) He was one of Chicago's most prominent bowlers. Died after a short illness. Buried St Adalbert Cemetery, Niles IL.

Nick Kahl—1 Year Infielder (b. 10 Apr 1879 Coulterville IL–d. 13 Jul 1959 Sparta IL) After spending 20 years in organized baseball as a player and minor league manager he became a minister, serving in a number of churchs in southern Illinois. Buried Coulterville Cemetery, Coulterville IL.

Bob Kahle—8 Games Pinch Hitter (b. 23 Nov 1915 Newcastle IN–d. 16 Dec 1988 Inglewood CA) He was a painter on movie sets for 33 years. Died from lung cancer. Buried Holy Cross Cemetery, Culver City CA.

George Kahler—5 Years Pitcher (b. 6 Sep 1889 Athens OH–d. 7 Feb 1924 Battle Creek Sanitarium, Battle Creek MI) He was an osteopath at Osteopathic Hospital in Detroit MI. Died from complications of diabetes. Buried West Union Street Cemetery, Athens OH.

Owen Kahn—1 Game Pinch Runner (b. 5 Jun 1905 Richmond VA–d. 17 Jan 1981 Richmond VA) Much of his life he was an examiner for the Virginia Department of Taxation, retiring about 1971. Served in the U.S. Navy during World War II. Buried Maury Cemetery, Richmond VA.

Mike Kahoe—11 Years Catcher (b. 3 Sep 1873 Yellow Springs OH–d. 14 May 1949 St Thomas Hospital, Akron OH) He lived in Akron 30 years and worked for Northern Ohio Traction and Light Company. Died after being ill only a few days. Buried Holy Cross Cemetery, Akron OH.

Al Kaiser—3 Years Outfielder (b. 3 Aug 1886 Cincinnati OH–d. 11 Apr 1969 St Francis Hospital, Cincinnati OH) He was a detective for the Cincinnati Police Department from 1915 until retiring in 1945. Died following an extended illness. Buried St Joseph Old Catholic Cemetery, Cincinnati OH.

George Kaiserling—2 Years Pitcher (b. 15 Aug 1890 Steubenville OH–d. 2 Mar 1918 Steubenville OH) Died from pulmonary tuberculosis. Buried Union Cemetery, Steubenville OH.

John Kalahan—1 Year Catcher (b. 30 Sep 1878 Philadelphia PA–d. 20 Jun 1952 Philadelphia PA) Buried Holy Cross Cemetery, Yeadon PA.

Charlie Kalbfus—1 Year Outfielder (b. 28 Dec 1864 Washington DC–d. 18 Nov 1941 Washington DC) He was a retired post office clerk. Died from uremic poisoning. Buried Oak Hill Cemetery, Washington DC.

Bill Kalfass—1 Year Pitcher (b. 3 Mar 1916 New York City NY–d. 8 Sep 1968 Brooklyn NY) Buried Germonds Presbyterian Cemetery, New City NY.

Frank Kalin—2 Years Outfielder (b. 3 Oct 1917 Steubenville OH–d. 12 Jan 1975 Weirtown WV) Served in the U.S. Army during World War II. He was dead-on-arrival from natural causes at General Hospital. Buried St Paul Catholic Church Cemetery, Weirton WV.

Rudy Kallio—3 Years Pitcher (b. 14 Dec 1892 Portland OR–d. 6 Apr 1979 Pacific Communities Hospital, Newport OR) Buried Lone Fir Cemetery, Portland OR.

Willie Kamm—13 Years Infielder (b. 2 Feb 1900 San Francisco CA–d. 21 Dec 1988 Convalescent Hospital, Belmont CA) He managed in the Pacific Coast League. An avid horse racing fan and fisherman, he lived at Burlingame CA since 1955. Died from congestive heart failure. Cremated. Buried Cypress Lawn Memorial Park, Colma CA.

Ike Kamp—2 Years Pitcher (b. 5 Sep 1900 Roxbury MA–d. 25 Feb 1955 Peter Bent Brigham Hospital, Boston MA) He managed the Boston Auto Park. Died after a brief illness. Buried Mount Calvary Cemetery, Roslindale MA.

Alex Kampouris—9 Years Infielder (b. 13 Nov 1912 Sacramento CA–d. 29 May 1993 Sacramento CA) He worked in the Sacramento County, CA, marshall's office and later handled the concessions at Sacramento Memorial Auditorium. Died following a heart attack. Buried St Mary's Cemetery, Sacramento CA.

Frank Kane—2 Years Outfielder (b. 9 Mar 1895 Whitman MA–d. 2 Dec 1962 at his home in Brockton MA) Served in the U.S. Army during World War I. He made hundreds of appearances as a singer while working as an accountant for a large Boston accounting firm. Active in civic affairs, he was a city selectman and town accountant. Died from a heart attack. Buried Calvary Cemetery, Brockton MA.

Harry Kane—4 Years Pitcher (b. 27 Jul 1883 Hamburg AR–d. 15 Sep 1932 at the Cornelius Hotel in Portland OR) He was a Pacific Coast League umpire. Found dead from a heart attack after umpiring that day's game.

Jim Kane—1 Year Infielder (b. 27 Nov 1881 Scranton PA–d. 2 Oct 1947 at his home in Omaha NE) For 20 years he was a government inspector at the Omaha stockyards. Buried Holy Sepulchre Cemetery, Omaha NE.

John Kane—1 Year Infielder (b. 19 Feb 1900 Chicago IL–d. 25 Jul 1956 Chicago IL).

Johnny Kane—4 Years Outfielder (b. 24 Sep 1882 Chicago IL–d. 28 Jan 1934 on the Yellowstone Hwy near St Anthony ID) He owned a pool and billiard parlor in St Anthony. Killed instantly when a car he was riding in skidded on ice and overturned. Buried Riverview Cemetery, St Anthony ID.

Tom Kane—1 Year Infielder (b. 15 Dec 1906 Chicago IL–d. 26 Nov 1973 Chicago IL) Buried St Joseph Cemetery, River Grove IL.

Erv Kantlehner—3 Years Pitcher (b. 31 Jul 1892 San Jose CA–d. 3 Feb 1990 Valle Verde Healthcare, Santa Barbara CA) He taught 30 years in the Esparto CA schools. Died from pneumonia and complications of arteriosclerosis and diabetes. Cremated. Buried Capay Cemetery, Capay CA.

Heinie Kappel—3 Years Infielder (b. 1862 Philadelphia PA–d. 27 Aug 1905 Philadelphia PA).

Joe Kappel—2 Years Outfielder (b. 1857 Philadelphia PA–d. 8 Jul 1929 Philadelphia PA) Buried Holy Redeemer Cemetery, Philadelphia PA.

Paul Kardow—1 Year Pitcher (b. 19 Sep 1915 Humble TX–d. 27 Apr 1968 San Antonio TX) A plumber, he lived in San Antonio 45 years. Died from cancer. Buried Mission Burial Park, San Antonio TX.

Ed Karger—6 Years Pitcher (b. 6 May 1883 San Angelo TX–d. 9 Sep 1957 Thomas' Resthaven Nursing Home in Delta CO) He was a construction engineer and lived for a number of years in Canada. Buried Delta Cemetery, Delta CO.

Andy Karl—5 Years Pitcher (b. 8 Apr 1914 Mount Vernon NY–d. 8 Apr 1989 Scripps Memorial Hospital, Encinitas CA) He owned and operated a heating and plumbing firm in Fairfield CT for 25 years. Died from kidney failure five weeks after a surgery. Buried Mission San Luis Rey Cemetery, San Luis Rey CA.

Bill Karlon—1 Year Outfielder (b. 21 Jan 1909 Palmer MA–d. 7 Dec 1964 near Monson MA) He worked for the U.S. Rubber Company, Fisk Division. Died from a heart attack while hunting. Buried St Anne's Cemetery, Palmer MA.

Bill Karns—1 Year Pitcher (b. 28 Dec 1875 Richmond IA–d. 15 Nov 1941 Seattle WA).

Marty Karow—1 Year Infielder (b. 18 Jul 1904 Braddock PA–d. 27 Apr 1986 at a hospital in Bryan TX) He coached college baseball at the University of Texas for ten years, at Texas A & M before and after World War II, and at Ohio State University for 25 years. He also coached the U.S. baseball team in the 1967 Pan-American Games. Buried City Cemetery, College Station TX.

Herb Karpel—1 Year Pitcher (b. 27 Dec 1917 Brooklyn NY–d. 24 Jan 1995 Kaiser Hospital, San Diego CA) Died from pneumonia ten days after suffering a stroke, but suffered from diabetes, hypertension and dementia. Buried Eden Memorial Park, Mission Hills CA.

Benn Karr—6 Years Pitcher (b. 28 Nov 1893 Mount Pleasant MI–d. 8 Dec 1968 Veteran's

Hospital, Memphis TN) Served in the U.S. Army during World War I. He pitched several years in the Southern League before retiring from baseball to Earle AR where he was a planter. Buried Crittendon Memorial Park, Marion AR.

John Karst—1 Year Infielder (b. 15 Oct 1893 Philadelphia PA–d. 21 May 1976 Cape May Court House NJ) He retired as vice-president of Harleysville Insurance Company. Buried Sunset Memorial Park, Philadelphia PA.

John Katoll—4 Years Pitcher (b. 24 Jun 1872 Germany–d. 18 Jun 1955 Hartland IL).

Bob Katz—1 Year Pitcher (b. 30 Jan 1911 Lancaster PA–d. 15 Dec 1962 Memorial Hospital, St Joseph MI) He worked for Auto Specialties, Inc. Died from cancer. Buried Resurrection Catholic Cemetery, St Joseph MI.

Benny Kauff—8 Years Outfielder (b. 5 Jan 1890 Pomeroy OH–d. 17 Nov 1961 Grant Hospital, Columbus OH) World War I veteran. He was a baseball scout 22 years before becoming a salesman for John R Lyman Company. Buried Union Cemetery, Columbus OH.

Dick Kauffman—2 Years Infielder (b. 22 Jun 1888 East Lewisburg PA–d. 17 Apr 1948 Evangelical Hospital, Lewisburg PA) He was sales manager for Southern Baking Company before returning to Union County, PA, as a sales rep for a Kansas firm. Died from a heart ailment. Buried Lewisburg Cemetery, Lewisburg PA.

Ewing M Kauffman—(b. 21 Sep 1916 near Garden City MO–d. 1 Aug 1993 Mission Hills KS) He was a drug salesman before founding Marion Laboratories in 1950. He owned the Kansas City Royals from 1969 until his death. Died from bone cancer. Buried Marion Visitor's Center, Kansas City MO.

Tony Kaufmann—12 Years Pitcher (b. 16 Dec 1900 Chicago IL–d. 4 Jun 1982 St Joseph Hospital, Elgin IL) He worked his entire life in baseball as a player, pitching coach, scout and minor league manager, retiring in 1962. Died from cancer. Buried Mount Emblem Cemetery, Elmhurst IL.

Charlie Kavanagh—5 Games Pinch Hitter (b. 9 Jun 1892 Chicago IL–d. 6 Sep 1973 at his home in Reedsburg WI) He was a bailiff at the Cook County Court in Chicago. World War I veteran. Buried Calvary Cemetery, Reedsburg WI.

Leo Kavanagh—1 Year Infielder (b. 9 Aug 1894 Chicago IL–d. 10 Aug 1950 Chicago IL) Buried Mount Carmel Cemetery, Hillside IL.

Marty Kavanagh—5 Years Infielder (b. 13 Jun 1891 Harrison NJ–d. 28 Jul 1960 Taylor MI) Died from a heart attack. Buried Mount Olivet Cemetery, Detroit MI.

Bill Kay—1 Year Outfielder (b. 14 Feb 1878 New Castle VA–d. 3 Dec 1945 Roanoke VA) Buried Albany NY.

Johnny Keane—6 Years Manager (b. 3 Nov 1911 St Louis MO–d. 6 Jan 1967 at his home in Houston TX) He spent his entire life in baseball as a manager, administrator and minor league player. Died from a heart attack. Buried Memorial Oaks Cemetery, Houston TX.

Ted Kearns—2 Years Infielder (b. 1 Jan 1900 Trenton NJ–d. 21 Dec 1949 at his home in Trenton NJ) He was also a professional basketball player. An active democrat, he ran for public office several times, served in many appointed positions and was a Trenton city commissioner for part of a term. Died from a heart attack. Buried St Mary's Cemetery, Trenton NJ.

Tom Kearns—3 Years Infielder (b. 1860 Rochester NY–d. 7 Dec 1938 Buffalo NY) Buried Rochester NY.

Eddie Kearse—1 Year Catcher (b. 23 Feb 1916 San Francisco CA–d. 15 Jul 1968 St Joseph Hospital, Eureka CA) He worked in a lumber mill at Eureka. Died from lung cancer. Buried Holy Sepulchre Cemetery, Hayward CA.

Ed Keas—1 Year Pitcher (b. 2 Jan 1863 Dubuque IA–d. 12 Jan 1940 at his home in Dubuque IA) In 1889 a leg injury ended his baseball career. He was a painter, and was well-known in the Dubuque area, where he lived his entire life, as a fancy ice skater. Died suddenly. Buried Mount Olivet Cemetery, Dubuque IA.

Chick Keating—4 Years Infielder (b. 8 Aug 1891 Philadelphia PA–d. 13 Jul 1959 Philadelphia PA) Buried Holy Sepulchre Cemetery, Philadelphia PA.

Ed Keating—1 Year Pitcher (b. abt 1866 Springfield MA–d. 19 Jan 1922 at his home in Springfield MA) He was the inventor and manufacturer of the Keating bicycle, among other things. Died after a short illness. Buried St Michael's Cemetery, Springfield MA.

Ray Keating—7 Years Pitcher (b. 21 Jul 1893 Bridgeport CT–d. 28 Dec 1963 Sutter Memorial Hospital, Sacramento CA) He operated a tavern in Sacramento for 25 years before retiring in 1958. Died from kidney disease and heart failure. Buried St Mary's Cemetery, Sacramento CA.

Cactus Keck—2 Years Pitcher (b. 13 Jan 1899 St Louis MO–d. 6 Feb 1981 Kirkwood MO) He was assistant Chief/Fire Marshall at Kirkwood. Died from leukemia. Cremated. Buried Bellerive Heritage Gardens, Creve Coeur MO.

Bob Keefe—3 Years Pitcher (b. 16 Jun 1882 Folsom CA–d. 6 Dec 1964 at his home in Sacramento CA) He was the postmaster at Folsum for 11 years. Died from a heart attack. Buried St John's Cemetery, Folsum CA.

Dave Keefe—5 Years Pitcher (b. 9 Jan 1897 Williston VT–d. 4 Feb 1978 St Mary's Hospital, Kansas City MO) He spent 50 years in baseball, 13 as a player, pitching in the American Association, Pacific Coast League, Eastern League, Piedmont League and the Southern League. He was also a coach, batting practice pitcher and traveling secretary for the A's. Buried Holy Rosary Cemetery, Richmond VT.

George Keefe—6 Years Pitcher (b. 7 Jan 1867 Washington DC–d. 24 Aug 1935 Providence Hospital, Washington DC) He worked at the Navy yard in Washington DC for several years, but was a gardener at Eastern High School when he died. Died from an infection incurred when he scraped his leg while getting out of a car. Buried Cedar Hill Cemetery, Suitland MD.

John Keefe—1 Year Pitcher (b. 5 May 1867 Fitchburg MA–d. 9 Aug 1937 Burbank Hospital, Fitchburg MA) He was the proprietor of a gasoline filling station in Fitchburg. Died after a very short illness. Buried St Bernard's Church Cemetery, Fitchburg MA.

Tim Keefe—14 Years Pitcher Hall of Fame (b. 1 Jan 1857 Cambridge MA–d. 23 Apr 1933 at his home in Cambridge MA) He was involved in real estate at Cambridge. Buried Cambridge Cemetery, Cambridge MA.

Willie Keeler—19 Years Outfielder Hall of Fame (b. 3 Mar 1872 Brooklyn NY–d. 1 Jan 1923 at his home in Brooklyn NY) Involved in an unsuccessful real estate endeaver, he died penniless. Died from heart disease. Buried Calvary Cemetery, Woodside NY.

Burt Keeley—2 Years Pitcher (b. 2 Nov 1888 Wilmington IL–d. 4 May 1952 Ely MN) Died from complications following a fracture. Buried Ely Cemetery, Ely MN.

Bill Keen—1 Year Infielder (b. 16 Aug 1892 Oglethorpe GA–d. 16 Jul 1947 South Point OH) He formerly worked for the Kaiser-Frazer automobile plant in Detroit MI and had just started working for Houdaille-Hershey Corporation in Huntington WV when he was killed in a car-train crash. Buried Ferncliff Cemetery, Springfield OH.

Vic Keen—8 Years Pitcher (b. 16 Mar 1899 Bel Air MD–d. 10 Dec 1976 Peninsula General Hospital, Salisbury MD) He was a poultryman in Pocomoke City MD. Died after a long illness. Buried First Baptist Church Cemetery, Pocomoke City MD.

Jim Keenan—10 Years Catcher (b. 25 May 1858 New Haven CT–d. 21 Sep 1926 St Mary's Hospital, Cincinnati OH) At one time he owned a saloon near the baseball park. He was a former city councilman. Died from a stroke of apoplexy. Buried Spring Grove Cemetery, Cincinnati OH.

Jim Keenan—2 Years Pitcher (b. 25 May 1899 Avon NY–d. 5 Jun 1980 Seminole FL) He worked on the docks at Lorain OH for U.S. Steel, retiring to Florida in 1962. Cremated.

Kid Keenan—1 Year Pitcher (b. 1875 Louisville KY–d. 11 Jun 1903 at his brother's home in Covington KY).

Harry Keener—1 Year Pitcher (b. 1869 Easton PA–d. 5 Mar 1912 Easton PA).

Jim Keesey—2 Years Infielder (b. 27 Oct 1903 Perryville MD–d. 5 Sep 1951 St Alphonsus Hospital, Boise ID) He worked in baseball his entire life, managing several minor league teams and scouting for some major league teams. Suffered from myoloma, a form of cancer, but died from a heart attack. Buried Lincoln Memorial Park, Portland OR.

Frank Keffer—1 Year Pitcher (b. 19 Oct 1859 Philadelphia PA–d. 1 Oct 1932 at his home in Chicago IL) Died after an illness of three weeks.

Chet Kehn—1 Year Pitcher (b. 30 Oct 1921 San Diego CA–d. 5 Apr 1984 San Diego CA) He was the manager at a Handyman hardware store. Died from a heart attack in the stadium parking lot. Cremated.

Katie Keifer—1 Year Pitcher (b. 3 Sep 1891 California PA–d. 19 Feb 1927 Outwood KY).

Bill Keister—7 Years Infielder (b. 17 Aug 1874 Baltimore MD–d. 19 Aug 1924 Baltimore MD).

George Kelb—1 Year Pitcher (b. 17 Jul 1870 Toledo OH–d. 20 Oct 1936 at his home in Toledo OH) He was a bridge operator for the City of Toledo for ten years. Died from heart disease. Buried Forest Cemetery, Toledo OH.

Mickey Keliher—2 Years Infielder (b. 11 Jan 1890 Washington DC–d. 7 Sep 1930 Emergency Hospital, Washington DC) He managed minor league baseball. Died from injuries suffered when he was mysteriously thrown from a moving car near Alexandria VA. Buried Mount Olivet Cemetery, Washington DC.

Duke Kelleher—1 Year Catcher (b. 30 Sep 1893 New York City NY–d. 28 Sep 1947 Staten Island NY).

Frankie Kelleher—2 Years Outfielder (b. 22 Aug 1916 San Francisco CA–d. 12 Apr 1979 Stockton CA) He was a self-employed tool distributor. Died from a heart attack. Cremated.

Hal Kelleher—4 Years Pitcher (b. 24 Jun 1914 Philadelphia PA–d. 27 Aug 1989 Tomlin Mem Hosp, Cape May Court House NJ) Buried St Mary's Cemetery, Cold Springs NJ.

John Kelleher—6 Years Infielder (b. 13 Sep 1893 Brookline MA–d. 21 Aug 1960 Chestnut Hill MA) Served in the U.S. Army during World War I. He coached baseball at Harvard and Brown. From 1941 until his death he was a general foreman for the Brookline Highway Department. Buried Walnut Hills Cemetery, Brookline MA.

Charlie Keller—13 Years Outfielder (b. 12 Sep 1916 Middletown MD–d. 23 May 1990 at his home near Frederick MD) He became a successful harness race horse breeder. He was an avid golfer. Died from colon cancer. Buried United Church of Christ Cemetery, Middletown MD.

Frank Kellert—4 Years Infielder (b. 6 Jul 1924 Oklahoma City OK–d. 19 Nov 1976 at his home in Oklahoma City OK) Served in the U.S. Army Air Corps during World War II. The managing director of Wilson Credit Union in Oklahoma City, he was also a member of the Oklahoma City Chamber of Commerce. Died from lymphoma. Buried Rose Hill Burial Park, Oklahoma City OK.

Al Kellett—2 Years Pitcher (b. 30 Oct 1901 Red Bank NJ–d. 14 Jul 1960 New York City NY).

Red Kellett—1 Year Infielder (b. 15 Jul 1909 Brooklyn NY–d. 3 Nov 1970 Holy Cross Hospital, Fort Lauderdale FL) He coached college football and worked as a television executive before becoming general manager of the Baltimore Colts NFL team in 1953, retiring to Florida in 1966. Died from a heart attack. Buried Druid Ridge Cemetery, Pikesville MD.

Dick Kelley—2 Years Pitcher (b. 8 Jan 1940 Boston MA–d. 11 Dec 1991 Northridge Hospital, Northridge CA) He was a loan officer for Bay County Mortgage Company. Died from heart disease. Cremated.

Harry Kelley—6 Years Pitcher (b. 13 Feb 1906 Parkin AR–d. 23 Mar 1958 at his home in Parkin AR) He managed his family's farming interests in the Parkin area. Died after a long illness. Buried Cogbill Cemetery, Wynne AR.

Joe Kelley—17 Years Outfielder 5 Years Manager Hall of Fame (b. 9 Dec 1871 Cambridge MA–d. 14 Aug 1943 at his home in Baltimore MD) He was a scout for the Yankees and managed some minor league baseball. Died after being ill about a year. Buried New Cathedral Cemetery, Baltimore MD.

Mike Kelley—1 Year Infielder (b. 2 Dec 1876 Otter River MA–d. 6 Jun 1955 Minneapolis MN) He spent 52 years in organized baseball as a player, minor league manager and owner. Died from the shock of the injuries caused by a fall, and its subsequent surgery. Buried Lakewood Cemetery, Minneapolis MN.

Frank Kelliher—1 Game Pinch Hitter (b. 23 May 1899 Somerville MA–d. 4 Mar 1956 Somerville MA).

Alex Kellner—12 Years Pitcher (b. 26 Aug 1924 Tucson AZ–d. 2 May 1996 at his home in Tucson AZ) Served in the U.S. Navy. He was a construction worker. Died in his sleep. Cremated.

Al Kellogg—1 Year Pitcher (b. 9 Sep 1886 Providence RI–d. 21 Jul 1953 Portland OR) For 25 years he was a buyer for the sporting goods department of Meir and Frank Company in Portland. He was an ardent fly-fisherman and trap-shooter. Died from pneumonia. Buried Lincoln Memorial Park, Portland OR.

Bill Kellogg—1 Year Infielder (b. 25 May 1884 Albany NY–d. 12 Dec 1971 Baltimore MD) Buried New Cathedral Cemetery, Baltimore MD.

Win Kellum—3 Years Pitcher (b. 11 Apr 1876 Waterford, Ontario, Canada–d. 10 Aug 1951 Big Rapids MI) He managed minor league baseball and pitched a minor league game at age 55. After retiring from baseball he farmed and enjoyed fishing. He had a heart attack while fishing and was dead-on-arrival at Community Hospital.

Bill Kelly—4 Years Catcher (b. 1 May 1886 Baltimore MD–d. 3 Jun 1940 Harper Hospital, Detroit MI) He worked for the Detroit Edison Company. Buried Lakeside Cemetery, Port Huron MI.

Bill Kelly—2 Years Infielder (b. 28 Dec 1898 Syracuse NY–d. 8 Apr 1990 Syracuse NY) He retired in 1979 after 55 years in baseball as a player, coach, minor league manager and scout, the last 15 years with the Mets. Buried St Agnes Cemetery, Syracuse NY.

Bob Kelly—3 Years Outfielder (b. 1 Feb 1884 Bloomfield NJ–d. 10 Apr 1961 Kingsport TN).

Ed Kelly—1 Year Pitcher (b. 10 Dec 1889 Providence RI–d. 4 Nov 1928 Red Lodge MT) He was a miner. Died during emergency surgery performed in an effort to save his life after 36 hours of critical illness.

George Kelly—16 Years Infielder Hall of Fame (b. 10 Sep 1895 San Francisco CA–d. 13 Oct 1984 Peninsula Hospital, Burlingame CA) He owned and managed minor league baseball teams until 1954 when he retired to a life of fishing and working with youth. Died from complications of a stroke suffered a week earlier. Buried Holy Cross Catholic Cemetery, Colma CA.

Herb Kelly—2 Years Pitcher (b. 4 Jun 1892 Mobile AL–d. 18 May 1973 Medical Convalescent Center, Torrance CA) He was an insurance agent for 20 years. Died from a cancerous salivary gland. Buried Pine Crest Cemetery, Mobile AL.

Honest John Kelly—1 Year Catcher 1 Year Manager (b. 31 Oct 1856 New York City NY–d. 27 Mar 1926 at the home of a friend in New York City NY) He umpired baseball, refereed prize fights, operated gambling houses until they were made illegal, operated race tracks, and was a well known gambler and bookmaker on horse races. Died from pneumonia. Buried Calvary Cemetery, Woodside NY.

Joe Kelly—5 Years Outfielder (b. 23 Sep 1886 Weir City KS–d. 16 Aug 1977 at a hospital in St Joseph MO) Served in the U.S. Navy during World War I. He played professional baseball for 25 years. He lived at St Joseph since 1910 and was a retired employee of the Sheridan-Clayton Paper Company. He was also an avid baseball historian. Buried Mount Olivet Cemetery, St Joseph MO.

Joe Kelly—2 Years Outfielder (b. 23 Apr 1900 New York City NY–d. 24 Nov 1967 Long Beach Memorial Hospital, Lynbrook NY) He owned and operated a filling station in Lynbrook from 1931 until a year before he died. Died after an extended illness. Buried Rockville Cemetery, Lynbrook NY.

John Kelly—1 Year Outfielder (b. 13 Mar 1879 Clifton Heights PA–d. 19 Mar 1944 Baltimore MD) Buried Baltimore Cemetery, Baltimore MD.

King Kelly—3 Years Catcher (b. 1859 Paterson NJ–d. 13 Apr 1908 at his home in Paterson NJ) He worked a long time for Alex Hughes in Paterson before opening a cafe there. Died from complications of diabetes. Buried Holy Sepulchre Cemetery, Totowa NJ.

King Kelly—16 Years Outfielder 2 Years Manager Hall of Fame (b. 31 Dec 1857 Troy NY–d. 8 Nov 1894 at the emergency hospital in Boston MA) He played the vaudeville circuit as a singer and wit. Died from pneumonia that developed from a slight cold just a few days earlier. Buried Mount Hope Cemetery, Boston MA.

Ray Kelly—Hall of Fame (b. abt 1914–d. 22 Nov 1988 Nazareth Hospital, Philadelphia PA) A sportswriter, he worked 50 years for the *Philadelphia Bulletin*, covering the Athletics from 1948 to 1955 and the Phillies from 1956 until he retired in 1979. Cremated.

Red Kelly—1 Year Outfielder (b. 15 Nov 1884 Union IL–d. 4 Feb 1961 Zephyrhills FL).

Ren Kelly—1 Year Pitcher (b. 18 Nov 1899 San Francisco CA–d. 24 Aug 1963 Serra Hospital, Millbrae CA) He was a longshoreman 31 years for the Pacific Maritime Association. Died from pneumonia and heart disease. Buried Oak Hill Memorial Park, San Jose CA.

Speed Kelly—1 Year Infielder (b. 12 Aug 1884 Goshen IN–d. 6 May 1949 Goshen Hospital, Goshen IN) He owned Kelly Foundry amd Machine Company in Goshen for several years. Died from complications of pneumonia and a kidney infection. Buried Violett Cemetery, Goshen IN.

Billy Kelsey—1 Year Catcher (b. 24 Aug 1881 Covington OH–d. 25 Apr 1968 Community Hospital, Springfield OH) He managed Cappel's House Furnishing Company in Springfield. Cremated.

Ken Keltner—13 Years Infielder (b. 31 Oct 1916 Milwaukee WI–d. 12 Dec 1991 at his home in New Berlin WI) He was a member of the Wisconsin Hall of Fame. Died from a heart attack. Buried Wisconsin Memorial Park, Brookfield WI.

Bill Kemmer—1 Year Infielder (b. 15 Nov 1873 PA–d. 8 Jun 1945 Home for Incurables, Washington DC) Buried Milford OH.

Rudy Kemmler—8 Years Catcher (b. 1860 Chicago IL–d. 20 Jun 1909 Chicago IL) Buried Concordia Cemetery, Forest Park IL.

Dutch Kemner—1 Year Pitcher (b. 4 Mar 1899 Quincy IL–d. 16 Jan 1988 at the Sunset Home in Quincy IL) He was a carpenter for the Rose Construction Company until his retirement in 1972. Buried Calvary Cemetery, Quincy IL.

Ed Kenna—1 Year Catcher (b. 30 Sep 1897 San Francisco CA–d. 21 Aug 1972 St Luke's Hospital, San Francisco CA) World War I veteran. He was a retired employee of the San Francisco Department of Public Works. Died from a pulmonary embolism. Buried Olivet Memorial Park, Colma CA.

Ed Kenna—1 Year Pitcher (b. 17 Oct 1877 Charleston WV–d. 22 Mar 1912 Grant FL) He was an editor for the *Charleston Gazette* newspaper and colonel on the staff of the West Virginia Governor. Died suddenly from heart failure after spending two months in Florida for a nervous stomach disorder. Buried Spring Hill Cemetery, Charleston WV.

Bill Kennedy—8 Years Pitcher (b. 14 Mar 1921 Carnesville GA–d. 9 Apr 1983 Seattle WA) Served in the U.S. Army during World War II. He was a bartender at the Ballard Eagle's Lodge. Died from lung cancer. Buried Evergreen-Washelli Cemetery, Seattle WA.

Bill Kennedy—3 Years Pitcher (b. 22 Dec 1918 Alexandria VA–d. 20 Aug 1995 Alexandria Hospital, Alexandria VA) Served in Europe as an army paratrooper during World War II. He was a brakeman and conductor for the Richmond, Fredericksburg and Potomac Railroad, retiring in 1982. Buried Mount Comfort Cemetery, Alexandria VA.

Brickyard Kennedy—12 Years Pitcher (b. 7 Oct 1868 Bellaire OH–d. 23 Sep 1915 at his brother's home in Bellaire OH) Died from tuberculosis. Buried Rose Hill Cemetery, Bellaire OH.

Doc Kennedy—5 Years Catcher (b. 11 Aug 1855 Brooklyn NY–d. 23 May 1920 Swains NY) He lived on a farm near Swains for several years.

Ed Kennedy—4 Years Outfielder (b. 1 Apr 1856 Carbondale PA–d. 20 May 1905 New York City NY).

Ed Kennedy—1 Year Infielder (b. 5 Apr 1861 Bellevue KY–d. 22 Dec 1912 Cheyenne WY) He farmed and operated a newspaper at Cedar Bluffs NE for 12 years. Died from heart failure in a Cheyenne alley. He was in the process of moving to Cheyenne to take a job in the mechanical department of a Cheyenne newspaper. Buried Cedar Bluffs NE.

Jim Kennedy—1 Year Manager (b. 1867 New York City NY–d. 20 Apr 1904 Brighton Beach NY) A newspaperman and promoter of sporting events, he managed the Seaside Athletic Club on Coney Island, as well as several boxers. He also promoted bicycle races and other prominent sporting events. Died suddenly on a commute train. Buried Calvary Cemetery, Woodside NY.

John Kennedy—1 Year Infielder (b. 12 Oct 1926 Jacksonville FL–d. 27 Apr 1998 Jacksonville FL) He played in the Nergo Leagues. Died after a long illness. Buried Evergreen Cemetery, Jacksonville FL.

Monte Kennedy—8 Years Pitcher (b. 11 May 1922 Amelia VA–d. 1 Mar 1997 Midlothian VA) Served in the U.S. Army Air Corps during World War II. He retired as a detective for the Richmond VA Police Department. Buried Dale Memorial Park, Chesterfield VA.

Ray Kennedy—1 Game Pinch Hitter (b. 19 May 1895 Pittsburgh PA–d. 18 Jan 1969 Winter Park Hospital, Winter Park FL) He had a long career in baseball as a player, minor league manager, executive and a scout for the Mets. Died of complications from influenza. Buried Glen Haven Memorial Park, Winter Park FL.

Snapper Kennedy—1 Year Outfielder (b. 1 Nov 1878 Conneaut OH–d. 15 Aug 1945 Pasadena TX).

Ted Kennedy—2 Years Pitcher (b. Feb 1865 Henry IL–d. 31 Oct 1907 St Louis MO).

Vern Kennedy—12 Years Pitcher (b. 20 Mar 1907 Kansas City MO–d. 28 Jan 1993 Mendon MO) An all-around athlete, he participated in baseball, football and track at Central Missouri State University and the football stadium there was named after him in 1954. He was killed instantly when a building he was tearing down collapsed and fell on him. Buried Old Mendon Cemetery, Mendon MO.

Maury Kent—2 Years Pitcher (b. 17 Sep 1885 Marshalltown IA–d. 19 Apr 1966 at a nursing home in Iowa City IA) After his playing career he coached basketball and baseball at a number of midwest colleges, including Iowa, Iowa State, Wisconsin and 21 years at Northwestern. Died following a lingering illness. Cremated.

Duke Kenworthy—4 Years Infielder (b. 3 Jul 1886 Hopewell OH–d. 21 Sep 1950 Eureka CA) He managed and coached in the Pacific Coast League and was part owner of the Portland team. Dropping out of baseball for a while, he worked in the contracting business, but was coach of the freshman baseball team at St Mary's College when he died. Drowned with three companions in the Pacific Ocean when his boat capsized. Buried Mountain View Cemetery, Oakland CA.

Gus Keriazakos—3 Years Pitcher (b. 28 Jul 1931 West Orange NJ–d. 4 May 1996 at his home in Hilton Head SC) He was vice-president of sales and marketing for Essex Chemical Corporation in Clifton NJ. Cremated.

John Kerins—7 Years Infielder 1 Year Manager (b. 22 Dec 1858 Indianapolis IN–d. 15 Sep 1919 City Hospital, Louisville KY) Died unfriended and without funds. A fund drive was established to give him a Christian burial. Buried Cave Hill Cemetery, Louisville KY.

Bill Kerksieck—1 Year Pitcher (b. 6 Dec 1913 Ulm AR–d. 11 Mar 1970 Stuttgart AR) He farmed and raised registered Angus cattle. He was also a farm implement dealer. Buried Lone Tree Cemetery, Stuttgart AR.

Orie Kerlin—1 Year Catcher (b. 23 Jan 1891 Summerfield LA–d. 29 Oct 1974 Heritage Manor Nursing Home, Shreveport LA) Buried Arlington Cemetery, Homer LA.

Dickie Kerr—4 Years Pitcher (b. 3 Jul 1893 St Louis MO–d. 4 May 1963 at his home in Houston TX) He won two games for the White Sox in the infamous World Series of 1919 and managed minor league baseball before working ten years in the cotton business. He lived in Houston 30 years and was a retired office manager for B and M Electrical Company. Died from cancer. Buried Forest Park of Lawndale, Houston TX.

Doc Kerr—2 Years Catcher (b. 17 Jan 1882 Dellroy OH–d. 9 Jun 1937 Baltimore MD) An educated medical doctor, he owned and operated a drug store in Baltimore his last 20 years. Buried Richmond Cemetery, Richmond OH.

John Kerr—8 Years Infielder (b. 26 Nov 1898 San Francisco CA–d. 19 Oct 1993 Royal Care Convalescent Hosp, Long Beach CA) He played for years in the Pacific Coast League. He was a grip in the motion picture industry, retiring in 1963. Died from a heart attack, but suffered from leukemia. Cremated. Buried All Souls Cemetery, Long Beach CA.

Mel Kerr—1 Game Pinch Runner (b. 22 May 1903 Souris, Manitoba, Canada–d. 9 Aug 1980 Indian River Memorial Hosp, Vero Beach FL) He was a salesman for Kraft Foods Company, retiring to Vero Beach in 1980. Cremated.

Dan Kerwin—1 Year Outfielder (b. 9 Jul 1879 Philadelphia PA–d. 13 Jul 1960 Philadelphia PA) Buried Holy Cross Cemetery, Yeadon PA.

Henry Kessler—2 Years Infielder (b. 1847 Brooklyn NY–d. 9 Jan 1900 at the County Poor Farm in Sugarcreek PA) He took to drinking and ended up serving a term in the Western Penitentiary for arson. After his release he returned to drink again and was destitute when he died. Died from heart failure. Buried County Poor Farm Cemetery, Sugarcreek PA.

Fred Ketcham—2 Years Outfielder (b. 27 Jul 1875 Elmira NY–d. 12 Mar 1908 Cortland NY) He dropped dead from a heart attack while at the height of his baseball career.

Gus Ketchum—1 Year Pitcher (b. 21 Mar 1898 Rockwall TX–d. 6 Sep 1980 Oklahoma City OK).

Phil Ketter—1 Year Catcher (b. 13 Apr 1884 St Louis MO–d. 9 Apr 1965 St Louis MO) Buried St Paul Churchyard, St Louis MO.

Hank Keupper—1 Year Pitcher (b. 24 Jun 1887 Staunton IL–d. 14 Aug 1960 Marion Memorial Hospital, Marion IL) He operated a variety store in Shawneetown IL for several years. Died from a heart ailment. Buried Lake View Cemetery, Johnston City IL.

E Lee Keyser—(b. abt 1885 St Louis MO–d. 26 Apr 1950 St John's Hospital, St Louis MO) He was minor league secretary for the St Louis Browns. Known as the "Father of Night Baseball," he introduced night games to professional baseball in 1925 when he owned the Des Moines club of the Western League. Died from a cerebral thrombosis after being in ill health a year. Buried Glendale Cemetery, Des Moines IA.

Hod Kibbie—1 Year Infielder (b. 18 Jul 1903 Fort Worth TX–d. 19 Oct 1975 at a hospital in Fort Worth TX) Served in the U.S. Army during World War II. A physician, he had a general practice of medicine in Fort Worth from 1933 until shortly before his death. For many years he was the company doctor for the Fort Worth city employees and for the Santa Fe Railway. Buried Rose Hill Memorial Park, Fort Worth TX.

Jack Kibble—1 Year Infielder (b. 2 Jan 1892 Seatonville IL–d. 13 Dec 1969 Memorial Hospital, Roundup MT) Served in the U.S. Army during World War I. He worked in the coal mines near Roundup before opening a sporting goods store there in 1922, operating it until shortly before his death. Buried Custer Battlefield National Cemetery, Crow Ageny MT.

Joe Kiefer—3 Years Pitcher (b. 19 Jul 1899 West Leyden NY–d. 5 Jul 1975 Faxton Hospital, Utica NY) He worked for Savage Arms Corporation before spending 20 years at Niagara Mohawk Power Corporation, retiring in 1964. Died after a brief illness. Buried Mount Olivet Cemetery, Whitesboro NY.

Leo Kiely—7 Years Pitcher (b. 30 Nov 1929 Hoboken NJ–d. 18 Jan 1984 Mountainside Hospital, Montclair NJ) He was a mechanic for Finkle Trucking Company for five years, retiring in 1974. Died from cancer. Buried Holy Cross Cemetery, North Arlington NJ.

John Kiernan—Hall of Fame (b. 1892 Kingsbridge NY–d. 10 Dec 1981 Rockport MA) Served in France for the U.S. Army during World War I. He was a sportswriter for a number of New York City newspapers from 1915 to 1944. He was also a noted naturalist, author and panelist on radio and television. Died from a heart attack. Buried Beech Grove Cemetery, Rockport MA.

Pete Kilduff—5 Years Infielder (b. 4 Apr 1893 Weir City KS–d. 14 Feb 1930 Mount Carmel Hospital, Pittsburg KS) He was a minor league manager. Died following an operation for appendicitis. Buried St Mary's Cemetery, Pittsburg KS.

Darryl Kile—12 Years Pitcher (b. 1968 Garden Grove CA–d. 22 Jun 2002 Westin Hotel, Chicago IL) Died at the height of his career, apparently from a heart condition. He was found dead in his bed at the hotel where his team, the Cardinals, was staying during a series with the Cubs. Cremated.

John Kiley—2 Years Outfielder (b. Jul 1859 South Dedham MA–d. 18 Dec 1940 Norwood MA) He was a former town clerk at Norwood. Buried Highland Cemetery, Norwood MA.

Pat Kilhullen—1 Year Catcher (b. 10 Jul 1890 Carbondale PA–d. 2 Nov 1922 Oakland CA).

Bill Killefer—13 Years Catcher 9 Years Manager (b. 10 Oct 1887 Bloomingdale MI–d. 2 Jul 1960 V A Hospital, Elsmere DE) He spent 45 years in baseball as a player, coach, manager and scout, finishing as a scout for the Dodgers and Indians. Buried Prospect Hill Cemetery, Paw Paw MI.

Red Killefer—7 Years Outfielder (b. 13 Apr 1884 Bloomingdale MI–d. 4 Sep 1958 at his home in Palos Verdes CA) He managed minor league baseball, including five teams in the Pacific Coast League, retiring in 1942. Died from cancer of the peritoneum. Cremated.

Frank Killen—10 Years Pitcher (b. 30 Nov 1870 Pittsburgh PA–d. 3 Dec 1939 Pittsburgh PA) He umpired minor league baseball before opening a hotel and tavern in Pittsburgh. Found dead in his car from a heart attack.

Ed Killian—8 Years Pitcher (b. 12 Nov 1876 Racine WI–d. 18 Jul 1928 at his home in Detroit MI) He worked in the body plant of the Lincoln Motor Company. Died from cancer. Buried Woodlawn Cemetery, Detroit MI.

Jack Killilay—1 Year Pitcher (b. 24 May 1887 Leavenworth KS–d. 21 Oct 1968 at the Albany Hotel in Tulsa OK) He worked in the soft drink business in Kansas for several years and was in the hotel business at Miami OK ten years before retiring to Tulsa in 1955. Buried Memorial Park, Tulsa OK.

Matt Kilroy—10 Years Pitcher (b. 21 Jun 1866 Philadelphia PA–d. 2 Mar 1940 Temple Hospital, Philadelphia PA) He operated a taproom across the street from Shibe Park. Died after an illness of two years. Buried Holy Sepulchre Cemetery, Philadelphia PA.

Mike Kilroy—2 Years Pitcher (b. 4 Nov 1872 Philadelphia PA–d. 2 Oct 1960 Philadelphia PA) Buried New Cathedral Cemetery, Philadelphia PA.

Sam Kimber—2 Years Pitcher (b. 29 Oct 1852 Philadelphia PA–d. 7 Nov 1925 Philadelphia PA) Died after a short illness. Buried Westminster Cemetery, Bala Cynwyd PA.

Henry Kimbro—(b. abt 1911–d. 13 Jul 1999 Nashville TN) He founded Bill's Cab, a taxi service in Nashville. Known as the "Black Ty Cobb," he played in the negro leagues from 1934 to 1951. Buried Greenwood Cemetery, Nashville TN.

Hal Kime—1 Year Pitcher (b. 15 Mar 1900 West Salem OH–d. 16 May 1939 White Cross Hospital, Columbus OH) He was a judge in the Franklin County (OH) Court of Common Pleas. Died from a malignant brain tumor. Buried Union Cemetery, Cincinnati OH.

Wally Kimmick—6 Years Infielder (b. 30 May 1897 Turtle Creek PA–d. 24 Jul 1989 at his home in Boswell PA) Served in the U.S. Army during World War I. He was a retired employee of Westinghouse Electric Corporation. Buried William Penn Memorial Cemetery, Pittsburgh PA.

Chad Kimsey—6 Years Pitcher (b. 6 Aug 1905 Copperhill TN–d. 2 Dec 1942 near Pryor OK) He worked with his brother in the trucking business in Pryor. Killed instantly when the dump truck he was driving collided with a concrete bridge two miles south of Pryor. Buried Fairview Cemetery, Pryor OK.

Ellis Kinder—12 Years Pitcher (b. 26 Jul 1914 Atkins AR–d. 16 Oct 1968 Baptist Memorial Hospital, Memphis TN) World War II veteran. He worked at various jobs—as a house painter, a taxi-cab driver and repairman. Died three weeks after undergoing open heart surgery. Buried Highland Memorial Gardens, Jackson TN.

Lee King—2 Years Outfielder (b. 24 Jan 1894 New Britain CT–d. 7 Sep 1938 Newton Centre MA).

Lee King—7 Years Outfielder (b. 23 Dec 1892 Hundred WV–d. 16 Sep 1967 at his home in Shinnstown WV) World War I veteran. He worked 30 years for Matthiessen Hegeler Zinc Company at Spelter WV. Buried Shinnstown Masonic Cemetery, Shinnstown WV.

Lynn King—3 Years Outfielder (b. 28 Nov 1908 Clarinda IA–d. 11 May 1972 Atlantic IA) He played quarterback for Drake University and is a member of the Iowa Hall of Fame. Died after being in failing health for some time. Buried Villisca Cemetery, Villisca IA.

Sam King—1 Year Infielder (b. 17 May 1852 Peabody MA–d. 11 Aug 1922 at his home in Peabody MA).

Silver King—10 Years Pitcher (b. 11 Jan 1868 St Louis MO–d. 19 May 1938 Lutheran Hospital, St Louis MO) He was a brick contractor. Died following surgery for gall stones and appendicitis. Buried New St Marcus Cemetery, St Louis MO.

Wes Kingdon—1 Year Infielder (b. 4 Jul 1900 Los Angeles CA–d. 19 Apr 1975 Bevery Manor Conv Hosp, Capistrano Beach CA) He owned and operated a retail hardware store for 20 years. Died from a heart attack. Cremated.

Henry Kingman—1 Year Infielder (b. 3 Apr 1892 Tientsin, China–d. 27 Dec 1982 Piedmont Gardens Infirmary, Oakland CA) For 20 years he was executive secretary at Stiles Hall for the YMCA. Suffered from dementia and died from a heart attack. Cremated.

Walt Kinney—4 Years Pitcher (b. 9 Sep 1894 Denison TX–d. 1 Jul 1971 Escondido CA) For 15 years he was a boilermaker in steel construction. Died from a heart attack. Cremated.

Bob Kinsella—2 Years Outfielder (b. 5 Jan 1899 Springfield IL–d. 30 Dec 1951 Los Angeles CA) He was a self-employed ice cream salesman. Died from congestive heart failure. Buried Calvary Cemetery, Springfield IL.

Ed Kinsella—2 Years Pitcher (b. 15 Jan 1880

Lexington IL–d. 17 Jan 1976 Hawthorne Lodge, Bloomington IL) He operated a restaurant for a number of years before farming near Towanda IL. Buried St Mary's Cemetery, Bloomington IL.

Tom Kinslow—10 Years Catcher (b. 12 Jan 1866 Washington DC–d. 22 Feb 1901 at his home in Washington DC) Died from consumption.

Walt Kinzie—2 Years Infielder (b. 16 Mar 1857 KY–d. 5 Nov 1909 Chicago IL) Buried Graceland Cemetery, Chicago IL.

Ed Kippert—1 Year Outfielder (b. 3 Jan 1880 Detroit MI–d. 3 Jun 1960 Receiving Hospital, Detroit MI) Buried Evergreen Cemetery, Detroit MI.

Clay Kirby—8 Years Pitcher (b. 25 Jun 1948 Washington DC–d. 11 Oct 1991 at his mother's home in Arlington VA) He was a self-employed financial securities broker. Died after a heart attack. Buried National Memorial Park, Falls Church VA.

John Kirby—5 Years Pitcher (b. 13 Jan 1865 St Louis MO–d. 6 Oct 1931 St Louis MO) Buried Sunset Memorial Park, Affton MO.

LaRue Kirby—3 Years Outfielder (b. 30 Dec 1889 Eureka MI–d. 10 Jun 1961 at a hospital in Lansing MI) World War I veteran. He lived in Lansing 40 years, working for the city parks department there, and was a school patrol officer seven years. Buried Eureka Cemetery, Eureka MI.

Mike Kircher—3 Years Pitcher (b. 30 Sep 1897 Rochester NY–d. 26 Jun 1972 Genesee Hospital, Rochester NY) Worked as a security guard at Kodak Park for Eastman-Kodak until he retired in 1962. Died from a stroke. Buried Irondequoit Cemetery, Irondequoit NY.

Tom Kirk—1 Game Pinch Hitter (b. 27 Sep 1927 Philadelphia PA–d. 1 Aug 1974 Nazareth Hospital, Philadelphia PA) He worked for the Philadelphia Redevelopment Authority and served on the city's Zoning Board of Adjustment. Buried Resurrection Cemetery, Bensalem PA.

Jay Kirke—7 Years Outfielder (b. 16 Jun 1888 Fleichmans NY–d. 31 Aug 1968 New Orleans LA) Died in his sleep. Buried Machpelah Cemetery, Pascagoula MS.

Enos Kirkpatrick—4 Years Infielder (b. 8 Dec 1885 Pittsburgh PA–d. 14 Apr 1964 St Joseph's Hospital, Pittsburgh PA) He sold real estate for 20 years before becoming an inspector for the Pittsburgh city law department. Buried Calvary Cemetery, Pittsburgh PA.

Harry Kirsch—1 Year Pitcher (b. 17 Oct 1889 Fair Haven PA–d. 25 Dec 1925 at his home in Pittsburgh PA).

Ernie Kish—1 Year Infielder (b. 6 Feb 1918 Washington DC–d. 21 Dec 1993 Western Reserve Health Center, Kirtland OH) Served in the U.S. Coast Guard during World War II. He worked 40 years for his mother's dress shops with stores in Akron and Cleveland Heights. He took over the operation of the business in 1963 and retired in 1989, closing the shops. Buried Lake View Cemetery, Cleveland OH.

Bill Kisinger—3 Years Pitcher (b. 15 Aug 1871 Dayton KY–d. 21 Apr 1929 Cincinnati OH) Worked as a clothing designer. Died from a heart attack. Buried Evergreen Cemetery, Southgate KY.

Rube Kisinger—2 Years Pitcher (b. 13 Dec 1876 Adrian MI–d. 17 Jul 1941 Huron OH) For 35 years he was a mechanical engineer for New York Central Railroad. Killed instantly when he was struck by a train. Buried Oakwood Cemetery, Adrian MI.

Frank Kitson—10 Years Pitcher (b. 11 Apr 1872 Watson MI–d. 14 Apr 1930 Allegan MI) He spent his entire life in the Allegan area. Died at his home shortly after retiring for the night. Buried Hudson Corners Cemetery, Allegan MI.

Mal Kittredge—16 Years Catcher 1 Year Manager (b. 12 Oct 1869 Clinton MA–d. 23 Jun 1928 Methodist Hospital, Gary IN) He owned the Worcester MA baseball club and worked in sales for National Cash Register Company and as a salesman of peanut and popcorn vending machines. Died from a cerebral hemorrhage while on a sales trip. Buried Bucksport ME.

Hugo Klaerner—1 Year Pitcher (b. 15 Oct 1908 Fredericksburg TX–d. 3 Feb 1982 Hill Country Mem Hosp, Fredericksburg TX) Served as sheriff of Gillespie County, TX, from 1950 to 1980. A music lover, he performed in a local old-time band. Buried Der Stadt Friedhof, Fredericksburg TX.

Al Klawitter—3 Years Pitcher (b. 12 Apr 1888 Wilkes-Barre PA–d. 2 May 1950 Milwaukee WI).

Ollie Klee—1 Year Outfielder (b. 20 May 1900 Piqua OH–d. 9 Feb 1977 at his home in, Toledo OH) He coached and taught commercial subjects at the high school level in Maryland, Port Clinton OH and Toledo, retiring in 1967. Buried Memorial Park Cemetery, Dayton OH.

Chuck Klein—17 Years Outfielder Hall of Fame (b. 7 Oct 1904 Indianapolis IN–d. 28 Mar 1958 Indianapolis IN) He operated a tavern. Found dead from a cerebral hemorrhage in the flooded bathroom of his home. Buried Holy Cross Cemetery, Indianapolis IN.

Hal Klein—2 Years Pitcher (b. 8 Jun 1923 St Louis MO–d. 10 Dec 1957 St Louis MO) Buried Resurrection Cemetery, St Louis MO.

Lou Klein—5 Years Infielder 3 Years Manager (b. 22 Oct 1918 New Orleans LA–d. 20 Jun 1976 Metairie LA) Buried St Louis Cemetery # 3, New Orleans LA.

Ted Kleinhans—4 Years Pitcher (b. 8 Apr 1899 Deer Park WI–d. 24 Jul 1985 Redington Beach FL) Served in the U.S. Army during both World War I and World War II. Coached baseball about 20 years at Syracuse University, retiring in 1966. He was also commissioner of Parks and Recreation at Syracuse NY. Buried Serenity Gardens Memorial Park, Largo FL.

Nub Kleinke—2 Years Pitcher (b. 19 May 1911 Fond du Lac WI–d. 16 Mar 1950 off the Pacific Coast near Marin County, CA) A bartender in Oakland CA, he died from a heart attack while fishing. Buried Mountain View Cemetery, Oakland CA.

Red Kleinow—8 Years Catcher (b. 20 Jul 1879 Milwaukee WI–d. 9 Oct 1929 at his home in New York City NY) Buried Lutheran Cemetery, Middle Village NY.

Bill Klem—Hall of Fame (b. abt 1874–d. 16 Sep 1951 at his home in Miami Beach FL) He was known as the "Dean of Baseball umpires" and the " Old Arbitrator." Died from a heart attack after suffering from serious internal and respiratory disorders for two years. Buried Graceland Memorial Park, Coral Gables FL.

Ed Klepfer—6 Years Pitcher (b. 17 Mar 1888 Summerville PA–d. 9 Aug 1950 at a hospital in Tulsa OK) Served with the American Expeditionary Forces in France during World War I and was gassed. Was an independent oil operator before going to work as a broker for C W Titus, a Tulsa oilman, in 1946. Died after a lengthy illness. Buried Rose Hill Memorial Park, Tulsa OK.

Eddie Klieman—8 Years Pitcher (b. 21 Mar 1918 Norwood OH–d. 15 Nov 1979 Homosassa FL).

Bob Kline—5 Years Pitcher (b. 9 Dec 1909 Enterprise OH–d. 16 Mar 1987 Manor Care Nursing Center, Westerville OH) Scouted for the Cardinals and Atletics. Worked for the State of Ohio Administrative Office and the State Highway Department. Died from cancer. Buried Green Lawn Memorial Cemetery, Columbus OH.

Bill Kling—3 Years Pitcher (b. 14 Jan 1867 Kansas City MO–d. 25 Aug 1934 at his home in Kansas City MO) After baseball he entered business and was vice-president of Balto Recreation Company. He had been ill for six months when he died. Buried Calvary Cemetery, Kansas City MO.

Johnny Kling—13 Years Catcher 1 Year Manager (b. 13 Feb 1875 Kansas City MO–d. 31 Jan 1947 Kansas City MO) An expert billiard player, he won the national pocket billiard championship one year. He owned a hotel and billiard parlor in Kansas City. From 1933 to 1937 he owned the Kansas City Blues in the American Association with the understanding that visiting teams would stay at his hotel. Died from a cerebral hemorrhage following a heart attack. Buried Mount Moriah Cemetery, Kansas City MO.

Rudy Kling—1 Year Infielder (b. 23 Mar 1870 St Louis MO–d. 14 Mar 1937 St Louis MO) Buried Old St Marcus Cemetery, St Louis MO.

Bob Klinger—8 Years Pitcher (b. 4 Jun 1908 Allenton (between Pacific and Eureka) MO–d. 19 Aug 1977 Villa Ridge MO) Veteran of World War II. Killed in an automobile accident. Buried Allen Cemetery, Allenton MO.

Joe Klinger—2 Years Infielder (b. 2 Aug 1902 Canonsburg PA–d. 31 Jul 1960 at a hospital in Little Rock AR) He played in the Southern Association. When he died he was working in the service department of an automobile agency. Buried Pine Crest Memorial Park, Alexander AR.

Fred Klobedanz—5 Years Pitcher (b. 13 Jun 1871 Waterbury CT–d. 12 Apr 1940 Waterbury Hospital, Waterbury CT) Worked as a clerk at the Connecticut Hotel in Waterbury for several years until he became ill and died after a lingering illness. Buried New Pine Grove Cemetery, Waterbury CT.

Stan Klopp—1 Year Pitcher (b. 22 Dec 1910 Womelsdorf PA–d. 7 Mar 1980 Hershey Medical Center, Hershey PA) He worked for the Parish Division of Dana Corporation in Reading PA before retiring in 1971. Buried St Daniels Cemetery, Robesonia PA.

Nap Kloza—2 Years Outfielder (b. 2 Sep 1903 Poland–d. 11 Jun 1962 County Emergency Hospital, Milwaukee WI) He was an instructor in the Milwaukee municipal baseball program. Died from a heart attack. Buried Holy Cross Cemetery, Milwaukee WI.

Joe Klugman—4 Years Infielder (b. 26 Mar 1895 St Louis MO–d. 18 Jul 1951 Woodland Hospital, Moberly MO) He played and managed in the Southern Association before becoming Chief of Police at Moberly in 1932, sheriff of Randolph County, MO, in 1940, and Missouri State Recreation Director in 1946. Died following a heart attack. Buried Oakland Cemetery, Moberly MO.

Elmer Klumpp—2 Years Catcher (b. 26 Aug 1906 St Louis MO–d. 18 Oct 1996 Community Memorial Hosp, Menomonee Falls WA) He worked in the welding and machine division of Falk Corporation, retiring in 1973. Died following a heart attack. Buried Pinelawn Memorial Park, Milwaukee WI.

Billy Klusman—2 Years Infielder (b. 24 Mar 1865 Cincinnati OH–d. 24 Jun 1907 Cincinnati OH) He managed minor league baseball before opening a cafe in Cincinnati. Died from consumption.

Ted Kluszewski—15 Years Infielder (b. 10 Sep 1924 Argo IL–d. 29 Mar 1988 Bethesda North Hospital, Cincinnati OH) He operated a chain of restaurants in the Cincinnati area while still working as hitting instructor for the Reds. Died after suffering a heart attack. Buried Gate of Heaven Cemetery, Cincinnati OH.

Clyde Kluttz—9 Years Catcher (b. 12 Dec 1917 Rockwell NC–d. 12 May 1979 Salisbury NC) He worked his entire life in baseball and was Director of Player Development for the Orioles when he died. He had been in declining health three years and seriously ill two and a half weeks. Buried Rowan Memorial Park, Salisbury NC.

Otto Knabe—11 Years Infielder 2 Years Manager (b. 12 Jun 1884 Carrick PA–d. 17 May 1961 at his home in Philadelphia PA) Buried New Cathedral Cemetery, Philadelphia PA.

Cotton Knaupp—2 Years Infielder (b. 13 Aug 1889 San Antonio TX–d. 5 Jul 1967 V A Hospital, New Orleans LA) World War I veteran. He was a retired rodman. Died from uremia and generalized arteriosclerotic heart disease. Buried Mission Burial Park South, San Antonio TX.

Rudy Kneisch—1 Year Pitcher (b. 10 Apr 1899 Baltimore MD–d. 6 Apr 1965 Church Home Hospital, Baltimore MD) He worked in Baltimore as a steamfitter in construction. Died after being ill nearly a month. Buried Lorraine Park Cemetery, Baltimore MD.

Phil Knell—6 Years Pitcher (b. 12 Mar 1865 San Francisco CA–d. 5 Jun 1944 Santa Monica CA) Died from a heart attack. Cremated.

Charlie Knepper—1 Year Pitcher (b. 18 Feb 1871 Anderson IN–d. 6 Feb 1946 Ball Hospital, Muncie IN) Worked 25 years in the heat treatment department at Warner Gear Company, retiring in 1935. Died following a long illness. Buried Beech Grove Cemetery, Muncie IN.

Lou Knerr—3 Years Pitcher (b. 21 Aug 1921 Strasburg PA–d. 23 Mar 1980 at his home in Denver PA) An avid golfer, he worked for a service station in Denver from 1951 until he died suddenly from a heart attack. Buried Fairview Cemetery, Denver PA.

Elmer Knetzer—8 Years Pitcher (b. 22 Jul 1885 Carrick PA–d. 3 Oct 1975 St Joseph's Hospital, Pittsburgh PA) For 16 years he was a watchman for the Joseph Horne Company, retiring in 1954. Buried St Wendelin Cemetery, Brentwood PA.

Austin Knickerbocker—1 Year Outfielder (b. 15 Oct 1918 Bangall NY–d. 18 Feb 1997 at his home in Clinton Corners NY) Served in France, Germany, Italy and Africa for the U.S. Army during World War II. He managed minor league baseball before settling in Clinton Corners where he was a self-employed carpenter and was active in local politics. Died after a long illness. Buried Stanford Cemetery, Stanfordville NY.

Bill Knickerbocker—10 Years Infielder (b. 29 Dec 1911 Los Angeles CA–d. 8 Sep 1963 Palm Drive Hospital, Sebastopol CA) Served in the U.S. Army during World War II. Died following a heart attack. Buried Golden Gate National Cemetery, San Bruno CA.

Jack Knight—4 Years Pitcher (b. 12 Jan 1895 Pittsboro MS–d. 30 Jul 1976 San Antonio TX).

Joe Knight—2 Years Outfielder (b. 26 Sep 1859 Point Stanley, Ontario, Canada–d. 18 Oct 1938 Lynhurst, Ontario, Canada).

John Knight—8 Years Infielder (b. 6 Oct 1885 Philadelphia PA–d. 19 Dec 1965 John Muir Hospital, Walnut Creek CA) He managed minor league baseball for a short while before becoming an auditor and office manager for a San Francisco corporation. Cremated. Buried Chapel of the Chimes, Oakland CA.

Lon Knight—7 Years Outfielder 1 Year Manager (b. 16 Jun 1853 Philadelphia PA–d. 23 Apr 1932 Hahnemann Hospital, Philadelphia PA) Died from gas poisoning after a line to his gas heater broke. Buried Laurel Hill Cemetery, Philadelphia PA.

Pete Knisely—4 Years Outfielder (b. 11 Aug 1883 Waynesburg PA–d. 1 Jul 1948 General Hospital, Brownsville PA) He was a retired employee of the Vesta Number 4 mine. Died from head injuries received when he fell 15 feet to a concrete highway from a railroad bridge at the Vesta Number 6 mine. Buried Hewitt Cemetery, Rice's Landing PA.

Mike Knode—1 Year Outfielder (b. 8 Nov 1895 Westminster MD–d. 20 Dec 1980 Memorial Hospital, South Bend IN) He was a practicing pediatrician for nearly 60 years, specializing in pediatric allergies. Died following an extended illness. Buried Violett Cemetery, Goshen IN.

Ray Knode—4 Years Infielder (b. 28 Jan 1901 Westminster MD–d. 13 Apr 1982 Community Hospital, Battle Creek MI) He was an auditor for U.S. Fidelity and Guaranty Company in Cleveland before coaching baseball, football and basketball in Findlay OH and Battle Creek. Later he worked in personnel departments for a number of companies. Buried Memorial Park Cemetery, Battle Creek MI.

Punch Knoll—1 Year Outfielder (b. 7 Oct 1881 Evansville IN–d. 8 Feb 1960 Deaconess Hospital, Evansville IN) He played and managed in several minor leagues. For a short time he ran a tavern in Evansville. He also owned an orchard near Chandler IN. Died from a lingering illness. Buried Locust Hill Cemetery, Evansville IN.

Hub Knolls—1 Year Pitcher (b. 18 Dec 1883 Valparaiso IN–d. 1 Jul 1946 Chicago IL) Commercial agent for Railway Express. Buried Waldheim Jewish Cemetery, Forest Park IL.

Fritz Knothe—2 Years Infielder (b. 1 May 1903 Passaic NJ–d. 27 Mar 1963 General Hospital, Passaic NJ) He was a patrolman for the Passaic Police Department from 1935 until his death. Died after suffering a heart attack ten days earlier. Buried Holy Cross Cemetery, North Arlington NJ.

George Knothe—1 Year Infielder (b. 12 Jan 1900 Bayonne NJ–d. 3 Jul 1981 Dover NJ).

Jack Knott—11 Years Pitcher (b. 2 Mar 1907 Dallas TX–d. 13 Oct 1981 Brownwood Regional Hospital, Brownwood TX) Served in the U.S. Army during World War II and was the recipient of a purple heart. He was the first manager of the Brownwood Coliseum and a former executive of the Downtown Brownwood Merchant's Association. Died after a lengthy illness. Buried Greenleaf Cemetery, Brownwood TX.

Joe Knotts—1 Year Catcher (b. 3 Mar 1884 Greensboro PA–d. 15 Sep 1950 Philadelphia PA).

Ed Knouff—5 Years Pitcher (b. Jun 1868 Philadelphia PA–d. 14 Sep 1900 German Hospital, Philadelphia PA) A Philadelphia city fireman, his back was broken when a heavy stone fell on him in 1897 while fighting a fire. He had been hospitalized since. Died from kidney trouble.

Tom Knowlson—1 Year Pitcher (b. 23 Apr 1895 Pittsburgh PA–d. 11 Apr 1943 Miami Shores FL) Moving from Pittsburgh to Miami about 1924, he was the owner and originator of the Gulf Stream Fishing Lodge at Key Largo. Buried Woodlawn Park Cemetery, Miami FL.

Bill Knowlton—1 Year Pitcher (b. 18 Aug 1892 Philadelphia PA–d. 25 Feb 1944 Philadelphia PA) A Philadelphia policeman, he dropped dead from a heart attack while disembarking from a trolley. Buried Fernwood Cemetery, Fernwood PA.

Andy Knox—1 Year Infielder (b. 5 Jan 1864 Philadelphia PA–d. 14 Sep 1940 at his home in Philadelphia PA) For 23 years he was a detective for the Philadelphia Police Department before spending 20 years as a special officer for the Pennsylvania Bottler's Protective Association. Died after a lengthy illness. Buried Lawnview Cemetery, Rockledge PA.

Cliff Knox—1 Year Catcher (b. 7 Jan 1902 Coalville IA–d. 24 Sep 1965 Mahaska Hospital, Oskaloosa IA) His major league career came to an end in 1924 when he broke a finger and an ankle, but he played several more years in the minors. Later he was a football official, working games in the Big Eight and Missouri Valley conferences. He officiated several Sugar Bowl games. Died after a lingering illness. Buried Forest Cemetery, Oskaloosa IA.

Barney Koch—1 Year Infielder (b. 23 Mar 1923 Campbell NE–d. 6 Jun 1987 at his home in Tacoma WA) He was a building materials salesman. Cremated.

Brad Kocher—3 Years Catcher (b. 16 Jan 1888 White Haven PA–d. 13 Feb 1965 at his home in White Haven PA) He was a funeral director. Died after being ill three years. Buried St John's Cemetery, Dallas PA.

Ben Koehler—2 Years Outfielder (b. 26 Jan 1877 Schoerndorn, Germany–d. 21 May 1961 at his home in South Bend IN) He worked for the School City and for many years was the groundskeeper and caretaker of School Field. Died after a five-month illness. Buried Highland Cemetery, South Bend IN.

Pip Koehler—1 Year Outfielder (b. 16 Jan 1902 Gilbert PA–d. 8 Dec 1986 at his home in Tacoma WA) Also a professional basketball player, he managed minor league baseball for several years. Died from a heart attack and complications from diabetes. Buried Calvary Cemetery, Tacoma WA.

Len Koenecke—3 Years Outfielder (b. 18 Jan 1904 Baraboo WI–d. 17 Sep 1935 Toronto, Ontario, Canada) Died at the height of his baseball career. Killed by an airman who was defending himself when Koenecke attempted to take over the airplane, while intoxicated, flying over Toronto. Buried Mount Repose Cemetery, Friendship WI.

Mark Koenig—12 Years Infielder (b. 19 Jul 1904 San Francisco CA–d. 22 Apr 1993 Willow View Convalescent Center, Willows CA) Died from lung cancer, congestive heart failure and pneumonia. Cremated.

Willis Koenigsmark—1 Year Pitcher (b. 27 Feb 1896 Waterloo IL–d. 1 Jul 1972 Memorial Hospital, Belleville IL) Worked as a salesman, living many years in Alabama, and in Murphysboro IL. Buried Waterloo City Cemetery, Waterloo IL.

Elmer Koestner—2 Years Pitcher (b. 30 Nov 1885 Piper City IL–d. 27 Oct 1959 Fairbury Hospital, Fairbury IL) Operated a restaurant and pool hall in Piper City IL. Died following a long illness. Buried Calvary Cemetery, Piper City IL.

Joe Kohlman—2 Years Pitcher (b. 28 Jan 1913 Philadelphia PA–d. 16 Mar 1974 Philadelphia PA).

Dick Kokos—5 Years Outfielder (b. 28 Feb 1928 Chicago IL–d. 9 Apr 1986 Chicago IL) Buried St Adalbert Cemetery, Niles IL.

Don Kolloway—12 Years Infielder (b. 4 Aug 1918 Posen IL–d. 30 Jun 1994 St Francis Hospital, Blue Island IL) Served in the U.S. Army during World War II. He owned and operated a tavern in Blue Island from 1956 to 1969. Later he worked in voter registration for Cook County. Buried Cedar Park Cemetery, Chicago IL.

Ray Kolp—12 Years Pitcher (b. 1 Oct 1894 New Berlin OH–d. 29 Jul 1967 Good Samaritan Hospital, Cincinnati OH) He managed minor league baseball. Buried St Stephen Cemetery, Fort Thomas KY.

Karl Kolsth—1 Year Infielder (b. 25 Dec 1892 Somerville MA–d. 3 May 1956 at his home in Bowling Green MD) He was a well-known horse trainer. Buried St Peter's and St Paul's Cemetery, Cumberland MD.

Fred Kommers—2 Years Outfielder (b. 31 Mar 1886 Chicago IL–d. 14 Jun 1943 Chicago IL) Buried Cedar Park Cemetery, Chicago IL.

Ed Konetchy—15 Years Infielder (b. 3 Sep 1885 LaCrosse WI–d. 27 May 1947 Fort Worth TX) He lived 22 years in Fort Worth. Buried Greenwood Memorial Park, Fort Worth TX.

Alex Konikowski—3 Years Pitcher (b. 8 Jun 1928 Troop PA–d. 28 Sep 1997 at his home in Seymour CT) Buried St Augustine Cemetery, Seymour CT.

Mike Konnick—2 Years Catcher (b. 13 Jan 1889 Glen Lyon PA–d. 9 Jul 1971 at his home in Wilkes-Barre PA) He managed and umpired minor league baseball and was a scout for the Braves and Phillies. He retired as a truckdriver for Stegmeier Brewing Company. Buried St Mary's Cemetery, Wilkes-Barre PA.

Bruce Konopka—3 Years Infielder (b. 16 Sep

1919 Hammond IN–d. 27 Sep 1996 Denver CO) Served in the U.S. Navy during World War II. He worked for Coors Brewery, Burns Realty and DuPont Stocks and Bonds. Cremated.

Jim Konstanty—11 Years Pitcher (b. 2 Mar 1917 Strykersville NY–d. 11 Jun 1976 Fox Hospital, Oneonta NY) He owned and operated a sporting goods store in Oneonta from 1948 until retiring in 1973. Died after a brief illness. Buried Maple Grove Cemetery, Worcester NY.

Ernie Koob—4 Years Pitcher (b. 11 Sep 1893 Keeler MI–d. 12 Nov 1941 Mount St Rose Sanitarium, Lemay MO) Pitched a no-hit game against the White Sox in 1917, winning 1 to 0. He was a foreman at a St Louis manufacturing firm. Died from tuberculosis. Buried Calvary Cemetery, St Louis MO.

Cal Koonce—10 Years Pitcher (b. 18 Nov 1940 Fayetteville NC–d. 28 Oct 1993 Baptist Hospital, Winston-Salem NC) He coached high school and college baseball and was a minor league team executive. Active in civic affairs, he was the Hope Mills NC town manager and a member of the town board of commissioners. Died from cancer. Buried Lafayette Memorial Park, Fayetteville NC.

Larry Kopf—10 Years Infielder (b. 3 Nov 1890 Bristol CT–d. 15 Oct 1986 at a nursing home in Hamilton County OH) A real estate developer and home builder, he was responsible for building many of the homes in the Watch Hill area of Cincinnati. Died from pneumonia and a heart attack. Buried Mount Moriah Cemetery, Withamsville OH.

Wally Kopf—1 Year Infielder (b. 10 Jul 1899 Stonington CT–d. 30 Apr 1979 Bethesda Hospital, Cincinnati OH) World War I veteran. He was a principal in a realty and building firm in Cincinnati from 1923 until he retired in 1975. Died from septicemia. Buried Calvary Cemetery, Cincinnati OH.

Merlin Kopp—3 Years Outfielder (b. 2 Jan 1892 Toledo OH–d. 7 May 1960 at his home in Sacramento CA) World War I veteran. For over 30 years he was a warehouseman for a wholesale hardware company. Died from a heart attack. Buried St Mary's Cemetery, Sacramento CA.

George Kopshaw—1 Year Catcher (b. 5 Jul 1895 Passaic NJ–d. 26 Dec 1934 Memorial Hospital, Lynchburg VA) He was an umpire in the Piedmont League. Died from typhoid fever. Buried St Mary's Cemetery, East Orange NJ.

Art Kores—1 Year Infielder (b. 22 Jul 1886 Milwaukee WI–d. 26 Mar 1974 Milwaukee WI) He worked over 25 years for the Wisconsin Gas Company. Buried Wisconsin Memorial Park, Brookfield WI.

Jim Korwan—2 Years Pitcher (b. 4 Mar 1874 Brooklyn NY–d. 24 Jul 1899 Brooklyn NY).

Clem Koshorek—2 Years Infielder (b. 20 Jun 1925 Royal Oak MI–d. 8 Sep 1991 Royal Oak MI).

Dave Koslo—12 Years Pitcher (b. 31 Mar 1920 Menasha WI–d. 1 Dec 1975 Theda Clark Memorial Hospital, Menasha WI) World War II veteran. Worked for George Banta Company at Menasha WI. Died unexpectedly. Buried St John Cemetery, Menasha WI.

Joe Kostal—1 Year Pitcher (b. 17 Mar 1876 Guelph, Ontario, Canada–d. 10 Oct 1933 Guelph, Ontario, Canada).

Fred Koster—1 Year Outfielder (b. 21 Dec 1905 Louisville KY–d. 24 Apr 1979 Suburban Hospital, St Matthews KY) He was a star athlete at the University of Louisville, playing football, basketball, baseball and track and is a member of the University of Louisville Hall of Fame. He was one of the top football officials in the South. Active in the automobile business for 35 years, he owned the Buick dealership in Louisville. Died from a heart attack. Buried Cave Hill Cemetery, Louisville KY.

Joe Koukalik—1 Year Pitcher (b. 3 Mar 1880 Chicago IL–d. 27 Dec 1945 Chicago IL).

Lou Koupal—6 Years Pitcher (b. 19 Dec 1898 Tabor SD–d. 8 Dec 1961 Community Hospital, San Gabriel CA) A carpenter for various contractors for 16 years, he died from lung cancer. Buried Resurrection Cemetery, San Gabriel CA.

Fabian Kowalik—3 Years Pitcher (b. 22 Apr 1908 Falls City TX–d. 14 Aug 1954 Karnes City TX) A wholesale beer distributor, he died from cirrhosis of the liver. Buried Falls City Cemetery, Falls City TX.

Joe Kracher—1 Year Catcher (b. 4 Nov 1913 Philadelphia PA–d. 24 Dec 1981 Shannon Hospital, San Angelo TX) Buried Lawnhaven Memorial Gardens, San Angelo TX.

Clarence Kraft—1 Year Infielder (b. 9 Jun

1887 Evansville IN–d. 26 Mar 1958 Fort Worth TX) He was a retired county judge. Buried Greenwood Memorial Park, Fort Worth TX.

Joe Krakauskas—7 Years Pitcher (b. 28 Mar 1915 Montreal, Quebec, Canada–d. 8 Jul 1960 Hamilton, Ontario, Canada) Died from pneumonia. Buried Holy Sepulchre Cemetery, Burlington, Ontario, Can.

Jack Kramer—12 Years Pitcher (b. 5 Jan 1918 New Orleans LA–d. 18 May 1995 Metairie LA).

Gene Krapp—4 Years Pitcher (b. 12 May 1888 Rochester NY–d. 13 Apr 1923 Deaconess Hospital, Detroit MI) Principal in the Krapp Brothers Auto Sale Company. Died following surgery for intestinal cancer. Buried Woodmere Cemetery, Detroit MI.

Tex Kraus—3 Years Pitcher (b. 26 Apr 1918 San Antonio TX–d. 2 Jan 1976 San Antonio TX) Buried Fort Sam Houston National Cemetery, San Antonio TX.

Charlie Krause—1 Year Infielder (b. 2 Oct 1873 Detroit MI–d. 30 Mar 1948 Eloise MI).

Harry Krause—5 Years Pitcher (b. 12 Jul 1888 San Francisco CA–d. 23 Oct 1940 Mary's Help Hospital, San Francisco CA) Died from skull injuries suffered 11 days earlier in a head-on automobile accident. Buried Holy Cross Catholic Cemetery, Colma CA.

Lew Krausse—2 Years Pitcher (b. 8 Jun 1912 Media PA–d. 6 Sep 1988 Sarasota FL) Served in the U.S. Army during World War II. He coached, scouted and managed minor league baseball, retiring from baseball in 1970. Buried Palms Memorial Park, Sarasota FL.

Mike Kreevich—12 Years Outfielder (b. 10 Jun 1908 Mount Olive IL–d. 25 Apr 1994 Community Hospital, Pana IL) He was a coal miner, but was last employed at a tool and die factory in Aurora IL. Buried Union Miners Cemetery, Mount Olive IL.

Charlie Krehmeyer—2 Years Outfielder (b. 5 Jul 1857 St Louis MO–d. 10 Feb 1926 City Hospital, St Louis MO) He was a sawyer in a planing mill. Died from pneumonia. Buried New St Marcus Cemetery, St Louis MO.

Ralph Kreitz—1 Year Catcher (b. 13 Nov 1885 Plum Creek NE–d. 20 Jul 1941 Portland OR) He was a gasoline distributor. Died from a heart attack shortly after participating in an old-timer's game. Buried Lincoln Memorial Park, Portland OR.

Ray Kremer—10 Years Pitcher (b. 23 Mar 1893 Oakland CA–d. 8 Feb 1965 Pinole CA) Buried Sunset View Cemetery, El Cerrito CA.

Red Kress—14 Years Infielder (b. 2 Jan 1905 Columbia CA–d. 29 Nov 1962 at his home in Canoga Park CA) He worked in baseball his entire life, coaching for several teams and managing some minor league baseball. Died from a heart attack. Buried Forest Lawn Memorial Park, Glendale CA.

Paul Krichell—2 Years Catcher (b. 19 Dec 1882 New York City NY–d. 4 Jun 1957 at his home in New York City NY) He was the chief scout for the Yankees for 37 years, signing over 200 of the players who made up the Yankee dynasty. He also operated a saloon in the Bronx NY. Buried Kensico Cemetery, Valhalla NY.

Bill Krieg—4 Years Catcher (b. 29 Jan 1859 Mount Pulaski IL–d. 25 Mar 1930 at his home in Chillicothe IL) He managed minor league baseball until about 1918 when he went to work for the Santa Fe Railroad Company in Chillicothe. Died from a complication of illnesses. Buried Chillicothe Cemetery, Chillicothe IL.

Kurt Krieger—2 Years Pitcher (b. 16 Sep 1926 Traisen, Austria–d. 16 Aug 1970 St Mary's Hospital, St Louis MO) Worked as a batting practice pitcher for the Cardinals. Died from cancer. Buried Sunset Memorial Park, Affton MO.

Howie Krist—6 Years Pitcher (b. 28 Feb 1916 West Henrietta NY–d. 23 Apr 1989 Veteran's Hospital, Buffalo NY) Served in the U.S. Army during World War II. Owned and operated a furniture store for 32 years. Died after a long illness. Buried Delevan Cemetery, Delevan NY.

Ray Kroc—(b. 5 Oct 1902 IL–d. 14 Jan 1984 Scripps Clinic, La Jolla CA) He was the founder and owner of the MacDonald hamburger empire and the owner of the Padres. Died from a heart attack and complications of diabetes. Cremated. Buried El Camino Memorial Park, San Diego CA.

Gus Krock—3 Years Pitcher (b. 9 May 1866 Milwaukee WI–d. 22 Mar 1905 at his home in Pasadena CA) A contractor, he died from consumption.

Rube Kroh—6 Years Pitcher (b. 25 Aug 1886 Friendship NY–d. 17 Mar 1944 New Orleans LA) Buried Garden of Memories, Metairie LA.

Jack Krol—2 Years Manager (b. 5 Jul 1936 Chicago IL–d. 30 May 1994 at his home in Winston-Salem NC) He was involved in professional baseball 41 years, mostly as a minor league manager where he had over 1000 wins. He was also a coach for the Cardinals and Padres. Buried Parklawn Memorial Gardens, Winston-Salem NC.

John Kroner—4 Years Infielder (b. 13 Nov 1908 St Louis MO–d. 26 Aug 1968 Christian Hospital Northwest, St Louis MO) He was a newspaper carrier for the *St Louis Post-Dispatch*. Buried Memorial Park Cemetery, St Louis MO.

Art Krueger—4 Years Outfielder (b. 16 Mar 1881 San Antonio TX–d. 28 Nov 1949 near Hondo CA) Died after a series of strokes. Buried Holy Cross Cemetery, Culver City CA.

Ernie Krueger—8 Years Catcher (b. 27 Dec 1890 Chicago IL–d. 22 Apr 1976 Victory Memorial Hospital, Waukegan IL) He caught the longest game in major league history—26 innings. A carpet layer for Marshall Fields, he retired in 1947. Buried Oak Woods Cemetery, Chicago IL.

Otto Krueger—7 Years Infielder (b. 17 Sep 1876 Chicago IL–d. 20 Feb 1961 St Louis MO) Died from infirmities due to age. Buried Resurrection Cemetery, St Louis MO.

Henry Krug—1 Year Outfielder (b. 4 Dec 1876 San Francisco CA–d. 14 Jan 1908 San Francisco CA) Buried Cypress Lawn Memorial Park, Colma CA.

Marty Krug—2 Years Infielder (b. 10 Sep 1888 Coblenz, Germany–d. 26 Jun 1966 Memorial Hospital, Glendale CA) He worked 41 years in baseball as a coach, minor league manager and executive, retiring in 1951. He lived in Glendale 43 years. Died from a heart attack. Cremated. Buried Forest Lawn Memorial Park, Glendale CA.

Abe Kruger—1 Year Pitcher (b. 14 Feb 1885 Morris Run PA–d. 4 Jul 1962 Elmira NY).

Johnny Kucab—3 Years Pitcher (b. 17 Dec 1919 Olyphant PA–d. 26 May 1977 Youngstown OH) Served in Europe and the Far East during World War II. Associated with the Havanec Distributing Company in Youngstown for 10 years. Died from a heart attack. Buried St John's Catholic Cemetery, Campbell OH.

Bert Kuczynski—1 Year Pitcher (b. 8 Jan 1920 Philadelphia PA–d. 19 Jan 1997 Sacred Heart Hospital, Allentown PA) Served in the U.S. Army during World War II. He also played professional football. He taught history and coached football and baseball at Coatesville (PA) High School and Catasaugua (PA) High School, retiring in 1985. Buried Schoenersville Cemetery, Schoenersville PA.

Willie Kuehne—10 Years Infielder (b. 24 Oct 1858 Chicago IL–d. 27 Oct 1921 at his father-in-law's, Sulphur Springs OH) Died from lobar pneumonia, but he had been an invalid for many years. Buried Union Cemetery, Sulphur Springs OH.

Harvey Kuenn—15 Years Outfielder 3 Years Manager (b. 4 Dec 1930 Milwaukee WI–d. 28 Feb 1988 at his home in Peoria AZ) He spent his entire life working in baseball. Died from a variety of serious medical problems suffered since the mid-1970s. He had open-heart surgery in 1976 and a leg amputated just below the knee in 1980. Buried Sunland Memorial Park, Sun City AZ.

Joe Kuhel—18 Years Infielder 2 Years Manager (b. 25 Jun 1906 Cleveland OH–d. 26 Feb 1984 Univ of Kansas Med Center, Kansas City KS) He moved to the Kansas City area in 1926, retiring in 1971 after working 20 years as a district sales manager for Roper Sales Corporation. Buried Forest Hill Cemetery, Kansas City MO.

Bub Kuhn—1 Year Pitcher (b. 12 Oct 1899 Vicksburg MI–d. 20 Nov 1956 Henry Ford Hospital, Detroit MI) Coordinated agriculture and research extension programs for Michigan State University Extension Service from 1928 until his death. His last position was as a personnel officer. Died following an operation. Buried Evergreen Cemetery, Lansing MI.

Walt Kuhn—3 Years Catcher (b. 2 Feb 1884 Fresno CA–d. 14 Jun 1935 Fresno CA) Served in the U.S. Army during World War I where he suffered the loss of an eye. In 1919 and 1920 he was chief of detectives at Dallas TX, but a chronic illness prevented him from working after that. Believed to be despondent over ill health he took his own life by shooting himself with a 30-30 rifle. Buried Belmont Memorial Park, Fresno CA.

Charlie Kuhns—2 Years Infielder (b. Freeport PA–d. 15 Jul 1922 Pittsburgh PA).

John Kull—1 Year Pitcher (b. 24 Jun 1882 Shenandoah PA–d. 30 Mar 1936 County Almshouse, Schuylkill Haven PA) He died after being in failing health a number of years.

Bill Kunkel—3 Years Pitcher (b. 7 Jul 1936 Hoboken NJ–d. 4 May 1985 Riverview Medical Center, Red Bank NJ) He umpired in the American League from 1968 until his death, as well as officiating some in the National Basketball League. Died from cancer. Cremated.

Earl Kunz—1 Year Pitcher (b. 25 Dec 1899 Sacramento CA–d. 14 Apr 1963 at his home in Sacramento CA) Operated a night club near San Rafael CA during the 1930s and was a trainer and owner of race horses from the 1940s until he died from a heart attack. Buried St Mary's Cemetery, Sacramento CA.

Whitey Kurowski—9 Years Infielder (b. 19 Apr 1918 Reading PA–d. 9 Dec 1999 Reading PA) Buried Gethsemane Cemetery, Laureldale PA.

Ed Kusel—1 Year Pitcher (b. 15 Feb 1886 Cleveland OH–d. 20 Oct 1948 at his home in Cleveland OH) Worked as an accountant. Buried Brooklyn Heights Cemetery, Cleveland OH.

Emil Kush—6 Years Pitcher (b. 4 Nov 1916 Chicago IL–d. 25 Nov 1969 River Grove IL) Took his own life with carbon monoxide poisoning. Buried St Joseph Cemetery, River Grove IL.

Joe Kustus—1 Year Outfielder (b. 5 Sep 1882 Detroit MI–d. 27 Apr 1916 at his sister's home in Detroit MI) He quit baseball when he contracted tuberculosis. Died from the disease.

Joe Kutina—2 Years Infielder (b. 16 Jan 1885 Chicago IL–d. 13 Apr 1945 Chicago IL) Cremated.

Andy Kyle—1 Year Outfielder (b. 29 Oct 1889 Toronto, Ontario, Canada–d. 6 Sep 1971 Toronto, Ontario, Canada) Buried Park Lawn Cemetery, Toronto, Ontario, Can.

L

Chet Laabs—11 Years Outfielder (b. 30 Apr 1912 Milwaukee WI–d. 26 Jan 1983 Warren MI) He worked for the Spike Lawrence Trophy Company. Died from a pulmonary embolism. Buried St Clement Cemetery, Center Line MI.

Candy LaChance—12 Years Infielder (b. 15 Feb 1870 Waterbury CT–d. 18 Aug 1932 at his home in Waterbury CT) He was a watchman at the Chase plant in Waterville CT. Died after an illness of more than a year. Buried Calvary Cemetery, Waterbury CT.

George LaClaire—2 Years Pitcher (b. 18 Oct 1886 Milton VT–d. 10 Oct 1918 Farnham, Quebec, Canada) Died from influenza.

Guy Lacy—1 Year Infielder (b. 12 Jun 1897 Cleveland TN–d. 19 Nov 1953 at a hospital in Cleveland TN) He played minor league baseball for 30 years and also managed in the minors. Buried Triplett Cemetery, Cleveland TN.

Hi Ladd—1 Year Outfielder (b. 9 Feb 1870 Willimantic CT–d. 7 May 1948 Cranston RI) Buried Knotty Oak Cemetery, Coventry RI.

Flip Lafferty—2 Years Outfielder (b. 4 May 1854 Scranton PA–d. 8 Feb 1910 Wilmington DE) He was a freight conductor on the Delaware Division until 1905 when he went into business for himself at Wilmington. Died from fatty degeneration of the heart at his place of business. Buried Wilmington-Brandywine Cemetery, Wilmington DE.

Ed Lafitte—5 Years Pitcher (b. 7 Apr 1886 New Orleans LA–d. 12 Apr 1971 at his home in Jenkintown PA) Served overseas for the U.S. Army during World War I. Baseball helped him earn a degree in denistry, and he practiced denistry 42 years in Philadelphia PA, retiring in 1961. Buried Ivy Hill Cemetery, Philadelphia PA.

Ty LaForest—1 Year Infielder (b. 18 Apr 1919 Edmondston, New Brunswick, Canada–d. 5 May 1947 Symmes Hospital, Arlington MA) He died at the height of his career after a five-week battle with a heart condition that developed from an attack of pneumonia. Buried Mount Pleasant Cemetery, Arlington MA.

Ed Lagger—1 Year Pitcher (b. 14 Jul 1912 Joliet IL–d. 10 Nov 1981 St Joseph Hospital, Joliet IL) Retired from Olin Corporation in 1972. Buried Mount Olivet Cemetery, Joliet IL.

Dick Lajeskie—1 Year Infielder (b. 8 Jan 1926 Passaic NJ–d. 15 Aug 1976 at his home in Ramsey NJ) Served in the U.S. Marine Corps during World War II. He was the regional manager of the reference division of Encyclopedia Brittanica. Buried Maryrest Cemetery, Mahwah NJ.

Nap Lajoie—21 Years Infielder 5 Years Manager Hall of Fame (b. 5 Sep 1875 Woonsocket RI–d. 7 Feb 1959 Halifax Hospital, Daytona Beach FL) Died after a relapse during a bout with pneumonia. Buried Cedar Hill Memory Gardens, Daytona Beach FL.

Eddie Lake—11 Years Infielder (b. 18 Mar 1916 Antioch CA–d. 7 Jun 1995 Baywood Nursing Facility, Castro Valley CA) He coached baseball at St Mary's College in Moraga CA and scouted until his retirement in 1970. Died from generalized nodular Hodgkin's disease ten weeks after rectal surgery. Buried Holy Sepulchre Cemetery, Hayward CA.

Fred Lake—5 Years Catcher 3 Years Manager (b. 16 Oct 1866 Nova Scotia, Canada–d. 24 Nov 1931 Deaconess Hospital, Boston MA) He spent his entire life in baseball, managing minor league baseball, scouting, and coaching at Harvard and Tufts University. Died after an illness of two weeks. Buried Oak Grove Cemetery, Medford MA.

Joe Lake—6 Years Pitcher (b. 6 Dec 1881 Brooklyn NY–d. 30 Jun 1950 Brooklyn NY) Buried St John's Cemetery, Middle Village NY.

Al Lakeman—9 Years Catcher (b. 31 Dec 1918 Cincinnati OH–d. 25 May 1976 General Hospital, Spartanburg SC) He managed minor league baseball, coached and scouted before going to work for R O Pickens Sheet Metal and Roofing Company. Buried Roselawn Memorial Gardens, Inman SC.

Bud Lally—2 Years Outfielder (b. 12 Aug 1867 Jersey City NJ–d. 14 Apr 1936 Milwaukee County Hospital, Milwaukee WI) Buried Mount Olivet Cemetery, Milwaukee WI.

Frank Lamanna—3 Years Pitcher (b. 22 Aug 1919 Watertown PA–d. 1 Sep 1980 St Joseph Hospital, Syracuse NY) Buried St Mary's Cemetery, Syracuse NY.

Frank Lamanske—1 Year Pitcher (b. 30 Sep 1906 Oglesby IL–d. 4 Aug 1971 Richland Memorial Hospital, Olney IL) Died following a short illness. Buried Oak Hill Cemetery, Taylorville IL.

Bill Lamar—9 Years Outfielder (b. 21 Mar 1897 Rockville MD–d. 24 May 1970 at his home in Rockport MA) Veteran of both World Wars I and II. He was a real estate broker in Washington DC and Baltimore MD before retiring in 1956. Buried Baltimore National Cemetery, Baltimore MD.

Wayne LaMaster—2 Years Pitcher (b. 13 Feb 1907 Speed IN–d. 4 Aug 1989 Green Valley Conv Center, New Albany IN) He was a retired cashier for the old Marhoefer Packing Company in Jeffersonville IN. Buried Kraft Graceland Memorial Park, New Albany IN.

Lyman Lamb—2 Years Infielder (b. 17 Mar 1895 Lincoln NE–d. 5 Oct 1955 Fayetteville AR).

Clay Lambert—2 Years Pitcher (b. 26 Mar 1917 Summit IL–d. 3 Apr 1981 at his home in Ogden UT) Served in the U.S. Army Air Force during World War II. Worked as an inventory specialist at the Ogden UT Defense Depot. Died from cancer. Buried Aultorest Memorial Park, Ogden UT.

Otis Lambeth—3 Years Pitcher (b. 13 May 1890 Berlin KS–d. 5 Jun 1976 Moran KS) A World War I veteran, he was a retired mail carrier. Buried Moran Cemetery, Moran KS.

Pete Lamer—2 Years Catcher (b. 1874 Hoboken NJ–d. 24 Oct 1931 St John's Hospital, Brooklyn NY) He died after an illness of several weeks.

Fred Lamline—2 Years Pitcher (b. 14 Aug 1887 Port Huron MI–d. 20 Sep 1970 Port Huron MI) World War I veteran. Worked 23 years as an interviewer for the Michigan Employment Security Commission, retiring in 1959. Died from an apparent heart attack while mowing his lawn. Buried Mount Hope Catholic Cemetery, Port Huron MI.

Ray Lamonno—5 Years Catcher (b. 17 Nov 1919 Oakland CA–d. 9 Feb 1994 Alta Bates Hospital, Berkeley CA) Served in World War II. He was a parking attendant at Golden Gate Fields. Died from bladder cancer. Cremated.

Bobby LaMotte—5 Years Infielder (b. 15 Feb 1898 Savannah GA–d. 2 Nov 1970 St Joseph Hospital, Savannah GA) Served in Europe for the U.S. Army during World War I. His major league career was ended by an eye injury when he was hit by a ball. He was a minor league manager and executive for a few years, then managed the Savannah Airport several years. Later he operated a cigar store in a Savannah hotel. Died after a short illness. Buried Bonaventure Cemetery, Savannah GA.

Henry Lampe—2 Years Pitcher (b. 19 Sep 1872 Boston MA–d. 16 Sep 1936 at his home in Dorchester MA) He worked 36 years for the South Boston MA police force, the last 15 as a clerk at the station. Died when he failed to rally following a serious operation.

Dick Lanahan—4 Years Pitcher (b. 27 Sep 1913 Washington DC–d. 12 Mar 1975 Rochester MN).

Doc Land—1 Year Outfielder (b. 14 May 1903 Binnsville MA–d. 14 Apr 1986 at his home in Livingston AL) Buried Belmont Community Cemetery, Belmont AL.

Grover Land—6 Years Catcher (b. 22 Sep 1884 Frankfort KY–d. 22 Jul 1958 Phoenix Veteran's Hospital, Phoenix AZ) Served in World War I. He lived in Phoenix AZ from 1921 until his death. Buried Greenwood Memory Lawn, Phoenix AZ.

Ken Landenberger—1 Year Infielder (b. 29 Jul 1928 Lyndhurst OH–d. 28 Jul 1960 Cleveland OH) Died from a cerebral hemorrhage and acute leukemia. Buried Whitehaven Park, Mayfield Village OH.

Kenesaw Mountain Landis—Hall of Fame (b. 20 Nov 1866 Millville OH–d. 25 Nov 1944 St Luke's Hospital, Chicago IL) He was the first baseball commissioner, a position he held from 1920 until his death. Before that he was a Federal District Court Judge in the Northern Illinois district. Buried Oak Woods Cemetery, Chicago IL.

Jesse Landrum—1 Year Infielder (b. 31 Jul 1912 Crockett TX–d. 27 Jun 1983 at his home in Beaumont TX) He was a baseball scout until 1971 when he became a bailiff at the county courthouse. Buried Forest Lawn Memorial Park, Beaumont TX.

Chappy Lane—2 Years Infielder (b. Pittsburgh PA–d. 8 Mar 1896 at his son-in-law's home in Pittsburgh PA) He was a painter.

Frank Lane—(b. abt 1895–d. 19 Mar 1981 Richardson TX) An executive for the Reds, White Sox, Cardinals, A's and Indians, he was involved in over 400 player trades. Died after a long illness. Buried Restland Memorial Park, Dallas TX.

Hunter Lane—1 Year Infielder (b. 20 Jul 1900 Pulaski TN–d. 12 Sep 1994 at his home in Memphis TN) A retired attorney, he was active in many Memphis civic activities. Died from heart disease. Buried Elmwood Cemetery, Memphis TN.

Jerry Lane—3 Years Pitcher (b. 7 Feb 1926 Ashland NY–d. 24 Jul 1988 Chattanooga TN) Served in the U.S. Navy during World War II. Played for the Chattanooga Lookouts of the Southern League, and was inducted into the Chattanooga Oldtimer's Hall of Fame. Lived in Chattanooga for 35 years. Buried Chattanooga National Cemetery, Chattanooga TN.

Sam Lanford—1 Year Pitcher (b. 8 Jan 1886 Woodruff SC–d. 14 Sep 1970 Woodruff SC) Farmed in the Woodruff area. Died after a long illness. Buried Bethel Cemetery, Woodruff SC.

Walt Lanfranconi—2 Years Pitcher (b. 9 Nov 1916 Barre VT–d. 18 Aug 1986 at his home in Barre VT) Served in Germany for the U.S. Army during World War II. After retiring from baseball he operated a service station in Barre VT from 1951 until 1978. Died from cancer. Buried Hope Cemetery, Barre VT.

Marty Lang—1 Year Pitcher (b. 27 Sep 1905 Hooper NE–d. 13 Jan 1968 at his home in Lakewood CO) Worked as an industrial engineer for Boeing in Wichita KS for 16 years, and for Martin Marietta in Denver CO for 10 years. Died from cancer. Buried Crown Hill Cemetery, Denver CO.

Bill Lange—7 Years Outfielder (b. 6 Jun 1871 San Francisco CA–d. 23 Jul 1950 at his home in San Francisco CA) He was a real estate and insurance broker. Died from a heart attack. Buried Holy Cross Catholic Cemetery, Colma CA.

Erv Lange—1 Year Pitcher (b. 12 Aug 1887

Forest Park IL–d. 24 Apr 1971 Maywood IL) Buried Oakridge Cemetery, Hillside IL.

Frank Lange —4 Years Pitcher (b. 28 Oct 1883 Columbus WI–d. 26 Dec 1945 at a hospital in Madison WI) He was the proprietor of the Fountain Tavern in Columbus for 31 years. Died after an illness of several months. Buried Hillside Cemetery, Columbus WI.

Sam Langford —3 Years Outfielder (b. 21 May 1899 Briggs TX–d. 31 Jul 1993 Plainview TX).

Bob Langsford —1 Year Infielder (b. 5 Aug 1865 Louisville KY–d. 10 Jan 1907 City Hospital, Louisville KY) Took his own life by swallowing carbolic acid. 10 years earlier he had been beaned by a pitch while playing for Mobile in the Southern League, and friends said he had been unbalanced since then. Buried Cave Hill Cemetery, Louisville KY.

Johnny Lanning —11 Years Pitcher (b. 6 Sep 1910 Asheville NC–d. 8 Nov 1989 at a hospital in Asheville NC) Buried Tweed's Chapel Cemetery, Asheville NC.

Les Lanning —1 Year Outfielder (b. 13 May 1895 Harvard IL–d. 13 Jun 1962 Bristol CT) An executive for the New Departure Division of General Motors, he retired in 1958 after 40 years service. Died suddenly of natural causes while visiting a friend at the Bristol Hospital. Buried Pine Hill Cemetery, Westfield MA.

Tom Lanning —1 Year Pitcher (b. 22 Apr 1907 Asheville NC–d. 4 Nov 1967 at his home in Marietta GA) Worked as a salesman for Atlanta Motor Parts, Inc. Buried Georgia Memorial Park Cemetery, Marietta GA.

Gene Lansing —1 Year Pitcher (b. 11 Jan 1898 Albany NY–d. 18 Jan 1945 at his home in Rensselaer NY) He worked in the engineering department of the New York Power and Light Corporation. Buried Albany Rural Cemetery, Menands NY.

Pete Lapan —2 Years Catcher (b. 25 Jun 1891 Easthampton MA–d. 5 Jan 1953 V A Hospital, Norwalk CA) World War I veteran. He was an attendant at the State Hospital. Died from lung cancer. Buried Los Angeles National Cemetery, Los Angeles CA.

Andy Lapihuska —2 Years Pitcher (b. 1 Nov 1922 Delmont NJ–d. 17 Feb 1996 Millville RI).

Ralph LaPointe —2 Years Infielder (b. 8 Jan 1922 Winooski VT–d. 13 Sep 1967 at a hospital in Burlington VT) Served in the Army Air Corps during World War II. After retiring from baseball he was the varsity baseball coach at the University of Vermont. Died after a long illness. Buried St Stephen's Cemetery, Winooski VT.

Frank LaPorte —11 Years Infielder (b. 6 Feb 1880 Uhrichsville OH–d. 25 Sep 1939 Newcomerstown OH) He was a foreman in the forging department of Heller Brothers Company. Died from a heart attack. Buried Union Cemetery, Uhrichsville OH.

Jack Lapp —9 Years Catcher (b. 10 Sep 1884 Frazer PA–d. 6 Feb 1920 at his home in Philadelphia PA) He managed minor league baseball. Died from pneumonia after being in ill health four years. Buried Mount Peace Cemetery, Philadelphia PA.

Ring Lardner —Hall of Fame Sportswriter. Died 1933.

Ed Larkin —1 Year Catcher (b. 1 Jul 1885 Wyalusing PA–d. 28 Mar 1934 at his home in Wyalusing PA) Served in the U.S. Army Air Corps during World War I. He operated a shoe store in Wyalusing from 1919 until it was sold in 1927 and a Ford dealership from 1919 until his death. A civic leader, he was a member of the school board and the borough council. Died in his sleep following a heart attack. Buried St Peter and St Paul Cemetery, Towanda PA.

Henry Larkin —10 Years Infielder 1 Year Manager (b. 12 Jan 1860 Reading PA–d. 31 Jan 1942 St Joseph's Hospital, Reading PA) He was a boilermaker at the Reading Company shops for many years before working for the City of Reading in the City Park. Died after several days serious illness. Buried St Peter's Church Cemetery, Reading PA.

Steve Larkin —1 Year Pitcher (b. 9 Dec 1910 Cincinnati OH–d. 2 May 1969 at the YMCA in Norristown PA) Served in Greenland for the U.S. Army during World War II. He was a commuting supervisor for General Electric at King of Prussia PA. He died suddenly from a ruptured abdominal aneurysm while enroute from Cincinnati. Buried Cincinnati OH.

Terry Larkin —6 Years Pitcher (b. 1856 Brooklyn NY–d. 16 Sep 1894 Brooklyn NY) Took his own life by slitting his throat with a razor.

Bob Larmore —1 Year Infielder (b. 6 Dec 1896

Anderson IN–d. 15 Jan 1964 St Louis MO) Buried Oak Grove Cemetery, St Louis MO.

Harry LaRoss —1 Year Outfielder (b. 12 Jan 1888 Easton PA–d. 22 May 1954 Hines Memorial Hospital, Chicago IL).

Lyn Lary —12 Years Infielder (b. 28 Jan 1906 Armona CA–d. 9 Jan 1973 Community Hospital, Downey CA) He was an expeditor for North American Rockwell in the aircraft business. Died from a heart attack. Buried All Souls Cemetery, Long Beach CA.

Bill Lasley —1 Year Pitcher (b. 13 Jul 1902 Gallipolis OH–d. 21 Aug 1990 at his home in Seattle WA) In 1978 he retired from Lasley Knitting Company, a firm he founded. He was also associated with Washington Furniture Company and Lasley-Lynch Manufacturing Company. Cremated. Buried Acacia Cemetery, Seattle WA.

Arlie Latham —17 Years Infielder 1 Year Manager (b. 15 Mar 1860 West Lebanon NH–d. 29 Nov 1952 at his daughter's home in Garden City NY) He was a coach, scout, night club owner, actor and owner of a delicatessen. As a comedian, he was known for his comedy stunts while coaching baseball.

Juice Latham —4 Years Infielder (b. 6 Sep 1852 Utica NY–d. 26 May 1914 at a hospital in Utica NY) Died from an illness with complications.

Chick Lathers —2 Years Infielder (b. 22 Oct 1888 Dearborn MI–d. 26 Jul 1971 Little Traverse Hospital, Petoskey MI) World War I veteran. He operated a large dairy farm on Burt Lake, east of Brutus MI, from 1934 to 1962 and was active in civic and community affairs in the area. After selling his farm he spent winters in Florida. Buried Greenwood Cemetery, Petoskey MI.

Bill Lathrop —2 Years Pitcher (b. 12 Aug 1891 Hanover WI–d. 20 Nov 1958 Mercy Hospital, Janesville WI) A top notch amateur golfer, he headed the Lathrop Insurance Agency in Janesville WI. When he died he had been in failing health for two years and hospitalized one month. Buried Oak Hill Cemetery, Janesville WI.

Tacks Latimer —5 Years Catcher (b. 30 Nov 1877 Loveland OH–d. 23 Apr 1936 at his home in Loveland OH) A detective, he served six years in prison for a fatal shooting that occurred in Xenia OH in 1924. Died from a heart attack. Buried Greenlawn Cemetery, Milford OH.

Bill Latimore —1 Year Pitcher (b. 5 May 1884 Roxton TX–d. 30 Oct 1919 Colorado Springs CO) A successful clothing dealer, he co-owned the Thompson-Latimore store in Roxton. Buried Evergreen Cemetery, Paris TX.

Charlie Lau —11 Years Catcher (b. 12 Apr 1933 Romulus MI–d. 18 Mar 1984 at his home in Key Colony Beach FL) He worked his entire life in baseball as a player and coach and was considered by some to be the greatest hitting instructor of all time. Died from colon cancer. Buried Moreland Memorial Park, Parkville MD.

Billy Lauder —5 Years Infielder (b. 23 Feb 1874 New York City NY–d. 20 May 1933 at his home in Norwalk CT) He coached college baseball 15 years at Brown, Yale, Columbia and Williams before he was a coach and scout two years for the White Sox. He then went into the soap business in New York City. Died suddenly from heart failure. Buried Norwalk Cemetery, Norwalk CT.

Bill Lauterborn —2 Years Infielder (b. 9 Jun 1878 Hornell NY–d. 19 Apr 1965 Andover NY) He owned and operated a restaurant in Andover. Died after a long illness. Buried Hillside Cemetery, Andover NY.

Cookie Lavagetto —10 Years Infielder 5 Years Manager (b. 1 Dec 1912 Oakland CA–d. 10 Aug 1990 at his home in Orinda CA) He was best known for breaking up Bill Bevens' no-hitter in the 1947 World Series. Served in the U.S. Navy during World War II. He worked 34 years in baseball as a player, coach and scout until his retirement in 1967. He then assisted his wife with her therapy equipment business. Died in his sleep from a heart attack. Buried Holy Cross Cemetery, St Helena CA.

Doc Lavan —12 Years Infielder (b. 28 Oct 1890 Grand Rapids MI–d. 29 May 1952 Harper Hospital, Detroit MI) A practicing medical doctor, he was an officer in the U.S. Navy Medical Corps during both World War I and World War II, retiring with the rank of Commander, USNR. He was a city health officer in New York City, St Louis, Kansas City, Toledo, Kalamazoo and Grand Rapids and served as Director of Research for the National Foundation for Infantile Paralysis. Died after a brief illness. Buried Arlington National Cemetery, Arlington VA.

Jimmy Lavender —6 Years Pitcher (b. 25 Mar 1884 Montezuma GA–d. 12 Jan 1960 at a hospital in Cartersville GA) Connected with the Georgia State Highway Department until a few years before he died from a sudden heart attack. Buried Felton Cemetery, Montezuma GA.

Art LaVigne—1 Year Catcher (b. 26 Jan 1885 Worcester MA–d. 18 Jul 1950 at his home in Worcester MA) He ran a diner at Fitchburg MA and owned two diners in Worcester. During World War II he worked for General Electric in Fitchburg, retiring in 1947. A champion caliber bowler, he held the New England candle pin bowling championship for two years. Buried Hope Cemetery, Worcester MA.

Garland Lawing—1 Year Outfielder (b. 29 Aug 1918 Mount Holly NC–d. 27 Sep 1996 Grand Strand Hospital, Myrtle Beach SC) Served in the U.S. Army during World War II. Buried Sharon Memorial Park, Charlotte NC.

Mike Lawlor—2 Years Catcher (b. 11 Mar 1854 Utica NY–d. 3 Aug 1918 Troy NY) Died following a protracted illness. Buried St Mary's Cemetery, Troy NY.

Bill Lawrence—1 Year Outfielder (b. 11 Mar 1906 San Mateo CA–d. 15 Jun 1997 Hillsdale Manor, San Mateo CA) Died from a heart attack. Cremated. Buried Cypress Lawn Memorial Park, Colma CA.

Bob Lawrence—1 Year Pitcher (b. 14 Dec 1899 Brooklyn NY–d. 6 Nov 1983 Jamaica NY).

Otis Lawry—2 Years Infielder (b. 1 Nov 1893 Fairfield ME–d. 23 Oct 1965 China ME).

Al Lawson—1 Year Pitcher (b. 24 Mar 1869 London, England–d. 29 Nov 1954 San Antonio TX).

Bob Lawson—2 Years Pitcher (b. 23 Aug 1875 Brookneal VA–d. 28 Oct 1952 Watts Hospital, Chapel Hill NC) Served in the U.S. Army Medical Corps during World War I. Coached baseball, football, track and gymnastics at the University of North Carolina, and was the trainer for the university's athletic teams. Regarded as the "Father of Basketball" at the university. Associate Professor of Anatomy for the medical school from 1906 to 1936 and the physical education department from 1936 until he retired in 1949. Buried Chapel Hill Cemetery, Chapel Hill NC.

Roxie Lawson—9 Years Pitcher (b. 13 Apr 1906 Donnellson IA–d. 9 Apr 1977 at his home in Stockport IA) Served in the U.S. Navy during World War II. After his playing career he managed minor league teams, and umpired in the Three-I League. Buried Dibble Cemetery, Stockport IA.

Gene Layden—1 Year Outfielder (b. 14 Mar 1894 Pittsburgh PA–d. 12 Dec 1984 Forbes Hospice, Pittsburgh PA) World War I veteran. He was a retired supervisor for Moore Park in Brookline. Died from heart disease. Buried Queen of Heaven Cemetery, Bridgeville PA.

Pete Layden—1 Year Outfielder (b. 30 Dec 1919 Dallas TX–d. 18 Jul 1982 at his home near Edna TX) Served in the U.S. Army Air Corps during World War II. He was a rancher in Jackson County, TX, and served ten years as a county commissioner. Died in his sleep, apparently from a heart attack. He was buried on his ranch near Edna TX.

Herman Layne—1 Year Outfielder (b. 13 Feb 1901 New Haven WV–d. 27 Aug 1973 Gallipolis OH) The president of Mason County Bank in New Haven, he was active in real estate development, coal mining and produce marketing in the area. Buried Kirkland Memorial Gardens, Point Pleasant WV.

Tony Lazzeri—14 Years Infielder Hall of Fame (b. 6 Dec 1903 San Francisco CA–d. 6 Aug 1946 at his home in San Francisco CA) He was part-owner of a San Francisco cocktail lounge and sometime instructor for youth baseball camps. Died from a heart attack. Buried Sunset Mausoleum, Kensington CA.

Freddy Leach—10 Years Outfielder (b. 23 Nov 1897 Springfield MO–d. 10 Dec 1981 at his home in Bliss ID) He moved to Jerome ID in 1919, and to Bliss, where he operated a ranch, in 1933. Buried Hagerman Cemetery, Hagerman ID.

Tommy Leach—19 Years Outfielder (b. 4 Nov 1877 French Creek NY–d. 29 Sep 1969 Haines City FL) He was the last surviving player from the first World Series in 1903. He worked in minor league baseball in Florida, moving there in 1914.

Dan Leahy—1 Year Infielder (b. 8 Aug 1870 Knoxville TN–d. 30 Dec 1903 Knoxville TN) He was shot and killed by a friend at a bar where he was bartending. He and his friend had become involved in an argument over the abuse of another customer. Buried Calvary Cemetery, Knoxville TN.

Tom Leahy—4 Years Catcher (b. 2 Jun 1869

New Haven CT–d. 11 Jun 1951 at his home in New Haven CT) He worked a short time at the Hotel Taft in New Haven before becoming the assistant trainer at Yale University, a position he held for 32 years. Buried St Lawrence Cemetery, West Haven CT.

Fred Lear—4 Years Infielder (b. 7 Apr 1894 New York City NY–d. 13 Oct 1955 Veteran's Hospital, East Orange NJ) Served in the U.S. Navy during World War I. He scouted for the Pirates and White Sox. For a number of years he operated a restaurant at New Dorp NY and also worked for the American Legion restaurant at Stapleton, LI. Buried St Mary's Cemetery, Staten Island NY.

King Lear—2 Years Pitcher (b. 23 Jan 1891 Greencastle PA–d. 31 Oct 1976 Waynesboro Hospital, Waynesboro PA) He worked for the State and Federal Milk Consumer's Board as an auditor, and eight years as Franklin County (PA) Assessor. His last job was with the A G Crunkleton Electric Company. He had been in failing health for years, but not critically ill until his last six months. Buried Cedar Hill Cemetery, Greencastle PA.

Bill Leard—1 Year Infielder (b. 14 Oct 1885 Oneida NY–d. 15 Jan 1970 St Joseph's Hospital, San Francisco CA) He managed some in the Pacific Coast League, and later worked as a bartender. Died from cirrhosis of the liver. Cremated. Buried Cypress Lawn Memorial Park, Colma CA.

Frank Leary—1 Year Pitcher (b. 26 Feb 1881 Wayland MA–d. 4 Oct 1907 Natick MA).

John Leary—2 Years Infielder (b. 2 May 1891 Waltham MA–d. 18 Aug 1961 Waltham Hospital, Waltham MA) Served in the U.S. Navy during World War I. He coached football, baseball and was athletic director at Waltham High School from 1920 until retiring in 1960, winning three state football championships. Died after suffering a stroke a month earlier.

Hal Leathers—1 Year Infielder (b. 2 Dec 1898 Los Angeles CA–d. 12 Apr 1977 at his home in Modesto CA) Died after a brief illness. Cremated. Buried Lakewood Memorial Park, Hughson CA.

Emil Leber—1 Year Infielder (b. 15 May 1881 Cleveland OH–d. 6 Nov 1924 Cleveland OH) He was a mail carrier. Died from pulmonary tuberculosis. Buried Riverside Cemetery, Cleveland OH.

Bevo LeBourveau—5 Years Outfielder (b. 24 Aug 1896 Dana CA–d. 9 Dec 1947 Nevada City CA) World War I veteran. Died from a heart attack. Cremated.

George LeClair—2 Years Pitcher (b. 18 Oct 1886 Milton VT–d. 10 Oct 1918 Farnham, Quebec, Canada).

Razor Ledbetter—1 Year Pitcher (b. 8 Dec 1894 Rutherford College NC–d. 1 Feb 1969 St Mary's Hospital, West Palm Beach FL) A retired railway engineer. Buried Burke Memorial Park, Morganton NC.

Bill Lee—2 Years Outfielder (b. 9 Jan 1892 Bayonne NJ–d. 6 Jan 1984 St Joseph Hospital, West Hazleton PA) Served in the U.S. Army during World War I. He coached basketball, football and baseball at Bayonne High School, retiring to the Hazleton area in 1963. Buried Calvary Cemetery, Drums PA.

Bill Lee—14 Years Pitcher (b. 21 Oct 1909 Plaquemine LA–d. 15 Jun 1977 at his home in Plaquemine LA) Director in the Plaquemine Bank and Trust Company. Buried Protestant Cemetery, Plaquemine LA.

Cliff Lee—8 Years Outfielder (b. 4 Aug 1896 Lexington NE–d. 25 Aug 1980 St Anthony Hospital Central in Denver CO) He worked for the State of Colorado in surplus commodities. Cremated.

Dud Lee—5 Years Infielder (b. 22 Aug 1900 Denver CO–d. 7 Jan 1971 Denver General Hospital, Denver CO) Known as a slick fielding shortstop, he played baseball for 22 years. Died from a blood clot following brain surgery. Buried Fairmount Cemetery, Denver CO.

Hal Lee—7 Years Outfielder (b. 15 Feb 1905 Ludlow MS–d. 4 Sep 1989 Singing River Hospital, Pascagoula MS) He retired from Ingalls Shipbuilders and had served on the Moss Point MS school board. Buried Jackson County Memorial Park, Pascagoula MS.

Leonidas Lee—1 Year Outfielder (b. 13 Dec 1860 St Louis MO–d. 11 Jun 1912 Hendersonville NC) Died from a heart attack. Buried Rosehill Cemetery, Chicago IL.

Roy Lee—1 Year Pitcher (b. 28 Sep 1917 Elmira NY–d. 11 Nov 1985 Jewish Hospital, St Louis

MO) Head baseball coach at St Louis University from 1961 until 1967, and at Southern Illinois University-Edwardsville from 1968 until 1978. He retired as associate professor of physical education at SIUE in 1984. Died from a heart ailment. Buried Frieden's Evangelical Cemetery, Troy IL.

Thornton Lee—16 Years Pitcher (b. 13 Sep 1906 Sonoma CA–d. 9 Jun 1997 Tucson AZ) He worked over 25 years in Phoenix AZ for Bowen McGlothlin and for Garrett Research. He managed some minor league baseball and scouted 40 years for the Cardinals and Giants. He loved to fish and hunt. Died from complications related to Parkinson's disease.

Tom Lee—1 Year Pitcher (b. 9 Jun 1864 Milwaukee WI–d. 4 Mar 1886 Milwaukee WI) He contracted maleria while playing baseball in the south. This developed in quick consumption and, at the beginning of his career, he died.

Watty Lee—4 Years Outfielder (b. 12 Aug 1879 Lynch's Station VA–d. 6 Mar 1936 at his home in Washington DC) Died from heart disease. Buried Mount Olivet Cemetery, Washington DC.

George Lees—1 Year Catcher (b. 2 Feb 1895 Bethlehem PA–d. 2 Jan 1980 Harrisburg PA).

Sam Leever—13 Years Pitcher (b. 23 Dec 1871 Goshen OH–d. 19 May 1953 at his home in Goshen OH) Worked as a school teacher and was widely known as an expert trapshooter. Died following a week's illness. Buried Goshen Cemetery, Goshen OH.

Al Lefevre—1 Year Infielder (b. 16 Sep 1898 New York City NY–d. 21 Jan 1982 Glen Cove NY) Buried Calvary Cemetery, Woodside NY.

Wade Lefler—1 Year Outfielder (b. 5 Jun 1896 Cooleemee NC–d. 6 Mar 1981 at a hospital in Hickory NC) Served in the U.S. Army during World War I. Known as the "Dean of Newton Attorneys," he opened a law office in Newton NC in 1924. He later served as Newton City Attorney and clerk of the Catawba County (NC) Superior Court. Buried Eastview Cemetery, Newton NC.

Lou Legett—4 Years Catcher (b. 1 Jun 1901 New Orleans LA–d. 6 Mar 1988 Jo Ellen Smith Conv Center, New Orleans LA) A retired dentist, he was instrumental in forming the New Orleans Recreation Department baseball program. Died following a long illness. Buried Masonic Cemetery, New Orleans LA.

Regis Leheny—1 Year Pitcher (b. 5 Jan 1908 Pittsburgh PA–d. 2 Nov 1976 Pittsburgh PA).

Paul Lehner—7 Years Outfielder (b. 1 Jul 1920 Dolomite AL–d. 27 Dec 1967 at a hospital in Birmingham AL) Buried Highland Memorial Gardens, Bessemer AL.

Clarence Lehr—1 Year Outfielder (b. 16 May 1886 Escanaba MI–d. 31 Jan 1948 Highland Park General Hospital, Detroit MI) He was an attorney until 1933 when he became head of the Detroit Racing Association, a position he held until his death. He was an avid golfer and enjoyed hunting and fishing. Died after suffering a ruptured artery in his office. Buried Forest Hill Cemetery, Ann Arbor MI.

Norm Lehr—1 Year Pitcher (b. 28 May 1901 Rochester NY–d. 17 Jul 1968 Conesus Lake Nursing Home, Livonia NY) He was a state patrolman, retiring in 1966. Buried Leicester Cemetery, Leicester NY.

Hank Leiber—10 Years Outfielder (b. 17 Jan 1911 Phoenix AZ–d. 8 Nov 1993 Tucson AZ) His baseball career ended prematurely after he was hit in the head twice by pitched balls. He went into the real estate business in Tucson in the 1940s and opened his own real estate company in the 1950s. Buried East Lawn Cemetery, Tucson AZ.

Nemo Leibold—13 Years Outfielder (b. 17 Feb 1892 Butler IN–d. 4 Feb 1977 Detroit MI) He spent 40 years in baseball as a player, scout and minor league manager. Scouted for the Tigers, retiring in 1953. Died following a heart attack. Buried Holy Sepulchre Cemetery, Southfield MI.

Elmer Leifer—1 Year Outfielder (b. 23 May 1893 Clarington OH–d. 26 Sep 1948 at the Avon Hotel in Everett WA) For 18 years he was a night foreman for Robinson Manufacturing Company at Everett. Died following a short illness. Buried Pine City Cemetery, Pine City WA.

Lefty Leifield—12 Years Pitcher (b. 5 Sep 1883 Trenton IL–d. 10 Oct 1970 Alexandria VA).

John Leighton—1 Year Outfielder (b. 4 Oct 1861 Peabody MA–d. 31 Oct 1956 at a nursing home in Lynn MA) He worked as a maintenance man in buildings owned by an old friend. Died after a long illness. Buried Pine Grove Cemetery, Lynn MA.

Bill Leinhauser —1 Year Outfielder (b. 4 Nov 1893 Philadelphia PA–d. 14 Apr 1978 Rolling Hill Hospital, Elkins Park PA) Served in France for the U.S. Army during World War I. He retired as captain of the North Central Detective Division of the Philadelphia Police Department in 1959 after 41 years, 29 in the narcotics squad. He was a noted amateur welterweight boxer when he was younger. Buried Holy Cross Cemetery, Yeadon PA.

Ed Leip —4 Years Infielder (b. 29 Nov 1910 Trenton NJ–d. 24 Nov 1983 Zephyrhills FL) He worked for the Sheet Metal Workers Union in Trenton, retiring in 1976. Buried Princeton Memorial Park, Robbinsville NJ.

Jack Leiper —1 Year Pitcher (b. 23 Dec 1867 Chester PA–d. 23 Aug 1960 West Goshen PA) Buried Leiper Church Cemetery, Swarthmore PA.

Bill Leith—1 Year Pitcher (b. 31 May 1873 Matteawan NY–d. 16 Jul 1940 at his home in Beacon NY) Worked as assistant storekeeper at Sing Sing Prison. Died after an illness of about two years. Buried Fishkill Rural Cemetery, Fishkill NY.

Doc Leitner —1 Year Pitcher (b. 14 Sep 1865 Piermont NY–d. 18 May 1937 Columbia-Pres Medical Ctr, New York City NY) He used baseball to earn money for medical school, refusing to return to baseball after becoming a doctor. He was a leading physician and surgeon in the Hudson Valley and health officer in eight villages and townships in that area. He was also involved in politics and was a Democratic party leader in Rockland County, NY.

Dummy Leitner —2 Years Pitcher (b. 19 Jun 1871 Parkton MD–d. 20 Feb 1960 Bel Aire Nursing Home, Baltimore MD) A deaf-mute, he worked 30 years as a printer for the *Baltimore Sun* newspaper. Buried Loudon Park National Cemetery, Baltimore MD.

Frank Leja —3 Years Infielder (b. 7 Feb 1936 Holyoke MA–d. 4 May 1991 at the Logan Airport in Boston MA) He sold life insurance in Boston before going into business for himself, shipping lobster from Nahant MA. Died from a heart attack on his way to a golfing vacation in Alabama. Buried Greenlawn Cemetery, Nahant MA.

Larry LeJeune —2 Years Outfielder (b. 22 Jul 1885 Chicago IL–d. 21 Apr 1952 Eloise MI) Died from cancer of the tongue. Buried Our Lady-Mount Carmel Cemetery, Wyandotte MI.

Bill Lelivelt —2 Years Pitcher (b. 21 Oct 1884 Chicago IL–d. 14 Feb 1968 Chicago IL) Buried St Adalbert Cemetery, Niles IL.

Jack Lelivelt —6 Years Outfielder (b. 14 Nov 1885 Chicago IL–d. 20 Jan 1941 Maynard Hospital, Seattle WA) He managed minor league baseball up until he died, minutes after suffering a severe heart attack. Buried Grand View Memorial Park, Glendale CA.

Steve Lembo —2 Years Catcher (b. 13 Nov 1926 Brooklyn NY–d. 4 Dec 1989 Flushing NY) Buried St Charles Cemetery, Farmingdale NY.

Bob Lemon —15 Years Pitcher 8 Years Manager Hall of Fame (b. 22 Sep 1920 San Bernardino CA–d. 11 Jan 2000 Palmcrest Convalescent Hosp, Long Beach CA) He worked in baseball for 61 years. Died from a heart attack. Cremated.

Ed Lennon —1 Year Pitcher (b. 17 Aug 1897 Philadelphia PA–d. 13 Sep 1947 Philadelphia PA) Died suddenly from a heart attack. Buried Holy Cross Cemetery, Yeadon PA.

Ed Lennox —6 Years Infielder (b. 3 Nov 1885 Camden NJ–d. 26 Oct 1939 Cooper Hospital, Camden NJ) He was a minor league umpire and scouted for several teams. Died from rectal cancer. Buried Evergreen Cemetery, Camden NJ.

Andy Leonard —4 Years Outfielder (b. 1 Jun 1846 County Cavan, Ireland–d. 21 Aug 1903 Roxbury MA) Buried New Calvary Cemetery, Mattapan MA.

Buck Leonard —Hall of Fame (b. 8 Sep 1907 Rocky Mount NC–d. 27 Nov 1997 at a hospital in Rocky Mount NC) He played 17 years in the negro leagues and was known as the "Black Lou Gehrig." Died from complications of a stroke suffered more than a decade earlier. Buried Gardens of Gethsemane, Rocky Mount NC.

Dutch Leonard —20 Years Pitcher (b. 25 Mar 1909 Auburn IL–d. 17 Apr 1983 St John's Hospital, Springfield IL) He spent three years as a pitching coach for the Cubs, then worked for the Illinois Youth Commission from 1956 until 1974 when he retired. Died from heart failure. Buried Auburn Cemetery, Auburn IL.

Dutch Leonard—11 Years Pitcher (b. 16 Apr 1892 Birmingham OH–d. 11 Jul 1952 Fresno CA) He became a well-known California vineyardist, vintner and wine packer. He was also an expert left-handed golfer. Died from complications of a stroke suffered three days earlier. Buried Mountain View Cemetery, Fresno CA.

Elmer Leonard—1 Year Pitcher (b. 12 Nov 1888 Napa CA–d. 27 May 1981 Napa CA) In 1921 he established the Leonard Salt Water Taffy manufacturing business at Seaside OR and operated it until retiring in 1959. Died from a heart attack in the same house where he was born. Buried Tulocay Cemetery, Napa CA.

Joe Leonard—5 Years Infielder (b. 14 Nov 1893 Chicago IL–d. 1 May 1920 George Washington Hospital, Washington DC) Died from complications following an appendectomy.

Rudy Leopold—1 Year Pitcher (b. 27 Jul 1905 Grand Cane LA–d. 3 Sep 1965 Our Lady of the Lake Hosp, Baton Rouge LA) He was a captain with Copolymer Chemical Company. Buried Roselawn Memorial Park, Baton Rouge LA.

Pete LePine—1 Year Outfielder (b. 5 Sep 1876 Montreal, Quebec, Canada–d. 3 Dec 1949 at his home in Woonsocket RI) For ten years he was manager of the Princeton Clothing Store in Woonsocket and was a salesman for a liquor distributor for another ten years, retiring in 1942. Died following a brief illness. Buried Precious Blood Cemetery, Woonsocket RI.

Dutch Lerchen—1 Year Infielder (b. 4 Apr 1889 Detroit MI–d. 7 Jan 1962 Grace Hospital, Detroit MI) He owned a small chain of meat markets in Detroit before becoming a food inspector for the Detroit Department of Health. Buried Roseland Park Cemetery, Berkley MI.

Walt Lerian—2 Years Catcher (b. 10 Feb 1903 Baltimore MD–d. 22 Oct 1929 Baltimore MD) At the height of his baseball career he was killed when a truck and car collided, the truck running up on the sidewalk, crushing him against a brick wall. Buried New Cathedral Cemetery, Baltimore MD.

Louis LeRoy—3 Years Pitcher (b. 18 Feb 1879 Red Spring WI–d. 10 Oct 1944 Shawano WI).

Roy Leslie—3 Years Infielder (b. 23 Aug 1894 Bailey TX–d. 9 Apr 1972 Sherman TX) He retired from his grocery and lumber business in Bailey about 1962. Unable to talk the last year of his life, he died after a long illness. Buried Arledge Ridge Cemetery, Bailey TX.

Sam Leslie—10 Years Infielder (b. 26 Jul 1905 Moss Point MS–d. 21 Jan 1979 Singing River Hospital, Pascagoula MS) He was a retired hull foreman with Ingalls Shipbuilders. Died following a lengthy illness. Buried Jackson County Memorial Park, Pascagoula MS.

Charlie Letchas—4 Years Infielder (b. 3 Oct 1915 Thomasville GA–d. 14 Mar 1995 Town 'N Country Hospital, Tampa FL) World War II veteran. He worked at Southwestern State Hospital. Buried Laurel Hill Cemetery, Thomasville GA.

Walt Leverenz—3 Years Pitcher (b. 21 Jul 1888 Chicago IL–d. 19 Mar 1973 General Hospital, Atascadero CA) World War I veteran. He owned the Ford dealership at Atascadero from 1947 until he retired in 1958. Died following a stroke. Cremated. Buried Atascadero Cemetery, Atascadero CA.

Dixie Leverett—5 Years Pitcher (b. 29 Mar 1894 Georgetown TX–d. 17 Feb 1957 Beaverton OR) He was in the tree spraying business at Beaverton. Died from injuries suffered when he fell from a tree. Buried Riverview Abbey Mausoleum, Portland OR.

Hod Leverette—1 Year Pitcher (b. 4 Feb 1889 Shreveport LA–d. 10 Apr 1958 St Petersburg FL) He was a machine shop superintendent for Caterpiller Tractor Company in East Peoria IL, retiring to St Petersburg in 1954. Buried Parkview Cemetery, Peoria IL.

Jim Levey—4 Years Infielder (b. 13 Sep 1906 Pittsburgh PA–d. 14 Mar 1970 Dallas TX) Died from cancer. Buried Restland Memorial Park, Dallas TX.

Charlie Levis—2 Years Infielder 1 Year Manager (b. 21 Jun 1860 St Louis MO–d. 16 Oct 1926 St Louis MO) Buried Calvary Cemetery, St Louis MO.

Dutch Levsen—6 Years Pitcher (b. 29 Apr 1898 Wyoming IA–d. 12 Mar 1972 Minneapolis MN) He once pitched and won both games of a double-header. At one time he headed up the Iowa American Legion Baseball program. Buried Wyoming Cemetery, Wyoming IA.

Dan Lewandowski—1 Year Pitcher (b. 6 Jan 1928 Buffalo NY–d. 19 Jul 1996 Hamilton, Ontario, Canada).

Bert Lewis —1 Year Pitcher (b. 3 Oct 1895 Tonawanda NY–d. 24 Mar 1950 Tonawanda NY) Active politically, he was chairman of the Tonawanda Republican City Committee and for 15 years had been an Erie County, NY, deputy sheriff. Died from a heart attack. Buried Sweeney Cemetery, North Tonawanda NY.

Bill Lewis —3 Years Catcher (b. 15 Oct 1904 Ripley TN–d. 24 Oct 1977 at his home in Memphis TN) For several years he was a minor league manager and a scout for the Cardinals and Mets. Buried Memorial Park Cemetery, Memphis TN.

Duffy Lewis —11 Years Outfielder (b. 18 Apr 1888 San Francisco CA–d. 17 Jun 1979 at his home in Salem NH) For several years he was traveling secretary for the Braves. Buried Holy Cross Cemetery, Londonderry NH.

Fred Lewis —5 Years Outfielder (b. 13 Oct 1858 Utica NY–d. 5 Jun 1945 at a hospital in Utica NY) He worked a number of years for Foster Brothers in Utica and later worked in a variety of jobs for the City of Utica. Died after a brief illness. Buried Forest Hill Cemetery, Utica NY.

Jack Lewis —3 Years Infielder (b. 14 Feb 1884 Pittsburgh PA–d. 25 Feb 1956 Ohio Valley Hospital, Steubenville OH) He was the chief of plant protection at Follansbee Steel Corporation, retiring in 1954. Died from heart disease. Buried Mount Calvary Cemetery, Steubenville OH.

Phil Lewis —4 Years Infielder (b. 7 Oct 1883 Pittsburgh PA–d. 8 Aug 1959 at his home in Port Wentworth GA) World War I veteran. He retired as woodlands supervisor for Union Bag-Camp Paper Corporation. Died after a long illness. Buried Dorchester Cemetery, Dorchester GA.

Ted Lewis —6 Years Pitcher (b. 25 Dec 1872 Machynlleth, Wales–d. 24 May 1936 at his home in Durham NH) He was an educator at a number of eastern colleges, including Columbia University, Williams College, Massachusetts Agricultural College and the University of New Hampshire where he was president of the school from 1927 until his death.

Steve Libby —1 Year Infielder (b. 8 Dec 1853 Scarborough ME–d. 31 Mar 1935 at his home in Milford CT) He worked many years for the NY NH and H Railroad and took a great interest in public affairs. Died suddenly. Buried Evergreen Cemetery, New Haven CT.

Fred Lieb —Hall of Fame (b. 5 Mar 1888 Philadelphia PA–d. 2 Jun 1980 Houston TX) A sportswriter and baseball historian for nearly 70 years, he was the first sportswriter inducted into baseball's Hall of Fame. Cremated.

Dutch Lieber —2 Years Pitcher (b. 1 Feb 1910 Alameda CA–d. 31 Dec 1961 V A Hospital, Los Angeles CA) World War II veteran. He was a truck driver. Died from lung cancer. Buried Los Angeles National Cemetery, Los Angeles CA.

Glenn Liebhardt —4 Years Pitcher (b. 10 Mar 1883 Milton IN–d. 13 Jul 1956 Huron Road Hospital, Cleveland OH) He managed a paint store in Cleveland for Wagerman Paint Company. Died after a short illness. Buried Calvary Cemetery, Cleveland OH.

Glenn Liebhardt —3 Years Pitcher (b. 31 Jul 1910 Cleveland OH–d. 14 Mar 1992 Meadowbrook Manor, Winston-Salem NC) Buried Forsyth Memorial Park, Winston-Salem NC.

Fred Liese —5 Games Pinch Hitter (b. 7 Oct 1885 WI–d. 30 Jun 1967 Gramercy Drive Rest Home, Los Angeles CA) Died from medullary failure and thrombotic encephalomalacia (softening of the brain). Cremated.

Gene Lillard —3 Years Pitcher (b. 12 Nov 1913 Santa Barbara CA–d. 12 Apr 1991 Cottage Hospital, Santa Barbara CA) He was a rancher and farmer in the Goleta CA area. Died from lung cancer. Buried Goleta Cemetery, Santa Barbara CA.

Jim Lillie —4 Years Outfielder (b. 27 Jul 1861 New Haven CT–d. 9 Nov 1890 Kansas City MO) Died from peritonitis.

Rufino Linares —4 Years Outfielder (b. 28 Feb 1951 San Pedro de Macoris, Dominican Republic–d. 16 May 1998 San Pedro de Macoris, Dominican Republic.

Ezra Lincoln —1 Year Pitcher Born 17 Nov 1868 Raynham MA–d. 7 May 1951 Taunton MA) He owned and operated a blacksmith shop. Buried Pleasant Street Cemetery, Raynham MA.

Carl Lind —4 Years Infielder (b. 19 Sep 1904 New Orleans LA–d. 1 Aug 1946 New York City NY) Died after a lingering illness. Buried Hope Mausoleum, New Orleans LA.

Vive Lindaman —4 Years Pitcher (b. 28 Oct 1877 Charles City IA–d. 13 Feb 1927 Charles City IA) He was a dairy farmer near Charles City and a city mail carrier there. Died following a stroke of apoplexy. Buried Calvary Cemetery, Charles City IA.

Lyman Linde—2 Years Pitcher (b. 30 Sep 1920 Rolling Prairie WI–d. 24 Oct 1995 Hillside Hospital, Beaver Dam WI) Served as a Radar Signal Corps specialist for the U.S. Army during World War II. Over the years he worked for the Kirsh Foundry in Beaver Dam, the City of Beaver Dam Street Department and the Beaver Dam School District. Buried Leipsic Cemetery, Beaver Dam WI.

Johnny Lindell—12 Years Outfielder (b. 30 Aug 1916 Greeley CO–d. 27 Aug 1985 Hoag Memorial Hospital, Newport Beach CA) Died from lung cancer. Cremated.

Ernie Lindeman—1 Year Pitcher (b. 5 Jun 1881 Manhattan NY–d. 27 Dec 1951 at his home in Brooklyn NY) For many years he was a supervisor for Equitable Life Assurance Society, retiring in 1948. Died after a long illness. Buried Lutheran Cemetery, Middle Village NY.

Bob Lindemann—1 Year Outfielder (b. Chester PA–d. 19 Dec 1951 Williamsport Hospital, Williamsport PA) From 1910 until nearly up to his death he operated a laundry in Williamsport and used a horse-drawn carriage for his deliveries. He was also known for operating an animal refuge in Williamsport and a horse stable. Buried Mound Cemetery, Williamsport PA.

Bill Lindsay—1 Year Infielder (b. 24 Feb 1878 Madison NC–d. 14 Jul 1963 Wesley Long Hospital, Greensboro NC) He worked for the real estate branch of the Federal Land Bank of Columbia SC in Tampa FL. Died following a lengthy illness. Buried New Garden Cemetery, Greensboro NC.

Pinky Lindsay—2 Years Infielder (b. 24 Jul 1878 Monaca PA–d. 25 Jan 1941 Cleveland Clinic, Cleveland OH) Died from a heart attack. Buried Union Cemetery, Monaca PA.

Jim Lindsey—9 Years Pitcher (b. 24 Jan 1898 Greensburg LA–d. 25 Oct 1963 at his home in Jackson LA) His last 13 years he was the farm manager for the East Louisiana State Hospital. Buried Greensburg Cemetery, Greensburg LA.

Axel Lindstrom—1 Year Pitcher (b. 26 Aug 1895 Gustafsburg, Sweden–d. 24 Jun 1940 in a hospital in Asheville NC) He was a minor league umpire. Died from a brain concussion suffered when he fell near the Union Bus depot in Asheville. Buried Manchester NH.

Freddie Lindstrom—13 Years Infielder Hall of Fame (b. 21 Nov 1905 Chicago IL–d. 4 Oct 1981 Mercy Hospital, Chicago IL) In 1924, at age 18, he was the youngest player ever in a World Series game. He was the baseball coach at Northwestern University from 1948 to 1961, and postmaster at Evanston IL from 1961 until retiring in 1964. He lived the last ten years of his life at Port Richey FL. Buried All Saints Cemetery, Des Plaines IL.

Fred Link—1 Year Pitcher (b. 11 Mar 1887 Columbus OH–d. 22 May 1939 at his home in Houston TX) He worked 19 years in the general offices of the Texas Company in Houston. Buried Rosewood Park Cemetery, Houston TX.

Ed Linke—6 Years Pitcher (b. 9 Nov 1911 Chicago IL–d. 21 Jun 1988 Chicago IL) Died after a long illness.

Bob Linton—1 Year Catcher (b. 18 Apr 1902 Emerson AR–d. 3 Apr 1980 Destin FL) Buried Magnolia Memorial Park, Magnolia AR.

Johnny Lipon—9 Years Infielder 1 Year Manager (b. 10 Nov 1922 Martin's Ferry OH–d. 17 Aug 1998 Memorial Hospital, Houston TX) Served in the U.S. Navy during World War II. He managed in the minor leagues with over 2200 career wins, retiring in 1995. Buried Memorial Oaks Cemetery, Houston TX.

Tom Lipp—1 Year Pitcher (b. 4 Jun 1870 Baltimore MD–d. 30 May 1932 Maryland General Hospital, Baltimore MD) Buried New Freedom Cemetery, New Freedom PA.

Nig Lipscomb—1 Year Infielder (b. 24 Feb 1911 Rutherfordton NC–d. 28 Feb 1978 Huntersville Hospital, Huntersville NC) He worked at Highland Park Mills where he coached their semi-pro baseball team and was a warehouseman. When the mill closed in 1969 he drove truck for Brake Service Company until he retired. Buried Sharon Memorial Park, Charlotte NC.

Hod Lisenbee—8 Years Pitcher (b. 23 Sep 1898 Clarksville TN–d. 14 Nov 1987 Memorial Hospital, Clarksville TN) He played minor league baseball until the age of 51. After baseball he lived the life of a gentleman farmer on his 800 acre farm near Clarksville. Buried Liberty Cemetery, Clarksville TN.

Ad Liska—5 Years Pitcher (b. 10 Jul 1906 Dwight NE–d. 30 Nov 1998 Portland OR) He played 14 years for the Portland Beavers in the Pacific Coast League from 1936 to 1949. He then worked for the U.S. Post Office in Portland, retiring in 1971. Buried Mount Calvary Cemetery, Portland OR.

Pete Lister—1 Year Infielder (b. 21 Jul 1881 Savanna IL–d. 27 Feb 1947 St Petersburg FL).

Jack Little—1 Year Outfielder (b. 12 Mar 1891 Mart TX–d. 27 Jul 1961 at a hospital in Dallas TX) A Dallas resident 20 years, he was a representative for George L Dahl, Architects and Engineers. Died after a long illness. Buried Oakwood Cemetery, Waco TX.

Dick Littlefield—9 Years Pitcher (b. 18 Mar 1926 Detroit MI–d. 20 Nov 1997 Detroit MI) Buried Grand Lawn Cemetery, Detroit MI.

Carlisle Littlejohn—2 Years Pitcher (b. 6 Oct 1901 Mertens TX–d. 27 Oct 1977 Kansas City MO).

Jack Lively—1 Year Pitcher (b. 29 May 1885 Joppa AL–d. 5 Dec 1967 Arab Hospital, Arab AL) He was a retired employee of the American Cast Iron Pipe Company in Birmingham AL. Died after an extended illness. Buried Hebron Church of Christ Cemetery, Arab AL.

Wes Livengood—1 Year Pitcher (b. 18 Jul 1910 Spencer NC–d. 2 Sep 1996 Forsyth Memorial Hospital, Winston-Salem NC) Served in the U.S. Navy during World War II. He managed minor league baseball and was a scout for the Phillies from 1952 to 1982. He owned and operated Carolinas Men's Shop and, later, the Livengood Furniture Company. Buried Salem Cemetery, Winston-Salem NC.

Jake Livingston—1 Year Pitcher (b. 1 Jan 1886 Russia–d. 22 Mar 1949 Wassaic NY).

Mickey Livingston—10 Years Catcher (b. 15 Nov 1914 Prosperity SC–d. 3 Apr 1983 V A Hospital, Houston TX) Served in the U.S. Army during World War II. He managed minor league baseball in the Texas League. Buried Rosemont Cemetery, Newberry SC.

Paddy Livingston—7 Years Catcher (b. 14 Jan 1880 Cleveland OH–d. 19 Sep 1977 St John's Hospital, Cleveland OH) He worked 43 years in the City of Cleveland's bridge maintenance department, retiring in 1963. He was the last surviving player from the American League's inaugural year of 1901. Buried Calvary Cemetery, Cleveland OH.

Abel Lizotte—1 Year Infielder (b. 13 Apr 1870 Lewiston ME–d. 4 Dec 1926 at his home in Wilkes-Barre PA) He managed minor league baseball. Died from complications following a lingering illness. Buried St Mary's Cemetery, Wilkes-Barre PA.

Clem Llewellyn—1 Year Pitcher (b. 1 Aug 1895 Dobson NC–d. 27 Nov 1969 Charlotte NC) Buried Oakwood Cemetery, Concord NC.

Pop Lloyd—18 Years Infielder 11 Years Manager Hall of Fame (b. 25 Apr 1884 Palatka FL–d. 19 Mar 1964 at his home in Atlantic City NJ) Played in the negro leagues. He was a janitor at the Atlantic City Post Office and at a number of schools in Atlantic City. Died after a long illness. Buried Pleasantville Cemetery, Pleasantville NJ.

Mike Loan—1 Year Catcher (b. 27 Sep 1894 Philadelphia PA–d. 21 Nov 1966 Springfield PA).

Frank Lobert—1 Year Infielder (b. 26 Nov 1884 Williamsport PA–d. 29 May 1932 St Joseph's Hospital, Pittsburgh PA) He was an engineer for Allegheny County, PA. Died from peritonitis following surgery. Buried St George's Cemetery, Pittsburgh PA.

Hans Lobert—14 Years Infielder 2 Years Manager (b. 18 Oct 1881 Wilmington DE–d. 14 Sep 1968 Jeanes Hospital, Philadelphia PA) He spent his entire life in baseball as a player, coach and scout. He was the baseball coach at the U.S. Naval Academy from 1918 to 1925, coached for the Phillies and was a scout for the Giants.

Harry Lochhead—2 Years Infielder (b. 28 Mar 1876 Stockton CA–d. 22 Aug 1909 Stockton CA) He umpired minor league baseball until he became ill. Died at his mother's home from a long-lasting liver complaint, a month after suffering overexposure when he was lost on the desert near Bakersfield CA. Buried Rural Cemetery, Stockton CA.

Milo Lockwood—1 Year Pitcher (b. 7 Apr 1858 Solon OH–d. 9 Oct 1897 Economy Hotel, Economy PA) A barred attorney, he was a principal in the Lockwood-Taylor Hardware Company of Cleveland OH. He was also interested in a line of lake transports. Despondent over ill health, he took his own life by shooting himself in the temple. Buried Lake View Cemetery, Cleveland OH.

George Loepp —2 Years Outfielder (b. 11 Sep 1901 Detroit MI–d. 4 Sep 1967 Lincoln Convalescent Hosp, Los Angeles CA) He was a vacuum cleaner salesman for 15 years. Died from a heart attack. Cremated.

Dick Loftus —2 Years Outfielder (b. 7 Mar 1901 Concord MA–d. 21 Jan 1972 Sleepy Hollow Cemetery, Concord MA) Buried Sleepy Hollow Cemetery, Concord MA.

Frank Loftus —1 Year Pitcher (b. 10 Mar 1898 Scranton PA–d. 27 Oct 1980 at his home in Belchertown MA) He worked for the Belchertown Police Department and was active in civic matters. A selectman from 1966 to 1969, he was known as the "Mayor of Belchertown." Buried Mount Hope Cemetery, Belchertown MA.

Tom Loftus —2 Years Outfielder 9 Years Manager (b. 15 Nov 1856 St Louis MO–d. 16 Apr 1910 at his home in Dubuque IA) The last several years of his life he was a respected businessman in Dubuque. Died from throat cancer. Buried Mount Olivet Cemetery, Dubuque IA.

Bob Logan —5 Years Pitcher (b. 10 Feb 1910 Thompson NE–d. 21 May 1978 at his home in Indianapolis IN) He pitched several years in the American Association. He owned and operated Lefty Bob Logan's Service Station in Indianapolis from 1947 until retiring in 1972. Buried Oaklawn Memorial Gardens, Indianapolis IN.

Pete Lohman —1 Year Catcher (b. 21 Oct 1864 Lake Elmo MN–d. 21 Nov 1928 Los Angeles CA).

Howard Lohr —2 Years Outfielder (b. 3 Jun 1892 Philadelphia PA–d. 9 Jun 1977 Presbyterian Hospital, Philadelphia PA) For 40 years he was an accountant for the Pennsylvania Railroad, retiring in 1957. Buried Arlington Cemetery, Drexel Hill PA.

Sherm Lollar —18 Years Catcher (b. 23 Aug 1924 Durham AR–d. 24 Sep 1977 Cox Medical Center, Springfield MO) He owned a bowling alley in Springfield and was inducted into the Arkansas Sports Hall of Fame in 1972. Died from cancer. Buried Rivermonte Memorial Gardens, Springfield MO.

Ernie Lombardi —17 Years Catcher (b. 6 Apr 1908 Oakland CA–d. 26 Sep 1977 Dominican Hospital, Santa Cruz CA) For six years he was in charge of the press box at Candlestick Park in San Francisco, seeing that writers from all areas felt at home. Died from heart failure. Buried Mountain View Cemetery, Oakland CA.

Vic Lombardi —6 Years Pitcher (b. 20 Sep 1922 Reedley CA–d. 7 Dec 1997 Fresno Community Hospital, Fresno CA) Served in World War II. For 35 years he was a professional golfer. Died from heart failure four days after undergoing heart bypass surgery. Cremated. Buried Cemetery Tulare, Tulare CA.

Walt Lonergan —1 Year Infielder (b. 22 Sep 1885 Boston MA–d. 23 Jan 1958 at a hospital in Lexington MA) A retired post office worker, he worked at the South Postal Annex in Boston. Died after falling and fracturing his skull. Buried Mount Calvary Cemetery, Roslindale MA.

Dale Long —10 Years Infielder (b. 6 Feb 1926 Springfield MO–d. 27 Jan 1991 Memorial Hospital, Ormond Beach FL) He umpired five years in the minor leagues and later was a field representative for the National Association of Professional Baseball Leagues — the governing body of minor league baseball. Died after a long bout with cancer. Buried Cheshire Cemetery, Cheshire MA.

Dan Long —2 Years Outfielder (b. 27 Aug 1867 Boston MA–d. 30 Apr 1929 Sausalito CA) A scout for the White Sox, he managed in the Pacific Coast League before he became a court recorder in the police court in San Francisco CA. Killed when he slipped and fell under a commute train he was trying to board after it had started. Buried St Mary's Cemetery, Oakland CA.

Herman Long —16 Years Infielder (b. 13 Apr 1866 Chicago IL–d. 17 Sep 1909 at the Oakes Home in Denver CO) Died from tuberculosis. Buried Concordia Cemetery, Forest Park IL.

Jim Long —1 Year Catcher (b. 29 Jun 1898 Fort Dodge IA–d. 14 Sep 1970 Park Manor Nursing Home, Fort Dodge IA) Served in World War I. He followed baseball locally for several years, then worked for the Tobin Packing Plant and, later, for the City of Fort Dodge as a parking attendant. Died following an illness of two years. Buried Corpus Christi Cemetery, Fort Dodge IA.

Jim Long —2 Years Outfielder (b. 15 Nov 1862

Louisville KY–d. 12 Dec 1932 at his home in Louisville KY) He was a city meat inspector. Buried Resthaven Memorial Park, Louisville KY.

Lep Long—1 Year Pitcher (b. 12 Jul 1888 Summit NJ–d. 21 Oct 1958 at a hospital in Birmingham AL) Served in the U.S. Army during World War I. A civil engineer, he was vice-president in charge of sales and secretary of the Acipco Company in Birmingham, retiring in 1952. Died following a brief illness. Buried Oak Hill Memorial Cemetery, Birmingham AL.

Red Long—1 Year Infielder (b. 28 Sep 1876 Burlington, Ontario, Canada–d. 11 Aug 1929 Hamilton, Ontario, Canada).

Tom Long—1 Year Pitcher (b. 22 Apr 1898 Memphis TN–d. 16 Sep 1973 Louisville KY) Buried St Louis Cemetery, Louisville KY.

Tommy Long—5 Years Outfielder (b. 1 Jun 1890 Mitchum AL–d. 15 Jun 1972 Jackson AL).

Peter Loos—1 Year Pitcher (b. 23 Mar 1878 Philadelphia PA–d. 23 Feb 1956 Darby PA) Buried Mount Peace Cemetery, Philadelphia PA.

Ed Lopat—12 Years Pitcher 2 Years Manager (b. 21 Jun 1918 New York City NY–d. 15 Jun 1992 Darien CT) He was a scout for the Yankees. Died from pancreatic cancer. Buried St Mary's Cemetery, Greenwich CT.

Aurelio Lopez—11 Years Pitcher (b. 21 Sep 1948 Tecamachalco, Mexico–d. 22 Sep 1992 Matehuala, Mexico).

Ramon Lopez—1 Year Pitcher (b. 26 May 1933 Las Villas, Cuba–d. 4 Sep 1982 Miami FL) Buried Woodlawn Park North Cemetery, Miami FL.

Bris Lord—8 Years Outfielder (b. 21 Sep 1883 Upland PA–d. 13 Nov 1964 Annapolis MD) Buried Lawn Croft Cemetery, Linwood PA.

Carlton Lord—1 Year Infielder (b. 7 Jan 1900 Philadelphia PA–d. 15 Aug 1947 Chester PA).

Harry Lord—9 Years Infielder 1 Year Manager (b. 8 Mar 1882 Porter ME–d. 9 Aug 1948 at a hospital in Westbrook ME) He left baseball for a year over a salary dispute and found himself blacklisted when he tried to return. He managed several minor league teams before entering a number of business ventures in Portland ME. When he died he had been hospitalized four months. Buried Riverside Cemetery, Kezar Falls ME.

Lefty Lorenzen—1 Year Pitcher (b. 12 Jan 1893 Davenport IA–d. 5 Mar 1963 Davenport IA) He was a sheet metal worker and security guard. Died from a heart attack. Buried Fairmont Cemetery, Davenport IA.

Joe Lotz—1 Year Pitcher (b. 2 Jan 1891 Remsen IA–d. 1 Jan 1971 at his home in Castro Valley CA) He moved to California in 1940. Died following a long illness.

Art Loudell—1 Year Pitcher (b. 10 May 1882 Latham MO–d. 19 Feb 1961 Kansas City MO) Buried Mount Moriah Cemetery, Kansas City MO.

Baldy Louden—6 Years Infielder (b. 27 Aug 1885 Piedmont WV–d. 8 Dec 1935 Piedmont WV).

Charlie Loudenslager—1 Year Infielder (b. 21 May 1881 Baltimore MD–d. 31 Oct 1933 Baltimore MD) Died suddenly. Buried Loudon Park National Cemetery, Baltimore MD.

Slim Love—6 Years Pitcher (b. 1 Aug 1890 Love MO–d. 30 Nov 1942 Memphis TN) He worked with his brother at the Love Automatic Sprinkler Company. Died shortly after being struck by a car. Buried Calvary Cemetery, Memphis TN.

Tom Lovelace—1 Game Pinch Hitter (b. 19 Oct 1897 Wolfe City TX–d. 12 Jul 1979 Dallas TX) He was a salesman for Reynolds-Penland Company in the downtown Dallas and Richardson TX stores. Died after a lengthy illness. Buried Restland Memorial Park, Dallas TX.

John Lovett—1 Year Pitcher (b. 6 May 1877 Monday OH–d. 5 Dec 1937 Murray City OH) He operated a service station. Active in Republican Party politics, he was elected Hocking County (OH) Commissioner for two terms. Died from a heart attack. Buried Green Lawn Cemetery, Nelsonville OH.

Mem Lovett—1 Game Pinch Hitter (b. 15 Jun 1912 Chicago IL–d. 19 Sep 1995 Downer's Grove IL). Cremated.

Tom Lovett—6 Years Pitcher (b. 7 Dec 1863 Providence RI–d. 19 Mar 1928 Providence RI) He was a salesman for a time before becoming a watchman for the Outlet Company. Died suddenly from a heart attack while walking on the street. Buried St Ann's Cemetery, Cranston RI.

Fletcher Low—1 Year Infielder (b. 7 Apr 1893

Essex MA–d. 6 Jun 1973 at his home in Hanover NH) A professor of chemistry at Dartmouth College, he served in the New Hampshire House of Representatives from 1961 to 1966. Buried Dartmouth Cemetery, Hanover NH.

Grover Lowdermilk—9 Years Pitcher (b. 15 Jan 1885 Sandborn IN–d. 31 Mar 1968 Yaw Nursing Home, Odin IL) He was a coal miner. Buried Peaceful Valley Cemetery, Odin IL.

Lou Lowdermilk—2 Years Pitcher (b. 23 Feb 1887 Sandborn IN–d. 27 Dec 1975 St Mary's Hospital, Centralia IL) World War I veteran. He was a coal miner and artist. Buried Summit Prairie Cemetery, Salem IL.

Bobby Lowe—18 Years Infielder 1 Year Manager (b. 10 Jul 1868 Pittsburgh PA–d. 8 Dec 1951 Arnold Home, Detroit MI) He was the first man to hit four homeruns in one game. Buried Evergreen Cemetery, Detroit MI.

Dickie Lowe—1 Year Catcher (b. 28 Jan 1854 Evansville WI–d. 28 Jun 1922 Janesville WI).

George Lowe—1 Year Pitcher (b. 24 Apr 1895 Ridgefield Park NJ–d. 2 Sep 1981 Shore Memorial Hospital, Somers Point NJ) Buried Seaside Cemetery, Marmora NJ.

Peanuts Lowrey—13 Years Outfielder (b. 27 Aug 1917 Culver City CA–d. 2 Jul 1986 Daniel Freeman Hospital, Inglewood CA) World War II veteran. He spent 43 years in organized baseball as a player, coach and minor league manager, retiring in 1981 after a heart attack. Died from congestive heart failure after months of failing health. Buried Holy Cross Cemetery, Culver City CA.

Dwight Lowry—4 Years Catcher (b. 23 Oct 1957 Lumberton NC–d. 10 Jul 1997 Jamestown NY) Died from heart failure.

Sam Lowry—2 Years Pitcher (b. 25 Mar 1920 Philadelphia PA–d. 1 Dec 1992 at his home in Philadelphia PA) Served in Korea and the Philippines for the U.S. Army during World War II. He ran Sam's Dugout, a sports bar in Roxborough, for some years and later drove a cab in Philadelphia.

Hugh Luby—2 Years Infielder (b. 13 Jun 1913 Blackfoot ID–d. 4 May 1986 Sacred Heart General Hospital, Eugene OR) Served in the U.S. Navy during World War II. He worked in baseball most of his life as a minor league manager, general manager and league president. He owned a sporting goods store in Eugene from 1960 until closing it in 1985. Died following a cerebral hemorrhage. Buried Rest-Haven Memorial Park, Eugene OR.

Pat Luby—4 Years Pitcher (b. 22 Aug 1868 Charleston SC–d. 24 Apr 1899 at his home in Charleston SC) Died after a long illness.

Fred Lucas—1 Year Outfielder (b. 19 Jan 1903 Vineland NJ–d. 11 Mar 1987 Dorchester General Hospital, Cambridge MD) He owned Lucas and Fowler Office Supply Store in Cambridge from 1940 to 1950 and later operated a sporting goods store there. Active politically, he served one term in the Maryland House of Delegates and also as county treasurer. Died after being in failing health six months. Buried Dorchester Memorial Park, Cambridge MD.

Henry Lucas—2 Years Manager (b. 5 Sep 1857 St Louis MO–d. 15 Nov 1910 at the home of a niece in St Louis MO) An early owner of the St Louis Browns, he inherited a fortune and spent it trying to build a winning St Louis baseball team. After going broke in his baseball endeavor he worked as a St Louis street inspector for $75 a month. Died from blood poisoning after a fall. Buried Calvary Cemetery, St Louis MO.

Johnny Lucas—2 Years Outfielder (b. 10 Feb 1903 Glen Carbon IL–d. 31 Oct 1970 at his home in Maryville IL) He was the chief of police at Maryville for 36 years. Died from a heart attack. Buried Buck Road Cemetery, Glen Carbon IL.

Ray Lucas—5 Years Pitcher (b. 2 Oct 1908 Springfield OH–d. 9 Oct 1969 Harrison MI) Served in the U.S. Navy during World War II. He managed minor league baseball for a short while before spending the rest of his life as a scout for the Giants.

Red Lucas—16 Years Pitcher (b. 28 Apr 1902 Columbia TN–d. 9 Jul 1986 at his home in Nashville TN) He worked for the Tennessee State Motor Vehicle Division. Buried Spring Hill Cemetery, Nashville TN.

Frank Luce—1 Year Outfielder (b. 6 Dec 1896 Spencer OH–d. 3 Feb 1942 at his home in Milwaukee WI) He was known as a "Powerhouse" in the American Association where he played for several years. Later he was a floor manager at Schusters in Milwaukee. Died from a heart attack. Buried Forest Home Cemetery, Milwaukee WI.

Joe Lucey—2 Years Pitcher (b. 27 Mar 1897 Holyoke MA–d. 30 Jul 1980 Providence Hospital, Holyoke MA) Served in the U.S. Army during World War II. He operated a sporting goods store in Holyoke from 1925 until 1932 when he went to work for the Internal Revenue Service. In 1944 he was appointed city treasurer and held that post until he retired in 1972. Died following a long illness. Buried Calvary Cemetery, Holyoke MA.

Ron Luciano—(b. 1937 Binghamton NY–d. 18 Jan 1995 at his home in Endicott NY) He was an American League umpire from 1969 to 1980, and a television announcer after that. His death was ruled a suicide by carbon monoxide poisoning. Buried Calvary Cemetery, Johnson City NY.

Con Lucid—5 Years Pitcher (b. 24 Feb 1874 Dublin, Ireland–d. 25 Jun 1931 Houston TX) He managed some minor league baseball before coaching college baseball at Rice Institute, the University of Texas and Texas A & M. He also worked for the Texas Company. Died after a short illness. Buried Holy Cross Cemetery, Houston TX.

Fred Luderus—12 Years Infielder (b. 12 Sep 1885 Milwaukee WI–d. 4 Jan 1961 at his home near Three Lakes WI) He was a handy man at the Milwaukee (WI) Yacht Club and a member of the Wisconsin Hall of Fame. Died from a heart attack. Buried Pinelawn Memorial Park, Milwaukee WI.

Willie Ludolph—1 Year Pitcher (b. 21 Jan 1900 San Francisco CA–d. 8 Apr 1952 Oakland CA) One of the Pacific Coast League's great pitchers, he worked for his brother's milk trucking business. Died from a heart attack. Buried Holy Sepulchre Cemetery, Hayward CA.

Bill Ludwig—1 Year Catcher (b. 27 May 1882 Louisville KY–d. 5 Sep 1947 at his home in Louisville KY) He was a service station supervisor for Standard Oil of Kentucky for 22 years. Died from a cerebral hemorrhage. Buried Calvary Cemetery, Louisville KY.

Roy Luebbe—1 Year Catcher (b. 17 Sep 1901 Parkersburg IA–d. 21 Aug 1985 at a nursing home in Papillon NE) He was a superintendent for General Electric in Omaha. Buried Forest Lawn Memorial Park, Omaha NE.

Dick Luebke—1 Year Pitcher (b. 8 Apr 1935 Chicago IL–d. 4 Dec 1974 Alvarado Community Hospital, San Diego CA) He was a lending officer at Crocker National Bank for 15 years. Died from a heart attack. Cremated.

Henry Luff—3 Years Infielder (b. 14 Sep 1856 Philadelphia PA–d. 11 Oct 1916 Philadelphia PA) Buried North Laurel Hill Cemetery, Philadelphia PA.

Bill Luhrsen—1 Year Pitcher (b. 14 Apr 1884 Buckley IL–d. 18 Aug 1973 Little Rock AR) He was a retired employee of E L Bruce Company. Buried Edgewood Memorial Cemetery, North Little Rock AR.

Eddie Lukon—4 Years Outfielder (b. 5 Aug 1920 Burgettstown PA–d. 7 Nov 1996 Canonsburg PA) Served in the U.S. Army during World War II and fought at the Battle of the Bulge. He quit baseball in 1948 when his father was ill, returning home to run the family business, retiring in 1990. Buried Our Lady of Lourdes Cemetery, Burgettstown PA.

Harry Lumley—7 Years Outfielder 1 Year Manager (b. 29 Sep 1880 Forest City PA–d. 22 May 1938 City Hospital, Binghamton NY) He operated a tavern at Binghamton. Died following a long illness. Buried Floral Park Cemetery, Johnson City NY.

Jack Lundbom—1 Year Pitcher (b. 10 Mar 1877 Manistee MI–d. 31 Oct 1949 Manistee MI) For 33 years he was a mail carrier in Manistee, retiring in 1937. Buried Oak Grove Cemetery, Manistee MI.

Carl Lundgren—8 Years Pitcher (b. 16 Feb 1880 Marengo IL–d. 21 Aug 1934 Marengo IL) He was baseball coach at Princeton University from 1913 to 1914, University of Michigan from 1915 to 1921, and at University of Illinois from 1922 until his death. He was also assistant athletic director at the University of Illinois. Died from a heart attack. Buried Marengo Cemetery, Marengo IL.

Del Lundgren—3 Years Pitcher (b. 21 Sep 1899 Lindsborg KS–d. 19 Oct 1984 at his home in Lindsborg KS) He worked 35 years for Rodney Milling Company, retiring in 1965. Died after a short illness. Buried Elmwood Cemetery, Lindsborg KS.

Harry Lunte—2 Years Infielder (b. 15 Sep 1892 St Louis MO–d. 27 Jul 1965 St Louis MO) Buried St John's Cemetery, St Louis MO.

Dolf Luque—20 Years Pitcher (b. 4 Aug 1890 Havana, Cuba–d. 3 Jul 1957 Havana, Cuba) Died from a heart attack. Buried Christopher Columbus Necropolis, Havana, Cuba.

Billy Lush—7 Years Outfielder (b. 10 Nov 1873 Bridgeport CT–d. 28 Aug 1951 Hawthorne NY).

Ernie Lush—1 Year Outfielder (b. 31 Oct 1884 Bridgeport CT–d. 26 Feb 1937 at his home in Detroit MI) He worked 16 years in the engineering department for the City of Detroit after working in a similar job for the City of Bridgeport. Died from pneumonia after a brief illness. Buried St Michael's Cemetery, Bridgeport CT.

Johnny Lush—7 Years Pitcher (b. 8 Oct 1885 Williamsport PA–d. 18 Nov 1946 at his home in Beverly Hills CA) He operated gift shops in hotels at Monterey CA and Honolulu HI before World War II and was operating a gift shop in the Beverly Hills Hotel when he died. Died from a heart attack. Buried Calvary Cemetery, Los Angeles CA.

Charlie Luskey—1 Year Outfielder (b. 6 Apr 1876 Washington DC–d. 20 Dec 1962 Bethesda MD) Buried Fort Lincoln Cemetery, Brentwood MD.

Luke Lutenberg—1 Year Infielder (b. 4 Oct 1864 Quincy IL–d. 24 Dec 1938 Quincy IL) He operated saloons in Quincy until prohibition shut them down. After repeal he worked as a bartender until ill health forced his retirement. Buried Woodland Cemetery, Quincy IL.

Lyle Luttrell—2 Years Infielder (b. 22 Feb 1930 Bloomington IL–d. 11 Jul 1984 at a hospital in Chattanooga TN) He played for the Chattanooga Lookouts and moved to Chattanooga in 1970, working for Millwrights, Inc, his last eight years. Died from a heart attack. Buried Chattanooga National Cemetery, Chattanooga TN.

Red Lutz—1 Year Catcher (b. 17 Dec 1898 Cincinnati OH–d. 22 Feb 1984 Veteran's Hospital, Cincinnati OH) Served in the U.S. Navy during World War II. He was a retired employee of the New York Central Railroad. Buried St Stephen Cemetery, Fort Thomas KY.

Rube Lutzke—5 Years Infielder (b. 17 Nov 1897 Milwaukee WI–d. 6 Mar 1938 at his home in Milwaukee WI) A great defensive third baseman who couldn't hit, he played several years in the American Association. Buried Valhalla Memorial Cemetery, Milwaukee WI.

Jim Lyle—1 Year Pitcher (b. 24 Jul 1900 Lake MS–d. 10 Oct 1977 Divine Providence Hospital, Williamsport PA) He retired as a foreman from Bethlehem Steel Corporation in 1969. Buried Mount Carmel Cemetery, Williamsport PA.

Adrian Lynch—1 Year Pitcher (b. 9 Feb 1897 Laurens IA–d. 16 Mar 1934 Davenport IA) He was a salesman for Certain-teed Products Company. Killed instantly in an automobile accident on Hwy 61 when he drove his car into a ditch, one mile west of Davenport. Buried Glendale Cemetery, Des Moines IA.

Dummy Lynch—1 Year Infielder (b. 7 Feb 1927 Dallas TX–d. 30 Jun 1978 Plano TX) Killed when the car he was driving was struck by a cement-mixer truck. Buried Restland Memorial Park, Dallas TX.

Henry Lynch—1 Year Outfielder (b. 1866 Worcester MA–d. 23 Nov 1925 St Vincent Hospital, Worcester MA) Buried St John's Cemetery, Worcester MA.

Jack Lynch—7 Years Pitcher (b. 5 Feb 1855 New York City NY–d. 19 Apr 1923 Bronx NY) Buried Gate of Heaven Cemetery, Hawthorne NY.

Mike Lynch—1 Year Outfielder (b. 10 Sep 1875 St Paul MN–d. 2 Apr 1947 at his home in Jennings Lodge OR) He operated an orchard near Yakima WA before moving to Jennings Lodge five months before his death. Buried Terrace Heights Memorial Park, Yakima WA.

Mike Lynch—4 Years Pitcher (b. 28 Jun 1880 Holyoke MA–d. 2 Apr 1927 Garrison NY).

Thomas Lynch—1 Year Pitcher (b. 1862 Peru IL–d. 13 May 1923 Peru IL).

Tom Lynch—2 Years Outfielder (b. 3 Apr 1860 Bennington VT–d. 28 Mar 1955 Cohoes Memorial Hospital, Cohoes NY) He worked for the Cohoes Department of Public Works. He was said to be the oldest living former major leaguer when he died. Died from pulmonary edema and arteriosclerotic heart disease. Buried St Agnes Cemetery, Cohoes NY.

Walt Lynch—1 Year Catcher (b. 15 Apr 1897 Buffalo NY–d. 21 Dec 1976 Community Hospital, Daytona Beach FL) Served in Europe for the U.S. Army during World War I. He taught physical education in the Buffalo schools for 26 years, retiring to Daytona Beach in 1958. Buried Oakwood Cemetery, East Aurora NY.

Byrd Lynn—5 Years Catcher (b. 13 Mar 1889 Unionville IL–d. 5 Feb 1940 Victory Hospital, Napa CA) He was a well-known attendant at the Napa State Hospital. Died from a perforated ulcer and heart disease. Cremated.

Jerry Lynn—1 Year Infielder (b. 14 Apr 1916 Scranton PA–d. 25 Sep 1972 State General Hospital, Scranton PA) World War II veteran. He was a bartender prior to his retirement. Buried St Catherine's Cemetery, Moscow PA.

Red Lynn—3 Years Pitcher (b. 27 Dec 1913 Kenney TX–d. 27 Oct 1977 City Hospital, Bellville TX) Died after a one-year illness. Buried Oak Knoll Cemetery, Bellville TX.

Russ Lyon—1 Year Catcher (b. 26 Jun 1913 Ball Ground GA–d. 24 Dec 1975 Charleston SC).

Al Lyons—4 Years Pitcher (b. 18 Jul 1918 St Joseph MO–d. 20 Dec 1965 at his home in Inglewood CA) World War II veteran. He was a scout for the Mets. Died from a heart attack. Buried Inglewood Park Cemetery, Inglewood CA.

Denny Lyons—13 Years Infielder (b. 12 Mar 1866 Cincinnati OH–d. 2 Jan 1929 at his sister's home in West Covington, KY) Died from influenza. Buried St Joseph New Cemetery, Cincinnati OH.

George Lyons—2 Years Pitcher (b. 25 Jan 1891 Bible Grove IL–d. 12 Aug 1981 at a hospital in Nevada MO) World War I veteran. He retired from baseball in 1930, moving to Nevada where he farmed, owned a paint and wall paper store and sold cars and real estate. He served a four-year term as Vernon County (MO) Treasurer. He suffered from a respiratory ailment. Buried Newton Burial Park, Nevada MO.

Harry Lyons—6 Years Outfielder (b. 25 Mar 1866 Chester PA–d. 28 Jun 1912 Buckshutem NJ) He was an office clerk for the Philadelphia City Water Department. Died from an abdomonal disorder. Buried West Laurel Hill Cemetery, Bala Cynwyd PA.

Pat Lyons—1 Year Infielder (b. 1860 Canada–d. 20 Jan 1914 City Hospital, Springfield OH) He was a tinner in several Springfield factories. Died from chronic nephritis. Buried Calvary Cemetery, Springfield OH.

Ted Lyons—21 Years Pitcher 3 Years Manager Hall of Fame (b. 28 Dec 1900 Lake Charles LA–d. 25 Jul 1986 at a nursing home in Sulphur LA) Served as a major in the U.S. Marines during World War II. He retired to his favorite pastimes of golfing and hunting. Died from cancer. Buried Big Woods Cemetery, Edgerly LA.

Terry Lyons—1 Year Infielder (b. 14 Dec 1908 New Holland OH–d. 9 Sep 1959 Dayton OH) For 22 years he worked in inventory control for Frigidaire Division of General Motors Corporation in Dayton. Died in the dentist's office while having gas administered to him. Buried Memorial Park Cemetery, Dayton OH.

Toby Lyons—1 Year Pitcher (b. 27 Mar 1869 Cambridge MA–d. 27 Aug 1920 at his home in Boston MA) He umpired in the minor leagues a short while before spending 20 years on stage as an actor and comedian. Died after an illness of three weeks.

Bill Lyston—2 Years Pitcher (b. 1863 Baltimore MD–d. 4 Aug 1944 Baltimore MD) Buried Holy Redeemer Cemetery, Baltimore MD.

Pop Lytle—1 Year Outfielder (b. 14 May 1862 Racine WI–d. 21 Dec 1950 General Hospital, Los Angeles CA) He was a carpenter for a Hollywood motion picture studio. Died from congestive heart failure. Buried Sunnyside Cemetery, Long Beach CA.

M

Duke Maas—7 Years Pitcher (b. 31 Jan 1929 Utica MI–d. 7 Dec 1976 St Joseph's Hospital West, Mount Clemens MI) He worked for the Ford Motor Company. Died from complications of arthritis. Buried Utica Cemetery, Utica MI.

Mac MacArthur—1 Year Pitcher (b. 19 Jan 1862 Glasgow, Scotland–d. 18 Oct 1932 at his home in Detroit MI) For 30 years he was an inspector for the Department of Public Works. Buried Elmwood Cemetery, Detroit MI.

Bill MacDonald—2 Years Pitcher (b. 28 Mar 1929 Alameda CA–d. 4 May 1991 Shasta Lake CA) Served during the Korean War. In 1989 he retired to Redding CA from Sun Valley ID where he was a regional manager for Del Monte Corporation for 25 years. Died at a marina on Shasta Lake from a sudden heart attack. Cremated. Buried Memory Gardens Memorial Park, Concord CA.

Harvey MacDonald—1 Year Outfielder (b. 18 May 1898 New York City NY–d. 4 Oct 1965 Philadelphia PA) Buried Glenwood Memorial Gardens, Broomall PA.

Danny MacFayden—17 Years Pitcher (b. 10 Jun 1905 North Truro MA–d. 26 Aug 1972 Regional Memorial Hospital, Brunswick ME) He coached baseball and hockey at Bowdoin College for 23 years. Buried Old North Cemetery, North Truro MA.

Bill Mack—1 Year Pitcher (b. 12 Feb 1885 Elmira NY–d. 30 Sep 1971 Elmira NY) He retired as a claims superintendent for the Royal Indemnity Insurance Company in New York City. Buried St Peter and Paul's Cemetery, Elmira NY.

Connie Mack—11 Years Catcher 53 Years Manager Hall of Fame (b. 22 Dec 1862 East Brookfield MA–d. 8 Feb 1956 at his daughter's home in Philadelphia PA) The owner and manager of the Philadelphia Athletics for 50 years, he won and lost more games than any other manager. Died from complications of a broken hip suffered four months earlier. Buried Holy Sepulchre Cemetery, Philadelphia PA.

Denny Mack—4 Years Infielder (b. 1851 Easton PA–d. 10 Apr 1888 Wilkes-Barre PA) He did handy work for the proprietor of a hotel and cafe. Died from a hemorrhage after falling down the stairs of his home.

Earle Mack—3 Years Infielder (b. 1 Feb 1890 Spencerlphia MA–d. 5 Feb 1967 Delaware County Hospital, Drexel Hill PA) He played minor league baseball for years, managed minor league baseball and coached for the Athletics. He owned the Athletics from 1950 until they were sold in 1954. Died from a stroke while in the hospital for his annual physical checkup. Buried Morganton NC.

Frank Mack—3 Years Pitcher (b. 2 Feb 1900 Oklahoma City OK–d. 2 Jul 1971 at a nursing home in Dunedin FL) He was a retired printer and moved to Bradenton FL from Sacramento CA in 1966. Buried Mount Emblem Cemetery, Elmhurst IL.

Ray Mack—9 Years Infielder (b. 31 Aug 1916 Cleveland OH–d. 7 May 1969 University Hospital, Columbus OH) World War II veteran. He was sales manager for the Ohio Locomotive Crane Company in Bucyrus OH. Died from cancer. Buried Oakwood Cemetery, Bucyrus OH.

Reddy Mack—6 Years Infielder (b. 2 May 1866 Ireland–d. 30 Dec 1916 at his home in Newport KY) Died after falling and fracturing his skull.

Roy Mack—(b. 27 Aug 1888 Washington DC–d. 10 Feb 1960 Bryn Mawr Hospital, Bryn Mawr PA) He was co-owner of the Philadelphia Athletics. Died from a heart attack. Buried Calvary Cemetery, West Conshohocken PA.

Felix Mackiewicz—6 Years Outfielder (b. 20 Nov 1917 Chicago IL–d. 20 Dec 1993 at his home in Olivette MO) For more than 30 years he was a sales representative for Whiting Corporation, a manufacturer of heavy cranes and transportation equipment in Harvey IL. He retired as a regional sales manager in the early 1980s. Died from cancer. Buried Calvary Cemetery, St Louis MO.

Johnny Mackinson—2 Years Pitcher (b. 29 Oct 1923 Orange NJ–d. 17 Oct 1989 at his home in Reseda CA) World War II veteran. For 25 years he was a truck driver for Frito-Lay Corporation. Died from lung cancer. Cremated. Buried Riverside National Cemetery, Riverside CA.

Steve Macko—2 Years Infielder (b. 6 Sep 1954 Burlington IA–d. 15 Nov 1981 at a hospital in Arlington TX) Died from cancer at the height of his baseball career. Buried Moore Memorial Gardens, Arlington TX.

Max Macon—6 Years Pitcher (b. 14 Oct 1915 Pensacola FL–d. 5 Aug 1989 Jupiter FL) He spent 41 years in professional baseball as a player, scout and minor league manager. Buried Resthaven Memorial Park, Louisville KY.

Larry MacPhail —Hall of Fame (b. 3 Feb 1890 Cass City MI–d. 1 Oct 1975 V A Hospital, Miami FL) Wounded while serving in the U.S. Army at the Argonne front during World War I. He was an executive for the Yankees, Reds and Dodgers, and introduced night baseball to the major leagues. After retiring from baseball in 1947 he established one of the most successful thoroughbred breeding farms in Maryland. Died from pneumonia and old age. Buried Elkland Township Cemetery, Cass City MI.

Waddy MacPhee —1 Year Infielder (b. 23 Dec 1899 Brooklyn NY–d. 20 Jan 1980 Charlotte NC).

Jimmy Macullar —6 Years Infielder (b. 16 Jan 1855 Boston MA–d. 8 Apr 1924 Baltimore MD) Buried Baltimore Cemetery, Baltimore MD.

Bunny Madden —2 Years Outfielder (b. 31 Jul 1883 Philadelphia PA–d. 26 Jul 1930 Philadelphia PA) Buried Holy Sepulchre Cemetery, Philadelphia PA.

Frank Madden —1 Year Catcher (b. 17 Oct 1892 Pittsburgh PA–d. 30 Apr 1952 Pittsburgh PA).

Gene Madden —1 Game Pinch Hitter (b. 5 Jun 1890 Elm Grove WV–d. 5 Apr 1949 Utica NY).

Kid Madden —5 Years Pitcher (b. 22 Oct 1866 Portland ME–d. 16 Mar 1896 at his home in Portland ME) Buried Calvary Cemetery, South Portland ME.

Len Madden —1 Year Pitcher (b. 2 Jul 1890 Toledo OH–d. 9 Sep 1949 at his home in Toledo OH) He worked for the Toledo Fire Department from 1917 until retiring in 1948. He was promoted to lieutenant in 1941. Died following a long illness. Buried Calvary Cemetery, Toledo OH.

Tom Madden —3 Years Catcher (b. 14 Sep 1882 Boston MA–d. 20 Jan 1954 City Hospital, Cambridge MA) He was a retired employee of New England Telephone and Telegraph Company. Buried St Joseph's Cemetery, West Roxbury MA.

Clarence Maddern —4 Years Outfielder (b. 26 Sep 1921 Bisbee AZ–d. 9 Aug 1986 Tucson Medical Center, Tucson AZ) Served as a military policeman in the U.S. Army during World War II. He played baseball in the high minor leagues for 14 years and was an agent for Farmers Insurance Group. Buried Evergreen Cemetery, Bisbee AZ.

Nick Maddox —4 Years Pitcher (b. 9 Nov 1886 Gavanstown MD–d. 27 Nov 1954 Pittsburgh PA) Died after an illness of six weeks. Buried St Augustine Church Cemetery, Pittsburgh PA.

Tony Madigan —1 Year Pitcher (b. 1868 Washington DC–d. 4 Dec 1954 Providence Hospital, Washington DC) He worked for a Washington DC law firm until he could save enough to open a liquor store that he closed in 1914. He then went to work for Pabst Brewing Company for six years before finally working several years as a pressman for the U.S. Government Printing Office. Died after a six-week illness. Buried Mount Olivet Cemetery, Washington DC.

Art Madison —2 Years Infielder (b. 14 Jan 1872 Clarksburg MA–d. 27 Jan 1933 at his home in North Adams MA) He was a machinist for Hunter Machine Company in North Adams. Died after suffering a stroke two days earlier. Buried South View Cemetery, North Adams MA.

Dave Madison —3 Years Pitcher (b. 1 Feb 1921 Brooksville MS–d. 8 Dec 1985 Noxubee General Hospital, Macon MS) Served in the U.S. Army during World War II and the Korean War. He managed in the Yankee farm system and was a scout for several teams. Died after a lengthy illness. Buried Brooksville Cemetery, Brooksville MS.

Ed Madjeski —4 Years Catcher (b. 20 Jul 1908 Far Rockaway NY–d. 11 Nov 1994 Montgomery OH).

Sal Madrid —1 Year Infielder (b. 19 Jun 1920 El Paso TX–d. 24 Feb 1977 Fort Wayne IN) He was a print shop manager for North American Van Lines in Fort Wayne. He was dead-on-arrival at Lutheran Hospital. Buried Lindenwood Cemetery, Fort Wayne IN.

Bill Magee —5 Years Pitcher (b. 11 Jan 1868 Cambridge MA–d. 12 Aug 1922 Tuftonboro NH).

Lee Magee —9 Years Outfielder 1 Year Manager (b. 4 Jun 1889 Cincinnati OH–d. 14 Mar 1966 Columbus OH) He was the proprietor of the Commerce Coal Company. Buried St Joseph Cemetery, Lockbourne OH.

Sherry Magee —16 Years Outfielder (b. 6 Aug

1884 Clarendon PA–d. 13 Mar 1929 Philadelphia PA) He worked for a Philadelphia restaurant concern during the off-season while umpiring in the minor leagues and for the National League in 1928. Died from pneumonia. Buried Arlington Cemetery, Drexel Hill PA.

George Magerkurth—(b. 20 Dec 1888 McPherson KS–d. 7 Oct 1966 St Anthony's Hospital, Rock Island IL) He played some minor league baseball and logged 62 bouts as a professional fighter before he turned to umpiring. He was a National League umpire from 1929 to 1947. Died from a complication of problems including pneumonia and uremic poisoning. Buried Greenview Memorial Gardens, East Moline IL.

Harl Maggert—2 Years Outfielder (b. 13 Feb 1884 Cromwell IN–d. 7 Jan 1963 General Hospital, Fresno CA) He lived 50 years in Berkeley CA where he was in the feed and fuel business. Died from prostate cancer, pneumonia and congestive heart failure. Cremated. Buried Sunset Mausoleum, Kensington CA.

Harl Maggert—1 Year Outfielder (b. 4 May 1914 Los Angeles CA–d. 10 Jul 1986 Citrus Heights CA) He was a property manager for Vandenburg Properties in Sacramento CA. Died from lung cancer. Buried Calvary Cemetery, Sacramento CA.

Sal Maglie—10 Years Pitcher (b. 26 Apr 1917 Niagara Falls NY–d. 28 Dec 1992 Memorial Medical Center, Niagara Falls NY) Called "The Barber," he was never a barber, only working in a barber shop as a cleanup boy when he was a youngster. Died from pneumonia after three cerebral vascular accidents between 1982 and 1987 that debilitated him. Buried St Joseph's Cemetery, Niagara Falls NY.

John Magner—1 Year Outfielder (b. 5 Jan 1844 Appleby, England–d. 20 Jul 1923 at his home in St Louis MO) He came to the United State as a child and fought with an Ohio regiment in the Civil War. Moving to St Louis in 1876, he entered the contracting and building business, working in that line the rest of his life. He had been an invalid his last five years.

Stubby Magner—1 Year Infielder (b. 20 Feb 1888 Kalamazoo MI–d. 6 Sep 1956 Chillicothe OH).

Jim Magnuson—3 Years Pitcher (b. 18 Aug 1946 Marinette WI–d. 30 May 1991 Green Bay WI) Served in the U.S. Marine Corps. He was found dead from alcohol poisoning in his girl friend's apartment. Buried Forest Home Cemetery, Marinette WI.

George Magoon—5 Years Infielder (b. 27 Mar 1875 St Albans ME–d. 6 Dec 1943 at his home in Rochester NH) He coached baseball at the University of Maine from 1912 to 1913, and at the University of New Hampshire in 1915. Served as City Marshall for Rochester from 1917 to 1920, and was a policeman at different times. Died after suffering a heart attack.

Freddie Maguire—6 Years Infielder (b. 10 May 1899 Roxbury MA–d. 3 Nov 1961 St Elizabeth's Medical Center, Brighton MA) He coached college baseball at Boston College ten years before he joined the Red Sox as a scout in 1953. Buried St John's Cemetery, Worcester MA.

Jim Maguire—1 Year Infielder (b. 4 Feb 1875 Dunkirk NY–d. 27 Jan 1917 Municipal Hospital, Buffalo NY) He clerked at various clothing stores in Dunkirk and was an exempt fireman. Died after a long illness.

Jim Mahady—1 Year Infielder (b. 22 Apr 1901 Cortland NY–d. 9 Aug 1936 at a boarding house in Cortland NY) Died from an apparent heart attack while sleeping. Buried St Mary's Cemetery, Cortland NY.

Lou Mahaffey—1 Year Pitcher (b. 3 Jan 1874 KY–d. 26 Oct 1949 Harbor General Hospital, Torrance CA) He coached football at Kentucky State College and lived in Long Beach CA 39 years where he owned a fruit stand. Died from an intestinal hemorrhage. Buried Inglewood Park Cemetery, Inglewood CA.

Roy Mahaffey—9 Years Pitcher (b. 9 Feb 1904 Belton SC–d. 23 Jul 1969 Anderson Hospital, Anderson SC) He was a brick mason. Died after being in failing health three years and seriously ill six months. Buried Forest Lawn Memorial Park, Anderson SC.

Billy Maharg—2 Years Outfielder (b. 19 Mar 1881 Philadelphia PA–d. 20 Nov 1953 Philadelphia PA) Buried Holy Sepulchre Cemetery, Philadelphia PA.

Frank Mahar—1 Game Pinch Hitter (b. 4 Dec 1878 Natick MA–d. 5 Dec 1961 Somerville MA) Buried Forest Dale Cemetery, Malden MA.

Tom Maher—1 Game Pinch Runner (b. 6 Jul 1870 Philadelphia PA–d. 25 Aug 1929 Philadelphia PA).

Al Mahon—1 Year Pitcher (b. 23 Sep 1909 Albion NE–d. 26 Dec 1977 New Haven CT).

Chris Mahoney—1 Year Pitcher (b. 11 Jun 1885 Milton MA–d. 15 Jul 1954 Visalia CA) He was a graduate attorney but never practiced law. From 1924 to 1939 he worked for the Tulare CA Studebaker dealer. He was the steward at the Moose Hall in Tulare from 1939 until his death. Died from heart disease while working at the hall. Buried Visalia Cemetery, Visalia CA.

Dan Mahoney—2 Years Catcher (b. 20 Mar 1864 Springfield MA–d. 31 Jan 1904 Springfield MA) He worked only infrequently for tobacco growers and his habits were not steady. Died by his own hand by drinking carbolic acid. Buried St Michael's Cemetery, Springfield MA.

Danny Mahoney—1 Game Pinch Runner (b. 6 Sep 1888 Haverhill MA–d. 28 Sep 1960 St Luke's Memorial Hospital, Utica NY) Died after a long illness. Buried St Bernard's Cemetery, Waterville NY.

Mike Mahoney—2 Years Infielder (b. 5 Dec 1873 Boston MA–d. 3 Jan 1940 Carney Hospital, Boston MA) For nearly 40 years he was a policeman for the Boston Police Department. Died following a three-week illness. Buried Mount Calvary Cemetery, Roslindale MA.

Bob Maier—1 Year Outfielder (b. 16 Dec 1915 Dunellen NJ–d. 4 Aug 1993 at his home in South Plainfield NJ) For many years he was a pressman for Art Color Printing Company in Dunellen and ten years for Twin City Press Company in North Plainfield NJ, retiring in 1980. Buried Resurrection Cemetery, Piscataway NJ.

Duster Mails—7 Years Pitcher (b. 1 Oct 1895 San Quentin CA–d. 5 Jul 1974 Fort Miley Hospital, San Francisco CA) He was a longtime public relations man for the Giants. Died from prostate cancer, heart disease and complications from Parkinson's disease. Buried Mount Olivet Catholic Cemetery, San Rafael CA.

Alex Main—3 Years Pitcher (b. 13 May 1884 Montrose MI–d. 29 Dec 1965 William Beaumont Hospital, Royal Oak MI) He operated a Ford dealership at Harrisville, retiring in 1936. Buried Crestwood Memorial Cemetery, Grand Blanc MI.

Woody Main—4 Years Pitcher (b. 12 Feb 1922 Delano CA–d. 27 Jun 1992 Whittier Hospital, Whittier CA) Died from pneumonia two months after suffering a stroke. Buried North Kern Cemetery, Delano CA.

Jim Mains—1 Year Pitcher (b. 12 Jun 1922 Bridgton ME–d. 17 Mar 1969 Portland ME) Like his father, he manufactured bats from 1949 until his death. Died from cancer. Buried South High Street Cemetery, Bridgton ME.

Willard Mains—3 Years Pitcher (b. 7 Jul 1868 North Windham ME–d. 23 May 1923 at his home in Bridgton ME) During a 20 year minor league career between 1887 and 1906 he won 319 games while losing only 181. When he died unexpectedly from heart failure he was making baseball bats for a select line of customers who liked his particular pattern. Buried South High Street Cemetery, Bridgton ME.

Charlie Maisel—1 Year Catcher (b. 21 Apr 1894 Catonsville MD–d. 25 Aug 1953 at his home in Baltimore MD) Buried Lorraine Park Cemetery, Baltimore MD.

Fritz Maisel—6 Years Infielder (b. 23 Dec 1889 Catonsville MD–d. 22 Apr 1967 St Agnes Hospital, Baltimore MD) The chief of the Baltimore County Fire Department from 1938 to 1951, he was associated with the minor league Orioles 58 years as a player, manager, scout, director and stockholder. Died after a month's illness. Buried Lorraine Park Cemetery, Baltimore MD.

George Maisel—4 Years Outfielder (b. 12 May 1892 Catonsville MD–d. 20 Nov 1968 Union Memorial Hospital, Baltimore MD) Served as an ambulance driver for the U.S. Army during World War I. He was a supervisor for Consolidated Engineering Co, Inc, and later was an official for the Baltimore County Sanitation Bureau, retiring in 1965. Died after a short illness. Buried Baltimore National Cemetery, Baltimore MD.

Hank Majeski—13 Years Infielder (b. 13 Dec 1916 Staten Island NY–d. 9 Aug 1991 at his home in Staten Island NY) Served in the U.S. Coast Guard during World War II. He coached baseball at Wagnor College on Staten Island. He was a scout for several teams and was a batting instructor for the Astros. Died from cancer. Cremated.

Frank Makosky—1 Year Pitcher (b. 20 Jan 1912 Boonton NJ–d. 10 Jan 1987 Stroudsburg PA).

Dave Malarcher—12 Years Infielder 7 Years Manager (b. 18 Oct 1894 Whitehall LA–d. 11 May 1982 St Bernard Hospital, Chicago IL) World War I veteran. He played in the negro leagues and was a real estate broker and a published poet, writing three book-length epic poems and several shorter poems. Died after a brief illness. Buried Convent LA.

Bill Malarkey—1 Year Pitcher (b. 26 Nov 1878 Port Byron IL–d. 12 Dec 1956 St Joseph's Hospital, Phoenix AZ) He pitched several years in the high minor leagues. He lived in Uvalde TX before moving to Kingman AZ in 1933, retiring from Citizen's Utilities Company in 1951. Buried Mountain View Cemetery, Kingman AZ.

John Malarkey—6 Years Pitcher (b. 10 May 1872 Springfield OH–d. 29 Oct 1949 Cincinnati OH).

Charlie Malay—1 Year Infielder (b. 13 Jun 1879 Brooklyn NY–d. 18 Sep 1949 Brooklyn NY) He was well-known at the Brooklyn Parade Grounds where he coached teen-age boys in baseball. He worked for Berggren Machine Company in Brooklyn. Died after a brief illness. Buried Holy Cross Cemetery, Brooklyn NY.

Joe Malay—2 Years Infielder (b. 25 Oct 1905 Brooklyn NY–d. 19 Mar 1989 St Vincent's Medical Center, Bridgeport CT) He was a supervisor at the Bridgeport Brass Company. Buried St Michael's Cemetery, Bridgeport CT.

Cy Malis—1 Year Pitcher (b. 26 Feb 1907 Philadelphia PA–d. 12 Jan 1971 Valley Doctor's Hosp, North Hollywood CA) He was an actor for Metro-Goldwyn-Mayer Studio for 35 years. Died from a heart attack. Buried Valhalla Memorial Park, North Hollywood CA.

Les Mallon—4 Years Infielder (b. 21 Nov 1905 Sweetwater TX–d. 17 Apr 1991 Hood County Hospital, Granbury TX) Served in the U.S. Navy during World War II. An avid golfer, fisherman and card player, he was sales manager for White Rose Distributing. Buried Acton Cemetery, Acton TX.

Ben Mallonee—1 Year Outfielder (b. 31 Mar 1894 Baltimore MD–d. 19 Feb 1978 Union Memorial Hospital, Baltimore MD) Served in France for the U.S. Army during World War I. He worked 17 years for Bethlehem Steel Corp at Sparrows Point, retiring in 1955. Died after a long illness. Buried Druid Ridge Cemetery, Pikesville MD.

Jule Mallonee—1 Year Outfielder (b. 4 Apr 1900 Charlotte NC–d. 26 Dec 1934 Mercy Hospital, Charlotte NC) He worked with his brother in the Mallonee Company before moving to a Charlotte branch of the Home Owners Loan Corporation where he worked when he became ill. Died after an illness of three months. Buried Elmwood Cemetery, Charlotte NC.

Alex Malloy—1 Year Pitcher (b. 31 Oct 1886 Laurinburg NC–d. 1 Mar 1961 Ferris TX) Buried Park Cemetery, Ferris TX.

Herm Malloy—2 Years Pitcher (b. 1 Jun 1885 Massillon OH–d. 9 May 1942 Molly Stark Sanitarium, Massillon OH) He was a hotel clerk. Died from pulmonary tuberculosis. Buried St Joseph's Cemetery, Massillon OH.

Harry Malmberg—1 Year Infielder (b. 31 Jul 1925 Fairfield AL–d. 29 Oct 1976 V A Hospital, Martinez CA) Served in World War II. He was a car salesman in Antioch CA for 29 years. Died from pancreatic cancer. Buried Holy Cross Cemetery, Antioch CA.

Fergy Malone—2 Years Catcher 1 Year Manager (b. abt 1839 Ireland–d. 18 Jan 1905 Seattle WA) He was a special agent of the U.S. Treasury Department- Puget Sound District. Died from alcohol poisoning in the back of a hack near the Grand Opera House after a prolonged drinking spree. Buried New Cathedral Cemetery, Philadelphia PA.

Lew Malone—4 Years Infielder (b. 13 Mar 1897 Baltimore MD–d. 17 Feb 1972 Brooklyn NY) Buried St Patrick's Cemetery, Southold NY.

Pat Malone—10 Years Pitcher (b. 25 Sep 1902 Altoona PA–d. 13 May 1943 Mercy Hospital, Altoona PA) Served in the U.S. Army cavalry during World War I. Died from acute pancreatitis. Cremated. Buried Milan OH.

Billy Maloney—6 Years Outfielder (b. 5 Jun 1878 Lewiston ME–d. 2 Sep 1960 Stephens Memorial Hospital, Breckenridge TX) Died from prostate cancer. Buried St Mary's Cemetery, North Attleboro MA.

Charlie Maloney—1 Year Pitcher (b. 22 May 1886 Cambridge MA–d. 17 Jan 1967 Arlington

MA) He was an assistant deputy at the Massachusetts Reformatory at Concord MA.

Pat Maloney—1 Year Outfielder (b. 19 Jan 1888 Grosvenordale CT–d. 27 Jun 1979 Memorial Hospital, Cumberland RI) A wound suffered in France while serving in the U.S. Army during World War I shortened his baseball career. Buried St Joseph Cemetery, Berkeley RI.

Paul Maloy—1 Year Pitcher (b. 4 Jun 1892 Bascom OH–d. 18 May 1976 Sandusky OH).

Gordon Maltzberger—4 Years Pitcher (b. 4 Sep 1912 Utopia TX–d. 11 Dec 1974 Community Hospital, San Bernardino CA) World War II veteran. He was a coach, scout and minor league manager, working in baseball until 1973. Died from pancreatic cancer. Buried Hermosa Cemetery, Colton CA.

Al Mamaux—12 Years Pitcher (b. 30 May 1894 Pittsburgh PA–d. 31 Dec 1962 City Hospital, Santa Monica CA) He was a guard at Pacific Ocean Park, an amusement center, for several years. Died from a heart attack. Buried Forest Lawn-Hollywood Hills, Los Angeles CA.

Gus Mancuso—17 Years Catcher (b. 5 Dec 1905 Galveston TX–d. 26 Oct 1984 at a hospital in Houston TX) He coached and was a sportscaster in St Louis MO. A lifelong resident of Houston, he had been inducted into the Texas Sports Hall of Fame. Buried Forest Park of Lawndale, Houston TX.

Carl Manda—1 Year Infielder (b. 16 Nov 1886 Little River KS–d. 9 Mar 1983 Artesia General Hospital, Artesia NM) He played professional baseball for 15 years and moved to Artesia in 1928 where he farmed until retirement in 1972. Thought to be the oldest living professional baseball player when he died. Buried Woodbine Cemetery, Artesia NM.

Leo Mangum—7 Years Pitcher (b. 24 May 1896 Durham NC–d. 9 Jul 1974 St Rita's Hospital, Lima OH) He was a proprietor of a bowling alley in Lima for 31 years, retiring in 1968. Cremated.

George Mangus—1 Year Outfielder (b. 22 May 1890 Red Creek NY–d. 10 Aug 1933 Rutland MA).

Clyde Manion—13 Years Catcher (b. 30 Oct 1896 Jefferson City MO–d. 4 Sep 1967 Detroit MI) World War I veteran. For 42 years he was an agent for Equitable Life Assurance Society. Buried Holy Sepulchre Cemetery, Southfield MI.

Charlie Manlove—1 Year Catcher (b. 8 Oct 1862 Philadelphia PA–d. 12 Feb 1952 Mercy Hospital, Altoona PA) He operated a cigar store in Altoona for several years and worked as a machinist in the Pennsylvania Railroad Altoona shops for 25 years. Died after being ill for some time. Buried Oakridge Cemetery, Altoona PA.

Fred Mann—6 Years Outfielder (b. 1 Apr 1858 Windsor VT–d. 6 Apr 1916 Springfield Hospital, Springfield MA) He engaged in the hotel business in Springfield for 20 years until becoming ill. Died after an illness of one week. Buried Oak Grove Cemetery, Springfield MA.

Garth Mann—1 Game Pinch Runner (b. 16 Nov 1911 Brandon TX–d. 11 Sep 1980 Tenery Community Hospital, Italy TX) He owned and operated Associated Aircraft Supply Company with his two brothers in Dallas TX, retiring to Italy about 1965. There he owned the Black Meadow Farm where he raised thoroughbred horses. Buried Laurel Land Memorial Park, Dallas TX.

Johnny Mann—1 Year Infielder (b. 4 Feb 1898 Fontanet IN–d. 31 Mar 1977 Union Hospital, Terre Haute IN) Buried Calvary Cemetery, Terre Haute IN.

Les Mann—16 Years Outfielder (b. 18 Nov 1893 Lincoln NE–d. 14 Jan 1962 Pasadena CA) He was a sports specialist for the Los Angeles CA Parks and Recreation Department for six years. Died from a heart attack while driving his car. Cremated.

Ernie Manning—1 Year Pitcher (b. 9 Oct 1890 Florala AL–d. 28 Apr 1973 at a hospital in Pensacola FL) A lifelong resident of Florala, he was the postmaster there. Buried Greenwood Cemetery, Florala AL.

Jack Manning—9 Years Outfielder (b. 20 Dec 1853 Braintree MA–d. 15 Aug 1929 Boston MA) He was a theatrical mechanic in the performing arts industry. Died after being in ill health several months. Buried New Calvary Cemetery, Mattapan MA.

Jimmy Manning—5 Years Outfielder 1 Year Manager (b. 31 Jan 1862 Fall River MA–d. 21 Oct 1929 Houston TX) One of the original team owners in the American League, he moved to

Houston as a land appraiser for the Gulf Coast Lines division of the Missouri Pacific Railroad after selling the interest in his team. Buried North Burial Ground, Fall River MA.

Rube Manning—4 Years Pitcher (b. 29 Apr 1883 Chambersburg PA–d. 23 Apr 1930 Williamsport Hospital, Williamsport PA) He worked for the Lycoming Rubber Company in Williamsport. Died from a heart attack suffered two days earlier while bowling. Buried Wildwood Cemetery, Williamsport PA.

Tim Manning—4 Years Infielder (b. 3 Aug 1853 Henley, England–d. 11 Jun 1934 Oak Park IL) Buried Calvary Cemetery, Evanston IL.

Don Manno—2 Years Outfielder (b. 4 May 1915 Williamsport PA–d. 11 Mar 1995 Williamsport Home, Williamsport PA) Served in the U.S. Navy during World War II. He managed minor league baseball for a few years, then was an agent for Baltimore Life Insurance Company for many years. He retired as director of the insurance division for Little League Baseball, Inc. For 45 years he officiated local and collegiate baseball, football and basketball. Died after an extended illness. Buried Wildwood Cemetery, Williamsport PA.

John Mansell—1 Year Outfielder (b. 1861 Auburn NY–d. 20 Feb 1925 Willard NY).

Mike Mansell—5 Years Outfielder (b. 15 Jan 1858 Auburn NY–d. 4 Dec 1902 at his home in Auburn NY) He conducted a business at Auburn. Died from pneumonia. Buried St Joseph's Cemetery, Auburn NY.

Tom Mansell—3 Years Outfielder (b. 1 Jan 1855 Auburn NY–d. 6 Oct 1934 at the home of his sister in Auburn NY) He was a policeman at Kansas City KS, where he lived for 44 years. He became chief-of-police there. Buried St Joseph's Cemetery, Auburn NY.

Lou Manske—1 Year Pitcher (b. 4 Jul 1884 Milwaukee WI–d. 27 Apr 1963 at his home in Milwaukee WI) Buried Arlington Park Cemetery, Milwaukee WI.

Mickey Mantle—18 Years Outfielder Hall of Fame (b. 20 Oct 1931 Spavinaw OK–d. 13 Aug 1995 Baylor University Medical Center, Waco TX) Died from liver cancer. After his death his family became involved in organ transplant awareness programs. Buried Sparkman-Hillcrest Memorial Park, Dallas TX.

Moxie Manuel—2 Years Pitcher (b. 16 Oct 1881 Metroplis IL–d. 26 Apr 1924 St Joseph's Hospital, Memphis TN) He was active in the mercantile business at Pascola MO the last 24 years of his life. Died from peritonitis. Buried Kennett Cemetery, Kennett MO.

Frank Manush—1 Year Infielder (b. 18 Sep 1883 Tuscumbia AL–d. 5 Jan 1965 South Coast Community Hosp, Laguna Beach CA) For 35 years he owned and operated a cotton gin. Died from a pulmonary embolism. Buried Good Shepherd Cemetery, Huntington Beach CA.

Heinie Manush—17 Years Outfielder Hall of Fame (b. 20 Jul 1901 Tuscumbia AL–d. 12 May 1971 Extendicare Nursing Home, Sarasota FL) Died from throat cancer. Buried Sarasota Memorial Park, Sarasota FL.

Rolla Mapel—1 Year Pitcher (b. 9 Mar 1890 Lee's Summit MO–d. 6 Apr 1966 U.S. Naval Hospital, San Diego CA) World War I veteran. He was a clerk at a cigar store. Died from heart disease. Buried Fort Rosecrans National Cemetery, Point Loma CA.

Cliff Mapes—5 Years Outfielder (b. 13 Mar 1922 Sutherland NE–d. 5 Dec 1996 at his home in Pryor OK) Served in the U.S. Navy during World War II. He worked for John Deere and Nipak until the plant closed. He then worked for the State of Oklahoma at the Whitaker State Home. Died in his sleep. Buried Graham Memorial Cemetery, Pryor OK.

Howard Maple—1 Year Catcher (b. 20 Jul 1903 Adrian MO–d. 9 Nov 1970 Emanuel Hospital, Portland OR) Served in Alaska for the U.S. Army Corps of Engineers during World War II. Playing both professional baseball and football, he managed some minor league baseball and coached college football and baseball. He owned a sporting goods store in Salem OR and a car dealership at Bend OR. Later he worked for several Oregon city's chambers of commerce and managed the Oregon State Fair. Died from heart failure following a successful hip replacement. Buried Belcrest Memorial Park, Salem OR.

George Mappes—2 Years Infielder (b. 25 Dec 1865 St Louis MO–d. 20 Feb 1934 St Louis MO) Buried Calvary Cemetery, St Louis MO.

Rabbit Maranville—23 Years Infielder 1 Year Manager Hall of Fame (b. 11 Nov 1891 Springfield MA–d. 5 Jan 1954 at his home in New York

City NY) He played minor league baseball until he was 47 years old and managed minor league baseball for a number of years. Died from a heart attack while watching television. Buried St Michael's Cemetery, Springfield MA.

Firpo Marberry—14 Years Pitcher (b. 30 Nov 1898 Streetman TX–d. 30 Jun 1976 Memorial Hospital, Mexia TX) His baseball career was cut short by an automobile accident in which he lost his arm. Buried Birdston Cemetery, Streetman TX.

Walt Marbet—1 Year Pitcher (b. 13 Sep 1890 Plymouth County IA–d. 24 Sep 1956 Hohenwald TN) Buried Swiss Cemetery, Hohenwald TN.

Oliver Marcelle—13 Years Infielder (b. 24 Jun 1897 Thibedeaux LA–d. 12 Jun 1949 Denver CO) He played in the negro leagues.

Phil Marchildon—9 Years Pitcher (b. 25 Oct 1913 Penetanguishene, Ontario, Canada–d. 10 Jan 1997 Grace Hospital, Toronto, Ontario, Canada) Served in the Royal Canadian Air Force during World War II. Cremated.

Johnny Marcum—7 Years Pitcher (b. 9 Sep 1908 Campbellsburg KY–d. 10 Sep 1984 Jewish Hospital, Louisville KY) He lived at Eminence KY where he operated a dairy and tobacco farm. Buried Eminence Cemetery, Eminence KY.

Dan Marion—2 Years Pitcher (b. 31 Jul 1890 Cleveland OH–d. 19 Jan 1933 County Hospital, Milwaukee WI) He operated the Maple Leaf Roadhouse near Milwaukee. Died from a hemorrhage after he was found dying in a roominghouse. He was penniless and friends came to the rescue and provided funds for a funeral. Buried Mount Olivet Cemetery, Milwaukee WI.

Red Marion—2 Years Outfielder (b. 14 Mar 1914 Richburg SC–d. 12 Mar 1975 Valley Medical Center, San Jose CA) He managed minor league baseball until 1963 when he retired, ending a 30-year baseball career. Died from lactic acidosia and shock from hemorrhaging. Buried Cedar Lawn Memorial Park, Fremont CA.

Roger Maris—12 Years Outfielder (b. 10 Sep 1934 Hibbing MN–d. 14 Dec 1985 M D Anderson Hospital, Houston TX) He is best known for hitting 61 home runs in 1961. Died from lymphatic cancer. Buried Holy Cross Cemetery, Fargo ND.

Duke Markell—1 Year Pitcher (b. 17 Aug 1923 Paris, France–d. 14 Jun 1984 Fort Lauderdale FL).

Cliff Markle—5 Years Pitcher (b. 3 May 1894 Dravosburg PA–d. 24 May 1974 at his home in Temple City CA) He was warehouse foreman for Westinghouse-Parker, a manufacturing company, for ten years. Died from heart disease. Buried Resurrection Cemetery, San Gabriel CA.

Dick Marlowe—6 Years Pitcher (b. 27 Jun 1929 Hickory NC–d. 30 Dec 1968 City Hospital, Toledo OH) He was the plant manager for Perfect Measure Tape Company in Toledo for ten years. Died after a six-day illness. Buried Toledo Memorial Park, Sylvania OH.

Jim Maroney—3 Years Pitcher (b. 4 Dec 1885 Boston MA–d. 26 Feb 1929 Philadelphia PA).

Rube Marquard—18 Years Pitcher Hall of Fame (b. 9 Oct 1889 Cleveland OH–d. 1 Jun 1980 at his home in Pikesville MD) Died from cancer. Buried Hebrew Cemetery, Baltimore MD.

Ollie Marquardt—1 Year Infielder (b. 22 Sep 1902 Toledo OH–d. 7 Feb 1968 Magruder Hospital, Port Clinton OH) He managed minor league baseball for a while. For 20 years he owned Marquardt Construction Company in Toledo. Died from a heart attack while fishing off Rock Ledge in Lake Erie. Buried Toledo Memorial Park, Sylvania OH.

Gonzalo Marquez—3 Years Infielder (b. 31 Mar 1946 Carupano, Venezuela–d. 19 Dec 1984 Carcas, Venezuela).

Luis Marquez—2 Years Outfielder (b. 28 Oct 1925 Aguadilla, Puerto Rico–d. 1 Mar 1988 Aguadilla, Puerto Rico) Died after being shot during a family argument.

Jim Marquis—1 Year Pitcher (b. 18 Nov 1900 Yoakum TX–d. 5 Aug 1992 Amador Hospital, Jackson CA) He owned and operated a furniture store for 40 years. Died from an obstruction of the small bowell. Cremated.

Lefty Marr—4 Years Outfielder (b. 19 Sep 1862 Cincinnati OH–d. 11 Jan 1912 at his hotel room in New Britain CT) He was a bartender at a number of saloons in New Britain and was also a janitor at the hotel where he lived.

Bill Marriott—6 Years Infielder (b. 18 Apr 1893 Pratt KS–d. 11 Aug 1969 Elwood Convalescent Hospital, Berkeley CA) For ten years he was a foreman for Pacific Gas and Electric. Died from a heart attack. Buried Mountain View Cemetery, Oakland CA.

Buck Marrow—3 Years Pitcher (b. 29 Aug 1909 Tarboro NC–d. 21 Nov 1982 Riverside Hospital, Newport News VA) He served as a city councilman in Newport News and retired from the City Assessor's Office. He owned and operated a tire store in Newport News. Buried Peninsula Memorial Park, Newport News VA.

Ed Mars—1 Year Pitcher (b. 4 Dec 1866 Chicago IL–d. 9 Dec 1941 Chicago IL) Buried Oak Woods Cemetery, Chicago IL.

Armando Marsans—8 Years Outfielder (b. 3 Oct 1887 Matanzas, Cuba–d. 3 Sep 1960 Havana, Cuba) Buried Christopher Columbus Necropolis, Havana, Cuba.

Bill Marshall—2 Years Infielder (b. 14 Feb 1911 Dorchester MA–d. 5 May 1977 Sacramento CA) He was a scout for the Braves. Died from cirrhosis with anasarca. Buried St Mary's Cemetery, Sacramento CA.

Doc Marshall—5 Years Catcher (b. 22 Sep 1875 Butler PA–d. 11 Dec 1959 at his home in Clinton IL) He practiced medicine in Clinton IL for 46 years. Buried Woodlawn Cemetery, Clinton IL.

Joe Marshall—2 Years Outfielder (b. 19 Feb 1876 Audubon MN–d. 11 Sep 1931 Norwalk CA).

Max Marshall—3 Years Outfielder (b. 18 Sep 1913 Shenandoah IA–d. 16 Sep 1993 Salem OR) Served in the U.S. Navy during World War II. He was a retired recreation officer. Buried Belcrest Memorial Park, Salem OR.

Rube Marshall—4 Years Pitcher (b. 19 Jul 1890 Salineville OH–d. 11 Jun 1980 New Dawn Health Center, Dover OH) He was a scout for the Indians. A butcher, for 40 years he was a partner in Marsh and Marshall Meat Market in Dover. He also owned a bowling alley in New Philadelphia OH. Buried Evergreen Burial Park, New Philadelphia OH.

Marty Martel—2 Years Catcher (b. 29 Jan 1883 Weymouth MA–d. 11 Oct 1947 at his home in Washington DC) Served in the U.S. Army Medical Corps during World War I. He was a prominent surgeon and gynecologist in Washington DC and a professor of gynecology at Georgetown University. Buried Arlington National Cemetery, Arlington VA.

Babe Martin—6 Years Outfielder (b. 28 Mar 1920 Columbia SC–d. 31 Oct 1997 Columbia SC) Served in the U.S. Navy during World War II. He was a conductor on the Atlantic Coastline Railroad. Buried Greenlawn Memorial Park, Columbia SC.

Bill Martin—1 Year Infielder (b. 13 Feb 1894 Washington DC–d. 14 Sep 1949 Washington DC) He operated a tavern in Georgetown from 1934 until his death. Died following a stroke. Buried Cedar Hill Cemetery, Suitland MD.

Billy Martin—11 Years Infielder 16 Years Manager (b. 16 May 1928 Berkeley CA–d. 25 Dec 1989 Johnson City NY) He worked in baseball his entire life. Fired four times as manager of the Yankees, he quit once. Died from injuries suffered in an automobile accident. Buried Gate of Heaven Cemetery, Hawthorne NY.

Doc Martin—3 Years Pitcher (b. 23 Sep 1887 Roxbury MA–d. 15 Apr 1935 Milton MA) He practiced medicine in Roxbury from 1914 until his death. Died following an illness of six weeks. Buried Milton Cemetery, Milton MA.

Frank Martin—3 Years Infielder (b. 28 Feb 1879 Chicago IL–d. 30 Sep 1924 Chicago IL) Buried Calvary Cemetery, Evanston IL.

Freddie Martin—3 Years Pitcher (b. 27 Jun 1915 Williams OK–d. 11 Jun 1979 Northwestern Memorial Hospital, Evanston IL) Served in the U.S. Army during World War II. For 14 years he was a minor league instructor for the Cubs and Tigers. Died from lung cancer.

Herschel Martin—6 Years Outfielder (b. 19 Sep 1909 Birmingham AL–d. 17 Nov 1980 Cuba MO) For 17 years he was a scout for the Mets. Died after a long illness.

Jack Martin—2 Years Infielder (b. 19 Apr 1887 Plainfield NJ–d. 4 Jul 1980 Plainfield NJ) Buried Laurelton Cemetery, Laurelton NJ.

Joe Martin—1 Year Outfielder (b. 1 Jan 1876 Hollidaysburg PA–d. 25 May 1964 at his home in Altoona PA) For some years he was a partner in the Martin and Company feed business and later worked as a painter. Died after an extended illness. Buried Calvary Cemetery, Altoona PA.

Joe Martin—2 Years Infielder (b. 28 Aug 1911 Seymour MO–d. 28 Sep 1960 at the Buckingham Hotel in Buffalo NY) He operated a tavern in Buffalo and later worked at the New York Central terminal there.

Pat Martin—2 Years Pitcher (b. 13 Apr 1892 Brooklyn NY–d. 4 Feb 1949 Brooklyn NY).

Pepper Martin—13 Years Outfielder (b. 29 Feb 1904 Temple OK–d. 5 Mar 1965 McAlester OK) While operating a 970 acre ranch near McAlester, where he raised top quality Hereford beef cattle, he managed and coached minor league baseball until his death. Died from a heart attack. Buried Memorial Park Cemetery, Edmond OK.

Speed Martin—6 Years Pitcher (b. 15 Sep 1893 Wawawai WA–d. 14 Jun 1983 Cresta Loma Conv Hosp, Lemon Grove CA) Living in the San Diego CA area more than 60 years, he worked 20 years as a scheduler for General Dynamics. He was also a noted amateur golfer. Died from congestive heart failure. Cremated.

Stu Martin—8 Years Infielder (b. 17 Nov 1913 Rich Square NC–d. 11 Jan 1997 Severn NC).

Joe Martina—1 Year Pitcher (b. 8 Jul 1889 New Orleans LA–d. 22 Mar 1962 at his home in New Orleans LA) Known as "Iron Arm," he appeared in 211 games and 1313 innings for the New Orleans Pelicans of the Southern Association during a five year period between 1922 and 1927, with 108 wins and 50 losses. In a long minor league career that lasted from 1910 until 1931 he won 349 games while losing 277 and compiled an ERA of 3.22. Later he worked for the American Brewing Company. Died from a heart attack. Buried Greenwood Cemetery, New Orleans LA.

Tony Martinez—4 Years Infielder (b. 18 Mar 1940 Perico, Cuba 24–d. Aug 1991 Miami FL) Buried Vista Memorial Gardens, Hialeah FL.

Wedo Martini—1 Year Pitcher (b. 1 Jul 1913 Birmingham AL–d. 28 Oct 1970 at his home in Philadelphia PA) He drove a truck for the *Philadelphia Inquirer.* Buried St Peter and St Paul Cemetery, Springfield PA.

Joe Marty—5 Years Outfielder (b. 1 Sep 1913 Sacramento CA–d. 4 Oct 1984 Mercy Hospital, Sacramento CA) He owned and operated Joe Marty's El Chico restaurant and bar in Sacramento for 32 years, selling it in 1980. Died from a heart attack while recovering from surgery. Buried St Mary's Cemetery, Sacramento CA.

Harry Maskrey—1 Year Outfielder (b. 21 Dec 1861 Mercer PA–d. 17 Aug 1930 Mercer PA) In the hotel business with his brother, Leech, he operated a number of hotels, including the St Cloud Hotel, the Spier House and the Arlington Hotel in Greenville PA and the Sharon Hotel in Sharon PA. He also managed the Sharon Country Club. Died after a lingering illness. Buried Mercer Cemetery, Mercer PA.

Leech Maskrey—5 Years Outfielder 2 Years Manager (b. 16 Feb 1856 Mercer PA–d. 1 Apr 1922 Mercer PA) He conducted hotels in Kent OH, Warren OH and Mercer. Died from a heart attack. Buried Mercer Cemetery, Mercer PA.

Charlie Mason—1 Year Outfielder 3 Years Manager (b. 25 Jun 1853 New Orleans LA–d. 21 Oct 1936 at his home in Germantown PA) At one time a co-owner of the Athletics, he was the originator of "Ladies Day" and was the first to suggest that a batter hit by a pitch should be awarded first base. Buried Hillside Cemetery, Roslyn PA.

Del Mason—3 Years Pitcher (b. 29 Oct 1883 Newfane NY–d. 31 Dec 1962 at his home in Winter Park FL) He coached baseball at Rollins College ten years and was the former owner of Winter Park Auto Company. Buried Palm Cemetery, Winter Park FL.

Ernie Mason—1 Year Pitcher (b. New Orleans LA–d. 30 Jul 1904 Covington LA).

Bill Massey—1 Year Infielder (b. Jan 1871 Philadelphia PA–d. 9 Oct 1940 Manila, Philippines).

Mike Massey—1 Year Infielder (b. 28 Sep 1893 Galveston TX–d. 17 Oct 1971 Fairfield Hospital, Shreveport LA) Died following a lengthy illness. Buried Forest Park Cemetery, Shreveport LA.

Roy Massey—1 Year Outfielder (b. 9 Oct 1890 Sevierville TN–d. 23 Jun 1954 at a hospital in Atlanta GA) He was co-founder and chairman of the board of Massey and Fair Food Brokers of Atlanta. Died after a lengthy illness. Buried Westview Cemetery, Atlanta GA.

Walt Masters—3 Years Pitcher (b. 28 Mar 1907 Pen Argyl PA–d. 10 Jul 1992 Ottawa, Ontario, Canada).

Joe Mathes—3 Years Infielder (b. 28 Jul 1891 Milwaukee WI–d. 21 Dec 1978 St Louis MO).

Bill Mathews—1 Year Pitcher (b. 12 Jan 1878

Mahanoy City PA–d. 23 Jan 1946 at his home in Mount Carbon PA) Served in Puerto Rico during the Spanish-American War. He was a watchman for the Silver Creek Water Company. Died from complications following a short illness. Buried Calvary Cemetery, Pottsville PA.

Bobby Mathews—10 Years Pitcher (b. 21 Nov 1851 Baltimore MD–d. 17 Apr 1898 at his parent's home in Baltimore MD) Died from brain trouble and a complication of diseases after suffering from paresis brought on by a bout with syphilis.

Eddie Mathews—17 Years Infielder 3 Years Manager Hall of Fame (b. 13 Oct 1931 Texarkana TX–d. 18 Feb 2001 Scripps Memorial Hospital, La Jolla CA) Served in the military. He worked in a variety of posts for the Braves, Brewers and Athletics. Died from congestive heart failure, lung problems and pneumonia after being hospitalized five months. He had been in fragile health several years after he was pinned between a cruise ship and a pier while on a Caribbean cruise, crushing his pelvis. Cremated. Buried Santa Barbara Cemetery, Santa Barbara CA.

Christy Mathewson—17 Years Pitcher 3 Years Manager Hall of Fame (b. 12 Aug 1880 Factoryville PA–d. 7 Oct 1925 Saranac Lake NY) He was compelled to leave baseball when he contracted tuberculosis. Died from the dread disease after several years illness. Buried Lewisburg Cemetery, Lewisburg PA.

Henry Mathewson—2 Years Pitcher (b. 24 Dec 1886 Factoryville PA–d. 1 Jul 1917 Factoryville PA) Died from tuberculosis. Buried Factoryville Cemetery, Factoryville PA.

Jimmy Mathison—1 Year Infielder (b. Nov 1878 Baltimore MD–d. 4 Jul 1911 Mercy Hospital, Baltimore MD).

Leroy Matlock—9 Years Pitcher (b. 12 Mar 1907 Moberly MO–d. 6 Feb 1968 St Paul MN) He played in the negro leagues. Buried Elmhurst Cemetery, St Paul MN.

Al Mattern—5 Years Pitcher (b. 16 Jun 1883 West Rush NY–d. 6 Nov 1958 at his home in West Rush NY) He owned and operated an automobile dealership in West Rush. Buried Pine Hill Cemetery, Rush NY.

Henry Matteson—2 Years Pitcher (b. 7 Sep 1884 Guy's Mills PA–d. 8 Sep 1943 Westfield Hospital, Westfield NY) Died following a short illness. Buried Evergreen Cemetery, Portland NY.

Joe Matthews—1 Year Pitcher (b. 29 Sep 1898 Baltimore MD–d. 8 Feb 1968 Washington County Hospital, Hagerstown MD) World War I veteran. Buried Rose Hill Cemetery, Hagerstown MD.

Wid Matthews—3 Years Outfielder (b. 20 Oct 1896 Raleigh IL–d. 5 Oct 1965 at a hotel in West Hollywood CA) World War I veteran. He was a scout for the Cardinals from 1936 to 1943 and for the Dodgers from 1943 to 1950. He was player-personnel manager for the Cubs and Braves, and was later assistant general manager for the Mets. He was a scout for the Angels when he died. Died from a heart attack. Buried Roseland Park Cemetery, Hattiesburg MS.

Dale Matthewson—2 Years Pitcher (b. 15 May 1923 Catasauqua PA–d. 20 Feb 1984 Union General Hospital, Blairsville GA) Buried Union Memory Gardens, Blairsville GA.

Wally Mattick—3 Years Outfielder (b. 12 Mar 1887 St Louis MO–d. 5 Nov 1968 Sunny Terrace Conv Hospital, Sunnyvale CA) For 15 years he was an engineer for the City of St Louis. Died from lung cancer and hemorrhaging from a duadenal ulcer. Buried Calvary Cemetery, St Louis MO.

Mike Mattimore—4 Years Outfielder (b. 1859 Renova PA–d. 29 Apr 1931 Butte MT) Buried Holy Cross Cemetery, Butte MT.

Earl Mattingly—1 Year Pitcher (b. 4 Nov 1904 Newport MD–d. 8 Sep 1993 Brookeville MD) Buried Cedar Hill Cemetery, Suitland MD.

Ralph Mattis—1 Year Outfielder (b. 24 Aug 1890 Roxborough PA–d. 13 Sep 1960 Williamsport Hospital, Williamsport PA).

Cloy Mattox—1 Year Catcher (b. 21 Nov 1902 Leesville VA–d. 2 Sep 1985 Oak Grove Lodge, Chatham VA) Buried Greenpond Baptist Church Cemetery, Chatham VA.

Jim Mattox—2 Years Catcher (b. 17 Dec 1896 Leesville VA–d. 12 Oct 1973 Myrtle Beach SC).

Harry Matuzak—2 Years Pitcher (b. 27 Jan 1910 Omer MI–d. 16 Nov 1978 Fairhope AL) He was a retired equipment operator. Buried Belforest Catholic Cemetery, Belforest AL.

Hal Mauck—1 Year Pitcher (b. 6 Mar 1869

Princeton IN–d. 27 Apr 1921 at his home in Princeton IN) He umpired in the Three-I League and the Southern Association for a few years before becoming a special agent for the Southern Railroad. Later he was a marshall in Princeton. For nine years he was deputy fish and game commissioner of Indiana. Died following an illness of several weeks. Buried Warnock Cemetery, Patoka IN.

Al Maul—15 Years Pitcher (b. 9 Oct 1865 Philadelphia PA–d. 3 May 1958 Sharon Hall Nursing Home, Philadelphia PA) He scouted college teams and worked in the ticket departments of both the Athletics and Phillies. Buried Holy Redeemer Cemetery, Philadelphia PA.

Mark Mauldin—1 Year Infielder (b. 5 Nov 1914 Atlanta GA–d. 2 Sep 1990 Southwest Christian Hospice, Union City GA) A professional golfer, he retired as Fulton County, GA, parks superintendent. Died from colon cancer. Buried Forest Lawn Memorial Gardens, College Park GA.

Ernie Maun—2 Years Pitcher (b. 3 Feb 1901 Clearwater KS–d. 1 Jan 1987 at a hospital in Corpus Christi TX) He lived in Falfurrias TX since 1929, operating a farm there. Buried Falfurrias Burial Park, Falfurrias TX.

Dick Mauney—3 Years Pitcher (b. 26 Jan 1920 Concord NC–d. 6 Feb 1970 Albemarle NC) He worked for Wiscassett Mills Company. Died from a heart attack. Buried Fairview Memorial Park, Albemarle NC.

Harry Maupin—2 Years Pitcher (b. 11 Jul 1872 Wellsville MO–d. 25 Aug 1952 Parsons KS) He was a conductor for the Katy Railroad from 1907 until retiring in 1937. Died from a heart attack. Buried Oakwood Cemetery, Parsons KS.

Bert Maxwell—4 Years Pitcher (b. 17 Oct 1886 Texarkana AR–d. 10 Dec 1961 at his home in Brady TX) He operated a general store, lumberyard and cotton buying business from 1921 until retiring in 1954. Died in his sleep. Buried Rest Haven Cemetery, Brady TX.

Buckshot May—1 Year Pitcher (b. 13 Dec 1899 Bakersfield CA–d. 15 Mar 1984 Bakersfield CA) For 30 years he was an oil drilling superintendent in South America for Cabeen Exploration Corporation and Santa Fe Drilling Company. He retired to and lived his last 17 years in Bakersfield, his hometown. Died from pneumonia. Buried Greenlawn Memorial Park, Bakersfield CA.

Jakie May—14 Years Pitcher (b. 25 Nov 1895 Youngville NC–d. 3 Jun 1970 Wendell NC) Buried Montlawn Memorial Park, Raleigh NC.

Jerry May—10 Years Catcher (b. 14 Dec 1943 Staunton VA–d. 30 Jun 1996 Swoope VA) The president of Transit Mixed Concrete Corporation and owner of May Trucking, he also operated the family farm and was a former member of the Augusta County (VA) Board of Supervisors. Died when a tractor he was repairing fell off a jack, crushing him. Buried Presbyterian Church Cemetery, Churchville VA.

Ed Mayer—2 Years Infielder (b. 16 Aug 1866 Marshall IL–d. 18 May 1913 Chicago IL).

Erskine Mayer—8 Years Pitcher (b. 16 Jan 1890 Atlanta GA–d. 10 Mar 1957 at his home in Los Angeles CA) He was a refrigerator salesman. Died from a heart attack. Buried Forest Lawn Memorial Park, Glendale CA.

Sam Mayer—1 Year Outfielder (b. 28 Feb 1893 Atlanta GA–d. 1 Jul 1962 at his home in Atlanta GA) He was a real estate salesman for D L Stokes Realty Company in Atlanta. Buried Decatur Cemetery, Decatur GA.

Wally Mayer—7 Years Catcher (b. 8 Jul 1890 Cincinnati OH–d. 18 Nov 1951 Glen Lake Sanitorium, Minneapolis MN) Cremated. Buried Cincinnati OH.

Paddy Mayes—1 Year Outfielder (b. 17 Mar 1885 Locust Grove OK–d. 28 May 1962 Fayetteville AR).

Buster Maynard—4 Years Outfielder (b. 25 Mar 1913 Henderson NC–d. 7 Sep 1977 V A Hospital, Durham NC) World War II veteran. A retired textile worker, he lived at Henderson NC. Died after an illness of seven years. Buried Union Chapel Church Cemetery, Henderson NC.

Chick Maynard—1 Year Infielder (b. 2 Nov 1896 Turner Falls MA–d. 31 Jan 1957 at a hospital in Bangor ME) World War I veteran. He was superintendent of the ground wood department for Great Northern Paper Company. Died following a brief illness. Buried Millinocket Cemetery, Millinocket ME.

Al Mays—6 Years Pitcher (b. 17 May 1865 Canal Dover OH–d. 7 May 1905 Parkersburg

WV) Drowned in the Ohio River at the head of Blennerhassett Island. Buried Odd Fellows Cemetery, Parkersburg WV.

Carl Mays—15 Years Pitcher (b. 12 Nov 1891 Liberty KY–d. 4 Apr 1971 Valley Hospital, El Cajon CA) Served in the U.S. Army during World War I. He threw the pitch that killed Ray Chapman in 1920. He pitched the first game ever played at Yankee Stadium and was a scout for 20 years for the Indians and the Braves. Died from pneumonia and a heart ailment. Buried Riverview Cemetery, Portland OR.

Mel Mazzera—5 Years Outfielder (b. 31 Jan 1914 Stockton CA–d. 17 Dec 1997 St Joseph's Medical Center, Stockton CA) He was a Stockton police officer for 24 years. Died from a ruptured abdominal aortic aneurysm. Buried San Joaquin Catholic Cemetery, Stockton CA.

Jack McAdams—1 Year Pitcher (b. 17 Dec 1886 Benton AR–d. 21 May 1937 San Francisco CA) He worked for the Missouri Pacific Railroad. Buried Bryant Cemetery, Benton AR.

Bill McAfee—5 Years Pitcher (b. 7 Sep 1907 Smithville GA–d. 8 Jul 1958 Culpeper VA) He was the distributor for International Harvestor products in Albany GA. He was serving his second term as Albany mayor when he and three others were killed when their private airplane crashed, returning from the All-Star Baseball Game in Baltimore MD.

Jimmy McAleer—13 Years Outfielder 11 Years Manager (b. 10 Jul 1864 Youngstown OH–d. 29 Apr 1931 at his home in Youngstown OH) The majority stockholder in the Red Sox for a few years, he was one of the primary movers in the formation of the American League. Died from a self-inflicted gunshot wound to the head. Buried Oak Hill Cemetery, Youngstown OH.

John McAleese—2 Years Outfielder (b. 22 Aug 1877 Sharon PA–d. 15 Nov 1950 St Luke's Hospital, New York City NY) He operated the Albany Hotel in Youngstown OH before moving to Florida. He lived his last ten years in New York City. Died after a month's illness. Buried St Mary's Cemetery, Sharon PA.

Bill McAllester—1 Year Catcher (b. 29 Dec 1889 Chattanooga TN–d. 3 Mar 1970 at a hospital in Chattanooga TN) World War I veteran. His baseball career was shortened when he injured his arm in a sliding drill in spring training. He was a retired lawyer and hosiery mill executive.

Sport McAllister—7 Years Outfielder (b. 23 Jul 1874 Austin MS–d. 18 Jul 1962 Wyandotte General Hospital, Detroit MI) He was a stage actor. Died after a short illness. Buried Mount Olivet Cemetery, Detroit MI.

Dixie McArthur—1 Year Pitcher (b. 1 Feb 1892 Vernon AL–d. 31 May 1986 Clay County Medical Center, West Point MS) He owned a Ford dealership in Charleston IL for 31 years before retiring to Columbus MS in 1962. There he developed real estate until his death. Buried Friendship Cemetery, Columbus MS.

Ike McAuley—5 Years Infielder (b. 19 Aug 1891 Wichita KS–d. 6 Apr 1928 Des Moines IA) Died from a complication of diseases followed by influenza and pneumonia. Buried Maple Grove Cemetery, Wichita KS.

Gene McAuliffe—1 Year Catcher (b. 28 Feb 1872 Randolph MA–d. 29 Apr 1953 at his home in Randolph MA) He was the news dealer in Randolph for 25 years before going into real estate. Died after an illness of several months. Buried St Mary's Cemetery, Randolph MA.

Wickey McAvoy—6 Years Catcher (b. 20 Oct 1894 Rochester NY–d. 6 Jul 1973 Rochester NY) Died from a heart condition. Buried Holy Sepulchre Cemetery, Rochester NY.

Pryor McBee—1 Year Pitcher (b. 20 Jun 1901 Blanco OK–d. 19 Apr 1963 District Hospital, Roseville CA) He operated a lumber business for 25 years. Died from a heart attack. Buried Roseville Cemetery, Roseville CA.

Algie McBride—5 Years Outfielder (b. 23 May 1869 Washington DC–d. 10 Jan 1956 Georgetown OH) He was an express messenger for the Norfolk and Western Railroad. Died from injuries suffered in a fall six weeks earlier. Buried Greenlawn Cemetery, Portsmouth OH.

Dick McBride—1 Year Pitcher (b. 1845 Philadelphia PA–d. 10 Oct 1916 Philadelphia PA).

George McBride—16 Years Infielder 1 Year Manager (b. 20 Nov 1880 Milwaukee WI–d. 2 Jul 1973 St Mary's Hospital, Milwaukee WI) He was a major league coach and a member of the Wisconsin Hall of Fame. Died from complications of old age. Buried Holy Cross Cemetery, Milwaukee WI.

Pete McBride—2 Years Pitcher (b. 9 Jul 1875 Adams MA–d. 3 Jul 1944 North Adams MA) He established the McBride Funeral Home at North Adams in 1900 and worked there up until his death. At one time he was on the Adams Board of Health. Died from a coronary thrombosis at his funeral parlor. Buried Maple Cemetery, Adams MA.

Tom McBride—6 Years Outfielder (b. 2 Nov 1914 Bonham TX–d. 26 Dec 2001).

Bill McCabe—3 Years Outfielder (b. 28 Oct 1892 Chicago IL–d. 2 Sep 1966 Chicago IL) Buried Mount Carmel Cemetery, Hillside IL.

Dick McCabe—2 Years Pitcher (b. 21 Feb 1896 Mamaroneck NY–d. 11 Apr 1950 Sister's Hospital, Buffalo NY) He was a salesman for the William Simon Brewery at Buffalo, later becoming sales manager, then vice-president. Died following a stroke. Buried Mount Calvary Cemetery, Cheektowaga NY.

Ralph McCabe—1 Year Pitcher (b. 21 Oct 1918 Napanee, Ontario, Canada–d. 3 May 1974 Windsor, Ontario, Canada).

Swat McCabe—2 Years Outfielder (b. 20 Nov 1882 Towanda PA–d. 9 Dec 1944 Bristol Hospital, Bristol CT) Spanish-American War veteran. Died after a long illness. Buried St Joseph Cemetery, Bristol CT.

Tim McCabe—4 Years Pitcher (b. 19 Oct 1894 Ironton MO–d. 12 Apr 1977 Arcadia Valley Hospital, Ironton MO) He retired as a mill superintendent for Hanna Mining Company. Buried Arcadia Valley Memorial Park Cemetery, Ironton MO.

Harry McCaffrey—3 Years Outfielder (b. 25 Nov 1858 St Louis MO–d. 19 Apr 1928 St Louis MO) Buried Calvary Cemetery, St Louis MO.

Sparrow McCaffrey—1 Year Catcher (b. Philadelphia PA–d. 29 Apr 1894 at his parent's home in Philadelphia PA) Buried New Cathedral Cemetery, Philadelphia PA.

Bill McCahan—4 Years Pitcher (b. 7 Jun 1921 Philadelphia PA–d. 3 Jul 1986 at a hospital in Fort Worth TX) Served as a test pilot in the U.S. Army Air Corps during World War II. He managed minor league baseball for a short time, then worked 23 years for General Dynamics, retiring in 1978. During that time he headed the F-16 mockup project. Died from cancer. Buried Greenwood Memorial Park, Fort Worth TX.

Dutch McCall—1 Year Pitcher (b. 27 Dec 1920 Columbia TN–d. 8 Jan 1996 Little Rock AR) Served in the U.S. Army during World War II. He was a salesman at a number of mens clothing stores in Little Rock. Died after a year-long battle with cancer. Buried Little Rock National Cemetery, Little Rock AR.

Jack McCallister—1 Year Manager (b. 19 Jan 1879 Marietta OH–d. 18 Oct 1946 White Cross Hospital, Columbus OH) He coached for the Indians and scouted for several teams. Died from injuries suffered when he was struck by an automobile three months earlier. Buried Green Lawn Memorial Cemetery, Columbus OH.

Scott McCandless—2 Years Outfielder (b. 5 May 1891 Pittsburgh PA–d. 17 Aug 1961 Presbyterian Hospital, Pittsburgh PA).

Emmett McCann—3 Years Infielder (b. 4 Mar 1902 Philadelphia PA–d. 15 Apr 1937 Philadelphia PA) He managed minor league baseball. Died after shooting himself on the Karakung Golf Course in Cobbs Creek Park. He had been ill for some time. Buried Old Cathedral Cemetery, Philadelphia PA.

Gene McCann—2 Years Pitcher (b. 13 Jun 1876 Baltimore MD–d. 26 Apr 1943 Jamaica Hospital, New York City NY) He worked his entire life in baseball as a player, coach, scout, executive and minor league manager. When he died he was president of two Yankee farm teams. Died from a cerebral hemorrhage. Buried St John's Cemetery, Middle Village NY.

Roger McCardell—1 Year Catcher (b. 29 Aug 1932 Gorsuch Mills MD–d. 13 Nov 1996 Perry Point MD).

Bill McCarren—1 Year Infielder (b. 4 Nov 1895 Honesdale PA–d. 11 Sep 1983 Denver CO).

Alex McCarthy—8 Years Infielder (b. 12 May 1888 Chicago IL–d. 12 Mar 1978 at a nursing home in Salisbury MD) He worked in road construction and in the building trade in Salisbury, and later tended bar at the William Penn Hotel there. Died after a brief illness. Buried Parsons Cemetery, Salisbury MD.

Bill McCarthy—2 Years Catcher (b. abt 1885 Boston MA–d. 4 Feb 1928 Emergency Hospital, Washington DC) He was the prohibition administrator of the New England district and was known as the rum runner's scourge. Died from a heart attack. Buried Holyhood Cemetery, Brookline MA.

Bill McCarthy—1 Year Pitcher (b. 11 Apr 1882 Ashland MA–d. 29 May 1939 Massachusetts General Hospital, Boston MA) He worked at the Dennison and was in the painting business at Concord MA until he retired in 1932 because of ill health. Died following a serious operation performed three weeks earlier. Buried St Bernard's Parish Cemetery, Concord MA.

Jack McCarthy—12 Years Outfielder (b. 26 Mar 1869 Gilbertville MA–d. 11 Sep 1931 Chicago IL).

Jerry McCarthy—1 Year Infielder (b. 23 May 1923 Brooklyn NY–d. 3 Oct 1965 Oceanside NY) Served in the U.S. Army Air Force during World War II. He was an advertising salesman for the Army Times Publishing Company in New York City. Died from a heart attack. Buried Cemetery of Holy Rood, Westbury NY.

Joe McCarthy—24 Years Manager Hall of Fame (b. 21 Apr 1887 Philadelphia PA–d. 13 Jan 1978 Millard Fillmore Hospital, Buffalo NY) He spent his entire life in baseball as a player and manager, retiring in 1950. Died from pneumonia after entering the hospital for treatment of a lung disease. Buried Mount Olivet Cemetery, Buffalo NY.

Joe McCarthy—2 Years Catcher (b. 25 Dec 1881 Syracuse NY–d. 12 Jan 1937 Syracuse NY).

Johnny McCarthy—11 Years Infielder (b. 7 Jan 1910 Chicago IL–d. 13 Sep 1973 at his home in Mundelein IL) He worked for the Village of Mundelein where he lived for 25 years. Buried Ascension Cemetery, Libertyville IL.

Tom McCarthy—2 Years Pitcher (b. 22 May 1884 Fort Wayne IN–d. 28 Mar 1933 St Joseph Hospital, Mishawaka IN) Died following a long illness. Buried Catholic Cemetery, Fort Wayne IN.

Tommy McCarthy—13 Years Outfielder 1 Year Manager Hall of Fame (b. 24 Jul 1864 Boston MA–d. 5 Aug 1922 at his home in Dorchester MA) He coached baseball at Dartmouth, College of the Holy Cross and Boston College. Died from double pneumonia after an acute illness of more than a month. Buried Mount Calvary Cemetery, Roslindale MA.

Lew McCarty—9 Years Catcher (b. 17 Nov 1888 Milton PA–d. 9 Jun 1930 Reading PA) Died from a cerebral embolism. Buried Hillside Cemetery, Catawissa PA.

Al McCauley—3 Years Infielder (b. 4 Mar 1863 Indianapolis IN–d. 24 Aug 1917 Marion County Home, Indianapolis IN) Buried Crown Hill Cemetery, Indianapolis IN.

Bill McCauley—1 Year Infielder (b. 20 Dec 1869 Washington DC–d. 27 Jan 1926 Sibley Hospital, Washington DC) Buried Congressional Cemetery, Washington DC.

Jim McCauley—3 Years Catcher (b. 24 Mar 1863 Stanley NY–d. 14 Sep 1930 Memorial Hospital, Canandaigua NY) He was a prominent resident of Canandaigua. Died after a long illness. Buried Woodlawn Cemetery, Canandaigua NY.

Pat McCauley—3 Years Catcher (b. 10 Jun 1870 Ware MA–d. 17 Jan 1917 Hoboken NJ) He was a longshoreman. Died from pneumonia. Buried St Williams Cemetery, Ware MA.

Harry McChesney—1 Year Outfielder (b. 1 Jun 1880 Pittsburgh PA–d. 11 Aug 1960 at his home in Pittsburgh PA).

Pete McClanahan—7 Games Pinch Hitter (b. 24 Oct 1906 Coldspring TX–d. 28 Oct 1987 at his home in Mont Belvieu TX) He was a retired supervisor for Texas Producing Co. Buried Oakwood Cemetery, Coldspring TX.

Bill McClellan—8 Years Infielder (b. 22 Mar 1856 Chicago IL–d. 2 Jul 1929 Chicago IL) Buried Rosehill Cemetery, Chicago IL.

Harvey McClellan—6 Years Infielder (b. 22 Dec 1894 Cynthiana KY–d. 6 Nov 1925 Harrison Memorial Hospital, Cynthiana KY) Died at the height of his baseball career following surgery for liver cancer. He was a buyer for Liggett and Myers Tobacco Company during the off-season. Buried Battle Grove Cemetery, Cynthiana KY.

Gordon McClendon—(b. 8 Jun 1921 Paris TX–d. 14 Sep 1986 Lake Dallas TX) A sportscaster, he accumulated a fortune in precious metals, movie theatres, real estate and broadcasting. Calling himself "The Old Scotchman," in the 1950s he rebroadcast major league games over his Liberty Broadcasting System that included over 400 radio stations. Died from cancer of the esophagus.

Jeff McCleskey—1 Year Infielder (b. 6 Nov 1891 Americus GA–d. 11 May 1971 County Hospital, Americus GA) World War I veteran. He was associated with the McCleskey Mills in Americus for a number of years. Buried Oak Grove Cemetery, Americus GA.

Jim McCloskey—1 Year Pitcher (b. 26 May 1912 Danville PA–d. 18 Aug 1971 Medical Center, Jersey City NJ) He owned and operated the Bergen Bar in Jersey City. Died after a lengthy illness. Buried Holy Name Cemetery, Jersey City NJ.

John McCloskey—5 Years Manager (b. 4 Apr 1862 Louisville KY–d. 17 Nov 1940 City Hospital, Louisville KY) He worked in baseball his entire life. Starting as a bat boy, he became a player, coach, manager, scout and executive. He was instrumental in the formation of ten minor leagues and managed 47 different teams during his lifetime. Died following a series of strokes. Buried Calvary Cemetery, Louisville KY.

John McCloskey—2 Years Pitcher (b. 20 Aug 1882 Wyoming PA–d. 5 Jun 1919 Wilkes-Barre PA) He worked in the Black Diamond tunnel of the D and H Coal Company mine when kegs of powder exploded, killing him and nearly 100 other miners on a train going into the mine to work. Buried St Mary's Cemetery, Wilkes-Barre PA.

Hal McClure—1 Year Outfielder (b. 8 Aug 1859 Lewisburg PA–d. 1 Mar 1919 at his doctor's office in Lewisburg PA) An attorney, he served 20 years as judge of the Union-Snyder District. Active in civic, religious and business affairs he served on several boards. Died from neuralgia of the heart. Buried Lewisburg Cemetery, Lewisburg PA.

Larry McClure—1 Year Outfielder (b. 3 Oct 1885 Wayne WV–d. 31 Aug 1949 Huntington WV) He practiced law in Huntington. Buried Woodmere Memorial Park, Huntington WV.

Harry McCluskey—1 Year Pitcher (b. 29 May 1892 Clay Center OH–d. 7 Jun 1962 Maumee Valley Hospital, Toledo OH) For 14 years he was a switchman for the Baltimore and Ohio Railroad and he worked ten years in maintenance for Columbia Burner Company, retiring in 1955. Buried Forest Cemetery, Toledo OH.

Alex McColl—2 Years Pitcher (b. 29 Mar 1894 Eagleville OH–d. 6 Feb 1991 Kingsville OH).

Ralph McConnaughey—1 Year Pitcher (b. 5 Aug 1889 PA–d. 4 Jun 1966 Detroit MI) Buried Cadillac Memorial Gardens West, Berkley MI.

Amby McConnell—4 Years Infielder (b. 29 Apr 1882 Williamstown NY–d. 20 May 1942 at his home in Utica NY) He managed minor league baseball until 1923 and was part-owner of the Utica Braves in the Canadian-American League. Died unexpectedly from heart disease. Buried St Peter's Cemetery, Utica NY.

George McConnell—6 Years Pitcher (b. 16 Sep 1877 Wartrace TN–d. 10 May 1964 at a hospital in Chattanooga TN) He was the starting pitcher for the Cubs when Wrigley Field was dedicated. He founded The Success Portrait Company, a photo studio in Chattanooga, and operated it until his death. Buried Forest Hills Cemetery, Chattanooga TN.

Sammy McConnell—1 Year Infielder (b. 8 Jun 1895 Philadelphia PA–d. 27 Jun 1981 Phoenixville Hospital, Phoenixville PA) World War I veteran. He was a salesman for Hill-Chase Steel Distributors of Philadelphia, retiring in 1962.

Barry McCormick—10 Years Infielder (b. 25 Dec 1874 Maysville KY–d. 28 Jan 1956 Cincinnati OH) He was a National League umpire from 1919 to 1928. Collapsed and died on the street across from the YMCA where he had lived for 15 years. Buried St Joseph New Cemetery, Cincinnati OH.

Frank McCormick—13 Years Infielder (b. 9 Jun 1911 New York City NY–d. 21 Nov 1982 North Shore Hospital, Manhasset NY) He was director of group sales for the Yankees from 1975 until shortly before his death. Died after an extended bout with cancer. Buried Cemetery of Holy Rood, Westbury NY.

Harry McCormick—4 Years Pitcher (b. 25 Oct 1855 Syracuse NY–d. 8 Aug 1889 Syracuse NY) Died from cholera.

Jerry McCormick—2 Years Infielder (b. Philadelphia PA–d. 19 Sep 1905 Philadelphia PA).

Jim McCormick—10 Years Pitcher 2 Years Manager (b. 1856 Glasgow, Scotland–d. 10 Mar 1918 at his home in Paterson NJ) Died from cirrhosis of the liver. Buried Laurel Grove Memorial Park, Totowa NJ.

Jim McCormick—1 Year Infielder (b. 2 Nov 1868 Spencer MA–d. 1 Feb 1948 Saco ME).

Mike McCormick—1 Year Infielder (b. 1883 Jersey City NJ–d. 18 Nov 1953 at his home in Jersey City NJ) He was a scout for the Dodgers and a Hudson County (NJ) employee. Died suddenly. Buried Holy Name Cemetery, Jersey City NJ.

Mike McCormick—10 Years Outfielder (b. 6 May 1917 Angels Camp CA–d. 14 Apr 1976 Queen of Angel's Hospital, Los Angeles CA) Died from a heart attack he had suffered while attending a game at Dodger Stadium.

Moose McCormick—5 Years Outfielder (b. 28 Feb 1881 Philadelphia PA–d. 9 Jul 1962 Lewisburg PA) Served in the U.S. Army during both World Wars I and II. He coached baseball and basketball at Bucknell Univ from 1922 to 1926 and baseball at West Point from 1926 to 1937. He managed the veteran's housing at Bucknell from 1947 to 1958 when he retired. He had been in ill health for a year when he died. Buried Lewisburg Cemetery, Lewisburg PA.

Bill McCorry—1 Year Pitcher (b. 9 Jul 1887 Saranac Lake NY–d. 22 Mar 1973 at a hospital in Augusta GA) He was the traveling secretary for the Yankees for many years and was manager or general manager of several minor league teams, including the Augusta Yankees. Buried Westover Memorial Park, Augusta GA.

Barney McCosky—11 Years Outfielder (b. 11 Apr 1917 Coal Run PA–d. 6 Sep 1996 Venice FL) Buried Detroit MI.

Art McCoy—1 Year Infielder (b. 1865 Danville PA–d. 22 Mar 1904 Danville PA) He managed minor league baseball. Buried Odd Fellows Cemetery, Danville PA.

Frank McCrea—1 Year Catcher (b. 6 Sep 1896 Jersey City NJ–d. 25 Feb 1981 St Clare's Hospital, Denville NJ) Served in the U.S. Navy during World War I. He retired in 1962 after 30 years working in transportation at the Picatinny Arsenal. Buried Locust Hill Cemetery, Dover NJ.

Judge McCreedie—1 Year Outfielder (b. 9 Nov 1876 Manchester IA–d. 29 Jul 1934 Medical Hospital, Portland OR) He owned and managed the Portland team in the Pacific Coast League from 1904 until 1921. Cremated.

Ed McCreery—1 Year Pitcher (b. 24 Dec 1889 Cripple Creek CO–d. 19 Oct 1960 Mercy Hospital, Sacramento CA) He was a retail electrical salesman for 20 years. Died from lung cancer and heart failure. Buried Holy Sepulchre Cemetery, Hayward CA.

Tom McCreery—9 Years Outfielder (b. 19 Oct 1874 Beaver PA–d. 3 Jul 1941 at his home in Beaver PA) An executive for United States Steel Corporation, he retired in 1938 because of ill health. Died suddenly. Buried Beaver Cemetery, Beaver PA.

Frank McCue—1 Year Infielder (b. 4 Oct 1897 Chicago IL–d. 5 Jul 1953 Chicago IL) Buried St Mary Cemetery, Evergreen Park IL.

Clyde McCullough—15 Years Catcher (b. 3 Mar 1917 Nashville TN–d. 18 Sep 1982 St Francis Hotel, San Francisco CA) Served in the U.S. Navy during World War II. He managed minor league baseball and was a pitching coach for the Padres when he died. Died from heart disease. Buried Rosewood Memorial Park, Virginia Beach VA.

Paul McCullough—1 Year Pitcher (b. 28 Jul 1898 New Castle PA–d. 7 Nov 1970 Jameson Memorial Hospital, New Castle PA) He was a retired plant guard for Mesta Machine Company. Buried Oak Park Cemetery, New Castle PA.

Harry McCurdy—10 Years Catcher (b. 15 Sep 1900 Stevens Point WI–d. 21 Jul 1972 Houston TX) He was a scout for the Dodgers and an administrator for the Houston Independent School District. Died from cancer. Cremated.

Von McDaniel—2 Years Pitcher (b. 18 Apr 1939 Hollis OK–d. 20 Aug 1995 Comanche County Memorial Hosp, Lawton OK) Served in the U.S. Army Reserves. He farmed, preached at the Vinson Church of Christ and was a finance accountant in Hollis. Buried Dobson Cemetery, Dobson OK.

Mike McDermott—4 Years Pitcher (b. 7 Sep 1862 St Louis MO–d. 30 Jun 1943 St Louis MO) Buried Calvary Cemetery, St Louis MO.

Red McDermott—1 Year Outfielder (b. 12 Nov 1889 Philadelphia PA–d. 11 Sep 1964 Philadelphia PA).

Tom McDermott—1 Year Infielder (b. 15 Mar 1856 Zanesville OH–d. 23 Nov 1922 General Hospital, Mansfield OH) He umpired in the minor leagues and worked as a telegrapher. Died from cancer of the stomach and intestines.

Buried Mount Calvary Cemetery, Zanesville OH.

Ed McDonald—3 Years Infielder (b. 28 Oct 1886 Albany NY–d. 11 Mar 1946 St Peter's Hospital, Albany NY) He played minor league baseball for several years, mostly in the south. Later he was assistant cashier in the Albany City Treasurer's office. Died from a coronary occlusion. Buried St Agnes Cemetery, Menands NY.

Hank McDonald—2 Years Pitcher (b. 16 Jan 1911 Santa Monica CA–d. 17 Oct 1982 Valley Hospital, Hemet CA) For 20 years he was a manager for RCA Corporation. Died from a heart attack. Buried Inglewood Park Cemetery, Inglewood CA.

Jim McDonald—2 Years Infielder (b. 6 Aug 1860 San Francisco CA–d. 14 Sep 1914 San Francisco CA) He was an umpire. Buried Holy Cross Catholic Cemetery, Colma CA.

Joe McDonald—1 Year Infielder (b. 9 Apr 1888 Galveston TX–d. 30 May 1963 at a hospital in Baytown TX) He retired from Humble Oil Company in 1953 after working in the Plant Protection Department there many years. Buried Cedarcrest Cemetery, Baytown TX.

John McDonald—1 Year Pitcher (b. 27 Jan 1883 Throop PA–d. 9 Apr 1950 at his son's home in Roselle NJ) He practiced denistry in Throop and Olyphant PA several years before retiring. Buried Mount Carmel Cemetery, Dunmore PA.

Tex McDonald—4 Years Outfielder (b. 31 Jan 1891 Farmersville TX–d. 30 Mar 1943 Jeff Davis Hospital, Houston TX) He cleaned windows in Houston for a living until he became too ill. Died after an illness of several days. Buried Farmersville TX.

Webster McDonald—15 Years Pitcher 7 Years Manager (b. 1 Jan 1900 Wilmington DE–d. 12 Jun 1982 at his home in Philadelphia PA) He played in the negro leagues. Buried Fairview Cemetery, Willow Grove PA.

Jim McDonnell—3 Years Catcher (b. 15 Aug 1922 Gagetown MI–d. 24 Apr 1993 Detroit MI).

Ed McDonough—2 Years Catcher (b. 11 Sep 1886 Elgin IL–d. 2 Sep 1926 St Joseph Hospital, Elgin IL) He was an executive at the Van Sicklen Speedometer Company in Elgin and later was superintendent of the Stewart-Warner Speedometer plant in Chicago IL. Died from heart trouble. Buried Bluff City Cemetery, Elgin IL.

John McDougal—2 Years Pitcher (b. 21 May 1874 Buffalo NY–d. 2 Oct 1910 Buffalo NY).

John McDougal—2 Years Pitcher (b. 19 Sep 1871 Aledo IL–d. 28 Apr 1936 Cottage Hospital, Galesburg IL) He was the custodian at the Eagle's Lodge in Galesburg. Died following a lingering illness. Buried Aledo Cemetery, Aledo IL.

Jim McElroy—1 Year Pitcher (b. 1863 San Francisco CA–d. 24 Jul 1889 Needles CA) Took his own life with an overdose of morphine.

Pryor McElveen—3 Years Infielder (b. 5 Nov 1883 Atlanta GA–d. 27 Oct 1951 Pleasant Hill TN).

Lee McElwee—1 Year Infielder (b. 23 May 1894 La Mesa CA–d. 8 Feb 1957 Union ME).

Frank McElyea—1 Year Outfielder (b. 4 Aug 1918 Hawthorne Township IL–d. 19 Apr 1987 at his home in Evansville IN) He retired from the Evansville Police Department as a policeman in 1959. Buried Sunset Memorial Park Cemetery, Evansville IN.

Lou McEvoy—2 Years Pitcher (b. 30 May 1902 Williamsburg KS–d. 17 Dec 1953 Webster Groves MO) He was a sporting goods salesman. Died from cancer. Buried St Patrick's Cemetery, Williamsburg KS.

Barney McFadden—2 Years Pitcher (b. 22 Feb 1874 Eckley PA–d. 28 Apr 1924 Mauch Chunk PA).

Guy McFadden—1 Year Infielder (b. 3 Sep 1872 Topeka KS–d. 10 Mar 1911 Topeka KS) Died after a long term of sickness. Buried Topeka Cemetery, Topeka KS.

Alex McFarlan—1 Year Outfielder (b. 11 Nov 1866 KY–d. 2 Mar 1939 Pewee Valley Hospital, Pewee Valley KY) He owned a restaurant at Pewee Valley. Died from pneumonia. Buried Duncan Memorial Cemetery, Floydsburg KY.

Dan McFarlan—2 Years Pitcher (b. 5 Nov 1873 Valley View TX–d. 23 Sep 1924 Kings Daughter's Hospital, Louisville KY) He was paralized the last 11 years of his life after being hit in the head by a pitched ball. Died from acute indigestion, believed to have been caused by his paralysis. Buried Flat Rock Cemetery, Louisville KY.

Chappie McFarland—5 Years Pitcher (b. 13 Mar 1875 White Hill IL–d. 14 Dec 1924 Houston TX) He managed theatres in Houston and Fort Worth TX, and was the manager of a company that owned several theatres when he died. Died from a heart attack while golfing at River Oaks Country Club. Buried Glenwood Cemetery, Houston TX.

Claude McFarland—1 Year Outfielder (b. 17 Aug 1861 Fall River MA–d. 24 May 1918 at his home in New Bedford MA) He was prominent in the dry goods business in Fall River and New Bedford. Died from a severe attack of indigestion. Buried Oak Grove Cemetery, Fall River MA.

Ed McFarland—14 Years Catcher (b. 3 Aug 1874 Cleveland OH–d. 28 Nov 1959 Cleveland OH) Buried Lake View Cemetery, Cleveland OH.

Herm McFarland—5 Years Outfielder (b. 11 Mar 1870 Des Moines IA–d. 21 Sep 1935 at his home in Richmond VA) A well known amateur bowler, he managed a bowling alley and billiard parlor in Richmond. Buried Riverview Cemetery, Richmond VA.

Howie McFarland—1 Year Outfielder (b. 7 Mar 1910 El Reno OK–d. 7 Apr 1993 Wichita KS) He retired as stockroom and shipping manager at Cesna Aircraft Company in Wichita. Died from cancer. Buried Memorial Cemetery, Ringling OK.

Monte McFarland—2 Years Pitcher (b. 7 Nov 1872 White Hall IL–d. 15 Nov 1913 Proctor Hospital, Peoria IL) He played and managed in the Three-I League and umpired in the Wisconsin-Illinois League. Died from pneumonia. Buried White Hall Cemetery, White Hall IL.

Jack McFetridge—2 Years Pitcher (b. 25 Aug 1869 Philadelphia PA–d. 10 Jan 1917 at his home in Glenolden PA) He was a vice-president of John R McFetridge and Sons, a printing and publishing firm in Philadelphia. Died suddenly from a heart attack brought on by an attack of acute indigestion. Buried South Laurel Hill Cemetery, Glenolden PA.

Patsy McGaffigan—2 Years Infielder (b. 12 Sep 1888 Carlyle IL–d. 22 Dec 1940 Carlyle IL) World War I veteran. He taught school from 1926 until 1937 when he took a job as deputy county treasurer. Drowned in a creek near his home. Buried Carlyle Cemetery, Carlyle IL.

Ed McGamwell—1 Year Infielder (b. 10 Jan 1879 Buffalo NY–d. 26 May 1924 at his home in Albany NY) He conducted a confectionary store in Albany. Died from chronic myocarditis and nephritis. Buried St Agnes Cemetery, Menands NY.

Dan McGann—13 Years Infielder (b. 15 Jul 1872 Shelbyville KY–d. 13 Dec 1910 Louisville KY) He played baseball up until his death. Fatally shot himself through the heart in a Louisville hotel room. Buried Grove Hill Cemetery, Shelbyville KY.

Chippy McGarr—10 Years Infielder (b. 10 May 1863 Worcester MA–d. 6 Jun 1904 Worcester Insane Hospital, Worcester MA) Died from paresis after an illness of four years. Buried St John's Cemetery, Worcester MA.

Jim McGarr—1 Year Infielder (b. 9 Nov 1888 Philadelphia PA–d. 21 Jul 1981 Miami FL).

Dan McGarvey—1 Year Outfielder (b. 2 Dec 1887 Philadelphia PA–d. 7 Mar 1947 Philadelphia PA) He worked for Philadelphia Electric Company. Buried Holy Cross Cemetery, Yeadon PA.

Jack McGeachy—6 Years Outfielder (b. 23 May 1864 Clinton MA–d. 5 Apr 1930 City Hospital, Cambridge MA) He was engaged in business at Boston MA. Buried Woodlawn Cemetery, Clinton MA.

Bill McGee—8 Years Pitcher (b. 16 Nov 1909 Batchtown IL–d. 11 Feb 1987 Christian Hospital Northeast, St Louis MO) He farmed at Hardin IL after his baseball career was over. Buried St Norbett's Catholic Church Cemetery, Hardin IL.

Dan McGee—1 Year Infielder (b. 29 Sep 1911 New York City NY–d. 4 Dec 1991 Lakehurst NJ).

Tubby McGee—1 Year Infielder (b. 28 Apr 1899 Columbus OH–d. 30 Jan 1934 Mount Carmel Hospital, Columbus OH) He was an adjuster for a Columbus finance company. Died from lobar pneumonia. Buried St Joseph Cemetery, Lockbourne OH.

Connie McGeehan—1 Year Pitcher (b. 25 Aug 1882 Drifton PA–d. 4 Jul 1907 Hazleton PA).

Dan McGeehan—1 Year Infielder (b. 7 Jun 1885 Jeddo PA–d. 12 Jul 1955 at his home in

Hazleton PA) He was a retired boiler inspector for the Hartford Insurance Company. Died suddenly. Buried Calvary Cemetery, Drums PA.

Pat McGehee—1 Year Pitcher (b. 2 Jul 1888 Meadville MS–d. 30 Dec 1946 Illinois Central (Railroad), Paducah KY) World War I veteran. He lived at Paducah KY for 20 years where he was a foreman at the Illinois Central shops. Buried Maplelawn Park Cemetery, Paducah KY.

Bill McGhee—2 Years Outfielder (b. 5 Sep 1905 Shawmut AL–d. 10 Mar 1984 Decatur GA) Buried Bayview Memorial Park, Pensacola FL.

Ed McGhee—4 Years Outfielder (b. 29 Sep 1924 Perry AR–d. 13 Feb 1986 Memphis TN).

Bill McGill—1 Year Pitcher (b. 29 Jun 1880 McPherson KS–d. 7 Aug 1959 Alva General Hospital, Alva OK) He operated a furniture store in Alva until he retired in 1953. Died after a long illness. Buried Alva Municipal Cemetery, Alva OK.

Willie McGill—7 Years Pitcher (b. 10 Nov 1873 Atlanta GA–d. 29 Aug 1944 at his home in Indianapolis IN) He was the baseball coach and athletic trainer at Northwestern University and was also associated with the athletic department of Butler University. Later he worked for Indianapolis Power and Light and for American Compressed Steel Corporation. Buried Crown Hill Cemetery, Indianapolis IN.

John McGillen—1 Year Pitcher (b. 6 Aug 1917 Eddystone PA–d. 11 Aug 1987 Crozer-Chester Medical Center, Upland PA) He was a salesman for Wilco Plumbing and Heating Supply Company in Wilmington DE, retiring in 1982. Died from thyroid cancer. Buried St Peter and St Paul Cemetery, Springfield PA.

Bill McGilvray—2 Games Pinch Hitter (b. 28 Apr 1883 Portland OR–d. 23 May 1952 at his home in Denver CO)He worked for Continental Oil Company in Denver CO for 35 years. Died after a long illness. Buried Fairmount Cemetery, Denver CO.

Jim McGinley—2 Years Pitcher (b. 2 Oct 1878 Groveland MA–d. 20 Sep 1961 Hale Hospital, Haverhill MA) For nearly 50 years he managed a bank and was an officer in the bank. Buried Riverview Cemetery, Groveland MA.

Tim McGinley—1 Year Outfielder (b. Philadelphia PA–d. 2 Nov 1899 Oakland CA).

Frank McGinn—1 Year Outfielder (b. Cincinnati OH–d. 19 Nov 1897 Cincinnati OH).

Jumbo McGinnis—6 Years Pitcher (b. 22 Feb 1864 St Louis MO–d. 18 May 1934 at his home in St Louis MO) Died following a brief illness. Buried Calvary Cemetery, St Louis MO.

Joe McGinnity—10 Years Pitcher Hall of Fame (b. 19 Mar 1871 Rock Island IL–d. 14 Nov 1929 at his daughter's home in Brooklyn NY) He pitched minor league baseball until four years before his death. Buried Oak Hill Cemetery, McAlester OK.

John McGlone—3 Years Infielder (b. 1864 Brooklyn NY–d. 24 Nov 1927 Brooklyn NY).

Lynn McGlothen—11 Years Pitcher (b. 27 Mar 1950 Monroe LA–d. 14 Aug 1984 Dubach LA) Died from smoke inhalation in a mobile home fire.

Jim McGlothlin—9 Years Pitcher (b. 6 Oct 1943 Los Angeles CA–d. 23 Dec 1975 at his home in Union KY) Died at the height of his career from a rare strain of leukemia that would not respond to treatment. Buried Burlington Cemetery, Burlington KY.

Stoney McGlynn—3 Years Pitcher (b. 26 May 1872 Lancaster PA–d. 26 Aug 1941 at his home in Manitowoc WI) He was known as "Iron Man" due to his ability to pitch both games of double headers. He worked in the shipping department for Aluminum Goods Manufacturing Company. Died following an illness of four weeks. Buried Evergreen Cemetery, Manitowoc WI.

Art McGovern—1 Year Catcher (b. 27 Feb 1882 St John, New Brunswick, Canada–d. 14 Nov 1915 Thornton RI).

Bill McGowan—Hall of Fame (b. 18 Jan 1896 Wilmington DE–d. 9 Dec 1954 at his home in Silver Spring MD) He was an American League umpire from 1925 until his death. Died from a heart attack. Buried Cathedral Cemetery, Wilmington DE.

Frank McGowan—5 Years Outfielder (b. 8 Nov 1901 Branford CT–d. 6 May 1982 St Raphael's Hospital, New Haven CT) He was a scout for the Orioles for 30 years. Buried St Lawrence Cemetery, West Haven CT.

Howard McGraner—1 Year Pitcher (b. 11 Sep 1889 Hamley Run OH–d. 22 Oct 1952 at his home in Zaleski OH) World War I veteran. He was a brakeman for the Baltimore and Ohio Railroad for 25 years. Died from a heart attack. Buried West Union Street Cemetery, Athens OH.

Bob McGraw—9 Years Pitcher (b. 10 Apr 1895 La Veta CO–d. 2 Jun 1978 at the VA Hospital in Boise ID) Served in the U.S. Army during World War I. He lived in Long Beach CA and Seal Beach CA before moving to Boise ID in 1978. He was in the hospital, where he died, because of a broken hip. Buried Roselawn Cemetery, Pueblo CO.

Jim McGraw—1 Year Pitcher (b. 9 Sep 1891 Cleveland OH–d. 14 Nov 1918 Cleveland OH) He was a machinist for White Auto Company. Died from influenza. Buried St John's Cemetery, Cleveland OH.

John McGraw—16 Years Infielder 33 Years Manager Hall of Fame (b. 7 Apr 1873 Truxton NY–d. 25 Feb 1934 New Rochelle Hospital, New Rochelle NY) He worked in baseball his entire life. Died from uremic poisoning and prostate cancer. Buried New Cathedral Cemetery, Baltimore MD.

John McGraw—1 Year Pitcher (b. 8 Dec 1890 Intercourse PA–d. 24 Apr 1967 Torrance CA).

Slim McGrew—3 Years Pitcher (b. 5 Aug 1899 Yoakum TX–d. 21 Aug 1967 Houston TX) He lived in Houston 23 years. Buried Rosewood Park Cemetery, Houston TX.

Mark McGrillis—1 Year Infielder (b. 22 Oct 1872 Philadelphia PA–d. 16 May 1935 Philadelphia PA) Buried Old Cathedral Cemetery, Philadelphia PA.

Joe McGuckin—1 Year Outfielder (b. 1862 Paterson NJ–d. 31 Dec 1903 Yonkers NY).

John McGuinness—3 Years Infielder (b. 1857 Ireland–d. 19 Dec 1916 at his daughter's home in Binghamton NY) Died after a week's illness. Buried St Patrick Cemetery, Johnson City NY.

Deacon McGuire—26 Years Catcher 6 Years Manager (b. 2 Nov 1865 Youngstown OH–d. 31 Oct 1936 at his home on Duck Lake near Springport MI) He retired to a quiet farm overlooking Duck Lake where he raised chickens and fished. Died from pneumonia, but had suffered from poor health the last five years, and had a stroke a few weeks earlier. Buried Riverside Cemetery, Albion MI.

Murray McGuire—1 Year Pitcher (b. 19 Jan 1872 Richmond VA–d. 10 Sep 1945 Baltimore MD) A well-known lawyer in Richmond from 1896 until his death, he was president of the Richmond Bar Association at one time. Died suddenly while enroute home to Richmond from a vacation in New Hampshire. Buried Hollywood Cemetery, Richmond VA.

Tom McGuire—2 Years Pitcher (b. 1 Feb 1892 Chicago IL–d. 7 Dec 1959 Phoenix AZ) World War I veteran. He was a grain broker on the Chicago Board of Trade for 37 years. Died while recuperating from a recent surgery. Buried Holy Sepulchre Cemetery, Worth IL.

Bill McGunnigle—3 Years Outfielder 6 Years Manager (b. 1 Jan 1855 East Stoughton MA–d. 9 Mar 1899 at his home in Brockton MA) He owned and operated a store in Brockton. His death came after an illness of several years, but was hastened by injuries received when his carriage was run over by an electric car some months earlier. Buried St Patrick's Cemetery, Brockton MA.

Bob McHale—1 Year Outfielder (b. 25 Feb 1872 Michigan Bluff CA–d. 9 Jun 1952 at his home in Sacramento CA) He was a retired carpenter for Pacific Gas and Electric. Died from a heart attack. Buried St Mary's Cemetery, Sacramento CA.

Jim McHale—1 Year Outfielder (b. 17 Dec 1875 Miners Mills PA–d. 18 Jun 1959 St John of God Sanitarium, Los Angeles CA) He was a machinist for Lockheed Aircraft. Died from a heart attack. Buried San Gabriel Mission Cemetery, San Gabriel CA.

Marty McHale—6 Years Pitcher (b. 30 Oct 1888 Stoneham MA–d. 7 May 1979 Hempstead NY) Buried Cemetery of Holy Rood, Westbury NY.

Austin McHenry—5 Years Outfielder (b. 22 Sep 1895 Wrightsville OH–d. 27 Nov 1922 Blue Creek OH) Died at the height of his career following surgery to remove a brain tumor. Buried Moore's Chapel Cemetery, Blue Creek OH.

Vance McIlree—1 Year Pitcher (b. 14 Oct 1897 Riverside IA–d. 6 May 1959 Kansas City MO).

Irish McIlveen—3 Years Outfielder (b. 27 Jul 1880 Belfast, Ireland–d. 18 Oct 1960 St Joseph Hospital, Lorain OH) He was athletic director at Penn State University for several years before moving to Arizona where he was active in construction and mining. Returning to Lorain, he was associated with the City of Lorain 14 years as a civil engineer. Died after a short illness. Buried Ridge Hill Memorial Park, Lorain OH.

Stover McIlwain—2 Years Pitcher (b. 22 Sep 1939 Savannah GA–d. 15 Jan 1966 Buffalo NY) Died after shooting himself in the temple.

Stuffy McInnis—19 Years Infielder 1 Year Manager (b. 19 Sep 1890 Gloucester MA–d. 16 Feb 1960 Cable Memorial Hospital, Ipswich MA) He managed minor league baseball and coached college baseball at Amherst, Norwich and Harvard, retiring in 1955. Died following a prolonged illness, climaxed by a fall, breaking a hip, a few days before his death. Buried Rosedale Cemetery, Manchester by the Sea MA.

Frank McIntyre—1 Year Pitcher (b. abt 1860 Detroit MI–d. 7 Jul 1887 at his sister's home in Detroit MI) Buried Mount Elliott Cemetery, Detroit MI.

Harry McIntyre—9 Years Pitcher (b. 11 Jan 1879 Winchester IN–d. 9 Jan 1949 Daytona Beach FL) Died from a heart attack while fishing from a pier. Buried Woodland Cemetery, Dayton OH.

Matty McIntyre—10 Years Outfielder (b. 12 Jun 1880 Stonington CT–d. 2 Apr 1920 St Mary's Hospital, Detroit MI) Died from influenza and Bright's disease.

Otto McIver—1 Year Outfielder (b. 26 Jul 1884 Greenville TX–d. 4 May 1954 at a hospital in Dallas TX) For 28 years he was superintendent of the West Texas warehouses for Underwood and Compres Warehouse Company, retiring in 1953. Buried Greenwood Cemetery, Dallas TX.

Doc McJames—6 Years Pitcher (b. 27 Aug 1873 Williamsburg SC–d. 23 Sep 1901 Francis Xavier Infirmary, Charleston SC) He quit baseball to study medicine, but after graduating and practicing medicine for a short while he returned to baseball. Died from injuries suffered in a buggy runaway a month earlier.

Archie McKain—6 Years Pitcher (b. 12 May 1911 Delphos KS–d. 21 May 1985 Asbury Hospital, Salina KS) He farmed and did carpentry work in Minneapolis KS where he lived most of his life and was active in youth baseball activities. Buried Highland Cemetery, Minneapolis KS.

Hal McKain—5 Years Pitcher (b. 10 Jul 1906 Logan IA–d. 24 Jan 1970 Medical Center, Sacramento CA) He was the sales manager at Fuller Lumber Company in Sacramento for 11 years. Died from a heart attack. Buried Cedar Lawn Cemetery, Council Bluffs IA.

Reeves McKay—1 Year Pitcher (b. 16 Nov 1881 Morgan City TX–d. 18 Jan 1946 Dallas TX) Spanish-American War veteran. Buried Restland Memorial Park, Dallas TX.

Ed McKean—13 Years Infielder (b. 6 Jun 1864 Grafton OH–d. 16 Aug 1919 Cleveland OH).

Bill McKechnie—11 Years Infielder 25 Years Manager Hall of Fame (b. 7 Aug 1886 Wilkinsburg PA–d. 29 Oct 1965 Memorial Hospital, Bradenton FL) He spent 50 years in baseball as a player, manager and executive. Died from pneumonia and leukemia. Buried Manasota Memorial Park, Bradenton FL.

Red McKee—4 Years Catcher (b. 20 Jul 1890 Shawnee OH–d. 5 Aug 1972 Osteopathic Hospital, Saginaw MI) He was a patrolman in plant production for Eaton Manufacturing Company, retiring in 1959. Died following a brief illness. Buried Forest Lawn Cemetery, Saginaw MI.

Jim McKeever—1 Year Catcher (b. 19 Apr 1861 Newfoundland, Canada–d. 19 Aug 1897 at his home in Boston MA) Died after a five-week illness of brain fever.

Stephen McKeever—(b. 31 Oct 1853 Brooklyn NY–d. 7 Mar 1938 at his home in New York City NY) A plumbing contractor, he became associated with the Brooklyn Robins (later Dodgers) in 1912 when he loaned money to Charley Ebbets to build Ebbets Field. He was part-owner of the team from 1912 until Ebbets' death in 1925, and principal owner until his own death in 1938. Buried Holy Cross Cemetery, Brooklyn NY.

Tim McKeithan—3 Years Pitcher (b. 2 Nov 1906 Lawndale NC–d. 20 Aug 1969 Forest City NC) He was murdered.

Russ McKelvey—2 Years Outfielder (b. 8 Sep 1856 Swissvale PA–d. 19 Oct 1915 at his home in Omaha NE) He worked for Pacific Express Company in Omaha. Died from a complication of heart and kidney diseases. Buried Forest Lawn Memorial Park, Omaha NE.

Kit McKenna—2 Years Pitcher (b. 10 Feb 1873 Lynchburg VA–d. 31 Mar 1941 at his home in

Lynchburg VA) He operated a tinning business in Lynchburg. Died from pneumonia. Buried Holy Cross Cemetery, Lynchburg VA.

Limb McKenry—2 Years Pitcher (b. 13 Aug 1888 Piney Flat TN–d. 1 Nov 1956 at his apartment in Fresno CA) He farmed near Selma CA. Died from a self-inflicted blast to the head from a shotgun. He suffered from chronic arthritis. Buried Mountain View Cemetery, Oakland CA.

Larry McKeon—3 Years Pitcher (b. 25 Mar 1866 Indianapolis IN–d. 18 Jul 1915 City Hospital, Indianapolis IN) Died from pulmonary tuberculosis and excessive drinking. Buried Port Jarvis NY.

Dave McKeough—2 Years Catcher (b. 1 Dec 1864 Utica NY–d. 11 Jul 1901 at his home in Utica NY) He conducted a plumbing business with his brother in Utica. Died from a cerebral hemorrhage.

Bob McKinney—1 Year Infielder (b. 4 Oct 1875 McSherrystown PA–d. 19 Aug 1946 General Hospital, Hanover PA) He was a cigar packer for the Anton H Bock Company in Hanover. Died after being ill two weeks. Buried Church of the Annunciation Cemetery, Hanover PA.

Alex McKinnon—4 Years Infielder (b. 14 Aug 1856 Boston MA–d. 24 Jul 1887 Charlestown MA) Died at the height of his career from typhoid fever. Buried Lowell Cemetery, Lowell MA.

Denny McKnight—1 Year Manager (b. 1847 Pittsburgh PA–d. 5 May 1900 Pittsburgh PA).

Jim McKnight—2 Years Outfielder (b. 1 Jun 1936 Bee Branch AR–d. 24 Feb 1994 near Choctaw AR) He was a pipefitter. Killed instantly in a head-on collision with a van while negoiating a curve. Buried Blackwell Cemetery, Bee Branch AR.

Ed McLane—1 Year Outfielder (b. 20 Aug 1881 Weston MA–d. 21 Aug 1975 Baltimore MD).

Art McLarney—1 Year Infielder (b. 20 Dec 1908 Fort Worden WA–d. 20 Dec 1984 Swedish Hospital, Seattle WA) He coached high school basketball in Washington for years and was the head basketball coach at the Univ of Washington in 1949 and 1950. He was the recreation director for Fort Worden Diagnostic Center and also worked in the King County, WA, assessor's office. Died from heart-related problems. Buried Laurel Grove Cemetery, Port Townsend WA.

Polly McLarry—2 Years Infielder (b. 25 Mar 1891 Leonard TX–d. 4 Nov 1971 Allen Memorial Hospital, Bonham TX) He umpired minor league baseball ten years before spending 33 years in the real estate business. Buried Leonard Cemetery, Leonard TX.

Barney McLaughlin—3 Years Infielder (b. 1857 Ireland–d. 13 Feb 1921 at his home in Lowell MA) Buried St Patrick's Cemetery, Lowell MA.

Frank McLaughlin—3 Years Infielder (b. 19 Jun 1856 Lowell MA–d. 5 Apr 1917 at his brother's home in Lowell MA) Buried St Patrick's Cemetery, Lowell MA.

Jim McLaughlin—1 Year Infielder (b. 1860 Cleveland OH–d. 16 Nov 1895 Cleveland OH) He was a printer. Killed when the streetcar he was riding in plunged 100 feet off a viaduct into the Cuyahoga River below. Buried Riverside Cemetery, Cleveland OH.

Jim McLaughlin—1 Year Infielder (b. 3 Jan 1902 St Louis MO–d. 18 Dec 1968 Good Samaritan Hospital, Mount Vernon IL) He played in the Pacific Coast League for several years. Active in politics, he was a leader in the Democratic Party in Illinois, and was elected to three terms as Clerk of the Illinois State Appeals Court-5th District. Died after being in failing health for a long time. Buried Oakwood Cemetery, Mount Vernon IL.

Jud McLaughlin—3 Years Pitcher (b. 24 Mar 1912 Brighton MA–d. 27 Sep 1964 Belmont MA) World War II veteran. Buried Belmont Cemetery, Belmont MA.

Kid McLaughlin—1 Year Outfielder (b. 12 Apr 1888 Randolph NY–d. 17 Nov 1934 at his home in Allegany NY) He was a mathematics professor at St Bonaventure College for 19 years. Died after an illness of long duration. Buried St Bonaventure Cemetery, St Bonaventure NY.

Tom McLaughlin—5 Years Infielder (b. 28 Mar 1860 Louisville KY–d. 21 Jul 1921 SS Mary & Elizabeth Hospital, Louisville KY) He worked for the Standard and Sanitary Manufacturing Company in Louisville. Died following an illness of a year. Buried St Michael Cemetery, Louisville KY.

Warren McLaughlin —3 Years Pitcher (b. 22 Jan 1876 North Plainfield NJ–d. 22 Oct 1923 Muhlenberg Hospital, Plainfield NJ) He was a craftsman. Died from pneumonia. Buried Hillside Cemetery, Plainfield NJ.

Ralph McLaurin —1 Year Outfielder (b. 23 May 1885 Kissimmee FL–d. 11 Feb 1943 at his home in McColl SC) He coached 10 years at McColl High School, then pursued farming. Later he was a land surveyor. Died after an illness of several months. Buried McColl Cemetery, McColl SC.

Al McLean —1 Year Pitcher (b. 20 Sep 1912 Chicago IL–d. 29 Sep 1990 Brian Center, Asheboro NC) Served in the U.S. Army Air Corps during World War II. Buried Guilford Memorial Park, Greensboro NC.

Larry McLean —13 Years Catcher (b. 18 Jul 1881 Cambridge MA–d. 14 Mar 1921 Boston MA) Shot to death by a bartender during an argument.

Jim McLeod —3 Years Infielder (b. 12 Sep 1908 Jones LA–d. 3 Aug 1981 Little Rock AR) World War II veteran. He played and managed in the higher minor leagues for several years and retired as a clerk from the Pulaski County, AR, tax assessor's office. Buried Roselawn Memorial Park, Little Rock AR.

Sam McMackin —1 Year Pitcher (b. abt 1872 Cleveland OH–d. 11 Feb 1903 at his home in Columbus OH) Died from pneumonia at the height of his career. Buried Cleveland OH.

Doc McMahon —1 Year Pitcher (b. 19 Dec 1886 Woburn MA–d. 11 Dec 1929 at his home in Woburn MA) He was a prominent dentist in Woburn. Died suddenly from a heart attack. Buried Calvary Cemetery, Woburn MA.

Don McMahon —18 Years Pitcher (b. 4 Jan 1930 Brooklyn NY–d. 22 Jul 1987 Queen of Angels Medical Ctr, Los Angeles CA) He worked his entire life in baseball, coaching and scouting after his playing days were over. Died from a heart attack suffered while pitching batting practice for the Dodgers. Buried Good Shepherd Cemetery, Huntington Beach CA.

Jack McMahon —2 Years Infielder (b. 15 Oct 1869 Waterbury CT–d. 30 Dec 1894 at his parent's home in Bridgeport CT) Died at the height of his career after a year's illness from complications of bladder stones. Buried St Michael's Cemetery, Bridgeport CT.

Sadie McMahon —9 Years Pitcher (b. 19 Sep 1867 Wilmington DE–d. 20 Feb 1954 Wilmington DE) Died following surgery on a foot. Buried St Joseph on the Brandywine Cemetery, Wilmington DE.

John McMakin —1 Year Pitcher (b. 6 Mar 1878 Spartanburg SC–d. 26 Sep 1956 at his home near Lyman SC) Died after a long illness. Buried Wood Memorial Park, Greer SC.

Frank McManus —3 Years Catcher (b. 21 Sep 1875 Lawrence MA–d. 1 Sep 1923 Syracuse NY) He was murdered.

George McManus —1 Year Manager (b. 28 Jun 1846 Ireland–d. 2 Oct 1918 Park Hospital, New York City NY) A retired theatrical manager, he died suddenly.

Joe McManus —1 Year Pitcher (b. 7 Sep 1887 Palmyra IL–d. 23 Dec 1955 Beckley WV) He was a bookkeeper and weighmaster for the New River Company at Skelton WV. Died from the effects of a stroke suffered a month earlier. Buried Sunset Memorial Park, Beckley WV.

Marty McManus —15 Years Infielder 2 Years Manager (b. 14 Mar 1900 Chicago IL–d. 18 Feb 1966 Cochran Veteran's Hospital, St Louis MO) He was a hotel detective in Chicago. Died following surgery for cancer. Buried Calvary Cemetery, St Louis MO.

Pat McManus —1 Year Pitcher (b. Ireland–d. 6 Oct 1917 Brooklyn NY).

Norm McMillan —5 Years Infielder (b. 5 Oct 1895 Latta SC–d. 28 Sep 1969 Marion SC) He owned and operated a drug store in Latta and also owned a farm near there. Buried Magnolia Cemetery, Latta SC.

Roy McMillan —16 Years Infielder 2 Years Manager (b. 16 Jul 1929 Bonham TX–d. 2 Nov 1997 Northeast Medical Center, Bonham TX) He was active in baseball 51 years as a player, coach, scout and manager. Died from a heart attack. Buried Willow Wild Cemetery, Bonham TX.

Tommy McMillan —4 Years Infielder (b. 17 Apr 1888 Pittston PA–d. 15 Jul 1966 Orlando FL) World War I veteran. He moved to Orlando from Atlanta GA about 1922. Buried Woodlawn Cemetery, Winter Garden FL.

Hugh McMullen —4 Years Catcher (b. 16 Dec 1901 La Cygne KS–d. 23 May 1986 Whittier

Medical Center, Whittier CA) Died from a ruptured aortic aneurysm. Buried Rose Hills Memorial Park, Whittier CA.

Fred McMullin —6 Years Infielder (b. 13 Oct 1891 Scammon KS–d. 20 Nov 1952 at his home in Los Angeles CA) He was banned from baseball for his involvement in the Black Sox Scandal. For years he worked in the office of the U.S. Marshall. Died from a cerebral hemorrhage. Buried Inglewood Park Cemetery, Inglewood CA.

Edgar McNabb —1 Year Pitcher (b. 24 Oct 1865 Mount Vernon OH–d. 28 Feb 1894 Pittsburgh PA) Died from a self-inflicted gunshot wound after shooting his lover at the Hotel Eiffel. He had just learned he was dying from tuberculosis. His girlfriend died the next day. Buried Mound View Cemetery, Mount Vernon OH.

Eric McNair —14 Years Infielder (b. 12 Apr 1909 Meridian MS–d. 11 Mar 1949 Rush Memorial Hospital, Meridian MS) He managed minor league baseball and was a scout for the A's. Died from a heart attack. Buried Magnolia Cemetery, Meridian MS.

Hurley McNair —11 Years Outfielder (b. 28 Oct 1888 Marshall TX–d. 2 Dec 1948 Kansas City MO) He played in the negro leagues.

Mike McNally —10 Years Infielder (b. 13 Sep 1893 Minooka PA–d. 29 May 1965 St Luke's Hospital, Bethlehem PA) He was the first player to steal home in a World Series game. He scouted for the Indians and was the head of their farm system for several years. Died from a heart attack after suffering a virus attack while visiting relatives. Buried St Joseph Parish Cemetery, Minooka PA.

Dinny McNamara —2 Years Outfielder (b. 16 Sep 1905 Lexington MA–d. 20 Dec 1963 Lexington MA) A football coach, he was an assistant at Fordham Univ and Boston College before becoming head coach at Boston College in 1935. Died when he was hit by an automobile while walking near his home. Buried St Bernard's Parish Cemetery, Concord MA.

George McNamara —1 Year Outfielder (b. 11 Jan 1901 Chicago IL–d. 12 Jun 1990 Hinsdale IL) He retired as fire chief of Chicago's 25th Battalion and was also the mutual manager of the Chicago area race tracks. Buried Holy Sepulchre Cemetery, Worth IL.

Tim McNamara —5 Years Pitcher (b. 20 Nov 1898 Millville MA–d. 5 Nov 1994 at his home in North Smithfield RI) He owned Mack Buick, an automobile dealership, 40 years before retiring in the late 1980s. Buried St Charles Cemetery, Blackstone MA.

Tom McNamara —1 Game Pinch Hitter (b. 5 Nov 1895 Roxbury MA–d. 5 May 1974 at his home in Danvers MA) Served in the U.S. Navy during World War I. He coached and taught 17 years at Salem High School, retiring in 1952. Died suddenly. Buried Annunciation Cemetery, Danvers MA.

Gordon McNaughton —1 Year Pitcher (b. 31 Jul 1910 Chicago IL–d. 6 Aug 1942 Chicago IL) Shot to death by a jilted girlfriend in another woman's hotel room. Buried Calvary Cemetery, Evanston IL.

Harry McNeal —1 Year Pitcher (b. 11 Aug 1877 Iberia OH–d. 11 Jan 1945 Auditorium Hotel, Cleveland OH) He was a Cleveland attorney. Died from a self-inflicted gunshot wound. Buried Ferndale Cemetery, Johnstown NY.

Earl McNeely —8 Years Outfielder (b. 12 May 1898 Sacramento CA–d. 16 Jul 1971 Sutter Memorial Hospital, Sacramento CA) World War I veteran. He managed some minor league baseball. Retiring from the farming and cattle business in 1959, he was active in many civic activities. Died from lung cancer. Buried Mount Vernon Memorial Park, Fair Oaks CA.

Norm McNeil —1 Year Catcher (b. 22 Oct 1892 Chicago IL–d. 11 Apr 1942 Sister's Hospital, Buffalo NY) He managed minor league baseball. Died after being ill his last few weeks.

Ed McNichol —1 Year Pitcher (b. 10 Jan 1879 Martins Ferry OH–d. 1 Nov 1952 City Hospital, East Liverpool OH) He was a coal operator in the mines. Died from burns and shock suffered when he was trapped in his burning house. Buried Woodland Cemetery, Salineville OH.

Pat McNulty —5 Years Outfielder (b. 27 Feb 1899 Cleveland OH–d. 4 May 1963 at his home in Los Angeles CA) World War I veteran. He was a jig builder for the Lockheed Aircraft Company. Died from heart disease. Buried Good Shepherd Cemetery, Huntington Beach CA.

Frank McPartlin —1 Year Pitcher (b. 16 Feb 1872 Hoosick Falls NY–d. 13 Nov 1943 New York City NY).

Bid McPhee—18 Years Infielder 2 Years Manager Hall of Fame (b. 1 Nov 1859 Massena NY–d. 3 Jan 1943 San Diego CA) Died from a heart attack. Cremated. Buried Cypress View Cemetery, San Diego CA.

John McPherson—2 Years Pitcher (b. 9 Mar 1869 Easton PA–d. 30 Sep 1941 Easton PA) He was a retired bricklayer and had been ill seven years. Buried Easton Heights Cemetery, Easton PA.

Herb McQuaid—2 Years Pitcher (b. 29 Mar 1899 San Francisco CA–d. 4 Apr 1966 Kaiser Hospital, Richmond CA) For several years he was a security guard for a San Francisco company. Died from kidney cancer. Buried Chapel of the Chimes, Oakland CA.

Marty McQuaid—1 Year Infielder (b. 28 Jun 1861 Chicago IL–d. 5 Mar 1928 Chicago IL) Died after an illness of about a month. Buried Calvary Cemetery, Evanston IL.

Mox McQuery—5 Years Infielder (b. 28 Jun 1861 Garrard County KY–d. 12 Jun 1900 Cincinnati OH) A Covington KY policeman, he was shot in the line of duty, and died from blood poisoning as a result of his wounds. Buried Linden Grove Cemetery, Covington KY.

George McQuillan—10 Years Pitcher (b. 1 May 1885 Brooklyn NY–d. 30 Mar 1940 at his home in Columbus OH) He was a furniture salesman for F R Lazarus Company. Died from pulmonary heart disease. Buried Paterson NJ.

Hugh McQuillan—10 Years Pitcher (b. 15 Sep 1897 New York City NY–d. 26 Aug 1947 Queens General Hospital, New York City NY) Buried Calvary Cemetery, Woodside NY.

Glenn McQuillen—5 Years Outfielder (b. 19 Apr 1915 Strasburg VA–d. 8 Jun 1989 at his home in Gardenville MD) Served in the U.S. Navy during World War II. Playing minor league baseball until 1957, he managed some minor league baseball and worked in the catering business. Died from heart failure.

George McQuinn—12 Years Infielder (b. 29 May 1909 Arlington VA–d. 24 Dec 1978 Alexandria Hospital, Alexandria VA) For many years he was a coach, scout and minor league manager. Died from a massive heart attack and stroke. Cremated.

Pete McShannic—1 Year Infielder (b. 20 Mar 1864 Pittsburgh PA–d. 30 Nov 1946 St Vincent Hospital, Toledo OH) He lived 34 years in Toledo. Died after a brief illness. Buried Toledo Memorial Park, Sylvania OH.

John McSherry—(b. 4 Sep 1944 Bronx NY–d. 1 Apr 1996 University Hospital, Cincinnati OH) He was a National League umpire from 1971 until his death. Died from a heart attack suffered during the opening day game of the 1996 season. Buried Gate of Heaven Cemetery, Hawthorne NY.

Trick McSorley—3 Years Infielder (b. 6 Dec 1858 St Louis MO–d. 9 Feb 1936 at his home in St Louis MO) He started playing in 1874 for the St Louis Red Stockings, one of the earliest professional teams, and worked for the St Louis Police Department from 1901 until he retired in 1931. Died from apoplexy. Buried Calvary Cemetery, St Louis MO.

Paul McSweeney—1 Year Infielder (b. 3 Apr 1867 St Louis MO–d. 12 Aug 1951 St Louis MO) He was an outstanding all-around athlete, starring during his youth in soccer, football, baseball, hockey, boxing and track. He officiated soccer games in the St Louis area for 40 years and was a bookkeeper at the St Louis Country Club for many years. Buried Calvary Cemetery, St Louis MO.

Jim McTamany—7 Years Outfielder (b. 4 Jul 1863 Philadelphia PA–d. 16 Apr 1916 Lenni PA).

Bill McTigue—3 Years Pitcher (b. 3 Jan 1892 Nashville TN–d. 6 May 1920 Nashville TN) Died from tuberculosis. Buried Calvary Cemetery, Nashville TN.

Cal McVey—4 Years Infielder 3 Years Manager (b. 30 Aug 1850 Montrose IA–d. 19 Aug 1926 San Francisco CA) He ran a cigar store in San Francisco at the time of the 1906 earthquake and later was a night watchman for the Loop Lumber Company. Died after an illness of several months. Cremated.

George McVey—1 Year Infielder (b. 1864 Port Jervis NY–d. 3 May 1896 St Mary Hospital, Quincy IL) Died from consumption. Buried Columbus OH.

Doug McWeeny—8 Years Pitcher (b. 17 Aug 1896 Chicago IL–d. 1 Jan 1953 Chicago IL) For years he operated a filling station in Chicago and later worked for Public Service Company of Northern Illinois. Died after a three-week illness. Buried All Saints Cemetery, Des Plaines IL.

Bill McWilliams —(b. 28 Nov 1910 Dubuque IA–d. 21 Jan 1997 Garland TX) He also played professional football. Living in Chicago IL for 65 years, he retired as playground director for the City of Chicago Park District. Cremated.

Johnny Meador —1 Year Pitcher (b. 4 Dec 1892 Madison NC–d. 11 Apr 1970 Baptist Hospital, Winston-Salem NC) He was a retired employee of R J Reynolds Tobacco Company. Buried Forsyth Memorial Park, Winston-Salem NC.

Lee Meadows —15 Years Pitcher (b. 12 Jul 1894 Oxford NC–d. 29 Jan 1963 Halifax Hospital, Daytona Beach FL) He was the first man to wear glasses while playing major league baseball. He was a deputy collector for the Internal Revenue Service. Died from a stroke. Buried Resthaven Garden of Memories, Decatur GA.

Rufe Meadows —1 Year Pitcher (b. 25 Aug 1907 Chase City VA–d. 10 May 1970 Wichita KS) He moved from Tyler TX to Wichita in 1940 and was a mechanic at the Boeing plant there. Buried Resthaven Gardens of Memory, Wichita KS.

George Meakim —4 Years Pitcher (b. 11 Jul 1865 Brooklyn NY–d. 17 Feb 1923 at his home in Queens NY) He was a retired milk dealer. Died after a brief illness. Buried Mount Olivet Cemetery, Maspeth NY.

Pat Meaney —1 Year Infielder (b. 1892 Philadelphia PA–d. 20 Oct 1922 Philadelphia PA) Died from a complication of diseases. Buried Holy Cross Cemetery, Yeadon PA.

Tom Meany —Hall of Fame (b. 21 Sep 1903 Brooklyn NY–d. 11 Sep 1964 New York City NY) He was a sportswriter and raconteur for a number of New York City newspapers for nearly 40 years. He also did promotion work for the Yankees, Mets and Sugar Ray Robinson. Buried Holy Cross Cemetery, Brooklyn NY.

Charlie Meara —1 Year Outfielder (b. 16 Apr 1891 New York City NY–d. 8 Feb 1962 Kingsbridge NY) Buried Long Island National Cemetery, Farmingdale NY.

Irv Medlinger —2 Years Pitcher (b. 18 Jun 1927 Chicago IL–d. 3 Sep 1975 Wheeling IL).

Joe Medwick —17 Years Outfielder Hall of Fame (b. 24 Nov 1911 Carteret NJ–d. 21 Mar 1975 Bayfront Medical Center, St Petersburg FL) He engaged in the insurance business in St Louis MO from 1950 to 1966, but in 1966 returned to baseball as the minor league hitting instructor for the Cardinals. Died from a heart attack. Buried St Lucas Cemetery, Sappington MO.

Tommy Mee —1 Year Infielder (b. 18 Mar 1890 Chicago IL–d. 16 May 1981 Rush-Presbyterian St Luke Hosp, Chicago IL) He was the founder and owner of a medical supply company and directed Ethicon, Inc, a Johnson and Johnson subsidiary. Buried Holy Sepulchre Cemetery, Worth IL.

Pete Meegan —2 Years Pitcher (b. 13 Nov 1863 San Francisco CA–d. 15 Mar 1905 San Francisco CA) Buried Holy Cross Catholic Cemetery, Colma CA.

Bill Meehan —1 Year Pitcher (b. 4 Sep 1889 Osceola Mills PA–d. 8 Oct 1982 Michael Manor, Douglas WY) Served in the U.S. Navy during World War I. He was a detective for the Reading Railroad, retiring in 1954. He was the first president of the Railway Patrolman's Union and national chairman of that union. In 1971 he moved to Wyoming to be near his son. Buried Douglas Park Cemetery, Douglas WY.

Dad Meek —2 Years Catcher (b. abt 1867 St Louis MO–d. 26 Dec 1922 St Louis MO) Cremated. Buried New Picker's Cemetery, Lemay MO.

Roy Meeker —3 Years Pitcher (b. 15 Sep 1900 Lead Mines MO–d. 25 Mar 1929 in his hotel room in Orlando FL) Died from a heart attack suffered two hours after a spring training workout. Buried Memorial Park Cemetery, Kansas City KS.

Jouett Meekin —10 Years Pitcher (b. 21 Feb 1867 New Albany IN–d. 14 Dec 1944 St Edward's Hospital, New Albany IN) He worked more than 25 years for the New Albany Fire Department. Died from a heart attack after injuring himself in a fall. Buried Fairview Cemetery, New Albany IN.

Russ Meers —3 Years Pitcher (b. 28 Nov 1918 Tilton IL–d. 16 Nov 1994 General Hospital, Lancaster PA) Served in the U.S. Navy during World War II. For 31 years he worked for Ford Motor Company, retiring in 1981 as manager of the parts distribution center at Atlanta GA. Died following a brief illness.

Dutch Meier—1 Year Outfielder (b. 30 Mar 1879 St Louis MO–d. 23 Mar 1948 at his home in Chicago IL) The baseball coach at Princeton University from 1908 to 1910, he was widely known in the sporting goods business and in bowling circles.

Heinie Meine—7 Years Pitcher (b. 1 May 1896 St Louis MO–d. 18 Mar 1968 Alexian Brothers' Hospital, St Louis MO) Served in the U.S. Army during World War II. He operated a saloon in south St Louis for many years and supported sandlot baseball in that area. Died from cancer. Buried St Trinity Lutheran Cemetery, St Louis MO.

Walt Meinert—1 Year Outfielder (b. 11 Dec 1890 New York City NY–d. 9 Nov 1958 Decatur IL) He was a millwright for A E Staley Manufacturing Company in Decatur. He was working on the 7th floor of an old starch building when he accidently fell five floors to his death. Buried Fairlawn Cemetery, Decatur IL.

Bob Meinke—1 Year Infielder (b. 25 Jun 1887 Chicago IL–d. 29 Dec 1952 Chicago IL) Buried Acacia Park Cemetery, Chicago IL.

Frank Meinke—2 Years Infielder (b. 18 Oct 1862 Chicago IL–d. 8 Nov 1931 at his home in Chicago IL) He was a street department foreman for a Chicago ward. Buried Montrose Cemetery, Chicago IL.

Charlie Meisel—1 Year Catcher (b. 21 Apr 1894 Catonsville MD–d. 25 Aug 1953 at his home in Baltimore MD) Buried Lorraine Park Cemetery, Baltimore MD.

George Meister—1 Year Infielder (b. 5 Jun 1864 Ellenbock, Germany–d. 24 Aug 1908 at his home in Pittsburgh PA) He conducted a hotel in Pittsburgh for several years.

John Meister—2 Years Infielder (b. 10 May 1863 Philadelphia PA–d. 17 Jan 1923 Episcopal Hospital, Philadelphia PA) He was engaged in the hotel and cafe business in Allentown PA with his brother. After selling his business there he opened a shoe store in Philadelphia that he operated until his death. Died from pneumonia that developed from grippe. Buried Union Cemetery, Allentown PA.

Karl Meister—1 Year Outfielder (b. 15 May 1891 Marietta OH–d. 15 Aug 1967 Selby General Hospital, Marietta OH) He was a mechanic and a lifelong resident of Marietta. Buried East Lawn Memorial Park, Marietta OH.

Moxie Meixel—2 Games Pinch-Hitter (b. 18 Oct 1887 Lake Crystal MN–d. 17 Aug 1982 V A Medical Center, Los Angeles CA) He was a game warden in Wisconsin for 17 years. Died from tuberculosis and congestive heart failure. Cremated.

Dutch Mele—1 Year Outfielder (b. 11 Jan 1915 New York City NY–d. 12 Feb 1975 Hollywood FL).

Oscar Melillo—12 Years Infielder (b. 4 Aug 1899 Chicago IL–d. 14 Nov 1963 at his home in Chicago IL) He coached and scouted for several teams and managed minor league baseball. Died from a heart attack. Buried Holy Sepulchre Cemetery, Worth IL.

Joe Mellana—1 Year Infielder (b. 11 Mar 1905 Oakland CA–d. 1 Nov 1969 Marin General Hospital, San Rafael CA) For 25 years he was a bartender and at one time owned Joe's Village Patio Restaurant in Corte Madera CA. Died from esophageal bleeding and cirrhosis of the liver. Buried Mount Tamalpais Cemetery, San Rafael CA.

Bill Mellor—1 Year Infielder (b. 6 Jun 1874 Camden NJ–d. 5 Nov 1940 Bridgeton RI) Buried Acote Hill Cemetery, Chepachet RI.

Paul Meloan—2 Years Outfielder (b. 23 Aug 1888 Paynesville MO–d. 11 Feb 1950 at his home in Taft CA) He was a rigbuilder for Standard Oil Company, living in California 38 years and in Taft 25 years. Died from a heart attack. Cremated.

Steve Melter—1 Year Pitcher (b. 2 Jan 1886 Cherokee IA–d. 28 Jan 1962 at his home in Mishawaka IN) He retired to Mishawaka in 1960 after working for several newspapers in the Detroit MI area. Died after a one-year illness. Buried Mount Calvary Cemetery, Cherokee IA.

Cliff Melton—8 Years Pitcher (b. 3 Jan 1912 Brevard NC–d. 28 Jul 1986 St Joseph Hospital, Baltimore MD) For 20 years he was a truck driver for Lou Grasmick Lumber Company. Died from cancer. Buried Most Holy Redeemer Memorial Park, Baltimore MD.

Rube Melton—6 Years Pitcher (b. 27 Feb 1917 Cramerton NC–d. 11 Sep 1971 Greer SC) He was a salesman for Chastain's, Inc. He and his wife were killed in an automobile accident. Buried Woodlawn Memorial Park, Greenville SC.

Jock Menefee—9 Years Pitcher (b. 15 Jan 1868

WV–d. 11 Mar 1953 Restful Acres Nursing Home, Belle Vernon PA) He was a former Monessen PA businessman and public official. Buried Cochran Cemetery, Dawson PA.

Mike Menosky—9 Years Outfielder (b. 16 Oct 1894 Glen Campbell PA–d. 11 Apr 1983 Mount Carmel Hospital, Detroit MI) He was a retired Detroit probation officer. Buried Holy Sepulchre Cemetery, Southfield MI.

Ed Mensor—3 Years Outfielder (b. 7 Nov 1886 Woodville, Ontario, Canada–d. 20 Apr 1970 at a hospital in Salem OR) Buried Buena Vista Cemetery, Independence OR.

Ted Menze—1 Year Outfielder (b. 4 Nov 1897 St Louis MO–d. 23 Dec 1969 St Louis MO) After retiring from baseball he became a top amateur bowler, rolling a 300 game in 1957. Died from a cerebral hemorrhage. Buried St Peter's Cemetery, St Louis MO.

Mike Meola—2 Years Pitcher (b. 19 Oct 1905 New York City NY–d. 1 Sep 1976 Memorial Hospital, Fair Lawn NJ) He was a partner in P Meola and Sons, a demolition contractor in New York City. Politically active in the Republican Party, he was a former county committeeman in the party and a member of the Fair Lawn Planning Board. Buried Calvary Cemetery, Paterson NJ.

Jack Mercer—1 Year Pitcher (b. 10 Mar 1889 Zanesville OH–d. 25 Jun 1945 Dayton OH).

John Mercer—1 Year Pitcher (b. 22 Jun 1892 Taylortown LA–d. 22 Dec 1982 Live Oak Retirement Center, Shreveport LA) Buried Greenwood Cemetery, Shreveport LA.

Sid Mercer—Hall of Fame (b. 1883 Paxton IL–d. 19 Jun 1945 at his home in New York City NY) For 40 years he was a sportswriter for, first, the *New York Globe,* and later, the *New York Evening Journal.* Died after a six-month illness. Cremated.

Win Mercer—9 Years Pitcher (b. 20 Jun 1874 Chester WV–d. 12 Jan 1903 at the Occidental Hotel in San Francisco CA) He committed suicide by gassing himself while barnstorming with a team in California. Buried Riverview Cemetery, East Liverpool OH.

Spike Merena—1 Year Pitcher (b. 18 Nov 1909 Paterson NJ–d. 8 Mar 1977 St Vincent's Medical Center, Bridgeport CT) He worked in factories at Bridgeport until 1944 when he joined the Bridgeport Police Department, working there 32 years before retiring in 1976. Buried St Michael's Cemetery, Bridgeport CT.

Art Merewether—1 Game Pinch Hitter (b. 7 Jul 1902 East Providence RI–d. 2 Feb 1997 Bayside NY).

Fred Merkle—16 Years Infielder (b. 20 Dec 1888 Watertown WI–d. 2 Mar 1956 Daytona Beach FL) He is best remembered for the "Merkle Boner" that cost the Giants the National League pennant in 1908. Died in bed from natural causes. Buried Cedar Hill Memory Gardens, Daytona Beach FL.

Ed Merrill—2 Years Infielder (b. 1860 Chicago IL–d. 18 Aug 1924 Chicago IL).

Bill Merritt—8 Years Catcher (b. 30 Jul 1870 Lowell MA–d. 17 Nov 1937 St John's Hospital, Lowell MA) He spent his entire life in baseball as a player, minor league manager and scout. Died after being ill several months. Buried St Patrick's Cemetery, Lowell MA.

George Merritt—3 Years Outfielder (b. 14 Apr 1880 Paterson NJ–d. 21 Feb 1938 St Joseph's Hospital, Memphis TN) He played in the Southern League and lived in West Memphis AR while working for Federal Compress and Warehouse Company. Died from a coronary thrombosis. Buried Memorial Park Cemetery, Memphis TN.

Herm Merritt—1 Year Infielder (b. 12 Nov 1900 Independence KS–d. 26 May 1957 Kansas City MO).

Howard Merritt—1 Year Outfielder (b. 6 Oct 1894 Plantersville MS–d. 3 Nov 1955 at his home in Tupelo MS) He served 20 years as the Tupelo City Clerk, after which he was a partner in a men's clothing store in Tupelo and in the *Lee County* (MS) *Tribune.* He worked his last two years as a deputy clerk in the county courthouse. Died from a kidney ailment. Buried Glenwood Cemetery, Tupelo MS.

Sam Mertes—10 Years Outfielder (b. 6 Aug 1872 San Francisco CA–d. 11 Mar 1945 near Guerneville CA) Died from a heart attack. Cremated. Buried Woodlawn Memorial Park, Daly City CA.

Steve Mesner—6 Years Infielder (b. 13 Jan 1918 Los Angeles CA–d. 6 Apr 1981 at his home in San Diego CA) Died from a heart attack. Buried Greenwood Memorial Park, San Diego CA.

Bobby Messenger—4 Years Outfielder (b. 19 Mar 1884 Bangor ME–d. 10 Jul 1951 at his home in Bath ME) He was the sheriff of Lincoln County (ME) for 15 years after serving several years as tax collector and deputy sheriff. Buried Richmond Cemetery, Richmond ME.

Bud Messenger—1 Year Pitcher (b. 1 Feb 1898 Grand Blanc MI–d. 4 Nov 1971 at a hospital in Lansing MI) He played 18 years in the Indian farm system and operated service station at Vernon MI until 1970. Buried Roselawn Cemetery, Perry MI.

Tom Messitt—1 Year Catcher (b. 27 Jul 1874 Philadelphia PA–d. 22 Sep 1934 Chicago IL) He was a conductor on the Chicago elevated lines. Died from a heart attack while on the job. Buried Calvary Cemetery, Evanston IL.

Scat Metha—1 Year Infielder (b. 13 Dec 1913 Los Angeles CA–d. 2 Mar 1975 Community Hospital, Fountain Valley CA) He worked at the Long Beach CA Naval Shipyard. Died from lung cancer that had spread to the liver. Buried Rose Hills Memorial Park, Whittier CA.

Dewey Metivier—3 Years Pitcher (b. 6 May 1898 Cambridge MA–d. 2 Mar 1947 at his home in Cambridge MA) He was a foreman for the Cambridge Street Department from 1939 until his death. Died from a lingering illness. Buried St Paul's Cemetery, Arlington MA.

Catfish Metkovich—10 Years Outfielder (b. 8 Oct 1920 Angels Camp CA–d. 17 May 1995 Port Bay Convalescent Hosp, Costa Mesa CA) Died from acute respiratory arrest. Buried El Toro Memorial Park, Lake Forest CA.

Lenny Metz—3 Years Infielder (b. 6 Jul 1899 Louisville CO–d. 24 Feb 1953 Veteran's Hospital, Denver CO) He was the town marshall at Lafayette CO and operated a sporting goods store there. Died after being in failing health for some time. Buried Mountain View Cemetery, Boulder CO.

Alex Metzler—6 Years Outfielder (b. 4 Jan 1903 Fresno CA–d. 29 Nov 1973 Hy Lond Convalescent Hospital, Fresno CA) He was a self-employed grape farmer for 37 years. Died from liver cancer. Buried Mountain View Cemetery, Fresno CA.

Bob Meusel—11 Years Outfielder (b. 19 Jul 1896 San Jose CA–d. 28 Nov 1977 Kaiser Hospital, Bellflower CA) For 12 years he was a civilian security officer for the U.S. Navy. Died from a heart attack. Cremated. Buried Rose Hills Memorial Park, Whittier CA.

Irish Meusel—11 Years Outfielder (b. 9 Jun 1893 Oakland CA–d. 1 Mar 1963 Pacific Hospital, Long Beach CA) He was a gateman at the Los Angeles Turf Club for 15 years. Died from a heart attack after a short illness. Buried Inglewood Park Cemetery, Inglewood CA.

Benny Meyer—4 Years Outfielder (b. 21 Jan 1885 Hematite MO–d. 6 Feb 1974 Jefferson Memorial Hospital, Festus MO) He spent nearly 70 years in baseball as a player, coach and scout. Cremated. Buried Hillcrest Abbey, St Louis MO.

Billy Meyer—3 Years Catcher 5 Years Manager (b. 14 Jan 1892 Knoxville TN–d. 31 Mar 1957 Presbyterian Hospital, Knoxville TN) He worked in baseball for 43 years and was one of the few men to be named Manager of the Year in both the major and minor leagues. Died from uremic poisoning and heart disease. Buried Lynnhurst Cemetery, Knoxville TN.

George Meyer—1 Year Infielder (b. 3 Aug 1909 Chicago IL–d. 3 Jan 1992 Hoffman Estates IL) Buried Memory Gardens Cemetery, Arlington Heights IL.

Jack Meyer—7 Years Pitcher (b. 23 Mar 1932 Philadelphia PA–d. 9 Mar 1967 Jefferson Hospital, Philadelphia PA) He worked for Regal Corrugated Box Company. Collapsed from a heart attack while watching a basketball game on television and died later at the hospital.

Russ Meyer—13 Years Pitcher (b. 25 Oct 1923 Peru IL–d. 16 Nov 1998 Oglesby IL).

Levi Meyerle—3 Years Infielder (b. Jul 1845 Philadelphia PA–d. 4 Nov 1921 Philadelphia PA).

Bert Meyers—3 Years Infielder (b. 8 Apr 1874 Frederick MD–d. 12 Dec 1915 Washington DC).

Chief Meyers—9 Years Catcher (b. 29 Jul 1880 Riverside CA–d. 25 Jul 1971 Community Hospital, San Bernardino CA) He served 25 years as Chief of Police for the Indian Service of Southern California. Died from chronic brain syndrome and generalized arteriosclerosis. Buried Green Acres Memorial Park, Bloomington CA.

Henry Meyers—1 Year Infielder (b. 1860 Philadelphia PA–d. 25 Jun 1898 at his home in

Harrisburg PA) He was a hotelkeeper in Harrisburg. Died from an overdose of a combination of liquor, opium and perhaps other poisons. May have been a sucide.

Lew Meyers—1 Year Catcher (b. 9 Dec 1859 Cincinnati OH–d. 30 Nov 1920 General Hospital, Cincinnati OH) He was a porter. Took his own life with strychnine poison. Buried Spring Grove Cemetery, Cincinnati OH.

Cass Michaels—12 Years Infielder (b. 4 Mar 1926 Detroit MI–d. 12 Nov 1982 Bon Secours Hospital, Grosse Pointe MI) He retired from baseball after suffering a fractured skull when hit by a pitch. He was a manufacturer's representative. Died following a lingering illness. Buried Mount Olivet Cemetery, Detroit MI.

John Michaels—1 Year Pitcher (b. 10 Jul 1907 Bridgeport CT–d. 18 Nov 1996 Sebring FL) He worked for Sikorsky Aircraft in Bridgeport until retiring to Florida in 1970. Buried St Michael's Cemetery, Bridgeport CT.

Ralph Michaels—3 Years Infielder (b. 3 May 1902 Etna PA–d. 5 Aug 1988 Forbes Regional Hospital, Monroeville PA) He was the police chief of Etna. Died from a heart attack. Buried St Mary's Cemetery, O'Hara PA.

John Michaelson—1 Year Pitcher (b. 12 Aug 1893 Taivalkoski, Oulu, Finland–d. 16 Apr 1968 Woodruff WI) He was a painting contractor. Died from a heart attack while dumping rubbish at the city dump. Buried Marenisco Cemetery, Marenisco MI.

Jim Middleton—2 Years Pitcher (b. 28 May 1899 Argos IN–d. 12 Jan 1974 at his home in Argos IN) He played and managed in the Pacific Coast League, Texas League and American Association. He worked for the Marshall County (IN) Highway Department. Died following a lengthy illness. Buried Maple Grove Cemetery, Argos IN.

John Middleton—1 Year Pitcher (b. 11 Apr 1900 Mount Calm TX–d. 3 Nov 1986 Amarillo TX) Served in the U.S. Army during both World Wars I and II. He taught 20 years in the Amarillo Public School System and also owned and managed Middleton Cafe Supply Company. Buried Llano Cemetery, Amarillo TX.

Dick Midkiff—1 Year Pitcher (b. 28 Sep 1914 Gonzales TX–d. 30 Oct 1956 Veteran's Hospital, Temple TX) Served in the U.S. Army artillery during World War II. He was an accountant at Del Rio TX for several years. Buried Memorial Park, Gonzales TX.

Ezra Midkiff—3 Years Infielder (b. 13 Nov 1882 Salt Rock WV–d. 20 Mar 1957 Huntington WV) Active politically in the Huntington area, he served as justice of the peace, constable and Cabell County (WV) sheriff. Died following a long illness. Buried Woodmere Memorial Park, Huntington WV.

John Mihalic—3 Years Infielder (b. 13 Nov 1911 Cleveland OH–d. 24 Apr 1987 Fort Oglethorpe GA) He was a group executive for Avco Corporation, a division of Textron, retiring after 35 years. Buried Woodlawn Memorial Park, Nashville TN.

Clyde Milan—16 Years Outfielder 1 Year Manager (b. 25 Mar 1887 Linden TN–d. 3 Mar 1953 Orange Memorial Hospital, Orlando FL) Spending his entire life in baseball as a player, coach, scout and manager, he was associated with the Senators from 1907 until his death. Died following a heart attack during spring training. Buried Clarksville Cemetery, Clarksville TX.

Horace Milan—2 Years Outfielder (b. 7 Apr 1894 Linden TN–d. 29 Jun 1955 St Michael's Hospital, Texarkana TX) World War I veteran. He was a scout for the Senators. Buried Fairview Cemetery, Clarksville TX.

Dee Miles—7 Years Outfielder (b. 15 Feb 1909 Kellerman AL–d. 2 Nov 1976 Birmingham AL) Served in the U.S. Navy during World War II. He was retired from Fruehauf Corporation. Buried Elmwood Cemetery, Birmingham AL.

Mike Miley—2 Years Infielder (b. 30 Mar 1953 Yazoo City MS–d. 6 Jan 1977 Baton Rouge LA) He was killed instantly, at the height of his baseball career, in a one-car accident when his car skidded out of control, hitting several road posts and turned over on top of him. Buried Garden of Memories, Metairie LA.

Johnny Miljus—7 Years Pitcher (b. 30 Jun 1895 Pittsburgh PA–d. 11 Feb 1976 Fort Harrison Veteran's Hospital, Polson MT) He struck out Babe Ruth in the 1927 World Series with the bases loaded. He supervised the athletic department at Northrup Company. He lived at Bigfork MT from 1967 to 1970 when he moved to St Petersburg FL for two years, then back to

Montana where he lived at Polson until his death. Cremated.

Frank Millard—1 Year Infielder (b. 4 Jul 1865 East Saint Louis IL–d. 4 Jul 1892 Galveston TX).

Bert Miller—1 Year Pitcher (b. 26 Oct 1875 Riley MI–d. 14 Jun 1937 Hurley Hospital, Flint MI).

Bill Miller—1 Year Pitcher (b. 12 Apr 1910 Hannibal MO–d. 26 Feb 1982 at his home in Hannibal MO) He owned Whitney Automotive in Hannibal. Buried Holy Family Cemetery, Hannibal MO.

Bill Miller—1 Year Outfielder (b. 23 May 1879 Bad Schwalbach, Germany–d. 8 Sep 1957 Ashtabula OH).

Bing Miller—16 Years Outfielder (b. 30 Aug 1894 Vinton IA–d. 7 May 1966 Presbyterian Hospital, Philadelphia PA) He spent his entire life in baseball as a scout and hitting instructor, working for the Tigers, Red Sox, White Sox and Athletics. Died from a heart attack after suffering injuries in an automobile accident. Buried Calvary Cemetery, West Conshohocken PA.

Bob Miller—17 Years Pitcher (b. 18 Feb 1939 St Louis MO–d. 6 Aug 1993 Rancho Bernardo CA) Served in the military. He scouted and coached for the Giants. Died instantly in an automobile crash. Buried Dearborn Memorial Park, Poway CA.

Charlie Miller—1 Year Infielder (b. 4 Jan 1892 Warrensburg MO–d. 23 Apr 1972 Warrensburg MO) Served in the U.S. Army during World War II. He taught at Hannibal MO for several years before returning to Warrensburg, working there as a master carpenter. He served several years there on the school board and as a city councilman. Buried Sunset Hills Cemetery, Warrensburg MO.

Charlie Miller—1 Game Pinch Hitter (b. 30 Dec 1877 Conestoga Center PA–d. 13 Jan 1951 at his home in Millersville PA) He worked in a silk mill and was foreman in a cigar factory, retiring in 1942 because of ill health. Died after a long illness. Buried Millersville Mennonite Cemetery, Millersville PA.

Charlie Miller—2 Years Outfielder (b. 18 Sep 1889 Woodville OH–d. 16 Jun 1961 Houston TX) World War I veteran. He lived in Houston 40 years and was a design engineer for the City of Houston public works department. Buried Forest Park of Lawndale, Houston TX.

Cyclone Miller—2 Years Pitcher (b. 24 Sep 1859 Springfield MA–d. 13 Oct 1916 Lawrence Hospital, New London CT).

Dakin Miller—1 Year Outfielder (b. 2 Sep 1877 Malvern IA–d. 20 Apr 1950 at a hospital in Stockton CA) After being in business in Kansas City MO he moved to California in 1924, opening a tourist camp, service station and grocery near Manteca CA. Later he opened a service station in Manteca. Buried Rural Cemetery, Stockton CA.

Doc Miller—5 Years Outfielder (b. 1883 Chatham, Ontario, Canada–d. 31 Jul 1938 Jersey City NJ) He was a physician with a practice in New York City. He committed suicide by jumping from a third story, apparently despondent over the death of a wife two years earlier. Cremated.

Doggie Miller—13 Years Catcher (b. 15 Aug 1864 Brooklyn NY–d. 6 Apr 1909 Brooklyn NY) Died from Bright's disease.

Dots Miller—12 Years Infielder (b. 9 Sep 1886 Kearny NJ–d. 5 Sep 1923 Saranac Lake NY) Died from tuberculosis.

Dusty Miller—7 Years Outfielder (b. 10 Sep 1868 Oil City PA–d. 3 Sep 1945 at his home in Memphis TN) Buried Forest Hill Cemetery, Memphis TN.

Ed Miller—3 Years Infielder (b. 24 Nov 1888 Annville PA–d. 17 Apr 1980 V A Medical Center, South Lebanon PA) World War I veteran. Buried Mount Annville Cemetery, Annville PA.

Eddie Miller—14 Years Infielder (b. 26 Nov 1916 Pittsburgh PA–d. 31 Jul 1997 Lake Worth FL) He taught at various baseball schools throughout the country, including his own. Becoming a scratch golfer, he supplemented his retirement income at the Palm Beach and Newport jai alai frontons for many years. Buried Union Dale Cemetery, Pittsburgh PA.

Elmer Miller—7 Years Outfielder (b. 28 Jul 1888 Sandusky OH–d. 28 Nov 1944 at his home in Beloit WI) Died suddenly from a heart attack. Buried Eastlawn Cemetery, Beloit WI.

Elmer Miller—1 Year Pitcher (b. 17 Apr 1903 Detroit MI–d. 8 Jan 1987 Circle City Hospital, Corona CA) For 20 years he was a machinist for Chrysler Corporation. Died from a heart attack. Cremated.

Frank Miller—7 Years Pitcher (b. 13 Mar 1886 Salem MI–d. 19 Feb 1974 Allegan General Hospital, Allegan MI) He bought a farm near Allegan in 1923 and lived there the rest of his life. Buried Rowe Cemetery, Allegan MI.

Fred Miller—1 Year Pitcher (b. 28 Jun 1886 Fairfield IN–d. 2 May 1953 Brookville IN) He farmed in Franklin County, IN. Died in his sleep. Buried Maple Grove Cemetery, Brookville IN.

George Miller—2 Years Catcher 1 Year Manager (b. 19 Feb 1853 Newport KY–d. 25 Jul 1929 at his home in Norwood OH) He was a machinist at Allis Chalmers. Died from a heart attack. Buried Spring Grove Cemetery, Cincinnati OH.

Hack Miller—6 Years Outfielder (b. 1 Jan 1894 Chicago IL–d. 16 Sep 1971 Kaiser Hospital, Oakland CA) He was a longshoreman for 25 years. Died from a pulmonary embolism. Buried St Mary's Cemetery, Oakland CA.

Hack Miller—2 Years Catcher (b. 13 Feb 1911 Celeste TX–d. 21 Nov 1966 Dallas TX).

Hughie Miller—3 Years Infielder (b. 28 Dec 1887 St Louis MO–d. 24 Dec 1945 Veteran's Hospital, Jefferson Barracks MO) He was wounded in action while serving in the U.S. Marines in World War I. This ended his baseball career. Buried Jefferson Barracks National Cemetery, St Louis MO.

Jake Miller—1 Year Outfielder (b. 1 Dec 1895 Baltimore MD–d. 24 Aug 1974 Towson MD).

Jake Miller—9 Years Pitcher (b. 28 Feb 1898 Wagram OH–d. 20 Aug 1975 at a nursing home in Venice FL) He was a civil engineer for Interpack Company of New Jersey, retiring in 1959. Cremated.

Jim Miller—1 Year Infielder (b. 2 Oct 1880 Pittsburgh PA–d. 8 Feb 1937 Pittsburgh PA) He managed minor league baseball. Died following a short illness.

Joe Miller—2 Years Infielder (b. 17 Feb 1861 Baltimore MD–d. 23 Apr 1928 North Hospital, Wheeling WV) He worked in the water works department for the City of Wheeling, retiring in 1925. He had a leg amputated two years before he died. Died following surgery for the removal of the other leg. Buried Mount Calvary Cemetery, Wheeling WV.

Kohley Miller—2 Years Infielder (b. Jan 1874 Cumru Township PA–d. 29 Mar 1951 at his son's home in Reading PA) For 17 years he was a mailman for the Carpenter Steel Company, retiring in 1950. Buried Gethsemane Cemetery, Laureldale PA.

Otto Miller—13 Years Catcher (b. 1 Jun 1889 Minden NE–d. 29 Mar 1962 Brooklyn NY) He scouted for the Dodgers and Red Sox. Later he worked in Wall Street and managed the Edison Bar near Ebbets Field in Brooklyn. Died when he plunged from an office on the fourth floor of a building where he had undergone eye surgery two days earlier.

Otto Miller—4 Years Infielder (b. 2 Feb 1901 Belleville IL–d. 26 Jul 1959 St Elizabeth Hospital, Belleville IL) He worked in the insurance business and later as a steamfitter. Served eight two-year terms as a representative in the Illinois General Assembly. Died from complications that followed a serious illness of two months. Buried Walnut Hill Cemetery, Belleville IL.

Ralph Miller—3 Years Infielder (b. 29 Feb 1896 Fort Wayne IN–d. 18 Mar 1939 St Joseph Hospital, Fort Wayne IN) Served in France and Germany as a sergeant in the U.S. Army during World War I. He also played professional basketball. Died from peritonitis following surgery for appendicitis. Buried Catholic Cemetery, Fort Wayne IN.

Ralph Miller—1 Year Pitcher (b. 14 Jan 1899 Vinton IA–d. 18 Feb 1967 at his home in White Bear Lake MN) He operated Miller's Nursery at White Bear Lake. He lived at White Bear Lake for 28 years. Buried Sunset Memorial Park, Minneapolis MN.

Ralph Miller—2 Years Pitcher (b. 15 Mar 1873 Cincinnati OH–d. 7 May 1973 Hyde Park Villa Nursing Home, Cincinnati OH) He was a shipping department manager for Ault and Wilborg Company in Cincinnati for 25 years. Buried Spring Grove Cemetery, Cincinnati OH.

Ray Miller—1 Year Infielder (b. 9 Apr 1888 Pittsburgh PA–d. 7 Apr 1927 at his mother's home in Pittsburgh PA) Served in the U.S. Navy during World War I. Died after a prolonged illness. Buried St Mary's Cemetery, Pittsburgh PA.

Red Miller—1 Year Pitcher (b. 11 Feb 1897 Philadelphia PA–d. 20 Oct 1973 Orlando FL).

Roger Miller—1 Year Pitcher (b. 1 Aug 1954 Connellsville PA–d. 26 Apr 1993 Mill Run PA)

He was a welder for Commercial Stone, Inc, at Mill Run. Killed, while at work, from an explosion that occurred as he was preparing to weld on some tanks. Buried Indian Creek Baptist Cemetery, Mill Run PA.

Ronnie Miller—1 Year Pitcher (b. 28 Aug 1918 Mason City IA–d. 6 Jan 1998 Ferguson MO).

Roscoe Miller—4 Years Pitcher (b. 2 Dec 1876 Greenville IN–d. 18 Apr 1913 at his home in Corydon IN) When his health failed him he left baseball to work in his father's grocery store in Corydon. Died from pneumonia, but suffered from tuberculosis. Buried Cedar Hill Cemetery, Corydon IN.

Rudy Miller—1 Year Infielder (b. 12 Jul 1900 Kalamazoo MI–d. 22 Jan 1994 Kalamazoo MI) He founded the Miller and Boerman Sporting Goods Company. Buried Mountain Home Cemetery, Kalamazoo MI.

Russ Miller—2 Years Pitcher (b. 25 Mar 1900 Pataskala OH–d. 30 Apr 1962 Community Hospital, Bucyrus OH) He served 28 years as Crawford County, OH, agriculture extension agent. Died from a heart attack. Buried Glen Rest Memorial Estates, Reynoldsburg OH.

Tom Miller—2 Years Pinch Hitter (b. 5 Jul 1897 Powhatan Court House VA–d. 13 Aug 1980 Richmond VA)For 28 years he was a clerk in Hustings Court in Richmond. Served in the U.S. Navy during World War I and in the Naval Reserve during World War II. Died from a self-inflicted gunshot wound to the head after being despondent over ill health.

Walt Miller—1 Year Pitcher (b. 19 Oct 1884 Spiceland IN–d. 1 Mar 1956 Marion General Hospital, Marion IN) He owned and operated a gasoline station and grocery store in Red Bridge IN. He had been in ill health the last years of his life. Buried Riverside Cemetery, Jonesboro IN.

Ward Miller—8 Years Outfielder (b. 5 Jul 1884 Mount Carroll IL–d. 3 Sep 1958 K S B Hospital, Dixon IL) He served two terms as Lee County (IL) sheriff, one term as chief deputy sheriff and a term as county treasurer. He was then Chief of Police at Dixon State School for 15 years. Died following a short illness. Buried Oakwood Cemetery, Dixon IL.

Warren Miller—2 Years Outfielder (b. 14 Jul 1885 Philadelphia PA–d. 12 Aug 1956 at his home in Philadelphia PA) He was a private investigator. Died suddenly. Buried Holy Sepulchre Cemetery, Philadelphia PA.

Whitey Miller—1 Year Pitcher (b. 2 May 1915 St Louis MO–d. 3 Apr 1991 St Louis MO) He retired from Anheuser Busch Company. Buried Our Redeemer Cemetery, Affton MO.

Wally Millies—6 Years Catcher (b. 18 Oct 1906 Chicago IL–d. 28 Feb 1995 Oak Lawn IL) He was a scout for the Astros. Buried Chapel Hill Gardens South, Worth IL.

Bill Milligan—2 Years Pitcher (b. 19 Aug 1878 Buffalo NY–d. 14 Oct 1928 at his home in Buffalo NY) He was a foreman for the Buffalo Department of Streets. Died from heart failure. Buried Holy Cross Cemetery, Lackawanna NY.

Jocko Milligan—10 Years Catcher (b. 8 Aug 1861 Philadelphia PA–d. 30 Aug 1923 at his home in Philadelphia PA) For 15 years he was a tipstaff in Quarter Sessions Court at Philadelphia City Hall. Died after he had been ill five months and had recently undergone surgery. Buried Mount Moriah Cemetery, Philadelphia PA.

John Milligan—5 Years Pitcher (b. 22 Jan 1904 Schuylerville NY–d. 15 May 1972 at his home in Fort Pierce FL) He moved to Fort Pierce about 1947 and worked five years in the maintenance department of the St Lucie County (FL) School District before retiring. Buried Fort Pierce Cemetery, Fort Pierce FL.

Art Mills—2 Years Pitcher (b. 2 Mar 1903 Utica NY–d. 23 Jul 1975 St Luke's Memorial Hospital, Utica NY) He coached and managed in the minor leagues and was a scout for the Phillies. He also worked for General Electric in Utica, retiring in 1968. Died after a long illness. Buried Forest Hill Cemetery, Utica NY.

Buster Mills—7 Years Outfielder 1 Year Manager (b. 16 Sep 1908 Ranger TX–d. 1 Dec 1991 at his home in Arlington TX) He was a coach and scout for the Yankees. He was also on the Board of Directors of the Ranger Savings and Loan Association. Buried Oakwood Cemetery, Waco TX.

Everett Mills—1 Year Infielder (b. 1845 Newark NJ–d. 22 Jun 1908 Newark NJ) He worked at the courthouse. Died from chronic heart disease. Buried Fairmount Cemetery, Newark NJ.

Frank Mills—1 Year Catcher (b. 13 May 1895 Knoxville OH–d. 31 Aug 1983 South Side Hospital, Youngstown OH) He worked for U.S. Steel Corporation from 1917 until he retired in 1960, working his way up from a clerk in the personnel department to salesman for the slag division in 1929, to sales manager of the slag division in 1953. He was also a well-known bird watcher. Buried Forest Lawn Memorial Park, Youngstown OH.

Jack Mills —1 Year Infielder (b. 23 Oct 1889 South Williamstown MA–d. 3 Jun 1973 Washington Hospital Center, Washington DC) Served in France for the U.S. Army during World War I. He practiced law in Washington DC from the early 1920s until his death. He took up competitive figure skating at age 55. Died from injuries suffered in a fire. Cremated.

Lefty Mills —5 Years Pitcher (b. 12 May 1910 Dedham MA–d. 23 Sep 1982 Community Hospital, Riverside CA) For 27 years he was a manager for Air-Research Aviation, an aircraft modification company. Died from lymphoma. Buried Green Hills Memorial Park, Rancho Palos Verdes CA.

Rupert Mills —1 Year Infielder (b. 12 Oct 1892 Newark NJ–d. 20 Jul 1929 Lake Hopatcong NJ) He was an under-sheriff in Essex County, NJ. Died when he accidentally drowned while swimming. Buried St Mary's Cemetery, East Orange NJ.

Willie Mills —1 Year Pitcher (b. 15 Aug 1877 Schenevus NY–d. 5 Jul 1914 Norwood NY) Killed when he was run over by a train, probably while in an intoxicated condition.

John Milner —12 Years Infielder (b. 28 Dec 1949 Atlanta GA–d. 6 Jan 2000 Atlanta GA) Died from cancer. Buried College Park Cemetery, College Park GA.

Mike Milosevich—2 Years Infielder (b. 13 Jan 1915 Zeigler IL–d. 3 Feb 1966 East Chicago IN) Died from heart disease.

George Milstead —3 Years Pitcher (b. 26 Sep 1903 Cleburne TX–d. 9 Aug 1977 Johnson County Memorial Hosp, Cleburne TX) Buried Godley Cemetery, Godley TX.

Larry Milton —1 Year Pitcher (b. 4 May 1879 Owensboro KY–d. 16 May 1942 Hannibal MO).

Cotton Minahan —1 Year Pitcher (b. 10 Dec 1882 Springfield OH–d. 20 May 1958 at his home in East Orange NJ) A general contractor in Orange NJ, he retired in 1933. Died after a long illness. Buried St John's Cemetery, Orange NJ.

Dan Minahan —1 Year Infielder (b. 28 Nov 1865 Troy NY–d. 8 Aug 1929 at his home in Troy NY) He worked for the New York State Department of Highways. Died following an illness of five months. Buried St Joseph's Cemetery, Troy NY.

Ray Miner —1 Year Pitcher (b. 4 Apr 1897 Glen Falls NY–d. 15 Sep 1963 Glen Ridge Hospital, Glenville NY) World War I veteran. Buried St Mary's Cemetery, South Glens Falls NY.

Willie Miranda —9 Years Infielder (b. 24 May 1926 Velasco, Cuba–d. 7 Sep 1996 Baltimore MD) Buried Gardens of Faith Memorial Gardens, Baltimore MD.

John Misse —1 Year Infielder (b. 30 May 1885 Highland KS–d. 18 Mar 1970 Sister's Hospital, St Joseph MO) A partner in a general store at Highland from 1912 to 1924 and the Highland postmaster from 1932 to 1934, he helped at the local funeral home several years. He was also a part-owner of the St Joseph minor league baseball team and a real estate broker. Died following several years of failing sight and health. Buried Highland Cemetery, Highland KS.

Bobby Mitchell —4 Years Pitcher (b. 6 Feb 1856 Cincinnati OH–d. 1 May 1933 Chronic Disease Hospital, Cincinnati OH) Died from generalized heart disease. Buried Oak Hill Cemetery Park, Cincinnati OH.

Clarence Mitchell —18 Years Pitcher (b. 22 Feb 1891 Franklin NE–d. 6 Nov 1963 at a hospital in Grand Island NE) He was the batter that hit into the only unassisted triple play in World Series history. World War I veteran. He managed minor league baseball before operating a tavern in Aurora NE. He had been in ill health five years and was a double amputee because of a circulatory problem. A wheelchair was his means of getting around. Died from a heart ailment. Buried Aurora Cemetery, Aurora NE.

Dale Mitchell —11 Years Outfielder (b. 23 Aug 1921 Cloud Chief OK–d. 5 Jan 1987 at his home in Tulsa OK) World War II veteran. He was the CEO of Rocky Mountain Cement and was later president of Martin Marietta's Cement-Western Division. Died from a heart attack. Buried Cloud Chief Cemetery, Cloud Chief OK.

Fred Mitchell—7 Years Pitcher 7 Years Manager (b. 5 Jun 1878 Cambridge MA–d. 13 Oct 1970 Newton MA) Buried Mount Calvary Cemetery, Roslindale MA.

Johnny Mitchell—5 Years Infielder (b. 9 Aug 1894 Detroit MI–d. 4 Nov 1965 Lourdes Convalescent Home, Pontiac MI) He worked for the Detroit Water Board until retiring in 1959. Buried Mount Olivet Cemetery, Detroit MI.

Mike Mitchell—8 Years Outfielder (b. 12 Dec 1879 Springfield OH–d. 16 Jul 1961 at his home in Phoenix AZ) After baseball he managed parimutual machines at several tracks in the midwest and west before retiring to Phoenix in 1954. Buried St Francis Catholic Cemetery, Phoenix AZ.

Monroe Mitchell—1 Year Pitcher (b. 11 Sep 1901 Starkville MS–d. 4 Sep 1976 Valdosta GA) He retired from the Owens-Illinois Paper Company. Died after a short illness. Buried Riverview Memorial Gardens, Valdosta GA.

Roy Mitchell—7 Years Pitcher (b. 19 Apr 1885 Belton TX–d. 8 Sep 1959 at a hospital in Temple TX) He managed minor league baseball for a few years. He was a retired stockfarmer and long-time director of the First National Bank. Died after an extended illness. Buried North Belton Cemetery, Belton TX.

Willie Mitchell—11 Years Pitcher (b. 1 Dec 1889 Sardis MS–d. 23 Nov 1973 North Panola County Hospital, Sardis MS) He was a machine gunner in France during World War I. Buried Rose Hill Cemetery, Sardis MS.

Ralph Mitterling—1 Year Outfielder (b. 19 Apr 1890 Freeburg PA–d. 22 Jan 1956 Veteran's Hospital, Pittsburgh PA) Served in the U.S. Army during World War I. He coached baseball at a number of different colleges including the University of Pittsburgh from 1938 to 1955. Died after suffering a heart attack nine months earlier. Buried Freeburg Cemetery, Freeburg PA.

Johnny Mize—15 Years Infielder Hall of Fame (b. 7 Jan 1913 Demorest GA–d. 2 Jun 1993 at his home in Demorest GA) He was almost reclusive at his Georgia mountain home during his last years. Contended with prostate cancer, heart bypass surgery and knee replacements, but was not thought to be in failing health when he died in his sleep from cardiac arrest. Buried Yonah Memorial Gardens, Demorest GA.

Vinegar Bend Mizell—9 Years Pitcher (b. 13 Aug 1930 Leakesville MS–d. 21 Feb 1999 at a hospital in Kerrville TX) He served as a North Carolina congressman from 1969 to 1975 and as a senior official for the Ford and Reagan administrations. Died after suffering a heart attack four months earlier. Buried Faith Missionary Alliance Church Cem, Winston-Salem NC.

Bill Mizeur—2 Years Pinch Hitter (b. 22 Jun 1897 Nokomis IL–d. 27 Aug 1976 Decatur Memorial Hospital, Decatur IL) He played in the Three-I League and drove a school bus for St Thomas School in Decatur. Buried Calvary Cemetery, Decatur IL.

Mike Modak—1 Year Pitcher (b. 18 May 1922 Campbell OH–d. 12 Dec 1995 Regional Health Center, Lakeland FL) Served in the U.S. Army during World War II. He was an executive foreman for Youngstown Steel Corporation in Ohio, retiring to Florida in 1985. Died from heart disease, complicated by diabetes. Buried Tod Homestead Cemetery, Youngstown OH.

Danny Moeller—7 Years Outfielder (b. 23 Mar 1885 DeWitt IA–d. 14 Apr 1951 E C M Hospital, Florence AL) He worked for the Muscle Shoals Auto Parts Company. Buried Forest Hill Cemetery, Memphis TN.

Sam Moffett—3 Years Outfielder (b. 14 Mar 1857 Wheeling WV–d. 5 May 1907 Butte MT) Buried Greenwood Cemetery, Wheeling WV.

George Mogridge—15 Years Pitcher (b. 18 Feb 1889 Rochester NY–d. 4 Mar 1962 at his home in Rochester NY) He pitched the first no-hitter ever by a Yankee. He operated an inn from 1927 to 1934, then owned a sporting goods store until 1942. He then went to work for Weathermaster, a manufacturer of storm windows, retiring in 1960. Died from a heart attack. Buried Holy Sepulchre Cemetery, Rochester NY.

John Mohardt—1 Year Outfielder (b. 21 Jan 1898 Pittsburgh PA–d. 24 Nov 1961 at his home in La Jolla CA) World War II veteran. He was a self-employed medical doctor for 35 years. Died from a self-inflicted laceration of his groin, bleeding to death. Cremated.

George Mohart—2 Years Pitcher (b. 6 Mar 1892 Buffalo NY–d. 2 Oct 1970 Silver Creek NY) Buried Glenwood Cemetery, Silver Creek NY.

Kid Mohler—1 Year Infielder (b. 13 Dec 1874 Oneida IL–d. 4 Nov 1961 San Francisco CA).

Johnny Mokan—7 Years Outfielder (b. 23 Sep 1895 Buffalo NY–d. 10 Feb 1985 Buffalo NY) He was a light equipment operator for the State Thruway Authority from 1949 to 1969 when he retired. He also served as director for the Buffalo Municipal League. Buried St Augustine Cemetery, Lancaster NY.

Carlton Molesworth—1 Year Pitcher (b. 15 Feb 1876 Frederick MD–d. 25 Jul 1961 Glen Merrie Nursing Home, Frederick MD) He worked 53 years in organized baseball as a player, minor league manager and scout, 21 years as a scout for the Pirates. Died after being in declining health a number of years. Buried Mount Olivet Cemetery, Frederick MD.

Fred Mollenkamp—1 Year Infielder (b. 15 Mar 1890 Cincinnati OH–d. 1 Nov 1948 Good Samaritan Hospital, Cincinnati OH) He was a partner in the Mollenkamp Furniture Company. Died following a long illness. Buried St Mary Cemetery, Cincinnati OH.

Fritz Mollwitz—7 Years Infielder (b. 6 Jun 1891 Kolberg, Germany–d. 3 Oct 1967 at his home in Bradenton FL) He worked 22 years for the Shorewood WI Police Dept, retiring to Bradenton in 1955. Buried Wisconsin Memorial Park, Brookfield WI.

Vince Molyneaux—2 Years Pitcher (b. 17 Aug 1888 Lewiston NY–d. 4 May 1950 Stamford CT).

Freddie Moncewicz—1 Year Infielder (b. 1 Sep 1903 Brockton MA–d. 23 Apr 1969 Cushing Hospital, Brockton MA) Served in the Pacific for the U.S. Navy during World War II. He was assistant baseball coach at Boston College while earning his law degree. He then practiced law until he was appointed as state comptroller in 1946, serving in that position until he retired. Buried Calvary Cemetery, Brockton MA.

Ed Monroe—2 Years Pitcher (b. 22 Feb 1895 Louisville KY–d. 29 Apr 1969 Veteran's Hospital, Louisville KY) Served in the U.S. Army during World War I. He was a clerk for the Indiana and Kentucky Terminal Railroad, retiring in 1959. Buried Calvary Cemetery, Louisville KY.

John Monroe—1 Year Infielder (b. 24 Aug 1898 Farmersville TX–d. 19 Jun 1956 Conroe TX).

Ed Montague—4 Years Infielder (b. 24 Jul 1905 San Francisco CA–d. 17 Jun 1988 at his home in Daly City CA) For 40 years he was a scout for the Giants. Died from prostate cancer. Buried Holy Cross Catholic Cemetery, Colma CA.

Aurelio Monteagudo—7 Years Pitcher (b. 19 Nov 1943 Caibarien, Cuba–d. 10 Nov 1990 Saltillo, Mexico).

Rene Monteagudo—4 Years Pitcher (b. 12 Mar 1916 Santa Clara, Cuba–d. 14 Sep 1973 Hialeah FL).

Al Montgomery—1 Year Catcher (b. 3 Jul 1920 Loving NM–d. 26 Apr 1942 Waverly VA) Died at the height of his baseball career in a three-car accident in which five others died. Buried Los Angeles CA.

Dan Monzon—2 Years Infielder (b. 17 May 1946 Bronx NY–d. 21 Jan 1996 Santo Domingo, Dominican Republic).

George Moolic—1 Year Catcher (b. 1865 Lawrence MA–d. 19 Feb 1915 Methuen MA) He conducted a liquor establishment in Lawrence. Died from blood poisoning during a blood transfusion following a routine surgery. Buried St Mary's Cemetery, Lawrence MA.

Leo Moon—1 Year Pitcher (b. 22 Jun 1899 Belmont NC–d. 26 Aug 1970 New Orleans LA) His baseball career was shortened by the loss of sight in one eye. He had been totally blind since 1958. Died after a lengthy illness. Buried Greenwood Cemetery, New Orleans LA.

Jim Mooney—4 Years Pitcher (b. 4 Sep 1906 Mooresburg TN–d. 27 Apr 1979 Memorial Hospital, Johnson City TN) He was the baseball coach at East Tennessee State Univ for nearly 30 years. Died from an apparent heart attack. Buried Fairview Cemetery, Johnson City TN.

Al Moore—2 Years Outfielder (b. 4 Aug 1902 Brooklyn NY–d. 29 Nov 1974 New York City NY) He worked in the public relations department of Rheingold Beer until his retirement in 1973. Died from a heart attack. Buried Plain Lawn Cemetery, Roslyn Heights NY.

Anse Moore—1 Year Outfielder (b. 22 Sep 1917 Delphi LA–d. 29 Oct 1993 at his home in Pearl MS) Served in the U.S. Army during World War II. He owned and operated Moore's Fabrics in Pearl for many years. Died from cancer. Buried Union Baptist Church Cemetery, Puckett MS.

Bill Moore—2 Years Catcher (b. 12 Dec 1901 Kansas City MO–d. 24 May 1972 St Mary's Hospital, Kansas City MO) He retired from the Kansas City Fire Department in 1966 after 32 years service, 20 as Captain. Buried Calvary Cemetery, Kansas City MO.

Bill Moore—1 Year Pitcher (b. 3 Sep 1902 Corning NY–d. 24 Jan 1984 Corning NY) He retired as a captain from the Corning Police Dept. Buried St Mary's Cemetery, Corning NY.

Carlos Moore—1 Year Pitcher (b. 13 Aug 1906 Clinton TN–d. 2 Jul 1958 New Orleans LA).

Charley Moore—1 Year Infielder (b. 1 Dec 1884 Jackson County IN–d. 29 Jul 1970 at a nursing home in Portland OR) He worked at the Port of Portland from 1923 until he retired in 1950. Buried Skyline Memorial Gardens, Portland OR.

Cy Moore—6 Years Pitcher (b. 7 Feb 1905 Elberton GA–d. 28 Mar 1972 V A Hospital, Augusta GA) World War II veteran. He operated a clothing store in Elberton for ten years before farming in Ogelthorpe County, GA, for 13 years. Buried Stevens Family Cemetery, Sandy Cross GA.

Dee Moore—4 Years Catcher (b. 6 Apr 1914 Hedley TX–d. 2 Jul 1997 Bethel Lutheran Home, Williston ND) Served in Guam for the U.S. Marine Corps during World War II. He managed minor league baseball before becoming assistant manager for the El Rancho Motel in Williston, retiring in 1981. Buried Riverview Cemetery, Williston ND.

Donnie Moore—9 Years Pitcher (b. 13 Feb 1954 Lubbock TX–d. 18 Jul 1989 Anaheim CA) Died from a self-inflicted gunshot wound during his baseball career after attempting to kill his wife. Buried Peaceful Gardens Memorial Park, Woodrow TX.

Earl Moore—14 Years Pitcher (b. 29 Jul 1878 Pickerington OH–d. 28 Nov 1961 Columbus OH) He was a clerk in the sporting goods department of a Cleveland department store. Buried Glen Rest Memorial Estates, Reynoldsburg OH.

Eddie Moore—10 Years Infielder (b. 18 Jan 1899 Barlow KY–d. 10 Feb 1976 Fort Myers FL).

Euel Moore—3 Years Pitcher (b. 27 May 1908 Reagan OK–d. 12 Feb 1989 Johnston Memorial Hospital, Tishomingo OK) Served in the U.S. Army during World War II. For 27 years he was a game ranger. Buried Tishomingo City Cemetery, Tishomingo OK.

Ferdie Moore—1 Year Infielder (b. 21 Feb 1896 Camden NJ–d. 6 May 1947 City Hospital, Atlantic City NJ) Served in the U.S. Navy during World War II. He was a detective for the Atlantic City Police Department and at one time was the head of the vice squad. He fatally shot a cigar store proprietor, then took his own life with a bullet to the head. A dispute over money was the alleged cause of the row. Buried Laurel Memorial Park, Pomona NJ.

Gene Moore—14 Years Outfielder (b. 26 Aug 1909 Lancaster TX–d. 12 Mar 1978 St Dominic's Hospital, Jackson MS) He owned and operated Laurel Iron Works, an iron and junk business in Laurel MS, from 1946 until his death. Buried Lake Park Cemetery, Laurel MS.

Gene Moore—3 Years Pitcher (b. 9 Nov 1885 Lancaster TX–d. 31 Aug 1938 at his home in Lancaster TX) Died after several years of ill health. Buried Edgewood Cemetery, Lancaster TX.

George Moore—1 Year Pitcher (b. 25 Nov 1872 Cambridge MA–d. 4 Nov 1948 Hyannis MA).

Jerry Moore—2 Years Catcher (b. Detroit MI–d. 26 Sep 1908 Wayne MI).

Jim Moore—2 Years Outfielder (b. 24 Apr 1903 Paris TN–d. 7 Mar 1986 Memphis TN) Buried Memorial Park Cemetery, Memphis TN.

Jim Moore—5 Years Pitcher (b. 14 Dec 1904 Prescott AR–d. 19 May 1973 Seattle WA) Died from cancer. Buried Fairmount Cemetery, Denver CO.

Johnny Moore—10 Years Outfielder (b. 23 Mar 1902 Waterville CT–d. 4 Apr 1991 Blake Memorial Hospital, Bradenton FL) He was the west coast scout for the Braves and Expos, retiring to Bradenton in 1971. Buried Manasota Memorial Park, Sarasota FL.

Jo-Jo Moore—12 Years Outfielder (b. 25 Dec 1908 Gause TX–d. 1 Apr 2001 Gause TX) He used his baseball earnings to buy a ranch near Gause and ranched there.

Randy Moore—10 Years Outfielder (b. 21 Jun 1906 Naples TX–d. 12 Jun 1992 Titus County

Mem Hosp, Mount Pleasant TX) At one time he was the majority owner in the Lone Star State Bank at Lone Star TX. He and a partner in the oil business had two major oil discoveries in Titus County, TX. Buried Omaha Cemetery, Omaha TX.

Ray Moore—11 Years Pitcher (b. 1 Jun 1926 Meadows MD–d. 2 Mar 1995 Southern Maryland Hospital, Clinton MD) Served in the Pacific for the U.S. Army during World War II. He operated a farm near Upper Marlboro MD. Died from cancer. Buried Cedar Hill Cemetery, Suitland MD.

Roy Moore—4 Years Pitcher (b. 26 Dec 1898 Austin TX–d. 5 Apr 1951 Seattle WA).

Scrappy Moore—1 Year Infielder (b. 16 Dec 1892 St Louis MO–d. 13 Oct 1964 Little Rock AR) A veteran of World War I, he also served in the U.S. Navy during World War II. He played several years in the higher minor leagues, officiated football games in Arkansas and worked for the Arkansas Highway Department. Buried Roselawn Memorial Park, Little Rock AR.

Terry Moore—11 Years Outfielder 1 Year Manager (b. 27 May 1912 Vernon AL–d. 29 Mar 1995 at his home in Collinsville IL) He coached for the Cardinals until 1958, except for a short managerial stint with the Phillies. Died after a long illness. Buried Holy Cross Lutheran Cemetery, Collinsville IL.

Whitey Moore—7 Years Pitcher (b. 10 Jun 1912 Tuscarawas OH–d. 10 Dec 1987 Aultman Hospital, Canton OH) Served with the combat engineers in the U.S. Army during World War II. He was an assembler for Warner-Swasey Company in New Philadelphia OH, retiring in 1977. Died after being ill two months. Buried Union Cemetery, Uhrichsville OH.

Wilcy Moore—6 Years Pitcher (b. 20 May 1897 Bonita TX–d. 29 Mar 1963 Hollis OK) He farmed just east of Hollis. Died following a lengthy illness. Buried Fairmount Cemetery, Hollis OK.

Bob Moorhead—2 Years Pitcher (b. 23 Jan 1938 Chambersburg PA–d. 3 Dec 1986 at his home in Lemoyne PA) He was a retired employee of Roadway Express. Buried Parklawns Memorial Gardens, Chambersburg PA.

Bob Moose—10 Years Pitcher (b. 9 Oct 1947 Export PA–d. 9 Oct 1976 Martins Ferry OH) He lived in Monroeville PA. Killed at the height of his baseball career in an automobile accident. While returning home from a golf tournament he lost control of his car, hitting another car headon. Buried Twin Valley Memorial Park, Delmont PA.

Jake Mooty—7 Years Pitcher (b. 13 Apr 1913 Bennett TX–d. 20 Apr 1970 at a hospital in Fort Worth TX) He was a retired grocer. Buried Mount Olivet Cemetery, Fort Worth TX.

Bill Moran—2 Years Catcher (b. 18 Oct 1868 Joliet IL–d. 7 Apr 1916 St Joseph Hospital, Joliet IL) He operated a construction company in Joliet. Buried St Patrick's Cemetery, Joliet IL.

Charley Moran—2 Years Catcher (b. 22 Feb 1878 Nashville TN–d. 14 Jun 1949 at his home in Horse Cave KY) He coached football at Centre College in Danville KY before umpiring in the National League for 23 years, retiring in 1939. After that he operated a farm near Danville KY. Died from a heart ailment. Buried Horse Cave Municipal Cemetery, Horse Cave KY.

Charlie Moran—3 Years Infielder (b. 26 Mar 1879 Washington DC–d. 11 Apr 1934 at his home in Washington DC) He worked for the U.S. Commerce Department until 1912 when he became athletic director and baseball coach at Catholic University, a post he held until 1930. Died from a heart attack. Buried Mount Olivet Cemetery, Washington DC.

Harry Moran—3 Years Pitcher (b. 2 Apr 1889 Thayer WV–d. 28 Nov 1962 Beckley WV) Served in the U.S. Navy during World War I. He had extensive coal interests in the east and was president of Leccony Smokeless Fuel Company in Beckley. Buried High Lawn Memorial Park, Oak Hill WV.

Herbie Moran—7 Years Outfielder (b. 16 Feb 1884 Costello PA–d. 21 Sep 1954 at his home in Clarkson NY) He was a guard at Bausch and Lomb from 1940 until he retired in 1953. Died unexpectedly. Buried Eulalia Cemetery, Coudersport PA.

Hiker Moran—2 Years Pitcher (b. 1 Jan 1912 Rochester NY–d. 7 Jan 1998 Saratoga Springs NY) He worked 35 years for the Otis Elevator Company and enjoyed golfing, hunting and fishing. Buried Greenridge Cemetery, Saratoga Springs NY.

Pat Moran—14 Years Catcher 9 Years Manager (b. 7 Feb 1876 Fitchburg MA–d. 7 Mar 1924 Orange General Hospital, Orlando FL) Died at the height of his managerial career from acute nephritis. Buried St Bernard's Church Cemetery, Fitchburg MA.

Roy Moran—1 Year Outfielder (b. 17 Sep 1884 Iona IN–d. 18 Jul 1966 Atlanta GA) Buried Westview Cemetery, Atlanta GA.

Sam Moran—1 Year Pitcher (b. 16 Sep 1870 Rochester NY–d. 27 Aug 1897 City Hospital, Rochester NY) Died from a lingering illness that developed into dropsy. Buried Holy Sepulchre Cemetery, Rochester NY.

Forrest More—1 Year Pitcher (b. 30 Sep 1883 Hayden IN–d. 17 Aug 1968 Bartholomew County Hospital, Columbus IN) Buried Hillcrest Cemetery, North Vernon IN.

Ray Morehart—3 Years Infielder (b. 2 Dec 1899 near Abner TX–d. 13 Jan 1989 at his home in Dallas TX) He was an accountant for Sun Oil Company in Dallas, retiring in 1964. Died from a heart attack while reading the newspaper in his rocking chair. Buried Restland Memorial Park, Dallas TX.

Lew Moren—6 Years Pitcher (b. 4 Aug 1883 Pittsburgh PA–d. 2 Nov 1966 Pittsburgh PA) He was a retired electrician helper. Died when he slit his throat with a razor. Buried Homewood Cemetery, Pittsburgh PA.

Julio Moreno—4 Years Pitcher (b. 28 Jan 1921 Guines, Cuba–d. 2 Jan 1987 Miami FL).

Dave Morey—1 Year Pitcher (b. 25 Feb 1889 Malden MA–d. 4 Jan 1986 Martha's Vineyard Hospital, Oak Bluffs MA) He coached football at Middlebury College, Auburn Univ, Bates College and Lowell Tech in a coaching career that spanned more than 40 years when he retired in 1960. Died after a long illness. Buried Oak Grove Cemetery, Vineyard Haven MA.

Chet Morgan—2 Years Outfielder (b. 6 Jun 1910 Cleveland MS–d. 20 Sep 1991 Pasadena TX).

Cy Morgan—10 Years Pitcher (b. 10 Nov 1878 Pomeroy OH–d. 28 Jun 1962 Wheeling WV) For 26 years he was a minor league umpire. Died when he slashed his throat with a razor. Buried Riverview Cemetery, Martins Ferry OH.

Cy Morgan—2 Years Pitcher (b. 11 Dec 1896 Lakeville MA–d. 11 Sep 1946 at his home in Lakeville MA) He sold caskets before going to work at the Bethlehem shipyards in Fall River MA during World War II. Died after a long illness. Buried East Harwich Cemetery, East Harwich MA.

Ed Morgan—7 Years Infielder (b. 22 May 1904 Cairo IL–d. 9 Apr 1980 New Orleans LA) He lived at Kenner LA for 68 years. Buried Garden of Memories, Metairie LA.

Eddie Morgan—2 Years Outfielder (b. 19 Nov 1914 Brady Lake OH–d. 27 Jun 1982 Lakewood OH) He worked in construction for the Cleveland Housing Authority. Cremated. Buried Hillcrest Memorial Park Cemetery, Bedford Heights OH.

Ray Morgan—8 Years Infielder (b. 14 Jun 1889 Baltimore MD–d. 15 Feb 1940 Baltimore MD) Died from pneumonia and heart disease. Buried Cecilton MD.

Red Morgan—1 Year Infielder (b. 6 Oct 1883 Neola IA–d. 25 Mar 1981 New York City NY).

Tom Morgan—12 Years Pitcher (b. 20 May 1930 El Monte CA–d. 13 Jan 1987 Anaheim CA) He was a pitching coach for the Angels. Died from complications of a stroke suffered a week earlier. Buried Green Hills Memorial Park, Rancho Palos Verdes CA.

Vern Morgan—2 Years Infielder (b. 8 Aug 1928 Emporia VA–d. 8 Nov 1975 Univ of Minnesota Hospital, Minneapolis MN) He managed minor league baseball and coached for the Twins. Died from complications of a kidney transplant surgery and rejection of the transplanted kidney. Buried Emporia Cemetery, Emporia VA.

Bill Moriarty—1 Year Infielder (b. 1883 Chicago IL–d. 25 Dec 1916 Chicago IL) Buried Mount Olivet Cemetery, Chicago IL.

Ed Moriarty—2 Years Infielder (b. 12 Oct 1912 Holyoke MA–d. 29 Sep 1991 Holyoke Hospital, Holyoke MA) Served in the U.S. Navy during World War II. A former superintendent of the Holyoke public schools, he worked 44 years in the Holyoke schools as teacher, department head, principal and administrator. Buried Calvary Cemetery, Holyoke MA.

George Moriarty—13 Years Infielder 2 Years Manager (b. 7 Jul 1884 Chicago IL–d. 8 Apr 1964 at his home in Coral Gables FL) He was an American League umpire from 1917 to 1940, except for 1927 and 1928 when he managed the Tigers. Buried St Mary Cemetery, Evergreen Park IL.

Bill Morley—1 Year Infielder (b. 23 Jan 1890 Holland MI–d. 13 May 1985 Methodist Hospital, Lubbock TX) World War I veteran. He was athletic director and head football coach at Ouachita College in Arkadelphia AR from 1912 to 1926, athletic director and head football coach at Baylor University from 1926 to 1941, athletic director at Texas Tech from 1941 to 1952 and the head of the physical education department there until he retired in 1966. Died after a lengthy illness. Buried Lubbock City Cemetery, Lubbock TX.

Jim Moroney—3 Years Pitcher (b. 4 Dec 1883 Boston MA–d. 26 Feb 1929 Philadelphia PA).

Bill Morrell—3 Years Pitcher (b. 9 Apr 1900 Boston MA–d. 5 Aug 1975 Birmingham AL) He retired from the U.S. Army as a Lieutenant Colonel.

John Morrill—15 Years Infielder 8 Years Manager (b. 19 Feb 1855 Boston MA–d. 2 Apr 1932 at his home in Brookline MA) He was general manager and treasurer for Wright and Ditson, a Boston sporting goods store, for 39 years, retiring in 1931. Died from double pneumonia. Buried Holyhood Cemetery, Brookline MA.

Bugs Morris—2 Years Pitcher (b. 19 Apr 1892 Weir City KS–d. 21 Nov 1957 Noel MO).

Doyt Morris—1 Year Outfielder (b. 15 Jul 1916 Stanley NC–d. 4 Jul 1984 Gaston Memorial Hospital, Stanley NC) He was a retired employee of Duke Power Company. Buried Stanley Cemetery, Stanley NC.

Ed Morris—7 Years Pitcher (b. 29 Sep 1859 Brooklyn NY–d. 12 Apr 1937 Allegheny General Hospital, Pittsburgh PA) Died after an eight-week illness caused by an infected toe. Buried Union Dale Cemetery, Pittsburgh PA.

Ed Morris—5 Years Pitcher (b. 7 Dec 1899 Foshee AL–d. 3 Mar 1932 Tuberville Hospital, Century FL) Died at the height of his career of complications from knife wounds received three days earlier in a schuffle at a party given in his honor. Buried Oak Grove Cemetery, Flomation AL.

Walter Morris—1 Year Infielder (b. 30 Jan 1880 Rockwall TX–d. 2 Aug 1961 Baylor Hospital, Dallas TX) An educated lawyer, he opted to make his living from baseball. Known as "Mr Baseball" in the southwest for over 50 years he was a player, manager, club executive and league president. He organized 14 different minor leagues. Died from a heart attack following surgery. Buried Restland Memorial Park, Dallas TX.

Bill Morrisette—3 Years Pitcher (b. 17 Jan 1893 Baltimore MD–d. 25 Mar 1966 Virginia Beach VA) He was a retired civil service employee. Buried Rosewood Memorial Park, Virginia Beach VA.

Guy Morrison—2 Years Pitcher (b. 29 Aug 1898 Hinton WV–d. 14 Aug 1934 at his home in Grand Rapids MI) He was director of physical education in the public schools and the head of the Grand Rapids city recreation program. Took his own life with a self-inflicted gunshot wound to the head. Buried Sunset Memorial Park, South Charleston WV.

Hank Morrison—1 Year Pitcher (b. 22 May 1866 Olneyville RI–d. 30 Sep 1927 at his home in Attleboro MA) A jeweler by trade, he worked in several factories in the Attleboro area. Buried St John Cemetery, Attleboro MA.

Johnny Morrison—10 Years Pitcher (b. 22 Oct 1895 Pelleville KY–d. 20 Mar 1966 Veteran's Hospital, Louisville KY) World War I veteran. Died following a long illness. Buried Rosehill Cemetery, Owensboro KY.

Mike Morrison—3 Years Pitcher (b. 2 Feb 1869 Erie PA–d. 16 Jun 1955 St Mary's Home, Erie PA) He conducted a grocery store in Erie until he retired about 1935. Buried Trinity Cemetery, Erie PA.

Phil Morrison—1 Year Pitcher (b. 18 Oct 1894 Rockport IN–d. 18 Jan 1955 Veteran's Hospital, Lexington KY).

Deacon Morrissey—2 Years Pitcher (b. 5 May 1876 Baltimore MD–d. 22 Feb 1939 at his home in Baltimore MD) Died suddenly. Buried New Cathedral Cemetery, Baltimore MD.

Jack Morrissey—2 Years Infielder (b. 2 May 1876 Lansing MI–d. 30 Oct 1936 at his home in Lansing MI) He was active in local baseball at Lansing before operating a tobacco store there for several years. He later became active in county politics in the Democratic Party in Ingham County, MI, and ran for county sheriff in

1935. Buried Mount Hope Cemetery, Lansing MI.

John Morrissey—2 Years Infielder (b. abt 1855 Janesville WI–d. 30 Apr 1884 at the home of his parents in Janesville WI) He umpired a short while before dying from consumption. Buried Mount Olivet Cemetery, Janesville WI.

Jo-Jo Morrissey—3 Years Infielder (b. 16 Jan 1904 Warren RI–d. 2 May 1950 at his home in Worcester MA) He worked for Boeing in Seattle WA before returning to Worcester in 1940. There he delivered special delivery mail for the post office for a year before becoming a stampman in the production control department at Wyman-Gordon Company. Buried St John's Cemetery, Worcester MA.

Tom Morrissey—1 Year Infielder (b. 1861 Janesville WI–d. 23 Sep 1941 Mercy Hospital, Janesville WI) For 27 years he was a Janesville policeman, including a term as chief of police. Died after a long illness. He had been confined to his bed his last 11 years. Buried Mount Olivet Cemetery, Janesville WI.

Bud Morse—1 Year Infielder (b. 4 Sep 1904 Berkeley CA–d. 6 Apr 1987 at a care center in Sparks NV) World War II veteran. He was an attorney for the Veteran's Administration. Cremated.

Hap Morse—1 Year Infielder (b. 6 Dec 1886 St Paul MN–d. 19 Jun 1974 St Paul MN) Buried Forest Lawn Memorial Park, St Paul MN.

Jake Morse—1 Year Manager (b. 7 Jun 1860 Concord NH–d. 12 Apr 1937 at his home in Brookline MA) He worked 25 years for the *Boston Herald*, part of that time as sports editor. He also wrote sports for the *Boston Traveler* and had been engaged in the insurance business, as well as being active in civic matters. Died from a sudden heart attack. Cremated.

Carl Morton—8 Years Pitcher (b. 18 Jan 1944 Kansas City MO–d. 12 Apr 1983 at his parent's home in Tulsa OK) Died from a heart attack after jogging with his son. Buried Memorial Park, Tulsa OK.

Charlie Morton—3 Years Outfielder 3 Years Manager (b. 12 Oct 1854 Kingsville OH–d. 9 Dec 1921 Massillon State Hospital, Massillon OH) Died from generalized paralysis of the insane. Buried Akron OH.

Guy Morton—11 Years Pitcher (b. 1 Jun 1893 Vernon AL–d. 18 Oct 1934 at his home in Sheffield AL) World War I veteran. Died from an acute heart attack. Buried Vernon AL.

Walt Moryn—8 Years Outfielder (b. 12 Apr 1926 St Paul MN–d. 21 Jul 1996 Central DuPage Hospital, Winfield IL) Served on an ammunition ship during World War II. He managed a tavern in Cicero IL and worked as a sporting goods manager for a department store. Buried Assumption Cemetery, Glenwood IL.

Earl Moseley—4 Years Pitcher (b. 7 Sep 1887 Middleburg OH–d. 1 Jul 1963 City Hospital, Alliance OH) Served overseas in the U.S. Army two years during World War I. He coached the Mount Union College baseball team from 1922 to 1932, then owned and managed a clothing store in Alliance from 1923 to 1937. Died from cancer. Buried Alliance City Cemetery, Alliance OH.

Walter Moser—2 Years Pitcher (b. 27 Feb 1886 Concord NC–d. 10 Dec 1946 Presbyterian Hospital, Philadelphia PA) For 23 years he was superintendent of automotive equipment for Gulf Refining Company. Buried West Laurel Hill Cemetery, Bala Cynwyd PA.

Wally Moses—17 Years Outfielder (b. 8 Oct 1910 Uvalda GA–d. 10 Oct 1990 Meadows Memorial Hospital, Vidalia GA) He spent his entire life in baseball as a player, coach and scout, retiring in 1970. Died following an extended illness. Buried Pinecrest Cemetery, Vidalia GA.

Doc Moskiman—1 Year Infielder (b. 20 Dec 1878 Oakland CA–d. 11 Jan 1953 at his home in San Leandro CA) He was a retired salesman. Died after a lengthy illness. Buried Holy Sepulchre Cemetery, Hayward CA.

Jim Mosolf—4 Years Outfielder (b. 21 Aug 1905 Puyallup WA–d. 28 Dec 1979 Dallas OR) He worked for Sears-Roebuck in Tacoma WA from 1938 to 1948 and managed the Sears store at Salem OR from 1948 until he retired in 1964. Died from a heart attack. Buried Woodbine Cemetery, Puyallup WA.

Charlie Moss—3 Years Catcher (b. 20 Mar 1911 Meridian MS–d. 9 Oct 1991 Meridian MS) He managed minor league baseball in the Three-I League for several years. Died from complications of Alzheimer's disease. Buried Magnolia Cemetery, Meridian MS.

Howie Moss—2 Years Outfielder (b. 17 Oct 1918 Gastonia NC–d. 7 May 1989 at his home in Baltimore MD) He played in the International League until 1958 and later operated a tavern and sold cars for a Buick dealership until retiring in 1985. Died from natural causes. Buried Dulaney Valley Memorial Garden, Timonium MD.

Mal Moss—1 Year Pitcher (b. 18 Apr 1905 Sullivan IN–d. 5 Feb 1983 Memorial Medical Center, Savannah GA) Served in the U.S. Navy during World War II. He was an attorney with a Chicago IL law firm. Died from a heart attack. Buried Beaufort National Cemetery, Beaufort SC.

Ray Moss—6 Years Pitcher (b. 5 Dec 1901 Chattanooga TN–d. 9 Aug 1998 at his home in Chattanooga TN) He founded and operated a dairy farm and plant known as Ray Moss Farms and Golden Gallon Stores. Buried Hamilton Memorial Gardens, Chattanooga TN.

Earl Mossor—1 Year Pitcher (b. 21 Jul 1925 Forbus TN–d. 29 Dec 1988 Batavia OH).

Johnny Mostil—10 Years Outfielder (b. 1 Jun 1896 Chicago IL–d. 10 Dec 1970 at a nursing home in Midlothian IL) He was a White Sox instructor and scout until illness forced his retirement in 1968. Died after a long illness, suffering from circulatory problems and arthritis. Buried Mount Mercy Cemetery, Gary IN.

Frank Motz—3 Years Infielder (b. 1 Oct 1868 Freeburg PA–d. 18 Mar 1944 City Hospital, Akron OH) He was a stage hand at theatres in Akron, where he lived for 68 years. Died from pneumonia and lung cancer. Buried Rose Hill Burial Park, Fairlawn OH.

Glen Moulder—3 Years Pitcher (b. 28 Sep 1917 Cleveland OK–d. 27 Nov 1994 Decatur GA) Served in the U.S. Army Air Corps during World War II. He worked in the scrap metal business in Albany GA, Thomasville GA and Dayton OH. From 1970 until retiring in 1980 he worked in various industrial positions in Atlanta GA. Died from colon cancer. He donated his body to medical science research.

Ollie Moulton—1 Year Infielder (b. 16 Jan 1886 Medway MA–d. 10 Jul 1968 Peabody MA).

Frank Mountain—7 Years Pitcher (b. 17 May 1860 Fort Edward NY–d. 19 Nov 1939 Schenectady NY) He retired as assistant fire chief for General Electric Corporation. Buried Most Holy Redeemer Cemetery, Schenectady NY.

Billy Mountjoy—3 Years Pitcher (b. 1857 Port Huron MI–d. 19 May 1894 London, Ontario, Canada) Died from consumption.

Ray Mowe—1 Year Infielder (b. 12 Jul 1889 Rochester IN–d. 14 Aug 1968 Sarasota FL).

Mike Mowrey—13 Years Infielder (b. 20 Apr 1884 Brown's Mill PA–d. 20 Mar 1947 at his home in Chambersburg PA) He managed minor league baseball for a few years, then was employed as a night watchman at Wilson College. During World War II he worked at the Letter Kenny Ordinance plant. Died after a four-month illness. Buried Lincoln Cemetery, Chambersburg PA.

Joe Mowry—3 Years Outfielder (b. 6 Apr 1908 St Louis MO–d. 9 Feb 1994 at his home in St Louis MO) After managing minor league baseball in the 1930s and the early 1940s, he worked 30 years for the Mobil Oil Company in East St Louis IL, retiring in 1975 as safety director. Died after a long illness. Buried Resurrection Cemetery, St Louis MO.

Charlie Moyer—1 Year Pitcher (b. 15 Aug 1885 Andover OH–d. 18 Nov 1962 at a hospital in Jacksonville FL) He was a retired physician. Died after a brief illness. Cremated.

Mike Moynahan—4 Years Infielder (b. 1856 Chicago IL–d. 9 Apr 1899 Chicago IL) Buried Mount Olivet Cemetery, Chicago IL.

Emmett Mueller—4 Years Infielder (b. 20 Jul 1912 St Louis MO–d. 3 Oct 1986 Orlando FL) World War II veteran. He moved to Orlando from St Louis in 1978. Buried Woodlawn Cemetery, Winter Garden FL.

Heinie Mueller—11 Years Outfielder (b. 16 Sep 1899 Creve Coeur MO–d. 23 Jan 1975 at his home in Desoto MO) He was an electrician for Hussmann Refrigeration Company, retiring in 1964. He also maintained an interest in a South St Louis flower shop with Phil Todt. Died from cancer. Buried Park Lawn Cemetery, St Louis MO.

Ray Mueller—14 Years Catcher (b. 8 Mar 1912 Pittsburg KS–d. 29 Jun 1994 Village Teresa Nurs Hm, Lower Paxton Twp PA) Served in the U.S. Army during World War II. He managed minor league baseball and was a scout for the Phillies and Indians. In his later years he was a tipstaff at the Dauphin County, PA, courthouse. Buried Harrisburg Cemetery, Harrisburg PA.

Walter Mueller—4 Years Outfielder (b. 6 Dec 1894 Central MO–d. 16 Aug 1971 St Louis MO) He was a long-time employee of the Alton Brick Company. Died from cancer. Buried Mount Lebanon Cemetery, St Ann MO.

Joe Muich—1 Year Pitcher (b. 23 Nov 1903 St Louis MO–d. 2 Jul 1993 Altenheim Retirement Home, St Louis MO) From 1930 until he retired in 1966 he worked for the St Louis Police Department, mostly in the traffic department. Buried SS Peter and Paul Cemetery, St Louis MO.

Joe Muir—2 Years Pitcher (b. 26 Nov 1922 Oriole MD–d. 25 Jun 1980 Baltimore MD) For 25 years he was a Maryland State Policeman. He had undergone open heart surgery and complications resulted in the amputation of a leg. Died from kidney failure due to an aneurysm. Buried Oriole Cemetery, Oriole MD.

Tony Mullane—13 Years Pitcher (b. 20 Feb 1859 Cork, Ireland–d. 25 Apr 1944 at his home in Chicago IL) He gained fame as an ambidextrous pitcher, learning to throw with his left arm after injuring his right arm. He worked for the Chicago Police Department from 1903 until he retired in 1924. Buried Holy Sepulchre Cemetery, Worth IL.

Greg Mulleavy—3 Years Infielder (b. 25 Sep 1905 Detroit MI–d. 1 Feb 1980 Santa Teresite Hospital, Duarte CA) He managed minor league baseball for the Dodgers from 1946 to 1950 and from 1954 to 1957. He was a scout for the Dodgers until his death. Died from a chronic pulmonary condition. Buried Queen of Heaven Cemetery, Rowland Heights CA.

Billy Mullen—5 Years Infielder (b. 23 Jan 1896 St Louis MO–d. 4 May 1971 St Louis MO) Buried Jefferson Barracks National Cemetery, St Louis MO.

Charlie Mullen—5 Years Infielder (b. 15 Mar 1888 Seattle WA–d. 6 Jun 1963 Swedish Hospital, Seattle WA) He managed minor league baseball for a short while before becoming a securities broker for H M Herrin Company. Buried Evergreen-Washelli Cemetery, Seattle WA.

Freddie Muller—2 Years Infielder (b. 21 Dec 1907 Newark CA–d. 20 Oct 1976 at his home in Davis CA) He was a supervisor 36 years for Andco Farms. Died from prostate cancer. Cremated.

Dick Mulligan—3 Years Pitcher (b. 18 Mar 1918 Swoyersville PA–d. 15 Dec 1992 Victoria TX) Served in the U.S. Army Air Corps during World War II. He was district manager for Houston American Life Insurance in Victoria. He also sold sporting goods there and worked three years for a local radio station. Buried Resurrection Cemetery, Victoria TX.

Eddie Mulligan—5 Years Infielder (b. 27 Aug 1894 St Louis MO–d. 15 Mar 1982 Hillhaven Convalescent Hosp, San Rafael CA) He spent 62 years in baseball as a player, minor league manager, owner and executive. He still holds many Pacific Coast League records for third baseman. Died from a heart attack. Buried Holy Cross Catholic Cemetery, Colma CA.

Joe Mulligan—1 Year Pitcher (b. 31 Jul 1913 East Weymouth MA–d. 5 Jun 1986 West Roxbury MA) Buried St Joseph's Cemetery, West Roxbury MA.

George Mullin—14 Years Pitcher (b. 4 Jul 1880 Toledo OH–d. 7 Jan 1944 at his home in Wabash IN) Died after four weeks serious illness. Buried Falls Cemetery, Wabash IN.

Jim Mullin—2 Years Infielder (b. 16 Oct 1883 New York City NY–d. 24 Jan 1925 St Joseph Hospital, Philadelphia PA) Died from a complication of diseases believed to have come from a spiking received in baseball.

Dominic Mulrenan—1 Year Pitcher (b. 18 Dec 1893 Woburn MA–d. 27 Jul 1964 Melrose-Wakefield Hospital, Melrose MA) He worked for the Melrose Fire Department from 1927 until retiring as captain in 1960. After that he was a guard at the Transitron Co. Died after a short illness. Buried Wyoming Cemetery, Melrose MA.

Frank Mulroney—1 Year Pitcher (b. 8 Apr 1903 Mallard IA–d. 11 Nov 1985 at a hospital in Aberdeen WA) He worked for Phillips Oil Company in Texas, moving to Portland OR in 1944, then to Aberdeen WA where he lived 40 years and was a marine supervisor for Union Oil Company many years. Later he worked for Bay City Fuel Company before retiring. He enjoyed woodworking, making much of his own furniture. Buried Fern Hill Cemetery, Aberdeen WA.

Joe Mulvey—12 Years Infielder (b. 27 Oct 1858 Providence RI–d. 21 Aug 1928 Philadelphia PA) Died suddenly. Buried Magnolia Cemetery, Philadelphia PA.

John Munce—1 Year Outfielder (b. 18 Nov 1857 Philadelphia PA–d. 15 Mar 1917 Philadelphia PA) Buried Holy Cross Cemetery, Yeadon PA.

Jake Munch—1 Year Outfielder (b. 16 Nov 1890 Morton PA–d. 8 Jun 1966 at his home in Lansdowne PA) For 33 years he was the manager of the Emergency Road Service of Keystone Automobile Club, retiring in 1965. Buried Arlington Cemetery, Drexel Hill PA.

Bob Muncrief—12 Years Pitcher (b. 28 Jan 1916 Madill OK–d. 6 Feb 1996 Duncanville TX) He played professional baseball 25 years, retiring from the game in 1955. Buried Cedarlawn Memorial Park, Sherman TX.

George Mundinger—1 Year Catcher (b. 20 Nov 1854 New Orleans LA–d. 12 Oct 1910 Covington LA).

Bill Mundy—1 Year Infielder (b. 28 Jun 1889 Salineville OH–d. 23 Sep 1958 Kalamazoo MI).

Red Munger—10 Years Pitcher (b. 4 Oct 1918 Houston TX–d. 23 Jul 1996 Houston TX) He was a veteran of World War II. Buried Forest Park of Lawndale, Houston TX.

Van Lingle Mungo—14 Years Pitcher (b. 8 Jun 1911 Pageland SC–d. 12 Feb 1985 Pageland SC) Buried First Baptist Church Cemetery, Pageland SC.

Les Munns—3 Years Pitcher (b. 1 Dec 1908 Fort Bragg CA–d. 28 Feb 1997 West Ridge Care Center, Cedar Rapids IA) Died after a long illness. Buried Oakdale Cemetery, Crookston MN.

Joe Munson—2 Years Outfielder (b. 6 Nov 1899 Renovo PA–d. 24 Feb 1991 Drexel Hill PA).

Red Munson—1 Year Catcher (b. 31 Jul 1883 Cincinnati OH–d. 19 Feb 1957 St Joseph Hospital, Mishawaka IN) He was a salesman for Silvertone Supply Company in Cincinnati OH, retiring in 1954. Died while visiting his sister in Mishawaka. Buried Silverton OH.

Thurman Munson—11 Years Catcher (b. 7 Jun 1947 Akron OH–d. 2 Aug 1979 Canton OH) Died in a private airplane crash, at the height of his career, while piloting his own jet airplane, practicing touch-and-go landings. Buried Sunset Hills Burial Ground, Canton OH.

John Munyan—3 Years Catcher (b. 14 Nov 1860 Chester PA–d. 18 Feb 1945 Ideal Hospital, Endicott NY) Buried Riverhurst Memorial Cemetery, Endicott NY.

Simmy Murch—3 Years Infielder (b. 21 Nov 1881 Castine ME–d. 6 Jun 1939 Exeter NH) He was the baseball and basketball coach at Middlebury College before serving 16 years as baseball coach and trainer at Phillip's Exeter Academy.

Tim Murchison—2 Years Pitcher (b. 8 Oct 1896 Liberty NC–d. 20 Oct 1962 Liberty NC) He managed some minor league baseball before scouting for the Cubs and Giants. Buried Fairview Cemetery, Liberty NC.

Wilbur Murdock—1 Year Outfielder (b. 14 Mar 1875 Avon NY–d. 29 Oct 1941 St Catherine's Hospital, Santa Monica CA) He was an ice cream salesman. Died from a cerebral hemorrhage. Buried Valhalla Memorial Park, North Hollywood CA.

Tim Murnane—4 Years Infielder 1 Year Manager Hall of Fame (b. 4 Jun 1852 Naugatuck CT–d. 7 Feb 1917 Boston MA) He was a Hall of Fame sportswriter and editor for the *Boston Globe* for 30 years. Dropped dead from a sudden heart attack as he was entering the Shubert Theatre in downtown Boston. Buried Old Dorchester Burial Ground, Dorchester MA.

Buzz Murphy—2 Years Outfielder (b. 26 Apr 1895 Denver CO–d. 11 May 1938 at his home in Denver CO) He quit baseball, giving up a promising career, because he did not like riding on trains. Died from natural causes. Buried Mount Olivet Cemetery, Wheat Ridge CO.

Con Murphy—2 Years Pitcher (b. 15 Oct 1863 Worcester MA–d. 1 Aug 1914 at his home in Worcester MA) He was a salesman for the Thomas Ward Company of New York. Died from heart disease. Buried St John's Cemetery, Worcester MA.

Connie Murphy—2 Years Catcher (b. 1 Nov 1870 Northfield MA–d. 14 Dec 1945 at his home in New Bedford MA) For many years he owned a restaurant in New Bedford, retiring in 1944.

Danny Murphy—1 Year Catcher (b. 10 Sep 1864 Brooklyn NY–d. 14 Dec 1915 Brooklyn NY).

Danny Murphy—16 Years Infielder (b. 11 Aug 1876 Philadelphia PA–d. 22 Nov 1955 Medical Center, Jersey City NJ) He managed minor league baseball and was a scout for the Athletics. Later he worked for Hudson County, NJ. Died after a two-year illness. Buried Norwich CT.

Dave Murphy—1 Year Infielder (b. 4 May 1876 North Adams MA–d. 8 Apr 1940 at his sister's home in Adams MA) He coached baseball at St Michael's College and Hamilton College, and worked at the Strong Hewat Mill in Briggsville MA. Died from complications of diabetes. Buried Maple Cemetery, Adams MA.

Dummy Murphy—1 Year Infielder (b. 18 Dec 1886 Olney IL–d. 9 Aug 1962 at his home in Tallahassee FL) He was in the construction business. Buried Laurel Hill Cemetery, Thomasville GA.

Ed Murphy—4 Years Pitcher (b. 22 Jan 1877 Auburn NY–d. 29 Jan 1935 Whitten Nursing Home, Weedsport NY) He owned and operated a haberdashery with his brother in Auburn for 28 years until two disastrous fires closed the store. He had been an invalid seven years when he died. Buried St Joseph's Cemetery, Auburn NY.

Ed Murphy—1 Year Infielder (b. 23 Aug 1918 Joliet IL–d. 10 Dec 1991 St Joseph Medical Center, Joliet IL) Served in the U.S. Army during World War II. He managed minor league baseball for the Phillies and coached the College of St Francis baseball teams. Buried St John's Cemetery, Joliet IL.

Eddie Murphy—11 Years Outfielder (b. 2 Oct 1891 Hancock NY–d. 20 Feb 1969 at his home in Dunmore PA) He served in the USO during World War II and supervised the recreation division of the WPA in Lackawanna County, PA, for a number of years. Buried Queen of Peace Cemetery, Hawley PA.

Frank Murphy—1 Year Outfielder (b. 1880 Hackensack NJ–d. 2 Nov 1912 Central Islip NY).

Howard Murphy—1 Year Outfielder (b. 1 Jan 1882 Birmingham AL–d. 5 Oct 1926 at his home in Fort Worth TX) He worked in the sand and gravel business. Buried Mount Olivet Cemetery, Fort Worth TX.

Joe Murphy—2 Years Pitcher (b. 7 Sep 1866 St Louis MO–d. 28 Mar 1951 at his home in Coral Gables FL) The sports editor for the *St Louis Globe-Democrat* and the *Chicago Tribune* and a well-known horse race track official, he retired to Florida about 1936. Buried Calvary Cemetery, St Louis MO.

John Murphy—2 Years Infielder (b. 1879 New Haven CT–d. 20 Apr 1949 Andover MA) He worked for the City of Lawrence MA, retiring a few years before his death. Died suddenly from a heart condition while visiting his daughter. Buried Immaculate Conception Cemetery, Lawrence MA.

Johnny Murphy—13 Years Pitcher (b. 14 Jul 1908 New York City NY–d. 14 Jan 1970 Roosevelt Hospital, New York City NY) Known as baseball's first fully glamourous relief pitcher, he directed the Red Sox minor league operations before moving to the Mets in 1961, later becoming their general manager. Died after a heart attack. Buried Woodlawn Cemetery, Bronx NY.

Leo Murphy—1 Year Catcher (b. 7 Jan 1889 Terre Haute IN–d. 12 Aug 1960 Racine WI) He worked 25 years in organized baseball, including four years as manager of the Racine Belles of the All-American Girl's Baseball League in the 1940s.

Mike Murphy—2 Years Catcher (b. 19 Aug 1888 Forestville PA–d. 26 Oct 1952 Wilson Memorial Hospital, Johnson City NY) He umpired minor league baseball and managed a semipro team in the Johnson City area. Buried Calvary Cemetery, Johnson City NY.

Morg Murphy—11 Years Catcher (b. 12 Feb 1867 East Providence RI–d. 3 Oct 1938 Providence RI) Buried St Francis Cemetery, Pawtucket RI.

Pat Murphy—4 Years Catcher (b. 2 Jan 1857 Auburn MA–d. 16 May 1927 at his daughter's home in Worcester MA) For ten years he was a policeman for the Worcester Police Department before spending 20 years as a special police officer for the Plaza Theatre, retiring in 1925. Died after a month's illness. Buried St John's Cemetery, Worcester MA.

Walter Murphy—1 Year Pitcher (b. 27 Sep 1907 New York City NY–d. 23 Mar 1976 Houston TX) He was a retired director of industrial relations for Aero-Jet General Corporation in Pasadena CA. Died from cancer. Buried Memorial Oaks Cemetery, Houston TX.

Yale Murphy—3 Years Infielder (b. 11 Nov 1869 Southville MA–d. 14 Feb 1906 Southville MA).

Amby Murray—1 Year Pitcher (b. 4 Jun 1913 Fall River MA–d. 6 Feb 1997 Port Salerno FL).

Bill Murray—3 Years Manager (b. 13 Apr 1864 Peabody MA–d. 17 Mar 1937 at a hospital in Youngstown OH) He managed the Strand Theater in Youngstown. Died from cardiac failure. Buried Salem MA.

Bill Murray—1 Year Infielder (b. 6 Sep 1893 Vinalhaven ME–d. 14 Sep 1943 Boston MA).

Bobby Murray—1 Year Infielder (b. 4 Jul 1894 St Albans VT–d. 4 Jan 1979 at a hospital in Nashua NH) Served in the U.S. Army during World War I. He stayed active in baseball his entire life, scouting for the Braves, Red Sox, and Yankees. He managed some minor league baseball and worked with youth groups. Buried Edgewood Cemetery, Nashua NH.

Ed Murray—1 Year Infielder (b. 8 May 1895 Mystic CT–d. 8 Nov 1970 at his home in Cheyenne WY) World War I veteran. He moved to Cheyenne in 1920 where he spent the rest of his life working in insurance. Buried Olivet Cemetery, Cheyenne WY.

George Murray—6 Years Pitcher (b. 23 Sep 1898 Charlotte NC–d. 18 Oct 1955 Memphis TN) Served in the U.S. Army during World War I. He was a minor league umpire for a few years, and worked for a blueprint company in Memphis his last 15 years. Buried Oakwood Cemetery, Brownsville TN.

Jim Murray—3 Years Outfielder (b. 16 Jan 1878 Galveston TX–d. 25 Apr 1945 Galveston TX) World War I veteran. He worked as a night clerk at a funeral home. Buried Episcopal Cemetery, Galveston TX.

Jim Murray—1 Year Pitcher (b. 31 Dec 1900 Scranton PA–d. 15 Jul 1973 New York City NY) He was the general manager of the Scranton minor league team before becoming director of group sales for the Mets in 1962, a job he held until his death. Died from injuries received in an automobile accident on the George Washington Bridge in New York City. Buried St Catherine's Cemetery, Moscow PA.

Miah Murray—4 Years Catcher (b. 1 Jan 1865 Boston MA–d. 11 Jan 1922 at his home in North Dorchester MA) He umpired minor league baseball before operating a billiard and pool parlor in Boston for 30 years. He had been in failing health two years when he died. Buried Holyhood Cemetery, Brookline MA.

Pat Murray—1 Year Pitcher (b. 18 Jul 1897 Scottsville NY–d. 5 Nov 1983 Rochester NY) Buried St John's Cemetery, Spencerport NY.

Red Murray—11 Years Outfielder (b. 4 Mar 1884 Arnot PA–d. 4 Dec 1958 Robert Packer Hospital, Sayre PA) He was the retired director of recreation for the City of Elmira NY.

Tony Murray—1 Year Outfielder (b. 30 Apr 1904 Chicago IL–d. 19 Mar 1974 Columbus Hospital, Chicago IL) He was a Chicago police sergeant, attorney and hearing officer for the zoning board. Buried All Saints Cemetery, Des Plaines IL.

Danny Murtaugh—9 Years Infielder 15 Years Manager (b. 8 Oct 1917 Chester PA–d. 2 Dec 1976 Chester PA) He spent his entire life in baseball as a player, manager, coach and minor league manager. Died after a stroke. Buried St Peter and St Paul Cemetery, Springfield PA.

Paul Musser—2 Years Pitcher (b. 24 Jun 1889 Millheim PA–d. 7 Jul 1973 Centre Community Hospital, State College PA) He retired as a guard from the Rockview Correctional Institution. Buried Fairview Cemetery, Millheim PA.

Alex Mustaikis—1 Year Pitcher (b. 26 Mar 1909 Chelsea MA–d. 17 Jan 1970 State General Hospital, Scranton PA) Died shortly after he was admitted to the hospital. Buried Cathedral Cemetery, Scranton PA.

Jim Mutrie—9 Years Manager (b. 13 Jun 1851 Chelsea MA–d. 24 Jan 1938 Cancer Institute, New York City NY) He started the New York Metropolitans (later to become the Giants), owning them from 1882 to 1890. After that he entered the hotel business in Elmira NY, and later ran a newstand in Staten Island NY. Died from cancer. Buried Moravian Cemetery, Staten Island NY.

Glenn Myatt—16 Years Catcher (b. 9 Jul 1897 Argenta AR–d. 9 Aug 1969 at his home in Houston TX) Served in the U.S. Navy during World War I. He lived in Houston 60 years and worked as a grocery checker. Died after a lengthy illness. Buried Forest Park of Lawndale, Houston TX.

Buddy Myer—17 Years Infielder (b. 16 Mar 1904 Ellisville MS–d. 31 Oct 1974 Doctor's Memorial Hospital, Baton Rouge LA) Buried Greenoaks Memorial Park, Baton Rouge LA.

Al Myers—8 Years Infielder (b. 22 Oct 1863 Danville IL–d. 24 Dec 1927 at his home in Marshall IL) Died from chronic nephritis. Buried Highland Lawn Cemetery, Terre Haute IN.

Billy Myers—7 Years Infielder (b. 14 Aug 1910 Enola PA–d. 10 Apr 1995 Cumberland County Nursing Home, Carlisle PA) He retired as a locomotive engineer for the Pennsylvania Railroad. Buried Rolling Green Memorial Park, Camp Hill PA.

Elmer Myers—8 Years Pitcher (b. 2 Mar 1894 York Springs PA–d. 29 Jul 1976 Collingwood NJ) Died after suffering a stroke a month earlier. Buried Sunnyside Cemetery, York Springs PA.

George Myers—6 Years Catcher (b. 13 Nov 1860 Buffalo NY–d. 14 Dec 1926 Buffalo NY).

Hap Myers—5 Years Infielder (b. 8 Apr 1888 San Francisco CA–d. 30 Jun 1967 Notre Dame Hospital, San Francisco CA) World War I veteran. He worked 35 years as director of an automobile finance company. Died from a heart attack. Cremated.

Henry Myers—3 Years Infielder 1 Year Manager (b. May 1858 Philadelphia PA–d. 18 Apr 1895 Philadelphia PA).

Hy Myers—14 Years Outfielder (b. 27 Apr 1889 East Liverpool OH–d. 1 May 1965 at his home in Minerva OH) He owned an automobile dealership in Kensington OH for several years before going to work for the Kensington State Bank. Buried Hanoverton Cemetery, Hanoverton OH.

Joe Myers—1 Year Pitcher (b. 18 Mar 1882 Wilmington DE–d. 11 Feb 1956 Delaware City DE) An ardent fisherman and outdoors man, he conducted a taproom in Wilmington. Buried Cathedral Cemetery, Wilmington DE.

N

Jack Nabors—3 Years Pitcher (b. 19 Nov 1887 Montevallo AL–d. 20 Nov 1923 Wilton AL).

Bill Nagel—3 Years Infielder (b. 19 Aug 1915 Memphis TN–d. 8 Oct 1981 Freehold NJ).

Lou Nagelsen—1 Year Catcher (b. 29 Jun 1887 Piqua OH–d. 21 Oct 1965 Lutheran Hospital, Fort Wayne IN) He lived in Fort Wayne except for a period from 1940 to 1955 when he was in Detroit MI. Died after being a patient in the hospital for three weeks. Buried Catholic Cemetery, Fort Wayne IN.

Judge Nagle—1 Year Pitcher (b. 10 Mar 1880 Santa Rosa CA–d. 26 May 1971 Memorial Hospital, Santa Rosa CA) A well-known politician, promoter and author in the Santa Rosa area, he was instrumental in bringing outside businesses to Sonoma County, CA. He served as county clerk from 1935 to 1950. Died from congestive heart failure. Cremated. Buried Santa Rosa Memorial Park, Santa Rosa CA.

Tom Nagle—2 Years Catcher (b. 30 Oct 1865 Milwaukee WI–d. 9 Mar 1946 Milwaukee WI) Buried Calvary Catholic Cemetery, Milwaukee WI.

Frank Naleway—1 Year Infielder (b. 4 Jul 1901 Chicago IL–d. 28 Jan 1949 Chicago IL) Died from the effects of multiple sclerosis. Buried Resurrection Cemetery, Justice IL.

Kid Nance—4 Years Outfielder (b. 2 Aug 1877 Fort Worth TX–d. 28 May 1958 Fort Worth TX) He managed minor league baseball briefly and coached baseball at Texas Christian University from 1918 to 1923. He had lost a leg before he died. Buried Rose Hill Memorial Park, Fort Worth TX.

Buddy Napier—4 Years Pitcher (b. 18 Dec 1889 Byronville GA–d. 29 Mar 1968 Dallas TX) Living in Hutchins TX since 1891, he owned and operated Napier's Mobil Service there from 1931 until his death. Buried Hutchins Cemetery, Hutchins TX.

Bill Narleski—2 Years Infielder (b. 9 Jun 1899

Perth Amboy NJ–d. 22 Jul 1964 Laurel Springs NJ) Died suddenly. Buried Beverly National Cemetery, Beverly NJ.

Sam Narron—3 Years Catcher (b. 25 Aug 1913 Middlesex NC–d. 31 Dec 1996 Middlesex NC) In addition to spending 31 years in organized baseball he was a farmer, hunter, fisherman and volunteer fireman. Buried Antioch Baptist Church Cemetery, Middlesex NC.

Billy Nash—15 Years Infielder 1 Year Manager (b. 24 Jun 1865 Richmond VA–d. 15 Nov 1929 East Orange NJ) He was a hospital attendant in Massachusetts. Died from a heart attack while inspecting a health department building. Buried Boston MA.

Ken Nash—2 Years Infielder (b. 14 Jul 1888 South Weymouth MA–d. 16 Feb 1977 Epsom NH) He served as a state representative and a state senator from Weymouth MA and was a judge 52 years, including seven as Chief Justice of the Massachusetts district courts, retiring in 1970. Died after a long illness. Buried Highland Cemetery, Weymouth MA.

Sandy Nava—5 Years Catcher (b. 12 Apr 1850 San Francisco CA–d. 15 Jun 1906 Baltimore MD).

Frank Navin—(b. 18 Apr 1871 Adrian MI–d. 13 Nov 1935 Detroit MI) Making his fortune in the insurance business, he bought controlling interest in the Detroit Tigers in 1903, owning them until his death. Died from a heart attack while horeseback riding. Buried Mount Olivet Cemetery, Detroit MI.

Earl Naylor—3 Years Outfielder (b. 19 May 1919 Kansas City MO–d. 16 Jan 1990 Winter Haven FL).

Rollie Naylor—7 Years Pitcher (b. 4 Feb 1892 Ponder TX–d. 18 Jun 1966 Fort Worth TX) World War I veteran. He was a retired minor league umpire. Buried Odd Fellows Cemetery, Denton TX.

Jack Neagle—3 Years Pitcher (b. 2 Jan 1858 Syracuse NY–d. 20 Sep 1904 Syracuse NY).

Charlie Neal—8 Years Infielder (b. 30 Jan 1931 Longview TX–d. 18 Nov 1996 Baylor Medical Center, Dallas TX) Died from heart failure. Buried Grace Hill Cemetery, Longview TX.

Joe Neal—4 Years Pitcher (b. 7 May 1867 Wadsworth OH–d. 30 Dec 1913 at his home in Akron OH) He was a flagman on highway construction. Died from a heart attack four months after being run over by a car while at work. Buried Mount Peace Cemetery, Akron OH.

Offa Neal—1 Year Infielder (b. 5 Jun 1876 Logan IL–d. 11 Apr 1950 Mount Vernon IL).

Greasy Neale—8 Years Outfielder (b. 5 Nov 1891 Parkersburg WV–d. 2 Nov 1973 Darcy Hall Nursing Home, Lake Worth FL) The only man to play in a World Series, coach a college football team in the Rose Bowl and coach a world champ NFL team, he coached football at seven colleges from 1919 to 1940 before coaching the Philadelphia Eagles from 1941 to 1950. He was inducted in both the College Football Hall of Fame and the Professional Football Hall of Fame. Buried Odd Fellows Cemetery, Parkersburg WV.

Jim Nealon—2 Years Infielder (b. 13 Dec 1884 San Francisco CA–d. 2 Apr 1910 at his father's home in San Francisco CA) He retired from baseball shortly before his death, and was working at the county clerk's office in San Francisco when he died. Died from typhoid pneumonia. Buried Holy Cross Catholic Cemetery, Colma CA.

Tom Needham—11 Years Catcher (b. 17 May 1879 Steubenville OH–d. 14 Dec 1926 at his home in Steubenville OH) He owned his own tailoring company after working as a skilled glassworker. Died from injuries received when he accidentally fell while trying to rescue a child from an oncoming car. Buried Mount Calvary Cemetery, Steubenville OH.

Doug Neff—2 Years Infielder (b. 8 Oct 1891 Harrisonburg VA–d. 23 May 1932 Cape Charles VA) Drowned when he fell from a boat.

Jim Neher—1 Year Pitcher (b. 5 Feb 1889 Rochester NY–d. 11 Nov 1951 Meyer Memorial Hospital, Buffalo NY) Forced to leave baseball because of a broken leg, he worked for Hotel Statler in Buffalo NY for 38 years, first as an elevator repairman, then as a house officer and, finally, as an electrician. Died after a four-month illness. Buried Forest Lawn Cemetery, Buffalo NY.

Art Nehf—15 Years Pitcher (b. 31 Jul 1892 Terre Haute IN–d. 18 Dec 1960 at his home in Phoenix AZ) He once pitched 20 innings in a game without yielding a run. He lived in

Phoenix for 35 years where he was an insurance executive. He is a member of the Arizona Sports Hall of Fame. Died from cancer. Cremated.

Bob Neighbors—1 Year Infielder (b. 9 Nov 1917 Talahina OK–d. 8 Aug 1952 North Korea) He was missing in action and presumed dead during the Korean War. He also served in World War II.

Cy Neighbors—1 Year Outfielder (b. 23 Sep 1880 MO–d. 20 May 1964 at a hospital in Tacoma WA) He was a carpenter and lived in Tacoma 60 years. Buried Mountain View Memorial Park, Tacoma WA.

Tommy Neill—2 Years Outfielder (b. 7 Nov 1919 Hartselle AL–d. 22 Sep 1980 Houston TX) Buried Earthman Rest Haven, Houston TX.

Bernie Neis—8 Years Outfielder (b. 26 Sep 1895 Bloomington IL–d. 29 Nov 1972 Inverness FL) He moved to Florida about 1942 and was a fishing guide there. Buried Oak Ridge Cemetery, Inverness FL.

Ernie Neitzke—1 Year Outfielder (b. 13 Nov 1894 Toledo OH–d. 27 Apr 1977 Flower Hospital, Sylvania OH) Served in France for the U.S. Army during World War I. For 20 years he was a bartender and was manager of the VFW canteen, retiring in 1962. An avid bowler, he averaged over 200. Buried Union Hill Cemetery, Bowling Green OH.

Bots Nekola—2 Years Pitcher (b. 10 Dec 1906 New York City NY–d. 11 Mar 1987 Rockville Centre NY).

Bill Nelson—1 Year Pitcher (b. 28 Sep 1863 Terre Haute IN–d. 23 Jun 1941 Terre Haute IN) He umpired minor league baseball for a number of years until he lost a leg in an accident. Died at the New National Hotel where he had lived several years. Buried St Joseph's Cemetery, Terre Haute IN.

Candy Nelson—9 Years Infielder (b. 12 Mar 1854 Portland ME–d. 4 Sep 1910 at his home in Brooklyn NY) Died from heart disease.

Emmett Nelson—2 Years Pitcher (b. 26 Feb 1905 Viborg SD–d. 25 Aug 1967 Sioux Valley hospital, Sioux Falls SD) He worked for Jack Rabbit Bus Lines in Sioux Falls and owned a fuel oil business in Viborg for a few years before going into the drugstore business at Garretson SD in 1946, retiring in 1965. Died after a long illness. Buried Zion Lutheran Church Cemetery, Garretson SD.

Lindsey Nelson—Hall of Fame (b. 25 May 1919 near Campbellsville TN–d. 10 Jun 1995 Emory University Hospital, Atlanta GA) Served in Europe and North Africa for the U.S. Army during World War II. He was a sportscaster for NBC, CBS, the Mets and the Giants. Died from complications of Parkinson's disease and pneumonia. Buried Polk Memorial Gardens, Columbia TN.

Luke Nelson—1 Year Pitcher (b. 4 Dec 1893 Cable IL–d. 14 Nov 1985 Public Hospital, Moline IL) He was a coal miner before going to work at the International Harvestor-Farmall plant in 1934, retiring in 1962. Buried St John's Cemetery, Viola IL.

Lynn Nelson—7 Years Pitcher (b. 24 Feb 1905 Sheldon ND–d. 15 Feb 1955 at his home in Kansas City MO) He was an electrician and had been in failing health three years when he died. Died from colon cancer. Buried Mount St Mary's Cemetery, Kansas City MO.

Ray Nelson—1 Year Infielder (b. 4 Aug 1875 Holyoke MA–d. 8 Jan 1961 Mount Vernon NY).

Red Nelson—4 Years Pitcher (b. 19 May 1886 Cleveland OH–d. 26 Oct 1956 Morton Plant Hospital, Clearwater FL) Died after suffering a heart attack. Buried Woodlawn Memory Gardens, St Petersburg FL.

Tom Nelson—1 Year Infielder (b. 1 May 1917 Chicago IL–d. 24 Sep 1973 Hillside Hospital, San Diego CA) He owned and operated a hotel restaurant supply company. Died from injuries suffered in an accidental fall at his home four days earlier. Cremated.

Jack Ness—2 Years Infielder (b. 11 Nov 1885 Chicago IL–d. 3 Dec 1957 at his home in De Land FL) He was found by police, dead from natural causes.

Milo Netzel—1 Year Infielder (b. 12 May 1887 Olean NY–d. 18 Mar 1938 at his home in Oxnard CA) Died from a heart attack, but suffered from cirrhosis of the liver. Buried Los Angeles National Cemetery, Los Angeles CA.

Otto Neu—1 Year Infielder (b. 24 Sep 1894 Springfield OH–d. 19 Sep 1932 at his home in Kenton OH) He was a self-employed wholesale rug merchant. Died from intestinal influenza. Buried Ferncliff Cemetery, Springfield OH.

Hal Neubauer—1 Year Pitcher (b. 13 May 1902 Hoboken NJ–d. 9 Sep 1949 Providence RI) He was sales manager for Fiegenspan Brewing Company of Newark NJ and Blatz Brewing Company of Milwaukee WI before taking a similar position with the James Hanley Company in Providence. Died from a heart attack after a golf match. Buried Swan Point Cemetery, Providence RI.

Tex Neuer—1 Year Pitcher (b. 8 Jun 1877 Freemont OH–d. 14 Jan 1966 County Hospital, Northumberland PA) Served in the U.S. Army Infantry during the Spanish-American War. He worked in the engineering department of Bendix Aviation Corporation at Greene NY, retiring in 1942. Died after being in failing health several years and hospitalized his last seven months. Buried West Side Cemetery, Shamokin Dam PA.

Johnny Neun—6 Years Infielder 3 Years Manager (b. 28 Oct 1900 Baltimore MD–d. 28 Mar 1990 Union Memorial Hospital, Baltimore MD) He was a scout and player development specialist for the Yankees for years. He was a scout for the Brewers when he died. Died from pancreatic cancer. Buried Immanuel Lutheran Cemetery, Baltimore MD.

Ernie Nevel—3 Years Pitcher (b. 17 Aug 1919 Charleston MO–d. 10 Jul 1988 Cox Medical Center, Springfield MO) He lived in the Branson MO area for 29 years, and was affiliated with a baseball school and camp there. Died following a long illness. Buried Ozarks Memorial Park, Branson MO.

Ernie Nevers—3 Years Pitcher (b. 11 Jun 1902 Willow River MN–d. 3 May 1976 Marin General Hospital, San Rafael CA) Served in the U.S. Marines during World War II. A college football All-American from Stanford University and a member of the College Football Hall of Fame, he also played professional football. He coached college football for a short time, then was a public relations and sales representative for a wholesale liquor firm, retiring in 1968. Died from a kidney disorder. Cremated.

John Newell—1 Year Infielder (b. 14 Jan 1868 Wilmington DE–d. 28 Jan 1919 Wilmington DE) Buried Cathedral Cemetery, Wilmington DE.

Hal Newhouser—17 Years Pitcher Hall of Fame (b. 20 May 1921 Detroit MI–d. 10 Nov 1998 at a hospital in Southfield MI) He suffered from emphysema and heart ailments. Buried Oakland Hills Memorial Gardens, Novi MI.

Floyd Newkirk—1 Year Pitcher (b. 16 Jul 1908 Norris City IL–d. 15 Apr 1976 Clayton MO) Buried Jefferson Barracks National Cemetery, St Louis MO.

Joel Newkirk—2 Years Pitcher (b. 1 May 1896 Kyana IN–d. 22 Jan 1966 Pearce Hospital, Eldorado IL) World War I veteran. He was a custodian at the American Legion Hall. Buried Wolf Creek Cemetery, Eldorado IL.

Maury Newlin—2 Years Pitcher (b. 22 Jun 1914 Bloomingdale IN–d. 14 Aug 1978 V A Hospital, Houston TX) He was a retired salesman. Buried Brookside Memorial Park, Houston TX.

Charlie Newman—1 Year Outfielder (b. 5 Nov 1868 Platteville WI–d. 23 Nov 1947 San Diego CA) He was a retired chief of police. Died from a heart attack. Cremated.

Fred Newman—6 Years Pitcher (b. 21 Feb 1942 Boston MA–d. 24 Jun 1987 Union Hospital, Framingham MA) He worked for the Brookline Fire Department from 1970 to 1978. He then moved to Holliston MA where he painted houses until his death. Died from injuries received in an automobile accident. Buried Walnut Hills Cemetery, Brookline MA.

Pat Newnam—2 Years Infielder (b. 10 Dec 1880 Hemstead TX–d. 20 Jun 1938 at his home in San Antonio TX) He played, managed and umpired in the Texas League for 19 years. Died after an illness of several months. Buried St Mary's Cemetery, San Antonio TX.

Bobo Newsom—20 Years Pitcher (b. 11 Aug 1907 Hartsville SC–d. 7 Dec 1962 at a hospital in Orlando FL) He pitched in the minor leagues until 1953, retiring to Winter Park FL at that time. Died from cirrhosis of the liver. Buried Magnolia Cemetery, Hartsville SC.

Dick Newsome—3 Years Pitcher (b. 13 Dec 1909 Ahoskie NC–d. 15 Dec 1965 Ahoskie NC).

Skeeter Newsome—12 Years Infielder (b. 18 Oct 1910 Phenix City AL–d. 31 Aug 1989 Oak Manor Nursing Home, Columbus GA) He managed minor league baseball 13 years before becoming an account executive for a television station in Columbus, retiring in 1974. Buried Parkhill Cemetery, Columbus GA.

Doc Newton—8 Years Pitcher (b. 26 Oct 1877

Indianapolis IN–d. 14 May 1931 at his home in Memphis TN) A graduate from medical school, he never practiced medicine, preferring to play baseball. He later was a superintendent at a warehouse. Died from food poisoning following a nervous breakdown. Buried Crown Hill Cemetery, Indianapolis IN.

Sam Nichol—2 Years Outfielder (b. 20 Apr 1869 Ireland–d. 19 Apr 1937 at the home of a niece in Steubenville OH) He conducted a tavern in Wheeling WV until prohibition shut him down. He then went into the hotel business in Akron OH and Barbarton OH. Buried Mount Calvary Cemetery, Steubenville OH.

Simon Nicholls—6 Years Infielder (b. 17 Jul 1882 Germantown MD–d. 12 Mar 1911 Union Protestant Infirmary, Baltimore MD) Died at the height of his baseball career from peritonitis and typhoid fever following surgery. Buried Holy Cross Cemetery, Yeadon PA.

Art Nichols—6 Years Catcher (b. 14 Jul 1871 Manchester NH–d. 9 Aug 1945 Memorial Hospital, Willimantic CT) He coached baseball at Windham High School and at the University of Connecticut. Died four days after surgery for a ruptured stomach ulcer. Buried St Joseph's Cemetery, Windham CT.

Chet Nichols—6 Years Pitcher (b. 2 Jul 1897 Woonsocket RI–d. 11 Jul 1982 Memorial Hospital, Lincoln RI) Served in the U.S. Navy during World War I. A laborer for the Slater Dyer Works, Inc, in Pawtucket RI, he retired in 1965. Buried Union Cemetery, North Smithfield RI.

Chet Nichols—9 Years Pitcher (b. 22 Feb 1931 Pawtucket RI–d. 27 Mar 1995 Lincoln RI) Served in the U.S. Army during the Korean War. He went into the banking business, but returned to baseball as a minor league pitching coach for the Orioles. For 25 years he worked for a Rhode Island bank in a number of capacities, including lending officer and branch manager, retiring in 1987 as a vice-president. Buried Union Cemetery, North Smithfield RI.

Dolan Nichols—1 Year Pitcher (b. 28 Feb 1930 Tishomingo MS–d. 20 Nov 1989 North Mississippi Medical Center, Tupelo MS) He was a salesman for VWR Furniture Company in Tupelo. Buried Oak Hill Cemetery, Water Valley MS.

Kid Nichols—15 Years Pitcher 2 Years Manager Hall of Fame (b. 14 Sep 1869 Madison WI–d. 11 Apr 1953 Menorah Hospital, Kansas City MO) An expert amateur bowler, he was the assistant manager of a bowling alley. Died from a malignant growth on his neck. Buried Mount Moriah Cemetery, Kansas City MO.

Tricky Nichols—5 Years Pitcher (b. 26 Jul 1850 Bridgeport CT–d. 2 Feb 1918 at his sister's home in Bridgeport CT) Buried Lakeview Cemetery, Bridgeport CT.

Bill Nicholson—16 Years Outfielder (b. 11 Dec 1914 Chestertown MD–d. 8 Mar 1986 Chestertown MD).

Frank Nicholson—1 Year Pitcher (b. 29 Aug 1889 Berlin PA–d. 10 Nov 1972 at his home in Jersey Shore PA) A retired welder for the New York Central Railroad, he worked in the shops at Avis PA and Albany NY. Buried Jersey Shore Cemetery, Jersey Shore PA.

Fred Nicholson—5 Years Outfielder (b. 1 Sep 1894 Honey Grove TX–d. 23 Jan 1972 at his home in Kilgore TX) He lived in Kilgore from 1936 until his death and had an ownership-managerial relationship in the old East Texas League. Died after a brief illness. Buried Lakeview Cemetery, Marietta OK.

Ovid Nicholson—1 Year Outfielder (b. 30 Dec 1888 Salem IN–d. 24 Mar 1968 Washington County Memorial Hosp, Salem IN) Buried Crown Hill Cemetery, Salem IN.

Parson Nicholson—3 Years Infielder (b. 14 Apr 1862 Blaine OH–d. 28 Feb 1917 at his home in Bellaire OH) He owned a shoe store in Bellaire and was active politically, having been elected mayor on one occasion. Died from bronchopneumonia. Buried Rose Hill Cemetery, Bellaire OH.

George Nicol—3 Years Outfielder (b. 17 Oct 1870 Barry IL–d. 10 Aug 1924 at his home in Milwaukee WI) He was a machinist and worked on the night shift. Died suddenly from the effects of diabetes shortly after returning home from work one night. Buried Milwaukee WI.

Hugh Nicol—10 Years Outfielder 1 Year Manager (b. 1 Jan 1858 Campsie, Scotland–d. 27 Jun 1921 Home Hospital, Lafayette IN) He owned and managed a team in the Three-I League for several years before becoming the first athletic director at Purdue University, a position he held ten years. Died from gangrene and diabetes.

Buried Meadowlawn Memorial Gardens, New Port Richey FL.

Al Niehaus—1 Year Infielder (b. 1 Jun 1899 Cincinnati OH–d. 14 Oct 1931 St Mary's Hospital, Cincinnati OH) He played in the Southern Association and the American Association. Died from bronchopneumonia. Buried St Joseph Old Catholic Cemetery, Cincinnati OH.

Dick Niehaus—4 Years Pitcher (b. 24 Oct 1892 Covington KY–d. 12 Mar 1957 V A Hospital, Atlanta GA) For a dozen years he was trainer for the Atlanta Crackers in the Southern Association, retiring in 1950 because of ill health. Died after suffering several years from lung cancer and a heart condition. Buried Woodbury GA.

Bert Niehoff—6 Years Infielder (b. 13 May 1884 Louisville CO–d. 8 Dec 1974 St Joseph Hospital, Burbank CA) He was a scout for the Angels. Died from prostate cancer. Buried Inglewood Park Cemetery, Inglewood CA.

Bob Nieman—12 Years Outfielder (b. 26 Jan 1927 Cincinnati OH–d. 10 Mar 1985 at his home in Corona CA) He was a substitute high school teacher in Orange County, CA, and often spoke at banquets and programs throughout Southern California. Buried Fairhaven Memorial Park, Santa Ana CA.

Butch Nieman—3 Years Outfielder (b. 8 Feb 1918 Herkimer KS–d. 2 Nov 1993 at a nursing home in Topeka KS) He managed minor league baseball for a short time. For 30 years he was a foreman in the shipping department for Goodyear Tire and Rubber Company. Buried Topeka Cemetery, Topeka KS.

Jack Niemes—1 Year Pitcher (b. 19 Oct 1919 Cincinnati OH–d. 4 Mar 1966 Mercy Hospital, Hamilton OH) Served in the South Pacific for the U.S. Navy during World War II. He owned a plumbing contracting company. Killed when his car ran off the road, striking a 12-foot ditch embankment. Buried Oak Hill Cemetery Park, Cincinnati OH.

Al Niemiec—2 Years Infielder (b. 18 May 1911 Meriden CT–d. 29 Oct 1995 at a convalescent center in Kirkland WA) Served in the U.S. Navy during World War II. An avid golfer and gardener, he was the teaching pro at Juanita, Bellevue and Redmond golf courses before retiring in the 1970s. Buried Sunset Hills Memorial Park, Bellevue WA.

Johnny Niggeling—9 Years Pitcher (b. 10 Jul 1903 Remsen IA–d. 16 Sep 1963 Grand Central Hotel, Le Mars IA) Hung himself in his hotel room. Buried St Mary's Catholic Church Parish Cemetery, Remsen IA.

Tom Niland—1 Year Outfielder (b. 14 Apr 1870 Brookfield MA–d. 30 Apr 1950 at his home in Lynn MA) He served on the Massachusetts State Boxing Commission from 1929 to 1935. Died following a brief illness. Buried St Mary's Cemetery, Lynn MA.

Billy Niles—1 Year Infielder (b. 11 Jan 1867 Covington KY–d. 3 Jul 1936 Springfield OH) Living in Springfield 50 years, he worked about 25 years for French and Hecht, Inc. there. Buried Ferncliff Cemetery, Springfield OH.

Harry Niles—5 Years Outfielder (b. 10 Sep 1880 Buchanan MI–d. 18 Apr 1953 Memorial Hospital, Sturgis MI) Died following a stroke. Buried Oak Lawn Cemetery, Sturgis MI.

Rabbit Nill—5 Years Infielder (b. 14 Jul 1881 Fort Wayne IN–d. 24 May 1962 St Joseph Hospital, Fort Wayne IN) He operated a garage in Fort Wayne before becoming associated with Fort Wayne Tool and Die Company, retiring in 1954. Died following a six-month illness. Buried Catholic Cemetery, Fort Wayne IN.

Otho Nitcholas—1 Year Pitcher (b. 13 Sep 1908 McKinney TX–d. 11 Sep 1986 North Texas Medical Center, McKinney TX) He was the first chief of police at Plano TX and retired as chief of police at McKinney. Buried Altoga Cemetery, McKinney TX.

Al Nixon—9 Years Outfielder (b. 11 Apr 1886 Atlantic City NJ–d. 9 Nov 1960 at a hospital in Lafayette LA) He lived in Opelousas LA 35 years and worked with the Little League program there. Buried Myrtle Grove Cemetery, Opelousas LA.

Williard Nixon—9 Years Pitcher (b. 17 Jun 1928 Taylorsville TX–d. 10 Dec 2000 Rome GA) Buried East View Cemetery, Rome GA.

Ray Noble—3 Years Catcher (b. 15 Mar 1919 Central Hatillo, Cuba–d. 9 May 1998 Cabrini Medical Center, New York City NY) He owned a liquor store in Brooklyn NY. Died from complications of diabetes.

George Noftsker—1 Year Outfielder (b. 24 Aug 1859 Shippensburg PA–d. 8 May 1931 at his home in Shippensburg PA) He conducted a carriage factory in Shippensburg until about 1920. He was also secretary of the Centennial Fire Insurance Company from 1904 until his death. Died from an internal hemorrhage. Buried Spring Hill Cemetery, Shippensburg PA.

The Only Nolan—5 Years Pitcher (b. 7 Nov 1857 Paterson NJ–d. 18 May 1913 at his home in Paterson NJ) He was a patrolman for the Paterson Police Department from 1887 until his death. Died from chronic heart disease and nephritis. Buried Holy Sepulchre Cemetery, Totowa NJ.

Pete Noonan—3 Years Catcher (b. 24 Nov 1881 West Stockbridge MA–d. 11 Feb 1965 Fairview Hospital, Great Barrington MA) A lawyer by education, he had controlling interest in a minor league team until it folded because of World War I. He then went into the hotel business in New York City, retiring as assistant manager of the Roosevelt Hotel in 1954. Buried St Peter's Cemetery, Great Barrington MA.

Jerry Nops—6 Years Pitcher (b. 23 Jun 1875 Toledo OH–d. 27 Mar 1937 West Jersey Hospital, Camden NJ) At various times he was a proprietor of a taproom and a bartender. Died two days after suffering a cerebral hemorrhage. Buried St Paul's Catholic Cemetery, Norwalk OH.

Lou Nordyke—1 Year Infielder (b. 7 Aug 1876 Brighton IA–d. 27 Sep 1945 Methodist Hospital, Los Angeles CA) He was a security guard at a bank. Died from a heart attack. Cremated.

Bill Norman—2 Years Outfielder 2 Years Manager (b. 16 Jul 1910 St Louis MO–d. 21 Apr 1962 St Luke's Hospital, Milwaukee WI) He worked in baseball his entire life. Died from a heart attack while in Milwaukee, scouting the Milwaukee Braves for the White Sox. Buried Calvary Cemetery, St Louis MO.

Leo Norris—2 Years Infielder (b. 17 May 1908 Bay Saint Louis MS–d. 13 Feb 1987 Zachary LA).

Lou North—7 Years Pitcher (b. 15 Jun 1889 Elgin IL–d. 15 May 1974 Long Hill Convalescent Home in Shelton CT) Served in the U.S. Army during World War I. He was a machinist at United Shoe Machine in Shelton. Buried Pine Grove Cemetery, Ansonia CT.

Hub Northen—3 Years Outfielder (b. 16 Aug 1885 Atlanta TX–d. 1 Oct 1947 Tri-State Sanitarium, Shreveport LA) He managed in the minor leagues and scouted up until his death. He was also in the automobile business at Atlanta TX during the offseason. Died from a nervous condition. Buried Pine Crest Cemetery, Atlanta TX.

Ron Northey—12 Years Outfielder (b. 26 Apr 1920 Frackville PA–d. 16 Apr 1971 Passavant Hospital, Pittsburgh PA) Served in the U.S. Medical Corps during World War II. He worked in the promotional department of the Pittsburgh Brewing Company. Collapsed and died suddenly from a heart attack. Buried Fairfield Memorial Park, Stamford CT.

Jake Northrop—2 Years Pitcher (b. 5 Mar 1888 Monroeton PA–d. 16 Nov 1945 at his home in Monroeton PA) He taught school and worked at the Ingersoll-Rand plant at Athens PA. Died suddenly from a heart attack. Buried Monroeton Cemetery, Monroeton PA.

Elisha Norton—2 Years Pitcher (b. 17 Aug 1873 Conneaut OH–d. 5 Mar 1950 at his home in Aspinwall PA) Buried Conneaut OH.

Chet Nourse—1 Year Pitcher (b. 7 Aug 1887 Ipswich MA–d. 20 Apr 1958 at his son's home in Clearwater FL) A retired industrial engineer, he was on the executive board of H P Hood Company from 1924 to 1948. He spent his last eight winters at Clearwater. Buried Oak Hill Cemetery, Newburyport MA.

Lou Novikoff—5 Years Outfielder (b. 12 Oct 1915 Glendale AZ–d. 30 Sep 1970 St Francis Hospital, Lynwood CA) He was a longshoreman for the Pacific Maritime Association for 15 years. Died from a heart attack. Buried New Russian Cemetery.

Rube Novotney—1 Year Catcher (b. 5 Aug 1924 Streator IL–d. 16 Jul 1987 South Bay Hospital, Redondo Beach CA) Served in World War II. For 30 years he was an assistant superintendent for the Los Angeles Times. Died from lung disease. Buried Holy Cross Cemetery, Culver City CA.

Win Noyes—3 Years Pitcher (b. 16 Jun 1889 Pleasanton NE–d. 8 Apr 1969 Cashmere Nursing Home, Cashmere WA) Served in Europe for the U.S. Army during World War I. He operated a pharmacy at Sumas WA for 14 years before moving to Cashmere where he operated the Rexall Drug store seven years before retiring in 1949. Died following a lingering illness. Buried Cashmere Cemetery, Cashmere WA.

Les Nunamaker—12 Years Catcher (b. 25 Aug 1889 Aurora NE–d. 14 Nov 1938 Mary Lanning Memorial Hospital, Hastings NE) A player/manager in the minor leagues for several years, he worked the last six years with his brother in a market at Hastings. Died from thyroid cancer. Buried Aurora Cemetery, Aurora NE.

Emory Nusz—1 Year Outfielder (b. 2 Apr 1866 Frederick MD–d. 3 Aug 1893 Point of Rocks MD) He had recently taken a job as a traveling salesman for a York PA company when he was crushed by an oncoming train as he disembarked from a train moving in the other direction. Buried Mount Olivet Cemetery, Frederick MD.

Dizzy Nutter—1 Year Outfielder (b. 27 Aug 1893 Roseville OH–d. 25 Jul 1958 Battle Creek MI) He was a cab driver in Battle Creek. He was dead-on-arrival at a Battle Creek hospital after being in ill health for two years. Buried Rose Hill Cemetery, Roseville OH.

Charlie Nyce—1 Year Infielder (b. 1 Jul 1870 Philadelphia PA–d. 9 May 1908 Philadelphia PA) Buried Westminster Cemetery, Bala Cynwyd PA.

O

Billy O'Brien—5 Years Infielder (b. 16 Apr 1860 Albany NY–d. 26 May 1911 at his home in Kansas City MO) He was a fireman in Kansas City before working as a policeman for 18 years. Died from heart disease. Buried Mount St Mary's Cemetery, Kansas City MO.

Buck O'Brien—3 Years Pitcher (b. 9 May 1882 Brockton MA–d. 25 Jul 1959 at Lawley's Shipyard in Boston MA) He worked for the Boston Park's Department until World War II when he became a guard. Later he was a custodian at the Charlestown Boy's Club, retiring in 1955. Buried New Calvary Cemetery, Mattapan MA.

Darby O'Brien—6 Years Outfielder (b. 1 Sep 1863 Peoria IL–d. 15 Jun 1893 at his home in Peoria IL) Died from consumption.

Darby O'Brien—4 Years Pitcher (b. 15 Apr 1867 Troy NY–d. 11 Mar 1892 at his home in Troy NY) Died at the height of his career from pneumonia. Buried St Patrick's Cemetery, Watervliet NY.

George O'Brien—1 Year Catcher (b. 4 Nov 1889 Cleveland OH–d. 24 Mar 1966 Lutheran Senior City, Columbus OH) He was athletic director at Mount Union College before becoming associated with the Ohio Chamber of Commerce. Buried Calvary Cemetery, West Conshohocken PA.

Jack O'Brien—8 Years Catcher (b. 12 Jun 1860 Philadelphia PA–d. 2 Nov 1910 Philadelphia PA).

Jack O'Brien—3 Years Outfielder (b. 5 Feb 1873 Watervliet NY–d. 10 Jun 1933 Watervliet NY) He was a policeman for the Watervliet Police Department, serving at one time as its chief. Died from kidney disease. Buried St Agnes Cemetery, Menands NY.

Jerry O'Brien—1 Year Infielder (b. 2 Feb 1864 NY–d. 4 Jul 1911 Binghamton NY) Died from drowning.

John O'Brien—6 Years Infielder (b. 14 Jul 1870 St John, New Brunswick, Canada–d. 13 May 1913 at a hospital in Lewiston ME) After retiring from baseball he umpired local baseball games and refereed boxing and wrestling matches. Died from kidney trouble after an illness of about a month. Buried Mount Hope Cemetery, Lewiston ME.

John O'Brien—1 Year Outfielder (b. 22 Oct 1851 Columbus OH–d. 31 Dec 1914 at his sister-in-law's house, Fall River MA) He worked 41 years for the Fall River Fire Department, rising to the rank of captain. Died after being ill several weeks. Buried St Patrick's Cemetery, Fall River MA.

Mickey O'Brien—1 Year Catcher (b. 13 Sep 1894 San Francisco CA–d. 4 Nov 1971 Garfield Hospital, Monterey Park CA) He was head cashier at Santa Anita Turf Club for 47 years. Died from a heart attack. Buried Willamette National Cemetery, Portland OR.

Pete O'Brien—3 Years Infielder (b. 16 Jun 1867 Chicago IL–d. 30 Jun 1937 near Donners Grove IL) He was the founder and owner of O'Brien Paving Company in Chicago. Died from a heart attack while golfing at the Butterfield Country Club. Buried All Saints Cemetery, Des Plaines IL.

Pete O'Brien—3 Years Infielder (b. 17 Jun 1877 Binghamton NY–d. 31 Jan 1917 St Francis Hospital, Jersey City NJ) Died from lobar pneumonia. Buried St Mary's Cemetery, Portland NY.

Ray O'Brien—1 Year Outfielder (b. 31 Oct 1892 St Louis MO–d. 31 Mar 1942 St Louis MO) Buried Calvary Cemetery, St Louis MO.

Tom O'Brien—4 Years Outfielder (b. 20 Feb 1873 Verona PA–d. 4 Feb 1901 at the Hardwick Hotel in Phoenix AZ) Died at the height of his career from pneumonia. Buried St Mary's Cemetery, Pittsburgh PA.

Tom O'Brien—6 Years Infielder (b. abt 1863 Worcester MA–d. 21 Apr 1921 City Hospital, Worcester MA) He managed minor league baseball and scouted for the Indians and Athletics. Died from acute appendicitis and generalized peritonitis. Buried St John's Cemetery, Worcester MA.

Tommy O'Brien—5 Years Outfielder (b. 19 Dec 1918 Anniston AL–d. 5 Nov 1978 Stringfellow Hospital, Anniston AL) Buried Edgemont Cemetery, Anniston AL.

Danny O'Connell—10 Years Infielder (b. 21 Jan 1927 Paterson NJ–d. 2 Oct 1969 Clifton NJ) Served in the U.S. Army during the Korean War. He was a representative of the Whippany Paper Works. Killed when his car left the road and hit a utility pole after he had suffered a heart attack. Buried Immaculate Conception Cemetery, Montclair NJ.

Jimmy O'Connell—2 Years Outfielder (b. 11 Feb 1901 Sacramento CA–d. 11 Nov 1976 Mercy Hospital, Bakersfield CA) He was banned from baseball for "slacking off" during the 1924 season. He worked 34 years for Atlantic Richfield in Bakersfield, last serving as a general storekeeper. Died from a heart attack. Buried Greenlawn Memorial Park, Bakersfield CA.

John O'Connell—2 Years Infielder (b. 16 May 1872 Lawrence MA–d. 14 May 1908 at his sister's home in Derry NH) He was a successful dentist at Danville IL. Died from cirrhosis of the liver. Buried Immaculate Conception Cemetery, Lawrence MA.

John O'Connell—2 Years Catcher (b. 13 Jun 1904 Verona PA–d. 17 Oct 1992 Canton OH).

Pat O'Connell—2 Years Outfielder (b. 10 Jun 1861 Lewiston ME–d. 24 Jan 1943 at his home in Lewiston ME) He worked for the Lewiston police force for several years before working for the Lewiston Bleachery. He had been in poor health for a long time. Buried Mount Hope Cemetery, Lewiston ME.

Andy O'Connor—1 Year Pitcher (b. 14 Sep 1884 Roxbury MA–d. 26 Sep 1980 Norwood MA) Buried St Joseph's Cemetery, West Roxbury MA.

Dan O'Connor—1 Year Infielder (b. Aug 1868 Guelph, Ontario, Canada–d. 3 Mar 1942 Guelph, Ontario, Canada).

Frank O'Connor—1 Year Pitcher (b. 15 Sep 1869 Keeseville NY–d. 26 Dec 1913 at his office in Brattleboro VT) He was a prominent physician and surgeon at Brattleboro. Died from a heart attack. Buried Catholic Cemetery, Brattleboro VT.

Jack O'Connor—21 Years Catcher 1 Year Manager (b. 3 Mar 1867 St Louis MO–d. 14 Nov 1937 at his home in St Louis MO) He promoted boxing matches in the St Louis area. Died following a brief illness. Buried Calvary Cemetery, St Louis MO.

Johnny O'Connor —1 Year Catcher (b. 1 Dec 1891 Cahirciveen, Ireland–d. 30 May 1982 Bonner Springs KS).

Paddy O'Connor —6 Years Catcher (b. 4 Aug 1879 Windsor Locks CT–d. 17 Aug 1950 Mercy Hospital, Springfield MA) He managed minor league baseball and coached a short while for the Yankees. Later he was in business at Springfield. Buried St Michael's Cemetery, Springfield MA.

Hank O'Day —7 Years Pitcher 2 Years Manager (b. 8 Jul 1863 Chicago IL–d. 2 Jul 1935 Chicago IL) He was a National League umpire 1888 to 1889, 1893, 1895 to 1911, 1913 and 1915 to 1926. Buried Calvary Cemetery, Evanston IL.

Ken O'Dea —12 Years Catcher (b. 16 Mar 1913 Lima NY–d. 17 Dec 1985 Lima NY) Buried St Agnes Cemetery, Avon NY.

Paul O'Dea —2 Years Outfielder (b. 3 Jul 1920 Cleveland OH–d. 11 Dec 1978 Cleveland OH) He worked 40 years for the Indians as a player, scout and director of minor league operations. Died from a heart attack. Buried Myrtle Hill Cemetery, Valley City OH.

Harry O'Donnell —1 Year Catcher (b. 2 Apr 1894 Philadelphia PA–d. 31 Jan 1958 Philadelphia PA) Buried St Dominic Cemetery, Philadelphia PA.

Lefty O'Doul —11 Years Outfielder (b. 4 Mar 1897 San Francisco CA–d. 7 Dec 1969 French Hospital, San Francisco CA) Served in the U.S. Navy during World War I. He spent over 20 years as a manager in the Pacific Coast League. Died from a heart attack after suffering a stroke a month earlier. Buried Cypress Lawn Memorial Park, Colma CA.

John O'Dowd —1 Year Infielder (b. 3 Jan 1891 South Waymouth MA–d. 31 Jan 1981 Fort Lauderdale FL).

Bob O'Farrell —21 Years Catcher 2 Years Manager (b. 19 Oct 1896 Waukegan IL–d. 20 Feb 1988 St Theresa Medical Center, Waukegan IL) He owned and operated O'Farrell's Recreation in Waukegan from 1927 to 1961. Buried Northshore Garden of Memories, North Chicago IL.

Hal O'Hagan —2 Years Infielder (b. 30 Sep 1873 Washington DC–d. 14 Jan 1913 Newark NJ) He was an electrician. Died from acute gastritis. Buried Holy Sepulchre Cemetery, East Orange NJ.

Bill O'Hara —2 Years Outfielder (b. 14 Aug 1883 Toronto, Ontario, Canada–d. 15 Jun 1931 Plaza Hotel, Jersey City NJ) Died from heart disease. Buried Toronto, Canada.

Kid O'Hara —1 Year Outfielder (b. 19 Dec 1875 Wilkes-Barre PA–d. 1 Dec 1954 Canton OH) He worked his way through medical school while playing baseball, and practiced medicine in Canton 44 years. Died from the effects of a heart attack. Buried Calvary Catholic Cemetery, Canton OH.

Tom O'Hara —2 Years Outfielder (b. 13 Jul 1885 Waverly NY–d. 8 Jun 1954 St Anthony Hospital, Denver CO) He was a scout for several major league teams and represented Pierce Arrow in Kansas City MO before moving to Denver about 1942. Buried Mount Olivet Cemetery, Wheat Ridge CO.

Charley O'Leary —11 Years Infielder (b. 15 Oct 1882 Chicago IL–d. 6 Jan 1941 Woodlawn Hospital, Chicago IL) He was a coach for the Yankees until 1930. After that he worked for the Chicago Sanitary District. Died from peritonitis. Buried Mount Olivet Cemetery, Chicago IL.

Dan O'Leary —5 Years Outfielder 1 Year Manager (b. 22 Oct 1856 Detroit MI–d. 24 Jun 1922 St Joseph's Hospital, Chicago IL) For 35 years he was a free lance police reporter. Buried Mount Carmel Cemetery, Hillside IL.

Walter O'Malley —(b. 9 Oct 1903 New York City NY–d. 9 Aug 1979 Methodist Hospital, Rochester MN) An attorney, he began as legal counsel for the Dodgers in 1943 and by 1950 had become their majority owner. He started baseball's expansion to the west by moving the team to Los Angeles in 1958. Died from heart failure while being treated for cancer. Cremated. Buried Holy Cross Cemetery, Culver City CA.

Ollie O'Mara —6 Years Infielder (b. 8 Mar 1891 St Louis MO–d. 24 Oct 1989 at his home in Reno NV) He moved from Las Vegas NV to Reno in 1968. Buried All Saints Cemetery, Kenosha WI.

Tom O'Meara—2 Years Catcher (b. 12 Dec 1872 Chicago IL–d. 16 Feb 1902 at his home in Fort Wayne IN) He ran a saloon in Fort Wayne. Died from rheumatism and water on the brain. Buried Catholic Cemetery, Fort Wayne IN.

Skinny O'Neal—2 Years Pitcher (b. 2 May 1899 Gatewood MO–d. 2 Jun 1981 St John's Medical Center, Springfield MO) He was a retired salesman. Died following a long illness. Buried Evergreen Cemetery, Republic MO.

Dennie O'Neil—1 Year Infielder (b. 10 Apr 1860 Tralee, Ireland–d. 18 May 1926 at his home in Holyoke MA) A diverse businessman, he owned minor league baseball teams, engaged in the paper business, built a cigar-making firm and was in the hotel business. He was also president of the Eastern League at its creation and was active in county and city politics. Died from pneumonia, brought on by a long bout with diabetes. Buried St Jerome Cemetery, Holyoke MA.

Ed O'Neil—1 Year Pitcher (b. 11 Mar 1859 Fall River MA–d. 30 Sep 1892 Fall River MA).

Mickey O'Neil—9 Years Catcher (b. 12 Apr 1900 St Louis MO–d. 8 Apr 1964 at his home in St Louis MO) He managed minor league baseball. Buried Calvary Cemetery, St Louis MO.

Bill O'Neill—2 Years Outfielder (b. 22 Jan 1880 St John, New Brunswick, Canada–d. 27 Jul 1920 St John, New Brunswick, Canada).

Emmett O'Neill—4 Years Pitcher (b. 13 Jan 1918 San Mateo CA–d. 11 Oct 1993 Sparks Family Hospital, Sparks NV) He worked in the Nevada gaming industry from 1955 until retiring in 1992. He managed Stateline Country in Lake Tahoe, worked 12 years for the Regency Casino in Laughlin and was a co-owner of the Silver Club in Sparks and the River Inn at Reno. Cremated.

Fred O'Neill—1 Year Outfielder (b. 1865 London, Ontario, Canada–d. 7 Mar 1892 London, Ontario, Canada).

Harry O'Neill—1 Year Catcher (b. 8 May 1917 Philadelphia PA–d. 6 Mar 1945 Iwo Jima, Volcano Islands) Killed in the battle for Iwo Jima during World War II.

Harry O'Neill—2 Years Pitcher (b. 19 Feb 1897 Ridgetown, Ontario, Canada–d. 5 Sep 1969 Ridgetown, Ontario, Canada).

Jack O'Neill—5 Years Catcher (b. 10 Jan 1873 Maam, Ireland–d. 29 Jun 1935 Moses Taylor Hospital, Scranton PA) He worked in the Keyser Valley shops of the Lackawanna Railroad for a number of years. Active in civic affairs, he was one of the founders of the Minooka Volunteer Fire Department. Died from pneumonia after being ill two weeks. Buried St Joseph's Cemetery, Minooka PA.

Jim O'Neill—2 Years Infielder (b. 23 Feb 1893 Minooka PA–d. 5 Sep 1976 at a hospital in Chambersburg PA) He was personnel manager for Anaconda Wire and Cable Company at Hastings-on-the-Hudson NY. Buried St Joseph's Church Cemetery, Minooka PA.

Mike O'Neill—5 Years Pitcher (b. 7 Sep 1877 Galway, Ireland–d. 12 Aug 1959 at his home in Dunmore PA) He coached baseball at Scranton University and was a scout for the Phillies. Died after a brief illness. Buried St Joseph's Cemetery, Minooka PA.

Peaches O'Neill—1 Year Catcher (b. 30 Aug 1879 Anderson IN–d. 2 Aug 1955 St John's Hospital, Anderson IN) He was baseball coach at Indiana University for one year before beginning a law practice in Anderson that lasted more than 40 years. An active Democrat, he served two terms as city attorney. Died following an illness of several weeks. Buried East Maplewood Cemetery, Anderson IN.

Steve O'Neill—17 Years Catcher 14 Years Manager (b. 6 Jul 1891 Minooka PA–d. 26 Jan 1962 Huron Road Hospital, Cleveland OH) He retired from baseball in 1954 and worked the last few years of his life for the Cleveland City Recreation Department. Died from a heart attack suffered five days earlier. Buried St Joseph's Cemetery, Scranton PA.

Steve O'Neill—(b. abt 1900–d. 29 Aug 1983 Cleveland OH) He owned interests in the trucking and transportation business, and bought an interest in the Indians in 1961, selling it in 1973 to buy an interest in the Yankees. Later he was the majority owner of the Indians from 1978 until his death. Died from a heart attack. Buried Calvary Cemetery, Cleveland OH.

Tip O'Neill —10 Years Outfielder (b. 25 May 1858 Woodstock, Ontario, Canada–d. 31 Dec 1915 Montreal, Ontario, Canada).

Don O'Riley —2 Years Pitcher (b. 12 Mar 1945 Topeka KS–d. 2 May 1997 Kansas City MO) He was an avid golfer. Died after being shot during a holdup. Buried Floral Hills Memorial Gardens, Kansas City MO.

Frank O'Rourke —14 Years Infielder (b. 28 Nov 1891 Hamilton, Ontario, Canada–d. 14 May 1986 King James Nursing Home, Chatham NJ) He managed some minor league baseball before scouting 40 years for the Yankees. He was the oldest active scout in the major leagues when he died. Buried Graceland Memorial Park, Kenilworth NJ.

Jim O'Rourke —19 Years Outfielder 5 Years Manager Hall of Fame (b. 24 Aug 1852 Bridgeport CT–d. 8 Jan 1919 at his home in Bridgeport CT) He owned and managed minor league teams and was president of two minor leagues in the Northeast. Died from pneumonia. Buried St Michael's Cemetery, Bridgeport CT.

Joe O'Rourke —3 Games Pinch Hitter (b. 28 Oct 1904 Philadelphia PA–d. 27 Jun 1990 at his home in Philadelphia PA) He spent 44 years in organized baseball as a player, minor league manager and scout before opening O'Rourke's Shortstop Cafe in Port Richmond in 1982. Buried Holy Sepulchre Cemetery, Philadelphia PA.

John O'Rourke —3 Years Outfielder (b. 1853 Bridgeport CT–d. 23 Jun 1911 Boston MA).

Patsy O'Rourke —1 Year Infielder (b. 13 Apr 1881 Philadelphia PA–d. 18 Apr 1956 at his home in Philadelphia PA) He spent 50 years in baseball as a player, minor league manager, coach and scout. He was the chief scout 13 years for the Phillies, resigning in 1939. He then was a scout for several other teams before retiring. Died after being ill three months. Buried Holy Sepulchre Cemetery, Philadelphia PA.

Queenie O'Rourke —1 Year Outfielder (b. 26 Dec 1889 Bridgeport CT–d. 22 Dec 1955 Sparrows Point MD) Buried Oak Lawn Cemetery, Baltimore MD.

Tim O'Rourke —5 Years Infielder (b. 18 May 1864 Chicago IL–d. 20 Apr 1938 Seattle WA) Buried Calvary Cemetery, Seattle WA.

Tom O'Rourke —3 Years Catcher (b. 1862 New York City NY–d. 19 Jul 1929 New York City NY) He was secretary for the Board of Water Supply in New York City. Died from heart trouble. Buried Calvary Cemetery, Woodside NY.

Marty O'Toole —5 Years Pitcher (b. 27 Nov 1888 Lost Creek PA–d. 18 Feb 1949 Aberdeen WA) He umpired minor league baseball for a while before moving to Washington where he sold books, clerked in a cigar store and worked for Harbor Plywood Company for a time. During the war he worked for Boeing Aircraft Company in Seattle, and was a dispatcher for a cab company when he died. Killed in a fall down some stairs, his body wedged between two buildings. Buried Fern Hill Cemetery, Aberdeen WA.

Rebel Oakes —7 Years Outfielder 2 Years Manager (b. 17 Dec 1886 Homer LA–d. 29 Feb 1948 at a sanitarium in Shreveport LA) He was an independent oil operator in Shreveport. Died from pneumonia following a week's illness. Buried Rocky Springs Cemetery, Lisbon LA.

Prince Oana —3 Years Pitcher (b. 22 Jan 1908 Waipahu HI–d. 19 Jun 1976 at his home in Austin TX) He managed minor league baseball and was a captain at the Correctional Division of the Travis County, TX, sheriff's department. Blind at one time, he had his sight restored by a number of surgeries, and was a supervisor for the Travis Association for the Blind. Died from a heart attack. Buried Oakwood Cemetery, Austin TX.

Henry Oberbeck —2 Years Outfielder (b. 17 May 1858 MO–d. 26 Aug 1921 St Louis MO) Buried Bellefontaine Cemetery, St Louis MO.

Doc Oberlander —1 Year Pitcher (b. 12 May 1864 Waukegan IL–d. 14 Nov 1922 Pryor MT).

Frank Oberlin —4 Years Pitcher (b. 29 Mar 1876 Elsie MI–d. 5 Jan 1952 at his home in Ashley IN) Died from a heart condition. Buried Hamilton Cemetery, Hamilton IN.

Whitey Ock—1 Year Catcher (b. 17 Mar 1912 Brooklyn NY–d. 18 Mar 1975 Mount Kisco NY).

Walter Ockey—1 Year Pitcher (b. 4 Jul 1920 New York City NY–d. 4 Dec 1971 Staten Island NY).

Ted Odenwald—2 Years Pitcher (b. 4 Jan 1902 Hudson WI–d. 23 Oct 1965 St Francis Hospital, Shakopee MN) He was a shipping clerk for Reis Bottling Company and was active in civic affairs at Shakopee. Died following a stroke. Buried St Mary's Cemetery, Minneapolis MN.

Dave Odom—1 Year Pitcher (b. 5 Jun 1918 Dunuba CA–d. 19 Nov 1987 at his home in Myrtle Beach SC) Served in the U.S. Army Corps of Engineers during World War II. He played both professional football and baseball. He worked 30 years for A T & T in Greensboro NC, 25 years as plant manager. He retired to Myrtle Beach where he was active in real estate. Died from a heart attack.

Heinie Odom—1 Year Infielder (b. 13 Oct 1900 Rusk TX–d. 31 Aug 1970 Rusk TX) He was a bookkeeper. Died suddenly. Buried Cedar Hill Cemetery, Rusk TX.

Fred Odwell—4 Years Outfielder (b. 25 Sep 1872 Downsville NY–d. 19 Aug 1948 Stevens Hospital, Downsville NY) He was the postmaster at Downsville for 14 years. Died after an illness of two months. Buried Paige Cemetery, Downsville NY.

Joe Oeschger—12 Years Pitcher (b. 24 May 1892 Chicago IL–d. 29 Jul 1986 Petaluma CA) He is best known for pitching the longest game in major league history—a 1 to 1 tie after 26 innings in 1920. He was a teacher at Portola Junior High School in San Francisco CA for 27 years. Died from a heart attack. Cremated. Buried Holy Cross Catholic Cemetery, Colma CA.

Curly Ogden—5 Years Pitcher (b. 24 Jan 1901 Ogden PA–d. 6 Aug 1964 Chester Hospital, Chester PA) He taught and coached 18 years at Penns Grove (NJ) High School. Died following a heart attack. Buried Lawn Croft Cemetery, Linwood PA.

Jack Ogden—5 Years Pitcher (b. 5 Nov 1897 Ogden PA–d. 9 Nov 1977 Lankenau Hospital, Philadelphia PA) He spent his entire life in baseball as a player, minor league manager, general manager, minor league team owner and scout, retiring in 1970. Buried Oxford Cemetery, Oxford PA.

Jim Oglesby—1 Year Infielder (b. 10 Aug 1905 Schofield MO–d. 1 Sep 1955 at his apartment in Tulsa OK) He managed minor league baseball for a short while and was a security guard at the Douglas Aircraft Company when he shot himself in the head with a shotgun. He had been in ill health for five years. Buried Memorial Park, Tulsa OK.

Brusie Ogrodowski—2 Years Catcher (b. 17 Feb 1912 Hoytville PA–d. 5 Mar 1956 at his home in San Francisco CA) Disabled his last few years, he died from pulmonary tuberculosis. Buried Cypress Lawn Memorial Park, Colma CA.

Joe Ogrodowski—1 Year Pitcher (b. 20 Nov 1906 Hoytville PA–d. 24 Jun 1959 Elmira NY).

Joe Ohl—1 Year Pitcher (b. 10 Jan 1888 Jobstown NJ–d. 18 Dec 1951 Cooper Hospital, Camden NJ) He was active in hunting and fishing clubs. Died after a brief illness. Buried Springfield Cemetery, Jobstown NJ.

Frank Okrie—1 Year Pitcher (b. 28 Oct 1896 Detroit MI–d. 16 Oct 1959 Detroit MI) Died after a lingering illness. Buried Mount Olivet Cemetery, Detroit MI.

David Oldfield—3 Years Catcher (b. 18 Nov 1864 Kensington PA–d. 28 Aug 1939 Philadelphia PA) Buried Oakland Cemetery, Philadelphia PA.

Red Oldham—7 Years Pitcher (b. 15 Jul 1893 Zion MD–d. 28 Jan 1961 Hoag Memorial Hospital, Newport Beach CA) World War I veteran. For 20 years he was a security officer. Died from cancer of the larynx. Cremated.

Rube Oldring—13 Years Outfielder (b. 30 May 1884 New York City NY–d. 9 Sep 1961 at his home near Roadstown NJ) He farmed in Cumberland County, NJ, and ran for county sheriff in 1948. Died suddenly from heart disease. Buried Cohansey Baptist Cemetery, Roadstown NJ.

Frank Olin —2 Years Outfielder (b. 9 Jan 1860 Woodford VT–d. 21 May 1951 Barnes Hospital, St Louis MO) Earning a fortune in explosives, he founded Olin Industries, and was reputed to be one of the wealthiest men in the Mississippi Valley. Died from heart disease. Buried Oak Grove Cemetery, St Louis MO.

Steve Olin —4 Years Pitcher (b. 4 Oct 1965 Portland OR–d. 22 Mar 1993 Little Lake Nellie FL) He was killed instantly when a speedboat he was riding in smashed into a dock at a high rate of speed. Cremated. Buried Skyline Memorial Gardens, Portland OR.

Jose Oliva —2 Years Infielder (b. 3 Mar 1971 San Pedro de Macoris, Dominican Republic–d. 22 Dec 1997 San Cristobal, Dominican Republic).

Tom Oliver —4 Years Outfielder (b. 15 Jan 1903 Montgomery AL–d. 26 Feb 1988 at his home in Montgomery AL) Served in the U.S. Navy during World War II. He managed minor league baseball six years for the Athletics, coached six years for the Athletics and Orioles and was a scout 17 years for the Twins and Phillies. Buried Greenwood Cemetery, Montgomery AL.

Chi Chi Olivo —4 Years Pitcher (b. 18 May 1926 Guayubin, Dominican Republic–d. 3 Feb 1977 Guayubin, Dominican Republic).

Diomedes Olivo —3 Years Pitcher (b. 22 Jan 1919 Guayubin, Dominican Republic–d. 15 Feb 1977 Santo Domingo, Dominican Republic).

Fred Olmstead —4 Years Pitcher (b. 3 Jul 1883 Grand Rapids MI–d. 22 Oct 1936 at a hospital in Muskogee OK) He operated the Majestic Hotel in Wagoner OK. Died from pneumonia and injuries suffered in an automobile accident ten months earlier. Buried Elmwood Cemetery, Wagoner OK.

Hank Olmsted —1 Year Pitcher (b. 12 Jan 1879 Sak Bay MI–d. 6 Jan 1969 Manatee Memorial Hospital, Bradenton FL) A chiropractor in Jackson MI for 32 years, he also was a scout for the Tigers and Indians. Buried Manasota Memorial Park, Bradenton FL.

Barney Olsen —1 Year Outfielder (b. 11 Sep 1919 Everett MA–d. 30 Mar 1977 Whidden Memorial Hospital, Everett MA) Served in the U.S. Navy during World War II. He was a truck driver for Standard Electric Supply Company. Buried Holy Cross Cemetery, Malden MA.

Ole Olsen —2 Years Pitcher (b. 12 Sep 1894 South Norwalk CT–d. 12 Sep 1980 Norwalk Hospital, Norwalk CT) Served in the U.S. Navy during World War I. Active politically, he was chairman of the Republican Town Committee in Norwalk and was liquor inspector for Fairfield County, CT. Buried Rowayton Union Cemetery, Norwalk CT.

Vern Olsen —5 Years Pitcher (b. 16 Mar 1918 Hillsboro OR–d. 13 Jul 1989 Loyola University Medical Ctr, Maywood IL) Served in the U.S. Navy during World War II. He sold cars for a number of west suburban Chicago IL automobile dealers, retiring in 1979. Buried Arlington Cemetery, Elmhurst IL.

Ivy Olson —14 Years Infielder (b. 14 Oct 1885 Kansas City MO–d. 1 Sep 1965 Park View Hospital, Los Angeles CA) For 20 years he was a customer service representative at an automobile dealership. Died from complications of diabetes. Cremated.

Marv Olson —3 Years Infielder (b. 28 May 1907 Gayville SD–d. 5 Feb 1998 St Michael's Hospital, Tyndall SD) He managed minor league baseball and scouted for the Athletics and Twins, retiring in 1986. Buried Gayville Cemetery, Gayville SD.

Ted Olson —3 Years Pitcher (b. 27 Aug 1912 Quincy MA–d. 9 Dec 1980 South Shore Hospital, Weymouth MA) He was an independent insurance broker. Died following a heart attack. Buried Church of St John the Evangelist, Hingham MA.

Ralph Onis —1 Year Catcher (b. 24 Oct 1908 Tampa FL–d. 4 Jan 1995 Tampa FL) Served in the U.S. Coast Guard during World War II. He retired from the City of Tampa Fire Department. Buried Centro Asturiano Cemetery, Tampa FL.

Eddie Onslow —4 Years Infielder (b. 17 Feb 1893 Meadville PA–d. 8 May 1981 Twin City Hospital, Dennison OH) He played in the International League for years and managed some minor league baseball before working for Scio Pottery in Scio OH. Died from a hemorrhage. Buried Grandview Cemetery, Scio OH.

Jack Onslow—2 Years Catcher 2 Years Manager (b. 13 Oct 1888 Scottdale PA–d. 22 Dec 1960 Concord MA) He spent his entire life in baseball as a player, manager, coach and scout. He was a scout for the Red Sox when he died from a heart attack. Buried Grandview Cemetery, Scio OH.

Tony Ordenana—1 Year Infielder (b. 30 Oct 1918 Guanabacoa, Havana, Cuba–d. 29 Sep 1988 Miami FL) He played both baseball and basketball in Cuba where he was known as "Mosquito" because of his quickness. Considered as one of Cuba's greatest atheletes, he lived in New York until 1959 when he returned to Cuba to work as a public works inspector. Going back to New York in 1971, he worked as a busboy and maintenance man, retiring to Miami in the late 1970s. Died from a heart attack. Buried Dade Memorial Park-South, Miami FL.

Joe Orengo—6 Years Infielder (b. 29 Nov 1914 San Francisco CA–d. 24 Jul 1988 at his home in San Francisco CA) He was director of the Speaker's Bureau for the Giants for 30 years. Died from a heart attack. Buried Italian Cemetery, Daly City CA.

George Orme—1 Year Outfielder (b. 16 Sep 1891 Lebanon IN–d. 16 Mar 1962 Indianapolis IN) He was a structural iron worker for 40 years, retiring in 1957. Died from a heart attack suffered at his union hall. Buried Floral Park Cemetery, Indianapolis IN.

Jess Orndorff—1 Year Catcher (b. 15 Jan 1881 Chicago IL–d. 28 Sep 1960 at his home in Cardiff-By-The-Sea CA) He was a self-employed realtor for 45 years. Died from chronic heart and kidney disease. Cremated.

Bill Orr—2 Years Infielder (b. 22 Apr 1891 San Francisco CA–d. 10 Mar 1967 City Hospital, St Helena CA) He was a deputy for the Contra Costa County (CA) Sheriff's Department for five years. Died from a heart attack. Buried Holy Cross Catholic Cemetery, Colma CA.

Dave Orr—8 Years Infielder 1 Year Manager (b. 29 Sep 1859 New York City NY–d. 2 Jun 1915 at the home of a niece in Richmond Hill NY) Died from heart disease. Buried Woodlawn Cemetery, Bronx NY.

Joe Orrell—3 Years Pitcher (b. 6 Oct 1917 National City CA–d. 12 Jan 1993 Scripps Memorial Hospital, Chula Vista CA) For 20 years he was self-employed in the swimming pool maintenance business. Died from pneumonia but suffered from chronic lymphatic leukemia. Cremated. Buried La Vista Memorial Park, National City CA.

Ernie Orsatti—9 Years Outfielder (b. 8 Sep 1902 Los Angeles CA–d. 4 Sep 1968 at his home in Canoga Park CA) He operated a bail bond business in Van Nuys CA. Died from a heart attack. Buried San Fernando Mission Cemetery, Mission Hills CA.

Al Orth—15 Years Pitcher (b. 5 Sep 1872 Sedalia MO–d. 8 Oct 1948 at his home in Lynchburg VA) He was a National League umpire in 1901 and from 1912 to 1917. During World War I he went overseas with the YMCA. Later he coached baseball at Washington and Lee University and at Virginia Military Institute. Died after an illness of eight weeks. Buried Spring Hill Cemetery, Lynchburg VA.

Baby Ortiz—1 Year Pitcher (b. 5 Dec 1919 Camaguey, Cuba–d. 27 Mar 1984 Central Senado, Camaguey, Cuba).

Roberto Ortiz—6 Years Outfielder (b. 30 Jun 1915 Camaguey, Cuba–d. 15 Sep 1971 Cedars of Lebanon Hospital, Miami FL) He was a milk salesman for Borden Dairy in Miami. Died from cancer. Buried Flagler Memorial Park, Miami FL.

Ossie Orwoll—2 Years Pitcher (b. 17 Nov 1900 Portland OR–d. 8 May 1967 Smith Memorial Hospital, Decorah IA) World War I veteran. He taught school at Kiester MN during World War II, then worked 18 years for the Rath Packing Company in Waterloo IA. Died from cancer. Buried Lutheran Cemetery, Decorah IA.

Bob Osborn—6 Years Pitcher (b. 17 Apr 1903 San Diego TX–d. 19 Apr 1960 at his home in Paris AR) He played several years in the Texas League and was a street foreman for the City of

Paris for six years. Died from a heart attack. Buried Oakwood Cemetery, Paris AR.

Fred Osborn—3 Years Outfielder (b. 28 Nov 1883 Sycamore OH–d. 2 Sep 1954 Wyandot Memorial Hosp, Upper Sandusky OH) He operated the Bon Ton Restaurant in Upper Sandusky for 34 years, retiring in 1949 when heart trouble forced him to quit. Died from a heart attack. Buried Oak Hill Cemetery, Upper Sandusky OH.

Tiny Osborne—4 Years Pitcher (b. 9 Apr 1893 Porterdale GA–d. 5 Jan 1969 at a hospital in Atlanta GA) Buried Riverview Memorial Park, Smyrna GA.

Wayne Osborne—2 Years Pitcher (b. 11 Oct 1912 Watsonville CA–d. 13 Mar 1987 Vancouver WA) He was a color announcer for the Cubs in the 1940s, and in public relations for WOPA in Illinois, retiring in 1981. Moving to Vancouver, he would visit nursing homes, playing recorded music of an earlier era for the patients. Cremated.

Harry Ostdiek—2 Years Catcher (b. 12 Apr 1881 Ottumwa IA–d. 6 May 1956 Minneapolis MN) Buried St Mary's Cemetery, Minneapolis MN.

Champ Osteen—4 Years Infielder (b. 24 Feb 1876 Brevard NC–d. 14 Dec 1962 at his son's home in Piedmont SC) He managed minor league baseball for a few years before going to work as a blacksmith and welder for the street department of the City of Greenville SC. He had been ill several years when he died, and partially blind most of that time. Buried Rose Hill Cemetery, Piedmont SC.

Fred Ostendorf—1 Year Pitcher (b. 5 Aug 1890 Baltimore MD–d. 2 Mar 1965 Kecoughtan Hospital, Hampton VA) Buried Woodlawn Cemetery, Baltimore MD.

Red Ostergard—12 Games Pinch Hitter (b. 16 May 1896 Denmark WI–d. 13 Jan 1977 Valley Hospital, Hemet CA) He worked 30 years in the real estate and insurance business before retiring to Hemet in 1963. World War I veteran. Died from a heart attack. Buried San Jacinto Valley Cemetery, San Jacinto CA.

Charlie Osterhout—1 Year Outfielder (b. 1857 Syracuse NY–d. 21 May 1933 Syracuse NY).

Fritz Ostermueller—15 Years Pitcher (b. 15 Sep 1907 Quincy IL–d. 17 Dec 1957 St Mary Hospital, Quincy IL) Served in the U.S. Navy during World War II. He owned and operated the Diamond Motel in Quincy. Died from cancer. Buried Calvary Cemetery, Quincy IL.

Johnny Ostrowski—7 Years Outfielder (b. 17 Oct 1917 Chicago IL–d. 13 Nov 1992 at his home in Chicago IL) He drove a truck for Material Service Corporation before retiring in 1980. Buried Resurrection Cemetery, Justice IL.

Reggie Otero—1 Year Infielder (b. 7 Sep 1915 Havana, Cuba–d. 21 Oct 1988 at his home in Hialeah FL) Considered one of the best first basemen in Cuban baseball history, he was inducted into the Cuban Baseball Hall of Fame. He coached for the Reds and was the Latin American scout for the Dodgers up until his death. Died from heart failure. Buried Vista Memorial Gardens, Hialeah FL.

Bill Otey—3 Years Pitcher (b. 19 Dec 1886 Dayton OH–d. 22 Apr 1931 State Hospital, Dayton OH) He was an automobile mechanic for Penn-Ohio Electric Company in Youngstown OH. Died from generalized paralysis. Buried Brunstetter Cemetery, Austintown OH.

Bill Otis—1 Year Outfielder (b. 24 Dec 1889 Scituate MA–d. 15 Dec 1990 Jensen Nursing Home, Duluth MN) The oldest living former professional baseball player when he died, he worked for a Duluth newspaper before going into the insurance business. In 1958 he started his own insurance agency and retired in 1967. Buried Forest Hill Cemetery, Duluth MN.

Harry Otis—1 Year Pitcher (b. 5 Oct 1886 West New York NJ–d. 29 Jan 1976 Holy Name Hospital, Ridgefield NJ) He was a former West New York police captain and an exempt fireman of the West New York Fire Department. Buried George Washington Memorial Park, Paramus NJ.

Mel Ott—22 Years Outfielder 7 Years Manager Hall of Fame (b. 2 Mar 1909 Gretna LA–d. 21 Nov 1958 Touro Infirmary, New Orleans LA) He worked with the Giants farm system and managed minor league baseball until 1952 when he went into the building construction business, returning to baseball in 1955 as an announcer. Died from injuries suffered in an auto accident a week earlier. Buried Metairie Cemetery, Metairie LA.

Billy Otterson —1 Year Infielder (b. 4 May 1862 Pittsburgh PA–d. 21 Sep 1940 Pittsburgh PA) Buried Union Dale Cemetery, Pittsburgh PA.

Johnny Oulliber —1 Year Outfielder (b. 24 Feb 1911 New Orleans LA–d. 26 Dec 1980 Touro Infirmary, New Orleans LA) An attorney, he worked for the First National Bank of Commerce in New Orleans from 1935 until he retired in 1973, serving as president 1958 to 1969, and chairman of the board from 1969 to 1973. Active in civic affairs, he was elected Chairman of the Board of Trustees of Loyola University Law School in 1975. Buried Metairie Cemetery, Metairie LA.

Chick Outen —1 Year Catcher (b. 17 Jun 1905 Mount Holly NC–d. 11 Sep 1961 V A Hospital, Durham NC) Buried Mount Holly Cemetery, Mount Holly NC.

Orval Overall —7 Years Pitcher (b. 2 Feb 1881 Visalia CA–d. 14 Jul 1947 at a hospital in Fresno CA) He was vice-president and manager of the main Fresno branch of Security-First National Bank of Los Angeles. Died from a heart attack. Cremated.

Stubby Overmire —10 Years Pitcher (b. 16 May 1919 Moline MI–d. 3 Mar 1977 General Hospital, Lakeland FL) He managed minor league baseball and was a scout for the Tigers. Died two months after suffering a heart attack, never regaining consiousness during that time. Cremated. Buried Grand Rapids MI.

Ernie Ovitz —1 Year Pitcher (b. 7 Oct 1885 Mineral Point WI–d. 11 Sep 1980 Bellin Hospital, Green Bay WI) He lived in the Laona WI area for 66 years, and was a pioneer country doctor there for 32 years. Died after a short illness. Buried Laona Cemetery, Laona WI.

Frank Owen —8 Years Pitcher (b. 23 Dec 1879 Ypsilanti MI–d. 24 Nov 1942 Dearborn Hotel, Dearborn MI) Buried Grand Lawn Cemetery, Detroit MI.

Marv Owen —9 Years Infielder (b. 22 Mar 1906 Agnew CA–d. 22 Jun 1991 Mountain View Conv Hosp, Mountain View CA) He managed minor league baseball and scouted for the Tigers until retiring in the mid–1970s. Died from Alzheimer's disease and generalized arteriosclerosis. Buried Santa Clara Mission Cemetery, Santa Clara CA.

Frank Owens —4 Years Catcher (b. 26 Jan 1886 Toronto, Ontario, Canada–d. 2 Jul 1958 at a hospital in Minneapolis MN) Died after suffering a severe hemorrhage the day before. Cremated.

Jack Owens —1 Year Catcher (b. 6 Jun 1910 Converse SC–d. 14 Nov 1958 at a hospital in Greenville SC) World War II veteran. He worked at the Glenwood Mill in Easley SC and served a term on the Easley City Council. Died after an illness of two years. Buried Westview Cemetery, Easley SC.

Red Owens —2 Years Infielder (b. 1 Nov 1874 Pottsville PA–d. 21 Aug 1952 Harrisburg PA) Served in the U.S. Army during the Spanish-American War. He managed minor league baseball. When he died he was a night watchman at the Moose Lodge in Harrisburg. Died after an illness of several months. Buried Prospect Hill Cemetery, Harrisburg PA.

Henry Oxley —1 Year Catcher (b. 4 Jan 1858 Covehead, Prince Edward Island, Canada–d. 12 Oct 1945 Somerville MA).

Andy Oyler —1 Year Infielder (b. 5 May 1880 Newville PA–d. 24 Oct 1970 Holy Spirit Hospital, Cumberland County, PA) A retired civil engineer, he worked for the Pennsylvania State Highway Department and the Pennsylvania Turnpike Commission. Buried Rolling Green Memorial Park, Camp Hill PA.

Ray Oyler —6 Years Infielder (b. 4 Aug 1938 Indianapolis IN–d. 26 Jan 1981 at his home in Redmond WA) Served in the U.S. Marines. He coached for a while, retiring from baseball in 1973. He was working for Boeing Aircraft Company in Seattle when he died. Died from a heart attack. Buried Sunset Hills Memorial Park, Bellevue WA.

Doc Ozmer —1 Year Pitcher (b. 25 May 1901 Atlanta GA–d. 28 Dec 1970 Atlanta GA) Buried Crest Lawn Memorial Park, Atlanta GA.

P

Ed Pabst—1 Year Outfielder (b. 1868 St Louis MO–d. 19 Jun 1940 St Louis MO).

Gene Packard—8 Years Pitcher (b. 13 Jul 1887 Colorado Springs CO–d. 18 May 1959 Community Hospital, Riverside CA) He worked 11 years as a stock clerk in a San Francisco CA men's clothing store before retiring to Riverside. Died from a heart attack. Buried Evergreen Memorial Park, Riverside CA.

Dick Padden—9 Years Infielder (b. 22 Sep 1870 Wheeling WV–d. 31 Oct 1922 at his home in Martins Ferry OH) Died from diabetes mellitus. Buried St Mary's Cemetery, Martins Ferry OH.

Tom Padden—7 Years Catcher (b. 6 Oct 1908 Manchester NH–d. 11 Jun 1973 Manchester NH) He was a coach before serving as a steward at the Daniel F O'Connell Club in Manchester NH. Died after a brief illness. Buried St Joseph's Cemetery, Bedford NH.

Del Paddock—1 Year Infielder (b. 8 Jun 1887 Volga SD–d. 6 Feb 1952 at his cabin on Rice Lake near Remer MN) Served in World War I. Died from a heart attack after suffering from ten years of heart trouble. Buried Ditson Cemetery, Girard IL.

Don Padgett—8 Years Catcher (b. 5 Dec 1911 Caroleen NC–d. 9 Dec 1980 High Point NC).

Ernie Padgett—5 Years Infielder (b. 1 Mar 1899 Philadelphia PA–d. 15 Apr 1957 Veteran's Hospital, East Orange NJ) Buried Northwood Cemetery, Philadelphia PA.

Joe Page—8 Years Pitcher (b. 28 Oct 1917 Cherry Valley PA–d. 21 Apr 1980 Latrobe Hospital, Latrobe PA) Died from heart failure. Buried Greenwood Memorial Park, Lower Burrell PA.

Phil Page—4 Years Pitcher (b. 23 Aug 1905 Springfield MA–d. 27 Jun 1958 Springfield Hospital, Springfield MA) He managed minor league baseball and was a scout for the Yankees. Buried Hillcrest Park Cemetery, Springfield MA.

Vance Page—4 Years Pitcher (b. 15 Sep 1903 Elm City NC–d. 14 Jul 1951 Wilson NC) Died from injuries suffered when he fell from the roof of his barn. Buried Cedar Grove Cemetery, Elm City NC.

Pat Paige—1 Year Pitcher (b. 5 May 1883 Paw Paw MI–d. 8 Jun 1939 Berlin Memorial Hospital, Berlin WI) After baseball he worked as a burnisher in a band instrument factory for a year before taking a job as a brakeman for the New York Central Railroad. He was later promoted to conductor. He loved hunting, fishing and other outdoor sports. Died from a heart ailment, after a lingering illness, while visiting his son in Wautoma WI. Buried Rice Cemetery, Elkhart IN.

Satchel Paige—6 Years Pitcher Hall of Fame (b. 7 Jul 1906 Mobile AL–d. 8 Jun 1982 at his home in Kansas City MO) He was perhaps the greatest pitcher of all time, not getting a chance to pitch in the majors until he was in his 40s. He pitched three innings of shutout baseball for the A's at age 59 and is said to have pitched in over 2500 games in the negro leagues, winning over 2000 of them. Died from a heart attack. Buried Forest Hill Cemetery, Kansas City MO.

Phil Paine—6 Years Pitcher (b. 8 Jun 1930 Chepachet RI–d. 19 Feb 1978 Veteran's Hospital, Lebanon PA) He owned and operated the Warwick Hotel. Died after a lengthy illness. Buried Hummelstown Cemetery, Hummelstown PA.

Erv Palica—10 Years Pitcher (b. 9 Feb 1928 Lomita CA–d. 29 May 1982 St Mary Medical Center, Long Beach CA) For 19 years he was a stevedore for the Pacific Maritime Association. Died from a heart attack. Buried Holy Cross Cemetery, Culver City CA.

Eddie Palmer—1 Year Infielder (b. 1 Jun 1893 Petty TX–d. 9 Jan 1983 Marlow OK) World War I veteran. He was an umpire and farmed in the Marlow area. Died after a long illness. Buried Marlow Cemetery, Marlow OK.

Emilio Palmero—5 Years Pitcher (b. 13 Jun 1895 Havana, Cuba–d. 15 Jul 1970 St Vincent Hospital, Toledo OH) For 20 years he was an assembler for DeVilbiss Company in Toledo, retiring in 1960. He was an avid tournament caliber bridge player. Buried Ottawa Hills Memorial Park, Toledo OH.

Joe Palmisano—1 Year Catcher (b. 19 Nov 1902 West Point GA–d. 5 Nov 1971 at a hospital in Albuquerque NM) He played in the Pacific Coast League and the Southern League and managed a minor league team that won 46 of its last 47 games. Buried Gate of Heaven Cemetery, Albuquerque NM.

Al Papai—4 Years Pitcher (b. 7 May 1917 Divernon IL–d. 7 Sep 1995 St John's Hospice, Springfield IL) Served in Africa and Europe for the U.S. Army during World War II, earning a purple heart, as well as several other honors. Buried Brush Creek Cemetery, Divernon IL.

Larry Pape—3 Years Pitcher (b. 21 Jul 1883 Norwood OH–d. 21 Jul 1918 Swissvale PA) He was a draftsman for Westinghouse Electric Company in Pittsburgh PA. Died from internal injuries suffered eight years earlier in a baseball game. Buried Spring Grove Cemetery, Cincinnati OH.

Frank Papish—6 Years Pitcher (b. 21 Oct 1917 Pueblo CO–d. 30 Aug 1965 Pueblo CO) He worked for the Gilmore Trucking Company in Pueblo until shortly before his death when he had joined the Pueblo County (CO) sheriff's department as a deputy. Died from a heart attack while walking on the street.

John Pappalau—1 Year Pitcher (b. 3 Apr 1875 Albany NY–d. 12 May 1944 Albany NY) Buried Albany Rural Cemetery, Menands NY.

Freddy Parent—12 Years Infielder (b. 25 Nov 1875 Biddeford ME–d. 2 Nov 1972 Hillcrest Manor, Sanford ME) Buried St Ignatius Cemetery, Sanford ME.

Tony Parisse—2 Years Catcher (b. 25 Jun 1911 Philadelphia PA–d. 2 Jun 1956 at his home in Philadelphia PA) He worked for the Midvale Company in Philadelphia. Died following a heart attack. Buried Holy Sepulchre Cemetery, Philadelphia PA.

Jim Park—3 Years Pitcher (b. 10 Nov 1892 Richmond KY–d. 17 Dec 1970 at his home in Lexington KY) A prominent Lexington lawyer and a long-time leader in the Republican Party, he served in several local offices and ran for U.S. Senate in 1944. Died after a long illness. Buried Lexington Cemetery, Lexington KY.

Dan Parker—(b. 1894 Waterbury CT–d. 20 May 1967 St Mary's Hospital, Waterbury CT) He was the editor and sports columnist for the *New York Daily Mirror* from its start in 1924 until it closed in 1963.Died from cancer. Buried New St Joseph's Cemetery, Waterbury CT.

Dixie Parker—1 Year Catcher (b. 24 Apr 1895 Forest Home AL–d. 15 May 1972 Druid City Hospital, Tuscaloosa AL) Buried Green Pond Cemetery, Green Pond AL.

Doc Parker—4 Years Pitcher (b. 14 Jun 1874 Theresa NY–d. 3 Mar 1941 North Chicago Hospital, Chicago IL) As a medical doctor he was a well-known nerve specialist. He was also a prominent billiard instructor. Buried All Saints Cemetery, Des Plaines IL.

Jay Parker—1 Year Pitcher (b. 8 Jul 1874 Theresa NY–d. 8 Jun 1935 Hartford MI) He managed minor league baseball and umpired college and semi-pro baseball. Died after a year's illness with heart trouble. Buried Maple Hill Cemetery, Hartford MI.

Pat Parker—1 Year Outfielder (b. 22 May 1893 Somerville MA–d. 21 Mar 1967 Claremont General Hospital, Claremont NH) He was director of physical education and coach at Stevens High School in Claremont NH for 35 years. Buried Mountain View Cemetery, Claremont NH.

Roy Parker—1 Year Pitcher (b. 29 Feb 1996 Union MO–d. 17 May 1954 Tulsa OK).

Salty Parker—1 Year Infielder 2 Years Manager (b. 8 Jul 1913 East St Louis IL–d. 27 Jul 1992 Houston TX) He spent his entire life in baseball, 19 years as a minor league manager and 16 years as a major league coach. Died from pancreatic cancer. Buried Forest Park Westheimer Cemetery, Houston TX.

Frank Parkinson—4 Years Infielder (b. 23 Mar 1895 Dickson City PA–d. 4 Jul 1960 Helene Fuld Hospital, Trenton NJ) World War I veteran. He was a custodian at a junior high school in Trenton. Died after a long illness. Buried Beverly National Cemetery, Beverly NJ.

Art Parks—2 Years Outfielder (b. 1 Nov 1911 Paris AR–d. 6 Dec 1989 Little Rock AR) A chiropractor in Paris, he served on the Arkansas State Board of Examiners for Chiropractors. Buried Oakwood Cemetery, Paris AR.

Bill Parks—1 Year Outfielder (b. 4 Jun 1849 Easton PA–d. 10 Oct 1911 Easton PA) Civil War veteran for the Union. He was a self-employed barber. Died while sitting in a comfortable position in his barber shop. Buried Easton Cemetery, Easton PA.

Slicker Parks —1 Year Pitcher (b. 10 Nov 1895 Dallas MI–d. 21 Feb 1978 Royal Oak MI).

Roy Parmelee —10 Years Pitcher (b. 25 Apr 1907 Lambertville MI–d. 31 Aug 1981 Mercy Hospital, Monroe MI) For a short while he was a tool and die maker for Doehler-Jarvis before becoming a sales representative for the Auto Club of Michigan and, later, manager of the Monroe office of the auto club. Retired in 1971. Buried Toledo Memorial Park, Sylvania OH.

Rube Parnham —2 Years Pitcher (b. 1 Feb 1894 Heidelberg PA–d. 25 Nov 1963 McKeesport PA) Died suddenly. Buried Mount Vernon Cemetery, McKeesport PA.

Sam Parrilla —1 Year Outfielder (b. 12 Jun 1943 Santurce, Puerto Rico–d. 9 Feb 1994 Brooklyn NY) Died from a self-inflicted gunshot wound.

Jiggs Parrott —4 Years Infielder (b. 14 Jul 1871 Portland OR–d. 14 Apr 1898 Phoenix City Hospital, Phoenix AZ) Died from edema of the lungs. Buried Lone Fir Cemetery, Portland OR.

Tom Parrott —4 Years Outfielder (b. 10 Apr 1868 Portland OR–d. 1 Jan 1932 at his home in Newberg OR) An accomplished musician, he played the clarinet in bands and orchestras all over the country. Buried Lone Fir Cemetery, Portland OR.

Jiggs Parson —2 Years Pitcher (b. 27 Dec 1885 Parker SD–d. 19 May 1967 Morningside Hospital, Los Angeles CA) For 45 years he was a storekeeper at Williamsport Technical Institute. Died from emphysema and heart disease. Cremated.

Charlie Parsons —3 Years Pitcher (b. 18 Jul 1863 Cherry Flats PA–d. 24 Mar 1936 Mansfield PA) Buried Cherry Flats Cemetery, Cherry Flats PA.

Dixie Parsons —3 Years Catcher (b. 12 May 1916 Talladega AL–d. 31 Oct 1991 Longview TX).

Stan Partenheimer —2 Years Pitcher (b. 21 Oct 1922 Chicopee Falls MA–d. 28 Jan 1989 North Carolina Memorial Hospital, Wilson NC) He was a teacher and coach. Buried Evergreen Memorial Garden, Wilson NC.

Steve Partenheimer —1 Year Infielder (b. 30 Aug 1891 Greenfield MA–d. 16 Jun 1971 Mansfield OH) For 53 years he worked in tire manufacturing technology for Fisk Rubber Company, B F Goodrich and, finally, Mansfield Tire and Rubber Company. He was responsible for many innovations in tire development. Died after being in failing health for several years. Buried Green River Cemetery, Greenfield MA.

Jay Partridge —2 Years Infielder (b. 15 Nov 1902 Mountville GA–d. 14 Jan 1974 Parkview Hospital, Nashville TN) Buried Woodlawn Memorial Park, Nashville TN.

Ben Paschal —8 Years Outfielder (b. 13 Oct 1895 Enterprise AL–d. 10 Nov 1974 Charlotte NC) He worked many years in Charlotte for Cunningham Wholesale Company. Buried Sharon Memorial Park, Charlotte NC.

Johnny Pasek —2 Years Catcher (b. 25 Jun 1905 Niagara Falls NY–d. 13 Mar 1976 St Petersburg FL) Buried Holy Trinity Roman Catholic Cemetery, Lewiston NY.

Dode Paskert —15 Years Outfielder (b. 28 Aug 1881 Cleveland OH–d. 12 Feb 1959 St John's Hospital, Cleveland OH) He worked for the Gabriel Snwbber Company in Cleveland. Died from a heart attack after suffering a cerebral hemorrhage. Buried St Mary's Cemetery, Cleveland OH.

Mike Pasquariello —1 Year Infielder (b. 7 Nov 1898 Philadelphia PA–d. 5 Apr 1965 at his home in Bridgeport CT) Served in the U.S. Marines during World War I. He managed minor league baseball and worked many years for the Nothnagle Furniture Company in Bridgeport. Buried St Michael's Cemetery, Bridgeport CT.

Jim Pastorius —4 Years Pitcher (b. 12 Jul 1881 Pittsburgh PA–d. 10 May 1941 St Joseph's Hospital, Pittsburgh PA) He worked 20 years for the Allegheny County (PA) Highway Department. Died after a six-week illness. Buried South Side Cemetery, Pittsburgh PA.

Joe Pate —2 Years Pitcher (b. 6 Jun 1894 Alice TX–d. 26 Dec 1948 at his home in Fort Worth TX) He won 176 games and lost only 51 in eight seasons for Fort Worth in the Texas League. He umpired minor league baseball and later operated a newsstand and domino parlor in Fort Worth. Died from a heart attack. Buried West Oakwood Cemetery, Fort Worth TX.

Van Patrick—(b. abt 1916–d. 29 Sep 1974 St Joseph Hospital, South Bend IN) A broadcaster for the Detroit Tigers from 1952 to 1959, He participated in the first national broadcast of the World Series in 1948. He also broadcasted Notre Dame and Lion football games. Died from complications following cancer surgery. Buried Northview Cemetery, Dearborn MI.

Harry Pattee—1 Year Infielder (b. 17 Jan 1882 Charlestown MA–d. 17 Jul 1971 Guggenheimer Memorial Hosp, Lynchburg VA) He coached baseball 10 years at Brown University before opening an insurance agency in Providence RI in 1921, retiring from the insurance business in 1935. Died from complications 10 days after breaking his hip. Buried Princess Hill Cemetery, Barrington RI.

Casey Patten—8 Years Pitcher (b. 7 May 1876 Westport NY–d. 31 May 1935 Rochester NY).

Claire Patterson—1 Year Outfielder (b. 5 Oct 1887 Arkansas City KS–d. 28 Mar 1913 Mohave CA) Died at the height of his career from tuberculosis. Buried Riverview Cemetery, Arkansas City KS.

Ham Patterson—1 Year Infielder (b. 13 Oct 1877 Belleville IL–d. 25 Nov 1945 at his home in East St Louis IL) He managed minor league baseball and at one time owned the Dallas team of the Texas League. He was well known as an amateur bowler. Died following a six-month illness. Buried Walnut Hill Cemetery, Belleville IL.

Hank Patterson—1 Year Catcher (b. 17 Jul 1907 San Francisco CA–d. 30 Sep 1970 Kaiser Hospital, Panorama City CA) He was superintendent for the Los Angeles Water and Power Company. Died from a heart attack. Buried San Fernando Mission Cemetery, Mission Hills CA.

Pat Patterson—1 Year Infielder (b. 29 Jan 1897 Belleville IL–d. 1 Oct 1977 St Louis MO) He retired from Famous Barr Department Store. Buried Resurrection Cemetery, St Louis MO.

Roy Patterson—7 Years Pitcher (b. 17 Dec 1876 Stoddard WI–d. 14 Apr 1953 St Croix Falls WI) He played 14 years for the Minneapolis Millers of the American Association. Died from a heart attack while driving near his home. Buried St Croix Falls Cemetery, St Croix Falls WI.

Jimmy Pattison—1 Year Pitcher (b. 18 Dec 1908 Bronx NY–d. 22 Feb 1991 Holmes Regional Med Center, Melbourne FL) Cremated.

Bill Patton—1 Year Catcher (b. 7 Oct 1912 Cornwall PA–d. 15 Mar 1986 Chestnut Hill Hospital, Philadelphia PA) He taught and coached at schools in Highspire PA and Souderton PA and retired as administrator of Indian Crest Junior High School in Souderton. Buried George Washington Memorial Park, Paramus NJ.

Harry Patton—1 Year Pitcher (b. 29 Jun 1884 Gillespie IL–d. 9 Jun 1930 St Louis MO).

Gabe Paul—(b. 4 Jan 1910 Rochester NY–d. 26 Apr 1998 at a hospital in Tampa FL) He was an executive with the Reds, Astros, Indians and Yankees, and part-owner of the Yankees after 1973. Died after a series of strokes.

Carlos Paula—3 Years Outfielder (b. 28 Nov 1927 Havana, Cuba–d. 25 Apr 1983 Miami FL).

Gene Paulette—6 Years Infielder (b. 26 May 1892 Centralia IL–d. 8 Feb 1966 Little Rock AR) He retired as the yardmaster in Little Rock for the Missouri Pacific Lines. Buried Calvary Cemetery, Little Rock AR.

Gil Paulsen—1 Year Pitcher (b. 14 Nov 1902 Graettinger IA–d. 2 Apr 1994 Harlan IA).

Si Pauxtis—1 Year Catcher (b. 20 Jul 1885 Pittston PA–d. 13 Mar 1961 at his home in Philadelphia PA) He was a practicing attorney for 50 years in WilkesBarre PA and Philadelphia, retiring in 1955. He also coached college football 36 years at Dickenson College, Univ of Pennsylvania amd Pennsylvania Military College. Buried St Peter and St Paul Cemetery, Springfield PA.

Ted Pawelek—1 Year Catcher (b. 15 Aug 1920 Chicago Heights IL–d. 12 Feb 1964 Chicago Heights IL) Served in the U.S. Marines during World War II. He was a material control checker at the Ford Motor Company stamping plant near Chicago Heights. He was a scout for the Tigers and was involved in local baseball events with the parks department and American Legion. He and his wife were killed instantly when his car was struck by a tanker truck. Buried Holy Cross Cemetery, Calumet City IL.

Fred Payne—6 Years Catcher (b. 2 Sep 1880 Camden NY–d. 16 Jan 1954 at the home of a niece in Camden NY) He is believed to be the only batter to pinch hit for Ty Cobb. In 1906 Cobb had struck out four straight times when Payne hit for him. For 27 years he was a construction inspector for the City of Detroit MI. Died after a long illness. Buried Mexico Village Cemetery, Mexico NY.

George Payne—1 Year Pitcher (b. 23 May 1890 Mount Vernon KY–d. 24 Jan 1959 Veteran's Hospital, Bellflower CA) World War I veteran. Died from a heart attack. Buried Westminster Memorial Park, Westminster CA.

Harley Payne—4 Years Pitcher (b. 9 Jan 1866 Windsor OH–d. 29 Dec 1935 Orwell OH) He was a farmer. Died from chronic heart disease. Buried Windsor OH.

George Paynter—1 Year Outfielder (b. 6 Jul 1871 Cincinnati OH–d. 1 Oct 1950 Cincinnati OH) Buried Spring Grove Cemetery, Cincinnati OH.

Joan Whitney Payson—(b. 5 Feb 1903 New York City NY–d. 4 Oct 1975 New York Hospital, New York City NY) She inherited a $100 million fortune in the 1920s, and lived in royal splendor her entire life, investing in racing stables, art museums, hospitals and the New York Mets of whom she was the principal owner. Died following a long illness after suffering a stroke four months earlier. Buried Pine Grove Cemetery, Falmouth ME.

Johnny Peacock—9 Years Catcher (b. 10 Jan 1910 Fremont NC–d. 17 Oct 1981 Memorial Hospital, Wilson NC) He operated lumber companies in Wilson and Fremont, a grain company in Fremont and supply companies in Fremont and Stantonsburg NC. He was also vice-chairman of the Wayne Community College Board of Trustees. Buried Fremont Cemetery, Fremont NC.

Elias Peak—1 Year Infielder (b. 23 May 1859 Philadelphia PA–d. 17 Dec 1916 Philadelphia PA) Died suddenly. Buried Fernwood Cemetery, Fernwood PA.

Dickey Pearce—2 Years Infielder 2 Years Manager (b. 2 Jan 1836 Brooklyn NY–d. 12 Oct 1908 Wareham MA).

Ducky Pearce—2 Years Catcher (b. 17 Mar 1885 Corning OH–d. 22 May 1933 at his home in Brownstown IN) He played in the Three-I League, American Association and Pacific Coast League. He operated a lunch counter in Brownstown and, later, a filling station there. Died from a heart attack. Buried Crown Hill Cemetery, Indianapolis IN.

Frank Pearce—3 Years Pitcher (b. 31 Aug 1905 Middletown KY–d. 3 Sep 1950 Memphis NY) Served in the U.S. Navy during World War II. He had just gone into a partnership in the Memphis Inn when he went on a drinking spree and shot himself in the heart at the inn, dying immediately. Buried Eastwood Cemetery, Eastwood KY.

Frank Pearce—1 Year Pitcher (b. 30 Mar 1860 Louisville KY–d. 13 Nov 1926 at his apartment in Louisville KY) Died from dilation of the heart. Buried Cave Hill Cemetery, Louisville KY.

George Pearce—6 Years Pitcher (b. 10 Jan 1888 Aurora IL–d. 11 Oct 1935 Silver Cross Hospital, Joliet IL) He operated a billiard parlor in Plainfield IL. Died from a perforated gastric ulcer and peritonitis. Buried Plainfield Township Cemetery, Plainfield IL.

Harry Pearce—3 Years Infielder (b. 12 Jul 1889 Philadelphia PA–d. 8 Jan 1942 at his home in Philadelphia PA) He also played soccer and was known as one of the greatest goalies ever developed in Philadelphia. Buried Holy Sepulchre Cemetery, Philadelphia PA.

Frank Pears—2 Years Pitcher (b. 30 Aug 1866 KY–d. 29 Nov 1923 at the city sanitarium in St Louis MO) Buried Calvary Cemetery, St Louis MO.

Alex Pearson—2 Years Pitcher (b. 9 Mar 1877 Greensboro PA–d. 30 Oct 1966 Rochester Hospital, Rochester PA) He managed minor league baseball. A retired employee of Koppers Company, Kobuta Plant, near Monaca PA, he served three terms as a Rochester burgess and was an avid hunter and fisher. Buried Irvin Cemetery, Rochester PA.

Ike Pearson—6 Years Pitcher (b. 1 Mar 1917 Grenada MS–d. 17 Mar 1985 Sarasota FL).

Monte Pearson—10 Years Pitcher (b. 2 Sep 1909 Oakland CA–d. 27 Jan 1978 City Hospital, Fowler CA) He was a real estate salesman for 20 years. Died from pancreatic cancer. Cremated.

Marv Peasley—1 Year Pitcher (b. 16 Jul 1890 Jonesport ME–d. 27 Dec 1948 San Francisco CA) World War I veteran. He was a machinist.

Died from pneumonia and liver disease. Buried Golden Gate National Cemetery, San Bruno CA.

George Pechiney—3 Years Pitcher (b. 20 Sep 1861 Cincinnati OH–d. 14 Jul 1943 Cincinnati OH) He was a toolmaker. Died from a cerebral hemorrhage. Buried Spring Grove Cemetery, Cincinnati OH.

Charlie Pechous—3 Years Infielder (b. 5 Oct 1896 Chicago IL–d. 13 Sep 1980 St Catherine's Hospital, Kenosha WI) After his baseball career was over he returned to Loyola Medical School for his medical degree. He was a family doctor in the Kenosha WI area for 45 years. Died after a three-month illness. Buried All Saints Cemetery, Kenosha WI.

Hal Peck—7 Years Outfielder (b. 20 Apr 1917 Big Bend WI–d. 13 Apr 1995 Milwaukee WI) He worked many years for Atlantic Richfield Company, retiring to Sunsites AZ. Cremated.

Roger Peckinpaugh—17 Years Infielder 8 Years Manager (b. 5 Feb 1891 Wooster OH–d. 17 Nov 1977 Hanna House Hospital, Cleveland OH) He was a manufacturer's representative for Cleveland Oak Belting Company. Died from a respiratory problem, but had been suffering from cancer and heart disease. Buried Acacia Masonic Memorial Park, Cleveland OH.

Chick Pedroes—1 Year Outfielder (b. 27 Oct 1869 Chicago IL–d. 6 Aug 1927 Chicago IL) Buried Montrose Cemetery, Chicago IL.

Steve Peek—1 Year Pitcher (b. 30 Jul 1914 Springfield MA–d. 20 Sep 1991 Syracuse NY).

Homer Peel—5 Years Outfielder (b. 10 Oct 1902 Port Sullivan TX–d. 8 Apr 1997 Shreveport LA).

Jack Peerson—2 Years Infielder (b. 28 Aug 1910 Brunswick GA–d. 23 Oct 1966 City Hospital, Fort Walton Beach FL) He owned and managed Standard Marine, Inc, in Fort Walton Beach from 1956 until he died suddenly. Buried Beal Memorial Cemetery, Fort Walton Beach FL.

Red Peery—2 Years Pitcher (b. 15 Aug 1906 Payson UT–d. 6 May 1985 Holy Cross Hospital, Salt Lake City UT) He coached for several teams before working 35 years for the Utah State Department of Transportation. Buried Payson City Cemetery, Payson UT.

Charlie Peete—1 Year Outfielder (b. 22 Feb 1931 Franklin VA–d. 27 Nov 1956 Caracas, Venezuela) Died at the height of his career in an airplane crash.

Heinie Peitz—16 Years Catcher (b. 28 Nov 1870 St Louis MO–d. 23 Oct 1943 General Hospital, Cincinnati OH) Died from stomach cancer. Buried St Mary Cemetery, Cincinnati OH.

Joe Peitz—1 Year Outfielder (b. 8 Nov 1869 St Louis MO–d. 4 Dec 1919 St Louis MO) Died from tuberculosis. Buried Calvary Cemetery, St Louis MO.

Bill Pelouze—1 Year Outfielder (b. 12 Sep 1865 Washington DC–d. 20 Jun 1943 at his summer home in Lake Geneva WI) Served in the U.S. Army as a Colonel during World War I. Died from heart trouble following an illness of about seven weeks. Buried Oak Woods Cemetery, Chicago IL.

Barney Pelty—10 Years Pitcher (b. 10 Sep 1880 Farmington MO–d. 24 May 1939 State Hospital, Farmington MO) Active in the Republican Party, he was appointed to a position in the Missouri State Pure Food and Drug Department, remaining there for several years. Died following a cerebral hemorrhage. Buried Masonic Cemetery, Farmington MO.

John Pelz—3 Years Outfielder (b. 23 Apr 1861 New Orleans LA–d. 26 Feb 1906 at his home in New Orleans LA) Died from consumption. Buried Valence Street Cemetery, New Orleans LA.

Roberto Pena—6 Years Infielder (b. 17 Apr 1940 Santo Domingo, Dominican Republic–d. 23 Jul 1982 Santiago, Dominican Republic).

Elmer Pence—1 Year Outfielder (b. 17 Aug 1900 Valley Springs CA–d. 17 Sep 1968 Mount Zion Hospital, San Francisco CA) He was an electrician for 35 years. Died from a cerebral hemorrhage. Cremated. Buried Olivet Memorial Park, Colma CA.

Russ Pence—1 Year Pitcher (b. 11 Mar 1900 Marine IL–d. 11 Aug 1971 at a hospital in Hot Springs AR) He played a number of years in the Southern Association before retiring to Hot Springs where he lived for 20 years. Buried Marine City Cemetery, Marine IL.

Jim Pendleton—8 Years Outfielder (b. 7 Jan 1924 St Charles MO–d. 20 Mar 1996 Houston TX) Buried Houston National Cemetery, Houston TX.

Ken Penner—2 Years Pitcher (b. 24 Apr 1896 Booneville IN–d. 28 May 1959 at his home in Sacramento CA) He worked in baseball more than 40 years as a player, coach, scout and minor league manager. Died from Lou Gehrig's disease. He had been paralyzed and unable to move a muscle for eight months. Cremated.

Kewpie Pennington—1 Year Pitcher (b. 24 Sep 1896 New York City NY–d. 3 May 1953 Beth Israel Hospital, Newark NJ) He was a claims adjuster for Globe Indemnity Insurance Company and for Norwich Union Fire Insurance Company before becoming manager of Banker's Indemnity Insurance Company in Newark. His last six years he worked as a private adjuster. Died after a week's illness. Buried Restland Memorial Park, East Hanover NJ.

Herb Pennock—22 Years Pitcher Hall of Fame (b. 10 Feb 1894 Kennett Square PA–d. 30 Jan 1948 New York City NY) Working his entire life in baseball, he was general manager of the Phillies when he died. Died from a cerebral hemorrhage. Buried Union Hill Cemetery, Kennett Square PA.

Jimmy Peoples—6 Years Catcher (b. 8 Oct 1863 Big Beaver MI–d. 29 Aug 1920 at his home in Detroit MI) He umpired for several years before going into real estate sales in Detroit. Died from heart failure.

Henry Peploski—1 Year Infielder (b. 15 Sep 1905 Garlin, Poland–d. 28 Jan 1982 Dover NJ).

Pepper Peploski—1 Year Infielder (b. 12 Sep 1891 Brooklyn NY–d. 13 Jul 1972 New York City NY).

Bill Pepper—1 Year Pitcher (b. 2 Sep 1865 KY–d. 5 Nov 1903 Webb City MO) Died from miner's consumption and stomach cancer. Buried Webb City Cemetery, Webb City MO.

Bob Pepper—1 Year Pitcher (b. 3 May 1895 Rosston PA–d. 8 Apr 1968 at his home in Ford Cliff PA) Injured while pitching for the Athletics when he was age 18, he had been an invalid since. Buried Ford City Cemetery, Ford City PA.

Ray Pepper—5 Years Outfielder (b. 5 Aug 1905 Decatur AL–d. 24 Mar 1996 at his home in Mooresville AL) He owned and operated Pepper and Howell Menswear in Decatur for 20 years. After selling the shop he worked 20 years for Monsanto before retiring. Buried Athens City Cemetery, Athens AL.

Hub Perdue—5 Years Pitcher (b. 7 Jun 1882 Bethpage TN–d. 31 Oct 1968 Shady Grove Nursing Home, Gallatin TN) He managed for a short time in the Southern League. Buried Bethpage Cemetery, Bethpage TN.

Louis Perini—(b. 29 Nov 1903 Framingham MA–d. 16 Apr 1972 West Palm Beach FL) The owner of the Boston and Milwaukee Braves from 1946 to 1962, he was the first owner to shift cities, moving the Braves from Boston to Milwaukee in 1953. He owned a controlling interest in the Boston-based Perini Corp, one of the largest construction companies in the nation. He also had extensive real estate holdings. Died after a lengthy illness. Buried Woodlawn Cemetery, Wellesley MA.

Charlie Perkins—2 Years Pitcher (b. 9 Sep 1905 Birmingham AL–d. 25 May 1988 Salem OR) He was a professional golfer. Cremated and his ashes scattered over the Willamette Valley.

Cy Perkins—17 Years Catcher (b. 27 Feb 1896 Gloucester MA–d. 2 Oct 1963 Harston Hall Conv Home, Philadelphia PA) He coached for the Tigers and Phillies, spending 36 years in major league baseball. He also coached at Valley Forge Military Academy for three years. Died after being ill with a virus. Buried Oak Grove Cemetery, Gloucester MA.

Hub Pernoll—2 Years Pitcher (b. 14 Mar 1888 Applegate OR–d. 18 Feb 1944 Josephine General Hospital, Grants Pass OR) He operated the Owl Billiard Parlor in Grants Pass for over 25 years. Died following a heart attack suffered six weeks earlier. Buried Hillcrest Memorial Park, Grants Pass OR.

Bill Perrin—1 Year Pitcher (b. 23 Jun 1911 New Orleans LA–d. 30 Jun 1974 Obhsner Foundation Hospital, New Orleans LA) Died from post-surgical complications. Buried Hope Mausoleum, New Orleans LA.

Jack Perrin—1 Year Outfielder (b. 4 Feb 1893 Escanaba MI–d. 24 Jun 1969 Detroit MI) Buried Lakeview Cemetery, Escanaba MI.

Nig Perrine—1 Year Infielder (b. 14 Jan 1885 Clinton WI–d. 13 Aug 1948 at his home in Kansas City MO) Buried Memorial Park Cemetery, Kansas City MO.

George Perring—5 Years Infielder (b. 13 Aug 1884 Sharon WI–d. 20 Aug 1960 at a hospital in Beloit WI) He was an insurance underwriter.

Active in Beloit civic affairs for 40 years, he participated in Red Cross, Salvation Army, Boy Scouts and Community Chest. Buried Eastlawn Cemetery, Beloit WI.

Pol Perritt—10 Years Pitcher (b. 3 Aug 1892 Arcadia LA–d. 15 Oct 1947 at a hospital in Shreveport LA) He engaged in the oil business and was well known in the Texas, Arkansas and Louisiana area. Died from tuberculosis. Buried Arcadia Cemetery, Arcadia LA.

Boyd Perry—1 Year Infielder (b. 21 Mar 1914 Snow Camp NC–d. 29 Jun 1990 Central Piedmont Conv Center, Burlington NC) He was a retired dairy farmer. Buried Spring Friend Cemetery, Snow Camp NC.

Clay Perry—1 Year Infielder (b. 18 Dec 1881 Clayton WI–d. 13 Jan 1954 at his home in Rice Lake WI) He played several years in the Southern League and the Texas League and operated a bottling plant at Rice Lake. He had been in failing health for some time. Buried Nora Cemetery, Rice Lake WI.

Hank Perry—1 Year Outfielder (b. 28 Jul 1886 Howell MI–d. 18 Jul 1956 Pontiac MI).

Scott Perry—7 Years Pitcher (b. 17 Apr 1891 Dennison TX–d. 27 Oct 1959 General Hospital, Kansas City MO) He was a short-order cook in restaurants. When he died he had lived in Kansas City about ten years and had been ill for a month. Buried St Mary's Cemetery, Kansas City MO.

Parson Perryman—1 Year Pitcher (b. 24 Oct 1888 Everette Springs GA–d. 12 Sep 1966 at a hospital in Starke FL) World War I veteran. He was a lawyer and served 20 years as a county judge in Bradford County, FL. Died following a short illness. Buried Crosby Lake Cemetery, Starke FL.

Bill Pertica—4 Years Pitcher (b. 17 Aug 1898 Santa Barbara CA–d. 28 Dec 1967 Los Angeles CA) World War II veteran. He was a bartender. Died from a heart attack. Buried Willamette National Cemetery, Portland OR.

John Peters—4 Years Catcher (b. 14 Jul 1893 Kansas City KS–d. 21 Feb 1932 Kansas City MO) He played professional baseball for 22 years, up until his death. Died from a heart attack while preparing for another spring training with the Kansas City Blues of the American Association, where he had played the last five years. Buried Memorial Park Cemetery, Kansas City MO.

Johnny Peters—9 Years Infielder (b. 8 Apr 1850 Louisiana MO–d. 4 Jan 1924 at his home in St Louis MO) He worked for the St Louis Parks Department. Buried Old St Marcus Cemetery, St Louis MO.

Rube Peters—2 Years Pitcher (b. 15 Mar 1885 Grantfork IL–d. 7 Feb 1965 Chilton Memorial Hosp, Pompton Plains NJ) He retired from the Federal Shipyards at Kearney NJ about 1949. Buried Bay View-New York Bay Cemetery, Jersey City NJ.

Bob Peterson—2 Years Catcher (b. 16 Jul 1884 Philadelphia PA–d. 27 Nov 1962 Evesham Township NJ).

Cap Peterson—8 Years Outfielder (b. 15 Aug 1942 Tacoma WA–d. 17 May 1980 Tacoma WA) He joined the family construction business, Peterson Building Company, as president. Died after a long illness. Buried Mountain View Memorial Park, Tacoma WA.

Jim Peterson—3 Years Pitcher (b. 18 Aug 1908 Philadelphia PA–d. 8 Apr 1975 Palm Beach FL) He owned and operated the Taboo Restaurant in Palm Beach from 1955 to 1975. Buried Our Lady Queen of Peace Cemetery, Royal Palm Beach FL.

Kent Peterson—8 Years Pitcher (b. 21 Dec 1925 Goshen UT–d. 27 Apr 1995 LDS Hospital, Salt Lake City UT) Inducted into the Utah Sports Hall of Fame, he was involved in community activities and was an avid golfer. Died from complications resulting from an automobile accident in Highland UT. Buried Orem City Cemetery, Orem UT.

Ted Petoskey—2 Years Outfielder (b. 5 Jan 1911 St Charles MI–d. 30 Nov 1996 Elgin SC).

Pat Pettee—1 Year Infielder (b. 10 Jan 1863 Natick MA–d. 9 Oct 1934 Leonard Morse Hospital, Natick MA) Died after a long and painful illness. Buried St Patrick's Cemetery, Natick MA.

Ned Pettigrew—2 Games Pinch Hitter (b. 25 Aug 1881 Honey Grove TX–d. 20 Aug 1952 at his home in Duncan OK) He managed minor league baseball and was a scout for the White Sox and Tigers. Died following a long illness. Buried Duncan Cemetery, Duncan OK.

Bob Pettit—3 Years Outfielder (b. 19 Jul 1861 Williamstown MA–d. 1 Nov 1910 at his home in

Derby CT) For 13 years he was a foreman for the Silver Plate Cutlery Company. Died suddenly from a hemorrhage after being in poor health the last three years. Buried Oak Cliff Cemetery, Derby CT.

Leon Pettit —2 Years Pitcher (b. 23 Jun 1902 Waynesburg PA–d. 11 Nov 1974 Maury County Hospital, Columbia TN) He was a retired employee of Pure-Vav Dairy Products Corporation. Buried Memorial Park Cemetery, Memphis TN.

Jesse Petty —7 Years Pitcher (b. 23 Nov 1894 Orr OK–d. 23 Oct 1971 General Hospital, St Paul MN) Died from a heart attack. Buried Fort Snelling National Cemetery, Minneapolis MN.

Bruce Petway —8 Years Catcher 4 Years Manager (b. abt 1883 Nashville TN–d. 27 Jun 1941 Cook County Hospital, Chicago IL) He played in the negro leagues and managed some kitchenette apartments the last 15 years of his life. He had been sick for several months. Buried Burr Oak Cemetery, Chicago IL.

Larry Pezold —1 Year Infielder (b. 22 Jun 1893 New Orleans LA–d. 22 Oct 1957 General Hospital, Baton Rouge LA) Buried Greenoaks Memorial Park, Baton Rouge LA.

Pretzel Pezzullo —2 Years Pitcher (b. 10 Dec 1910 Bridgeport CT–d. 16 May 1990 Dallas TX) He worked for Chance-Vought Aircraft in Dallas where he designed aircraft and missile models, some of which are on display at the Smithsonian Institute in Washington DC. Later he owned and operated Gulf Industries in Grand Prairie TX where he continued to build models for the aircraft industry. Died from cancer. Buried Holy Redeemer Cemetery, DeSoto TX.

Bill Pfann —1 Year Pitcher (b. Jun 1863 Hamilton, Ontario, Canada–d. 3 Jun 1904 Hamilton, Ontario, Canada).

Big Jeff Pfeffer —6 Years Pitcher (b. 31 Mar 1881 Champaign IL–d. 19 Dec 1954 State Hospital, Kankakee IL) He was a real estate agent. Buried St Mary's Cemetery, Champaign IL.

Fred Pfeffer —16 Years Infielder 1 Year Manager (b. 17 Mar 1860 Louisville KY–d. 10 Apr 1932 at his home in Chicago IL) For years he ran a tavern in Chicago. Later he was in charge of the press boxes at Chicago's race tracks. Died from heart disease. Buried All Saints Cemetery, Des Plaines IL.

Jeff Pfeffer —13 Years Pitcher (b. 4 Mar 1888 Seymour IL–d. 15 Aug 1972 Chicago IL).

Monte Pfeiffer —1 Year Infielder (b. 1891 New York City NY–d. 27 Sep 1941 New York City NY).

Jack Pfiester —8 Years Pitcher (b. 24 May 1878 Cincinnati OH–d. 3 Sep 1953 at his home in Twightwee OH) Buried Union Cemetery, Montgomery OH.

George Pfister —1 Year Catcher (b. 4 Sep 1918 Bound Brook NJ–d. 14 Aug 1997 St Joseph MO) Buried Bound Brook Cemetery, Bound Brook NJ.

Monte Pfyl —1 Year Infielder (b. 11 May 1886 St Louis MO–d. 18 Oct 1945 San Francisco CA) He was an electrician. Died from cancer of the larynx. Buried Park View Cemetery, Manteca CA.

Bill Phebus —3 Years Pitcher (b. 2 Aug 1909 Cherryvale KS–d. 11 Oct 1989 Bartow FL) For 30 years he was a maintenance worker for the City of Bartow. Buried Wildwood Cemetery, Bartow FL.

Art Phelan —5 Years Infielder (b. 14 Aug 1887 Niantic IL–d. 27 Dec 1964 at his home in Fort Worth TX) He managed some minor league baseball. Living 45 years in Fort Worth, he was a deputy clerk in the Tarrant County, TX, tax office when he died. Cremated.

Dan Phelan —1 Year Infielder (b. Jul 1865 Thomaston CT–d. 7 Dec 1945 at his home in West Haven CT) He worked for the American Brass Company in Waterbury CT until he retired in 1927. Buried St Lawrence Cemetery, West Haven CT.

Dick Phelan —2 Years Infielder (b. 10 Dec 1854 Towanda PA–d. 13 Feb 1931 at his home in San Antonio TX) Died after a long illness. Buried St Mary's Cemetery, San Antonio TX.

Babe Phelps —11 Years Catcher (b. 19 Apr 1908 Odenton MD–d. 10 Dec 1992 at his home in Odenton MD) He worked 17 years for National Plastics Company. Died after a year-long battle with cancer. Buried Bethel Methodist Church Cemetery, Odenton MD.

Ed Phelps —11 Years Catcher (b. 3 Mar 1879 Albany NY–d. 31 Jan 1942 at his home in East Greenbush NY) Died after a long illness. Buried Greenbush Reformed Church Cemetery, East Greenbush NY.

Neal Phelps—1 Year Outfielder (b. 19 Nov 1840 New York City NY–d. 12 Feb 1885 New York City NY) He died from pneumonia. Buried Greenwood Cemetery, Brooklyn NY.

Ray Phelps—5 Years Pitcher (b. 11 Dec 1903 Dunlap TN–d. 7 Jul 1971 Fort Pierce Memorial Hosp, Fort Pierce FL) He moved from New York to Fort Pierce about 1941 and was connected with the Pitts Gas Company there. Buried Fort Pierce Cemetery, Fort Pierce FL.

Deacon Phillippe—13 Years Pitcher (b. 23 May 1872 Rural Retreat VA–d. 30 Mar 1952 at his daughter's home in Avalon PA) From 1935 until his death he was a tipstaff at the Allegheny County (PA) Courthouse. Died while he was watching television. Buried Allegheny County Memorial Park, Allison Park PA.

Bill Phillips—10 Years Infielder (b. 1857 St John, New Brunswick, Canada–d. 6 Oct 1900 Chicago IL) Buried Graceland Cemetery, Chicago IL.

Bill Phillips—7 Years Pitcher 2 Years Manager (b. 9 Nov 1868 Allenport PA–d. 25 Oct 1941 at his home in Charleroi PA) Buried Mount Auburn Cemetery, Fayette City PA.

Bubba Phillips—10 Years Infielder (b. 24 Feb 1928 West Point MS–d. 22 Jun 1993 at his home in Hattiesburg MS) In private business in Hattiesburg, he also instructed tennis at Mississippi State University. Buried Cedar Lawn Cemetery, Philadelphia MS.

Buz Phillips—1 Year Pitcher (b. 25 May 1904 Newton NC–d. 6 Nov 1964 Baltimore MD).

Dick Phillips—4 Years Infielder (b. 24 Nov 1931 Racine WI–d. 29 Mar 1998 Burnaby, British Columbia, Canada) Coached one year.

Eddie Phillips—6 Years Catcher (b. 17 Feb 1901 Worcester MA–d. 26 Jan 1968 at his home in Buffalo NY) For 20 years he played, coached or managed in baseball. He worked for Curtiss-Wright and, later, for Curbell Plastics, Inc. Died from a heart attack. Buried Mount Calvary Cemetery, Cheektowaga NY.

John Phillips—1 Year Pitcher (b. 24 May 1921 St Louis MO–d. 16 Jun 1958 St Louis MO) Died suddenly. Buried Resurrection Cemetery, St Louis MO.

Lefty Phillips—3 Years Manager (b. 16 May 1919 Los Angeles CA–d. 12 Jun 1972 St Jude Hospital, Fullerton CA) He spent his entire life in baseball as a minor league player, coach, scout and executive. Died from a heart attack after a severe attack of chronic asthma. Buried Mount Sinai Cemetery, Los Angeles CA.

Marr Phillips—3 Years Infielder (b. 16 Jun 1862 Pittsburgh PA–d. 1 Apr 1928 Pittsburgh PA) He worked in the Sanitary Division of the Pittsburgh City Department of Health. Died after a brief illness.

Red Phillips—2 Years Pitcher (b. 3 Nov 1908 Pauls Valley OK–d. 1 Feb 1988 Wichita KS) He was a retired employee of Boeing in Wichita. Buried Old Mission Cemetery, Wichita KS.

Tom Phillips—4 Years Pitcher (b. 1 Apr 1889 Philipsburg PA–d. 12 Apr 1929 at his mother's home in Philipsburg PA) Buried Philipsburg Cemetery, Philipsburg PA.

Bill Phyle—4 Years Pitcher (b. 25 Jun 1875 Duluth MN–d. 6 Aug 1953 General Hospital, Los Angeles CA) He was an umpire in the Pacific Coast League from 1913 until 1931. Died from heart disease and prostate cancer. Buried Holy Cross Cemetery, Culver City CA.

Wiley Piatt—6 Years Pitcher (b. 13 Jul 1874 Blue Creek OH–d. 20 Sep 1946 Good Samaritan Hospital, Cincinnati OH) He taught school at Mount Tabor OH and Otway OH. During World War II he did defense work at Patterson Field. Buried Heck's Cemetery, Augusta KY.

Nick Picciuto—1 Year Infielder (b. 27 Aug 1921 Newark NJ–d. 10 Jan 1997 Winchester Medical Center, Winchester VA) Served in the U.S. Army during World War II. A paving contractor, he owned and operated Picciuto and Sons of Livingston NJ for 40 years. Cremated.

Val Picinich—18 Years Catcher (b. 8 Sep 1896 New York City NY–d. 5 Dec 1942 Nobleboro ME) He was director of personal service and morale at Bath Iron Works. Died from pneumonia. Buried Dunbar Cemetery, Nobleboro ME.

Charlie Pick—6 Years Infielder (b. 12 Apr 1888 Roxboro NC–d. 26 Jun 1954 Memorial Hospital, Lynchburg VA) For several years he was attendance officer for the Rustburg school board. Died from a heart attack. Buried Spring Hill Cemetery, Lynchburg VA.

Eddie Pick—3 Years Infielder (b. 7 May 1899 Attleboro MA–d. 13 May 1967 Santa Monica

CA) World War I veteran. He was vice-president of Riss and Company, a transportation related firm. Died from prostate cancer. Cremated.

Ollie Pickering —8 Years Outfielder (b. 9 Apr 1870 Olney IL–d. 20 Jan 1952 at his home in Vincennes IN) Died after a long illness. Buried Fairview Cemetery, Vincennes IN.

Urbane Pickering —2 Years Infielder (b. 3 Jun 1899 Hoxie KS–d. 13 May 1970 at a hospital in Modesto CA) Served in the U.S. Army during World War II. He worked for the Modesto police department 20 years, including seven years as Chief of Police from 1945 to 1952. He then spent ten years as a jailor for the Stanislaus County, CA, sheriff's department before retiring in 1964. He also served 18 years on the Selective Service Board. Died after a brief illness. Buried Lakewood Memorial Park, Hughson CA.

Charlie Pickett —1 Year Pitcher (b. 1 Mar 1883 Delaware OH–d. 20 May 1969 Springfield OH) He was a salesman for Midland Grocery Company, retiring in 1959. Died after several months of failing health. Buried Glen Haven Memorial Gardens, Donnelsville OH.

Dave Pickett —1 Year Outfielder (b. 26 May 1874 Brookline MA–d. 22 Apr 1950 at his home in Easton MA) Died after a short illness. Buried Holyhood Cemetery, Brookline MA.

John Pickett —3 Years Infielder (b. 20 Feb 1866 Chicago IL–d. 4 Jul 1922 Mercy Hospital, Chicago IL) He worked his last 24 years for the Spaulding Sporting Goods Company. Died following an operation. Buried Calvary Cemetery, Evanston IL.

Clarence Pickrel —2 Years Pitcher (b. 28 Mar 1911 Gretna VA–d. 4 Nov 1983 Rocky Mount VA) He owned the Circle Lunch Cafe in Rocky Mount. Buried Gretna Burial Park, Gretna VA.

Ty Pickup —1 Year Outfielder (b. 29 Oct 1897 Philadelphia PA–d. 2 Aug 1974 Philadelphia PA) Buried St Dominic Cemetery, Philadelphia PA.

Al Piechota —2 Years Pitcher (b. 19 Jan 1914 Chicago IL–d. 13 Jun 1996 Methodist Hospital, Chicago IL) He retired after working about 25 years for the Chicago Police Department. Buried St Adalbert Cemetery, Niles IL.

Cy Pieh —3 Years Pitcher (b. 29 Sep 1886 Wannikee WI–d. 13 Sep 1945 at a hospital in Jacksonville FL) He lived in Jacksonville three years and worked in the George Washington Hotel there. Died after a brief illness. Buried Enderlin Community Cemetery, Enderlin ND.

Gracie Pierce —3 Years Infielder (b. New York City NY–d. 28 Aug 1894 New York City NY).

Ray Pierce —3 Years Pitcher (b. 6 Jun 1897 Emporia KS–d. 4 May 1963 at a hospital in Denver CO) Served in both World Wars I and II. Buried Topeka Cemetery, Topeka KS.

Andy Piercy —1 Year Infielder (b. Aug 1856 San Jose CA–d. 27 Dec 1932 County Hospital, San Jose CA) He was a retired rancher. Died from a heart attack. Buried Woodlawn Memorial Park, Daly City CA.

Bill Piercy —6 Years Pitcher (b. 2 May 1896 El Monte CA–d. 28 Aug 1951 at a hospital in Long Beach CA) During World War II he served as administrator of war shipping. Died from a heart attack. Cremated.

Marino Pieretti —6 Years Pitcher (b. 23 Sep 1920 Lucca, Italy–d. 30 Jan 1981 at his home in San Francisco CA) For years a fan favorite in the Pacific Coast League, he worked for a freight company in San Francisco. Died after a three-year bout with pancreatic cancer. Buried Holy Cross Catholic Cemetery, Colma CA.

Al Pierotti —2 Years Pitcher (b. 24 Oct 1895 Boston MA–d. 12 Feb 1964 Revere MA) He was a public school teacher in Chelsea MA. Buried Glenwood Cemetery, Everett MA.

Bill Pierson —3 Years Pitcher (b. 13 Jun 1899 Atlantic City NJ–d. 20 Feb 1959 City Hospital, Atlantic City NJ) He was an electrician 30 years for the Atlantic City Electric Company. Died after a short illness. Buried Holy Cross Cemetery, Yeadon PA.

Dave Pierson —1 Year Catcher (b. 20 Aug 1855 Wilkes-Barre PA–d. 11 Nov 1922 City Hospital, Newark NJ) He was a prison keeper. Died from gall bladder cancer. Buried Fairmount Cemetery, Newark NJ.

Dick Pierson —1 Year Infielder (b. 24 Oct 1857 Newark NJ–d. 20 Jul 1922 at his home in Newark NJ) Died from chronic nephritis and heart disease. Buried Fairmount Cemetery, Newark NJ.

Tony Piet —8 Years Infielder (b. 7 Dec 1906 Berwick PA–d. 1 Dec 1981 Hinsdale Hospital, Hinsdale IL) A prominent auto dealer on Chicago's southside, he opened Tony Piet Motors in 1938 and operated it until his death. Buried Resurrection Cemetery, Justice IL.

Sandy Piez —1 Year Outfielder (b. 13 Oct 1888 New York City NY–d. 29 Dec 1930 Atlantic City NJ) He was a salesman for a gas heater company. Drowned when the car he was riding in ran off a bridge. Buried Pleasantville NJ.

Jess Pike —1 Year Outfielder (b. 31 Jul 1915 Dustin OK–d. 28 Mar 1984 Mercy Hospital, San Diego CA) He was a horseman in the race horse industry for 30 years. Died from adenocarcinoma and multiple organ carcinomatosis. Buried Glen Abbey Memorial Park, Bonita CA.

Lip Pike —5 Years Outfielder 3 Years Manager (b. 25 May 1845 New York City NY–d. 10 Oct 1893 Brooklyn NY) Buried Salem Fields Cemetery, Brooklyn NY.

George Piktuzis —1 Year Pitcher (b. 3 Jan 1932 Chicago IL–d. 28 Nov 1993 V A Medical Center, Long Beach CA) Served in the military. For 15 years he was a sheet metal worker for a steel manufacturer. Died from a heart attack, but suffered from liver and kidney disease. Cremated.

Herman Pillette —4 Years Pitcher (b. 26 Dec 1896 St Paul OR–d. 30 Apr 1960 Mercy Hospital, Sacramento CA) For 13 years he was a pressman for the California State Printing Office in Sacramento. Died from a cerebral embolism. Buried St Mary's Cemetery, Sacramento CA.

Squiz Pillion —1 Year Pitcher (b. 13 Apr 1894 Hartford CT–d. 30 Sep 1962 at his home in Pittsburgh PA) He was a retired insurance adjuster. Died from a heart attack. Buried Homewood Cemetery, Pittsburgh PA.

Andy Pilney —3 Games Pinch Hitter (b. 19 Jan 1913 Frontenac KS–d. 15 Sep 1996 Kenner LA).

George Pinckney —10 Years Infielder (b. 11 Jan 1859 Peoria IL–d. 9 Nov 1926 St Francis Hospital, Peoria IL) He worked in the auditing department of the Peoria and Pekin Union Railroad for 30 years, retiring in 1925. Died after several years of failing health. Buried Springdale Cemetery, Peoria IL.

Babe Pinelli —8 Years Infielder (b. 18 Oct 1895 San Francisco CA–d. 22 Oct 1984 Villa Convalescent Hospital, Daly City CA) A National League umpire from 1935 to 1956, his last game behind the plate was in the 1956 World Series when Don Larsen pitched his perfect game. Died from pneumonia brought on by influenza. Buried Holy Cross Catholic Cemetery, Colma CA.

Ed Pinnance —1 Year Pitcher (b. 22 Oct 1879 Walpoli Island, Ontario, Canada–d. 12 Dec 1944 Walpole Island, Ontario, Canada).

Vada Pinson —18 Years Outfielder (b. 11 Aug 1938 Memphis TN–d. 21 Oct 1995 Summit Medical Center, Oakland CA) He spent his entire life in baseball as a player and coach, coaching for a number of teams up until his death. Died from a heart attack after suffering a stroke three weeks earlier. Buried Rolling Hills Memorial Park, Richmond CA.

Lerton Pinto —2 Years Pitcher (b. 8 Apr 1899 Chillicothe OH–d. 13 May 1983 St John's Medical Center, Oxnard CA) He was a psychiatric technician at Camarillo State Hospital for 22 years. Died from a heart attack. Buried Ivy Lawn Memorial Park, Ventura CA.

Ed Pipgras —1 Year Pitcher (b. 15 Jun 1904 Schleswig IA–d. 13 Apr 1964 two miles east of Currie MN) Died in an automobile accident when he lost control of his car. Buried Restland Memory Gardens, Slayton MN.

George Pipgras —11 Years Pitcher (b. 20 Dec 1899 Ida Grove IA–d. 19 Oct 1986 Gainesville FL) Cremated. Buried Memorial Park Cemetery, St Petersburg FL.

Wally Pipp —15 Years Infielder (b. 17 Feb 1893 Chicago IL–d. 11 Jan 1965 at a nursing home in Grand Rapids MI) Lou Gehrig replaced Pipp in the Yankee lineup when he started his consecutive game streak. Pipp was a manufacturer's agent for Rockford Screw Products Company of Rockford IL. Died from a heart attack. Buried Woodlawn Cemetery, Grand Rapids MI.

Cotton Pippen —3 Years Pitcher (b. 2 Apr 1911 Cisco TX–d. 15 Feb 1981 Valley West Hospital, Williams CA) He lived in the San Francisco East Bay area 30 years before taking the job of caretaker and manager of the Capitol Outing Club near Colusa CA in 1978. Died from lung cancer. Buried Sierra View Cemetery, Marysville CA.

Jim Pirie —1 Year Infielder (b. 31 Mar 1853 Ontario, Canada–d. 2 Jun 1934 Dundas, Ontario, Canada).

Jake Pitler—2 Years Infielder (b. 22 Apr 1894 New York City NY–d. 3 Feb 1968 Binghamton General Hospital, Binghamton NY) He managed in the minor leagues and was a Dodger scout from 1947 to 1957. Buried Riverside Cemetery, Endicott NY.

Pinky Pittenger—7 Years Infielder (b. 24 Feb 1899 Hudson MI–d. 4 Nov 1977 Fort Lauderdale FL).

Togie Pittinger—8 Years Pitcher (b. 12 Jan 1872 Greencastle PA–d. 14 Jan 1909 at his mother's home in Greencastle PA) He operated a restaurant and grocery store in Carlisle PA for a short while. He became ill at the height of his baseball career and died two years later from diabetes. Buried Cedar Hill Cemetery, Greencastle PA.

Stan Pitula—1 Year Pitcher (b. 23 Mar 1931 Hackensack NJ–d. 15 Aug 1965 Hackensack NJ) Served in the U.S. Army. He was a machinist for a sheet metal company. Died from self-inflicted carbon monoxide poisoning, being despondent over a recent divorce. Buried Hackensack Cemetery, Hackensack NJ.

Herman Pitz—1 Year Catcher (b. 18 Jul 1865 Brooklyn NY–d. 3 Sep 1924 St Joseph Hospital, Far Rockaway NY) He was in the cafe business for 29 years in Brooklyn. Died following a stroke suffered four months earlier. Buried Evergreen Cemetery, Brooklyn NY.

Emil Planeta—1 Year Pitcher (b. 13 Jan 1909 Higganum CT–d. 2 Feb 1963 at his home in Rocky Hill CT) For 22 years he was a serviceman for P Ballantine and Sons in Wethersfield CT. Buried Rose Hill Memorial Park, Rocky Hill CT.

Eddie Plank—17 Years Pitcher Hall of Fame (b. 31 Aug 1875 Gettysburg PA–d. 24 Feb 1926 at his home in Gettysburg PA) He retired to his home in Gettysburg where he spent 11 inactive years. Died two days after suffering a stroke. Buried Evergreen Cemetery, Gettysburg PA.

Don Plarski—1 Year Outfielder (b. 9 Nov 1929 Chicago IL–d. 29 Dec 1981 Barnes Hospital, St Louis MO) He was the sports editor for the *Daily Interlake* at Kalispell MT until 1959 when he moved to the *Alton (IL) Telegraph*. There he was sports editor from 1962 until his death. Died after a long illness. Cremated.

Elmo Plaskett—2 Years Catcher (b. 27 Jun 1938 Frederiksted, Virgin Islands–d. 2 Nov 1998 Christianstad, Virgin Islands).

Whitey Platt—5 Years Outfielder (b. 21 Aug 1920 West Palm Beach FL–d. 27 Jul 1970 at his home in West Palm Beach FL) World War II veteran. Died from a sudden heart attack. Buried Hillcrest Memorial Park, West Palm Beach FL.

Al Platte—1 Year Outfielder (b. 13 Apr 1890 Grand Rapids MI–d. 29 Aug 1976 Michigan Veteran Hospital, Grand Rapids MI) World War I veteran. He played in the Western League, Three-I League, Southern Association and American Association. His last 12 years were spent as a patient at the veteran's facility. Buried Holy Trinity Cemetery, Grand Rapids MI.

Norman Plitt—2 Years Pitcher (b. 21 Feb 1893 York PA–d. 1 Feb 1954 New York City NY) He was connected with the Read-Standard Corporation in York. He was found dead from natural causes in a bed in his son's room at a Columbia University dormitory while visiting there. Buried Prospect Hill Cemetery, York PA.

Walter Plock—1 Year Outfielder (b. 2 Jul 1869 Philadelphia PA–d. 28 Apr 1900 Richmond VA) He worked for the Philadelphia police force for a time before taking a job as a construction worker. Killed while working on an elevated track in downtown Richmond when the crane and a steam engine fell from the track, killing or injuring several workers. It was his first day on the job. Buried Philadelphia PA.

Ray Poat—6 Years Pitcher (b. 19 Dec 1917 Chicago IL–d. 29 Apr 1990 at his home in Oak Lawn IL) He was a chemist at Corn Products, retiring in 1979. Buried Chapel Hill Gardens South, Worth IL.

Bud Podbielan—9 Years Pitcher (b. 6 Mar 1924 Curlew WA–d. 26 Oct 1982 Veteran's Hospital, Syracuse NY) World War II veteran. Died after a long illness. Buried St Mary's Cemetery, Syracuse NY.

Johnny Podgajny—5 Years Pitcher (b. 10 Jun 1920 Chester PA–d. 2 Mar 1971 Sacred Heart Hospital, Chester PA) He switched from job to job, sometimes working in sales, and at one time worked in a steel plant. Died from a heart attack. Buried St Francis of De Sales Cemetery, Lenni PA.

Joe Poetz—1 Year Pitcher (b. 30 Nov 1895 St Louis MO–d. 7 Feb 1942 St Louis MO) He played in the Piedmont League and International League. Died from heart disease. Buried SS Peter and Paul Cemetery, St Louis MO.

Jimmy Pofahl—3 Years Infielder (b. 18 Jun 1917 Faribault MN–d. 14 Sep 1984 Owatonna City Hospital, Owatonna MN) He was a partner in Gopher Athletic Company. Buried Maple Lawn Cemetery, Faribault MN.

Jennings Poindexter—2 Years Pitcher (b. 30 Sep 1910 Pauls Valley OK–d. 3 Mar 1983 Municipal Hospital, Norman OK) Buried Mount Olivet Cemetery, Pauls Valley OK.

Hugh Poland—5 Years Catcher (b. 19 Jan 1910 Tompkinsville KY–d. 30 Mar 1984 at his home in Guthrie KY) World War II veteran. He was a five term member of the Western Kentucky University Board of Regents and an executive for the San Francisco Giants. Died from a heart attack. Buried Guthrie Highland Cemetery, Guthrie KY.

Lou Polchow—1 Year Pitcher (b. 14 Mar 1881 Mankato MN–d. 15 Aug 1912 Good Thunder MN) He was a barber. Died from Bright's disease. Buried Mankato MN.

Mark Polhemus—1 Year Outfielder (b. 4 Oct 1860 Brooklyn NY–d. 12 Nov 1923 Lynn Hospital, Lynn MA) He was an inspector in the meter department for General Electric at Lynn. Died from a heart attack suffered while attending a boxing match. Buried New York City NY.

Gus Polidar—7 Years Infielder (b. 26 Oct 1961 Caracas, Venezuela–d. 28 Apr 1995 Caracas, Venezuela) He was murdered by drug dealers.

Ken Polivka—1 Year Pitcher (b. 21 Jan 1921 Chicago IL–d. 23 Jul 1988 Copley Memorial Hospital, Aurora IL) Served in the South Pacific for the U.S. Navy during World War II. He retired from Zenith Corporation and worked part-time for Strictly Golf in Naperville IL. Buried SS Peter and Paul Cemetery, Naperville IL.

Howie Pollet—14 Years Pitcher (b. 26 Jun 1921 New Orleans LA–d. 8 Aug 1974 at a hospital in Houston TX) Served in the U.S. Army Air Force during World War II. He was a pitching coach for the Cardinals and Astros, and was engaged in the insurance business in Houston for 24 years. Died after a lengthy illness.

Nick Polly—2 Years Infielder (b. 18 Apr 1917 Chicago IL–d. 17 Jan 1993 Chicago IL).

John Pomorski—1 Year Pitcher (b. 30 Dec 1905 Brooklyn NY–d. 6 Dec 1977 Brampton, Ontario, Canada).

Arlie Pond—4 Years Pitcher (b. 19 Jan 1872 Rutland VT–d. 19 Sep 1930 Cebu, Philippines) A medical doctor, he served in the U.S. Army during the Spanish-American War. After the war he stayed in the Philippines, devoting the rest of his life, except for a short time during World War I when he was Assistant Surgeon General of the U.S. Army with the rank of Colonel, to combating disease there.

Ralph Pond—1 Year Outfielder (b. 4 May 1888 Eau Claire WI–d. 8 Sep 1947 at his home in Cleveland OH) He worked for Allied Products Company until about 1922 when he formed his own road construction company. Died from a heart attack. Cremated.

Elmer Ponder—4 Years Pitcher (b. 26 Jun 1893 Reed OK–d. 20 Apr 1974 at a hospital in Albuquerque NM) World War I veteran. He lived his last 34 years in Albuquerque where he was an independent automobile dealer, and was involved in real estate financing and insurance. Buried Fairview Memorial Park, Albuquerque NM.

Harlin Pool—2 Years Outfielder (b. 12 Mar 1908 Lakeport CA–d. 15 Feb 1963 at his home in Rodeo CA) Buried Golden Gate National Cemetery, San Bruno CA.

Ed Poole—5 Years Pitcher (b. 7 Sep 1873 Canton OH–d. 11 Mar 1920 at his home in Malvern OH) He was a merchant. Died from diabetes mellitus. Buried Bethlehem Cemetery, Malvern OH.

Jim Poole—3 Years Infielder (b. 12 May 1895 Taylorsville NC–d. 2 Jan 1975 at his home in Hickory NC) He and a former umpire conducted clinics for players and umpires in Newton NC. Died unexpectedly. Buried Linney's Grove Church Cemetery, Hiddenite NC.

Tom Poorman—6 Years Outfielder (b. 14 Oct 1857 Lock Haven PA–d. 18 Feb 1905 at his sister's home in Lock Haven PA) He engaged in the dry goods business in Cortland NY before becoming ill. Died from consumption after suffering for more than a year. Buried Highland Cemetery, Lock Haven PA.

Dave Pope—4 Years Outfielder (b. 17 Jun 1925 Talladaga AL–d. 28 Aug 1999 Cleveland OH) Buried Lake View Cemetery, Cleveland OH.

Bill Popp—1 Year Pitcher (b. 7 Jun 1877 St Louis MO–d. 5 Sep 1909 St Louis MO) Buried Calvary Cemetery, St Louis MO.

Ed Porray—1 Year Pitcher (b. 15 Dec 1888 Brooklyn NY–d. 13 Jul 1954 Lackawaxen PA).

Dick Porter—6 Years Outfielder (b. 30 Dec 1901 Allen MD–d. 24 Sep 1974 Veteran's Hospital, Philadelphia PA) Served as a chief in the U.S. Coast Guard during World War II. He managed minor league baseball and later was a sports promotion director for Scott and Grauer, a Philadelphia beer distributor, retiring in 1971. Buried Asbury Methodist Church Cemetery, Allen MD.

Henry Porter—6 Years Pitcher (b. 1861 Vergennes VT–d. 30 Dec 1906 at his home in Brockton MA) He worked in a shoe factory in Brockton. Died after an illness of long duration. Buried Calvary Cemetery, Brockton MA.

Irv Porter—1 Year Outfielder (b. 17 May 1888 Lynn MA–d. 19 Feb 1971 Lynn Hospital, Lynn MA) He was a clerical worker in the Everett plant of General Electric, retiring in 1955. Died after a brief illness. Buried St Joseph Cemetery, Lynn MA.

Jim Porter—1 Year Pitcher (b. 24 Jul 1877 Borden IN–d. 3 May 1903 at his home near Borden IN) Died from lung trouble. Buried Pleasant Ridge Cemetery, Borden IN.

Ned Porter—2 Years Pitcher (b. 6 May 1905 Apalachicola FL–d. 30 Jun 1968 University Hospital, Gainesville FL) He was executive personnel manager for St Joe Paper Company. Died from injuries suffered in a boating accident two weeks earlier. Buried Magnolia Cemetery, Apalachicola FL.

Bob Porterfield—12 Years Pitcher (b. 10 Aug 1923 Newport VA–d. 28 Apr 1980 Presbyterian Hospital, Charlotte NC) Served in the U.S. Army during World War II. For eight years he was a welder for Westinghouse Corporation. Died from lymphoma. Buried Sharon Memorial Park, Charlotte NC.

Arnie Portocarrero—7 Years Pitcher (b. 5 Jul 1931 New York City NY–d. 21 Jul 1986 Kansas City KS) Cremated.

Bill Posedel—5 Years Pitcher (b. 2 Aug 1906 San Francisco CA–d. 28 Nov 1989 V A Hospital, Livermore CA) World War II veteran. He spent 38 years in organized baseball, working as pitching coach for seven big league teams and retiring in 1974. Died following a long battle with colon cancer and was confined to a wheel chair his last few years. Cremated and his ashes scattered at sea.

Lou Possehl—5 Years Pitcher (b. 12 Apr 1926 Chicago IL–d. 7 Oct 1997 Sarasota FL).

Lew Post—1 Year Outfielder (b. 12 Apr 1875 Hastings MI–d. 21 Aug 1944 Chicago IL) Buried All Saints Cemetery, Des Plaines IL.

Sam Post—1 Year Infielder (b. 17 Nov 1896 Richmond VA–d. 31 Mar 1971 Portsmouth VA) Buried Oak Grove Cemetery, Portsmouth VA.

Wally Post—15 Years Outfielder (b. 9 Jul 1929 St Wendelin OH–d. 6 Jan 1982 at the home of a son in St Henry OH) He was an executive for the Minster Canning Company in Minster OH. Died from cancer. Buried St Henry Catholic Cemetery, St Henry OH.

Nellie Pott—1 Year Pitcher (b. 16 Jul 1899 Cincinnati OH–d. 3 Dec 1963 Cincinnati OH) He was a salesman for Niser Ice Cream Company. Buried Baltimore Pike Cemetery, Cincinnati OH.

Nels Potter—12 Years Pitcher (b. 23 Aug 1911 Mount Morris IL–d. 30 Sep 1990 at his home in Mount Morris IL) He owned and operated Town and Country Lanes in Mount Morris and was a township supervisor for 13 years. Died from a heart attack. Buried Oakwood Cemetery, Mount Morris IL.

Squire Potter—1 Year Pitcher (b. 18 Mar 1902 Flatwoods KY–d. 27 Jan 1983 at his home in Ashland KY) Died following an extended illness. Buried Bellefonte Memorial Gardens, Flatwoods KY.

John Potts—1 Year Outfielder (b. 6 Feb 1887 Tipp City OH–d. 5 Sep 1962 Hanna House Hospital, Cleveland OH) Served as a naval aviator during World War I. A lawyer, he was secretary and legal counsel for W F Ryan Corporation. Died from cancer.

Bill Pounds—1 Year Pitcher (b. 11 Mar 1878 Paterson NJ–d. 7 Jul 1936 General Hospital, Paterson NJ) He was a beer merchant. Died from cancer of the tongue. Buried Laurel Grove Memorial Park, Totowa NJ.

Shirley Povich—Hall of Fame (b. 15 Jul 1905

Bar Harbor ME–d. 4 Jun 1998 at his home in Washington DC) He was sports editor for the *Washington Post* for 74 years, during which time he wrote some 15000 articles. Died from a heart attack. Buried Elesavetrograd Cemetery, Washington DC.

Abner Powell—2 Years Outfielder (b. 15 Dec 1860 Shenandoah PA–d. 7 Aug 1953 Baptist Hospital, New Orleans LA) He worked over 40 years in baseball as a player, manager and owner. At one time he owned four teams in the Southern Association at the same time. Known as the originator of rain checks and lady's day, he retired about 1920. Died from a heart attack. Buried Hope Mausoleum, New Orleans LA.

Bill Powell—4 Years Pitcher (b. 8 May 1885 Grafton WV–d. 28 Sep 1967 City Hospital, East Liverpool OH) He threw the first strike at Pittsburgh's Forbes Field. He was a real estate broker. Buried Columbiana County Memorial Park, East Liverpool OH.

Grover Powell—1 Year Pitcher (b. 10 Oct 1940 Sayre PA–d. 21 May 1985 Raleigh NC) He was a salesman for Johnson-Lambe Sporting Goods and for ten years was a branch manager for First Citizens Bank and Trust in Raleigh. Died from leukemia. Buried Camptown Cemetery, Wyomissing PA.

Jack Powell—16 Years Pitcher (b. 9 Jul 1874 Bloomington IL–d. 17 Oct 1944 Chicago IL) Buried Mount Carmel Cemetery, Hillside IL.

Jack Powell—1 Year Pitcher (b. 17 Aug 1891 Holcomb MO–d. 12 Mar 1930 St Joseph's Hospital, Memphis TN) Died suddenly when he choked on a piece of steak. Buried Memphis National Cemetery, Memphis TN.

Jake Powell—11 Years Outfielder (b. 15 Jul 1908 Silver Spring MD–d. 4 Nov 1948 Washington DC) Died from a self-inflicted gunshot wound to the head while being interrogated by police about a bad check charge. Buried St John's Cemetery, Forest Glen MD.

Martin Powell—5 Years Infielder (b. 25 Mar 1856 Fitchburg MA–d. 5 Feb 1888 Fitchburg MA) He worked in the wood and coal business with his brother in Fitchburg. Died from complications of malaria. Buried St Bernard's Church Cemetery, Fitchburg MA.

Ray Powell—9 Years Outfielder (b. 20 Nov 1888 Siloam Springs AR–d. 16 Oct 1962 at a hospital in Chillicothe MO) He worked in baseball 40 years, scouting for several teams until retiring in 1950. Died from a respiratory ailment. Buried Mount Zion Cemetery, Bogard MO.

Willie Powell—9 Years Pitcher (b. 30 Oct 1903 Eutah AL–d. 16 May 1987 Three Rivers Manor, Three Rivers MI) He played in the negro leagues and worked 30 years for a Chicago tannery. Buried Parkville Cemetery, Three Rivers MI.

Tom Power—1 Year Infielder (b. abt 1868 San Francisco CA–d. 25 Feb 1898 at his home in San Francisco CA) Died at the height of his career from consumption. Buried Holy Cross Catholic Cemetery, Colma CA.

Ike Powers—2 Years Pitcher (b. 13 Mar 1906 Hancock MD–d. 22 Dec 1968 War Memorial Hospital, Hancock MD) He worked for the Pennsylvania Glass Sand Corporation. Buried Hancock Methodist Church Cemetery, Hancock MD.

Jim Powers—1 Year Pitcher (b. 1868 New York City NY–d. 13 Feb 1943 New York City NY).

Les Powers—2 Years Infielder (b. 5 Nov 1909 Seattle WA–d. 13 Nov 1978 St John's Hospital, Santa Monica CA) He was a teacher in the Santa Monica public schools for 30 years. Died from complications of Parkinson's disease. Buried Holy Cross Cemetery, Culver City CA.

Mike Powers—2 Years Outfielder (b. 2 Mar 1906 Crestwood KY–d. 2 Dec 1983 Hillcreek Manor Nursing Home, Louisville KY) He played baseball for 20 years, including time in the American Association, Southern League and Pacific Coast League. He managed a Southern States seed store. Buried Floydsburg Cemetery, Crestwood KY.

Mike Powers—11 Years Catcher (b. 22 Sep 1870 Pittsfield MA–d. 26 Apr 1909 Northwestern Hospital, Philadelphia PA) He was a medical doctor. Died from heart failure following surgery to relieve a bowell obstruction. Buried New Cathedral Cemetery, Philadelphia PA.

Pat Powers—2 Years Manager (b. 27 Jun 1860 Trenton NJ–d. 29 Aug 1925 Belmar NJ) He promoted sporting events in the Jersey City NJ area. Died from an infection caused by a carbuncle. Buried St Mary's Cemetery, Trenton NJ.

Phil Powers—7 Years Catcher (b. 26 Jul 1854

New York City NY–d. 22 Dec 1914 at his home in New York City NY) Buried Raymond Hill Cemetery, Pleasantville NY.

Johnny Pramesa—4 Years Catcher (b. 28 Aug 1925 Barton OH–d. 9 Sep 1996 Los Angeles CA).

Al Pratt—2 Years Manager (b. 19 Nov 1848 Pittsburgh PA–d. 21 Nov 1937 at his home in Pittsburgh PA) Served in the Civil War. He managed Pittsburgh's first major league team.

Del Pratt—13 Years Infielder (b. 10 Jan 1888 Walhalla SC–d. 30 Sep 1977 Abbe Nursing Home, Texas City TX) He managed minor league baseball until 1935 when he retired to live in Galveston TX. Cremated.

Frank Pratt—1 Game Pinch Hitter (b. 24 Aug 1897 Blocton AL–d. 8 Apr 1974 Bibb County Nursing Home, Centreville AL) For 17 years he was superintendent of the Bibb County, AL, school system. Buried Pineland Memorial Park, Centreville AL.

Larry Pratt—2 Years Catcher (b. 8 Oct 1887 Gibson City IL–d. 8 Jan 1969 Peoria IL).

Tom Pratt—1 Year Manager (b. 1844 Worcester MA–d. 28 Sep 1908 Philadelphia PA).

Mel Preibisch—2 Years Outfielder (b. 23 Nov 1914 Sealy TX–d. 12 Apr 1980 at a hospital in Dallas TX) He owned and operated the Preibisch Furniture Store in Sealy for many years. Died following a heart attack. Buried Sealy Cemetery, Sealy TX.

Jim Prendergast—1 Year Pitcher (b. 23 Aug 1917 Brooklyn NY–d. 23 Aug 1994 at his home in Amherst NY) Served in Europe for the U.S. Army during World War II. He worked in sales for a number of brewing companies including William Simon Brewery, Carling Brewing Co and Ballantine Brewing Co, retiring in the mid 1970s. He then went into real estate, founding Parade of Homes Realty Company. Active in civic affairs, he served a term as a city supervisor and a term as a state representative. Died after a long illness. Buried Mount Olivet Cemetery, Buffalo NY.

Mike Prendergast—6 Years Pitcher (b. 15 Dec 1888 Arlington IL–d. 18 Nov 1967 Omaha NE) Buried Calvary Cemetery, Omaha NE.

George Prentiss—2 Years Pitcher (b. 10 Jun 1876 Wilmington DE–d. 8 Sep 1902 Wilmington DE) Died from typhoid fever.

Tot Pressnell—5 Years Pitcher (b. 8 Aug 1906 Findlay OH–d. 6 Jan 2001 at his home in Findlay OH).

Jackie Price—1 Year Infielder (b. 13 Nov 1912 Winborn MS–d. 2 Oct 1967 San Francisco CA) World War II veteran. For seven years he was a bartender at the J and J Bar in San Francisco. He hung himself when he was intoxicated. Cremated.

Jim Price—1 Year Manager (b. 1847 New York City NY–d. 6 Oct 1931 Chicago IL).

Joe Price—1 Year Outfielder (b. 10 Apr 1897 Milligan College TN–d. 15 Jan 1961 George Washington Univ Hosp, Washington DC) He was president of Watauga Oil Company in Johnson City TN and a prominent Democratic Party leader. Died from a heart ailment. Buried Monte Vista Burial Park, Johnson City TN.

Bob Prichard—1 Year Infielder (b. 21 Oct 1917 Paris TX–d. 25 Sep 1991 at a hospital in Abilene TX) He owned and operated a radio station in Stamford TX from 1958 until his death and was mayor of Stamford from 1983 to 1989. Buried Highland Memorial Cemetery, Stamford TX.

Gerry Priddy—11 Years Infielder (b. 9 Nov 1919 Los Angeles CA–d. 3 Mar 1980 at his home in Studio City CA) For six years he was in executive sales for a plastic tubing manufacturer. Died from heart disease. Buried Holy Cross Cemetery, Culver City CA.

Johnnie Priest—2 Years Infielder (b. 23 Jun 1886 St Joseph MO–d. 5 Nov 1979 Washington DC) Buried Oakwood Cemetery, Falls Church VA.

Ray Prim—6 Years Pitcher (b. 30 Dec 1906 Salitpa AL–d. 29 Apr 1995 Sebastopol Convalescent Hosp, Sebastopol CA) Died from lung cancer. Buried Calvary Cemetery, Los Angeles CA.

Bob Prince—Hall of Fame (b. abt 1916–d. 10 Jun 1985 Presbyterian-University Hosp, Pittsburgh PA) He was the broadcaster for the Pittsburgh Pirates from 1948 to 1975. Died from pneumonia a month after surgery for throat cancer. Cremated. Buried Westminster Presbyterian Church, Upper St Clair PA.

Walter Prince—2 Years Infielder (b. 9 May 1861 Amherst NH–d. 2 Mar 1938 Bristol NH)

For 25 years he was the general foundry superintendent for the International Steam Pump Company. Died after a lingering illness. Buried Homeland Cemetery, Bristol NH.

Red Proctor—1 Year Pitcher (b. 27 Oct 1900 Williamsburg VA–d. 17 Dec 1954 at his home in Williamsburg VA) He was a painter. He lived in Richmond eight years and had just returned to live in his hometown. Buried Cedar Grove Cemetery, Williamsburg VA.

George Proeser—2 Years Outfielder (b. 30 May 1864 Cincinnati OH–d. 14 Oct 1941 New Burlington OH) He was a farmer. Died from chronic heart disease. Buried Spring Grove Cemetery, Cincinnati OH.

Jake Propst—1 Game Pinch Hitter (b. 10 Mar 1895 Kennedy AL–d. 24 Feb 1967 at his doctor's office in Columbus MS) He raised cattle and timber and served as mayor of Columbus from 1934 to 1935, 1953 to 1957 and 1961 to 1965. Served overseas in the U.S. Army during World War I.From 1940 to 1944 he was also county sheriff. Died from a heart attack. Buried Friendship Cemetery, Columbus MS.

Doc Prothro—5 Years Infielder 3 Years Manager (b. 16 Jul 1893 Memphis TN–d. 14 Oct 1971 Memphis TN) He was a dentist and the father of Tommy Prothro, the famous college and professional football coach. Buried Memorial Park Cemetery, Memphis TN.

Bill Prough—1 Year Pitcher (b. 28 Nov 1887 Markle IN–d. 29 Dec 1936 Indiana State Hospital, Richmond IN) Died following a two-week illness. Buried Hoverstock Cemetery, Zanesville IN.

Augie Prudhomme—1 Year Pitcher (b. 20 Nov 1902 Frierson LA–d. 4 Oct 1992 Shreveport LA).

Gibby Pruess—1 Year Outfielder (b. 2 Apr 1895 Chicago IL–d. 28 Aug 1979 Chicago IL) Buried Irving Park Cemetery, Chicago IL.

Hub Pruett—7 Years Pitcher (b. 1 Sep 1900 Malden MO–d. 28 Jan 1982 at his home in Ladue MO) Known for his ability to strike out Babe Ruth, Ruth fanned 10 of the first 13 times he faced Pruett, and was only 4 for 30 when Pruett was pitching, striking out 15 times. He became a doctor, and was a general practitioner from 1932 until 1972. Died from cancer. Buried Bellefontaine Cemetery, St Louis MO.

Tex Pruiett—2 Years Pitcher (b. 10 Apr 1883 Osgood IN–d. 6 Feb 1953 at his home in Ojai CA) He worked for Tidewater Oil Company. Died from heart disease. Cremated.

George Puccinelli—4 Years Outfielder (b. 22 Jun 1907 San Francisco CA–d. 16 Apr 1956 San Francisco CA) He operated a television shop in San Francisco. Died from a heart attack while golfing at Harding Park. Buried Holy Cross Catholic Cemetery, Colma CA.

Troy Puckett—1 Year Pitcher (b. 10 Dec 1889 Winchester IN–d. 13 Apr 1971 Randolph Nursing Home, Winchester IN) He operated Puckett's Dairy in Randolph County, IN, for a number of years and was a highly decorated Mason. Buried Fountain Park Cemetery, Winchester IN.

John Puhl—2 Years Infielder (b. 1875 Bayonne NJ–d. 24 Aug 1900 at his home in Bayonne NJ).

Harry Clay Pulliam—(b. 8 Feb 1868 Scottsville KY–d. 23 Jul 1909 New York City NY) Starting as a laborer in a raisin packing plant in Fresno CA, he became a baseball writer in Louisville KY and eventually president of the National League. Died the morning following a self-inflicted gunshot wound to the head. Buried Cave Hill Cemetery, Louisville KY.

Spence Pumpelly—1 Year Pitcher (b. 11 Apr 1893 Owego NY–d. 5 Dec 1973 Sayre PA).

Blondie Purcell—12 Years Outfielder 1 Year Manager (b. 16 Mar 1854 Paterson NJ–d. 20 Feb 1912 Trenton NJ) He was a retired cabinet maker. Died from acute peritonotis caused by a bowell obstruction. Buried Greenmount Cemetery, Philadelphia PA.

Pid Purdy—4 Years Outfielder (b. 15 Jun 1904 Beatrice NE–d. 16 Jan 1951 Ingleside State Hospital near Hastings NE) He played professional football for the Green Bay Packers before playing baseball. He did odd jobs, but battled alcoholism his entire life. Died from a heart attack. Buried Evergreen Home Cemetery, Beatrice NE.

Jesse Purnell—1 Year Infielder (b. 11 May 1879 Glenside PA–d. 4 Jul 1966 Philadelphia PA) Buried Oakland Cemetery, Philadelphia PA.

Billy Purtell—5 Years Infielder (b. 6 Jan 1886 Columbus OH–d. 17 Mar 1962 at a rest home in Bradenton FL) He managed and coached in the minor leagues before he was a landscape engineer for the State of Ohio for ten years. Buried Mansion Memorial Park, Ellenton FL.

Ambrose Puttmann—4 Years Pitcher (b. 9 Sep 1880 Cincinnati OH–d. 21 Jun 1936 Jamaica NY) He operated a shoe store in Cincinnati for 17 years, retiring in 1930. After that he was a clerk in a state liquor store. Died from a heart attack while on a vacation in New York. Buried St Joseph Old Catholic Cemetery, Cincinnati OH.

Harlan Pyle—1 Year Pitcher (b. 29 Nov 1905 Burchard NE–d. 13 Jan 1993 Good Samaritan Center, Beatrice NE) He farmed near Burchard ten years, owned and operated a grocery store in Liberty NE 13 years, and was a meat cutter in Wymore NE 13 years before retiring in 1980. Buried Liberty Cemetery, Liberty NE.

Shadow Pyle—2 Years Pitcher (b. 30 Oct 1861 Reading PA–d. 26 Dec 1908 at his home in Reading PA) Believed to have died from internal hemorrhages, he was found dead in his bed. He had been ill for some time. Buried Charles Evans Cemetery, Reading PA.

Frankie Pytlak—12 Years Catcher (b. 30 Jul 1908 Buffalo NY–d. 8 May 1977 Millard Fillmore Hospital, Buffalo NY) Served in the U.S. Navy during World War II. He coached high school baseball and worked at a sporting goods store. Died after a three-month illness. Buried St Stanislaus Cemetery, Buffalo NY.

Q

Bill Quarles—2 Years Pitcher (b. 1869 Petersburg VA–d. 25 Mar 1897 at his home in Petersburg VA) Died suddenly, at the height of his baseball career, a week following a delicate surgery. Buried Blandford Cemetery, Petersburg VA.

Mel Queen—8 Years Pitcher (b. 4 Mar 1918 Maxwell PA–d. 4 Apr 1982 Fort Smith AR).

George Quellich—1 Year Outfielder (b. 10 Feb 1906 Johnsville CA–d. 31 Aug 1958 near Johnsville CA) For 29 years he was a police officer in the Traffic Division of the Oakland CA Police Department, retiring earlier in 1958 due to a heart condition. Killed when his jeep overturned, plunging 400 feet, on a mountain trail while he was prospecting. Cremated. Buried Chapel of the Chimes, Oakland CA.

Joe Quest—9 Years Infielder (b. 16 Nov 1852 New Castle PA–d. 14 Nov 1924 San Diego CA) He umpired in the National League in 1886 and 1887.

Ed Quick—1 Year Pitcher (b. Baltimore MD–d. 19 Jun 1913 in his room at Rocky Ford CO) He was pitching for the Rocky Ford minor league team when he died in his room in the Gobin block after an illness of short duration.

Jim Quick—1 Year Infielder (b. 14 Oct 1917 Rome, Italy–d. 9 Mar 1974 Castle Haven Convalescent Ctr, Swansea IL) He retired as a lieutenant colonel from the U.S. Air Force after serving 25 years, including World War II, the Korean War and the Vietnam War. He received Bronze Stars in both World War II and the Vietnam War. Died from emphysema and a heart ailment. Buried Leavenworth National Cemetery, Leavenworth KS.

Lee Quillin—2 Years Infielder (b. 5 May 1882 North Branch MN–d. 14 Mar 1965 St Paul MN) Buried Oakland Cemetery, St Paul MN.

Finners Quinlan—2 Years Outfielder (b. 21 Oct 1887 Scranton PA–d. 17 Feb 1966 Mercy Heights Hospital, Scranton PA) Serving for the U.S. Army during World War I, he was injured in France and unable to continue his baseball career. He turned to politics and held several Lackawanna County (PA) and Scranton City offices including County Commissioner, Registrar of Wills and City Council. Died after ailing four months. Buried St Catherine's Cemetery, Moscow PA.

Frank Quinlan—1 Year Outfielder (b. 9 Mar 1869 Marlboro MA–d. 4 May 1904 in his room at City Hotel in Brockton MA) He worked as a laster at a shoe factory. Died from heart failure. Buried Immaculate Conception Cemetery, Marlboro MA.

Frank Quinn—1 Year Outfielder (b. Grand Rapids MI–d. 17 Feb 1920 Camden IN).

Frank Quinn—2 Years Pitcher (b. 27 Nov 1927 Springfield MA–d. 11 Jan 1993 Boynton Beach FL).

Jack Quinn—23 Years Pitcher (b. 5 Jul 1883 Jeanesville PA–d. 17 Apr 1946 Good Samaritan Hospital, Pottsville PA) He played minor league baseball until he was age 51. Died from a liver infection. Buried Charles Baber Cemetery, Pottsville PA.

Joe Quinn—1 Year Outfielder (b. 1851 Chicago IL–d. 2 Jan 1909 Chicago IL) Buried Calvary Cemetery, Evanston IL.

Joe Quinn—17 Years Infielder 2 Years Manager (b. 25 Dec 1864 Sydney, Australia–d. 12 Nov 1940 Alexian Brothers' Hospital, St Louis MO) He owned and operated a funeral home the last 45 years of his life. Died from hardening of the arteries. Buried Calvary Cemetery, St Louis MO.

John Quinn—1 Year Catcher (b. 12 Sep 1885 Framingham MA–d. 9 Apr 1956 Marlboro Hospital, Marlboro MA) He worked as an engineer for the Framingham Hat Co, retiring in 1955. Died after suffering a heart attack. Buried St Mary's Cemetery, Mansfield MA.

Robert Quinn—(b. 14 Feb 1870 Anderson IN–d. 12 Mar 1954 at a hospital in Providence RI) He was owner of the Red Sox, and general manager for the Boston Bees (later Braves), Browns and Dodgers. Died from the effects of a stroke. Buried St Joseph Cemetery, Lockbourne OH.

Tad Quinn—2 Years Pitcher (b. 21 Sep 1882 Torrington CT–d. 6 Aug 1946 St Mary's Hospital, Waterbury CT) For 35 years he was a cost accountant for the Chase Brass and Copper Company. Buried Hillside Cemetery, Torrington CT.

Tom Quinn—3 Years Catcher (b. 25 Apr 1864 Pittsburgh PA–d. 24 Jul 1932 at his home in Swissvale PA) He worked in the Department of Factory Inspection for the State of Pennsylvania. Died from septic poisoning. Buried Braddock Catholic Cemetery, Pittsburgh PA.

Wimpy Quinn—1 Year Pitcher (b. 14 May 1918 Birmingham AL–d. 1 Sep 1954 V A Hospital, Los Angeles CA) World War II veteran. Died from cancer. Buried Woodlawn Cemetery, Santa Monica CA.

Dan Quisenberry—12 Years Pitcher (b. 7 Feb 1953 Santa Monica CA–d. 30 Sep 1998 at his home in Leawood KS) A published poet, he was also known for his charitable activities. Died from a malignant brain tumor.

R

Joe Rabbitt—1 Year Outfielder (b. 15 Jan 1901 Frontenac KS–d. 5 Dec 1969 Norwalk Hospital, Norwalk CT) He retired from the Hat Corporation of America in 1968. Died after a short illness. Buried St John's Cemetery, Norwalk CT.

George Radbourn—1 Year Pitcher (b. 8 Apr 1856 Bloomington IL–d. 1 Jan 1904 at his home in Bloomington IL) He was a deputy sheriff for a short while before engaging in cigar making. Died from dropsy. Buried Evergreen Memorial Cemetery, Bloomington IL.

Old Hoss Radbourn—12 Years Pitcher Hall of Fame (b. 11 Dec 1854 Rochester NY–d. 5 Feb 1897 at his home in Bloomington IL) He lost an eye in a gun shot accident two years before he died from convulsions and paralysis brought on by syphilis. Buried Evergreen Memorial Cemetery, Bloomington IL.

Alec Radcliff—16 Years Infielder (b. 26 Jul 1905 Mobile AL–d. 18 Jul 1983 Chicago IL) He played in the negro leagues.

Rip Radcliff—10 Years Outfielder (b. 19 Jan 1906 Kiowa OK–d. 23 May 1962 at his home in Enid OK) Served in the U.S. Navy during World

War II. He worked for Western Bridge and Supply Company in Enid before moving to the Bert Smith Road Machinery Company there. Died from a heart attack after being ill for some time. Buried Memorial Park Cemetery, Enid OK.

Roy Radebaugh—1 Year Pitcher (b. 22 Feb 1884 Champaign IL–d. 17 Jan 1945 in a hospital in Cedar Rapids IA) He was a deputy sheriff for Linn County, IA, for 22 years. Died from a heart ailment after an illness of seven days. Buried Linwood Cemetery, Cedar Rapids IA.

Don Rader—2 Years Infielder (b. 5 Sep 1893 Wolcott IN–d. 28 Jun 1983 at his home in Walla Walla WA) World War I veteran. He was a sales clerk at a hardware store prior to his retirement. Cremated.

Drew Rader—1 Year Pitcher (b. 14 May 1901 Elmira NY–d. 5 Jun 1975 Catskill NY).

Paul Radford—12 Years Outfielder (b. 14 Oct 1861 Roxbury MA–d. 21 Feb 1945 at his home in Hyde Park MA).

Jack Rafter—1 Year Catcher (b. 20 Feb 1875 Troy NY–d. 4 Jan 1943 Leonard Hospital, Troy NY) He worked 46 years for United Traction Company, first during the off-season as a conductor, then as an inspector before entering the claims department, retiring in 1942. Died after several month's illness. Buried St John's Cemetery, Troy NY.

Tom Raftery—1 Year Outfielder (b. 5 Oct 1881 Haverhill MA–d. 1 Jan 1955 Boston MA).

Pat Ragan—11 Years Pitcher (b. 15 Nov 1888 Blanchard IA–d. 4 Sep 1956 Briorwood Terr Sanitarium, Los Angeles CA) He was a security guard for an aircraft company. Died from kidney cancer. Buried Forest Lawn Memorial Park, Glendale CA.

Rip Ragan—1 Year Pitcher (b. 5 Jun 1878 Lincoln IL–d. 8 Jun 1953 at his home in Kansas City MO) A painter and decorator for the William Rockhill Nelson estate, he had lived in Kansas City since 1887. Buried Forest Hill Cemetery, Kansas City MO.

Frank Ragland—2 Years Pitcher (b. 26 May 1904 Water Valley MS–d. 28 Jul 1959 Paris MS).

Larry Raines—2 Years Infielder (b. 9 Mar 1930 St Albans WV–d. 28 Jan 1978 at a hospital in Lansing MI) He lived 15 years in Lansing. Buried Mount Hope Cemetery, Lansing MI.

John Rainey—2 Years Outfielder (b. 26 Jul 1864 Birmingham MI–d. 11 Nov 1912 at the home of a sister in Detroit MI) He worked for Swift Brothers meat packers in Chicago. Died from phthisis pulmonalis. Buried Birmingham Cemetery, Birmingham MI.

John Raleigh—2 Years Pitcher (b. 21 Apr 1890 Elkhorn WI–d. 24 Aug 1955 at his home in Escondido CA) He retired as part owner and operator of the Ontario Bowling Academy at Ontario CA in 1951, moving to Escondido. Died from a heart attack. Buried Oakhill Memorial Park, Escondido CA.

Doc Ralston—1 Year Outfielder (b. 3 Aug 1885 Pierpont OH–d. 29 Aug 1950 at his home in Lancaster PA) A noted amateur golfer, he practiced denistry in Pittsburgh PA 35 years and one year in Lancaster before he became ill. Died after an illness of one month. Cremated.

Pep Rambert—2 Years Pitcher (b. 1 Aug 1916 Cleveland OH–d. 16 Nov 1974 West Palm Beach FL) Buried Royal Palm Memorial Gardens, West Palm Beach FL.

Pete Rambo—1 Year Pitcher (b. 1 Nov 1906 Thorofare NJ–d. 19 Jun 1991 Cooper Medical Center, Camden NJ) He was a guard at the duPont Repauno Works in Gibbstown NJ. Buried Eglington Cemetery, Clarksboro NJ.

Chucho Ramos—1 Year Outfielder (b. 12 Apr 1918 Maturin, Venezuela–d. 2 Sep 1977 Caracas, Venezuela).

Willie Ramsdell—5 Years Pitcher (b. 4 Apr 1916 Williamsburg KS–d. 8 Oct 1969 Wesley Hospital, Wichita KS) Moving to Wichita in 1954, he was a salesman when his health permitted. Died following a long illness. Buried Kiowa Cemetery, Kiowa KS.

Toad Ramsey—6 Years Pitcher (b. 8 Aug 1864 Indianapolis IN–d. 27 Mar 1906 Deaconess Hospital, Indianapolis IN) Died from pneumonia. Buried Crown Hill Cemetery, Indianapolis IN.

Dick Rand—3 Years Catcher (b. 7 Mar 1931 South Gate CA–d. 22 Jan 1996 at his home in Moreno Valley CA) He drove a bus 27 years for the Los Angeles Rapid Transit District. Died from stage III lymphoma. Cremated and his ashes scattered at sea.

Newt Randall—1 Year Outfielder (b. 3 Feb

1880 New Lowell, Ontario, Canada–d. 3 May 1955 Duluth MN) He was a deputy sheriff at Hibbing MN. Buried Park Hill Cemetery, Duluth MN.

Earl Rapp—3 Years Outfielder (b. 20 May 1921 Corunna MI–d. 13 Feb 1992 Swedesboro NJ) Served in North Africa for the U.S. Army during World War II. Spent 50 years in baseball as a player and scout, scouting for the Astros, Royals, Expos and Reds, retiring in 1989. Buried St Joseph's Cemetery, Swedesboro NJ.

Goldie Rapp—3 Years Infielder (b. 6 Feb 1894 Cincinnati OH–d. 1 Jul 1966 Little Flower Haven, La Mesa CA) A retired chief petty officer in the U.S. Navy, he served in both World Wars I and II and lived in San Diego County, CA, 17 years. Died from a heart attack. Buried Fort Rosecrans National Cemetery, Point Loma CA.

Bill Rariden—12 Years Catcher (b. 5 Feb 1888 Bedford IN–d. 28 Aug 1942 Dunn Memorial Hospital, Bedford IN) A retired filling station operator in Bedford, he had been in failing health for years, but died from a heart attack. Buried Green Hill Cemetery, Bedford IN.

Vic Raschi—10 Years Pitcher (b. 28 Mar 1919 West Springfield MA–d. 14 Oct 1988 at his home in Groveland NY) He owned and operated Valley Liquor Store in Geneseo NY from the early 1960s until about 1983. Died from a heart attack. Cremated.

Henry Rasmussen—1 Year Pitcher (b. 18 Apr 1895 Chicago IL–d. 1 Jan 1949 Chicago IL) Buried All Saints Cemetery, Des Plaines IL.

Morrie Rath—6 Years Infielder (b. 25 Dec 1887 Mobeetie TX–d. 18 Nov 1945 Upper Darby PA) Died from a self-inflicted gunshot wound. Buried Arlington Cemetery, Drexel Hill PA.

Tommy Raub—2 Years Catcher (b. 1 Dec 1870 Raubsville PA–d. 16 Feb 1949 at his home in Phillipsburg NJ) He worked many years at the Standard Silk Mill in Phillipsburg, retiring in 1935. Died two days after suffering a stroke. Buried Fairmount Cemetery, Phillipsburg NJ.

Johnny Rawlings—12 Years Infielder (b. 17 Aug 1892 Bloomfield IA–d. 16 Oct 1972 Daniel Freeman Memorial Hosp, Inglewood CA) He worked 15 years in the ticket department at the Los Angeles Sports Center. Died from emphysema. Cremated.

Carl Ray—2 Years Pitcher (b. 31 Jan 1889 Danbury NC–d. 2 Apr 1970 Haven Nursing Home, Lexington NC) He was a former sheriff of Stokes County, NC. Buried Highland Memorial Park.

Farmer Ray—1 Year Pitcher (b. 17 Sep 1886 Fort Lyon CO–d. 11 Mar 1963 Hillcrest Haven Home, Electra TX) He was an oil well pumper for Texaco. Died from cerebral arteriosclerosis. Buried New Electra Cemetery, Electra TX.

Irv Ray—4 Years Infielder (b. 22 Jan 1864 Harrington ME–d. 21 Feb 1948 Harrington ME).

Fred Raymer—3 Years Infielder (b. 12 Nov 1875 Leavenworth KS–d. 11 Jun 1957 Lincoln Park Retreat, Los Angeles CA) World War I veteran. He owned and operated a resort. Died from heart disease. Cremated.

Bugs Raymond—6 Years Pitcher (b. 24 Feb 1882 Chicago IL–d. 7 Sep 1912 in his room in the Veley Hotel, Chicago IL) He was a pressman. Believed to have died from a combination of intoxication and hot weather. Buried Montrose Cemetery, Chicago IL.

Harry Raymond—5 Years Infielder (b. 20 Feb 1866 Utica NY–d. 21 Mar 1925 San Diego CA).

Lou Raymond—1 Year Infielder (b. 11 Dec 1894 Buffalo NY–d. 2 May 1979 Rochester NY) He was a policeman. Buried Holy Sepulchre Cemetery, Rochester NY.

George A Reach—(b. abt 1868–d. 7 Dec 1954 Methodist Hospital, Philadelphia PA). The president of the Reach Company, a sporting goods manufacturer, he introduced the cork-centered "lively" baseball in 1910 and invented the first boxing glove.

Jerry Reardon—1 Year Pitcher (b. 1866 St Louis MO–d. 25 Feb 1891 Hoosick Falls NY) Died at the height of his career from consumption.

Phil Reardon—1 Year Outfielder (b. 3 Oct 1883 Brooklyn NY–d. 28 Sep 1920 St Mary's Hospital, Brooklyn NY) He was associated with his father in the building materials business in Brooklyn. Died from pleurisy. Buried Holy Cross Cemetery, Brooklyn NY.

Bill Reccius—2 Years Manager (b. 1847 Frankfurt-on-Main, Germany–d. 25 Jan 1911 Norton Memorial Infirmary, Louisville KY) A machinist by trade, he had a toy and sporting goods business in Louisville KY, and conducted a store there after 1873. Died following surgery for intestinal trouble. Buried Cave Hill Cemetery, Louisville KY.

John Reccius—2 Years Outfielder (b. 7 Jun 1862 Louisville KY–d. 1 Sep 1930 at his home in Louisville KY) Although best known for his baseball activities around Louisville, he was also well known as a doll maker. He operated a doll store and doll hospital. Died from pneumonia that developed after a stroke. Buried Cave Hill Cemetery, Louisville KY.

Phil Reccius—8 Years Infielder (b. 7 Jun 1862 Louisville KY–d. 15 Feb 1903 Central KY Insane Asylum, Lakeland KY) Died as a result of an injury incurred nine years earlier when he was hit in the head by a batted ball, pressing a portion of his skull into his brain. Buried Cave Hill Cemetery, Louisville KY.

Phil Redding—2 Years Pitcher (b. 25 Jan 1890 Crystal Springs MS–d. 30 Mar 1929 at his home in Greenwood MS) He was a bookkeeper for the Humphrey Cotton Company in Greenwood. Died from pneumonia after being ill ten days. Buried Terry Cemetery, Terry MS.

Johnny Reder—1 Year Infielder (b. 24 Sep 1909 Lublin, Poland–d. 12 Apr 1990 Fall River MA) World War II veteran. Died from arteriosclerotic heart disease. Buried St Patrick's Cemetery, Fall River MA.

Buck Redfern—2 Years Infielder (b. 7 Apr 1902 Asheville NC–d. 8 Sep 1964 in a hospital in Asheville NC) Served in the U.S. Navy during World War II. For 25 years he was a salesman for Ideal Cement Company. Died following a brief illness. Buried Riverside Cemetery, Asheville NC.

Harry Redmond—1 Year Infielder (b. 13 Sep 1887 Cleveland OH–d. 10 Jul 1960 Deaconess Hospital, Cleveland OH) He was secretary-treasurer for 40 years for the George Redmond Company in Cleveland. Buried Holy Cross Cemetery, Cleveland OH.

Jack Redmond—1 Year Catcher (b. 3 Sep 1910 Florence AZ–d. 27 Jul 1968 Garland TX) Buried Mesa Cemetery, Mesa AZ.

Howie Reed—10 Years Pitcher (b. 21 Dec 1936 Dallas TX–d. 7 Dec 1984 at a hospital in Corpus Christi TX) He operated a cotton and grain farm near Mathis TX where he had lived the last nine years. Died from cancer. Buried Robstown Memorial Park, Robstown TX.

Milt Reed—4 Years Infielder (b. 4 Jul 1890 Atlanta GA–d. 27 Jul 1938 V A Hospital, Atlanta GA) Served in the U.S. Army during World War I. He was the wholesale representative for Hudson Motors in the Atlanta area. Died after a long illness. Buried Crest Lawn Memorial Park, Atlanta GA.

Ted Reed—1 Year Infielder (b. 18 Oct 1890 Beaver PA–d. 16 Feb 1959 at his home in Beaver PA) Served in the U.S. Army artillery during World War I. He was president of Standard Collapsible Tube Company of Rochester PA. Buried Beaver Cemetery, Beaver PA.

Nick Reeder—1 Year Infielder (b. 22 Mar 1867 Louisville KY–d. 26 Sep 1894 in his room at Louisville KY) Died from brain fever at the height of his career. Buried Cave Hill Cemetery, Louisville KY.

Stan Rees—1 Year Pitcher (b. 23 Feb 1899 Cynthiana KY–d. 29 Aug 1937 St Joseph's Hospital, Lexington KY) He was president of Wombwell Automotive Parts Company of Lexington. Died following a heart attack he suffered while playing baseball with friends. Buried Battle Grove Cemetery, Cynthiana KY.

Andy Reese—4 Years Outfielder (b. 7 Feb 1904 Tupelo MS–d. 10 Jan 1966 North Mississippi Community Hosp, Tupelo MS) He worked at the Gulf Ordinance Plant during World War II, then for several years in Memphis TN for Herb Sadler Distributing Company. When his health failed he was working for the Pennsylvania Tire Company plant in Tupelo. Died from cancer after being in failing health several months. Buried Glenwood Cemetery, Tupelo MS.

Jimmie Reese—3 Years Infielder (b. 1 Oct 1901 New York City NY–d. 13 Jul 1994 Santa Ana CA) He was a World War II veteran. He spent his entire life in baseball, coaching for the San Diego Padres in the Pacific Coast League until they became a National League team, then for the Angels until his death. Died from generalized arteriosclerosis and respiratory failure. Cremated. Buried Westwood Memorial Park, Los Angeles CA.

Pee Wee Reese—16 Years Infielder Hall of Fame (b. 23 Jul 1918 Ekron KY–d. 14 Aug 1999 at his home in Louisville KY) He coached for the Dodgers one year, then spent the next ten years as a radio/TV announcer. After that he did promotional work for the Hillerich and Bradsby bat company. He also owned and operated a bowling alley in Louisville. Died from lung cancer. Buried Resthaven Memorial Park, Louisville KY.

Bobby Reeves—6 Years Infielder (b. 24 Jun 1904 Hill City TN–d. 4 Jun 1993 at a hospital in Chattanooga TN) Served in the antiaircraft division of the U.S. Army in World War II. A lifelong resident of Chattanooga, he retired as a supervisor for the heating and air conditioning division of the Electric Power Board. Buried Chattanooga National Cemetery, Chattanooga TN.

Bill Regan—6 Years Infielder (b. 23 Jan 1899 Pittsburgh PA–d. 11 Jun 1968 Divine Providence Hospital, Pittsburgh PA) He worked 24 years for the Allegheny County, PA, police force. Buried Calvary Cemetery, Pittsburgh PA.

Joe Regan—1 Year Outfielder (b. 12 Jan 1872 Seymour CT–d. 18 Nov 1948 St Francis Hospital, Hartford CT) Served in the U.S. Army during World War I. An engineering consultant, he was associated 25 years with E Horton & Sons, Inc, machine tool manufacturers in Hartford. Retired in 1948 as their general manager and president. Buried St Francis Cemetery, Southington CT.

Mike Regan—3 Years Pitcher (b. 19 Nov 1887 Phoenix NY–d. 22 May 1961 V A Hospital, Albany NY) Served in the U.S. Army during World War I. He worked in the Oklahoma oil fields prior to and after his days as a ballplayer. Later he was a supervisor at the paint and pigment division of General Electric at Schenectady NY. He retired in 1948 after breaking a hip, and had been in declining health since then.

Tony Rego—2 Years Catcher (b. 31 Oct 1897 Wailuku HI–d. 6 Jan 1978 Tulsa OK) Served in the U.S. Navy during World War I. He owned and managed minor league baseball teams for a number of years before working eight years for Tulsa Video Theatres, a movie theatre chain. In the 1950s he owned a theatre at Boynton OK. Died following arterial surgery. Buried Calvary Cemetery, Tulsa OK.

Wally Rehg—7 Years Outfielder (b. 31 Aug 1888 Summerfield IL–d. 5 Apr 1946 Burbank CA).

Dick Reichle—2 Years Outfielder (b. 23 Nov 1896 Lincoln IL–d. 13 Jun 1967 St Louis MO) Died from cancer. Buried Resurrection Cemetery, St Louis MO.

Joe Reichler—Hall of Fame (b. 1915–d. 12 Dec 1988 Roslyn Heights NY) A sportswriter 22 years for the Associated Press until 1966, he then became the public relations director for the baseball commissioner's office for 12 years. He was the editor of *The Baseball Enclyclodedia* and a vice-president of Major League Productions until retiring in 1985. Died from cancer. Buried Kensico Cemetery, Valhalla NY.

Billy Reid—2 Years Infielder (b. 17 May 1857 London, Ontario, Canada–d. 26 Jun 1940 London, Ontario, Canada).

Earl Reid—1 Year Pitcher (b. 8 Jun 1913 Bangor AL–d. 11 May 1984 Cullman AL) Served in the U.S. Army during World War II. Retired from O'Neal Steel. Buried Holly Pond Cemetery, Holly Pond AL.

Bill Reidy—6 Years Pitcher (b. 9 Oct 1875 Cleveland OH–d. 14 Oct 1915 at his sister's home in Cleveland OH) He managed in the Pacific Coast League before working as a coach and scout for the Cleveland Naps (later Indians). Died from cirrhosis of the liver. Buried St John's Cemetery, Cleveland OH.

Duke Reilley—1 Year Outfielder (b. 25 Aug 1884 Chicago IL–d. 4 Mar 1968 at a nursing home in Indianapolis IN) He played baseball 24 years, most of them in the American Association. He then was a bartender before becoming ill. Died following a long illness. Buried Holy Cross Cemetery, Indianapolis IN.

Arch Reilly—1 Year Infielder (b. 17 Aug 1891 Alton IL–d. 29 Nov 1963 Columbus OH) He was president of Leckie Coal Sales Company, working 42 years for the company. Died from a heart attack at his office. Buried St Joseph Cemetery, Lockbourne OH.

Barney Reilly—1 Year Infielder (b. 7 Feb 1885 Brockton MA–d. 15 Nov 1934 at his home in St Joseph MO) He had a brilliant career as a criminal attorney in St Joseph and was active in the Democratic Party there. Died after an illness of two years. Buried Mount Olivet Cemetery, St Joseph MO.

Charlie Reilly—8 Years Infielder (b. 24 Jun 1855 New Brunswick NJ–d. 16 Dec 1937 Los Angeles CA) He managed minor league baseball, including the first Los Angeles team in the Pacific Coast League from 1901 to 1903. Buried Calvary Cemetery, Los Angeles CA.

Hal Reilly—1 Year Outfielder (b. 1 Apr 1894 Oshkosh WI–d. 24 Dec 1957 Chicago IL) He worked for the Cook County (IL) Treasurer's Office. Buried Holy Sepulchre Cemetery, Worth IL.

Josh Reilly—1 Year Infielder (b. 1868 San Francisco CA–d. 13 Jun 1938 San Francisco CA) Died from a heart attack. Buried Holy Cross Catholic Cemetery, Colma CA.

Long John Reilly—10 Years Infielder (b. 5 Oct 1858 Cincinnati OH–d. 31 May 1937 at his home in Cincinnati OH) He was a commercial artist. Died from heart disease. Buried Spring Grove Cemetery, Cincinnati OH.

Tom Reilly—3 Years Infielder (b. 3 Aug 1884 St Louis MO–d. 19 Oct 1918 New Orleans LA) He worked for the Godchaux Sugar Company in New Orleans. Died from pneumonia caused by influenza. Buried St Louis Cemetery # 3, New Orleans LA.

Art Reinhart—5 Years Pitcher (b. 29 May 1899 Ackley IA–d. 11 Nov 1946 at a hospital in Houston TX) World War I veteran. He worked for the Ajax Distribution Company. Died from cancer. Buried Oakwood Cemetery, Ackley IA.

Art Reinholz—1 Year Infielder (b. 27 Jan 1903 Detroit MI–d. 29 Dec 1980 New Port Richey FL) He was a retired employee of Chrysler Corporation. Buried Cadillac Memorial Gardens, Westland MI.

Charlie Reipschlager—5 Years Catcher (b. 11 Jun 1864 New York City NY–d. 19 Sep 1960 at a hospital in St Petersburg FL) For 49 years he was a foreman-supervisor for the New York City street railway system and helped build the old elevated lines and subways. Buried St Michael's Cemetery, East Elmhurst NY.

Bobby Reis—6 Years Pitcher (b. 2 Jan 1909 Woodside NY–d. 1 May 1973 St Paul MN) During the 1935 season he played every position—the first major leaguer to do so. After his baseball career he worked for the Fleishman distillery. Died after an illness of several months. Buried Willow River Cemetery, Hudson WI.

Jack Reis—1 Year Pitcher (b. 14 Jun 1891 Cincinnati OH–d. 20 Jul 1939 Cincinnati OH) He was a steamfitter. Died from pulmonary tuberculosis. Buried Vine Street Hill Cemetery, Cincinnati OH.

Laurie Reis—2 Years Pitcher (b. 20 Nov 1858 IL–d. 24 Jan 1921 Chicago IL) Buried Mount Greenwood Cemetery, Chicago IL.

Pete Reiser—10 Years Outfielder (b. 17 Mar 1919 St Louis MO–d. 25 Oct 1981 Eisenhower Hospital, Rancho Mirage CA) Known for his exciting and reckless style of play, he worked in baseball his entire life as a player, coach and scout. Died from respiratory arrest caused by years of smoking. Buried Desert Memorial Park, Cathedral City CA.

Bugs Reisigl—1 Year Pitcher (b. 12 Dec 1887 Brooklyn NY–d. 24 Feb 1957 St Mary's Hospital, Amsterdam NY) He worked for the Mohawk Power Corp for 30 years, 18 as a lineman and 12 as a collector, retiring in 1952. Buried St Mary's Cemetery, Fort Johnson NY.

Charlie Reising—1 Year Outfielder (b. 28 Aug 1861 IN–d. 26 Jul 1915 at his mother's home in Louisville KY) Buried Cave Hill Cemetery, Louisville KY.

Doc Reisling—4 Years Pitcher (b. 25 Jul 1874 Martins Ferry OH–d. 4 Mar 1955 at his daughter's home in Tulsa OK) He conducted a dental practice in Tulsa from 1918 to 1946 and in Gravette AR from 1950 until his death. Died from a heart ailment. Buried Rose Hill Memorial Park, Tulsa OK.

Al Reiss—1 Year Infielder (b. 8 Jan 1909 Elizabeth NJ–d. 13 May 1989 Riverview Medical Center, Red Bank NJ) He was a policeman in Elizabeth for 30 years, retiring in 1971. Buried Rosedale Cemetery, Linden NJ.

Heinie Reitz—7 Years Infielder (b. 29 Jun 1867 Chicago IL–d. 9 Nov 1914 Sacramento CA) He was a laborer. Died from a fractured skull suffered in an automobile accident. Buried Chicago IL.

Butch Rementer—1 Year Catcher (b. 14 Mar 1878 Philadelphia PA–d. 23 Sep 1922 Philadelphia PA) Buried Holy Cross Cemetery, Yeadon PA.

Alex Remneas—2 Years Pitcher (b. 21 Jul 1886 Minneapolis MN–d. 27 Aug 1975 Phoenix AZ).

Wally Renecker—1 Year Infielder (b. 21 Apr 1890 Pittsburgh PA–d. 18 Apr 1957 Pittsburgh PA).

Erwin Renfer—1 Year Pitcher (b. 12 Dec 1893 Elgin IL–d. 26 Oct 1957 Sycamore Municipal Hospital, Sycamore IL) He was employed by Anaconda Wire and Cable Company from 1918 to 1948, working his way up to mill manager. Later he was production manager for Nehring Electrical Works in Dekalb IL from 1948 until his death. Buried Bluff City Cemetery, Elgin IL.

Marshall Renfroe—1 Year Pitcher (b. 25 May 1936 Century FL–d. 10 Dec 1970 Pensacola FL) Died from burns received two and a half weeks earlier when his pickup truck was rammed by a gasoline tank truck on the Pensacola Bay Bridge. Buried Bayview Memorial Park, Pensacola FL.

Jim Reninger—2 Years Pitcher (b. 7 Mar 1915 Aurora IL–d. 23 Aug 1993 at his home in North Fort Myers FL) Served in the U.S. Navy during World War II. He was a manufacturer's agent for sporting goods, retiring to Florida in 1986. Cremated.

Tony Rensa—6 Years Catcher (b. 29 Sep 1901 Parsons PA–d. 4 Jan 1987 Summitt health Care Center, Wilkes-Barre PA) He worked in the coal mines at the Huber Colliery, retiring in 1960. Buried St Mary's Cemetery, Wilkes-Barre PA.

Rip Repulski—9 Years Outfielder (b. 4 Oct 1928 Sauk Rapids MN–d. 10 Feb 1993 Waite Park Nursing Home, Waite Park MN) Buried Trinity Lutheran Church Cemetery, Sauk Rapids MN.

George Rettger—2 Years Pitcher (b. 29 Jul 1868 Cleveland OH–d. 5 Jun 1921 Lakewood OH) He was a master automobile mechanic. Died from pulmonary tuberculosis. Buried Calvary Cemetery, Cleveland OH.

Otto Rettig—1 Year Pitcher (b. 29 Jan 1894 New York City NY–d. 16 Jun 1977 at his home in Stuart FL) He owned and managed a theatre in East Orange NJ for 45 years. Cremated.

Ed Reulbach—13 Years Pitcher (b. 1 Dec 1882 Detroit MI–d. 17 Jul 1961 at his home in Glens Falls NY) He pitched four consecutive shutouts in 1908 and also pitched two shutouts in a doubleheader that year. Buried Immaculate Conception Cemetery, Montclair NJ.

Nap Reyes—4 Years Infielder (b. 24 Niv 1919 San Luis, Cuba–d. 15 Sep 1995 Miami FL) One of Cuba's most popular players, he worked as a minor league manager and as a manager of Latin American teams in Cuba, Mexico and Puerto Rico. He was also a scout for the Reds. Died after being ill some time. Buried Vista Memorial Gardens, Hialeah FL.

Allie Reynolds—13 Years Pitcher (b. 10 Feb 1917 Bethany OK–d. 26 Dec 1994 St Anthony Hospital, Oklahoma City OK) He was one of few pitchers to throw two no-hitters in the same season. He was the owner and president of Atlas Mud Company and regional president of Newpark Drilling Fluids after it acquired his company in 1980. Died from complications of lymphoma and diabetes. Buried Memorial Park Cemetery, Oklahoma City OK.

Bill Reynolds—2 Years Catcher (b. 14 Aug 1883 Eastland TX–d. 5 Jun 1924 at his home in Carnegie OK) He managed minor league baseball until a malignant tumor on his lower left jaw ended his career and his life. Buried Carnegie Cemetery, Carnegie OK.

Carl Reynolds—13 Years Outfielder (b. 1 Feb 1903 LaRue TX–d. 29 May 1978 Methodist Hospital, Houston TX) A retired rancher and farmer, he was inducted into the Texas Sports Hall of Fame. Died following an extended illness. Buried Wharton City Cemetery, Wharton TX.

Charlie Reynolds—1 Year Catcher (b. 1 May 1865 Williamsburgh IN–d. 3 Jul 1944 Denver CO) Buried Fairmount Cemetery, Denver CO.

Charlie Reynolds—1 Year Pitcher (b. 31 Jul 1857 Allegany NY–d. 1 May 1913 Buffalo NY).

Ross Reynolds—2 Years Pitcher (b. 20 Aug 1887 Barksdale TX–d. 23 Jun 1970 at a hospital in Ada OK) World War I veteran. He worked in the oil industry and lived in Los Angeles CA from 1942 until 1960 when he moved to Ada. Died after a lengthy illness. Buried Rosedale Cemetery, Ada OK.

Bobby Rhawn—3 Years Infielder (b. 13 Feb 1919 Catawissa PA–d. 9 Jun 1984 Geisinger Medical Center, Danville PA) He was a World War II veteran. Buried Elan Memorial Cemetery, Lime Ridge PA.

Cy Rheam—2 Years Infielder (b. 28 Sep 1893 Pittsburgh PA–d. 23 Oct 1947 Pittsburgh PA) He served as a city councilman at Bellevue PA. Buried Allegheny Cemetery, Pittsburgh PA.

Billy Rheil—4 Years Infielder (b. 16 Aug 1900 Youngstown OH–d. 16 Aug 1946 at his sister's home in Youngstown OH) He managed the

VFW canteen in Warren OH for ten years. Died from heart disease while visiting his sister. Buried Calvary Cemetery, Youngstown OH.

Flint Rhem—12 Years Pitcher (b. 24 Jan 1901 Rhems SC–d. 30 Jul 1969 at a hospital in Columbia SC) Buried Wood Memorial Park, Greer SC.

Billy Rhines—9 Years Pitcher (b. 14 Mar 1869 Ridgway PA–d. 30 Jan 1922 at his home in Ridgway PA) He operated a taxi in Ridgway. He loved to hunt and was considered by some to be the best shot in Pennsylvania. Died from heart disease after an 18-month illness, the last eight months confined to his bed. Buried Ridgway Cemetery, Ridgway PA.

Bob Rhoads—8 Years Pitcher (b. 5 Oct 1875 Wooster OH–d. 12 Feb 1967 County Hospital, San Bernardino CA) He retired from a civilian job for the U.S. Marine Corps Supply Center at 29 Palms CA. Died from pulmonary tuberculosis. Buried Mountain View Memorial Park, Barstow CA.

Charlie Rhodes—3 Years Pitcher (b. 7 Apr 1885 Caney KS–d. 26 Oct 1918 at his home in Caney KS) Died from pneumonia caused by a bout with the flu. Buried Sunnyside Cemetery, Caney KS.

Gordon Rhodes—8 Years Pitcher (b. 11 Aug 1907 Winnemucca NV–d. 22 Mar 1960 V A Hospital, Bellflower CA) World War II veteran. He was a kitchen helper at a hotel. Died from cancer. Buried Los Angeles National Cemetery, Los Angeles CA.

Hal Rhyne—7 Years Infielder (b. 30 Mar 1899 Paso Robles CA–d. 7 Jan 1971 Orangevale CA) He was a guard at Folsum Prison in Folsum CA for 21 years. Died from a heart attack and emphysema. Cremated. Buried East Lawn Memorial Park, Sacramento CA.

Bob Rice—1 Year Infielder (b. 28 May 1899 Philadelphia PA–d. 20 Feb 1986 Elizabethtown PA).

Del Rice—17 Years Catcher 1 Year Manager (b. 27 Oct 1922 Portsmouth OH–d. 26 Jan 1983 Los Coyotes Country Club, Buena Park CA) He worked his entire life in baseball and was a scout for the Giants when he died from lung cancer. He was in the process of receiving an award at a testimonial in his honor when he collapsed and died. Cremated.

Grantland Rice—Hall of Fame (b. 1 Nov 1880 Murfreesboro TN–d. 13 Jul 1954 Roosevelt Hospital, New York City NY) For 53 years he was a sportswriter, the last 43 in New York City. Died from the effects of a stroke. Buried Woodlawn Cemetery, Bronx NY.

Hal Rice—7 Years Outfielder (b. 11 Feb 1924 Morganette WV–d. 22 Dec 1997 St Augustine FL).

Harry Rice—10 Years Outfielder (b. 22 Nov 1901 Ware Station IL–d. 1 Jan 1971 Portland OR) Buried Riverview Abbey Mausoleum, Portland OR.

Len Rice—2 Years Catcher (b. 2 Sep 1918 Lead SD–d. 13 Jun 1992 Community Hospital, Sonora CA) For 20 years he was an estimator for a paving contractor. Died from lung cancer. Buried Buena Vista Cemetery, Murphys CA.

Sam Rice—20 Years Outfielder Hall of Fame (b. 20 Feb 1890 Morocco IN–d. 13 Oct 1974 at his home in Rossmoor MD) Died from cancer after being ill for some time. Cremated. Buried St Mark's Cemetery, Highland MD.

Woody Rich—4 Years Pitcher (b. 9 Mar 1916 Morganton NC–d. 18 Apr 1983 Valdese General Hospital, Morganton NC) Served in the U.S. Marines during World War II. Died from natural causes. Buried South Mountain Baptist Church Cemetery, Morganton NC.

Paul Richards—8 Years Catcher 12 Years Manager (b. 21 Nov 1908 Waxahachie TX–d. 4 May 1986 at the country club in Waxahachie TX) He got the key hit that beat the Cubs in the seventh game of the 1945 World Series. Spending a lifetime in the game, he was a well-known baseball authority and evaluator of talent. Buried Hillcrest Burial Park, Waxahachie TX.

Bill Richardson—1 Year Infielder (b. 8 Oct 1877 near Osgood IN–d. 11 Apr 1954 Margaret Mercy Hospital, Batesville IN) Died after being in ill health the last four years. Buried Greendale Cemetery, Osgood IN.

Bill Richardson—1 Year Infielder (b. 24 Sep 1878 Salem IN–d. 6 Nov 1949 Sullivan IN).

Danny Richardson—11 Years Infielder 1 Year Manager (b. 25 Jan 1863 Elmira NY–d. 12 Sep 1926 at the Hofbrau Restaurant, New York City NY) He was a buyer for Sheehan, Bean and Company, a department store chain in Elmira. Died from a heart attack while having lunch on a business trip for his company. Buried Elmira NY.

Hardy Richardson—14 Years Infielder (b. 21 Apr 1855 Clarksboro NJ–d. 14 Jan 1931 at a hospital in Utica NY) He worked several years for the Remington Typewriter Company at Ilion NY and was an avid hunter and fisherman. Died after a brief illness. Buried Forest Hill Cemetery, Utica NY.

Jack Richardson—2 Years Pitcher (b. 3 Oct 1892 Central City IL–d. 18 Jan 1970 Marion IL).

Ken Richardson—2 Years Infielder (b. 2 May 1915 Orleans IN–d. 7 Dec 1987 Motion Picture Hospital, Woodland Hills CA) He was a grip in the motion picture industry for 20 years. Died from a heart attack, but suffered from prostate cancer. Cremated.

Nolen Richardson—6 Years Infielder (b. 18 Jan 1903 Chattanooga TN–d. 25 Sep 1951 at a hospital in Athens GA) He owned and operated a clothing store in Athens before becoming baseball coach at the University of Georgia for one year in 1950. Died after being ill several months. Buried Oconee Hill Cemetery, Athens GA.

Tom Richardson—1 Game Pinch Hitter (b. 7 Aug 1883 Louisville IL–d. 15 Nov 1939 at his home in Onawa IA) He was a landscape gardener and left, as a fitting monument, the landscaping at the county fairgrounds. Died from a heart attack. Buried Graceland Cemetery, Onawa IA.

Lance Richbourg—8 Years Outfielder (b. 18 Dec 1897 DeFuniak Springs FL–d. 10 Sep 1975 on his farm near Crestview FL) A cattle rancher, he served in elected offices for Okaloosa County, FL, from 1949 to 1964. Died from a heart attack while loading cattle for market. Buried Live Oak Park Memorial, Crestview FL.

Lew Richie—8 Years Pitcher (b. 23 Aug 1883 Ambler PA–d. 15 Aug 1936 State Sanitarium, South Mountain PA).

Milton Richman—Hall of Fame (b. 29 Jan 1922–d. 9 Jun 1986 New York City NY) A minor league player in the Browns' organization during World War II, he was a sports columnist for UPI 42 years and was their sports editor from 1964 to 1985. Died from a heart attack. Buried Mount Ararat Cemetery, Farmingdale NY.

Beryl Richmond—2 Years Pitcher (b. 24 Aug 1907 Glen Easton WV–d. 24 Apr 1980 at his home in Cameron WV) Buried Highland Cemetery, Cameron WV.

Don Richmond—4 Years Infielder (b. 27 Oct 1919 Gillett PA–d. 24 May 1981 St Joseph's Hospital, Elmira NY) Served in the U.S. Army during World War II. He owned Mid-State Beverage Company in Elmira. Buried St Peter and Paul's Cemetery, Elmira NY.

Lee Richmond—6 Years Pitcher (b. 5 May 1857 Sheffield OH–d. 1 Oct 1929 Toledo OH) A professor and dean of men at the University of Toledo, he had been a noted educator in the Toledo area since 1890. Died from a heart attack five weeks after suffering a stroke. Buried Woodlawn Cemetery, Toledo OH.

Ray Richmond—2 Years Pitcher (b. 5 Jun 1896 Fillmore IL–d. 21 Dec 1969 DeSoto MO) Buried Glendale Cemetery, Fillmore IL.

John Richter—1 Year Infielder (b. 8 Feb 1873 Louisville KY–d. 4 Oct 1927 Deaconess Hospital, Louisville KY) Buried St Louis Cemetery, Louisville KY.

Reggie Richter—1 Year Pitcher (b. 14 Sep 1888 Dusseldorf, Germany–d. 2 Aug 1934 at his home in Winfield IL) His baseball career ended prematurely when he was hit by a pitch. He worked at a clerical position for Western Electric in Hawthorne. Buried Oak Hill Cemetery, Chicago IL.

Joe Rickert—2 Years Outfielder (b. 12 Dec 1876 London OH–d. 15 Oct 1943 at his home in Springfield OH) He entered business at New Orleans LA and retired to Springfield several years before his death. Died from a heart attack. Buried St Bernard Cemetery, Springfield OH.

Marv Rickert—6 Years Outfielder (b. 8 Jan 1921 Longbranch WA–d. 3 Jun 1978 at his home in Oakville WA) Served in the U.S. Coast Guard during World War II. He was a park supervisor for Pierce County, WA, Parks and Recreation Department, retiring to his farm near Oakville in 1975. Cremated.

Dick Ricketts—1 Year Pitcher (b. 4 Dec 1933 Pottstown PA–d. 6 Mar 1988 Genesee Hospital, Rochester NY) He played both professional baseball and basketball and was personnel director at Eastman-Kodak's Apparatus Division. Died from leukemia. Buried Pughtown Baptist Cemetery, Pughtown PA.

Branch Rickey—4 Years Catcher 10 Years Manager Hall of Fame (b. 20 Dec 1881 Stockdale OH–d. 9 Dec 1965 Columbia MO) Best known for breaking baseball's color barrier by signing Jackie Robinson to a major league contract, he was one of the most successful general managers and administrators in baseball. He suffered a fatal heart attack while addressing the Missouri State Hall of Fame, accepting his induction into the hall. Buried Rushtown Cemetery, Rushtown OH.

Chris Rickley—1 Year Infielder (b. 7 Oct 1859 Philadelphia PA–d. 25 Oct 1911 Philadelphia PA) Buried Greenmount Cemetery, Philadelphia PA.

Art Rico—2 Years Catcher (b. 23 Jul 1896 Roxbury MA–d. 3 Jan 1919 Massachusetts General Hospital, Boston MA) Served in the U.S. Navy during World War I. Died at the height of his baseball career from peritonitis caused by appendicitis. Buried Holyhood Cemetery, Brookline MA.

Harry Riconda—6 Years Infielder (b. 17 Mar 1897 New York City NY–d. 15 Nov 1958 Mahopac NY).

Elmer Riddle—10 Years Pitcher (b. 31 Jul 1914 Columbus GA–d. 14 May 1984 St Francis Hospital, Columbus GA) He was a salesman for the United Oil Company and a scout for the Athletics. Buried Parkhill Cemetery, Columbus GA.

Dorsey Riddlemoser—1 Year Pitcher (b. 25 Mar 1875 Frederick MD–d. 11 May 1954 Memorial Hospital, Frederick MD) He was the janitor at the Frederick City Hall for a number of years. Buried Mount Olivet Cemetery, Frederick MD.

Jack Ridgeway—1 Year Pitcher (b. 23 Jul 1889 Philadelphia PA–d. 23 Feb 1928 Philadelphia PA) Died in an automobile accident. Buried Westminster Cemetery, Bala Cynwyd PA.

Elmer Rieger—1 Year Pitcher (b. 25 Feb 1889 Perris CA–d. 21 Oct 1959 Cedars of Lebanon Hospital, Los Angeles CA) He was a painter at a motion picture studio. Died from a heart attack. Cremated. Buried Inglewood Park Cemetery, Inglewood CA.

Joe Riggert—3 Years Outfielder (b. 11 Dec 1886 Janesville WI–d. 10 Dec 1973 at his home in Kansas City MO) He played professional baseball for 20 years, including 12 for the St Paul Saints of the American Association. He operated the cigar stand in the Jackson County (MO) Courthouse for ten years and worked as a clerk for the Wilson Sporting Goods Company for ten years. Buried Calvary Cemetery, Kansas City MO.

Lew Riggs—10 Years Infielder (b. 22 Apr 1910 Mebane NC–d. 12 Aug 1975 V A Hospital, Durham NC) World War II veteran. Died after being ill several months. Buried Rock Creek Methodist Church Cemetery, Graham NC.

Billy Rigney—8 Years Infielder 18 Years Manager (b. 29 Jan 1918 Alameda CA–d. 20 Feb 2001) Served in the U.S. Navy during World War II. He worked his entire life in baseball as a manager, coach and special assistant. He was a broadcaster and special assistant for the Athletics from 1982 until his death. Died after being hospitalized three months with pneumonia following a year-long struggle with lymphoma.

Johnny Rigney—8 Years Pitcher (b. 28 Oct 1914 Oak Park IL–d. 23 Oct 1984 at a convalescent home in Lombard IL) Served in the U.S. Navy during World War II. Married to the daughter of Charlie Comiskey, he headed the White Sox farm system for several years before becoming a Sox vice-president. He also owned some of Florida's top thoroughbred race horses. Buried Queen of Heaven Cemetery, Hillside IL.

Topper Rigney—6 Years Infielder (b. 7 Jan 1897 Groveton TX–d. 6 Jun 1972 at a hospital in San Antonio TX) Buried Sunset Memorial Park, San Antonio TX.

Billy Riley—1 Year Outfielder (b. Nov 1853 Philadelphia PA–d. 9 Nov 1887 Cincinnati OH) Died from peritonitis. Buried St Joseph New Cemetery, Cincinnati OH.

Jim Riley—2 Years Infielder (b. 25 May 1895 Bayfield, New Brunswick, Canada–d. 25 May 1969 Guadalupe Valley Hospital, Seguin TX) He worked in public relations for a distillery, retiring to Sequin in 1960. Died from lung cancer. Buried Guadalupe Valley Memorial Park, Sequin TX.

Jimmy Riley—1 Year Outfielder (b. 10 Nov 1886 Buffalo NY–d. 25 Mar 1949 Our Lady of Victory Hospital, Buffalo NY) He was a clerk at the Buffalo City Law Department. Died after a two-week illness. Buried Holy Cross Cemetery, Lackawanna NY.

Lee Riley—1 Year Outfielder (b. 20 Aug 1906 Princeton NE–d. 13 Sep 1970 St Clare's Hospital, Schenectady NY) He managed minor league baseball before operating a variety store in Scotia NY. He also coached high school baseball a few years. Buried Most Holy Redeemer Cemetery, Schenectady NY.

Jimmy Ring—12 Years Pitcher (b. 15 Feb 1895 Brooklyn NY–d. 6 Jul 1965 at his summer home in Breezy Point NY) Died from a heart attack. Buried St John's Cemetery, Middle Village NY.

Frank Ringo—4 Years Catcher (b. 12 Oct 1860 Parkville MO–d. 12 Apr 1889 at the home of his parents, Kansas City MO) He played baseball up until his death and operated a cigar store in Kansas City. An alcoholic, during one of his drunken binges he ended his own life by taking 40 grams of morphine. Buried Elmwood Cemetery, Kansas City MO.

Juan Rios—1 Year Infielder (b. 14 Jun 1942 Mayaquez, Puerto Rico–d. 28 Aug 1995 Mayaquez, Puerto Rico).

Cal Ripken, Sr—2 Years Manager (b. 17 Dec 1935 Aberdeen MD–d. 25 Mar 1999 Johns Hopkins Oncology Center, Baltimore MD) He worked 36 years in baseball, all in the Oriole organization as a minor league player, scout, coach and manager, retiring in 1992. Died from lung cancer. Buried Baker Cemetery, Aberdeen MD.

Walt Ripley—1 Year Pitcher (b. 26 Nov 1916 Worcester MA–d. 7 Oct 1990 Sturdy Memorial Hospital, Attleboro MA) Served in the U.S. Army Air Corps during World War II. He worked for L G Balfour Company and later was a scout for the Giants. Died after a long illness. Buried Massachusetts National Cemetery, Bourne MA.

Charlie Ripple—3 Years Pitcher (b. 1 Dec 1921 Bolton NC–d. 6 May 1979 New Hanover Memorial Hosp, Wilmington NC) Buried Whiteville Memorial Cemetery, Whiteville NC.

Jimmy Ripple—7 Years Outfielder (b. 14 Oct 1909 Export PA–d. 16 Jul 1959 Westmoreland Hospital, Greensburg PA) Died following surgery for acute pancreatitis. Buried Eastview Union Cemetery, Delmont PA.

Swede Risberg—4 Years Infielder (b. 13 Oct 1894 San Francisco CA–d. 13 Oct 1975 Ceadars Convalescent Hospital, Red Bluff CA) He was banned from baseball for his involvement in the Black Sox Scandal. He worked in a paper mill. Died from a cardio-respiratory arrest, but he suffered from cancer of the esophagus. Buried Mount Shasta Memorial Park, Mount Shasta CA.

Pop Rising—1 Year Outfielder (b. Jan 1877 PA–d. 28 Jan 1938 Rochester PA).

Claude Ritchey—13 Years Infielder (b. 5 Oct 1873 Emlenton PA–d. 8 Nov 1951 at his home in Emlenton PA) He had an interest in a clothing store in Emlenton and later worked for the Emlenton Refining Company, retiring in 1941. Buried Emlenton Cemetery, Emlenton PA.

Floyd Ritter—1 Year Catcher (b. 1 Jun 1870 Dorset OH–d. 7 Feb 1943 West Klickitat General Hosp, Stevenson WA) He was a retired carpenter. Died from a hemorrhaging stomach ulcer. Buried White Salmon Cemetery, White Salmon WA.

Hank Ritter—4 Years Pitcher (b. 12 Oct 1893 McCoysville PA–d. 3 Sep 1964 Akron General Hospital, Akron OH) Served in the U.S. Army during World War I. He was president of Wreitz Coal Company in Windber PA and director of public relations for Ruhlin Construction Company of Akron. Buried Rose Hill Burial Park, Fairlawn OH.

Lou Ritter—7 Years Catcher (b. 7 Sep 1875 Liverpool PA–d. 27 May 1952 at his home in Harrisburg PA) He was a retired insurance agent. Died after an illness of more than a year. Buried Liverpool Cemetery, Liverpool PA.

Ed Ritterson—1 Year Catcher (b. 26 Apr 1855 Philadelphia PA–d. 28 Jul 1917 Sellersville PA) Buried Reform Cemetery, Perkasie PA.

Jim Ritz—1 Year Infielder (b. 1874 Pittsburgh PA–d. 10 Nov 1896 Mercy Hospital, Pittsburgh PA) Died at the height of his career from typhoid fever.

Tink Riviere—2 Years Pitcher (b. 2 Aug 1899 Liberty TX–d. 27 Sep 1965 Kersting Hospital, Liberty TX) Served in the U.S. Army during World War II. For 30 years he was an agent for Southland Life Insurance Company. Died following a heart attack. Buried Catholic Cemetery, Liberty TX.

Eppa Rixey—21 Years Pitcher Hall of Fame (b. 3 May 1891 Culpeper VA–d. 28 Feb 1963 Christ Hospital, Cincinnati OH) He owned a successful insurance business in Cincinnati. Died after suffering a heart attack earlier in the day. Buried Greenlawn Cemetery, Milford OH.

Johnny Rizzo—5 Years Outfielder (b. 30 Jul 1912 Houston TX–d. 4 Dec 1977 Houston TX) Buried Calvary Cemetery, Houston TX.

John Roach—1 Year Pitcher (b. Farrensville PA–d. 1 Mar 1915 Sandusky OH).

Mike Roach—1 Year Catcher (b. 1876 New York City NY–d. 12 Nov 1916 at his brother's home in New York City NY) He played, coached and managed in the minor leagues for several years, and was a part owner of the Binghamton NY baseball club. He also owned the MacDonald Hotel in Binghamton, and later owned the Cadillac Hotel there. Buried Renovo PA.

Roxy Roach—4 Years Infielder (b. 28 Nov 1882 Morrisdale Mines PA–d. 26 Dec 1947 Samaritan Hospital, Bay City MI) He worked for the National Gypsum plant at National City MI and was an expert trap shooter, avid fisherman and a raiser of championship dogs. Died from a heart attack. Buried Tawas City Cemetery, Tawas City MI.

Skel Roach—1 Year Pitcher (b. 20 Oct 1871 Chicago IL–d. 9 Mar 1958 at his home in Oak Park IL) He played several years in the Pacific Coast League before coaching baseball at the University of Michigan and Indiana University. He used his baseball earnings to work his way through Northwestern University, becoming an attorney. He then practiced law several years in Chicago IL. Buried Concordia Cemetery, Forest Park IL.

Fred Roat—2 Years Infielder (b. 10 Feb 1867 Oregon IL–d. 24 Sep 1913 Oregon IL) Buried River View Cemetery, Oregon IL.

Tony Robello—2 Years Infielder (b. 9 Feb 1913 San Leandro CA–d. 25 Dec 1994 at a care center in Fort Worth TX) He spent 65 years in baseball as a player, coach, minor league manager and scout, his last 30 years as a scout for the Reds. Buried Mount Olivet Cemetery, Fort Worth TX.

Curt Roberts—3 Years Infielder (b. 16 Aug 1929 Pineland TX–d. 14 Nov 1969 Kaiser Hospital, Oakland CA) For five years he was a policeman at the University of California's Lawrence Radiation Lab in Berkeley CA. Died from a fractured skull suffered when he was struck by a blunt instrument at a freeway onramp. Buried Evergreen Cemetery, Oakland CA.

Jim Roberts—2 Years Pitcher (b. 13 Oct 1895 Artesia MS–d. 24 Jun 1984 Columbus Hospital, Columbus MS) Served in the U.S. Navy during World War I. He entered the hardware business at Artesia before becoming a Mississippi highway patrolman in 1938. In 1947 he became a Columbus policeman, serving as chief of police from 1947 to 1951, and retiring in 1867. He was an avid fisherman and hunter. Buried Friendship Cemetery, Columbus MS.

Ray Roberts—1 Year Pitcher (b. 24 Aug 1895 Cruger MS–d. 30 Jan 1962 Cruger MS).

Skipper Roberts—2 Years Catcher (b. 11 Jan 1888 Wardner ID–d. 24 Dec 1963 St Mary's Hospital, Long Beach CA) He was an operator at an oil refinery for Shell Oil. Died from heart disease. Buried All Souls Cemetery, Long Beach CA.

Charlie Robertson—8 Years Pitcher (b. 31 Jan 1897 Sherman TX–d. 23 Aug 1984 Fort Worth TX) Buried Palo Pinto Cemetery, Palo Pinto TX.

Dave Robertson—9 Years Outfielder (b. 25 Sep 1889 Portsmouth VA–d. 5 Nov 1970 at his home in Virginia Beach VA) For 28 years he was a game warden before spending ten years selling real estate. Died after being in poor health for some time. Buried Forest Lawn Cemetery, Norfolk VA.

Dick Robertson—3 Years Pitcher (b. 1891 Washington DC–d. 2 Oct 1944 New Orleans LA) Buried St Joseph Cemetery # 2, New Orleans LA.

Gene Robertson—9 Years Infielder (b. 25 Dec 1899 St Louis MO–d. 21 Oct 1981 Fallon NV).

Jerry Robertson—2 Years Pitcher (b. 13 Oct 1943 Winchester KS–d. 24 Mar 1996 Coffey County Hospital, Burlington KS) He worked for the Topeka KS YMCA from 1965 until his death, except from 1982 until 1989 when he headed the Washburn University athletic department. He was active in civic matters and was president of the YMCA when he died. Died shortly after a headon collision when he drove his car into oncoming traffic. Cremated.

Sherry Robertson—10 Years Outfielder (b. 1 Jan 1919 Montreal, Quebec, Canada–d. 23 Oct 1970 Houghton SD) He was the farm director for the Twins from 1956 until his death. Killed when his car left the road and hit a tree while on a hunting trip with other Twins personnel and players. He died from a multiple fracture of the skull suffered in the accident. There was no sign of a heart attack. Buried Lakewood Cemetery, Minneapolis MN.

Aaron Robinson —8 Years Catcher (b. 23 Jun 1915 Lancaster SC–d. 9 Mar 1966 at his home in Lancaster SC) Served in the U.S. Coast Guard during World War II. He managed minor league baseball for a year, then was an electrical appliance salesman. Died from lung cancer. Buried Zions Methodist Church Cemetery, Lancaster SC.

Charlie Robinson —2 Years Catcher (b. 27 Jul 1856 Westerly RI–d. 18 May 1913 at his home in Providence RI) He conducted a livery stable in Providence from the 1880s until his death. Buried River Bend Cemetery, Westerly RI.

Fred Robinson —1 Year Infielder (b. 6 Jul 1856 South Acton MA–d. 18 Dec 1933 Hudson MA) He worked as a janitor at a bank in Hudson. Died from a heart attack while clearing snow in front of the bank.

Hank Robinson —6 Years Pitcher (b. 16 Aug 1889 Floyd AR–d. 3 Jul 1965 at his home in North Little Rock AR) In a career spanning 22 years he won 304 games as a pitcher in both the major and minor leagues, 208 of them in the Southern Association. He played 13 years for the Little Rock Travelers. He retired from the Arkansas Highway Department in 1959. Buried Edgewood Memorial Cemetery, North Little Rock AR.

Jack Robinson —1 Year Catcher (b. 15 Jul 1880 Portland ME–d. 22 Jul 1921 Macon GA) He owned and operated the Acme Welding Company in Macon GA. His death was ruled a suicide. He drank a solution of potassium cyandide, a chemical used in welding. Buried Riverside Cemetery, Macon GA.

Jackie Robinson —10 Years Infielder Hall of Fame (b. 31 Jan 1919 Cairo GA–d. 24 Oct 1972 Stamford CT) He broke baseball's color barrier in 1947. Died from a heart attack after suffering from diabetes for years. Buried Cypress Hills Cemetery, Brooklyn NY.

Ken Robinson —1 Year Pitcher (b. abt 1969 Akron OH–d. 28 Feb 1999 Tucson AZ) Killed, at the height of his career, in an alcohol-related automobile accident when the car in which he was a passenger left the road and overturned. Buried Oaklawn Cemetery, Jacksonville FL.

Rabbit Robinson —3 Years Infielder (b. 5 Mar 1882 Wellsburg WV–d. 9 Apr 1915 Waterbury Hospital, Waterbury CT) Died after a short illness.

Wilbert Robinson —17 Years Catcher 19 Years Manager Hall of Fame (b. 2 Jun 1863 Bolton MA–d. 8 Aug 1934 Atlanta GA) He worked his entire life in baseball as a player, coach, manager and executive. When he died from a brain hemorrhage he was president of the Atlanta Crackers in the Southern Association. Buried New Cathedral Cemetery, Baltimore MD.

Yank Robinson —10 Years Infielder (b. 19 Sep 1859 Philadelphia PA–d. 25 Aug 1894 St Louis MO) Died from pulmonary problems. Buried Calvary Cemetery, St Louis MO.

Frank Robison —(b. abt 1852 Pittsburgh PA–d. 25 Sep 1908 Bratenahl OH) He owned several streetcar companies and was co-owner of the Cleveland Naps (later Indians). Died from a cerebral hemorrhage. Buried Cleveland OH.

Matt Robison —1 Year Manager (b. 30 Mar 1859 Pittsburgh PA–d. 24 Mar 1911 at the home of his sis-in-law, Cleveland OH) He owned the St Louis Cardinals and a majority of the stock in the trolley line of Cleveland OH. He and his brothers bought the Cleveland National League team in 1889 and moved them to St Louis MO in 1899. Died from a heart condition. Buried Lake View Cemetery, Cleveland OH.

Chick Robitaille —2 Years Pitcher (b. 2 Mar 1879 Whitehall NY–d. 30 Jul 1947 Cohoes NY) Buried St Joseph's Cemetery, Waterford NY.

Rafael Robles —3 Years Infielder. (b. 20 Oct 1947 San Pedro de Macoris, Dominican Republic–d. 13 Aug 1998 New York City NY).

Mickey Rocco —4 Years Infielder Born 2 Mar 1916 St Paul MN–d. 1 Jun 1997 St Paul MN) A longtime employee of Distillers Distributing and Old Peoria, he coached American Legion baseball ten years. Buried Roselawn Cemetery, Roseville MN.

Jack Roche —3 Years Catcher (b. 22 Nov 1890 Los Angeles CA–d. 30 Mar 1983 at his home in Peoria AZ) A retired breeder of greyhound dogs, he had moved to Arizona in 1980. Buried Resthaven Park Cemetery, Glendale AZ.

Ben Rochefort—1 Year Infielder (b. 15 Aug 1896 Camden NJ–d. 2 Apr 1981 Red Bank NJ).

Lou Rochelli—1 Year Infielder (b. 11 Jan 1919 Staunton IL–d. 23 Oct 1992 Victoria TX) He managed minor league baseball and moved to Victoria in 1957 when he managed the minor league team there. He worked for Radio Shack in Victoria when he died. Buried Resurrection Cemetery, Victoria TX.

Les Rock—1 Year Infielder (b. 19 Aug 1912 Springfield MN–d. 9 Sep 1991 Driftwood Convalescent Hospital, Davis CA) Served in the U.S. Army Air Force during World War II. He retired in 1972 after eight years as a custodian at U C Davis. Died from an attack of acute bronchitis, but suffered from cardiovascular heart disease. Cremated.

Ike Rockenfeld—2 Years Infielder (b. 3 Nov 1876 Omaha NE–d. 21 Feb 1927 San Diego CA) Cremated.

Bill Rodgers—2 Years Outfielder (b. 18 Apr 1887 Amberly Village OH–d. 24 Dec 1978 Goliad Nursing Home, Goliad TX) He owned and managed minor league baseball teams. Died following a long illness. Buried Berclair Cemetery, Berclair TX.

Eric Rodin—1 Year Outfielder (b. 5 Feb 1930 Orange NJ–d. 4 Jan 1991 Somerset Medical Center, Somerville NJ) He operated a ministorage and warehouse company in Clinton NJ until retiring in 1985. Buried Prospect Hill Cemetery, Flemington NJ.

Jose Rodriguez—3 Years Infielder (b. 23 Feb 1894 Havana, Cuba–d. 21 Jan 1953 Havana, Cuba).

Clay Roe—1 Year Pitcher (b. 27 Mar 1901 Greenbrier TN–d. 3 Apr 1956 at his mother-in-law's home in Cleveland MS) He worked 25 years for the Federal Compress Company at Cleveland before taking a job as foreman for Central Delta Warehouse Company his last few years. Buried Cleveland Cemetery, Cleveland MS.

Oscar Roettger—4 Years Infielder (b. 19 Feb 1900 St Louis MO–d. 4 Jul 1986 St John's Mercy Hospital, St Louis MO) Known as the "tailor to the baseball stars", he played in the American Association and the International League, and managed in the International League and the Southern Association. In 1941 he went to work for the Rawlings Sporting Goods Company where he designed baseball attire. Died from a heart attack after suffering an aneurysm. Buried Bethlehem Cemetery, Bellefontaine Neighbors MO.

Wally Roettger—8 Years Outfielder (b. 28 Aug 1902 St Louis MO–d. 14 Sep 1951 at his home in Champaign IL) He was baseball coach at the University of Illinois for 16 years. Despondent over ill health, he took his own life by slashing his wrists and throat with a razor. Buried Riverview Cemetery, Streator IL.

Ed Roetz—1 Year Infielder (b. 6 Aug 1905 Philadelphia PA–d. 16 Mar 1965 at his home in Philadelphia PA) Buried Beverly National Cemetery, Beverly NJ.

Joe Rogalski—1 Year Pitcher (b. 16 Jul 1912 Ashland WI–d. 20 Nov 1951 at a hospital in Ashland WI) Served in the U.S. Army Medical Corps during World War II. He worked at the Kalamazoo Vegetable Parchment Company in Kalamazoo MI. Died from Lou Gehrig's disease. Buried Duquesne Cemetery, Duquesne PA.

Bullet Joe Rogan—12 Years Pitcher Hall of Fame (b. 28 Jul 1889 Oklahoma City OK–d. 4 Mar 1967 Kansas City MO) Playing in the negro leagues for the Kansas City Monarchs, he was both a pitcher, with 113 wins and 45 losses, and an infielder, with a lifetime batting average of .343. Buried Blue Ridge Lawn Memorial Gardens, Kansas City MO.

Jay Rogers—1 Year Catcher (b. 3 Aug 1888 Sandusky NY–d. 1 Jul 1964 Carlisle Hospital, Carlisle PA) Served in the U.S. Army infantry during World War I. Buried Temple Hill Cemetery, Genesseo NY.

Jim Rogers—2 Years Infielder 1 Year Manager (b. 9 Apr 1872 Hartford CT–d. 21 Jan 1900 at his mother-in-law's home, Bridgeport CT) Died at the height of his career from kidney trouble complications. Buried St Michael's Cemetery, Bridgeport CT.

Lee Rogers—1 Year Pitcher (b. 8 Oct 1913 Holt AL–d. 23 Nov 1995 Little Rock NJ) Served in the U.S. Army during World War II. He owned and operated the Spaulding athletic goods store in Little Rock from 1939 to 1980 and officiated high school games and Southwest Conference college games for 15 years. Died from complications of a heart attack suffered a month earlier at an Arkansas-Auburn football game. Buried Roselawn Memorial Park, Little Rock AR.

Packy Rogers—1 Year Infielder (b. 26 Apr 1913 Swoyersville PA–d. 15 May 1998 at his home in Elmira NY) Served in the U.S. Navy during World War II. He spent 45 years in organized baseball as a player, minor league manager and scout, retiring in 1980. Buried Woodlawn National Cemetery, Elmira NY.

Tom Rogers—4 Years Pitcher (b. 12 Feb 1891 Scottville KY–d. 7 Mar 1936 at a hospital in Nashville TN) He pitched several years in the Southern League. After his playing days were over he worked as baseball director for the Nashville Dupont rayon plant where he was in charge of their amateur team. Died from pneumonia. Buried Spring Hill Cemetery, Nashville TN.

Clint Rogge—2 Years Pitcher (b. 19 Jul 1889 Memphis MI–d. 6 Jan 1969 at his home in Mount Clemens MI) World War I veteran. A practicing attorney, he was active in the Republican Party and widely known for his work for veteran's organizations. Died from a heart attack. Buried Memphis Cemetery, Memphis MI.

Saul Rogovin—8 Years Pitcher (b. 10 Oct 1923 Brooklyn NY–d. 23 Jan 1995 New York City NY) He sold liquor for several years when he decided to resume his education. He then taught school in New York City for 12 years. Died from cancer. Buried Beth David Cemetery, Elmont NY.

George Rohe—4 Years Infielder (b. 15 Sep 1875 Cincinnati OH–d. 10 Jun 1957 General Hospital, Cincinnati OH) He managed minor league baseball before becoming a commercial photographer, retiring after World War II. Died from the effects of a stroke suffered three months earlier. Buried Walnut Hills Cemetery, Cincinnati OH.

Ray Rohwer—2 Years Outfielder (b. 5 Jun 1895 Dixon CA–d. 24 Jan 1988 Sutter-Davis Hospital, Davis CA) For 35 years he was an appraiser of agricultural land for the Federal Land Bank in Woodland CA and for the Production Credit Association in Woodland, retiring in 1965. Died from congestive heart failure. Cremated. Buried Dixon Cemetery, Dixon CA.

Stan Rojek—8 Years Infielder (b. 21 Apr 1919 North Tonawanda NY–d. 9 Jul 1997 DeGraff Memorial Hospital, N Tonawanda NY) Served in the U.S. Army Air Corps during World War II. For 25 years he ran Rojek's Park Manor Bowling Lanes in North Tonawanda. Died after a long illness. Buried Mount Olivet Cemetery, Buffalo NY.

Red Rolfe—10 Years Infielder 4 Years Manager (b. 17 Oct 1908 Penacook NH–d. 8 Jul 1969 Gilford NH) He coached basketball and baseball at Yale University before serving as athletic director at Dartmouth College from 1954 until 1967. Died from cancer. Buried Woodlawn Cemetery, Penacook NH.

Ray Rolling—1 Year Infielder (b. 8 Sep 1886 Martinsburg MO–d. 25 Aug 1966 St Paul MN) Buried Lakewood Cemetery, Minneapolis MN.

Red Rollings—3 Years Infielder (b. 31 Mar 1904 Mobile AL–d. 31 Dec 1964 at his home in Mobile AL) He operated the Budweiser Beer distributorship at Mobile. Died unexpectedly. Buried Pine Crest Cemetery, Mobile AL.

Jim Romano—1 Year Pitcher (b. 6 Apr 1927 Brooklyn NY–d. 12 Sep 1990 New York City NY).

Dutch Romberger—1 Year Pitcher (b. 26 May 1927 Klingerstown PA–d. 26 May 1983 Weikert PA) A butcher by trade, he owned and operated Romberger's Hotel in Klingerstown from 1962 until his death. Died from natural causes at his mountain cabin. Buried St Michael's Church Cemetery, Klingerstown PA.

Eddie Rommel—13 Years Pitcher (b. 13 Sep 1897 Baltimore MD–d. 26 Aug 1970 at his home in Baltimore MD) He managed minor league baseball for a short while before umpiring in the American League from 1938 to 1959. After leaving umpiring he owned a duckpin alley in Baltimore and worked seven years as a clerk in the Maryland governor's office. Buried New Cathedral Cemetery, Baltimore MD.

Henri Rondeau—3 Years Outfielder (b. 5 May 1887 Danielson CT–d. 28 May 1943 Woonsocket Hospital, Woonsocket RI) He operated a cafe in Woonsocket for ten years. Buried Precious Blood Cemetery, Woonsocket RI.

George Rooks—1 Year Outfielder (b. 21 Oct 1863 Chicago IL–d. 11 Mar 1935 Chicago IL)

Buried Waldheim Jewish Cemetery, Forest Park IL.

Frank Rooney—1 Year Infielder (b. 12 Oct 1894 Austria–d. 6 Apr 1977 Grand View Hospital, Ironwood MI) He worked several years for the Charbonneau Furniture Store in Hurley WI. Buried Hurley Cemetery, Hurley WI.

Charlie Root—17 Years Pitcher (b. 17 Mar 1899 Middletown OH–d. 5 Nov 1970 Hazel Hawkins Hospital, Hollister CA) He gave up the "called" home run to Babe Ruth in the 1932 World Series. He owned a cattle ranch near Hollister, and was an antique dealer there. Died from pneumonia and eosinophilic leukemia. Cremated.

Buddy Rosar—13 Years Catcher (b. 3 Jul 1914 Buffalo NY–d. 13 Mar 1994 Strong Memorial Hospital, Rochester NY) He was an engineer in the powerhouse at the Ford stamping plant in Woodlawn, retiring in the late 1970s. Died after becoming ill on a visit to the Rochester area. Buried Mount Calvary Cemetery, Cheektowaga NY.

Chuck Rose—1 Year Pitcher (b. 1 Sep 1885 Macon MO–d. 4 Aug 1961 St John's Hospital, Salina KS) A retired construction superintendent, he lived at Salina from 1942 until his death. Buried Mount Olivet Cemetery, Marceline MO.

Zeke Rosebraugh—2 Years Pitcher (b. 8 Sep 1870 Charleston IL–d. 16 Jul 1930 at his home in Fresno CA) He was an engineer and rancher. Died from a self-inflicted gunshot wound to the breast. Buried Washington Colony Cemetery, Fresno CA.

Chief Roseman—7 Years Outfielder 1 Year Manager (b. 1856 New York City NY–d. 4 Jul 1938 at his home in Brooklyn NY) He worked 36 years for the New York City Bureau of Sewers, retiring in 1934. Buried St John's Cemetery, Middle Village NY.

Goody Rosen—6 Years Outfielder (b. 28 Aug 1912 Toronto, Ontario, Canada–d. 6 Apr 1994 Toronto, Ontario, Canada).

Harry Rosenberg—1 Year Outfielder (b. 22 Jun 1909 San Francisco CA–d. 13 Apr 1997 St Francis Pavilion, Daly City CA) For 25 years he was self-employed in the construction business. Died from a heart attack, but suffered from prostate cancer. Cremated. Buried Hills of Eternity Memorial, Colma CA.

Lou Rosenberg—1 Year Infielder (b. 5 Mar 1904 San Francisco CA–d. 8 Sep 1991 U C Medical Center, San Francisco CA) For 55 years he was the proprietor of Garden Supply Nursery. Died from a ruptured abdominal aortic aneurysm. Buried Eternal Home Cemetery, Daly City CA.

Max Rosenfeld—3 Years Outfielder (b. 23 Dec 1902 New York City NY–d. 10 Mar 1969 Miami FL) An avid bowler and fisherman, he lived in Miami 50 years and was a realtor. Buried Graceland Memorial Park, Coral Gables FL.

Larry Rosenthal—8 Years Outfielder (b. 21 May 1910 St Paul MN–d. 4 Mar 1992 Woodbury Healthcare Center, Woodbury MN) He worked for Schmidt Brewery and later drove trucks for Mobil Oil Company, retiring in 1978. After retiring he was a parking attendant at the Commercial State Bank parking lot in St Paul. Buried Resurrection Cemetery, St Paul MN.

Si Rosenthal—2 Years Outfielder (b. 13 Nov 1903 Boston MA–d. 7 Apr 1969 Veteran's Hospital, West Roxbury MA) World War II veteran. He suffered a serious spinal injury when his ship struck a mine off the Normandy coast shortly after D-Day. He spent the rest of his life in a wheelchair. Died from a heart attack. Buried Beth El Cemetery, West Roxbury MA.

Jack Roser—1 Year Outfielder (b. 15 Nov 1901 St Louis MO–d. 6 May 1979 at a convalescent home in Rocky Hill CT) He managed minor league baseball and was a scout for the Giants before working 20 years for United Technologies Corporation in East Hartford CT, retiring in 1959. Buried Rose Hill Memorial Park, Rocky Hill CT.

Buck Ross—10 Years Pitcher (b. 3 Feb 1915 Norwood NC–d. 23 Nov 1978 Charlotte NC).

Buster Ross—3 Years Pitcher (b. 1 Apr 1917 Buffalo NY–d. 24 Apr 1982 Community Hospital, Mayfield KY) Buried Maplewood Cemetery, Mayfield KY.

Chet Ross—6 Years Outfielder (b. 1 Apr 1917 Buffalo NY–d. 21 Feb 1989 Veteran's Hospital, Buffalo NY) Served in the U.S. Navy during World War II. Died after a long illness. Buried Holy Cross Cemetery, Lackawanna NY.

Don Ross—7 Years Infielder (b. 16 Jul 1914 Pasadena CA–d. 28 Mar 1996 Methodist Hospital, Arcadia CA) He was a salesman at a retail liquor store for 15 years. Died from complications four weeks after knee replacement surgery. Buried Resurrection Cemetery, San Gabriel CA.

Ernie Ross—1 Year Pitcher (b. 31 Mar 1880 Toronto, Ontario, Canada–d. 28 Mar 1950 Wellesley Hosp, Toronto, Ontario, Canada) Buried Necropolis Cemetery, Toronto, Ontario, Can.

George Ross—1 Year Pitcher (b. 28 Jun 1893 San Rafael CA–d. 22 Apr 1935 Amityville NY) Died from pneumonia.

Claude Rossman—5 Years Infielder (b. 17 Jun 1881 Philmont NY–d. 16 Jan 1928 Poughkeepsie NY) Stricken with a nervous breakdown at the height of his baseball career, he had been ill some time and his death was not unexpected. Buried Mellenville NY.

Frank Rosso—1 Year Pitcher (b. 1 Mar 1921 Agawam MA–d. 26 Jan 1980 Mercy Hospital, Springfield MA) Served in the U.S. Marines during World War II. He coached football, baseball and basketball at Westfield High School and was athletic director there from 1956 until 1978 when poor health forced his retirement. Buried St Thomas Cemetery, West Springfield MA.

Braggo Roth—8 Years Outfielder (b. 29 Aug 1892 Chicago IL–d. 11 Sep 1936 St Luke's Hospital, Chicago IL) He enjoyed life, fishing, golfing and visiting with friends. Died from a fractured skull suffered in an automobile accident earlier that day. Buried St Mary's Cemetery, Burlington WI.

Frank Roth—6 Years Catcher (b. 11 Oct 1878 Chicago IL–d. 27 Mar 1955 at his home in Burlington WI) He played, coached and scouted baseball 31 years, then umpired for several more. Buried St Charles Cemetery, Burlington WI.

Bob Rothel—1 Year Infielder (b. 17 Sep 1923 Columbia Station OH–d. 21 Mar 1984 Huron OH) He was the president of State Sales, Inc, in Elyria OH. Died from a self-inflicted gunshot wound. Buried York Chapel Cemetery, Bellevue OH.

Bobby Rothermel—1 Year Infielder (b. 18 Dec 1870 Fleetwood PA–d. 11 Feb 1927 Detroit MI).

Jack Rothfuss—1 Year Infielder (b. 18 Apr 1872 Newark NJ–d. 20 Apr 1947 Basking Ridge NJ).

Claude Rothgeb—1 Year Outfielder (b. 1 Jan 1880 Milford IL–d. 6 Jul 1944 Manitowoc WI).

Jack Rothrock—11 Years Outfielder (b. 14 Mar 1905 Long Beach CA–d. 2 Feb 1980 County Medical Center, San Bernardino CA) He managed some minor league baseball before working 20 years as a foreman for the San Bernardino County, CA, street department, retiring in 1970. Died from a heart attack. Buried Montecito Memorial Park, Colton CA.

Edd Roush—18 Years Outfielder Hall of Fame (b. 8 May 1893 Oakland City IN–d. 21 Mar 1988 Bradenton FL) He retired to Bradenton in 1935 and was a winter visitor there until his death. Died from a heart attack suffered while attending a spring training game. At the time of his death he was the oldest living member of baseball's Hall of Fame. Buried Montgomery Cemetery, Oakland City IN.

Phil Routcliffe—1 Year Outfielder (b. 24 Oct 1870 Oswego NY–d. 4 Oct 1918 at his home in Oswego NY) He was a member of the Oswego Police Department. Died from influenza during the great flu epidemic of 1918.

Dave Rowan—1 Year Infielder (b. 6 Dec 1882 Eananoque, Ontario, Canada–d. 30 Jul 1955 Toronto, Ontario, Canada).

Jack Rowan—7 Years Pitcher (b. 16 Jun 1886 New Castle PA–d. 29 Sep 1966 Crestview Nursing Home, Dayton OH) He was a mail carrier in Dayton from 1919 until he retired in 1950. Buried Memorial Park Cemetery, Dayton OH.

Dave Rowe—7 Years Outfielder 2 Years Manager (b. 9 Oct 1854 Harrisburg PA–d. 9 Dec 1930 Glendale CA).

Harland Rowe—1 Year Infielder (b. 20 Apr 1896 Springvale ME–d. 26 May 1969 at his home in Springvale ME) Served in the U.S. Army during World War I. He was a cashier at Springvale National Bank for 48 years, retiring in 1966. Died unexpectedly. Buried Riverside Cemetery, Springvale ME.

Jack Rowe—12 Years Infielder 1 Year Manager (b. 18 Dec 1856 Harrisburg PA–d. 26 Apr 1911 St Louis MO) Buried Bellefontaine Cemetery, St Louis MO.

Schoolboy Rowe—15 Years Pitcher (b. 11 Jan 1910 Waco TX–d. 8 Jan 1961 El Dorado AR) Served in the U.S. Navy during World War II. He got his name when he was in high school, pitching against a local semi-pro team in Texas. The next day a newspaper reported, "Schoolboy beats local nine." From that time on he was known as "Schoolboy". He won 16 straight games in 1934. He coached and scouted for several major league teams. Died from a heart attack. Buried Arlington Cemetery, El Dorado AR.

Bama Rowell—6 Years Infielder (b. 13 Jan 1916 Citronelle AL–d. 16 Aug 1993 at his home in Citronelle AL) World War II veteran. Buried New Home Cemetery, Citronelle AL.

Ed Rowen—3 Years Catcher (b. 22 Oct 1857 Bridgeport CT–d. 22 Feb 1892 at his parent's home in Bridgeport CT) Died from general debility and hemorrhages of the lungs.

Chuck Rowland—1 Year Catcher (b. 23 Jul 1899 Warrenton NC–d. 21 Jan 1992 Wake Medical Center, Raleigh NC) He was a retired electrical machinist. Buried Greenmount Cemetery, Wendell NC.

Pants Rowland—4 Years Manager (b. 12 Feb 1879 Platteville WI–d. 17 May 1969 Terrace Nursing Home, Chicago IL) He was a minor league manager and executive and an American League umpire from 1923 to 1927. Later he was president of the Pacific Coast League. Buried Holy Sepulchre Cemetery, Worth IL.

Jim Roxburgh—2 Years Catcher (b. 17 Jan 1858 San Francisco CA–d. 21 Feb 1934 San Francisco CA) Died from internal injuries suffered two weeks earlier when he was struck by a car on a San Francisco street. Buried Holy Cross Catholic Cemetery, Colma CA.

Charlie Roy—1 Year Pitcher (b. 22 Jun 1884 Beaulieu MN–d. 10 Feb 1950 at his home southeast of Blackfoot ID) A half-blood Chippewa Indian, he worked in dairying at a number of Indian schools, before farming the last 15 years of his life near Fort Hall ID. Died from a heart attack. Buried Gibson Mission Cemetery, Blackfoot ID.

Emil Roy—1 Year Pitcher (b. 26 May 1907 Brighton MA–d. 5 Jan 1997 Cypress Cove Care Center, Crystal River FL) Served in the U.S. Navy during World War II. He worked for Schenley Distillers Corporation of New York as national sales manager for military and special accounts, retiring to Florida in 1972. Cremated.

Luther Roy—4 Years Pitcher (b. 29 Jul 1902 Ooltewah TN–d. 24 Jul 1963 Blodgett Hospital, Grand Rapids MI) He lived 12 years in Grand Rapids, working for Packaging Corporation of America. Died after a lingering illness. Buried Rest Lawn Memorial Park, Grand Rapids MI.

Al Rubeling—4 Years Infielder (b. 10 May 1913 Baltimore MD–d. 28 Jan 1988 Baltimore MD) Buried Parkwood Cemetery, Baltimore MD.

Art Ruble—2 Years Outfielder (b. 11 Mar 1903 Knoxville TN–d. 1 Nov 1983 Chilhowee Nursing Center, Maryville TN) He retired from ALCOA in 1967 after more than 25 years service. A Maryville College alumnus, he is honored on their Wall of Fame. Buried Logan's Chapel Cemetery, Maryville TN.

Johnny Rucker—6 Years Outfielder (b. 15 Jan 1917 Crabapple GA–d. 7 Aug 1985 Colquitt Medical Center, Moultrie GA) He worked for a company in Moultrie that made company uniforms and rose to the position of executive vice-president. Died from the complications of Alzheimer's disease after falling and breaking a hip and contracting pneumonia. Buried Rucker Family Cemetery, Crabapple GA.

Nap Rucker—10 Years Pitcher (b. 30 Sep 1884 Crabapple GA–d. 19 Dec 1970 St Joseph Hospital, Atlanta GA) Buried Roswell Presbyterian Church Cemetery, Roswell GA.

John Rudderham—1 Year Outfielder (b. 30 Aug 1863 Quincy MA–d. 3 Apr 1942 Randolph MA) He was a trainer for professional boxers and for the Phillies from 1907 to 1914. After that he was the trainer for the football and track teams at the Univ of Illinois. He also umpired some minor league baseball. Died after he was in failing health for many years. Buried St Mary's Cemetery, Randolph MA.

Dick Rudolph—13 Years Pitcher (b. 25 Aug 1887 New York City NY–d. 20 Oct 1949 Bronx NY) He was a coach for several seasons. Died from the effects of a heart attack suffered two months earlier. Buried Woodlawn Cemetery, Bronx NY.

Don Rudolph—6 Years Pitcher (b. 16 Aug 1931 Baltimore MD–d. 12 Sep 1968 Encino Hospital, Encino CA) He was a corporate vice-president of Underground Utilities, Inc, an installer of underground electric and telephone conduit. Died from injuries suffered in an automobile accident. Buried Forest Lawn-Hollywood Hills, Los Angeles CA.

Dutch Rudolph—2 Years Outfielder (b. 10 Jul 1882 Natrona PA–d. 17 Apr 1967 Natrona PA).

Muddy Ruel—19 Years Catcher 1 Year Manager (b. 20 Feb 1896 St Louis MO–d. 13 Nov 1963 Palo Alto CA) He was active in baseball 43 years as a player, coach, manager and executive. Died from a heart attack while driving his car. Buried Alta Mesa Memorial Park, Palo Alto CA.

Dutch Ruether—11 Years Pitcher (b. 13 Sep 1893 Alameda CA–d. 16 May 1970 at a hospital in Phoenix AZ) For 25 years he was a scout for the Giants and lived in Los Angeles CA. Died after a year-long illness. Cremated.

Red Ruffing—22 Years Pitcher Hall of Fame (b. 3 May 1904 Granville IL–d. 17 Feb 1986 Hillcrest Hospital, Mayfield Heights OH) Considered to be the best hitting pitcher of his time, he was a scout for the Indians, White Sox and Mets, and coached one year for the Mets. He had a stroke 13 years before his death and spent those last years of his life in a wheel chair. Died from heart failure. Buried Hillcrest Memorial Park Cemetery, Bedford Heights OH.

Chico Ruiz—8 Years Infielder (b. 5 Dec 1938 Santo Domingo, Cuba–d. 9 Feb 1972 Palomar Memorial Hospital, Escondido CA) Killed in a one-car accident when he lost control of his car, hitting a signpost on I 15 near Escondido. Buried El Camino Memorial Park, San Diego CA.

Joe Rullo—2 Years Infielder (b. 16 Jun 1916 New York City NY–d. 28 Oct 1969 St Agnes Hospital, Philadelphia PA) He worked in the maintenance division of General Electric in Philadelphia. Buried Holy Cross Cemetery, Yeadon PA.

Bill Rumler—3 Years Catcher (b. 27 Mar 1891 Milford NE–d. 26 May 1966 Veteran's Hospital, Lincoln NE) World War I veteran. He spent 30 years in police work, including time as the chief of police at Milford. He also served as Justice of the Peace and was a draft board member after retiring from police work in 1964. Buried Blue Mound Cemetery, Milford NE.

Pete Runnels—14 Years Infielder 1 Year Manager (b. 28 Jan 1928 Lufkin TX–d. 20 May 1991 Bayshore Hospital, Pasadena TX) Served in the U.S. Marines. He was the founder and co-owner of Highland Lakes Athletic Association and Camp Champions, a summer camp for boys and girls. Died after suffering a heart attack. Buried Forest Park East, Houston TX.

Damon Runyon—Hall of Fame (b. 4 Oct 1884 Manhattan KS–d. 10 Dec 1946 Memorial Hospital, New York City NY) Served in the U.S. Army during World War I. Worked as a syndicated columnist for nearly 35 years, covering a wide variety of subjects, including sports. Died from cancer. Cremated.

Jacob Ruppert—(b. 5 Aug 1867 New York City NY–d. 13 Jan 1939 at his home in New York City NY) The owner of the brewery founded by his father in 1851, he bought the Yankees in 1915 and owned them until his death. He also owned a stable of thoroughbred race horses. Died from a complication of ailments, including phlebitis. Buried Kensico Cemetery, Valhalla NY.

Andy Rush—1 Year Pitcher (b. 26 Dec 1889 Longton KS–d. 16 Mar 1969 Fresno CA) He was the owner and operator of a gas station in Fresno. Died from a heart attack. Buried Washington Colony Cemetery, Fresno CA.

Amos Rusie—10 Years Pitcher Hall of Fame (b. 30 May 1871 Mooresville IN–d. 6 Dec 1942 Ballard General Hospital, Seattle WA) He lived on a ranch near Auburn WA until a few years before his death. Buried Acacia Cemetery, Seattle WA.

Allan Russell—11 Years Pitcher (b. 31 Jul 1893 Baltimore MD–d. 20 Oct 1972 Baltimore MD) Died suddenly. Buried Loudon Park National Cemetery, Baltimore MD.

Harvey Russell—2 Years Catcher (b. 10 Jan 1887 Marshall VA–d. 8 Jan 1980 The Hermitage, Alexandria VA) Served in France for the U.S. Army during World War I. He operated a farm near Marshall and was the postmaster at Marshall from 1937 until he retired in 1957. He was also a volunteer for the Marshall Fire Department. Buried Ivy Hill Cemetery, Upperville VA.

Jack Russell—15 Years Pitcher (b. 24 Oct 1905 Paris TX–d. 3 Nov 1990 Morton Plant Hospital, Clearwater FL) He founded Jack Russell Oil Company in Clearwater about 1940 and operated it until he turned it over to his son. A civic leader, he was a city commissioner from 1951 to 1955 and an avid golfer. Buried Sylvan Abbey Memorial Park, Clearwater FL.

Jim Russell—10 Years Outfielder (b. 1 Oct 1918 Fayette City PA–d. 24 Nov 1987 Pittsburgh PA) He scouted nine years for the Dodgers and Senators. Moving to Florida in 1978, he was a salesman there for Smith-Corona Typewriter Company, retiring in 1987. Died from a heart attack on a plane from Tampa FL to Pittsburgh where he was to visit family for Thanksgiving. Buried Mount Auburn Cemetery, Fayette City PA.

John Russell—4 Years Pitcher (b. 20 Oct 1894 San Mateo CA–d. 19 Nov 1930 Ely NV) World War I veteran. He worked his last five years in a club in Ely. Died unexpectedly in his hotel room after retiring for the night. Buried Cypress Lawn Memorial Park, Colma CA.

Lefty Russell—3 Years Pitcher (b. 8 Jul 1890 Baltimore MD–d. 22 Jan 1962 Baltimore MD) He managed minor league baseball for a short while before going to work on the Baltimore waterfront. Buried Dulaney Valley Memorial Garden, Timonium MD.

Lloyd Russell—2 Games Pinch Runner (b. 10 Apr 1913 Atoka OK–d. 24 May 1968 Goodall-Witcher Hospital, Clifton TX) Served in both the Atlantic and Pacific for the U.S. Navy during World War II. He was athletic director and head football coach at St Mary's College in San Antonio TX and at North Texas State University in Denton TX before becoming chairman of the Health, Physical Education and Recreation Department at Baylor University in Waco TX. He was also a Waco city councilman. Died from a heart attack. Buried Oakwood Cemetery, Waco TX.

Reb Russell—9 Years Pitcher (b. 12 Apr 1889 Jackson MS–d. 30 Sep 1973 at a nursing home in Indianapolis IN) He once struck Babe Ruth out on three straight pitches, and faced Ruth four times, always getting him out. For 25 years he was a guard at Kingan and Company and at Hygrade Food Products Company, both in Indianapolis, retiring in 1959. Buried St Joseph Cemetery, Indianapolis IN.

Rip Russell—6 Years Infielder (b. 26 Jan 1915 Los Angeles CA–d. 26 Sep 1976 at his home in Los Alamitos CA) He was a salesman for a wholesale beer distributor for 18 years. Died from a heart attack. Buried Holy Cross Cemetery, Culver City CA.

Babe Ruth—22 Years Outfielder Hall of Fame (b. 6 Feb 1895 Baltimore MD–d. 16 Aug 1948 New York City NY) In addition to his feats as a prolific homerun hitter, he was also an outstanding pitcher, winning 94 games early in his career. Died from throat cancer. Buried Gate of Heaven Cemetery, Hawthorne NY.

Jim Rutherford—1 Year Outfielder (b. 26 Sep 1886 Stillwater MN–d. 18 Sep 1956 Lakewood Hospital, Cleveland OH) An ardent golfer, he worked 40 years for Phoenix Mutual Life Insurance Company. Buried Lakewood Park Cemetery, Cleveland OH.

Blondy Ryan—6 Years Infielder (b. 4 Jan 1906 Lynn MA–d. 28 Nov 1959 at his home in Swampscott MA) Served in the U.S. Navy during World War II. Before the war he was a deputy collector for the Internal Revenue Service. Later he was an officer in a warehouse firm. Died from a heart attack. Buried St Joseph Cemetery, Lynn MA.

Bud Ryan—2 Years Outfielder (b. 6 Oct 1885 near Plainville KS–d. 9 Jul 1956 Mercy Hospital, Sacramento CA) He managed minor league baseball and operated a service station near the ballpark in Sacramento. Died from a stroke. Buried St Mary's Cemetery, Sacramento CA.

Connie Ryan—12 Years Infielder 2 Years Manager (b. 27 Feb 1920 New Orleans LA–d. 3 Jan 1996 Metairie LA) Coached four years.

Cyclone Ryan—2 Years Infielder (b. 1866 Capperwhite, Ireland–d. 30 Jan 1917 Medfield MA).

Ellis Ryan—(b. abt 1904 Cleveland OH–d. 11 Aug 1966 Holy Cross Hospital, Fort Lauderdale FL) A baseball executive, he was president and part-owner of the Cleveland Indians from 1949 to 1952. Buried Knollwood Cemetery, Mayfield OH.

Jack Ryan—1 Year Outfielder (b. 5 May 1905 Mineral KS–d. 2 Sep 1967 Rochester MN).

Jack Ryan—3 Years Pitcher (b. 19 Sep 1884 Lawrenceville IL–d. 16 Oct 1949 Handsboro MS) Buried Evergreen Cemetery, Gulfport MS.

Jimmy Ryan—18 Years Outfielder (b. 11 Feb 1863 Clinton MA–d. 26 Oct 1923 Chicago IL)

After he grew tired of the strenuous schedule of major league baseball he managed semi-pro teams in the Chicago area. Buried Calvary Cemetery, Evanston IL.

John Ryan —13 Years Catcher (b. 12 Nov 1869 Haverhill MA–d. 21 Aug 1952 Jamaica Plain MA) He coached college baseball at the Univ of Washington and the Univ of Virginia. During World War I he took a job with the government as an athletic instructor. He also managed some minor league baseball and coached for the Red Sox and Senators. Buried St James Cemetery, Haverhill MA.

Johnny Ryan —2 Years Outfielder (b. abt 1852 Philadelphia PA–d. 22 Mar 1902 Philadelphia PA) For his last nine years he was a policeman for the Philadelphia Police Department. Died while on duty from heart failure during a struggle with an unruly saloon patron. Buried New Cathedral Cemetery, Philadelphia PA.

Rosy Ryan —10 Years Pitcher (b. 15 Mar 1898 Worcester MA–d. 10 Dec 1980 Scottsdale Memorial Hospital, Scottsdale AZ) His baseball career spanned nearly 50 years as a player, coach, minor league manager and executive. He was the first National League pitcher to hit a home run in a World Series game. Died from cancer. Buried St John's Cemetery, Worcester MA.

Mike Ryba —10 Years Pitcher (b. 9 Jun 1903 DeLancey PA–d. 13 Dec 1971 Brookline Station MO) One year in the minor leagues he played every game of the season, either as a pitcher or catcher, and led the league in hitting. Later he managed, coached and was a scout for the Red Sox and Cardinals. Died from injuries he suffered when he fell from a ladder while trimming a tree at his home. Buried Resurrection Cemetery, Springfield MO.

Gene Rye —1 Year Outfielder (b. 15 Nov 1906 Chicago IL–d. 21 Jan 1980 Park Ridge IL).

S

By Saam —Hall of Fame (b. 11 Sep 1914 Fort Worth TX–d. 16 Jan 2000 Devon Manor, Devon PA) The popular radio announcer for the Phillies and the Philadelphia Athletics, he called more than 8000 games during a 38-year career, retiring in 1975. Died following a stroke. Buried Calvary Cemetery, West Conshohocken PA.

Frank Sacka —2 Years Catcher (b. 30 Aug 1924 Romulus MI–d. 7 Dec 1994 Dearborn MI) Buried Michigan Memorial Park Cemetery, Flat Rock MI.

Bill Sadler —(b. abt 1909–d. 10 Nov 1987 Christiana Hospital, Delaware City DE) He played in the Negro Leagues and for 20 years was a laborer for the Delaware State Division of Highways, retiring in 1974. Died from heart failure. Buried Gracelawn Memorial Park, New Castle DE.

Ed Sadowski —5 Years Catcher (b. 19 Jan 1931 Pittsburgh PA–d. 6 Nov 1993 Orange Grove Conv Hosp, Garden Grove CA) Served in the military. He was an assistant press operator for a paper container manufacturer for 20 years. Died from respiratory failure after suffering two years with Lou Gehrig's disease. Buried Holy Sepulchre Cemetery, Orange CA.

Ted Sadowski —3 Years Pitcher (b. 1 Apr 1936 Pittsburgh PA–d. 18 Jul 1993 at his home in Shaler PA) He gave traveling baseball clinics for the Allegheny County (PA) Parks and Recreation Department from 1966 to 1978. Later he worked for a sporting goods business, was a house painter and worked for a cleaning service. He officiated sporting events throughout the area for 25 years. Died from cancer. Buried Allegheny Cemetery, Pittsburgh PA.

Harry Sage —1 Year Catcher (b. 16 Mar 1864 Rock Island IL–d. 27 May 1947 at his home in Rock Island IL) For 25 years he was a machinist at the Rock Island Arsenal, leaving there in 1921 to work in a number of theatres in the Rock Island area. He retired from the theatre business in 1941. Died following a three-month illness. Buried Calvary Cemetery, Rock Island IL.

Bus Saidt—Hall of Fame (b. abt 1920 Bordentown NJ–d. 8 Apr 1989 Helene Fuld Medical Center, Trenton NJ) An accountant by education, from 1940 to 1965 he was an accountant for the City of Trenton. From 1947 to 1969 he was sports director for radio stations in the Trenton area, and from 1967 until his death he was a sportswriter for the *Trenton Times* newspaper. Died from a heart attack. Buried Riverview Cemetery, Trenton NJ.

Vic Saier—8 Years Infielder (b. 4 May 1891 Lansing MI–d. 14 May 1967 at his home in East Lansing MI) World War I veteran. His baseball career was cut short by a compound ankle fracture. Buried Mount Hope Cemetery, Lansing MI.

Freddy Sale—1 Year Pitcher (b. 2 May 1902 Chester SC–d. 27 May 1956 at his home in Hermosa Beach CA) He was an advertising executive for a beverage company. Cremated.

Ed Sales—1 Year Infielder (b. 1861 Harrisburg PA–d. 10 Aug 1912 at a friend's home in New Haven CT) Died from tuberculosis. Buried Mount Calvary Cemetery, Harrisburg PA.

Bill Salisbury—1 Year Pitcher (b. 12 Nov 1876 Algona IA–d. 17 Jan 1952 Rowena OR) Spanish-American War veteran. He was a printer for The Dalles Chronicle newspaper, as well as working at a number of other print shops in the area. Buried Odd Fellows Cemetery, The Dalles OR.

Harry Salisbury—2 Years Pitcher (b. 15 May 1855 Providence RI–d. 29 Mar 1933 at his home in Chicago IL).

Bill Salkeld—6 Years Catcher (b. 8 Mar 1917 Pocatello ID–d. 22 Apr 1967 at his home in Los Angeles CA) He was a furniture salesman at a Los Angeles department store. Died from rectal cancer. Buried Forest Lawn-Hollywood Hills, Los Angeles CA.

Slim Sallee—14 Years Pitcher (b. 3 Feb 1885 Higginsport OH–d. 22 Mar 1950 Higginsport OH) He won a game and lost a game in the infamous World Series of 1919 when his team, the Reds, played the White Sox. He operated a tavern in Higginsport for several years. Died from a heart attack. Buried Confidence Cemetery, Georgetown OH.

Roger Salmon—1 Year Pitcher (b. 11 May 1891 Newark NJ–d. 17 Jun 1974 Belfast ME) For many years he was the court stenographer at Newark. Buried Belfast Grove Cemetery, Belfast ME.

H G Salsinger—Hall of Fame (d. 27 Nov 1958). Sportswriter.

Jack Saltzgaver—6 Years Infielder (b. 23 Jan 1905 Croton IA–d. 2 Feb 1978 in a hospital at Keokuk IA) He managed the Keokuk Skating Rink for several years and was superintendent of the Oakland Cemetery in Keokuk. Buried Greenglade Cemetery, Farmington IA.

Gus Salve—1 Year Pitcher (b. 29 Dec 1885 Boston MA–d. 29 Mar 1971 Providence RI) Buried Thomas Cemetery, Swansea MA.

Jack Salveson—5 Years Pitcher (b. 5 Jan 1914 Fullerton CA–d. 28 Dec 1974 Metropolitan State Hospital, Norwalk CA) He pitched for years in the Pacific Coast League. Died from cancer of the liver and Alzheimer's disease. Buried Loma Vista Memorial Park, Fullerton CA.

Manny Salvo—5 Years Pitcher (b. 30 Jun 1912 Sacramento CA–d. 7 Feb 1997 Vallejo CA) Served in Japan for the U.S. Army during World War II. He was a Sacramento County, CA, deputy marshall for 17 years. Died from congestive heart failure and interstitial lung disease. Buried St Mary's Cemetery, Sacramento CA.

Ike Samuels—1 Year Infielder (b. 20 Feb 1876 Chicago IL–d. 1 Jan 1942 Cedar of Lebanon Hospital, Los Angeles CA) He owned and operated of a lady's clothing store. Died from a heart attack. Buried Rosemont Park Cemetery, Chicago IL.

Joe Samuels—1 Year Pitcher (b. 21 Mar 1905 Scranton PA–d. 28 Oct 1996 Bath NY).

Gus Sanberg—2 Years Catcher (b. 23 Feb 1895 Long Island City NY–d. 3 Feb 1930 California Lutheran Hosp, Los Angeles CA) Died from burns suffered when his car's gas tank exploded. Cremated.

Celerino Sanchez—2 Years Infielder (b. 3 Feb 1944 Veracruz, Mexico–d. 1 May 1992 Leon, Mexico) Died from an aneurysm.

Heinie Sand—6 Years Infielder (b. 3 Jul 1897 San Francisco CA–d. 3 Nov 1958 St Mary's Hospital, San Francisco CA) World War I veteran. He was an active member in one of San Francisco's oldest plumbing contracting firms. Died from respiratory failure. Cremated.

Ben Sanders—5 Years Pitcher (b. 16 Feb 1865 Catharpin VA–d. 29 Aug 1930 Baptist Memorial Hospital, Memphis TN) He was a civil engineer. Died from a gall bladder infection. Buried Sudley Methodist Church Cemetery, Catharpin VA.

Ray Sanders—7 Years Infielder (b. 4 Dec 1916 Bonne Terre MO–d. 28 Oct 1983 Washington MO) Killed in an automobile accident. Buried Mount Hope Mausoleum, St Louis MO.

Roy Sanders—2 Years Pitcher (b. 1 Aug 1892 Stafford KS–d. 17 Jan 1950 at his home in Kansas City MO) Buried Calvary Cemetery, Kansas City MO.

Roy Sanders—2 Years Pitcher (b. 10 Jun 1894 Pittsburg KS–d. 8 Jul 1963 St Joseph Infirmary, Louisville KY) He worked for Oertel Brewing Company 25 years, retiring in 1960. Buried Louisville Memorial Gardens, Louisville KY.

War Sanders—2 Years Pitcher (b. 2 Aug 1877 Maynardville TN–d. 3 Aug 1962 at his home in Chattanooga TN) Buried Forest Hills Cemetery, Chattanooga TN.

Ed Sanicki—2 Years Outfielder (b. 7 Jul 1923 Wallington NJ–d. 6 Jul 1998 Raritan Bay Medical Center, Old Bridge NJ) Served as a signalman for the U.S. Navy during World War II. For 30 years he was a special education teacher in Clifton NJ. Buried Holy Cross Burial Park, East Brunswick NJ.

Louis Santop—11 Years Catcher (b. 17 Jan 1890 Tyler TX–d. 6 Jan 1942 Philadelphia PA) He played in the negro leagues.

Ed Santry—1 Year Infielder (b. 1861 Chicago IL–d. 6 Mar 1899 Chicago IL) Buried Calvary Cemetery, Evanston IL.

Joe Sargent—1 Year Infielder (b. 24 Sep 1893 Rochester NY–d. 5 Jul 1950 at his home in Rochester NY) World War I veteran. He operated a smokehouse in Rochester and was an outstanding bowler and a better than average amateur golfer. He had suffered from blinding headaches for years. Buried Holy Sepulchre Cemetery, Rochester NY.

Bill Sarni—5 Years Catcher (b. 19 Sep 1927 Los Angeles CA–d. 15 Apr 1983 St John's Mercy Hospital, Creve Coeur MO) His baseball career was shortened by a heart attack suffered at age 29. He was a general partner in a brokerage firm in St Louis. Died from a heart attack.

Ed Sauer—4 Years Outfielder (b. 3 Jan 1919 Pittsburgh PA–d. 1 Jul 1988 Los Robles Hospital, Thousand Oaks CA) Died from a ruptured aortic aneurysm. Cremated.

Hank Sauer—15 Years Outfielder (b. 17 Mar 1917 Pittsburgh PA–d. 24 Aug 2001 Burlingame CA) Served in the U.S. Coast Guard during World War II. Died from a heart attack while golfing.

Rusty Saunders—1 Year Outfielder (b. 12 Mar 1906 Trenton NJ–d. 24 Nov 1967 Community Memorial Hospital, Toms River NJ) Served in the U.S. Navy during World War II. Also a professional basketball player, he was a corrections officer at the New Jersey State Prison in Trenton from 1939 until his death. Buried Greenwood Cemetery, Trenton NJ.

Don Savage—2 Years Infielder (b. 5 Mar 1919 Bloomfield NJ–d. 25 Dec 1961 Mountainside Hospital, Montclair NJ) He worked for the Boylis Company of Bloomfield NJ and for the Otis Elevator Company. Died after a year-long illness complicated by a longstanding diabetic condition. Buried Mount Olivet Cemetery, Newark NJ.

Hal Savage—3 Years Outfielder (b. 29 Aug 1883 Southington CT–d. 26 Jun 1940 New Castle Hospital, New Castle PA) He owned and operated the Savage Hotel in New Castle. Died from a heart attack after being ill the past year. Buried Southington CT.

Don Savidge—1 Year Pitcher (b. 28 Aug 1908 Berwick PA–d. 22 Mar 1983 Cottage Hospital, Santa Barbara CA) He was a real estate broker for 28 years. Died from complications of a perforated duadenal ulcer. He donated his body to the UCLA Medical School.

Ralph Savidge—2 Years Pitcher (b. 3 Feb 1879 Jerseytown PA–d. 22 Jul 1959 at his home in Berwick PA) He was the foreman of the freight department for ACF Industries in Berwick until he retired in 1944. When he died he had been ill four years and bedfast his last two months. Buried Pine Grove Cemetery, Berwick PA.

Carl Sawatski—1 Year Catcher (b. 4 Nov 1927 Shickshinny PA–d. 24 Nov 1991 Little Rock AR) He spent his entire life in baseball as an executive, receiving the *Sporting News* executive of the year award in 1970. When he died he was president of the Texas League and was formerly general manager of the Arkansas Travelers baseball team. Buried Pine Crest Memorial Park, Alexander AR.

Carl Sawyer—2 Years Infielder (b. 19 Oct 1890 Seattle WA–d. 17 Jan 1957 Good Samaritan Hospital, Los Angeles CA) One of the first baseball clowns, he was vice-president of a wholesale stationery operation. Died from stomach cancer. Buried Forest Lawn Memorial Park, Glendale CA.

Eddie Sawyer—8 Years Manager (b. 10 Sep 1910 Westerly RI–d. 22 Sep 1997 Phoenixville PA) Died from a combination of respiratory problems and kidney failure. He donated his body to the Pennsylvania Medical Society for research.

Will Sawyer—1 Year Pitcher (b. 29 Jul 1863 Brimfield OH–d. 5 Jan 1936 Kent OH) He was a mechanical engineer for a steel company. Died from a heart attack. Buried Standing Rock Cemetery, Kent OH.

Ollie Sax—1 Year Infielder (b. 5 Nov 1904 Branford CT–d. 21 Mar 1982 St Michael's Medical Center, Newark NJ) He worked for duPont, Inc, in Kearny NJ before spending ten years with Egyptian Lacquer Company in Kearny, retiring in 1971. Buried Arlington Cemetery, Kearny NJ.

Jimmy Say—3 Years Infielder (b. 1862 Baltimore MD–d. 23 Jun 1894 at his home in Baltimore MD) Died after a lingering illness.

Lew Say—4 Years Infielder (b. 4 Feb 1854 Baltimore MD–d. 5 Jun 1930 Fallston MD).

Bill Sayles—2 Years Pitcher (b. 27 Jul 1917 Portland OR–d. 20 Nov 1996 Lincoln City OR) Served in the U.S. Army during World War II. After the war he managed minor league baseball until 1956 when he became a minor league executive until 1962. From 1962 until 1982 he was a scouting supervisor for the Cardinals. From 1982 to 1995 he owned and operated a men's clothing store. Cremated.

Phil Saylor—1 Year Pitcher (b. 2 Jan 1871 Van Wert County OH–d. 23 Jul 1937 at his home in West Alexandria OH) He practiced law in Preble County, OH, from 1906 until his death. He served two terms in the state legislature and one term as prosecuting attorney for Preble County. Died following a long illness. Buried Fairview Cemetery, West Alexandria OH.

Jerry Scala—3 Years Outfielder (b. 27 Sep 1924 Bayonne NJ–d. 14 Dec 1993 Fallston MD) Buried Lorraine Park Cemetery, Baltimore MD.

Frank Scalzi—1 Year Infielder (b. 16 Jun 1913 Lafferty OH–d. 25 Aug 1984 Highland Park V A Hospital, Pittsburgh PA) Served in the U.S. Navy during World War II. He managed minor league baseball until a tragic auto accident in 1960 ended his baseball career and left him partially invalided. He spent his last few years in a wheelchair. Buried Upland Cemetery, Yorkville OH.

Johnny Scalzi—2 Games Pinch Hitter (b. 22 Mar 1907 Stamford CT–d. 27 Sep 1962 Port Chester NY).

Doc Scanlan—8 Years Pitcher (b. 7 Mar 1881 Syracuse NY–d. 29 May 1949 at his home in Brooklyn NY) He practiced general medicine in the Park Slope section of Brooklyn for 38 years. Died after an illness of several months. Buried St Joseph's Cemetery, Stockbridge MA.

Frank Scanlan—1 Year Pitcher (b. 28 Apr 1890 Syracuse NY–d. 9 Apr 1969 Brooklyn NY) Buried St John's Cemetery, Middle Village NY.

Mort Scanlan—1 Year Infielder (b. 18 Mar 1861 Chicago IL–d. 29 Dec 1928 at his home in Chicago IL) Buried Calvary Cemetery, Evanston IL.

Mike Scanlon—2 Years Manager (b. Nov 1843 Cork, Ireland–d. 18 Jan 1929 Georgrtown Hospital, Washington DC) Served in the Union Army during the Civil War. He conducted a billiard parlor in Washington DC. Died from the effects of a fall suffered a few weeks earlier. Buried Mount Olivet Cemetery, Washington DC.

Pat Scantlebury—1 Year Pitcher (b. 11 Nov 1917 Gatun, Panama–d. 24 May 1991 Mountainside Hospital, Glen Ridge NJ) He played in the Negro Leagues. Buried Glendale Cemetery, Bloomfield NJ.

Ray Scarborough—10 Years Pitcher (b. 23 Jul 1917 Mount Gilead NC–d. 1 Jul 1982 at his home in Mount Olive NC) Served in the U.S. Navy during World War II. He owned and operated Scarborough Oil and Supply Company in Mount Olive. He was also a scout for several teams. Died from a heart attack. Buried Martin-Price Cemetery, Mount Olive NC.

Russ Scarritt—4 Years Outfielder (b. 14 Jan 1903 Pensacola FL–d. 4 Dec 1994 Pensacola FL) Buried St John's Cemetery, Pensacola FL.

Les Scarsella—5 Years Infielder (b. 23 Nov 1913 Santa Cruz CA–d. 16 Dec 1958 Moffitt Hospital, San Francisco CA) He owned a liquor store in Alameda CA for ten years. Died from heart disease. Buried Oakmont Memorial Park, Lafayette CA.

Al Schacht—3 Years Pitcher (b. 11 Nov 1892 New York City NY–d. 14 Jul 1984 Waterbury Hospital, Waterbury CT) The "Clown Prince of Baseball", he was best known as a clown at baseball games after his baseball career was over. Died after a brief illness. Buried Beth El Cemetery, Waterbury CT.

Sid Schacht—2 Years Pitcher (b. 3 Feb 1918 Bogota NJ–d. 30 Mar 1991 Fort Lauderdale FL) Buried Cedar Park Cemetery, Paramus NJ.

Germany Schaefer—15 Years Infielder (b. 4 Feb 1882 Chicago IL–d. 16 May 1919 Saranac Lake NY) Known as a comedian of the diamond, he coached and scouted for the Senators and Giants up until his death. Died from an internal hemorrhage while enroute by train to Lake Placid NY. Buried St Boniface Cemetery, Chicago IL.

Harry Schafer—3 Years Infielder (b. 14 Aug 1846 Philadelphia PA–d. 28 Feb 1935 at his home in Philadelphia PA) Died from a lingering illness caused by an accident suffered a few years earlier. Buried Fernwood Cemetery, Fernwood PA.

Ray Schalk—18 Years Catcher 2 Years Manager Hall of Fame (b. 12 Aug 1892 Harvel IL–d. 19 May 1970 Wesley Memorial Hospital, Chicago IL) He was an assistant baseball coach at Purdue University and owned a bowling alley. Died from cancer. Buried Evergreen Cemetery, Evergreen Park IL.

Biff Schaller—2 Years Outfielder (b. 23 Sep 1889 Chicago IL–d. 9 Oct 1939 Emeryville CA) He operated a restaurant in Emeryville CA. Died from a sudden heart attack. Buried Mountain View Cemetery, Oakland CA.

Bobby Schang—3 Years Catcher (b. 7 Dec 1886 Wales Center NY–d. 29 Aug 1966 Mercy Hospital, Sacramento CA) For 25 years he was an assistant storekeeper for the State of California Division of Highways, retiring in 1956. Died from bladder cancer. Buried St Mary's Cemetery, Sacramento CA.

Wally Schang—19 Years Catcher (b. 22 Aug 1889 South Wales NY–d. 6 Mar 1965 St Luke's Hospital, St Louis MO) He owned and operated a farm outside Dixon MO. Died from a blood clot following surgery. Buried Dixon Cemetery, Dixon MO.

Charley Schanz—5 Years Pitcher (b. 8 Jun 1919 Anacortes WA–d. 28 May 1992 at his home in Sacramento CA) Died from coronary artery disease. Buried East Lawn Memorial Park, Sacramento CA.

Jack Schappert—1 Year Pitcher (b. Brooklyn NY–d. 29 Jul 1916 Rockaway Beach NY).

Bill Schardt—2 Years Pitcher (b. 20 Jan 1886 Cleveland OH–d. 26 Jul 1964 at his home in Vermilion OH) He worked for the personnel department of White Motor Company in Cleveland from 1916 to 1926. After that he owned and operated four service stations in the Cleveland area, retiring in 1944 and moving to Vermilion. Died from a heart attack. Buried Lutheran Cemetery, Cleveland OH.

Art Scharein—3 Years Infielder (b. 30 Jun 1905 Decatur IL–d. 2 Jul 1969 at a hospital in San Antonio TX) He worked 25 years for the Pearl Brewery. Died from a heart attack. Buried Sunset Memorial Park, San Antonio TX.

George Scharein—4 Years Infielder (b. 21 Nov 1914 Decatur IL–d. 23 Dec 1981 at his home in Decatur IL) World War II veteran. He played in the International League and the American Association and retired from Superior Welding Company. Buried Fairlawn Cemetery, Decatur IL.

Nick Scharf—2 Years Outfielder (b. 1859 Baltimore MD–d. 12 May 1937 Baltimore MD) Died from pneumonia. Buried New Cathedral Cemetery, Baltimore MD.

Rube Schauer—5 Years Pitcher (b. 19 Mar 1891 Odessa, Russia–d. 15 Apr 1957 Minneapolis MN) Buried St Mary's Cemetery, Minneapolis MN.

Al Scheer—3 Years Outfielder (b. 21 Oct 1888 Dayton OH–d. 6 May 1959 at his home in Logansport IN) He operated a tavern in Logansport. Buried Mount Hope Cemetery, Logansport IN.

Heinie Scheer—2 Years Infielder (b. 31 Jul 1900 New York City NY–d. 21 Mar 1976 Yale-New Haven Hospital, New Haven CT) For 24 years he was a liquor salesman for Eder Brothers Liquor Distributors, retiring in 1966. Buried Congregation Sinai Memorial Park, Allington CT.

Fritz Scheeren—2 Years Outfielder (b. 1 Jul 1891 Kokomo IN–d. 17 Jun 1973 Oil City PA).

Owen Scheetz—1 Year Pitcher (b. 24 Dec 1913 New Bedford OH–d. 28 Sep 1994 Pine Kirk Nursing Home, Kirkersville OH) He managed minor league baseball and worked for Columbus Bolt Works. He retired from the Reynoldsburg OH Water Department. Died from a heart attack. Buried Glen Rest Memorial Estates, Reynoldsburg OH.

Bob Scheffing—8 Years Catcher 6 Years Manager (b. 11 Aug 1915 Overland MO–d. 26 Oct 1985 St Joseph's Hospital, Phoenix AZ) He was active in baseball for 51 years as a player, manager, announcer and administrator. Buried St Francis Catholic Cemetery, Phoenix AZ.

Ted Scheffler—2 Years Outfielder (b. 5 Apr 1864 New York City NY–d. 24 Feb 1949 Jamaica NY).

Lefty Schegg—1 Year Pitcher (b. 29 Aug 1889 Leesville OH–d. 27 Feb 1963 Niles OH).

Frank Scheibeck—8 Years Infielder (b. 28 Jun 1865 Detroit MI–d. 22 Oct 1956 St Joseph's Hospital, Detroit MI) Buried Mount Elliott Cemetery, Detroit MI.

John Scheible—2 Years Pitcher (b. 16 Feb 1866 Youngstown OH–d. 9 Aug 1897 Mahoning Valley Hospital, Youngstown OH) Died from typhoid fever. Buried Oak Hill Cemetery, Youngstown NC.

Danny Schell—2 Years Outfielder (b. 26 Dec 1927 Fostoria MI–d. 11 May 1972 Mayville MI).

Jim Schelle—1 Year Pitcher (b. 13 Apr 1917 Baltimore MD–d. 4 May 1990 South Shore Hospital, South Weymouth MA) Served in the U.S. Army during World War II. He worked in sales and marketing for a number of firms including Chem-Tex and Madison Chemical Company of Boston, Peter Pan of New York, Maidenform, Playtex and Mona Lisa. Later he was a manufacturing representative for Scripto of Boston. Buried Massachusetts National Cemetery, Bourne MA.

Al Schellhase—2 Years Catcher (b. 13 Sep 1864 Evansville IN–d. 3 Jan 1919 at his home in Evansville IN) His baseball career ended when a foul ball struck him in the left eye, blinding the one eye. He conducted a saloon in Evansville until prohibition shut him down. As a hobby he raised race horses. Died from a complication of diseases. Buried Oak Hill Cemetery, Evansville IN.

Fred Schemanske—1 Year Pitcher (b. 28 Apr 1903 Detroit MI–d. 18 Feb 1960 Detroit MI) He collapsed and died from a heart attack. Buried Woodmere Cemetery, Detroit MI.

Mike Schemer—2 Years Infielder (b. 20 Nov 1917 Baltimore MD–d. 22 Apr 1983 General Hospital, North Miami FL) He lived in Miami 50 years, working 27 years for the Miami Parks Department, retiring in 1975. Buried Southern Memorial Park, North Miami FL.

John Scheneberg—2 Years Pitcher (b. 20 Nov 1887 Guyandotte WV–d. 26 Sep 1950 at a hospital in Huntington WV) Buried Highland Cemetery, Huntington WV.

Hank Schenz—6 Years Infielder (b. 11 Apr 1919 New Richmond OH–d. 12 May 1988 Christ Hospital, Cincinnati OH) Served in the U.S. Navy during World War II. Died after suffering a massive heart attack. Buried Green Mound Cemetery, New Richmond OH.

Joe Schepner—1 Year Infielder (b. 10 Aug 1895 Aliquippa PA–d. 25 Jul 1959 Mobile AL) World War I veteran. Buried Pine Crest Cemetery, Mobile AL.

Dutch Schesler—1 Year Pitcher (b. 1 Jun 1900 Frankfurt, Germany–d. 19 Nov 1953 Harrisburg Hospital, Harrisburg PA) World War I veteran. Buried Harrisburg Cemetery, Harrisburg PA.

Lou Schettler—1 Year Pitcher (b. 12 Jun 1886 Pittsburgh PA–d. 1 May 1960 South Side Hospital, Youngstown OH) His baseball career ended by a broken leg incurred in a train wreck in 1916. He worked for Republic Steel Corporation from 1917 until he retired in 1957. Died from a heart ailment. Buried Forest Lawn Memorial Park, Youngstown OH.

Lou Schiappacasse—1 Year Outfielder (b. 29 Mar 1881 Ann Arbor MI–d. 20 Sep 1910 at his home in Ann Arbor MI) Died from typhoid fever at the height of his career. Buried St Thomas Catholic Cemetery, Ann Arbor MI.

Morrie Schick—1 Year Outfielder (b. 17 Apr 1892 Chicago IL–d. 25 Oct 1979 Hazel Crest IL).

Red Schillings—1 Year Pitcher (b. 29 Mar 1900 Deport TX–d. 7 Jan 1954 Veteran's Hospital, Oklahoma City OK) He worked for the Oklahoma City Fire Department from 1930 to 1944 when an accident forced his retirement. Died from cancer. Buried Memorial Park Cemetery, Oklahoma City OK.

Bill Schindler—1 Year Catcher (b. 10 Jul 1896 Perryville MO–d. 6 Feb 1979 Perry County Memorial Hosp, Perryville MO) World War I veteran. He was a retired soda bottling factory worker. Buried Mount Hope Cemetery, Perryville MO.

Dutch Schirick—1 Game Pinch Hitter (b. 15 Jun 1890 Ruby NY–d. 12 Nov 1968 Kingston NY) An attorney, he was a New York State Supreme Court justice from 1935 to 1961. Buried Mount Marion Cemetery, Mount Marion NY.

Harry Schlafly—4 Years Infielder 2 Years Manager (b. 20 Sep 1878 Port Washington OH–d. 27 Jun 1919 at his home in Beach City OH) He managed and umpired minor league baseball. Died from tubercular meningitis and pulmonary tuberculosis. Buried Grandview Union Cemetery, Strasburg OH.

Admiral Schlei—8 Years Catcher (b. 12 Jan 1878 Cincinnati OH–d. 24 Jan 1958 at his home in Huntington WV) He was a retired employee of Standard Printing and Publishing Company in Huntington. Died after a long illness. Buried Ridgelawn Memorial Park, Barboursville WV.

Dutch Schliebner—1 Year Infielder (b. 19 May 1891 Charlottenburg, Germany–d. 15 Apr 1975 Mercy Hospital, Toledo OH) For 28 years he was a machinist for National Supply Company in Toledo, retiring in 1956. Buried Toledo Memorial Park, Sylvania OH.

Biff Schlitzer—3 Years Pitcher (b. 4 Dec 1884 Rochester NY–d. 4 Jan 1948 Wellesley Hills MA) He was a sales representative for the Armstrong Cork Company. Died after a year's illness. Buried Forest Hill Cemetery, Utica NY.

Ray Schmandt—6 Years Infielder (b. 25 Jan 1896 St Louis MO–d. 2 Feb 1969 St Mary's Hospital, St Louis MO) He worked in the insurance and real estate business. Died from a heart attack. Buried Calvary Cemetery, St Louis MO.

George Schmees—1 Year Outfielder (b. 6 Sep 1924 Cincinnati OH–d. 30 Oct 1998 Alexian Brother's Hospital, San Jose CA) Served in World War II. Died from a heart attack but suffered from prostate cancer and chronic obstructive lung disease. Cremated. Buried Oak Hill Memorial Park, San Jose CA.

Gus Schmelz—11 Years Manager (b. 26 Sep 1850 Columbus OH–d. 13 Oct 1925 at his son's home in Columbus OH) He was a merchant in Springfield OH. Died from heart trouble and Bright's disease. Buried Green Lawn Memorial Cemetery, Columbus OH.

Boss Schmidt—6 Years Catcher (b. 12 Sep 1880 Coal Hill AR–d. 14 Nov 1932 at his doctor's home in Altus AR) Died from an intestinal disorder after a short illness. Buried St Mary's Catholic Cemetery, Altus AR.

Butch Schmidt—4 Years Infielder (b. 19 Jul 1887 Baltimore MD–d. 4 Sep 1952 Baltimore MD) He was a meat dealer at Baltimore. Died suddenly from a heart attack after collapsing while inspecting cattle at the Union Stockyards. Buried Druid Ridge Cemetery, Pikesville MD.

Henry Schmidt—1 Year Pitcher (b. 26 Jun 1873 Brownsville TN–d. 23 Apr 1926 at his home in Nashville TN) He was a pipe fitter for the Nashville, Chattanooga and St Louis Railway. Died from a heart attack. Buried Spring Hill Cemetery, Nashville TN.

Pete Schmidt—1 Year Pitcher (b. 23 Jul 1890 Lowden IA–d. 11 Mar 1973 Pembroke, Ontario, Canada).

Walter Schmidt—10 Years Catcher (b. 20 Mar 1887 Coal Hill AR–d. 4 Jul 1973 at a hospital in Modesto CA) He lived 35 years in Ceres CA. Died after a brief illness. Buried St Stanislaus Catholic Cemetery, Modesto CA.

Crazy Schmit—5 Years Pitcher (b. 13 Feb 1866 Chicago IL–d. 5 Oct 1940 Chicago IL) Buried Mount Greenwood Cemetery, Chicago IL.

Charlie Schmutz—2 Years Pitcher (b. 1 Jan 1891 San Diego CA–d. 27 Jun 1962 Seattle WA) Served in the U.S. Army during World War I. For 37 years he was an outstanding salesman for Graybar Electric Company, retiring in 1957. Cremated.

Frank Schneiberg—1 Year Pitcher (b. 12 Mar 1882 Milwaukee WI–d. 18 May 1948 at his home in Milwaukee WI) He worked in an asbestos plant in Milwaukee. Buried Wanderer's Rest Cemetery, Milwaukee WI.

Pete Schneider—6 Years Pitcher (b. 20 Aug 1895 Los Angeles CA–d. 1 Jun 1957 at his home in Los Angeles CA) Died from a heart attack. Buried Inglewood Park Cemetery, Inglewood CA.

Karl Schnell—2 Years Pitcher (b. 20 Sep 1899 Los Angeles CA–d. 31 May 1992 Lytton Gardens, Palo Alto CA) World War I veteran. He was a superintendent for Richfield Oil Corporation for 40 years. Died from congestive heart failure. Cremated. Buried Alta Mesa Memorial Park, Palo Alto CA.

Jumbo Schoeneck—3 Years Infielder (b. 3 Mar 1862 Chicago IL–d. 20 Jan 1930 Chicago IL) Buried Mount Emblem Cemetery, Elmhurst IL.

Otto Schomberg—3 Years Infielder (b. 14 Nov 1864 Milwaukee WI–d. 3 May 1927 Ottawa KS) He was a retired real estate dealer and lumberman. Died from a heart attack on a train enroute from Pasadena CA, where he had spent the winter, to Milwaukee, where he lived. Buried Fairview.

Ed Schorr—1 Year Pitcher (b. 16 Feb 1891 Bremen OH–d. 12 Sep 1969 Atlantic City Hospital, Atlantic City NJ) He was a trucking executive. Buried Holy Cross Cemetery, Mays Landing NJ.

Gene Schott—5 Years Pitcher (b. 14 Jul 1913 Batavia OH–d. 16 Nov 1992 Sun City Center FL) Buried Garden of Memories, Tampa FL.

Ossee Schreckengost—11 Years Catcher (b. 11 Apr 1875 New Bethlehem PA–d. 9 Jul 1914 Northwestern General Hosp, Philadelphia PA) He played baseball up until two years before he died. Died from a complication of diseases, including uremia. Buried Kittanning Cemetery, Kittanning PA.

Barney Schreiber—1 Year Pitcher (b. 8 May 1882 Waverly OH–d. 6 Oct 1964 Chillicothe Hospital, Chillicothe OH) He owned a confectionary in Chillicothe for a short time before going to work for the Mead Corporation, first as a yard worker and later in their security department, retiring in 1952. Died unexpectedly after a brief illness. Buried Floral Hills Memory Gardens, Chillicothe OH.

Hank Schreiber—5 Years Infielder (b. 12 Jul 1891 Cleveland OH–d. 19 Feb 1968 Indianapolis IN) World War I veteran. He worked for the Indianapolis Salvage Corps and the Diamond Chain Company. Found dead, apparently from a heart attack, in his home several days after his death. Buried Holy Cross Cemetery, Indianapolis IN.

Paul Schreiber—3 Years Pitcher (b. 8 Oct 1902 Jacksonville FL–d. 28 Jan 1982 Sarasota Memorial Hospital, Sarasota FL) He coached for the Yankees and Red Sox and was a scout for the Red Sox. Buried Riverside Memorial Park, Jacksonville FL.

Pop Schriver—14 Years Catcher (b. 11 Jun 1866 Brooklyn NY–d. 27 Dec 1932 Brooklyn NY).

Heinie Schuble—7 Years Infielder (b. 1 Nov 1906 Houston TX–d. 2 Oct 1990 Baytown TX) He was the first player to be married at home plate. Died the same day that his wife of 63 years was buried. Buried Forest Park of Lawndale, Houston TX.

Wes Schulmerich—4 Years Outfielder (b. 21 Aug 1902 Hillsboro OR–d. 26 Jun 1985 Corvallis OR) Served in the U.S. Navy during World War II, reaching the rank of Lieutenant Commander. He was a river guide at Beaver OR. From 1947 to 1958 he was a commissioner in Tillamook County, OR, and from 1958 to 1960 he owned the Albany Golf Course at Albany OR. Died from cancer. Buried Valley Memorial Park, Hillsboro OR.

Fred Schulte—11 Years Outfielder (b. 13 Jan 1901 Belvidere IL–d. 20 May 1983 Northwoods Healthcare Centre, Belvidere IL) He managed minor league teams and was a scout for several years. Died following a long illness. Cremated.

Ham Schulte—1 Year Infielder (b. 1 Sep 1912 St Louis MO–d. 21 Dec 1993 at his home in St Charles MO) Served in the U.S. Army during World War II. He was a co-owner of St Charles Bowling Lanes 34 years, retiring in 1977. Died from cancer. Buried St Peter's Catholic Church Cemetery, St Charles MO.

Johnny Schulte—5 Years Catcher (b. 8 Sep 1896 Fredericktown MO–d. 28 Jun 1978 St Louis MO) He was a coach and scout. Died from cancer. Buried Calvary Cemetery, St Louis MO.

Len Schulte—3 Years Infielder (b. 5 Dec 1916 St Charles MO–d. 6 May 1986 Orlando FL) He moved to Orlando from St Louis MO in 1957 and was a maintenance worker for the public schools. Buried Glen Haven Memorial Park, Winter Park FL.

Wildfire Schulte—15 Years Outfielder (b. 17 Sep 1882 Cohocton NY–d. 17 Aug 1975 Mount Clemens General Hosp, Roseville MI) He was a salesman for the Eagle Picher Lead Company. Buried Resurrection Cemetery, Mount Clemens MI.

Bob Schultz—4 Years Pitcher (b. 27 Nov 1923 Louisville KY–d. 31 Mar 1979 General Hospital, Nashville TN) He had a 25–6 record for the Nashville Vols of the Southern League in 1950, but never had another good year. He was a house painter. Shot and killed in a brawl at a bar in the VFW Hall. Buried Nashville National Cemetery, Nashville TN.

Joe Schultz—11 Years Outfielder (b. 24 Jul 1893 Pittsburgh PA–d. 13 Apr 1941 Providence Hospital, Columbia SC) He managed minor league baseball and coached for the Cardinals before becoming director of the Pirate farm system in 1939. Died from ptomaine poisoning while on a scouting trip. Buried Calvary Cemetery, St Louis MO.

Joe Schultz—9 Years Catcher 2 Years Manager (b. 29 Aug 1918 Chicago IL–d. 10 Jan 1996 St Louis MO) Spent his entire life in baseball as a player, coach, manager and scout. Cremated.

Webb Schultz—1 Year Pitcher (b. 31 Jan 1898 Wautoma WI–d. 26 Jul 1986 at his home in Delevan WI) Served in the U.S. Army during World War I. Died from natural causes. Buried Spring Grove Cemetery, Delevan WI.

Al Schulz—5 Years Pitcher (b. 12 May 1889 Toledo OH–d. 14 Dec 1931 Ohio Hospital for Epileptics, Gallipolis OH) He was a salesman. Died from a cerebral hemorrhage. Buried Toledo Memorial Park, Sylvania OH.

Walt Schulz—1 Year Pitcher (b. 16 Apr 1900 St Louis MO–d. 27 Feb 1928 Prescott AZ) Buried Sunset Memorial Park, Affton MO.

Hal Schumacher—13 Years Pitcher (b. 23 Nov 1910 Hinckley NY–d. 21 Nov 1993 Cooperstown NY).

Hack Schumann—1 Year Pitcher (b. 13 Aug 1884 Buffalo NY–d. 25 Mar 1946 Mill Grove NY).

Ferdie Schupp—10 Years Pitcher (b. 16 Jan 1890 Louisville KY–d. 16 Dec 1971 White Memorial Hospital, Los Angeles CA) Died from pneumonia and heart disease. Buried Calvary Cemetery, Los Angeles CA.

Bill Schuster—5 Years Infielder (b. 4 Aug 1912 Buffalo NY–d. 28 Jun 1987 Community Hospital, El Monte CA) Known for his clowning on the field, he was the MVP twice in the Pacific Coast League while playing for the Los Angeles Angels. A retired *Los Angeles Times* employee, he was an avid golfer. Died from heart disease. Buried Live Oak Memorial Park, Monrovia CA.

Blackie Schwamb—1 Year Pitcher (b. 6 Aug 1926 Lancaster CA–d. 21 Dec 1989 Los Angeles CA) He was a gardener. Died from lung cancer. Cremated.

Bill Schwartz—1 Year Infielder (b. 22 Apr 1884 Cleveland OH–d. 29 Aug 1961 Baptist Hospital, Nashville TN) Associated with Vanderbilt University for 38 years, he was on two occasions the baseball coach there, and was the business manager of the Vanderbilt Athletic Assn from 1926 to 1942. Died from a heart attack. Buried Woodlawn Memorial Park, Nashville TN.

Pop Schwartz—2 Years Catcher (b. 3 Apr 1864 Jamestown KY–d. 22 Dec 1940 at his home in Newport KY) He caught before baseball players used gloves. As a result, he had crippled fingers and hands. Buried Evergreen Cemetery, Southgate KY.

Bill Schwarz—1 Year Catcher (b. 30 Jan 1891 Birmingham AL–d. 24 Jun 1949 at a hospital in Jacksonville FL) A resident of Jacksonville for 30 years, he was connected with Gulf Life Insurance Company. Buried Jewish Temple Cemetery, Jacksonville FL.

Al Schweitzer—4 Years Outfielder (b. 23 Dec 1882 Cincinnati OH–d. 27 Jan 1969 Licking County Memorial Hospital, Newark OH) He worked 24 years for the Health Pure Oil refinery, retiring in 1948. Buried Cedar Hill Cemetery, Newark OH.

Rudy Schwenck—1 Year Pitcher (b. 6 Apr 1884 Louisville KY–d. 27 Nov 1941 at his home in Louisville KY) Buried Cave Hill Cemetery, Louisville KY.

Hal Schwenk—1 Year Pitcher (b. 23 Aug 1890 Schuylkill Haven PA–d. 3 Sep 1955 Veteran's Hospital, Kansas City MO) Lived at Sedalia MO for 41 years where he worked as a painter and wallpaper hanger. Served in the U.S. Army. Played the bass drum in the Army Band and in the Sedalia City Band. Buried Memorial Park Cemetery, Sedalia MO.

Pius Schwert—2 Years Catcher (b. 22 Nov 1892 Angola NY–d. 11 Mar 1941 Washington DC) He was in his second term as a Congressman from Buffalo NY when he died from a heart attack shortly after making a short speech at a dinner party in the Annapolis Hotel. Buried Forest Avenue Cemetery, Angola NY.

Art Schwind—1 Year Infielder (b. 4 Nov 1889 Fort Wayne IN–d. 13 Jan 1968 Sullivan IL).

Lou Scoffic—1 Year Outfielder (b. 20 May 1913 Herrin IL–d. 28 Aug 1997 Herrin IL).

Jim Scoggins—1 Year Pitcher (b. 19 Jul 1891 Killeen TX–d. 16 Aug 1923 Columbia Hospital, Columbia SC) World War I veteran. Died from a brain injury six weeks after he was beaned by a baseball. Buried Winters TX.

Dick Scott—1 Year Pitcher (b. 5 Feb 1883 Bethel OH–d. 18 Jan 1911 Chicago IL) He was in the insurance business in Chicago when he took his own life by cutting his throat with a razor. Buried Bethel OH.

Ed Scott—2 Years Pitcher (b. 12 Aug 1870 Toledo OH–d. 1 Nov 1933 at his home in Toledo OH) He was a security policeman at Interlake Iron and Steel Corporation for ten years. Died from acute nephritis. Buried Toledo Memorial Park, Sylvania OH.

Everett Scott—13 Years Infielder (b. 19 Nov 1892 Bluffton IN–d. 2 Nov 1960 Parkview Memorial Hospital, Fort Wayne IN) He held the consecutive game record of 1307 games that was broken by Lou Gehrig. He owned and managed two bowling alleys in Fort Wayne. Died following a long illness. Buried Elm Grove Cemetery, Bluffton IN.

Jack Scott—12 Years Pitcher (b. 18 Apr 1892 Ridgeway NC–d. 30 Nov 1959 Duke Hospital, Durham NC) He was the police chief at Warrenton NC. Died while undergoing surgery. Buried Fairview Cemetery, Warrenton NC.

Jim Scott—1 Year Infielder (b. 22 Sep 1888 Shenandoah PA–d. 12 May 1972 South Pasadena FL) He worked as an electrician for Ford Motor Company. Buried Woodlawn Memory Gardens, St Petersburg FL.

Jim Scott—9 Years Pitcher (b. 23 Apr 1888 Deadwood SD–d. 7 Apr 1957 Jacumba Hotel, Jacumba CA) World War I veteran. Known as "Death Valley Jim", he was an electrician in the motion picture studios. Died from congestive heart failure and arteriosclerotic heart disease. Cremated. Buried Inglewood Park Cemetery, Inglewood CA.

Lefty Scott—1 Year Pitcher (b. 15 Jul 1915 Roswell NM–d. 3 Mar 1964 Houston TX) Buried Glenwood Cemetery, Groveton TX.

LeGrand Scott—1 Year Outfielder (b. 25 Jul 1910 Cleveland OH–d. 12 Nov 1993 Birmingham AL) He scouted 15 years for the Tigers and Athletics. Buried Elmwood Cemetery, Birmingham AL.

Milt Scott—4 Years Infielder (b. 17 Jan 1866 Chicago IL–d. 3 Nov 1938 Baltimore MD) Died suddenly. Buried Loudon Park National Cemetery, Baltimore MD.

Pete Scott—3 Years Outfielder (b. 21 Dec 1898 Woodland CA–d. 3 May 1953 Daly City CA) He owned a farm at Oakdale CA and was a bartender at the Tanforan race track. Died from a heart attack. Buried Cypress Lawn Memorial Park, Colma CA.

Rod Scurry—8 Years Pitcher (b. 17 Mar 1956 Sacramento CA–d. 5 Nov 1992 Reno NV) A promising career cut short by cocaine, he died in an intensive care unit shortly after a scuffle with a police officer.

Ken Sears—2 Years Catcher (b. 6 Jul 1917 Streator IL–d. 17 Jul 1968 Bridgeport TX).

Tom Seaton—6 Years Pitcher (b. 30 Aug 1887 Blair NE–d. 10 Apr 1940 at a hospital in El Paso TX) He was a foreman at the smelter in the cottrell plant and the arsenic plant at El Paso. He excelled as an amateur bowler. Buried Evergreen Cemetery, El Paso TX.

Tom Seats—2 Years Pitcher (b. 24 Sep 1910 Farmington NC–d. 10 May 1992 San Ramon Medical Center, San Ramon CA) Died from pneumonia and chronic obstructive lung disease. Buried Woodlawn Memorial Park, Daly City CA.

Dick Seay—16 Years Infielder (b. 30 Nov 1904 West New York NJ–d. 6 Apr 1981 at his home in Jersey City NJ) He played in the negro leagues and worked for the Jersey City Department of Recreation.

Jimmy Sebring—5 Years Outfielder (b. 25 Mar 1882 Liberty PA–d. 22 Dec 1909 Williamsport Hospital, Williamsport PA) Died at the height of his baseball career from Bright's disease. Buried Wildwood Cemetery, Williamsport PA.

Doc Sechrist—1 Year Pitcher (b. 10 Feb 1876 Williamstown KY–d. 2 Apr 1950 Kentucky Baptist Hospital, Louisville KY) He worked for the Louisville and Nashville Railroad for 35 years, retiring in 1948 as assistant superintendent of machinery. Buried Somerset Cemetery, Somerset KY.

Frank Secory—5 Years Outfielder (b. 24 Aug 1912 Mason City IA–d. 7 Apr 1995 Port Huron MI) He umpired in the National League from 1952 to 1970. Cremated.

Duke Sedgwick—2 Years Pitcher (b. 1 Jun 1899 Martins Ferry OH–d. 4 Dec 1982 Clearwater FL) Served in the U.S. Army during World War I. He was a sheet metal specialist for the Pennsylvania Railroad.

Charlie See—3 Years Outfielder (b. 13 Oct 1896 Pleasantville NY–d. 19 Jul 1948 Bridgeport CT) He was an automobile salesman. Died aboard his boat, the "Loretta".

Bob Seeds—9 Years Outfielder (b. 24 Feb 1907 Ringgold TX–d. 28 Oct 1993 Erick OK).

Pat Seerey—7 Years Outfielder (b. 17 Mar 1923 Wilburton OK–d. 28 Apr 1986 at his home in Jennings MO) He was one of the few players to hit four home runs in a single game. Died after an extended illness. Buried Calvary Cemetery, St Louis MO.

Emmett Seery—9 Years Outfielder (b. 13 Feb 1861 Princeville IL–d. 7 Aug 1930 Saranac NY).

Socks Seibold—9 Years Pitcher (b. 31 May 1896 Philadelphia PA–d. 21 Sep 1965 Philadelphia PA).

Kip Selbach—13 Years Outfielder (b. 24 Mar 1872 Columbus OH–d. 17 Feb 1956 St Anthony Hospital, Columbus OH) One of Columbus' top bowlers, he organized the city's first bowling team in 1896 and was a bowling alley proprietor until he retired in 1943. Died after a four-month illness. Buried Green Lawn Memorial Cemetery, Columbus OH.

Frank Selee—16 Years Manager Hall of Fame (b. 26 Oct 1858 Amherst NH–d. 5 Jul 1909 at the Oakes Home in Denver CO) He engaged in the grocery business in Melrose MA. He spent the last few years of his life in Denver for his deteriorating health. Died from tuberculosis. Buried Wyoming Cemetery, Melrose MA.

George Selkirk—9 Years Outfielder (b. 4 Jan 1908 Huntsville, Ontario, Canada–d. 19 Jan 1987 North Ridge Hospital, Fort Lauderdale FL) Served as an aerial gunner in the U.S. Navy during World War II. He spent 46 years in baseball as a player, minor league manager and scout. He was an avid golfer and hunter. Died after a long illness. Buried Harrisonville PA.

Epp Sell—2 Years Pitcher (b. 26 Apr 1897 Llewellyn PA–d. 19 Feb 1961 at his home in Reading PA) He was a city policeman in Reading from 1943 to 1951 and after that was a detective for the county district attorney, retiring in 1961 because of ill health. Buried Forest Hills Memorial Park, Reading PA.

Rube Sellers—1 Year Outfielder (b. 7 Mar 1881 Duquesne PA–d. 13 Jan 1952 St Joseph's Hospital, Pittsburgh PA) He was a steel mill crane operator for Homestead Steel, retiring in 1945. Buried Jefferson Memorial Park, Pleasant Hills PA.

Carey Selph—2 Years Infielder (b. 5 Dec 1901 Donaldson AR–d. 24 Feb 1976 Memorial Hospital, Houston TX) He managed some minor league baseball. Living in Houston 49 years, he worked in insurance. Later he was president of Big John Can Company. Died after an extended illness. Buried Pleasant Hill Cemetery, Donaldson AR.

Paul Sentelle—2 Years Infielder (b. 27 Aug 1879 New Orleans LA–d. 27 Apr 1923 Good Samaritan Hospital, Cincinnati OH) He was a National League umpire from 1922 until his death. Died from acute gangrenous appendicitis. Buried St Louis Cemetery # 3, New Orleans LA.

Steve Senteney—1 Year Pitcher (b. 7 Aug 1957 Indianapolis IN–d. 18 Jun 1989 near Williams CA) Served in the U.S. military. He was a fencing contractor near Sacramento CA. Died instantly in a head-on collision when the car he was driving crossed over the centerline into oncoming traffic. Buried Sylvan Cemetery, Citrus Heights CA.

Billy Serad—4 Years Pitcher (b. 1863 Philadelphia PA–d. 1 Nov 1925 Chester PA) He umpired in the minor leagues before going to work at the pipe mill in Chester. Later he worked 24 years for the South Chester Tube Company. Died after being ill one week.

Bill Serena—6 Years Infielder (b. 2 Oct 1924 Alameda CA–d. 17 Apr 1996 at his home in Hayward CA) He was a teamster for Lucky Stores. For 50 years he was a scout for the Braves and Marlins, retiring in 1994. Died from lung cancer. Cremated.

Walt Sessi—2 Years Outfielder (b. 23 Jul 1918 Finleyville PA–d. 18 Apr 1998 at a hospital in Mobile AL) Buried Memorial Gardens, Mobile AL.

Merle Settlemire—1 Year Pitcher (b. 19 Jan 1903 Santa Fe OH–d. 12 Jun 1988 at his home in Russell's Point OH) Buried Mount Tabor Cemetery, Gutman OH.

Hank Severeid—15 Years Catcher (b. 1 Jun 1891 Story City IA–d. 17 Dec 1968 at his home in San Antonio TX) He managed minor league baseball and was a scout for the Red Sox. Died in his sleep. Buried Sunset Memorial Park, San Antonio TX.

Ed Seward—6 Years Pitcher (b. 29 Jun 1867 Cleveland OH–d. 30 Jul 1947 at his home in Cleveland OH) He worked for the Cleveland Fire Department from 1894 until he retired in 1932.

Joe Sewell—14 Years Infielder Hall of Fame (b. 9 Oct 1898 Titus AL–d. 6 Mar 1990 at his son's home in Mobile AL) He struck out only 114 times in over 7000 times at bat during his 14 year baseball career. He worked in public relations for Dairy Fresh. Buried Tuscaloosa Memorial Park, Tuscaloosa AL.

Luke Sewell—20 Years Catcher 10 Years Manager (b. 5 Jan 1901 Titus AL–d. 14 May 1987 Akron General Hospital, Akron OH) He co-owned Seville Centrifugal Bronz, Inc., retiring in 1970. Buried Rose Hill Burial Park, Fairlawn OH.

Rip Sewell—13 Years Pitcher (b. 11 May 1907 Decatur AL–d. 3 Sep 1989 South Florida Baptist Hosp, Plant City FL) He was known for his "blooper pitch" that took a 25-foot arc on its way to the plate. A shotgun blast seriously injured him in 1941, later leading to circulation problems that resulted in the amputation of both legs below the knees in 1972. Died from pneumonia and kidney failure after a lengthy illness. Buried Oaklawn Cemetery, Plant City FL.

Tommy Sewell—1 Game Pinch Hitter (b. 16 Apr 1906 Titus AL–d. 28 Jul 1956 Montgomery AL) He was manager of a Montgomery radio station. Drowned accidentally in Lake Jordan. Buried Greenwood Cemetery, Montgomery AL.

Frank Sexton—1 Year Pitcher (b. 8 Jul 1872 Brockton MA–d. 4 Jan 1938 Brighton MA) He coached college baseball at the University of Michigan, University of Pennsylvania, Brown and Harvard. In 1910 he left baseball and began practicing medicine, first at Brockton, then North Easton MA, and finally at Boston MA. Died suddenly. Buried St Patrick's Cemetery, Brockton MA.

Tom Sexton—1 Year Infielder (b. 14 Mar 1865 Milwaukee WI–d. 8 Feb 1934 at his home in Rock Island IL) Buried Calvary Cemetery, Rock Island IL.

Socks Seybold—9 Years Outfielder (b. 23 Nov 1870 Washingtonville OH–d. 21 Dec 1921 Greensburg PA) He was the steward of the Eagles Club in Jeannette PA. Died from a broken neck suffered in a car accident when his car ran off the road over an embankment.

Cy Seymour—16 Years Outfielder (b. 9 Dec 1872 Albany NY–d. 20 Sep 1919 New York City NY) He played in the International League until 1916, and even tried out for the Yankees in 1919 at age 46. He worked in the shipyards during World War I. Died from tubercular phthisis. Buried Albany Rural Cemetery, Menands NY.

Tom Seymour—1 Year Pitcher (b. 1858 Pittsburgh PA–d. 17 Feb 1916 near Boise ID) His body was found on a trail leading to West Mountain, where he was hiking. Died from exposure.

Ralph Shafer—1 Game Pinch Hitter (b. 17 Mar 1894 Cincinnati OH–d. 5 Feb 1950 City Hospital, Akron OH) Served in the U.S. Army during World War I. He was a high school coach and physical education teacher in Akron and

Cleveland. Died after an illness of five months. Cremated. Buried New Ulm MN.

Tillie Shafer —4 Years Infielder (b. 22 Mar 1889 Los Angeles CA–d. 10 Jan 1962 at his home in Los Angeles CA) World War I veteran. He was a prominent real estate operator and one of Southern California's top amateur golfers. He was also a partner in a wholesale produce operation. Died from prostate cancer. Buried Holy Cross Cemetery, Culver City CA.

John Shaffer —2 Years Pitcher (b. 18 Feb 1864 Lock Haven PA–d. 21 Nov 1926 at his home in Endicott NY) He worked at the plant of the Demorest Sewing Machine Company in Williamsport PA until about 1914 when he moved to Endicott. Died suddenly, but had been in ill health for ten years. Buried Highland Cemetery, Lock Haven PA.

Gus Shallix —2 Years Pitcher (b. 29 Mar 1858 Bielfeld, Germany–d. 28 Oct 1937 at his home in Cincinnati OH) He was a policeman in Cincinnati for 29 years. Died from a heart attack and chronic Bright's disease. Buried St Joseph Old Catholic Cemetery, Cincinnati OH.

Wally Shaner —4 Years Outfielder (b. 24 May 1900 Lynchburg VA–d. 13 Nov 1992 Las Vegas NV) World War II veteran. He was a stage manager at the Stardust Hotel in Las Vegas. Buried Paradise Memorial Gardens, Las Vegas NV.

Howard Shanks —14 Years Outfielder (b. 21 Jul 1890 Chicago IL–d. 30 Jul 1941 at his home in Monaca PA) He managed minor league baseball for a year, then worked for the County Real Estate department. Died suddenly from a heart attack. Buried Old Monaca Cemetery, Monaca PA.

Doc Shanley —1 Year Infielder (b. 30 Jan 1889 Granbury TX–d. 14 Dec 1934 St Anthony's Hospital, St Petersburg FL) He was a dentist. Died from a heart attack. Buried Royal Palm Cemetery, St Petersburg FL.

Jim Shanley —1 Year Outfielder (b. New York City NY–d. 4 Nov 1904 Brooklyn NY).

Warren Shannabrook —1 Year Infielder (b. 30 Nov 1885 Massillon OH–d. 10 Mar 1964 North Canton OH) Buried Massillon Cemetery, Massillon OH.

Bill Shanner —1 Year Pitcher (b. 4 Nov 1894 Oakland City IN–d. 18 Dec 1986 Welborn Baptist Hospital, Evansville IN) World War I veteran. For 33 years he was an accountant for Standard Oil of Indiana. Later he was an accountant for Hahn, Inc. Buried Sunset Memorial Park Cemetery, Evansville IN.

Dan Shannon —3 Years Infielder 2 Years Manager (b. 23 Mar 1865 Bridgeport CT–d. 25 Oct 1913 Bridgeport CT) He umpired for a short time, operated a cafe in Bridgeport and worked for the City of Bridgeport. His last four years he was a messenger for the Yost Typewriter Company. Died after not being ill very long. Buried St Michael's Cemetery, Bridgeport CT.

Frank Shannon —2 Years Infielder (b. 3 Dec 1873 San Francisco CA–d. 27 Feb 1934 Boston MA).

Joe Shannon —1 Year Outfielder (b. 11 Feb 1895 Jersey City NJ–d. 28 Jul 1955 Jersey City NJ).

Owen Shannon —2 Years Catcher (b. 22 Dec 1885 Omaha NE–d. 10 Apr 1918 Wise Memorial Hospital, Omaha NE) Buried Holy Sepulchre Cemetery, Omaha NE.

Red Shannon —7 Years Infielder (b. 11 Feb 1895 Jersey City NJ–d. 12 Apr 1970 St Francis Health Center, Jersey City NJ) He was a retired employee of the Jersey City Department of Recreation. Buried Holy Cross Cemetery, North Arlington NJ.

Spike Shannon —5 Years Outfielder (b. 7 Feb 1876 Pittsburgh PA–d. 16 May 1940 Minneapolis MN) He umpired in the Federal League in 1914 and 1915 and in the American Association and other minor leagues. Buried St Mary's Cemetery, Minneapolis MN.

Wally Shannon —2 Years Infielder (b. 23 Jan 1933 Cleveland OH–d. 8 Feb 1992 St John's Mercy Hospital, Creve Coeur MO) For 13 years he owned Shannon Associates, a brokerage firm that represented manufacturers. He was also a scout for the Mets.

Billy Shantz —3 Years Catcher (b. 31 Jul 1927 Pottstown PA–d. 13 Dec 1993 Lauderhill FL) Associated 29 years with Webster's Sport Centers, he retired to enjoy his greatest passion—golf. Died from cancer. Cremated.

Ralph Sharman —1 Year Outfielder (b. 11 Apr 1895 South Norwood OH–d. 24 May 1918 Camp Sheridan AL) He was serving in the U.S.

Army during World War I when he drowned while swimming in the Alabama River while on an outing. Buried Spring Grove Cemetery, Cincinnati OH.

Bud Sharpe—2 Years Infielder (b. 6 Aug 1881 West Chester PA–d. 31 May 1916 Haddock GA) Died from tuberculosis after being an invalid for several years, living in the rural home of George Stallings. Buried Greenmount Cemetery, West Chester PA.

Mike Sharperson—8 Years Infielder (b. 4 Oct 1961 Orangeburg SC–d. 26 May 1996 Las Vegas NV) Died at the height of his career from massive head and internal injuries suffered in a single car accident at the intersection of I15 and I215. Just hours earlier he had been recalled to play for the Padres.

George Sharrott—2 Years Pitcher (b. 2 Nov 1869 Staten Island NY–d. 5 Jan 1932 Mary Immaculate Hospital, Jamaica NY) For 20 years he was a foreman for a Brooklyn newspaper. Died after an operation. Buried Silver Mount Cemetery, Staten Island NY.

John Sharrott—4 Years Pitcher (b. 13 Aug 1869 Bangor ME–d. 31 Dec 1927 Los Angeles CA) He was an elevator operator. Died from a stroke. Cremated.

Bill Sharsig—8 Years Manager (b. 1855 Philadelphia PA–d. 1 Feb 1902 at his home in Philadelphia PA) He was involved in executive positions in baseball his entire life and was general manager of the Athletics when he died. Buried Mount Vernon Cemetery, Philadelphia PA.

Shag Shaughnessy—2 Years Outfielder (b. 8 Apr 1883 Montreal, Quebec, Canada–d. 15 May 1969 Montreal, Quebec, Canada) He was football coach at McGill College and president of the International League. He originated baseball's playoff system, known as the Shaugnessy playoffs. Died from an aortic aneurysm.

Joe Shaute—13 Years Pitcher (b. 1 Aug 1899 Peckville PA–d. 21 Feb 1970 Moses Taylor Hospital, Scranton PA) Active in Lackawanna County, PA, politics, he served four years as County Treasurer and some time as County Sheriff before becoming a sales representative for Zipsy Motors in Peckville. Buried St Catherine's Cemetery, Moscow PA.

Al Shaw—4 Years Catcher (b. 3 Oct 1874 Burslem, England–d. 25 Mar 1958 Twin City Nursing Home, Uhrichsville OH) He was a moldmaker at East Liverpool OH for some time, but was working at the Twin City Greenhouse when he died following a 19-day illness. Buried Union Cemetery, Uhrichsville OH.

Al Shaw—5 Years Outfielder (b. 1 Mar 1881 Rardin IL–d. 30 Dec 1974 Danville Care Nursing Home, Danville IL) He had been a patient at the nursing home three years. Buried Greasy Point Cemetery, Rardin IL.

Ben Shaw—2 Years Infielder (b. 18 Jun 1893 La Center KY–d. 16 Mar 1959 St Luke's Hospital, Aurora OH) He had his own real estate development and building company. Buried Aurora Cemetery, Aurora OH.

Dupee Shaw—6 Years Pitcher (b. 31 May 1859 Charlestown MA–d. 11 Jun 1938 Everett MA).

Jim Shaw—9 Years Pitcher (b. 13 Aug 1893 Pittsburgh PA–d. 27 Jan 1962 Georgetown Hospital, Washington DC) For many years he was an agent for the Internal Revenue Service, stationed at Herndon VA. Buried St Mary's Cemetery, Alexandria VA.

Royal Shaw—1 Game Pinch Hitter (b. 29 Sep 1884 Yakima WA–d. 3 Jul 1969 at his home in Yakima WA) He was a stockholder in a funeral home. Died after an extended illness. Buried Terrace Heights Memorial Park, Yakima WA.

Bob Shawkey—15 Years Pitcher 1 Year Manager (b. 4 Dec 1890 Sigel PA–d. 31 Dec 1980 Veteran's Hospital, Syracuse NY) Served in the U.S. Navy during World War I. He coached baseball at Dartmouth College and was the pitching coach for the Yankees for many years. Buried Oakwood-Morningside Cemetery, Syracuse NY.

Danny Shay—4 Years Infielder (b. 8 Nov 1876 Kansas City MO–d. 1 Dec 1927 Kansas City MO) Committed suicide. Buried St Mary's Cemetery, Kansas City MO.

Marty Shay—2 Years Infielder (b. 25 Apr 1896 Boston MA–d. 20 Feb 1951 Worcester MA) Served in the U.S. Navy during World War I. He worked for Parker and Harper Manufacturing Company. Buried Mount Calvary Cemetery, Roslindale MA.

Gerry Shea—1 Year Catcher (b. 26 Jul 1881 St Louis MO–d. 4 May 1964 Berkeley MO) Buried Calvary Cemetery, St Louis MO.

John Shea—1 Year Pitcher (b. 27 Dec 1904 Everett MA–d. 30 Nov 1956 at his home in Malden MA) In the brokerage business in Boston MA for several years, he worked his last 12 years as a night foreman at the Everett General Electric plant. Died in his sleep from a heart attack. Buried Holy Cross Cemetery, Malden MA.

Merv Shea—11 Years Catcher (b. 5 Sep 1900 San Francisco CA–d. 27 Jan 1953 Mercy Hospital, Sacramento CA) He coached and managed minor league baseball until 1952 when stomach trouble forced him to quit. Died from a peptic abscess after a year's illness. Buried St Mary's Cemetery, Sacramento CA.

Nap Shea—1 Year Catcher (b. 23 May 1874 Ware MA–d. 8 Jul 1968 Bloomfield Hills MI) He owned the Commercial Hotel in Ware before working several years as a supervisor for Fisk Rubber Company. Later he was an inspector for Uni-Royal Tire. Died from prostate cancer. Buried St Mary's Cemetery, Ware MA.

Red Shea—3 Years Pitcher (b. 29 Nov 1898 Ware MA–d. 17 Nov 1981 Stafford Springs CT).

William Shea—(b. 21 Jun 1907 New York City NY–d. 3 Oct 1991 at his home in New York City NY) A New York City attorney and politician, he was largely responsible for creating the Mets in an effort to bring National League baseball back to New York. Died from complications of a stroke suffered two years earlier.

Al Shealy—2 Years Pitcher (b. 24 May 1900 Chapin SC–d. 7 Mar 1967 Washington County Hospital, Hagerstown MD) A retired school teacher, he had been the baseball coach and athletic director for the Chester County schools in South Carolina. Died from a heart attack enroute to the hospital. Buried Grand View Memorial Park, Rock Hill SC.

Dave Shean—9 Years Infielder (b. 23 May 1878 Ware MA–d. 22 May 1963 Massachusetts General Hospital, Boston MA) He was president of Nathan Robbins Company, a poultry firm in the Boston market district. Died from injuries suffered in an automobile accident a week earlier. Buried St Paul's Cemetery, Arlington MA.

Ray Shearer—1 Year Outfielder (b. 19 Sep 1929 Jacobus PA–d. 21 Feb 1982 Memorial Osteopathic Hospital, York PA) He worked for Preston Trucking Company in York. Buried Salem Union Cemetery, Jacobus PA.

John Shearon—2 Years Outfielder (b. 9 May 1854 Ireland–d. 1 Feb 1923 at his home in Bradford PA) He engaged in pipe line work from 1876 until he retired in 1919, working for McKean Pipe Line first, then its successor, New York Transit Company. Died following a long period of illness. Buried St Bernard's Cemetery, Bradford PA.

George Shears—1 Year Pitcher (b. 13 Apr 1890 Minneapolis MN–d. 12 Nov 1978 at his home west of Loveland CO) He was a chiropractor. Died following a brief illness. He was cremated and his ashes scattered over Sunrise Ranch.

Jimmy Sheckard—17 Years Outfielder (b. 23 Nov 1878 Upper Chanceford PA–d. 15 Jan 1947 General Hospital, Lancaster PA) He managed minor league baseball from time to time and was working at a service station when he was hit by a car while walking to work. Died from injuries received in the accident. Buried Laurel Hill Memorial Gardens, Columbia PA.

Biff Sheehan—2 Years Outfielder (b. 13 Feb 1868 Hartford CT–d. 21 Oct 1923 Hartford CT) Buried St Patrick's Cemetery, Hartford CT.

Jack Sheehan—2 Years Infielder (b. 15 Apr 1893 Chicago IL–d. 29 May 1987 at a nursing home in West Palm Beach FL) He worked 64 years in baseball, 19 of them as farm director for the Cubs. He was a scout for the Senators and Rangers, retiring in 1977. Buried Royal Palm Memorial Gardens, West Palm Beach FL.

Tom Sheehan—6 Years Pitcher 1 Year Manager (b. 31 Mar 1894 Grand Ridge IL–d. 29 Oct 1982 Chillicothe OH).

Tommy Sheehan—3 Years Infielder (b. 6 Nov 1877 Sacramento CA–d. 22 May 1959 Panama City, Panama).

Bud Sheely—3 Years Catcher (b. 26 Nov 1920 Spokane WA–d. 17 Oct 1985 at his home in Sacramento CA) He owned and operated the Pancake Parade restaurants in Sacramento, selling them in 1983. Died from kidney failure. Cremated.

Earl Sheely—9 Years Infielder (b. 12 Feb 1893 Bushnell IL–d. 16 Sep 1952 at his home in Seattle WA) He worked in baseball 41 years in almost every capacity including scout, coach, minor league manager and minor league general manager. Died from a heart attack. Buried East Lawn Memorial Park, Sacramento CA.

Charlie Sheerin—1 Year Infielder (b. 17 Apr 1911 Brooklyn NY–d. 27 Sep 1986 Valley Stream NY) Buried Cemetery of Holy Rood, Westbury NY.

Frank Shellenback—2 Years Pitcher (b. 16 Dec 1898 Joplin MO–d. 17 Aug 1969 at his home in Newton MA) Banned from the major leagues because he threw the outlawed spitball, he won 315 games while losing 192 in the minor leagues between 1917 and 1938. He coached and scouted in the majors until his retirement in 1965. Buried Newton Cemetery, Newton MA.

Hugh Shelley—1 Year Outfielder (b. 26 Oct 1910 Rogers TX–d. 16 Jun 1978 St Elizabeth Hospital, Beaumont TX) He was a clerk for the Terrell Hardware Company. Buried Magnolia Cemetery, Beaumont TX.

Skeeter Shelton—1 Year Outfielder (b. 29 Jun 1888 Huntington WV–d. 9 Jan 1954 Huntington WV) He worked for the State of West Virginia Liquor Commission and was later manager of the Huntington Elk's Club. Died from self-inflicted gunshot wounds to the head after being despondent over a heart condition. Buried Spring Hill Cemetery, Huntington WV.

Steve Shemo—2 Years Infielder (b. 9 Apr 1915 Swoyersville PA–d. 13 Apr 1992 Morehead Memorial Hospital, Eden NC) Buried Wilson Primitive Baptist Church Cem, Walnut Cove NC.

Jack Shepard—4 Years Catcher (b. 13 May 1931 Clovis CA–d. 31 Dec 1994 Stanford Medical Center, Palo Alto CA) For 27 years he was a self-employed consultant for the electronics industry. Died from a heart attack while undergoing treatment for tongue cancer. Cremated.

Ray Shepherdson—1 Year Catcher (b. 3 May 1897 Little Falls NY–d. 8 Nov 1975 Little Falls NY).

Bill Sherdel—15 Years Pitcher (b. 15 Aug 1896 McSherrystown PA–d. 14 Nov 1968 at his home in McSherrystown PA) Served in the U.S. Army during World War I. He was the steward at the Moose Club in Hanover PA. Died following a long illness during which he had been hospitalized several times. Buried Annunciation Church Cemetery, McSherrystown PA.

Roy Sherid—3 Years Pitcher (b. 25 Jan 1907 Norristown PA–d. 28 Feb 1982 at his home in Parker Ford PA) He retired from the National Liberty Insurance Company at Valley Forge PA in 1975. Buried Oak Grove Cemetery, Parker Ford PA.

Red Sheridan—2 Years Infielder (b. 14 Nov 1896 Brooklyn NY–d. 25 Nov 1975 Queens NY).

Ed Sherling—4 Games Pinch Hitter (b. 18 Jul 1897 Coalburg AL–d. 16 Nov 1965 at his home in Enterprise AL)He was a prominent banking official in Enterprise until his retirement about 1964. Died suddenly. Buried Meadowlawn Memorial Park, Enterprise AL.

Monk Sherlock—1 Year Infielder (b. 26 Oct 1904 Buffalo NY–d. 26 Nov 1985 Millard Fillmore Hospital, Buffalo NY) He was an administrator at Erie Community College and Lafayette General Hospital. Buried Forest Lawn Cemetery, Buffalo NY.

Vince Sherlock—1 Year Infielder (b. 27 Mar 1910 Buffalo NY–d. 11 May 1997 Cheektowaga NY) He worked for the Buffalo Police Department from 1942 until he retired in 1972, working in the Traffic Division, Youth Division and, finally, at headquarters where he had been promoted to detective. Died after a long illness. Buried Mount Olivet Cemetery, Buffalo NY.

Babe Sherman—1 Year Pitcher (b. 9 May 1890 Hubbardsville NY–d. 16 Sep 1955 Highland Park MI) Buried White Chapel Memorial Cemetery, Troy MI.

Joe Sherman—1 Year Pitcher (b. 4 Nov 1890 Yarmouth MA–d. 21 Dec 1987 Cape Coral FL) He retired from Rhode Island to Cape Coral in 1963. Buried River Bend Cemetery, Westerly RI.

Fred Sherry—1 Year Pitcher (b. 13 Jun 1889 Honesdale PA–d. 27 Jul 1975 Wayne County Memorial Hosp, Honesdale PA) Served in the U.S. Army during World War I. Died after being hospitalized two weeks. Buried St John's Lutheran Cemetery, Honesdale PA.

Bill Shettsline—5 Years Manager (b. 25 Oct 1863 Philadelphia PA–d. 22 Feb 1933 at his home in Philadelphia PA) For 43 years he was a Phillie executive, retiring in 1927. He died from a heart attack with a cigar in his hand and a smile on his face. Buried Chelten Hills Cemetery, Philadelphia PA.

John Shetzline—1 Year Infielder (b. 1850 Philadelphia PA–d. 15 Dec 1892 Philadelphia PA).

Jimmy Shevlin—3 Years Infielder (b. 9 Jul 1909 Cincinnati OH–d. 30 Oct 1974 at his home in Fort Lauderdale FL) He owned and operated Shevlin Restaurant in Cincinnati before retiring to Florida in 1952. Buried Our Lady Queen of Heaven Cemetery, North Lauderdale FL.

Benjamin F Shibe—(b. 23 Jan 1838–d. 14 Jan 1922 at his daughter's home in Philadelphia PA) Starting as a horsecar driver, he became interested in baseball and started a baseball manufacturing business. As it grew and prospered he was able to buy half-interest in the Athletics when they were formed in 1901 and held a controlling interest until his death. In 1920 he had an automobile accident that left him invalided. Died from complications of that accident. Buried West Laurel Hill Cemetery, Bala Cynwyd PA.

Thomas S Shibe—(b. 13 Jan 1866 Philadelphia PA–d. 16 Feb 1936 St Agnes Hospital, Philadelphia PA)The owner and president of the Philadelphia Athletics from 1922 until his death, he also owned A J Reach Company, the manufacturer of baseballs for the American League. Died from a heart ailment. Buried West Laurel Hill Cemetery, Bala Cynwyd PA.

Ben Shields—4 Years Pitcher (b. 17 Jun 1903 Huntersville NC–d. 23 Jan 1982 Woodruff SC) He was the retired owner of Shield's Appliance and Services in Woodruff. Buried Hopewell Church Cemetery, Huntersville NC.

Charlie Shields—2 Years Pitcher (b. 10 Dec 1879 Jackson TN–d. 27 Aug 1953 at his home in Memphis TN) He operated the elevator in the Shelby County (TN) Courthouse. Died from cancer. Buried Elmwood Cemetery, Memphis TN.

Pete Shields—1 Year Infielder (b. 21 Sep 1891 Swiftwater MS–d. 11 Feb 1961 V A Hospital, Jackson MS) World War I veteran. For his last ten years he was a cotton classer for the U.S. Department of Agriculture-Cotton Division. Died after a long illness. Buried Greenwood Cemetery, Jackson MS.

Vince Shields—1 Year Pitcher (b. 18 Nov 1900 Fredericton, New Brunswick, Canada–d. 17 Oct 1952 Plaster Rock, New Brunswick, Canada).

Jim Shilling—1 Year Infielder (b. 14 May 1915 Tulsa OK–d. 12 Sep 1986 Tulsa OK) Buried Memorial Park, Tulsa OK.

Ginger Shinault—2 Years Catcher (b. 6 Sep 1892 Memphis TN–d. 29 Dec 1930 Fitzsimmon's General Hospital, Denver CO) He played baseball up until the year he died. Died from tuberculosis-meningitis. Buried Forest Hill Cemetery, Memphis TN.

Bill Shindle—13 Years Infielder (b. 1860 Gloucester City NJ–d. 3 Jun 1936 at his home in Lakeland NJ) He worked for MacAndrews and Forbes Company in Camden NJ. Died from chronic nephritis and heart disease. Buried Union Cemetery, Gloucester City NJ.

Ralph Shinners—3 Years Outfielder (b. 4 Oct 1895 Monches WI–d. 23 Jul 1962 at his home in Brookfield WI) A beaning in 1922 shortened his career. Died from a heart attack. Buried Holy Cross Cemetery, Milwaukee WI.

Tim Shinnick—2 Years Infielder (b. 6 Nov 1867 Exeter NH–d. 18 May 1944 Exeter Hospital, Exeter NH) Died after being in the hospital for six weeks.

Bill Shipke—4 Years Infielder (b. 18 Nov 1882 St Louis MO–d. 10 Sep 1940 at a hospital in Omaha NE) He managed minor league baseball and was a scout for the Reds and Indians. Died from leakage of the heart and high blood pressure. Buried West Lawn Cemetery, Omaha NE.

Art Shires—4 Years Infielder (b. 13 Aug 1906 Milford TX–d. 13 Jul 1967 at his home in Italy TX) He operated a food establishment in Dallas. Died from lung cancer. Buried Italy Cemetery, Italy TX.

Duke Shirey—1 Year Pitcher (b. 20 Jun 1898 Jersey Shore PA–d. 1 Sep 1962 Washington County Hospital, Hagerstown MD) He worked his last ten years at the York Cycle Company. Buried Rose Hill Cemetery, Hagerstown MD.

Mule Shirley—2 Years Infielder (b. 24 May 1901 Snow Hill NC–d. 3 Aug 1955 Wayne Memorial Hospital, Goldsboro NC) He managed minor league baseball. Buried Willow Dale Cemetery, Goldsboro NC.

Tex Shirley—5 Years Pitcher (b. 25 Apr 1918 Birthright TX–d. 7 Nov 1993 DeSoto TX) He was retired from the Valero Energy Company. Died from cancer. Buried Red Oak Cemetery, Red Oak TX.

Ivey Shiver—2 Years Outfielder (b. 22 Jan 1906 Sylvester GA–d. 31 Aug 1972 at his home in Savannah GA) He coached basketball and football at Armstrong Junior College and at Savannah High School from 1935 to 1951 when he went into the insurance business. Died from a heart attack. Buried Bonaventure Cemetery, Savannah GA.

George Shoch—11 Years Outfielder (b. 6 Jan 1859 Philadelphia PA–d. 30 Sep 1937 Philadelphia PA) Buried East Cedar Hill Cemetery, Philadelphia PA.

Urban Shocker—13 Years Pitcher (b. 22 Aug 1890 Cleveland OH–d. 9 Sep 1928 St Luke's Hospital, Denver CO) He played baseball up to the year he died, pitching a month earlier in a semi-pro game for the Piggly Wiggly team in Denver. Died from heart disease and pneumonia. Buried Calvary Cemetery, St Louis MO.

Charlie Shoemaker—3 Years Infielder (b. 10 Aug 1939 Los Angeles CA–d. 31 May 1990 at his home in Mount Penn PA) He was a salesman for A-C Industries of Philadelphia. Died in his backyard from a self-inflicted gunshot from a hunting rifle. Buried Aulenbach's Cemetery, Mount Penn PA.

Milt Shoffner—7 Years Pitcher (b. 13 Nov 1905 Sherman TX–d. 19 Jan 1978 Madison OH) Served in Europe for the U.S. Army during World War II. For 17 years he was an assembler for Picker-XRay in Cleveland, retiring to Madison in 1973. Died after suffering a heart attack. Cremated. Buried Madison Memorial Cemetery, Madison OH.

Strick Shofner—1 Year Infielder (b. 23 Jul 1919 Crawford TX–d. 10 Oct 1998 Crestview Retirement Center, Crawford TX) He worked for W A Holt in Houston TX and for B and B Sporting Goods in Waco TX. Buried Crawford Cemetery, Crawford TX.

Ray Shook—1 Game Pinch Runner(b. 18 Nov 1890 Perry OH–d. 16 Sep 1970 Cardinal Nursing Home, South Bend IN) He was partowner of F and S Transit Company in South Bend from 1924 to 1956, and when it was sold to Navajo Freight Lines he took over as general manager until retiring in 1961. Died after a four-year illness. Buried Riverview Cemetery, South Bend IN.

Ernie Shore—7 Years Pitcher (b. 24 Mar 1891 East Bend NC–d. 24 Sep 1980 at his home in Winston-Salem NC) Served in the U.S. Navy during World War I. He sold cars and insurance for a while before he was elected Forsyth County (NC) Sheriff in 1936, a job he held until 1970. Buried Forsyth Memorial Park, Winston-Salem NC.

Ray Shore—3 Years Pitcher (b. 9 Jun 1921 Cincinnati OH–d. 13 Aug 1996 St Louis MO).

Bill Shores—6 Years Pitcher (b. 26 May 1904 Abilene TX–d. 19 Feb 1984 Municipal Hospital, Purcell OK) He was a retired salesman. Died after an extended illness. Buried Lexington Cemetery, Lexington OK.

Chris Short—15 Years Pitcher (b. 19 Sep 1937 Milford DE–d. 1 Aug 1991 Brandywine Convalescent Ctr, Wilmington DE) Died after being in a coma three years following a ruptured brain aneurysm. Buried Union Cemetery, Georgetown DE.

Dave Short—2 Years Outfielder (b. 11 May 1917 Magnolia AR–d. 22 Nov 1983 Shreveport LA).

Robert Short—(b. 20 Jul 1917 Minneapolis MN–d. 20 Nov 1982 St Mary's Minneapolis MN) The owner of the Washington Senators, he moved the team to Texas where they became the Texas Rangers in 1972. He also owned the Lakers basketball team, and moved them from Minneapolis to Los Angeles. Died from lung cancer. Buried Resurrection Cemetery, Mendota Heights MN.

Chick Shorten—8 Years Outfielder (b. 19 Apr 1892 Scranton PA–d. 23 Oct 1965 Scranton PA) Served in the U.S. Navy during World War I. In business with his son in the operation of Shorten's Market in Scranton, he was also a scout for the Indians, retiring in 1959. Died after three years of ill health. Buried Abington Hills Cemetery, Scranton PA.

Burt Shotton—14 Years Outfielder 11 Years Manager (b. 18 Oct 1884 Brownhelm OH–d. 29 Jul 1962 at his home in Lake Wales FL) He worked over 40 years in baseball as a player, coach and manager, retiring in 1950. His last six years were spent fishing and relaxing in Florida. Died from a heart attack.

Clyde Shoun—14 Years Pitcher (b. 20 Mar 1912 Mountain City TN–d. 20 Mar 1968 Mountain Home Vet's Hosp, Johnson City TN) Served in the U.S. Navy during World War II. Died after an illness of eight months. Buried Sunset Cemetery, Mountain City TN.

John Shoupe—3 Years Infielder (b. 30 Sep 1851 Cincinnati OH–d. 13 Feb 1920 at his home in Cincinnati OH) Died from acute bronchitis. Buried Linden Grove Cemetery, Covington KY.

John Shovlin—3 Years Infielder (b. 14 Jan 1891 Drifton PA–d. 16 Feb 1976 Suburban Hospital, Bethesda MD) He retired from the Jeddo-Highland Coal Company. Buried St Ann's Cemetery, Freeland PA.

Eric Show—11 Years Pitcher (b. 19 May 1956 Riverside CA–d. 16 Mar 1994 Rancho L'Abri Retreat, Dulzura CA) Died from an accidental self-administered overdose of heroin and cocaine. Buried Olivewood Cemetery, Riverside CA.

Lev Shreve—3 Years Pitcher (b. 14 Jan 1869 Louisville KY–d. 12 Nov 1942 at his home in Detroit MI) Living 45 years in Michigan, he retired about 1927 as an executive for the Ford Motor Company. Buried Cave Hill Cemetery, Louisville KY.

Harry Shriver—2 Years Pitcher (b. 2 Sep 1896 Wadestown WV–d. 21 Jan 1970 West Virginia Univ Hosp, Morgantown WV) Buried Wadestown Cemetery, Wadestown WV.

Frank Shugart—8 Years Infielder (b. 10 Dec 1866 Luthersburg PA–d. 9 Sep 1944 Clearfield PA) Died after a long illness. Buried Luthersburg Cemetery, Luthersburg PA.

Toots Shultz—2 Years Pitcher (b. 10 Oct 1888 Homestead PA–d. 30 Jan 1959 McKeesport PA).

Harry Shuman—3 Years Pitcher (b. 5 Mar 1915 Philadelphia PA–d. 25 Oct 1996 Philadelphia PA) Active polictically, he worked as a constable for Philadelphia City, supervisor of sales tax collections for the State Department of Revenue and for the City Veteran's Advisory Council. His last five years he worked for the Democratic City Committee. Died at his desk at work from a heart attack. Buried Haym Salomon Memorial Park, Frazer PA.

Vince Shupe—1 Year Infielder (b. 5 Sep 1921 East Canton OH–d. 5 Apr 1962 Canton OH) He was a salesman for Pure Oil Company. Died from a heart attack suffered while bowling. Buried Mapleton Cemetery, East Canton OH.

Eddie Sicking—5 Years Infielder (b. 30 Mar 1897 St Bernard OH–d. 30 Aug 1978 Woodside Manor Nursing Home, Cincinnati OH) Served in the U.S. Army during World War I. He operated the Sportsman's Cafe in St Bernard for 25 years. Died from arterioscelrotic heart disease. Buried St Mary Cemetery, Cincinnati OH.

Dick Siebert—11 Years Infielder (b. 19 Feb 1912 Fall River MA–d. 9 Dec 1978 University Hospital, Minneapolis MN) He was the head baseball coach at the University of Minnesota for 31 years, leading the Golden Gophers to 11 Big Ten titles and NCAA championships in 1956, 1960 and 1964. Died from pneumonia and other complications a month following ulcer surgery and spleen removal. Buried Lakewood Cemetery, Minneapolis MN.

Fred Siefke—1 Year Infielder (b. 27 Mar 1870 New York City NY–d. 18 Apr 1893 New York City NY) Died from pneumonia. Buried Greenwood Cemetery, Brooklyn NY.

Johnny Siegle—2 Years Outfielder (b. 8 Jul 1874 Columbus OH–d. 12 Feb 1968 Mercy Memorial Hospital, Urbana OH) He was elected sheriff of Champaign County, OH, in 1917 and was postmaster at Urbana from 1921 to 1933. An expert bowler, he managed a bowling alley for seven years. He also worked for both the state highway department and the county highway department. Buried Oakdale Cemetery, Urbana OH.

Oscar Siemer—2 Years Catcher (b. 14 Aug 1901 St Louis MO–d. 5 Dec 1959 St Louis MO) Buried Calvary Cemetery, St Louis MO.

Ed Siever—7 Years Pitcher (b. 2 Apr 1877 Goodard KS–d. 4 Feb 1920 Detroit MI) He managed a cigar stand in the Grand Cafe in Detroit. Later he was appointed as inspector for the department of public works. Fell dead, suddenly, from heart disease after leaving a street car on his way home from work.

Frank Siffel—2 Years Catcher (b. 1860 Germany–d. 26 Oct 1909 at his home in Philadelphia PA) Died suddenly. Buried Greenmount Cemetery, Philadelphia PA.

Frank Sigafoos—3 Years Infielder (b. 21 Mar 1904 Easton PA–d. 12 Apr 1968 Indianapolis IN) He was a popular player in the American Association for several years. For 30 years he was a special assistant in the engineering department of Citizen's Gas and Coke Utility. Died from a heart attack while working in the backyard of his home. Cremated.

Paddy Siglin—3 Years Infielder (b. 24 Sep

1891 Aurelia IA–d. 5 Aug 1956 V A Hospital, Oakland CA) World War I veteran. He was a watchman and janitor. Died from colon cancer. Buried Santa Clara Mission Cemetery, Santa Clara CA.

Tripp Sigman —2 Years Outfielder (b. 17 Jan 1899 Mooresville NC–d. 8 Mar 1971 at a hospital in Augusta GA) World War I veteran. He managed the sports program at Republic Mills in Great Falls SC and later operated the Sky View Driving Range in Augusta GA. Died from a heart condition. Buried Westover Memorial Park, Augusta GA.

Walter Signer —2 Years Pitcher (b. 12 Oct 1910 New York City NY–d. 23 Jul 1974 Greenwich CT) Buried Gate of Heaven Cemetery, Hawthorne NY.

Seth Sigsby —1 Year Pitcher (b. 30 Apr 1874 Cobleskill NY–d. 15 Sep 1953 Schenectady NY).

Eddie Silber —2 Years Outfielder (b. 6 Jun 1914 Philadelphia PA–d. 26 Oct 1976 Dunedin FL) He was a detective on the Philadelphia Police Dept for 23 years before retiring to Florida about 1963. Buried Sylvan Abbey Memorial Park, Clearwater FL.

Ed Silch—1 Year Outfielder (b. 22 Feb 1865 St Louis MO–d. 14 Jan 1895 at his home in St Louis MO) He was a motorman on the St Louis Street Car Line. Died from consumption. Buried Calvary Cemetery, St Louis MO.

Danny Silva —1 Year Infielder (b. 5 Oct 1896 Everett MA–d. 4 Apr 1974 Cape Cod Hospital, Hyannis MA) A veteran of both World Wars I and II, he taught, coached and umpired 24 years in the Everett area high schools. He retired to the Cape Cod area in 1955 where he was a minor league administrator and umpire almost until his death. Died following a short illness. Buried Mosswood Cemetery, Cotuit MA.

Ken Silvestri —8 Years Catcher 1 Year Manager (b. 3 May 1916 Chicago IL–d. 31 Mar 1992 at his home in Tallahassee FL) Served in the U.S. Army during World War II, earning three Bronze Battle Stars. He spent his entire life in baseball as a player, coach, scout, manager and minor league manager. Buried Mount Carmel Cemetery, Hillside IL.

Al Sima —4 Years Pitcher (b. 7 Oct 1921 Mahwah NY–d. 17 Aug 1993 Suffern NY).

Al Simmons —20 Years Outfielder Hall of Fame (b. 22 May 1902 Milwaukee WI–d. 26 May 1956 Milwaukee WI) Died from a heart attack in front of the Athletic Club where he was living. Buried St Adalbert's Cemetery, Milwaukee WI.

Hack Simmons —4 Years Infielder (b. 29 Jan 1885 Brooklyn NY–d. 26 Apr 1942 at his sons's home in Arverne NY) He was a general inspector for 26 years at B M T. Died from injuries suffered in an automobile accident.

Joe Simmons —1 Year Manager (b. 13 Jun 1845 New York NY–d. 10 Dec 1888 at his home in Brooklyn NY) Died from blood poisoning caused by a spiking in a game several months earlier.

Lew Simmons —3 Years Manager (b. 27 Aug 1838 New Castle PA–d. 2 Sep 1911 Jamestown PA).

Pat Simmons —2 Years Pitcher (b. 29 Nov 1908 Watervliet NY–d. 3 Jul 1968 Albany NY) Buried St Patrick's Cemetery, Watervliet NY.

Henry Simon —2 Years Outfielder (b. 25 Aug 1862 Hawkinsville NY–d. 1 Jan 1925 Albany NY) He was a cigar maker. Died from a heart attack while waiting for a train when he was enroute from his home in Utica NY to visit his sister in Connecticut.

Mike Simon —7 Years Catcher (b. 13 Apr 1883 Hayden IN–d. 10 Jun 1963 General Hospital, Los Angeles CA) He was a truck driver for a dry cleaning company. Died from a cardiovascular collapse, pneumonia and inanition. Buried Loma Vista Memorial Park, Fullerton CA.

Syl Simon —2 Years Infielder (b. 14 Dec 1897 Evansville IN–d. 28 Feb 1973 near Chandler IN) He worked for Wesselman's in Evanston until 1971 when he retired to his orchard near Chandler. Took his own life by hanging himself in his barn. Buried Locust Hill Cemetery, Evansville IN.

Mel Simons —2 Years Outfielder (b. 1 Jul 1900 Carlyle IL–d. 10 Nov 1974 Lourdes Hospital, Paducah KY) He worked in baseball until 1941, after which he operated the Simons Paint Store in Fulton KY. Buried Greenlea Cemetery, Fulton KY.

Harry Simpson —8 Years Outfielder (b. 3 Dec 1925 Dalton GA–d. 3 Apr 1979 at his home in

Akron OH) Served in the U.S. Army during World War II. He was a machinist for Goodyear Aerospace until his retirement in 1976. Died from a heart attack. Buried West Hill Cemetery, Dalton GA.

Steve Simpson —1 Year Pitcher (b. 30 Aug 1948 St Joseph MO–d. 2 Nov 1989 Omaha NE) Buried Memorial Park Cemetery, Topeka KS.

Pete Sims —1 Year Pitcher (b. 24 May 1891 Crown City OH–d. 2 Dec 1968 Dallas TX) He was a retired real estate agent. Buried Forest Rose Cemetery, Lancaster OH.

Bert Sincock —1 Year Pitcher (b. 8 Sep 1887 Barkerville, British Columbia, Canada–d. 1 Aug 1946 Houghton MI) For 25 years he was assistant manager for the New Lawrence Hotel in Chicago, and manager of the Douglas House, a hotel in Houghton, for one year. Died from a heart attack shortly after taking the job in Houghton. Buried Lake View Cemetery, Calumet MI.

Hosea Siner —1 Year Infielder (b. 20 Mar 1885 Shelburn IN–d. 10 Jun 1948 Mary Sherman Hospital, Sullivan IN) A prominent farmer and dairyman in Sullivan County, IN, he was active in community affairs, serving as a county councilman and on the hospital board. Died from a heart condition. Buried Mount Zion Cemetery, New Lebanon IN.

Elmer Singleton —8 Years Pitcher (b. 26 Jun 1918 Ogden UT–d. 5 Jan 1996 at his home in Plain City UT) After retiring from baseball in 1964 he was active in civic affairs in the Ogden area. Buried Plain City Cemetery, Plain City UT.

John Singleton —1 Year Pitcher (b. 27 Nov 1896 Gallipolis OH–d. 23 Oct 1937 Soldier's Hospital, Dayton OH) Served in the U.S. Marine Corps during World War I. Died from complications of diabetes. Buried Vine Street Hill Cemetery, Cincinnati OH.

Dick Sisler —8 Years Infielder 2 Years Manager (b. 2 Nov 1920 St Louis MO–d. 20 Nov 1998 Lakeshore Nursing Home, Nashville TN) World War II veteran. He managed minor league baseball and coached for several teams before becoming staff director of recreation for the Tennessee Department of Corrections. Buried Woodlawn Memorial Park, Nashville TN.

George Sisler —15 Years Infielder 3 Years Manager Hall of Fame (b. 24 Mar 1893 Manchester OH–d. 26 Mar 1973 St Mary's Health Center, St Louis MO) He was commissioner of the National Baseball Congress, the governing organization for semi-pro baseball, before returning to the major leagues as a scout. Later he was a batting instructor, and was also a minor league executive. Cremated.

Carl Sitton —1 Year Pitcher (b. 22 Sep 1882 Pendleton SC–d. 11 Sep 1931 Valdosta GA) He worked for a powder company in Brunswick GA, and spent much of his time hunting and fishing. He was found at the fairgrounds where he died from a self-inflicted gunshot wound to the heart. Buried Walhalla SC.

Ed Sixsmith—1 Year Catcher (b. 26 Feb 1863 Philadelphia PA–d. 12 Dec 1926 at his home in Philadelphia PA) Buried North Cedar Hill Cemetery, Philadelphia PA.

Frank Skaff—2 Years Infielder 1 Year Manager (b. 30 Sep 1913 LaCrosse WI–d. 12 Apr 1988 Towson MD) He worked 33 years as a manager, coach and scout for the Tigers. Died from a heart attack after leaving a college baseball game. Buried Dulaney Valley Memorial Garden, Timonium MD.

Dave Skeels —1 Year Pitcher (b. 29 Dec 1892 WA–d. 2 Dec 1926 at a sanitarium in Spokane WA) Buried Chewelah Cemetery, Spokane WA.

Bud Sketchley —1 Year Outfielder (b. 30 Mar 1919 Virden, Manitoba, Canada–d. 19 Dec 1979 Los Angeles CA) Buried Forest Lawn Memorial Park, Glendale CA.

Bill Skiff—2 Years Catcher (b. 16 Oct 1895 New Rochelle NY–d. 25 Dec 1976 Bronxville NY) A long-time Yankee scout, he spent 55 years in organized baseball as a player, coach, minor league manager and farm director.

Camp Skinner —2 Years Outfielder (b. 25 Jun 1897 Douglasville GA–d. 4 Aug 1944 Douglasville GA) Buried Douglasville City Cemetery, Douglasville GA.

John Skopec —2 Years Pitcher (b. 8 May 1880 Chicago IL–d. 12 Oct 1912 Chicago IL).

Gordon Slade —6 Years Infielder (b. 9 Oct 1904 Salt Lake City UT–d. 2 Jan 1974 at his home in Long Beach CA) He was manager of the health club at a private club. Died from a heart attack. Cremated.

Art Sladen —1 Year Outfielder (b. 28 Oct 1860 Dracut MA–d. 1 Mar 1914 at his home in Dracut MA) Buried Edson Cemetery, Lowell MA.

Jimmy Slagle —10 Years Outfielder (b. 11 Jul 1873 Worthville PA–d. 10 May 1956 at his home in Chicago IL) He owned a laundry in Chicago until he retired in 1946. Buried Oakridge Cemetery, Hillside IL.

Walt Slagle —1 Year Pitcher (b. 15 Dec 1878 Kenton OH–d. 14 Jun 1974 San Marino Manor, San Gabriel CA) At the time of his death he was the oldest living former major league ballplayer. He was an oil field worker for Standard Oil for 20 years. Died from heart disease. Buried Rose Hills Memorial Park, Whittier CA.

Cy Slapnicka —2 Years Pitcher (b. 23 Mar 1886 Cedar Rapids IA–d. 20 Oct 1979 Cedar Rapids IA) He was a scout, general manager and vice-president for the Cleveland Indians and a member of the Iowa Hall of Fame. Died after a long illness. Buried Cedar Memorial Park Cemetery, Cedar Rapids IA.

John Slappey —1 Year Pitcher (b. 8 Aug 1898 Albany GA–d. 10 Jun 1957 Marietta GA) He was general manager of the Kennesaw Memorial Park Cemetery. Died following a heart attack. Buried Oakview Cemetery, Albany GA.

Jack Slattery —4 Years Catcher 1 Year Manager (b. 6 Jan 1877 Boston MA–d. 17 Jul 1949 City Hospital, Boston MA) He graduated from college with a degree in denistry, but never practiced the profession, coaching baseball at Tufts, Harvard and Boston College. His last 20 years was spent as an associate with his brothers in the leather firm of Slattery Brothers. Died from a heart affliction. Buried St Joseph's Cemetery, West Roxbury MA.

Mike Slattery —5 Years Outfielder (b. 28 Oct 1865 Boston MA–d. 16 Oct 1904 Carney Hospital, Boston MA) He was the head salesman in a clothing store in Boston. Died after a short illness of stomach trouble.

Phil Slattery —1 Year Pitcher (b. 25 Feb 1893 Harper IA–d. 10 Mar 1968 St Mary's Hospital, Long Beach CA) He was a hotel clerk for 30 years. Died from a heart attack. Buried Westminster Memorial Park, Westminster CA.

Barney Slaughter —1 Year Pitcher (b. 6 Oct 1884 Smyrna DE–d. 17 May 1961 Lankenau Hospital, Philadelphia PA) He worked more than 35 years in the secretary's office of the Pennsylvania Railroad, retiring in 1956. Buried Glenwood Memorial Gardens, Broomall PA.

Scottie Slayback —1 Year Infielder (b. 5 Oct 1901 Paducah KY–d. 30 Nov 1979 General Hospital, Cincinnati OH) He worked for Seagram's distillery in Lawrenceburg KY.

Steve Slayton —1 Year Pitcher (b. 26 Apr 1902 Barre VT–d. 20 Dec 1984 Elliot Hospital, Manchester NH) He coached high school baseball. Died following a brief illness. Buried Hope Cemetery, Barre VT.

Bruce Sloan —1 Year Outfielder (b. 4 Oct 1914 McAlester OK–d. 24 Sep 1973 Mercy Hospital, Oklahoma City OK) Buried Chapel Hill Memorial Gardens, Oklahoma City OK.

Tod Sloan —3 Years Outfielder (b. 24 Dec 1890 Madisonville TN–d. 12 Sep 1956 Akron OH) Served in the U.S. Navy during World War I. He retired from Goodyear Tire and Rubber Company as a supervisor. Died after a brief illness. Buried Chestnut Hill Memorial Park, Cuyahoga Falls OH.

Charlie Small —1 Year Outfielder (b. 24 Oct 1905 Auburn ME–d. 14 Jan 1953 Damon Nursing Home, Auburn ME) He played and/or managed minor league baseball up until he became ill, two years before his death. Buried Lower Gloucester Cemetery, New Gloucester ME.

Will Smalley —2 Years Infielder (b. 27 Jun 1871 Oakland CA–d. 11 Oct 1891 Bay City MI) Died at the height of his baseball career from stomach trouble, presumably cancer. Buried CA.

Walt Smallwood —2 Years Pitcher (b. 24 Apr 1893 Dayton MD–d. 29 Apr 1967 Baltimore MD) Buried New Cathedral Cemetery, Baltimore MD.

Joe Smaza —1 Year Outfielder (b. 7 Jul 1923 Detroit MI–d. 30 May 1979 Beaumont Hospital, Royal Oak MI) He was a Detroit police officer. Died two weeks after suffering a heart attack while on duty at traffic court. Buried St Hedwig Cemetery, Dearborn Heights MI.

Bill Smiley —1 Year Infielder (b. 1856 Baltimore MD–d. 11 Jul 1884 Baltimore MD) Buried St Patrick's Cemetery, Baltimore MD.

Al Smith —12 Years Pitcher (b. 12 Oct 1907 Belleville IL–d. 28 Apr 1977 Valley Grande Manor, Brownsville TX) Cremated.

Al Smith—1 Year Pitcher (b. 13 Dec 1903 Norristown PA–d. 11 Aug 1995 S D Hospice Care Facility, San Diego CA) He owned an oil drilling business for ten years. Died from lung cancer.

Art Smith—1 Year Pitcher (b. 21 Jun 1906 Boston MA–d. 22 Nov 1995 Norwalk CT).

Bill Smith—3 Years Pitcher (b. 8 Jun 1934 Washington DC–d. 30 Mar 1997 Clinton MD) Buried Resurrection Cemetery, Clinton MD.

Bill Smith—1 Year Outfielder (b. Cleveland OH–d. 9 Aug 1886 Toronto, Ontario, Canada) Died after breaking his back in a diving accident.

Bob Smith—15 Years Pitcher (b. 22 Apr 1898 Rogersville TN–d. 19 Jul 1987 Baptist Village, Waycross GA) He managed minor league baseball for a few years. Died after a lengthy illness. Buried Westview Cemetery, Atlanta GA.

Bob Smith—3 Years Pitcher (b. 20 Jul 1890 Woodbury VT–d. 27 Dec 1965 V A Hospital, West Los Angeles CA) Served in World War I. He was a self-employed real estate broker for 15 years. Died from arteriosclerotic heart disease. Cremated.

Broadway Aleck Smith—9 Years Catcher (b. 1871 New York City NY–d. 9 Jul 1919 New York City NY) Buried Woodlawn Cemetery, Bronx NY.

Bull Smith—3 Years Outfielder (b. 20 Aug 1880 Plum WV–d. 1 May 1928 Charleston WV).

C Arnholt Smith—(b. 13 Mar 1899 WA–d. 8 Jun 1996 Casa Palmero Care Center, Del Mar CA) The owner of the San Diego Padres from 1955 to 1974, he helped bring major league baseball to San Diego. He was also a banker, hotel owner, farm owner, transportation entrepreneur and the owner of tuna clippers. Died from congestive heart failure. Buried Greenwood Memorial Park, San Diego CA.

Carr Smith—2 Years Outfielder (b. 8 Apr 1901 Kernersville NC–d. 14 Apr 1989 Miami FL).

Charley Smith—10 Years Infielder (b. 15 Sep 1937 Charleston SC–d. 29 Nov 1994 at his home in Reno NV) An avid hunter and fisherman, he was a street maintenance worker for the City of Sparks NV. Died from a blood clot following knee surgery. Cremated.

Charlie Smith—10 Years Pitcher (b. 20 Apr 1880 Cleveland OH–d. 3 Jan 1929 at a sanitarium in Wickliff OH) He suffered a sunstroke a few years before he died and never fully recovered. Died from lobar pneumonia. Buried St Joseph Cemetery, Cleveland OH.

Chick Smith—1 Year Pitcher (b. 2 Dec 1892 Dayton KY–d. 11 Oct 1935 at his home in Dayton KY) He was an engineer. Buried St Stephen Cemetery, Fort Thomas KY.

Dave Smith—2 Years Pitcher (b. 17 Dec 1914 Sellers SC–d. 1 Apr 1998 Whiteville NC) Buried Whiteville Memorial Cemetery, Whiteville NC.

Doug Smith—1 Year Pitcher (b. 25 May 1892 Millers Falls MA–d. 18 Sep 1973 Franklin Nursing Home in Greenfield MA) World War I veteran. He retired after working 43 years for the Millers Falls Paper Company. Buried Highland Cemetery, Millers Falls MA.

Earl Smith—7 Years Outfielder (b. 20 Jan 1891 Oak Hill OH–d. 13 Mar 1943 General Hospital, Portsmouth OH) He was a plumber. Died from an intestinal obstruction. Buried Memorial Burial Park, Wheelersburg OH.

Earl Smith—12 Years Catcher (b. 14 Feb 1897 Sheridan AR–d. 9 Jun 1963 at a hospital in Little Rock AR) World War I veteran. He managed minor league baseball for five years before retiring to Hot Springs AR in 1940. Died after a long illness. Buried Little Rock National Cemetery, Little Rock AR.

Ed Smith—1 Year Pitcher (b. 21 Feb 1879 Mentone IN–d. 20 Mar 1955 Tarpon Springs FL).

Eddie Smith—10 Years Pitcher (b. 14 Dec 1913 Mansfield NJ–d. 2 Jan 1994 Rancocas Hospital, Willingboro NJ) Served in the U.S. Army during World War II. Buried New Jersey Veteran's Memorial Cemetery, New Egypt NJ.

Edgar Smith—4 Years Outfielder (b. 12 Jun 1862 Providence RI–d. 3 Nov 1892 Providence RI) Died from a pulmonary hemorrhage. Buried Swan Point Cemetery, Providence RI.

Elmer Smith—14 Years Outfielder (b. 23 Mar 1868 Pittsburgh PA–d. 3 Nov 1945 at his home in Pittsburgh PA) He retired from his job as inspector for the Pittsburgh Bureau of Highways in 1931. Buried Union Dale Cemetery, Pittsburgh PA.

Elmer Smith—10 Years Outfielder (b. 21 Sep 1892 Sandusky OH–d. 3 Aug 1984 Summit

Manor Nursing Home, Columbia KY) World War I veteran. In 1920 he was the first player to hit a grandslam home run in a World Series game. He worked for an engineering firm in Ohio from the 1930s until retiring in 1959. Cremated.

Ernie Smith—1 Year Infielder (b. 11 Oct 1901 Paterson NJ–d. 6 Apr 1973 Brooklyn NY).

Frank Smith—1 Year Catcher (b. 24 Nov 1857 Canada–d. 11 Oct 1928 at his home in Canandaigua NY) Died after a long illness. Buried Woodlawn Cemetery, Canandaigua NY.

Frank Smith—11 Years Pitcher (b. 28 Oct 1879 Pittsburgh PA–d. 3 Nov 1952 at his home in Pittsburgh PA) Buried Minersville Cemetery, Pittsburgh PA.

Fred Smith—4 Years Infielder (b. 29 Jul 1886 Cleveland OH–d. 28 May 1961 Cleveland OH) Hw worked 24 years for the Internal Revenue Service before spending five years as a real estate salesman in Cleveland. Died from a heart attack. Buried Calvary Cemetery, Cleveland OH.

Fred Smith—1 Year Pitcher (b. 25 Mar 1863 Greene NY–d. 9 Jan 1941 Syracuse NY).

Fred Smith—1 Year Pitcher (b. 24 Nov 1879 New Diggins WI–d. 4 Feb 1964 at his home in Los Angeles CA) He was a welder for Southern Pacific Railroad. Died from heart disease. Buried Inglewood Park Cemetery, Inglewood CA.

George Smith—4 Years Infielder (b. 7 Jul 1938 St Petersburg FL–d. 15 Jun 1987 Bayfront Medical Center, St Petersburg FL) He was a physical education teacher at Bay Point Middle School in St Petersburg and a recreation aide at a community center. He was also a maintenance supervisor at a bank. Died from cancer. Buried Lincoln Cemetery, Gulfport FL.

George Smith—8 Years Pitcher (b. 31 May 1892 Byram CT–d. 7 Jan 1965 Greenwich Hospital, Greenwich CT) He taught mathematics at Greenwich High School from 1919 until 1957 when he retired as the department head. Buried Greenwood Union Cemetery, Rye NY.

George Smith—5 Years Pitcher (b. 27 Oct 1901 Louisville KY–d. 26 May 1981 Richmond VA) He was a retired employee of the U.S. Tobacco Company. Buried Sunset MeZmorial Park, Richmond VA.

Germany Smith—15 Years Infielder (b. 21 Apr 1863 Pittsburgh PA–d. 1 Dec 1927 Altoona Hospital, Altoona PA) He was a watchman for the Pennsylvania Railroad. Died from a fractured skull after he was hit by a car as he was walking to catch a trolley on his way home from work. Buried Calvary Cemetery, Altoona PA.

Hal Smith—4 Years Pitcher (b. 30 Jun 1902 Creston IA–d. 27 Sep 1992 Fort Lauderdale FL) Cremated. Buried Parkview Cemetery, Peoria IL.

Hap Smith—1 Year Outfielder (b. 14 Jul 1883 Coquille OR–d. 26 Feb 1961 at his home in San Jose CA) He retired from Carl N Swenson Construction Company in 1959, after 24 years. After retirement he was a night watchman on weekends. Died from a heart seizure. Buried Oak Hill Memorial Park, San Jose CA.

Harry Smith—2 Years Infielder (b. 5 Feb 1856 North Vernon IN–d. 4 Jun 1898 Queensville IN).

Harry Smith—10 Years Catcher 1 Year Manager (b. 31 Oct 1874 Yorkshire, England–d. 17 Feb 1933 at his home in Salem NJ) He managed some minor league baseball. From 1919 until shortly before his death he was a machinist for duPont Company. He was working for Salem Glass when he died. Died suddenly from a heart attack. Buried Lawnside Cemetery, Woodstown NJ.

Harry Smith—4 Years Catcher (b. 15 May 1890 Baltimore MD–d. 1 Apr 1922 at a hospital in Charlotte NC) Died at the height of his career following a two-day illness from influenza and pneumonia. Buried Oak Lawn Cemetery, Baltimore MD.

Harry Smith—1 Year Pitcher (b. 15 Aug 1889 Avoca NE–d. 27 Jul 1964 at his home in Dunbar NE) He was a carpenter. Died after an illness of many months. Buried Wyuka Cemetery, Nebraska City NE.

Harvey Smith—1 Year Infielder (b. 24 Jul 1871 Union Deposit PA–d. 12 Nov 1962 at his home in Harrisburg PA) A noted physician and surgeon, he was known as Harrisburg's "grand old man of medicine". He practiced surgery from 1899 until retiring in 1961, sometimes performing nearly 1000 surgeries a year. Died after a six-month illness. Buried Harrisburg Cemetery, Harrisburg PA.

Heinie Smith—6 Years Infielder 1 Year Manager (b. 4 Mar 1870 Pittsburgh PA–d. 25 Jun

1939 Sister's Hospital, Buffalo NY) An avid bowler, he managed bowling alleys for several years. At one time he held the Buffalo City Bowling Championship. Died after a long illness. Buried Elmlawn Cemetery, Kenmore NY.

Hilton Smith—13 Years Pitcher Hall of Fame (b. 27 Feb 1907 Giddings TX–d. 18 Nov 1983 Moriah Medical Center, Kansas City MO) He pitched in the negro leagues from 1932 to 1948 and was a foreman for Armco Inc for 30 years, retiring in 1978. He lived in the Kansas City area for 40 years. Buried Mount Moriah Cemetery, Kansas City MO.

Jack Smith—1 Year Infielder (b. 8 Aug 1893 Oswayo PA–d. 4 Dec 1962 New York City NY).

Jack Smith—15 Years Outfielder (b. 23 Jun 1895 Chicago IL–d. 2 May 1972 Westchester IL) Buried Forest Home Cemetery, Forest Park IL.

Jake Smith—1 Year Pitcher (b. 10 Jun 1887 Dravosburg PA–d. 7 Nov 1948 East McKeesport PA).

Jimmy Smith—8 Years Infielder (b. 15 May 1895 Pittsburgh PA–d. 1 Jan 1974 Mercy Hospital, Pittsburgh PA) He was the general manager of National Distilleries Co before founding Hillcrest Coal Co of Foxburg PA. Later he worked for the Pennsylvania State Inheritance Tax Office. He was the father-in-law of fighter Billy Conn. Buried Calvary Cemetery, Pittsburgh PA.

Joe Smith—1 Year Catcher (b. 29 Dec 1893 New York City NY–d. 12 Jan 1974 Yonkers NY).

John Smith—1 Year Infielder (b. 6 Apr 1858 Ireland–d. 6 Jan 1899 San Francisco CA) Buried Holy Cross Catholic Cemetery, Colma CA.

John Smith—1 Year Infielder (b. 27 Sep 1906 Washington DC–d. 9 May 1982 Holy Cross Hospital, Silver Spring MD) Buried Parklawn Memorial Park, Rockville MD.

Jud Smith—4 Years Infielder (b. 13 Jan 1869 Brighton MI–d. 7 Dec 1947 at his home in Los Angeles CA) He left baseball in 1909 to enter a denistry practice. Died from pneumonia after suffering a stroke. Cremated.

Ken Smith—Hall of Fame (d. 1 Mar 1991 Palatine Bridge NY). He was a sportswriter.

Klondike Smith—1 Year Outfielder (b. 4 Jan 1887 London, England–d. 15 Nov 1959 Springfield MA) An avid golfer, he retired several years earlier from Stone and Webster Company. Died from a heart attack while visiting friends in Springfield. Buried Bellevue Cemetery, Lawrence MA.

Leo Smith—1 Year Infielder (b. 13 May 1859 Brooklyn NY–d. 30 Aug 1935 Brooklyn NY) Buried Riverview Cemetery, Trenton NJ.

Mayo Smith—1 Year Outfielder 9 Years Manager (b. 17 Jan 1915 New London MO–d. 24 Nov 1977 Boynton Beach FL) He worked 36 years in professional baseball, retiring in 1970.

Mike Smith—1 Year Outfielder (b. 16 Nov 1904 Norfolk VA–d. 31 May 1981 Chesapeake VA) He served in a number of public offices in Norfolk County, VA, and Chesapeake from 1942 until he retired, including deputy clerk of the circuit court, deputy treasurer and county commissioner. He was the first real estate assessor in Chesapeake. Buried Riverside Memorial Park, Norfolk VA.

Milt Smith—1 Year Infielder (b. 26 Mar 1929 Columbus GA–d. 11 Apr 1997 San Diego CA) Died from a heart attack. Buried Greenwood Memorial Park, San Diego CA.

Paddy Smith—1 Year Catcher (b. 16 May 1894 Pelham NY–d. 2 Dec 1990 New Rochelle Medical Ctr, New Rochelle NY) Served in the U.S. Navy during World War I. He and two brothers ran Smith Construction Company in Pelham, doing mainly excavation work in the eastern states. Buried Gate of Heaven Cemetery, Hawthorne NY.

Paul Smith—1 Year Outfielder (b. 7 May 1891 Mount Zion IL–d. 3 Jul 1958 Decatur IL) Served in the U.S. Army during World War I. He worked for the U.S. Fish and Wildlife Service from 1941 to 1951. Died from a heart attack. Buried Mount Zion Cemetery, Mount Zion IL.

Phenomenal Smith—8 Years Pitcher (b. 12 Dec 1864 Strasbourg, Alsace-Lorraine–d. 3 Apr 1952 at a hospital in Manchester NH) Best known for finding Christy Mathewson, he worked for the Myrna Shoe Factory in Manchester. Died following an illness of several weeks.

Pop Smith—12 Years Infielder (b. 12 Oct 1856 Digby, Nova Scotia, Canada–d. 18 Apr 1927 Allston MA).

Pop Boy Smith—3 Years Pitcher (b. 23 May

1892 Newport TN–d. 16 Feb 1924 Sweetwater TX) World War I veteran. He was called "Pop Boy" because he sold pop in the stands as a boy before starting his pitching career. Died from a pulmonary hemorrhage. Buried Elmwood Cemetery, Birmingham AL.

Red Smith—2 Years Catcher (b. 11 Apr 1892 Logansport IN–d. 17 Jul 1972 Noblesville IN).

Red Smith—1 Year Infielder (b. 17 Jul 1900 Ashley IL–d. 19 Feb 1961 Los Angeles CA) A veteran of both World Wars I and II, he was a scout. Died from heart disease. Buried Fort Rosecrans National Cemetery, Point Loma CA.

Red Smith—1 Year Catcher (b. 18 May 1904 Brokaw WI–d. 8 Mar 1978 Flower Hospital, Toledo OH) He was general manager of the Toledo Mud Hens of the American Association from 1952 to 1955 when he became general manager for Buckeye Brewing Company in Toledo. He was an executive for Buckeye Brewing until it closed in 1972. Buried Calvary Cemetery, Toledo OH.

Red Smith—9 Years Infielder (b. 6 Apr 1890 Greenville SC–d. 10 Oct 1966 Atlanta GA) Buried Westview Cemetery, Atlanta GA.

Red Smith—(b. 25 Sep 1905–d. 15 Jan 1982 Stamford Hospital, Stamford CT) He was Pulitzer Prize winning sports columnist for the *New York Times*. Hall of Fame Died from heart failure after a brief illness.

Rufus Smith—1 Year Pitcher (b. 24 Jan 1905 Guilford College NC–d. 22 Aug 1984 at his home in Aiken SC) He was a contractor. Buried St Paul Church Cemetery, New Ellenton SC.

Sherry Smith—14 Years Pitcher (b. 18 Feb 1891 Monticello GA–d. 12 Sep 1949 at his home in Reidsville GA) He was the chief of police of Madison GA until shortly before his death when he took a job at Tattnall State Prison in Reidsville. Died from a heart attack. Buried Mansfield GA.

Skyrocket Smith—1 Year Infielder (b. 19 Mar 1868 St Louis MO–d. 26 Apr 1916 St Louis MO) He worked for the St Louis Fire Department. Buried Calvary Cemetery, St Louis MO.

Syd Smith—5 Years Catcher (b. 31 Aug 1883 Smithville SC–d. 5 Jun 1961 Regional Hospital, Orangeburg SC) He worked for the South Carolina Employment Security Commission. A versatile athlete, he was a top golfer, tennis player, polo player and coach. Buried Camden SC.

Tom Smith—1 Year Infielder (b. 1851 Guelph, Ontario, Canada–d. 28 Mar 1889 St Mary's Hospital, Detroit MI) He was an example of a promising baseball career wasted to excesses. Died from consumption. Buried London, Ontario, Canada.

Tom Smith—4 Years Pitcher (b. 5 Dec 1871 Boston MA–d. 1 Mar 1929 Dorchester MA) A Boston police officer since 1900, he was assigned to duty at the Board of Health in 1927. Died after a long illness. Buried Mount Calvary Cemetery, Roslindale MA.

Tony Smith—3 Years Infielder (b. 14 May 1884 Chicago IL–d. 27 Feb 1964 St Mary's Infirmary, Galveston TX) For 33 years he was a secretary at the University of Texas Medical Branch at Galveston. Buried Galveston Memorial Park, Hitchcock TX.

Vinnie Smith—2 Years Catcher (b. 7 Dec 1915 Richmond VA–d. 14 Dec 1979 Virginia Beach VA) Served in the U.S. Navy during World War II. His baseball career cut short by a knee injury, he umpired in the National League from 1956 to 1966. Died from cancer. His body was donated to the Medical College of Virginia for cancer research.

Wally Smith—3 Years Infielder (b. 13 Mar 1889 Philadelphia PA–d. 10 Jun 1930 Pinal County Hospital, Florence AZ) He was a railroad dispatcher. Died from pulmonary tuberculosis after being hospitalized four months. Buried Ray AZ.

Wendell Smith—Hall of Fame (b. abt 1914 Detroit MI–d. 26 Nov 1972 St Joseph's Hospital, Chicago IL) He was a black sportswriter for the *Chicago American* from 1947 to 1963 when he became a sportscaster for WGN TV in Chicago. He continued to write a column for the *Chicago Sun-Times*. Died after an extended illness. Buried Burr Oak Cemetery, Chicago IL.

Wib Smith—1 Year Catcher (b. 30 Aug 1886 Evart MI–d. 18 Nov 1959 at a hospital in Fargo ND) He worked 25 years for Allis-Chalmers Manufacturing Company, the last 15 as manager of the Fargo branch, retiring in 1954. Buried Lakewood Cemetery, Minneapolis MN.

Lefty Smoll—1 Year Pitcher (b. 17 Apr 1914 Quakertown PA–d. 31 Aug 1985 Quakertown PA).

Homer Smoot—5 Years Outfielder (b. 26 Mar 1878 Galestown MD–d. 25 Mar 1928 at his home in Salisbury MD) He owned and operated a feed business in Salisbury and managed minor league baseball. Died after a brief illness. Buried Galestown Cemetery, Galestown MD.

Henry Smoyer—1 Year Infielder (b. 25 Apr 1890 Fredericksburg PA–d. 28 Feb 1958 Maple Ave Hospital, Du Bois PA) Served in the U.S. Army field artillery during World War I. He retired in 1945 as a machinist for National Foundry. Died after an illness of five months. Buried Morningside Cemetery, Du Bois PA.

Frank Smykal—1 Year Infielder (b. 13 Oct 1889 Chicago IL–d. 11 Aug 1950 Chicago IL) He was an associate professor at the Chicago Medical School and the senior physician at the municipal tuberculosis sanitarium. Buried Bohemian National Cemetery, Chicago IL.

Red Smyth—4 Years Outfielder (b. 30 Jan 1891 Holly Springs MS–d. 14 Apr 1958 V A Hospital, West Los Angeles CA) World War I veteran. He was a bookkeeper for Simmons Bed Company, a mattress manufacturer. Died from complications following a fall in which he broke his leg, but he suffered from Parkinson's disease. Buried Holy Cross Cemetery, Culver City CA.

Harry Smythe—3 Years Pitcher (b. 24 Oct 1904 Augusta GA–d. 28 Aug 1980 in a hospital in Augusta GA) He worked for the rationing board during World War II. He was district circulation manager for the *Augusta Herald* from 1945 to 1965, and worked for the *Augusta Chronicle* five years. He had a newspaper route until 1979 and operated a vending machine business. Died from cancer. Buried Westover Memorial Park, Augusta GA.

John Sneed—3 Years Outfielder (b. Columbus OH–d. 4 Jan 1899 Memphis TN).

Charlie Snell—1 Year Catcher (b. 29 Nov 1892 Hampstead MD–d. 4 Apr 1988 St Joseph Hospital, Reading PA) He was a railway mail clerk for the Railway Mail Service, retiring in 1959. Buried East Harrisburg Cemetery, Harrisburg PA.

Wally Snell—1 Year Catcher (b. 19 Apr 1889 West Bridgewater MA–d. 23 Jul 1980 Rhode Island Hospital, Providence RI) Between 1920 and 1940 he coached every sport, at one time or the other, at Brown University and served as athletic director for a time. But it was as a botanist that he received international fame and was recognized as the world's leading authority on the boletus mush-Broom. He was a retired professor of natural history and head of the botany department at Brown University. Died from a metabolic encephalopathy. Cremated.

Roxy Snipes—1 Game Pinch Hitter (b. 28 Oct 1896 Marion SC–d. 1 May 1941 V A Hospital, Fayetteville NC) He was an attorney at Marion and was serving as a state senator from Marion County, SC, when he died. Served in the U.S. Navy during World War I. Died from pneumonia after being ill several months. Buried Rose Hill Cemetery, Marion SC.

Chappie Snodgrass—1 Year Outfielder (b. 18 Mar 1870 Springfield OH–d. 9 Sep 1951 New York City NY).

Fred Snodgrass—9 Years Outfielder (b. 19 Oct 1887 Ventura CA–d. 5 Apr 1974 Community Memerial Hospital, Ventura CA) He is best remembered as the man who dropped a fly ball in the 1912 World Series, costing the Giants the championship. For over 25 years he owned and operated an appliance store in Oxnard CA, and was mayor of Oxnard for a short time. He was also a citrus fruit grower. Died from a heart attack, emphysema and kidney failure. Cremated.

Colonel Snover—1 Year Pitcher (b. 16 May 1895 Hallstead PA–d. 30 Apr 1969 Rochester NY).

Bill Snyder—2 Years Pitcher (b. 28 Jan 1898 Mansfield OH–d. 8 Oct 1934 Franklin Memorial Hospital, Vicksburg MI) He worked for Kalamazoo Vegetable Parchment Company in Kalamazoo MI. Died from pneumonia. Buried Vicksburg Cemetery, Vicksburg MI.

Charlie Snyder—1 Year Outfielder (b. Camden NJ–d. 3 Mar 1901 Pennsylvania Hotel, Philadelphia PA) Died from a fractured skull suffered when he was ejected from the St Albans Hotel in Philadelphia.

Cooney Snyder—1 Year Catcher (b. Toronto, Ontario, Canada–d. 9 May 1917 Toronto, Ontario, Canada).

Frank Snyder—16 Years Catcher (b. 27 May 1893 San Antonio TX–d. 5 Jan 1962 at a hospital in San Antonio TX) He managed minor league baseball and coached briefly for the Giants before working in the public relations department of the Lone Star Brewery in San Antonio. Buried Fort Sam Houston National Cemetery, San Antonio TX.

Gene Snyder —1 Year Pitcher (b. 31 Mar 1931 York PA–d. 2 Jun 1996 Colonial Manor Nursing Center, York PA) He retired after 29 years as a salesman for Edgcomb Metals Company. He then worked part-time for Schaeffer Florist. Died from natural causes after a brief illness. Buried Mount Zion Cemetery, York PA.

George Snyder —1 Year Pitcher (b. 1849 Philadelphia PA–d. 2 Aug 1895 Philadelphia PA).

Jack Snyder —2 Years Catcher (b. 6 Oct 1886 Lincoln Township PA–d. 13 Dec 1981 Brownsville PA).

Pop Snyder —15 Years Catcher 4 Years Manager (b. 6 Oct 1854 Washington DC–d. 29 Oct 1924 Washington DC) Buried Glenwood Cemetery, Washington DC.

Redleg Snyder —2 Years Outfielder (b. 12 Dec 1854 Camden NJ–d. 24 Nov 1932 Camden NJ) Committed suicide by inhaling illuminating gas. Buried St Peter's Cemetery, Riverside NJ.

Louis Sockalexis —3 Years Outfielder (b. 24 Oct 1871 Old Town ME–d. 24 Dec 1913 Burlington ME) He was an American Indian who showed great promise as a ballplayer, but could not control his appetite for booze and the bright lights, so had a shortened career. He umpired some in the minor leagues. Died suddenly from heart disease at a logging camp. Buried St Anne's Church Cemetery, Old Town ME.

Bill Sodd —1 Game Pinch Hitter (b. 18 Sep 1914 Fort Worth TX–d. 14 May 1998 at a hospital in Fort Worth TX) A CPA, he worked for Consolidated Aircraft before becoming the owner of six supermarkets in the Fort Worth area, retiring in 1977. Served in the U.S. Army during World War II. Buried Mount Olivet Cemetery, Fort Worth TX.

Tony Solaita —7 Years Infielder (b. 15 Jan 1947 Nuuuli, American Samoa–d. 10 Feb 1990 Tafuna, American Samoa) Died when he was shot in an altercation with a relative.

Eddie Solomon —10 Years Pitcher (b. 9 Feb 1951 Perry GA–d. 12 Jan 1986 Macon GA) He was a car salesman for Huckabee Buick-Cadillac in Macon. Died instantly when he lost control of his car and hit a utility pole. Buried King Chapel Cemetery, Perry GA.

Moe Solomon —1 Year Outfielder (b. 8 Dec 1900 New York City NY–d. 25 Jun 1966 Miami FL) He also played professional football. Moving to Florida in 1937, he formed the firm of M Solomon General Contractors. He personally supervised the construction of over 200 Royal Castle hamburger stands throughout the South. Died from heart failure. Buried Mount Nebo Memorial Gardens, Miami FL.

Moose Solters —9 Years Outfielder (b. 22 Mar 1906 Pittsburgh PA–d. 28 Sep 1975 Mercy Hospital, Pittsburgh PA) Operating a tavern in Beltzhoover, he was partially blind because of a blow to his head by a baseball. Buried Calvary Cemetery, Pittsburgh PA.

Jack Somerlott —2 Years Infielder (b. 26 Oct 1882 Flint IN–d. 21 Apr 1965 Sheehy Nursing Home, Butler IN) He farmed in Steuben County, IN, until 1937 when he sold his farm and bought a business in Bronson IN, retiring from it in 1947. Buried Metz Cemetery, Metz IN.

Kid Somers —1 Year Outfielder (b. abt 1868 Toronto, Ontario, Canada–d. 16 Oct 1895 Toronto, Ontario, Canada) Died at the height of his baseball career. He had contracted malarial fever the year before his death when he was playing in the Southern Association, but he died from a blood clot on the brain caused by a fall at his home. Buried Saint James Cemetery, Toronto, Ontario, Can.

Ed Somerville —1 Year Infielder (b. Philadelphia PA–d. 30 Sep 1877 Toronto, Ontario, Canada).

Joe Sommer —10 Years Outfielder (b. 20 Nov 1858 Covington KY–d. 16 Jan 1938 Deaconess Hospital, Cincinnati OH) He was a hotel proprietor in Covington for several years. Died from chronic heart disease. Buried Highland Cemetery, Fort Mitchell KY.

Pete Sommers —4 Years Catcher (b. 26 Oct 1866 Cleveland OH–d. 22 Jul 1908 at his home in Cleveland OH) Well known as a bowler, he was the first to build a bowling alley in Cleveland (about 1898) and was known as the "Father of Bowling in Cleveland". Died after an illness lasting over a year.

Rudy Sommers —4 Years Pitcher (b. 30 Oct

1888 Cincinnati OH–d. 18 Mar 1949 at his home in Louisville KY) He was a molder at B F Avery Company in Louisville. Died from a blood ailment. Buried Calvary Cemetery, Louisville KY.

Andy Sommerville—1 Year Pitcher (b. 6 Feb 1876 Brooklyn NY–d. 16 Jun 1931 Richmond Hill NY).

Don Songer—4 Years Pitcher (b. 31 Jan 1899 Walnut KS–d. 3 Oct 1962 at his home in Kansas City MO) One year he won 31 games for Enid (OK) in the Western Association. He lived at Kansas City for 60 years, where he owned Billy-Don's Restaurant. Buried Mount Moriah Cemetery, Kansas City MO.

Vic Sorrell—10 Years Pitcher (b. 9 Apr 1901 Morrisville NC–d. 4 May 1972 Rex Hospital, Raleigh NC) He worked in the Wilmington NC shipyards during World War II before coaching baseball at North Carolina State University from 1946 to 1966. He was a member of the North Carolina State athletic staff until his death. Died following a long illness. Buried Raleigh Memorial Park, Raleigh NC.

Chick Sorrells—1 Year Infielder (b. 31 Jul 1896 Stringtown OK–d. 20 Jul 1983 Terrell TX).

Denny Sothern—5 Years Outfielder (b. 20 Jan 1904 Washington DC–d. 7 Dec 1977 Durham NC).

Allen Sothoron—11 Years Pitcher 1 Year Manager (b. 29 Apr 1893 Bradford OH–d. 17 Jun 1939 St John's Hospital, St Louis MO) He won 30 games with Portland in the Pacific Coast League in 1916 and later managed in the minor leagues. Died from heart trouble, acute hepatitis and alcoholism. Buried NY.

Clyde Southwick—1 Year Catcher (b. 3 Nov 1886 Maxwell IA–d. 14 Oct 1961 at a hospital in Freeport IL) He was an auto mechanic, and later worked in the supply department of Crum and Forster in Freeport. Buried Chapel Hill Memorial Park, Freeport IL.

Billy Southworth—13 Years Outfielder 13 Years Manager (b. 9 Mar 1893 Harvard NE–d. 15 Nov 1969 Riverside Hospital, Columbus OH) He worked his entire life in baseball. Died from emphysema. Buried Green Lawn Memorial Cemetery, Columbus OH.

Bill Sowders—3 Years Pitcher (b. 29 Nov 1864 Louisville KY–d. 2 Feb 1951 at his home in Indianapolis IN) He coached at Wabash College and ran a seafood stand at City Market in Indianapolis until his retirement in 1936. A Republican Party worker, he was also employed at the City Board of Health and the City Street Department. Buried Crown Hill Cemetery, Indianapolis IN.

John Sowders—3 Years Pitcher (b. 10 Dec 1866 Louisville KY–d. 26 Sep 1909 Indianapolis IN) Buried Crown Hill Cemetery, Indianapolis IN.

Len Sowders—1 Year Outfielder (b. 29 Jun 1861 Louisville KY–d. 21 Nov 1888 Indianapolis IN) Buried Crown Hill Cemetery, Indianapolis IN.

Bob Spade—4 Years Pitcher (b. 4 Jan 1877 Akron OH–d. 7 Sep 1924 Seton Hospital, Cincinnati OH) He conducted a saloon in Cincinnati until prohibition shut it down. After that he dealt in bootleg whiskey. Died from atrophic cirrhosis of the liver. Buried Springfield Center Cemetery, Akron OH.

Al Spalding—3 Years Pitcher 2 Years Manager Hall of Fame (b. 2 Sep 1850 Byron IL–d. 9 Sep 1915 at his home in Point Loma CA) He is famed for starting the Spalding Sporting Goods Company. Died from a stroke of apoplexy. Cremated and his ashes scattered over Point Loma.

Dick Spalding—2 Years Outfielder (b. 13 Oct 1893 Philadelphia PA–d. 3 Feb 1950 at his home in Philadelphia PA) He coached and was a scout for the Phillies and Cubs. Buried Northwood Cemetery, Philadelphia PA.

Tully Sparks—12 Years Pitcher (b. 12 Dec 1874 Aetna GA–d. 15 Jul 1937 at his home in Anniston AL) He entered the cotton business in Louisiana and Mississippi for a few years. From 1911 to 1914 he engaged in real estate at Chattanooga TN. He mined bauxite ore in Tennessee and Georgia until 1918, then worked the rest of his life in the insurance business at Anniston. Died from a heart ailment. Buried Edgemont Cemetery, Anniston AL.

Joe Sparma—7 Years Pitcher (b. 4 Feb 1942 Massillon OH–d. 14 May 1986 Columbus GA) Died from heart disease.

Tris Speaker—22 Years Outfielder 8 Years Manager Hall of Fame (b. 4 Apr 1888 Hubbard TX–d. 8 Dec 1958 Whitney TX) Died from a heart attack after returning from a fishing trip at his lodge on Lake Whitney. Buried Fairview Cemetery, Hubbard TX.

Byron Speece—4 Years Pitcher (b. 6 Jan 1897 West Baden IN–d. 29 Sep 1974 at his home in Elgin OR) Buried Elgin Cemetery, Elgin OR.

Floyd Speer—2 Years Pitcher (b. 27 Jan 1913 Booneville AR–d. 22 Mar 1969 Little Rock AR) He lived at North Little Rock AR for 35 years and was a clerk at a pharmacy. Buried Carolan Cemetery, Booneville AR.

Kid Speer—1 Year Pitcher (b. 16 Jun 1886 Corning MO–d. 13 Jan 1946 Edmonton, Alberta, Canada).

Harry Spence—1 Year Manager (b. 2 Feb 1856 New York City NY–d. 17 May 1908 Chicago IL) Buried Elmwood Cemetery, River Grove IL.

Stan Spence—9 Years Outfielder (b. 20 Mar 1915 South Portsmouth KY–d. 9 Jan 1983 Lenoir Memorial Hospital, Kinston NC) He worked for Gardner Construction Company in Kinston. Buried Maplewood Cemetery, Kinston NC.

Ben Spencer—1 Year Outfielder (b. 15 May 1890 Patapsco MD–d. 1 Sep 1970 Finksburg MD).

Chet Spencer—1 Year Outfielder (b. 2 Mar 1883 South Webster OH–d. 10 Nov 1938 Mercy Hospital, Portsmouth OH) He was a timekeeper for the Ohio State Highway Department. Died from chronic nephritis and a heart attack. Buried Greenlawn Cemetery, Portsmouth OH.

Fred Spencer—1 Year Pitcher (b. 25 Apr 1885 St Cloud MN–d. 5 Feb 1969 Minneapolis MN) Buried Sunset Memorial Park, Minneapolis MN.

Glenn Spencer—5 Years Pitcher (b. 11 Sep 1905 Corning NY–d. 30 Dec 1958 City Hospital, Binghamton NY) World War II veteran. He was a salesman for E B Gale, Inc. Died from a heart attack. Buried Vestal Hills Memorial Park, Vestal NY.

Jim Spencer—15 Years Infielder (b. 30 Jul 1947 Hanover PA–d. 11 Feb 2002 Fort Lauderdale FL) Died from a heart attack.

Roy Spencer—12 Years Catcher (b. 22 Feb 1900 Scranton NC–d. 8 Feb 1973 St Joseph's Hospital, Port Charlotte FL) Buried Gulf Pines Memorial Park, Englewood FL.

Tubby Spencer—9 Years Catcher (b. 26 Jan 1884 Oil City PA–d. 1 Feb 1945 San Francisco CA) Died from a cerebral hemorrhage. Cremated. Buried Woodlawn Memorial Park, Daly City CA.

Vern Spencer—1 Year Outfielder (b. 24 Feb 1894 Wixom MI–d. 3 Jun 1971 Wixom MI) He owned a dairy and farmed near Wixom. He developed the Spencer Airfield there and was active in the Flying Farmers organization. Died following an illness of three years. Buried New Hudson Cemetery, New Hudson MI.

Paul Speraw—1 Year Infielder (b. 5 Oct 1893 Annville PA–d. 22 Feb 1962 Cedar Rapids IA) He worked for Allis-Chalmers in Cedar Rapids IA. Died following a sudden illness. Buried Linwood Cemetery, Cedar Rapids IA.

Ed Sperber—2 Years Outfielder (b. 21 Jan 1895 Cincinnati OH–d. 5 Jan 1976 Cincinnati OH) Buried Spring Grove Cemetery, Cincinnati OH.

Stan Sperry—2 Years Infielder (b. 19 Feb 1914 Evansville WI–d. 27 Sep 1962 St Clare Hospital, Monroe WI) He was a deputy for the Rock County, WI, sheriff's department, and later operated a restaurant and tavern in Evansville. Died after a brief illness. Buried Maple Hill Cemetery, Evansville WI.

Harry Spies—1 Year Infielder (b. 12 Jun 1866 New Orleans LA–d. 7 Jul 1942 Georgia Street Hospital, Los Angeles CA) Died after being struck by an automobile five days earlier. Buried Inglewood Park Cemetery, Inglewood CA.

Al Spink—(b. abt 1853–d. 27 May 1928 at his home in Oak Park IL) A sportswriter, he founded the *Sporting News*. At one time he owned the *St Louis World*, a daily newspaper. Died after a lengthy illness. Buried Woodlawn Cemetery, Forest Park IL.

J G Taylor Spink—Hall of Fame (b. 1888–d. 7 Dec 1962 at his home in St Louis MO) He was publisher and editor of the *Sporting News* from 1914 until shortly before his death. Died following a long illness. Buried Bellefontaine Cemetery, St Louis MO.

Al Spohrer—8 Years Catcher (b. 3 Dec 1902 Philadelphia PA–d. 17 Jul 1972 Sceva Speare Memorial Hospital, Plymouth NH) He was a field representative for a national company. Died after a brief illness. Buried Trinity Cemetery, Holderness NH.

Carl Spongburg—1 Year Pitcher (b. 21 May 1884 Idaho Falls ID–d. 21 Jul 1938 at his home in Los Angeles CA) He was a grocery store manager. Died from a pulmonary hemorrhage. Buried Forest Lawn Memorial Park, Glendale CA.

Karl Spooner—2 Years Pitcher (b. 23 Jun 1931 Oriskany Falls NY–d. 10 Apr 1984 Indian River Memorial Hosp, Vero Beach FL) He was a packing house manager for Hatfield Citrus Corporation. Died from cancer. Buried Crestlawn Cemetery, Vero Beach FL.

Jim Spotts—1 Year Catcher (b. 10 Apr 1909 Honeybrook PA–d. 15 Jun 1964 at his home in Medford NJ) Buried Mount Laurel Cemetery, Mount Laurel NJ.

Charlie Sprague—3 Years Outfielder (b. 10 Oct 1864 Cleveland OH–d. 31 Dec 1912 Des Moines IA) Died from a head injury.

Harry Spratt—2 Years Infielder (b. 10 Jul 1887 Broadford VA–d. 3 Jul 1969 Washington DC).

Brad Springer—2 Years Pitcher (b. 9 May 1904 Detroit MI–d. 4 Jan 1970 William Beaumont Hospital, Royal Oak MI) For 20 years he was a commercial agent for Standard Oil Company, retiring in 1964. Buried Holy Sepulchre Cemetery, Southfield MI.

Ed Springer—1 Year Pitcher (b. 8 Feb 1867 CA–d. 24 Apr 1926 Los Angeles CA).

Joe Sprinz—3 Years Catcher (b. 3 Aug 1902 St Louis MO–d. 11 Jan 1994 at his son's home in Fremont CA) He was best known for failing to catch a ball dropped from a blimp during the World's Fair on Treasure Island in 1939. Died from a heart attack. Buried Holy Cross Catholic Cemetery, Colma CA.

Charlie Sproull—1 Year Pitcher (b. 9 Jan 1919 Taylorsville GA–d. 13 Jan 1980 Rockford Memorial Hospital, Rockford IL) For 30 years he was a tool and die maker for National Lock Company, retiring in 1978. Buried Greenwood Cemetery, Rockford IL.

Freddy Spurgeon—4 Years Infielder (b. 9 Oct 1901 Wabash IN–d. 5 Nov 1970 Bronson Hospital, Kalamazoo MI) A broken arm, suffered in a mishap, ended his baseball career. He was a sales representative for Gooderham and Worts, Inc, of Detroit, and was also a well-known sports official. Died following a lengthy illness. Buried Grand Prairie Cemetery, Kalamazoo MI.

Ed Spurney—1 Year Infielder (b. 19 Jan 1872 Cleveland OH–d. 11 Oct 1932 Cleveland Heights OH) He was an attorney. Died following his third stroke of apoplexy. Buried Woodland Cemetery, Cleveland OH.

Ebba St Claire—4 Years Catcher (b. 5 Aug 1921 Whitehall NY–d. 22 Aug 1982 at his home in Whitehall NY) Served in the U.S. Army during World War II. He owned and operated an insurance office in Whitehall. Died after a long illness. Buried Our Lady of Angels Cemetery, Whitehall NY.

Jim St Vrain—1 Year Pitcher (b. 6 Jun 1871 Ralls County MO–d. 12 Jun 1937 at his home in Butte MT) An electrician for Anaconda Company, he had lived in Butte 12 years. Died after a brief illness. Buried Mountain View Cemetery, Butte MT.

Eddie Stack—5 Years Pitcher (b. 24 Oct 1887 Chicago IL–d. 28 Aug 1958 Chicago IL) Buried Mount Carmel Cemetery, Hillside IL.

General Stafford—1 Year Outfielder (b. 9 Jul 1868 Webster MA–d. 18 Sep 1923 Memorial Hospital, Worcester MA) He operated his farm near Dudley MA. Died a week after undergoing surgery. Buried Calvary Cemetery, Dudley MA.

Heinie Stafford—1 Game Pinch Hitter (b. 1 Nov 1891 Orleans VT–d. 29 Jan 1972 Lake Worth FL).

John Stafford—1 Year Pitcher (b. 8 Apr 1870 Dudley MA–d. 3 Jul 1940 Memorial Hospital, Worcester MA) He used his earnings from baseball to work his way through optometry school, and was a successful optometrist in Dudley until a few weeks before his death when illness forced his retirement. Buried Calvary Cemetery, Dudley MA.

Chick Stahl—10 Years Outfielder 1 Year Manager (b. 10 Jan 1873 Fort Wayne IN–d. 28 Mar 1907 West Baden IN) At the height of his career, during spring training, he took his own life by drinking carbolic acid. Buried Lindenwood Cemetery, Fort Wayne IN.

Jake Stahl—9 Years Infielder 4 Years Manager (b. 13 Apr 1879 Elkhart IN–d. 19 Sep 1922 at his cottage near Monrovia CA) He was the president of a Chicago IL bank until he moved to California in an attempt to save himself from tuberculosis, from which he finally died. Buried Oak Woods Cemetery, Chicago IL.

Tuck Stainback—13 Years Outfielder (b. 4 Aug 1911 Los Angeles CA–d. 29 Nov 1992 at a hospital in Camarillo CA) Died after suffering a stroke. Cremated.

Gale Staley—1 Year Infielder (b. 2 Jun 1899 DePere WI–d. 19 Apr 1989 John Muir Medical Center, Walnut Creek CA) Served in World War I. For 35 years he was an assistant secretary for Standard Oil Company. Died from pneumonia. Buried Oakmont Memorial Park, Lafayette CA.

Harry Staley—8 Years Pitcher (b. 3 Nov 1866 Jacksonville IL–d. 12 Jan 1910 Nichols Hospital, Battle Creek MI) Died following surgery performed a week earlier. Buried Oak Hill Cemetery, Battle Creek MI.

Virgil Stallcup—7 Years Infielder (b. 3 Jan 1922 Ravensford NC–d. 2 May 1989 Greenville SC) Served in the U.S. Navy during World War II. He was a supervisor for Texize Chemical Company when he retired. Died from a self-inflicted gunshot wound. Buried Greenville Memorial Gardens, Greenville SC.

George Staller—1 Year Outfielder (b. 1 Apr 1916 Rutherford Heights PA–d. 3 Jul 1992 Harrisburg Hospital, Harrisburg PA) Served in the U.S. Marine Corps during World War II. He retired as a coach for the Orioles. Buried Hershey Cemetery, Hershey PA.

George Stallings—3 Years Catcher 13 Years Manager (b. 17 Nov 1866 Augusta GA–d. 13 May 1929 at his plantation home near Haddock GA) He spent his entire life in baseball as a player, manager and executive. He managed and owned minor league teams, including the Montreal team in the International League when he quietly died in his sleep. Buried Riverside Cemetery, Macon GA.

Oscar Stanage—14 Years Catcher (b. 17 Mar 1883 Tulare CA–d. 11 Nov 1964 Detroit MI).

Charley Stanceu—2 Years Pitcher (b. 9 Jan 1916 Canton OH–d. 3 Apr 1969 at his home in Canton OH) He was manager of the industrial relations department at Monarch Rubber Company where he worked 20 years. Died from a heart attack. Buried Forest Hill Cemetery, Canton OH.

Jerry Standaert—3 Years Infielder (b. 2 Nov 1901 Chicago IL–d. 4 Aug 1964 Chicago IL) Buried St Mary Cemetery, Evergreen Park IL.

Pete Standridge—2 Years Pitcher (b. 25 Apr 1891 Seattle WA–d. 2 Aug 1963 St Mary's Hospital, San Francisco CA) He was a clerk at the Green Cigar Company in Seattle for 30 years. Died from emphysema. Buried Holy Cross Catholic Cemetery, Colma CA.

Tom Stankard—1 Year Infielder (b. 20 Mar 1882 Waltham MA–d. 13 Jun 1958 Waltham Hospital, Waltham MA) Buried Calvary Cemetery, Waltham MA.

Eddie Stanky—11 Years Infielder 8 Years Manager (b. 3 Sep 1916 Philadelphia PA–d. 6 Jun 1999 at a hospital in Fairhope AL) He was the head baseball coach 14 years at the University of South Alabama. Died from a heart attack. Buried Catholic Cemetery, Mobile AL.

Buck Stanley—1 Year Pitcher (b. 13 Nov 1889 Washington DC–d. 13 Aug 1940 Norfolk VA) World War I veteran. He was a detective for the Norfolk Police Department from 1923 until his death. Buried Forest Lawn Cemetery, Norfolk VA.

Joe Stanley—7 Years Outfielder (b. 2 Apr 1881 Washington DC–d. 13 Sep 1967 Detroit MI) Buried Mount Olivet Cemetery, Washington DC.

John Stansbury—1 Year Infielder (b. 6 Dec 1885 Phillipsburg NJ–d. 26 Dec 1970 Causa Convalescent Home, Easton PA) He was a retired employee of Magnolia Refinery Company in Beaumont TX. Buried Fairmount Cemetery, Phillipsburg NJ.

Buck Stanton—1 Year Outfielder (b. 19 Jun 1906 Stantonsburg NC–d. 1 Jan 1992 San Antonio TX).

Tom Stanton—1 Year Catcher (b. 25 Oct 1874 St Louis MO–d. 17 Jan 1957 St John's Hospital, St Louis MO) He played in the Texas League and worked 32 years for the Internal Revenue Office, retiring in 1946. He had been hospitalized for one month with a broken hip when he died. Buried Calvary Cemetery, St Louis MO.

Willie Stargell—21 Years Outfielder Hall of Fame (b. 6 Mar 1940 Earlsboro OK–d. 9 Apr 2001 New Hanover Medical Center, Wilmington NC) He worked his entire life in baseball for the Pirates and Braves. Died from a stroke two weeks after undergoing gall bladder surgery, but suffered his last three years from a kidney disorder. Buried Oleander Memorial Gardens, Wilmington NC.

Dolly Stark—4 Years Infielder (b. 19 Jan 1885 Ripley MS–d. 1 Dec 1924 Memphis TN) He managed minor league teams. Shot to death by a drunk friend at a roadhouse that he operated. Buried Elmwood Cemetery, Memphis TN.

Con Starkell—1 Year Pitcher (b. 16 Nov 1880 Red Oak IA–d. 19 Jan 1933 at his home in Tacoma WA) He owned the Starkell Smoke House in Tacoma for many years. Died from a heart attack. Buried New Tacoma Memorial Park, Tacoma WA.

George Starnagle—1 Year Catcher (b. 6 Oct 1873 Belleville IL–d. 15 Feb 1946 at his home in Belleville IL) He was a brick mason before becoming associated with his son in Canfield Laboratories. Died from a stroke. Buried Walnut Hill Cemetery, Belleville IL.

Bill Starr—2 Years Catcher (b. 16 Feb 1911 Brooklyn NY–d. 12 Aug 1991 at his home in La Jolla CA) He owned the minor league San Diego Padres from 1944 to 1955. A self-employed real estate developer, he built condos and shopping centers in the San Diego area. Died from gastrointestinal cancer. Buried Cypress View Cemetery, San Diego CA.

Charlie Starr—3 Years Infielder (b. 30 Aug 1878 Pike County, OH–d. 18 Oct 1937 Pasadena CA) He was a metal lather in the construction business. Died following surgery for appendicitis. Cremated.

Ray Starr—7 Years Pitcher (b. 23 Apr 1906 Nowata OK–d. 9 Feb 1963 at his home in Baylis IL) He operated a restaurant in Baylis while working as an oil contractor and developer there. Died from a heart attack. Buried Carlyle Cemetery, Carlyle IL.

Joe Start—11 Years Infielder (b. 14 Oct 1842 New York City NY–d. 27 Mar 1927 Providence RI).

Jigger Statz—8 Years Outfielder (b. 20 Oct 1897 Waukegan IL–d. 16 Mar 1988 at his home in Corona Del Mar CA) The Pete Rose of the minors, between 1920 and 1942 he played a record 18 years for one minor league team, the Los Angeles Angels of the Pacific Coast League. He played in 3473 professional games, collecting 4093 hits. He was then a scout for 25 years. Died from prostate cancer. Buried Holy Cross Cemetery, Culver City CA.

Ed Stauffer—2 Years Pitcher (b. 10 Jan 1898 Emsworth PA–d. 2 Jul 1979 at a nursing home in St Petersburg FL) He was general sales manager in Pittsburgh PA for the Frigidaire Division of General Motors, retiring and moving to St Petersburg in 1962. Died after a seven-month illness. Cremated.

Turkey Stearnes—18 Years Outfielder Hall of Fame (b. 8 May 1901 Nashville TN–d. 4 Sep 1979 Harper Hospital, Detroit MI) He played in the negro leagues for the Detroit Stars, among other teams, and worked 30 years in the foundry at the Ford Motor Company Rouge plant. Buried Lincoln Memorial Park, Mount Clemens MI.

Dan Stearns—7 Years Infielder (b. 17 Oct 1861 Buffalo NY–d. 28 Jun 1944 at his home in Glendale CA) Buried Calvary Cemetery, Los Angeles CA.

Bill Steele—5 Years Pitcher (b. 5 Oct 1885 Milford PA–d. 19 Oct 1949 Overland MO) He was a maintenance man at the A & P bakeries. Killed when hit by a streetcar. Buried Memorial Park Cemetery, St Louis MO.

Bob Steele—4 Years Pitcher (b. 29 Mar 1894 Cassburn, Ontario, Canada–d. 27 Jan 1962 Munroe Memorial Hospital, Ocala FL) He operated a motel. Buried Burlington Cemetery, Burlington WI.

Elmer Steele—5 Years Pitcher (b. 17 May 1884 Muitzeskill NY–d. 9 Mar 1966 Rhinebeck NY) He was a mail carrier for the post office in Poughkeepsie from 1923 until retiring in 1953. Died after a long illness. Buried Poughkeepsie Rural Cemetery, Poughkeepsie NY.

Farmer Steelman—4 Years Catcher (b. 29 Jun 1875 Millville NJ–d. 16 Sep 1944 at his home in Merchantville NJ) He was a retired Camden NJ policeman.

Bill Steen—4 Years Pitcher (b. 11 Nov 1887 Pittsburgh PA–d. 13 Mar 1979 St Christopher Conv Center, Signal Hill CA) Died from a heart attack. Cremated.

Milt Steengrafe—2 Years Pitcher (b. 26 May 1900 San Francisco CA–d. 2 Jun 1977 St Anthony Hospital, Oklahoma City OK) He umpired in the minor leagues from 1935 until retiring in 1953. He had the longest service of any player-manager-umpire in the Texas League. Died following a short illness. Buried Chapel Hill Memorial Gardens, Oklahoma City OK.

Fred Steere—1 Year Infielder (b. 16 Aug 1872 South Scituate RI–d. 13 Mar 1942 Maurice Hotel, San Francisco CA) He was a retired real estate broker. Died from senile dementia and heart disease. Cremated.

Ed Stein—8 Years Pitcher (b. 5 Sep 1869 Detroit MI–d. 10 May 1928 Providence Hospital, Detroit MI) He was a manufacturer's representative for a cigar maker for a time. He served in Detroit as police court clerk, deputy city clerk, chief deputy sheriff and county treasurer. He was sheriff of Wayne County, MI, when he died. Died from pneumonia that developed from a throat infection. Buried Elmwood Cemetery, Detroit MI.

Irv Stein—1 Year Pitcher (b. 21 May 1911 Madisonville LA–d. 7 Jan 1981 Covington LA) Buried Dendinger Memorial Cemetery, Madisonville LA.

Justin Stein—1 Year Infielder (b. 9 Aug 1911 St Louis MO–d. 1 May 1992 Creve Coeur MO) Buried Calvary Cemetery, St Louis MO.

Hank Steinbacher—3 Years Outfielder (b. 22 Mar 1913 Sacramento CA–d. 3 Apr 1977 at his home in Sacramento CA) World War II veteran. He worked 23 years as a police officer in Sacramento, retiring in 1969. Died from a heart attack. Buried St Mary's Cemetery, Sacramento CA.

Gene Steinbrenner—1 Year Infielder (b. 16 Nov 1892 Pittsburgh PA–d. 25 Apr 1970 Presbyterian-University Hosp, Pittsburgh PA) He was a retired Pittsburgh city fireman. Died from a heart attack suffered while watching a baseball game on television. Buried Union Dale Cemetery, Pittsburgh PA.

Bill Steinecke—1 Year Catcher (b. 7 Feb 1907 Cincinnati OH–d. 20 Jul 1986 Flagler Hospital, St Augustine FL) He managed minor league baseball and was on special assignment with the Expos when he died. Buried San Lorenzo Cemetery, St Augustine FL.

Ray Steineder—2 Years Pitcher (b. 13 Nov 1895 Salem NJ–d. 25 Aug 1982 Newcomb Hospital, Vineland NJ) He was a self-employed mason contractor. An active Democrat, he once ran for city commissioner. Died following a brief illness. Buried Siloam Cemetery, Vineland NJ.

Ben Steiner—3 Years Infielder (b. 28 Jul 1921 Alexandria VA–d. 27 Oct 1988 Venice CA).

Harry Steinfeldt—14 Years Infielder (b. 29 Sep 1876 St Louis MO–d. 17 Aug 1914 at his home in Bellevue KY) He worked with his father-in-law for Lockwood Manufacturing Company, makers of baker's utensils. Died from a stroke of paralysis. Buried Evergreen Cemetery, Southgate KY.

Bill Stellbauer—1 Year Outfielder (b. 20 Mar 1894 Bremond TX–d. 16 Feb 1974 at a hospital in Houston TX) Buried Bremond Cemetery, Bremond TX.

Bill Stellberger—1 Year Pitcher (b. 22 Apr 1865 Detroit MI–d. 9 Nov 1936 Jennings Hospital, Detroit MI) He retired from the real estate business in 1926. Died after a long illness. Buried Woodmere Cemetery, Detroit MI.

Fred Stem—2 Years Infielder (b. 22 Sep 1885 Oxford NC–d. 5 Sep 1964 Darlington SC).

Bill Stemmyer—4 Years Pitcher (b. 6 May 1865 Cleveland OH–d. 3 May 1945 at his home in Cleveland OH) He operated a cafe in Cleveland for more than 20 years. Died after a long illness. Buried Lakewood Park Cemetery, Cleveland OH.

Casey Stengel—14 Years Outfielder 25 Years Manager Hall of Fame (b. 30 Jul 1890 Kansas City MO–d. 29 Sep 1975 Glendale CA) He was a player, coach or manager for 17 professional teams. Died from cancer of the lymph glands. Buried Forest Lawn Memorial Park, Glendale CA.

Jake Stenzel—9 Years Outfielder (b. 24 Jun 1867 Cincinnati OH–d. 6 Jan 1919 at his home in Cincinnati OH) He conducted a cafe across from the baseball park until about 1916 when he went to work as a night guard. Died from congestion of the brain after suffering from influenza for two weeks.

Bryan Stephens—2 Years Pitcher (b. 14 Jul 1920 Fayetteville AR–d. 21 Nov 1991 Coastal Community Hospital, Santa Ana CA) Served in World War II. For 35 years he was a plate maker for the *Los Angeles Times* newspaper. Died from kidney cancer. Buried Pacific View Memorial Park, Newport Beach CA.

Clarence Stephens—3 Years Pitcher (b. 19 Aug 1863 Cincinnati OH–d. 28 Feb 1947 Cincinnati OH) Buried Spring Grove Cemetery, Cincinnati OH.

George Stephens—3 Years Pitcher (b. 28 Sep 1867 Romeo MI–d. 5 Aug 1896 Armada MI) Died from consumption.

Jack Stephens—17 Years Infielder (b. 10 Feb 1900 Pleasureville PA–d. 5 Feb 1981 York Hospital, York PA) Played in the negro leagues. He was a York County, PA, deputy sheriff and a notary public in York. Buried Mount Zion Cemetery, York PA.

Jim Stephens—6 Years Catcher (b. 10 Dec 1883 Salineville OH–d. 2 Jan 1965 at his home in Oxford AL) He was a retired employee of Alabama Power Company. Died suddenly. Buried Oxford Cemetery, Oxford AL.

Vern Stephens—15 Years Infielder (b. 23 Oct 1920 McAlister NM–d. 4 Nov 1968 Memorial Hospital, Long Beach CA) He was a sales manager for an industrial rigging company. Died from a heart attack. Buried Sunnyside Cemetery, Long Beach CA.

Dummy Stephenson—1 Year Outfielder (b. 22 Sep 1869 Petersburg NJ–d. 1 Dec 1924 City Hospital, Trenton NJ) He was a sanitary presser for Fernwood Pottery. Died from pulmonary tuberculosis. Buried South Dennis NJ.

Riggs Stephenson—14 Years Outfielder (b. 5 Jan 1898 Akron AL–d. 15 Nov 1985 at his home in Tuscaloosa AL) He operated a Chrysler dealership for a number of years, and had a lumber yard in Akron. Buried Tuscaloosa Memorial Park, Tuscaloosa AL.

Walter Stephenson—3 Years Catcher (b. 27 Mar 1911 Saluda NC–d. 4 Jul 1993 Shreveport LA).

Dutch Sterrett—2 Years Outfielder (b. 1 Oct 1889 Milroy PA–d. 9 Dec 1965 Mount Sinai Hospital, Baltimore MD) Served in the U.S. Navy during World War I. He was associated with the advertising division of Standard Oil of New Jersey for a number of years. He retired in 1958 as an advertising executive for the National Auto Dealer's Association at Washington DC. Died after being ill one day. Buried Church Hill Cemetery, Reedsville PA.

Jim Stevens—1 Year Pitcher (b. 25 Aug 1889 Williamsburg MD–d. 25 Sep 1966 General Hospital, Baltimore MD) Buried Druid Ridge Cemetery, Pikesville MD.

Ace Stewart—1 Year Infielder (b. 14 Feb 1869 Terre Haute IN–d. 17 Apr 1912 at the home of a sister in Terre Haute IN) He tended bar, worked on the police force and in mills at Terre Haute. Died from rheumatism and a complication of diseases. Buried Highland Lawn Cemetery, Terre Haute IN.

Bill Stewart—(b. 1895 Fitchburg MA–d. 18 Feb 1964 Veteran's Hospital, Jamaica Plain MA) Served in the U.S. Navy during World War I. A National League umpire from 1934 to 1955, he was also a coach in the National Hockey League. Died after a recent stroke. Buried St Joseph's Cemetery, West Roxbury MA.

Glen Stewart—3 Years Infielder (b. 29 Sep 1912 Tullahoma TN–d. 11 Feb 1997 at his home in Memphis TN) He managed several minor league teams before going to work for the U.S. Postal Service. Died from heart failure. Buried Forest Hill Cemetery Midtown, Memphis TN.

Joe Stewart—1 Year Pitcher (b. 11 Mar 1879 Monroe NC–d. 10 Feb 1913 City Hospital, Youngstown OH) He tended bar and oversaw pool rooms in Niles OH and Youngstown. Died from injuries received when he fell from a second story window at a hotel where he was working. Buried Monroe NC.

Lefty Stewart—10 Years Pitcher (b. 23 Sep 1900 Sparta TN–d. 23 Sep 1974 Fort Sanders Hospital, Knoxville TN) He lived at Crossville TN where he owned a furniture store. Buried Green Acres Memory Gardens, Crossville TN.

Mack Stewart—2 Years Pitcher (b. 23 Sep 1914 Stevenson AL–d. 21 Mar 1960 Macon GA) He co-owned the Toole and Stewart Service Station in Macon for several years. Died after a long illness. Buried Macon Memorial Park, Macon GA.

Mark Stewart—1 Year Catcher (b. 11 Oct 1889 Whitlock TN–d. 17 Jan 1932 Baptist Memorial Hospital, Memphis TN) He was a civil engineer for S and W Construction Company in Memphis TN. Died from a fractured skull and internal injuries suffered when hit by a car while he was walking. Buried Maplewood Cemetery, Paris TN.

Neb Stewart—1 Year Outfielder (b. 21 May

1918 South Charleston OH–d. 8 Jun 1990 Madison County Hospital, London OH) He was a retired farmer. Died following an eight-month illness. Buried Kirkwood Cemetery, London OH.

Stuffy Stewart —8 Years Infielder (b. 31 Jan 1894 Jasper FL–d. 30 Dec 1980 Veteran's Hospital, Lake City FL) Served in the field artillery for the U.S. Army during World War I. He managed minor league baseball. Died after a brief illness. Buried Oaklawn Cemetery, Lake City FL.

Tuffy Stewart —2 Years Outfielder (b. 31 Jul 1883 Chicago IL–d. 18 Nov 1934 Chicago IL) Buried Oakridge Cemetery, Hillside IL.

Fred Stiely —3 Years Pitcher (b. 1 Jun 1901 Pillow PA–d. 6 Jan 1981 at his home in Valley View PA) Buried St Andrews Church Cemetery, Valley View PA.

Archie Stimmel —3 Years Pitcher (b. 30 May 1873 Woodsboro MD–d. 17 Aug 1958 Memorial Hospital, Frederick MD) He lived his entire life in the same house where he was born. Buried Mount Hope Cemetery, Woodsboro MD.

Carl Stimson —1 Year Pitcher (b. 18 Jul 1894 Hamburg IA–d. 9 Nov 1936 at a hospital in Omaha NE) An electrician, he had lived in Omaha 20 years. Died from a heart ailment. Buried Forest Lawn Memorial Park, Omaha NE.

Harry Stine —1 Year Pitcher (b. 20 Feb 1864 Shenandoah PA–d. 6 Jun 1924 at his home in Niagara Falls NY) A druggist, he owned and operated a drugstore in Niagara Falls from 1899 until his death. Died from a general breakdown in health aggravated by a fall down a stairway in his home. Buried Oakwood Cemetery, Niagara Falls NY.

Snuffy Stirnweiss —10 Years Infielder (b. 26 Oct 1918 New York City NY–d. 15 Sep 1958 Newark Bay NJ) He was a foreign freight agent for Caldwell and Company in New York City. Died in a commuter train accident on his way home from work. Buried Mount Olivet Cemetery, Middletown NJ.

Jack Stivetts —11 Years Pitcher (b. 31 Mar 1868 Ashland PA–d. 18 Apr 1930 Ashland PA) He did carpenter work around Ashland. Died from heart failure after falling in a stairway.

Milt Stock —14 Years Infielder (b. 11 Jul 1893 Chicago IL–d. 16 Jul 1977 at his home in Montrose AL) He worked his entire life in baseball as a player, coach, minor league manager and team owner. Died while watching television. Buried Catholic Cemetery, Mobile AL.

Otis Stockdale —4 Years Pitcher (b. 7 Aug 1871 Arcadia MD–d. 15 Mar 1933 Pennsville NJ) He was a security guard. Died from valvular heart disease. Buried Arcadia MD.

J Roy Stockton —Hall of Fame (b. abt 1893 St Louis MO–d. 24 Aug 1972 St Petersburg FL) Served in the U.S. Army during World War I. For 41 years he was the sports editor for the *St Louis Post-Dispatch,* retiring to Florida in 1958. Cremated and scattered.

Len Stockwell —3 Years Outfielder (b. 25 Aug 1859 Cordova IL–d. 28 Jan 1905 Niles CA).

Al Stokes —2 Years Catcher (b. 1 Jan 1900 Chicago IL–d. 19 Dec 1986 Grantham NH).

Art Stokes —1 Year Pitcher (b. 13 Sep 1896 Emmitsburg MD–d. 3 Jun 1962 at his home in Titusville PA) World War I veteran. He worked a number of years at the Pennzoil plant in Rouseville PA. Later he became co-owner of the East Titusville Mill. Buried Jamison Corners Cemetery, Titusville PA.

Arnie Stone —2 Years Pitcher (b. 19 Dec 1892 North Creek NY–d. 29 Jul 1948 at his home in Hudson Falls NY) He was a salesman at Griffin Lumber Company. Died suddenly. Buried Union Cemetery, Fort Edward NY.

Dick Stone —1 Year Pitcher (b. 5 Dec 1911 Oklahoma City OK–d. 18 Feb 1980 Oklahoma City OK) He was a manufacturer in Oklahoma City. Died from a heart attack. Buried Rose Hill Burial Park, Oklahoma City OK.

Dwight Stone —2 Years Pitcher (b. 2 Aug 1886 Holt County NE–d. 3 Jul 1976 Dreier's Sanitarium, Glendale CA) He worked 30 years for a retail lumber company. Died from lung cancer. Buried Valhalla Memorial Park, North Hollywood CA.

Ed Stone —14 Years Outfielder (b. abt 1909–d. 20 Mar 1983 New York City NY) He played in the negro leagues.

George Stone —7 Years Outfielder (b. 7 Sep 1877 Lost Nation IA–d. 6 Jan 1945 Clinton IA) A banker at Coleridge NE, he was president of the Cedar County (NE) Banker's Association.

In 1941 he moved to Clinton and operated a bowling alley there. Died in his sleep. Buried Coleridge Cemetery, Coleridge NE.

John Stone—11 Years Outfielder (b. 10 Oct 1905 Lynchburg TN–d. 30 Nov 1955 Shelbyville TN) He founded, owned and managed Shelbyville Pure Milk Company until selling it two years before his death. Died from a sudden heart attack. Buried Odd Fellows-Masonic Cemetery, Lynchburg TN.

Rocky Stone—1 Year Pitcher (b. 23 Aug 1918 Redding CA–d. 12 Nov 1986 City Hospital, Fountain Valley CA) He was a truck driver for 31 years. Died from a heart attack. Buried Fresno Memorial Gardens, Fresno CA.

Tige Stone—1 Year Outfielder (b. 18 Sep 1906 Macon GA–d. 1 Jan 1960 at a hospital in Jacksonville FL) World War II veteran. He worked many years for Cohen Brothers in Jacksonville. Buried Riverside Memorial Park, Jacksonville FL.

Toni Stone—(b. abt 1921–d. 2 Nov 1996 Alameda CA) She was the first woman to play on a big league professional team, the 1953 Indianapolis Clowns in the negro leagues. Died from heart failure.

Horace Stoneham—(b. 10 Jul 1903 Jersey City NJ–d. 7 Jan 1990 at a nursing home in Scottsdale AZ) The principal owner of the Giants for 40 years, he moved them from New York to San Francisco in 1958. He was one of the last owners with no business interests outside of baseball. Died from natural causes. Cremated. Buried St Francis Catholic Cemetery, Phoenix AZ.

Lil Stoner—9 Years Pitcher (b. 28 Feb 1899 Bowie TX–d. 25 Jun 1966 at a hospital in Enid OK) He worked for Champlin Refining Company. Buried Memorial Park Cemetery, Enid OK.

Howie Storie—2 Years Catcher (b. 15 May 1911 Pittsfield MA–d. 27 Jul 1968 Pittsfield MA) In the restaurant business in Pittsfield, he owned and/or operated a number of restaurants there. Died from a heart attack while working at a restaurant. Buried St Joseph's Cemetery, Pittsfield MA.

Alan Storke—4 Years Infielder (b. 27 Sep 1884 Auburn NY–d. 19 Mar 1910 at a friend's home in Newton MA) A third year law student at Harvard University, he died after an operation on his lungs, suffering from a complication of diseases, including a severe attack of the grippe. Buried Fort Hill Cemetery, Auburn NY.

Lin Storti—4 Years Infielder (b. 5 Dec 1906 Santa Monica CA–d. 24 Jul 1982 Doctor's Hospital, Montclair CA) He was the golf pro at La Mancha Golf Course for 30 years. Died from a heart attack. Buried Bellevue Memorial Gardens, Ontario CA.

Carl Stotz—(b. 20 Feb 1910 Williamsport PA–d. 4 Jun 1992 Williamsport Hospital, Williamsport PA) The founder of Little League baseball, he worked for various businesses over the years and served more than two decades as a township tax collector. Died from a heart attack. Buried Twin Hills Memorial Park, Muncy PA.

Tom Stouch—1 Year Infielder (b. 2 Dec 1870 Perryville OH–d. 7 Oct 1956 at his home in Lancaster PA) He managed minor league baseball in the south from 1903 to 1919 and coached at four colleges. From 1919 until he retired in 1952 he worked for the Lancaster newspapers, last in the circulation department. Buried Riverview Cemetery, Lancaster PA.

Allyn Stout—6 Years Pitcher (b. 31 Oct 1904 Peoria IL–d. 22 Dec 1974 Sikeston MO) Moving to Sikeston in 1967, he had been confined to a wheelchair for 15 years due to rheumatoid arthritis. Died from a heart attack enroute to Missouri Community Hospital. Buried Garden of Memories Cemetery, Sikeston MO.

George Stovall—12 Years Infielder 5 Years Manager (b. 23 Nov 1878 Independence MO–d. 5 Nov 1951 Burlington IA) Died following a heart attack. Buried Aspen Grove Cemetery, Burlington IA.

Jesse Stovall—2 Years Pitcher (b. 24 Jul 1875 Independence MO–d. 12 Jul 1955 U.S. Naval Hospital, San Diego CA) Spanish-American War veteran. Died from complications of a perforated appendix following surgery for an intestinal obstruction. Buried Long Beach CA.

Harry Stovey—14 Years Outfielder 2 Years Manager (b. 20 Dec 1856 Philadelphia PA–d. 20 Sep 1937 New Bedford MA) Retiring from the New Bedford Police Department as a captain in 1923, he had been disabled several years. Buried Oak Grove Cemetery, New Bedford MA.

Dick Strahs—1 Year Pitcher (b. 4 Dec 1923 Evanston IL–d. 26 May 1988 Las Vegas NV).

Paul Strand—4 Years Outfielder (b. 19 Dec 1893 Carbonado WA–d. 2 Jul 1974 Salt Lake City UT) After injuring his arm as a pitcher, he returned to the major leagues as an outfielder nine years later. Buried Salt Lake City Cemetery, Salt Lake City UT.

Johnny Strands—1 Year Infielder (b. 5 Dec 1885 Chicago IL–d. 19 Jan 1957 Forest Park IL) Buried Chapel Hill Gardens West, Oakbrook Terrace IL.

Sammy Strang—10 Years Infielder (b. 16 Dec 1876 Chattanooga TN–d. 13 Mar 1932 Erlanger Hospital, Chattanooga TN) He owned the Chattanooga Lookouts of the Southern League. Died from a ruptured gastric ulcer. Buried Chattanooga National Cemetery, Chattanooga TN.

Alan Strange—5 Years Infielder (b. 7 Nov 1906 Philadelphia PA–d. 27 Jun 1994 at a hospital in Seattle WA) He coached and managed in the minor leagues until 1959 when he went to work for the King County, WA, auditor's office, retiring in 1975. Cremated. Buried Calvary Cemetery, Seattle WA.

Asa Stratton—1 Year Infielder (b. 10 Feb 1853 Grafton MA–d. 14 Aug 1925 at his home in Fitchburg MA) An attorney, he also was the editor and/or proprietor of a number of newspapers in Massachusetts. Died from complications of a stroke. Buried Grafton MA.

Monty Stratton—5 Years Pitcher (b. 21 May 1912 Celeste TX–d. 29 Sep 1982 Citizen's General Hospital, Greenville TX) He lost a leg in a hunting accident in 1938 and in 1946 made a comeback, winning minor league games. He ran his 52 acre ranch near Greenville. Died after a lengthy bout with cancer. Buried Memoryland Memorial Park, Greenville TX.

Scott Stratton—8 Years Pitcher (b. 2 Oct 1869 Campbellsburg KY–d. 8 Mar 1939 Louisville KY) He operated a farm near Bloomfield KY. Died from a heart attack. Buried Valley Cemetery, Taylorsville KY.

Joe Straub—3 Years Catcher (b. 19 Jan 1858 Milwaukee WI–d. 13 Feb 1929 at his home in Pueblo CO) Buried Roselawn Cemetery, Pueblo CO.

Joe Strauss—3 Years Outfielder (b. 17 Mar 1844 Gecse, Hungary–d. 25 Jun 1906 Cincinnati OH).

Gabby Street—8 Years Catcher 6 Years Manager (b. 30 Sep 1882 Huntsville AL–d. 6 Feb 1951 St John's Hospital, Joplin MO) Awarded the Purple Heart for his service during World War I. He worked his entire life in baseball as a player, manager, coach and broadcaster. He once caught a ball dropped from the top of the Washington Monument. Died from cancer. Buried Ozark Memorial Park Cemetery, Joplin MO.

Sam Streeter—15 Years Pitcher (b. 17 Sep 1900 New Market AL–d. 9 Aug 1985 Pittsburgh PA) He played in the negro leagues.

Oscar Streit—2 Years Pitcher (b. 7 Jul 1873 Florence AL–d. 10 Oct 1935 Birmingham AL).

Ed Strelecki—3 Years Pitcher (b. 10 Apr 1908 Newark NJ–d. 9 Jan 1968 Beth Israel Hospital, Newark NJ) He was a patrolman for the Newark Police Department from 1942 until his death. Buried Gate of Heaven Catholic Cemetery, East Hanover NJ.

Phil Stremmel—2 Years Pitcher (b. 16 Apr 1880 Zanesville OH–d. 26 Dec 1947 Chicago IL) Killed in his home by gas from a faulty stove. Buried Cedar Park Cemetery, Chicago IL.

Cub Stricker—11 Years Infielder (b. 15 Feb 1860 Philadelphia PA–d. 19 Nov 1937 Philadelphia PA) Buried West Laurel Hill Cemetery, Bala Cynwyd PA.

Elmer Stricklett—4 Years Pitcher (b. 29 Aug 1876 Glasco KS–d. 7 Jun 1964 Loma Linda Nursing Sanit, Santa Cruz CA) Purported to be the inventer of the spitball, he was an orchardist for several years. In 1936 he moved to Santa Cruz and retired as a surveyor about 1949. Died from a cerebral hemorrhage. Cremated.

George Strief—5 Years Infielder (b. 16 Oct 1856 Cincinnati OH–d. 1 Apr 1946 at his home in Cleveland OH) For 20 years he was a bailiff in the U.S. Federal Court in Cleveland, retiring in 1943.

Joe Stripp—11 Years Infielder (b. 3 Feb 1903 Harrison NJ–d. 10 Jun 1989 Orlando FL) He moved to Orlando from East Orange NJ in 1939. Buried Woodlawn Cemetery, Winter Garden FL.

Allie Strobel—2 Years Infielder (b. 11 Jun 1884 Dorchester MA–d. 10 Feb 1955 Hollywood FL) He owned the Sagimon Spring Golf Club at Lynnfield MA until retiring to Florida in 1951. Buried Memorial Gardens Cemetery, Hollywood FL.

Floyd Stromme—1 Year Pitcher (b. 1 Aug 1916 Cooperstown ND–d. 7 Feb 1993 Central Washington Hospital, Wenatchee WA) For several years he worked for Georgia Pacific at Coos Bay OR, retiring in 1977. Died after a brief illness. Buried Sunset Memorial Park Cemetery, Coos Bay OR.

Jim Stroner—1 Year Infielder (b. 29 May 1904 Chicago IL–d. 16 Nov 1971 Chicago IL) Buried St Mary Cemetery, Evergreen Park IL.

Sailor Stroud—3 Years Pitcher (b. 15 May 1885 Ironia NJ–d. 11 Apr 1970 at a hospital in, Stockton CA) Buried East Lawn Memorial Park, Sacramento CA.

Amos Strunk—17 Years Outfielder (b. 22 Nov 1889 Philadelphia PA–d. 22 Jul 1979 at his home in Llanerch PA) He observed his 50th anniversary as an insurance broker shortly before his death. Died following a brief illness. Buried Greenmount Cemetery, Philadelphia PA.

Steamboat Struss—1 Year Pitcher (b. 24 Feb 1909 Riverdale IL–d. 12 Sep 1985 Grand Rapids MI).

Dutch Stryker—2 Years Pitcher (b. 29 Jul 1895 Atlantic Highlands NJ–d. 5 Nov 1964 Riverview Hospital, Red Bank NJ) Served in France for the U.S. Army during World War I. He was a pari-mutuel clerk at various New Jersey race tracks. Buried Mount Olivet Cemetery, Middletown NJ.

Bill Stuart—2 Years Infielder (b. 28 Aug 1873 Boalsburg PA–d. 14 Oct 1928 Fort Worth TX) Buried State College PA.

Johnny Stuart—4 Years Pitcher (b. 27 Apr 1901 Clinton TN–d. 13 May 1970 General Hospital, Charleston WV) At one time he operated five Humble service stations. Later he was associated with the Gasoline Dealers Association. Died after a brief illness. Buried Mountain View Memorial Park, Dunbar WV.

Luke Stuart—1 Year Infielder (b. 23 May 1892 Alamance County NC–d. 15 Jun 1947 Winston-Salem NC) He was a scout for the Yankees and worked 20 Years in real estate for Pilot Real Estate Company in Winston-Salem. He had been in ill health when he died at his office from a self-inflicted gunshot wound. Buried Guilford College Cemetery, Guilford College NC.

Marlin Stuart—6 Years Pitcher (b. 8 Aug 1918 Paragould AR–d. 16 Jun 1994 Arkansas Methodist Hospital, Paragould AR) Buried Wood's Chapel Cemetery, Paragould AR.

George Stueland—4 Years Pitcher (b. 2 Mar 1899 Renwick IA–d. 9 Sep 1964 Onawa IA).

George Stultz—1 Year Pitcher (b. 30 Jun 1873 Louisville KY–d. 19 Mar 1955 General Hospital, Lousiville KY) He played minor league baseball 15 years. Later he was a policeman, deputy sheriff, jail guard and assessor. He also worked in the railroad yards for the Louisville and Nashville Railroad and the Indiana and Kentucky Terminal Railroad.

Bill Stumpf—2 Years Infielder (b. 21 Mar 1892 Baltimore MD–d. 14 Feb 1966 Crownsville MD) Buried Loudon Park Cemetery, Baltimore MD.

George Stumpf—4 Years Outfielder (b. 15 Dec 1910 New Orleans LA–d. 6 Mar 1993 Metairie LA).

Guy Sturdy—2 Years Infielder (b. 7 Aug 1899 Sherman TX–d. 4 May 1965 Memorial Hospital, Marshall TX) He managed minor league baseball for years and was a scout for several major league teams. He was also business manager for the local Steamfitters and Plumbers Union in Marshall where he lived from 1938 until his unexpected death. Buried Colonial Gardens, Marshall TX.

Dean Sturgis—1 Year Catcher (b. 1 Dec 1892 Beloit KS–d. 4 Jun 1950 Uniontown Hospital, Uniontown PA) He was wounded during World War I while serving in the U.S. Army. A corporation lawyer of exceptional ability, he was well-known in the Pennsylvania Superior and Supreme courts and also in the U.S. Supreme Court. His death came unexpectedly, although he had been in failing health for several months. Buried Oak Lawn Cemetery, Uniontown PA.

George Stutz—1 Year Infielder (b. 12 Feb 1893 Philadelphia PA–d. 29 Dec 1930 at his home in Philadelphia PA) He was still playing baseball up until he suddenly keeled over dead. Buried Hillside Cemetery, Roslyn PA.

Lena Styles—5 Years Catcher (b. 27 Nov 1899 Gurley AL–d. 14 Mar 1956 Fifth Avenue Hospital, Huntsville AL) He worked at Anniston AL in a tire recapping business before retiring to a farm at Gurley. Buried Gurley Cemetery, Gurley AL.

Neil Stynes—1 Year Catcher (b. 10 Dec 1868 Arlington MA–d. 26 Mar 1944 at his home in Somerville MA) He retired as a foreman at the Somerville Water Dept.

Luis Suarez—1 Year Infielder (b. 24 Aug 1916 Alto Songo, Cuba–d. 5 Jun 1991 Havana, Cuba).

Charley Suche—1 Year Pitcher (b. 5 Aug 1915 Cranes Mill TX–d. 11 Feb 1984 San Antonio TX) Served in the Signal Corps during World War II. He was an engineer for Southwestern Bell Telephone, retiring after 37 years. Buried Sunset Memorial Park, San Antonio TX.

Tony Suck—2 Years Catcher (b. 11 Jun 1858 Chicago IL–d. 29 Jan 1895 Chicago IL) Buried Oak Woods Cemetery, Chicago IL.

Willie Sudhoff—10 Years Pitcher (b. 17 Sep 1874 St Louis MO–d. 25 May 1917 St Louis MO) Died from paralysis at the city sanitarium where he had been a patient since since 1913. His trouble started when the Browns, who he played for, were involved in a train wreck. This led to a nervous breakdown, and he was never the same again. Buried Bethany Cemetery, St Louis MO.

William Suero—2 Years Infielder (b. 7 Nov 1966 Santo Domingo, Dominican Republic–d. 30 Nov 1995 Santo Domingo, Dominican Republic).

Joe Sugden—13 Years Catcher (b. 31 Jul 1870 Philadelphia PA–d. 28 Jun 1959 Philadelphia PA) Buried North Cedar Hill Cemetery, Philadelphia PA.

George Suggs—8 Years Pitcher (b. 7 Jul 1883 Kinston NC–d. 4 Apr 1949 at his home in Kinston NC) He once picked seven runners off base in a single game. He operated a sporting goods store in Kinston before spending 20 years as storage house manager and factory foreman for E V Webb Tobacco Company. Died following a four-month illness. Buried Maplewood Cemetery, Kinston NC.

Clyde Sukeforth—10 Years Catcher 1 Year Manager (b. 30 Nov 1901 Washington ME–d. 3 Sep 2000).

Ernie Sulik—1 Year Outfielder (b. 7 Jul 1910 San Francisco CA–d. 31 May 1963 Kaiser Hospital, Oakland CA) He was a retired Oakland fireman. Died from liver disease. Buried Holy Sepulchre Cemetery, Hayward CA.

Andy Sullivan—1 Year Infielder (b. 30 Aug 1884 Southborough MA–d. 14 Feb 1920 Framingham MA).

Bill Sullivan—1 Year Outfielder (b. 4 Jul 1853 Holyoke MA–d. 13 Nov 1884 at his saloon in Holyoke MA) A bricklayer, he also owned a saloon in Holyoke, had served two years as a city councilman and was a volunteer fireman. Died suddenly from a stroke.

Billy Sullivan—16 Years Catcher 1 Year Manager (b. 1 Feb 1875 Fort Atkinson WI–d. 28 Jan 1965 Newberg OR) He invented the first chest protector, and was the first catcher to set up behind the batter in the position catchers still use. In 1914 he retired to a 20 acre farm near Newberg where he spent the rest of his life. Died from heart failure. Buried St James Cemetery, McMinnville OR.

Billy Sullivan—12 Years Catcher (b. 23 Oct 1910 Chicago IL–d. 4 Jan 1994 Sarasota FL).

Charlie Sullivan—3 Years Pitcher (b. 23 May 1903 Yadkin Valley NC–d. 28 May 1935 Maiden NC) He was killed instantly while still in his baseball career when a Carolina and Northwestern passenger train hit his car at a crossing. It was reported that he had been drinking before the accident. Buried Yadkin Valley NC.

Chub Sullivan—3 Years Infielder (b. 12 Jan 1856 Boston MA–d. 12 Sep 1881 Boston MA).

Dan Sullivan—5 Years Catcher (b. 9 May 1857 Providence RI–d. 25 Oct 1893 at his brother-in-law's home, Providence RI) Died from consumption and Bright's disease.

Denny Sullivan—4 Years Outfielder (b. 28 Sep 1882 Hillsboro WI–d. 2 Jun 1956 V A Hospital, Los Angeles CA) A veteran of both World Wars I and II, he was a medical doctor. Buried Los Angeles National Cemetery, Los Angeles CA.

Denny Sullivan—2 Years Infielder (b. 26 Jun 1858 Boston MA–d. 31 Dec 1925 Boston MA) Ordained to the Catholic priesthood in 1884, he served in a number of positions in the Boston area and was pastor at St Patrick's Church in Roxbury his last ten years. Died after an illness of several months. Buried New Calvary Cemetery, Mattapan MA.

Fleury Sullivan—1 Year Pitcher (b. 1862 East St Louis IL–d. 15 Feb 1897 East St Louis IL).

Harry Sullivan—1 Year Pitcher (b. 12 Apr

1888 Rockford IL–d. 22 Sep 1919 at his parent's home in Rockford IL) World War I veteran. He was a medical doctor in Rockford. Died from septicemia and pneumonia that developed after a bout with influenza. Buried St Marys/St James Cemetery, Rockford IL.

Jackie Sullivan —1 Year Infielder (b. 22 Feb 1918 Princeton TX–d. 15 Oct 1992 Humana Hospital, Dallas TX) World War II veteran. He managed in the minor leagues until 1955 when he became a McKinney TX policeman. He was also a Dallas County, TX, deputy sheriff for a year. Died from complications of heart disease. Buried Ridgeview Memorial Park, Allen TX.

Jim Sullivan —4 Years Pitcher (b. 25 Apr 1869 Charlestown MA–d. 29 Nov 1901 at his home in Roxbury MA) Buried Malden MA.

Jim Sullivan —3 Years Pitcher (b. 5 Apr 1894 Mine Run VA–d. 12 Feb 1972 Burtonville MD).

Joe Sullivan —4 Years Infielder (b. 6 Jan 1870 Charlestown MA–d. 2 Nov 1897 at his home in Charlestown MA) Died at the height of his baseball career from consumption after an illness of nearly a year. Buried Holy Cross Cemetery, Malden MA.

Joe Sullivan —5 Years Pitcher (b. 26 Sep 1910 Mason City IL–d. 8 Apr 1985 at his home in Sequim WA) He worked at the Puget Sound Naval Shipyard from 1945 to 1970, first as a pipefitter and retiring as fire chief. He moved to Sequim in 1975. Died from cancer. Cremated and his ashes scattered in Okanogan County.

John Sullivan —2 Years Catcher (b. 16 Feb 1873 IL–d. 5 Jun 1924 at Shaw Field in St Paul MN) He dropped dead from a heart attack while playing in a practice game. Buried Minneapolis MN.

John Sullivan —2 Years Outfielder (b. 21 Mar 1890 Williamsport PA–d. 1 Apr 1966 Lewisburg Community Hospital, Lewisburg PA) He retired from Williamsport Wire Rope Corp in 1958. Buried Harmony Cemetery, Milton PA.

John Sullivan —1 Year Pitcher (b. 31 May 1894 Chicago IL–d. 7 Jul 1958 Chicago IL) Buried St Mary Cemetery, Evergreen Park IL.

Lefty Sullivan —1 Year Pitcher (b. 7 Sep 1916 Nashville TN–d. 1 Nov 1988 Scottsdale Memorial Hospital, Scottsdale AZ) He was a real estate salesman. Buried Paradise Memorial Gardens, Scottsdale AZ.

Marty Sullivan —5 Years Outfielder (b. 20 Oct 1862 Lowell MA–d. 6 Jan 1894 at his home in Lowell MA) Buried St Patrick's Cemetery, Lowell MA.

Mike Sullivan —1 Year Outfielder (b. 10 Jun 1860 Philadelphia PA–d. 21 Mar 1929 Webster MA).

Mike Sullivan —11 Years Pitcher (b. 23 Oct 1866 Boston MA–d. 14 Jun 1906 City Hospital, Boston MA) A lawyer, he went into politics and was elected to the State House of Representatives and the State Senate. He had been a member of the Governor's Council three years when he died. Died from a brain hemorrhage five days after suffering a heart attack. Buried Mount Calvary Cemetery, Roslindale MA.

Pat Sullivan —1 Year Infielder (b. 22 Dec 1862 Milwaukee WI–d. 29 Mar 1886 West Roxbury MA).

Sleeper Sullivan —4 Years Catcher (b. abt 1849 St Louis MO–d. 25 Sep 1899 Camden NJ) He managed minor league baseball and was a well-known saloonkeeper in Camden. Buried New Cathedral Cemetery, Philadelphia PA.

Suter Sullivan —2 Years Infielder (b. 14 Oct 1872 Baltimore MD–d. 19 Apr 1925 at his home in Baltimore MD) Buried St Mary's Cemetery, Baltimore MD.

Ted Sullivan —1 Year Outfielder 3 Years Manager (b. 1852 County Clare, Ireland–d. 5 Jul 1929 Washington DC).

Tom Sullivan —1 Year Catcher (b. 19 Dec 1906 Nome AK–d. 16 Aug 1944 Seattle WA) Served in the U.S. Army during World War II. Died from epilepsy in his cell at the Seattle city jail. He had been booked that day for drunkedness and the failure to carry his draft card. Buried Calvary Cemetery, Seattle WA.

Tom Sullivan —1 Year Pitcher (b. 18 Oct 1897 Boston MA–d. 23 Sep 1962 Veteran's Hospital, Boston MA) World War I veteran. Died after a long illness. Buried Mount Hope Cemetery, Boston MA.

Tom Sullivan —4 Years Pitcher (b. 1 Mar 1860 New York City NY–d. 12 Apr 1947 General Hospital, Cincinnati OH) He operated an advertising agency. Died from a skull fracture and other injuries suffered when he was struck by a car. Buried Oak Hill Cemetery Park, Cincinnati OH.

Homer Summa—10 Years Outfielder (b. 3 Nov 1898 Gentry MO–d. 29 Jan 1966 Memorial Hospital, Glendale CA) He was an assistant cashier at a bank for 33 years. Died from lung cancer. Buried Grand View Memorial Park, Glendale CA.

Bill Summers—(b. 10 Nov 1895–d. 12 Sep 1966 Upton MA) He gave up professional boxing for a career as an umpire, umpiring in the American League from 1933 to 1959. Buried Lakeview Cemetery, Upton MA.

Ed Summers—5 Years Pitcher (b. 5 Dec 1884 Ladoga IN–d. 12 May 1953 at his home in Indianapolis IN) An ambidextrous pitcher, rheumatism forced his retirement from baseball. For 32 years he was a welder for Prest-O-Lite Corporation, retiring in 1950. Died from a stroke. Buried Ladoga Cemetery, Ladoga IN.

Billy Sunday—8 Years Outfielder (b. 19 Nov 1862 Ames IA–d. 6 Nov 1935 Chicago IL) He is best known as an evangelist after his playing days were over. Buried Forest Home Cemetery, Forest Park IL.

Steve Sundra—9 Years Pitcher (b. 27 Mar 1910 Luxor PA–d. 23 Mar 1952 at his home in Cleveland OH) Served in the U.S. Army during World War II. Died from rectal cancer. Buried Calvary Cemetery, Cleveland OH.

Max Surkont—9 Years Pitcher (b. 16 Jun 1922 Central Falls RI–d. 8 Oct 1986 at his home in Largo FL) Served in the U.S. Navy during World War II. He owned and operated Surkont's Cafe in Pawtucket RI for 21 years before moving to Florida in 1984. Buried Notre Dame Cemetery, Pawtucket RI.

George Susce—8 Years Catcher (b. 13 Aug 1908 Pittsburgh PA–d. 25 Feb 1986 Manatee Memorial Hospital, Bradenton FL) He coached in the major leagues for three decades. Died following a lengthy illness. Buried Sarasota Memorial Park, Sarasota FL.

Pete Susko—1 Year Infielder (b. 2 Jul 1904 Laura OH–d. 22 May 1978 Jacksonville FL).

Butch Sutcliffe—1 Year Catcher (b. 22 Jul 1915 Fall River MA–d. 2 Mar 1994 Fall River MA) Served in the Pacific for the U.S. Army during World War II. He worked several years in Trinidad for the Walsh-Driscoll Construction Company before spending ten years as head of the marine department of the J O'Neil Hardware Company in Fall River. He retired in 1978 after working five years as a route salesman for the Fall River News Company. Buried Oak Grove Cemetery, Fall River MA.

Sy Sutcliffe—7 Years Catcher (b. 15 Apr 1862 Wheaton IL–d. 13 Feb 1893 at his home in Wheaton IL) Died at the height of his career from Bright's disease.

Rube Suter—1 Year Pitcher (b. 15 Sep 1887 Independence MO–d. 24 Jul 1971 at his home in Topeka KS) World War I veteran. Moving to Topeka from Salina KS in 1947, he was a plumbing and heating engineer for the Kansas State architect's office, retiring in 1963. Buried Assaria Cemetery, Assaria KS.

Dizzy Sutherland—1 Year Pitcher (b. 9 Apr 1923 Washington DC–d. 26 Aug 1979 Washington DC) Buried Maryland Veteran's Cemetery, Cheltenham MD.

Suds Sutherland—1 Year Pitcher (b. 20 Feb 1894 Coburg OR–d. 11 May 1972 St Vincent Hospital, Portland OR) He was a retired mechanic from Safeway Scaffolding Co. Cremated. Buried Pioneer Cemetery, Portland OR.

Jack Sutthoff—6 Years Pitcher (b. 29 Jun 1873 Cincinnati OH–d. 3 Aug 1942 Cincinnati OH) He was an oil station attendent. Died from cancer of the tongue and larynx. Buried St Joseph New Cemetery, Cincinnati OH.

Ezra Sutton—13 Years Infielder (b. 17 Sep 1850 Palmyra NY–d. 20 Jun 1907 at a hospital in Braintree MA) He lost heavily in an ice business venture in Palmyra NY in 1890, shortly before he was seized with locomotor ataxia, from which he suffered until his death.

Harry Swacina—4 Years Infielder (b. 22 Aug 1881 St Louis MO–d. 21 Jun 1944 at his home in Birmingham AL) Buried Elmwood Cemetery, Birmingham AL.

Cy Swaim—2 Years Pitcher (b. 11 Mar 1874 Cadwallader OH–d. 27 Dec 1945 Eustis FL).

Andy Swan—1 Year Infielder (b. 11 May 1845 Tewsbury MA–d. 27 Aug 1885 Lawrence MA) A businessman in Lawrence, he had interests in a bobbin factory and in the beginnings of a telephone exchange in Massachusetts and New Hampshire. He was shot to death by an irrate investor in the telephone exchange. Buried Bellevue Cemetery, Lawrence MA.

Ducky Swan—1 Year Pitcher (b. 11 Aug 1888 Lancaster PA–d. 9 May 1946 at his home in Pittsburgh PA) He was a teacher at Westinghouse High School. Died from a heart attack. Buried Smithfield East End Cemetery, Pittsburgh PA.

Pinky Swander—2 Years Outfielder (b. 4 Jul 1880 Portsmouth OH–d. 24 Oct 1944 Springfield MA) He was a dentist at Springfield for 30 years. Died suddenly from a heart attack in his office. Buried Greenlawn Cemetery, Portsmouth OH.

Bill Swanson—1 Year Infielder (b. 12 Oct 1888 New York City NY–d. 16 Oct 1954 Wickersham Hospital, New York City NY) He worked 27 years for the construction division of the New York State Department of Labor. Buried Calvary Cemetery, Woodside NY.

Evar Swanson—5 Years Outfielder (b. 15 Oct 1902 DeKalb IL–d. 17 Jul 1973 Cottage Hospital, Galesburg IL) He was a production planner for Butler Manufacturing Company in Galesburg and was postmaster at Galesburg from 1958 to 1972. He also served in elected positions for the city and county. Died from a heart condition. Buried Oak Lawn Memorial Gardens, Galesburg IL.

Ed Swartwood—9 Years Outfielder (b. 12 Jan 1859 Rockford IL–d. 15 May 1924 Presbyterian Hospital, Pittsburgh PA) He was a National League umpire from 1894 to 1900. For 19 years he worked in the Allegheny County, PA, sheriff's office and was the official hangman of the county. He was so well known in that capacity that his services were often requested by surrounding counties in western Pennsylvania. Died following an extended illness.

Bud Swartz—1 Year Pitcher (b. 13 Jun 1931 Tulsa OK–d. 24 Jun 1991 UCLA Medical Center, Los Angeles CA) For 20 years he was a self-employed realtor. Died from kidney cancer five years after kidney transplant surgery. Buried Hillside Memorial Park, Los Angeles CA.

Dazzy Swartz—1 Year Pitcher (b. 1 Jan 1897 Farmersville OH–d. 13 Jan 1980 at his home in Germantown OH) World War I veteran. He operated the restaurant at the Shawnee Inn at Sunbury OH for many years. Later he was a bailiff in the Montgomery County, OH, court system for 31 years, retiring in 1974. Buried Germantown Cemetery, Germantown OH.

Parke Swartzel—1 Year Pitcher (b. 21 Nov 1865 Knightstown IN–d. 3 Jan 1940 at his home in Los Angeles CA) For 24 years he was a clerk at a retail hardware store. Died from pneumonia brought on by influenza. Cremated.

Charlie Sweasy—2 Years Infielder 1 Year Manager (b. 2 Nov 1847 Newark NJ–d. 30 Mar 1908 City Hospital, Newark NJ) He was a laborer. Died from heart disease and senility. Buried Evergreen Cemetery, Hillside NJ.

Bill Sweeney—3 Years Infielder (b. 29 Dec 1903 Cleveland OH–d. 18 Apr 1957 Mercy Hospital, San Diego CA) He managed minor league baseball, including several teams in the Pacific Coast League. Died from complications of a peptic ulcer. Buried Resurrection Cemetery, San Gabriel CA.

Bill Sweeney—8 Years Infielder (b. 6 Mar 1886 Covington KY–d. 26 May 1948 Mount Auburn Hospital, Cambridge MA) For several years he was engaged in the insurance business in Boston MA. Buried St Joseph's Cemetery, West Roxbury MA.

Bill Sweeney—2 Years Pitcher (b. 1858 Philadelphia PA–d. 13 Apr 1908 Paterson NJ).

Charlie Sweeney—1 Year Outfielder (b. 15 Apr 1890 Philadelphia PA–d. 13 Mar 1955 Shadyside Hospital, Pittsburgh PA) He was equipment manager for the Pirates and Steelers for several years. Before that he was one of Pittsburgh's first motorcycle policemen. Died from a heart attack. Buried St Mary's Cemetery, Pittsburgh PA.

Charlie Sweeney—6 Years Pitcher (b. 13 Apr 1863 San Francisco CA–d. 3 Apr 1902 San Francisco CA) Died from consumption. Buried Cypress Lawn Memorial Park, Colma CA.

Dan Sweeney—1 Year Outfielder (b. 28 Jan 1868 Philadelphia PA–d. 13 Jul 1913 at his home in Louisville KY) Died from gastritis. Buried St John Cemetery, Louisville KY.

Hank Sweeney—1 Year Infielder (b. 28 Dec 1915 Franklin TN–d. 6 May 1980 Maury County Hospital, Columbia TN) World War II veteran. He was a yard foreman for Monsanto Chemical Company. Buried Leiper's Fork Cemetery, Columbia TN.

Jeff Sweeney—9 Years Catcher (b. 19 Jul 1888 Chicago IL–d. 4 Jul 1947 Chicago IL) Buried Mount Carmel Cemetery, Hillside IL.

Jerry Sweeney—1 Year Infielder (b. 1860 Boston MA–d. 25 Aug 1891 Boston MA) Buried Mount Calvary Cemetery, Roslindale MA.

Pete Sweeney—3 Years Infielder (b. 31 Dec 1863 CA–d. 22 Aug 1901 San Francisco CA) Buried Holy Cross Catholic Cemetery, Colma CA.

Rooney Sweeney—3 Years Catcher (b. 1860–d. 1 Jun 1889 New York City NY).

Les Sweetland—5 Years Pitcher (b. 15 Aug 1901 St Ignace MI–d. 4 Mar 1974 Brevard Hospital, Melbourne FL) He lived in Detroit MI until 1964.

Augie Swentor—1 Year Catcher (b. 21 Nov 1899 Seymour CT–d. 10 Nov 1969 at the Medicare Pavilion in Waterbury CT) He worked in Europe and South America for the U.S. Department of Agriculture, retiring in 1967. Died after a long illness. Buried Waterside Cemetery, Marblehead MA.

Steve Swetonic—6 Years Pitcher (b. 13 Aug 1903 Mount Pleasant PA–d. 22 Apr 1974 General Hospital, Canonsburg PA) He was a sales representative for Blaw-Knox Company.

Pop Swett—1 Year Catcher (b. 16 Apr 1870 San Francisco CA–d. 22 Nov 1934 San Francisco CA) Died after a short illness. Buried Holy Cross Catholic Cemetery, Colma CA.

Bill Swift—11 Years Pitcher (b. 10 Jan 1908 Elmira NY–d. 23 Feb 1969 Polk General Hospital, Bartow FL) He owned and operated Swift Shoe Repair Company. Buried Oakhill Burial Park, Lakeland FL.

Bob Swift—14 Years Catcher 1 Year Manager (b. 6 Mar 1915 Salina KS–d. 17 Oct 1966 Henry Ford Hospital, Detroit MI) He worked in baseball his entire life as a player, coach, scout or manager. Died from lung cancer. Buried Roselawn Memorial Park, Salina KS.

Oad Swigart—2 Years Pitcher (b. 13 Feb 1915 Archie MO–d. 8 Aug 1997 at his home in St Joseph MO) For 32 years he was an agent for the Missouri Dept of Conservation and was instrumental in developing the Honey Creek Wildlife Area. Cremated. Buried Mount Olivet Cemetery, St Joseph MO.

Ad Swigler—1 Year Pitcher (b. 21 Sep 1895 Philadelphia PA–d. 5 Feb 1975 Mercy Medical Center, Philadelphia PA) Served in the U.S. Army Dental Corps during World War I. A dental surgeon for 24 years, he was forced to give up his practice in 1948 because of failing eyesight. Buried Arlington Cemetery, Drexel Hill PA.

Charlie Swindell—1 Year Catcher (b. 26 Oct 1877 Rockford IL–d. 22 Jul 1940 at his home in Portland OR) He practiced law at Bellingham WA until 1911 when he moved his law office to Portland where he was a prominent attorney. Buried Portland Memorial, Portland OR.

Josh Swindell—2 Years Pitcher (b. 5 Jul 1883 Rose Hill KS–d. 19 Mar 1969 Lower Valley Hospital, Fruita CO) He farmed in Mesa County, CO, for several years. Buried Memorial Gardens Cemetery, Grand Junction CO.

Tom Swope—(b. abt 1888 Georgetown OH–d. 11 Feb 1969 Cincinnati OH) A sportswriter for the *Cincinnati Post* from 1915 until ten days before his death, he was recognized as the ultimate authority on rules, records and statistics. He helped draft modern scoring rules in 1949. Buried Rest Haven Memorial Park, Cincinnati OH.

Len Swormstedt—3 Years Pitcher (b. 6 Oct 1878 Cincinnati OH–d. 19 Jul 1964 Salem MA) Buried Harmony Grove Cemetery, Salem MA.

T

John Taber—1 Year Pitcher (b. 28 Jun 1868 Acushnet MA–d. 21 Feb 1940 Boston MA).

Lefty Taber—2 Years Pitcher (b. 11 Jan 1900 Rock Island IL–d. 5 Nov 1983 Lincoln NE) A manufacturer's representative, he had lived in Lincoln since 1930. Buried Wyuka Cemetery, Lincoln NE.

Jim Tabor—9 Years Infielder (b. 5 Nov 1916

Owens Crossroads AL–d. 22 Aug 1953 County Hospital, Sacramento CA) Served in the U.S. Army during World War II. He worked briefly for a construction company in Sacramento after retiring from baseball in 1951. Died after suffering a heart attack five days earlier. Buried Beason Hill Cemetery, Gurley AL.

John Taff—1 Year Pitcher (b. 3 Jun 1890 Austin TX–d. 15 May 1961 at a hospital in Houston TX) He retired from the insurance business. Buried Oakwood Cemetery, Austin TX.

Doug Taitt—4 Years Outfielder (b. 3 Aug 1902 Bay City MI–d. 12 Dec 1970 at a nursing home in Portland OR) He worked 19 years for the Supercargoes and Checkers Union before retiring. Buried Riverview Abbey Mausoleum, Portland OR.

Vito Tamulis—6 Years Pitcher (b. 11 Jul 1911 Cambridge MA–d. 5 May 1974 Veteran's Hospital, Nashville TN) Served in the U.S. Army during World War II. He played baseball for 16 years. He worked for a beer distributor and was a part-time grocery clerk. Buried Nashville National Cemetery, Nashville TN.

Leo Tankersley—1 Year Catcher (b. 8 Jun 1901 Terrell TX–d. 18 Sep 1980 Dallas TX) Buried College Mound Cemetery, Terrell TX.

Jesse Tannehill—15 Years Pitcher (b. 14 Jul 1874 Dayton KY–d. 22 Sep 1956 Speers Hospital, Dayton KY) He worked at a machine shop after retiring from baseball in 1911. Died following a stroke. Buried Evergreen Cemetery, Southgate KY.

Lee Tannehill—10 Years Infielder (b. 26 Oct 1880 Dayton KY–d. 16 Feb 1938 Live Oak FL) For ten years he was a salesman for Libby, McNeill and Libby in Indiana. Died from kidney ailments. Buried Antioch Baptist Church Cemetery, Live Oak FL.

El Tappe—6 Years Catcher 2 Years Manager (b. 21 May 1927 Quincy IL–d. 11 Oct 1998 at his home in Quincy IL) He coached for the Cubs from 1958 to 1965 and scouted for them until 1975. He operated a sporting goods store in Quincy and for 25 years was a radio play-by-play announcer for a Quincy radio station. He also did some TV work. Died after a five-year battle with pancreatic cancer. Buried Quincy Memorial Park, Quincy IL.

Walter Tappen—1 Year Infielder (b. 8 Oct 1890 Carlinville IL–d. 19 Dec 1967 St Francis Hospital, Lynwood CA) For 50 years he was a cattle buyer for a packing company. Died from a heart attack. Cremated.

Arlie Tarbert—2 Years Outfielder (b. 10 Sep 1904 Cleveland OH–d. 27 Nov 1946 Hanna House Hospital, Cleveland OH) He was the New York representative for B F Goodrich Company. Died after an 18-month bout with heart disease. Buried Lake View Cemetery, Cleveland OH.

Al Tate—1 Year Pitcher (b. 1 Jul 1918 Coleman OK–d. 8 May 1993 at his home in Bountiful UT) Served in the U.S. Army during World War II. He worked 33 years for the Chevron refinery. He loved to fish and golf. Died after a lingering illness. Buried Lakeview Memorial Estates, Bountiful UT.

Bennie Tate—10 Years Catcher (b. 3 Dec 1901 Whitwell TN–d. 27 Oct 1973 Union Hospital, West Frankfort IL) He served a term as Franklin County, IL, treasurer. He had been ill about two years, but suffered a heart attack the week he died. Buried Boner Cemetery, West Frankfort IL.

Hugh Tate—1 Year Outfielder (b. 19 May 1880 Everett PA–d. 7 Aug 1956 at his home in Greenville PA) He engaged in sign painting and decorating in the Greenville area. Died from a heart attack. Buried St Michael's Cemetery, Greenville PA.

Pop Tate—6 Years Catcher (b. 22 Dec 1860 Richmond VA–d. 25 Jun 1932 at his home in Richmond VA) He was a bailiff at Richmond City Police Court. Died from a heart attack. Buried Riverview Cemetery, Richmond VA.

Tommy Tatum—2 Years Outfielder (b. 16 Jul 1919 Boyd TX–d. 7 Nov 1989 Oklahoma City OK) He managed the Oklahoma City Indians in the Texas League four years before becoming an insurance broker. Buried Resurrection Memorial Cemetery, Oklahoma City OK.

Fred Tauby—2 Years Outfielder (b. 27 Mar 1906 Canton OH–d. 23 Nov 1955 Concord CA) Served in the U.S. Navy during World War II. He was a salesman for a wholesale liquor company. Buried Golden Gate National Cemetery, San Bruno CA.

Walt Tauscher—2 Years Pitcher (b. 22 Nov

1901 LaSalle IL–d. 27 Nov 1992 Winter Park FL) He moved to Central Florida in 1947. Buried Woodlawn Memorium, Orlando FL.

Jackie Tavener —6 Years Infielder (b. 27 Dec 1897 Celina OH–d. 14 Sep 1969 Fort Worth TX) A well-known bowling proprietor in Fort Worth, he owned four different bowling lanes from 1931 until 1969 when he retired. He was inducted into the Fort Worth Bowling Hall of Fame. Buried Greenwood Memorial Park, Fort Worth TX.

Arlas Taylor —1 Year Pitcher (b. 16 Mar 1896 Warick County IN–d. 10 Sep 1968 Dade City FL).

Ben Taylor —1 Year Pitcher (b. 2 Apr 1889 Paoli IN–d. 3 Nov 1946 near Shoals IN) He was an interior decorator at Bedford IN. Died from a broken neck when he lost control of his car and collided with an embankment on Hwy 50 near Shoals. Buried Green Hill Cemetery, Bedford IN.

Ben Taylor —10 Years Infielder 5 Years Manager (b. 1888 Anderson SC–d. 24 Jan 1953 Provident Hospital, Baltimore MD) He played in the negro leagues and left baseball after losing his right arm in a fall. Died following an illness of little more than a month. Buried Arbutus Memorial Park, Baltimore MD.

Billy Taylor —7 Years Pitcher (b. 1857 Washington DC–d. 14 May 1900 at his home in Jacksonville FL) After being ill several months, he died peacefully, as though just going to sleep. Buried Evergreen Cemetery, Jacksonville FL.

Chink Taylor —1 Year Outfielder (b. 9 Feb 1898 Burnet TX–d. 7 Jul 1980 at a hospital in Temple TX) He was a wholesale agent for Mobil Oil Company for 32 years. Died following a long illness. Buried Burnet Cemetery, Burnet TX.

Danny Taylor —9 Years Outfielder (b. 23 Dec 1900 Lash PA–d. 11 Oct 1972 Latrobe Hospital, Latrobe PA) He managed minor league baseball. Buried West Newton Cemetery, West Newton PA.

Dummy Taylor —9 Years Pitcher (b. 21 Feb 1875 Oskaloosa KS–d. 22 Aug 1958 Our Savior's Hospital, Jacksonville IL) A deaf and dumb ballplayer, he was once thrown out of a game when he hadn't said anything. He coached baseball at schools for the deaf in Kansas, Iowa and Illinois. Died after suffering a stroke 11 days earlier. Buried Baldwin City Cemetery, Baldwin City KS.

Eddie Taylor —1 Year Infielder (b. 17 Nov 1901 Chicago IL–d. 30 Jan 1992 Pardise Valley Hospital, Chula Vista CA) He was a scout for the Cardinals. Died from cardio-respiratory arrest. Cremated. Buried Mount Greenwood Cemetery, Chicago IL.

George Taylor —2 Years Outfielder (b. 3 Feb 1855 Belfast ME–d. 19 Feb 1888 San Francisco CA) Died at the height of his career from a lung complaint. Buried Laurel Hill Cemetery, San Francisco CA.

Harry Taylor —1 Year Infielder (b. 26 Dec 1907 McKeesport PA–d. 27 Apr 1969 Flower Hospital, Toledo OH) Served in the U.S. Navy during World War II. For 14 years he was a checker for the Lakefront Dock Company and for six years a personnel manager for Toledo Steel Products Company. Buried Woodlawn Cemetery, Toledo OH.

Harry Taylor —4 Years Infielder (b. 4 Apr 1866 Halsey Valley NY–d. 12 Jul 1955 Buffalo General Hospital, Buffalo NY) He served as a Justice in County Court, New York State Supreme Court and United States Appeals Court for 40 years. Died from arteriosclerotic heart disease. Cremated.

Harry Taylor —6 Years Pitcher (b. 20 May 1919 East Glenn IN–d. 5 Nov 2000 Union Hospital, Terre Haute IN) Served in the U.S. Army during World War II. He farmed in the Shirkieville IN area and worked for Bemis and Visqueen, and later for St Mary-of-the-Woods. Died after an extended illness. Buried Shepherd's Cemetery, Shepherdsville IN.

Jack Taylor —10 Years Pitcher (b. 14 Jan 1874 New Straitsville OH–d. 4 Mar 1938 White Cross Hospital, Columbus OH) He was a coal miner. Died from cancer of the sigmoid and liver. Buried Green Lawn Memorial Cemetery, Columbus OH.

Jack Taylor —9 Years Pitcher (b. 23 May 1873 Staten Island NY–d. 7 Feb 1900 Staten Island NY) Died from Bright's disease.

Joe Taylor —4 Years Outfielder (b. 2 Mar 1926 Chapman AL–d. 18 Mar 1993 Veteran's Hospital, Pittsburgh PA) Buried Greenwood Cemetery, Pittsburgh PA.

Leo Taylor—2 Games Pinch Runner (b. 13 May 1901 Walla Walla WA–d. 20 May 1982 Seattle WA) He was retired from Pacific Northwest Bell. Buried Mount Pleasant Cemetery, Seattle WA.

Rube Taylor—1 Year Pitcher (b. 23 Mar 1877 Palestine TX–d. 30 Jan 1912 Dallas TX) He was a blacksmith with a shop in Dallas. Killed intantly when he was hit by a streetcar. Buried Greenwood Cemetery, Dallas TX.

Tommy Taylor—1 Year Infielder (b. 17 Sep 1895 Mexia TX–d. 5 Apr 1956 Greenville Hospital, Greenville MS) World War I veteran. He managed minor league baseball until 1935. He operated a service station and later engaged in the auto parts business in Greenville. He also served two terms as Justice of the Peace. Died from a bleeding ulcer. Buried Greenville Cemetery, Greenville MS.

Wally Taylor—1 Year Infielder (b. 1872 Pittsburgh PA–d. 13 Sep 1905 Cincinnati OH).

Wiley Taylor—4 Years Pitcher (b. 18 Mar 1888 Wamego KS–d. 8 Jul 1954 Westmoreland KS) He lived his entire life in Pottawatomie County, KS, and served in public offices there throughout his life. Buried Louisville Cemetery, Louisville KS.

Zack Taylor—16 Years Catcher 5 Years Manager (b. 27 Jul 1898 Yulee FL–d. 19 Sep 1974 Orlando FL) Buried Woodlawn Cemetery, Orlando FL.

Bud Teachout—3 Years Pitcher (b. 27 Feb 1904 Los Angeles CA–d. 11 May 1985 Gardens Convalescent Hosp, Laguna Beach CA) He was a school teacher in the Glendale CA Unified School District for 30 years. Died from bronchopneumonia and generalized heart disease. Cremated.

Birdie Tebbetts—14 Years Catcher 11 Years Manager (b. 10 Nov 1912 Burlington VT–d. 24 Mar 1999 Bradenton FL) Cremated. Buried St Bernard Church Memorial Gardens, Holmes Beach FL.

Patsy Tebeau—13 Years Infielder 11 Years Manager (b. 5 Dec 1864 St Louis MO–d. 15 May 1918 St Louis MO) He owned a saloon in downtown St Louis. He suffered from heart disease and was having a more difficult time getting around when he died from a self-inflicted gunshot wound to the right temple. Buried Calvary Cemetery, St Louis MO.

Pussy Tebeau—1 Year Outfielder (b. 22 Feb 1870 Worcester MA–d. 25 Mar 1950 at his home in Pittsfield MA) He retired from General Electric in 1933 after long service. Active in civic matters, he was a city alderman and a member of the Board of Health many years. Died after a long illness. Buried St Joseph's Cemetery, Pittsfield MA.

White Wings Tebeau—6 Years Outfielder (b. 26 Dec 1862 St Louis MO–d. 4 Feb 1923 St Luke's Hospital, Denver CO) He owned several minor league teams and baseball parks. Died from diabetes. Buried Crown Hill Cemetery, Denver CO.

Al Tedrow—1 Year Pitcher (b. 14 Dec 1891 Westerville OH–d. 23 Jan 1958 Westerville Convalscent Ctr, Westerville OH) A pressman more than 30 years for the Columbus Dispatch, he retired in 1956. Died following a heart attack. Buried Pioneer Cemetery, Westerville OH.

Johnny Temple—13 Years Infielder (b. 8 Aug 1927 Lexington NC–d. 9 Jan 1994 at his son's home in Anderson SC) Served in the U.S. Navy during World War II. He played lots of golf. Died from pancreatic cancer. Cremated.

Chuck Templeton—2 Years Pitcher (b. 1 Jun 1932 Detroit MI–d. 9 Oct 1997 Irving TX).

John Tener—4 Years Pitcher (b. 25 Jul 1863 Tyrone County, Ireland–d. 19 May 1946 Pittsburgh PA) He was governor of Pennsylvania from 1911 to 1915 and president of the National League from 1913 to 1918. He served in Congress one term before becoming governor. When he died he was a bank president and a partner in an insurance company. Died from a heart attack suffered three weeks earlier. Buried Homewood Cemetery, Pittsburgh PA.

Jim Tennant—1 Year Pitcher (b. 3 Mar 1908 Shepherdstown WV–d. 16 Apr 1967 Trumbull CT) He retired after 25 years with the FBI, mostly spent in the Bridgeport CT office. He then was a bank security officer. Died a short while after suffering a heart attack while golfing. Buried Lakeview Cemetery, Bridgeport CT.

Tom Tennant—2 Games Pinch Hitter (b. 3 Jul 1882 Monroe WI–d. 15 Feb 1955 at his daughter's home in San Carlos CA) He worked 30 years for the Pelton Water Wheel Company of San Francisco CA, retiring in 1950. Died from a heart attack. Buried Holy Cross Cemetery, Menlo Park CA.

Fred Tenney—17 Years Infielder 4 Years Manager (b. 26 Nov 1871 Georgetown MA–d. 3 Jul 1952 Massachusetts General Hospital, Boston MA) He worked 37 years in the Boston office of Equitable Life Assurance of New York, retiring in 1949. Died after a long illness. Buried Harmony Cemetery, Georgetown MA.

Fred Tenney—1 Year Outfielder (b. 9 Jul 1854 Marlboro NH–d. 15 Jun 1919 Truesdale Hospital, Fall River MA) An educator, he was superintendent at a number of schools in Southern Massachusetts and was also manager of the educational department at a publishing company. Died from Bright's disease. Buried Holliston MA.

Tom Terrell—1 Year Outfielder (b. abt 1870 Louisville KY–d. 9 Jul 1893 at his home in Louisville KY) Died from consumption. Buried St John Cemetery, Louisville KY.

Adonis Terry—14 Years Pitcher (b. 7 Aug 1864 Westfield MA–d. 24 Feb 1915 at his home in Milwaukee WI) He was nationally known as the proprietor of the Second Street Alleys, a bowling establishment in Milwaukee. Died from pneumonia. Buried Westfield MA.

Bill Terry—14 Years Infielder 10 Years Manager Hall of Fame (b. 30 Oct 1898 Atlanta GA–d. 9 Jan 1989 Jacksonville FL) In 1930 he was the last National League batter to hit over .400. He owned and operated the Bill Terry Buick dealership in Jacksonville until shortly before his death. Died following a brief illness. Buried Evergreen Cemetery, Jacksonville FL.

John Terry—2 Years Pitcher (b. 1 Nov 1879 Waterbury CT–d. 27 Apr 1933 Kansas City MO) Buried Forest Hill Cemetery, Kansas City MO.

Yank Terry—5 Years Pitcher (b. 11 Feb 1911 Bedford IN–d. 4 Nov 1979 Bloomington Hospital, Bloomington IN) He played in the Pacific Coast League and the Southern Association and operated Yank's Sportsman's Store in Bedford. Died from cancer. Buried Cresthaven Cemetery, Bedford IN.

Zeb Terry—7 Years Infielder (b. 17 Jun 1891 Denison TX–d. 14 Mar 1988 Cedars-Sinai Medical Center, Los Angeles CA) World War I veteran. He graduated from Stanford Univ in 1914 and was married to the same woman for 71 years. For 50 years he was self-employed in the oil leasing business. Died from a heart attack. Cremated.

Dick Terwilliger—1 Year Pitcher (b. 27 Jun 1906 Sand Lake MI–d. 21 Jan 1969 United Memorial Hospital, Greenville MI) World War II veteran. He worked for Gibson Products Corporation. Buried Rest Haven Memory Gardens, Belding MI.

Al Tesch—1 Year Infielder (b. 27 Jan 1891 Jersey City NJ–d. 3 Aug 1947 Medical Center, Jersey City NJ) He was an industrial engineer for The Insurance Company of North America in Manhattan. Died after a short illness. Buried Bay View-New York Bay Cemetery, Jersey City NJ.

Jeff Tesreau—7 Years Pitcher (b. 5 Mar 1889 Ironton MO–d. 24 Sep 1946 Hanover NH) He was baseball coach at Dartmouth College for 27 years. Died following a stroke suffered on a fishing trip at Reservoir Pond. Buried Pine Hill Cemetery, Hanover NH.

George Textor—2 Years Catcher (b. 27 Dec 1889 Newport KY–d. 10 Mar 1954 City Hospital, Massillon OH) He worked from 1916 to 1941 in the plant protection department of Central Steel Company in Massillon. A doctor, he was known throughout Ohio for his manipulative therapy and treatment of athletic injuries. Died after an illness of four days. Buried West Lawn Cemetery, Canton OH.

Moe Thacker—5 Years Catcher (b. 21 May 1934 Louisville KY–d. 13 Nov 1997 at his home near Louisville KY) He was a retired partner and superintendent for L M Kapfhammer Associates that owned several Long John Silver franchises. Died from cancer. Cremated.

Grant Thatcher—2 Years Pitcher (b. 23 Feb 1877 Maytown PA–d. 17 Mar 1936 Lancaster PA) He worked for Dutt's Restaurant in Manheim PA. Died from a complication of diseases after a two-week illness. Buried Woodward Hill Cemetery, Lancaster PA.

Jack Theis—1 Year Pitcher (b. 23 Jul 1891 Georgetown OH–d. 6 Jul 1941 at his mother's home in Georgetown OH) Served in the U.S. Army during World War I. He was a tobacco buyer for Liggett and Myers Tobacco Company. Died from pulmonary heart disease. Buried Confidence Cemetery, Georgetown OH.

Tommy Thevenow—15 Years Infielder (b. 6

Sep 1903 Madison IN–d. 29 Jul 1957 King's Daughter's Hospital, Madison IN) He assisted in the management of the Moose Home at Fairmount IN before opening a grocery store in Madison. Died from a cerebral hemorrhage. Buried Springdale Cemetery, Madison IN.

Henry Thielman—2 Years Pitcher (b. 30 Oct 1880 St Cloud MN–d. 2 Sep 1942 St Vincent's Hospital, New York City NY) He was an assistant coach at Notre Dame High School in South Bend IN and at Manhattan College in New York City before becoming a dentist. He practiced denistry in New York City from 1906 until his death, except from 1911 to 1913 when he had an office in St Cloud. Died after being ill a week. Buried Calvary Cemetery, St Cloud MN.

Jake Thielman—4 Years Pitcher (b. 20 Mar 1879 St Cloud MN–d. 28 Jan 1928 Minneapolis General Hosp, Minneapolis MN) Died from a cerebral hemorrhage. Buried Calvary Cemetery, St Cloud MN.

Bill Thomas—1 Year Outfielder (b. 8 Dec 1877 Norristown PA–d. 14 Jan 1950 Evansburg PA) Buried Montgomery Cemetery, Norristown PA.

Blaine Thomas—1 Year Pitcher (b. 1888 Glendora CA–d. 21 Aug 1915 Glendora CA).

Claude Thomas—1 Year Pitcher (b. 15 May 1890 Stanberry MO–d. 6 Mar 1946 Veteran's Hospital, Sulphur OK) World War I veteran. He served as undersheriff of Canadian County, OK, and was an officer at the El Reno (OK) Reformatory before becoming involved with the draft board during World War II. Buried El Reno Cemetery, El Reno OK.

Danny Thomas—2 Years Outfielder (b. 9 May 1951 Birmingham AL–d. 12 Jun 1980 Mobile AL) Hung himself in his cell while in jail awaiting trial on charges of sexually assaulting a 12 year old girl.

Fay Thomas—4 Years Pitcher (b. 10 Oct 1903 Holyrood KS–d. 12 Aug 1990 at his home in Chatsworth CA) He was a stagehand in the television and movie industry for 30 years. Died from a self-inflicted gunshot wound to the head. Cremated.

Fred Thomas—3 Years Infielder (b. 19 Dec 1892 Milwaukee WI–d. 15 Jan 1986 Rice Lake Convalescent Home, Rice Lake WI) He owned and operated the Fred Thomas Resort at Birchwood WI from 1925 until retiring in 1960. Cremated.

Frosty Thomas—1 Year Pitcher (b. 23 May 1881 Faucett MO–d. 18 Mar 1970 at his home in Fulton MO) A medical doctor with a private practice, he retired in 1965. He also served on the St Joseph State Hospital staff 25 years, was a medic in the State Guard, was chief examiner on the Selective Service Board during World War II and was Buchanan County, MO, coroner for two terms. Buried Memorial Park Cemetery, St Joseph MO.

Herb Thomas—3 Years Outfielder (b. 26 May 1902 Sampson City FL–d. 4 Dec 1991 Bradford Hospital, Starke FL) Served in both World Wars I and II. He engaged in the timber business and later operated Herb's Restaurant in Starke. Died after a long illness. Buried Oak Hill Cemetery, Palatka FL.

Ira Thomas—10 Years Catcher (b. 22 Jan 1881 Ballston Spa NY–d. 11 Oct 1958 Nazareth Hospital, Philadelphia PA) He worked in baseball as a scout and trouble shooter, mostly for the Athletics, but the last few years for the Yankees, retiring in 1956 because of arthritis. Died after a five-week stay in the hospital. Buried Holy Sepulchre Cemetery, Philadelphia PA.

Kite Thomas—2 Years Outfielder (b. 27 Apr 1923 Kansas City KS–d. 7 Jan 1995 Rocky Mount NC) Served in the U.S. Navy during World War II. During the 1950s he owned the popular Kite's Tavern in Manhattan KS and was said to dispense more beer than any other tavern in Kansas. After moving to North Carolina he owned the franchise for 37 Pizza Huts in the eastern Carolinas. Died from cancer. Buried Abilene Cemetery, Abilene KS.

Lefty Thomas—2 Years Pitcher (b. 4 Oct 1903 Abingdon VA–d. 19 Mar 1952 University Hospital, Charlottesville VA) He was a chemist at the duPont powder plant in Grove NJ. Buried Knollkreg Memorial Park, Abington VA.

Myles Thomas—5 Years Pitcher (b. 22 Oct 1897 State College PA–d. 12 Dec 1963 at his home in Toledo OH) He managed some minor league baseball and was sales manager at Trilby Motor Sales in Toledo. Died from a heart attack. Buried Woodlawn Cemetery, Toledo OH.

Pinch Thomas—10 Years Catcher (b. 24 Jan 1888 Camp Point IL–d. 24 Dec 1953 Modesto CA).

Ray Thomas—1 Year Catcher (b. 9 Jul 1910 Dover NH–d. 6 Dec 1993 Wilson NC) Served as a lieutenant commander in the U.S. Navy during World War II. He managed minor league baseball before managing the Raleigh Country Club and, later, the Holiday Inn at Wilson. Cremated.

Red Thomas—1 Year Outfielder (b. 25 Apr 1898 Hargrove AL–d. 29 Mar 1962 Fremont OH).

Roy Thomas—13 Years Outfielder (b. 24 Mar 1874 Norristown PA–d. 20 Nov 1959 at his home in Norristown PA) He coached baseball at Penn from 1909 to 1919. As a player he was so skilled at hitting foul balls that the present day rule of the first two fouls counting as strikes was made. Buried Riverside Cemetery, Norristown PA.

Tom Thomas—2 Years Pitcher (b. 27 Dec 1873 Syracuse OH–d. 23 Sep 1942 Shawnee OH) He was a miner and did odd jobs around Shawnee. Died from a heart attack. Buried Shawnee Cemetery, Shawnee OH.

Tommy Thomas—12 Years Pitcher (b. 23 Dec 1899 Baltimore MD–d. 27 Apr 1988 Dallastown PA) Buried Druid Ridge Cemetery, Pikesville MD.

Walt Thomas—1 Year Infielder (b. 28 Apr 1884 Altoona PA–d. 6 Jun 1950 at his home in Altoona PA) He retired from the passenger car shop of the Altoona Works earlier in the year. Died unexpectedly. Buried Alto Reste Park Cemetery, Altoona PA.

Art Thomason—1 Year Outfielder (b. 12 Feb 1889 Liberty MO–d. 1 May 1944 Research Medical Hospital, Kansas City MO) He was clerk of the County Court of Clay County, MO, for five years after serving three terms as City Marshall at Liberty. He loved hunting and fishing, but froze his foot on a hunting trip in 1939, causing amputation of the foot. Died of complications following a surgery. Buried Fairview Cemetery, Liberty MO.

Bill Thompson—1 Year Pitcher (b. 30 Aug 1870 Pittsburgh PA–d. 9 Jun 1962 Pittsburgh PA) He was a medical doctor. Buried Homewood Cemetery, Pittsburgh PA.

Danny Thompson—7 Years Infielder (b. 1 Feb 1947 Wichita KS–d. 10 Dec 1976 Rochester MN) Died from complications of leukemia at the height of his baseball career. Buried Capron Cemetery, Capron OK.

Dave Thompson—2 Years Pitcher (b. 3 Mar 1918 Mooresville NC–d. 26 Feb 1979 Memorial Hospital, Charlotte NC) He managed the men's department at the J C Penney store in Statesville NC for 19 years. Died after being in declining health two years. Buried Iredell Memorial Gardens, Statesville NC.

Frank Thompson—1 Year Infielder (b. 2 Jul 1895 Springfield MO–d. 27 Jun 1940 Jasper County TB Hospital, Webb City MO) He was a lineman for the telephone company and, later, was an electrician for Empire District Electric Company. Died from tuberculosis. Buried Fairview Cemetery, Joplin MO.

Fresco Thompson—9 Years Infielder (b. 6 Jun 1902 Centreville AL–d. 20 Nov 1968 St Jude Hospital, Fullerton CA) He worked 45 years in baseball as a player and executive, and had recently been named general manager of the Dodgers. Died following kidney surgery. Buried Queen of Heaven Cemetery, Rowland Heights CA.

Fuller Thompson—1 Year Pitcher (b. 1 May 1889 Los Angeles CA–d. 21 Feb 1972 California Hospital, Los Angeles CA) He was a self-employed stock investor for 50 years. Died from gall bladder cancer. Cremated.

Gus Thompson—2 Years Pitcher (b. 22 Jun 1877 Humboldt IA–d. 28 Mar 1958 Kalispell MT) He pitched for Pittsburgh in the first World Series, and was believed to be the last survivor of that event. He operated a pool hall in Kalispell for several years. Buried Conrad Memorial Cemetery, Kalispell MT.

Hank Thompson—9 Years Infielder (b. 8 Dec 1925 Oklahoma City OK–d. 30 Sep 1969 V A Hospital, Fresno CA) World War II veteran. In 1963 he was sentenced to a ten year prison term for armed robbery, but was paroled before serving the entire term. He was a playground director for the Fresno Parks and Recreation Department when he died. Died after suffering a heart seizure. Buried Odd Fellows Cemetery, Fresno CA.

Harry Thompson—1 Year Pitcher (b. 9 Sep 1889 Nanticoke PA–d. 14 Feb 1951 at a hospital in Reno NV) World War I veteran. He tended bar eight years at the Fort Sutter Club in Sacramento CA prior to his recent retirement. Buried

Golden Gate National Cemetery, San Bruno CA.

Homer Thompson —1 Year Catcher (b. 1 Jun 1892 Spring City TN–d. 12 Sep 1957 at his home in Atlanta GA) Served in the U.S. Army Air Corps during World War I. He was a national representative for the Coca-cola Company. Died from a heart attack. Buried Westview Cemetery, Atlanta GA.

Jocko Thompson —4 Years Pitcher (b. 17 Jan 1920 Beverly MA–d. 3 Feb 1988 Olney MD) He was a sales representative in the book binding industry. Cremated.

Lee Thompson —1 Year Pitcher (b. 26 Feb 1898 Smithfield UT–d. 17 Feb 1963 Santa Barbara CA) Served in the U.S. Army during World War I and in the U.S. Navy Seabees during World War II. He also served on the Santa Barbara Police and Fire Commission. He worked in real estate and, later, was a foreman at the Construction Center at Port Hueneme CA. Died from a heart attack the same day as an older brother. Buried Oak Hill Cemetery, Solvang CA.

Sam Thompson —15 Years Outfielder Hall of Fame (b. 5 Mar 1860 Danville IN–d. 7 Nov 1922 at his home in Detroit MI) Served as a U.S. Marine during World War I. He invested in Detroit real estate, and was said to be in comfortable circumstances. He was a crier at the courthouse. Died from a heart attack. Buried Elmwood Cemetery, Detroit MI.

Shag Thompson —3 Years Outfielder (b. 29 Apr 1893 Haw River NC–d. 7 Jan 1990 at his home in Black Mountain NC) He was president of General Building Products in Asheville NC for several years. Buried Linwood Cemetery, Graham NC.

Tommy Thompson —6 Years Outfielder (b. 19 May 1910 Elkhart IL–d. 24 May 1971 Placer Hospital, Auburn CA) He managed some minor league baseball and worked for the Jacobs Distributing Company in Auburn CA. Died from seminoma and throat cancer. Cremated.

Tommy Thompson —1 Year Pitcher (b. 7 Nov 1889 Spring City TN–d. 16 Jan 1963 at his home in La Jolla CA) He was an executive for Coca-Cola in Atlanta for 40 years. Died from heart disease. Cremated.

Jack Thoney —6 Years Outfielder (b. 8 Dec 1879 Fort Thomas KY–d. 24 Oct 1948 St Elizabeth Hospital, Covington KY) He was a guard for Brink's Armoured Car Service. Died after a long illness. Buried St Stephen Cemetery, Fort Thomas KY.

Hank Thormahlen —6 Years Pitcher (b. 5 Jul 1896 Jersey City NJ–d. 6 Feb 1955 at his home in Los Angeles CA) He was a security guard at a bank. Died from colon cancer. Buried Fairview Cemetery, Fairview NJ.

John Thornton —3 Years Pitcher (b. 1870 Washington DC–d. 31 Aug 1893 Pensacola FL).

Walter Thornton —4 Years Outfielder (b. 18 Feb 1875 Lewiston ME–d. 14 Jul 1960 at his home in Los Angeles CA) Died from heart disease. Cremated.

Bob Thorpe —1 Year Pitcher (b. 12 Jan 1935 San Diego CA–d. 17 Mar 1960 U.S. Naval Hospital, San Diego CA) An electrician for Standard Electric Company in San Diego, he was accidentally electrocuted while splicing a 2400 volt electric line. Buried Greenwood Memorial Park, San Diego CA.

Bob Thorpe —3 Years Outfielder (b. 19 Nov 1926 Caryville FL–d. 30 Oct 1996 Waveland MS) Served in the U.S. Navy during World War II. He owned Captain Bob's Seafood and Emerald Cut Lawn Care in Waveland.

Jim Thorpe —6 Years Outfielder (b. 28 May 1888 Prague OK–d. 28 Mar 1953 Los Angeles CA) He was better known as an Olympic athlete and also played professional football. Died from a heart attack. Buried Jim Thorpe Monument, Jim Thorpe PA.

Buck Thrasher —2 Years Outfielder (b. 6 Aug 1889 Watkinsville GA–d. 12 Jun 1938 at his home in Cleveland TN) He was a cotton buyer for Anderson-Clayton Company in Cedartown GA. Died from a coronary thrombosis. Buried Fort Hill Cemetery, Cleveland TN.

Marv Throneberry —7 Years Infielder (b. 2 Sep 1933 Collierville TN–d. 23 Jun 1994 Fisherville TN) "Marvelous Marv". Mediocre batting & poor base running made him a symbol of early Met's ineptitide. Died from cancer. Buried Fisherville Cemetery, Fisherville TN.

Sloppy Thurston —9 Years Pitcher (b. 2 Jun 1899 Fremont NE–d. 14 Sep 1973 at his home in Los Angeles CA) He gave up three home runs to Babe Ruth in Ruth's 60 home run season. He managed some minor league baseball and was a scout for the Pirates and White Sox. Died from a self-inflicted gunshot wound to the head. Buried Holy Cross Cemetery, Culver City CA.

Eddie Tiemeyer—3 Years Infielder (b. 9 May 1885 Cincinnati OH–d. 27 Sep 1946 General Hospital, Cincinnati OH) He was a pipe cutter for Mutual Manufacturing and Supply Company. Died after an illness of eight months. Buried Vine Street Hill Cemetery, Cincinnati OH.

Mike Tiernan—13 Years Outfielder (b. 21 Jan 1867 Trenton NJ–d. 7 Nov 1918 Bellevue Hospital, New York City NY) Died from tuberculosis.

Bill Tierney—2 Years Outfielder (b. 14 May 1858 Boston MA–d. 21 Sep 1898 Boston MA) Buried Mount Calvary Cemetery, Roslindale MA.

Cotton Tierney—6 Years Infielder (b. 10 Feb 1894 Kansas City KS–d. 18 Apr 1953 at his home in Kansas City MO) Served in France during World War I. He operated the Tierney-Wheat Recreation Company that owned bowling alleys. Buried Calvary Cemetery, Kansas City MO.

Les Tietje—6 Years Pitcher (b. 11 Sep 1910 Fayette IA–d. 2 Oct 1996 St Mary's Hospital, Rochester MN) He operated a produce business in Kasson MN for many years, then went to work for Crenlo in Rochester, retiring in 1979. Active in civic affairs, he served on the Kasson City Council and on the Fair Board. Buried Maple Grove Cemetery, Kasson MN.

Ray Tift—1 Year Pitcher (b. 21 Jun 1884 Fitchburg MA–d. 29 Mar 1945 Verona NJ).

Johnny Tillman—1 Year Pitcher (b. 6 Oct 1893 Bridgeport CT–d. 7 Apr 1964 at a hospital in Harrisburg PA) World War I veteran. He was a retired employee of Model City Cleaners in Harrisburg. Buried Flat Brook Cemetery, Canaan NY.

Ben Tincup—5 Years Pitcher (b. 14 Dec 1894 Adair OK–d. 5 Jul 1980 Claremore OK) The first Oklahoma Indian to play major league baseball, he was inducted into the Oklahoma Baseball Hall of Fame. He coached and scouted for several teams. Found dead from natural causes in his hotel room. Buried Rose Hill Memorial Park, Tulsa OK.

Joe Tinker—15 Years Infielder 4 Years Manager Hall of Fame (b. 27 Jul 1880 Muscotah KS–d. 27 Jul 1948 Orange Memorial Hospital, Orlando FL) He managed minor league baseball and was active in real estate in the Orlando area, often given credit for developing Central Florida. Later he operated a tavern and bowling alley in Orlando. He had a leg removed because of diabetes a year before his death. Died from congestive heart failure. Buried Greenwood Cemetery, Orlando FL.

Bud Tinning—4 Years Pitcher (b. 12 Mar 1906 Pilger NE–d. 17 Jan 1961 Evansville State Hospital, Evansville IN) He lived in Terre Haute IN before being admitted to the State Hospital in 1949. Buried Pilger Cemetery, Pilger NE.

Dan Tipple—1 Year Pitcher (b. 13 Feb 1890 Rockford IL–d. 26 Mar 1960 Omaha NE) Buried Hillcrest Memorial Park, Omaha NE.

Joe Tipton—7 Years Catcher (b. 18 Feb 1922 McCaysville GA–d. 1 Mar 1994 Birmingham AL) Buried Pleasant Grove Methodist Cemetery, Pleasant Grove AL.

Jack Tising—1 Year Pitcher (b. 9 Oct 1903 High Point MO–d. 5 Sep 1967 St Vincent Hospital, Leadville CO) He played baseball for 23 years before moving to Buena Vista CO in 1947. There he owned and operated a cafe and lounge. Buried Memorial Gardens Cemetery, Colorado Springs CO.

Cannonball Titcomb—5 Years Pitcher (b. 21 Aug 1866 West Baldwin ME–d. 9 Jun 1950 Kingston NH) He was an agent for United Shoe Machinery Corporation. Buried Greenwood Cemetery, Kingston NH.

John Titus—11 Years Outfielder (b. 21 Feb 1876 St Clair PA–d. 8 Jan 1943 at his home in St Clair PA) Spanish-American War veteran. Died after being in failing health three months, and critical the last few days. Buried Odd Fellows Cemetery, St Clair PA.

Bill Tobin—1 Year Infielder (b. 10 Oct 1854 Hartford CT–d. 10 Oct 1912 Hartford CT) He was a Hartford policeman from 1889 until he retired in 1904. Died from pneumonia and other complications. Buried Mount St Benedict Cemetery, Bloomfield CT.

Jack Tobin—13 Years Outfielder (b. 4 May 1892 St Louis MO–d. 10 Dec 1969 St John's Mercy Hospital, Creve Coeur MO) Died from pneumonia. Buried Calvary Cemetery, St Louis MO.

Jim Tobin—9 Years Pitcher (b. 27 Dec 1912 Oakland CA–d. 19 May 1969 Providence Hospital, Oakland CA) A pitcher who hit three consecutive home runs in one game in 1942, he owned a tavern in Oakland his last six years. Died from a heart attack following vascular surgery. Buried Holy Sepulchre Cemetery, Hayward CA.

Johnny Tobin—1 Game Pinch Hitter (b. 15 Sep 1906 Jamaica Plain MA–d. 6 Aug 1983 Rhinebeck NY).

Johnny Tobin—1 Year Infielder (b. 8 Jan 1921 Oakland CA–d. 18 Jan 1982 in his apartment in Oakland CA) He umpired in the Pacific Coast League before becoming a storeroom clerk for Pacific Gas and Electric. Died from a heart attack. Buried Holy Sepulchre Cemetery, Hayward CA.

Pat Tobin—1 Year Pitcher (b. 28 Jan 1916 Hermitage AR–d. 21 Jan 1975 Doctor's Hospital, Shreveport LA) He was the district manager for Union Banker's Insurance Company. Died from a heart attack. Buried Forest Park Cemetery, Shreveport LA.

Al Todd—11 Years Catcher (b. 7 Jan 1904 Troy NY–d. 8 Mar 1985 St Joseph's Hospital, Elmira NY) He managed minor league baseball nine years before owning a liquor store for over 40 years while working as a salesman for Consolidated Brick and for Van Brunt Motors. Died after being ill several months. Buried Maple Grove Cemetery, Horseheads NY.

Frank Todd—1 Year Pitcher (b. 18 Oct 1869 Aberdeen MD–d. 11 Aug 1919 Havre de Grace MD).

Phil Todt—8 Years Infielder (b. 9 Aug 1901 St Louis MO–d. 15 Nov 1973 St Louis MO) He played and managed in the American Association, as well as other minor leagues. He ran a flower shop in St Louis. Buried SS Peter and Paul Cemetery, St Louis MO.

Chick Tolson—5 Years Infielder (b. 6 Nov 1898 Washington DC–d. 16 Apr 1965 Washington DC) Buried Harmony Cemetery, Landover MD.

George Tomer—1 Game Pinch Hitter (b. 26 Nov 1895 Perry IA–d. 15 Dec 1984 Rowley Masonic Home, Perry IA) He retired as an engineer for the Milwaukee Railroad in 1965. World War I veteran. Buried Violet Hill Cemetery, Perry IA.

Phil Tomney—3 Years Infielder (b. 17 Jul 1863 Reading PA–d. 18 Mar 1892 at his home in Reading PA) Died at the height of his baseball career from a lung infection. Buried Aulenbach's Cemetery, Mount Penn PA.

Chuck Tompkins—1 Year Pitcher (b. 1 Sep 1889 Prescott AR–d. 20 Sep 1975 Prescott AR) He was an attorney. Buried DeAnn Cemetery, DeAnn AR.

Fred Toney—12 Years Pitcher (b. 11 Dec 1888 Nashville TN–d. 11 Mar 1953 at his home in Nashville TN) In a minor league game he struck out 19 batters while pitching a 17 inning no-hit game. For the Cincinnati Reds he once pitched both games of a double header, giving up three hits in each game. In 1917 he pitched a 10 inning no-hit game in which neither team got a hit in the first nine innings. After baseball he was a court officer in Davidson County, TN. Died from a heart attack. Buried Spring Hill Cemetery, Nashville TN.

Doc Tonkin—1 Year Pitcher (b. 11 Aug 1881 Concord NH–d. 30 May 1959 Miami FL).

Tony Tonneman—1 Year Catcher (b. 10 Sep 1881 Chicago IL–d. 4 Aug 1951 Pioneer's Home in Prescott AZ) He moved to Jerome AZ in 1914, and was an accountant there until his retirement in 1949. Buried Greenwood Memory Lawn, Phoenix AZ.

Steve Toole—4 Years Pitcher (b. 9 Apr 1859 New Orleans LA–d. 28 Mar 1919 at his home in Pittsburgh PA) Active in Pittsburgh politics, he was elected to two terms as county commissioner. Died following a stroke of apoplexy suffered four months earlier.

Bert Tooley—2 Years Infielder (b. 30 Aug 1886 Howell MI–d. 17 Aug 1976 Provincial House, Marshall MI) For many years he was a machinist for the Carbon Coated Paper Company in Sturgis MI. Buried Mount Ever-Rest Cemetery, Kalamazoo MI.

Specs Toporcer—8 Years Infielder (b. 9 Feb 1899 New York City NY–d. 17 May 1989 Huntington Hospital, Huntington Station NY) The first major league infielder to wear glasses, he had been blind since 1951. He managed minor league baseball and was the farm director for the Red

Sox until failing eyesight forced him out of baseball. Died after falling down a flight of stairs to his cellar. Buried Melville Cemetery, Melville NY.

Dan Topping—(b. 11 Jun 1912–d. 18 May 1974 Miami Heart Institute, Miami FL) Served in the Pacific for the U.S. Marines during World War II. He was part-owner of the Yankees from 1945 to 1965. Died from long-standing lung disease and adherent complications. Buried Woodlawn Cemetery, Bronx NY.

Earl Torgeson—15 Years Infielder (b. 1 Jan 1924 Snohomish WA–d. 8 Nov 1990 at his home in Everett WA) Served in the U.S. Army during World War II. He managed minor league baseball. Active in civic affairs, he was director of Snohomish County (WA) Department of Emergency Management eight years, a county commissioner four years and served on many other county, city and state boards. Cremated. Buried Grand Army of the Republic Cemetery, Snohomish WA.

Red Torkelson—1 Year Pitcher (b. 19 Mar 1894 Chicago IL–d. 22 Sep 1964 Chicago IL) Buried Mount Olive Cemetery, Chicago IL.

Red Torphy—1 Year Infielder (b. 6 Nov 1891 Fall River MA–d. 11 Feb 1980 Fall River MA) He was a mechanic for the Eastern Massachusetts Street Railway Company, retiring in 1964. Died after a brief illness. Buried St Patrick's Cemetery, Fall River MA.

Gil Torres—4 Years Infielder (b. 23 Aug 1915 Regla, Cuba–d. 10 Jan 1983 Regla, Cuba).

Ricardo Torres—3 Years Catcher (b. 16 Apr 1891 Regla, Cuba–d. 17 Apr 1960 Regla, Cuba).

Lou Tost—3 Years Pitcher (b. 1 Jul 1911 Cumberland WA–d. 21 Feb 1967 at a rest home in Santa Clara CA) Served in the U.S. Navy during World War II. He was a machinist at Westinghouse Electric Corporation for 16 years. Died from lung cancer. Buried Golden Gate National Cemetery, San Bruno CA.

Paul Toth—3 Years Pitcher (b. 30 Jun 1935 McRoberts KY–d. 24 Mar 1999 Erie MI).

Clay Touchstone—3 Years Pitcher (b. 24 Jan 1903 Moore PA–d. 28 Apr 1949 at his home in Beaumont TX) He managed minor league baseball for a short while before owning and operating the Service Amusement Club in Beaumont. Died unexpectedly. Buried Forest Lawn Memorial Park, Beaumont TX.

Cesar Tovar—12 Years Outfielder (b. 3 Jul 1940 Caracas, Venezuela–d. 14 Jul 1994 Caracas, Venezuela) Died from pancreatic cancer.

Babe Towne—1 Year Catcher (b. 12 Mar 1880 Coon Rapids IA–d. 29 Oct 1938 Coon Rapids IA) Died from a heart attack while sitting in his car in the business district. Buried Riverside Cemetery, Spencer IA.

George Townsend—4 Years Catcher (b. 4 Jun 1867 Hartsdale NY–d. 15 Mar 1930 New Haven CT) He was a physician in Brandford CT. Buried Alderbrook Cemetery, Guilford CT.

Ira Townsend—2 Years Pitcher (b. 9 Jan 1894 Weimar TX–d. 21 Jul 1965 Von Minden Hotel, Schulenburg TX) World War I veteran. Died from a heart attack. Buried Masonic Cemetery, Weimar TX.

Jack Townsend—6 Years Pitcher (b. 9 Apr 1879 Townsend DE–d. 21 Dec 1963 Delaware Hospital, Wilmington DE) He worked 15 years for the Department of Public Safety before retiring in 1953. Died from a heart condition. Buried Townsend Cemetery, Townsend DE.

Leo Townsend—2 Years Pitcher (b. 15 Jan 1891 Mobile AL–d. 3 Dec 1976 at a hospital in Mobile AL) Buried Catholic Cemetery, Mobile AL.

Jim Toy—2 Years Infielder (b. 20 Feb 1858 Beaver Falls PA–d. 13 Mar 1919 Cresson Sanitorium, Cresson PA).

Bill Tozer—1 Year Pitcher (b. 3 Jul 1882 St Louis MO–d. 23 Feb 1955 Campbell Sanitarium, Belmont CA) He was a retired employee of the U.S. Mint in San Francisco CA. Died from a heart attack. Cremated. Buried Cypress Lawn Memorial Park, Colma CA.

Bill Traffley—5 Years Catcher (b. 21 Dec 1859 Staten Island NY–d. 23 Jun 1908 Des Moines IA) Died from tuberculosis. Buried Woodland Cemetery, Des Moines IA.

John Traffley—1 Year Outfielder (b. 1862 Chicago IL–d. 13 Jul 1900 Baltimore MD) Died from a brain injury. Buried Mount Olivet Cemetery, Baltimore MD.

Walt Tragesser—7 Years Catcher (b. 14 Jun 1887 Lafayette IN–d. 14 Dec 1970 St Elizabeth Hospital, Lafayette IN) Served in the U.S. Navy during World War I. He was superintendent of the service department of Indiana Gas Company from 1924 until he retired in 1953. Buried St Boniface Cemetery, Lafayette IN.

Red Tramback—1 Year Outfielder (b. 1 Nov 1915 Iselin PA–d. 28 Dec 1979 Buffalo NY).

Fred Trautman—1 Year Pitcher (b. 24 Mar 1892 Bucyrus OH–d. 15 Feb 1964 Community Hospital, Bucyrus OH) He owned and operated a tire and battery shop in Bucyrus before becoming manager of the Crawford County (OH) Automobile Club. He was also deputy registrar of automobiles for 30 years. Died from a heart attack. Buried Oakwood Cemetery, Bucyrus OH.

George Trautman—(b. 1890 Bucyrus OH–d. 24 Jun 1963 Columbus OH) He was the president of the National Association of Professional Baseball Leagues (minor leagues) from 1947 to 1963. Died from cancer. Cremated.

Allan Travers—1 Year Pitcher (b. 7 May 1892 Philadelphia PA–d. 21 Apr 1968 Misericordia Hospital, Philadelphia PA) A catholic priest, in 1912 he volunteered his St Joseph College team to play the Athletics when the Tigers walked off the field to protest a Ty Cobb suspension. He pitched, giving up 24 runs, 10 unearned. He taught eight years at St Francis Xavier High School in New York, was Dean of Men at St Joseph's College from 1934 to 1943, and taught Spanish and religion at St Joseph's Prep School from 1943 until his death. Buried Jesuit Novitiate Cemetery, Wernersville PA.

Jim Tray—1 Year Catcher (b. 14 Feb 1860 Jackson MI–d. 28 Jul 1905 Jackson MI) Found dead in his room from heart trouble. Buried St John's Cemetery, Jackson MI.

Pie Traynor—17 Years Infielder 6 Years Manager Hall of Fame (b. 11 Nov 1899 Framingham MA–d. 16 Mar 1972 Shadyside Hospital, Pittsburgh PA) He was a local sports broadcaster in Pittsburgh and was a familiar figure on television commercials. Died after a three-year battle with a number of illnesses. Buried Homewood Cemetery, Pittsburgh PA.

George Treadway—4 Years Outfielder (b. 11 Nov 1866 Greenup County KY–d. 5 Nov 1928 County Hospital, Riverside CA) He was a prospector. Died from nephritis. Buried Evergreen Memorial Park, Riverside CA.

Ray Treadway—1 Year Infielder (b. 31 Oct 1907 Ragland AL–d. 12 Oct 1935 Newell Sanitarium, Chattanooga TN) Died at the height of his baseball career from complications following the amputation of his left leg. He was shot in the leg during a barroom brawl in Jul 1935, and that resulted in the amputation that caused his death. Buried Birmingham AL.

Red Treadway—2 Years Outfielder (b. 28 Apr 1920 Athlone NC–d. 26 May 1994 Atlanta GA) Buried Arlington Memorial Park, Sandy Springs GA.

Frank Trechock—1 Year Infielder (b. 24 Dec 1915 Windber PA–d. 16 Jan 1989 at his home in Minneapolis MN) Served in the South Pacific for the U.S. Army during World War II. Died from leukemia. Buried Fort Snelling National Cemetery, Minneapolis MN.

Harry Trekell—1 Year Pitcher (b. 18 Nov 1892 Buda IL–d. 4 Nov 1965 V A Hospital, Spokane WA) Served in the U.S. Marine Corps during World War I. He was a representative of Sun Life Assurance of Canada for 30 years. Buried Forest Cemetery, Coeur d'Alene ID.

Overton Tremper—2 Years Outfielder (b. 22 Mar 1906 Brooklyn NY–d. 9 Jan 1996 Carrington Place Nursing Home, Largo FL) He was a high school math teacher on Long Island, NY, Retiring to Florida in 1977. Cremated.

Ted Trent—13 Years Pitcher (b. 17 Dec 1903 Jacksonville FL–d. 10 Jan 1944 Chicago IL) He played in the negro leagues.

Mike Tresh—12 Years Catcher (b. 23 Feb 1914 Hazleton PA–d. 4 Oct 1966 Detroit MI) Died from cancer. Buried Michigan Memorial Park Cemetery, Flat Rock MI.

Bob Trice—3 Years Pitcher (b. 28 Aug 1926 Newton GA–d. 16 Sep 1988 Weirton Medical Center, Weirton WV) Served in the U.S. Navy during World War II. He retired from the Weirton Steel Corporation where he worked in the Strip Steel Department's 54 inch skin mill. Buried St Paul Catholic Church Cemetery, Weirton WV.

Ken Trinkle—5 Years Pitcher (b. 15 Dec 1919 Paoli IN–d. 10 May 1976 Paoli IN) Served in the U.S. Army during World War II. He owned a package store near Paoli Square in Paoli. He had a heart attack at the store and was dead-on-arrival at Orange County Hospital. Buried Stamper's Creek Cemetery, Paoli IN.

Coaker Triplett—6 Years Outfielder (b. 18 Dec 1911 Boone NC–d. 30 Jan 1992 Boone NC).

Hal Trosky—11 Years Infielder (b. 11 Nov 1912 Norway IA–d. 18 Jun 1979 Mercy Hospital, Cedar Rapids IA) He worked for 25 years in farm real estate sales and was a member of the Iowa Sports Hall of Fame. Died after a sudden illness. Buried St Michael's Cemetery, Norway IA.

Mike Trost—2 Years Catcher (b. 1866 Philadelphia PA–d. 24 Mar 1901 Philadelphia PA).

Sam Trott—8 Years Catcher 1 Year Manager (b. 1858 Washington DC–d. 5 Jun 1925 at his home in Catonsville MD) He was in the cigar manufacturing business. Died after being in ill health several months. Buried Loudon Park National Cemetery, Baltimore MD.

Bill Trotter—7 Years Pitcher (b. 10 Aug 1908 Cisne IL–d. 26 Aug 1984 St Mary's Hospital, Evansville IN) He worked for the Caterpiller Tractor Company in Peoria IL. Buried Maple Hill Cemetery, Fairfield IL.

Quincy Trouppe—1 Year Catcher (b. 25 Dec 1912 Dublin GA–d. 12 Aug 1993 St John's Mercy Hospital, Creve Coeur MO) He played and managed in the negro leagues. The first black scout for the Cardinals, he scouted for them during the 1950s and 1960s.

Dizzy Trout—15 Years Pitcher (b. 29 Jun 1915 Sandcut IN–d. 28 Feb 1972 Ingall's Hospital, Harvey IL) He was a pitching instructor for the White Sox and later joined the team's public relations staff. Died from cancer of the stomach. Buried Homewood Memorial Gardens, Homewood IL.

Bob Trowbridge—5 Years Pitcher (b. 27 Jun 1930 Hudson NY–d. 3 Apr 1980 Hudson NY) Died from a heart attack.

Bun Troy—1 Year Pitcher (b. 22 Aug 1888 Germany–d. 7 Oct 1918 Meuse, France) He was a World War I casualty.

Dasher Troy—5 Years Infielder (b. 8 May 1856 New York City NY–d. 30 Mar 1938 at his home in Ozone Park NY) He managed minor league baseball until 1890 when he went into the cafe business. Later he opened a saloon in Manhattan, retiring several years before prohibition. Died after being ill three months. Buried Calvary Cemetery, Woodside NY.

Fred Truax—1 Year Outfielder (b. 1868–d. 18 Dec 1899 Omaha NE).

Harry Truby—2 Years Infielder (b. 12 May 1870 Ironton OH–d. 21 Mar 1953 at his home in Ironton OH) He managed minor league baseball and umpired in the National League in 1909. Died after a brief illness. Buried Woodland Cemetery, Ironton OH.

Frank Truesdale—4 Years Infielder (b. 31 Mar 1884 St Louis MO–d. 27 Aug 1943 Albuquerque NM) He moved to Albuquerque shortly before his death. Buried Sunset Memorial Park, Albuquerque NM.

Ollie Tucker—2 Years Outfielder (b. 27 Jan 1902 Radiant VA–d. 13 Jul 1940 at his home in Radiant VA) He operated a general merchandise store at Burndt Tree VA from 1935 until his death. Died following surgery for removal of a brain tumor. Buried Tucker Family Cemetery, Radiant VA.

Thurman Tucker—9 Years Outfielder (b. 26 Sep 1917 Gordon TX–d. 7 May 1993 Oklahoma City OK) Served in the U.S. Navy during World War II. He was an insurance agent for Phoenix Mutual Life Insurance Co. Buried Gordon Cemetery, Gordon TX.

Tommy Tucker—13 Years Infielder (b. 28 Oct 1865 Holyoke MA–d. 22 Oct 1935 Farren Memorial Hospital, Montague MA) Died after being confined to the hospital six months. Buried Calvary Cemetery, Holyoke MA.

Tom Tuckey—2 Years Pitcher (b. 7 Oct 1883 CT–d. 17 Oct 1950 New York City NY).

Oscar Tuero—3 Years Pitcher (b. 17 Dec 1892 Havana, Cuba–d. 21 Oct 1960 Houston TX).

George Turbeville—3 Years Pitcher (b. 24 Aug 1914 Turbeville SC–d. 5 Oct 1983 Salisbury NC) Served in the U.S. Army Air Corps during World War II. Buried Greenlawn Memorial Park, Columbia SC.

Jerry Turbidy—1 Year Infielder (b. 4 Jul 1852 Dudley MA–d. 5 Sep 1920 Webster MA) He retired from his liquor business in Webster after 25 years. Died following a long illness. Buried Calvary Cemetery, Dudley MA.

Eddie Turchin—1 Year Infielder (b. 10 Feb 1917 New York City NY–d. 8 Feb 1982 Brookhaven NY).

Pete Turgeon—1 Year Infielder (b. 3 Jan 1897 Minneapolis MN–d. 23 Jan 1977 at his home in Wichita Falls TX) World War I veteran. He was a retired package store owner, having owned two liquor stores in Wichita Falls. Buried Crestview Memorial Park, Wichita Falls TX.

Lucas Turk—1 Year Pitcher (b. 2 May 1898 Homer GA–d. 11 Jan 1994 at his home in Homer GA) He practiced industrial medicine in Atlanta GA from 1927 until he retired to his hometown in 1963. There he continued to practice medicine until he was in his 80s, while also operating a poultry and cattle farm that had been in his family four generations. Died in his sleep in the same house where he was born. Buried Presbyterian Church Cemetery, Homer GA.

Hy Turkin—(b. 9 Jul 1915 New York City NY–d. 24 Jun 1955 New York City NY) A sportswriter for the *New York Daily News* for 19 years and author, he was co-editor of the first *Official Baseball Encyclopedia*. Suffered from muscular dystropy.

Jim Turner—9 Years Pitcher (b. 6 Aug 1903 Antioch TN–d. 29 Nov 1998 Nashville TN) He coached for a number of teams until retiring in 1973. He played, managed or coached baseball 51 straight years. Died after a long illness. Buried Woodlawn Memorial Park, Nashville TN.

Ted Turner—1 Year Pitcher (b. 4 May 1892 Laurenceburg KY–d. 4 Feb 1958 Good Samaritan Hospital, Lexington KY) Died after a brief illness. Buried Lexington Cemetery, Lexington KY.

Terry Turner—17 Years Infielder (b. 28 Feb 1881 Sandy Lake PA–d. 18 Jul 1960 Mount Sinai Hospital, Cleveland OH) Died five days after suffering a stroke. Buried Knollwood Cemetery, Mayfield OH.

Tink Turner—1 Year Pitcher (b. 20 Feb 1890 Swarthmore PA–d. 25 Feb 1962 Philadelphia PA) Died suddenly. Buried West Laurel Hill Cemetery, Bala Cynwyd PA.

Tom Turner—5 Years Catcher (b. 8 Sep 1916 Custer County OK–d. 14 May 1986 at his home in Kennewick WA) He was a construction inspector at Phoenix AZ before moving to Kennewick in 1984. Died from cancer. Cremated.

Tuck Turner—6 Years Outfielder (b. 13 Feb 1873 Brighton NY–d. 17 Jul 1945 Staten Island NY) Died from a heart ailment.

Bill Tuttle—11 Years Outfielder (b. 4 Jul 1929 Elwood IL–d. 27 Jul 1998 Anoka MN) He spent the last four years of his life campaigning against the dangers of smokeless tobacco for the National Spit Tobacco Education Program. Died of complications from oral cancer. Cremated.

Elmer Tutwiler—1 Year Pitcher (b. 19 Nov 1905 Carbon Hill AL–d. 3 May 1976 Pensacola FL).

Guy Tutwiler—2 Years Infielder (b. 17 Jul 1889 Coalburg AL–d. 15 Aug 1930 Birmingham AL) Died in a train accident. Buried Elmwood Cemetery, Birmingham AL.

Twink Twining—1 Year Pitcher (b. 30 May 1894 Lansdale PA–d. 14 Jun 1973 at his home in Lansdale PA) He was a retired Philadelphia dermatologist and one-time president of the Philadelphia Dermatology Association. Died after a long illness. Buried Forest Hills Cemetery, Philadelphia PA.

Larry Twitchell—9 Years Outfielder (b. 18 Feb 1864 Cleveland OH–d. 23 Apr 1930 Cleveland OH) He was an inspector. Died from heart disease. Buried Lakewood Park Cemetery, Cleveland OH.

Babe Twombly—2 Years Outfielder (b. 18 Jan 1896 Jamaica Plain MA–d. 23 Nov 1974 San Clemente CA) He was a sales engineer for the Torrance Brass Foundry. Died from emphysema and respiratory failure. Buried Oakdale Memorial Park, Glendora CA.

Cy Twombly—1 Year Pitcher (b. 15 Jun 1897 Groveland MA–d. 3 Dec 1974 Memorial Medical Center, Savannah GA) He was swimming and golf coach at Washington and Lee University from 1921 to 1973, and athletic director from 1954 to 1969. Died from a heart attack while visiting friends at Savannah. Buried Stonewall Jackson Cemetery, Lexington VA.

George Twombly—5 Years Outfielder (b. 4 Jun 1892 Boston MA–d. 17 Feb 1975 Lexington MA).

Jim Tyack—1 Year Outfielder (b. 9 Jan 1911 Florence MT–d. 3 Jan 1995 Bakersfield CA) He owned and operated a retail tire store for 20 years. Died from cardiovascular heart disease. Buried Hillcrest Memorial Park, Bakersfield CA.

Fred Tyler—1 Year Catcher (b. 16 Dec 1891 Derry NH–d. 14 Oct 1945 Alexander-Eastman

Hospital, East Derry NH) World War I veteran. Buried Forest Hill Cemetery, Derry NH.

Johnnie Tyler—2 Years Outfielder (b. 30 Jul 1906 Mount Pleasant PA–d. 11 Jul 1972 Mount Pleasant PA) Served in the U.S. Army during World War II. Buried Transfiguration Cemetery, Mount Pleasant PA.

Lefty Tyler—12 Years Pitcher (b. 14 Dec 1889 Derry NH–d. 29 Sep 1953 at his home in Lowell MA) Died unexpectedly. Buried St Patrick's Cemetery, Lowell MA.

Jim Tyng—2 Years Pitcher (b. 27 Mar 1856 Philadelphia PA–d. 30 Oct 1931 Roosevelt Hospital, New York City NY) A prominent golfer in the pioneer days of golf, he was an attorney for several years before entering the insurance business where he worked for 30 years. Died from pneumonia. Cremated. Buried Fresh Pond NY.

Earl Tyree—1 Year Catcher (b. 4 Mar 1890 Huntsville IL–d. 17 May 1954 Culbertson Memorial Hospital, Rushville IL) He worked briefly in a men's clothing store at Rushville before spending 30 years in the monument business. Buried Rushville Cemetery, Rushville IL.

Dave Tyriver—1 Year Pitcher (b. 31 Oct 1937 Oshkosh WI–d. 28 Oct 1988 at his home in Oshkosh WI) He was the manager of a clothing store. Died from a heart attack. Buried Peace Lutheran Cemetery, Oshkosh WI.

Ty Tyson—3 Years Outfielder (b. 1 Jun 1892 Wilkes-Barre PA–d. 16 Aug 1953 while walking near his home in Buffalo NY) He worked more than 20 years for duPont deNemours Co, Inc. Died from a heart attack.

U

Jimmy Uchrinscko—1 Year Pitcher (b. 20 Oct 1900 West Newton PA–d. 17 Mar 1995 Harmon House, Mount Pleasant PA) He was a retired coal miner from Mathies Mine. Buried West Newton Cemetery, West Newton PA.

Bob Uhl—2 Years Pitcher (b. 17 Sep 1913 San Francisco CA–d. 21 Aug 1990 Memorial Hospital, Santa Rosa CA) Served in World War II. He was a truck driver for 30 years. Died from cerebral vascular heart disease. Buried Cypress Hill Memorial Park, Petaluma CA.

George Uhle—17 Years Pitcher (b. 18 Sep 1898 Cleveland OH–d. 26 Feb 1985 Lakewood Hospital, Lakewood OH) He was one of the few players who never played in the minor leagues. He was a manufacturer's representative for Arrow Aluminum Company. Died from emphysema after suffering from it for about 20 years. Buried Lakewood Park Cemetery, Cleveland OH.

Maury Uhler—1 Year Outfielder (b. 14 Dec 1886 Pikesville MD–d. 4 May 1918 Baltimore MD) Died after a lingering illness. Buried Druid Ridge Cemetery, Pikesville MD.

Charlie Uhlir—1 Year Outfielder (b. 30 Jul 1912 Chicago IL–d. 9 Jul 1984 at his home in Spirit Lake IA) He was a reporter for the Chicago Tribune and later became superintendent of the pork plant at Estherville IA. Buried Lakeview Cemetery, Spirit Lake IA.

Dutch Ulrich—3 Years Pitcher (b. 18 Nov 1899 Baltimore MD–d. 12 Feb 1929 Baltimore MD) Died from pneumonia at the height of a promising baseball career. Buried Oak Hill Cemetery.

Jim Umbricht—5 Years Pitcher (b. 17 Sep 1930 Chicago IL–d. 8 Apr 1964 M D Anderson Hospital, Houston TX) Died at the height of his baseball career from cancer that originated in his groin. He was cremated and his ashes scattered in the Astrodome.

Frank Umont—(b. abt 1917–d. 20 Jun 1991 Fort Lauderdale FL). He umpired in the American League from 1954 to 1973 and was famous for wearing glasses during the latter years of his career as an umpire.

Willie Underhill—2 Years Pitcher (b. 6 Sep 1904 Bay City TX–d. 26 Oct 1970 Matagorda General Hospital, Bay City TX) He was a retired oil worker. Died from acute respiratory failure. Buried Roselawn Memorial Cemetery, Van Vleck TX.

Fred Underwood—1 Year Pitcher (b. 14 Oct 1868 Kansas City MO–d. 26 Jan 1906 at his home in Kansas City MO) He owned a saloon in Kansas City. Died from pneumonia. Buried Mount St Mary's Cemetery, Kansas City MO.

Bob Unglaub—6 Years Infielder 1 Year Manager (b. 31 Jul 1881 Baltimore MD–d. 29 Nov 1916 Baltimore MD) Died from injuries received when he was struck by a train in the Orangeville yards of the Pennsylvania Railroad. Buried Loudon Park National Cemetery, Baltimore MD.

Al Unser—4 Years Catcher (b. 12 Oct 1912 Morrisonville IL–d. 7 Jul 1995 Decatur IL) He managed minor league baseball for the Braves and Indians. For 32 years he coached St Thomas Grade School basketball teams and officiated high school baseball and basketball teams in the Decatur area. He also farmed and raised livestock. Died from natural causes. Buried Calvary Cemetery, Decatur IL.

Woody Upchurch—2 Years Pitcher (b. 13 Apr 1911 Buies Creek NC–d. 23 Oct 1971 Buies Creek NC) He farmed in the Buies Creek area. Buried Buies Creek Cemetery, Buies Creek NC.

Bill Upham—2 Years Pitcher (b. 4 Apr 1888 Akron OH–d. 14 Sep 1959 Martland Medical Center, Newark NJ) He was a checker at the General Motor's plant in Bloomfield NJ, retiring in 1952. Died from a stroke.

Jerry Upp—1 Year Pitcher (b. 10 Dec 1883 Sandusky OH–d. 30 Jun 1937 Providence Hospital, Sandusky OH) He was a watchman at the city park. Died from a heart attack. Buried Oakland Cemetery, Sandusky OH.

Dixie Upright—9 Games Pinch Hitter (b. 30 May 1926 Kannapolis NC–d. 13 Nov 1986 Concord NC) He was a furniture salesman. Died from cancer. Buried Greenlawn Cemetery, China Grove NC.

Cecil Upshaw—9 Years Pitcher (b. 22 Oct 1942 Spearsville LA–d. 7 Feb 1995 Lawrenceville GA) Died after a heart attack. Buried Eternal Hills Memory Gardens, Snellville GA.

Bill Upton—1 Year Pitcher (b. 18 Jun 1929 Esther MO–d. 2 Jan 1987 Kaiser Foundation Hospital, San Diego CA) He was a self-employed drywall contractor for 15 years. Died from relapse of the cardio valves. Cremated.

Luke Urban—2 Years Catcher (b. 22 Mar 1898 Fall River MA–d. 7 Dec 1980 Somerset MA) He also played professional football and basketball. He coached at Canisius College ten years and from 1940 to 1960 coached baseball, basketball and football at Durfee High School in Fall River. He retired as athletic director at the high school in 1967. Buried Notre Dame Cemetery, Fall River MA.

Billy Urbanski—7 Years Infielder (b. 5 Jun 1903 Staten Island NY–d. 12 Jul 1973 General Hospital, Perth Amboy NJ) He owned the Shortstop Cafe in Perth Amboy from 1941 until retiring in 1966. Died from a heart attack. Buried Holy Trinity Church Cemetery, Perth Amboy NJ.

Lou Ury—1 Year Infielder (b. abt 1874 Fort Scott KS–d. 4 Mar 1918 at his home in Kansas City MO) He managed in the minor leagues and was responsible for discovering Rogers Hornsby. He worked in the mail department at Union Station in Kansas City. Died from pneumonia. Buried Evergreen Cemetery, Fort Scott KS.

Dutch Ussat—2 Years Infielder (b. 11 Apr 1904 Dayton OH–d. 29 May 1959 Dayton OH) He was a circulation distributor for the *Dayton Journal Herald* newspaper while also involved in youth baseball programs. Died from a heart attack while delivering newspapers. Buried Memorial Park Cemetery, Dayton OH.

V

Tex Vache—1 Year Outfielder (b. 17 Nov 1889 Santa Monica CA–d. 11 Jun 1953 Los Angeles CA) World War I veteran. He was Chief of Police at Universal Studios in Hollywood. Died from a heart attack. Buried Overton Cemetery, Overton TX.

Gene Vadeboncoeur—1 Year Catcher (b. Syracuse NY–d. 16 Oct 1935 at his daughter's home in Haverhill MA) He farmed and was a shoe worker. Buried St Joseph Cemetery, Haverhill MA.

Harry Vahrenhorst—1 Game Pinch Hitter (b. 13 Feb 1885 St Louis MO–d. 10 Oct 1943 St Louis MO).Buried Bethlehem Cemetery, Bellefontaine Neighbors MO.

Bob Vail—1 Year Pitcher (b. 24 Sep 1881 Linneus ME–d. 22 Mar 1942 Philadelphia PA) He was a machinist. Buried Chelten Hills Cemetery, Philadelphia PA.

John Valentine—1 Year Pitcher (b. 21 Nov 1855 Brooklyn NY–d. 10 Oct 1903 Central Islip NY).

Elmer Valo—20 Years Outfielder (b. 5 Mar 1921 Ribnik, Czechoslovakia–d. 19 Jul 1998 Palmerton Hospital, Palmerton PA) Served in the U.S. Army Medical Corps during World War II. Scouted for the Phillies from 1970 until he retired in 1982. Died from cardiopulmonary arrest. Buried Sacred Heart New Cemetery, Palmerton PA.

Clay Van Alstyne—2 Years Pitcher (b. 24 May 1900 Stuyvesant NY–d. 5 Jan 1960 Columbia Memorial Hospital, Hudson NY) He was associated with the Connecticut General Life Insurance Company of Hartford CT, and was a retired town clerk of Stuyvesant. Died from a heart condition. Buried Firwood Cemetery, Stuyvesant NY.

Russ Van Atta—7 Years Pitcher (b. 21 Jun 1906 Augusta NJ–d. 10 Oct 1986 Andover Nursing Home, Andover NJ) He was the sheriff of Sussex County, NJ, during the 1940s and owned V and H Oil Company from 1949 until he retired in 1971. Buried Frankford Plains Cemetery, Newton NJ.

Deacon Van Buren—1 Year Outfielder (b. 14 Dec 1870 La Salle County IL–d. 29 Jun 1957 at his home in Portland OR) He did carpenter work and odd-jobs in Portland. Cremated.

Al Van Camp—3 Years Outfielder (b. 7 Sep 1903 Moline IL–d. 2 Feb 1981 Davenport IA) He was president of Al Van Camp Agency, a Davenport insurance firm. Buried Mount Calvary Cemetery, Davenport IA.

Chris Van Cuyk—3 Years Pitcher (b. 13 Jan 1927 Kimberly WI–d. 3 Nov 1992 at his home in Hudson FL) Served in the U.S. Navy during World War II. Cremated. Buried Florida National Cemetery, Bushnell FL.

Ben Van Dyke—2 Years Pitcher (b. 15 Aug 1888 Clintonville PA–d. 22 Oct 1973 at a nursing home in Sarasota FL) Buried Sarasota Memorial Park, Sarasota FL.

Bill Van Dyke—3 Years Outfielder (b. 15 Dec 1863 Paris IL–d. 5 May 1933 City-County Hospital, El Paso TX) In destitute circumstances, he lived at the County Poor Farm and died from a combination of senility, arteriosclerosis and malnutrition. Buried Concordia Cemetery, El Paso TX.

Roy Van Graflan—(b. abt 1894–d. 4 Sep 1953 Rochester NY) An American League umpire from 1927 to 1933, he was behind the plate in the 1932 World Series when Babe Ruth "called his shot" against Charlie Root. He also umpired in the International League and coached girl's basketball and baseball teams. Died from injuries suffered in an automobile accident six weeks earlier in Toronto, Canada. Buried Mount Hope Cemetery, Rochester NY.

George Van Haltren—17 Years Outfielder 2 Years Manager (b. 30 Mar 1866 St Louis MO–d. 29 Sep 1945 at his home in Oakland CA) He was a lather in building construction. Died from a heart attack. Buried St Mary's Cemetery, Oakland CA.

Maurice Van Robays—6 Years Outfielder (b. 15 Nov 1914 Detroit MI–d. 1 Mar 1965 Detroit MI).

Ike Van Zandt—3 Years Outfielder (b. 1877 Brooklyn NY–d. 14 Sep 1908 Nashua NH) Died from a self-inflicted gunshot wound to the heart. Buried NY.

Dick Van Zant—1 Year Infielder (b. Nov 1864 Richmond IN–d. 6 Aug 1912 Richmond IN) He played several years in the Pacific Coast League. Died in the county infirmary where he had been taken after suffering a heart attack a few days earlier. Buried Earlham Cemetery, Richmond IN.

Dazzy Vance—16 Years Pitcher Hall of Fame (b. 4 Mar 1891 Orient IA–d. 18 Feb 1961 at his home in Homosassa Springs FL) He operated a hotel and fishing camp in Homosassa Springs. Died in bed from a heart attack. Buried Stage Stand Cemetery, Homosassa Springs FL.

Joe Vance—3 Years Pitcher (b. 16 Sep 1905 Devine TX–d. 4 Jul 1978 Devine TX) He was a civil service employee at Kelley Field. He played one year of professional football. Buried St Joseph Cemetery, Devine TX.

Carl Vandagrift—1 Year Infielder (b. 22 Apr 1883 Cantrall IL–d. 9 Oct 1920 Fort Wayne IN) He operated a bowling and billiards establishment in Fort Wayne. Died following surgery to remove his appendix. Buried Catholic Cemetery, Fort Wayne IN.

Hy Vandenberg—7 Years Pitcher (b. 17 Mar 1906 Abilene KS–d. 31 Jul 1994 at his home in Bloomington MN) He was a liquor salesman, worked for a sprinkler manufacturer in Minneapolis and was an engineering technician for the Hennepin County (MN) Highway Department, retiring about 1969. Died from cancer. Buried Lakewood Cemetery, Minneapolis MN.

Johnny Vander Meer—13 Years Pitcher (b. 2 Nov 1914 Prospect Park NJ–d. 6 Oct 1997 St Joseph Hospital, Tampa FL) He pitched two consecutive no-hitters in 1938, the second one in the first night game played at Ebbets Field in Brooklyn. Served in the South Pacific for the U.S. Navy during World War II. He managed minor league baseball several years, then became a sales rep for Schlitz Brewing Company, dealing primarily with military bases. Died from an abdominal aneurysm. Buried Myrtle Hill Cemetery, Tampa FL.

Elam Vangilder—11 Years Pitcher (b. 23 Apr 1896 Cape Girardeau MO–d. 30 Apr 1977 St Francis Medical Ctr, Cape Girardeau MO) He played professional baseball for 19 years. World War I veteran. Died following surgery. He had been in failing health his last year. Buried Fairmount Cemetery, Cape Girardeau MO.

John Vann—1 Game Pinch Hitter (b. 7 Jun 1890 Fairland OK–d. 10 Jun 1958 at his home in Shreveport LA) He was a detective for the Shreveport Police Detective Bureau from 1934 to 1953. World War I veteran. Died following a long illness. Buried Forest Park Cemetery, Shreveport LA.

Andy Varga—2 Years Pitcher (b. 11 Dec 1930 Chicago IL–d. 4 Nov 1992 Orlando FL) He was an internal auditor for the Churchill Downs race track. Cremated.

Bill Vargus—2 Years Pitcher (b. 11 Nov 1899 North Scituate MA–d. 12 Feb 1979 Cape Cod Hospital, Hyannis MA) He was an insurance underwriter 35 years for John Hancock Insurance Company in Quincy MA, retiring in 1966. Died after a short illness. Buried Mount Wollaston Cemetery, Quincy MA.

Dike Varney—1 Year Pitcher (b. 9 Aug 1880 Dover NH–d. 23 Apr 1950 Long Island City NY).

Moses Vasbinder—1 Year Pitcher (b. 19 Jul 1880 Scio OH–d. 22 Dec 1950 Cadiz OH) Buried Cadiz Cemetery, Cadiz OH.

Arky Vaughan—14 Years Infielder (b. 9 Mar 1912 Clifty AR–d. 30 Aug 1952 near Eagleville CA) He purchased a ranch near Eagleville CA in 1949. He and a companion drowned in Lost Lake when their boat capsized while fishing. Buried Eagleville Cemetery, Eagleville CA.

Bobby Vaughn—2 Years Infielder (b. 4 Jun 1885 Stamford NY–d. 11 Apr 1965 Seattle WA) He was a retired self-employed civil engineer and building contractor, and had lived in Seattle since 1935. Buried New Tacoma Memorial Park, Tacoma WA.

Clarence Vaughn—1 Year Pitcher (b. 4 Sep 1911 Sedalia MO–d. 1 Mar 1937 Martinsville VA).

Farmer Vaughn—13 Years Catcher (b. 1 Mar 1863 Ruraldale OH–d. 21 Feb 1914 Cincinnati OH) Died from lobar pneumonia. Cremated.

Fred Vaughn—2 Years Infielder (b. 18 Oct 1918 Coalinga CA–d. 2 Mar 1964 Lake Wales FL).

Hippo Vaughn—13 Years Pitcher (b. 9 Apr 1888 Weatherford TX–d. 29 May 1966 Chicago IL) The losing pitcher in baseball's only double no-hit game, he played semi-pro baseball in the Chicago area until he was age 47.

Al Veach—1 Year Pitcher (b. 6 Aug 1909 Maylene AL–d. 6 Sep 1990 Charlotte NC) He was a conductor for the Southern Railway out of Selma AL. Buried Live Oak Cemetery, Selma AL.

Bobby Veach—14 Years Outfielder (b. 29 Jun 1888 St Charles KY–d. 7 Aug 1945 at his home in Detroit MI) He went into business in Detroit. Died following a long illness. Buried White Chapel Memorial Cemetery, Southfield MI.

Peek-A-Boo Veach—3 Years Infielder (b. 15 Jun 1863 Indianapolis IN–d. 12 Nov 1937 Veterans Hospital, Indianapolis IN) Spanish-American War veteran. Died from pneumonia. Buried Floral Park Cemetery, Indianapolis IN.

Lou Vedder—1 Year Pitcher (b. 20 Apr 1897 Oakville MI–d. 9 Mar 1990 Lake Placid Medical Center, Lake Placid FL) He was a labor relations director for Fisher Body before retiring to Florida. Cremated.

Bill Veeck—Hall of Fame (b. 9 Feb 1914 Hinsdale IL–d. 2 Jan 1986 Chicago IL) At different times he owned three major league teams, the Indians, St Louis Browns and White Sox (twice). He was known as the "Barnum of Baseball" because of his flair and abilities as a showman. A World War II vet, he had his right leg amputated below the knee in 1946 as a result of injuries suffered on Bougainville during the war. He subsequently had 32 other surgeries on the leg. Died from a heart attack. Cremated.

Bucky Veil—2 Years Pitcher (b. 2 Aug 1881 Tyrone PA–d. 16 Apr 1931 Mercy Hospital, Altoona PA) He was a clerk for the Pennsylvania Railroad from 1910 to 1921, and the Justice of Peace of Cresson PA from 1925 until his death. Died from a heart attack. Buried Wildwood Cemetery, Williamsport PA.

Art Veltman—6 Years Catcher (b. 24 Mar 1906 Mobile AL–d. 1 Oct 1980 San Antonio TX) He was active in San Antonio amateur baseball, and in youth groups in general. Buried Sunset Memorial Park, San Antonio TX.

Emil Verban—7 Years Infielder (b. 27 Aug 1915 Lincoln IL–d. 8 Jun 1989 Blessing Hospital, Quincy IL) He worked in the construction business in Lincoln for a while before opening a real estate office, specializing in commercial and farm properties. Buried St Mary's Cemetery, Lincoln IL.

Al Verdel—1 Year Pitcher (b. 10 Jun 1921 Punxsutawney PA–d. 16 Apr 1991 Sarasota FL) Served in the U.S. Army during World War II. He was a high school teacher and football coach, retiring to Florida in 1985. Cremated. Buried St Mary's Cemetery, Hamilton NJ.

Tommy Vereker—1 Year Pitcher (b. 15 Dec 1893 Baltimore MD–d. 2 Apr 1974 Baltimore MD) Served in France for the U.S. Army during World War I. He was a bookkeeper for Baltimore Gas and Electric and for the Davidson Chemical Division of W R Grace and Co, retiring about 1959. Died suddenly after an illness of several months. Buried St John's Catholic Church Cemetery, Hydes MD.

Johnny Vergez—6 Years Infielder (b. 9 Jul 1906 Oakland CA–d. 15 Jul 1991 U C Davis Medical Center, Sacramento CA) He coached baseball at St Mary's College in Moraga CA from 1946 to 1950. He was then a wholesale liquor salesman in the Bay Area until he retired in 1973. Died following surgery a month earlier for an aneurysm. Cremated.

Joe Vernon—2 Years Pitcher (b. 25 Nov 1889 Mansfield MA–d. 13 Mar 1955 Philadelphia PA) He was the Philadelphia representative for Soft Lite Lens Company of New York. Died from a heart attack. Buried Milltown Rural Cemetery, Brewster NY.

Zoilo Versalles—12 Years Infielder (b. 18 Dec 1939 Vedado, Cuba–d. 9 Jun 1995 at his home in Bloomington MN) After baseball he could not hold a job, partly because he had never learned English. He held a number of menial jobs, but eventually lost his home in foreclosure and had to sell his MVP trophy, his all-star rings and his gold glove award in order to eat. Cremated.

Bob Veselic—2 Years Pitcher (b. 27 Sep 1955 Pittsburgh PA–d. 26 Dec 1995 Kaiser Hospital, Fontana CA) He was a pitching coach at Cal Poly in Pomona CA and a warehouseman for Ralph's Grocery Store. Died from melanoma. Buried Crestlawn Memorial Park, Riverside CA.

Lee Viau—5 Years Pitcher (b. 5 Jul 1868 Hanover NH–d. 17 Dec 1947 Wayne NJ).

Ernie Vick—4 Years Catcher (b. 2 Jul 1900 Toledo OH–d. 16 Jul 1980 University of Michigan Hosp, Ann Arbor MI) He was an All-American football player at the Univ of Michigan and was associated with University of Michigan athletics for more than six decades and a Big Ten official 21 years. Died following a stroke. Buried Washtenong Memorial Park, Ann Arbor MI.

Sammy Vick—5 Years Outfielder (b. 12 Apr 1895 Batesville MS–d. 17 Aug 1986 Baptist Hospital, Memphis TN) World War I veteran. He played several years in the Southern League. After baseball he retired to his 820 acre farm near Pope MS where he raised peaches and cattle. He was a member of the Mississippi Sports Hall of Fame. Buried Forrest Memorial Park, Batesville MS.

Rube Vickers—5 Years Pitcher (b. 17 May 1879 Pittsford MI–d. 9 Dec 1958 Sumpter Convalescent Home, Wayne MI) Buried Leonardson Memorial Cemetery, Pittsford MI.

Tom Vickery—4 Years Pitcher (b. 5 May 1867 Milford MA–d. 18 Mar 1921 Burlington County Hospital, Mount Holly NJ) Died from chronic nephritis. Buried Odd Fellows Cemetery, Burlington NJ.

George Vico—2 Years Infielder (b. 9 Aug 1923 San Fernando CA–d. 13 Jan 1994 Torrance CA) Buried United Serbian Cemetery, East Los Angeles CA.

Bob Vines—2 Years Pitcher (b. 25 Feb 1897 Waxahachie TX–d. 18 Oct 1982 Orlando FL) Buried Evergreen Cemetery.

Rube Vinson—3 Years Outfielder (b. 20 Mar 1879 Dover DE–d. 12 Oct 1951 Chester Hospital, Chester PA) He was a toolmaker until retiring in 1941. Died from injuries received at home when he fell from a second story window he was washing. Buried Lawn Croft Cemetery, Linwood PA.

Bill Vinton—2 Years Pitcher (b. 27 Apr 1865 Winthrop MA–d. 3 Sep 1893 at his father's home in Pawtucket RI) He was studying law at Lynn MA when he died after suffering from dysentery for some weeks.

Jim Viox—5 Years Infielder (b. 30 Dec 1890 Lockland OH–d. 6 Jan 1969 at his home in Erlanger KY) He was a parts assembler for General Motors Corp. Buried Forest Lawn Memorial Park, Erlanger KY.

Jake Virtue—5 Years Infielder (b. 2 Mar 1865 Philadelphia PA–d. 3 Feb 1943 at his son's home in Camden NJ) He suffered a stroke shortly after his baseball career was ended by an injury in 1895. Died following a two-week illness. Buried Mount Vernon Cemetery, Philadelphia PA.

Joe Vitelli—2 Years Pitcher (b. 12 Apr 1908 McKees Rocks PA–d. 7 Feb 1967 Veteran's Hospital, Pittsburgh PA) He worked for Allegheny County, PA, for years, serving as head of its baseball clinics. Buried St Mary's Cemetery, McKees Rocks PA.

Ossie Vitt—10 Years Infielder 3 Years Manager (b. 4 Jan 1890 San Francisco CA–d. 31 Jan 1963 Merritt Hospital, Oakland CA) He managed minor league baseball until his retirement in 1943. Died from complications of a stroke suffered earlier in the month. Buried Mountain View Cemetery, Oakland CA.

Otto Vogel—2 Years Outfielder (b. 26 Oct 1899 Mendota IL–d. 19 Jul 1969 University Hospital, Iowa City IA) Served in the U.S. Navy during World War II. He was the head baseball coach at the University of Iowa for 38 years. Died after a lengthy illness. Buried Memory Gardens Cemetery, Iowa City IA.

Ollie Voigt—1 Year Pitcher (b. 21 Jan 1899 Wheaton IL–d. 7 Apr 1970 Good Samaritan Hospital, Phoenix AZ) Served in the U.S. Army during World War I. He was a sales representative for Spaulding and McGregor Sporting Goods Company, retiring to Scottsdale AZ in 1963. Buried Greenwood Memory Lawn, Phoenix AZ.

Jake Volz—3 Years Pitcher (b. 4 Apr 1878 San Antonio TX–d. 11 Aug 1962 at his home in San Antonio TX) Buried St Joseph's Society Cemetery, San Antonio TX.

Chris Von Der Ahe—4 Years Manager (b. 7 Nov 1851 Hille, Germany–d. 7 Jun 1913 St Louis MO) An early owner of the St Louis Browns, he ran a butcher shop, a grocery store and a saloon when he bought the Browns. Died from cirrhosis of the liver. Buried Bellefontaine Cemetery, St Louis MO.

Hon Von Fricken—1 Year Pitcher (b. 30 May 1870 Brooklyn NY–d. 22 Mar 1947 at his home in Troy NY) Died in his sleep from a coronary occlusion. Buried St Peter's Cemetery, Troy NY.

Fritz Von Kolnitz—3 Years Infielder (b. 20 May 1893 Charleston SC–d. 18 Mar 1948 at his home in Mount Pleasant SC) Served in the U.S. Army during both World War I and II. He was a real estate and insurance executive for a Charleston firm. An amateur naturalist, he wrote several books on Low Country history. Died from a heart attack. Buried Magnolia Cemetery, Charleston SC.

Cy Vorhees—1 Year Pitcher (b. 30 Sep 1874 Lodi OH–d. 8 Feb 1910 State Hospital, Massillon OH) He was a salesman. Died from generalized paralysis and dementia. Buried Woodlawn Cemetery, Wadsworth OH.

Joe Vosmik—13 Years Outfielder (b. 4 Apr 1910 Cleveland OH–d. 27 Jan 1962 University Hospital, Cleveland OH) He managed minor league baseball and was a scout for the Indians before he was a salesman of automobiles and appliances. Died from pneumonia ten days after surgery for lung cancer. Buried Highland Park Cemetery, Cleveland OH.

Alex Voss—1 Year Pitcher (b. 1855 Roswell GA–d. 31 Aug 1906 Cincinnati OH).

Rip Vowinkel—1 Year Pitcher (b. 18 Nov 1884 Oswego NY–d. 13 Jul 1966 Oswego NY) He was, perhaps, the only person to pitch a no-run/no-hit game, bowl a 300 game and hit a hole-in-one. The Oswego County (NY) Coroner and manufacturer of patent medicines, he owned and operated the Chocolate Shop in Oswego for many years. Died unexpectedly shortly after reporting to work at the Oswego County Highway Dept. Buried St Paul's Cemetery, Oswego NY.

Phil Voyles—1 Year Outfielder (b. 12 May 1900 Murphy NC–d. 3 Nov 1972 Marlboro Hospital, Marlboro MA) Served in the U.S. Navy during both World Wars I and II. He was an electrician at the Boston MA Navy Shipyard, retiring in 1964. Buried Lakeview Cemetery, South Weymouth MA.

W

Paul Wachtel—1 Year Pitcher (b. 30 Apr 1888 Myersville MD–d. 15 Dec 1964 at a hospital in San Antonio TX) The winner of 232 games over 13 seasons in the Texas League, he was banned from the major leagues because he threw a spitball. Died following a heart attack. Buried Sunset Memorial Park, San Antonio TX.

Charlie Wacker—1 Year Pitcher (b. 8 Dec 1883 Jeffersonville IN–d. 7 Aug 1948 Wellborn Baptist hospital, Evansville IN) He worked for a number of years at Bosse Field, the baseball park at Evansville. Buried Oak Hill Cemetery, Evansville IN.

Rube Waddell—13 Years Pitcher Hall of Fame (b. 13 Oct 1876 Bradford PA–d. 1 Apr 1914 San Antonio TX) Died at the zenith of his career in a sanitarium, attempting to recover from the ravages of tuberculosis and other ailments. Buried Mission Burial Park, San Antonio TX.

Frank Waddey—1 Year Outfielder (b. 21 Aug 1905 Memphis TN–d. 21 Oct 1990 Shannondale Health Care Ctr, Knoxville TN) He was a retired engineer for Firestone Tire and Rubber Company. Buried Memorial Park Cemetery, Memphis TN.

Ham Wade—1 Year Outfielder (b. 20 Dec 1880 Spring City PA–d. 21 Jul 1968 Zurbrugg Memorial Hospital, Riverside NJ) He retired from Public Service Electric and Gas Company.

Rip Wade—1 Year Outfielder (b. 12 Jan 1898 Duluth MN–d. 15 Jun 1957 at a hospital in Duluth MN) He managed minor league baseball in Superior MN and Duluth.

Jack Wadsworth—4 Years Pitcher (b. 17 Dec 1867 Wellington OH–d. 8 Jul 1941 Elyria OH) He operated a restaurant in Wellington. Known for his skill as a hunter and marksman, he had trained hundreds of bird dogs. Buried Greenwood Cemetery, Wellington OH.

Woody Wagenhorst—1 Year Infielder (b. 3 Jun 1863 Kutztown PA–d. 14 Feb 1946 at his home in Washington DC) Buried Glenwood Cemetery, Washington DC.

Bill Wagner—5 Years Catcher (b. 2 Jan 1894 Jessup IA–d. 11 Jan 1951 St Francis Hospital, Waterloo IA) Died from a heart and lung ailment that had kept him bedridden much of his last few years. Buried Calvary Cemetery, Waterloo IA.

Bull Wagner—2 Years Pitcher (b. 1 Jan 1888 Lilley MI–d. 2 Oct 1967 Mercy Hospital, Muskegon MI) Served in the U.S. Army during World War I. For 30 years he was chief of plant protection at Continental Motors Corporation, retiring in 1960. Buried Oakwood Cemetery, Muskegon MI.

Butts Wagner—1 Year Infielder (b. 17 Sep 1869 Carnegie PA–d. 26 Nov 1928 at his doctor's office in Pittsburgh PA) Died from a stroke of apoplexy. Buried Chartiers Cemetery, Carnegie PA.

Hal Wagner—12 Years Catcher (b. 2 Jul 1915 East Riverton NJ–d. 7 Aug 1979 Zurbrugg Memorial Hospital, Riverside NJ) He was a sales representative for G and W H Corson, Inc, lime manufacturers in Gibbsboro NJ. Buried Lakeview Memorial Park, Cinnaminson NJ.

Heinie Wagner—12 Years Infielder 1 Year Manager (b. 23 Sep 1881 New York City NY–d. 20 Mar 1943 at his home in New Rochelle NY) He was a superintendent at a lumber yard in New Rochelle. Died from a heart ailment.

Honus Wagner—21 Years Infielder 1 Year Manager Hall of Fame (b. 24 Feb 1874 Carnegie PA–d. 6 Dec 1955 at his home in Carnegie PA) He coached 19 years for the Pirates, retiring in 1951. He also had an interest in a sporting goods store in Pittsburgh. Being bedfast since a recent fall in his home, he died in his sleep. Buried Jefferson Memorial Park, Pleasant Hills PA.

Joe Wagner—1 Year Infielder (b. 24 Apr 1889 New York City NY–d. 15 Nov 1948 Bronx NY).

Kermit Wahl—5 Years Infielder (b. 18 Nov 1922 Columbia SD–d. 16 Sep 1987 at his home in Tucson AZ) World War II veteran. He worked in coaching and college admissions in South Dakota from 1954 until 1975. After that he worked for nine years at a Tucson business college. Died from cancer. Buried Lakeview Cemetery, Columbia SD.

Eddie Waitkus—11 Years Infielder (b. 4 Sep 1919 Cambridge MA–d. 15 Sep 1972 Veteran's Hospital, Jamaica Plain MA) Served in the Pacific for the U.S. Army during World War II. Buried Cambridge Cemetery, Cambridge MA.

Charlie Waitt—3 Years Outfielder (b. 14 Oct 1853 Hallowell ME–d. 21 Oct 1912 County Hospital, San Francisco CA) He was a window washer. Died from blood poisoning that developed from an arm injury he had suffered in a fall from a window. Buried Sunset Cemetery, San Francisco CA.

Dick Wakefield—9 Years Outfielder (b. 6 May 1921 Chicago IL–d. 26 Aug 1985 at a nursing home in Wayne County, MI) Served two stints in the U.S. Navy during World War II. He worked in the Oakland County, MI, probate court, sold insurance and promoted goods made in Michigan. He was active in politics, twice falling short in bids for the Republican nomination for U.S. Congressman. Died from heart disease. Buried Resthaven Memory Garden, Avon OH.

Howard Wakefield—3 Years Catcher (b. 2 Apr 1884 Bucyrun OH–d. 16 Apr 1941 Chicago IL) Buried Calvary Cemetery, Evanston IL.

Rube Walberg—15 Years Pitcher (b. 27 Jul 1896 Pine City MN–d. 27 Oct 1978 at his home in Mesa AZ) He worked with youth groups for the Miami (FL) Recreational Department before retiring to Mesa in 1973. Cremated.

Ed Walczak—1 Year Infielder (b. 21 Sep 1915 Arctic RI–d. 10 Mar 1998 Backus Hospital, Norwich CT) Served in the U.S. Army Air Corps during World War II. He was an electrician for General Dynamics Electric Boat Division at Groton CT from 1951 until he retired in 1980. Buried St Mary's Cemetery, Lisbon CT.

Doc Waldbauer—1 Year Pitcher (b. 22 Feb 1892 Richmond VA–d. 16 Jul 1969 Fountain Nursing Home, Yakima WA) He was a retired laborer. Died from bronchopneumonia. Buried Terrace Heights Memorial Park, Yakima WA.

Fred Walden—1 Year Catcher (b. 25 Jun 1890 Fayette MO–d. 27 Sep 1955 Veteran's Hospital, Jefferson Barracks MO) He was a printer for the *St Louis Post-Dispatch* newspaper. Died following a stroke. Buried Memorial Park Cemetery, St Louis MO.

Irv Waldron—1 Year Outfielder (b. 21 Jan 1876 Hillside NY–d. 22 Jul 1944 Worcester MA) He was a nightwatchman for American Optical Company. Buried Oak Ridge Cemetery, Southbridge MA.

Bill Walker—10 Years Pitcher (b. 7 Oct 1903 East St Louis IL–d. 14 Jun 1966 Christian Welfare Hosp, East St Louis IL) He operated a tavern. Active in local democratic politics, he served as a deputy sheriff, county treasurer and probate clerk. Died from cancer. Buried Valhalla Gardens of Memory, Belleville IL.

Curt Walker—12 Years Outfielder (b. 3 Jul 1896 Beeville TX–d. 9 Dec 1955 at his home in Beeville TX) Served in the U.S. Army during both World Wars I and II. He operated the Walker Funeral Home in Beeville with his brother from 1932 to 1946, and served as justice of the peace there from 1954 until his death. Died from a stroke suffered a few weeks earlier. Buried Glenwood Cemetery, Beeville TX.

Dixie Walker—18 Years Outfielder (b. 24 Sep 1910 Villa Rica GA–d. 17 May 1982 Birmingham AL) He worked his entire life in baseball, 52 years as a player, coach, batting instructor and minor league manager, retiring in 1980. Died from cancer. Buried Elmwood Cemetery, Birmingham AL.

Dixie Walker—4 Years Pitcher (b. 1 Jun 1887 Brownsville PA–d. 14 Nov 1965 at a hospital in Leeds AL) Buried Elmwood Cemetery, Birmingham AL.

Ed Walker—2 Years Pitcher (b. 11 Aug 1874 Cambois, England–d. 29 Sep 1947 at his daughter's home in Akron OH) He was a school custodian, retiring in 1942 because of poor health. Died after a long illness. Buried Greenlawn Cemetery, Akron OH.

Ernie Walker—3 Years Outfielder (b. 17 Sep 1890 Blossburg AL–d. 1 Apr 1965 at his home in Pell City AL) Buried Fraternal Cemetery, Birmingham AL.

Fleet Walker—1 Year Catcher (b. 7 Oct 1856 Mount Pleasant OH–d. 11 May 1924 City Hospital, Cleveland OH) The first black player to play in the major leagues, 63 years before Jackie Robinson, he worked for the U.S. Postal Service before operating a nickelodeon in Cardiz OH. Died from lobar pneumonia. Buried Union Cemetery, Steubenville OH.

Frank Walker—5 Years Outfielder (b. 22 Sep 1894 Enoree SC–d. 16 Sep 1974 Memorial Hall, Bristol TN) He lived at Rocky Mount NC before moving to Bristol in 1969. Died after a brief illness. Buried Glenwood Shelby Hills Cemetery Mausoleum, Bristol TN.

Gee Walker—15 Years Outfielder (b. 19 Mar 1908 Gulfport MS–d. 20 Mar 1981 Whitfield MS).

Harry Walker—11 Years Outfielder 9 Years Manager (b. 22 Oct 1918 Pascagoula MS–d. 8 Aug 1999 Birmingham AL) Served in World War II.

Hub Walker—5 Years Outfielder (b. 17 Aug 1906 Gulfport MS–d. 26 Nov 1982 O'Connor Hospital, San Jose CA) Died from pneumonia and organic brain syndrome. Buried Santa Clara Mission Cemetery, Santa Clara CA.

Joe Walker—1 Year Infielder (b. 23 Jan 1898 Munhall PA–d. 20 Jun 1959 at his home in West Mifflin PA) Died suddenly. Buried Jefferson Memorial Park, Pleasant Hills PA.

Johnny Walker—3 Years Infielder (b. 11 Dec 1896 Toulon IL–d. 19 Aug 1976 Hollywood FL) Cremated.

Marty Walker—1 Year Pitcher (b. 27 Mar 1899 Philadelphia PA–d. 24 Apr 1978 Philadelphia PA) Buried Northwood Cemetery, Philadelphia PA.

Mysterious Walker—4 Years Pitcher (b. 21 Mar 1884 Utica NE–d. 31 Jan 1958 at his home in Oak Park IL) He coached football and basketball at several colleges before going into the securities business about 1936. Died from a heart attack.

Oscar Walker—4 Years Outfielder (b. 18 Mar 1854 Brooklyn NY–d. 20 May 1889 Brooklyn NY) Buried Evergreen Cemetery, Brooklyn NY.

Roy Walker—6 Years Pitcher (b. 13 Apr 1893 Lawrenceburg TN–d. 10 Feb 1962 New Orleans LA) He lived in New Orleans 48 years. Buried Garden of Memories, Metairie LA.

Rube Walker—11 Years Catcher (b. 16 May 1926 Lenoir NC–d. 12 Dec 1992 at his home in Lenoir NC) He spent 49 years in baseball as a player, coach, minor league manager and scout. Died following a lengthy illness. Buried Blue Ridge Memorial Park, Lenoir NC.

Tilly Walker—13 Years Outfielder (b. 4 Sep 1887 Telford TN–d. 21 Sep 1959 at his brother's home in Unicoi TN) He was a retired highway patrolman. Buried Urbana Cemetery, Limestone TN.

Tom Walker—3 Years Pitcher (b. 1 Aug 1881 Philadelphia PA–d. 10 Jul 1944 at his home in Woodbury Heights NJ) Buried Fernwood Cemetery, Fernwood PA.

Walt Walker—1 Year Outfielder (b. 12 Mar 1860 Berlin MI–d. 28 Feb 1922 Pontiac MI).

Welday Walker—1 Year Outfielder (b. 27 Jul 1859 Steubenville OH–d. 23 Nov 1937 at his home in Steubenville OH) Died from pneumonia. Buried Union Cemetery, Steubenville OH.

Jim Walkup—6 Years Pitcher (b. 14 Dec 1909 Havana AR–d. 7 Feb 1997 Danville AR).

Jim Walkup—1 Year Pitcher (b. 3 Nov 1895 Havana AR–d. 12 Jun 1990 at a nursing home in Duncan OK) Served in the U.S. Army during World War I. He retired from Haliburton Services. Buried Duncan Cemetery, Duncan OK.

Joe Wall—2 Years Catcher (b. 24 Jul 1873 Brooklyn NY–d. 17 Jul 1936 at his home in Brooklyn NY) He managed minor league baseball and conducted baseball schools for youth. For 20 years he coached and played ball at the Prospect Park Parade Grounds in Brooklyn, and promoted games around New York City almost every year after the major league season was over. Died from a heart attack.

Murray Wall—4 Years Pitcher (b. 19 Sep 1926 Dallas TX–d. 8 Oct 1971 Lone Oak TX) He was a vice-president of First Federal Savings and Loan in Dallas. Shot to death while hunting rabbits on his farm near Lone Oak. His death was ruled a suicide. Buried Restland Memorial Park, Dallas TX.

Bobby Wallace—25 Years Infielder 3 Years Manager Hall of Fame (b. 4 Nov 1873 Pittsburgh PA–d. 3 Nov 1960 Del Amo Sanitarium, Torrance CA) He was a scout for the Reds. Died from a heart attack. Buried Inglewood Park Cemetery, Inglewood CA.

Doc Wallace—1 Year Infielder (b. 20 Sep 1893 Church Hill MD–d. 31 Dec 1964 Haverford PA) Served in the U.S. Army during World War I. He was a teacher and coach at Haverford school from 1927 until 1956, and athletic director there from 1934 until he retired in 1959.

Huck Wallace—1 Year Pitcher (b. 27 Jul 1882 Richmond IN–d. 6 Jul 1951 Cleveland OH).

Jack Wallace—1 Year Catcher (b. 6 Aug 1890 Winnfield LA–d. 15 Oct 1960 Winnfield Hospital, Winnfield LA) He worked for the Louisiana State Insurance Department. Died after a long illness. Buried Winnfield Cemetery, Winnfield LA.

Jim Wallace—1 Year Outfielder (b. 14 Nov 1881 Boston MA–d. 16 May 1953 Revere MA) He was a retired printer. Died from a heart attack suffered three days earlier. Buried St Mary's Cemetery, Lynn MA.

Lefty Wallace—3 Years Pitcher (b. 12 Aug 1921 Evansville IN–d. 28 Jul 1982 St Mary's Medical Center, Evansville IN) Served in the U.S. Army during World War II. He played in the American Association. He worked for the Evansville Police Department from 1953 to 1974, and for the Vanderburgh County (IN) Sheriff's Department from 1974 to 1979. He was known as an expert in polygraph tests, fingerprinting, crime lab procedures, crime scene preservation and gathering evidence at crime scenes. Buried Sunset Memorial Park Cemetery, Evansville IN.

Jack Wallaesa—5 Years Infielder (b. 30 Aug 1919 Easton PA–d. 27 Dec 1986 Easton Hospital, Easton PA) Served in Italy and France for the U.S. Army during World War II. He worked more than 30 years for May's Men's Clothing Store in Easton, retiring in 1981. Buried St Anthony's Cemetery, Easton PA.

Red Waller—1 Year Pitcher (b. 16 Jun 1883 Washington DC–d. 9 Feb 1915 Secaucus NJ) Died from pulmonary tuberculosis. Buried Holy Name Cemetery, Jersey City NJ.

Lee Walls—10 Years Outfielder (b. 6 Jan 1933 San Diego CA–d. 11 Oct 1993 UCLA Medical Center, Los Angeles CA) Died from cardiopulmonary arrest while suffering from fungal sepsis and pneumonia. Cremated.

Augie Walsh—2 Years Pitcher (b. 17 Aug 1904 Wilmington DE–d. 12 Nov 1985 Marin General Hospital, San Rafael CA) He was the chief clerk for Pacific Far East Lines for 25 years. Died from prostate cancer. Cremated.

Austin Walsh—1 Year Outfielder (b. 1 Sep 1892 St Louis MO–d. 26 Jan 1955 Glenridge CA) World War I veteran. He was a sales agent for a life insurance company. Buried San Fernando Mission Cemetery, Mission Hills CA.

Connie Walsh—1 Year Pitcher (b. 23 Apr 1882

St Louis MO–d. 5 Apr 1953 St Louis MO) He worked for the St Louis Police Department. Buried Calvary Cemetery, St Louis MO.

Dee Walsh—3 Years Outfielder (b. 28 Mar 1890 St Louis MO–d. 14 Jul 1971 St Louis MO) Buried Calvary Cemetery, St Louis MO.

Ed Walsh—14 Years Pitcher Hall of Fame (b. 14 May 1881 Plains PA–d. 26 May 1959 at a friend's home in Pompano Beach FL) He won 40 games in 1908, managed minor league baseball, scouted, umpired a year in the American League and coached baseball at Notre Dame University. For many years he worked at a water plant in Meriden CT. Died from a kidney infection and prostate cancer after being bedfast for a year. Buried Forest Lawn Memorial Gardens, Pompano Beach FL.

Ed Walsh—4 Years Pitcher (b. 11 Feb 1905 Meriden CT–d. 31 Oct 1937 at his parent's home in Meriden CT) Died at the height of his career from the effects of rheumatic fever after being in a coma for a week. Buried Sacred Heart Cemetery, Meriden CT.

Jim Walsh—1 Year Pitcher (b. 10 Jul 1894 Roxbury MA–d. 13 May 1967 Brighton MA) Died suddenly. Buried New Calvary Cemetery, Mattapan MA.

Jimmy Walsh—6 Years Infielder (b. 25 Mar 1886 Lima OH–d. 21 Jan 1947 at his home in Baltimore MD) He owned and operated a restaurant at Catonsville MD. Died after an illness that had kept him confined six months. Buried New Cathedral Cemetery, Baltimore MD.

Jimmy Walsh—6 Years Outfielder (b. 22 Sep 1885 Kallila, Ireland–d. 3 Jul 1962 Syracuse NY) He was a foreman for the Syracuse City Department of Public Works. Died after suffering a heart attack while golfing. Buried St Agnes Cemetery, Syracuse NY.

Joe Walsh—1 Year Infielder (b. 5 Nov 1864 Baton Rouge LA–d. 8 Aug 1911 St Catherine's Hospital, Omaha NE) Died from paralysis. Buried Holy Sepulchre Cemetery, Omaha NE.

Joe Walsh—2 Years Catcher (b. 14 Oct 1887 Waterbury CT–d. 6 Jan 1967 Buffalo NY).

Joe Walsh—1 Year Infielder (b. 13 Mar 1917 Boston MA–d. 5 Oct 1996 Boston MA) He was a custodian for the Boston Police Department-District 14 in Brighton. Buried Walnut Hills Cemetery, Brookline MA.

John Walsh—1 Year Infielder (b. 25 Mar 1879 Wilkes-Barre PA–d. 25 Apr 1947 at his home in Wilkes-Barre NY) He worked several years for the Socony-Vacuum Oil Company. Died following a heart attack. Buried St Mary's Cemetery, Wilkes-Barre PA.

Junior Walsh—5 Years Pitcher (b. 7 Mar 1919 Arlington NJ–d. 12 Nov 1990 at his home in Olyphant PA) Served in the U.S. Army during World War II. Retiring from Associated Transport, he also worked for the Scranton (PA) Country Club. Buried St Joseph's Cemetery, Throop PA.

Mike Walsh—1 Year Manager (b. 6 Aug 1852 Baltimore MD–d. 2 Feb 1924 Louisville KY) Buried St Louis Cemetery, Louisville KY.

Tom Walsh—1 Year Catcher (b. 28 Feb 1885 Davenport IA–d. 16 Mar 1963 Naples FL) An industrialist, realtor and construction executive, he was chairman of the board of Walsh Construction Company. The company had been in business 65 years with offices in Chicago, New York City and San Francisco, and built railroads, buildings, tunnels and dams throughout the world. They helped erect the United Nations Building in New York City. Died after suffering a cerebral hemorrhage. Buried Mount Calvary Cemetery, Davenport IA.

Walt Walsh—2 Games Pinch Runner (b. 30 Apr 1897 Newark NJ–d. 15 Jan 1966 Fitkin Hospital, Neptune NJ) He was an industrial engineer for Westinghouse Corporation in Newark. Served in the U.S. Navy during World War I. Died after a long illness. Buried St Catharine's Cemetery, Wall NJ.

Bernie Walter—1 Year Pitcher (b. 15 Aug 1908 Dover TN–d. 30 Oct 1988 St Thomas Hospital, Nashville TN) He pitched only one inning in the majors, facing only three batters and striking out one of them. Buried Hillcrest Cemetery, Dover TN.

Bucky Walters—19 Years Pitcher 2 Years Manager (b. 19 Apr 1909 Philadelphia PA–d. 20 Apr 1991 Memorial Hospital, Abington PA) Died from unreported causes. Buried Whitemarsh Memorial Cemetery, Prospectville PA.

Fred Walters—1 Year Catcher (b. 4 Sep 1912 Laurel MS–d. 1 Feb 1980 Laurel General Hospital, Laurel MS) He served as sheriff of Jones County, MS, from 1956 to 1960. He refereed basketball and football in the Southeast Conference for 22 years and was part-owner of the Holiday Inn at Laurel. Died following a brief illness. Buried Hickory Grove Cemetery, Laurel MS.

Roxy Walters—11 Years Catcher (b. 5 Nov 1892 San Francisco CA–d. 3 Jun 1956 at his home in Alameda CA) Died from a heart attack. Buried Olivet Memorial Park, Colma CA.

Bill Wambsganss—13 Years Infielder (b. 19 Mar 1894 Garfield Heights OH–d. 8 Dec 1985 Lakewood Hospital, Lakewood OH) He is best known for an unassisted triple play in the 1920 World Series. He coached in the professional girl's baseball league and worked in sales for Tru-Fit Screw Products Corporation in Lakewood. Died from heart disease. Buried Calvary Cemetery, Cleveland OH.

Lloyd Waner—18 Years Outfielder Hall of Fame (b. 16 Mar 1906 Harrah OK–d. 22 Jul 1982 Presbyterian Hospital, Oklahoma City OK) Known as "Little Poison", he and his Hall of Fame brother, Paul, played in the same outfield for the Pirates. For many years he was a foreman for the city of Oklahoma City. Died from emphysema. Buried Rose Hill Burial Park, Oklahoma City OK.

Paul Waner—20 Years Outfielder Hall of Fame (b. 16 Apr 1903 Harrah OK–d. 29 Aug 1965 at his home in Sarasota FL) Known as "Big Poison," he and his Hall of Fame brother, Lloyd, played in the same outfield for the Pirates. He was an avid hunter, fisher and golfer. Died from a chronic respiratory ailment. Buried Manasota Memorial Park, Bradenton FL.

Jack Wanner—1 Year Infielder (b. 29 Nov 1885 Geneseo IL–d. 28 May 1919 at his parent's home in Geneseo IL) He was an inspector at the Rock Island Arsenal. Died from tuberculosis of the spine. Buried Oakwood Cemetery, Genesco IL.

Pee Wee Wanninger—2 Years Infielder (b. 12 Dec 1902 Birmingham AL–d. 7 Mar 1981 at his home in North Augusta SC) Buried Forest Hill Cemetery, Birmingham AL.

Dick Wantz—1 Year Pitcher (b. 11 Apr 1940 South Gate CA–d. 14 May 1965 Daniel Freeman Hospital, Inglewood CA) Died without regaining consiousness after surgery to remove a cancerous brain tumor. He was in his first major league season when he died, having pitched only one inning in the Angel's home opener. Buried Forest Lawn Memorial Park, Cypress CA.

Aaron Ward—12 Years Infielder (b. 28 Aug 1896 Booneville AR–d. 30 Jan 1961 V A Hospital, New Orleans LA) He worked for Southern Bell Telephone and Telegraph. Later he owned and operated a tire retreading business in New Orleans. Buried St Louis Cemetery # 3, New Orleans LA.

Arch Ward—(b. 27 Dec 1896 Irwin IL–d. 9 Jul 1955 at his home in Chicago IL) He worked 30 years for the *Chicago Tribune,* starting as a copy editor, rising to international renown as a sports editor, author, commentator and promoter. He was the originator of the annual Baseball All-Star game. Buried All Saints Cemetery, Des Plaines IL.

Chuck Ward—6 Years Infielder (b. 30 Jul 1894 St Louis MO–d. 4 Apr 1969 at his home in Indian Rocks FL) World War I veteran. He coached baseball at Rutgers University from 1938 to 1949 before scouting for the Braves, Phillies and Reds. Cremated.

Dick Ward—2 Years Pitcher (b. 21 May 1909 Herrick SD–d. 30 May 1966 Freeland WA).

Hap Ward—1 Year Outfielder (b. 15 Nov 1885 Leesburg NJ–d. 13 Sep 1979 Elmer NJ).

Jim Ward—1 Year Catcher (b. Mar 1855 Boston MA–d. 4 Jun 1886 Boston MA) Buried Mount Benedict Cemetery, West Roxbury MA.

Joe Ward—3 Years Infielder (b. 2 Sep 1884 Philadelphia PA–d. 11 Aug 1934 Frankford Hospital, Philadelphia PA) He managed minor league baseball. Died from injuries suffered in an automobile accident four days earlier. Buried Westminster Cemetery, Bala Cynwyd PA.

Monte Ward—17 Years Infielder 6 Years Manager Hall of Fame (b. 3 Mar 1860 Bellefonte PA–d. 4 Mar 1925 at a hospital in Augusta GA) He was a noted New York City lawyer and one of the leading amateur golfers in the country. He contracted a cold on a hunting trip that turned into pneumonia, while spending the winter in the Augusta area, and died. Buried Babylon Cemetery, Babylon NY.

Piggy Ward—6 Years Outfielder (b. 16 Apr 1867 Chambersburg PA–d. 23 Oct 1912 Altoona

PA) Died from paresis, the result of a fall from a telephone pole in 1909. Buried Cedar Grove Cemetery, Chambersburg PA.

Rube Ward—1 Year Outfielder (b. 6 Feb 1879 New Lexington OH–d. 17 Jan 1945 Akron OH) A retired clothing merchant from New Lexington, he came to Akron to work for the war effort at the Goodyear Aircraft plant. Died from a heart attack while at work. Buried Maplewood Cemetery, New Lexington OH.

Buzzy Wares—2 Years Infielder (b. 23 Mar 1886 Vandalla MI–d. 26 May 1964 at his home in South Bend IN) He coached for the Cardinals from 1930 to 1952. Buried Riverview Cemetery, South Bend IN.

Frank Warfield—13 Years Infielder 5 Years Manager (b. 1895 Indianapolis IN–d. 24 Jul 1932 Bailey Hotel, Pittsburgh PA) He played in the negro leagues and lived in Baltimore MD. Died in his hotel room after his team, the Washington DC Pilots, had closed a series with the Pittsburgh Crawfords. Died from an internal hemorrhage. Buried Mount Auburn Cemetery, Baltimore MD.

Jack Warhop—8 Years Pitcher (b. 4 Jul 1884 Hinton WV–d. 4 Oct 1960 at a hospital in Freeport IL) He gave up the first home run Babe Ruth hit. Died after an extended illness. Buried Lanark Cemetery, Lanark IL.

Cy Warmoth—3 Years Pitcher (b. 2 Feb 1893 Bone Gap IL–d. 20 Jun 1957 Wabash General Hospital, Mount Carmel IL) He pitched in the Three-I League, Southern Association and American Association. He was a switchman for the New York Central Railroad. Died after a brief illness. Buried Highland Memorial Cemetery, Mount Carmel IL.

Lon Warneke—15 Years Pitcher (b. 28 Mar 1909 Mount Ida AR–d. 23 Jun 1976 at his home in Hot Springs AR) After retiring as a player he was a National League umpire for ten years. Later he served as a county judge in Garland County, AR, for ten years. Died from a heart attack. Buried Owly Cemetery, Mount Ida AR.

Ed Warner—1 Year Pitcher (b. 29 Dec 1888 Fitchburg MA–d. 5 Feb 1954 Metropolitan Hospital, New York City NY) He was the office manager for Abercrombie and Fitch in New York City. Buried Forest Hill Cemetery, Fitchburg MA.

Fred Warner—5 Years Infielder (b. 1855 Philadelphia PA–d. 13 Feb 1886 Philadelphia PA).

Hooks Warner—4 Years Infielder (b. 29 May 1895 Del Rio TX–d. 19 Feb 1947 San Francisco CA) World War I veteran. Died from a subdural hematoma and liver disease. Buried Del Rio TX.

Jack Warner—8 Years Infielder (b. 29 Aug 1903 Evansville IN–d. 13 Mar 1986 Good Samaritan Hospital, Mount Vernon IL) He retired in 1982, following a 61-year baseball career as a player, coach, scout and minor league manager. Buried Memorial Gardens, Mount Vernon IL.

Jack Warner—14 Years Catcher (b. 15 Aug 1872 New York City NY–d. 21 Dec 1943 Queens NY).

Hal Warnock—1 Year Outfielder (b. 6 Jan 1912 New York City NY–d. 8 Feb 1997 Tucson AZ) He was a naval officer during World War II. A lawyer, he was an investigator for the U.S. Department of Agriculture for a short while before working over 50 years for a Tucson legal firm, retiring in 1993. He was president of the Pima County (AZ) Bar Association for a time and was active in other legal societies.

Bennie Warren—6 Years Catcher (b. 2 Mar 1912 Elk City OK–d. 11 May 1994 Oklahoma City OK) Served in the U.S. Navy during World War II. He was a deputy policeman in Oklahoma City for 21 years. Buried Ames Cemetery, Ames OK.

Bill Warren—2 Years Catcher (b. 11 Feb 1883 MO–d. 28 Jan 1960 at his home in Whiteville TN) Buried Melrose Cemetery, Whiteville TN.

Tommy Warren—1 Year Pitcher (b. 5 Jul 1917 Tulsa OK–d. 2 Jan 1968 at a southside motel in Tulsa OK) Serving in the U.S. Navy during World War II, he was wounded during troop landings in North Africa. He managed some minor league baseball and was a deputy sheriff for the Tulsa County, OK, sheriff's office. He was known for his work with youth groups. Died from a self-inflicted shotgun blast to the chest, leaving a note citing ill health as the reason. Buried Memorial Park, Tulsa OK.

Rabbit Warstler—11 Years Infielder (b. 13 Sep 1903 North Canton OH–d. 31 May 1964 at his home in North Canton OH) He worked in the shipping department of Hoover Company in

North Canton from 1943 until his death. Died from cancer. Buried North Canton Cemetery, North Canton OH.

Bill Warwick—3 Years Catcher (b. 26 Nov 1897 Philadelphia PA–d. 19 Dec 1984 San Antonio TX).

Jimmy Wasdell—11 Years Outfielder (b. 15 May 1914 Cleveland OH–d. 6 Aug 1983 Community Hospital, New Port Richey FL) He ran "The Dugout", a tavern in Cleveland for 25 years, retiring to Holiday FL in 1974. Died from kidney failure. Buried Meadowlawn Memorial Gardens, New Port Richey FL.

Link Wasem—1 Year Catcher (b. 30 Jan 1911 Birmingham OH–d. 6 Mar 1979 South Coast Medical Center, Laguna Beach CA) For 15 years he was a handyman, doing minor repairs on houses. Died from a heart attack. Cremated.

George Washburn—1 Year Pitcher (b. 6 Oct 1914 Solon ME–d. 5 Jan 1979 General Hospital, Baton Rouge LA) Buried Resthaven Gardens of Memory, Baton Rouge LA.

Libe Washburn—2 Years Outfielder (b. 16 Jun 1874 Lyme NH–d. 22 Mar 1940 at his home in Malone NY) Active in civic affairs, he operated a flour and feed mill in Malone before becoming manager of the Old Line Coal Company there. Died after several weeks' illness. Buried Morningside Cemetery, Malone NY.

Buck Washer—1 Year Pitcher (b. 11 Oct 1882 Akron OH–d. 8 Dec 1955 Akron OH).

George Washington—2 Years Outfielder (b. 7 Jun 1907 Linden TX–d. 17 Feb 1985 Municipal Hospital, Linden TX) He was a farmer. Died from a heart attack after suffering a broken hip. Buried New Colony Cemetery, Linden TX.

Fred Waters—2 Years Pitcher (b. 2 Feb 1927 Benton MS–d. 28 Aug 1989 W Florida Regional Med Center, Pensacola FL) For 32 years he was a teacher, administrator and coach at high schools in Pensacola. He was also a scout for the Twins. Died from pancreatic cancer. Buried Roseland Park Cemetery, Hattiesburg MS.

Bill Watkins—1 Year Infielder 9 Years Manager (b. 5 May 1858 Brantford, Ontario, Canada–d. 9 Jun 1937 General Hospital, Port Huron MI) Thought to be the first manager to take his team south for training, he took his 1886 Detroit team there. He managed minor and major league teams 40 years. After retiring from baseball he became active in civic affairs in Port Huron, working in the Chamber of Commerce, and was elected Justice of the Peace once. Died from diabetes. Buried Lakeside Cemetery, Port Huron MI.

Ed Watkins—1 Year Outfielder (b. 21 Jun 1877 Philadelphia PA–d. 29 Mar 1933 Kelvin AZ) He worked in the mines. Died in the mine of the Florence Lead and Silver Company from heart disease. Buried Ray AZ.

George Watkins—7 Years Outfielder (b. 4 Jun 1902 Palestine TX–d. 1 Jun 1970 at a hospital in Austin TX) Served in the U.S. Navy. He was a retired laborer. Buried Broyles Chapel Cemetery, Palestine TX.

Art Watson—2 Years Catcher (b. 11 Jan 1884 Jeffersonville IN–d. 9 May 1950 Buffalo NY).

Doc Watson—3 Years Pitcher (b. 30 Jan 1885 Kensington OH–d. 30 Dec 1949 at his home in San Diego CA) He was a steel worker. Died from a heart attack. Cremated.

Johnny Watson—1 Year Infielder (b. 16 Jan 1908 Tazewell VA–d. 29 Apr 1965 Huntington WV) Served in the U.S. Navy during World War II. He worked 28 years for the Veteran's Administration in Huntington as an administration officer, training specialist and, finally, as a vocational rehabilitation specialist. Died at his desk from a heart attack. Buried Woodmere Memorial Park, Huntington WV.

Milt Watson—4 Years Pitcher (b. 19 Jan 1891 Floville GA–d. 10 Apr 1962 Jefferson Hospital, Pine Bluff AR) He was a guard at the Jacksonville (AR) Ordinance Plant and a fireman at the Pine Bluff Arsenal. Buried Bellwood Cemetery, Pine Bluff AR.

Mother Watson—1 Year Pitcher (b. 27 Jan 1865 Middleport OH–d. 23 Nov 1898 Middleport OH) Murdered in a saloon at the height of his career. Buried Middleport Hill Cemetery, Middleport OH.

Mule Watson—7 Years Pitcher (b. 15 Oct 1896 Homer LA–d. 25 Aug 1949 Charity Hospital, Shreveport LA) Died from a heart attack. Buried Arlington Cemetery, Homer LA.

Allie Watt—1 Year Infielder (b. 12 Dec 1899 Philadelphia PA–d. 15 Mar 1968 Norfolk VA) A retired Norfolk police lieutenant, he had lived in

Norfolk 46 years. Buried Rosewood Memorial Park, Virginia Beach VA.

Frank Watt—1 Year Pitcher (b. 15 Dec 1902 Washington DC–d. 31 Aug 1956 Emergency Hospital, Washington DC) He worked for the Washington DC Police Department from 1932 to 1951, and for the Capitol Police from 1951 until his death. Died from a heart attack. Buried Fort Lincoln Cemetery, Brentwood MD.

Cliff Watwood—6 Years Outfielder (b. 17 Aug 1905 Alexander City AL–d. 1 Mar 1980 Goodwater AL).

Bob Way—1 Year Infielder (b. 2 Apr 1906 Emlenton PA–d. 20 Jun 1974 Pittsburgh PA) He was a retired shipping foreman for Fisher Food Company in Pittsburgh. Buried Hickory Grove Cemetery, Polk PA.

Frank Wayenberg—1 Year Pitcher (b. 27 Aug 1897 Franklin KS–d. 16 Apr 1975 Good Samaritan Medical Ctr, Zanesville OH) He operated the Wayenberg Texaco Service Station in Zanesville for a number of years, retiring in 1964. Died after a four-year illness. Buried Mount Olive Cemetery, Zanesville OH.

Roy Weatherly—10 Years Outfielder (b. 25 Feb 1915 Warren TX–d. 19 Jan 1991 Holiday Pines Manor, Woodville TX) Cremated.

Art Weaver—4 Years Catcher (b. 7 Apr 1879 Wichita KS–d. 23 Mar 1917 St Joseph's Hospital, Denver CO) He played baseball until asthma ended his career. Died from asthma. Buried Fairmount Cemetery, Denver CO.

Buck Weaver—9 Years Infielder (b. 18 Aug 1890 Pottstown PA–d. 31 Jan 1956 Chicago IL) He was banned from baseball for his involvement in the Black Sox Scandal. He played semipro baseball in the Chicago area and worked in the parimutual department of Chicago race tracks. He collapsed and died on the street from a heart attack. Buried Mount Hope Cemetery, Chicago IL.

Farmer Weaver—7 Years Outfielder (b. 23 Mar 1865 Parkersburg WV–d. 23 Jan 1943 at his home in Akron OH) He worked for Goodyear Tire and Rubber Company in Akron. Died from cardio-vascular renal disease. Buried Memorial Park Cemetery, Akron OH.

Harry Weaver—5 Years Pitcher (b. 26 Feb 1892 Clarendon PA–d. 30 May 1983 Rochester NY) Buried Holy Sepulchre Cemetery, Rochester NY.

Jim Weaver—8 Years Pitcher (b. 25 Nov 1903 Fulton KY–d. 12 Dec 1983 Regional Medical Center, Lakeland FL) He worked 18 years for the Kentucky State Department of Corrections, where he was recreation director at the LaGrange Reformatory and later a probation officer at Burlington, retiring to Lakeland in 1974. Buried Forest Lawn Memorial Park, Erlanger KY.

Monte Weaver—9 Years Pitcher (b. 15 Jun 1906 Helton NC–d. 14 Jun 1994 Orlando FL) Served for the U.S. Army Air Corps during World War II. He was a retired citrus grower.

Orlie Weaver—2 Years Pitcher (b. 4 Jun 1886 Newport KY–d. 28 Nov 1970 New Orleans LA) Buried Garden of Memories, Metairie LA.

Sam Weaver—5 Years Pitcher (b. 20 Jul 1855 Philadelphia PA–d. 1 Feb 1914 at his home in Philadelphia PA) He was a patrolman for the Philadelphia Police Dept from 1887 until he retired in 1908 following a serious operation. Died suddenly from heart disease while sitting in his parlor reading the newspaper.

Bill Webb—1 Year Pitcher (b. 12 Dec 1913 Atlanta GA–d. 1 Jun 1994 Cobb General Hospital, Austell GA) He retired in 1974 after 27 years as a fireman for the Atlanta Fire Department. Buried Cheatham Hill Memorial Park, Marietta GA.

Billy Webb—1 Year Infielder (b. 25 Jun 1895 Chicago IL–d. 12 Jan 1943 Chicago IL) A minor league manager and long-time White Sox coach, he worked in baseball his entire life. He was director of the White Sox farm system when he died from a heart attack while driving to work. Buried Mount Olivet Cemetery, Chicago IL.

Del Webb—(b. abt 1899 Fresno CA–d. 4 Jul 1974 Mayo Clinic, Rochester MN) Part-owner of the New York Yankees from 1945 to 1964, he was the owner of one of the country's largest construction companies. Died from complications following surgery for lung cancer. He was cremated and his ashes scattered over Arizona.

Earl Webb—7 Years Outfielder (b. 17 Sep 1899 Bon Air TN–d. 23 May 1965 at his home in Jamestown TN) He played baseball for 18 years. Buried Taylor Place Cemetery, Jamestown TN.

Lefty Webb—1 Year Pitcher (b. 1 Mar 1885

Mount Gilead OH–d. 12 Jan 1958 Berger Hospital, Circleville OH) He taught school and coached sports, as well as being superintendent of schools. Later he was supervisor of game management for the Ohio Division of Wildlife. Died following a heart attack. Buried Forest Cemetery, Circleville OH.

Red Webb—2 Years Pitcher (b. 25 Sep 1924 Washington DC–d. 7 Feb 1996 Hyattsville MD) Buried Cheltenham Veteran's Cemetery, Cheltenham MD.

Skeeter Webb—12 Years Infielder (b. 4 Nov 1909 Meridian MS–d. 8 Jul 1986 Riley Memorial Hospital, Meridian MS) He was a sales representative for Dickey Clay. Buried Magnolia Cemetery, Meridian MS.

Joe Webber—1 Year Catcher (b. 15 Feb 1862 Hamilton, Ontario, Canada–d. 15 Dec 1921 Hamilton, Ontario, Canada).

Les Webber—6 Years Pitcher (b. 6 May 1915 Lakeport CA–d. 13 Nov 1986 Valley Community Hospital, Santa Maria CA) He was a real estate broker for 35 years. Died from pneumonia and heart disease. Cremated. Buried Dudley-Hoffman Columbarium, Santa Maria CA.

Charlie Weber—1 Year Pitcher (b. 22 Oct 1868 Cincinnati OH–d. 13 Jun 1914 Beaumont TX) He owned the San Antonio team in the Texas League for a short time before opening a bar in Beaumont. Shot to death in an argument while eating dinner. Buried Magnolia Cemetery, Beaumont TX.

Pete Weckbecker—2 Years Catcher (b. 30 Aug 1864 Butler PA–d. 16 May 1935 Hampton VA).

Charlie Weeden—1 Game Pinch Hitter (b. 21 Dec 1882 Northwood NH–d. 7 Jan 1939 at his home in Northwood NH) He was a manager in the minor leagues before opening a lunch room in Northwood NH. Died from a heart attack.

Johnny Weekly—3 Years Outfielder (b. 14 Jun 1937 Waterproof LA–d. 24 Nov 1974 Walnut Creek CA) He was the assistant director for a Pittsburg CA boy's club for a number of years. Killed when he lost control of his car, hitting a utility pole. Buried Oak View Cemetery, Antioch CA.

Biggs Wehde—2 Years Pitcher (b. 23 Nov 1906 Holstein IA–d. 21 Sep 1970 V A Hospital, Sioux Falls SD) Died from a lung abscess. Buried Calvary Cemetery, Sioux City IA.

Herm Wehmeier—13 Years Pitcher (b. 18 Feb 1927 Cincinnati OH–d. 21 May 1973 Dallas TX) He was a district terminal manager for Midland Trans-National Trucking Company. Died from a heart attack while testifying in a federal theft trial in Dallas. Buried St John Cemetery, Cincinnati OH.

Ralph Weigel—3 Years Catcher (b. 2 Oct 1921 Coldwater MI–d. 15 Apr 1992 St Francis Hospital, Memphis TN) Served in the U.S. Coast Guard during World War II. He was a retired General Motors employee. Buried West Tennessee Veteran's Cemetery, Memphis TN.

Podgie Weihe—2 Years Outfielder (b. 13 Nov 1862 Cincinnati OH–d. 16 Apr 1914 Cincinnati OH) He was a saloonkeeper in Cincinnati. Died from an acute cellulitis of the neck. Buried Spring Grove Cemetery, Cincinnati OH.

Dick Weik—5 Years Pitcher (b. 17 Nov 1927 Waterloo IA–d. 21 Apr 1991 Harvey IL).

Bob Weiland—12 Years Pitcher (b. 14 Dec 1905 Chicago IL–d. 9 Nov 1988 Resurrection Hosp Care Center, Chicago IL) He sold auto parts for a number of companies before retiring in 1976. During the last 20 years of his life he had both legs amputated. Died from congestive heart failure. Buried Mount Emblem Cemetery, Elmhurst IL.

Ed Weiland—2 Years Pitcher (b. 26 Nov 1914 Evanston IL–d. 12 Jul 1971 Chicago IL) Buried Memorial Park Cemetery, Skokie IL.

Carl Weilman—8 Years Pitcher (b. 29 Nov 1889 Hamilton OH–d. 25 May 1924 Mercy Hospital, Hamilton OH) He was a scout for the St Louis Browns. Died from tuberculosis of the throat. Buried Greenwood Cemetery, Hamilton OH.

Jake Weimer—7 Years Pitcher (b. 29 Nov 1873 Ottumwa IA–d. 19 Jun 1928 South Shore Hospital, Chicago IL) Buried Mount Olivet Cemetery, Chicago IL.

Lefty Weinert—9 Years Pitcher (b. 21 Apr 1901 Philadelphia PA–d. 17 Apr 1973 Rockledge FL) Entered defense work during World War II. He coached baseball at Villanova University from 1946 to 1949 and was a scout for the Phillies, Dodgers and Indians. In 1960 he went to work for the New Jersey Highway Dept, retiring in 1970. Died, possibly from a heart attack, in a one-car accident on I95 when his car overturned in the median. Buried Lakeview Memorial Park, Cinnaminson NJ.

Phil Weintraub — 7 Years Infielder (b. 12 Oct 1907 Chicago IL–d. 21 Jun 1987 Desert Hospital, Palm Springs CA) Died from a heart attack, but suffered four years from lymphoma. Buried Desert Memorial Park, Cathedral City CA.

Roy Weir — 4 Years Pitcher (b. 25 Feb 1911 Portland ME–d. 30 Sep 1989 at his home in Anaheim CA) World War II veteran. He was an executive at A T & T for 27 years. Died from congestive heart failure after suffering for years from chronic obstructive pulmonary disease. Buried Rose Hills Memorial Park, Whittier CA.

Butch Weis — 4 Years Outfielder (b. 2 Mar 1901 St Louis MO–d. 4 May 1997 St Louis MO) Buried New St Marcus Cemetery, St Louis MO.

Bud Weiser — 2 Years Outfielder (b. 8 Jan 1891 Shamokin PA–d. 31 Jul 1961 State Hospital, Shamokin PA) Buried Odd Fellows Cemetery, Shamokin PA.

George Weiss — Hall of Fame (b. 23 Jun 1894 New Haven CT–d. 13 Aug 1972 Greenwich CT) He developed championship teams in both the minor and major leagues from 1916 to 1966 and was general manager of the Yankees from 1947 to 1960. From 1961 to 1966 he was the first president of the Mets. Died after being in ill health for some time. Buried Evergreen Cemetery, New Haven CT.

Joe Weiss — 1 Year Infielder (b. 27 Jan 1894 Chicago IL–d. 7 Jul 1967 Mount Vernon IA) He played in the Texas League and the American Association, and for 45 years was a senior industrial engineer for People's Gas Light and Coke Company, retiring in 1959. Died from a heart attack. Cremated.

Curt Welch — 10 Years Outfielder (b. 11 Feb 1862 East Liverpool OH–d. 29 Aug 1896 East Liverpool OH) Died from consumption. Buried St Aloysius Cemetery, East Liverpool OH.

Frank Welch — 9 Years Outfielder (b. 10 Aug 1897 Birmingham AL–d. 25 Jul 1957 Birmingham AL) Buried Elmwood Cemetery, Birmingham AL.

Herb Welch — 1 Year Infielder (b. 19 Oct 1898 RoEllen TN–d. 13 Apr 1967 Baptist Hospital, Memphis TN) He played baseball for about 25 years, and operated a restaurant at Dyersburg TN his last 12 years. Buried Fairview Cemetery, Dyersburg TN.

Johnny Welch — 9 Years Pitcher (b. 2 Dec 1906 Washington DC–d. 2 Sep 1940 Koch Hospital, St Louis MO) Died after a two-year bout with cancer. Buried Calvary Cemetery, St Louis MO.

Mickey Welch — 13 Years Pitcher Hall of Fame (b. 4 Jul 1859 Brooklyn NY–d. 30 Jul 1941 Nashua NH) He worked for the New York Giants for several years in a number of different jobs. Died after an illness of some weeks while visiting a grandson in New Hampshire. Buried Calvary Cemetery, Woodside NY.

Ted Welch — 1 Year Pitcher (b. 17 Oct 1892 Coyville KS–d. 6 Jan 1943 St Rose Hospital, Great Bend KS) He was the production foreman for Carter Oil Company. Died following a heart attack. Buried Woodland Cemetery, Cleveland OK.

Harry Welchonce — 1 Year Outfielder (b. 20 Nov 1883 North Point PA–d. 26 Feb 1977 Huntington Convalescent Hosp, Arcadia CA) For 32 years he was an auditor for the Los Angeles City Water Department. Died from kidney failure. Buried Mount Olivet Cemetery.

Mike Welday — 2 Years Outfielder (b. 19 Dec 1879 Conway IA–d. 28 May 1942 at a tavern in Leavenworth KS) Buried Mount Muncie Cemetery, Lansing KS.

Ollie Welf — 1 Game Pinch Runner (b. 17 Jan 1889 Cleveland OH–d. 15 Jun 1967 Euclid-Glenville Hospital, Cleveland OH) He was a veterinarian at Mantua OH before spending 36 years as legal counsel for the Workman's Compensation Division of the Industrial Commission of Ohio. Served in the U.S. Army during World War I. Buried Lake View Cemetery, Cleveland OH.

Bob Wellman — 2 Years Outfielder (b. 15 Jul 1925 Norwood OH–d. 20 Dec 1994 at his home in Villa Hills KY) Served in the U.S. Navy during World War II. He managed minor league baseball and scouted for the Mets. Died from cancer. Buried Gate of Heaven Cemetery, Cincinnati OH.

Ed Wells — 11 Years Pitcher (b. 7 Jun 1900 Ashland OH–d. 1 May 1986 Baptist Medical Center, Birmingham AL) He retired from the oil business. Died from a heart attack. Buried Greenwood Cemetery, Montgomery AL.

Jake Wells—2 Years Catcher (b. 9 Aug 1863 Memphis TN–d. 16 Mar 1927 Hendersonville NC) He was a prominent hotel and theater owner in the southern states. Took his own life by shooting himself in the head with a pistol. He was said to be despondent over the ill health of both he and his wife. Some said he had lost health, friends and money. Buried St Mary's Cemetery, Norfolk VA.

John Wells—1 Year Pitcher (b. 25 Nov 1922 Junction City KS–d. 23 Oct 1993 Olean NY) An avid hunter and fisherman, he worked for Stroehmann Brothers Company bakery before his retirement. Died from a heart attack. Cremated.

Willie Wells—20 Years Infielder Hall of Fame (b. 10 Aug 1908 Austin TX–d. 22 Jan 1989 Austin TX) He played in the negro leagues. Died from heart trouble. Buried Evergreen Cemetery, Austin TX.

Jimmy Welsh—6 Years Outfielder (b. 9 Oct 1902 Oakland CA–d. 30 Oct 1970 Providence Hospital, Oakland CA) For 20 years he was a teamster for Hawkey Transportation. Died from a massive internal hemorrhage. Buried Holy Sepulchre Cemetery, Hayward CA.

Tony Welzer—2 Years Pitcher (b. 5 Apr 1899 Germany–d. 18 Mar 1971 St Francis Hospital, Milwaukee WI) He worked for International Harvestor Company. Died after a brief illness. Buried St Adalbert's Cemetery, Milwaukee WI.

Lew Wendell—5 Years Catcher (b. 22 Mar 1892 New York City NY–d. 11 Jul 1953 Bronx NY) Buried Woodlawn Cemetery, Bronx NY.

Jack Wentz—1 Year Infielder (b. 4 Mar 1863 Louisville KY–d. 14 Sep 1907 at his home in Louisville KY) Died from pneumonia contracted following surgery for stomach trouble. Buried St Louis Cemetery, Louisville KY.

Stan Wentzel—1 Year Outfielder (b. 13 Jan 1917 Lorane PA–d. 28 Nov 1991 at his home in St Lawrence PA) He managed minor league baseball for a number of years before he was a routeman for ARA Services of Reading PA for 20 years, retiring in 1978. Died from natural causes. Buried Forest Hills Memorial Park, Reading PA.

Julie Wera—2 Years Infielder (b. 9 Feb 1902 Winona MN–d. 12 Dec 1975 Rochester MN) He was a butcher for Piggly Wiggly for 25 years. Died from a heart attack. Buried St Mary's Cemetery, Winona MN.

Perry Werden—7 Years Infielder (b. 21 Jul 1865 St Louis MO–d. 9 Jan 1934 Minneapolis MN) He hit 45 home runs for the Minneapolis Millers of the American Association in 1895—the record for organized baseball until it was broken by Babe Ruth in 1920. During a 20-year minor league career, between 1884 and 1908, he compiled a lifetime .341 batting average and hit 171 home runs during the "deadball" era of baseball. Died from a heart attack. Buried Bellefontaine Cemetery, St Louis MO.

Joe Werrick—4 Years Infielder (b. 25 Oct 1861 St Paul MN–d. 10 May 1943 State Hospital, St Peter MN) He was a harness maker by trade. Died from generalized arteriosclerosis and cardio-vascular disease. Buried State Hospital Cemetery, St Peter MN.

Johnny Werts—4 Years Pitcher (b. 20 Apr 1898 Pomaria SC–d. 24 Sep 1990 at his home in Newberry SC) He was a machinist for Newberry Mill, retiring in 1970. Died from a heart attack. Buried St Paul's Lutheran Church Cemetery, Pomaria SC.

Del Wertz—1 Year Infielder (b. 11 Oct 1888 Canton OH–d. 26 May 1958 Sarasota Memorial Hospital, Sarasota FL) He worked for the Studebaker Auto Manufacturing Company in South Bend IN, retiring to Sarasota in 1953. Buried City Cemetery, South Bend IN.

Vic Wertz—17 Years Outfielder (b. 9 Feb 1925 York PA–d. 7 Jul 1983 Harper Hospital, Detroit MI) He played for 17 seasons, eight of them after recovering from polio in 1955, and is enshrined in the sports halls of fame in Michigan, Ohio and Pennsylvania. He operated a beer distributorship in suburban Detroit, buying it in 1955 and building it into one of the largest in the state, employing 102 workers. Died following emergency open heart surgery, two weeks after a heart attack. Buried Holy Sepulchre Cemetery, Southfield MI.

Billy West—1 Year Infielder (b. 21 Aug 1840 Philadelphia PA–d. 18 Aug 1891 at his home in Radnor PA) An attorney, he served two terms as Philadelphia City Solicitor. He was also a vice-president of the Commonwealth Title and Trust Company. Although in excellent health, he took ill in the morning and died that day from heart disease.

Buck West—2 Years Outfielder (b. 29 Aug 1860 Spring Mill OH–d. 13 Jan 1929 at his home in Mansfield OH) He was a purchasing agent for a wholesale liquor business in Columbus OH before moving to Mansfield where he opened a liquor store. Later he opened a restaurant there. Died from influenza and pneumonia. Buried Mansfield Cemetery, Mansfield OH.

Dick West—6 Years Catcher (b. 24 Nov 1915 Louisville KY–d. 13 Mar 1996 Parkview Memorial Hospital, Fort Wayne IN) Served in the U.S. Navy during World War II. He retired from the wholesale lumber business and was the co-founder of the Kelly Box and Packaging Company. Buried Lindenwood Cemetery, Fort Wayne IN.

Frank West—1 Year Pitcher (b. Jan 1874 Johnstown PA–d. 6 Sep 1932 Wilmerding PA) He worked more than 20 years for Westinghouse Corp. Died following an illness of heart trouble and dropsy. Buried Grandview Cemetery, Johnstown PA.

Hi West—2 Years Pitcher (b. 8 Aug 1884 Roseville IL–d. 24 May 1963 Toluca Lake Conv Hosp, North Hollywood CA) He worked in the sales department of Standard Oil Company, retiring in 1950. Died from pneumonia following a cerebral thrombosis. Cremated.

Lefty West—2 Years Pitcher (b. 3 Sep 1915 Gibsonville NC–d. 23 Jul 1979 Hendersonville NC) He was a retired employee of Miller's Laundry and Cleaners in Hendersonville. Buried Forest Lawn Memorial Park, Hendersonville NC.

Max West—2 Years Outfielder (b. 14 Jul 1904 Sunset TX–d. 25 Apr 1971 Houston TX) He lived in Houston 29 years. Buried Earthman Rest Haven, Houston TX.

Sammy West—16 Years Outfielder (b. 5 Oct 1904 Longview TX–d. 23 Nov 1985 Methodist Hospital, Lubbock TX) World War II veteran. He was a partner in Jarrett-West Drug Store in Lubbock until 1945, and operated the sports center in Lubbock until his retirement in 1970. Buried Resthaven Memorial Park, Lubbock TX.

Oscar Westerberg—1 Year Infielder (b. 8 Jul 1882–d. 17 Apr 1909 at his home in Alameda CA) Died at the height of his career after an illness of several months. Buried Mountain View Cemetery, Oakland CA.

Al Weston—3 Games Pinch Hitter (b. 11 Dec 1905 Lynn MA–d. 12 Nov 1997 Sharp Cabrillo Hospital, San Diego CA) He owned and operated Paramount Laundry for 30 years. Died from throat cancer. Cremated.

Buzz Wetzel—2 Years Outfielder (b. 7 Jul 1893 Columbus IN–d. 5 Mar 1942 at his home in Burbank CA) World War I veteran. He was an electrician at a motion picture studio. Died from heart disease. Cremated.

Buzz Wetzel—1 Year Pitcher (b. 25 Aug 1894 Jay OK–d. 7 Mar 1941 Gila County Hospital, Globe AZ) He lived in the Miami AZ area for about two years where he was a carpenter. Died following blood poisoning. Buried Pinal Cemetery, Globe AZ.

Shorty Wetzel—1 Year Pitcher (b. 1868 Philadelphia PA–d. 24 Feb 1899 Deaconess Hospital, Dayton OH) Died at the height of his career from Bright's disease. Buried Syracuse NY.

Gus Weyhing—14 Years Pitcher (b. 29 Sep 1866 Louisville KY–d. 3 Sep 1955 at his home in Louisville KY) He played baseball for 18 years and was a manager and umpire in the minor leagues. He retired as a night watchman at the Louisville Water Company at age 86. Buried Calvary Cemetery, Louisville KY.

John Weyhing—2 Years Pitcher (b. 24 Jun 1869 Louisville KY–d. 20 Jun 1890 Louisville KY) Died from consumption early in his career. Buried Eastern Cemetery, Louisville KY.

Bill Whaley—1 Year Outfielder (b. 10 Feb 1899 Indianapolis IN–d. 3 Mar 1943 Methodist Hospital, Indianapolis IN) He played in the Pacific Coast League, and was a special delivery postman. Died following an illness of more than a year. Buried Crown Hill Cemetery, Indianapolis IN.

Bert Whaling—3 Years Catcher (b. 22 Jun 1888 Los Angeles CA–d. 21 Jan 1965 V A Hospital, Los Angeles CA) World War I veteran. Died from metastatic adenocarcinoma. Buried Los Angeles National Cemetery, Los Angeles CA.

Mack Wheat—7 Years Catcher (b. 9 Jun 1893 Polo MO–d. 14 Aug 1979 Los Banos Convalescent Hosp, Los Banos CA) He was a manager for Pacific Gas and Electric for 46 years. Died from lung cancer and emphysema. Buried Los Banos Cemetery, Los Banos CA.

Zack Wheat—19 Years Outfielder Hall of Fame (b. 23 May 1888 Hamilton MO–d. 11 Mar 1972 Bothwell Hospital, Sedalia MO) Died following a heart attack suffered at his home. Buried Forest Hill Cemetery, Kansas City MO.

Charlie Wheatley—1 Year Pitcher (b. 27 Jun 1893 Rosedale KS–d. 10 Dec 1982 at a hospital in Tulsa OK) A Tulsa inventor and businessman, he pioneered the invention of industrial valve equipment. He worked as a salesman and then a free agent for his brother's valve company before organizing his own firm to invent and build valves in the 1950s. Selling his business for $10M in 1970, he was still active as a consultant up until his death at age 89. Buried Memorial Park, Tulsa OK.

Woody Wheaton—2 Years Outfielder (b. 3 Oct 1914 Philadelphia PA–d. 11 Dec 1995 Lancashire Hall, Lancaster PA) He managed minor league baseball and coached baseball at Franklin and Marshall College from 1961 to 1970. He worked for Prestige Color, Inc, and was a guard at World Industries, Inc, retiring in 1980. He was also a singer of note. Died after a long illness. Buried Arlington Cemetery, Drexel Hill PA.

Dick Wheeler—1 Year Outfielder (b. 14 Jan 1898 Keene NH–d. 12 Feb 1962 Lexington MA).

Ed Wheeler—1 Year Infielder (b. 15 Jun 1879 Sherman MI–d. 15 Aug 1960 Fort Worth TX) He lived 27 years at Fort Worth and was the area sales representative for Carey Salt Company of Hutchinson KS, retiring in 1948. He was an avid hunter and fisher. Buried Greenwood Memorial Park, Fort Worth TX.

Ed Wheeler—1 Year Infielder (b. 24 May 1915 Los Angeles CA–d. 4 Aug 1983 at his home in Centralia WA) He coached and managed minor league baseball before working as a salesman for Rexall Drug Company. He later owned and operated Garrison's Rexall Drug Store in Centralia 19 years, retiring in 1978. Died from leukemia.

George Wheeler—3 Games Pinch Hitter (b. 10 Nov 1881 Shelburn IN–d. 13 Jun 1918 at his home in Clinton IN) He worked in the mines near Clinton. Died from tuberculosis.

George Wheeler—4 Years Pitcher (b. 30 Jul 1869 Methuen MA–d. 21 Mar 1946 Community Hospital, Santa Ana CA) He worked in the bakery business. Died from a cerebral hemorrhage. Cremated.

Harry Wheeler—6 Years Outfielder 1 Year Manager (b. 3 Mar 1858 Versailles IN–d. 9 Oct 1900 at his home in Cincinnati OH) Died after being ill a number of years. Buried Spring Grove Cemetery, Cincinnati OH.

Rip Wheeler—4 Years Pitcher (b. 2 Mar 1898 Marion KY–d. 18 Sep 1968 Crittenden County Hospital, Marion KY) He managed some minor league baseball before becoming a businessman in Marion. He also was a Kentucky Conservation officer for 21 years, retiring in 1963. Died following a lengthy illness. Buried Mapleview Cemetery, Marion KY.

Bobby Wheelock—3 Years Infielder (b. 6 Aug 1864 Charlestown MA–d. 13 Mar 1928 Boston MA) He was a well-known chef in many of the leading resort hotels of the United States. Died from pneumonia. Buried Mount Auburn Cemetery, Cambridge MA.

Jim Whelan—1 Game Pinch Hitter (b. 11 May 1890 Kansas City MO–d. 29 Nov 1929 Dayton OH)He was an executive for the Delco Light Company. Died from lymphoma. Buried Calvary Cemetery, Dayton OH.

Tom Whelan—1 Year Infielder (b. 3 Jan 1894 Lynn MA–d. 26 Jun 1957 Baker Memorial Hospital, Boston MA) Served in the Aviation Corps of the U.S. Navy during World War I. He also played professional football. He coached at English High School in Lynn from 1926 to 1942 and was principal there from 1942 until his death. Died after an illness of two years. Buried St Joseph Cemetery, Lynn MA.

Pete Whisenant—8 Years Outfielder (b. 14 Dec 1929 Asheville NC–d. 22 Mar 1996 Port Charlotte FL) Served in the U.S. Navy during the Korean War. He owned and operated several successful businesses including an arcade, an insulation business, a bar and package store and a vending machine business. Died after an extended illness. Cremated.

Lew Whistler—4 Years Infielder (b. 10 Mar 1868 St Louis MO–d. 30 Dec 1959 St Louis MO) Buried Bethany Cemetery, Pagedale MO.

Pat Whitaker—2 Years Pitcher (b. 1865 St

Louis MO–d. 15 Jul 1902 St Louis MO) Died from phthisis pulmonarius.

Bob Whitcher—1 Year Pitcher (b. 29 Apr 1917 Berlin NH–d. 8 May 1997 Akron OH).

Abe White—1 Year Pitcher (b. 16 May 1906 Winder GA–d. 1 Oct 1978 Atlanta GA) Buried Zion Cemetery, Brazelton GA.

Bill White—4 Years Infielder (b. 1 May 1860 Bellaire OH–d. 29 Dec 1924 Bellaire OH) He was a security guard for Riverside Tube Mill. Died from lobar pneumonia. Buried Rose Hill Cemetery, Bellaire OH.

Charlie White—2 Years Catcher (b. 12 Aug 1928 Kinston NC–d. 26 May 1998 Seattle WA).

Deacon White—15 Years Infielder 1 Year Manager (b. 2 Dec 1847 Caton NY–d. 7 Jul 1939 near St Charles IL) At the time of his death, at his daughter's summer cottage, he was the oldest living former major leaguer. Buried Restland Cemetery, Mendota IL.

Deke White—1 Year Pitcher (b. 8 Sep 1872 Albany NY–d. 5 Nov 1957 Ilion NY).

Doc White—13 Years Pitcher (b. 9 Apr 1879 Washington DC–d. 17 Feb 1969 at his home in Silver Spring MD) He practiced medicine in suburban Washington DC. Buried Rock Creek Cemetery, Washington DC.

Don White—2 Years Outfielder (b. 8 Jan 1919 Everett WA–d. 15 Jun 1987 Carlsbad CA).

Ed White—1 Year Outfielder (b. 6 Apr 1926 Anniston AL–d. 28 Sep 1982 Regional Medical Center, Lakeland FL) Living in Lakeland since 1950, he was a coach at Lakeland High School. Buried Lakeland Memorial Gardens, Lakeland FL.

Ernie White—7 Years Pitcher (b. 5 Sep 1916 Pacolet Mills SC–d. 22 May 1974 Veteran's Hospital, Augusta GA) World War II veteran. He was a coach for the Braves and Mets. Died following surgery to remove cartilage and bone chips from a knee. Buried Pacolet Memorial Gardens, Pacolet SC.

Hal White—12 Years Pitcher (b. 18 Mar 1919 Utica NY–d. 21 Apr 2001 Sarasota FL) Served in the U.S. Navy during World War II. Buried Florida National Cemetery, Bushnell FL.

Jack White—2 Years Infielder (b. 31 Aug 1905 New York City NY–d. 19 Jun 1971 Flushing NY) Buried St Raymond Cemetery, Bronx NY.

John White—1 Year Outfielder (b. 19 Jan 1878 Indianapolis IN–d. 30 Sep 1963 General Hospital, Indianapolis IN) He worked ten years for the Van Camp Hardware Company and 16 years for the Ford Motor Company. Buried Floral Park Cemetery, Indianapolis IN.

Jo-Jo White—9 Years Outfielder 1 Year Manager (b. 1 Jun 1909 Red Oak GA–d. 9 Oct 1986 Tacoma WA) Died from a pulmonary embolism. Cremated.

Kirby White—3 Years Pitcher (b. 3 Jan 1884 Hillsboro OH–d. 22 Apr 1943 at his home in Hillsboro OH) He was a furniture finisher and was well known as a fine woodworker and refinisher of antique furniture. Died from a heart attack. Buried Hillsboro Cemetery, Hillsboro OH.

Sam White—1 Year Catcher (b. 23 Aug 1892 Greater Preston, England–d. 11 Nov 1929 Philadelphia PA) Buried East Cedar Hill Cemetery, Philadelphia PA.

Sammy White—11 Years Catcher (b. 7 Jul 1927 Wenatchee WA–d. 4 Aug 1991 at his home in Princeville HI) He ran a successful bowling establishment in the Brighton section of Boston before moving to Hawaii where he operated a golf course. Died from a heart attack.

Steve White—1 Year Pitcher (b. 21 Dec 1884 Dorchester MA–d. 29 Jan 1975 Braintree Nursing Home, Braintree MA) He taught and coached at South Boston (MA) High School from 1925 to 1954. Buried St Mary's Cemetery, Randolph MA.

Will White—10 Years Pitcher 1 Year Manager (b. 11 Oct 1854 Caton NY–d. 31 Aug 1911 Port Carling, Ontario, Canada) Died from drowning.

Burgess Whitehead—9 Years Infielder (b. 29 Jun 1910 Tarboro NC–d. 25 Nov 1993 at his home in Windsor NC) Served in the U.S. Army Air Corps during World War II. Buried St Thomas Church Cemetery, Windsor NC.

John Whitehead—7 Years Pitcher (b. 27 Apr 1909 Coleman TX–d. 20 Oct 1964 M and S Hospital, Bonham TX) He farmed and ranched in Fannin County, TX. Buried Carson Cemetery, Ector TX.

Milt Whitehead—1 Year Infielder (b. 1862 Canada–d. 15 Aug 1901 Highland CA).

Earl Whitehill—17 Years Pitcher (b. 7 Feb 1900 Cedar Rapids IA–d. 22 Oct 1954 St Joseph's Hospital, Omaha NE) He traveled for a sporting goods firm for several years. Died from a hemorrhage from a basal skull fracture suffered in an automobile accident a week earlier. Buried Cedar Memorial Park Cemetery, Cedar Rapids IA.

Charlie Whitehouse—3 Years Pitcher (b. 25 Jan 1894 Charleston IL–d. 19 Jul 1960 V A Hospital, Indianapolis IN) Veteran of both World War I and World War II. For 40 years he was a yardman for the New York Central Railroad in Indianapolis. Buried Crown Hill Cemetery, Indianapolis IN.

Gil Whitehouse—2 Years Outfielder (b. 15 Oct 1893 Somerville MA–d. 14 Feb 1926 Brewer ME) Died suddenly while attending to his duties at the Eastern Manufacturing Company where he worked during the off-season.

Gurdon Whiteley—2 Years Outfielder (b. 5 Oct 1859 Ashaway RI–d. 24 Nov 1924 Cranston RI).

George Whiteman—3 Years Outfielder (b. 23 Dec 1882 Peoria IL–d. 10 Feb 1947 at his home in Houston TX) He managed minor league baseball before becoming a deputy constable in Harris County, TX, living in Houston 40 years. Died from a heart attack. Buried Hollywood Cemetery, Houston TX.

Jesse Whiting—3 Years Pitcher (b. 30 May 1879 Philadelphia PA–d. 28 Oct 1937 Philadelphia PA) He was a scout for the Athletics from 1905 to 1915, then became a conductor for Philadelphia Rapid Transit. Died suddenly. Buried Greenmount Cemetery, Philadelphia PA.

Frank Whitman—2 Years Infielder (b. 15 Aug 1924 Marengo IN–d. 6 Feb 1994 Anderson Hospital, Maryville IL) Served in the U.S. Army during World War II and was awarded the bronze star. He coached high school basketball in Illinois from 1949 until 1958 when he became a self-employed marketing analyst. Buried St John's Evangelical Cemetery, Troy IL.

Art Whitney—11 Years Infielder (b. 16 Jan 1858 Brockton MA–d. 15 Aug 1943 Lowell MA) He had a business in Fitchburg MA and for many years was associated with a large sporting house in the manufacture and supply of sporting equipment and supplies. Buried Edson Cemetery, Lowell MA.

Frank Whitney—1 Year Outfielder (b. 18 Feb 1856 Brockton MA–d. 30 Oct 1943 Baltimore MD) Buried Green Mount Cemetery, Baltimore MD.

Jim Whitney—10 Years Pitcher (b. 10 Nov 1857 Conklin NY–d. 21 May 1891 Binghamton NY) Died at the height of his baseball career after a long and painful struggle with the dread consumption. Buried Spring Forest Cemetery, Binghamton NY.

Pinky Whitney—12 Years Infielder (b. 2 Jan 1905 San Antonio TX–d. 1 Sep 1987 at his home in Center TX) He worked for the Lone Star Brewery in San Antonio before retiring to Center. Buried Mission Burial Park South, San Antonio TX.

Bill Whitrock—4 Years Pitcher (b. 4 Mar 1870 Cincinnati OH–d. 26 Jul 1935 at his home in Derby CT) He worked many years for Cameron Electrical Company in Ansonia CT. Died from a heart attack. Buried Cincinnati OH.

Walt Whittaker—1 Year Pitcher (b. 11 Jun 1894 Chelsea MA–d. 7 Aug 1965 Pembroke MA) He was a dentist in Somerville MA. Died from a heart attack while having tire trouble with his car. Buried Mount Pleasant Cemetery, Bryantville MA.

Possum Whitted—11 Years Outfielder (b. 4 Feb 1890 Durham NC–d. 16 Oct 1962 James Walker Memorial Hosp, Wilmington NC) World War I veteran. He was the baseball coach at Duke University for several years and athletic director at the Wilmington shipyards from 1942 until his death. Died following a short illness. Buried Wilmington National Cemetery, Wilmington NC.

Bob Wicker—6 Years Pitcher (b. 25 May 1878 Bedford IN–d. 22 Jan 1955 Evanston IL) Buried Forest Home Cemetery, Forest Park IL.

Kemp Wicker—4 Years Pitcher (b. 13 Aug 1906 Kernersville NC–d. 11 Jun 1973 at his home in Kernersville NC) He managed minor league baseball for a short while before opening a restaurant in Burlington Mills, retiring in 1967. Buried United Methodist Church Cemetery, Kernersville NC.

Al Wickland—5 Years Outfielder (b. 27 Jan 1888 Chicago IL–d. 14 Mar 1980 Heritage Nursing Home, Port Washington WI) He was a tool and die maker. Cremated.

Wild Bill Widner—5 Years Pitcher (b. 3 Jun 1867 Cincinnati OH–d. 10 Dec 1908 at his home in Cincinnati OH) He was a fireman and an inspector for the City of Cincinnati and later worked for Russell and Jemson Contracting Company. Died from diabetes.

Charlie Wiedemeyer—1 Year Pitcher (b. 31 Jan 1914 Chicago IL–d. 27 Oct 1979 at his home in Lake Geneva FL) World War II veteran. An educator, he was one of the first professors at Santa Fe Community College in 1966 and at one time was senator director of the east campus. Buried Keystone Heights Cemetery, Keystone Heights FL.

Stump Wiedman—9 Years Pitcher (b. 17 Feb 1861 Rochester NY–d. 2 Mar 1905 New York Hospital, New York City NY) He umpired in the National League in 1896. Died following surgery to remove a tumor from his throat. Buried Holy Sepulchre Cemetery, Rochester NY.

Jack Wieneke—1 Year Pitcher (b. 10 Mar 1894 Saltsburg PA–d. 16 Mar 1933 Pleasant Ridge MI) He was an experimental engineer at Ford Motor Company from 1928 until his death. Died from heart disease. Buried Roseland Park Cemetery, Berkley MI.

Alan Wiggins—7 Years Outfielder (b. 17 Feb 1958 Los Angeles CA–d. 6 Jan 1991 Cedars-Sinai Hospital, Los Angeles CA) Died from complications of AIDS and had a history of drug abuse. Buried Rose Hills Memorial Park, Whittier CA.

Jimmy Wiggs—3 Years Pitcher (b. 1 Sep 1876 Trondhjem, Norway–d. 20 Jan 1963 Green Memorial Hospital, Xenia OH) He pitched a 24 inning game for Oakland against San Francisco — the longest game in Pacific Coast League history. He was the national re-insurance manager for Fireman's Fund Insurance Company in San Francisco. Died following a brief illness. Cremated.

Fred Wigington—1 Year Pitcher (b. 16 Dec 1897 Rogers NE–d. 8 May 1980 Mesa Lutheran Hospital, Mesa AZ) He was an automobile dealer in Schuyler NE for 35 years before retiring to Mesa in 1960. He is a member of the Nebraska Baseball Hall of Fame. Buried Mountain View Memorial Gardens, Mesa AZ.

Claude Wilburn—1 Year Outfielder (b. 1 Sep 1912 Woodsdale NC–d. 13 Nov 1992 Person Memorial Hospital, Roxboro NC) He was a retired farmer. Buried Bethel Hill Baptist Church Cemetery, Bethel Hill NC.

Harry Wilhelm—1 Year Pitcher (b. 7 Apr 1874 Uniontown PA–d. 20 Feb 1944 at his sister-in-law's home in Republic PA) Buried Oak Grove Cemetery, Uniontown PA.

Kaiser Wilhelm—9 Years Pitcher 2 Years Manager (b. 26 Jan 1874 Wooster OH–d. 22 May 1936 Rochester NY) Buried Wooster OH.

Spider Wilhelm—1 Year Infielder (b. 23 May 1929 Baltimore MD–d. 20 Oct 1992 Venice FL) Buried Dulaney Valley Memorial Garden, Timonium MD.

Joe Wilhoit—4 Years Outfielder (b. 20 Dec 1888 Hiawatha KS–d. 25 Sep 1930 Cottage Hospital, Santa Barbara CA) He was the owner and operator of the Wilhoit Luggage Store in Santa Barbara. Died from respiratory failure. Buried Calvary Cemetery, Santa Barbara CA.

Denney Wilie—3 Years Outfielder (b. 22 Sep 1890 Mount Calm TX–d. 20 Jun 1966 Barrett Convalescent Hospital, Hayward CA) Died from inanition, debilitation and congestive heart failure. Cremated.

Harry Wilke—1 Year Infielder (b. 14 Dec 1900 Cincinnati OH–d. 21 Jun 1991 Schroder Manor, Hamilton OH) He owned and operated Wilke's Cafe for a number of years, retiring in 1962. Buried St Stephen's Cemetery, Hamilton OH.

Lefty Wilkie—3 Years Pitcher (b. 30 Oct 1914 Zealandia, Saskatchewan, Canada–d. 5 Aug 1992 at a hospital in Tualatin OR) Served on a mortar team at the Battle of the Bulge for the U.S. Army during World War II. For many years he was a self-employed cabinet maker, retiring in 1979. He raised poultry and was a superintendent and judge for 12 years at the Oregon State Fair. He was also a past-president of the Newberg (OR) Rod and Gun Club. Died from heart problems. Cremated.

Ed Wilkinson—1 Year Outfielder (b. 20 Jun 1890 Jacksonville OR–d. 9 Apr 1918 at a sanitarium in Tucson AZ) Died at the height of his career from pulmonary tuberculosis after being ill five years. Buried Jacksonville Cemetery, Jacksonville OR.

Roy Wilkinson—5 Years Pitcher (b. 8 May 1893 Canandaigua NY–d. 2 Jul 1956 Louisville KY).

Ted Wilks—10 Years Pitcher (b. 13 Nov 1915 Fulton NY–d. 21 Aug 1989 Houston TX) Buried Forest Park East, Houston TX.

Ed Willett—10 Years Pitcher (b. 7 Mar 1884 Norfolk VA–d. 10 May 1934 at his home in Wellington KS) He listed his occupation as carpenter, and was known to work on construction jobs. Died from a heart attack. Buried Caldwell Cemetery, Caldwell KS.

Al Williams—2 Years Pitcher (b. 11 May 1914 Valhermosa Springs AL–d. 19 Jul 1969 Doctor's Hospital, Groves TX) World War II veteran. He was a pumper at Gulf Oil in Port Arthur TX for 27 years. Died from injuries suffered in an automobile accident a week earlier. Buried Shilo Cemetery, San Augustine TX.

Art Williams—1 Year Outfielder (b. 26 Aug 1877 Somerville MA–d. 16 May 1941 at his home in Arlington VA).

Art Williams—(b. 24 Feb 1934 AR–d. 8 Feb 1979 San Joaquin Community Hosp, Bakersfield CA) A National League umpire from 1973 to 1977, he was the first black umpire in the National League. He drove a bus after being dismissed by the National League in 1977. Died six weeks after undergoing brain surgery. Buried Union Cemetery, Bakersfield CA.

Bob Williams—3 Years Catcher (b. 27 Apr 1894 Monday OH–d. 6 Aug 1962 Mount St Mary Hospital, Nelsonville OH) He was a well-known cafe owner in Nelsonville. Died after being in declining health several years. Buried Green Lawn Cemetery, Nelsonville OH.

Buff Williams—7 Years Catcher (b. 31 Jan 1882 Carthage IL–d. 23 Jul 1933 Graham Hospital, Keokuk IA) After retiring from baseball he returned to his farm near Hamilton IL where he farmed and was active in local baseball until poor health prevailed. Buried Moss Ridge Cemetery, Carthage IL.

Cy Williams—19 Years Outfielder (b. 21 Dec 1887 Wadena IN–d. 23 Apr 1974 Eagle River Memorial Hosp, Eagle River WI) He was a four-time National League home run leader. A renowned architect, he lived at Three Lakes WI for 56 years. Buried Three Lakes Cemetery, Three Lakes WI.

Dale Williams—1 Year Pitcher (b. 6 Oct 1855 Ludlow KY–d. 22 Oct 1939 at his home in Covington KY) He was a railroad car repairman and a building contractor, retiring in 1933.

Dave Williams—1 Year Pitcher (b. 7 Feb 1881 Scranton PA–d. 25 Apr 1918 Army and Navy Hospital, Hot Springs AR) Died from pneumonia while serving in the U.S. Army during World War I. Buried Dunmore Cemetery, Dunmore PA.

Denny Williams—4 Years Outfielder (b. 13 Dec 1899 Portland OR–d. 24 Mar 1929 near San Clemente CA) He was killed at the height of his career in a hit-and-run automobile accident while enroute from San Diego CA to Los Angeles CA with other members of the Portland OR Pacific Coast League baseball team. Buried Mount Calvary Cemetery, Portland OR.

Dib Williams—6 Years Infielder (b. 19 Jan 1910 Greenbrier AR–d. 2 Apr 1992 Searcy AR) Served in the U.S. Army during World War II. Buried Thorn Cemetery, Greenbrier AR.

Don Williams—1 Year Pitcher (b. 2 Sep 1935 Los Angeles CA–d. 20 Dec 1991 Torrey Pines Convalescent Hosp, La Jolla CA) Served in the military. For 23 years he was a retail salesman for Hartz Corporation. Died from lung cancer. Cremated.

Earl Williams—1 Year Catcher (b. 27 Jan 1903 Cumberland Gap TN–d. 10 Mar 1958 St Mary's Hospital, Knoxville TN) World War II veteran. He played baseball in the Eastern League, Sally League and Southern League, and was a collector for the U.S. Internal Revenue Service for 20 years. Apparently died from a heart attack. Buried Highland Memorial Cemetery, Knoxville TN.

Edward Bennett Williams—(b. 31 May 1920 Hartford CT–d. 13 Aug 1988 Georgetown Hospital, Washington DC) A prominent Washington DC trial lawyer, he owned the Washington Redskins 14 years and the Baltimore Orioles nine years. Died from colon cancer. Buried St Gabriel's Cemetery, Potomac MD.

Gus Williams—5 Years Outfielder (b. 7 May 1888 Omaha NE–d. 16 Apr 1964 Morrison Community Hospital, Morrison IL) He and his wife were chiropractors in Sterling IL. Later he was a game warden. Died from a heart attack. Buried Calvary Cemetery, Sterling IL.

Gus Williams—1 Year Pitcher (b. 1870 New York City NY–d. 14 Oct 1890 New York City NY).

Harry Williams—2 Years Infielder (b. 23 Jun 1890 Omaha NE–d. 21 Dec 1963 Community Hospital, Huntington Park CA) He was president of the Pacific Coast League for a time, and worked 20 years as a yardman for a feed yard. Died from acute leukemia. Buried Holy Sepulchre Cemetery, Omaha NE.

Jimmy Williams—3 Years Manager (b. 3 Jan 1848 Columbus OH–d. 24 Oct 1918 North Hempstead NY) At one time he was president of the American Association. Later he was the clerk of the Columbus Board of Education. Buried Green Lawn Memorial Cemetery, Columbus OH.

Jimmy Williams—11 Years Infielder (b. 20 Dec 1876 St Louis MO–d. 16 Jan 1965 at a hospital in St Petersburg FL) He retired from the City of Minneapolis (MN) Health Department. Buried Lakewood Cemetery, Minneapolis MN.

Johnny Williams—1 Year Pitcher (b. 16 Jul 1889 Honolulu HI–d. 8 Sep 1963 Kaiser Hospital, Los Angeles CA) World War I veteran. He retired to Hawaii where he lived until shortly before his death. For 25 years he was a collector for the city and county of Honolulu. Died from a heart attack and complications of diabetes. Buried San Fernando Mission Cemetery, Mission Hills CA.

Ken Williams—14 Years Outfielder (b. 28 Jun 1890 Grants Pass OR–d. 22 Jan 1959 Grants Pass OR) World War I veteran. He owned the Owl Billiard Parlor in Grants Pass where he had lived his entire life. Died from a heart condition. Cremated.

Lefty Williams—7 Years Pitcher (b. 9 Mar 1893 Aurora MO–d. 4 Nov 1959 at his home in Laguna Beach CA) He was banned from baseball for his involvement in the Black Sox Scandal. He was a self-employed nurseryman. Died from Hodgkin's disease. Cremated. Buried Melrose Abbey Cemetery, Orange CA.

Leon Williams—1 Year Pitcher (b. 2 Dec 1905 Macon GA–d. 20 Nov 1984 Piedmont Hospital, Atlanta GA) He was an account executive for Gulf Oil Corporation. Buried Arlington Memorial Park, Sandy Springs GA.

Marsh Williams—1 Year Pitcher (b. 21 Feb 1893 Faison NC–d. 22 Feb 1935 at his home in Tucson AZ) Served in the U.S. Army during World War I. He was gassed during the war and died from the effects of that gassing. He had been undergoing treatments for years. Buried Faison NC.

Mutt Williams—2 Years Pitcher (b. 31 Jul 1891 Ozark AR–d. 30 Mar 1962 Fayetteville AR) Veteran of World War I. Died after a long illness. Buried National Cemetery, Ozark AR.

Otto Williams—4 Years Infielder (b. 2 Nov 1877 Newark NJ–d. 19 Mar 1937 St Joseph's Hospital, Omaha NE) He managed minor league baseball, coached and was athletic trainer at Creighton University. Died from lobar pneumonia after an eight-day battle. Buried Graceland Park Cemetery, Omaha NE.

Papa Williams—1 Year Outfielder (b. 17 Jul 1913 Meridian MS–d. 2 Nov 1993 Jeff Anderson Medical Center, Meridian MS) He was a retired engineer for Southern Railway. Buried Memorial Park, Meridian MS.

Pop Williams—3 Years Pitcher (b. 19 May 1874 Bowdoinham ME–d. 4 Aug 1959 Topsham ME) He taught school at Topsham ME and was a selectman, serving the Topsham community for over 40 years. Died following a long illness. Buried Riverview Cemetery, Topsham ME.

Rinaldo Williams—1 Year Infielder (b. 18 Dec 1893 Santa Cruz CA–d. 24 Apr 1966 Lawrence Memorial Hospital, Cottonwood AZ) He played professional baseball for more than 20 years. Died while visiting friends in Cottonwood. Buried Beverly Hills CA.

Smokey Joe Williams—12 Years Pitcher Hall of Fame (b. 6 Apr 1885 Sequin TX–d. 12 Mar 1946 New York City NY) He pitched in the Negro Leagues from 1910 to 1932 and is credited with a .624 winning percentage. Buried Lincoln Memorial Cemetery, Suitland MD.

Steamboat Williams—2 Years Pitcher (b. 31 Jan 1892 Cascade MT–d. 29 Jun 1979 Homestead Nursing Home, Deer River MN) He owned a resort. Buried Olivet Cemetery, Deer River MN.

Tom Williams—2 Years Pitcher (b. 19 Aug 1870 Minersville OH–d. 27 Jul 1940 Black Rest Home, Columbus OH) He was a coal miner. Died from a heart attack. Buried New Straitsville Joint Cemetery, New Straitsville OH.

Wash Williams—2 Years Outfielder (b. Philadelphia PA–d. 9 Aug 1892 Philadelphia PA).

Woody Williams—4 Years Infielder (b. 21 Aug 1912 Pamplin VA–d. 24 Feb 1995 Appomattox Health Care Ctr, Appomattox VA) He owned and operated the Williams Grocery Store in Pamplin for 30 years. Buried Pamplin Community Cemetery, Pamplin VA.

Al Williamson—1 Year Pitcher (b. 20 Feb 1900 Buckville AR–d. 29 Nov 1978 at his home in Hot Springs AR) He worked for the Hot Springs Water Company, retiring in 1969. Buried Memorial Gardens Cemetery, Hot Springs AR.

Howie Williamson—10 Games Pinch Hitter (b. 23 Dec 1904 Little Rock AR–d. 15 Aug 1969 in a nursing home in Texarkana AR) Buried Hillcrest Cemetery, Texarkana AR.

Ned Williamson—13 Years Infielder (b. 24 Oct 1857 Philadelphia PA–d. 3 Mar 1894 Mountain Valley AR) Died from dropsy of the stomach. Buried Rosehill Cemetery, Chicago IL.

Julius Willigrod—1 Year Outfielder (b. 27 Oct 1857 Marshalltown IA–d. 27 Nov 1906 San Francisco CA) He worked 30 years for the Southern Pacific Railroad, first in Los Angeles CA, and the last 15 years in San Francisco. He held the position of claim agent when he died. Died suddenly from a gastric hemorrhage of a stomach ulcer. Buried Riverside Cemetery, Marshalltown IA.

Hugh Willingham—4 Years Infielder (b. 30 May 1906 Dalhart TX–d. 15 Jun 1988 at his home in El Reno OK) He was a scout for the White Sox before serving as under-sheriff for Canadian County, OK, from 1958 to 1976. He then worked for First National Bank until 1980. Died from cancer. Buried El Reno Cemetery, El Reno OK.

Joe Willis—3 Years Pitcher (b. 9 Apr 1890 Coal Grove OH–d. 3 Dec 1966 Lawrence County Hospital, Ironton OH) He was an oven foreman for Ironton Semet-Solvay Division of Allied Chemical Corporation. Died after a three-year illness. Buried Woodland Cemetery, Ironton OH.

Lefty Willis—3 Years Pitcher (b. 4 Nov 1905 Leetown WV–d. 10 May 1962 Bethesda MD) He owned and operated the Willis Market in Leetown. Buried Edge Hill Cemetery, Charles Town WV.

Les Willis—1 Year Pitcher (b. 17 Jan 1908 Nacogdoches TX–d. 22 Jan 1982 at a hospital in Jasper TX) He owned Star Cleaners in Jasper where he lived 50 years. Active in civic matters, he served on the city council and was mayor. Died from a cardio-vascular accident. Buried Memorial Park Cemetery, Jasper TX.

Ron Willis—5 Years Pitcher (b. 12 Jul 1943 Willisville TN–d. 21 Nov 1977 St Joseph Hospital-East, Memphis TN) He was a self-employed housewares salesman at Memphis. Died from cancer. Buried Zion Cemetery, Obion TN.

Vic Willis—13 Years Pitcher Hall of Fame (b. 12 Apr 1876 Wilmington DE–d. 3 Aug 1947 Union Hospital, Elkton MD) He was the proprietor of the Washington House in Newark DE. Died after suffering a stroke.

Claude Willoughby—7 Years Pitcher (b. 14 Nov 1898 Buffalo KS–d. 14 Aug 1973 Memorial Hospital, McPherson KS) A retired pump mechanic for NCRA, he moved to McPherson from Chanute KS in 1948. Buried Buffalo Cemetery, Buffalo KS.

Dave Wills—1 Year Infielder (b. 26 Jan 1877 Charlottesville VA–d. 12 Oct 1959 at his home in Washington DC) Served as a major and chief paymaster of the U.S. Marines during World War I. He directed a real estate business in Washington DC. Buried Arlington National Cemetery, Arlington VA.

Kid Willson—2 Years Outfielder (b. 3 Nov 1895 Bloomington IL–d. 17 Apr 1964 St Elizabeth Hospital, Union Gap WA) He was a deputy sheriff in Snohomish County, WA, and in Clark County, WA. He also worked for the Washington State Patrol in the weighing division at Vancouver WA and for the transportation service at McCord Air Force Base until he retired in 1961.

Walt Wilmot—10 Years Outfielder (b. 18 Oct 1863 Plover WI–d. 1 Feb 1929 Chicago IL) He promoted automobile shows from 1903 until his death. Died after a long illness. Buried Plover WI.

Whitey Wilshere—3 Years Pitcher (b. 3 Aug 1912 Poplar Ridge NY–d. 23 May 1985 at his home in Cooperstown NY) Served in the U.S. Navy during World War II. He coached baseball at Evansville (IN) High School, and later at Cooperstown (NY) Central School. He also worked in sales for a number of years. Buried Lakewood Cemetery, Cooperstown NY.

Art Wilson—14 Years Catcher (b. 11 Dec 1885

Macon IL–d. 12 Jun 1960 in his hotel room in Chicago IL) Died from a heart attack.

Bill Wilson—3 Years Catcher (b. 28 Oct 1867 Hannibal MO–d. 9 May 1924 St Paul MN) He was believed to be a member of organized crime and had served two prison sentences. Died from ten stab wounds to the chest and neck while trying to break up a robbery at a soft drink parlor. It was said that his death was a hit job to get rid of him. Buried Calvary Cemetery, St Paul MN.

Bill Wilson—5 Years Pitcher (b. 21 Sep 1942 Pomeroy OH–d. 11 Aug 1993 at his home in Broken Arrow OK) He coached for the Phillies before becoming a superintendent for a construction company. Died from cancer. Cremated.

Bob Wilson—1 Year Outfielder (b. 22 Feb 1925 Dallas TX–d. 23 Apr 1985 Dallas TX) World War II veteran. He was a laborer. Buried Lincoln Memorial Cemetery, Dallas TX.

Charlie Wilson—4 Years Infielder (b. 13 Jan 1905 Clinton SC–d. 19 Dec 1970 Rochester NY).

Chink Wilson—1 Year Pitcher (b. 7 Jan 1884 Columbus OH–d. 28 Oct 1925 Seattle WA) Cremated.

Don Wilson—9 Years Pitcher (b. 12 Feb 1945 Monroe LA–d. 5 Jan 1975 at his home in Houston TX) He pitched two no-hitters. He and his five-year-old son died from what was ruled an accidental carbon monoxide poisoning. Buried Forest Lawn Memorial Park, Covina CA.

Eddie Wilson—2 Years Outfielder (b. 7 Sep 1909 New Haven CT–d. 11 Apr 1979 Hilltop House, Hamden CT) Served in the U.S. Merchant Marines during World War II. He was a school teacher. Buried St Lawrence Cemetery, West Haven CT.

Fin Wilson—2 Years Pitcher (b. 9 Dec 1889 East Cork KY–d. 9 Mar 1959 Coral Gables FL) He served as a Kentucky legislator; prohibition administrator for Tennessee, Arkansas and Louisiana, from Memphis TN; and was the U.S. District Court Clerk for Western Tennessee before retiring to Florida about 1934. Buried Auburn Cemetery, Auburn KY.

Frank Wilson—4 Years Outfielder (b. 19 Apr 1901 Malden MA–d. 25 Nov 1974 at his home in Leicester MA) For 18 years he was a thread grinder for John Bath and Company, retiring in 1964. Buried Pine Grove Cemetery, Leicester MA.

Gary Wilson—1 Year Infielder (b. 12 Jan 1877 Baltimore MD–d. 1 May 1969 Randallstown MD) He worked in the freight department of the Baltimore and Ohio Railroad until he retired in 1958. Buried New Cathedral Cemetery, Baltimore MD.

Hack Wilson—12 Years Outfielder Hall of Fame (b. 26 Apr 1900 Elwood City PA–d. 23 Nov 1948 Baltimore MD) He did a number of odd jobs, including work at a sporting goods store, a night club impresario, bartending and was a laborer for the Baltimore City Parks Department when he died. Died from internal hemorrhaging and pneumonia. Buried Druid Ridge Cemetery, Pikesville MD.

Hickie Wilson—1 Year Outfielder (b. abt 1860 Brooklyn NY–d. 28 Nov 1914 Kings' County Hospital, Brooklyn NY) Died from Bright's disease. Buried Cypress Hills Cemetery, Brooklyn NY.

Highball Wilson—4 Years Pitcher (b. 9 Aug 1878 Philadelphia PA–d. 16 Oct 1934 Havre de Grace MD) Buried North Cedar Hill Cemetery, Philadelphia PA.

Icehouse Wilson—1 Game Pinch Hitter (b. 14 Sep 1912 Maricopa CA–d. 13 Oct 1973 Alta Bates Hospital, Berkeley CA) He was a retired Lieutenant Commander from the U.S. Navy Reserve and an administrator at Berkeley High School for 34 years. Died from prostate cancer. Buried St Joseph Cemetery, San Pablo CA.

Jack Wilson—9 Years Pitcher (b. 12 Apr 1912 Portland OR–d. 19 Apr 1995 Edmonds WA) Buried Holyrood Cemetery, Seattle WA.

Jim Wilson—12 Years Pitcher (b. 20 Feb 1922 San Diego CA–d. 2 Sep 1986 at his home in Newport Beach CA) He was a baseball scout. Died from lung cancer. Buried Pacific View Memorial Park, Newport Beach CA.

Jimmie Wilson—18 Years Catcher 9 Years Manager (b. 23 Jul 1900 Philadelphia PA–d. 31 May 1947 at a hospital in Bradenton FL) Retiring from baseball a year before his death, he had just gone into the citrus and vegetable produce business in Bradenton. Died from a heart attack suffered in a sandwich shop. Buried Manasota Memorial Park, Bradenton FL.

John Wilson—1 Year Pitcher (b. 15 Jun 1890 Boonsboro MD–d. 23 Sep 1954 Anne Arundel General Hospital, Annapolis MD) He worked in the physical education department at the U.S. Naval Academy 34 years and was the head basketball coach there for 20 years, retiring in 1953. Died from a heart condition. Buried Cedar Bluff Cemetery, Annapolis MD.

John Wilson—2 Years Pitcher (b. 25 Apr 1905 Coal City AL–d. 27 Aug 1980 at a hospital in Chattanooga TN) World War II veteran. He was a retired Chattanooga carpet salesman. Buried Chattanooga National Cemetery, Chattanooga TN.

Jud Wilson—24 Years Infielder (b. 28 Feb 1899 Remington VA–d. 26 Jun 1963 Washington DC) He played in the negro leagues. Buried Arlington National Cemetery, Arlington VA.

Les Wilson—1 Year Outfielder (b. 17 Jul 1885 St Louis MI–d. 4 Apr 1969 at his home in Edmonds WA) He worked 25 years for Yost Auto Company at Edmonds, then for seven years was a partner in Edmonds Motor Company, retiring in 1953. Died from a heart attack. Buried Floral Hills Cemetery, Lynnwood WA.

Maxie Wilson—2 Years Pitcher (b. 3 Jun 1916 Haw River NC–d. 2 Jan 1977 at his home in Greensboro NC) He worked for S and W Distributors in Greensboro where he had lived 23 years. Buried Pine Hill Cemetery, Burlington NC.

Mike Wilson—1 Year Catcher (b. 2 Dec 1896 Consumnes PA–d. 16 May 1978 Boynton Beach FL) Served in the U.S. Marines during both World Wars I and II. He played professional football before there was an NFL. He was an assistant to football commissioner Bert Bell and retired in 1962 as supervisor of NFL officials. Cremated. Buried Boynton Beach Cemetery, Boynton Beach FL.

Mutt Wilson—1 Year Pitcher (b. 20 Jul 1896 Kiser NC–d. 31 Aug 1962 Wildwood FL) Served in the U.S. Army during World War I. He worked for the Seaboard Airline Railroad. Died from encephalitis, also known as sleeping sickness. Buried Lone Oak Cemetery, Leesburg FL.

Owen Wilson—9 Years Outfielder (b. 21 Aug 1883 Austin TX–d. 22 Feb 1954 Bertram TX) He lived at Bertram 37 years and was a prominent farmer and rancher there. Died suddenly while working in his pasture. Buried Austin Memorial Park Cemetery, Austin TX.

Parke Wilson—7 Years Catcher (b. 26 Oct 1867 Keithsburg IL–d. 20 Dec 1934 Hermosa Beach CA) Buried Inglewood Park Cemetery, Inglewood CA.

Pete Wilson—2 Years Pitcher (b. 9 Oct 1885 Springfield MA–d. 5 Jun 1957 at his home in St Petersburg FL) He was a machinist for Manning, Maxwell and Moore Company in Stratford CT, retiring to St Petersburg in 1953. Buried Memorial Park Cemetery, St Petersburg FL.

Roy Wilson—1 Year Pitcher (b. 13 Sep 1896 Foster IA–d. 3 Dec 1969 at his home in Clarion IA) He served as sheriff of Wright County, IA, from 1937 to 1950 and two terms as mayor of Clarion. He was also an investigator for the Iowa State Department of Taxation. Died in his sleep. Buried Clarion City Cemetery, Clarion IA.

Squanto Wilson—2 Years Catcher (b. 29 Mar 1889 Old Town ME–d. 26 Mar 1967 Augusta General Hospital, Augusta ME) He taught high school before he founded Wilson's Dollar Stores. Buried Glenside Cemetery, Winthrop ME.

Ted Wilson—3 Years Outfielder (b. 30 Aug 1925 Cherryville NC–d. 29 Oct 1974 Gastonia NC) Buried Morningside Park Cemetery, Mount Holly NC.

Tex Wilson—1 Year Pitcher (b. 8 Jul 1901 Trenton TX–d. 15 Sep 1946 Sulphur Springs TX) He was an agent for Texaco. Died from a heart attack. Buried Burns Cemetery, Trenton TX.

Tom Wilson—1 Year Catcher (b. 3 Jun 1890 Fleming KS–d. 7 Mar 1953 San Pedro CA) He was a longshoreman. Died from cancer. Buried Green Hills Memorial Park, Rancho Palos Verdes CA.

Walter Wilson—1 Year Pitcher (b. 24 Nov 1913 Glenn GA–d. 17 Apr 1994 Meadowbrook Manor, Bremen GA) Served in the U.S. Army during World War II. He was a retired dairy farmer. Died after several months of declining health. Buried Glenn Cemetery, Glenn GA.

Zeke Wilson—5 Years Pitcher (b. 24 Dec 1869 Benton AL–d. 26 Apr 1928 at a hospital in Montgomery AL) Died after an extended illness. Buried Oakwood Cemetery, Montgomery AL.

Hal Wiltse—4 Years Pitcher (b. 6 Aug 1903 Clay City IL–d. 2 Nov 1983 at his home in

Bunkie LA) He worked for the Sid Richardson Oil Company, and was an avid golfer. Died from a self-inflicted gunshot wound. Buried Pythian Cemetery, Bunkie LA.

Hooks Wiltse—12 Years Pitcher (b. 7 Sep 1880 Hamilton NY–d. 21 Jan 1959 Long Beach NY).

Snake Wiltse—3 Years Pitcher (b. 5 Dec 1871 Bouckville NY–d. 25 Aug 1928 at his home in Harrisburg PA) He was a foreman in the service department of the Underwood Typewriter Company from 1913 until his death. Died when he accidentally severed an artery in his leg with a pruning knife. Buried Paxtang Cemetery, Harrisburg PA.

Fred Winchell—1 Year Pitcher (b. 23 Jan 1882 Arlington MA–d. 8 Aug 1958 Toronto, Ontario, Canada).

Bill Windle—2 Years Infielder (b. 13 Dec 1904 Galena KS–d. 8 Dec 1981 at a hospital in Corpus Christi TX) He lived in Corpus Christi 46 years, owning and operating Koronado Courts on North Beach until his retirement. Buried Seaside Cemetery, Corpus Christi TX.

Ed Wineapple—1 Year Pitcher (b. 10 Aug 1905 Boston MA–d. 23 Jul 1996 Delray Beach FL).

Ralph Winegarner—6 Years Pitcher (b. 29 Oct 1909 Benton KS–d. 14 Apr 1988 Wesley Medical Center, Wichita KS) He managed minor league baseball, and for eight years was a supervisor of toll collections for the Kansas Turnpike Authority, retiring in 1965. Buried Benton Cemetery, Benton KS.

Jim Winford—6 Years Pitcher (b. 9 Oct 1909 Shelbyville TN–d. 16 Dec 1970 Heritage House Nursing Home, Miami OK) Served in the U.S. Navy during World War II. He managed minor league baseball before becoming a fireman in Oklahoma City OK. He was also a security guard there. Buried New Hope Cemetery, Meeker OK.

Ernie Wingard—4 Years Pitcher (b. 17 Oct 1900 Prattville AL–d. 17 Jan 1977 Prattville AL) Died unexpectedly. Buried Oak Hill Cemetery, Prattville AL.

Ted Wingfield—5 Years Pitcher (b. 7 Aug 1899 Bedford VA–d. 18 Jul 1975 Memorial Hospital, Johnson City TN) World War I veteran. He played in the Southern League and the Appalachian League. He was the first president of the Appalachian League. He had lived at Elizabethton TN since 1920 and was retired from the U.S. Postal Service. Died after a brief illness. Buried Happy Valley Memorial Park, Elizabethton TN.

Al Wingo—6 Years Outfielder (b. 6 May 1898 Norcross GA–d. 9 Oct 1964 Allen Park MI) He was a truck driver for Ford Motor Company. Killed in a truck collision.

Ed Wingo—1 Year Catcher (b. 8 Oct 1895 Ste Anne, Quebec, Canada–d. 6 Dec 1964 Lachine, Quebec, Canada).

Ivy Wingo—17 Years Catcher 1 Year Manager (b. 8 Jul 1890 Gainesville GA–d. 1 Mar 1941 at his home in Norcross GA) Died from chronic bronchitis. Buried Norcross Cemetery, Norcross GA.

Lave Winham—2 Years Pitcher (b. 1881 Brooklyn NY–d. 11 Sep 1951 Brooklyn NY) He worked 47 years for the BMT Division of the City Transit System, most of that time as an assistant foreman. Buried Evergreen Cemetery, Brooklyn NY.

George Winkelman—1 Year Outfielder (b. 18 Feb 1865 Washington DC–d. 19 May 1960 Washington Hospital Center, Washington DC) He worked for the postal service from 1892 until he retired in 1932. Afterward he worked as a gateman at Griffith Stadium in Washington DC. Died after a brief illness. Buried Mount Olivet Cemetery, Washington DC.

George Winn—3 Years Pitcher (b. 26 Oct 1897 Perry GA–d. 1 Nov 1969 Roberta GA) He was a retired car salesman having worked for Dunlap Chevrolet and Steve M Solomon Motor Company in Macon GA. Buried Orange Hill Cemetery, Hawkinsville GA.

Tom Winsett—7 Years Outfielder (b. 24 Nov 1909 McKenzie TN–d. 20 Jul 1987 Veteran's Medical Center, Memphis TN) Served in the U.S. Army Air Corps during World War II. He was a retired real estate salesman. Died from cancer. Buried Memorial Park Cemetery, Memphis TN.

Hank Winston—2 Years Pitcher (b. 15 Jun 1904 Youngsville NC–d. 7 Feb 1974 Jacksonville FL) Living in Jacksonville since 1952, he retired from the shipyards there in 1967. Buried Restlawn Memorial Park, Jacksonville FL.

George Winter—8 Years Pitcher (b. 27 Apr 1878 New Providence PA–d. 26 May 1951 Franklin Lakes NJ).

Clarence Winters—1 Year Pitcher (b. 7 Sep 1898 Detroit MI–d. 29 Jun 1945 at his home in Detroit MI).

Jesse Winters—5 Years Pitcher (b. 22 Dec 1893 Stephenville TX–d. 5 Jun 1986 at his home in Abilene TX) He owned and operated D and W Tire Company, a wholesale tire firm in Abilene, and was mayor of Abilene from 1957 to 1959. Buried Elmwood Memorial Park, Abilene TX.

Kettle Wirtz—4 Years Catcher (b. 31 Oct 1897 Edge Hill PA–d. 12 Jul 1968 Mercy Hospital, Sacramento CA) He was a wine distributor before spending 15 years as a real estate salesman. Died from lung cancer. Buried St Mary's Cemetery, Sacramento CA.

Archie Wise—1 Year Pitcher (b. 31 Jul 1912 Waxahachie TX–d. 2 Feb 1978 St Paul Hospital, Dallas TX) Served in the U.S. Navy during World War II. A retired postal employee, he was also a scout for the White Sox, Astros and Braves. Buried Hillcrest Burial Park, Waxahachie TX.

Bill Wise—3 Years Pitcher (b. 15 Mar 1861 Washington DC–d. 5 May 1940 at his home in Washington DC) Buried Glenwood Cemetery, Washington DC.

Hughie Wise—1 Year Catcher (b. 9 Mar 1906 Campbellsville KY–d. 21 Jul 1987 Plantation FL) He stayed active in baseball 50 years, designing ballfields and scouting talent in the Caribbean and in Venezuela, retiring about 1977. Cremated.

Nick Wise—1 Year Outfielder (b. 15 Jun 1866 Boston MA–d. 15 Jan 1923 Boston MA).

Sam Wise—12 Years Infielder (b. 18 Aug 1857 Akron OH–d. 22 Jan 1910 Akron OH) He was a foreman at a rubber company in Akron. Died from appendicitis. Buried Glendale Cemetery, Akron OH.

John Wisner—4 Years Pitcher (b. 5 Nov 1899 Grand Rapids MI–d. 15 Dec 1981 Foote Hospital East, Jackson MI) He played several years in the American Association and was involved in minor league baseball for many years. He retired as a corrections officer at the Michigan Prison in 1970. Buried Oakridge Cemetery, Marshall MI.

Phil Wisner—1 Year Infielder (b. Jul 1869 Washington DC–d. 5 Jul 1936 Washington DC).

Whitey Wistert—1 Year Pitcher (b. 20 Feb 1912 Chicago IL–d. 23 Apr 1985 Painesville OH).

Tex Wisterzil—2 Years Infielder (b. 7 Mar 1891 Detroit MI–d. 27 Jun 1964 at his home in San Antonio TX) Buried Odd Fellows Cemetery, San Antonio TX.

Mickey Witek—7 Years Infielder (b. 19 Dec 1915 Luzerne PA–d. 24 Aug 1990 Nesbitt Memorial Hospital, Kingston PA) He retired in 1980 as sales manager for the Lion Brewery in Wilkes-Barre PA. Buried St John's Cemetery, Dallas PA.

Roy Witherup—3 Years Pitcher (b. 26 Jul 1886 North Washington PA–d. 23 Dec 1941 New Bethlehem PA).

Frank Withrow—2 Years Catcher (b. 14 Jun 1891 Greenwood MO–d. 5 Sep 1966 Omaha NE).

Whitey Witt—10 Years Outfielder (b. 28 Sep 1895 Orange MA–d. 14 Jul 1988 at his home in Alloway NJ) He farmed near Alloway and operated Whitey's Irish Bar in Salem NJ until 1948. Buried St Joseph's Church Cemetery, Woodstown NJ.

Andy Woehr—2 Years Infielder (b. 4 Feb 1896 Fort Wayne IN–d. 24 Jul 1990 at the Lutheran Home, Fort Wayne IN) World War I veteran. In 1964 he retired from International Harvestor in Fort Wayne after 30 years. Buried Greenlawn Memorial Park, Fort Wayne IN.

Joe Woerlin—1 Year Infielder (b. 9 Oct 1864 France–d. 22 Jun 1919 St Louis MO) Buried Calvary Cemetery, St Louis MO.

Pete Wojey—3 Years Pitcher (b. 1 Dec 1919 Stowe PA–d. 23 Apr 1991 Mobile AL).

Chicken Wolf—11 Years Outfielder 1 Year Manager (b. 12 May 1862 Louisville KY–d. 16 May 1903 City Hospital, Louisville KY) He worked for the Louisville Fire Department where he was injured in an accident that hastened his demise. A part of his last few years were spent in the state mental hospital. Buried Cave Hill Cemetery, Louisville KY.

Ernie Wolf—1 Year Pitcher (b. 2 Feb 1889 Newark NJ–d. 23 May 1964 Atlantic Highlands NJ) Buried Glendale Cemetery, Bloomfield NJ.

Lefty Wolf—1 Year Pitcher (b. 10 Jun 1900 Hartford CT–d. 25 Sep 1971 New Orleans LA) Buried Metairie Cemetery, Metairie LA.

Ray Wolf—1 Year Infielder (b. 15 Jul 1904 Chicago IL–d. 6 Oct 1979 at a hospital in Fort Worth TX) He coached football at Texas Christian University, Tulane University, the University of North Carolina and the University of Florida. Buried Oak Grove Cemetery, Graham TX.

Bill Wolfe—4 Years Pitcher (b. 9 Jan 1876 Independence PA–d. 27 Feb 1953 Charleroi-Monessen Hosp, Belle Vernon PA) For 30 years he was a watchman for Pittsburgh Steel Corporation. Buried Mount Auburn Cemetery, Fayette City PA.

Chuck Wolfe—1 Year Pitcher (b. 15 Feb 1897 Wolfsburg PA–d. 27 Nov 1957 Schellsburg PA) Buried Schellsburg Cemetery, Schellsburg NY.

Harry Wolfe—1 Year Outfielder (b. 24 Nov 1888 Worcester MA–d. 28 Jul 1971 Fort Wayne IN).

Polly Wolfe—2 Years Outfielder (b. 1 Sep 1888 Knoxville IL–d. 21 Nov 1938 Morris Hospital, Morris IL) He played in the Three-I League and the Western League, living at Morris IL 25 years. Died after being in failing health a number of years. Buried Mount Carmel Cemetery, Morris IL.

Roger Wolff—7 Years Pitcher (b. 10 Apr 1911 Evansville IL–d. 23 Mar 1994 St Ann's Healthcare Center, Chester IL) Over the years he was a butcher in his father's grocery store, a salesman for Schulze-Burch, athletic director at the Menard Penitentiary and toll taker at the Chester Bridge. Buried St Mary's Catholic Cemetery, Chester IL.

Mellie Wolfgang—5 Years Pitcher (b. 20 Mar 1890 Albany NY–d. 30 Jun 1947 Albany NY) At 5' 6" and 155 lbs, he was one of the smallest pitchers to perform in the major leagues. Buried St Agnes Cemetery, Menands NY.

Abraham Wolstenholme—1 Year Catcher (b. 4 Mar 1861 Philadelphia PA–d. 4 Mar 1916 Philadelphia PA) Buried North Cedar Hill Cemetery, Philadelphia PA.

Harry Wolter—7 Years Outfielder (b. 11 Jul 1884 Monterey CA–d. 6 Jul 1970 at his home in Palo Alto CA) He was the head baseball coach at Stanford University in 1916 and from 1923 to 1949. Died from heart disease. Buried Hollister Cemetery, Hollister CA.

Harry Wolverton—9 Years Infielder 1 Year Manager (b. 6 Dec 1873 Mount Vernon OH–d. 4 Feb 1937 Oakland CA) He was a special police officer for the Oakland Police Department. Died while walking his beat. He had suffered minor injuries a few hours earlier in an automobile accident. Buried Cypress Lawn Memorial Park, Colma CA.

Sid Womack—1 Year Catcher (b. 2 Oct 1896 Greensburg LA–d. 8 Aug 1958 Jackson MS).

Bob Wood—7 Years Catcher (b. 28 Jul 1865 Thorn Hill OH–d. 22 May 1943 Churchill OH) He was a blacksmith for Youngstown Sheet and Tube Company. Died from acute appendicitis. Buried Churchill Cemetery, Churchill OH.

Doc Wood—1 Year Infielder (b. 28 Feb 1900 Batesville MS–d. 3 Nov 1974 New Orleans LA) He was a practicing medical doctor. Buried Metairie Cemetery, Metairie LA.

Fred Wood—2 Years Catcher (b. abt 1859 Detroit MI–d. 28 Aug 1933 Flower Hospital, New York City NY) He was the general manager for the Shredded Wheat Co in Niagara Falls NY before becoming the Eastern representative for *The Billiards Magazine*. Died from injuries suffered a week earlier when he was hit by a car while walking across the street.

George Wood—13 Years Outfielder 1 Year Manager (b. 9 Nov 1858 Boston MA–d. 4 Apr 1924 at his home in Harrisburg PA) He was a clerk in the State Department for the State of Pennsylvania and later was a marshall for the Public Service Commission of the state. Died from a heart attack. Buried Franklin MA.

Harry Wood—1 Year Outfielder (b. 10 Feb 1881 Waterville ME–d. 18 May 1955 Bethesda MD) In 1918 he established a practice as a general surgeon in Washington DC, working at that trade until his death. Died following a brief illness. Buried Rock Creek Cemetery, Washington DC.

Joe Wood—1 Year Infielder (b. 3 Oct 1919 Houston TX–d. 26 Mar 1985 Houston TX) Served in the U.S. Navy during World War II. A lifelong resident of Houston, he had retired from Cameron Iron Works. Buried Forest Park of Lawndale, Houston TX.

Pete Wood—2 Years Pitcher (b. 1 Feb 1867 Hamilton, Ontario, Canada–d. 15 Mar 1923 Chicago IL).

Roy Wood—3 Years Outfielder (b. 29 Aug 1892 Monticello AR–d. 6 Apr 1974 at his home in Fayetteville AR) Served as a naval aviator in World War I. He was prominent in civic affairs at Fayetteville, and was co-owner of Campbell-Bell Dry Goods Company there. Buried Evergreen Cemetery, Fayetteville AR.

Smokey Joe Wood—14 Years Pitcher (b. 25 Oct 1889 Kansas City MO–d. 27 Jul 1985 West Haven CT) Although best known as a pitcher, he was also a good hitter and played over 400 games as an outfielder. He coached baseball at Yale University from 1923 until 1942, when he retired. Buried Wood Family Cemetery, Shohola PA.

Spades Wood—2 Years Pitcher (b. 13 Jan 1909 Spartanburg SC–d. 18 May 1986 Wichita KS) He was a vice-president at Kansas Milling Company. Buried Twin Grove Cemetery, Severy KS.

Larry Woodall—10 Years Catcher (b. 26 Jul 1894 Staunton VA–d. 6 May 1963 Santa Maria Hospital, Boston MA) World War I veteran. He managed some minor league baseball and worked for the Red Sox from 1942 until his death as a coach, scout and publicity director. Died following a long illness.

Gene Woodburn—2 Years Pitcher (b. 20 Aug 1886 Bellaire OH–d. 18 Jan 1961 Good Samaritan Hospital, Sandusky OH) He worked 36 years for the Sandusky City Street Department. Buried Oakland Cemetery, Sandusky OH.

Fred Woodcock—1 Year Pitcher (b. 17 May 1868 Winchendon MA–d. 11 Aug 1943 at his home in Ashburnham MA) He worked more than 50 years in the insurance business in Boston, 40 with New England Mutual Insurance Co. Buried New Cemetery, Ashburnham MA.

George Woodend—1 Year Pitcher (b. 9 Dec 1917 Hartford CT–d. 6 Feb 1980 Hartford Hospital, Hartford CT) He worked many years at Han-Dee Spring in Hartford, and his last ten years as a tool and die maker at Connecticut Spring and Manufacturing. Died suddenly. Buried Fairview Cemetery, Hartford CT.

Red Woodhead—1 Year Infielder (b. Jul 1851 Chelsea MA–d. 7 Sep 1881 Boston MA).

Dan Woodman—2 Years Pitcher (b. 8 Jul 1893 Danvers MA–d. 14 Dec 1962 Danvers MA) He was a World War I veteran. Buried Riverview Cemetery, Groveland MA.

Orville Woodruff—2 Years Infielder (b. 27 Dec 1876 Chilo OH–d. 22 Jul 1937 Cincinnati OH) He was a real estate broker. Died from rectal cancer. Buried Spring Grove Cemetery, Cincinnati OH.

Clarence Woods—1 Year Pitcher (b. 11 Jun 1891 Ohio County IN–d. 2 Jul 1969 at his home in Rising Sun IN) World War I veteran. He was a rural mail carrier 35 years before going into real estate in 1954, retiring shortly before his death. Buried Rising Sun New Cemetery, Rising Sun IN.

John Woods—1 Year Pitcher (b. 18 Jan 1898 Princeton WV–d. 4 Oct 1946 Norfolk VA) He worked for the Norfolk Police Department from 1929 until his death, and was the chief of police after 1938. Died instantly when his police car ran into the back of a wrecking truck. Buried Forest Lawn Cemetery, Norfolk VA.

Pinky Woods—3 Years Pitcher (b. 22 May 1915 Waterbury CT–d. 30 Oct 1982 Los Angeles CA) He played several years in the Pacific Coast League. Cremated and his ashes scattered at sea.

Walt Woods—3 Years Pitcher (b. 28 Apr 1875 Rye NH–d. 30 Oct 1951 at his home in Portsmouth NH) He played baseball for 21 years and was called the "Sunday School Pitcher" because he would not pitch on Sunday. He coached baseball at the University of New Hampshire from 1897 to 1899 and at Dartmouth College from 1912 to 1915. For 20 years he was a mail carrier at Portsmouth. Buried Newington Cemetery, Newington NH.

Frank Woodward—5 Years Pitcher (b. 17 May 1894 New Haven CT–d. 11 Jun 1961 Grace Haven Hospital, New Haven CT) Died after suffering a series of heart attacks. Buried East Lawn Cemetery, East Haven CT.

Fred Worden—1 Year Pitcher (b. 4 Sep 1894 St Louis MO–d. 9 Nov 1941 St Louis MO) He worked for the U.S. Postal Service. Buried Calvary Cemetery, St Louis MO.

Chuck Workman—6 Years Outfielder (b. 6 Jan 1915 Leeton MO–d. 3 Jan 1953 St Luke's Hospital, Kansas City MO) He taught mathematics and coached basketball and football at Central High School in Kansas City. Died from an internal hemorrhage. Buried Sunset Hills Cemetery, Warrensburg MO.

Hoge Workman—1 Year Pitcher (b. 25 Sep 1899 Huntington WV–d. 20 May 1972 Fort Myers FL) Cremated.

Ralph Works—5 Years Pitcher (b. 16 Mar 1888 Payson IL–d. 8 Aug 1941 at his home in Pasadena CA) He was a salesman. Died from a self-inflicted gunshot wound to the head. Buried Mountain View Cemetery, Altadena CA.

Red Worthington—4 Years Outfielder (b. 24 Apr 1906 Alhambra CA–d. 8 Dec 1963 V A Hospital, Los Angeles CA) World War II veteran. He was a brewer for Lucky Brewing Company. Died from pneumonia following surgery for an esophageal ulcer. Buried San Gabriel Mission Cemetery, San Gabriel CA.

Chuck Wortman—3 Years Infielder (b. 5 Jan 1892 Baltimore MD–d. 19 Aug 1977 at a hospital in Las Vegas NV) He was a retired postal worker who had lived in Las Vegas for 30 years. Buried Memory Gardens Cemetery, Las Vegas NV.

Jimmy Woulfe—1 Year Outfielder (b. 25 Nov 1856 New Orleans LA–d. 20 Dec 1924 New Orleans LA) Buried Metairie Cemetery, Metairie LA.

Ab Wright—2 Years Outfielder (b. 16 Nov 1905 Teriton OK–d. 23 May 1995 Muskogee OK) For over 50 years he was a member of the Plumbers and Steamfitters Union Local in Muskogee. Buried Memorial Park Cemetery, Muskogee OK.

Al Wright—1 Year Manager (b. 30 Mar 1842 Cedar Grove NJ–d. 20 Apr 1905 at his home in New York City NY).

Bob Wright—1 Year Pitcher (b. 13 Dec 1891 Greensburg IN–d. 30 Jul 1993 Brittany Health Care Center, Carmichael CA) Served in World War I. He was the oldest former major leaguer when he died. Died from pneumonia one month after surgery for a perforated gastric ulcer. Cremated. Buried South Park Cemetery, Greensburg IN.

Ceylon Wright—1 Year Infielder (b. 16 Aug 1893 Minneapolis MN–d. 7 Nov 1947 Hines Memorial Hospital, Chicago IL).

Clarence Wright—4 Years Pitcher (b. 11 Dec 1878 Cleveland OH–d. 29 Oct 1930 Barberton OH) Died from a heart attack. Buried Lakewood Cemetery, Akron OH.

Dave Wright—2 Years Pitcher (b. 27 Aug 1875 Dennison OH–d. 18 Jan 1946 at his home in Dennison OH) He was a machinist for the Pennsylvania Railroad. Died five days after suffering a heart attack. Buried Union Cemetery, Uhrichsville OH.

Dick Wright—1 Year Catcher (b. 5 May 1890 Worcester NY–d. 24 Jan 1952 at his home in Fountain Hill PA) He was the superintendent of the Number 2 open hearth at Bethlehem Steel. Died after an illness of several days. Buried Holy Savior Cemetery, Bethlehem PA.

Ed Wright—5 Years Pitcher (b. 15 May 1919 Dyersburg TN–d. 19 Nov 1995 Methodist Hospital, Dyersburg TN) He owned and operated Wright's Exxon Station in Dyersburg. Died from cancer. Buried Fairview Cemetery, Dyersburg TN.

George Wright—7 Years Infielder 1 Year Manager Hall of Fame (b. 28 Jan 1847 Yonkers NY–d. 21 Aug 1937 at his home in Dorchester MA) He founded the Wright and Ditson sporting goods store in 1871 and was active in its operation almost up until his death. Died after being ill nearly a year. Buried Holyhood Cemetery, Brookline MA.

Glenn Wright—11 Years Infielder (b. 6 Feb 1901 Archie MO–d. 6 Apr 1984 Good Samaritan Nursing Center, Olathe KS) One of the few players to make an unassisted triple play, he managed minor league baseball five years and was a scout for the Red Sox. He had been in ill health since suffering a stroke two years earlier. Cremated.

Harry Wright—2 Years Outfielder 23 Years Manager Hall of Fame (b. 10 Jan 1835 Sheffield, England–d. 3 Oct 1895 Atlantic City Sanitorium, Atlantic City NJ) He was chief of umpires in the National League when he died. Died from catarrhal pneumonia. Buried West Laurel Hill Cemetery, Bala Cynwyd PA.

Jim Wright—2 Years Pitcher (b. 19 Sep 1900 Hyde, England–d. 11 Apr 1963 Kaiser Hospital, Oakland CA) Served in the U.S. Marines during World War I. He operated a tavern in Richmond CA for a number of years before becoming a supervisor for the Richmond Parks Department. Died from colon cancer. Buried Golden Gate National Cemetery, San Bruno CA.

Lucky Wright—1 Year Pitcher (b. 21 Feb 1880 Watersville OH–d. 8 Jul 1941 at his home in Tontogany OH) He was a painter. His health failed in later years, necessitating the removal of a leg. Died from a malignant growth on his neck. Buried Tontogany Cemetery, Tontogany OH.

Mel Wright—4 Years Pitcher (b. 11 May 1928 Manila AR–d. 16 May 1983 Houston TX).

Pat Wright—1 Year Infielder (b. 5 Jul 1865 Pottsville PA–d. 29 May 1943 St John's Hospital, Springfield IL) At various times he was a park policeman at Washinton and Lincoln parks in Springfield. Buried Calvary Cemetery, Springfield IL.

Rasty Wright—1 Year Outfielder (b. 31 Jan 1863 Birmingham MI–d. 14 Oct 1922 at his home at Duluth MN) He worked in the brokerage business in Grand Rapids MI. Died after an illness of nine months. Buried Calvary Cemetery, Duluth MN.

Rasty Wright—5 Years Pitcher (b. 5 Nov 1895 Ceredo WV–d. 12 Jun 1948 University Hospital, Columbus OH) He was the head baseball coach at Ohio State University from 1929 to 1931 and part-time assistant coach from 1932 until his death. He was associated with Standard Oil Company during that time. Died after an illness of a year. Buried Union Cemetery, Columbus OH.

Sam Wright—3 Years Infielder (b. 25 Nov 1848 New York City NY–d. 6 May 1928 Dorchester MA).

Taffy Wright—9 Years Outfielder (b. 10 Aug 1911 Tabor City NC–d. 22 Oct 1981 Orlando FL) World War II veteran. He owned and operated a bar in Orlando for several years. Buried Meadowbrook Cemetery, Lumberton NC.

Russ Wrightstone—9 Years Infielder (b. 18 Mar 1893 Bowmansdale PA–d. 25 Feb 1969 Blue Ridge Haven Conv Home, Harrisburg PA) He owned and operated the Wrightstone Hardware Company in New Cumberland PA. Buried Woodlawn Memorial Gardens, Harrisburg PA.

Philip K Wrigley—(b. 5 Dec 1894 Chicago IL–d. 12 Apr 1977 Lakeland Hospital, Elkhorn WI) Served during World War I at Great Lakes Naval Training Center as an officer, training aviation mechanics. A chewing gum magnate, he was owner of the Cubs from 1932, when his father died, until his own death. Died from acute gastro-intestinal hemorrhaging. Cremated. Buried Forest Lawn Memorial Park, Glendale CA.

Zeke Wrigley—4 Years Infielder (b. 18 Jan 1874 Philadelphia PA–d. 28 Sep 1952 Philadelphia PA) Buried Holy Cross Cemetery, Yeadon PA.

William Wrigley, Jr—(b. 30 Sep 1861–d. 26 Jan 1932) He was owner of the Chicago Cubs. Buried Forest Lawn Memorial Park, Glendale CA.

Yats Wuestling—2 Years Infielder (b. 18 Oct 1903 St Louis MO–d. 26 Apr 1970 St Louis MO) Died from heart disease. Buried Oak Grove Cemetery, St Louis MO.

Frank Wurm—1 Year Pitcher (b. 27 Apr 1924 Cambridge NY–d. 19 Sep 1993 Glens Falls NY) Served in the North African-Sicilian campaigns for the U.S. Army during World War II. A special education teacher at Fort Edward NY for many years, he also scouted for the Dodgers and Pirates. Died after a long illness. Buried Glens Falls Cemetery, Glens Falls NY.

Joe Wyatt—1 Year Outfielder (b. 6 Apr 1901 Petersburg IN–d. 5 Dec 1970 near Oblong IL) He was a dealer for Texaco gasoline, and managed the Firestone store at Vincennes IN. Later he worked for a beer distributor. Died from a heart attack while hunting 12 miles north of Oblong IL. Buried Mount Calvary Cemetery, Vincennes IN.

John Wyatt—9 Years Pitcher (b. 19 Apr 1935 Chicago IL–d. 6 Apr 1998 at his home in Omaha NE) Played in the negro leagues. He lived in Kansas City MO, where he was a real estate developer, until moving to Omaha in 1987. Died from a heart attack. Cremated.

Whit Wyatt—16 Years Pitcher (b. 27 Sep 1907 Kensington GA–d. 16 Jul 1999) Buried Buchanan City Cemetery, Buchanan GA.

John Wyckoff—6 Years Pitcher (b. 25 Dec 1893 Williamsport PA–d. 8 May 1961 at his home in Sheboygan Falls WI) He worked for Kohler-Joa Company in Sheboygan Falls WI. Collapsed and died while working in his yard.

Buried Sheboygan Falls Cemetery, Sheboygan Falls WI.

Ren Wylie—1 Year Outfielder (b. 14 Dec 1861 Elizabeth PA–d. 17 Aug 1951 at his home in Wilkinsburg PA) A one-time state legislator and bank founder, his primary activity was real estate, where he remained active until his death. Buried Homewood Cemetery, Pittsburgh PA.

Frank Wyman—1 Year Outfielder (b. 10 May 1862 Haverhill MA–d. 4 Feb 1916 Everett MA).

Early Wynn—23 Years Pitcher Hall of Fame (b. 6 Jan 1929 Hartford AL–d. 4 Apr 1999 at a nursing home in Venice FL) Died from the complications of a stroke. Cremated.

Bill Wynne—1 Year Pitcher (b. 27 Mar 1869 Neuse NC–d. 7 Aug 1951 Raleigh NC) A champion trick bicycle rider in his youth, he built the first truck to appear on Raleigh streets, operated Raleigh's first telephone company, started Raleigh's first radio station and operated a radio repair shop in Raleigh from 1922 until his death. He had been ill for some time. Buried Oakwood Cemetery, Raleigh NC.

Johnny Wyrostek—11 Years Outfielder (b. 12 Jul 1919 Fairmont City IL–d. 12 Dec 1986 Barnes Hospital, St Louis MO) Served in the U.S. Army during World War II. He worked in construction and served as mayor of Fairmont City for 20 years. Died from cancer. Buried Lake View Memorial Gardens, Belleville IL.

Biff Wysong—3 Years Pitcher (b. 13 Apr 1905 Clarksville OH–d. 8 Aug 1951 McClelland Hospital, Xenia OH) Died from cirrhosis of the liver after being in failing health three years. Buried Clarksville Cemetery, Clarksville OH.

Y

Henry Yaik—1 Year Outfielder (b. 1 Mar 1864 Detroit MI–d. 21 Sep 1935 Detroit MI) Buried Mount Elliott Cemetery, Detroit MI.

Ad Yale—1 Year Infielder (b. 17 Apr 1870 Bristol CT–d. 27 Apr 1948 at his home in Bridgeport CT) He worked 34 years for the Jenkin's Valve Company. Died suddenly. Buried Park Cemetery, Bridgeport CT.

George Yantz—1 Year Catcher (b. 27 Jul 1886 Louisville KY–d. 26 Feb 1967 St Joseph Infirmary in Louisville KY) Playing baseball for 15 years, he had a hit in his only major league at bat. He was a brick mason contractor. Buried St Michael Cemetery, Louisville KY.

Rusty Yarnall—1 Year Pitcher (b. 22 Oct 1902 Chicago IL–d. 9 Oct 1985 St Joseph Hospital, Lowell MA) Served in the U.S. Navy during World War II. He was associated with Lowell University, coaching football there from 1927 to 1947, baseball 39 years, basketball 20 years and teaching economics from 1935 to 1960. He was athletic director there from 1960 until he retired in 1973. Buried Fairview Cemetery, Westford MA.

Rube Yarrison—2 Years Pitcher (b. 9 Mar 1896 Montgomery PA–d. 22 Apr 1977 Williamsport Home, Williamsport PA) World War I veteran. He retired as a draftsman from the Pennsylvania Department of Highways. Buried St John's Brick Church Cemetery, Montgomery PA.

Yam Yaryan—2 Years Catcher (b. 5 Nov 1892 Knowlton IA–d. 16 Nov 1964 at a hospital in Birmingham AL) Died after a short illness. Buried Elmwood Cemetery, Birmingham AL.

Tom Yawkey—Hall of Fame (b. 2 Feb 1903 Detroit MI–d. 9 Jul 1976 New England Baptist Hospital, Boston MA) He inherited vast holdings in mines, mineral interests, timberlands, lumber and paper mills and owned the Red Sox from 1933 until his death. Died in his sleep from leukemia. Cremated.

Emil Yde—5 Years Pitcher (b. 28 Jan 1900 Great Lakes IL–d. 4 Dec 1968 Leesburg FL) Served in the U.S. Navy during World War I. He moved to Leesburg from Freeport IL about 1928 and became a well-known real estate dealer there. Died after a long illness. Cremated.

Bert Yeabsley—3 Games Pinch Hitter (b. 17 Dec 1893 Philadelphia PA–d. 8 Feb 1961 University Hospital, Philadelphia PA) For 20 years he was a manufacturer's representative for Grove Nylons and United Container. Buried St Timothy's Church Cemetery, Philadelphia PA.

George Yeager—6 Years Catcher (b. 5 Jun 1874 Cincinnati OH–d. 5 Jul 1940 Cincinnati OH) He was a switch tender for the Southern Railroad Company. Died from a cerebral hemorrhage. Buried Spring Grove Cemetery, Cincinnati OH.

Joe Yeager—10 Years Infielder (b. 28 Aug 1875 Philadelphia PA–d. 29 Jun 1937 at his home in Detroit MI) He is best known for inventing the squeeze play. For 18 years he worked for the City of Detroit. Died following a long illness. Buried Woodmere Cemetery, Detroit MI.

Jim Yeargin—2 Years Pitcher (b. 16 Oct 1902 Mauldin SC–d. 8 May 1937 at a hospital in Greenville SC) He umpired minor league baseball. Died after an illness of a week. Buried Cross Roads Baptist Church Cemetery, Greer SC.

Archie Yelle—3 Years Catcher (b. 11 Jun 1892 Saginaw MI–d. 2 May 1983 Woodland Skilled Nursing Fac, Woodland CA) He worked 20 years for the Woodland Police Department. Died from prostate cancer. Buried Monument Hill Memorial Park, Woodland CA.

Chief Yellowhorse—2 Years Pitcher (b. 28 Jan 1898 Pawnee OK–d. 10 Apr 1964 Pawnee OK) The first full-blooded Indian in the major leagues, he worked several years for the Oklahoma State Highway Department at Stillwater OK. Buried North Indian Cemetery, Pawnee OK.

Carroll Yerkes—5 Years Pitcher (b. 13 Jun 1903 McSherrystown PA–d. 20 Dec 1950 Kaiser Hospital, Oakland CA) He was a Bay Area creamery worker. Died from a fractured skull suffered in a fall at a club meeting. Buried St Joseph Cemetery, San Pablo CA.

Stan Yerkes—3 Years Pitcher (b. 28 Nov 1874 Cheltonham PA–d. 27 Jul 1940 Boston MA).

Steve Yerkes—7 Years Infielder (b. 15 May 1888 Hatboro PA–d. 31 Jan 1971 North Penn Hospital, Lansdale PA) He owned and operated Glenside Bowling Lanes. Buried Holy Sepulchre Cemetery, Philadelphia PA.

Ed Yewell—1 Year Infielder (b. 22 Aug 1862 Washington DC–d. 15 Sep 1940 Emergency Hospital, Washington DC) He was a patent attorney in Washington DC. Died after an illness of a week. Buried Glenwood Cemetery, Washington DC.

Earl Yingling—5 Years Pitcher (b. 29 Oct 1888 Chillicothe OH–d. 2 Oct 1962 University Hospital, Columbus OH) Buried Lebanon Cemetery, Lebanon OH.

Joe Yingling—2 Years Infielder (b. 26 Jul 1866 Westminster MD–d. 24 Oct 1946 Manchester MD).

Bill Yohe—1 Year Infielder (b. 2 Sep 1878 Mount Elere IL–d. 24 Dec 1938 Bremerton WA) He operated a hotel in Bremerton. Buried Ivy Green Cemetery, Bremerton WA.

Lefty York—2 Years Pitcher (b. 1 Nov 1892 West Fork AR–d. 9 Apr 1961 York Hospital, York PA) Served in the U.S. Army during World War I. He was a guard at the York Naval Ordinance Plant. Buried Mount Rose Cemetery, York PA.

Rudy York—13 Years Infielder 1 Year Manager (b. 17 Aug 1913 Ragland AL–d. 5 Feb 1970 Floyd County Hospital, Rome GA) For a short while he was a minor league manager and he coached a year for the Red Sox. Then he was a painter and forester in Georgia. Died from lung cancer. Buried Sunset Memory Gardens, Cartersville GA.

Tom York—10 Years Outfielder (b. 13 Jul 1851 Brooklyn NY–d. 17 Feb 1936 New York City NY).

Tony York—1 Year Infielder (b. 27 Nov 1912 Irene TX–d. 18 Apr 1970 Hillsboro TX) He was the parts and service manager for Doheney Motors in Hillsboro. Died after suffering a heart attack the day before. Buried Fairview Cemetery, Hubbard TX.

Gus Yost—1 Year Pitcher (b. Toronto, Ontario, Canada–d. 16 Oct 1895 Toronto, Ontario, Canada).

Elmer Yoter—4 Years Infielder (b. 26 Jun 1900 Carlisle PA–d. 26 Jul 1966 at his home in Camp Hill PA) He was a scout for the Red Sox. Buried Pittsburgh Memorial Cemetery.

Babe Young—8 Years Infielder (b. 1 Jul 1915 Astoria NY–d. 25 Dec 1983 Everett MA) Buried Veteran's Memorial Cemetery, Windsor CT.

Bobby Young—8 Years Infielder (b. 22 Jan 1925 Granite MD–d. 28 Jan 1985 Baltimore MD).

Charlie Young—1 Year Pitcher (b. 12 Jan 1893 Philadelphia PA–d. 12 May 1952 at his home in Riverside NJ) He conducted a printing business from his home. Died suddenly. Buried Lakeview Memorial Park, Cinnaminson NJ.

Cliff Young—3 Years Pitcher (b. 2 Aug 1964 Willis TX–d. 4 Nov 1993 Willis TX) Died from head trauma when the truck he was driving slammed into a tree and flipped over. He was the third Indian pitcher to be accidentally killed in 1993. Buried Ebenizer Cemetery, Willis TX.

Cy Young—22 Years Pitcher 1 Year Manager Hall of Fame (b. 29 Mar 1867 Gilmore OH–d. 4 Nov 1955 Peoli OH) He won more games (511) and lost more games (313) than any other pitcher. Buried Peoli Cemetery, Peoli OH.

Del Young—4 Years Infielder (b. 18 May 1910 Cleveland OH–d. 8 Dec 1979 General Hospital, San Francisco CA) He was a shipping clerk for the Pacific Maritime Association for ten years. Died from a heart attack. Buried Olivet Memorial Park, Colma CA.

Del Young—3 Years Outfielder (b. 24 Oct 1885 Macon MO–d. 17 Dec 1959 Charity Hospital, Cleveland OH) He was a deputy sheriff for Cuyahoga County, OH. Buried Calvary Cemetery, Cleveland OH.

Dick Young—Hall of Fame (b. abt 1918–d. 31 Aug 1987 Montefiore Hospital, New York City NY) He worked 45 years for the *New York Daily News,* the last 40 as a sportswriter. In 1982 he moved to the *New York Post.* Died from complications of intestinal surgery three months earlier.

George Young—2 Games Pinch Hitter (b. 1 Apr 1890 Brooklyn NY–d. 13 Mar 1950 at his home in Brightwaters NY) Served as a pilot in the U.S. Air Service during World War I. He was a high school physical education instructor for 27 years. Died from a heart attack.

Harley Young—1 Year Pitcher (b. 28 Sep 1883 Portland IN–d. 26 Mar 1975 Jacksonville FL) Died suddenly. Buried Evergreen Cemetery, Jacksonville FL.

Herman Young—1 Year Infielder (b. 14 Apr 1886 Roxbury MA–d. 13 Dec 1966 Cable Memorial Hospital, Ipswich MA) A machinist, he retired to the Ipswich area about 1948. Buried Mount Hope Cemetery, Boston MA.

Irv Young—6 Years Pitcher (b. 21 Jul 1877 Columbia Falls ME–d. 14 Jan 1935 at his nephew's home in Brewer ME) Died from arteriosclerotic heart disease. Buried Great Hill Cemetery, Columbia Falls ME.

Pep Young—10 Years Infielder (b. 29 Aug 1907 Jamestown NC–d. 14 Jan 1962 Jamestown NC) Died from a heart attack. Buried Guilford Memorial Park, Greensboro NC.

Ralph Young—9 Years Infielder (b. 19 Sep 1890 Philadelphia PA–d. 24 Jan 1965 Lankenau Hospital, Philadelphia PA) He coached baseball. Died after a brief illness.

Russ Young—1 Year Catcher (b. 15 Sep 1902 Bryan OH–d. 13 May 1984 Roseville Convalescent Center, Roseville CA) For ten years he was a public housing manager in Dayton OH before retiring 23 years before his death and moving to Roseville. Died from lung cancer. Buried Camellia Memorial Lawn, Sacramento CA.

Chief Youngblood—1 Year Pitcher (b. 13 Jun 1900 Hillsboro TX–d. 6 Jul 1968 at his home in Amarillo TX) A veteran of both World Wars I and II. He owned the Big State Auction in Amarillo. Died from a heart attack. Buried Llano Cemetery, Amarillo TX.

Henry Youngman—1 Year Infielder (b. 1865 Indiana PA–d. 24 Jan 1936 Pittsburgh PA).

Ross Youngs—10 Years Outfielder Hall of Fame (b. 10 Apr 1897 Shiner TX–d. 22 Oct 1927 Physicians & Surgeons Hosp, San Antonio TX) Died at the peak of his career from Bright's disease. Buried Mission Burial Park, San Antonio TX.

Ducky Yount—1 Year Pitcher (b. 7 Dec 1885 Iredell County, NC–d. 7 May 1970 Baptist Hospital, Winston-Salem NC) He founded Newton Glove Company at Newton NC in 1917 and was chairman of the board of directors when he died. The company grew from ten employees to three plants and over 800 employees in 53 years. Buried Eastview Cemetery, Newton NC.

Eddie Yount—2 Years Outfielder (b. 19 Dec 1916 Newton NC–d. 26 Oct 1973 Newton NC) Served in the U.S. Army during World War II. Buried Eastview Cemetery, Newton NC.

Carl Yowell—2 Years Pitcher (b. 20 Dec 1902 Madison VA–d. 27 Jul 1985 at a hospital in Jacksonville TX) He was a rancher and real estate operator. Buried Berryman Family Cemetery, Alto TX.

H Barringer Distributing Company before working his last several years for Jones Bakeries, Inc. Buried Forsyth Memorial Park, Winston-Salem NC.

Eddie Yuhas—2 Years Pitcher (b. 5 Aug 1924 Youngstown OH–d. 6 Jul 1986 Forsyth Memorial Hospital, Winston-Salem NC) Served in Europe during World War II. He worked for R

Z

Zip Zabel—3 Years Pitcher (b. 18 Feb 1891 Wetmore KS–d. 31 May 1970 Beloit Memorial Hospital, Beloit WI) He pitched 18 1/3 innings of relief in a game in 1915. He was the foundry superintendent at Fairbanks Morse, and was active in city and county politics. Buried Mount Thabor Cemetery, Beloit WI.

Tom Zachary—19 Years Pitcher (b. 7 May 1896 Graham NC–d. 24 Jan 1969 Alamance County Hospital, Burlington NC) He threw the pitch that Babe Ruth hit for his 60th home run in 1927. Died from a stroke. Buried Alamance Memorial Park, Burlington NC.

Elmer Zacher—1 Year Outfielder (b. 17 Sep 1883 Buffalo NY–d. 20 Dec 1944 General Hospital, Buffalo NY) Educated as a pharmacist, he was supervisor of Buffalo City playgrounds for 22 years. He also served one year as assistant Secretary of State for New York State. Died after a two-month illness.

George Zackert—2 Years Pitcher (b. 24 Dec 1884 St Joseph MO–d. 18 Feb 1977 Burlington Medical Center, Burlington IA) For years he operated the Zackert Grocery Store in Burlington. Buried Aspen Grove Cemetery, Burlington IA.

Fred Zahner—2 Years Catcher (b. 5 Jun 1870 Louisville KY–d. 24 Jul 1900 Louisville KY) Drowned in the Ohio River after falling from a boat enroute from Jeffersonville IN to Louisville. Buried St Louis Cemetery, Louisville KY.

Paul Zahniser—5 Years Pitcher (b. 6 Sep 1896 Sac City IA–d. 26 Sep 1964 Klamath Falls OR) He lived in Klamath Falls eight years. Died from a self-inflicted gunshot wound. Buried Oakland Cemetery, Sac City IA.

Frankie Zak—3 Years Infielder (b. 22 Feb 1922 Passaic NY–d. 6 Feb 1972 St Mary's Hospital, Passaic NJ) He worked for United Wool Company of Passaic. Died after a heart attack. Buried St Michael's Cemetery, South Hackensack NJ.

Jack Zalusky—1 Year Catcher (b. 22 Jun 1879 Minneapolis MN–d. 11 Aug 1935 at his home in Minneapolis MN) He worked some as an umpire and was an avid stamp collector. Died following seven months of heart complaint. Buried St Mary's Cemetery, Minneapolis MN.

Carl Zamloch—1 Year Pitcher (b. 6 Oct 1889 Oakland CA–d. 19 Aug 1963 Cottage Hospital, Santa Barbara CA) He managed minor league baseball and coached baseball and was director of intra-mural activities during a 16-year tenure at the University of California. He worked 29 years in public relations for Signal Oil and Gas Company. He was also a noted amateur magician. Died from complications of diabetes. Buried Sunset View Cemetery, El Cerrito CA.

Al Zarilla—10 Years Outfielder (b. 1 May 1919 Los Angeles CA–d. 4 Sep 1996 Honolulu HI).

Dave Zearfoss—5 Years Catcher (b. 1 Jan 1868 Schenectady NY–d. 12 Sep 1945 Delaware Hospital, Wilmington DE) He managed some minor league baseball before working 29 years for Delaware Power and Light Company, retiring in 1939. Died after being in the hospital ten weeks. Buried Northwood Cemetery, Philadelphia PA.

Polly Zeider—9 Years Infielder (b. 16 Nov 1883 Auburn IN–d. 12 Sep 1967 Garrett Community Hospital, Garrett IN) He played in the Pacific Coast League. For several years he operated Polly's Tavern in Garrett, selling and retiring in 1959. Died from a complication of illnesses suffered for five years. Buried Woodlawn Cemetery, Auburn IN.

Matt Zeiser—1 Year Pitcher (b. 25 Sep 1888 Chicago IL–d. 10 Jun 1942 Norwood Park IL).

George Zettlein—1 Year Pitcher (b. 18 Jul 1844 Brooklyn NY–d. 22 May 1905 Patchogue NY) Served in both the Army and the Navy during the Civil War. Died from Bright's disease. Buried Evergreen Cemetery, Brooklyn NY.

Charlie Ziegler—2 Years Infielder (b. 2 Feb 1875 Canton OH–d. 16 Mar 1904 Canton OH) Died from typhoid fever.

George Ziegler—1 Year Pitcher (b. 1872 Chicago IL–d. 22 Jul 1916 Kankakee IL) Died from sunstroke. Buried Waldheim Jewish Cemetery, Forest Park IL.

Benny Zientara—4 Years Infielder (b. 14 Feb 1918 Chicago IL–d. 16 Apr 1985 Mission Valley Med Center, Lake Elsinore CA) He spent his entire life in baseball as a player, coach, scout and minor league manager, retiring to Lake Elisnore in 1982. Died from a heart attack. Buried Riverside National Cemetery, Riverside CA.

Chief Zimmer—19 Years Catcher 1 Year Manager (b. 23 Nov 1860 Marietta OH–d. 22 Aug 1949 at his daughter's home in Cleveland OH) He was a building inspector for some time before he opened a cigar store and became a cigar maker. Died after being in ill health for eight months. Buried Crown Hill Cemetery, Twinsburg OH.

Bill Zimmerman—1 Year Outfielder (b. 20 Jan 1889 Kengen, Germany–d. 4 Oct 1952 Newark NJ) He and his wife operated three candy stores in Newark, selling them in 1948. He then operated an apartment house in Vailsburg. Buried Hollywood Memorial Park, Union NJ.

Eddie Zimmerman—2 Years Infielder (b. 4 Jan 1883 Oceanic NJ–d. 6 May 1945 Allentown Hospital, Allentown PA) He was a security guard at the Mack Manufacturing Corp and manager of the Emmaus PA AA. Died after a three-day illness. Buried Northwood Cemetery, Emmaus PA.

Heinie Zimmerman—13 Years Infielder (b. 9 Feb 1887 New York City NY–d. 14 Mar 1969 New York City NY) He is most famous for the error that cost the New York Giants the 1917 World Series. He was suspended from baseball in 1919 for gambling. During prohibition he was associated with a speakeasy, after which he became a steamfitter. Buried Woodlawn Cemetery, Bronx NY.

Jerry Zimmerman—8 Years Catcher (b. 21 Sep 1934 Omaha NE–d. 9 Sep 1998 at his home in Neskowin OR) He coached and scouted for the Twins, Expos, Yankees and Orioles, retiring a year before his death. Found dead at his home from a heart attack. Cremated.

Roy Zimmerman—1 Year Outfielder (b. 13 Sep 1913 Pine Grove PA–d. 22 Nov 1991 Pine Grove PA) He was a retired carpenter. Cremated.

Walt Zink—1 Year Pitcher (b. 21 Nov 1899 Pittsfield MA–d. 12 Jun 1964 Quincy City Hospital, Quincy MA) The meat merchandising manager of the New England division of A & P Tea Company, he was the originator of the modern self-service meat department. Died after a long illness. Buried Blue Hill Cemetery, Braintree MA.

Frank Zinn—1 Year Catcher (b. 21 Dec 1865 Phoenixville PA–d. 12 May 1936 at his home in Manayunk PA) A former police lieutenant, he worked 28 years for the Philadelphia Police Department before World War I. He then became secretary for the Knights of Columbus in Philadelphia and later worked for the Mercantile Appraiser's office. Died from heart disease. Buried Westminster Cemetery, Bala Cynwyd PA.

Guy Zinn—5 Years Outfielder (b. 13 Feb 1887 Hallbrook WV–d. 3 Oct 1949 Clarksburg WV) Buried Greenlawn Masonic Cemetery, Clarksburg WV.

Jimmy Zinn—5 Years Pitcher (b. 21 Jan 1895 Benton AR–d. 26 Feb 1991 Veteran's Medical Center, Memphis TN) Served as an ambulance driver in Europe during World War I. He coached and managed in the minor leagues until 1949 when he went to work for the Arkansas Highway Department, retiring in 1962. Died after a long illness. Buried Oakland Cemetery, Little Rock AR.

Bill Zinser—1 Year Pitcher (b. 6 Jan 1918 Astoria NY–d. 16 Feb 1993 Englewood FL) Served in the U.S. Coast Guard and the Merchant Marine Corps during World War II. He was an operating engineer for Grumman Aircraft in New York before retiring to Florida in 1974. Died from a heart attack. Cremated.

Billy Zitzmann—6 Years Outfielder (b. 19 Nov 1897 Long Island City NY–d. 29 May 1985 Passaic NJ).

Ed Zmich—2 Years Pitcher (b. 1 Oct 1884

Cleveland OH–d. 20 Aug 1950 Cleveland OH) Buried St Mary's Cemetery, Cleveland OH.

Sam Zoldak —9 Years Pitcher (b. 8 Dec 1918 Brooklyn NY–d. 25 Aug 1966 Nassau Hospital, Mineola NY) Died from cancer. Buried Cemetery of Holy Rood, Westbury NY.

Bill Zuber —11 Years Pitcher (b. 26 Mar 1913 Middle Amana IA–d. 2 Nov 1982 Mercy Hospital, Cedar Rapids IA) He ran a restaurant in the Amana colonies. Died following a brief illness. Buried Middle Amana Cemetery, Middle Amana IA.

Dutch Zwilling —4 Years Outfielder (b. 2 Nov 1888 St Louis MO–d. 27 Mar 1978 at his home in La Crescenta CA) He was a scout for the Mets. Died from a heart attack. Cremated.

Appendix: Ballplayers by Cemetery

Alabama

Anniston

Edgemont Cemetery: Tommy O'Brien, Tully Sparks

Arab

Hebron Church of Christ Cemetery: Jack Lively

Athens

Athens City Cemetery: Dick Coffman, Ray Pepper

Belforest

Belforest Catholic Cemetery: Harry Matuzak

Belmont

Belmont Community Cemetery: Doc Land

Bessemer

Highland Memorial Gardens: Paul Lehner
Valhalla Cemetery: Hugh East

Birmingham

Elmwood Cemetery: Ben Chapman, Joe Conzelman, Piper Davis, Spud Davis, Sammy Hairston, Lum Harris, Bill Hughes, Dee Miles, LeGrand Scott, Pop Boy Smith, Harry Swacina, Guy Tutwiler, Dixie Walker, Dixie Walker, Frank Welch, Yam Yaryan
Forest Hill Cemetery: Lloyd Christenbury, Ernie Cox, Pee Wee Wanninger
Fraternal Cemetery: Ernie Walker
Oak Hill Memorial Cemetery: Lep Long

Centreville

Pineland Memorial Park: Frank Pratt

Citronelle

New Home Cemetery: Bama Rowell

Clanton

Clanton Cemetery: Jackie Hayes

Enterprise

Meadowlawn Memorial Park: Ed Sherling

Flomation

Oak Grove Cemetery: Ed Morris

Florala

Greenwood Cemetery: Ernie Manning

Gordo

Gordo Cemetery: Verdo Elmore

Gosport

Gosport Cemetery: Grant Gillis

Green Pond

Green Pond Cemetery: Dixie Parker

Gurley

Beason Hill Cemetery: Jim Tabor
Gurley Cemetery: Lena Styles

Holly Pond

Holly Pond Cemetery: Earl Reid

Lafayette

Chapel Hill Cemetery: Hal Finney, Lou Finney

Mobile

Catholic Cemetery: Tommie Aaron, Barney Graham, Eddie Stanky, Milt Stock, Leo Townsend
Magnolia Cemetery: Orville Armbrust, Pickles Dillhoefer, Charlie Duffee, Charlie Fritz, George Jumonville
Memorial Gardens: Walt Sessi
Pine Crest Cemetery: Tommie Agee, Stew Bolen, Herb Kelly, Red Rollings, Joe Schepner

Montgomery

Greenwood Cemetery: Gus Felix, Bill Higdon, Jim Hitchcock, Tom Oliver, Tommy Sewell, Ed Wells

Oakwood Cemetery: Slim Foster, Zeke Wilson

Oak Grove

Oak Grove Baptist Church Cemetery: Kyle Graham

Oxford

Oxford Cemetery: Jim Stephens

Pinson

Marvin's Chapel Cemetery: Tom Drake

Pleasant Grove

Pleasant Grove Methodist Cemetery: Joe Tipton

Prattville

Oak Hill Cemetery: George Grant, Ernie Wingard

Quinton

Shanghi Cemetery: Ivy Andrews

Red Level

Fairmount Memorial Cemetery: Sam Barnes

Selma

Live Oak Cemetery: Al Veach

Suggsville

Suggsville Cemetery: Red Barnes

Sylacauga

Evergreen Memorial Cemetery: Walt Cruise

Talladega

Oak Hill Cemetery: Art Decatur

Tuscaloosa

Memory Hill Gardens Cemetery: Danny Boone

Tuscaloosa Memorial Park: Ike Boone, Joe Sewell, Riggs Stephenson

Tuskegee

Tuskegee Cemetery: Dana Fillingim

Arizona

Bisbee

Evergreen Cemetery: John Henry, Clarence Maddern

Camille (south of Elgin)

Black Oak Cemetery: Mal Eason

Clarkdale

Valley View Cemetery: Bert Graham

Glendale

Resthaven Park Cemetery: Jack Roche

Globe

Pinal Cemetery: Buzz Wetzel

Kingman

Mountain View Cemetery: George Grantham, Bill Malarkey

Mesa

Mesa Cemetery: Jack Redmond

Mountain View Memorial Gardens: Fred Wigington

Nogales

Nogales City Cemetery: Alex Beam

Phoenix

East Resthaven Park Cemetery: Les Barnhart

Greenwood Memory Lawn: Earl Grace, Grover Land, Tony Tonneman, Ollie Voigt

St Francis Catholic Cemetery: Bill DeLancey, Mike Mitchell, Bob Scheffing, Horace Stoneham

Scottsdale

Green Acres Cemetery: Jocko Conlan, Lee Daney

Paradise Memorial Gardens: Lefty Sullivan

Sun City

Sunland Memorial Park: George Darrow, Harvey Kuenn

Tucson

East Lawn Cemetery: Gordon Cobbledick, Hank Leiber

Evergreen Cemetery: Lou Criger, Rags Faircloth

Holy Hope Cemetery: Ray Bates, Herb Herring

Arkansas

Alexander

Pine Crest Memorial Park: Grady Adkins, Marv Blaylock, Earl Browne, Lindsay Deal, Joe Klinger, Carl Sawatski

Altus

St Mary's Catholic Cemetery: Boss Schmidt

Atkins

Atkins City Cemetery: Fred Bennett, Leo Dickerman

Bee Branch

Blackwell Cemetery: Jim McKnight

Benton

Bryant Cemetery: Jack McAdams

Booneville

Carolan Cemetery: Floyd Speer

Clarksville
Oakland Cemetery: Paul Dean

DeAnn
DeAnn Cemetery: Chuck Tompkins

Donaldson
Pleasant Hill Cemetery: Carey Selph

El Dorado
Arlington Cemetery: Dave Davenport, Odell Hale, Schoolboy Rowe
Woodlawn Cemetery: Sherman Edwards

Fayetteville
Evergreen Cemetery: Sid Benton, Roy Wood

Fort Smith
Rose Lawn Cemetery: Harry Feldman

Greenbrier
Spring Hill Cemetery: Otis Brannan
Thorn Cemetery: Dib Williams

Hot Springs
Calvary Cemetery: Mike Cvengros
Memorial Gardens Cemetery: George Earnshaw, Al Williamson

Huntsville
Huntsville Cemetery: Joe Berry

Little Rock
Calvary Cemetery: Gene Paulette
Little Rock National Cemetery: Witt Guise, Dutch McCall, Earl Smith
Oakland Cemetery: Jimmy Zinn
Roselawn Memorial Park: Bob Allen, Bill Dickey, George Dickey, Tom Gulley, Art Jahn, Jim McLeod, Scrappy Moore, Lee Rogers

Magnolia
Magnolia Memorial Park: Bob Linton
New Hope Cemetery: George Harper

Marion
Crittendon Memorial Park: Benn Karr

Mount Ida
Owly Cemetery: Lon Warneke

Mountain Home
Tucker Memorial Cemetery: Red Evans

Murfeesboro
Oakdale Cemetery: Red Bird

North Little Rock
Edgewood Memorial Cemetery: Bill Luhrsen, Hank Robinson

Ozark
National Cemetery: Mutt Williams

Paragould
Linwood Cemetery: Orlin Collier
Wood's Chapel Cemetery: Marlin Stuart

Paris
Oakwood Cemetery: Bob Osborn, Art Parks

Pea Ridge
Pea Ridge Cemetery: Pea Ridge Day

Pine Bluff
Bellwood Cemetery: Milt Watson

Stuttgart
Lone Tree Cemetery: Bill Kerksieck

Texarkana
Hillcrest Cemetery: Howie Williamson

Waldo
Waldo Cemetery: Travis Jackson

Wynne
Cogbill Cemetery: Billy Bowers, Wes Flowers, Harry Kelley

California

Alpine
Alpine Cemetery: Bob Christian

Altadena
Mountain View Cemetery: Dick Cox, Reddy Grey, Don Heffner, Ralph Works

Antioch
Holy Cross Cemetery: Harry Malmberg
Oak View Cemetery: Johnny Weekly

Aptos
Calvary Cemetery: Harry Hooper

Atascadero
Atascadero Cemetery: Walt Leverenz

Bakersfield
Greenlawn Memorial Park: Buckshot May, Jimmy O'Connell
Hillcrest Memorial Park: Jim Tyack
Union Cemetery: Jack Burnett, Art Williams

Banning
Banning-Cabazon Cemetery: Joe Hoover

Barstow
Mountain View Memorial Park: Bob Rhoads

Bell Gardens
Park Lawn Memorial Park: Al Benton

Big Pine
Big Pine Cemetery: Bert Griffith

Bloomington
Green Acres Memorial Park: Chief Meyers

Bonita
Glen Abbey Memorial Park: Dick Aylward, Dain Clay, Jess Pike

Camarillo
Conejo Mountain Memorial Park: Alex Ferguson

Capay
Capay Cemetery: Cliff Garrison, Erv Kantlehner

Cathedral City
Desert Memorial Park: Pete Reiser, Phil Weintraub

Chico
Glen Oaks Memorial Park: Jim Battle

Citrus Heights
Sylvan Cemetery: Steve Senteney

Coachella
Coachella Valley Cemetery: Mays Copeland

Coalinga
Pleasant View Cemetery: Frenchy Bordagaray

Colfax
Colfax Cemetery: Ed Hutchinson

Colma
Cypress Lawn Memorial Park: Tommy Beals, Dolph Camilli, Bert Cole, George Crosby, Paul Fagan, Chicken Hawks, Willie Kamm, Henry Krug, Bill Lawrence, Bill Leard, Lefty O'Doul, Brusie Ogrodowski, John Russell, Pete Scott, Charlie Sweeney, Bill Tozer, Harry Wolverton

Hills of Eternity Memorial: Harry Rosenberg

Holy Cross Catholic Cemetery: Bob Blakiston, Ping Bodie, Julio Bonetti, Jim Byrnes, John Caulfield, Ike Caveney, Joe Chamberlain, Italo Chelini, Joe Corbett, Roy Corhan, Marty Creegan, John Cullen, Bill Cunningham, Mike DePangher, Joe DiMaggio, Mike Dupaugher, Cy Falkenberg, Joe Fogarty, Charlie Gagus, Joe Giannini, Charlie Graham, Ed Hallinan, Ham Iburg, Youngy Johnson, George Kelly, Harry Krause, Bill Lange, Jim McDonald, Pete Meegan, Ed Montague, Eddie Mulligan, Jim Nealon, Joe Oeschger, Bill Orr, Marino Pieretti, Babe Pinelli, Tom Power, George Puccinelli, Josh Reilly, Jim Roxburgh, John Smith, Joe Sprinz, Pete Standridge, Pete Sweeney, Pop Swett

Olivet Memorial Park: Heinie Heitmiller, Ed Kenna, Elmer Pence, Roxy Walters, Del Young

Colton
Hermosa Cemetery: Cam Carreon, Gordon Maltzberger

Montecito Memorial Park: Jay Dahl, Freddie Fitzsimmons, Ken Hubbs, Jack Rothrock

Colusa
Colusa Cemetery: Charlie Beville

Compton
Angeles Abbey Memorial Park: Shags Horan

Woodlawn Memorial Park: George Decker

Concord
Memory Gardens Memorial Park: Bill MacDonald

Corning
Sunset Hill Cemetery: Lee Grissom

Corona
Corona Cemetery: Jesse Hill

Costa Mesa
Harbor Rest Memorial Park: Al Demaree

Covina
Forest Lawn Memorial Park: George Gerken, Don Wilson

Culver City
Holy Cross Cemetery: Fred Baczewski, Johnny Berardino, Johnny Bero, Al Boucher, Frank Burke, Mike Gazella, Walt Golvin, Fred Haney, Bob Kahle, Art Krueger, Peanuts Lowrey, Rube Novotney, Walter O'Malley, Erv Palica, Bill Phyle, Les Powers, Gerry Priddy, Rip Russell, Tillie Shafer, Red Smyth, Jigger Statz, Sloppy Thurston

Cypress
Forest Lawn Memorial Park: Kit Carson, Dick Wantz

Daly City
Eternal Home Cemetery: Lou Rosenberg

Greenlawn Memorial Park: Truck Eagan

Italian Cemetery: Joe Orengo

Woodlawn Memorial Park: Jim Asbell, Win Ballou, Charlie Dorman, Sam Mertes, Andy Piercy, Tom Seats, Tubby Spencer

Delano
North Kern Cemetery: Woody Main

Dixon
Dixon Cemetery: George Darby, Ray Rohwer

Eagleville
Eagleville Cemetery: Arky Vaughan

East Los Angeles
United Serbian Cemetery: George Vico

EL CERRITO

Sunset View Cemetery: Tom Hafey, Ray Kremer, Carl Zamloch

ESCONDIDO

Oakhill Memorial Park: John Raleigh

FAIR OAKS

Mount Vernon Memorial Park: Bill Conroy, Art Garibaldi, Earl McNeely

FAIRFIELD

Suisun-Fairfield Cemetery: Cliff Aberson

FOLSUM

St John's Cemetery: Bob Keefe

FREMONT

Cedar Lawn Memorial Park: Red Marion

FRESNO

Belmont Memorial Park: Herb Hall, Joe Jenkins, Earl Jones, Walt Kuhn
Fresno Memorial Gardens: Rocky Stone
Mountain View Cemetery: Ned Garvin, Dutch Leonard, Alex Metzler
Odd Fellows Cemetery: Hank Thompson
Washington Colony Cemetery: Zeke Rosebraugh, Andy Rush

FULLERTON

Loma Vista Memorial Park: Al Campanis, Jack Salveson, Mike Simon

GARDEN GROVE

Magnolia Memorial Park: Jim Baxes

GLENDALE

Forest Lawn Memorial Park: Clyde Barfoot, Joe Brown, Ray Brown, Cleo Carlyle, Harvey Cotter, Babe Dahlgren, Pop Dillon, Chuck Dressen, Don Drysdale, Ed Halbriter, Babe Herman, Tom Hughes, Red Kress, Marty Krug, Erskine Mayer, Pat Ragan, Carl Sawyer, Bud Sketchley, Carl Spongburg, Casey Stengel, Philip K Wrigley, William Wrigley, Jr
Grand View Memorial Park: Walt Judnich, Jack Lelivelt, Homer Summa

GLENDORA

Oakdale Memorial Park: Curt Davis, Babe Twombly

GRASS VALLEY

St Patrick's Cemetery: Mitch Chetkovich

HAYWARD

Chapel of the Chimes: Art Delaney
Holy Sepulchre Cemetery: Stu Clarke, Ed Fernandes, Ray French, Eddie Kearse, Eddie Lake, Willie Ludolph, Ed McCreery, Doc Moskiman, Ernie Sulik, Jim Tobin, Johnny Tobin, Jimmy Welsh

HOLLISTER

Hollister Cemetery: Harry Wolter

HORNBROOK

Henly-Hornbrook Cemetery: Ivan Howard

HUGHSON

Lakewood Memorial Park: Buddy Gremp, Hal Leathers, Urbane Pickering

HUNTINGTON BEACH

Good Shepherd Cemetery: Jess Buckles, Connie Creeden, Vern Freiburger, Frank Manush, Don McMahon, Pat McNulty

INGLEWOOD

Inglewood Park Cemetery: Beals Becker, Steve Behel, Wally Berger, Curt Bernard, Tony Boeckel, Lyman Bostock, Bobby Brooks, Walter Carlisle, Doc Crandall, Sam Crawford, Wheezer Dell, Bill Essick, Curt Flood, Jim "Junior" Gilliam, Russ Hall, Charlie Hartman, Art Herman, Oris Hockett, Al Lyons, Lou Mahaffey, Hank McDonald, Fred McMullin, Irish Meusel, Bert Niehoff, Elmer Rieger, Pete Schneider, Jim Scott, Fred Smith, Harry Spies, Bobby Wallace, Parke Wilson

JACKSON

Jackson Catholic Cemetery: Luke Glavenich

KENSINGTON

Sunset Mausoleum: Russ Christopher, Tony Lazzeri, Harl Maggert

KINGSBURG

Kingsburg Cemetery: Dutch Hinrichs

LAFAYETTE

Oakmont Memorial Park: Les Scarsella, Gale Staley

LAKE ELSINORE

Elsinore Valley Cemetery: Homer Hillebrand

LAKE FOREST

El Toro Memorial Park: Catfish Metkovich

LODI

Cherokee Memorial Park: Lloyd Johnson

LONG BEACH

All Souls Cemetery: Allen Conkwright, Marty Griffin, John Kerr, Lyn Lary, Skipper Roberts
Sunnyside Cemetery: George Caster, Pop Lytle, Vern Stephens

LOS ANGELES

Calvary Cemetery: Jim Ball, Shad Barry, Hi Bell,

Charlie Chech, Tom Daley, Lefty Gervais, Specs Harkness, Johnny Lush, Ray Prim, Charlie Reilly, Ferdie Schupp, Dan Stearns

Forest Lawn-Hollywood Hills: Gene Autry, Roy Campanella, Ralph Capron, Leo Durocher, Al Mamaux, Don Rudolph, Bill Salkeld

Hillside Memorial Park: Ike Danning, Murray Franklin, Hank Greenberg, Bud Swartz

Hollywood Memorial Park Cemetery: Bert Adams

Los Angeles National Cemetery: Percy Coleman, Mike Dejan, Heinie Elder, Scott Hastings, Ed Hearn, Bill James, Bill Johnson, Pete Lapan, Dutch Lieber, Milo Netzel, Gordon Rhodes, Denny Sullivan, Bert Whaling

Mount Sinai Cemetery: Lefty Phillips

Rosedale Cemetery: Johnny Butler, Frank Chance, Byron Houck

Westwood Memorial Park: Jimmie Reese

Los Banos

Los Banos Cemetery: Mack Wheat

Lower Lake

Lower Lake Cemetery: Ted Easterly

Manteca

Park View Cemetery: Milo Candini, Monte Pfyl

Marysville

Sierra View Cemetery: Cotton Pippen

Menlo Park

Holy Cross Cemetery: Tom Tennant

Mission Hills

Eden Memorial Park: Herb Karpel

San Fernando Mission Cemetery: Gilly Campbell, Chuck Connors, Ernie Orsatti, Hank Patterson, Austin Walsh, Johnny Williams

Modesto

St Stanislaus Catholic Cemetery: Jack Gilligan, Walter Schmidt

Monrovia

Live Oak Memorial Park: Dick Conger, Bill Schuster

Monterey

San Carlos Catholic Cemetery: Ed Burns

Mount Shasta

Mount Shasta Memorial Park: Swede Risberg

Murphys

Buena Vista Cemetery: Len Rice

Napa

Tulocay Cemetery: Pat Bohen, Pete Dagila, Lou Guisto, Elmer Leonard

National City

La Vista Memorial Park: Joe Orrell

Newhall

Eternal Valley Memorial Park: Vic Harris

Newport Beach

Pacific View Memorial Park: Dale Coogan, Bert Delmas, Bryan Stephens, Jim Wilson

North Hollywood

Valhalla Memorial Park: Fred Abbott, Harry Berte, Vince DiMaggio, George Hildebrand, Cy Malis, Wilbur Murdock, Dwight Stone

Novato

Valley Memorial Park: Joe Gantenbein

Oakland

Chapel of the Chimes: Dick Bartell, John Knight, Herb McQuaid, George Quellich

Evergreen Cemetery: Curt Roberts

Mountain View Cemetery: Link Blakely, Babe Borton, Bill Brenzel, Glenn Burke, Bernie DeViveiros, Duke Kenworthy, Nub Kleinke, Ernie Lombardi, Bill Marriott, Limb McKenry, Biff Schaller, Ossie Vitt, Oscar Westerberg

St Mary's Cemetery: Bud Connolly, Tom Fitzsimmons, Dan Long, Hack Miller, George Van Haltren

Oceanside

Eternal Hills Memorial Park: Buster Adams

Ontario

Bellevue Memorial Gardens: Bill Collins, Lin Storti

Orange

Holy Sepulchre Cemetery: Harry Gaspar, Ed Sadowski

Melrose Abbey Cemetery: Jimmy Austin, Gavvy Cravath, Earl Hamilton, Lefty Williams

Oroville

Memorial Park Cemetery: Bill James

Palm Springs

Welwood Murray Cemetery: Carter Elliott

Palo Alto

Alta Mesa Memorial Park: Johnny Couch, Muddy Ruel, Karl Schnell

Paradise

Paradise Cemetery: Fritz Coumbe

Pasadena

Pasadena Mausoleum: Charlie Deal

Petaluma

Cypress Hill Memorial Park: Billy Hulen, Bob Uhl

Placerville

Westwood Hills Memorial Park: Tracy Baker

Point Loma

Fort Rosecrans National Cemetery: Jack Albright, Howard Craghead, Bud Hardin, Rolla Mapel, Goldie Rapp, Red Smith

Pomona

Pomona Cemetery: Jesse Baker, Roy Hitt

Poway

Dearborn Memorial Park: Deron Johnson, Bob Miller

Rancho Palos Verdes

Green Hills Memorial Park: Nanny Fernandez, Lefty Mills, Tom Morgan, Tom Wilson

Redondo Beach

Pacific Crest Cemetery: John Halla

Richmond

Rolling Hills Memorial Park: Vada Pinson

Riverside

Crestlawn Memorial Park: Bob Veselic

Evergreen Memorial Park: George Cobb, Tom Dowse, Gene Packard, George Treadway

Olivewood Cemetery: Eric Show

Riverside National Cemetery: Cecil Garriott, Johnny Mackinson, Benny Zientara

Roseville

Roseville Cemetery: Pryor McBee

Rowland Heights

Queen of Heaven Cemetery: Jesse Flores, Greg Mulleavy, Fresco Thompson

Sacramento

Calvary Cemetery: Orval Grove, Harl Maggert

Camellia Memorial Lawn: Russ Young

City Cemetery: George Borchers

East Lawn Memorial Park: Cliff Daringer, Joe Gedeon, Hal Rhyne, Charley Schanz, Earl Sheely, Sailor Stroud

East Lawn Sierra Hill Memorial Park: Gordon Jones

Masonic Lawn Cemetery: Bill Hanlon

Memorial Lawn Cemetery: Bill Clemensen, Bruce Edwards

Southeast Lawn Memorial Park: Nippy Jones

St Joseph's Cemetery: Charlie Enwright, Jim Hughes

St Mary's Cemetery: Ernie Bonham, Vince Castino, Tony Freitas, Alex Kampouris, Ray Keating, Merlin Kopp, Earl Kunz, Bill Marshall, Joe Marty, Bob McHale, Herman Pillette, Bud Ryan, Manny Salvo, Bobby Schang, Merv Shea, Hank Steinbacher, Kettle Wirtz

San Bruno

Golden Gate National Cemetery: Grover Baichley, Jim Begley, Eddie Brown, Kid Butler, Joe Connolly, Babe Ellison, John Grimes, Chris Hartje, Fred Hofmann, Bill Knickerbocker, Marv Peasley, Harlin Pool, Fred Tauby, Harry Thompson, Lou Tost, Jim Wright

San Diego

Cypress View Cemetery: Alex Carson, Roy Hutson, Bid McPhee, Bill Starr

El Camino Memorial Park: Cedric Durst, Bob Jones, Ray Kroc, Chico Ruiz

Greenwood Memorial Park: Earle Brucker, Bill Dalrymple, Bob Elliott, Steve Mesner, C Arnholt Smith, Milt Smith, Bob Thorpe

Holy Cross Cemetery: Bill Burns

Mount Hope Cemetery: Hick Carpenter

San Francisco

Home of Peace Cemetery: Walter Haas, Jr

Laurel Hill Cemetery: George Taylor

Mount Calvary Cemetery: Willard Brown

Odd Fellows Columbarium: Fred Carroll

San Francisco National Cemetery: Rowdy Elliott, Charlie Flanagan

Sunset Cemetery: Charlie Waitt

San Gabriel

Resurrection Cemetery: Lou Koupal, Cliff Markle, Don Ross, Bill Sweeney

San Gabriel Mission Cemetery: Hank Aguire, Jim McHale, Red Worthington

San Jacinto

San Jacinto Valley Cemetery: Red Ostergard

San Jose

Los Gatos Memorial Park: Al Gould

Oak Hill Memorial Park: Frank Arellanes, Hal Chase, Herb Gorman, Happy Hogan, Frank Jelincich, Ren Kelly, George Schmees, Hap Smith

San Luis Obispo

Odd Fellows Cemetery: Pug Cavet, Lafayette Henion

San Luis Rey

Mission San Luis Rey Cemetery: Andy Karl

San Mateo

Skylawn Memorial Park: Chub Feeney

St Johns Cemetery: Mike Fitzgerald

San Pablo

St Joseph Cemetery: Jim Cronin, Augie Galan, Bud Hafey, Icehouse Wilson, Carroll Yerkes

San Rafael

Mount Olivet Catholic Cemetery: Duster Mails
Mount Tamalpais Cemetery: Flame Delhi, Lefty Gomez, Russ Hodges, Joe Mellana

Santa Ana

Fairhaven Memorial Park: Chick Brandom, Harry DeMiller, Sam Dungan, Hank Edwards, Bill Hughes, Ernie Johnson, Bob Nieman

Santa Barbara

Calvary Cemetery: Joe Wilhoit
Goleta Cemetery: Gene Lillard
Santa Barbara Cemetery: Eddie Mathews

Santa Clara

Santa Clara Mission Cemetery: Herb Hippauf, Marv Owen, Paddy Siglin, Hub Walker

Santa Cruz

Holy Cross Cemetery: Joe Brovia

Santa Maria

Dudley-Hoffman Columbarium: Les Webber

Santa Monica

Woodlawn Cemetery: Johnny Bassler, Guy Cooper, Wimpy Quinn

Santa Rosa

Chapel of the Chimes: Sam Agnew, Chick Autry
Santa Rosa Memorial Park: Carl Holling, Judge Nagle

Shingletown

Inwood/Ogburn Cemetery: Joe Hatten

Solvang

Oak Hill Cemetery: Lee Thompson

St. Helena

Holy Cross Cemetery: Chick Hafey, Cookie Lavagetto
St Helena Catholic Cemetery: Dick Egan
St Helena Cemetery: Chick Gandil

Stockton

Casa Bonita Mausoleum: Hap Collard
Rural Cemetery: George Harper, Harry Lochhead, Dakin Miller
San Joaquin Catholic Cemetery: LeRoy Hermann, Bob Joyce, Mel Mazzera

Susanville

Susanville Cemetery: Hardin Barry

Sutter

Sutter Cemetery: Dolly Gray

Tulare

Cemetery Tulare: Vic Lombardi

Vallejo

St Vincent's Cemetery: John Gillespie

Ventura

Ivy Lawn Memorial Park: Josh Clarke, Charley Hall, Lerton Pinto

Vina

Vina-Carter Cemetery: Roy Joiner

Visalia

Visalia Cemetery: Larry French, Mike Garcia, Willard Hershberger, Chris Mahoney

Westlake Village

Valley Oaks Memorial Park: Paul Edmondson

Westminster

Westminster Memorial Park: Jesse Barnes, George Blaeholder, Rex Cecil, Red Dorman, George Payne, Phil Slattery

Whittier

Rose Hills Memorial Park: Tod Davis, Rube Ellis, Art Fromme, Wally Hood, Hugh McMullen, Scat Metha, Bob Meusel, Walt Slagle, Roy Weir, Alan Wiggins

Woodland

Monument Hill Memorial Park: Archie Yelle

Yountville

Yountville Cemetery: Ernie Alten

Colorado

Boulder

Mountain View Cemetery: Lenny Metz

Colorado Springs

Memorial Gardens Cemetery: Jack Tising

Delta

Delta Cemetery: Ed Karger

Denver

Crown Hill Cemetery: Bill Everett, Bill Hubbell, Marty Lang, White Wings Tebeau
Fairmount Cemetery: Les Channell, Jake Gettman, Dud Lee, Bill McGilvray, Jim Moore, Charlie Reynolds, Art Weaver

Golden

Golden Cemetery: Roy Hartzell, Cowboy Jones

Grand Junction

Memorial Gardens Cemetery: Josh Swindell
Municipal Cemetery: Ray Boggs

Pueblo

Imperial Memorial Gardens: Jim Bivin

Roselawn Cemetery: Delos Brown, Bob McGraw, Joe Straub

Wheat Ridge

Mount Olivet Cemetery: Gus Alberts, Grant Bowler, Cobe Jones, Buzz Murphy, Tom O'Hara

Yellow Jacket

Fairview Cemetery: Al Brazle

Connecticut

Allington

Congregation Sinai Memorial Park: Heinie Scheer

Ansonia

Pine Grove Cemetery: Lou North

Bloomfield

Mount St Benedict Cemetery: Ed Beecher, Steve Brady, Ed Cotter, Ed Coughlin, Frank Gilmore, John Henry, Bill Tobin

Bridgeport

Lakeview Cemetery: George Curry, Bob Emmerich, Tricky Nichols, Jim Tennant
Mountain Grove Cemetery: Neal Ball, Royal Clark
Park Cemetery: Kiddo Davis, Ad Yale
St Michael's Cemetery: Howard Baker, Ernie Lush, Joe Malay, Jack McMahon, Spike Merena, John Michaels, Jim O'Rourke, Mike Pasquariello, Jim Rogers, Dan Shannon

Bristol

St Joseph Cemetery: Swat McCabe

Colchester

St Joseph's Cemetery: Gus Dugas

Darien

St John's Cemetery: Fred Demarais

Derby

Mount St Peter's Cemetery: Dennis Fitzgerald
Oak Cliff Cemetery: Bob Pettit

East Haven

East Lawn Cemetery: Jumping Jack Jones, Frank Woodward

Fairfield

Lawncroft Burial Cemetery: Ed Buckingham

Glastonbury

St Michael's Cemetery: Danny Hoffman

Greenwich

St Mary's Cemetery: Ed Lopat

Guilford

Alderbrook Cemetery: George Townsend

Hartford

Cedar Hill Cemetery: Morgan G Bulkeley
Fairview Cemetery: George Woodend
St Patrick's Cemetery: Biff Sheehan

Lisbon

St Mary's Cemetery: Ed Walczak

Manchester

East Cemetery: Bob Brady

Meriden

Sacred Heart Cemetery: Jack Barry, Ed Walsh

Middletown

St John's Cemetery: Jerry Dorgan

Naugatuck

St James Cemetery: Ray Foley

New Canaan

Lakeview Cemetery: Ed Connolly

New Haven

Evergreen Cemetery: Steve Libby, George Weiss
Grove Street Cemetery: Bart Giamatti

Norwalk

Norwalk Cemetery: Billy Lauder
Rowayton Union Cemetery: Ole Olsen
St John's Cemetery: Joe Rabbitt
St Mary's Cemetery: Jack Dunleavy

Norwich

Yantic Cemetery: Bill Hutchison

Pachaug

Pachaug Cemetery: Tommy Corcoran

Rocky Hill

Rose Hill Memorial Park: Monk Dubiel, Emil Planeta, Jack Roser

Seymour

St Augustine Cemetery: Alex Konikowski

Somers

West Cemetery: Herman Bronkie

Southington

St Francis Cemetery: Joe Regan

Stamford

Beth El Cemetery: Mel Allen
Fairfield Memorial Park: Ron Northey

Torrington

Hillside Cemetery: Tad Quinn

Waterbury

Beth El Cemetery: Al Schacht
Calvary Cemetery: Candy LaChance

New Pine Grove Cemetery: Fred Klobedanz
New St Joseph's Cemetery: Dan Parker
Old St Joseph's Cemetery: Ed Begley, Joe Connor, Roger Connor
St Joseph's Cemetery: Red Donahue
Jordan Cemetery: Jack Burns

West Haven

Oak Grove Cemetery: George Bone
St Bernard's Cemetery: Pete Falsey, Henry Gruber
St Lawrence Cemetery: Chick Bowen, Al Clauss, Tom Leahy, Frank McGowan, Dan Phelan, Eddie Wilson

Westport

Willowbrook Cemetery: Hezekiah Allen

Wethersfield

Emmanuel Cemetery: Reuben Ewing

Windham

St Joseph's Cemetery: Art Nichols

Windsor

Veteran's Memorial Cemetery: Babe Young

Delaware

Georgetown

Union Cemetery: Chris Short

Harrington

Hollywood Cemetery: Al Burris

Millsboro

Millsboro Cemetery: Huck Betts, Broadway Jones

New Castle

Gracelawn Memorial Park: Frank Bennett, Bill Bruton, Bill Sadler

Newark

All Saints Cemetery: Ed Cihocki

Townsend

Townsend Cemetery: Harry Hoch, Jack Townsend

Wilmington

Cathedral Cemetery: Pete Cassidy, Bill Day, Chick Hartley, Bill McGowan, Joe Myers, John Newell
Silverbrook Cemetery: Bill Higgins, Judy Johnson
St Joseph on the Brandywine Cemetery: Sadie McMahon
Wilmington-Brandywine Cemetery: Harry Anderson, Bill Hawke, Flip Lafferty

District of Columbia

Washington

Congressional Cemetery: Art Devlin, Bill McCauley
Elesavetrograd Cemetery: Shirley Povich
Glenwood Cemetery: Phil Baker, Gene DeMontreville, Walter Hewett, Holly Hollingshead, Sadie Houck, Pop Snyder, Woody Wagenhorst, Bill Wise, Ed Yewell
Mount Olivet Cemetery: Tom Cantwell, Harry Colliflower, Tom Crooks, John Gilroy, Pop Joy, Mickey Keliher, Watty Lee, Tony Madigan, Charlie Moran, Mike Scanlon, Joe Stanley, George Winkelman
Oak Hill Cemetery: Bob Barr, Tom Evers, Charlie Kalbfus
Rock Creek Cemetery: Doc White, Harry Wood

Florida

Apalachicola

Magnolia Cemetery: Ned Porter

Bartow

Wildwood Cemetery: Bill Phebus

Bay Pines

Bay Pines National Cemetery: Verne Clemons

Boca Raton

Boca Raton Cemetery: Lee Allen

Boynton Beach

Boynton Beach Cemetery: Mike Wilson
Eternal Light Memorial Gardens: Izzy Goldstein

Bradenton

Fogartyville Cemetery: Hank Johnson
Manasota Memorial Park: Bill McKechnie, Hank Olmsted, Paul Waner, Jimmie Wilson

Brandon

Limona Cemetery: George Foss

Bushnell

Florida National Cemetery: Chris Van Cuyk, Hal White

Clearwater

Sylvan Abbey Memorial Park: George Abrams, Gene Ford, Jack Russell, Eddie Silber

Cocoa

Brevard Memorial Park: Jake Early

Coral Gables

Graceland Memorial Park: Bill Klem, Max Rosenfeld

Crestview
Live Oak Park Memorial: Lance Richbourg

Daytona Beach
Bellevue Memory Gardens: Bill Burwell
Cedar Hill Memory Gardens: John Campbell, Nap Lajoie, Fred Merkle
Shadyrest Cemetery: Larry Cheney

De Land
Oakdale Cemetery: Horace Allen, Dave Fultz

Dunedin
Dunedin Cemetery: Watty Clark

Ellenton
Mansion Memorial Park: Billy Purtell

Englewood
Gulf Pines Memorial Park: Bunny Hearn, Roy Spencer

Fort Lauderdale
Evergreen Cemetery: Orth Collins
Forest Lawn Central: Jack Enright

Fort Myers
Fort Myers Memorial Gardens: Jean Dubuc, Fred Heimach
Memorial Gardens: Joe Coleman

Fort Pierce
Fort Pierce Cemetery: John Milligan, Ray Phelps

Fort Walton Beach
Beal Memorial Cemetery: Jack Peerson

Gainesville
Evergreen Cemetery: Charlie Harris
Forest Meadows Memorial Park Central: Bill Ferrazzi

Gulfport
Lincoln Cemetery: George Smith

Hialeah
Vista Memorial Gardens: Chet Covington, Pedro Dibut, Bobby Estalella, Tony Martinez, Reggie Otero, Nap Reyes

High Springs
High Springs Cemetery: Myril Hoag

Hollywood
Memorial Gardens Cemetery: Karl Drews, Allie Strobel

Holmes Beach
St Bernard Church Memorial Gardens: Birdie Tebbetts

Homosassa Springs
Stage Stand Cemetery: Dazzy Vance

Inverness
Oak Ridge Cemetery: Bernie Neis

Jacksonville
Evergreen Cemetery: Dixie Carroll, Joe Dobson, Bob Fisher, John Kennedy, Billy Taylor, Bill Terry, Harley Young
Jewish Temple Cemetery: Bill Schwarz
Oaklawn Cemetery: Don Bessent, John Chambers, Bob Gandy, Ken Robinson
Restlawn Memorial Park: Bob Adams, Hank Winston
Riverside Memorial Park: Jim Holmes, Paul Schreiber, Tige Stone
St Mary's Section-Evergreen Cemetery: Frank Butler, Ben Geraghty

Keystone Heights
Keystone Heights Cemetery: Charlie Wiedemeyer

Lake City
Oaklawn Cemetery: Stuffy Stewart

Lake Mary
Oaklawn Park Cemetery: Ed Chaplin

Lake Placid
Oak Hill Cemetery: Red Causey

Lake Worth
Pinecrest Cemetery: Jim Faulkner

Lakeland
Lakeland Memorial Gardens: Ed White
Oakhill Burial Park: Bill Swift

Lantana
Palm Beach Memorial Park: George Fallon

Largo
Serenity Gardens Memorial Park: Jack Aragon, Ted Kleinhans

Leesburg
Hillcrest Memorial Gardens: Frank Barrett
Lone Oak Cemetery: Mutt Wilson

Live Oak
Antioch Baptist Church Cemetery: Lee Tannehill

Miami
Dade Memorial Park-South: Tony Ordenana
Flagler Memorial Park: Jimmie Foxx, Mike Guerra, Roberto Ortiz
Miami Memorial Park: Ray Bare
Mount Nebo Memorial Gardens: Moe Solomon
Woodlawn Park Cemetery: Sandy Amoros, Max Carey, John Douglas, George Ferguson, Tom Knowlson

Woodlawn Park North Cemetery: Tiny Chaplin, Ramon Lopez
Woodlawn Park South Cemetery: Fred Frink, Charlie Gassaway

New Port Richey

Meadowlawn Memorial Gardens: Charlie Niebergall, Jimmy Wasdell

North Lauderdale

Our Lady Queen of Heaven Cemetery: John Happenny, Jimmy Shevlin
Star of David Memorial Gardens: Cal Abrams

North Miami

Southern Memorial Park: Mike Schemer

Orlando

Greenwood Cemetery: Joe Tinker
Woodlawn Cemetery: Tim Crews, Zack Taylor
Woodlawn Memorium: Dick Hahn, Walt Tauscher

Ormond Beach

Hillside Cemetery: Vern Duncan

Palatka

Oak Hill Cemetery: Herb Thomas
West View Cemetery: Weldon Henley

Palm Bay

Fountainhead Memorial Park: Ray Dandridge

Palm Harbor

Curlew Hills Memory Gardens: Joe Cicero, Bill DeKoning

Panama City

Forest Lawn Memorial Cemetery: Jack Bolling
Garden of Memories: Jack Franklin

Pensacola

Bayview Memorial Park: Wally Dashiell, Bill Henderson, Bill McGhee, Marshall Renfroe
Pfeiffer Cemetery: Bill Holden
St John's Cemetery: Russ Scarritt
St Michael's Cemetery: Tom Gettinger

Plant City

Oaklawn Cemetery: Rip Sewell

Pompano Beach

Forest Lawn Memorial Gardens: Dan Daniel, Ed Walsh

Royal Palm Beach

Our Lady Queen of Peace Cemetery: Jim Peterson

Sanford

All Souls Cemetery: Tom Delahanty

Sarasota

Manasota Memorial Park: Johnny Cooney, Johnny Moore
Palms Memorial Park: Lew Krausse
Sarasota Memorial Park: Heinie Manush, George Susce, Ben Van Dyke

St Augustine

San Lorenzo Cemetery: Lyle Judy, Bill Steinecke

St Petersburg

Memorial Park Cemetery: Larry Bearnarth, Hooks Iott, George Pipgras, Pete Wilson
Royal Palm Cemetery: Frank Fletcher, Doc Shanley
Woodlawn Memory Gardens: Spud Chandler, Red Nelson, Jim Scott

Starke

Crosby Lake Cemetery: Parson Perryman

Tallahassee

Meadowwood Memorial Park: Fred Hatfield
Tallahassee Memory Gardens: Dick Howser

Tampa

Centro Asturiano Cemetery: Charlie Cuellar, Ralph Onis
Garden of Memories: Jerry Akers, Johnny Burnett, Tony Cuccinello, Gene Schott
Myrtle Hill Cemetery: Johnny Vander Meer

Tarpon Springs

Cycadia Cemetery: Elliott Bigelow

Tequesta

Riverside Memorial Park: Billy Herman

Vero Beach

Crestlawn Cemetery: Karl Spooner

West Palm Beach

Evergreen Cemetery: Zinn Beck
Hillcrest Memorial Park: Bob Harris, Whitey Platt
Royal Palm Memorial Gardens: Hank Gornicki, Pep Rambert, Jack Sheehan
Woodlawn Cemetery: Ed Andrews

Winter Garden

Woodlawn Cemetery: Tommy McMillan, Emmett Mueller, Joe Stripp

Winter Park

Glen Haven Memorial Park: Harry Biemiller, Ray Kennedy, Len Schulte
Palm Cemetery: Del Mason

Georgia

Albany

Crown Hill Cemetery: Alf Anderson
Oakview Cemetery: John Slappey

Americus
Oak Grove Cemetery: Jeff McCleskey

Athens
Evergreen Memorial Park: Bobo Holloman
Oconee Hill Cemetery: Nolen Richardson

Atlanta
Crest Lawn Memorial Park: Doc Ozmer, Milt Reed
Greenwood Cemetery: Johnny Echols, Ray Francis
Hollywood Cemetery: Red Howell
Mount Parran Cemetery: Hugh Casey
Westview Cemetery: Jim Bagby, Bob Barrett, Joe Bean, Ed Crowley, Hack Eibel, Paul Gillespie, Roy Massey, Roy Moran, Bob Smith, Red Smith, Homer Thompson

Augusta
Westover Memorial Park: Bill McCorry, Tripp Sigman, Harry Smythe

Barnesville
Fredonia Church Cemetery: Bill Bankston

Blairsville
Union Memory Gardens: Dale Matthewson

Brazelton
Zion Cemetery: Abe White

Brunswick
Palmetto Cemetery: Bob Gilks

Buchanan
Buchanan City Cemetery: Whit Wyatt

Cartersville
Sunset Memory Gardens: Rudy York

Clarksville
Clarksville City Cemetery: Red Barron

Clayton
Clayton Cemetery: Claud Derrick

Clem
Mount Pleasant Church Cemetery: Carl East

College Park
College Park Cemetery: Al Cochran, John Milner
Forest Lawn Memorial Gardens: Mark Mauldin

Columbus
Parkhill Cemetery: Herb Bremer, Skeeter Newsome, Elmer Riddle

Crabapple
Rucker Family Cemetery: Johnny Rucker

Cumming
Sawnee View Memorial Gardens: Luke Appling

Dalton
West Hill Cemetery: Harry Simpson

Decatur
Decatur Cemetery: Sam Mayer
Resthaven Garden of Memories: Jim Galvin, Dave Harris, Lee Meadows

Demorest
Yonah Memorial Gardens: Johnny Mize

Dorchester
Dorchester Cemetery: Phil Lewis

Douglasville
Douglasville City Cemetery: John Hill, Camp Skinner

Duluth
White Chapel Memorial Gardens: Charlie Bishop

Glenn
Glenn Cemetery: Walter Wilson

Harrison
Baptist Church Cemetery: Phil Bedgood

Hawkinsville
Orange Hill Cemetery: George Winn

Homer
Presbyterian Church Cemetery: Lucas Turk

Jackson
Jackson City Cemetery: Larry Bradford

Lake Park
Lake Park Cemetery: Paul Carter

Macon
Macon Memorial Park: Mack Stewart
Mount Zion Baptist Church Cemetery: Doc Bass
Riverside Cemetery: King Bailey, Jack Robinson, George Stallings

Marietta
Cheatham Hill Memorial Park: Bill Webb
Georgia Memorial Park Cemetery: Tom Lanning
Marietta City Cemetery: Bob Hasty

McDonough
Bethany Baptist Church Cemetery: Tim Bowden

Meigs
New Bethel Cemetery: Bill Hall

Millen
Millen Cemetery: Jim Busby

Montezuma
Felton Cemetery: Jimmy Lavender

Newnan
Oakhill Cemetery: Bill Ayers

Norcross
Norcross Cemetery: Roy Carlyle, Ivy Wingo

Perry
King Chapel Cemetery: Eddie Solomon

Reidsville
Reidsville City Cemetery: Paul Easterling

Rockmart
Rose Hill Cemetery: Bill Calhoun, Harry Dean

Rome
East View Cemetery: Williard Nixon
Oaknoll Memorial Gardens: Leon Culberson

Roswell
Roswell Presbyterian Church Cemetery: Nap Rucker

Royston
Rose Hill Cemetery: Ty Cobb, Tinsley Ginn

Saint Simons Island
Christ Churchyard Cemetery: Charlie Butler

Sandy Cross
Stevens Family Cemetery: Cy Moore

Sandy Springs
Arlington Memorial Park: Red Treadway, Leon Williams

Savannah
Bonaventure Cemetery: Harry Hanson, Bobby LaMotte, Ivey Shiver
Catholic Cemetery: Mike Handiboe

Smyrna
Riverview Memorial Park: Tiny Osborne

Snellville
Eternal Hills Memory Gardens: Cecil Upshaw

Stockbridge
Fairview Memorial Gardens: Jim Hayes

Tallapoosa
Hollywood Cemetery: Ralph Head

Tazewell
Tazewell Cemetery: Brad Hogg

Thomasville
Laurel Hill Cemetery: Ken Holloway, Charlie Letchas, Dummy Murphy

Trenton
Lake Hills Memorial Gardens: Joe Bokina

Valdosta
Riverview Memorial Gardens: Monroe Mitchell

Vidalia
Pinecrest Cemetery: Wally Moses

White
White Cemetery: Paul Fittery

Hawaii

Honolulu
Nouanu Cemetery: Alexander J Cartwright

Kaneohe
Hawaiian Memorial Park Cemetery: Joe DeSa

Idaho

Blackfoot
Gibson Mission Cemetery: Charlie Roy

Boise
Morris Hill Cemetery: Paul Fitzke, Andy Harrington

Coeur d'Alene
Forest Cemetery: Harry Trekell
St Thomas Cemetery: Bill Burdick

Hagerman
Hagerman Cemetery: Freddy Leach

Jerome
Jerome Cemetery: Chick Fraser

Pocatello
Mountain View Cemetery: Bob Addy

Sandpoint
Pinecrest Memorial Park: Leon Cadore

St Anthony
Riverview Cemetery: Johnny Kane

Illinois

Aledo
Aledo Cemetery: John McDougal

Arlington Heights
Memory Gardens Cemetery: George Meyer

Ashmore
Ashmore Cemetery: Bill Cox

Atlanta
Atlanta Cemetery: Lee Dunham

Auburn
Auburn Cemetery: Dutch Leonard

Belleville
Lake View Memorial Gardens: Dutch Hoffman, Johnny Wyrostek

Mount Carmel Cemetery: Steve Biras
Valhalla Gardens of Memory: Al Glossop, Bill Walker
Walnut Hill Cemetery: Jess Doyle, Max Flack, Bob Groom, Otto Miller, Ham Patterson, George Starnagle

BLOOMINGTON

Evergreen Memorial Cemetery: George Radbourn, Old Hoss Radbourn
St Mary's Cemetery: Ed Kinsella

CALUMET CITY

Holy Cross Cemetery: Ted Pawelek

CARLYLE

Carlyle Cemetery: Patsy McGaffigan, Ray Starr

CARTHAGE

Moss Ridge Cemetery: Buff Williams

CHAMPAIGN

Roselawn Cemetery: George Huff
St Mary's Cemetery: Big Jeff Pfeffer

CHESTER

St Mary's Catholic Cemetery: Roger Wolff

CHICAGO

Acacia Park Cemetery: Red Faber, John Hollison, Otto Jacobs, Bob Meinke
Bohemian National Cemetery: George Caithamer, Larry Hoffman, Frank Smykal
Burr Oak Cemetery: Bruce Petway, Wendell Smith
Cedar Park Cemetery: Don Kolloway, Fred Kommers, Phil Stremmel
Graceland Cemetery: Bob Caruthers, Emil Gross, William A Hulbert, Walt Kinzie, Bill Phillips
Irving Park Cemetery: Babe Blackburn, Gibby Pruess
Lincoln Cemetery: Andrew "Rube" Foster
Montrose Cemetery: Frank Meinke, Chick Pedroes, Bugs Raymond
Mount Greenwood Cemetery: Norm Glockson, Laurie Reis, Crazy Schmit, Eddie Taylor
Mount Hope Cemetery: Roy Henshaw, Buck Weaver
Mount Olive Cemetery: Earl Juul, Red Torkelson
Mount Olivet Cemetery: Dick Attreau, Art Ball, Tony Cusick, Jack Farrell, Herb Juul, Bill Moriarty, Mike Moynahan, Charley O'Leary, Billy Webb, Jake Weimer
Oak Hill Cemetery: Reggie Richter
Oak Woods Cemetery: Henry Adkinson, Cap Anson, Frank Bishop, Pete Fries, Ernie Krueger, Kenesaw Mountain Landis, Ed Mars, Bill Pelouze, Jake Stahl, Tony Suck
Ridgelawn Cemetery: Milt Galatzer
Rosehill Cemetery: Jack Brickhouse, Harry Buker, Edward H Burns, Snipe Hansen, Nat Hudson, Leonidas Lee, Bill McClellan, Ned Williamson
Rosemont Park Cemetery: Ike Samuels
St Boniface Cemetery: Adam DeBus, Bill Geis, Emil Geis, Spencer Heath, Mike Hechinger, Jack Kading, Germany Schaefer

CHILLICOTHE

Chillicothe Cemetery: Bill Krieg

CLINTON

Woodlawn Cemetery: Doc Marshall

COLLINSVILLE

Glenwood Cemetery: Art Fletcher
Holy Cross Lutheran Cemetery: Terry Moore

COLONA

Dayton Corners Cemetery: Baby Doll Jacobson

COULTERVILLE

Coulterville Cemetery: Nick Kahl

CRETE

Trinity Lutheran Cemetery: Rube Ehrhardt

DECATUR

Calvary Cemetery: Bill Mizeur, Al Unser
Fairlawn Cemetery: Beany Jacobson, Walt Meinert, George Scharein
Lutheran Cemetery: Boom-Boom Beck

DES PLAINES

All Saints Cemetery: Harry Carey, John Carmichael, Cozy Dolan, Paddy Driscoll, Lew Fonseca, John Godar, Gabby Hartnett, Freddie Lindstrom, Doug McWeeny, Tony Murray, Pete O'Brien, Doc Parker, Fred Pfeffer, Lew Post, Henry Rasmussen, Arch Ward
Ridgewood Cemetery: Tom Asmussen

DIVERNON

Brush Creek Cemetery: Al Papai

DIXON

Oakwood Cemetery: Lou Bevil, Ward Miller

DUPO

St Joseph Cemetery: Ed Albrecht

EAST MOLINE

Greenview Memorial Gardens: George Magerkurth

EDWARDSVILLE

Sunset Hill Memorial Estates: John Bischoff

ELDORADO

Wolf Creek Cemetery: Joel Newkirk

Elgin

Bluff City Cemetery: Ed McDonough, Erwin Renfer

Elmhurst

Arlington Cemetery: Vern Olsen
Mount Emblem Cemetery: Tony Kaufmann, Frank Mack, Jumbo Schoeneck, Bob Weiland

Evanston

Calvary Cemetery: John Carbine, Charlie Comiskey, Grace Lou Comiskey, Tom Connelly, Harry Curtis, Lou Fiene, Pat Flaherty, Jimmy Hallinan, Marty Honan, John Horan, Tim Manning, Frank Martin, Gordon McNaughton, Marty McQuaid, Tom Messitt, Hank O'Day, John Pickett, Joe Quinn, Jimmy Ryan, Ed Santry, Mort Scanlan, Howard Wakefield

Evergreen Park

Evergreen Cemetery: Ray Schalk
St Mary Cemetery: Hank Butcher, Clem Clemens, Eddie Gaedel, Jim Hackett, Frank McCue, George Moriarty, Jerry Standaert, Jim Stroner, John Sullivan

Fairfield

Maple Hill Cemetery: Bill Trotter

Fillmore

Glendale Cemetery: Ray Richmond

Forest Park

Concordia Cemetery: Charlie Getzien, Rudy Kemmler, Herman Long, Skel Roach
Forest Home Cemetery: Ed Gastfield, Moxie Hengle, Jack Smith, Billy Sunday, Bob Wicker
Waldheim Jewish Cemetery: Hub Knolls, George Rooks, George Ziegler
Woodlawn Cemetery: Erv Dusak, Al Spink

Frankfort

Pleasant Hill Cemetery: Lou Boudreau

Freeport

Chapel Hill Memorial Park: Clyde Southwick
County Home Cemetery: Frank Harris

Galesburg

Oak Lawn Memorial Gardens: Evar Swanson

Genesco

Oakwood Cemetery: Jack Wanner

Girard

Ditson Cemetery: Del Paddock

Glen Carbon

Buck Road Cemetery: Johnny Lucas

Glenwood

Assumption Cemetery: Walt Moryn

Grand Detour

Grand Detour Cemetery: Stan Hack

Hardin

St Norbett's Catholic Church Cemetery: Bill McGee

Havana

Laurel Hills Cemetery: Fred Beck, Frank Donnelly

Herrick

Myers Cemetery: Joe Adams

Herrin

Herrin City Cemetery: Dallas Bradshaw

Hillside

Glen Oak Cemetery: Hank Erickson
Mount Carmel Cemetery: Lefty Atkinson, Henry Croft, Jack Hendricks, Ed Hughes, Leo Kavanagh, Bill McCabe, Dan O'Leary, Jack Powell, Ken Silvestri, Eddie Stack, Jeff Sweeney
Oakridge Cemetery: Ernie Gilmore, Erv Lange, Jimmy Slagle, Tuffy Stewart
Queen of Heaven Cemetery: Warren Brown, Dick Drott, Bob Elson, Nick Etten, Johnny Rigney

Homewood

Homewood Memorial Gardens: Dizzy Trout

Jerseyville

Oak Grove Cemetery: Ed Baecht, Larry Chappell

Johnston City

Lake View Cemetery: Hank Keupper

Joliet

Elmhurst Cemetery: Sweetbreads Bailey
Mount Olivet Cemetery: Ed Lagger
St John's Cemetery: Jack Himes, Ed Murphy
St Patrick's Cemetery: Bobby Burke, Bill Moran

Justice

Resurrection Cemetery: Sig Gryska, Ray Jablonski, Frank Naleway, Johnny Ostrowski, Tony Piet

Kewanee

Pleasant View Cemetery: Tom Drohan

Keyesport

Kendree Chapel Cemetery: Frank Harter

LaGrange Park

Parkholm Cemetery: Fred Beebe

Lacon

Lacon Cemetery: Bob Barnes

Lanark

Lanark Cemetery: Jack Warhop

Libertyville
Ascension Cemetery: Johnny Dickshot, Johnny McCarthy

Lincoln
St Mary's Cemetery: Emil Verban

Lockport
South Lockport Cemetery: Jim Donahue

Marengo
Marengo Cemetery: Carl Lundgren

Marine
Marine City Cemetery: Russ Pence

McLeansboro
IOOF Cemetery: Ray Blades

Mendota
Restland Cemetery: Deacon White

Moline
Riverside Cemetery: Warren Giles, Oscar Graham

Monmouth
Monmouth City Cemetery: Charles Dryden

Morris
Mount Carmel Cemetery: Polly Wolfe

Mount Carmel
Highland Memorial Cemetery: Cy Warmoth

Mount Morris
Oakwood Cemetery: Nels Potter

Mount Olive
Union Miners Cemetery: Mike Kreevich

Mount Pulaski
Mount Pulaski Cemetery: Ray Demmitt

Mount Vernon
Memorial Gardens: Jack Warner
Oakwood Cemetery: Jim McLaughlin

Mount Zion
Mount Zion Cemetery: Paul Smith

Murphysboro
Pleasant Grove Memorial Park: Gary Geiger
Tower Grove Cemetery: Joe Grace

Naperville
SS Peter and Paul Cemetery: Ken Polivka

New Athens
Oakridge Cemetery: Mickey Haefner

Niles
St Adalbert Cemetery: George Halas, Jake Kafora, Dick Kokos, Bill Lelivelt, Al Piechota

Norris City
Odd Fellows Cemetery: Lew Brockett

North Chicago
Northshore Garden of Memories: Bob O'Farrell

O'Fallon
O'Fallon City Cemetery: Ed Busch

Oakbrook Terrace
Chapel Hill Gardens West: Bill Donovan, Johnny Strands

Odell
St Paul Cemetery: Bud Clancy

Odin
Peaceful Valley Cemetery: Grover Lowdermilk

Oregon
River View Cemetery: Fred Roat

Ottawa
Ottawa Avenue Cemetery: Charlie Jaeger

Pana
Calvary Cemetery: John Dudra
West Mound Cemetery: Nin Alexander

Peoria
Parkview Cemetery: Harry Bay, Hod Leverette, Hal Smith
Springdale Cemetery: Charlie Bartson, Ben Caffyn, Norwood Gibson, Bill Jackson, George Pinckney

Piper City
Calvary Cemetery: Elmer Koestner

Plainfield
Plainfield Township Cemetery: George Pearce

Pleasant Hill
Crescent Heights Cemetery: Dave Altizer

Quincy
Calvary Cemetery: Dutch Kemner, Fritz Ostermueller
Quincy Memorial Park: El Tappe
St Peter's Cemetery: Jim Finigan
Woodland Cemetery: Luke Lutenberg

Rardin
Greasy Point Cemetery: Al Shaw

River Grove
Elmwood Cemetery: Harry Spence
St Joseph Cemetery: Otto Denning, Martin Glendon, Newt Halliday, Long Tom Hughes, Tom Kane, Emil Kush

Rock Island
Calvary Cemetery: Harry Sage, Tom Sexton
Memorial Park Cemetery: Joe Berger, Herb Crompton
Rock Island National Cemetery: Gene Baker

Rockford

Arlington Memorial Park Cemetery: Hal Carlson
Greenwood Cemetery: Ross Barnes, Charlie Sproull
St Marys/St James Cemetery: Mike Golden, Tom Griffin, Harry Sullivan
Willwood Burial Park: Varney Anderson

Rushville

Rushville Cemetery: Earl Tyree

Salem

Summit Prairie Cemetery: Lou Lowdermilk

Sheffield

Sheffield Cemetery: Red Gunkel

Sheridan

Elerding Cemetery: Si Johnson

Sherman

Brittin Cemetery: Jack Brittin

Skokie

Memorial Park Cemetery: Will Harridge, Arndt Jorgens, Ed Weiland

Sparta

Caledonia Cemetery: Earl Gardner

Springfield

Calvary Cemetery: Joe Bernard, Bob Kinsella, Pat Wright
Camp Butler National Cemetery: Jim Hamby
Oak Ridge Cemetery: Fred Donovan

Sterling

Calvary Cemetery: Gus Williams

Streator

Riverview Cemetery: Wally Roettger

Taylorville

Oak Hill Cemetery: Frank Lamanske

Toulon

Toulon Municipal Cemetery: Charlie Hall

Troy

Frieden's Evangelical Cemetery: Roy Lee
St John's Evangelical Cemetery: Frank Whitman

Viola

St John's Cemetery: Luke Nelson

Warren

Elmwood Cemetery: Abner Dalrymple

Waterloo

Waterloo City Cemetery: Willis Koenigsmark

West Frankfort

Boner Cemetery: Bennie Tate

West Peoria

St Joseph Cemetery: Jim Bluejacket

White Hall

White Hall Cemetery: Monte McFarland

Willow Springs

Fairmount Willow Hills Park: Don Hanski

Witt

Calvary Cemetery: Paul Chervinko

Worth

Chapel Hill Gardens South: Ira Hutchinson, Wally Millies, Ray Poat
Holy Sepulchre Cemetery: Joe Benz, Pep Conroy, Leo Dixon, Ike Fisher, Charlie Irwin, Tom McGuire, George McNamara, Tommy Mee, Oscar Melillo, Tony Mullane, Hal Reilly, Pants Rowland

Indiana

Anderson

East Maplewood Cemetery: Eli Cates, Tom Fisher, Peaches O'Neill

Argos

Maple Grove Cemetery: Jim Middleton

Auburn

Woodlawn Cemetery: Polly Zeider

Bedford

Cresthaven Cemetery: Yank Terry
Green Hill Cemetery: Bill Rariden, Ben Taylor

Bluffton

Elm Grove Cemetery: Everett Scott

Borden

Pleasant Ridge Cemetery: Jim Porter

Brookville

Maple Grove Cemetery: Fred Miller

Corydon

Cedar Hill Cemetery: Roscoe Miller

Crown Point

Maplewood Cemetery: Pete Henning

Elkhart

Rice Cemetery: Nig Cuppy, Pat Paige

Evansville

Locust Hill Cemetery: Buster Bray, Punch Knoll, Syl Simon
Oak Hill Cemetery: Al Schellhase, Charlie Wacker

Sunset Memorial Park Cemetery: Frank McElyea, Bill Shanner, Lefty Wallace

Fort Wayne

Catholic Cemetery: Cy Alberts, Tom McCarthy, Ralph Miller, Lou Nagelsen, Rabbit Nill, Tom O'Meara, Carl Vandagrift
Concordia Cemetery: Bill Brandt
Covington Memorial Gardens: Bill Chambers
Greenlawn Memorial Park: Bill Cramer, Pinky Hargrave, Hub Hart, Andy Woehr
Lindenwood Cemetery: Louie Heilbroner, Sal Madrid, Chick Stahl, Dick West

Frankfort

Bunnell Cemetery: Elmer Johnson

French Lick

Mount Lebanon Cemetery: Charlie Biggs

Gary

Mount Mercy Cemetery: Johnny Mostil

Goshen

Violett Cemetery: Speed Kelly, Mike Knode

Greencastle

Forest Hill Cemetery: Ed Eiteljorg

Greendale

Greendale Cemetery: Kirtley Baker, George Boehler, Walt Justis

Greensburg

South Park Cemetery: Bob Wright

Greenwood

Forest Lawn Memory Gardens: Oral Hildebrand
Greenwood Cemetery: Elmer Brown

Hamilton

Hamilton Cemetery: Frank Oberlin

Hammond

Holy Cross Cemetery: Phil Collins

Hayden

Hayden Cemetery: Rolla Daringer

Huntingburg

Fairmount Cemetery: Ray Blemker

Indianapolis

Crown Hill Cemetery: Paddy Baumann, John T Brush, Charlie Carr, Rex Dawson, Hod Eller, John Grim, Carmen Hill, Al McCauley, Willie McGill, Doc Newton, Ducky Pearce, Toad Ramsey, Bill Sowders, John Sowders, Len Sowders, Bill Whaley, Charlie Whitehouse
Floral Park Cemetery: Oscar Charleston, George Orme, Peek-A-Boo Veach, John White
Holy Cross Cemetery: Ownie Bush, Pete Daniels, Jim Duggan, Johnny Hutchings, Chuck Klein, Duke Reilley, Hank Schreiber
Memorial Park Cemetery: Wally Andrews, Fred Eichrodt
Oaklawn Memorial Gardens: Bob Logan
St Joseph Cemetery: Dom Dallessandro, Reb Russell
St Vincent Cemetery: Red Corriden
Washington Park East Cemetery: Charlie French

Ireland

Shiloh Cemetery: Bob Friedrichs

Jeffersonville

Walnut Ridge Cemetery: Red Fisher, Frank Friend

Jonesboro

Riverside Cemetery: Walt Miller

Kingston

Kingston Cemetery: Cy Bowen

Kouts

St Paul Lutheran Cemetery: Stew Hofferth

Ladoga

Ladoga Cemetery: Ed Summers

Lafayette

St Boniface Cemetery: Walt Tragesser

Ligonier

Oak Park Cemetery: Bert Inks

Logansport

Mount Hope Cemetery: Al Scheer

Lyons

Prairie Chapel Cemetery: Stump Edington

Madison

Springdale Cemetery: Tommy Thevenow
St Patrick's Cemetery: Dutch Distel

Marion

Grant Memorial Park: Art Herring

Merrillville

Calumet Park Cemetery: Charles O Finley

Metz

Metz Cemetery: Jack Somerlott

Muncie

Beech Grove Cemetery: Charlie Knepper
Elm Ridge Memorial Park: Buck Crouse

New Albany

Fairview Cemetery: Jouett Meekin
Kraft Graceland Memorial Park: Wayne LaMaster

New Lebanon
Mount Zion Cemetery: Hosea Siner

New Lisbon
New Lisbon Cemetery: Jot Goar

North Vernon
Hillcrest Cemetery: Forrest More

Oakland City
Montgomery Cemetery: Edd Roush

Osgood
Greendale Cemetery: Bill Richardson

Paoli
Stamper's Creek Cemetery: Ken Trinkle

Patoka
Warnock Cemetery: Hal Mauck

Pershing
Lutheran Cemetery: Glenn Chapman

Peru
St Charles Cemetery: Al Bergman

Portage
Calvary Cemetery: Billy Holm

Richmond
Earlham Cemetery: Claude Berry, Dick Van Zant

Rising Sun
Rising Sun New Cemetery: Clarence Woods

Salem
Crown Hill Cemetery: Ovid Nicholson

Shepherdsville
Shepherd's Cemetery: Harry Taylor

South Bend
Cedar Grove Cemetery: Harry Arndt
City Cemetery: Del Wertz
Highland Cemetery: Ben Koehler
Riverside Cemetery: George Beck
Riverview Cemetery: Ray Shook, Buzzy Wares
St Joseph Cemetery: Ollie Bejma, Stan Coveleski, Ed Hanyzewski

Spencer
Riverside Cemetery: Ban Johnson

Terre Haute
Calvary Cemetery: Johnny Mann
Highland Lawn Cemetery: Bruce Connatser, Harry Glenn, Al Myers, Ace Stewart
Roselawn Memorial Park: Emil Bildilli, Three Finger Brown, Bill Butland, Jumbo Elliott
St Joseph's Cemetery: Bill Nelson

Trinity Springs
Trinity Springs Cemetery: Vic Aldridge

Vincennes
Fairview Cemetery: Ollie Pickering
Mount Calvary Cemetery: Joe Wyatt

Wabash
Falls Cemetery: George Mullin

West Lafayette
Grand View Cemetery: Hugh Nicol

Westfield
Westfield Cemetery: Ray Boyd

Winchester
Fountain Park Cemetery: Troy Puckett

Zanesville
Hoverstock Cemetery: Bill Prough

Iowa

Ackley
Oakwood Cemetery: Art Reinhart

Alden
Alden Cemetery: Charlie Frisbee

Algona
Riverview Cemetery: Jesse Duryea

Boone
Sacred Heart Cemetery: Jimmy Archer

Burlington
Aspen Grove Cemetery: George Stovall, George Zackert

Cedar Rapids
Cedar Memorial Park Cemetery: Orie Arntzen, Cy Slapnicka, Earl Whitehill
Linwood Cemetery: Bill Hoffer, Roy Radebaugh, Paul Speraw
Mount Calvary Cemetery: Mike Chartak
Oak Hill Cemetery: Belden Hill

Charles City
Calvary Cemetery: Vive Lindaman

Cherokee
Mount Calvary Cemetery: Steve Melter

Clarion
Clarion City Cemetery: Roy Wilson

Council Bluffs
Cedar Lawn Cemetery: Hal McKain

Davenport
Fairmont Cemetery: Lefty Lorenzen
Mount Calvary Cemetery: Al Van Camp, Tom Walsh

DECORAH
Lutheran Cemetery: Ossie Orwoll

DES MOINES
Glendale Cemetery: Charlie Dexter, Art Ewoldt, E Lee Keyser, Adrian Lynch
Pine Hill Cemetery: Ed Hahn
St Ambrose Cemetery: Pat Donahue
Woodland Cemetery: Bill Traffley

DUBUQUE
Linwood Cemetery: Charlie Buelow
Mount Olivet Cemetery: Ed Keas, Tom Loftus

FARMINGTON
Greenglade Cemetery: Jack Saltzgaver

FORT DODGE
Corpus Christi Cemetery: Gene Ford, Jim Long

HAMPTON
Hampton Cemetery: Joe Jaeger

IOWA CITY
Memory Gardens Cemetery: Otto Vogel

KEOKUK
St Peter's Catholic Church Cemetery: Ralph Bell

LINN GROVE
Barnes Township Cemetery: Wattie Holm

MADRID
Mount Hope Cemetery: Jim Grant

MARSHALLTOWN
Riverside Cemetery: James C Dunn, Julius Willigrod

MIDDLE AMANA
Middle Amana Cemetery: Bill Zuber

NEOLA
Neola Township Cemetery: Red Downs

NEW HAMPTON
New Hampton City Cemetery: Duane Josephson

NORWAY
St Michael's Cemetery: Hal Trosky

ONAWA
Graceland Cemetery: Tom Richardson
Onawa Cemetery: Buster Brown

OSKALOOSA
Forest Cemetery: Cliff Knox

OXFORD JUNCTION
Mayflower Cemetery: Joe Hovlik

PERRY
Violet Hill Cemetery: George Tomer

REMSEN
St Mary's Catholic Church Parish Cemetery: Johnny Niggeling

SAC CITY
Oakland Cemetery: Paul Zahniser

SIOUX CITY
Calvary Cemetery: Biggs Wehde
Graceland Cemetery: Bob Black, George Clark
Memorial Park Cemetery: Red Anderson

SPENCER
Riverside Cemetery: Babe Towne

SPIRIT LAKE
Lakeland Memorial Gardens: Vern Fear
Lakeview Cemetery: Charlie Uhlir

STOCKPORT
Dibble Cemetery: Roxie Lawson

TOLEDO
Woodlawn Cemetery: King Cole

TRURO
Hartman Cemetery: Ducky Holmes

VILLISCA
Villisca Cemetery: Lynn King

WATERLOO
Calvary Cemetery: Bill Wagner

WYOMING
Wyoming Cemetery: Dutch Levsen

KANSAS

ABILENE
Abilene Cemetery: Kite Thomas

ARKANSAS CITY
Riverview Cemetery: Claire Patterson

ASSARIA
Assaria Cemetery: Rube Suter

BALDWIN CITY
Baldwin City Cemetery: Dummy Taylor

BENTLEY
Pleasant Valley Cemetery: Bull Durham

BENTON
Benton Cemetery: Ralph Winegarner

BUFFALO
Buffalo Cemetery: Claude Willoughby

CALDWELL
Caldwell Cemetery: Ed Willett

CANEY
Sunnyside Cemetery: Charlie Rhodes

CLAY CENTER
Greenwood Cemetery: Herb Bradley

CLEARWATER
Clearwater Cemetery: Lloyd Bishop

CLYDE
Mount Hope Cemetery: George Dockins

COLUMBUS
Columbus City Cemetery: Raleigh Aitchison

DOUGLASS
Douglass Cemetery: Jimmy Durham

FORT SCOTT
Evergreen Cemetery: Lou Ury

HIGHLAND
Highland Cemetery: John Misse

HOLTON
Holton Cemetery: Virgil Barnes

KANSAS CITY
Maple Hill Cemetery: Bob Grim
Memorial Park Cemetery: Pat Collins, Roy Meeker
Mount Calvary Cemetery: Joe Ellick

KIOWA
Kiowa Cemetery: Willie Ramsdell

LANSING
Mount Muncie Cemetery: Mike Welday

LAWRENCE
Oak Hill Cemetery: Bob Edmundson

LEROY
LeRoy Cemetery: Loren Bader

LEAVENWORTH
Leavenworth National Cemetery: Jim Quick
Sunset Memory Gardens: Murry Dickson

LENEXA
Resurrection Cemetery: Joe Bowman

LINDSBORG
Elmwood Cemetery: Del Lundgren

LOUISVILLE
Louisville Cemetery: Wiley Taylor

MCPHERSON
McPherson Cemetery: Harry Chapman

MINNEAPOLIS
Highland Cemetery: Archie McKain

MORAN
Moran Cemetery: Otis Lambeth

OSKALOOSA
LeRoy Cemetery: Deacon Jones

PARSONS
Memorial Lawn Cemetery: Gil Britton
Oakwood Cemetery: Harry Maupin

PITTSBURG
St Mary's Cemetery: Pete Kilduff

SALINA
Roselawn Memorial Park: Bob Swift

SEVERY
Twin Grove Cemetery: Spades Wood

SPRING HILL
Spring Hill Cemetery: Curly Brown

ST MARYS
Mount Calvary Cemetery: Frank Bushey

STERLING
Sterling Cemetery: Art Evans

TOPEKA
Memorial Park Cemetery: Charlie Bates, Steve Simpson
Mount Hope Cemetery: Dale Gear
Topeka Cemetery: Guy McFadden, Butch Nieman, Ray Pierce

WICHITA
Lakeview Cemetery: Lou Clinton
Maple Grove Cemetery: Ike McAuley
Old Mission Cemetery: Fred Brickell, Frank Isbell, Tex Jones, Red Phillips
Resthaven Gardens of Memory: Rufe Meadows
White Chapel Cemetery: Pat Hardgrove
Wichita Park Cemetery: Tom Angley, Gus Hetling

WILLIAMSBURG
St Patrick's Cemetery: Lou McEvoy

WINFIELD
St Mary's Cemetery: Fred Clarke

KENTUCKY

ADAIRVILLE
Greenwood Cemetery: Bob James

AUBURN
Auburn Cemetery: Fin Wilson

AUGUSTA
Heck's Cemetery: Wiley Piatt

BURLINGTON
Burlington Cemetery: Jim McGlothlin

COLUMBIA

Columbia City Cemetery: Cy Barger

COVINGTON

Linden Grove Cemetery: Mox McQuery, John Shoupe

CRESTWOOD

Floydsburg Cemetery: Mike Powers

CYNTHIANA

Battle Grove Cemetery: Harvey McClellan, Stan Rees

EASTWOOD

Eastwood Cemetery: Frank Pearce

EMINENCE

Eminence Cemetery: Johnny Marcum

ERLANGER

Forest Lawn Memorial Park: Jim Viox, Jim Weaver

FLATWOODS

Bellefonte Memorial Gardens: Squire Potter

FLOYDSBURG

Duncan Memorial Cemetery: Alex McFarlan

FORT MITCHELL

Highland Cemetery: Joe Sommer
St Mary's Cemetery: Neal Brady, Bob Clark, Joe Heving

FORT THOMAS

St Stephen Cemetery: Ray Kolp, Red Lutz, Chick Smith, Jack Thoney

FRANKFORT

Frankfort Cemetery: Dick Crutcher
Peak's Mill Cemetery: Eddie Bacon

FULTON

Greenlea Cemetery: Mel Simons

GUTHRIE

Guthrie Highland Cemetery: Kent Greenfield, Hugh Poland

HORSE CAVE

Horse Cave Municipal Cemetery: Charley Moran

LA FAYETTE

Powell Cemetery: Erv Brame

LEXINGTON

Lexington Cemetery: Ted Conovar, Jim Park, Ted Turner

LONDON

A R Dyche Memorial Park: Jim Jones

LOUISVILLE

Calvary Cemetery: John Bellman, Pat Callahan, Bill Ludwig, John McCloskey, Ed Monroe, Rudy Sommers, Gus Weyhing
Cave Hill Cemetery: George Boone, Pete Browning, Harry Camnitz, Howie Camnitz, Monk Cline, Billy Clingman, Hub Collins, Mordecai Davidson, John Dodge, Irv Hach, John Haldeman, John Kerins, Fred Koster, Bob Langsford, Frank Pearce, Harry Clay Pulliam, Bill Reccius, John Reccius, Phil Reccius, Nick Reeder, Charlie Reising, Rudy Schwenck, Lev Shreve, Chicken Wolf
Eastern Cemetery: Hercules Burnett, John Weyhing
Evergreen Cemetery: Arnold Carter, Mahlon Higbee, Irv Jeffries
Flat Rock Cemetery: Dan McFarlan
Louisville Memorial Gardens: Roy Sanders
Portland Cemetery: Burley Bayer
Resthaven Memorial Park: Woody Abernathy, Roy Bruner, Milt Gray, Jim Long, Max Macon, Pee Wee Reese
St John Cemetery: Dan Sweeney, Tom Terrell
St Louis Cemetery: John Heinzman, Tom Long, John Richter, Mike Walsh, Jack Wentz, Fred Zahner
St Michael Cemetery: Tom McLaughlin, George Yantz
Zachary Taylor National Cemetery: Dick Durning

MARION

Mapleview Cemetery: Rip Wheeler

MAYFIELD

Maplewood Cemetery: Buster Ross

MORGANFIELD

St Ann's Cemetery: Ed Johnson

MOUNT STERLING

Machpelah Cemetery: Tom Grubbs

NORTH MIDDLETOWN

North Middletown Cemetery: Vic Bradford

OWENSBORO

Rosehill Cemetery: Johnny Morrison

PADUCAH

Maplelawn Park Cemetery: Pat McGehee
Mount Carmel Cemetery: Ed Holley

RICHMOND

Richmond Cemetery: Earle Combs

SHELBYVILLE

Grove Hill Cemetery: Dan McGann

SOMERSET

Somerset Cemetery: Doc Sechrist

SOUTHGATE

Evergreen Cemetery: Still Bill Hill, Alamazoo Jennings, Bill Kisinger, Pop Schwartz, Harry Steinfeldt, Jesse Tannehill

TAYLORSVILLE

Valley Cemetery: Scott Stratton

VERSAILLES

Pisgah Presbyterian Church Cemetery: A B "Happy" Chandler

LOUISIANA

ARCADIA

Arcadia Cemetery: Pol Perritt

BATON ROUGE

Greenoaks Memorial Park: Buddy Myer, Larry Pezold

Resthaven Gardens of Memory: George Washburn

Roselawn Memorial Park: Roland Howell, Rudy Leopold

BERNICE

Shiloh Cemetery: Red Booles

BUNKIE

Pythian Cemetery: Hal Wiltse

EDGERLY

Big Woods Cemetery: Ted Lyons

GREENSBURG

Greensburg Cemetery: Jim Lindsey

HALL SUMMIT

Mount Zion Cemetery: Clint Courtney

HOMER

Arlington Cemetery: Orie Kerlin, Mule Watson

HOUMA

Garden of Memory Cemetery: Sid Gautreaux

JEANERETTE

McGowen Memorial Cemetery: Harvey Green

LAKE CHARLES

Graceland Cemetery: Johnny Berger

LISBON

Rocky Springs Cemetery: Rebel Oakes

MADISONVILLE

Dendinger Memorial Cemetery: Irv Stein

MARTIN

Holly Springs Cemetery: Joe Adcock

METAIRIE

Garden of Memories: Rube Kroh, Mike Miley, Ed Morgan, Roy Walker, Orlie Weaver

Metairie Cemetery: Zeke Bonura, Count Campau, Al Flair, John Humphries, Mel Ott, Johnny Oulliber, Lefty Wolf, Doc Wood, Jimmy Woulfe

MONROE

Monroe City Cemetery: Lou Jackson

Riverview Burial Park: Bob Harmon

NEW ORLEANS

Carrollton Cemetery: Tex Hoffman

Greenwood Cemetery: Hal Bevan, Jimmy Dygert, Larry Gilbert, Al Jurisich, Joe Martina, Leo Moon

Hope Mausoleum: Jake Atz, Ted Jourdan, Carl Lind, Bill Perrin, Abner Powell

Lake Lawn Mausoleum: Larry Bettencourt, Charlie Gilbert, Tookie Gilbert

Masonic Cemetery: Lou Legett

Soniat Street Cemetery: Joe Dowie

St Joseph Cemetery # 2: Dick Robertson

St Louis Cemetery # 3: Lou Klein, Tom Reilly, Paul Sentelle, Aaron Ward

Valence Street Cemetery: John Pelz

OPELOUSAS

Myrtle Grove Cemetery: Al Nixon

PLAQUEMINE

Protestant Cemetery: Bill Lee

RUSTON

Greenwood Cemetery: Johnny Jones

SHREVEPORT

Forest Park Cemetery: Al Baird, Mike Massey, Pat Tobin, John Vann

Greenwood Cemetery: Bill Fincher, John Mercer

SIBLEY

Sibley Cemetery: Bill Bagwell

WEST MONROE

Sardis Cemetery: Ed Head

WINNFIELD

Winnfield Cemetery: Jack Wallace

MAINE

AUGUSTA

Maine Veteran's Memorial Cemetery: Hy Gunning

BELFAST

Belfast Grove Cemetery: Roger Salmon

BRIDGTON

South High Street Cemetery: Jim Mains, Willard Mains

Columbia Falls
Great Hill Cemetery: Irv Young

Cornish
Riverside Cemetery: Eddie Files

Falmouth
Pine Grove Cemetery: Des Beatty, Frank Dupee, Joan Whitney Payson

Kennebunk
Hope Cemetery: Sid Graves

Kezar Falls
Riverside Cemetery: Harry Lord

Lewiston
Mount Hope Cemetery: John O'Brien, Pat O'Connell
Riverside Cemetery: Bill Carrigan

Millinocket
Millinocket Cemetery: Chick Maynard

New Gloucester
Lower Gloucester Cemetery: Charlie Small
New Gloucester Cemetery: Ben Houser

Nobleboro
Dunbar Cemetery: Val Picinich

Ogunquit
Riverside Cemetery: Bobby Coombs

Old Town
St Anne's Church Cemetery: Louis Sockalexis

Portland
Eastern Cemetery: Cuke Barrows

Richmond
Richmond Cemetery: Bobby Messenger

Rockland
Acorn Cemetery: Chummy Gray

Sanford
St Ignatius Cemetery: Freddy Parent

South Portland
Calvary Cemetery: Kid Madden

Springvale
Riverside Cemetery: Harland Rowe

Topsham
Riverview Cemetery: Pop Williams

Winthrop
Glenside Cemetery: Del Bissonette, Squanto Wilson

Maryland

Aberdeen
Baker Cemetery: Cal Ripken, Sr

Allen
Asbury Methodist Church Cemetery: Dick Porter

Annapolis
Cedar Bluff Cemetery: John Wilson

Baltimore
Arbutus Memorial Park: Leon Day, Ben Taylor
Baltimore Cemetery: Boze Berger, John Kelly, Jimmy Macullar
Baltimore National Cemetery: Bill Lamar, George Maisel
Cedar Hill Cemetery: Bill Hohman
Gardens of Faith Memorial Gardens: Ed Carroll, Willie Miranda
Govans Presbyterian Cemetery: Merwin Jacobson
Green Mount Cemetery: Stub Brown, Frank Whitney
Hebrew Cemetery: Rube Marquard
Holy Redeemer Cemetery: Bill Lyston
Immanuel Lutheran Cemetery: Johnny Neun
Lorraine Park Cemetery: Rex Barney, Rudy Kneisch, Charlie Maisel, Fritz Maisel, Charlie Meisel, Jerry Scala
Loudon Park Cemetery: Cupid Childs, Buttercup Dickerson, Dave Foutz, Bill Stumpf
Loudon Park National Cemetery: Harry Aubrey, Bill Byers, Dave Danforth, Ferd Eunick, Sam Frock, Slats Jordan, Dummy Leitner, Charlie Loudenslager, Allan Russell, Milt Scott, Sam Trott, Bob Unglaub
Most Holy Redeemer Memorial Park: Cliff Melton
Mount Auburn Cemetery: Frank Warfield
New Cathedral Cemetery: Charlie Eakle, Mike Gaule, Ned Hanlon, Joe Kelley, Bill Kellogg, Walt Lerian, John McGraw, Deacon Morrissey, Wilbert Robinson, Eddie Rommel, Nick Scharf, Walt Smallwood, Jimmy Walsh, Gary Wilson
Oak Lawn Cemetery: Harry Baldwin, Charlie Fitzberger, Queenie O'Rourke, Harry Smith
Parkwood Cemetery: Al Rubeling
St Mary's Cemetery: Jack Dunn, Frank Foreman, Suter Sullivan
St Patrick's Cemetery: Bill Smiley
Western Cemetery: Ed High
Woodlawn Cemetery: Steve Brodie, Harry Fanwell, Fred Ostendorf

Beltsville
St John's Cemetery: Johnny Beall

BRENTWOOD

Fort Lincoln Cemetery: Tom Brown, Dan Casey, Ed Fuller, Charlie Gooch, Calvin Griffith, Clark Griffith, Joe Haynes, Charlie Luskey, Frank Watt

CAMBRIDGE

Cambridge Cemetery: Jake Flowers
Dorchester Memorial Park: Fred Lucas

CHARLESTOWN

Charlestown Cemetery: Ted Cather

CHELTENHAM

Cheltenham Veteran's Cemetery: Red Webb
Maryland Veteran's Cemetery: Dizzy Sutherland

CLARKSVILLE

St Louis Cemetery: Buck Etchison

CLINTON

Resurrection Cemetery: Bill Smith

CUMBERLAND

St Peter's and St Paul's Cemetery: Joe Buskey, Karl Kolsth

DENTON

Denton Cemetery: Buck Herzog

EASTON

Spring Hill Cemetery: Frank Baker

FOREST GLEN

St John's Cemetery: Jake Powell

FREDERICK

Mount Olivet Cemetery: Clarence Berger, Clarence Blethen, Ormond Butler, Carlton Molesworth, Emory Nusz, Dorsey Riddlemoser
St John's Catholic Cemetery: Ray Gardner

FROSTBURG

Frostburg Memorial Park: Lefty Grove

GALESTOWN

Galestown Cemetery: Homer Smoot

GWYNN OAK

Woodlawn Cemetery: Max Bishop

HAGERSTOWN

Cedar Lawn Memorial Park: Clyde Barnhart
Rose Hill Cemetery: John Allen, Joe Matthews, Duke Shirey

HANCOCK

Hancock Methodist Church Cemetery: Ike Powers

HAVRE DE GRACE

Angel Hill Cemetery: Charlie Burns

HIGHLAND

St Mark's Cemetery: Sam Rice

HYATTSVILLE

George Washington Cemetery: Rollie Hemsley

HYDES

St John's Catholic Church Cemetery: Tommy Vereker

LANDOVER

Harmony Cemetery: Chick Tolson

MIDDLETOWN

United Church of Christ Cemetery: Charlie Keller

ODENTON

Bethel Methodist Church Cemetery: Babe Phelps

ORIOLE

Oriole Cemetery: Joe Muir

PARKVILLE

Moreland Memorial Park: Ray Flanigan, Charlie Lau

PIKESVILLE

Druid Ridge Cemetery: Boileryard Clarke, Red Kellett, Ben Mallonee, Butch Schmidt, Jim Stevens, Tommy Thomas, Maury Uhler, Hack Wilson

POCOMOKE CITY

First Baptist Church Cemetery: Vic Keen

PORT TOBACCO

St Ignatius Church Cemetery: Ed Edelen

POTOMAC

St Gabriel's Cemetery: Bob Addie, Edward Bennett Williams

ROCKVILLE

Parklawn Memorial Park: John Smith
Union Cemetery: Bill Eagle, Walter Johnson

SALISBURY

Parsons Cemetery: Alex McCarthy

SANDY SPRING

Friend Cemetery: Jack Bentley

SANDYMOUNT

Pleasant Grove Cemetery: Jack Flater

SILVER SPRING

Gate of Heaven Cemetery: Joe Giebel, Joe Judge

SUDLERSVILLE

Sudlersville Cemetery: Frank Brower

SUITLAND

Cedar Hill Cemetery: Earl Clark, George Keefe, Bill Martin, Earl Mattingly, Ray Moore
Lincoln Memorial Cemetery: Smokey Joe Williams

TIMONIUM

Dulaney Valley Memorial Garden: Elmer Burkart, Howie Moss, Lefty Russell, Frank Skaff, Spider Wilhelm

WAVERLY

St John's Cemetery: Chick Fewster

WOODSBORO

Mount Hope Cemetery: Archie Stimmel

WYE MILLS

Wye Cemetery: Nick Carter

MASSACHUSETTS

ADAMS

Maple Cemetery: Pete McBride, Dave Murphy

AMESBURY

Mount Prospect Cemetery: Leon Chagnon

ANDOVER

Spring Grove Cemetery: John Cameron

ARLINGTON

Mount Pleasant Cemetery: Ty LaForest

St Paul's Cemetery: Cozy Dolan, Mert Hackett, Dewey Metivier, Dave Shean

ASHBURNHAM

New Cemetery: Fred Woodcock

ATTLEBORO

St John Cemetery: Hank Morrison

BARNSTABLE

St Francis Xavier Cemetery: Joe Cronin

BELCHERTOWN

Mount Hope Cemetery: Frank Loftus

BELMONT

Belmont Cemetery: Jud McLaughlin

BEVERLY

St Mary's Cemetery: John Deering

BLACKSTONE

St Charles Cemetery: Joe Connolly, Tim McNamara

BOSTON

Forest Hills Cemetery: Tommy Bond, Lew Brown, Pep Deininger, George Haddock, Bob Hall

Mount Hope Cemetery: Charlie Daniels, John Irwin, King Kelly, Tom Sullivan, Herman Young

BOURNE

Massachusetts National Cemetery: Walt Ripley, Jim Schelle

BRAINTREE

Blue Hill Cemetery: Claude Davidson, Walt Zink

BRIGHTON

Evergreen Cemetery: Jack Burns

BROCKTON

Calvary Cemetery: Pat Creeden, Haddie Gill, Frank Kane, Freddie Moncewicz, Henry Porter

St Patrick's Cemetery: Bill McGunnigle, Frank Sexton

BROOKLINE

Holyhood Cemetery: John Bergh, Cannonball Crane, Bill McCarthy, John Morrill, Miah Murray, Dave Pickett, Art Rico, George Wright

Walnut Hills Cemetery: John Kelleher, Fred Newman, Joe Walsh

BRYANTVILLE

Mount Pleasant Cemetery: Walt Whittaker

CAMBRIDGE

Cambridge Cemetery: Bill Barrett, Walter Clarkson, Gid Gardner, Mack Hillis, Tim Keefe, Eddie Waitkus

Mount Auburn Cemetery: Dad Clarkson, John Clarkson, Doc Gautreau, Bobby Wheelock

CANTON

St Mary Cemetery: Olaf Henriksen

CHATHAM

People's Cemetery: John Andre

CHESHIRE

Cheshire Cemetery: Dale Long

CHICOPEE

Calvary Cemetery: Mike Hickey

CLINTON

Woodlawn Cemetery: Jack McGeachy

COHASSET

Woodside Cemetery: Dick Donovan

CONCORD

Sleepy Hollow Cemetery: Dick Loftus

St Bernard's Parish Cemetery: Bill McCarthy, Dinny McNamara

CONWAY

Howland Cemetery: Jack Chesbro

COTUIT

Mosswood Cemetery: Ed Gallagher, Danny Silva

DALTON

Fairview Cemetery: Jim Garry

DANVERS

Annunciation Cemetery: Tom McNamara
St Mary's Cemetery: Ed Caskin

DEDHAM

Brookdale Cemetery: Buck Danner, Hal Deviney

DORCHESTER

Old Dorchester Burial Ground: Tim Murnane

DUDLEY

Calvary Cemetery: General Stafford, John Stafford, Jerry Turbidy

EAST HARWICH

East Harwich Cemetery: Cy Morgan

EASTON

Immaculate Conception Cemetery: Mike Driscoll

EVERETT

Glenwood Cemetery: Al Pierotti
Woodlawn Cemetery: Al Blanche, Clarence Dow, Sam Gentile, Skinny Graham

FALL RIVER

North Burial Ground: Tom Gunning, Jimmy Manning
Notre Dame Cemetery: Art Butler, Luke Urban
Oak Grove Cemetery: Charlie Buffinton, Claude McFarland, Butch Sutcliffe
St Patrick's Cemetery: Frank Fennelly, Tommy Gastall, Joe Harrington, John O'Brien, Johnny Reder, Red Torphy

FITCHBURG

Forest Hill Cemetery: Ed Warner
St Bernard's Church Cemetery: Tom Hart, John Keefe, Pat Moran, Martin Powell

GEORGETOWN

Harmony Cemetery: Fred Tenney

GLOUCESTER

Oak Grove Cemetery: Al Doe, Cy Perkins

GREAT BARRINGTON

St Peter's Cemetery: Pete Noonan

GREENFIELD

Green River Cemetery: Steve Partenheimer

GROVELAND

Riverview Cemetery: Jim McGinley, Dan Woodman

HAMILTON

Hamilton Cemetery: Joe Batchelder

HAVERHILL

St James Cemetery: John Ryan
St Joseph Cemetery: Gene Vadeboncoeur

HINGHAM

Church of St John the Evangelist: Ted Olson

HOLYOKE

Calvary Cemetery: Dick Burns, Tommy Dowd, Joe Lucey, Ed Moriarty, Tommy Tucker
St Jerome Cemetery: Marty Barrett, Pat Conway, Skip Dowd, Jack Doyle, Bill Gleason, Jack Hannifin, John Hummel, Dennie O'Neil

IPSWICH

Highland Cemetery: Joe Burns

LAKEVILLE

Clark Cemetery: Jim Cudworth

LANCASTER

Eastwood Cemetery: Billy Hamilton
St John's Cemetery: Billy Burke

LAWRENCE

Bellevue Cemetery: Klondike Smith, Andy Swan
Immaculate Conception Cemetery: Johnny Broaca, Jocko Flynn, Mike Jordan, John Murphy, John O'Connell
St Mary's Cemetery: Dick Conway, John Crowley, Patsy Donovan, George Moolic

LEICESTER

Pine Grove Cemetery: Frank Wilson

LOWELL

Edson Cemetery: Bill Hawes, Art Sladen, Art Whitney
Lowell Cemetery: Alex McKinnon
St Patrick's Cemetery: Roscoe Coughlin, Shorty Dee, Ed Flanagan, Bob Ganley, John Grady, Barney McLaughlin, Frank McLaughlin, Bill Merritt, Marty Sullivan, Lefty Tyler

LYNN

Pine Grove Cemetery: Harry Agganis, Bernie Friberg, Barney Gilligan, John Leighton
St Joseph Cemetery: Tom Bannon, Les Hennessy, Irv Porter, Blondy Ryan, Tom Whelan
St Mary's Cemetery: Tom Niland, Jim Wallace

MALDEN

Forest Dale Cemetery: Frank Maher
Holy Cross Cemetery: Tony Conigliaro, Sam Curran, Leo Hafford, Barney Olsen, John Shea, Joe Sullivan

MANCHESTER BY THE SEA

Rosedale Cemetery: Stuffy McInnis

MANSFIELD

St Mary's Cemetery: John Quinn

MARBLEHEAD

Waterside Cemetery: Joe Graves, Augie Swentor

Marlboro

Immaculate Conception Cemetery: John Buckley, Duke Farrell, Frank Quinlan

Mattapan

New Calvary Cemetery: Denny Berran, Joe Callahan, John Connor, Bill Cooney, John Fitzgerald, Gene Good, Andy Leonard, Jack Manning, Buck O'Brien, Denny Sullivan, Jim Walsh

Medford

Oak Grove Cemetery: Tom Daly, Howard Fahey, Shanty Hogan, Fred Lake

Melrose

Wyoming Cemetery: Joe Harris, Dominic Mulrenan, Frank Selee

Milford

St Mary's Catholic Cemetery: Doc Curley

Millers Falls

Highland Cemetery: Doug Smith

Milton

Milton Cemetery: Elbie Fletcher, Doc Martin

Nahant

Greenlawn Cemetery: Frank Leja

Nantucket

St Mary's Cemetery: Tom Earley

Natick

St Patrick's Cemetery: Thomas Connolly, Sr, John Coveney, Pat Pettee

Needham

St Mary's Cemetery: Shano Collins

New Bedford

Oak Grove Cemetery: Daff Gammons, Harry Stovey

St Mary's Cemetery: Benny Bowcock, Jimmy Canavan

Newburyport

Oak Hill Cemetery: Chet Nourse

Newton

Newton Cemetery: Bill Cronin, Al Hubbard, Frank Shellenback

North Adams

Hillside Cemetery: Jim Curtiss

South View Cemetery: Art Madison

North Andover

Ridgewood Cemetery: Johnny Barrett

North Attleboro

St Mary's Cemetery: Billy Maloney

North Brookfield

St Joseph Cemetery: Marty Bergen

North Truro

Old North Cemetery: Danny MacFayden

Norwood

Highland Cemetery: Marty Callaghan, John Kiley

Oxford

St Roch's Cemetery: Al Javery

Palmer

St Anne's Cemetery: Bill Karlon

Peabody

Puritan Lawn Memorial Park: Harold Kaese

Pittsfield

St Joseph's Cemetery: Mark Belanger, Ed Connolly, Cy Ferry, Jack Ferry, Howie Storie, Pussy Tebeau

Quincy

Mount Wollaston Cemetery: Bill Dam, Charlie Ganzel, Bill Vargus

Pine Hill Cemetery: Tom Jenkins

Randolph

St Mary's Cemetery: Gene McAuliffe, John Rudderham, Steve White

Raynham

Pleasant Street Cemetery: Ezra Lincoln

Rockland

St Patrick's Cemetery: Dan Burke, Jim Hickey

Rockport

Beech Grove Cemetery: John Kiernan

Roslindale

Mount Calvary Cemetery: Frank Butler, John Butler, Dan Cronin, Steve Dignan, Hugh Duffy, Joe Dugan, Curry Foley, Jim Halpin, Andy Harrington, Ike Kamp, Walt Lonergan, Mike Mahoney, Tommy McCarthy, Fred Mitchell, Marty Shay, Tom Smith, Mike Sullivan, Jerry Sweeney, Bill Tierney

Salem

Harmony Grove Cemetery: Len Swormstedt

Sharon

Sharon Memorial Park: Judge Fuchs

South Weymouth

Lakeview Cemetery: Phil Voyles

Southbridge

Oak Ridge Cemetery: Irv Waldron

Spencer

Holy Rosary-St Mary's Cemetery: Frank Bird

SPRINGFIELD
Hillcrest Park Cemetery: Phil Page
Oak Grove Cemetery: George Hemming, Fred Mann
St Michael's Cemetery: Tom Burns, Snooks Dowd, Pete Gilbert, Pat Hanifin, Ed Keating, Dan Mahoney, Rabbit Maranville, Paddy O'Connor

STOCKBRIDGE
St Joseph's Cemetery: Doc Scanlan

STONEHAM
St Patrick's Cemetery: Joe Casey

SWAMPSCOTT
Swampscott Cemetery: Les Burke, Bump Hadley

SWANSEA
Thomas Cemetery: Gus Salve

TAUNTON
St Joseph Cemetery: George Bignal, Tim Donahue

UPTON
Lakeview Cemetery: Bill Summers

UXBRIDGE
St Mary's Cemetery: Frank Fahey

VINEYARD HAVEN
Oak Grove Cemetery: Dave Morey

WALTHAM
Calvary Cemetery: Tom Cotter, Law Daniels, Tom Stankard

WARE
Aspen Grove Cemetery: Candy Cummings
Mount Carmel Cemetery: Joe Giard
St Mary's Cemetery: Nap Shea
St Williams Cemetery: Pat McCauley

WATERTOWN
St Patrick's Cemetery: Dee Cousineau, Bob Daughters

WELLESLEY
Woodlawn Cemetery: Hank Camelli, Louis Perini

WEST ROXBURY
Beth El Cemetery: Si Rosenthal
Mount Benedict Cemetery: Dan Cotter, John Fox, Ed Gill, Jim Ward
St Joseph's Cemetery: Bob Brown, John Freeman, Hank Garrity, Tom Madden, Joe Mulligan, Andy O'Connor, Jack Slattery, Bill Stewart, Bill Sweeney

WEST SPRINGFIELD
St Thomas Cemetery: Conny Doyle, Frank Rosso

WESTFIELD
Pine Hill Cemetery: Les Lanning
St Mary's Cemetery: Ray Fitzgerald
Fairview Cemetery: Rusty Yarnall

WESTON
Linwood Cemetery: Eddie Collins

WEYMOUTH
Fairmount Cemetery: Buster Burrell
Highland Cemetery: Ken Nash
St Francis Xavier Cemetery: Dan Howley

WINCHESTER
Wildwood Cemetery: Hod Ford

WINTHROP
Winthrop Cemetery: Paul Howard

WOBURN
Calvary Cemetery: Doc McMahon

WORCESTER
Hope Cemetery: Freeman Brown, Bruno Haas, Art LaVigne
St John's Cemetery: Bill Bergen, Hugh Bradley, Kitty Bransfield, Jesse Burkett, Hugh Canavan, Pat Carney, Doc Carroll, John Gaffney, Chick Gagnon, Henry Lynch, Freddie Maguire, Chippy McGarr, Jo-Jo Morrissey, Con Murphy, Pat Murphy, Tom O'Brien, Rosy Ryan
Swedish Cemetery: John Anderson

MICHIGAN

ADRIAN
Oakwood Cemetery: Bill Carrick, Emil Huhn, Rube Kisinger

ALBION
Riverside Cemetery: Deacon McGuire

ALLEGAN
Hudson Corners Cemetery: Frank Kitson
Oakwood Cemetery: Dad Hale
Rowe Cemetery: Frank Miller

ALMA
Riverside Cemetery: Rex DeVogt

ANN ARBOR
Forest Hill Cemetery: Clarence Lehr
St Thomas Catholic Cemetery: Lou Schiappacasse
Washtenong Memorial Park: Ray Fisher, Ernie Vick

BATTLE CREEK
Floral Lawn Memorial Gardens: Charlie Grover
Memorial Park Cemetery: Ray Knode

Oak Hill Cemetery: Allan Collamore, Harry Staley

Bay City

Elm Lawn Park Cemetery: Ernie Gust

Belding

Rest Haven Memory Gardens: Dick Terwilliger

Bellevue

Riverside Cemetery: John Eubank

Berkley

Cadillac Memorial Gardens West: Ralph McConnaughey

Roseland Park Cemetery: Fred Goldsmith, Davy Jones, Dutch Lerchen, Jack Wieneke

Birmingham

Birmingham Cemetery: John Rainey

Calumet

Lake View Cemetery: Bert Sincock

Cass City

Elkland Township Cemetery: Larry MacPhail

Center Line

St Clement Cemetery: Chet Laabs

Clinton

Riverside Cemetery: Bunny Fabrique

Coldwater

Lester Cemetery: Jim Hughey

Concord

Maple Grove Cemetery: Ernie Baker

Dearborn

Northview Cemetery: Van Patrick

Dearborn Heights

St Hedwig Cemetery: Bernie Boland, Joe Smaza

Detroit

Elmwood Cemetery: Mac MacArthur, Ed Stein, Sam Thompson

Evergreen Cemetery: Ed Kippert, Bobby Lowe

Forest Lawn Cemetery: Augie Bergamo, Harry Daubert, Bert Hogg

Grand Lawn Cemetery: Irv Bartling, Gus Bono, Homer Davidson, Dick Littlefield, Frank Owen

Mount Elliott Cemetery: Ben Guiney, Frank McIntyre, Frank Scheibeck, Henry Yaik

Mount Olivet Cemetery: Jimmy Barrett, Doc Casey, Frank Fuller, Ed Gagnier, Marty Kavanagh, Sport McAllister, Cass Michaels, Johnny Mitchell, Frank Navin, Frank Okrie

Woodlawn Cemetery: Fred Andrus, Fritz Buelow, Red Downey, Pete Fox, Ed Killian

Woodmere Cemetery: Charlie Bennett, Nig Clarke, Wish Egan, Gene Krapp, Fred Schemanske, Bill Stellberger, Joe Yeager

Escanaba

Lakeview Cemetery: Jack Perrin

Eureka

Eureka Cemetery: LaRue Kirby

Flat Rock

Michigan Memorial Park Cemetery: Frank Sacka, Mike Tresh

Flint

New Calvary Catholic Cemetery: Gene Desautels

River Rest Cemetery: Dave Hoskins

Sunset Hills: Red Bluhm, Arnie Earley

Franklin

Franklin Cemetery: Fred Blanding

Grand Blanc

Crestwood Memorial Cemetery: Alex Main

Grand Ledge

Oakwood Cemetery: Jerry Byrne

Grand Rapids

Calvary Cemetery: Casey Hageman

Fair Plains Cemetery: Walter Anderson, Al DeVormer

Holy Trinity Cemetery: Al Platte

Rest Lawn Memorial Park: Luther Roy

Woodlawn Cemetery: Wally Pipp

Harrisville

St Ann's Cemetery: Kiki Cuyler

Hartford

Maple Hill Cemetery: Jay Parker

Hastings

Riverside Cemetery: Lady Baldwin

Holt

Maple Ridge Cemetery: Bill Graham

Howell

Lakeview Cemetery: Bill Crouch

Jackson

Roseland Memorial Gardens: Ed Hendricks

St John's Cemetery: Jim Tray

Woodland Cemetery: Benny Frey

Kalamazoo

Grand Prairie Cemetery: Freddy Spurgeon

Mount Ever-Rest Cemetery: Bob Burkam, Bert Tooley

Mount Olivet Cemetery: Harvey Freeman

Mountain Home Cemetery: John Fetzer, Rudy Miller
Riverside Cemetery: Hod Fenner

LANSING

Evergreen Cemetery: Bub Kuhn
Mount Hope Cemetery: Jack Morrissey, Larry Raines, Vic Saier

LAPEER

Oregon Township Cemetery: Ralph Judd

LIVONIA

Parkview Memorial Cemetery: Eddie Cicotte

LUDINGTON

Ludington Cemetery: Danny Claire

MANISTEE

Oak Grove Cemetery: Henry Jones, Jack Lundbom

MARENISCO

Marenisco Cemetery: John Michaelson

MARSHALL

Oakridge Cemetery: John Wisner

MEMPHIS

Memphis Cemetery: Clint Rogge

MOUNT CLEMENS

Lincoln Memorial Park: Turkey Stearnes
Resurrection Cemetery: Wildfire Schulte

MUSKEGON

Mona View Jewish Cemetery: John Dobb
Oakwood Cemetery: Monte Beville, Bull Wagner

NEW HUDSON

New Hudson Cemetery: Vern Spencer

NORTH BRANCH

Greenwood Cemetery: Glenn Crawford

NORTH STAR

North Star Cemetery: Jesse Altenburg

NOVI

Oakland Hills Memorial Gardens: Hal Newhouser

OKEMOS

East Lawn Memory Gardens: Luke Hamlin

OXFORD

Oxford Cemetery: Elijah Jones

PAW PAW

Prospect Hill Cemetery: Bill Killefer

PERRY

Roselawn Cemetery: Bud Messenger

PETOSKEY

Greenwood Cemetery: Chick Lathers

PITTSFORD

Leonardson Memorial Cemetery: Rube Vickers

PORT HURON

Lakeside Cemetery: Bill Kelly, Bill Watkins
Mount Hope Catholic Cemetery: Fred Lamline

ROCHESTER

Christian Memorial Cultural Cemetery: Roy Cullenbine

ROMEO

Romeo Cemetery: Frank Bowerman

SAGINAW

Forest Lawn Cemetery: Red McKee

SALINE

Oakwood Cemetery: Watch Burnham

SHERIDAN

Sheridan Cemetery: Ed Hemingway

SOUTHFIELD

Holy Sepulchre Cemetery: Jack Bracken, Walter O Briggs, Jr, Walter O Briggs, Sr, Al Cicotte, Charlie Gehringer, Mickey Harris, Harry Heilmann, Nemo Leibold, Clyde Manion, Mike Menosky, Brad Springer, Vic Wertz
White Chapel Memorial Cemetery: Bobby Veach

ST CLAIR

St Mary's Cemetery: Ted Goulait

ST JOSEPH

Resurrection Catholic Cemetery: Bob Katz

STURGIS

Oak Lawn Cemetery: Harry Niles

TAWAS CITY

Tawas City Cemetery: Roxy Roach

THREE RIVERS

Parkville Cemetery: Willie Powell

TROY

White Chapel Memorial Cemetery: Babe Sherman

UTICA

Utica Cemetery: Duke Maas

VICKSBURG

Vicksburg Cemetery: Bill Snyder

WAYNE

Glenwood Cemetery: Ed Fisher

WEST BLOOMFIELD

Pine Lake Cemetery: Norm Cash

WESTLAND

Cadillac Memorial Gardens: Tom Cafego, Art Reinholz

White Cloud

Big Prairie-Everitt Cemetery: Pete Fahrer

Wyandotte

Our Lady of Hope Cemetery: Leo Cristante

Our Lady-Mount Carmel Cemetery: Larry LeJeune

Minnesota

Austin

Calvary Cemetery: Lou Ciola

Avon

St Benedict's Catholic Church Cemetery: Showboat Fisher

Crookston

Oakdale Cemetery: Les Munns

Deer River

Olivet Cemetery: Steamboat Williams

Duluth

Calvary Cemetery: Rasty Wright
Forest Hill Cemetery: Bill Otis
Park Hill Cemetery: Newt Randall
Sunrise Memorial Park: Wally Gilbert

Ely

Ely Cemetery: Burt Keeley

Faribault

Maple Lawn Cemetery: Jimmy Pofahl

Hopkins

Grand-View Park Cemetery: Bill Carney

Jordan

Spirit Hill Cemetery: Ollie Fuhrman

Kasson

Maple Grove Cemetery: Les Tietje

LeSeuer

Mound Cemetery: Roger Denzer

Mendota Heights

Resurrection Cemetery: Robert Short

Minneapolis

Crystal Lake Cemetery: Bob Ingersoll
Fort Snelling National Cemetery: Bill Antonello, Whitey Hilcher, Jesse Petty, Frank Trechock
Hillside Cemetery: Ellis Johnson
Lakewood Cemetery: Buzz Arlett, Ossie Bluege, Bert Brenner, George Dumont, Elmer Foster, Spence Harris, Mike Kelley, Sherry Robertson, Ray Rolling, Dick Siebert, Wib Smith, Hy Vandenberg, Jimmy Williams
St Mary's Cemetery: Joe Crotty, Joe Fautsch, Bill Fox, Ted Odenwald, Harry Ostdiek, Rube Schauer, Spike Shannon, Jack Zalusky
Sunset Memorial Park: Fred Curtis, Lew Drill, Ralph Miller, Fred Spencer

Mora

Oakwood Cemetery: Rube Geyer

Olivia

St Aloysius Catholic Church Cemetery: Blix Donnelly

Rochester

Calvary Cemetery: Moonlight Graham

Roseville

Roselawn Cemetery: Mickey Rocco

Sauk Rapids

Trinity Lutheran Church Cemetery: Rip Repulski

Slayton

Restland Memory Gardens: Ed Pipgras

St Cloud

Calvary Cemetery: Henry Thielman, Jake Thielman

St Paul

Calvary Cemetery: Paul Castner, Tony Faeth, Bill Wilson
Elmhurst Cemetery: Leroy Matlock
Forest Lawn Memorial Park: Hap Morse
Oakland Cemetery: Lee Quillin
Resurrection Cemetery: Larry Rosenthal

St Peter

State Hospital Cemetery: Joe Werrick

Winona

St Mary's Cemetery: Julie Wera

Mississippi

Ackerman

Concord Cemetery: Aubrey Epps

Batesville

Forrest Memorial Park: Sammy Vick

Bond

Bond Cemetery: Dizzy Dean

Brooksville

Brooksville Cemetery: Dave Madison

Cleveland

Cleveland Cemetery: Clay Roe

Columbus

Friendship Cemetery: Dixie McArthur, Jake Propst, Jim Roberts

Greenville

Greenville Cemetery: Cecil Bolton, Tommy Taylor

Greenwood

Odd Fellows Cemetery: Hughie Critz

Gulfport

Evergreen Cemetery: Jack Ryan

Hattiesburg

Roseland Park Cemetery: Wid Matthews, Fred Waters

Jackson

Garden Memorial Park: Marshall Bridges
Greenwood Cemetery: Pete Shields

Laurel

Hickory Grove Cemetery: Fred Walters
Lake Park Cemetery: Gene Moore

Meadville

Mount Zion Cemetery: Dick Jones

Meridian

Magnolia Cemetery: Danny Clark, Eric McNair, Charlie Moss, Skeeter Webb
Memorial Park: Sammy Holbrook, Papa Williams

Moss Point

Griffin Cemetery: Red Bullock

Pascagoula

Jackson County Memorial Park: Hal Lee, Sam Leslie
Machpelah Cemetery: Jay Kirke

Philadelphia

Cedar Lawn Cemetery: Bubba Phillips

Pontotoc

Pontotoc Cemetery: Jim Joe Edwards

Puckett

Union Baptist Church Cemetery: Anse Moore

Sardis

Rose Hill Cemetery: Willie Mitchell

Shannon

Shannon Cemetery: Guy Bush

Sherman

Sherman Cemetery: Dode Criss

Terry

Terry Cemetery: Phil Redding

Tupelo

Glenwood Cemetery: Howard Merritt, Andy Reese

Water Valley

Oak Hill Cemetery: Dolan Nichols

Missouri

Affton

Our Redeemer Cemetery: Milt Byrnes, Whitey Miller
Sunset Memorial Park: August Busch, Jr, Hooks Dauss, John Kirby, Kurt Krieger, Walt Schulz

Allenton

Allen Cemetery: Bob Klinger

Anaconda

Anaconda Cemetery: Loy Hanning

Bellefontaine Neighbors

Bethlehem Cemetery: Bill Abstein, Bobby Hofman, Oscar Roettger, Howard Vahrenhorst

Blue Eye

Blue Eye Cemetery: Chuck Hostetler

Bogard

Mount Zion Cemetery: Ray Powell

Bowling Green

Memorial Garden Cemetery: Jack Graney

Branson

Ozarks Memorial Park: Ernie Nevel

Cape Girardeau

Fairmount Cemetery: Elam Vangilder

Columbia

Memorial Park Cemetery: Ed Barnhart

Creve Coeur

Bellerive Heritage Gardens: Cactus Keck

Diamond

Diamond Cemetery: Marc Hall

Dixon

Dixon Cemetery: Wally Schang

Farmington

Masonic Cemetery: Barney Pelty

Festus

Rose Lawn Memorial Gardens: Walter Holke

Freeman

Freeman Cemetery: George Gilpatrick

Hannibal

Holy Family Cemetery: Bill Miller
Riverside Cemetery: Jake Beckley

IBERIA

Iberia Cemetery: Bill Humphrey

INDEPENDENCE

Mount Washington Cemetery: Mack Allison, Fred House, John Houseman
Salem Cemetery: Mort Cooper

IRONTON

Arcadia Valley Memorial Park Cemetery: Tim McCabe

JOPLIN

Fairview Cemetery: Frank Thompson
Forest Park Cemetery: Dick Bayless
Ozark Memorial Park Cemetery: Ferrell Anderson, Gabby Street

KANSAS CITY

Blue Ridge Lawn Memorial Gardens: Bullet Joe Rogan
Calvary Cemetery: Jim Gleeson, Bill Kling, Bill Moore, Joe Riggert, Roy Sanders, Cotton Tierney
Elmwood Cemetery: Ren Deagle, Frank Ringo
Floral Hills Memorial Gardens: John Johnson, Don O'Riley
Forest Hill Cemetery: Ad Brennan, Joe Crisp, John Farrell, Joe Kuhel, Satchel Paige, Rip Ragan, John Terry, Zack Wheat
Highland Park Cemetery: Frank Duncan
Marion Visitor's Center: Ewing M Kauffman
Memorial Park Cemetery: Nig Perrine, John Peters
Mount Moriah Cemetery: Johnny Kling, Art Loudell, Kid Nichols, Hilton Smith, Don Songer
Mount Olivet Cemetery: Luther Harvel
Mount St Mary's Cemetery: Lynn Nelson, Billy O'Brien, Fred Underwood
St Mary's Cemetery: Frank Bonner, Scott Perry, Danny Shay

KENNETT

Kennett Cemetery: Moxie Manuel

LEMAY

New Picker's Cemetery: Dad Meek

LIBERTY

Fairview Cemetery: Art Thomason

MARCELINE

Mount Olivet Cemetery: Ernie Herbert, Chuck Rose

MARSHALL

Ridge Park Cemetery: Bob Clemens

MENDON

Old Mendon Cemetery: Vern Kennedy

MILAN

Oakwood Cemetery: Cal Hubbard

MOBERLY

Oakland Cemetery: Joe Klugman

MONTGOMERY CITY

Montgomery City Cemetery: Jim Bishop

NEOSHO

Gibson Cemetery: Ed Hawk

NEVADA

Newton Burial Park: George Lyons

PAGEDALE

Bethany Cemetery: Lew Whistler
Laurel Hill Memorial Gardens: Allen Elliott

PERRYVILLE

Mount Hope Cemetery: Bill Cissell, Bill Schindler

PURCELL

Friend's Cemetery: Ken Boyer

REPUBLIC

Evergreen Cemetery: Skinny O'Neal

ROLLA

Rolla Cemetery: Marv Breuer

SALEM

Cedar Grove Cemetery: Elmer Jacobs
North Lawn Cemetery: Ben Cantwell

SAPPINGTON

St Lucas Cemetery: Joe Medwick

SEDALIA

Memorial Park Cemetery: Hal Schwenk

SIKESTON

Garden of Memories Cemetery: Allyn Stout

SPRINGFIELD

Greenlawn Memorial Gardens: Herschel Bennett
Resurrection Cemetery: Mike Ryba
Rivermonte Memorial Gardens: Sherm Lollar

ST ANN

Mount Lebanon Cemetery: Walter Mueller

ST CHARLES

St Peter's Catholic Church Cemetery: Ham Schulte

ST JOSEPH

Memorial Park Cemetery: Bill Bishop, Fritzie Brickell, Frosty Thomas
Mount Olivet Cemetery: Joe Kelly, Barney Reilly, Oad Swigart

St Louis

Bellefontaine Cemetery: Philip DeCatesby Ball, Bill Bayne, Doug Crothers, Ned Cuthbert, Silver Flint, Ed Herr, Hugh High, Bill Joyce, Henry Oberbeck, Hub Pruett, Jack Rowe, J G Taylor Spink, Chris Von Der Ahe, Perry Werden
Bethany Cemetery: Willie Sudhoff
Calvary Cemetery: Hal Anderson, Tom Barry, Bill Beckman, Herman Besse, Joe Blong, Cliff Brady, Jimmy Burke, Bobby Byrne, Gus Creely, Creepy Crespi, Art Croft, Jumbo Davis, Walt Devoy, Tom Dolan, Jewel Ens, Frank Figgemeier, Tim Flood, Bill Gleason, Jack Gleason, Bill Goodenough, Jack Gorman, Egyptian Healy, Ducky Hemp, Phil Hensiek, Art Hoelskoetter, Pat Hynes, Ernie Koob, Charlie Levis, Henry Lucas, Felix Mackiewicz, George Mappes, Wally Mattick, Harry McCaffrey, Mike McDermott, Jumbo McGinnis, Marty McManus, Trick McSorley, Paul McSweeney, Joe Murphy, Bill Norman, Ray O'Brien, Jack O'Connor, Mickey O'Neil, Frank Pears, Joe Peitz, Bill Popp, Joe Quinn, Yank Robinson, Ray Schmandt, Johnny Schulte, Joe Schultz, Pat Seerey, Gerry Shea, Urban Shocker, Oscar Siemer, Ed Silch, Skyrocket Smith, Tom Stanton, Justin Stein, Patsy Tebeau, Jack Tobin, Connie Walsh, Dee Walsh, Johnny Welch, Joe Woerlin, Fred Worden
Hillcrest Abbey: Benny Meyer
Jefferson Barracks National Cemetery: Frank Biscan, Jack Buck, Harry Hanebrink, Hughie Miller, Billy Mullen, Floyd Newkirk
Lakewood Park Cemetery: John Brock
Memorial Park Cemetery: Maurice Archdeacon, Mutz Ens, Solly Hofman, John Kroner, Bill Steele, Fred Walden
Mount Hope Mausoleum: Ray Sanders
New St Marcus Cemetery: Coonie Blank, Greek George, Silver King, Charlie Krehmeyer, Butch Weis
Oak Grove Cemetery: William DeWitt, Charlie Jackson, Bob Larmore, Frank Olin, Yats Wuestling
Oakhill Cemetery: Charlie Hollocher
Old St Marcus Cemetery: Rudy Kling, Johnny Peters
Park Lawn Cemetery: Heinie Mueller
Resurrection Cemetery: Dan Adams, Jake Boultes, Pat Burke, Mark Christman, Bill Friel, Gene Green, Joe Hoerner, Binky Jones, Hal Klein, Otto Krueger, Joe Mowry, Pat Patterson, John Phillips, Dick Reichle
SS Peter and Paul Cemetery: Mike Drissel, Charlie Hautz, Red Juelich, Joe Muich, Joe Poetz, Phil Todt
St John's Cemetery: Harry Lunte
St Matthew Cemetery: Jimmy Hudgens
St Paul Churchyard: Phil Ketter
St Peter's Cemetery: Cool Papa Bell, Ted Breitenstein, Kid Durbin, Ted Menze
St Trinity Lutheran Cemetery: Heinie Meine
Valhalla Cemetery: Art Bader, Toots Coyne, Frank Decker, Ray Jansen

Stella

Macedonia Cemetery: Al Atkisson

Sullivan

IOOF Cemetery: Jim Bottomley

Tina

Van Horn Cemetery: John Jenkins

Warrensburg

Sunset Hills Cemetery: Lou Fette, Charlie Miller, Chuck Workman

Webb City

Mount Hope Cemetery: Al Gerheauser
Webb City Cemetery: Bill Pepper

Webster Groves

Evergreen Cemetery: Andy High

Willard

Rose Hill Cemetery: Ken Gables

Montana

Butte

Holy Cross Cemetery: Mike Mattimore
Mountain View Cemetery: Jim St Vrain

Crow Ageny

Custer Battlefield National Cemetery: Jack Kibble

Havre

Calvary Cemetery: Ed Doyle

Kalispell

Conrad Memorial Cemetery: Gus Thompson

Lewistown

Lewistown City Cemetery: Jim Crabb

Nebraska

Aurora

Aurora Cemetery: Clarence Mitchell, Les Nunamaker

Beatrice
Evergreen Home Cemetery: Pid Purdy

Belden
Alderson Family Cemetery: Dale Alderson

Coleridge
Coleridge Cemetery: George Stone

Diller
Prairie Home Cemetery: Lee Dressen

Falls City
Steele Cemetery: Charlie Abbey

Geneva
Geneva Cemetery: Fred Fussell

Grand Island
Grand Island Cemetery: Fred Glade

Liberty
Liberty Cemetery: Harlan Pyle

Lincoln
Calvary Cemetery: Pug Griffin
Wyuka Cemetery: Lefty Taber

Maxwell
Fort McPherson National Cemetery: Bob Harris

Milford
Blue Mound Cemetery: Bill Rumler

Nebraska City
Wyuka Cemetery: Harry Smith

Omaha
Calvary Cemetery: Loren Babe, Mike Prendergast
Forest Lawn Memorial Park: Kid Camp, Llewellan Camp, Henry Clarke, Billy Earle, Roy Luebbe, Russ McKelvey, Carl Stimson
Graceland Park Cemetery: Otto Williams
Hillcrest Memorial Park: Dan Tipple
Holy Sepulchre Cemetery: Joe Dolan, Jim Kane, Owen Shannon, Joe Walsh, Harry Williams
West Lawn Cemetery: Bill Shipke

Pilger
Pilger Cemetery: Bud Tinning

Randolph
Randolph Cemetery: Jim Buchanan

Raymond
Raymond Cemetery: Al Bool

Scottsbluff
Fairview Cemetery: Charlie Jackson

St Paul
Elmwood Cemetery: Grover Alexander

Waverly
Rose Hill Cemetery: Bill Davidson

Winnebago
Agency Cemetery: Chief Johnson

Nevada

Las Vegas
Memory Gardens Cemetery: Bob Boken, Chuck Wortman
Paradise Memorial Gardens: Wally Shaner

Reno
Sierra Memorial Gardens: Archie Campbell

New Hampshire

Bedford
St Joseph's Cemetery: Tom Padden

Bristol
Homeland Cemetery: Walter Prince

Claremont
Mountain View Cemetery: Pat Parker

Conway
Center Conway Cemetery: Rip Jordan

Derry
Forest Hill Cemetery: Bill Anderson, Fred Tyler

Hanover
Dartmouth Cemetery: Fletcher Low
Pine Hill Cemetery: Jeff Tesreau

Holderness
Trinity Cemetery: Al Spohrer

Kingston
Greenwood Cemetery: Cannonball Titcomb

Londonderry
Holy Cross Cemetery: Duffy Lewis

Manchester
Mount Calvary Cemetery: Ray Dobens
Pine Grove Cemetery: Jack Carney, Lew Cross

Nashua
Edgewood Cemetery: Bobby Murray

Newington
Newington Cemetery: Walt Woods

Ossipee
Ossipee Cemetery: Fred Brown

Penacook
Woodlawn Cemetery: Red Rolfe

Rochester

St Mary's Cemetery: Jimmy Bannon

New Jersey

Basking Ridge

Evergreen Cemetery: Ben DeMott

Bellmawr

St Mary's Cemetery: Mike Clark

Belvidere

Belvidere Cemetery: Charlie Berry

Beverly

Beverly National Cemetery: Bill Narleski, Frank Parkinson, Ed Roetz

Bloomfield

Glendale Cemetery: Pat Scantlebury, Ernie Wolf
Mount Olivet Cemetery: Larry Hesterfer

Bordentown

Christ Churchyard: Doc Imlay

Bound Brook

Bound Brook Cemetery: George Pfister

Burlington

Odd Fellows Cemetery: William Coons, Tom Vickery

Camden

Evergreen Cemetery: Ed Lennox
New Camden Cemetery: Danny Green

Cedar Run

Greenwood Cemetery: Doc Cramer

Cinnaminson

Lakeview Memorial Park: Jim Curry, Hal Wagner, Lefty Weinert, Charlie Young
Morgan Cemetery: Lena Blackburne

Clarksboro

Eglington Cemetery: Pete Rambo

Cold Springs

St Mary's Cemetery: Hal Kelleher

Colonia

St Gertrude's Cemetery: Pete Appleton, Frank Bruggy

Dover

Locust Hill Cemetery: Frank McCrea

East Brunswick

Holy Cross Burial Park: Ed Sanicki

East Hanover

Gate of Heaven Catholic Cemetery: Ownie Carroll, Double Joe Dwyer, Happy Finneran, Ed Strelecki
Restland Memorial Park: Kewpie Pennington

East Orange

Holy Sepulchre Cemetery: Larry Corcoran, Jack Farrell, John Farrow, Hal O'Hagan
St Mary's Cemetery: George Kopshaw, Rupert Mills

Egg Harbor City

Egg Harbor City Cemetery: Lou Bauer, Carl Husta

Elizabeth

Mount Olivet Cemetery: Charlie Berry

Englewood

Brookside Cemetery: Davy Force, Hugh Fullerton

Fairview

Fairview Cemetery: Willie Garoni, Gil Hatfield, Hank Thormahlen

Flemington

Prospect Hill Cemetery: Eric Rodin

Gibbsboro

Cedar Grove Cemetery: Bill Husted

Gloucester City

Union Cemetery: Bill Shindle

Hackensack

Hackensack Cemetery: Stan Pitula
Maple Grove Park Cemetery: Ed Goebel

Hamilton

St Mary's Cemetery: Al Verdel

Hillside

Evergreen Cemetery: Swede Carlstrom, Charlie Hamburg, Charlie Sweasy

Jamesburg

Fernwood Cemetery: Frankie Hayes

Jersey City

Bay View-New York Bay Cemetery: Rube Peters, Al Tesch
Holy Name Cemetery: Bert Daly, Ed Forsythe, Jim McCloskey, Mike McCormick, Red Waller
St Peter's Cemetery: Nat Hicks

Jobstown

Springfield Cemetery: Joe Ohl

Kearny

Arlington Cemetery: Ollie Sax

Kenilworth

Graceland Memorial Park: Frank O'Rourke

Keyport
St Joseph's Cemetery: John Burke

Lambertville
Harbourton Cemetery: Fred Green
Riverside Cemetery: Charlie Hargreaves
Riverview Cemetery: Andy Boswell

Laurelton
Laurelton Cemetery: Jack Martin

Layton
Hainesville Cemetery: Harry Harper

Linden
Rosedale Cemetery: Al Reiss

Lodi
St Nicholas Cemetery: Otto Huber

Lumberton
Evergreen Cemetery: Ed Holmes

Mahwah
Maryrest Cemetery: Dick Lajeskie

Marmora
Seaside Cemetery: George Lowe

Mays Landing
Holy Cross Cemetery: Ed Schorr

Middletown
Mount Olivet Cemetery: Snuffy Stirnweiss, Dutch Stryker

Montclair
Immaculate Conception Cemetery: Bert Daniels, Mule Haas, Danny O'Connell, Ed Reulbach

Moorestown
Mount Carmel Cemetery: Wid Conroy

Mount Laurel
Mount Laurel Cemetery: Jim Spotts

New Brunswick
St Peter's Cemetery: John Harkins

New Egypt
New Jersey Veteran's Memorial Cemetery: Eddie Smith

Newark
Fairmount Cemetery: John Day, Gus Falzer, Mike Goodfellow, Everett Mills, Dave Pierson, Dick Pierson
Mount Olivet Cemetery: Don Savage

Newton
Frankford Plains Cemetery: Russ Van Atta

North Arlington
Holy Cross Cemetery: Oyster Burns, Leo Kiely, Fritz Knothe, Red Shannon

Orange
Rosedale Cemetery: Cookie Cuccurullo
St John's Cemetery: Cotton Minahan

Paramus
Cedar Park Cemetery: Joe Bennett, Sid Schacht
George Washington Memorial Park: Walter Ancker, Harry Cheek, Jack Cusick, Emerson Dickman, Charlie Fuchs, Tom Gorman, Elston Howard, Harry Otis, Bill Patton

Paterson
Calvary Cemetery: Mike Meola

Pennsauken
Bethel Memorial Park: Pop Corkhill

Perth Amboy
Holy Trinity Church Cemetery: Billy Urbanski

Phillipsburg
Fairmount Cemetery: Ed Fitzpatrick, Tommy Raub, John Stansbury

Piscataway
Resurrection Cemetery: Bob Maier

Plainfield
Hillside Cemetery: Warren McLaughlin

Pleasantville
Greenwood Cemetery: Ty Helfrich
Pleasantville Cemetery: Ed Haigh, Pop Lloyd

Pomona
Laurel Memorial Park: Ferdie Moore

Princeton
Princeton Cemetery: Pop Foster

Ridgewood
Valleau Cemetery: Charlie Jamieson

Riverside
St Peter's Cemetery: Chubby Dean, Redleg Snyder

Roadstown
Cohansey Baptist Cemetery: Rube Oldring

Robbinsville
Princeton Memorial Park: Ed Leip

Salem
Baptist Cemetery: Goose Goslin

Somerville
Immaculate Conception Cemetery: Bob Hooper

South Hackensack
St Michael's Cemetery: Frankie Zak

Swedesboro
St Joseph's Cemetery: Earl Rapp

Tenafly

Mount Carmel Cemetery: Jack Doscher

Totowa

Holy Sepulchre Cemetery: Dick Cogan, King Kelly, The Only Nolan

Laurel Grove Memorial Park: Jim McCormick, Bill Pounds

Trenton

Ewing Church Cemetery: Ralph Caldwell, George Case

Greenwood Cemetery: Rusty Saunders

Our Lady of Loardes Cemetery: George Hennessey

Riverview Cemetery: Fred Gaiser, Bus Saidt, Leo Smith

St Mary's Cemetery: Joe Burns, Charlie Hanford, Ted Kearns, Pat Powers

Union

Hollywood Memorial Park: Ed Fallenstin, Bill Zimmerman

Vineland

Siloam Cemetery: Ray Steineder

Wall

St Catharine's Cemetery: Walt Walsh

Washington

Garden of Memories: Buddy Hassett

Wenonah

Wenonah Cemetery: Norm Baker

Westfield

Fairview Cemetery: Joe Collins

Williamstown

M E Church Cemetery: Bill Grevell

Woodstown

Lawnside Cemetery: Harry Smith

St Joseph's Church Cemetery: Whitey Witt

New Mexico

Albuquerque

Fairview Memorial Park: Elmer Ponder

Gate of Heaven Cemetery: Joe Palmisano

Mount Calvary Cemetery: Emmett Bowles, Rip Hagerman

Sunset Memorial Park: Rudy Bell, Frank Truesdale

Artesia

Woodbine Cemetery: Carl Manda

Carlsbad

Carlsbad Cemetery: Bob Clark

Santa Fe

Fairview Cemetery: Al Clancy

New York

Albany

Our Lady of Angels Cemetery: Mickey Devine

Amherst

White Chapel Memorial Park: Bill Duzen

Amsterdam

Hagamans Mills Cemetery: Roger Bowman

Andover

Hillside Cemetery: Bill Lauterborn

Angola

Forest Avenue Cemetery: Pius Schwert

Auburn

Fort Hill Cemetery: Alan Storke

St Joseph's Cemetery: Tug Arundel, Jerry Dorsey, Mike Mansell, Tom Mansell, Ed Murphy

Avon

St Agnes Cemetery: Ken O'Dea

Babylon

Babylon Cemetery: Leo Fishel, Monte Ward

Binghamton

Spring Forest Cemetery: Jim Whitney

Bolivar

Catholic Cemetery: Patsy Dougherty

Brewster

Milltown Rural Cemetery: Joe Vernon

Bronx

St Raymond Cemetery: Jack White

Woodlawn Cemetery: Frankie Frisch, Johnny Murphy, Dave Orr, Grantland Rice, Dick Rudolph, Broadway Aleck Smith, Dan Topping, Lew Wendell, Heinie Zimmerman

Bronxville

Christ Church Columbarium: Ford Frick

Brooklyn

Cypress Hills Cemetery: Bob Ferguson, Jackie Robinson, Hickie Wilson

Evergreen Cemetery: Bill Dahlen, Artie Dede, George Hall, Herman Pitz, Oscar Walker, Lave Winham, George Zettlein

Flatbush Cemetery: John Cassidy

Greenwood Cemetery: Billy Barnie, Josh Bunce, Bill Cammeyer, Henry Chadwick, Jack Chapman, Larry Ciaffone, Charlie Ebbets, Frank

Hankinson, Fred Jacklitsch, Neal Phelps, Fred Siefke
Holy Cross Cemetery: Larry Battam, Jack Burdock, Doc Bushong, Dick Cotter, Gil Hodges, Joe Hornung, Charlie Malay, Stephen McKeever, Tom Meany, Phil Reardon
Salem Fields Cemetery: Lip Pike

Buffalo
Forest Lawn Cemetery: Jim Neher, Monk Sherlock
Mount Olivet Cemetery: Scrappy Carroll, Jocko Halligan, Joe McCarthy, Jim Prendergast, Stan Rojek, Vince Sherlock
St Stanislaus Cemetery: Frank Drews, Stan Jok, Frankie Pytlak

Canaan
Flat Brook Cemetery: Johnny Tillman

Canandaigua
Woodlawn Cemetery: Jim McCauley, Frank Smith

Canisteo
Woodlawn Cemetery: Howard Armstrong, Mort Flohr

Cheektowaga
Mount Calvary Cemetery: Dick McCabe, Eddie Phillips, Buddy Rosar
Ridge Lawn Cemetery: Bill Hunter

Cohoes
St Agnes Cemetery: Tom Lynch

Cooperstown
Lakewood Cemetery: Whitey Wilshere

Corning
St Mary's Cemetery: Bill Moore

Cortland
St Mary's Cemetery: Jim Mahady

Delevan
Delevan Cemetery: Howie Krist

Downsville
Paige Cemetery: Fred Odwell

East Aurora
Oakwood Cemetery: Walt Lynch

East Elmhurst
St Michael's Cemetery: Charlie Reipschlager

East Greenbush
Greenbush Reformed Church Cemetery: Ed Phelps

Eastchester
Holy Mount Cemetery: Frank Graham

Elmira
St Peter and Paul's Cemetery: Bill Mack, Don Richmond
Woodlawn National Cemetery: Packy Rogers

Elmont
Beth David Cemetery: Happy Foreman, Saul Rogovin

Endicott
Riverhurst Memorial Cemetery: John Munyan
Riverside Cemetery: Jake Pitler

Falconer
Levant Cemetery: Hugh Bedient

Farmingdale
Long Island National Cemetery: Heinie Beckendorf, Art Gardiner, Les Howe, Charlie Meara
Mount Ararat Cemetery: Milton Richman
New Montefiore Cemetery: Sid Gordon
St Charles Cemetery: Steve Lembo

Fishkill
Fishkill Rural Cemetery: Bill Leith

Flushing
Flushing Cemetery: Frank Brill

Fort Edward
Union Cemetery: Arnie Stone

Fort Johnson
St Mary's Cemetery: Bugs Reisigl

Fort Plain
Fort Plain Cemetery: Moose Grimshaw

Fulton
St Mary's Cemetery: Honey Barnes

Genesseo
Temple Hill Cemetery: Jay Rogers

Geneva
St Patrick's Cemetery: Frank Dwyer

Glens Falls
Glens Falls Cemetery: Gene Derby, Frank Wurm

Gorham
Gorham Cemetery: Frank Hershey

Hartsdale
Ferncliff Cemetery: Clint Blume

Hastings on Hudson
Westchester Hills Cemetery: Jonah Goldman

Hawthorne
Gate of Heaven Cemetery: Bob Berman, Heywood C Broun, Howie Carter, Bill Froats, Billy Gilbert, Jack Lynch, Billy Martin, John

McSherry, Babe Ruth, Walter Signer, Paddy Smith

Honeoye Falls
Honeoye Falls Cemetery: Chet Carmichael

Hornell
Rural Cemetery: Vince Daily

Horseheads
Maple Grove Cemetery: Al Todd

Hudson
Cedar Park Cemetery: Jim Bedford

Hyde Park
St James Churchyard: Rube DeGroff

Irondequoit
Irondequoit Cemetery: Mike Kircher

Jamestown
Holy Cross Cemetery: Jack Harper

Johnson City
Calvary Cemetery: Doc Farrell, Wild Bill Hallahan, Ron Luciano, Mike Murphy
Floral Park Cemetery: Otis Johnson, Harry Lumley
St Patrick Cemetery: John McGuinness

Johnstown
Ferndale Cemetery: Harry McNeal
Mount Carmel Cemetery: George Burns

Jordan
St Patrick Cemetery: Fred Burchell

Kenmore
Elmlawn Cemetery: Herm Doscher, Jim Gillespie, Heinie Smith
Elmwood Cemetery: Walt Chipple

Kennedy
Riverside Cemetery: Harry Eccles

Kingston
St Mary's Cemetery: Bud Culloton, Dick Johnston

Lackawanna
Holy Cross Cemetery: Jimmy Collins, Mickey Corcoran, Dave Eggler, Huck Geary, Bill Milligan, Jimmy Riley, Chet Ross

Lakewood
Sunset Hill Cemetery: Leon Carlson, Eric Erickson

Lancaster
Lancaster Cemetery: George Davis
St Augustine Cemetery: Johnny Mokan

Leicester
Leicester Cemetery: Norm Lehr

Lestershire
Catholic Cemetery: Dennis Casey

Lewiston
Holy Trinity Roman Catholic Cemetery: Johnny Pasek

Lynbrook
Rockville Cemetery: Joe Kelly

Malone
Morningside Cemetery: Libe Washburn

Maspeth
Mount Olivet Cemetery: Bill Collins, Ed Dugan, John Hatfield, George Meakim

Melville
Melville Cemetery: Specs Toporcer

Menands
Albany Rural Cemetery: Gene Lansing, John Pappalau, Cy Seymour
St Agnes Cemetery: Jimmy Esmond, Joe Evers, Bill Fagan, Matty Fitzgerald, Ed McDonald, Ed McGamwell, Jack O'Brien, Mellie Wolfgang

Mexico
Mexico Village Cemetery: Ripper Collins, Fred Payne

Middle Village
Lutheran Cemetery: George Chalmers, Sam Crane, Ira Davis, Red Kleinow, Ernie Lindeman
St John's Cemetery: Tommy Clarke, Joe Lake, Gene McCann, Jimmy Ring, Chief Roseman, Frank Scanlan

Moravia
Indian Mound Cemetery: Lew Carr

Mount Marion
Mount Marion Cemetery: Dutch Schirick

New City
Germonds Presbyterian Cemetery: Bill Kalfass

Niagara Falls
Oakwood Cemetery: Harry Stine
St Joseph's Cemetery: Sal Maglie

North Collins
Holy Spirit Cemetery: Marion Fricano

North Tonawanda
Sweeney Cemetery: Bert Lewis

Oneonta
Oneonta Plains Cemetery: Dick Fowler

Ossining
Dale Cemetery: Chet Hoff

Oswego
St Paul's Cemetery: She Donahue, Rip Vowinkel

Phelps
St Francis Cemetery: Joe Gleason

Pleasantville
Raymond Hill Cemetery: Phil Powers

Portland
Evergreen Cemetery: Henry Matteson
St Mary's Cemetery: Pete O'Brien

Poughkeepsie
Poughkeepsie Rural Cemetery: Elmer Steele
St Peter's Cemetery: George Browne

Randolph
Randolph Cemetery: Ray Caldwell

Redfield
Redfield Cemetery: Bill Duggleby

Rhinebeck
Rhinebeck Cemetery: Myron Allen

Richfield Springs
Lake View Cemetery: Lou Bruce

Rochester
Holy Sepulchre Cemetery: Tom Carey, Paul Cook, Red Dooin, Tex Erwin, Ray Gordonier, Wickey McAvoy, George Mogridge, Sam Moran, Lou Raymond, Joe Sargent, Harry Weaver, Stump Wiedman
Mount Hope Cemetery: Elmer Eggert, Lew Groh, Roy Van Graflan

Roslyn Heights
Plain Lawn Cemetery: Al Moore

Royalton
Mount Ridge Cemetery: Carl Fischer

Rush
Pine Hill Cemetery: Al Mattern

Rye
Greenwood Union Cemetery: George Smith

Saranac Lake
St Bernard's Church Cemetery: Larry Doyle

Saratoga Springs
Greenridge Cemetery: Hiker Moran

Schellsburg
Schellsburg Cemetery: Chuck Wolfe

Schenectady
Most Holy Redeemer Cemetery: Frank Mountain, Lee Riley
Park View Cemetery: Johnny Grabowski
St John's Cemetery: Bill Cunningham

Sherrill
St Helena Church Cemetery: Ben Egan

Silver Creek
Glenwood Cemetery: George Mohart

South Glens Falls
St Mary's Cemetery: Bob Cooney, Jack Gilbert, Ray Miner

Southold
St Patrick's Cemetery: Lew Malone

Spencerport
St John's Cemetery: Pat Murray

St Bonaventure
St Bonaventure Cemetery: Kid McLaughlin

Stanfordville
Stanford Cemetery: Austin Knickerbocker

Staten Island
Moravian Cemetery: Jim Mutrie
Silver Mount Cemetery: George Sharrott
St Mary's Cemetery: Fred Lear
Valhalla Burial Park: John Cronin

Stuyvesant
Firwood Cemetery: Clay Van Alstyne

Syracuse
Assumption Cemetery: Bob Becker
Morningside Cemetery: Ensign Cottrell
Oakwood-Morningside Cemetery: Bob Shawkey
Sacred Heart Cemetery: Al Grabowski, Reggie Grabowski
St Agnes Cemetery: Jim Devine, Mike Dorgan, Jim Doyle, Bill Kelly, Jimmy Walsh
St Mary's Cemetery: Frank Lamanna, Bud Podbielan

Tannersville
Evergreen Cemetery: Slow Joe Doyle

Troy
Oakwood Cemetery: Marc Filley
St John's Cemetery: Fatty Briody, Jim Devlin, Jack Rafter
St Joseph's Cemetery: Henry Cote, Dan Minahan
St Mary's Cemetery: Johnny Evers, Hugh Hearne, Mike Lawlor
St Peter's Cemetery: Hon Von Fricken

Utica
Calvary Cemetery: George DeTore
Forest Hill Cemetery: Alonzo Breitenstein, Fred Lewis, Art Mills, Hardy Richardson, Biff Schlitzer

New Forest Cemetery: Sam Dodge, Jim Fairbank
St Agnes Cemetery: Bill Dinneen, Mike Griffin
St Peter's Cemetery: Amby McConnell

VALHALLA

Kensico Cemetery: Ed Barrow, Andy Coakley, Lou Gehrig, Paul Krichell, Joe Reichler, Jacob Ruppert

VESTAL

Vestal Hills Memorial Park: Glenn Spencer

WAPPINGER FALLS

St Mary's Cemetery: Dan Brouthers

WATERFORD

St Joseph's Cemetery: Chick Robitaille

WATERVILLE

St Bernard's Cemetery: Danny Mahoney

WATERVLIET

St Patrick's Cemetery: Tom Donovan, Darby O'Brien, Pat Simmons

WEBSTER

Webster Rural Cemetery: Walter Bernhardt

WESTBURY

Cemetery of Holy Rood: Bob Chipman, Zip Collins, Tom Gorman, Jerry McCarthy, Frank McCormick, Marty McHale, Charlie Sheerin, Sam Zoldak

WHITEHALL

Our Lady of Angels Cemetery: Ebba St Claire

WHITESBORO

Mount Olivet Cemetery: Bill Clancy, Joe Kiefer

WOODSIDE

Calvary Cemetery: Charlie Byrne, Dick Cannon, Jack Coffey, Pete Cregan, Mike Donovan, Frank Farrell, Bill Finley, Mickey Finn, Tim Hurst, Jim Hutchinson, Willie Keeler, Honest John Kelly, Jim Kennedy, Al Lefevre, Hugh McQuillan, Tom O'Rourke, Bill Swanson, Dasher Troy, Mickey Welch

WORCESTER

Maple Grove Cemetery: Jim Konstanty

NORTH CAROLINA

ALBEMARLE

Fairview Memorial Park: John Gaddy, Dick Mauney

ARCHDALE

Mount Vernon Methodist Church Cemetery: Gil English

ASHEVILLE

Riverside Cemetery: Buck Redfern
Tweed's Chapel Cemetery: Johnny Lanning

BEARSKIN

Crumpler Family Cemetery: Roy Crumpler

BETHEL HILL

Bethel Hill Baptist Church Cemetery: Claude Wilburn

BLACK MOUNTAIN

Western Carolina Veteran's Cemetery: George Bradshaw

BUIES CREEK

Buies Creek Cemetery: Woody Upchurch

BURLINGTON

Alamance Memorial Park: Tom Zachary
Pine Hill Cemetery: Bill Evans, Maxie Wilson

CHAPEL HILL

Chapel Hill Cemetery: Bob Lawson
New Hope Church Cemetery: James Johnston

CHARLOTTE

Elmwood Cemetery: Jule Mallonee
Evergreen Cemetery: Mike Garbark, Jim Hopper
Forest Lawn Cemetery: Jimmy Jordan
Sharon Memorial Park: Pat Cooper, Bill Harris, Garland Lawing, Nig Lipscomb, Ben Paschal, Bob Porterfield

CHINA GROVE

Greenlawn Cemetery: Dixie Upright

CHURCHLAND

Barnes Family Cemetery: Junie Barnes

CONCORD

Carolina Memorial Park: Ron Blackburn, Fred Chapman, Herman Fink
Mount Olivet Methodist Church Cemetery: Billy Goodman
Oakwood Cemetery: Willy Fetzer, Herm Holshouser, Clem Llewellyn

ELIZABETH CITY

New Hollywood Cemetery: Dick Burrus

ELM CITY

Cedar Grove Cemetery: Vance Page

ENKA

Forest Lawn Memorial Park: Noodles Hahn

FAYETTEVILLE

Lafayette Memorial Park: Cap Clark, Cal Koonce

FREMONT

Fremont Cemetery: Johnny Peacock

Gastonia
Oakwood Cemetery: Skipper Friday

Goldsboro
Willow Dale Cemetery: Bill Bell, Mule Shirley

Graham
Linwood Cemetery: Shag Thompson
Rock Creek Methodist Church Cemetery: Lew Riggs

Greensboro
Forest Lawn Cemetery: Johnny Allen, Sam Gibson
Guilford Memorial Park: Dave Barbee, Al McLean, Pep Young
Moriah Methodist Church Cemetery: Tom Glass
New Garden Cemetery: Rick Ferrell, Wes Ferrell, Bill Lindsay
New Goshen Church Cemetery: Tom Alston

Greenville
Brownhill Cemetery: Dave Barnhill

Guilford College
Guilford College Cemetery: Luke Stuart

Henderson
Union Chapel Church Cemetery: Buster Maynard

Hendersonville
Forest Lawn Memorial Park: Lefty West

Hertford
Cedarwood Cemetery: Catfish Hunter

Hiddenite
Linney's Grove Church Cemetery: Jim Poole

High Point
Floral Garden Park Cemetery: Dick Culler
Springfield Friends Church Cemetery: Woody Crowson

Huntersville
Hopewell Church Cemetery: Ben Shields

Jackson
Davis Family Cemetery: Ron Davis

Kenly
Kenly Cemetery: Al Evans, Gary Fortune

Kernersville
United Methodist Church Cemetery: Kemp Wicker

Kinston
Maplewood Cemetery: Stan Spence, George Suggs

Landis
West Lawn Memorial Park: Fred Archer

Laurinburg
Hillside Memorial Park: Willie Jones

Lenoir
Blue Ridge Memorial Park: Rube Walker

Liberty
Fairview Cemetery: Tim Murchison

Lillington
Westview Memorial Gardens: Dusty Cooke

Lumberton
Meadowbrook Cemetery: Taffy Wright

Maxton
Oak Grove Cemetery: Dutch Holland

Middlesex
Antioch Baptist Church Cemetery: Sam Narron

Monroe
Lakeland Memorial Park: Dave Coble

Morganton
Burke Memorial Park: Razor Ledbetter
South Mountain Baptist Church Cemetery: Woody Rich

Mount Holly
Morningside Park Cemetery: Ted Wilson
Mount Holly Cemetery: Chick Outen

Mount Olive
Martin-Price Cemetery: Ray Scarborough

New Bern
Cedar Grove Cemetery: Stu Flythe

Newton
Eastview Cemetery: Wade Lefler, Ducky Yount, Eddie Yount

Pinetops
Pinetops Cemetery: Herb Cobb

Raleigh
Montlawn Memorial Park: Bill Clarkson, Snake Henry, Jakie May
Oakwood Cemetery: Bill Wynne
Raleigh Memorial Park: Vic Sorrell

Rockingham
Leak Family Cemetery: Russ Ford

Rocky Mount
Gardens of Gethsemane: Buck Leonard

Rowland
Rowland Cemetery: Nate Andrews

Salemburg
Baptist Church Cemetery: Rube Benton

Salisbury
Chestnut Hills Cemetery: Buck Jordan
Rowan Memorial Park: Johnnie Heving, Clyde Kluttz

SNOW CAMP

Spring Friend Cemetery: Boyd Perry

SOUTHERN PINES

Mount Hope Cemetery: Joe DeBerry

SPINDALE

Sunset Memorial Park: Smoky Burgess

STANLEY

Stanley Cemetery: Doyt Morris

STATESVILLE

Iredell Memorial Gardens: Dave Thompson

STONY POINT

Stony Point Cemetery: Dave Jolly

TAYLORSVILLE

Friendship Church Cemetery: Charlie Frye

THOMASVILLE

Holly Hill Memorial Park: Cliff Bolton

WAKE FOREST

Wake Forest Cemetery: Lee Gooch

WALKERTOWN

Gardens of Memory: Rufe Gentry

WALNUT COVE

Wilson Primitive Baptist Church Cem: Steve Shemo

WARRENTON

Fairview Cemetery: Jack Scott

WENDELL

Greenmount Cemetery: Chuck Rowland

WHITEVILLE

Whiteville Memorial Cemetery: Charlie Ripple, Dave Smith

WILMINGTON

Oakdale Cemetery: Gus Brittain
Oleander Memorial Gardens: Willie Stargell
Wilmington National Cemetery: Possum Whitted

WILSON

Evergreen Memorial Garden: Red Barrett, Stan Partenheimer
Maplewood Cemetery: Bunny Hearn

WINDSOR

St Thomas Church Cemetery: Burgess Whitehead

WINSTON-SALEM

Faith Missionary Alliance Church Cem: Vinegar Bend Mizell
Forsyth Memorial Park: General Crowder, Don Hankins, Glenn Liebhardt, Johnny Meador, Ernie Shore, Eddie Yuhas
Parklawn Memorial Gardens: Jack Krol
Salem Cemetery: Fred Anderson, Wes Livengood

YOUNGSTOWN

Oak Hill Cemetery: John Scheible

NORTH DAKOTA

ENDERLIN

Enderlin Community Cemetery: Cy Pieh

FARGO

Holy Cross Cemetery: Ken Hunt, Roger Maris

WILLISTON

Riverview Cemetery: Dee Moore

OHIO

AKRON

Glendale Cemetery: Joe Battin, Sam Wise
Greenlawn Cemetery: Ed Walker
Holy Cross Cemetery: Mike Kahoe
Lakewood Cemetery: Clarence Wright
Memorial Park Cemetery: Farmer Weaver
Mount Peace Cemetery: Joe Neal
Springfield Center Cemetery: Bob Spade
St Vincent Cemetery: Scotty Ingerton

ALLIANCE

Alliance City Cemetery: Earl Moseley

ATHENS

West Union Street Cemetery: George Kahler, Howard McGraner

AURORA

Aurora Cemetery: Ben Shaw

AUSTINTOWN

Brunstetter Cemetery: Bill Otey

AVON

Elmhurst Park Cemetery: Harry Bemis, Bill Bonness
Resthaven Memory Garden: Dick Wakefield

BEDFORD HEIGHTS

Hillcrest Memorial Park Cemetery: Eddie Morgan, Red Ruffing

BELLAIRE

Rose Hill Cemetery: Brickyard Kennedy, Parson Nicholson, Bill White

BELLEVUE

York Chapel Cemetery: Bob Rothel

BELLVILLE

Bellville Cemetery: Scott Hardesty

Blue Creek

Moore's Chapel Cemetery: Austin McHenry

Bowling Green

Union Hill Cemetery: Ernie Neitzke

Bucyrus

Oakwood Cemetery: Ray Mack, Fred Trautman

Cadiz

Cadiz Cemetery: Moses Vasbinder

Cambridge

Northwood Cemetery: Welcome Gaston

Campbell

St John's Catholic Cemetery: Johnny Kucab

Canton

Calvary Catholic Cemetery: Kid O'Hara
Forest Hill Cemetery: Siggy Broskie, Ed Gremminger, Joe Houser, Charley Stanceu
St John's Cemetery: Bill Delaney
Sunset Hills Burial Ground: Thurman Munson
Warstler Church Cemetery: Joe Agler
West Lawn Cemetery: Bill Batsch, George Textor

Cedarville

North Cemetery: Bumpus Jones

Celina

North Grove Cemetery: Bruno Betzel

Chillicothe

Floral Hills Memory Gardens: Barney Schreiber
Greenlawn Cemetery: Danny Friend

Churchill

Churchill Cemetery: Bob Wood

Cincinnati

Arlington Memorial Gardens: Gordy Coleman, Claude Corbitt, Bob Geary
Baltimore Pike Cemetery: Charlie Bell, Red Ehret, Nellie Pott
Bridgetown Cemetery: Flea Clifton
Calvary Cemetery: Wally Kopf
Gate of Heaven Cemetery: Jim Beckman, Gus Bell, Eddie Hunter, Ted Kluszewski, Bob Wellman
Guardian Angel Cemetery: Roy Hughes
Longview Asylum Cemetery: Kid Baldwin
Mount Washington Cemetery: Buck Ewing, John Ewing
Oak Hill Cemetery Park: Ival Goodman, Johnny Hodapp, Bobby Mitchell, Jack Niemes, Tom Sullivan
Rest Haven Memorial Park: Bill Hart, Tom Swope
Spring Grove Cemetery: Les Backman, Frank Bancroft, Jim Blackburn, Billy Campbell, Charlie Case, Powel Crosley, Jr, Pat Deisel, Ernie Diehl, Charlie Gould, Heinie Groh, Emil Haberer, Crese Heismann, Bug Holliday, Waite Hoyt, Miller Huggins, Larry Jacobus, Jim Keenan, Lew Meyers, George Miller, Ralph Miller, Larry Pape, George Paynter, George Pechiney, George Proeser, Long John Reilly, Ralph Sharman, Ed Sperber, Clarence Stephens, Podgie Weihe, Harry Wheeler, Orville Woodruff, George Yeager
St Aloysius Cemetery: Ralph Brickner
St John Cemetery: Herm Wehmeier
St Joseph New Cemetery: Bill Bartley, Buzz Boyle, Eddie Boyle, Jack Boyle, Jim Boyle, Carney Flynn, Ed Glenn, Denny Lyons, Barry McCormick, Billy Riley, Jack Sutthoff
St Joseph Old Catholic Cemetery: Larry Benton, Ed Hug, Al Kaiser, Al Niehaus, Ambrose Puttmann, Gus Shallix
St Mary Cemetery: Ralph Birkofer, Tony Hellman, Marty Herrmann, Fred Mollenkamp, Heinie Peitz, Eddie Sicking
Union Cemetery: Hal Kime
Vine Street Hill Cemetery: Nick Altrock, Al Bashang, Red Bittmann, Chink Heileman, Jack Reis, John Singleton, Eddie Tiemeyer
Walnut Hills Cemetery: George Rohe
Wesleyan Cemetery: Frank Bell

Circleville

Forest Cemetery: Lefty Webb
Hitler-Ludwig Cemetery: Jack Compton

Clarksville

Clarksville Cemetery: Biff Wysong

Cleveland

Acacia Masonic Memorial Park: Les Fusselman, Roger Peckinpaugh
Brooklyn Heights Cemetery: Ed Kusel
Calvary Cemetery: George Anderson, Bill Bradley, Buttons Briggs, Dick Carroll, Ed Delahanty, Frank Delahanty, Jim Delahanty, Joe Delahanty, Harley Dillinger, Frank Doljack, Steve Evans, Lee Fohl, Tom Healy, Dutch Henry, Ken Hogan, Glenn Liebhardt, Paddy Livingston, Steve O'Neill, George Rettger, Fred Smith, Steve Sundra, Bill Wambsganss, Del Young
Highland Park Cemetery: Luke Easter, Joe Vosmik
Holy Cross Cemetery: Moxie Divis, Harry Redmond
Lake View Cemetery: Heinie Berger, Helene Bigsby, Alva Bradley, Ray Chapman, Pete Hotaling, Ernie Kish, Milo Lockwood, Ed Mc-

Farland, Dave Pope, Matt Robison, Arlie Tarbert, Ollie Welf
Lakewood Park Cemetery: Clint Brown, Jack Hardy, Jim Rutherford, Bill Stemmyer, Larry Twitchell, George Uhle
Lutheran Cemetery: Bill Schardt
Riverside Cemetery: Amos Cross, Frank Cross, Emil Leber, Jim McLaughlin
St John's Cemetery: Jim McGraw, Bill Reidy
St Joseph Cemetery: Charlie Smith
St Mary's Cemetery: Dode Paskert, Ed Zmich
Woodland Cemetery: Joe Ardner, Charlie Bohn, Ed Cermak, Ed Spurney

Clyde
McPherson Cemetery: Bill Coliver

Columbus
Forest Lawn Memorial Gardens: Ed Donalds
Green Lawn Memorial Cemetery: Harry Fritz, Wally Gerber, Jim Gifford, Newt Hunter, Bob Kline, Jack McCallister, Gus Schmelz, Kip Selbach, Billy Southworth, Jack Taylor, Jimmy Williams
Mount Calvary Cemetery: Ed Dundon
Union Cemetery: Hank Gowdy, Benny Kauff, Rasty Wright

Cuyahoga Falls
Chestnut Hill Memorial Park: Tod Sloan

Darrtown
Darrtown Cemetery: Walter Alston

Dayton
Beth Abraham Cemetery: Si Burick
Calvary Cemetery: Bernie Hungling, Jim Whelan
Memorial Park Cemetery: Ollie Klee, Terry Lyons, Jack Rowan, Dutch Ussat
Woodland Cemetery: Amos Booth, Ollie Caylor, Howard Freigau, Trader Horne, Harry McIntyre

Delaware
Oak Grove Cemetery: Cliff Curtis

Delta
Greenlawn Cemetery: Harvey Bailey

Donnelsville
Glen Haven Memorial Gardens: Charlie Pickett

Dowling
New Belleville Cemetery: Jim Bilbrey

Doylestown
Chestnut Hill Cemetery: Denny Galehouse

East Canton
Mapleton Cemetery: Vince Shupe

East Liverpool
Columbiana County Memorial Park: Bill Powell
Riverview Cemetery: Win Mercer
Spring Grove Cemetery: Scoops Carey
St Aloysius Cemetery: Curt Welch

Fairlawn
Rose Hill Burial Park: Frank Motz, Hank Ritter, Luke Sewell

Findlay
St Michael's Cemetery: Delos Drake

Fostoria
St Wendelin Church Cemetery: Pat Hilly

Fredonia
Fredonia Cemetery: Woody English

Galloway
Sunset Cemetery: John Galbreath

Genoa
Clay Township Cemetery: Babe Doty

Georgetown
Confidence Cemetery: Slim Sallee, Jack Theis

Germantown
Germantown Cemetery: Dazzy Swartz

Goshen
Goshen Cemetery: Sam Leever

Gutman
Mount Tabor Cemetery: Merle Settlemire

Hamilton
Greenwood Cemetery: Carl Weilman
St Stephen's Cemetery: Bill Hobbs, Harry Wilke

Hanoverton
Hanoverton Cemetery: Hy Myers

Hillsboro
Hillsboro Cemetery: Kirby White

Holgate
United Church of Christ Cemetery: Jack Hallett

Ironton
Woodland Cemetery: Harry Truby, Joe Willis

Jackson
Fairmount Cemetery: Pat Duncan

Johnsville
Shauck Cemetery: Palmer Hildebrand

Kent
Standing Rock Cemetery: Will Sawyer

Lancaster
Forest Rose Cemetery: Pete Sims

Lebanon

Lebanon Cemetery: Earl Yingling

Lima

Gethsemane Cemetery: Larry Cox
Woodlawn Cemetery: Frank Foutz

Lockbourne

St Joseph Cemetery: John Fluhrer, Chappie Geygan, Frank Gleich, Jim Handiboe, Bill Hinchman, Dick Hoover, Vic Janowicz, Lee Magee, Tubby McGee, Robert Quinn, Arch Reilly

London

Kirkwood Cemetery: Bob Bescher, Neb Stewart

Lorain

Calvary Cemetery: Dad Clarke
Ridge Hill Memorial Park: Irish McIlveen

Madison

Madison Memorial Cemetery: Milt Shoffner

Malvern

Bethlehem Cemetery: Ed Poole

Mansfield

Mansfield Catholic Cemetery: John Daley
Mansfield Cemetery: Ernie Beam, Buck West

Marietta

East Lawn Memorial Park: Karl Meister
Valley Cemetery: Dick Hoblitzell, Frank Jones

Marion

Marion Cemetery: George Hogan

Martins Ferry

Riverview Cemetery: Cy Morgan
St Mary's Cemetery: Dick Padden

Massillon

Massillon Cemetery: Earl Blackburn, Bob Fothergill, Warren Shannabrook
Rose Hill Memorial Park: Fred Bratchi, Dick Gossett
St Joseph's Cemetery: Herm Malloy

Mayfield

Knollwood Cemetery: Ernest Barnard, Herb Conyers, Billy Evans, Pete Johns, Ellis Ryan, Terry Turner

Mayfield Village

Whitehaven Park: Don Fisher, Ken Landenberger

McCutchenville

Bethel Cemetery: Luther Bonin

Middleport

Middleport Hill Cemetery: Mother Watson

Mifflin

Mifflin Cemetery: Nick Cullop

Milford

Greenlawn Cemetery: Ches Crist, Tacks Latimer, Eppa Rixey

Miltonville

Miltonville Cemetery: Ollie Johns

Minerva

East Lawn Cemetery: Ray Grimes, Roy Grimes

Montgomery

Union Cemetery: Bubbles Hargrave, Jack Pfiester

Mount Vernon

Mound View Cemetery: Edgar McNabb

Nelsonville

Green Lawn Cemetery: Estel Crabtree, John Lovett, Bob Williams

New Hampshire

Walnut Hill Cemetery: Bob Ewing

New Knoxville

German Protestant Cemetery: Al Huenke

New Lexington

Maplewood Cemetery: John Churry, Rube Ward

New Marshfield

New Marshfield Cemetery: Josh Devore

New Philadelphia

Evergreen Burial Park: Rube Marshall

New Richmond

Green Mound Cemetery: Hank Schenz

New Straitsville

New Straitsville Joint Cemetery: Tom Williams

Newark

Cedar Hill Cemetery: Al Schweitzer

North Canton

Greensburg Cemetery: Ossie France
North Canton Cemetery: Rabbit Warstler

North Eaton

Butternut Ridge Cemetery: Pit Gilman

North Hampton

Asbury Cemetery: Harvey Haddix

North Olmsted

Fairview Cemetery: Otto Hess
Sunset Memorial Park: Oscar Grimes

Norwalk

St Paul's Catholic Cemetery: Jerry Nops

Oberlin

Westwood Cemetery: Cayt Fauver

Overpeck
Hickory Flats Cemetery: Dan Daub

Peoli
Peoli Cemetery: Cy Young

Phillipsburg
Bethel Cemetery: Jesse "Pop" Haines

Piketon
Mound Cemetery: Wiley Dunham

Portsmouth
Greenlawn Cemetery: Harry Blake, Al Bridwell, Algie McBride, Chet Spencer, Pinky Swander

Reynoldsburg
Glen Rest Memorial Estates: Russ Miller, Earl Moore, Owen Scheetz

Richmond
Richmond Cemetery: Doc Kerr

Roseville
Rose Hill Cemetery: Dizzy Nutter

Rushtown
Rushtown Cemetery: Branch Rickey

Salineville
Woodland Cemetery: Ed McNichol

Sandusky
Calvary Cemetery: Al Halt
Oakland Cemetery: Jerry Upp, Gene Woodburn

Scio
Grandview Cemetery: Eddie Onslow, Jack Onslow

Shandon
Shandon Cemetery: Charlie DeArmond

Shawnee
Shawnee Cemetery: Tom Thomas

Springboro
Springboro Cemetery: Bert Hamric

Springfield
Calvary Cemetery: Jiggs Donahue, Joe Dunn, Pat Lyons
Ferncliff Cemetery: Dick Harley, Bill Keen, Otto Neu, Billy Niles
St Bernard Cemetery: Joe Rickert

St Henry
St Henry Catholic Cemetery: Wally Post

St Louisville
Wilson Cemetery: Paul Carpenter

Steubenville
Mount Calvary Cemetery: Jack Lewis, Tom Needham, Sam Nichol
Union Cemetery: Johnny Bates, Harry Hardy, George Kaiserling, Fleet Walker, Welday Walker

Strasburg
Grandview Union Cemetery: Harry Schlafly

Sulphur Springs
Union Cemetery: Willie Kuehne

Swanton
Swanton Cemetery: Roy Beecher

Sylvania
Toledo Memorial Park: Ralph Comstock, Harry Hinchman, Dick Marlowe, Ollie Marquardt, Pete McShannic, Roy Parmelee, Dutch Schliebner, Al Schulz, Ed Scott

Tiltonsville
Indian Mound Cemetery: Jack Easton

Toledo
Calvary Cemetery: Roger Bresnahan, Frank Gilhooley, Len Madden, Red Smith
Forest Cemetery: George Kelb, Harry McCluskey
Ottawa Hills Memorial Park: Garland Buckeye, Emilio Palmero
St Mary's Catholic Cemetery: Erve Beck
Woodlawn Cemetery: Rollin Cook, Lave Cross, Nig Fuller, Topsy Hartsel, Addie Joss, Lee Richmond, Harry Taylor, Myles Thomas

Tontogany
Tontogany Cemetery: Lucky Wright

Twinsburg
Crown Hill Cemetery: Bunk Congalton, Elmer Flick, Chief Zimmer

Uhrichsville
Union Cemetery: Frank LaPorte, Whitey Moore, Al Shaw, Dave Wright

Upper Sandusky
Oak Hill Cemetery: Fred Osborn

Urbana
Oakdale Cemetery: Johnny Siegle

Valley City
Myrtle Hill Cemetery: Paul O'Dea

Wadsworth
Woodlawn Cemetery: Cy Vorhees

Wapakoneta
New St Joseph Cemetery: Fred Houtz
Wheeler Cemetery: Whitey Guese

Warren
Oakwood Cemetery: Red Ames

Wellington
Greenwood Cemetery: Jack Wadsworth

Wellston
Ridgewood Cemetery: Lefty James

Wellsville
Spring Hill Cemetery: John Godwin

West Alexandria
Fairview Cemetery: Phil Saylor

West Lafayette
Fairfield Cemetery: Lem Hunter

Westerville
Pioneer Cemetery: Al Tedrow

Weston
Weston Cemetery: Dan Abbott

Wheelersburg
Memorial Burial Park: Earl Smith
St Peters Catholic Church Cemetery: Ed Hock

Withamsville
Mount Moriah Cemetery: Rube Bressler, Larry Kopf

Woodsfield
Oak Lawn Cemetery: Sad Sam Jones

Wooster
Wooster Cemetery: Harry Billiard, Guy Hecker

Yorkville
Upland Cemetery: Frank Scalzi

Youngstown
Calvary Cemetery: Nick Goulish, Pat Griffin, Marty Hogan, Billy Rheil
Forest Lawn Memorial Park: Frank Mills, Lou Schettler
Lake Park Cemetery: Charlie Conway
Oak Hill Cemetery: Ed Cartwright, Jimmy McAleer
Tod Homestead Cemetery: Mike Modak

Zanesville
Greenwood Cemetery: Buster Caton
Mount Calvary Cemetery: Tom McDermott
Mount Olive Cemetery: Frank Wayenberg

Oklahoma

Ada
Memorial Park Cemetery: Uke Clanton
Rosedale Cemetery: Ross Reynolds

Altus
Altus Cemetery: Mike Balenti

Alva
Alva Municipal Cemetery: Bill McGill

Ames
Ames Cemetery: Bennie Warren

Atoko
Atoko Cemetery: Ted Blankenship

Bartlesville
White Rose Cemetery: Bugs Bennett

Blackwell
IOOF Cemetery: Harry Huston

Bokoshe
Milton Cemetery: Rube Foster

Broken Arrow
Floral Haven Memorial Gardens: Jim Brewer

Capron
Capron Cemetery: Danny Thompson

Carnegie
Carnegie Cemetery: Bill Reynolds

Cleveland
Woodland Cemetery: Ted Welch

Cloud Chief
Cloud Chief Cemetery: Dale Mitchell

Connerville
Connerville Cemetery: Vallie Eaves

Dobson
Dobson Cemetery: Von McDaniel

Duncan
Duncan Cemetery: Peaches Davis, Joe Hassler, Ned Pettigrew, Jim Walkup

Edmond
Memorial Park Cemetery: Charlie Emig, Pepper Martin

El Reno
El Reno Cemetery: Claude Thomas, Hugh Willingham

Elk City
Fairlawn Cemetery: Cal Dorsett

Enid
Memorial Park Cemetery: Dudley Branom, Rip Radcliff, Lil Stoner

Fort Gibson
Citizen Cemetery: Jim Gladd

Hollis
Fairmount Cemetery: Wilcy Moore

Lexington
Lexington Cemetery: Bill Shores

MARIETTA
Lakeview Cemetery: Fred Nicholson

MARLOW
Marlow Cemetery: Eddie Palmer

MCALESTER
Oak Hill Cemetery: Joe McGinnity

MEEKER
New Hope Cemetery: Carl Hubbell, Jim Winford

MUSKOGEE
Greenhill Cemetery: Paul Hinson
Memorial Park Cemetery: Ab Wright

OKLAHOMA CITY
Chapel Hill Memorial Gardens: Bruce Sloan, Milt Steengrafe
Fairlawn Cemetery: Liz Funk
Memorial Park Cemetery: Allie Reynolds, Red Schillings
Resurrection Memorial Cemetery: Tommy Tatum
Rose Hill Burial Park: Frank Kellert, Dick Stone, Lloyd Waner
Sunny Lane Cemetery: John Hall

PAULS VALLEY
Mount Olivet Cemetery: Jennings Poindexter

PAWNEE
North Indian Cemetery: Chief Yellowhorse

PRYOR
Fairview Cemetery: Chad Kimsey
Graham Memorial Cemetery: Cliff Mapes

RINGLING
Memorial Cemetery: Howie McFarland

SAND SPRINGS
Woodland Cemetery: Jerry Adair

SAPULPA
South Heights Cemetery: Denver Grigsby

SEMINOLE
Maple Grove Cemetery: Hugh Alexander

SHAWNEE
Tecumseh Cemetery: Cy Blanton

SPERRY
Rest Haven Cemetery: Denny Burns

TISHOMINGO
Tishomingo City Cemetery: Euel Moore

TULSA
Calvary Cemetery: Jack Bradley, Tony Rego
Memorial Park: Bill Breckinridge, Cal Crum, Howie Gregory, Jack Killilay, Carl Morton, Jim Oglesby, Jim Shilling, Tommy Warren, Charlie Wheatley
Rose Hill Memorial Park: Ed Grimes, Ed Klepfer, Doc Reisling, Ben Tincup

WAGONER
Elmwood Cemetery: Chuck Corgan, Fred Olmstead

WYANDOTTE
Lofland Cemetery: Roy Jarvis

OREGON

BEND
Greenwood Cemetery: Paul Gehrman

CANBY
Zion Memorial Park: Ed Coleman, Harry Gardner

COOS BAY
Sunset Memorial Park Cemetery: Floyd Stromme

CORVALLIS
Oaklawn Cemetery: Oscar Harstad

ELGIN
Elgin Cemetery: Byron Speece

EUGENE
Laurel Hill Cemetery: Howie Fox
Rest-Haven Memorial Park: Hugh Luby

GRANTS PASS
Granite Hill Cemetery: Charlie Armbruster
Hillcrest Memorial Park: Mel Ingram, Hub Pernoll

HILLSBORO
Valley Memorial Park: Wes Schulmerich

INDEPENDENCE
Buena Vista Cemetery: Ed Mensor

JACKSONVILLE
Jacksonville Cemetery: Ed Wilkinson

LAGRANDE
Odd Fellows Cemetery: Pete Dowling

MCMINNVILLE
St James Cemetery: Billy Sullivan

MYRTLE CREEK
Odd Fellows Cemetery: Glenn Elliott

PORTLAND
Lincoln Memorial Park: Jim Keesey, Al Kellogg, Ralph Kreitz
Lone Fir Cemetery: Rudy Kallio, Jiggs Parrott, Tom Parrott

Mount Calvary Cemetery: Ad Liska, Denny Williams
Mount Scott Park Cemetery: Cliff Carroll, Carl Druhot
Pioneer Cemetery: Suds Sutherland
Portland Memorial: Charlie Babb, Charlie High, Syl Johnson, Fielder Jones, Charlie Swindell
Riverview Abbey Mausoleum: Dixie Leverett, Harry Rice, Doug Taitt
Riverview Cemetery: Gus Fisher, Carl Mays
Skyline Memorial Gardens: Charley Moore, Steve Olin
Sunset Hills Memorial Gardens: Tommy Heath
Willamette National Cemetery: Carson Bigbee, Joe Erautt, Howie Haworth, Bruce Hitt, Mickey O'Brien, Bill Pertica

SALEM

Belcrest Memorial Park: Howard Maple, Max Marshall
Restlawn Memory Gardens: Bill Bevans, Wally Flager

ST PAUL

St Paul Cemetery: Curt Coleman

SWEET HOME

Liberty Cemetery: Lyle Bigbee

THE DALLES

Odd Fellows Cemetery: Bill Salisbury

PENNSYLVANIA

ALLENTOWN

Arlington Memorial Park: Claude Hendrix
Cedar Hill Memorial Park: Johnny Bucha, Sam Fishburn
Union Cemetery: John Meister

ALLISON PARK

Allegheny County Memorial Park: Deacon Phillippe

ALTOONA

Alto Reste Park Cemetery: Walt Thomas
Calvary Cemetery: Tommy Irwin, Joe Martin, Germany Smith
Fairview Cemetery: John Gochnaur
Oakridge Cemetery: Charlie Manlove

ANNVILLE

Mount Annville Cemetery: Ed Miller

ATLANTIC

Atlantic Cemetery: Goat Anderson

BALA CYNWYD

West Laurel Hill Cemetery: Joe Berry, Pete Childs, Harry Diddlebock, Samuel "Butch" Jones, Harry Lyons, Walter Moser, Benjamin F Shibe, Thomas S Shibe, Cub Stricker, Tink Turner, Harry Wright
Westminster Cemetery: Joe Berry, Harry Davis, Sam Kimber, Charlie Nyce, Jack Ridgeway, Joe Ward, Frank Zinn

BEALLSVILLE

Beallsville Cemetery: Bob Coulson

BEAVER

Beaver Cemetery: Tom McCreery, Ted Reed

BEAVER FALLS

Grove Cemetery: Joe Hughes

BENSALEM

Resurrection Cemetery: Tom Kirk

BERWICK

Pine Grove Cemetery: Ralph Savidge

BETHLEHEM

Holy Savior Cemetery: Dick Wright

BRADFORD

Oak Hill Cemetery: Elmer Bliss
St Bernard's Cemetery: Petie Behan, John Shearon

BRENTWOOD

St Wendelin Cemetery: Elmer Knetzer

BRIDGEVILLE

Queen of Heaven Cemetery: Howie Gorman, Gene Layden

BRIER HILL

Lafayette Memorial Park: Bill Foreman

BROOMALL

Glenwood Memorial Gardens: Harvey MacDonald, Barney Slaughter

BURGETTSTOWN

Our Lady of Lourdes Cemetery: Eddie Lukon

CAMP HILL

Rolling Green Memorial Park: George Hunter, Billy Myers, Andy Oyler

CARBONDALE

St Rose Cemetery: Jack Fee, Pete Gillespie

CARNEGIE

Chartiers Cemetery: Butts Wagner

CATAWISSA

Hillside Cemetery: Lew McCarty

CHAMBERSBURG

Cedar Grove Cemetery: Piggy Ward

Corpus Christi Cemetery: Gus Dorner
Lincoln Cemetery: Mike Mowrey
Norland Cemetery: Charley Gelbert
Parklawns Memorial Gardens: Bob Moorhead

Cherry Flats

Cherry Flats Cemetery: Charlie Parsons

Chester

Chester Rural Cemetery: Dave Anderson

Clarion

Clarion Cemetery: Emmet Heidrick

Coatesville

East Cain Friend's Burying Ground: Walt Doane
Fairview Cemetery: John Jones

Columbia

Laurel Hill Memorial Gardens: Jimmy Sheckard

Coraopolis

Resurrection Cemetery: Frankie Gustine, Lee Handley

Coudersport

Eulalia Cemetery: Herbie Moran

Cranberry

Sunset Hill Memorial Gardens: Joe Harris

Dallas

St John's Cemetery: Brad Kocher, Mickey Witek

Danville

Odd Fellows Cemetery: Bill Banks, Bill Hoffner, Art McCoy

Dawson

Cochran Cemetery: Jock Menefee

Delmont

Eastview Union Cemetery: Jimmy Ripple
Twin Valley Memorial Park: Bob Moose

Denver

Fairview Cemetery: Lou Knerr

Dickson City

St Mary's Cemetery: Joe Glenn

Drexel Hill

Arlington Cemetery: Harry Barton, George Bausewine, Jack Clements, Monte Cross, Wes Curry, Joe Green, Walter Huntzinger, Jim Jackson, Howard Lohr, Sherry Magee, Jake Munch, Morrie Rath, Ad Swigler, Woody Wheaton

Drums

Calvary Cemetery: Bill Lee, Dan McGeehan

Du Bois

Morningside Cemetery: Lee Gamble, Henry Smoyer

Dunmore

Dunmore Cemetery: Dave Williams
Mount Carmel Cemetery: John McDonald

Duquesne

Duquesne Cemetery: Joe Rogalski

East McKeesport

St Joseph's Cemetery: Shine Cortazzo

Easton

Easton Cemetery: George Barclay, Frank Grube, Bill Parks
Easton Heights Cemetery: John McPherson
St Anthony's Cemetery: Jack Wallaesa

Elizabeth

Elizabeth Cemetery: Andy Bruckmiller

Emlenton

Emlenton Cemetery: Claude Ritchey

Emmaus

Northwood Cemetery: Eddie Zimmerman

Erie

Erie Cemetery: Lou Bierbauer, Ed Cushman
Trinity Cemetery: Dell Darling, Gussie Gannon, Mike Morrison

Everett

Everett Cemetery: Earl Howard

Factoryville

Factoryville Cemetery: Henry Mathewson

Fayette City

Mount Auburn Cemetery: Bill Phillips, Jim Russell, Bill Wolfe

Fernwood

Fernwood Cemetery: Charlie Brynan, George Craig, George Davis, Henry Easterday, Chick Fulmer, Bill Harbridge, Hardie Henderson, Bill Knowlton, Elias Peak, Harry Schafer, Tom Walker

Ford City

Ford City Cemetery: Bob Pepper

Fountain Springs

St Joseph's Cemetery: John Chapman

Frazer

Haym Salomon Memorial Park: Harry Shuman

Freeburg

Freeburg Cemetery: Ralph Mitterling

Freeland

St Ann's Cemetery: John Shovlin

Gettysburg

Evergreen Cemetery: Jake Boyd, Eddie Plank

Girard
Girard Cemetery: Jim Hart

Gladwyne
United Methodist Church Cemetery: Richie Ashburn

Glenolden
South Laurel Hill Cemetery: Jack McFetridge

Glenshaw
Mount Royal Cemetery: Whitey Alperman

Greencastle
Cedar Hill Cemetery: King Lear, Togie Pittinger

Greenville
St Michael's Cemetery: Hugh Tate

Hadley
Hadley Cemetery: Estey Chaney

Hanover
Church of the Annunciation Cemetery: Bob McKinney

Harrisburg
East Harrisburg Cemetery: Les Bell, Charlie Snell
Harrisburg Cemetery: John Brackinridge, Ray Mueller, Dutch Schesler, Harvey Smith
Mount Calvary Cemetery: Ed Sales
Paxtang Cemetery: Myrl Brown, Snake Wiltse
Prospect Hill Cemetery: Red Owens
Woodlawn Memorial Gardens: Russ Wrightstone

Havertown
St Dennis Church Cemetery: Joe Burns, John Castle, Jimmy Dykes, Jack Hayden

Hawley
Queen of Peace Cemetery: Eddie Murphy

Hazleton
St Gabriel's Cemetery: Gene Connell
Vine Street Cemetery: Charlie Jordan

Hershey
Hershey Cemetery: George Staller

Honesdale
St John's Lutheran Cemetery: Fred Sherry

Hummelstown
Hummelstown Cemetery: Phil Paine

Huntingdon
Riverview Cemetery: Gene Elliott

Indiana
Catholic Cemetery: Doc Gessler

Irwin
Brush Creek Cemetery: Buzz Clarkson

Jacobus
Salem Union Cemetery: Ray Shearer

Jefferson
Jefferson Cemetery: Art Goodwin

Jersey Shore
Jersey Shore Cemetery: Frank Nicholson

Jessup
St John's Cemetery: Ben Cardoni

Jim Thorpe
Evergreen Cemetery: Hob Hiller
Jim Thorpe Monument: Jim Thorpe

Johnstown
Grandview Cemetery: Elmer Cleveland, Frank West

Kennett Square
Union Hill Cemetery: Herb Pennock

Kittanning
Kittanning Cemetery: Ossee Schreckengost

Klingerstown
St Michael's Church Cemetery: Dutch Romberger

Kulpmont
St Casimer's Church Cemetery: Steve Filipowicz

Lancaster
Lancaster Cemetery: Whitey Gibson
Riverview Cemetery: Tom Stouch
Woodward Hill Cemetery: George Carman, Grant Thatcher

Latrobe
St Mary's Cemetery: Ed Abbaticchio
St Vincent's Cemetery: Andy Gilbert, Hal Haid

Laureldale
Gethsemane Cemetery: Whitey Kurowski, Kohley Miller

Lenni
St Francis of De Sales Cemetery: Johnny Podgajny

Lewisburg
Lewisburg Cemetery: Walter Blair, Dick Kauffman, Christy Mathewson, Hal McClure, Moose McCormick

Lime Ridge
Elan Memorial Cemetery: Bobby Rhawn

Linwood
Immaculate Heart of Mary Cemetery: Joe Cassidy
Lawn Croft Cemetery: Bert Cunningham, Bris Lord, Curly Ogden, Rube Vinson

Littlestown
Mount Carmel Cemetery: Cliff Heathcote

Liverpool
Liverpool Cemetery: Lou Ritter

Lock Haven
Highland Cemetery: Jim Brown, Davey Dunkle, Tom Poorman, John Shaffer
St Mark's Cemetery: Tom Donovan
St Mary's Cemetery: Jerry Donovan

Lower Burrell
Greenwood Memorial Park: Joe Page

Luthersburg
Luthersburg Cemetery: Frank Shugart

Mahanoy City
St Mary's Slovak Church Cemetery: Joe Boley

Marietta
Florin Cemetery: Snake Deal

McKees Rocks
Mount Calvary Cemetery: Mike Hopkins
St Mary's Cemetery: Joe Vitelli

McKeesport
Mount Vernon Cemetery: Rube Parnham

McSherrystown
Annunciation Church Cemetery: Bill Sherdel

Mercer
Mercer Cemetery: Harry Maskrey, Leech Maskrey

Middletown
Middletown Cemetery: Hinkey Haines

Mill Run
Indian Creek Baptist Cemetery: Roger Miller

Millersburg
Oakhill Cemetery: Sumner Bowman

Millersville
Millersville Mennonite Cemetery: Charlie Miller

Millheim
Fairview Cemetery: Paul Musser

Milton
Harmony Cemetery: John Sullivan

Minooka
St Joseph Parish Cemetery: Mike McNally
St Joseph's Cemetery: Jack O'Neill, Mike O'Neill
St Joseph's Church Cemetery: Jim O'Neill

Monaca
Old Monaca Cemetery: Howard Shanks
Union Cemetery: Pinky Lindsay

Monongahela
Monongahela Cemetery: Ody Abbott

Monroeton
Monroeton Cemetery: Jake Northrop

Montgomery
St John's Brick Church Cemetery: Rube Yarrison

Montoursville
Montoursville Cemetery: Adam Johnson

Moscow
St Catherine's Cemetery: Hughie Jennings, Jerry Lynn, Jim Murray, Finners Quinlan, Joe Shaute

Mount Penn
Aulenbach's Cemetery: Sam Field, Jack Fox, Charlie Shoemaker, Phil Tomney

Mount Pleasant
Transfiguration Cemetery: Johnnie Tyler

Mount Union
Mount Union Cemetery: Jake Eisenhart

Muncy
Twin Hills Memorial Park: Carl Stotz

Munhall
Homestead Cemetery: Alex Jones

Nanticoke
St Joseph Church Cemetery: Steve Bilko

New Bethlehem
New Bethlehem Cemetery: Marc Campbell

New Brighton
Grove Cemetery: Rube Dessau

New Castle
Oak Park Cemetery: Paul McCullough
St Phillip and James Church Cemetery: Chet Boak

New Freedom
New Freedom Cemetery: Tom Lipp

New Kensington
Plum Creek Cemetery: Bill Culp

Newport
Newport Cemetery: Billy Cox

Norristown
Montgomery Cemetery: Bill Thomas
Riverside Cemetery: Roy Thomas

O'Hara
St Mary's Cemetery: Ralph Michaels

Oil City
Calvary Cemetery: Leo Callahan
St Joseph's Cemetery: Frank Boyd

Oxford
Oxford Cemetery: Jack Ogden

Palmerton
Sacred Heart New Cemetery: Elmer Valo

Parker Ford
Oak Grove Cemetery: Roy Sherid
Parker Ford Baptist Cemetery: Jing Johnson

Peckville
St Cyril and Methodius Cemetery: Nestor Chylak

Perkasie
Reform Cemetery: Ed Ritterson

Philadelphia
Cedar Hill Cemetery: John Hanna
Chelten Hills Cemetery: Bill Shettsline, Bob Vail
East Cedar Hill Cemetery: Bill Black, George Shoch, Sam White
Eden Cemetery: Fats Jenkins
Forest Hills Cemetery: Charlie Eckert, Twink Twining
Greenmount Cemetery: Jersey Bakely, Blondie Purcell, Chris Rickley, Frank Siffel, Amos Strunk, Jesse Whiting
Holy Redeemer Cemetery: Bart Cantz, Joe Kappel, Al Maul
Holy Sepulchre Cemetery: Stan Baumgartner, Joe Daly, Bill Hallman, Fritz Henrich, Chick Keating, Matt Kilroy, Connie Mack, Bunny Madden, Billy Maharg, Warren Miller, Joe O'Rourke, Patsy O'Rourke, Tony Parisse, Harry Pearce, Ira Thomas, Steve Yerkes
Ivy Hill Cemetery: Bill Grey, Ed Lafitte
Laurel Hill Cemetery: Lon Knight
Magnolia Cemetery: Joe Mulvey
Monument Cemetery: Bill Fouser
Mount Moriah Cemetery: Pat Deasley, Bill Greenwood, Jocko Milligan
Mount Peace Cemetery: Horace Fogel, Bill Haeffner, Bill Hallman, Jack Lapp, Peter Loos
Mount Vernon Cemetery: Bill Sharsig, Jake Virtue
New Cathedral Cemetery: Pete Hasney, Mike Kilroy, Otto Knabe, Fergy Malone, Sparrow McCaffrey, Mike Powers, Johnny Ryan, Sleeper Sullivan
North Cedar Hill Cemetery: Harry Brooks, Bill Clymer, Izzy Hoffman, Ed Sixsmith, Joe Sugden, Highball Wilson, Abraham Wolstenholme
North Laurel Hill Cemetery: Henry Luff
Northwood Cemetery: George Bradley, Kid Gleason, Joe Gunson, George Hesselbacher, Ernie Padgett, Dick Spalding, Marty Walker, Dave Zearfoss
Oakland Cemetery: Bert Conn, David Oldfield, Jesse Purnell
Old Cathedral Cemetery: Ben Conroy, Dick Harley, Emmett McCann, Mark McGrillis
St Dominic Cemetery: Benny Bengough, Harry O'Donnell, Ty Pickup
St Mary's Cemetery: John Barthold, Bill Crowley
St Timothy's Church Cemetery: Bert Yeabsley
Sunset Memorial Park: John Karst

Philipsburg
Philipsburg Cemetery: Tom Phillips

Pittsburgh
Allegheny Cemetery: Josh Gibson, Don Hoak, Cy Rheam, Ted Sadowski
Braddock Catholic Cemetery: Tom Quinn
Calvary Cemetery: Pud Galvin, Enos Kirkpatrick, Bill Regan, Jimmy Smith, Moose Solters
Greenwood Cemetery: Joe Taylor
Homewood Cemetery: Jim Gardner, Bob Gibson, Jim Gray, Ad Gumbert, Billy Gumbert, Lew Moren, Squiz Pillion, John Tener, Bill Thompson, Pie Traynor, Ren Wylie
Minersville Cemetery: Frank Smith
North Side Catholic Cemetery: Jack Cummings, Gus Dundon, John Gruber
Smithfield East End Cemetery: Ducky Swan
South Side Cemetery: Jim Pastorius
St Augustine Church Cemetery: Nick Maddox
St George's Cemetery: Frank Lobert
St Martin's Cemetery: Marty Berghammer
St Mary's Cemetery: Chick Cargo, Ray Miller, Tom O'Brien, Charlie Sweeney
Union Dale Cemetery: Dave Black, Eddie Miller, Ed Morris, Billy Otterson, Elmer Smith, Gene Steinbrenner
West View Cemetery: Dick Buckley, Barney Dreyfuss, Florence Dreyfuss
William Penn Memorial Cemetery: Wally Kimmick

Plains
SS Peter and Paul Parish Cemetery: Pete Elko

Pleasant Hills
Jefferson Memorial Park: Bob Collins, Dutch Jordan, Rube Sellers, Honus Wagner, Joe Walker

Polk
Hickory Grove Cemetery: Bob Way

Port Royal
New Church Hill Cemetery: Fred Frankhouse

Pottstown
Pottstown Cemetery: Harry Gilbert, John Gilbert

Pottsville
Calvary Cemetery: Bill Mathews

Charles Baber Cemetery: Jake Daubert, Jack Quinn
Mount Laurel Cemetery: Frank Eustace
Queen of the Universe Cemetery: Joe Holden

PRINGLE

St Ignatius Cemetery: Adam Comorosky
St Mary's Annunciation Church Cemetery: Harry Dorish

PROSPECTVILLE

Whitemarsh Memorial Cemetery: Hugo Bezdek, Bucky Walters

PUGHTOWN

Pughtown Baptist Cemetery: Dick Ricketts

READING

Charles Evans Cemetery: Bill Dunlap, Jake Goodman, Shadow Pyle
Forest Hills Memorial Park: Carl Furillo, Epp Sell, Stan Wentzel
St Peter's Church Cemetery: Henry Larkin

REEDSVILLE

Church Hill Cemetery: Dutch Sterrett

RICE'S LANDING

Hewitt Cemetery: Pete Knisely

RIDGWAY

Ridgway Cemetery: Billy Rhines

ROBESONIA

St Daniels Cemetery: Stan Klopp

ROCHESTER

Irvin Cemetery: Alex Pearson
Sylvania Hills Memorial Park: Vern Hughes

ROCKLEDGE

Lawnview Cemetery: Andy Knox
Odd Fellows Cemetery: Fred Dunlap

ROSLYN

Hillside Cemetery: Chief Bender, Del Ennis, Charlie Mason, George Stutz

ROYERSFORD

Fernwood Cemetery: Ray Hartranft

SAEGERTOWN

Saegertown Cemetery: Sal Campfield

SCHOENERSVILLE

Schoenersville Cemetery: Bert Kuczynski

SCRANTON

Abington Hills Cemetery: Chick Shorten
Cathedral Cemetery: John Cavanaugh, Bill Coughlin, Alex Mustaikis
St Joseph's Cemetery: Steve O'Neill

SHAMOKIN

Odd Fellows Cemetery: Bud Weiser
Shamokin Cemetery: George Gilham
St Stanislaus Cemetery: Harry Coveleski

SHAMOKIN DAM

West Side Cemetery: Tex Neuer

SHARON

Oakwood Cemetery: Charlie Gibson
St Mary's Cemetery: John McAleese

SHARON HILL

Mount Lawn Cemetery: Phil Cockrell

SHAVERTOWN

Evergreen Cemetery: Buck Freeman
St Nicholas Cemetery: Bill Goeckel

SHIPPENSBURG

Spring Hill Cemetery: George Noftsker

SHOHOLA

Wood Family Cemetery: Smokey Joe Wood

SOUTH STERLING

Pine Grove Cemetery: Bill Herring
St Peter and St Paul Cemetery: Jim Baumer, Tom Ferrick, Wedo Martini, John McGillen, Danny Murtaugh, Si Pauxtis

ST CLAIR

Odd Fellows Cemetery: Eddie Delker, John Titus

ST MARYS

St Mary's Cemetery: Dan Costello

ST THOMAS

St Thomas Cemetery: Nellie Fox

SUGARCREEK

County Poor Farm Cemetery: Henry Kessler

SUMMIT HILL

GAR Cemetery: Ed Gormley

SUNBURY

Pomfret Manor Cemetery: Birdie Cree

SWARTHMORE

Leiper Church Cemetery: Jack Leiper

TAMAQUA

Odd Fellows Cemetery: Chick Fullis

THROOP

St Joseph's Cemetery: Junior Walsh

TITUSVILLE

Jamison Corners Cemetery: Art Stokes

TOWANDA

St Peter and St Paul Cemetery: Ed Larkin

TREMONT

Reformed Cemetery: Sparky Adams

Union City
Evergreen Cemetery: Fred Chapman

Uniontown
Oak Grove Cemetery: Harry Wilhelm
Oak Lawn Cemetery: Dean Sturgis

Upper Darby
Montrose Cemetery: Will Holland

Upper St Clair
Westminster Presbyterian Church: Bob Prince

Valley View
St Andrews Church Cemetery: Fred Stiely

Waynesburg
Greene County Memorial Park: Chuck Coles
Oakmont Cemetery: Art Haugher

Wernersville
Jesuit Novitiate Cemetery: Allan Travers

West Chester
Birmingham-Lafayette Cemetery: Henry Baldwin
Greenmount Cemetery: Bud Sharpe

West Conshohocken
Calvary Cemetery: Roy Mack, Bing Miller, George O'Brien, By Saam

West Newton
West Newton Cemetery: Danny Taylor, Jimmy Uchrinscko

Whitehall
Fairview Cemetery: Joe Connell

Wiconisco
Wiconisco Cemetery: Bill Hart

Wilkes-Barre
Hollenback Cemetery: Al Bauers
Maple Hill Cemetery: Tommy Hughes
Oak Lawn Cemetery: Dixie Howell
St Mary's Cemetery: Frank Crossin, Steamer Flanagan, Mike Konnick, Abel Lizotte, John McCloskey, Tony Rensa, John Walsh

Williamsport
Mound Cemetery: Ed Holly, Bob Lindemann
Mount Carmel Cemetery: Jim Lyle
Wildwood Cemetery: Fred Applegate, Asby Asbjornson, Rube Manning, Don Manno, Jimmy Sebring, Bucky Veil

Willow Grove
Fairview Cemetery: Webster McDonald

Woodside
St Ann's Cemetery: Matt Broderick

Wyomissing
Camptown Cemetery: Grover Powell

Yeadon
Holy Cross Cemetery: Charlie Bastian, Henry Boyle, Jim Brennan, Pat Carroll, Dan Coogan, Wild Bill Donovan, Jim Field, John Kalahan, Dan Kerwin, Bill Leinhauser, Ed Lennon, Dan McGarvey, Pat Meaney, John Munce, Simon Nicholls, Bill Pierson, Butch Rementer, Joe Rullo, Zeke Wrigley

York
Mount Rose Cemetery: Lefty York
Mount Zion Cemetery: Gene Snyder, Jack Stephens
Prospect Hill Cemetery: Bill Clay, Lefty George, Norman Plitt

York Springs
Sunnyside Cemetery: Elmer Myers

Rhode Island

Barrington
Princess Hill Cemetery: Harry Pattee

Berkeley
St Joseph Cemetery: Pat Maloney

Bristol
North Burial Ground: John Hamill

Central Falls
Moshassuck Cemetery: Charley Bassett

Chepachet
Acote Hill Cemetery: Bill Mellor

Coventry
Knotty Oak Cemetery: Hi Ladd

Cranston
St Ann's Cemetery: Jimmy Cooney, Jimmy Cooney, Rip Egan, Tom Lovett

Cumberland
Mount Calvary Cemetery: Ed Conley

North Smithfield
Union Cemetery: Chet Nichols, Chet Nichols

Oascoag
St Joseph Cemetery: Edward S Doherty, Jr

Pawtucket
Mount St Mary's Cemetery: Jim Connor
Notre Dame Cemetery: Max Surkont
St Francis Cemetery: John Flynn, Pat Friel, Dinty Gearin, Jim Hanley, Morg Murphy

Providence
Swan Point Cemetery: Bruce Caldwell, Cap Crowell, Eddie Eayrs, Hal Neubauer, Edgar Smith

WESTERLY
River Bend Cemetery: John Frill, Charlie Robinson, Joe Sherman

WOONSOCKET
Precious Blood Cemetery: Pete LePine, Henri Rondeau

SOUTH CAROLINA

ANDERSON
Forest Lawn Memorial Park: Roy Mahaffey

BEAUFORT
Beaufort National Cemetery: Mal Moss

BENNETTSVILLE
Sunset Hill Memorial Park: Norm Brown

BISHOPVILLE
Bethlehem Methodist Cemetery: Dan Griner

BLACKSTOCK
Presbyterian Church Cemetery: Ed Durham

CHARLESTON
Magnolia Cemetery: Art Brouthers, Fritz Von Kolnitz
St Lawrence Cemetery: Tom Colcolough

CLINTON
Pinelawn Memory Gardens: Cal Cooper
Rosemont Cemetery: Chick Galloway

COLUMBIA
Crescent Hill Memorial Gardens: Bob Hazle
Elmwood Cemetery: Rufe Clarke, Logan Drake, Kirby Higbe
Greenlawn Memorial Park: Babe Martin, George Turbeville

EASLEY
Westview Cemetery: Jack Owens

GREENVILLE
Graceland Cemetery: Pelham Ballenger, Walter Barbare
Greenville Memorial Gardens: Virgil Stallcup
Woodlawn Memorial Park: Blackie Carter, Joe Jackson, Rube Melton

GREENWOOD
Edgewood Cemetery: Elbert Andrews
Greenwood Memorial Gardens: Cal Drummond

GREER
Cross Roads Baptist Church Cemetery: Jim Yeargin
Wood Memorial Park: John McMakin, Flint Rhem

HARTSVILLE
Darlington Memory Gardens: Harry Byrd
Magnolia Cemetery: Bobo Newsom

INMAN
Roselawn Memorial Gardens: Al Lakeman

KERSHAW
Kershaw City Cemetery: Art Jones

LAKE CITY
Lake City Memorial Park: Clise Dudley

LANCASTER
Bethlehem Baptist Church Cemetery: Mike Cunningham
Zions Methodist Church Cemetery: Aaron Robinson

LATTA
Magnolia Cemetery: Norm McMillan

LEXINGTON
Old Lexington Baptist Church Cemetery: George Jeffcoat
Pilgrim Lutheran Church Cemetery: John Boozer

MARION
Rose Hill Cemetery: Roxy Snipes

MCCOLL
McColl Cemetery: Ralph McLaurin

NEW ELLENTON
St Paul Church Cemetery: Rufus Smith

NEWBERRY
Rosemont Cemetery: Mickey Livingston

PACOLET
Pacolet Memorial Gardens: George Banks, Ernie White

PAGELAND
First Baptist Church Cemetery: Van Lingle Mungo

PIEDMONT
Rose Hill Cemetery: Champ Osteen

POMARIA
St Paul's Lutheran Church Cemetery: Johnny Werts

ROCK HILL
Grand View Memorial Park: Al Shealy

SELLERS
Haselden Family Cemetery: Frank Ellerbe

SPARTANBURG
Zion Hill Baptist Church Cemetery: Jesse Fowler

WOODRUFF
Bethel Cemetery: Sam Lanford

South Dakota

Columbia
Lakeview Cemetery: Kermit Wahl

Garretson
Zion Lutheran Church Cemetery: Emmett Nelson

Gayville
Gayville Cemetery: Marv Olson

Rapid City
Mountain View Cemetery: George Disch

Tennessee

Athens
Cedar Grove Cemetery: Jim Baskette

Bethpage
Bethpage Cemetery: Hub Perdue

Bristol
Glenwood Shelby Hills Cemetery Mausoleum: Frank Walker

Brownsville
Oakwood Cemetery: George Murray

Carthage
Ridgewood Cemetery: Tommy Bridges

Chattanooga
Brainerd Methodist Cemetery: Doc Johnston
Chattanooga Memorial Park: George Cunningham, Kid Elberfeld
Chattanooga National Cemetery: Bill Akers, Jerry Lane, Lyle Luttrell, Bobby Reeves, Sammy Strang, John Wilson
Forest Hills Cemetery: Pat Dillard, John Dobbs, Joe Engel, Jimmy Johnston, George McConnell, War Sanders
Greenwood Cemetery: Bob Higgins
Hamilton Memorial Gardens: Ray Moss
Mizpah Cemetery: Fred Graff

Clarksville
Liberty Cemetery: Hod Lisenbee

Cleveland
Fort Hill Cemetery: Buck Thrasher
Triplett Cemetery: Guy Lacy

Columbia
Leiper's Fork Cemetery: Hank Sweeney
Polk Memorial Gardens: Lindsey Nelson

Covington
Munford Cemetery: Harvey Hendrick

Crossville
Crossville City Cemetery: Mel Bosser
Green Acres Memory Gardens: Lefty Stewart

Dandridge
Hillcrest Memorial Cemetery: Bill Bolden

Dover
Hillcrest Cemetery: Bernie Walter

Dyersburg
Fairview Cemetery: Herb Welch, Ed Wright

Elizabethton
Happy Valley Memorial Park: Ted Wingfield

Fisherville
Fisherville Cemetery: Marv Throneberry

Hohenwald
Swiss Cemetery: Walt Marbet

Jackson
Brown's Cemetery: Bill Hopper
Highland Memorial Gardens: Ellis Kinder

Jamestown
Taylor Place Cemetery: Earl Webb

Jellico
Jellico Cemetery: Larry Douglas

Johnson City
Fairview Cemetery: Jim Mooney
Monte Vista Burial Park: Joe Price

Kingsport
Oak Hill Cemetery: George Diehl, Lew Flick

Knoxville
Calvary Cemetery: Dan Leahy
Greenwood Cemetery: Bonnie Hollingsworth
Highland Memorial Cemetery: Frank Callaway, Earl Williams
Lynnhurst Cemetery: Bob Baird, Carl Doyle, Billy Meyer

Lawrenceburg
Lawrence County Memorial Gardens: George Bradley, Doc Cook

Limestone
Urbana Cemetery: Tilly Walker

Lynchburg
Odd Fellows-Masonic Cemetery: John Stone

Maryville
Logan's Chapel Cemetery: Art Ruble

Memphis
Calvary Cemetery: John Antonelli, Walter Burke, Dino Chiozza, Lou Chiozza, Slim Love

Elmwood Cemetery: Hunter Lane, Charlie Shields, Dolly Stark
Forest Hill Cemetery: Fritz Clausen, Charlie Frank, Jim Henry, Dusty Miller, Danny Moeller, Ginger Shinault
Forest Hill Cemetery Midtown: Glen Stewart
Memorial Park Cemetery: Bill Harper, Bill Lewis, George Merritt, Jim Moore, Leon Pettit, Doc Prothro, Frank Waddey, Tom Winsett
Memphis National Cemetery: Jack Powell
New Park Cemetery: Larry Brown
West Tennessee Veteran's Cemetery: Ralph Weigel

MILAN
Oakwood Cemetery: Turner Barber

MILLINGTON
Woodhaven Cemetery: Ross Grimsley

MOUNTAIN CITY
Sunset Cemetery: Clyde Shoun

NASHVILLE
Calvary Cemetery: Johnny Gill, Tiny Graham, Charlie Harding, Bill McTigue
Greenwood Cemetery: Henry Kimbro
Middle Tennessee Veteran's Cemetery: Hardin Cathey
Mount Olivet Cemetery: Johnny Beazley, Slim Embry, Johnny Gooch, Ben Harris, Claude Jonnard
Nashville National Cemetery: Bob Schultz, Vito Tamulis
Spring Hill Cemetery: Tony Jacobs, Red Lucas, Tom Rogers, Henry Schmidt, Fred Toney
Woodlawn Memorial Park: Harley Boss, Slick Castleman, Dory Dean, Kerby Farrell, John Mihalic, Jay Partridge, Bill Schwartz, Dick Sisler, Jim Turner

OBION
Zion Cemetery: Ron Willis

PARIS
Maplewood Cemetery: Mark Stewart

PULASKI
Maplewood Cemetery: Cyril Collins

SAVANNAH
Savannah Cemetery: Hank DeBerry

SOUTH PITTSBURG
City Cemetery: Harry Baumgartner

TRACY CITY
Tracy City Cemetery: Phil Douglas

TUSCULUM
Shiloh Cemetery: Dale Alexander

WHITEVILLE
Melrose Cemetery: Bill Warren

TEXAS

ABILENE
Elmwood Memorial Park: Bernie Duffy, Jesse Winters

ACTON
Acton Cemetery: Les Mallon

ALLEN
Ridgeview Memorial Park: Jackie Sullivan

ALTO
Berryman Family Cemetery: Carl Yowell

AMARILLO
Llano Cemetery: John Middleton, Chief Youngblood

ARLINGTON
Arlington Cemetery: Ed Appleton
Moore Memorial Gardens: Steve Macko

ATLANTA
Pine Crest Cemetery: Hub Northen

AUSTIN
Austin Memorial Park Cemetery: Bibb Falk, Chet Falk, Hunter Hill, Owen Wilson
Capitol Memorial Park: Tom Hamilton, Hank Helf
Evergreen Cemetery: Willie Wells
Hornsby Bend Cemetery: Rogers Hornsby
Oakwood Cemetery: Forrest Crawford, Ox Eckhardt, Prince Oana, John Taff

BAILEY
Arledge Ridge Cemetery: Roy Leslie

BALLINGER
Evergreen Cemetery: Stan Gray

BANGS
Bangs Cemetery: Slim Harriss

BAYTOWN
Cedarcrest Cemetery: Joe McDonald
Memory Gardens: Clem Hausmann

BEAUMONT
Forest Lawn Memorial Park: Jim Clark, Dutch Dietz, Les Fleming, Jesse Landrum, Clay Touchstone
Magnolia Cemetery: Hugh Shelley, Charlie Weber

BEEVILLE
Glenwood Cemetery: Curt Walker

Bellville
Oak Knoll Cemetery: Red Lynn

Belton
North Belton Cemetery: Roy Mitchell

Berclair
Berclair Cemetery: Bill Rodgers

Blum
Blum Cemetery: George Jackson

Bonham
Willow Wild Cemetery: Roy McMillan

Brady
Rest Haven Cemetery: Bert Maxwell

Bremond
Bremond Cemetery: Bill Stellbauer

Brownsville
Rose Lawn Memorial Gardens: Frank Jude

Brownwood
Greenleaf Cemetery: Jack Knott

Bryan
City Cemetery: Johnny Hudson
Restever Memorial Park: Beau Bell

Burnet
Burnet Cemetery: Chink Taylor

Byers
Byers Cemetery: Ray Harrell

Carrollton
Frankford Cemetery: George Dickerson

Chicota
Presbyterian Cemetery: Buck Frierson

Clarksville
Clarksville Cemetery: Clyde Milan
Fairview Cemetery: Horace Milan

Coldspring
Oakwood Cemetery: Pete McClanahan

College Station
City Cemetery: Rip Collins, Marty Karow

Comanche
Oakwood Cemetery: Tex Carleton
White Point Cemetery: Belve Bean

Concord
Concord Cemetery: Ray Benge

Corpus Christi
Rose Hill Memorial Park: Tim Hendryx
Seaside Cemetery: Bill Windle

Corsicana
Oakwood Cemetery: Harvey Grubb

Crawford
Crawford Cemetery: Strick Shofner

Cushing
Cushing Cemetery: Joe Gallagher

Dallas
Calvary Hill Cemetery: Dave Howard
Crown Hill Cemetery: Wingo Anderson
Greenwood Cemetery: Otto McIver, Rube Taylor
Grove Hill Memorial Park: Walt Alexander, Duff Cooley, Bob Finley, Jim Haislip, Percy Jones
Hillcrest Memorial Park: Jimmy Adair, Dusty Boggess, Lum Davenport, Pinky Higgins, Bubber Jonnard
Laurel Land Memorial Park: Jay Avrea, Ken Chase, Virgil Cheeves, Red Durrett, Uel Eubanks, Oscar Fuhr, Garth Mann
Lincoln Memorial Cemetery: Bob Wilson
Oakland Cemetery: Oscar DuGey, Walt Goldsby
Restland Memorial Park: Heinz Becker, Boob Fowler, Sal Gliatto, Ziggy Hasbrook, Marty Hopkins, Frank Lane, Jim Levey, Tom Lovelace, Dummy Lynch, Reeves McK , Ray Morehart, Walter Morris, Murray Wa
Sparkman-Hillcrest Memorial Park: ickey Mantle
Wheatland Cemetery: Snipe Conley

DeSoto
Holy Redeemer Cemetery: Pretzel Pezzu

Denison
Fairview Cemetery: Tex Covington
Oakwood Cemetery: Sam Covington

Denton
Odd Fellows Cemetery: Rollie Naylor

Detroit
Dodd Family Cemetery: Ona Dodd

Devine
St Joseph Cemetery: Bert Gallia, Jc ance

Douglasville
St Williams Cemetery: Bernie H rson

Eagle Lake
Masonic Cemetery: Howie Fitz d

Ector
Carson Cemetery: John Whi

Edgewc
Oak Hill Cemetery: Alex

F
Edna Cemetery: Fra n

o
B'nai Zion Cemet dy Cohen, Syd Cohen

Concordia Cemetery: Bill Van Dyke
Evergreen Cemetery: Red Hill, Tom Seaton
Evergreen East Cemetery: Astyanax Douglass

Electra
Electra Memorial Park: Dick Adkins
New Electra Cemetery: Farmer Ray

Elmo
Elmo Cemetery: Hank Griffin

Falfurrias
Falfurrias Burial Park: Ernie Maun

Falls City
Falls City Cemetery: Fabian Kowalik

Ferris
Park Cemetery: Alex Malloy

Fort Worth
Greenwood Memorial Park: Tom Baker, Eddie Chiles, Pete Donohue, Ed Konetchy, Clarence Kraft, Bill McCahan, Jackie Tavener, Ed Wheeler
Laurel Land Memorial Park: John Goodell
Mount Olivet Cemetery: Joe Bratcher, Cecil Coombs, Jake Mooty, Howard Murphy, Tony Robello, Bill Sodd
Rose Hill Memorial Park: Scotty Barr, Hod Kibbie, Kid Nance
West Oakwood Cemetery: Joe Pate

Fredericksburg
Der Stadt Friedhof: Hugo Klaerner

Galveston
Calvary Cemetery: Sig Jakucki
Episcopal Cemetery: Jim Murray

Gary
Mount Bethel Cemetery: Vic Frazier

Georgetown
Odd Fellows Cemetery: Bad News Galloway

Glen Rose
Squaw Creek Cemetery: Debs Garms

Godley
Godley Cemetery: George Milstead

Gonzales
Gonzales Memorial Park: Dick Midkiff

Gordon
Gordon Cemetery: Pat Caraway, Thurman Tucker

Graham
Oak Grove Cemetery: Ray Wolf
Pioneer Cemetery: Roy Easterwood

Grandview
Grandview Cemetery: Slim Harrell

Greenville
Memoryland Memorial Park: Gib Brack, Monty Stratton

Groveton
Glenwood Cemetery: Lefty Scott

Hitchcock
Galveston Memorial Park: Bob Cone, Tony Smith

Hondo
Oakridge Cemetery: Stan Hollmig

Houston
Brookside Memorial Park: Maury Newlin
Calvary Cemetery: Johnny Rizzo
Earthman Rest Haven: Pidge Browne, Tommy Neill, Max West
Forest Park Cemetery: John Glaiser
Forest Park East: Frank Barnes, Pete Runnels, Ted Wilks
Forest Park Westheimer Cemetery: Dick Farrell, Salty Parker
Forest Park of Lawndale: Frank Croucher, Dickie Kerr, Gus Mancuso, Charlie Miller, Red Munger, Glenn Myatt, Heinie Schuble, Joe Wood
Garden of Gethsemani: Eddie Dyer
Glenwood Cemetery: Chappie McFarland
Hollywood Cemetery: Gene Bailey, Jack Berly, George Whiteman
Holy Cross Cemetery: Jerry Denny, Con Lucid
Houston National Cemetery: Walt Bond, Willard Brown, Jim Pendleton
Memorial Oaks Cemetery: Pat Ankenman, Jeff Cross, Hoot Evers, Johnny Keane, Johnny Lipon, Walter Murphy
Paradise Cemetery: Jake Brown
Rosewood Park Cemetery: Fred Link, Slim McGrew
Woodlawn Garden of Memories: Neal Baker, Gordie Hinkle

Hubbard
Fairview Cemetery: Tris Speaker, Tony York

Hutchins
Hutchins Cemetery: Buddy Napier

Italy
Italy Cemetery: Art Shires

Jasper
Memorial Park Cemetery: Les Willis

Kenedy
Butler Family Cemetery: Al Baker
Kenedy City Cemetery: Everett Booe

Lancaster

Edgewood Cemetery: Gene Moore

Laredo

Laredo City Cemetery: Clarence Huber

Leonard

Leonard Cemetery: Polly McLarry

Liberty

Catholic Cemetery: Tink Riviere

Linden

New Colony Cemetery: George Washington

Longview

Grace Hill Cemetery: Charlie Neal
Lakeview Memorial Gardens: Joe Dawson
Memory Park Cemetery: Abe Bowman, Tex Jeanes
Spring Hill Cemetery: Homer Blankenship

Lubbock

Lubbock City Cemetery: Sled Allen, Bill Morley
Resthaven Memorial Park: Bill Brown, Sammy West
Restland Cemetery: George Edmondson

Luling

Luling City Cemetery: Gene Cocreham

Marshall

Colonial Gardens: Guy Sturdy

Mason

Gooch Cemetery: Lindsay Brown

McGregor

Harris Creek Cemetery: Sarge Connally

McKinney

Altoga Cemetery: Otho Nitcholas

Mesquite

Mesquite Cemetery: Turkey Gross

Mexia

Mexia City Cemetery: John Carden

Meyersville

Meyersville Cemetery: Marv Gudat

Mission

Laurel Hill Cemetery: Paul Johnson

Montgomery

Montgomery Cemetery: Norm Branch

Omaha

Omaha Cemetery: Randy Moore

Overton

Overton Cemetery: Tex Vache

Palestine

Broyles Chapel Cemetery: George Watkins
St Joseph Cemetery: Jack Coombs

Palo Pinto

Palo Pinto Cemetery: Charlie Robertson

Paris

Evergreen Cemetery: Bill Latimore
Providence Cemetery: Rick Adams

Pharr

Valley Memorial Gardens: Earl Caldwell

Plainview

Plainview Cemetery: Claude Cooper

Red Oak

Red Oak Cemetery: Tex Shirley

Robstown

Robstown Memorial Park: Claude Davenport, Howie Reed

Rusk

Cedar Hill Cemetery: Heinie Odom

San Angelo

Fairmount Cemetery: Jake Freeze
Lawnhaven Memorial Gardens: Joe Kracher

San Antonio

Fort Sam Houston National Cemetery: Tex Kraus, Frank Snyder
Holy Cross Cemetery: Bernie James
Mission Burial Park: Frank Browning, Homer Ezzell, Paul Kardow, Rube Waddell, Ross Youngs
Mission Burial Park South: Cotton Knaupp, Pinky Whitney
Odd Fellows Cemetery: Tex Wisterzil
San Fernando Archdiocesan Cemetery: Tim Greisenbeck
San Jose Burial Park: Harry Ables
St Joseph's Society Cemetery: Jake Volz
St Mary's Cemetery: Pat Newnam, Dick Phelan
Sunset Memorial Park: Del Baker, Gene Bedford, Charlie Engle, Ray Flaskamper, Cy Fried, Joe Hague, Fred Johnson, Topper Rigney, Art Scharein, Hank Severeid, Charley Suche, Art Veltman, Paul Wachtel

San Augustine

Shilo Cemetery: Al Williams

San Marcos

San Marcos Cemetery: Tex Hughson

Sealy

Sealy Cemetery: Mel Preibisch

Sequin

Guadalupe Valley Memorial Park: Jim Riley

Sherman

Cedarlawn Memorial Park: Bob Muncrief

Stamford
Highland Memorial Cemetery: Bob Prichard

Stephenville
Hucksby Cemetery: Don Flinn

Streetman
Birdston Cemetery: Firpo Marberry

Sulphur Springs
Restlawn Memorial Park: Buck Fausett

Teague
Greenwood Cemetery: Joel Hunt

Terrell
College Mound Cemetery: Leo Tankersley

Texarkana
Hillcrest Memorial Park: Footsie Blair

Throckmorton
Throckmorton Cemetery: Jimmie Coker

Trenton
Burns Cemetery: Tex Wilson

Tyler
Memorial Park Cemetery: Larry Drake
Oakwood Cemetery: Fred Johnston

Van Alstyne
Van Alstyne Cemetery: Sam Gray

Van Vleck
Roselawn Memorial Cemetery: Willie Underhill

Victoria
Resurrection Cemetery: Dick Mulligan, Lou Rochelli

Waco
Holy Cross Cemetery: Louis Drucke
Oakwood Cemetery: Buster Chatham, Jack Little, Buster Mills, Lloyd Russell
Rosemound Cemetery: Charlie Barnabe, Jack Conway

Waxahachie
Hillcrest Burial Park: Paul Richards, Archie Wise

Weimar
Masonic Cemetery: Ira Townsend
St Michael Catholic Cemetery: Ed Donnelly

Wharton
Wharton City Cemetery: Carl Reynolds

Wheeler
Wheeler Cemetery: Sammy Hale

Wichita Falls
Crestview Memorial Park: Pete Turgeon

Willis
Ebenizer Cemetery: Cliff Young

Wimberly
Wimberly Cemetery: Al Hollingsworth

Woodrow
Peaceful Gardens Memorial Park: Donnie Moore

Woodsboro
La Rosa Cemetery: Martin Autry

Utah

Bountiful
Bountiful City Park: Ed Heusser
Lakeview Memorial Estates: Al Tate

Holladay
Holladay Memorial Park: Ray Jacobs

Layton
Kaysville-Layton Memorial Park: Spencer Adams

Ogden
Aultorest Memorial Park: Clay Lambert
Ogden City Cemetery: Fred Clark, Ed Green

Orem
Orem City Cemetery: Kent Peterson

Payson
Payson City Cemetery: Red Peery

Plain City
Plain City Cemetery: Elmer Singleton

Salt Lake City
Salt Lake City Cemetery: Roy Castleton, Paul Strand

Vermont

Barre
Hope Cemetery: Walt Lanfranconi, Steve Slayton

Brattleboro
Catholic Cemetery: Frank O'Connor

Burlington
Lakeview Cemetery: Doc Hazleton
Memorial Gardens at St Paul's Cathedral: Larry Gardner

Colchester
Colchester Village Cemetery: Ray Collins

Essex Center
Mountain View Cemetery: Bert Abbey

Poultney
St Raphael Cemetery: Ed Donnelly

Richmond
Holy Rosary Cemetery: Dave Keefe

Rutland
Evergreen Cemetery: Harry Hulihan

Winooski
St Stephen's Cemetery: Ralph LaPointe

Virginia

Abington
Knollkreg Memorial Park: Lefty Thomas

Alexandria
Mount Comfort Cemetery: Harry Child, Bill Kennedy
St Mary's Cemetery: Jim Shaw

Amherst
Amherst Cemetery: Jackie Jensen

Arlington
Arlington National Cemetery: Charlie Becker, Lu Blue, Bill Dietrick, Abner Doubleday, William Eckert, Nemo Gaines, Gil Gallagher, Dale Jones, Doc Lavan, Marty Martel, Dave Wills, Jud Wilson
Columbia Gardens Cemetery: Eddie Foster

Catharpin
Sudley Methodist Church Cemetery: Ben Sanders

Chatham
Greenpond Baptist Church Cemetery: Cloy Mattox

Chesterfield
Dale Memorial Park: Monte Kennedy

Churchville
Presbyterian Church Cemetery: Jerry May

Danville
Highland Burial Park: Herb Brett

Draper
Grantham Cemetery: Doc Ayers

Dublin
Dublin Cemetery: Jim Brillheart

Edinburg
Cedar Wood Cemetery: Vance Dinges

Emporia
Emporia Cemetery: Vern Morgan

Falls Church
National Memorial Park: Al Cypert, Clay Kirby
Oakwood Cemetery: Johnnie Priest

Gretna
Gretna Burial Park: Clarence Pickrel

Hampton
Oakland Cemetery: Sis Hopkins

Hopewell
Appomattox Cemetery: Morrie Aderholt

La Crosse
Crestview Memorial Park: Bill Connelly

Lexington
Stonewall Jackson Cemetery: Cy Twombly

Lynchburg
Holy Cross Cemetery: Kit McKenna
Spring Hill Cemetery: Al Orth, Charlie Pick

Mathews
Gwynn's Island Cemetery: Reese Diggs

McKenney
Good Shepherd Church Cemetery: Don Black

Mount Sidney
Lebanon Church Cemetery: Jim Hulvey

Newport News
Peninsula Memorial Park: Buck Marrow

Norfolk
Forest Lawn Cemetery: John Gallagher, Dave Robertson, Buck Stanley, John Woods
Riverside Memorial Park: Abie Hood, Mike Smith
St Mary's Cemetery: Jake Wells
Woodlawn Memorial Gardens: Garland Braxton

North Garden
Zion Baptist Church Cemetery: Vern Bickford

Pamplin
Pamplin Community Cemetery: Woody Williams

Petersburg
Blandford Cemetery: Bill Quarles

Portsmouth
Oak Grove Cemetery: Sam Post

Radiant
Tucker Family Cemetery: Ollie Tucker

Richmond
Forestlawn Cemetery: Bucky Jacobs
Hollywood Cemetery: Murray McGuire
Holy Cross Cemetery: Joe Boehling
Maury Cemetery: Owen Kahn
Oakwood Cemetery: Reddy Foster
Riverview Cemetery: Bob Habenicht, Cy Hooker, Herm McFarland, Pop Tate
Sunset Memorial Park: George Smith
Westhampton Memorial Park: Harry Hedgepath

Upperville
Ivy Hill Cemetery: Harvey Russell

Vinton

Mountain View Cemetery: Red Cox

Virgilina

Christian Church Cemetery: Dixie Davis

Virginia Beach

Eastern Shore Chapel Cemetery: Bill Damman
Rosewood Memorial Park: Clyde McCullough, Bill Morrisette, Allie Watt

Williamsburg

Cedar Grove Cemetery: Red Proctor
Williamsburg Memorial Park: Bud Davis

Winchester

Mount Hebron Cemetery: Mul Holland

Washington

Aberdeen

Fern Hill Cemetery: Jack Fournier, Frank Mulroney, Marty O'Toole

Bellevue

Sunset Hills Memorial Park: Al Niemiec, Ray Oyler

Bremerton

Ivy Green Cemetery: Bill Yohe

Cashmere

Cashmere Cemetery: Win Noyes

Everett

Cypress Lawn Memorial Park: Karl Adams
Evergreen Cemetery: Bob Chesnes

Kent

Hillcrest Burial Park: Red Badgro

Lynnwood

Floral Hills Cemetery: Les Wilson

Olympia

Masonic Memorial Park: Ira Flagstead
Olympia Cemetery: Ray Callahan

Pine City

Pine City Cemetery: Elmer Leifer

Port Townsend

Laurel Grove Cemetery: Tom Baker, Art McLarney

Puyallup

Woodbine Cemetery: Jim Mosolf

Renton

Mount Olivet Cemetery: Fred Hutchinson

Seattle

Acacia Cemetery: Bill Bailey, Dick Gyselman, Irv Higginbotham, Bill Lasley, Amos Rusie
Calvary Cemetery: George Burns, Dan Dugdale, John Hickey, Tim O'Rourke, Alan Strange, Tom Sullivan
Evergreen-Washelli Cemetery: Joe Abreu, Andy Anderson, Bill Kennedy, Charlie Mullen
Holyrood Cemetery: Dick Barrett, Jack Wilson
Lake View Cemetery: Emil Frisk, Jeff Heath
Mount Pleasant Cemetery: Leo Taylor

Sequim

Dungeness Cemetery: Joe Coscarart

Snohomish

Grand Army of the Republic Cemetery: Earl Averill, Earl Torgeson

Spokane

Chewelah Cemetery: Dave Skeels
Fairmount Memorial Park: Ed Brandt
Greenwood Memorial Terrace: Moose Baxter, Harry Howell
Holy Cross Cemetery: Ham Hyatt

Steilacomm

West Washington State Hosp Cemetery: Charlie Faust

Tacoma

Calvary Cemetery: Eddie Hickey, Pip Koehler
Mountain View Memorial Park: Jesse Baker, Bob Johnson, Cy Neighbors, Cap Peterson
New Tacoma Memorial Park: Con Starkell, Bobby Vaughn

Trentwood

St Joseph Cemetery: Phil Geier

White Salmon

White Salmon Cemetery: Floyd Ritter

Yakima

Terrace Heights Memorial Park: Mike Lynch, Royal Shaw, Doc Waldbauer

West Virginia

Aurora

Aurora Cemetery: Al Braithwood

Barboursville

Barboursville Cemetery: George Baumgardner
Ridgelawn Memorial Park: Admiral Schlei

Beckley

Sunset Memorial Park: Sheriff Blake, Joe McManus

Bluewell

Woodlawn Memorial Park: Bob Bowman

CAMERON

Big Run Church Cemetery: Clarence Garrett
Highland Cemetery: Beryl Richmond

CHARLES TOWN

Edge Hill Cemetery: Lefty Willis

CHARLESTON

Spring Hill Cemetery: Hugh Hill, Ed Kenna

CLARKSBURG

Elk View Masonic Cemetery: Ken Ash
Greenlawn Masonic Cemetery: Guy Zinn

DUNBAR

Dunbar Memorial Park: Bill Hall
Mountain View Memorial Park: Babe Barna, Johnny Stuart

ELKINS

Maplewood Cemetery: Del Gainor

FAIRMONT

Woodlawn Cemetery: Sam Jones

HUNTINGTON

Highland Cemetery: John Scheneberg
Spring Hill Cemetery: Fred Bailey, Wayland Dean, Wilbur Fisher, Johnson Fry, Skeeter Shelton
Woodmere Memorial Park: Larry McClure, Ezra Midkiff, Johnny Watson

MORGANTOWN

East Oak Grove Cemetery: Piano Legs Hickman

OAK HILL

High Lawn Memorial Park: Harry Moran

PARKERSBURG

Odd Fellows Cemetery: Charlie Hastings, Al Mays, Greasy Neale

PECKS MILL

Forest Lawn Cemetery: Max Butcher

POINT PLEASANT

Kirkland Memorial Gardens: Herman Layne
Suncrest Cemetery: Clarence Fisher

PROSPERITY

Blue Ridge Memorial Gardens: Walter Craddock

SHINNSTOWN

Shinnstown Masonic Cemetery: Lee King

SOUTH CHARLESTON

Sunset Memorial Park: Guy Morrison

ST MARYS

Odd Fellows Cemetery: Frank Barron

WADESTOWN

Wadestown Cemetery: Harry Shriver

WEIRTON

St Paul Catholic Church Cemetery: Frank Kalin, Bob Trice

WELLSBURG

Brooke Cemetery: Gene Curtis

WHEELING

Greenwood Cemetery: Sam Moffett
Mount Calvary Cemetery: Bill George, Joe Miller
Peninsula Cemetery: Jack Glasscock

WISCONSIN

APPLETON

Riverside Cemetery: George Hogriever

BEAVER DAM

Leipsic Cemetery: Lyman Linde
Oakwood Cemetery: Pink Hawley

BELOIT

Calvary Cemetery: Patsy Gharrity
Eastlawn Cemetery: Frank Gregory, Roy Hansen, Elmer Miller, George Perring
Mount Thabor Cemetery: Jim Breton, Zip Zabel

BLACK RIVER FALLS

Riverside Cemetery: Phil Haugstad

BROOKFIELD

Wisconsin Memorial Park: Tom Dougherty, Happy Felsch, Doc Hamann, Ken Jungels, Ken Keltner, Art Kores, Fritz Mollwitz

BURLINGTON

Burlington Cemetery: Bob Steele
St Charles Cemetery: Frank Roth
St Mary's Cemetery: Braggo Roth

CLEAR LAKE

Clear Lake Cemetery: Burleigh Grimes

COLUMBUS

Hillside Cemetery: Frank Lange

CROSS PLAINS

St Francis Xavier Cemetery: Connie Grob

DELEVAN

Spring Grove Cemetery: Webb Schultz

EVANSVILLE

Maple Hill Cemetery: Cal Broughton, Stan Sperry

FRIENDSHIP

Mount Repose Cemetery: Len Koenecke

GALESVILLE

Pine Cliff Cemetery: Sam Brenegan

HUDSON
Willow River Cemetery: Otis Clymer, Phil Gallivan, Bobby Reis

HURLEY
Hurley Cemetery: Frank Rooney

JANESVILLE
Mount Olivet Cemetery: Joe Cantillon, John Morrissey, Tom Morrissey
Oak Hill Cemetery: Frank Bliss, Bill Lathrop

KENOSHA
All Saints Cemetery: Ollie O'Mara, Charlie Pechous
Green Ridge Cemetery: Ben Dyer
Sunset Ridge Memorial Park: Ed Corey, Press Cruthers

LAKEWOOD
Community Bible Church Cemetery: Milo Allison

LAONA
Laona Cemetery: Ernie Ovitz

MADISON
Resurrection Catholic Cemetery: Ed Barry, Art Bramhall

MANITOWOC
Evergreen Cemetery: Stoney McGlynn

MARINETTE
Forest Home Cemetery: Jim Magnuson

MAYVILLE
Graceland Cemetery: Bert Husting

MAZOMANIE
St Barnabas Cemetery: Gene Brabender

MENASHA
St John Cemetery: Dave Koslo

MILTON JUNCTION
Milton Junction Cemetery: Willis Cole

MILWAUKEE
Arlington Park Cemetery: Lou Manske
Calvary Catholic: Charlie Cushman, Tom Nagle
Evergreen Cemetery: Hi Ebright
Forest Home Cemetery: Charlie Dougherty, Frank Luce
Good Hope Cemetery: Al Eckert
Holy Cross Cemetery: Jap Barbeau, Nap Kloza, George McBride, Ralph Shinners
Mount Olivet Cemetery: Bud Lally, Dan Marion
Oakwood Cemetery: Bunny Brief
Pinelawn Memorial Park: Art Bues, Elmer Klumpp, Fred Luderus
St Adalbert's Cemetery: Bruno Block, Fabian Gaffke, Al Simmons, Tony Welzer
Union Cemetery: Anton Falch
Valhalla Memorial Cemetery: Pep Clark, Rube Lutzke
Wanderer's Rest Cemetery: Frank Schneiberg

OGEMA
Hillside Cemetery: Jack Boyle

OSHKOSH
Peace Lutheran Cemetery: Dave Tyriver

PARDEEVILLE
Pardeeville Cemetery: Claude Elliott

RACINE
West Lawn Memorial Park: Jimmy Grant

REEDSBURG
Calvary Cemetery: Charlie Kavanagh

RICE LAKE
Nora Cemetery: Clay Perry

ROCHESTER
Rochester Cemetery: Ginger Beaumont

SHEBOYGAN
Calvary Cemetery: Joe Hauser

SHEBOYGAN FALLS
Sheboygan Falls Cemetery: John Wyckoff

ST CROIX FALLS
St Croix Falls Cemetery: Roy Patterson

SUPERIOR
Calvary Cemetery: Russ Ennis
Greenwood Cemetery: Dave Bancroft, Jay Cashion
Hebrew Cemetery: Morrie Arnovich

THREE LAKES
Three Lakes Cemetery: Cy Williams

VIOLA
Viola Cemetery: Henry Benn

WATERLOO
Waterloo Cemetery: George Davies

WYOMING

CHEYENNE
Olivet Cemetery: Ed Murray

DOUGLAS
Douglas Park Cemetery: Bill Meehan

Non-U.S. Cities

Cuba

Cienfuegos

Cienfuegos Cemetery: Martin Dihigo

Havana

Christopher Columbus Necropolis: Mike Gonzalez, Dolf Luque, Armando Marsans

Ontario, Canada

Burlington

Holy Sepulchre Cemetery: Joe Krakauskas

Scarborough

Memorial Park Cemetery: Alex Hardy

Toronto

Necropolis Cemetery: Ernie Ross
Park Lawn Cemetery: Andy Kyle
Saint James Cemetery: Kid Somers

Bibliography

Reference Books

Burek, Deborah M., ed. *Cemeteries of the United States.* Detroit: Gale Research, 1994.

Reichler, Joseph L., ed. *The Baseball Encyclopedia.* New York: Macmillan, 1985.

Thorn, John, et al., eds. *Total Baseball.* New York: Total Sports, Inc., 1999.

Turkin, Hy, and S. C. Thompson. *The Official Encyclopedia of Baseball, Jubilee Edition.* New York: A. S. Barnes, 1951.

Wolff, Rick, et al., eds. *The Baseball Encyclopedia.* New York: Macmillan, 1990.

Other Sources

Newspapers, too numerous to mention individually, from all parts of the United States and parts of Canada.

Public records at county courthouses, primarily in California.

Telephone conversations with hundreds of cemetery caretakers and funeral directors from all across the country.